FLIGHT MANUAL
B-58A

T.O. 1B-58A-1

USAF SERIES AIRCRAFT

Contracts AF 33(600)36200
and F41608-68-C-2168

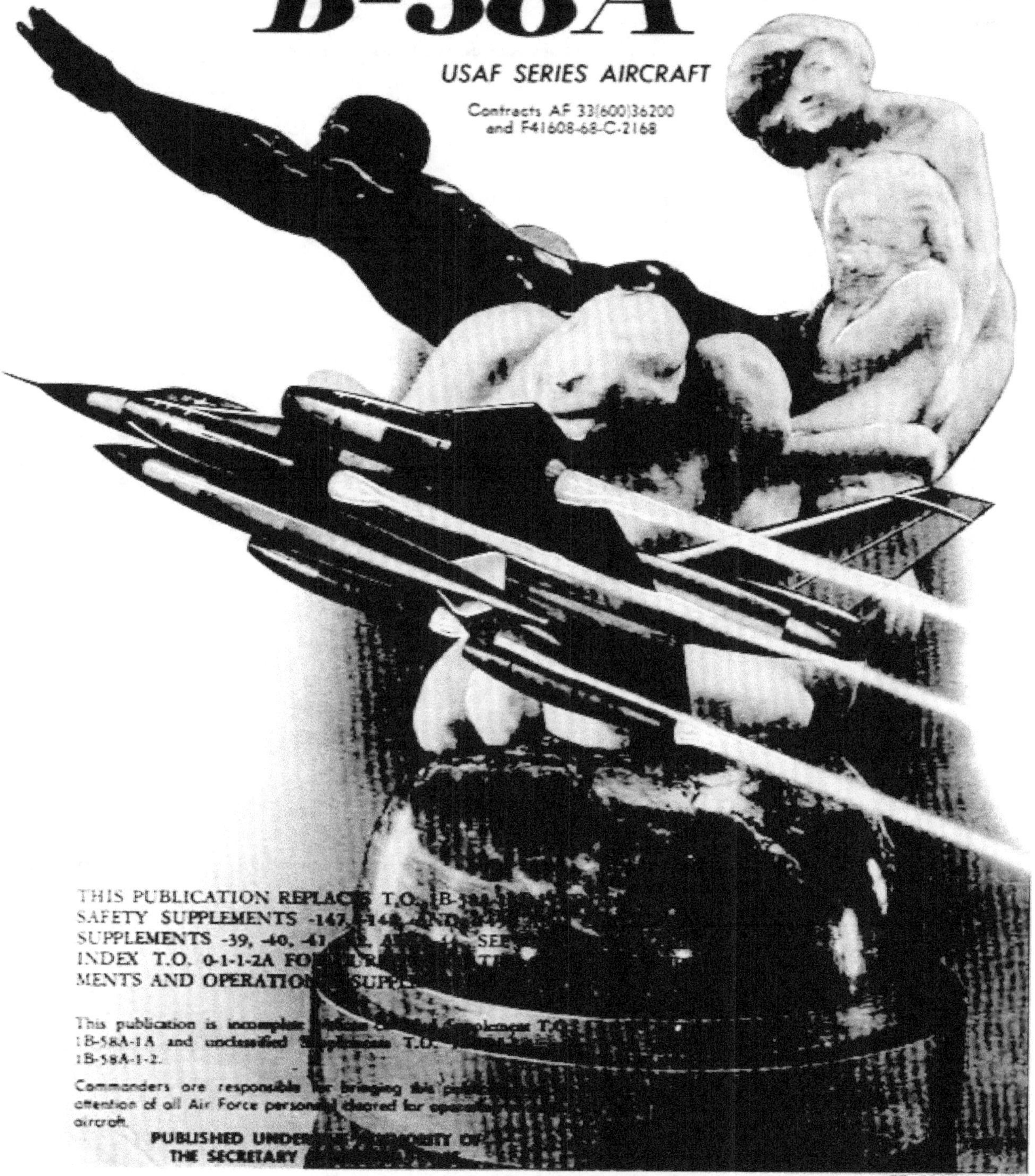

THIS PUBLICATION REPLACES T.O. 1B-58A-1
SAFETY SUPPLEMENTS -147, -148 AND
SUPPLEMENTS -39, -40, -41, -42, AND -43. SEE
INDEX T.O. 0-1-1-2A FOR CURRENT SAFETY
MENTS AND OPERATIONAL SUPPLEMENTS

This publication is incomplete without classified supplement T.O.
1B-58A-1A and unclassified supplement T.O.
1B-58A-1-2.

Commanders are responsible for bringing this publication to the
attention of all Air Force personnel cleared for operation of the
aircraft.

**PUBLISHED UNDER THE AUTHORITY OF
THE SECRETARY OF THE AIR FORCE**

AIR FORCE 240 5-13-69 — 1900

ISBN #978-1-937684-93-8

28 MARCH 1965

T.O. 1B-58A-1

Reproduction for nonmilitary use of the information or illustrations contained in this publication is not permitted without specific approval of the issuing service. The policy for use of Classified Publications is established for the Air Force in AFR 205-1.

LIST OF EFFECTIVE PAGES

INSERT LATEST CHANGED PAGES. DESTROY SUPERSEDED PAGES.

NOTE: The portion of the text affected by the changes is indicated by a vertical line in the outer margins of the page.

TOTAL NUMBER OF PAGES IN THIS PUBLICATION IS 578 CONSISTING OF THE FOLLOWING:

Page No.	Issue
Title	Original
A	Original
Supplement Flyleaf	Original
Blank	Original
TCTO Flyleaf	Original
Blank	Original
i thru iv	Original
1-1 thru 1-113	Original
1-114 Blank	Original
2-1 thru 2-80	Original
3-1 thru 3-52	Original
4-1 thru 4-118	Original
5-1 thru 5-33	Original
5-34 Blank	Original
6-1 thru 6-22	Original
7-1 thru 7-52	Original
8-1 thru 8-60	Original
9-1 thru 9-18	Original
A-1	Original
A-2 Blank	Original
1 thru 16	Original

This book has been digitally watermarked to prevent illegal duplication.

©2008-2012 Periscope Film LLC
All Rights Reserved
ISBN #978-1-937684-93-8

WWW.PERISCOPEFILM.COM

T.O. 1B-58A-1

FLIGHT MANUAL, SAFETY SUPPLEMENT, AND OPERATIONAL SUPPLEMENT STATUS

This page will be published with each Safety Supplement, Operational Supplement, Flight Manual Change, and Flight Manual Revision. It provides a comprehensive listing of the current Flight Manuals, Flight Crew Checklist, Safety Supplements, and Operational Supplements. The supplements you receive should follow in sequence. If you are missing one listed on this page, see your Publications Distribution Officer and get your copy. Periodically check weekly Safety Supplement Index T.O. 0-1-1-2A, T.O. 0-1-1-2, and supplements thereto to make sure you have the latest Supplements, Checklists, and Basic Manuals.

Current Flight Manual	*Date*	*Changed*
T.O. 1B-58A-1	28 March 69	—
T.O. 1B-58A-1-1	13 May 66	28 March 69
T.O. 1B-58A-1-2	28 Sep 62	10 May 68

Current Flight Crew Checklist		
T.O. 1B-58A-1CL-1	28 March 69	—
T.O. 1B-58A-1CL-2	28 March 69	—

CURRENT SAFETY SUPPLEMENTS

Number	*Date*	*Short Title*	*Flight Manual Pages Affected*
—	—	—	—

SAFETY SUPPLEMENTS INCORPORATED IN THIS REVISION

Number	*Date*	*Short Title*	*Flight Manual Pages Affected*
—147	31 May 68	Rotation for Takeoff	2-40
—148	23 July 68	Cartridge Starter Malfunction Instructions	2-19, 5-4
—149	3 Oct 68	Gear Damage/Emergency Ground Egress	3-3, 3-44, 3-45, 3-46

CURRENT OPERATIONAL SUPPLEMENTS

Number	*Date*	*Short Title*	*Flight Manual Pages Affected*
—43	20 Sep 69	Rescinded	—

OPERATIONAL SUPPLEMENTS INCORPORATED IN THIS REVISION

Number	*Date*	*Short Title*	*Flight Manual Pages Affected*
—39	18 July 68	Pilot Capsule Door Emergency Release	1-110
—40	19 July 68	Rotation Speed Callout	2-40, 2-42
—41	16 Sep 68	Escape Capsule Chute Manual Deployment	1-103, 1-104, 1-107, 1-110, 3-26
—42	17 Sep 68	Fuel Panel Variation/Before Lineup Checklist Change	2-37
—44	2 Oct 68	Bomb-Nav Procedures Change	8-16, 8-21

Supplement Flyleaf

T.O. 1B-58A-1

the B·58A airplane

THIS PAGE INTENTIONALLY LEFT BLANK

T.O. 1B-58A-1

AIRPLANE RETROFIT TECHNICAL ORDER INFORMATION.

Time Compliance Technical Order (TCTO) numbers, along with the signs "+" and "−", are used to distinguish between airplanes that have been modified and those that have not. This list includes the applicable TCTO numbers that have been issued up to the date of publication. Those issued after that date will appear in the next change/revision.

T.C.T.O. Flyleaf

T.O. 1B-58A-1

the B·58A airplane

THIS PAGE INTENTIONALLY LEFT BLANK

TABLE OF CONTENTS

SECTION I	description	1-1
SECTION II	normal procedures	2-1
SECTION III	emergency procedures	3-1
SECTION IV	auxiliary equipment	4-1
SECTION V	operating limitations	5-1
SECTION VI	flight characteristics	6-1
SECTION VII	systems operation	7-1
SECTION VIII	crew duties	8-1
SECTION IX	all weather operation	9-1
APPENDIX I	performance data	(See T.O. 1B-58A-1-1)
	alphabetical index	1

T.O. 1B-58A-1

The CRYSTAL BALL IS OUT OF DATE. READ THESE PAGES, DON'T TEMPT FATE!

SCOPE.

This manual contains the necessary information for safe and efficient operation of the B-58A. These instructions provide you with a general knowledge of the airplane, its characteristics, and specific normal and emergency operating procedures. Your flying experience is recognized, and therefore, basic flight principles are avoided.

SOUND JUDGMENT.

Instructions in this manual are for a crew inexperienced in the operation of this airplane. This manual provides the best possible operating instructions under most circumstances, but it is a poor substitute for sound judgment. Multiple emergencies, adverse weather, terrain, etc. may require modification of the procedures.

PERMISSIBLE OPERATIONS.

The Flight Manual takes a "positive approach" and normally states only what you can do. Unusual operations or configurations (such as asymmetrical loading) are prohibited unless specifically covered herein. Clearance must be obtained from SAAMA (SANEOF) before any questionable operation is attempted which is not specifically permitted in this manual.

HOW TO BE ASSURED OF HAVING LATEST DATA.

Refer to weekly Safety Supplement Index, T.O. 0-1-1-2A and T.O. 0-1-1-2 and supplements thereto for current listing of Flight Manuals, Safety Supplements, Operational Supplements, and Checklists.

STANDARDIZATION AND ARRANGEMENT.

Standardization assures that the scope and arrangement of all Flight Manuals are identical. The manual is divided into ten fairly independent sections to simplify reading it straight through or using it as a reference manual. The first three sections must be read thoroughly and fully understood before attempting to fly the airplane. The remaining sections provide important information for safe and efficient mission accomplishment.

SAFETY SUPPLEMENTS.

Information involving safety will be promptly forwarded to you by Safety Supplements. Supplements covering loss of life will get to you in 48 hours by TWX, and those concerning serious damage to equipment within 10 days by mail. The title page of the Flight Manual and the title block of each Safety Supplement should be checked to determine the effect they may have on existing supplements. You must remain constantly aware of the status of all supplements—current supplements must be complied with but there is no point in restricting your operation by complying with a replaced or rescinded supplement.

OPERATIONAL SUPPLEMENTS.

Information involving changes to operating procedures will be forwarded to you by Operational Supplements. The procedure for handling Operational Supplements is the same as for Safety Supplements.

CHECKLISTS.

The Flight Manual contains only amplified checklists. Abbreviated checklists have been issued as separate technical orders—see the back of the title page for T.O. number and date of your latest checklist. Line items in the Flight Manual and checklists are identical with respect to arrangement and item number. Formal supplements that require checklist changes will contain the changed checklist page(s) as part of the supplement.

HOW TO GET PERSONAL COPIES.

Each flight crew member is entitled to personal copies of the Flight Manual, Safety Supplements, Operational Supplements, and Check Lists. The required quantities should be ordered before you need them to assure their prompt receipt. Check with your supply personnel—it is their job to fulfill your Technical Order requests. Basically, you must order the required quantities on the Numerical Index and Requirements Table (NI & RT). Technical Orders 00-5-1 and 00-5-2 give detailed information for properly ordering these publications. Make sure a system is established at your base to deliver these publications to the flight crews immediately upon receipt.

FLIGHT MANUAL BINDERS.

Loose leaf binders and sectionalized tabs are available for use with your manual. These are obtained through local purchase procedures and are listed in the Federal Supply Schedule (FSC Group 75, Office Supplies, Part I). Check with your supply personnel for assistance in securing these items.

WARNINGS, CAUTIONS, AND NOTES.

The following definitions apply to "Warnings," "Cautions," and "Notes" found throughout the manual.

WARNING

Operating procedures, techniques, etc., which will result in personal injury or loss of life if not carefully followed.

CAUTION

Operating procedures, techniques, etc., which will result in damage to equipment if not carefully followed.

Note

An operating procedure, technique, etc., which is considered essential to emphasize.

YOUR RESPONSIBILITY — TO LET US KNOW.

Every effort is made to keep the Flight Manual current. Review conferences with operating personnel and a constant review of accident and flight test reports assure inclusion of the latest data in the manual. However, we cannot correct an error unless we know of its existence. In this regard, it is essential that you do your part. Comments, corrections, and questions regarding this manual or any phase of the Flight Manual program are welcomed. These should be forwarded through your Command Standardization Board to Hq SAAMA (SANEOF), Kelly AFB, Texas.

AIRPLANE DESIGNATION CODES.

Major differences between airplanes covered in this Manual are designated by number symbols which appear on illustrations and within the text. Symbol designations for individual aircraft, and groups of aircraft are as follows.

⑯ 58-1009	㊹ 59-2441	㊽ 60-1112	㊼ 61-2056
⑰ 58-1010	㊺ 59-2442	⑩ 60-1113	㊾ 61-2058
⑱ 58-1011	㊼ 59-2444	⑪ 60-1114	㊾ 61-2059
⑳ 58-1013	㊽ 59-2445	⑫ 60-1115	㊾ 61-2060
㉑ 58-1014	㊾ 59-2446	⑭ 60-1117	⑩ 61-2064
㉒ 58-1015	㊿ 59-2448	⑮ 60-1118	⑩ 61-2066
㉕ 58-1018	㊽ 59-2449	⑰ 60-1120	⑩ 61-2067
㉖ 58-1019	㊽ 59-2450	⑱ 60-1121	⑭ 61-2068
㉘ 58-1021	㊽ 59-2452	⑲ 60-1122	⑮ 61-2069
㉛ 59-2428	㊽ 59-2453	⑩ 60-1123	⑯ 61-2070
㉜ 59-2429	㊽ 59-2454	⑪ 60-1124	⑲ 61-2071
㉝ 59-2430	㊽ 59-2455	⑫ 60-1125	⑩ 61-2072
㉞ 59-2431	㊽ 59-2456	⑬ 60-1126	⑪ 61-2073
㉟ 59-2432	㊿ 59-2457	⑭ 60-1127	⑩ 61-2074
㊱ 59-2433	㊽ 59-2458	⑮ 60-1129	⑪ 61-2075
㊲ 59-2434	㊽ 59-2460	⑰ 61-2051	⑫ 61-2076
㊳ 59-2435	㊽ 59-2461	⑬ 61-2052	⑬ 61-2077
㊴ 59-2436	㊽ 59-2463	⑭ 61-2053	⑭ 61-2078
㊶ 59-2438	㊼ 60-1110	⑭ 61-2054	⑮ 61-2079
㊷ 59-2439	㊽ 60-1111	⑪ 61-2055	⑯ 61-2080
㊸ 59-2440			

♦ "through" or "and on"

+ "and those modified by" or "airplanes modified by"

− "unless modified by" or "airplanes not modified by"

T.O. 1B-58A-1

the B·58A airplane

TABLE OF CONTENTS.

	Page
The Airplane	1-1
Engines	1-5
Engine Afterburner System	1-14
Oil Supply System	1-15
Inlet Spike System	1-15
Fuel Supply System	1-17
Electrical Power Supply System	1-32
Hydraulic Power Supply System	1-56
Pneumatic Power Supply Systems	1-60
Flight Control System	1-60
Landing Gear System	1-76
Nose Wheel Steering System	1-81
Brake System	1-82
Drag Chute	1-85
Pitot-Static System	1-86
Air Data System	1-87
Instruments	1-87
Malfunction Indicator and Warning System	1-92
Emergency Equipment	1-95
Canopies	1-97
Escape Capsule	1-101
Safety Belt	1-113
Windshield and Window Glass Panels	1-113
Auxiliary Equipment	1-113

THE AIRPLANE.

The B-58A is a high-altitude, supersonic bomber manufactured by General Dynamics/Fort Worth, A Division of General Dynamics Corporation. The airplane is designed to carry externally attached weapons. The tactical mission is the destruction of surface objectives by bombs. After modification to carry a camera equipped pod the airplane also has the capability of performing daylight photographic reconnaissance missions.

AIRPLANE DIMENSIONS.

- Length (overall)   96 feet 9 inches
- Height (to top of fin)   29 feet 11 inches
- Wing Span   56 feet 10 inches
- Wing Area   1542 square feet
- Tread   13 feet 4 inches
- Wing Leading Edge Sweepback   60 degrees

Refer to Section II for turning radius and ground clearances.

GROSS WEIGHT.

- Weight empty without pod is approximately 58,000 pounds.
- The maximum gross weight varies with the weapon configuration attached. For information regarding the airplane maximum gross weight for a given weapon configuration, refer to "Weight Limitations" Section V.

FLIGHT CREW.

The flight crew consists of a pilot, a navigator, and a defensive system operator. The navigator located at the second crew station performs the duties of navigator and operates the bombing equipment. The defensive system operator at the third crew station operates the defensive ECM equipment and the remote-controlled tail turret and performs the duties of a performance engineer.

Section I
Description

T.O. 1B-58A-1

general arrangement diagram (typical)

1. Nose Boom
2. Air Refueling Receptacle
3. Search Radar RT Modulator Unit
4. Liquid Oxygen Containers
5. Single-Point Refueling Adapter
6. Pilot's Canopy
7. CG Calibrator
8. Navigation Unit
9. Navigator's Canopy
10. Yaw Amplifier Computer Assembly
11. DECM Equipment
12. DSO's Canopy
13. Primary Navigation Stabilization Computer
14. Primary Navigation Stabilization Unit
15. Astrotracker Amplifier Unit
16. Primary Navigation Computer Amplifier
17. Astrotracker Unit
18. Primary Navigation Stabilization Amplifier Unit
19. Primary Navigation Auxiliary Reference Unit
20. Yaw Rate Gyro Package
21. Rate Gyro and Accelerometer Package
22. Chaff Dispensers (Left and Right Wheel Wells)
23. Engine Starter Cart Receptacle
24. Ground Air Conditioning Receptacle
25. External Power and Ground Interphone Receptacles
26. Power Control Linkage Assembly
27. Radio Altimeter RT Amplifier Unit
28. Radar Track Breaker (Aft T4) Package
29. Doppler Electronics Unit
30. PI Beacon Receiver-Transmitter
31. RV Beacon Receiver-Transmitter
32. Fuel Dump Probe Assembly
33. Air-to-Ground IFF Transponder
34. Yaw Damper Servo
35. Remote Compass Transmitter
36. Fire Control System Frequency Control
37. Fire Control RF and Modulator Package
38. Fire Control System Controlled Line Platform
39. 20-MM Gatling-Type Gun
40. Tail Turret
41. Gun Feeder Assembly
42. Gun Control Package
43. Ammunition Box
44. Fire Control System Tracking Control Package
45. Drag Chute
46. Fire Control Computer Package
47. Bomb Damage Evaluation Camera Package
48. Nacelle Cooling and Fire Access Door (Two on Each Nacelle)
49. Hydraulic Oil Cooler Door
50. Yaw Gain Pressure Transducers
51. Starter Cartridge Loading Door
52. Starter Exhaust Door
53. Multiple Voltage Power Supply Unit
54. Battery
55. Air Navigation Data Recorder
56. Recorder Control Unit
57. Bomb Damage Evaluation Data Package
58. Air-to-Ground IFF Decoder Unit
59. Emergency UHF Receiver-Transmitter
60. UHF Command Radio (AN/ARC-34)
61. UHF Command Radio (AN/ARC-57)
62. Tactical Air Navigation System Package
63. Search Radar Photo Recorder
64. Radio Altimeter Unit
65. Autopilot Amplifier-Computer Assembly
66. Air Data Computer
67. Auxiliary Flight Reference System Directional Computer
68. Long Range Communication Receiver-Transmitter
69. Nose Wheel Well Canopy Control Valve
70. Secondary Pitot Probe
71. Temperature Probe
72. Landing and Taxi Lights
73. LRC Antenna Coupler Unit

Figure 1-1. (Sheet 1 of 2)

1-2

T.O. 1B-58A-1

Section I
Description

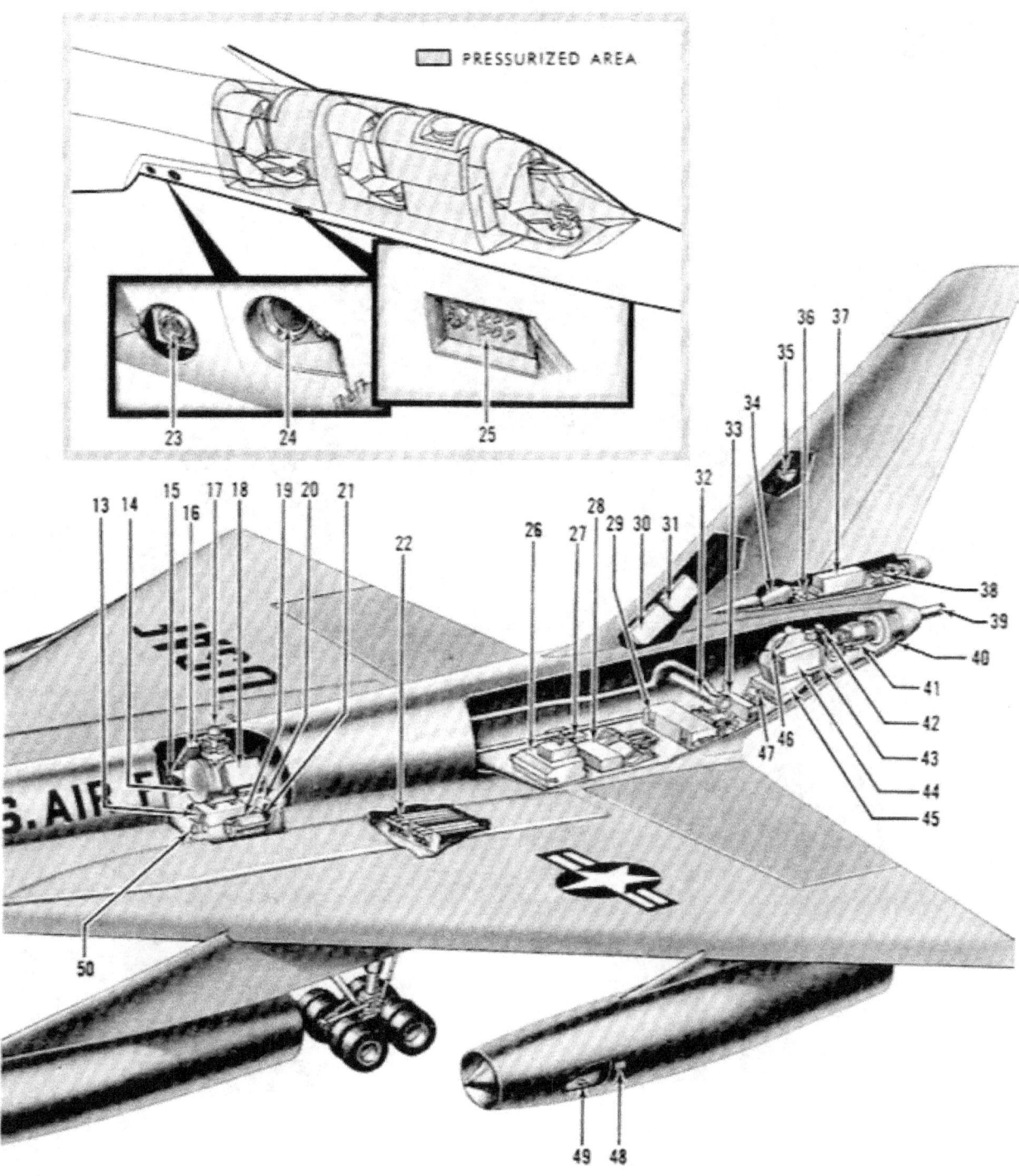

Figure 1-1. (Sheet 2 of 2)

Section 1
Description

T.O. 1B-58A-1

pilot's station (typical)

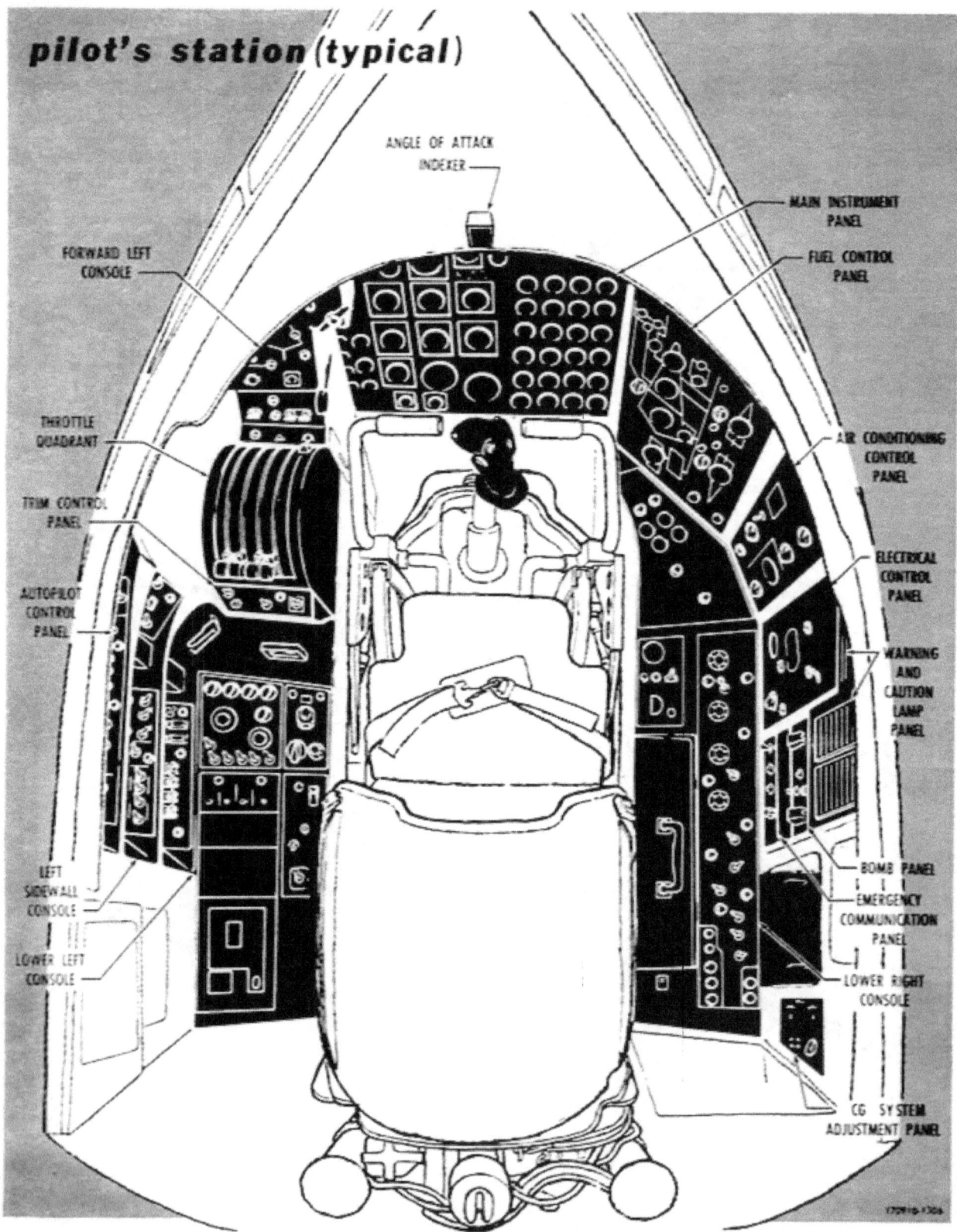

Figure 1-2.

1-4

CHARACTERISTICS AND FEATURES.

The airplane fuselage is area-rule designed and for the greatest part is covered with a bonded, beaded skin. The wing is a full cantilever, midwing, modified delta design with a cambered leading edge and a bonded honeycomb skin. The three-man crew sits in tandem in separate compartments. Entrance to their positions is made through individual power-actuated canopies. An air conditioning system maintains proper temperature, ventilation, and pressurization at all speeds and altitudes for crew compartments and temperature-limited equipment. The crew is also provided with a liquid oxygen system. Electrical power for the airplane is supplied through a two-bus a-c distribution system by three a-c generators which are driven by engines 1, 2, and 3 through constant-speed drive units. A portion of the a-c power is rectified to provide multiple voltages for d-c operated equipment; a 28-volt battery provides a limited source of d-c power for operation during extreme emergencies. The tricycle landing gear, brakes, nose wheel steering, tail turret, autopilot servos, search radar, air refueling door, chaff dispenser drive, and flight control system are actuated by a dual hydraulic system. The flight control surfaces consist of two elevons and a rudder. The airplane is not equipped with flaps. The flight control system has provisions for automatic flight control throughout the flight mission (except takeoff and landing). A pneumatic system provides for emergency operation of the landing gear and brakes. Normal actuation of the canopies, the drag chute, and the chaff dispensing system is is accomplished by separate pneumatic systems. Offensive armament consists of bombing equipment. Defensive armament consists of defensive ECM equipment and a remote-controlled tail turret equipped with a multi-barrel 20-mm cannon.

ENGINES.

Power is developed for the airplane by four General Electric J79-5 series engines. The approximate thrust rating of each engine at standard sea level static conditions is 15,600 pounds with maximum afterburner and 10,000 pounds at Military power. The engines are mounted in individual nacelles suspended beneath the wing and are numbered from left to right with the left outboard engine being No. 1. Each nacelle is equipped with a variable positioning spike which is used to maintain an efficient airflow to the engine throughout the speed range of the airplane. For further information on the spike refer to "Inlet Spike System" of this section. The engine is an axial-flow, reheat, turbojet engine consisting of a 17-stage compressor, 10 can-type combustion chambers, a three-stage turbine, an afterburner, and a variable exhaust nozzle. The amount of air entering the compressor is automatically controlled by variable positioning inlet guide vanes which act as an inlet air metering device. The first six stages of the compressor are equipped with variable positioning stator vanes which are positioned so that at a particular engine speed and compressor inlet temperature the inlet air strikes the vanes at the most effective angle of attack. The inlet guide vanes and variable stator vanes are connected externally and rotate in unison to control compressor pressure ratio and maintain an adequate stall margin under all operating conditions. The compressor and turbine, which are splined together, are supported by three bearings and rotate as a single unit. The exhaust nozzle functions as a variable restriction through which gases leaving the engine are accelerated to convert as much as possible of their pressure and temperature to velocity for thrust. Each engine is provided with a fuel control system, a main ignition system, and a starter system. Engine lubricating oil is provided by the oil supply system. Frontal areas of the engines are anti-iced by air from the anti-icing system (Refer to "Anti-Icing and Defogging Systems," Section IV). Engines 2 and 3 supply bleed air to the airplane air conditioning system and engines 1, 2, and 3 drive the electrical systems a-c generators.

ENGINE FUEL CONTROL SYSTEM.

The engine fuel control system consists of two separate systems—one for engine fuel control and one for afterburner fuel control. For information on the afterburner fuel control system, refer to "Engine Afterburner System" of this section. The primary function of the engine fuel control system (figure 1-3) is regulating engine speed by supplying and controlling fuel flow. The system also positions the inlet guide and variable stator vanes of the compressor section and initiates afterburner operation. Principal components of the system include a fuel strainer; a two-element, engine-driven fuel pump; a high pressure fuel filter; a fuel control unit; and a pressurizing and drain valve. Fuel flow is primarily controlled by the movement of the throttles. Movement of a throttle out of the OFF position opens the cutoff valve in the fuel control unit. Fuel is then supplied from the airplane fuel system through the strainer to the engine-driven fuel pump. (A fuel strainer bypass indicator is located inside the left fire access and ground cooling door. Strainer bypass is indicated by a red pop-up type button.) The fuel pump then delivers fuel under pressure to the main control unit. The basic control elements of this unit consist of an inlet guide and stator vane control unit, a bypass valve, an afterburner signal valve, and a metering valve. The inlet guide and stator vane control unit ports high pressure fuel to the inlet guide and stator vane actuators which position the vanes in proportion to engine speed and compressor inlet temperature. The bypass valve maintains a constant pressure to the metering valve by bypassing excess fuel back to the fuel pump inlet and controls actuating fuel pressure to open the afterburner ignition switch and the afterburner on-off valve. The metering valve automatically meters the optimum fuel flow for the particular flight condition (accelerating,

1-5

engine fuel control and variable exhaust nozzle system

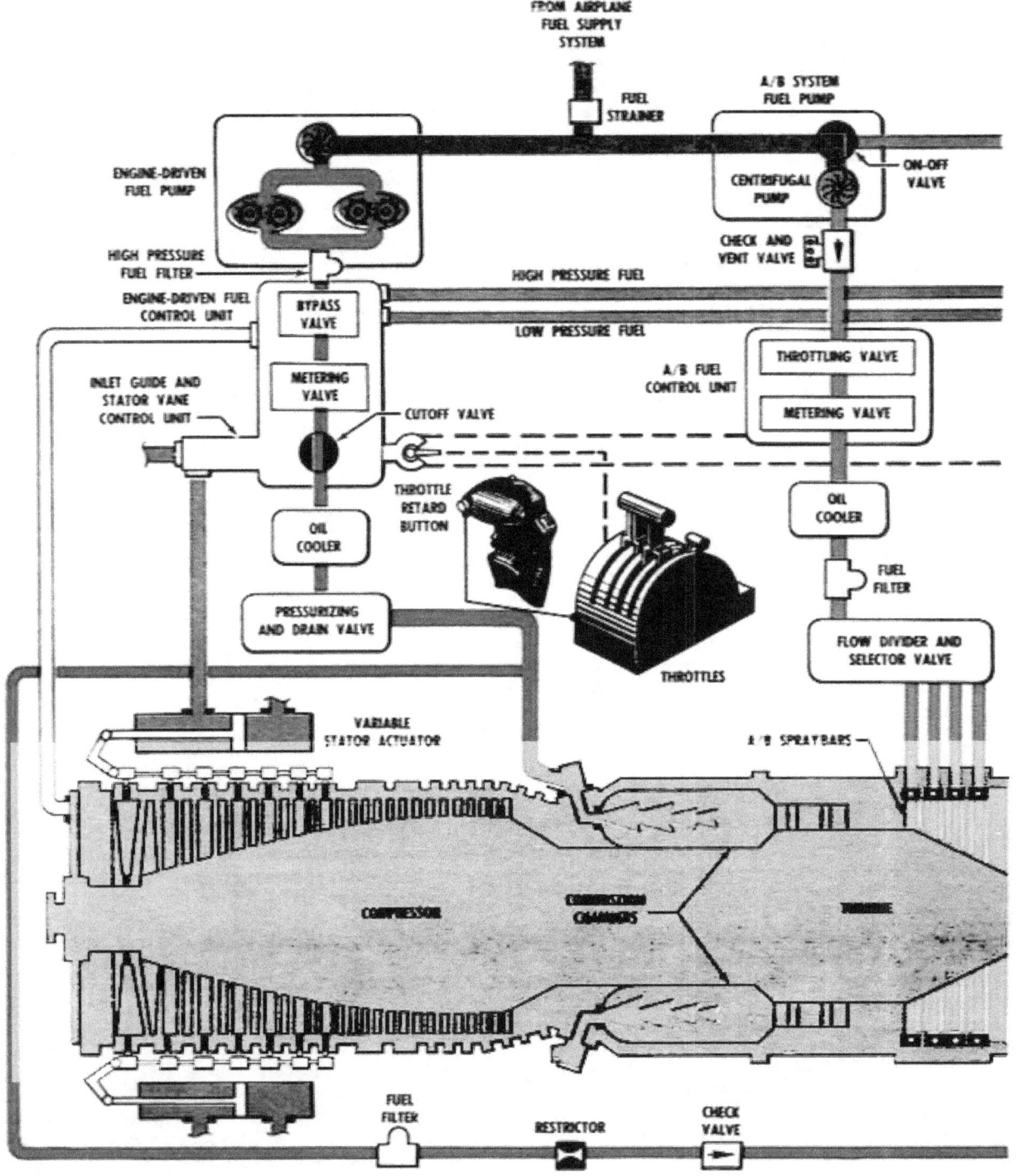

Figure 1-3. (Sheet 1 of 2)

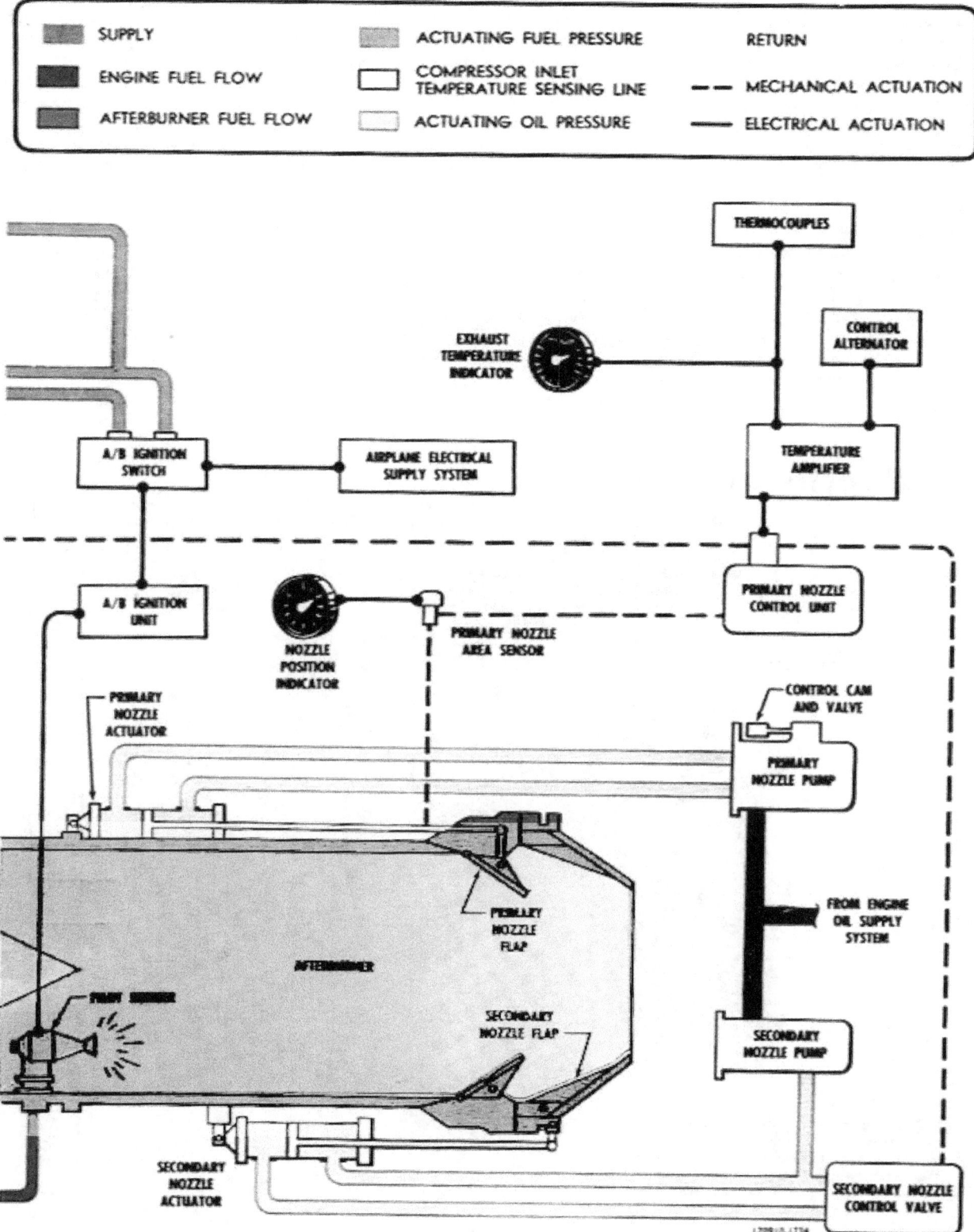

Figure 1-3. (Sheet 2 of 2)

decelerating, high altitude operation, etc.) in response to control signals received in terms of throttle position, engine speed, inlet air temperature, engine acceleration, and compressor discharge pressure. From the control unit the metered fuel flows first through an oil cooler, where it is used as the cooling medium, and then to the pressurizing and drain valve. This valve maintains pressure in the fuel control unit outlet line. The drain element of the valve serves to drain the engine burner manifold whenever the engine is shut down. From the pressurizing and drain valve the fuel enters the burner manifold, where it is directed to the nozzles. Each nozzle has an internal flow divider which sprays the fuel into the combustion chambers. The engine fuel control system also supplies fuel from the discharge side of the pressurizing and drain valve to the pilot burner for afterburner ignition. In addition to its normal function, the engine fuel control system incorporates a T_2 reset and cutback feature. The T_2 reset feature permits the engine to increase beyond rated engine speed (7460 rpm - 100 percent rpm) at high compressor inlet temperatures. The system consists of two temperature sensor elements. The compressor inlet temperature sensor converts inlet temperature variations into a mechanical signal to the engine fuel control system. The second sensor element compensates for temperature arising from the engine nacelle and produces a mechanical signal which opposes the compressor inlet temperature signal in the engine fuel control system. This combined signal is used by the engine fuel control system in establishing stator vane and acceleration fuel flow schedules, and in providing compressor inlet temperature resets of engine speed. An increase in engine speed beyond 100 percent is necessary to obtain air flow and thrust required for design speed. For additional information on T_2 reset and T_2 cutback, refer to "Engines", Section VII.

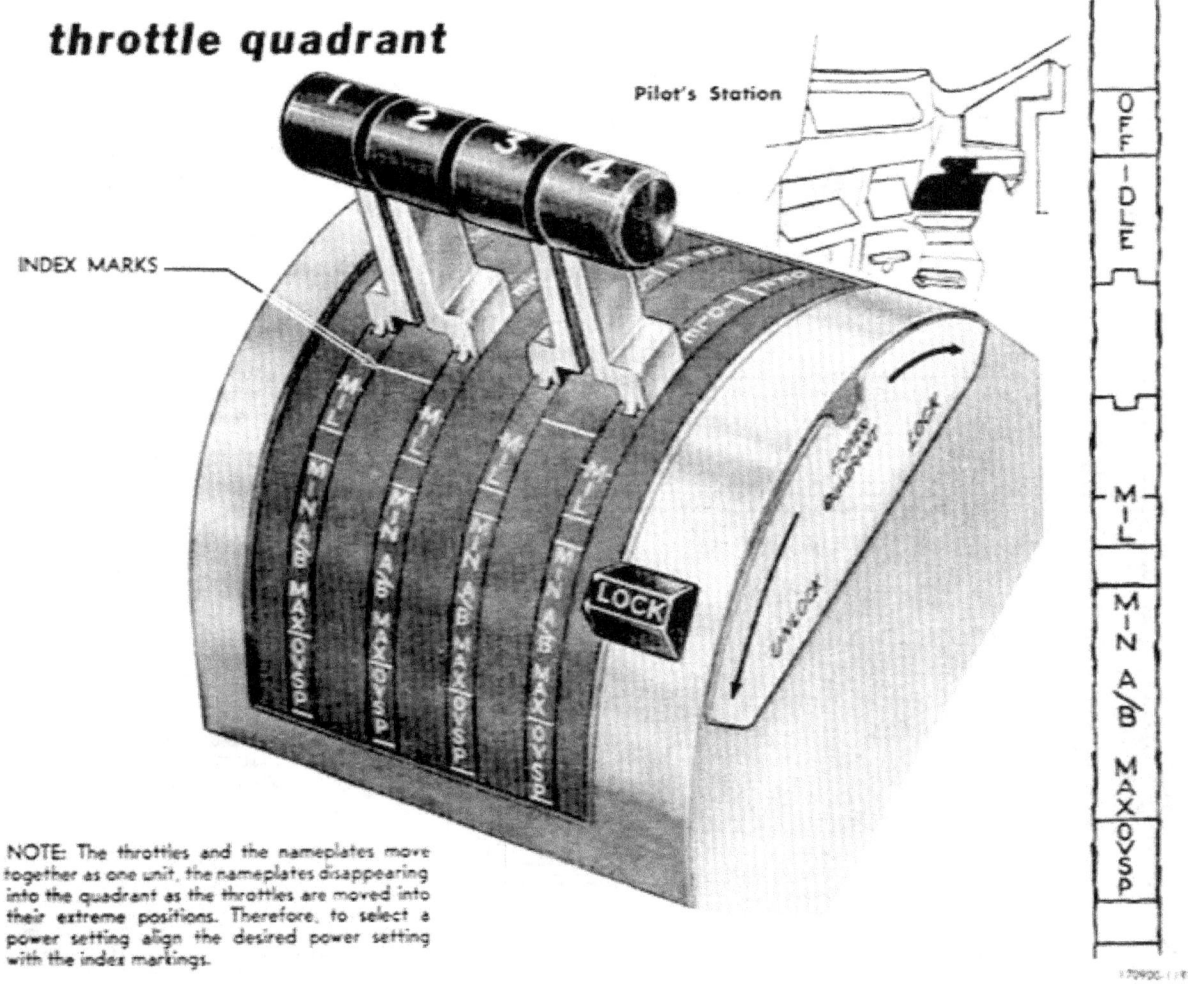

Figure 1-4.

Throttles.

Four throttles (figure 1-4), one for each engine, are located in a quadrant on the left side of the pilot's station. The throttles are mechanically linked to the control units of their respective engine and control engine speed, fuel flow, primary and secondary nozzle area, variable inlet guide and stator vane positioning, and afterburner operation. A throttle torque booster, installed on the input shaft side of the engine fuel control, aids in moving the throttles. Fuel pressures from zero to 900 psi are taken from the discharge side of the main fuel pump and routed to the torque booster. With no fuel pressure, the pilot must apply approximately 65 inch-pounds to the throttles for actuation. The quadrant is marked OFF, IDLE, MIL, MIN A/B, MAX A/B, and OVSP. Moving a throttle forward from OFF to IDLE mechanically opens the fuel cutoff valve in the engine fuel control unit. The ignition circuit is also energized for 75 ±10 seconds provided the corresponding engine start switch is in either the GROUND or AIR position. In order to restore ignition after 75 ±10 seconds have elapsed, the throttle must be retarded to OFF and then advanced to IDLE, or the engine start switch must be positioned to OFF and then to either GROUND or AIR. Advancing the throttle from IDLE to MIL increases engine speed from 67 to 100 percent rpm, closes secondary nozzle and positions the primary nozzle to maintain the required exhaust gas temperature for the power set. With an engine operating on the ground, rapidly advancing the throttle from IDLE to MIL causes the main fuel control to transmit a nozzle lock (off-speed) signal to the nozzle area control. This signal prevents the primary nozzle from closing on the mechanical schedule until engine rpm reaches 93.4 percent. At this point the signal ceases and the primary nozzle closes until the exhaust gas temperature (EGT) rises enough to cause temperature limiting to begin functioning. During this transit period, back pressure on the turbine increases, causing engine rpm to increase at a slower rate. Due to this condition, military thrust range may be reached prior to attaining military rpm. This is indicated by the leveling-off of fuel flow and obtaining military EGT and nozzle position. The engine should accelerate from IDLE to MIL thrust range within five seconds (at 16°C ram air temperature) from the time the throttle is advanced to the MIL position. As the throttle is moved from the MIL position through the afterburner transition range, it is raised through the action of a cam to indicate that afterburner operation is being initiated. When the throttle is passing through this range, a pressure signal opens the afterburner on-off valve, and permits fuel at airplane booster pump pressure to flow to the afterburner fuel pump. Minimum afterburner operation occurs when the throttle reaches the MIN A/B position. Advancing the throttle toward MAX A/B increases the number of afterburning fuel outlets until maximum fuel flow and afterburner power is reached at the MAX A/B position.

Moving the throttle into the OVSP position allows the engine to overspeed to 103.5 ±0.5 percent rpm providing the ram air temperature is above 10-16 degrees centigrade. However, this does not provide additional thrust to the engines until a higher ram air temperature is obtained. Thrust supplied by the engines in manual overspeed at temperatures below this particular ram air temperature is actually less than that in MAX A/B. The throttles must be raised and pushed forward before they can be placed in the OVSP position. The engines are stopped by placing the throttles in the OFF position. A stop is provided at the IDLE position to prevent inadvertent moving of the throttles to OFF. The throttles must be raised approximately 1/2 inch before they can be placed in the OFF position.

CAUTION

To prevent the possibility of jamming the throttle(s) against the cam and track assembly, the throttle(s) must not be raised when advancing the throttle(s) from the IDLE position or retarding the throttle(s) from the MAX A/B position.

Note

Throttle movement is controlled by the autopilot during the constant mach-altitude mode of automatic flight control. This control can be overridden by the pilot if required. For information on automatic control, refer to "Autopilot System," Section IV.

On engines 1, 2, and 3, the a-c generators are taken "off the line" when the respective throttle is retarded below idle. The throttle schedules the secondary nozzle open during idle and afterburner operation and closes the secondary nozzle as the throttle is moved through approximately 85 percent rpm toward the military range.

Throttle Lock Lever. The throttles are prevented from creeping by a lock lever (figure 1-4) located on the throttle quadrant. When the lever is in the UNLOCK position, the throttles are free to move. Moving the lever forward toward the LOCK position applies an increasing amount of friction to hold the throttles in the desired position.

Section I
Description

Throttle Retard Button. A guarded throttle retard button (1, figure 1-29) is located on the left side of the control stick grip to give the pilot the capability of reducing power while capsulated. To prevent inadvertent actuation of the throttles under critical conditions, the capsule doors must be closed before power is furnished to the circuit. When the button is depressed, power is furnished to drive a 115-volt a-c motor located under the throttle quadrant. Releasing the button breaks the circuit so that the pilot may stop the throttles where he desires. The motor unlocks the throttles in the motor's first 10 degrees of travel and then simultaneously retards all throttles to cruise power. This reduces engine rpm to approximately 91 percent. When the throttles reach cruise position, a microswitch opens to de-energize the circuit. The pilot can regain control of the throttles, when the capsule doors are opened, by manually moving the throttles to the desired position.

VARIABLE EXHAUST NOZZLE SYSTEM.

Each engine is equipped with a variable exhaust nozzle system (figure 1-3). The system controls the exhaust area to provide optimum thrust and specific fuel consumption for varying engine operating conditions. It also protects the engine from overheating. The system consists mainly of primary and secondary nozzle flaps, a primary nozzle control unit, primary and secondary nozzle pumps and actuators, thermocouples, a temperature amplifier, a control alternator, and a secondary nozzle control valve. The primary and secondary nozzle pumps, using oil from the oil supply system, supply hydraulic pressure for nozzle actuation. Each primary nozzle control unit and respective engine throttle is mechanically interconnected and synchronized so that throttle movement will automatically result in proper actuation of the primary nozzle. However, an electrical control is superimposed upon the mechanical linkage to prevent engine overheating. The temperature amplifier, acting through the primary nozzle control unit, automatically increases the nozzle area as necessary, regardless of throttle setting, to prevent turbine outlet over-temperature. Normally, at powers below military, the turbine outlet temperature has little effect on the primary nozzle area; however, at military power and above, turbine outlet temperature is the principal factor in determining the area. In the afterburner range, primary nozzle area is used to set power; however, fuel flow should also be monitored. An engine driven control alternator, independent of the airplane electrical power supply system, supplies a-c power to the temperature amplifier. The secondary nozzle flaps are used to provide maximum thrust and reduce drag during the cruise and military operating ranges. They are opened during idle and afterburner engine operation, and are closed for operation in the cruise and military ranges. This is accomplished automatically by throttle movement.

Nozzle Position Indicators.

Four nozzle position indicators (17, figure 1-5) are located on the right side of the pilot's main instrument panel. These instruments indicate the primary nozzle position in percent of travel of a teleflex cable which is used to transmit a feedback signal from the nozzle actuating pistons to a synchro transmitter. The nozzle position indicator is actuated by electrical signals from the synchro transmitter. The transmitter measures nozzle position over a range from 50 to 100 percent open only, since the nozzle is 50 percent open at its maximum closed position. The indicator dial is marked in ten equal major graduations from zero to 10. Indicator readings of approximately zero and 7.5 percent indicate that the nozzle is at its maximum closed and open positions, respectively. There are no indicators for the secondary nozzle positions; however, a momentary fluctuation may be noted on each engine oil pressure indicator when the nozzle moves to either the open or closed positions. The nozzle position indicators are used to set power when operating with afterburner. The indicators operate on 115-volt a-c power.

VARIABLE INLET GUIDE AND STATOR VANE SYSTEM.

The inlet guide vanes (IGV) and stator vanes of the compressor's first six stages are variable positioning to provide optimum engine performance throughout the engine speed range. The inlet guide vanes act as an inlet air metering device which controls the amount of air entering the compressor. The variable stator vanes are positioned so that at a particular engine speed and compressor inlet temperature the inlet air strikes the vanes at the most efficient angle of attack. The IGV and variable stator vanes are mechanically linked together externally and operate in unison. They are automatically modulated by the engine fuel control unit as a function of engine speed and compressor inlet temperature. In response to these factors, the inlet guide and stator vane control unit directs high pressure fuel to the two actuators which hydraulically position the vanes to their scheduled position. A mechanical feedback linkage transmits actual vane position to the servo piston in the main fuel control unit, thus eliminating vane angle error or overtravel of the vanes. The inlet guide and stator vane control unit is an integral part of the main engine fuel control unit. For additional information, refer to "Inlet Guide and Variable Stator Vane Operation," Section VII.

T.O. 1B-58A-1

Section I
Description

pilot's main instrument panel (typical)

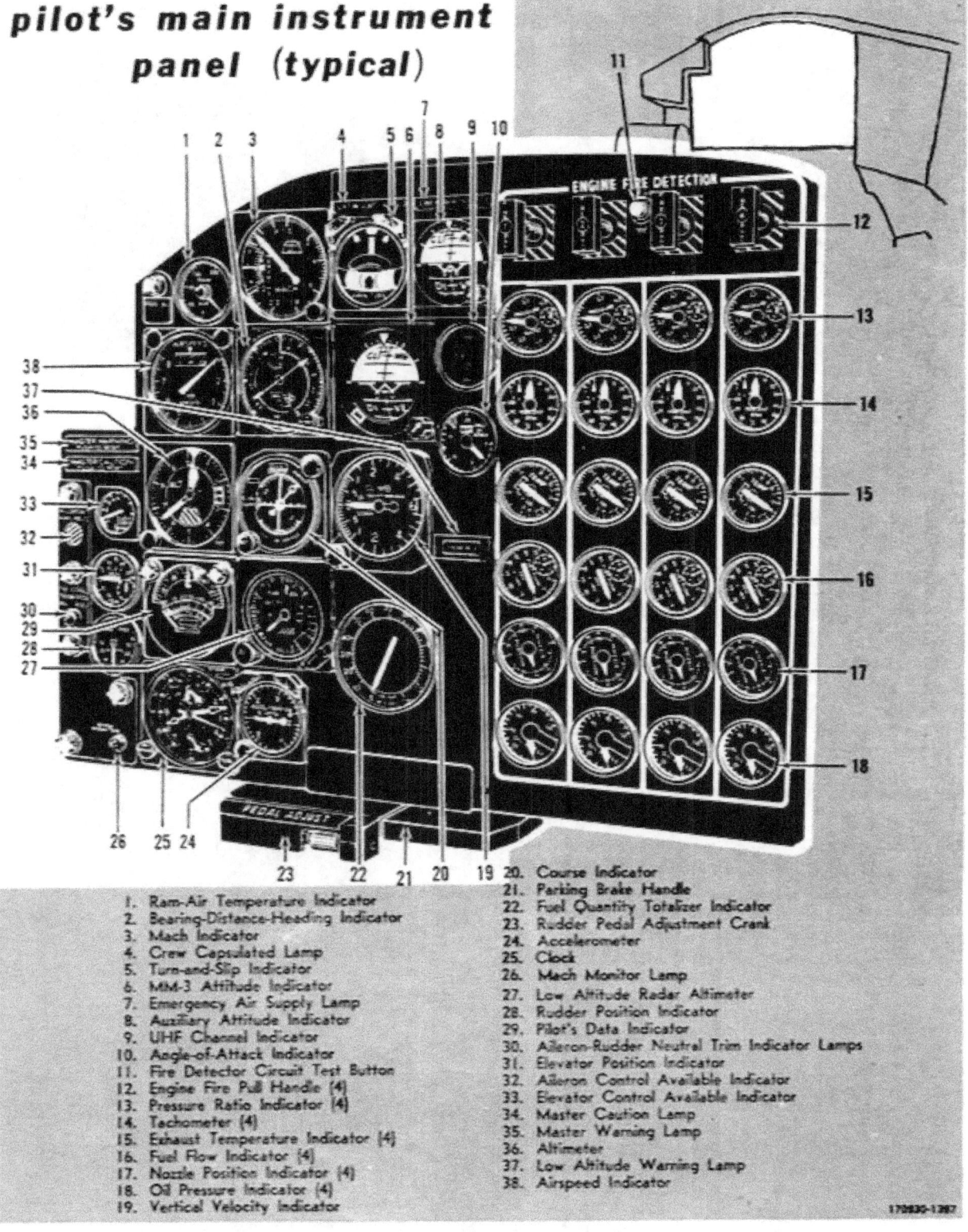

1. Ram-Air Temperature Indicator
2. Bearing-Distance-Heading Indicator
3. Mach Indicator
4. Crew Capsulated Lamp
5. Turn-and-Slip Indicator
6. MM-3 Attitude Indicator
7. Emergency Air Supply Lamp
8. Auxiliary Attitude Indicator
9. UHF Channel Indicator
10. Angle-of-Attack Indicator
11. Fire Detector Circuit Test Button
12. Engine Fire Pull Handle (4)
13. Pressure Ratio Indicator (4)
14. Tachometer (4)
15. Exhaust Temperature Indicator (4)
16. Fuel Flow Indicator (4)
17. Nozzle Position Indicator (4)
18. Oil Pressure Indicator (4)
19. Vertical Velocity Indicator
20. Course Indicator
21. Parking Brake Handle
22. Fuel Quantity Totalizer Indicator
23. Rudder Pedal Adjustment Crank
24. Accelerometer
25. Clock
26. Mach Monitor Lamp
27. Low Altitude Radar Altimeter
28. Rudder Position Indicator
29. Pilot's Data Indicator
30. Aileron-Rudder Neutral Trim Indicator Lamps
31. Elevator Position Indicator
32. Aileron Control Available Indicator
33. Elevator Control Available Indicator
34. Master Caution Lamp
35. Master Warning Lamp
36. Altimeter
37. Low Altitude Warning Lamp
38. Airspeed Indicator

Figure 1-5.

1-11

Section I
Description

T.O. 1B-58A-1

pilot's left sidewall console

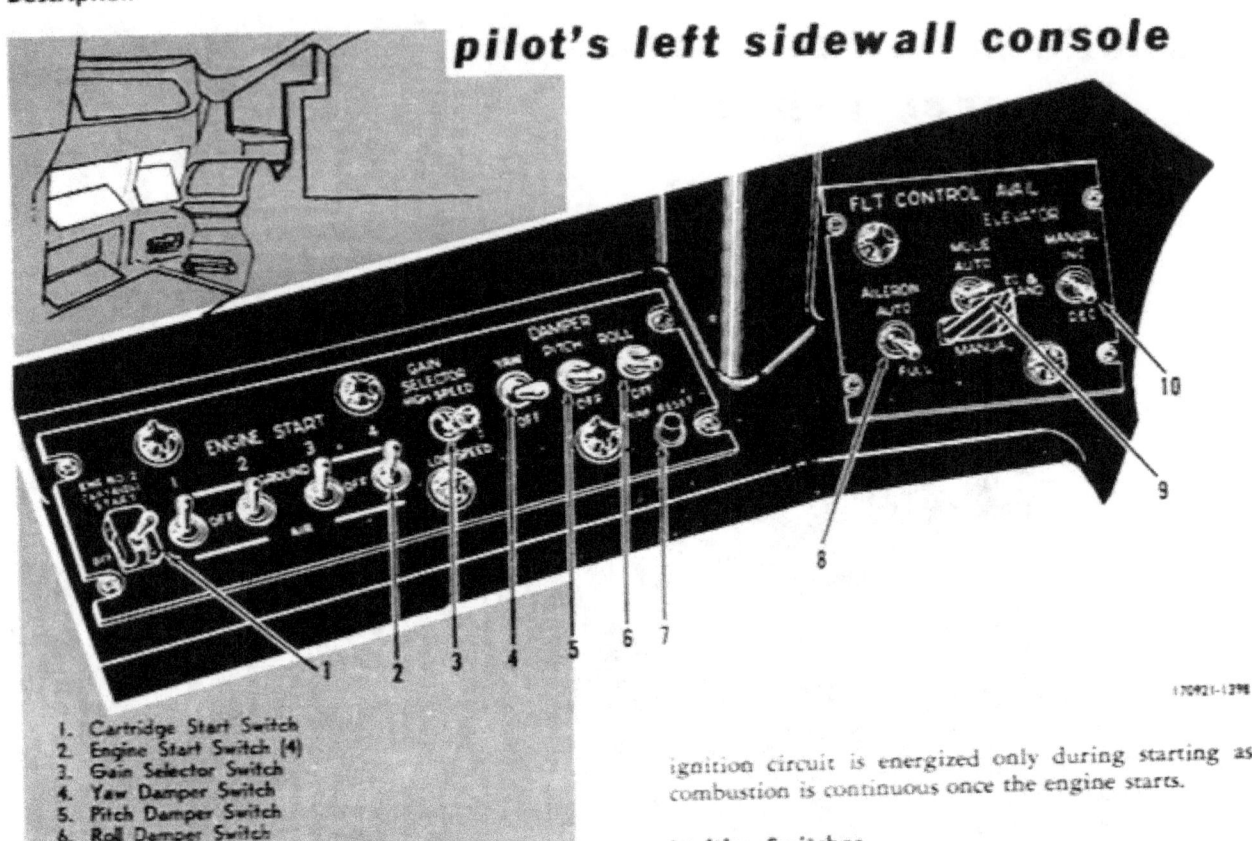

1. Cartridge Start Switch
2. Engine Start Switch (4)
3. Gain Selector Switch
4. Yaw Damper Switch
5. Pitch Damper Switch
6. Roll Damper Switch
7. Yaw Reset Button
8. Aileron Control Available Switch
9. Elevator Control Available Mode Selector Switch
10. Elevator Control Available Manual Adjust Switch

Figure 1-6.

MAIN IGNITION SYSTEM.

Each engine is equipped with two separate ignition systems—one main and one afterburner. (For information on afterburner ignition, refer to "Engine Afterburner System" of this section.) The main ignition system is a single-type, low-tension, capacitor discharge system. It consists of an ignition-relay, an ignition unit, a spark plug, a time delay relay, and an ignition switch actuated by the throttle. Power for ignition is obtained from the 28-volt d-c essential bus. Moving a throttle to the IDLE position completes a 28-volt d-c circuit from the ignition switch to the ignition relay, provided the corresponding engine start switch is actuated. The ignition relay supplies 28-volt direct current from the essential d-c bus to the ignition unit. This unit delivers high-voltage direct current to the spark plug in the No. 4 combustion chamber. The time delay relay, located in the circuit between the ignition switch and the ignition relay, automatically de-energizes the ignition relay after 75 ±10 seconds of continuous operation. This feature prevents the overheating of the ignition coils in the ignition unit if the start switch is inadvertently left energized. The

ignition circuit is energized only during starting as combustion is continuous once the engine starts.

Ignition Switches.

Four ignition switches, one for each engine, are located in the throttle quadrant and are actuated by throttle movement. Electrical power to the switches is controlled by the engine start switches. With an engine start switch positioned to GROUND or AIR, advancing the corresponding throttle to the IDLE position or beyond completes the ignition circuit and supplies high-voltage direct current to the spark plug in the No. 4 combustion chamber.

ENGINE STARTER SYSTEM.

The engines are started by means of a pneumatic starter system, or, engine no. 2 may be started by either a pneumatic or a cartridge starter system. When the pneumatic starter system is utilized an external source of compressed air is required. The system is designed so that the compressed air can be supplied from a ground cart to start any one or all of the engines. The system also provides for compressor bleed air from an operating inboard engine to be used in starting the remaining three engines. The system consists of four engine-mounted starters, four engine starter pressure regulating and shutoff valves, a receptacle located on the right side of fuselage below the wing leading edge for connecting the ground cart, and four engine start switches located at the pilot's station. The system also includes a cartridge start switch located at the pilot's station, a starter exhaust door, located near the bottom

1-12

of the no. 2 nacelle which must be unlatched before the engine can be started, (with start cart, bleed air, or cartridge starter) and an access door on the outboard side of the no. 2 engine nacelle for installing a cartridge in the starter. Four starter cartridges are stowed on the airplane in the crawlway immediately aft of bulkhead 3.0. The warm air manifold of the air conditioning system is used for directing the compressed air to the engine starters. Centrifugal switches control the starter valve to automatically disengage the pneumatic starter at approximately 47 percent engine rpm and the cartridge/pneumatic starter at approximately 37 percent engine rpm. Refer to "Engine Limitations," Section V, for limitations on the starter.

Engine Start Switches.

Four engine start switches (2, figure 1-6), one for each engine, are located on the pilot's left sidewall console. Each switch has three positions, marked AIR, GROUND, and OFF. When a switch is positioned to GROUND, 28-volt direct current is supplied to the starter relay. The energized relay directs 28-volt direct current to open the starter pressure regulating and shutoff valve. With the switch in this position, the ignition circuit is energized to the throttle ignition switch with 28-volt direct current. When the switch is placed to OFF, the starter valve closes, stopping starter operation; also, the ignition circuit is de-energized. The AIR position is used in flight to make a windmilling start and provides ignition only. When the switch is in this position, the ignition circuit is energized to the throttle ignition switches. With the start switch in the AIR or GROUND position, the ignition circuit will be de-energized after 75 ±10 seconds of continuous operation. In order to restore ignition, the throttle must be retarded to OFF and then advanced to IDLE, or the engine start switch must be positioned to OFF and then to either GROUND or AIR.

Cartridge Start Switch.

A cartridge start switch (1, figure 1-6) is located on the pilot's left sidewall console. The two-position toggle switch is marked OFF and ENG NO. 2 CARTRIDGE START. A guard prevents the switch from accidentally being placed in the START position. When the cartridge start switch is positioned to START, the No. 2 throttle to IDLE, and the No. 2 engine start switch is positioned to GROUND, 28-volt direct current energizes the cartridge start relay and ignites the starter cartridge, provided the starter exhaust door is unlatched. When in the OFF position, the switch does not interfere with normal operation of the engine start switches.

NACELLE COOLNG SYSTEM.

Secondary air for inflight nacelle cooling is provided by using part of the engine ram air. Ram air enters two scoops, located in the air inlet of each nacelle, and flows through bypass flaps and the hydraulic oil cooler and aft between the engine and nacelle to be expelled into the engine exhaust gases. During ground and low speed operation, secondary air for nacelle cooling is drawn in through two inward opening nacelle cooling and fire access doors by the pumping action of the ejector nozzle. At the same time, the lowered inlet pressure closes the flap valve at the rear of the hydraulic oil cooler and the bypass flap valves and opens the hydraulic oil cooler external door. This provides for hydraulic oil cooling under all nacelle pressure conditions and prevents reverse flow of air from the engine nacelle from going into the engine air inlet. The hydraulic oil cooler door and the two nacelle cooling and fire access doors are closed during flight by the differential air pressure across the doors. In addition, the nacelle heat during ground and inflight operations is reduced by routing seventeenth-stage seal leakage air overboard through two overboard dump openings, located on each side of the nacelle. The operation of the system is entirely automatic and no controls are provided.

ENGINE INSTRUMENTS.

Pressure Ratio Indicators.

Four pressure ratio indicators (13, figure 1-5) are located on the right side of the pilot's main instrument panel. These instruments give an indication of engine operation by showing the ratio of turbine outlet pressure to compressor inlet pressure. The indicators are used to set power when the afterburners are not being used. Inlet and outlet pressures are routed to a transmitter, located on the aft compressor case of each engine, where they are translated into an electrical signal. The signal is then transmitted to the indicator where it appears as a pressure ratio. The indicators operate on 115-volt a-c power.

Tachometers.

Four tachometers (14, figure 1-5), located on the pilot's main instrument panel, indicate engine speed in percent of military rpm (7460). The instruments receive power from tachometer generators which are mounted on the aft side of the rear gearcase; they are independent of the airplane electric system.

Fuel Flow Indicators.

The airplane is equipped with four individual fuel flow indicators (16, figure 1-5). The instruments are located on the pilot's main instrument panel and show fuel flow in pounds per hour. The indicators operate on 115-volt a-c power.

Fuel Flow Totalizer Indicator.

A fuel flow totalizer indicator reflects in pounds per hour the total fuel flow rate of all operating engines. The indicator is located on the DSO's main instrument panel (3, figure 4-66). It receives signals directly from the fuel flow transmitters and operates independent of the individual fuel flow indicators. In this manner, it

Section I
Description

will continue to read the total fuel flow rate in the event an individual fuel flow indicator becomes inoperative. The indicator operates on 115-volt a-c power.

Oil Pressure Indicators.

Four oil pressure indicators (18, figure 1-5) are located on the pilot's main instrument panel. They indicate oil pressure in pounds per square inch and operate on 28-volt a-c power.

Oil Low Level Caution Lamps.

Four oil low level caution lamps, one for each engine, are located on the pilot's caution lamp panel (figure 1-13). The caution lamps are marked OIL LOW 1, 2, 3, and 4 respectively. Each lamp will light when its respective engine oil level has been depleted to approximately one to two quarts. The lamps require 28-volt d-c power for operation.

Note

These lamps may light when electrical power is applied to the airplane. These lamps should go out when engines are started.

Ram Air Temperature Indicator.

A ram air temperature indicator (1, figure 1-5), located on the pilot's main instrument panel, indicates engine ram air temperature in degrees centigrade. This information is used when regulating airspeed so that excessive engine operating temperatures can be avoided. A resistance bulb-type probe located in the no. 2 engine ram air duct supplies control signals to the indicator. The indictaor operates on 28-volt d-c power.

Exhaust Temperature Indicators.

Four transistorized exhaust temperature indicators (15, figure 1-5), located on the pilot's main instrument panel, indicate turbine outlet temperature of each engine. Each indicator has a flag marked OFF that is visible when electrical power is removed from the indicator. The indicators operate on 115-volt a-c power and use 5-volt a-c power for integral lighting. In addition, 28-volt d-c battery power is connected thru a 115-volt a-c inverter to the number 2 engine EGT indicator, thereby furnishing a number 2 engine EGT indication for starting without the need for a generator or external power cart.

ENGINE AFTERBURNER SYSTEM.

Each engine is equipped with an afterburner system which provides an increase in engine thrust for maximum power. The afterburner system consists of an afterburner fuel control system, an ignition system, and the afterburner combustion section. The combustion section incorporates fuel spraybars and manifolds, a flame holder, a pilot burner, and a spark plug. Operation of the afterburners is controlled by the throttles. Moving the throttles through the afterburner transition range to MIN A/B initiates afterburner operation. For detailed information on the throttles, refer to "Engines" of this section.

AFTERBURNER FUEL CONTROL SYSTEM.

The afterburner of each engine is equipped with an independent fuel control system (figure 1-3). The system supplies fuel to the afterburner combustion section at a rate that varies between the minimum flow that will support afterburner combustion and the flow required to develop maximum thrust. Components of the system include an on-off valve, a centrifugal pump, a pilot burner, a check and vent valve, a fuel control unit, a flow divider and selector valve, and a partial burning and a full burning distribution system. The on-off valve is opened by fuel pressure from the engine fuel control unit as the throttle is advanced to the afterburner range. When the on-off valve opens, fuel is supplied to the afterburner fuel pump which in turn, supplies fuel to the afterburner fuel control unit. The pilot burner is supplied fuel continuously from the pressurizing and drain valve in the engine fuel control system, and therefore may continue to burn after initial A/B ignition and operation. The afterburner control unit meters fuel to the flow divider and selector valve as a function of throttle position and compressor discharge pressure. The flow divider and selector valve selects the spraybars of the partial or full burning distribution system according to the throttle position. The spraybars inject the fuel into the afterburner combustion section where it is ignited by the pilot burner. If the throttle is left at the point of switchover from the partial to the full burning distribution system, unstable afterburner operation may occur; therefore, the throttle should be moved through this range with a continuous motion. The check and vent valve aids in keeping the system primed when not in operation. It also allows fuel that seeps into the pumps to be vented overboard when the afterburner is not being used.

AFTERBURNER IGNITION SYSTEM.

The afterburner ignition system provides continuous ignition during afterburner operation. The system consists of an afterburner ignition switch, ignition unit, and a spark plug. When the throttle is advanced to the MIN A/B position and engine rpm is above 94 percent, the afterburner ignition switch is actuated by the fuel pressure differential between the on-off valve actuating line and the reference fuel pressure line. Both of these lines are connected to the ignition switch so that when afterburner operation is initiated, the pressure increase in the on-off valve actuating line will close the switch allowing 115-volt alternating current to flow to the ignition unit. This unit supplies continuous high-voltage direct pulsating current to the spark plug located in the pilot burner. The ignition system maintains a continuous flame in the pilot burner during afterburner operation.

OIL SUPPLY SYSTEM.

Each engine is equipped with an independent priority oil system which is contained within the engine nacelle. The operation of the system is entirely automatic and no controls are provided. The oil is used not only for engine lubrication and cooling, but it also serves as the actuating fluid in the variable exhaust nozzle system. In addition, on engines 1, 2, and 3 the oil lubricates and cools the constant-speed drive and a-c generator; it also serves as the working fluid in the constant-speed drive. The oil supply tank of each engine is installed around the upper right quadrant of the engine in the region of the front compressor case. The tank has a capacity of 4.5 gallons and adequate expansion space. For the oil specifications, see figure 1-47. The oil tank supplies oil to the engine, variable exhaust nozzle system and constant-speed drive unit on a priority basis so that any oil leakage in the constant-speed drive will not result in complete oil tank drainage. This is accomplished with an internal standpipe arrangement connected to the constant-speed drive oil supply line. Should a leak occur, in the constant speed drive system, the oil level in the tank will descend only to the level of the standpipe inlet allowing the remaining oil to circulate to the engine and variable exhaust nozzle system. Loss of oil quantity is normally indicated by the following sequence: generator frequency variation, generator abnormal caution lamp lights, oil low caution lamp lights, and low oil pressure indication. From the oil tank, oil flows to the constant-speed drive and to the two pressure elements of the gear-type oil pump. One element of the pump supplies oil to the variable exhaust nozzle system; the other element supplies pressurized oil for lubrication and cooling to the three main engine bearings, the transfer gear case and the rear gear case. During periods of peak demand, a crossover valve which connects the lines from the two pump elements will open and allow engine lubrication oil pressure to supplement the variable exhaust nozzle system. After the oil has passed through the engine bearings and gear cases and the exhaust nozzle system, it is scavenged by three pumps and returned to the oil tank through the main scavenge filter and two oil coolers. The oil supplied to the constant-speed drive is scavenged by the constant-speed drive scavenge pump, filtered and returned to the tank through the main scavenge filter and the two oil coolers. Under certain oil temperature conditions, the oil will bypass one or more of the coolers. In addition, a pressure relief valve, located in the bypass line connecting the constant-speed drive oil inlet and outlet lines, will open to allow oil to recirculate through the constant-speed drive in the event of excessive back pressure from the engine scavenge pumps. This produces a closed circulation that continues until the excessive back pressure is relieved and normal oil flow resumes. Deaeration of the scavenged oil takes place as the oil enters through the top and spills down the side of the tank. Each oil tank is pressurized by the scavenge pumps to reduce oil foaming and to insure a more positive flow to the oil pump and to the constant-speed drive. The pressure is maintained at approximately 3 to 4.5 psi above the ambient pressure at altitudes below 28,000 feet and at 5 to 6.5 psi above ambient pressure at altitudes above 28,000 feet. Up to 20,000 feet the pressurization is maintained by a tank pressurizing valve; above this altitude the tank valve is aided by a sump pressurizing valve. The tank pressurizing valve is mounted on the sump pressurizing valve which is located on the upper right side of the rear compressor casing. The sump pressurizing valve begins regulation at 20,000 feet and attains full regulation at 28,000 feet. The tank pressurizing valve also provides for venting ambient air into the tank during rapid descent. The oil system provides a continuous oil supply without flow interruption in any aircraft attitudes, including negative "G" conditions; however, only a maximum of 30 seconds negative "G" capability is provided. For information on the oil pressure indicators, refer to "Engines," this section.

INLET SPIKE SYSTEM.

A variable position inlet spike is located in each nacelle to maintain an efficient inlet airflow to the engine throughout the speed range of the airplane. At supersonic speeds, shock waves form at the engine air inlets. If the shock waves are not kept outside of the diffuser so that the air in the diffuser is subsonic, airflow to the engine will be greatly reduced. The inlet spike system prevents this from occurring by maintaining a constant ratio between two control pressures—a static pressure measured on the inner surface of the inlet lip and a total pressure measured on the spike tip. These pressures have no particular physical significance, but the ratio between them provides a sensitive means of controlling the inlet efficiency. The control system of each nacelle includes a transducer, an actuator, a control switch located at the pilot's station, and a control unit containing the amplifier and controlling relays of each of the four systems. Movement of the spike is forward and aft. During normal operation, control of this movement is completely automatic. The spike remains in the aft or retracted position until an airspeed of mach no. 1.42 is reached. At this speed, a switch in the air data computer closes and supplies a 28-volt direct current signal to the control unit, activating the system. The transducer receives the control pressures, computes their ratio, and produces an electrical error

Section I
Description

T.O. 1B-58A-1

pilot's lower left console (typical)

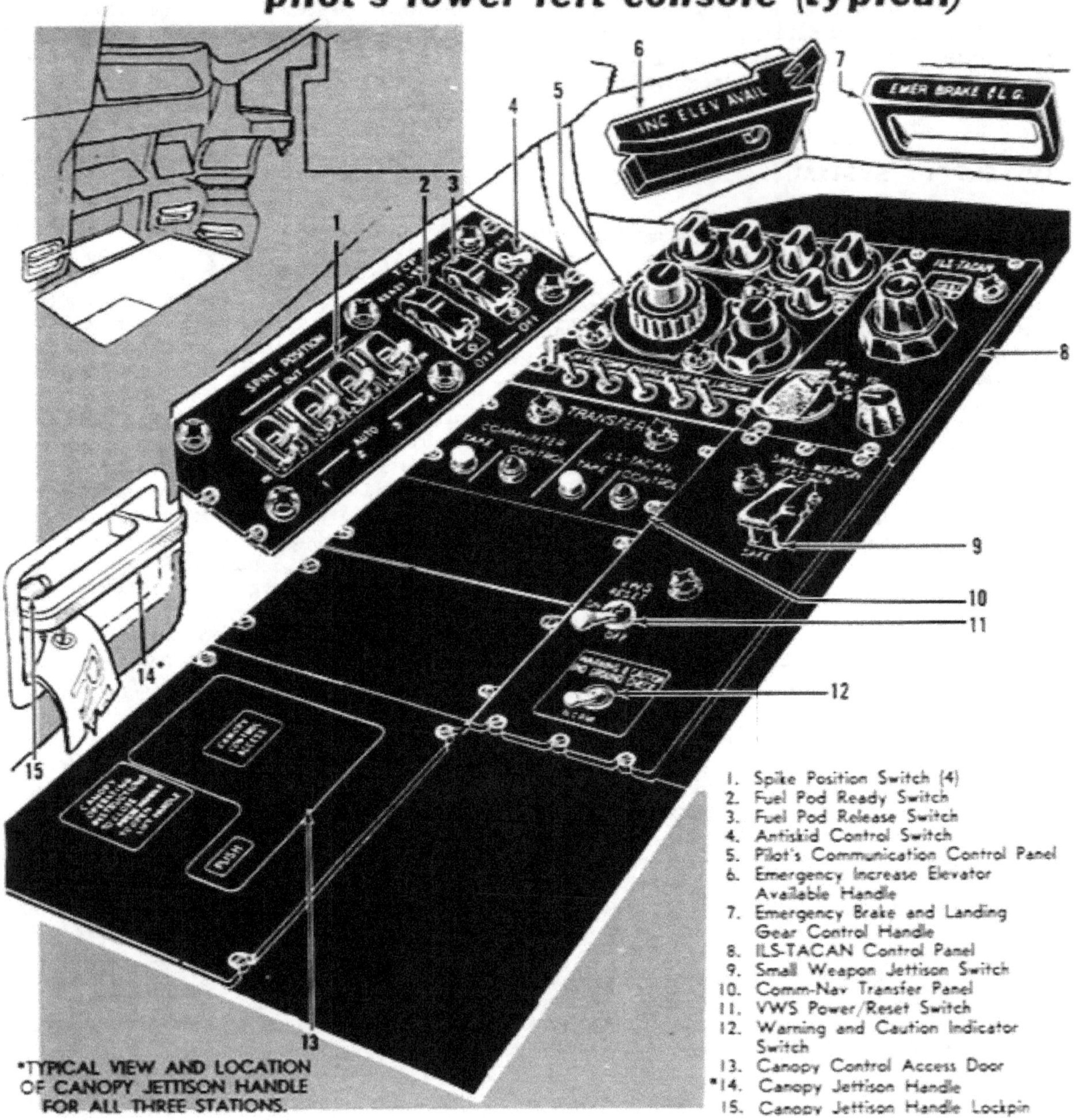

1. Spike Position Switch (4)
2. Fuel Pod Ready Switch
3. Fuel Pod Release Switch
4. Antiskid Control Switch
5. Pilot's Communication Control Panel
6. Emergency Increase Elevator Available Handle
7. Emergency Brake and Landing Gear Control Handle
8. ILS-TACAN Control Panel
9. Small Weapon Jettison Switch
10. Comm-Nav Transfer Panel
11. VWS Power/Reset Switch
12. Warning and Caution Indicator Switch
13. Canopy Control Access Door
*14. Canopy Jettison Handle
15. Canopy Jettison Handle Lockpin

*TYPICAL VIEW AND LOCATION OF CANOPY JETTISON HANDLE FOR ALL THREE STATIONS.

Figure 1-7.

signal when the computed ratio is incorrect. The amplifier receives the error signal from the transducer, amplifies it, and closes a relay which supplies 200-volt a-c power to the actuator. The actuator drives the spike in the proper direction. In event of malfunction in the automatic control system or engine during supersonic flight, the spike may be fully retracted by placing the spike position switch to IN. The positioning of the switch to OUT will be performed during ground maintenance only. No spike position indicators are provided.

SPIKE POSITION SWITCHES.

Four spike position switches (1, figure 1-7) are located on the pilot's lower left console. The switches have three positions marked AUTO, IN, and OUT. When a switch is in the AUTO position, the system is set up for automatic operation. In this condition, the system will become activated when an airspeed of mach no. 1.42 is reached. At speeds below mach no. 1.42, the spike will remain in its retracted position. Placing a switch

1-16

in the IN position moves its spike to the fully retracted position. The OUT position is a spring-loaded guarded position and is provided for ground checking purposes only (engine inoperative) except when following "Three Engine Subsonic Flight" emergency procedures, Section III. Holding the switch in the OUT position places the spike on the automatic schedule, but the mach no. 1.42 lockout is bypassed and the spike will extend. The spike position switch should be retained at the IN position during engine ground operations. Holding the switch to the OUT position will extend the spike and place an excessive structural load on the nacelle inner skin. This load is caused by the reduction in internal pressure resulting from the venturi effect (reduced flow area) with the spike extended.

FUEL SUPPLY SYSTEM.

The airplane is equipped with a fuel system (figure 1-8) which delivers fuel at booster pump pressure plus tank pressure to the fuel control system of the engines. The fuel system also transfers fuel as required for cg control. Fuel is contained in four airplane tanks and two pod tanks. Refer to figure 1-10 for fuel tank capacities. The fuel tanks of the airplane consist of a forward tank, an aft tank, a reservoir tank, and a balance tank. The forward and aft tanks each comprise a section of the wing and fuselage; the reservoir tank is located in the fuselage above the forward tank, and the balance tank is located in the aft portion of the fuselage. No provisions have been made to bullet-seal the tanks. Two types of booster pumps are used in the airplane and pod tanks. The forward tank has centrifugal-type pumps which have a single inlet while the aft, balance and reservoir tanks and both pod tanks have impeller-type pumps which have inlets at both the top and bottom. Fuel can be supplied directly to the engines from the aft, forward, and/or reservoir tank. The fuel supply in the reservoir tank is held on standby for direct engine supply if the pressure in either the right or left engine supply manifold drops too low to support the engines. Fuel in the balance tank and pod tanks cannot be supplied directly to the engine supply manifolds, but must be transferred to the aft, forward, and/or reservoir tanks for engine supply. Refer to Section VII for fuel management information. The fuel system is divided functionally into the following subsystems: engine supply, fuel transfer, vent and pressurization, fuel dump, fuel quantity measuring, single-point refueling, and air refueling. (Refer to Section IV for information on single-point and air refueling systems.) The system is operated from the fuel control panel (figure 1-11) at the pilot's station. Six fuel system maintenance test buttons, located on the upper exterior surface of the fuselage, provide a means of defueling the reservoir tank and for checking the operation of individual tank high level shut-off valves during refueling. For the specification of the fuel, see figure 1-47.

ENGINE SUPPLY SYSTEM.

The engine supply system delivers fuel at booster pump pressure plus tank pressure to the engines from the airplane forward, aft, and/or reservoir tank supply systems. Fuel is delivered to engines No. 1 and No. 2 through the left engine supply manifold and to engines No. 3 and No. 4 through the right engine supply manifold. A check valve in each engine supply manifold prevents total loss of aircraft fuel due to a fuel line break in the void area forward of the aft fuel tank. The two check valves are located in the manifold lines inside the aft fuel tank and prevent flow in these lines from the aft tank toward the forward and reservoir tanks. For identification, the fuel booster pumps are numbered 1 through 11. The forward tank supply system consists of booster pumps No. 1 and 2, and two booster pump low pressure caution lamps. The pumps are arranged so that booster pump No. 2 supplies the right manifold and booster pump No. 1 supplies the left manifold. In addition to supplying the engines, the forward tank pumps are used to transfer fuel to the balance and aft tanks for cg control. The aft tank supply system consists of booster pumps No. 6, 7, 8, and 9, and four booster pump low pressure caution lamps. The pumps are arranged so that booster pumps No. 8 and 9 supply the right manifold and booster pumps No. 6 and 7 supply the left manifold. In addition to supplying the engines, the aft tank pumps are used to transfer fuel to the forward tank for cg control. When the engines are being supplied from both the forward and aft tanks, booster pumps No. 6 and 7 supply the left engine manifold and booster pump No. 2 supplies the right engine manifold. The reservoir tank supply system consists of booster pumps No. 3, 4, and 5; right and left manifolds; and three booster pump low pressure caution lamps. Although the reservoir booster pumps can supply either the right or left manifold, the low pressure caution lamp for each is in conjunction with a specific manifold. Pumps 3 and 4 low pressure caution lamps operate from the left manifold and pump 5 low pressure caution lamp operates from the right manifold. Booster pumps No. 3 and 4 operate continuously, while booster pump No. 5 operates only when the right or left engine manifold pressure decreases to 19 ($\pm$1) psig. On airplane ㊲ ◆, at least

Section I
Description

T.O. 1B-58A-1

fuel supply system

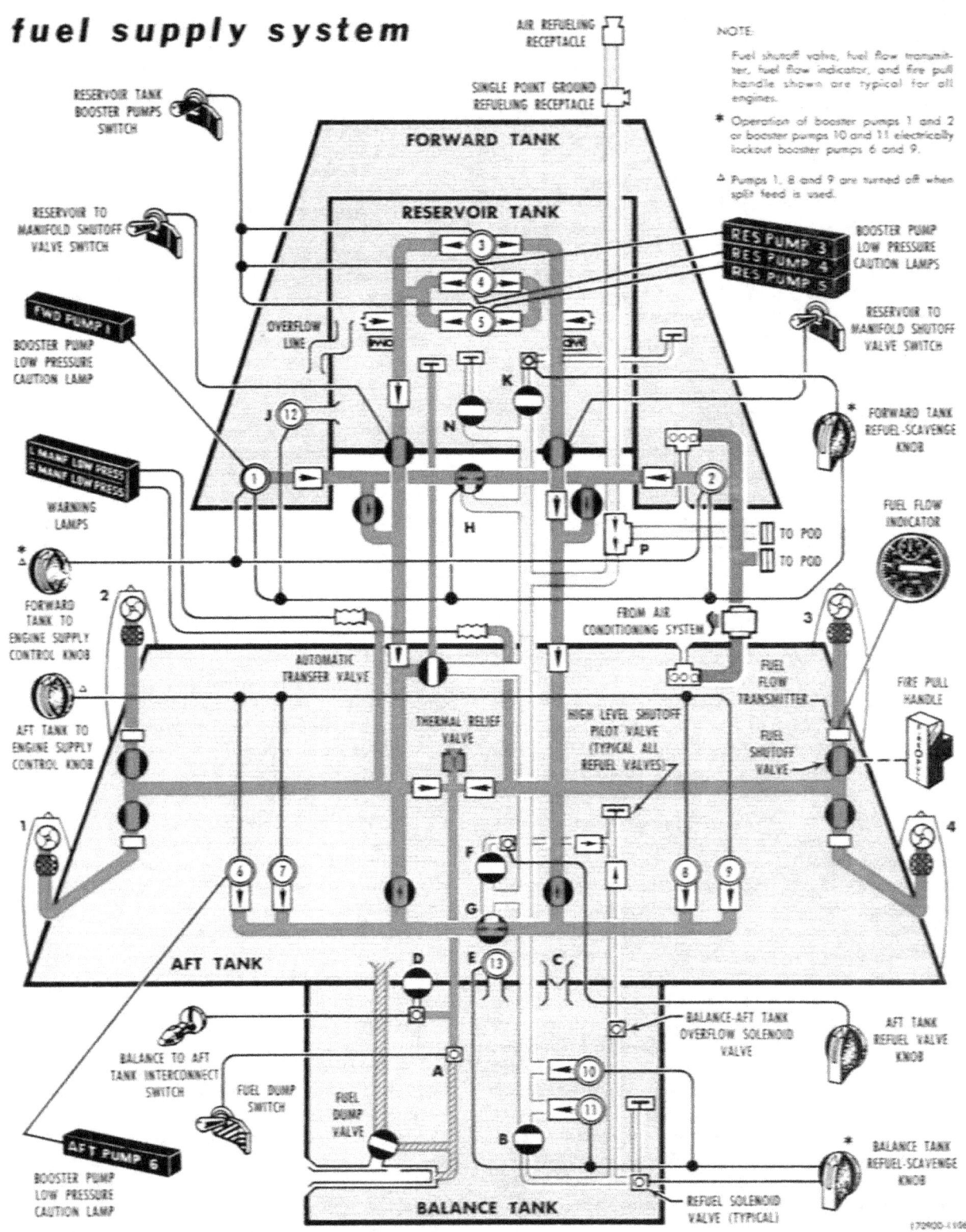

Figure 1-8. (Sheet 1 of 2)

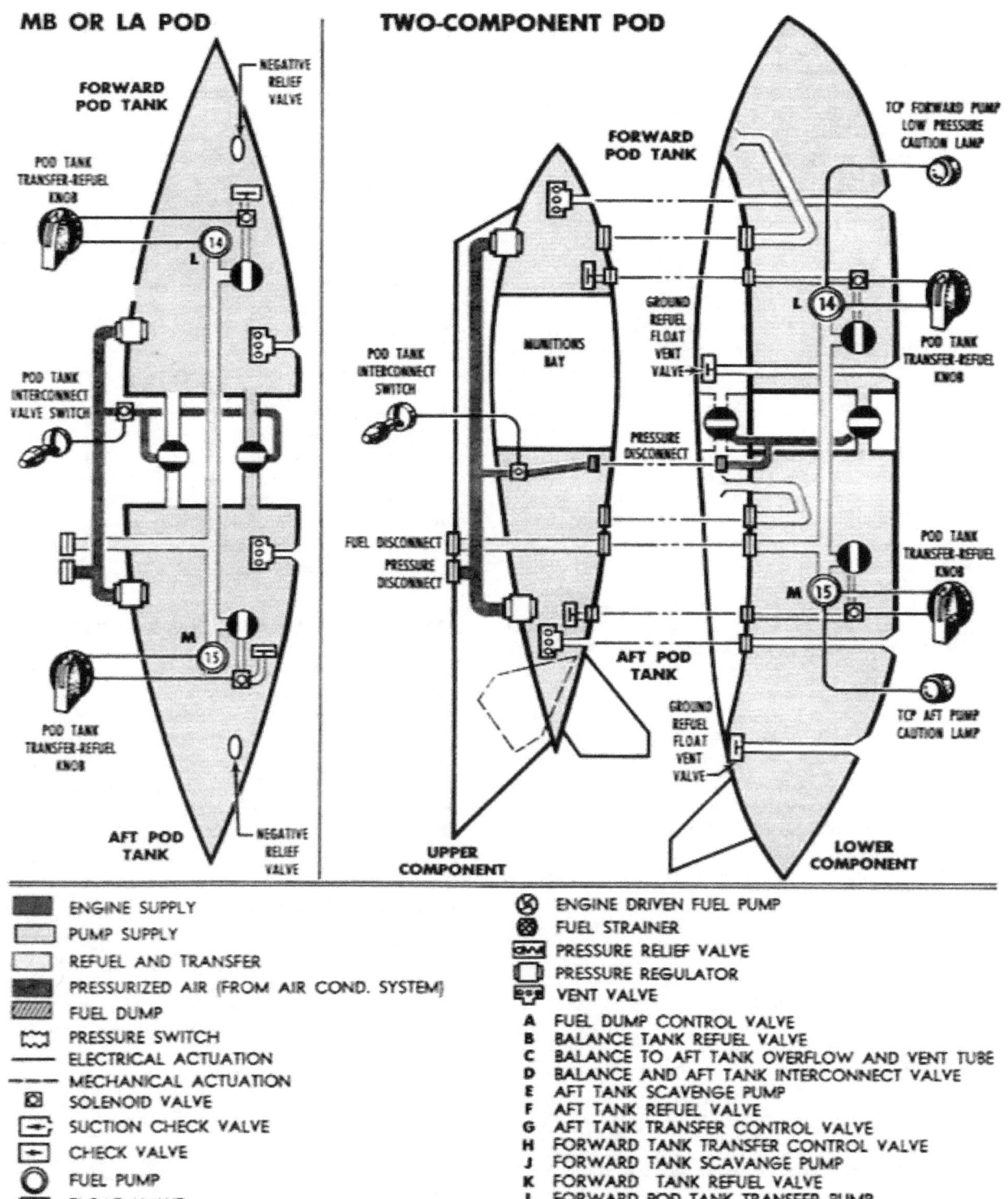

Figure 1-8. (Sheet 2 of 2)

Section I
Description

one reservoir to manifold switch must be in NORMAL to allow booster pump No. 5 to operate. This pump will come on regardless of pressure if both tanks to engine supply knobs are positioned to OFF and one or both reservoir to manifold switches are in NORMAL. The reservoir tank pumps insure a positive fuel supply to the engines during deceleration, descent, negative gravity conditions, or at any time engine supply manifold pressure drops too low to fulfill the engine requirements. Each reservoir manifold incorporates a pressure relief valve, a shutoff valve, a check valve, and a suction check valve. The arrangement of the pumps and reservoir manifolds is such that the upper outlet of pumps no. 3 and no. 4 and the lower outlet of pump no. 5 supplies the right manifold and the lower outlet of pumps no. 3 and no. 4 and the upper outlet of pump no. 5 supplies the left manifold. If the reservoir tank is not supplying the engines, fuel in the reservoir manifolds is recirculated back to the tank through the pressure relief valves. A shutoff valve in each reservoir tank manifold prevents loss of fuel from the reservoir tank if a break in an engine supply manifold should occur. The reservoir tank is automatically maintained full, and is the last fuel source to be depleted. In the event of total loss of electrical power, fuel is introduced by tank pressure into the reservoir tank manifolds through the suction check valves in sufficient quantities for the engine-driven fuel pumps to sustain afterburner operation of the engines at altitudes up to 6000 feet. Available fuel is limited to that in the reservoir tank plus any fuel that can be air pressure transferred from the forward tank. Refer to Section VII for the minimum forward tank fuel quantity available for air pressure transfer to reservoir tank at various deck angles. Antisuction valves incorporated in the engine supply manifolds prevent the suction of fuel or air from the forward and aft tanks in the event of electrical power failure. Four fuel shutoff valves, one for each engine, provide a means of shutting off the fuel to the engines in the event of a nacelle fire. The fuel shutoff valves are controlled by the engine fire pull handles. For additional information, refer to "Emergency Equipment" of this section.

FUEL TRANSFER SYSTEM.

The fuel transfer system is used for pod to airplane fuel transfer, reservoir tank automatic filling, center of gravity control, and fuel scavenging. For fuel system trouble shooting procedures refer to figure 7-11.

Pod-To-Airplane Fuel Transfer System.

The MB-1, LA-331A, and two component (BLU-2B) pod-to-airplane fuel transfer system is used to replenish fuel in the airplane forward, aft, and/or balance tanks.

The system consists primarily of two pod tank transfer-refuel knobs, two transfer pumps, a pod tank interconnect switch, and two pod tank interconnect valves. When either pod tank transfer-refuel knob is placed in the TRANS position, fuel in the pod is transferred to the airplane tanks preselected by the pilot. However, during a forward cg shift, the pod pumps are automatically locked out. In the event of a pod transfer pump failure, the interconnect valves between the two tanks may be actuated by placing the pod interconnect switch to INTERCONNECT. Pod pressurization air will open the two interconnect valves and allow fuel in the two tanks to seek a common level. Under these conditions, the remaining active transfer pump in the pod may be used to transfer fuel to the airplane tanks. Under certain conditions where crew compartment cooling air is not required, there is insufficient air pressure available at the pod air disconnect coupling to insure proper engagement. If the coupling is not engaged, there is no actuation air source available to the pod fuel tank interconnect valves. If pod tank interconnect switch is positioned to INTERCONNECT and there is no evidence of operation by a change of the pod fuel quantity gages, adequate air pressure can be supplied by operating the air conditioning system in the manual mode and selecting a colder temperature.

Reservoir Tank Automatic Filling System.

The reservoir tank automatic filling system, which consists of an automatic transfer valve and a float control valve, maintains the reservoir tank supply by several different methods with a different fuel quantity for each method. The following discussions explain the various filling methods and the approximate reservoir tank fuel quantities for each method. All quantities are for a ground attitude of —2.3 degrees unless otherwise specified.

Air Pressure Transfer. Fuel removed from the reservoir tank is replenished from the forward tank through the overflow-vent line. The transfer is accomplished from the forward tank by air pressure. Since the airflow-vent line maintains both tanks at the same pressure, transfer from forward to reservoir tank is initiated by the differential pressure caused by reducing the fuel quantity in the reservoir tank. Air pressure transfer will occur only as long as the overflow-vent-line in the forward tank is covered with fuel. The line is covered for forward tank fuel quantities greater than the following: approximately 19,000 pounds for a —2.3 degrees deck angle, approximately 12,900 pounds for a +2.5 degrees deck angle, and approximately 10,000 pounds for a +5.0 degrees deck angle. The reservoir tank fuel quantity will be 4100 to 4200 pounds.

1-20

center of gravity control system (typical)

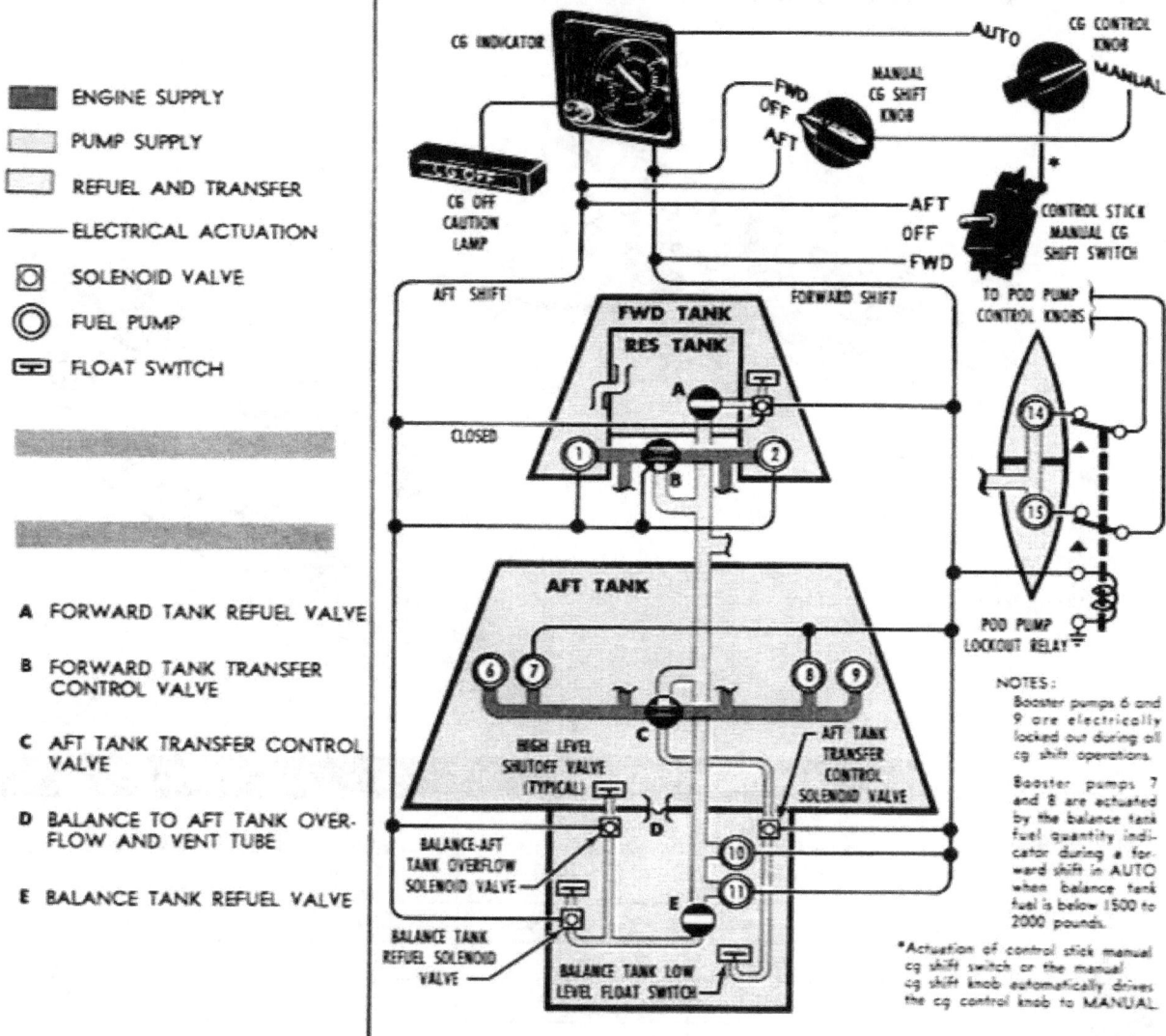

Figure 1-9.

Automatic Reservoir Filling. If air pressure transfer does not occur, fuel is routed into the reservoir tank through the autotransfer valve located in the line connecting the left engine supply manifold and the refuel manifold. Fuel will flow through the autotransfer valve into the reservoir tank if the left engine supply manifold pressure is greater than 18 ($\pm$1) psig and the reservoir fuel is below the float control valve. The autotransfer valve will close if the left engine supply manifold pressure drops below 18 ($\pm$1) psig. The float control valve will actuate, stopping the fuel transfer when the reservoir tank quantity reaches approximately 3600 pounds.

Refueling the Reservoir Tank. With the forward tank refuel-scavenge knob in the OFF position, fuel enters the reservoir tank from the refuel manifold through the refuel valve. The fuel source is from other airplane tanks or ground refueling. In this case, the reservoir tank fuel quantity will be determined by the high level refuel float which actuates at approximately 3900 pounds.

1-21

Section I
Description

T.O. 1B-58A-1

fuel quantity data

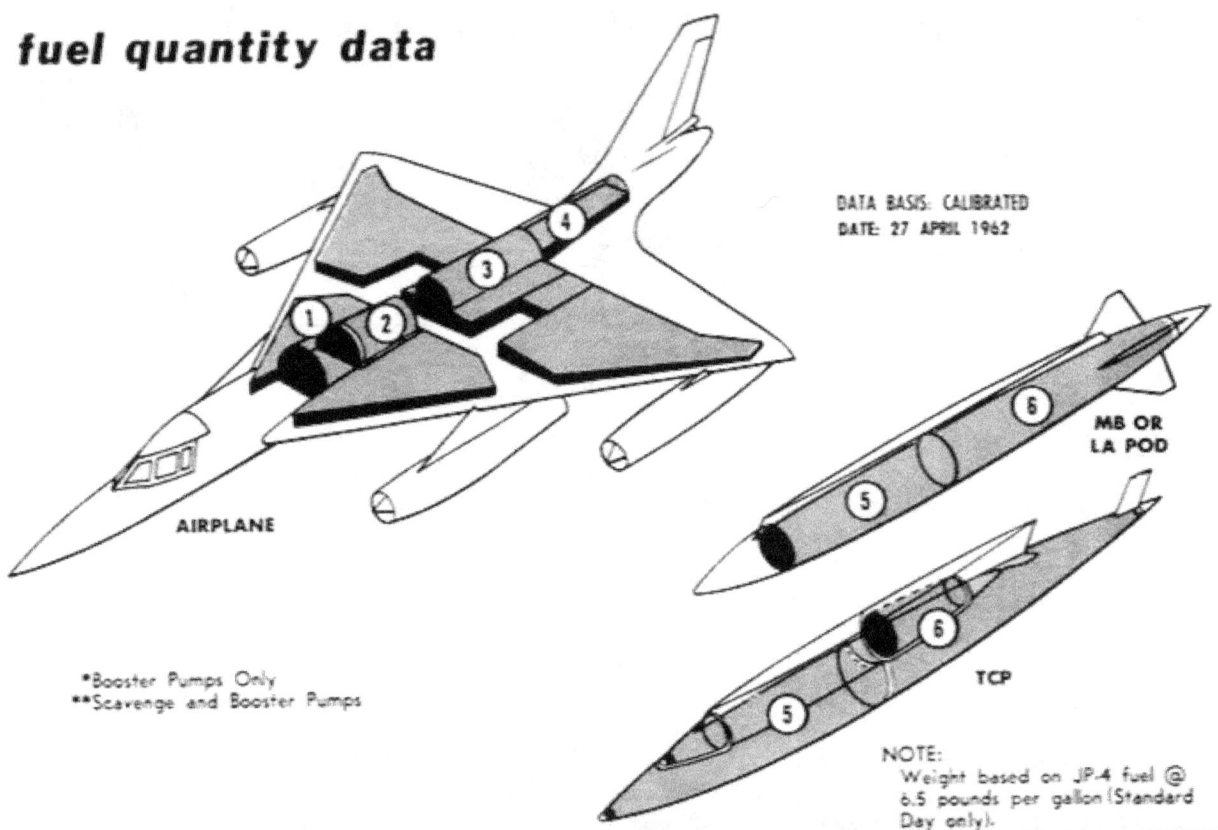

DATA BASIS: CALIBRATED
DATE: 27 APRIL 1962

*Booster Pumps Only
**Scavenge and Booster Pumps

NOTE:
Weight based on JP-4 fuel @ 6.5 pounds per gallon (Standard Day only).

	TANKS		GROUND-SERVICED				AIR-REFUELED			
			FULLY SERVICED IN GROUND ATTITUDE (2.3° Nose Down)		USABLE FUEL IN NORMAL FLIGHT ATTITUDE (2.5° Nose Up)		FULLY SERVICED AIR REFUELING ATTITUDE (6.5° Nose Up)		USABLE FUEL IN NORMAL FLIGHT ATTITUDE (2.5° Nose Up)	
			U. S. GALLONS	POUNDS	U. S. GALLONS	POUNDS	U. S. GALLONS	POUNDS	U. S. GALLONS	POUNDS
	FUEL LINES		103	672	32	211	120	781	32	211
AIRPLANE	1	FWD	3,202	20,811	*3,172 / **3,195	20,619 / 20,770	3,177	20,648	*3,147 / **3,170	20,456 / 20,607
	2	RES	610	3,963	607	3,945	640	4,163	638	4,145
	3	AFT	5,893	38,306	*5,816 / **5,884	38,000 / 38,245	6,122	39,794	*6,075 / **6,113	39,488 / 39,733
	4	BAL	1,219	7,925	1,206	7,839	1,261	8,195	1,248	8,109
MB OR LA POD	5	FWD	1,922	12,496	1,912	12,426	2,008	13,055	1,998	12,985
	6	AFT	2,250	14,625	2,244	14,585	2,306	14,991	2,300	14,951
TCP	5	FWD	1,844	11,988	1,837	11,941	1,870	12,154	1,863	12,107
	6	AFT	2,041	13,266	2,031	13,204	2,092	13,601	2,083	13,539

Figure 1-10.

Overflow. Once the reservoir tank is full, an overflow into the forward tank occurs. The overflow occurs during refueling or cg shifts. The amount of fuel in the reservoir tank when overflow occurs will be approximately 4100 to 4200 pounds.

Center of Gravity Indicating And Control System.

The location of the airplane center of gravity is controlled by transferring fuel either forward or aft. This may be accomplished automatically or manually. The system consists of a cg calibrator, a cg indicator, a cg repeater indicator, a cg system adjustment panel, a cg failure detector, a cg control knob, a control stick manual cg shift switch, a manual cg shift knob and various relays. These units operate in conjunction with components of the fuel system for transferring fuel forward or aft. The calibrator computes and displays the cg position in percent of the airplane mean aerodynamic chord (MAC). The cg indicating system electrically computes airplane cg in much the same manner as the weight and balance computer (cg slide rule). That is, certain constant values representing operational dry weight of the airplane, pod(s) and/or small weapons are set into the cg calibrator for a flight. (These compare to the basic moment index setting on the cg slide rule.) The calibrator also receives input signals from the fuel quantity indicators to compute changes in the cg due to use or transfer of fuel. The airplane values for weight and moment are manually set in by adjustment of two counters on the cg system adjustment panel (see figure 1-12).

Note

The numbers on the counters range from 000 through 999 to 000, the latter representing 1000. The numbers appearing on the counter have no direct relationship to the weight and moment. For example, 000 below 001 on the weight counter is equal to 53,000 pounds, and 000 above 999 is equal to 63,000 pounds. The moment adjustment is a function of the airplane operating weight and cg, relative to fuselage station 400, so the possibilities for variation are almost infinite.

When the pod selector switch is manually positioned to the proper pod setting, the pod dry weight values are set in automatically, upon attachment of the pod(s). In addition, values representing moment arms for the pod fuel are set in automatically. (This compares to the two sides of the slide of the balance computer, with the MB-1C on one side and the TCP on the other.) The small weapons values are also set in automatically, requiring no manual adjustment. Pod and/or small weapons inputs are then removed, automatically, by disengagement of the component. Two signals, representing fuel weight and mass, are fed from each of the pilot's individual fuel gages into the cg calibrator.

Summing networks in the calibrator add the weight signals to determine gross weight, and other networks determine moment from the fuel mass signal. The total moment is then electrically divided by the total weight and the result is displayed to the crew, expressed in percent MAC. An examination of the cg slide rule will show that the moment added by changing quantities of fuel in the tanks is non-linear and varies with attitude. The cg system compensates for non-linearity, but does not compensate for the variations due to attitude; all computations are at the single deck line attitude of 2.5 degrees nose up. The proven accuracy of the system is ±0.5 percent MAC (±0.6 percent MAC when the TCP or small weapons are attached), when compared to a machine calculation based on direct fuel gage readings and at plus 2.5 degrees deck attitude. When compared to the slide rule computations at +2.5 degrees nose up, the accuracy is ±0.8 percent MAC (0.9 percent with TCP or small weapons attached). At other attitudes between plus 0.5 and plus 6.5 degrees, demonstrations have shown that the system indication is accurate within ±1.5 percent MAC. At attitudes beyond plus 5.6 degrees, including equivalent attitudes due to acceleration and deceleration, there is a variable additional degradation, but not of sufficient magnitude to be cause for alarm. An additional error of ±0.2 percent MAC may occur at attitudes between 0.0 and 0.5 degrees.

Note

The values for chaff and ammunition are not included in the electrical computation of cg. Therefore, if ammunition and chaff are loaded the actual cg will be aft of the indicated cg. Normally, this error is negligible at high gross weights and will not exceed 1.0 percent MAC at low gross weights.

A cg failure detector and cg failed caution lamp are provided to detect and caution the pilot of a malfunction within the cg control system. When the cg failed lamp is lighted, automatic cg control is no longer possible, and the remainder of the flight must be accomplished in manual cg control.

Automatic CG Control. With the cg control system in the automatic mode, the cg indicator maintains the indicated cg within 0.5 ±0.1 percent MAC of the selected cg setting. A selector knob, located on the cg indicator provides a means of selecting the desired cg for a particular flight condition. If a cg is selected that is forward of the airplane cg, fuel will be transferred forward until the desired cg position is reached. Conversely, if a cg is selected that is aft of the airplane cg, fuel will be transferred aft. Fuel flows forward or aft in the same manner as during manual cg control except that the fuel transfer is automatically stopped. The cg repeater indicator is located at the DSO's sta-

Section I
Description

T.O. 1B-58A-1

fuel control panel (typical)

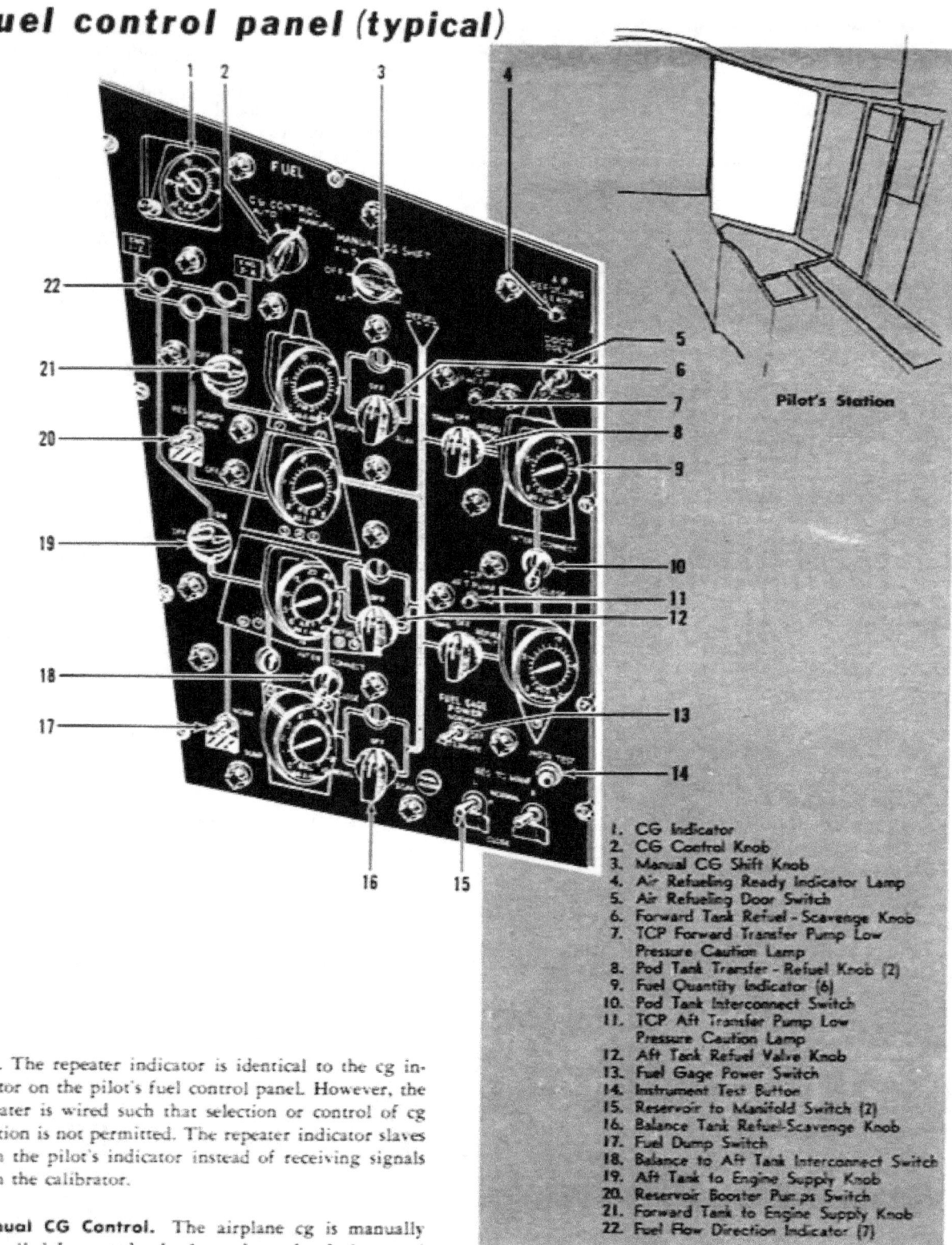

1. CG Indicator
2. CG Control Knob
3. Manual CG Shift Knob
4. Air Refueling Ready Indicator Lamp
5. Air Refueling Door Switch
6. Forward Tank Refuel - Scavenge Knob
7. TCP Forward Transfer Pump Low Pressure Caution Lamp
8. Pod Tank Transfer - Refuel Knob (2)
9. Fuel Quantity Indicator (6)
10. Pod Tank Interconnect Switch
11. TCP Aft Transfer Pump Low Pressure Caution Lamp
12. Aft Tank Refuel Valve Knob
13. Fuel Gage Power Switch
14. Instrument Test Button
15. Reservoir to Manifold Switch (2)
16. Balance Tank Refuel-Scavenge Knob
17. Fuel Dump Switch
18. Balance to Aft Tank Interconnect Switch
19. Aft Tank to Engine Supply Knob
20. Reservoir Booster Pumps Switch
21. Forward Tank to Engine Supply Knob
22. Fuel Flow Direction Indicator (7)

tion. The repeater indicator is identical to the cg indicator on the pilot's fuel control panel. However, the repeater is wired such that selection or control of cg location is not permitted. The repeater indicator slaves from the pilot's indicator instead of receiving signals from the calibrator.

Manual CG Control. The airplane cg is manually controlled by two knobs located on the fuel control panel: the cg control knob (2, figure 1-11) and the manual cg shift knob (3, figure 1-11), in addition to

Figure 1-11.

1-24

a manual cg shift switch located on the pilot's control stick (3, figure 1-29). For operation of this switch, refer to "Fuel System Controls and Indicators" of this section. With the cg control knob positioned to MANUAL and the manual cg shift knob positioned to AFT, booster pumps No. 1 and 2 will transfer fuel to the balance tank. If the balance tank becomes full before the desired cg is obtained, fuel will overflow into the aft tank, continuing to move the cg aft. The overflow and vent tube allows fuel to flow in only one direction from the balance to the aft tank. When the aft tank becomes full, transfer aft will cease. If fuel is transferred from the pod while the cg is being moved aft, the pod fuel will also be transferred aft. With the manual cg shift knob positioned to FWD and the aft tank to engine supply knob off, booster pump low pressure caution lamps No. 7, 8, 10, and 11 will blink and booster pumps No. 10 and 11 will transfer fuel through the forward tank refuel valve and into the reservoir tank. Fuel will then flow through the reservoir tank overflow line and into the forward tank. If the balance tank quantity becomes less than 1500 to 2000 pounds before the desired forward cg is attained, the aft tank transfer control valve will open allowing fuel in the aft tank to be transferred forward. The pod tank pumps are electrically locked out when the cg is being moved forward.

Scavenge System.

The scavenge system is used to scavenge fuel from the airplane forward and aft tanks to the reservoir tank. The system consists primarily of two scavenge pumps, associated tubing, and two tank scavenge switches. The system also utilizes the forward and balance tank booster pumps. The forward tank scavenge pump is located in the forward tank and has an outlet tube which extends into the bottom of the reservoir tank. The scavenge pump and forward tank booster pumps transfer fuel from the forward tank to the reservoir tank when the forward tank refuel-scavenge knob is positioned to SCAV. The aft tank scavenge pump is located in the aft tank and has an outlet tube which is routed into the balance tank. Placing the balance tank refuel-scavenge knob in the SCAV position energizes the aft tank scavenge pump and balance tank booster pumps. The scavenge pump transfers fuel from the aft tank to the balance tank where the balance tank booster pumps transfer the fuel to the reservoir tank.

VENT AND PRESSURIZATION SYSTEM.

The forward and aft tanks of the airplane and pod are provided with a vent and pressurization system to minimize vaporization. The reservoir and balance tanks are vented to the forward and aft tanks respectively and utilize the pressurization system. Pressurization of the tanks is accomplished by using air from the air conditioning system. The forward and aft tanks are equipped with a vent control valve which incorporates a pressure regulating valve. The regulating valve controls the flow of engine bleed air. When tank pressure is decreasing due to descent, transfer, or engine supply, sufficient air is introduced to hold the tank pressure at 5 psig. Whenever the tank pressure begins increasing due to climb, aerodynamic heating, or fuel transfer, the vent valve holds the tank pressure between 5 and 6 psig. Each vent valve also contains a float valve. When the vent valve is submerged in fuel due to the attitude of the airplane, the float valve prevents fuel from venting overboard until the tank pressure exceeds 11.5 psig. The vent control valve also provides the fuel tank with negative pressure relief and a high pressure relief valve. If the vent control valve becomes inoperative, the high pressure relief valve becomes independent to the vent control valve and will vent the tank when pressure reaches 12 psig. Each pod tank has an air pressure regulator valve that controls the air pressure. The regulator valve senses the pressure inside the tank. If the tank pressure drops below 4.4 psig the regulator valve will open and allow the tank pressure to build up to 4.7 psig. The regulator will then close. If the tank pressure builds up to 5 psig due to climb, refueling or aerodynamic heating, the vent control valve will open and relieve the tank pressure. The vent control valve will close when tank pressure has decreased to 4.75 psig. All pods are equipped with vent valves incorporating auxiliary relief valves. The auxiliary relief valve is a safety feature which will prevent damage to the pod if the vent valve fails to function normally. The auxiliary relief valves relieve pressure at 12 psig. If the airplane descends rapidly and the correct pressure cannot be maintained in the pod tanks, a negative relief valve in each tank will open and allow the tank pressure to adjust to ambient pressure. Operation of the system is completely automatic.

FUEL DUMP SYSTEM.

The fuel dump system provides an emergency means of reducing the gross weight of the airplane in flight. The system includes a control solenoid valve and a dump probe assembly. When it is necessary to jettison fuel, the control valve is opened by means of a guarded dump switch on the fuel control panel. The dump switch opens a control solenoid valve which allows engine supply manifold pressure to disengage the probe latch, to extend the probe, and to open the dump valve. The probe extends approximately two feet outward from the left side of the balance tank just aft of the

Section I
Description

T.O. 1B-58A-1

wing trailing edge. As the probe extends, it ruptures the thin cover over the dump probe port. When the probe reaches full extension, fuel in the aft tank is jettisoned by tank pressure and fuel head pressure. Any fuel that is desired to be dumped must be transferred to the aft tank. The dumping operation can be stopped any time by positioning the fuel dump switch to NORM. The probe can only be retracted manually and with the airplane on the ground.

FUEL QUANTITY MEASURING SYSTEM.

The fuel quantity measuring system is a capacitor-type indicating system which measures and indicates in pounds the quantity of fuel contained in the tanks of the airplane and pod. The system consists of capacitor-type tank units, six fuel quantity indicators, a fuel quantity totalizer indicator, and a transfer relay. In addition to indicating the individual tank fuel quantities, the system also totals and indicates, on the totalizer indicator, the number of pounds of fuel remaining in the airplane and pod tanks. The transfer relay consists of two relay units and two equivalent capacitors. When a pod is not attached to the airplane, the relays connect the capacitors into the pod indicator circuits to simulate empty tanks.

FUEL SYSTEM CONTROLS AND INDICATORS.

Tank to Engine Supply Knobs.

Two tank to engine supply knobs (19 and 21, figure 1-11), one for the forward tank and one for the aft tank, are located on the fuel control panel. The knobs have two positions marked ON and OFF. Placing either knob in the ON position supplies power to the respective tank booster pumps allowing one tank to supply both engine supply manifolds. Placing both knobs in the ON position supplies power to booster pumps No. 2, 6, and 7 so that the forward tank will supply the right manifold and the aft tank will supply the left manifold.

Reservoir Booster Pumps Switch.

A reservoir booster pumps switch (20, figure 1-11) is located on the fuel control panel. The switch has two positions marked NORM and OFF. Placing the switch in the NORM position energizes booster pumps No. 3 and 4 and supplies power to the left and right engine manifold pressure switches in the starting circuit of booster pump No. 5. Booster pump No. 5 will not become energized until the right or left engine supply manifold pressure decreases to 19 (±1) psig. On airplanes ⑰ ● at least one reservoir to manifold switch (15, figure 1-11) must be in NORMAL to allow booster pump No. 5 to operate.

Reservoir to Manifold Switches.

Two reservoir to manifold switches (15, figure 1-11), one for the right manifold and one for the left manifold, are located on the fuel control panel. The switches control 28-volt direct current to the manifold shutoff valves and have two positions marked NORMAL and CLOSE. Placing the switches in the NORMAL position opens the reservoir manifold shutoff valves allowing fuel in the reservoir tank to become available to the engine supply manifolds. Placing either switch in the CLOSE position isolates the reservoir tank from the respective engine supply manifold. The switches are guarded in the NORMAL position.

CG Control Knob.

A two-position rotary-type cg control knob (2, figure 1-11), located on the fuel control panel, is marked MANUAL and AUTO. In the MANUAL position, the knob directs 28-volt direct current to the manual cg shift knob contacts which control operation of the forward tank transfer control valve, aft tank transfer control valve, balance tank overflow solenoid valve, balance tank refuel valve, the forward tank refuel valve, and booster pumps 1, 2, 7, 8, 10, and 11. This enables fuel to be transferred forward or aft with the manual cg shift knob. In the AUTO position, the knob directs 28-volt direct current to the automatic cg control circuits which control operation of the components used to automatically transfer fuel either forward or aft. With the cg control knob in AUTO, placing either manual shift switch (on the control stick or on the fuel control panel) in the FWD or AFT position will automatically reposition the cg control knob from AUTO to MANUAL, and a cg shift will begin as selected. If automatic cg control is again desired after the manual shift has been completed, the cg control knob must be manually placed to the AUTO position.

Manual CG Shift Knob.

A three-position rotary-type manual cg shift knob, (3, figure 1-11), located on the fuel control panel, is marked FWD, OFF, and AFT. The knob is spring-loaded to the OFF position so that it must be held to the FWD or AFT position. The knob operates in conjunction with the cg control knob. With the cg control knob in the MANUAL position, the manual cg shift knob directs 28-volt direct current to the fuel system components which control the transfer of fuel either forward or aft. Placing the manual cg shift knob in the FWD position transfers fuel from the balance and aft tanks to the forward tank by energizing booster pumps No. 7, 8, 10, and 11; opening the aft tank transfer control solenoid valve and the forward tank refuel solenoid valve. However, the aft tank transfer control valve is prevented from opening until the fuel

1-26

level in the balance tank has decreased to approximately 1500 to 2000 pounds. At this point, fuel will bleed from the back side of the transfer control valve through the solenoid valve and the low level pilot valve, allowing booster pump pressure to overcome spring tension and open the poppet type valve. The FWD position also de-energizes the pod tank pumps and booster pumps No. 6 and 9. Placing the knob in the AFT position transfers fuel from the forward tank to the balance and aft tanks by opening the forward tank transfer control solenoid valve, the balance tank overflow solenoid valve, and the balance tank refuel solenoid valve; closing the forward tank refuel solenoid valve; energizing booster pumps No. 1 and 2 and de-energizing booster pumps No. 6 and 9. Opening the balance tank overflow solenoid valve allows the balance tank refuel valve to be controlled by the aft tank high level shutoff pilot valve. This prevents the balance tank refuel valve from closing when the balance tank becomes full. Fuel will then flow from the balance tank to the aft tank through the overflow and vent tube until the desired cg is reached, or until the aft tank becomes full. With the knob in the OFF position, the forward and aft tank transfer control solenoid valves, the forward and balance tank refuel solenoid valves, the balance tank overflow solenoid valve will close and booster pumps No. 10 and 11 will be de-energized. The OFF position also de-energizes booster pumps in the forward and aft tanks which are not being used to supply the engines.

Note

- The manual cg shift knob can be used to override the control stick manual cg shift switch in case of malfunction.

- If the cg control knob on the fuel control panel is in the AUTO position when the manual cg shift knob is actuated, the cg control knob will automatically drive to the MANUAL position, and a cg shift will begin as scheduled by the manual cg shift knob. If the automatic mode is again desired after the cg shift has been made, the cg control knob must be manually placed to the AUTO position.

Control Stick Manual CG Shift Switch.

A manual cg shift switch (3, figure 1-29) is located on the pilot's control stick. The switch has three positions marked FWD, OFF, and AFT, and is spring-loaded to the OFF position. The lock button, located in the center of the switch, must be depressed before the switch can be moved to either the FWD or AFT position. Whenever a cg shift is selected using the control stick manual cg shift switch, booster pump operation is the same as during an automatic cg shift.

Note

- If the cg control knob on the fuel control panel is in the AUTO position when the control stick manual cg shift switch is actuated, the cg control knob will automatically drive to the MANUAL position, and a cg shift will begin as scheduled by the control stick manual cg shift switch. If the automatic mode is again desired after the cg shift has been made, the cg control knob must be manually placed to the AUTO position.

- The control stick manual cg shift switch can be overridden by the manual cg shift knob on the fuel control panel.

- Should a malfunction occur, causing the control stick manual cg control switch to stick in either the forward or aft position, cg control may be regained by removing the cg control fuse from the 28-volt d-c power panel. With the cg control fuse removed, cg control is available in manual operation. Automatic cg control and the control stick manual cg control switch will be inoperative.

Pod Selector Switch Knob.

Prior to flight, the pod selector switch knob (figure 1-12), located on the cg system adjustment panel, must be in the correct position and need not be repositioned during the flight even upon release of the pod(s). The knob positions are marked and are to be used in conjunction with the pod configurations as follows:

Knob Position	Pod
OFF	Without Pod
1	MB-1 (with Warhead or Ballast) or LA-331A
2	TCP (BLU-2B) (with -39 Warhead)
3	TCP (BLU-2B) (with -53 Warhead or Ballast)

Positions 4, 5, and 6 are inoperative.

Note

- For use with upper pod only, with or without small weapons, the knob should be positioned to 2 or 3 as applicable for the warhead or ballast configuration.

1-27

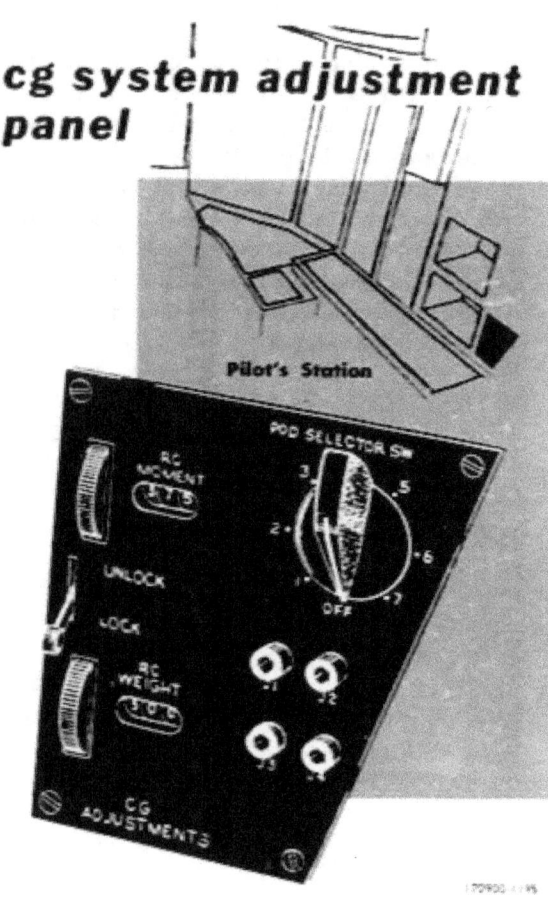

Figure 1-12.

● No adjustment of the knob is necessary for use with small weapons or the lower pod. The cg inputs are fed directly from the small weapon pylons or lower pod into the cg calibrator. The aft pylons have individual calibrator inputs and the forward pylons have a parallel input. That is, if either or both forward small weapons are attached, the cg calibrator input will be the same while an individual input is provided for each aft small weapon. The small weapon inputs to the cg calibrator are automatically removed when the small weapons are released.

Balance To Aft Tank Interconnect Switch.

The balance to aft tank interconnect switch (18, figure 1-11), with positions marked INTERCONNECT and CLOSE, controls a 28-volt d-c solenoid valve located on the balance tank. When the switch is in the INTERCONNECT position, the solenoid valve allows engine manifold pressure to open the interconnect valve which is located on the bulkhead separating the aft and balance tanks. This valve, when open, allows the fuel level in the aft and balance tanks to equalize.

Forward Tank Refuel-Scavenge Knob.

The forward tank refuel-scavenge knob (6, figure 1-11), located on the fuel control panel, has three positions marked REFUEL, SCAV and OFF. Placing the knob in the REFUEL position opens the forward tank refuel solenoid valve, allowing refueling pressure on the front side of the valve to overcome spring tension and open the refuel valve. Placing the knob in the SCAV position energizes booster pumps No. 1 and 2, and scavenge pump No. 12; opens the forward tank transfer control solenoid valve and closes the forward tank refuel solenoid valve. Fuel is then scavenged from the forward tank to the reservoir tank.

Balance Tank Refuel-Scavenge Knob.

The balance tank refuel-scavenge knob (16, figure 1-11), located on the fuel control panel, has three positions marked REFUEL, SCAV, and OFF. Placing the knob in the REFUEL position opens the balance tank refuel solenoid valve, allowing the refuel valve to be opened by manifold pressure. However, during air refueling, a float type switch in the aft tank prevents the balance tank refuel solenoid valve from opening before the aft tank becomes full. Placing the knob in the SCAV position energizes booster pumps No. 10 and 11, and scavenge pump No. 13; and closes the balance tank refuel solenoid valve. Fuel is then scavenged from the aft tank to the balance tank. From the balance tank, the fuel is then transferred to the reservoir tank by booster pumps No. 10 and 11.

Aft Tank Refuel Valve Knob.

The aft tank refuel valve knob (12, figure 1-11), located on the fuel control panel, has two positions marked REFUEL and OFF. Placing the knob in the REFUEL position opens the aft tank refuel solenoid valve, allowing manifold pressure to open the refuel valve. When the knob is positioned to OFF, the refuel valve closes and fuel flow into the tank is stopped.

Fuel Dump Switch.

The fuel dump switch (17, figure 1-11) is a two position switch marked DUMP and NORM. The switch is guarded and saftied in the NORM position. Placing the switch in the DUMP position opens the dump control solenoid valve which allows engine manifold pressure to actuate the dump probe assembly and to open the dump valve. Fuel is then dumped from the aft tank by tank pressure. The NORM position closes the dump control solenoid valve and stops the dumping operation. The probe cannot be retracted in flight.

Pod Tank Transfer-Refuel Knobs.

Two pod tank transfer-refuel knobs (8, figure 1-11), one for the forward tank of the pod and one for the aft tank of the pod, are located on the fuel control panel. The knobs have three positions marked TRANS, OFF and REFUEL-ONLY. When either knob is placed in the TRANS position, 28-volt direct current closes the respective pod refuel valve and the respective pod transfer pump is energized. This allows fuel in the pod tanks to be transferred to selected airplane tanks. Placing either knob in the REFUEL ONLY position, opens the respective pod refuel solenoid valve allowing refuel manifold pressure to open the refuel valve and refill the tank.

Pod Tank Interconnect Switch.

The pod tank interconnect switch (10, figure 1-11), with positions marked INTERCONNECT and CLOSE, controls the 28-volt d-c solenoid valve located in the pod pylon. When open, this valve allows air pressure from the pressurization system to open the two interconnect valves located on the bulkhead separating the forward and aft pod tanks. The lower valve, when open, allows fuel in the two tanks to seek a common level, and the upper valve allows air pressure in the two tanks to equalize.

Fuel Gage Power Switch.

A fuel gage power switch (13, figure 1-11), located on the fuel control panel, allows electrical power to be supplied to the fuel quantity and cg indicators from either the left or right a-c bus. The switch is a three position switch marked NORMAL, OFF, and ALTERNATE. Placing the switch in the NORMAL position supplies 115-volt a-c power to the indicators from the right a-c bus. Placing the switch in the ALTERNATE position supplies 115-volt a-c power to the indicators from the left a-c bus.

Instrument Test Button.

An instrument test button (14, figure 1-11) is provided for the fuel quantity indicators. The instrument test circuit is operative only when the cg control switch is positioned to MANUAL. When the button is depressed and fuel is in the tanks, movement of the indicator pointers toward zero indicates that the gages are functioning. Functioning of the totalizer indicator is indicated when the totalizer pointer follows the movement of the tank indicator pointers. The cg indicator may or may not move, dependent upon fuel loading conditions, when the instrument test button is depressed. If the cg indicator does move, the response time will be slow compared to the fuel gages and totalizer.

Note

Should the instrument test button fail or stick in the test position, all fuel gage indications will decrease to some intermediate position and the cg indicator will respond accordingly. Selecting "Auto" cg mode with CG control knob will remove power to the test circuit. The fuel gages and cg indicator will then function normally as long as the automatic cg mode is maintained.

Fuel Quantity Indicators.

Six fuel quantity indicators (9, figure 1-11), one for each tank of the airplane and the pod, are located on the fuel control panel and indicate the fuel quantity in pounds. An instrument test button is provided to test the operation of the indicators. All of the indicators require 115-volt a-c power only.

Note

- When a pod is released, capacitors are automatically connected to the affected indicator circuits to simulate empty tanks. These empty tank readings on the individual tank quantity indicators prevent the totalizer from giving erroneous indications.

- When electrical power to an indicator is interrupted for any reason, the pointer will remain in the position it was in before the power was interrupted. Since the totalizer gets its signals from the tank quantity indicators, power failure to an indicator will cause the totalizer to give an erroneous indication.

Fuel Quantity Repeater Indicators.

Six fuel quantity repeater indicators (4 and 5, figure 4-66), located on the DSO's main instrument panel, indicate the fuel quantity in each tank of the airplane and pod. These indicators are slaved directly to the pilot's indicators located on the fuel control panel and indicate to the DSO the individual tank fuel quantities in pounds. The repeater indicators should agree with the pilot's indicators within plus or minus one percent of full scale. The indicators operate on 115-volt a-c power only.

Fuel Quantity Totalizer Indicator.

A fuel quantity totalizer indicator (22, figure 1-5), located on the pilot's main instrument panel, indicates in pounds the total quantity of fuel remaining in the pod and airplane tanks. The totalizer indication should be within plus or minus 1300 pounds of the summation of the individual fuel gage readings. The system requires 115-volt a-c power only.

Section I
Description

T.O. 1B-58A-1

Note

When the indicator's electrical power is interrupted for any reason, the pointer remains in the position it was in before the power was interrupted.

CG Indicator.

A cg indicator (1, figure 1-11), located on the fuel control panel, indicates (in percent of the mean aerodynamic chord) the airplane center of gravity; and provides selection of the desired cg. The indicator has two pointers, a switching unit, and a selector knob. One of the indicator pointers shows the cg location. The other pointer is manually controlled with the selector knob, located on the face of the instrument. During automatic cg control, the desired cg is selected by adjusting this indicator pointer with the selector knob. The switching unit transmits signals to the fuel system for transferring fuel forward or aft as required to move and maintain the airplane cg at the selected position. When the preselected cg is obtained, the fuel transfer is stopped automatically. The airplane cg is maintained within 0.5 ±0.1 percent MAC of the selected cg setting. The cg indicator requires 115-volt a-c power and the switching unit requires 28-volt d-c power.

Note

The cg indication is based on the indicated fuel quantity and is computed from fuel moments at an airplane deck angle of plus 2.5 degrees.

CG Repeater Indicator.

A cg repeater indicator (7, figure 4-66), located on the DSO's main instrument panel, provides the DSO with an indication of the airplane cg location. The indicator has two pointers and a selector knob. One of the pointers shows the cg location and is slaved directly to the cg indicator on the fuel control panel. The repeater indicator and the pilot's indicator should agree within plus or minus 0.25 percent MAC. The other pointer is manually controlled with the selector knob and may be set to reference a desired cg; however, the pointer has no effect on automatic cg control. The indicator requires 115-volt a-c power.

Note

The repeater indicator is identical to the cg indicator on the fuel control panel except that the repeater indicator is not wired to control the cg.

Fuel Flow Direction Indicators.

Seven fuel flow direction indicators (22, figure 1-11), located on the fuel control panel, indicate routing of fuel for engine supply and transfer. When an indicator is energized it does not necessarily mean that fuel is flowing through the line as indicated, but only that the

system is electrically set up for flow in that direction. To determine if fuel is flowing as indicated it is necessary to monitor the respective fuel quantity indicator. The forward and aft tank to engine flow indicators operate whenever the selector knobs are positioned to ON. The reservoir tank to engine flow indicator operates whenever the reservoir pump switch is positioned to NORM, the reservoir to manifold switches are positioned to NORMAL and low manifold pressure requires fuel flow from the reservoir tank. The forward, aft, and balance tank refuel-transfer flow indicators operate only during cg shifts provided the flow direction is different from the selector knob positions. The indicators do not operate when the selector knobs are in REFUEL position and only the aft tank-balance tank flow indicator operates in the SCAV position. The aft tank-balance tank flow indicator also operates during aft cg shifts, whenever fuel overflows from the balance tank to the aft tank. The indicators operate on 28-volt d-c power.

Automatic CG Off Caution Lamp.

An automatic cg off caution lamp (figure 1-13), located on the caution panel, lights and displays "CG OFF" when the cg of the airplane is not within one percent of the desired location during automatic cg control. An additional automatic cg off caution lamp (6, figure 4-66) is located on the DSO's main instrument panel. The lamps may light when the cg is originally shifting to, but has not reached, the desired position, or when the cg is not maintained within $1 \begin{pmatrix} +0.3 \\ -0.1 \end{pmatrix}$ percent MAC of the selected setting. The opening differential of the switch which lights the lamps is 0.6 (±0.1) percent of MAC and is measured from the point where the lamps light toward the selected setting. For example, if the lamps light when the cg is precisely 1.0 percent MAC from the selected position, the lamps will remain lighted until the cg returns to between 0.5 and 0.3 percent of MAC from the selected value. The lamps are connected to the master caution lamp circuit and operate on 28-volt d-c power. For testing and dimming of the lamps, refer to the "Malfunction Indicator and Warning System" of this section.

CG Failed Caution Lamp.

A cg failed caution lamp, located on the pilot's caution lamp panel (figure 1-13), will light and display "CG FAILED" if the cg failure detector detects: (1) power failure to the pilot's cg indicator; (2) gear train failure or jamming of the gears within the pilot's cg indicator; or (3) degradation or loss of the amplifier within the pilot's cg indicator. When this lamp lights, automatic cg control is no longer possible. The cg failure detector cuts off 28-volt d-c power (for automatic cg control)

1-30

warning and caution lamp panels (typical)

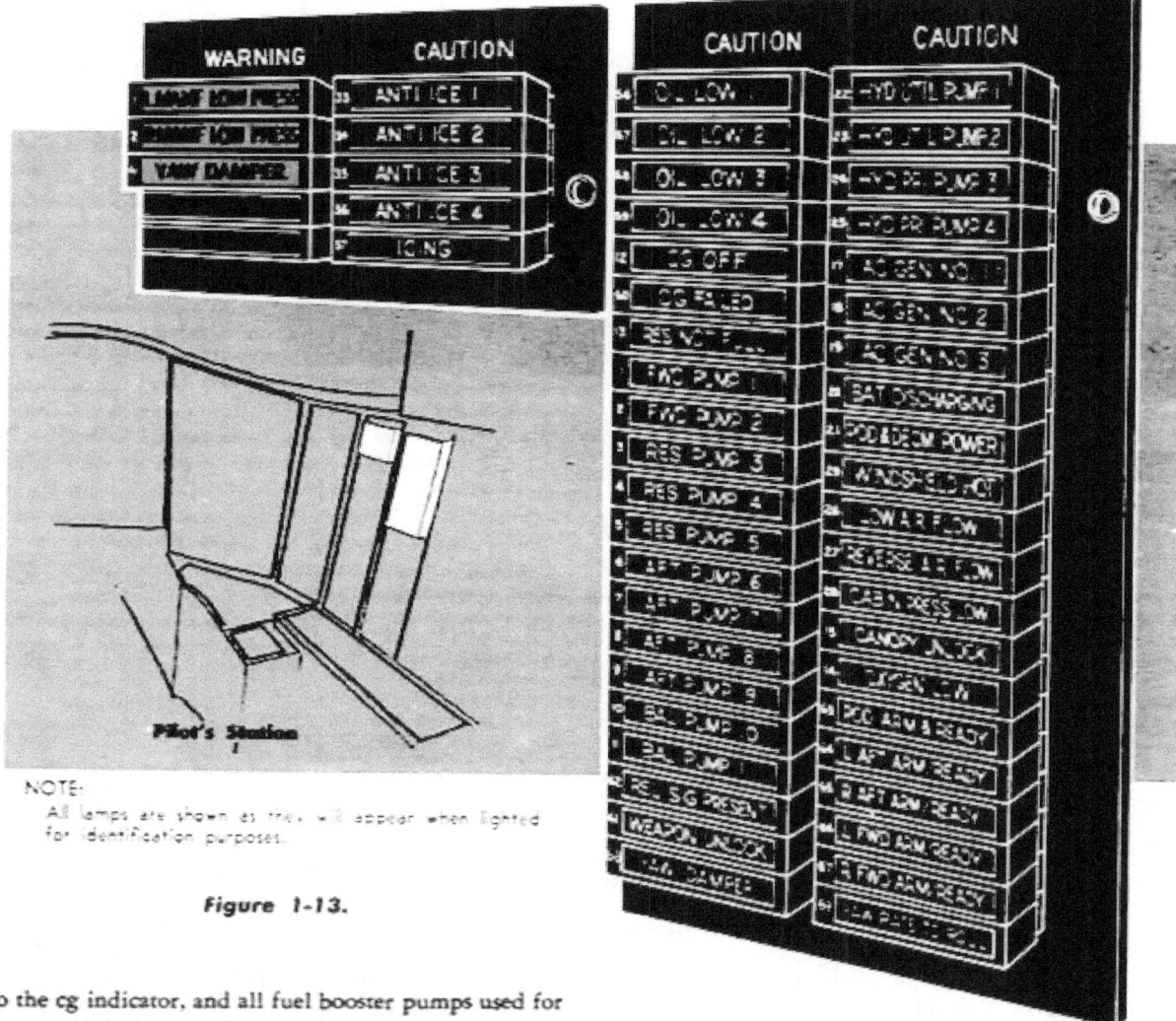

Figure 1-13.

to the cg indicator, and all fuel booster pumps used for automatic cg fuel transfers are de-energized. Fuel transfers are then possible only in manual cg control.

Manifold Low Pressure Warning Lamps.

Two manifold low pressure warning lamps (figure 1-13), located on the warning lamp panel, light and display "L MANF LOW PRESS" or "R MANF LOW PRESS" if the left or right engine supply manifold pressure drops below 11 ($\pm$.5) psi. The appropriate lamp will remain lighted until the manifold pressure increases to 13.5 psi. The warning lamps are connected to the master warning lamp circuit and operate on 28-volt d-c power. For testing and dimming of the lamps, refer to the "Malfunction Indicator and Warning System" of this section.

Booster Pump Low Pressure Caution Lamps.

Eleven booster pump low pressure caution lamps (figure 1-13), one each for pumps No. 1 through 11, are located on the caution lamp panel. Each lamp is operated by a fuel pressure switch which receives pressure from the discharge side of its respective fuel pump. The appropriate lamp will light when the discharge pressure of a booster pump falls below 10.5 ($\pm$.5) psig. The appropriate lamp will remain lighted until the pump discharge pressure increases to 12 psig.

1-31

Section I
Description

The caution lamps are connected to the master caution lamp circuit and operate on 28-volt d-c power. For testing and dimming of the lamps, refer to the "Malfunction Indicator and Warning System" of this section.

Note

Lighting of a booster pump caution lamp may also be due to a malfunctioning pressure sensing switch.

WARNING

Do not replace a blown booster pump fuse more than one time. Failure of a fuse more than once indicates a system malfunction which could result in fire or explosion. Qualified specialists should thoroughly check all electrical malfunctions associated with fuel tanks.

Pod Transfer Pump Low Pressure Caution Lamps.

Two pod transfer pump low pressure caution lamps (7 and 11, figure 1-11), one for each two component pod (BLU-2B) tank, are located on the fuel control panel. Each lamp is operated by a pressure switch located on the discharge side of the respective pump. The appropriate lamp will light when the discharge pressure drops below 10.5 ($\pm$0.5) psig. It will then remain lighted until the discharge pressure increases to 12 psig. The caution lamps are connected to the master caution lamp circuit and operate on 28-volt d-c power. These lamps are not energized when the MB or LA pod is installed. For testing and dimming of the lamps, refer to the "Malfunction Indicator and Warning System" of this section.

Reservoir Tank Not Full Caution Lamp.

A reservoir tank not full caution lamp (figure 1-13), located on the caution lamp panel, lights and displays "RES NOT FULL" when the reservoir tank fuel quantity has dropped below the full level. This level is approximately 3800 pounds for a deck angle of 14 degrees or 3200 pounds for a deck angle of −2.3 degrees. The lamp operates on 28-volt d-c power and is controlled by a float switch in the reservoir tank. The lamp is connected to the master caution lamp circuit. For testing and dimming of the lamps, refer to the "Malfunction Indicator and Warning System" of this section.

T.O. 1B-58A-1

ELECTRICAL POWER SUPPLY SYSTEM.

Electrical power for the airplane is generated by three engine-driven generators which supply 115/200-volt alternating current to an a-c bus network. The a-c buses supply power to eight d-c power units which deliver multiple voltages to a d-c bus network. A battery provides an emergency source of d-c power which can be connected to the 28-volt d-c essential bus with a battery switch. The a-c and d-c power systems are protected by fuses located in power panels (figures 1-16 through 1-19) at the navigator's and DSO's stations. Fuse location by airplane system is provided by figure 1-20. Spare fuses are provided for replacement in flight under favorable conditions of flight and accessibility. To aid the operator in locating fuses for a particular system, the fuse nameplates are color coded as follows: blue denotes electrical feeders, red denotes fuel system, green denotes engines and orange denotes autopilot, flight controls and air data system. All other fuse nameplates are gray. The letters A, B, and C on the a-c fuse nameplates denote the power phase to which the fuses are connected. Automatic and manual load-reducing features protect the a-c and d-c power sources in case of partial electrical failures. For ground operation, external power receptacles permit the use of an auxiliary power unit. Operation of the electrical power supply system is automatic when the electrical control panel is set up in the normal configuration.

A-C POWER SYSTEM.

Alternating current is distributed by the left and right main a-c buses. See figure 1-14. Each bus receives three-phase, 200-volt alternating current from a generator power source. The airplane is equipped with three oil-cooled, 40-KVA, 111-ampere generators driven by engines 1, 2, and 3. Each generator has an overload capacity of 166 amperes for five minutes. Each generator has a constant-speed drive which is connected to the engine by a drive shaft. The constant-speed drive maintains generator speed at 8000 rpm when engine speed is at idle or above. The generators are equipped with electro-mechanical constant speed drive decouplers. The decouplers enable continuing safe engine operation after a constant speed drive malfunction by decoupling the generator and drive assembly from the engine. Decoupling is accomplished mechanically by engine rotation and is electrically controlled from the pilot's station. Once decoupled, the decoupler cannot be reset inflight. In normal operation, the No. 1 generator energizes the left main a-c bus, the No. 3 generator energizes the right main a-c bus, and the No. 2 generator serves as a standby source on the bus crossfeed circuit. If a primary generator (No. 1 or No. 3) fails or the respective control switch placed to OFF, the standby generator (No. 2) is immediately connected to the applicable bus by automatic switching circuits. A single generator can

1-32

energize both a-c buses, but lockout circuits prevent two generators from energizing the same bus. The a-c power system is equipped with an automatic load-reducing safety feature. If a situation arises in which two generators fail or are taken out of operation, relays automatically cut off electrical power from the pod and DECM equipment. This prevents the a-c load from exceeding the capabilities of the remaining good generator. When necessary, power can be restored to the pod and DECM through the use of a pod and DECM power switch. All controls and indicators for the a-c power supply system are located on the electrical control panel (figure 1-15) at the pilot's station. Using the frequency meter and voltmeter on the electrical control panel to monitor the generators and the left and right a-c buses, the following values should be read: 115 ± 5 volts and 400 ± 6 cycles per second. These values include meter tolerances.

Generator Control Switches.

Three control switches (7, figure 1-15), one for each generator, are located on the electrical control panel. Each switch has two positions marked RESET, and OFF, and an unmarked ON (up) position. The switch is spring-loaded from RESET to OFF. While the switch is held momentarily in the RESET position, the respective field flashing circuits are closed and the voltage regulation circuits are connected to the generator. These actions excite the generator and place it in operation provided the engine rpm is at idle or above. When the switch is placed in the ON position, the associated power transfer contactor is electrically actuated, connecting the generator to its bus or crossfeed circuit. When the switch is placed in the OFF position, the power transfer contactor is electrically tripped, isolating the generator from its bus or crossfeed circuit. The generator control switches control 28-volt direct current to the actuation and trip coils of the power transfer contactors.

Note

When an abnormal voltage condition exists, protection circuits automatically override the switch circuits to isolate the malfunctioning generator. When an excessive current condition exists, a protection circuit automatically overrides the switch circuits to isolate both generator and bus.

Generator Drive Decoupler Switches.

Three generator drive decoupler switches (3, figure 1-28) are located on the pilot's lower right console. The switches marked NORM and DISC are spring-loaded to and guarded in the NORM position. Placing the switch to the DISC position energizes a solenoid in the decoupler which triggers a spring-loaded device allowing engine rotation to disconnect the generator and drive assembly from the engine.

Note

Once decoupled, the decoupler cannot be reset inflight.

A-C Meter Selector Knob.

An a-c system meter selector knob (9, figure 1-15), located on the electrical control panel, enables the pilot to monitor the generator and bus systems with the three instruments mounted on the panel. The rotary-type knob has positions marked GEN 1, L BUS, GEN 2, R BUS, and GEN 3. Placing the knob in a generator position connects the voltmeter, frequency meter, and ammeter to the respective generator. Placing the knob in a bus position connects the voltmeter and frequency meter to the respective a-c bus system.

Note

The ammeter is not operational when the meter selector knob is in a bus position.

Pod & DECM Power Switch.

The pod and DECM power switch (3, figure 1-15), located on the electrical control panel, provides a means of restoring electrical power to the pod and DECM equipment after it has been interrupted by the automatic load-reducing circuit. The switch has two positions marked AUTO LOAD REDUCTION and OVERRIDE. With the switch in the AUTO LOAD REDUCTION position, electrical power is available to the pod and DECM equipment until two generators fail, at which time the automatic load-reducing circuits remove power from the pod and DECM equipment. When the switch is placed in the OVERRIDE position during single generator operation, the automatic load-reducing circuits are overridden and electrical power is again restored to pod and DECM equipment. To move the switch out of the AUTO LOAD REDUCTION position, it is necessary to pull out on the handle.

CAUTION

Before placing the pod & DECM power switch to the OVERRIDE position, check that the restoration of pod and DECM power does not cause the total current load to exceed single generator capabilities. It may be necessary to de-energize other equipment using a-c power in order to safely restore pod and DECM power. For information on high amperage equipment refer to "Electrical System Emergency Operations," Section III.

Section I
Description

T.O. 1B-58A-1

a-c power distribution

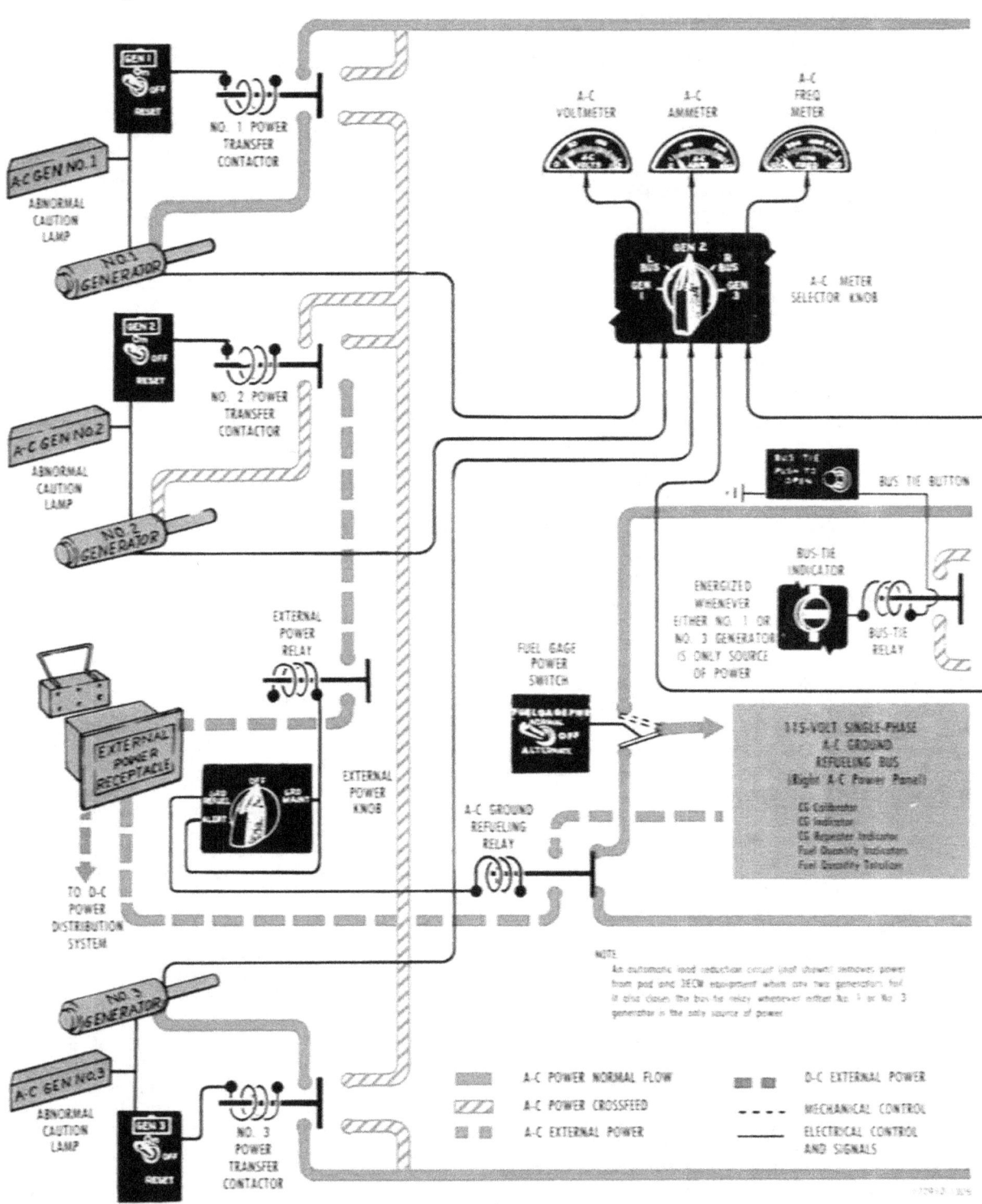

Figure 1-14. (Sheet 1 of 2)

1-34

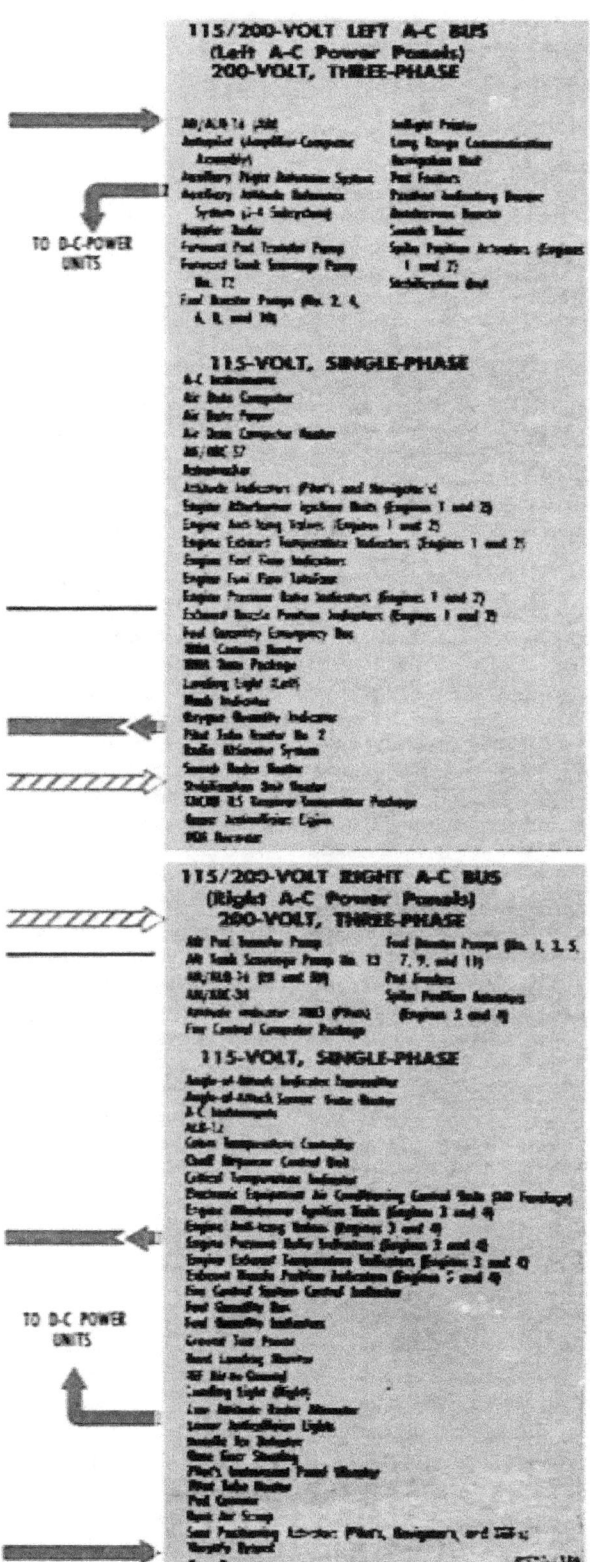

Figure 1-14. (Sheet 2 of 2)

A-C Voltmeter.

The a-c voltmeter (8, figure 1-15), located on the electrical control panel, is provided to enable the pilot to monitor the voltages delivered by the three generators and the two a-c bus systems. The meter scale is calibrated from 0 to 150 volts. With the meter selector knob in any one of the generator or bus positions, the normal indication should be 115 ±5 volts.

Frequency Meter.

The frequency meter (10, figure 1-15), located on the electrical control panel, enables the pilot to monitor frequencies of the generator and bus currents. The scale of this meter is calibrated from 380 to 420 cycles per second. With the meter selector knob in a generator or bus position, the normal meter indication should be 400 ±6 cycles per second.

A-C Ammeter.

The a-c ammeter (11, figure 1-15), located on the electrical control panel, enables the pilot to monitor the current loads being placed on the generators. The meter scale is calibrated from 0 to 250 amperes. With the meter selector knob in a generator position, the meter will indicate the current flow from the generator to the bus.

Note

The ammeter is not operational when the meter selector knob is in a bus position.

Bus Tie Button.

A bus tie button (4, figure 1-15), located on the electrical control panel, is marked PUSH TO OPEN. When No. 1 generator or No. 3 generator switch is placed to ON, the bus tie relay will close (bus tie indicator shows horizontal). Momentarily pressing the bus tie button will open the bus tie relay (bus tie indicator shows vertical), so that the other generator can be placed on its respective bus without the possibility of paralleling the two generators.

Power Flow Indicators.

Two power flow indicators (6, figure 1-15), located on the electrical control panel, indicate the flow of power from source to bus. Each indicator, one for each bus, is a three-position, dual-solenoid instrument. Right-angled white lines appear in the indicator window to show that the bus is being supplied by either a primary or the standby generator. If a bus is not energized or

Section I
Description

T.O. 1B-58A-1

electrical control panel (typical)

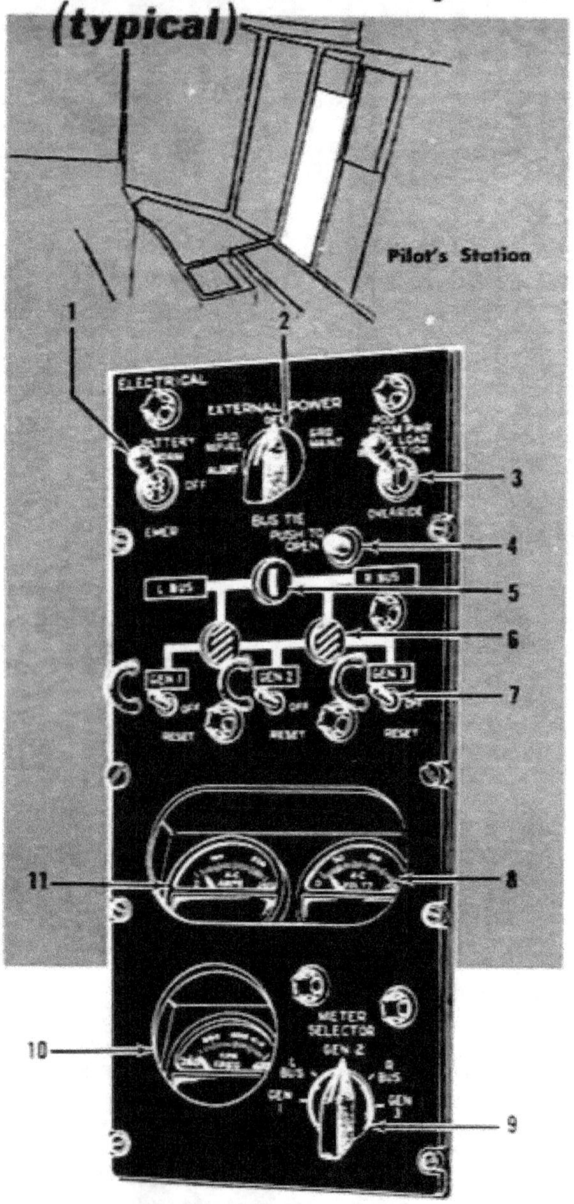

Pilot's Station

1. Battery Switch
2. External Power Knob
3. Pod and DECM Power Auto Load Reduction
4. Bus Tie Button
5. Bus Tie Indicator
6. Power Flow Indicator (2)
7. Generator Control Switch (3)
8. AC Voltmeter
9. AC Meter Selector Knob
10. Frequency Meter
11. AC Ammeter

Figure 1-15.

if power is being supplied through the bus-tie relay, diagonal stripes appear in the window.

Note

If a bus and generator are automatically isolated by an overcurrent condition, the power flow indicator will continue to show a right-angled white line.

A-C Generator Abnormal Caution Lamps.

Three a-c generator abnormal lamps (figure 1-13), one for each generator, are located on the warning and caution lamp panel and warn of abnormal conditions existing in the generator systems. The appropriate lamp will light and display "AC GEN NO. 1 (2, 3)" to indicate de-excitation, off-frequency, or overtemperature conditions in the respective generator. Overtemperature is caused by the loss of oil to the generator constant speed drive, the oil pressure sensing switch will actuate the a-c generator caution lamps earlier during the malfunction and increase the possibility for corrective action before the constant speed drive is damaged. When starting the engines, each lamp will light before the engine rpm reaches idle and will remain lighted until its generator is excited. When using external power, the warning and caution indicator switch must be placed to GROUND CHECK before power is available to the a-c generator abnormal caution lamps. When using external power, the abnormal lamps will not light until the respective generator engine is started and the rpm is increased toward idle. However, the master caution lamp may not light until idle rpm is reached. The lamps are connected to the master caution lamp circuit and operate on 28-volt d-c power. For dimming and testing of the lamps, and additional information relating to operation of the warning and caution indicator switch, refer to the "Malfunction Indicator and Warning System" of this section.

Bus Tie Indicator.

A two-position bus tie indicator (5, figure 1-15), located on the electrical control panel, indicates when the bus tie relay has closed. A horizontal white line appears in the indicator window to show that the bus tie relay has closed. The horizontal white line indication also serves as a warning device, since the bus tie relay closes automatically whenever either No. 1 or No. 3 generator is the only source of power. When the bus tie relay is open or the indicator is de-energized, a vertical white line appears in the indicator window.

1-36

T.O. 1B-58A-1

Section I
Description

left a-c power panels (typical)

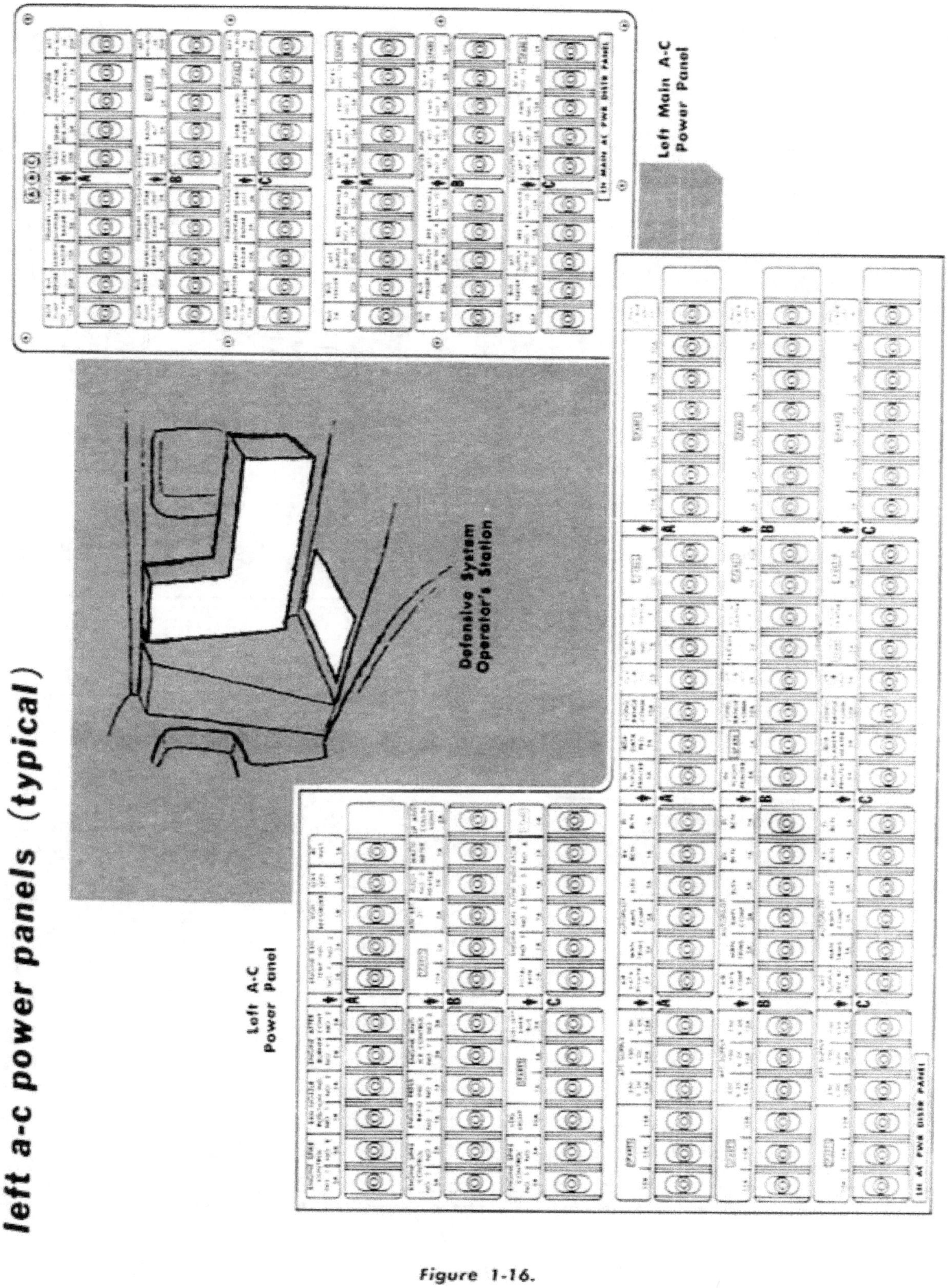

Figure 1-16.

1-37

Section I
Description

T.O. 1B-58A-1

right a-c and multiple weapons 28 volt d-c power panels (typical)

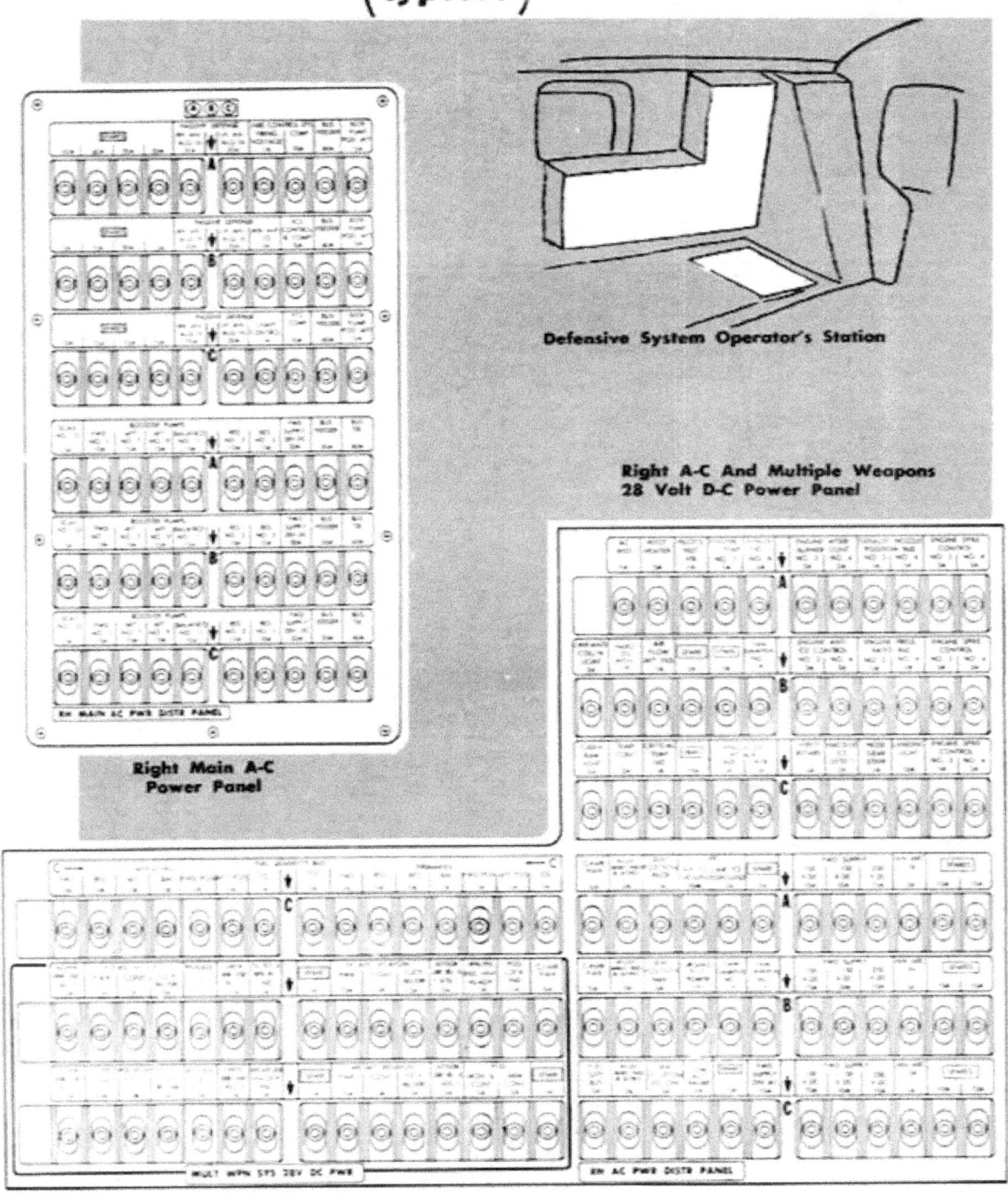

Figure 1-17.

T.O. 1B-58A-1

Section I
Description

Pod and DECM Power Caution Lamp.

A pod and DECM power caution lamp (figure 1-13), located on the warning and caution lamp panel, lights and displays "POD & DECM POWER" when the automatic load-reducing function has removed electrical power from the pod and DECM equipment. The lamp is connected to the master caution lamp and operates on 28-volt d-c power. For dimming and testing of the lamp, refer to the "Malfunction Indicator and Warning System," of this section.

D-C POWER SYSTEM.

Direct current is distributed by a network of d-c buses which receive power from eight multiple-voltage d-c power units and a battery. (Refer to figure 1-21.) The power units, which produce direct current by rectifying a-c power from the main a-c buses, are installed in a rack forward of the left console at the DSO's station. The eight units are equally divided into a forward and aft bank, and the individual units of the two banks are paired and wired in parallel. A pair of units produces one of the following voltages: 250-volt dc, 150-volt dc, negative 150-volt dc, and 28-volt dc. The 28-volt d-c power units also produce 28-volt a-c power for miscellaneous low-voltage a-c requirements. Each unit is marked on the front panel according to the voltage output (+250, —150, +150, or +28). The forward bank receives power from the right main a-c bus and the aft bank receives power from the left main a-c bus. If a power unit in either bank fails, the corresponding unit in the other bank assumes the full load for that voltage. During normal inflight operation, the power units are cooled by cabin air conditioning. During abnormal flight conditions, a cooling fan in each unit automatically limits operating temperatures. During ground operations, the cooling fans operate continuously whenever power is being supplied from an external source. The battery, located at the navigator's station, is provided for emergency d-c power and is connected directly to the battery bus. Under normal conditions, the two 28-volt d-c power units supply power to the non-essential bus which in turn supplies power to the essential bus, the interphone bus, and the multiple weapons bus. In the event that power from the nonessential bus is disrupted, the battery bus is automatically connected to the multiple weapons bus (if installed) and to the essential bus provided the battery switch is in the NORM or ON position. The battery bus can also be manually connected to the essential bus in the event of a failure of the automatic transfer system by placing the battery switch in the EMER position. Blocking diodes prevent the battery from supplying power to the non-essential bus and insure correct current flow in the charging circuit. Relays prevent the battery from supplying power to the multiple weapons bus whenever the non-essential bus is energized. The battery is charged, whenever, the battery switch is placed to NORM or ON and power is available from the 28-volt d-c power units. The battery is contained in a box which is connected to the air conditioning system and to an overboard vent line to provide force ventilation. Operation of the d-c power supply system is entirely automatic. A loadmeter, voltmeter, and rotary-type selector knob, mounted on the d-c system check panel (figure 1-22) at the upper aft end of the power unit rack, enable the DSO to monitor the d-c power units. When monitoring the d-c power units with the loadmeter, readings should fall within the following tolerances: —0.1 to 0.8 (28 volt units) and —0.1 to 0.7 (all other units). The loadmeter reading of a 28-volt unit should be within 0.85 of its parallel unit as observed on the loadmeter scale. All other units must be within 0.45 of their respective parallel units as observed on the loadmeter scale. (e.g. If a loadmeter is reading 0.1, its parallel 28-volt d-c pack must read between —0.1 and 0.8; its parallel unit on all other packs must read between —0.1 and 0.55).

Note

At low load values one unit may assume the entire load for that voltage. As a result the loadmeter may indicate a negative value for the opposite unit. A negative reading does not indicate a malfunctioning unit if the difference between the readings does not exceed the specified maximum difference between parallel units.

When using the voltmeter to monitor the power supplies, see figure 1-23 for the range voltages from no load to full load which should be indicated. The battery voltage should be a minimum of 23.1 volts.

Note

- To assure an accurate voltage check of a unit its parallel unit must be deactivated by pulling the a-c input fuses and then the d-c output fuses. The fuses must be reinserted in the same sequence. See figure 1-23.
- The voltmeter cannot be used to monitor the 28-volt a-c power.
- The above voltage values include meter tolerances.

Battery Switch.

The three-position battery switch (1, figure 1-15), located on the electrical control panel, has three positions marked NORM, OFF and EMER. The switch is me-

1-39

Section I
Description

T.O. 1B-58A-1

chanically latched in each position. When the switch is in the NORM position, the automatic transfer function is set up to automatically connect the battery to the essential bus in the event of a power failure of the non-essential bus. Placing the switch in the EMER position bypasses the automatic transfer circuits and connects the battery bus to the essential bus. With the battery switch in the OFF position, the battery cannot be connected to the essential bus by the automatic transfer circuit. To move the switch out of any position, it is necessary to pull out on the switch handle.

Battery Discharging Caution Lamp.

A battery discharging caution lamp (figure 1-13), located on the warning and caution panel, lights and displays "BAT DISCHARGING" when the battery is supplying power to the essential bus. The lamp is connected to the master caution lamp circuit and operates on battery power. For dimming and testing of the caution lamp, refer to the "Pilot's Indicator Lamp System," of this section.

D-C Meter Selector Knob.

The d-c meter selector knob (figure 1-22), located on the d-c system check panel at the DSO's station, permits the crew member to monitor each of the d-c power units. The rotary type knob has ten positions. The positions on the left and right side of the knob are marked 28VDC, 150VDC, 250VDC, and —150VDC. When the meter selector knob is placed in any one of the voltage positions on the left side, the loadmeter is connected to the respective power unit in the aft bank of the rack. With the knob in a voltage position on the right side, the loadmeter is connected to the respective power unit in the forward bank. The voltmeter reflects the respective combined voltages of both forward and aft banks at each voltage position.

D-C Voltmeter.

A voltmeter (figure 1-22) is located on the d-c system check panel at the DSO's station. The meter, which is connected to any one of the d-c buses through the d-c meter selector knob, is a direct-reading instrument. A single pointer moves over two scales. Voltages of the 28-volt d-c bus are read on the lower scale, which is marked from 0 to 30. Voltages of the other d-c buses are read on the upper scale, which is marked from 0 to 300.

Note

The d-c voltmeter cannot be used to monitor the 28-volt a-c power supply; nor can it be used as a reference to adjust the output voltage of the d-c power units.

D-C Loadmeter.

A loadmeter (figure 1-22) is located on the d-c system check panel at the DSO's station. This instrument is connected to any one of the power units through the d-c meter selector knob. When measuring a power unit amperage, the meter indicates current flow as a decimal fraction of the rated load. The loadmeter scale is marked from minus .1 to plus 1.25.

Note

The d-c loadmeter cannot be used to monitor the 28-volt a-c power supply.

ELECTRICALLY OPERATED EQUIPMENT.

For listings of electrically operated equipment, see figures 1-14 and 1-21.

EXTERNAL POWER SOURCE.

Electrical power for ground operations is supplied by an auxiliary power unit. The unit is connected to the external power receptacle located on the right side of the fuselage below the wing leading edge. When the auxiliary power unit is in use, 200-volt alternating current is routed to the bus crossfeed circuit to energize the main a-c buses.

CAUTION

To prevent possible damage to equipment, the electrical power should not be connected to the airplane unless air conditioning is available for equipment cooling except when following the Scramble Procedures in Section II or when power switches are positioned to OFF.

Direct current for ground operations is provided, as in normal flight operation, through the multiple voltage d-c power supply system, provided a main a-c bus is energized. A switch in the pilot's compartment enables servicing personnel to isolate the refueling buses for use with the external power source in single-point ground refueling operations. For such operations, the external source supplies 115-volt, single-phase a-c power and 28-volt d-c power to the isolated buses only.

Note

When using external power, the warning and caution indicator switch must be placed in the GROUND CHECK position before power is available to the warning and caution lamps. Refer to "Malfunction Indicator and Warning System" this section.

1-40

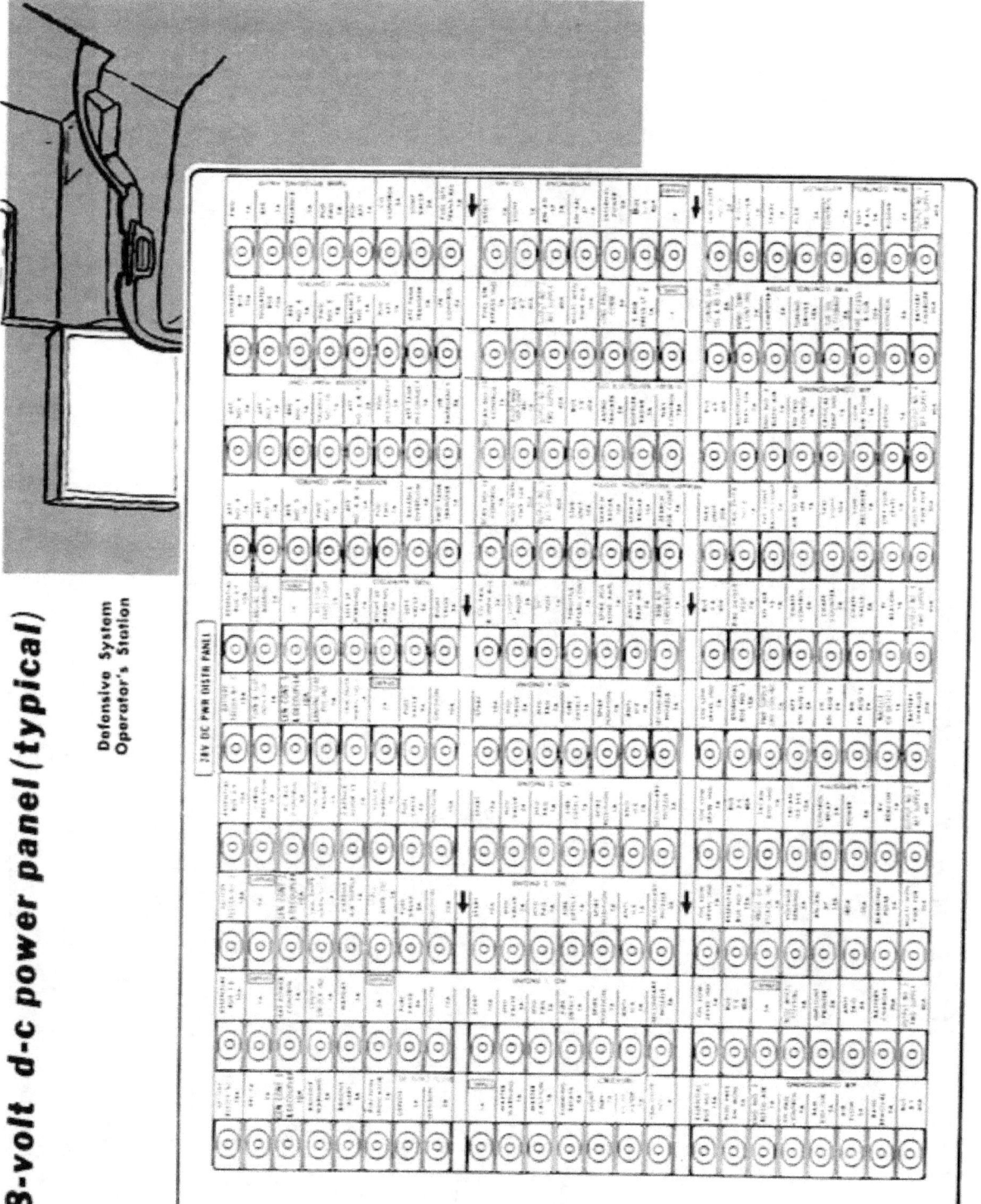

Figure 1-18. 28-volt d-c power panel (typical) — Defensive System Operator's Station

Section I
Description

T.O. 1B-58A-1

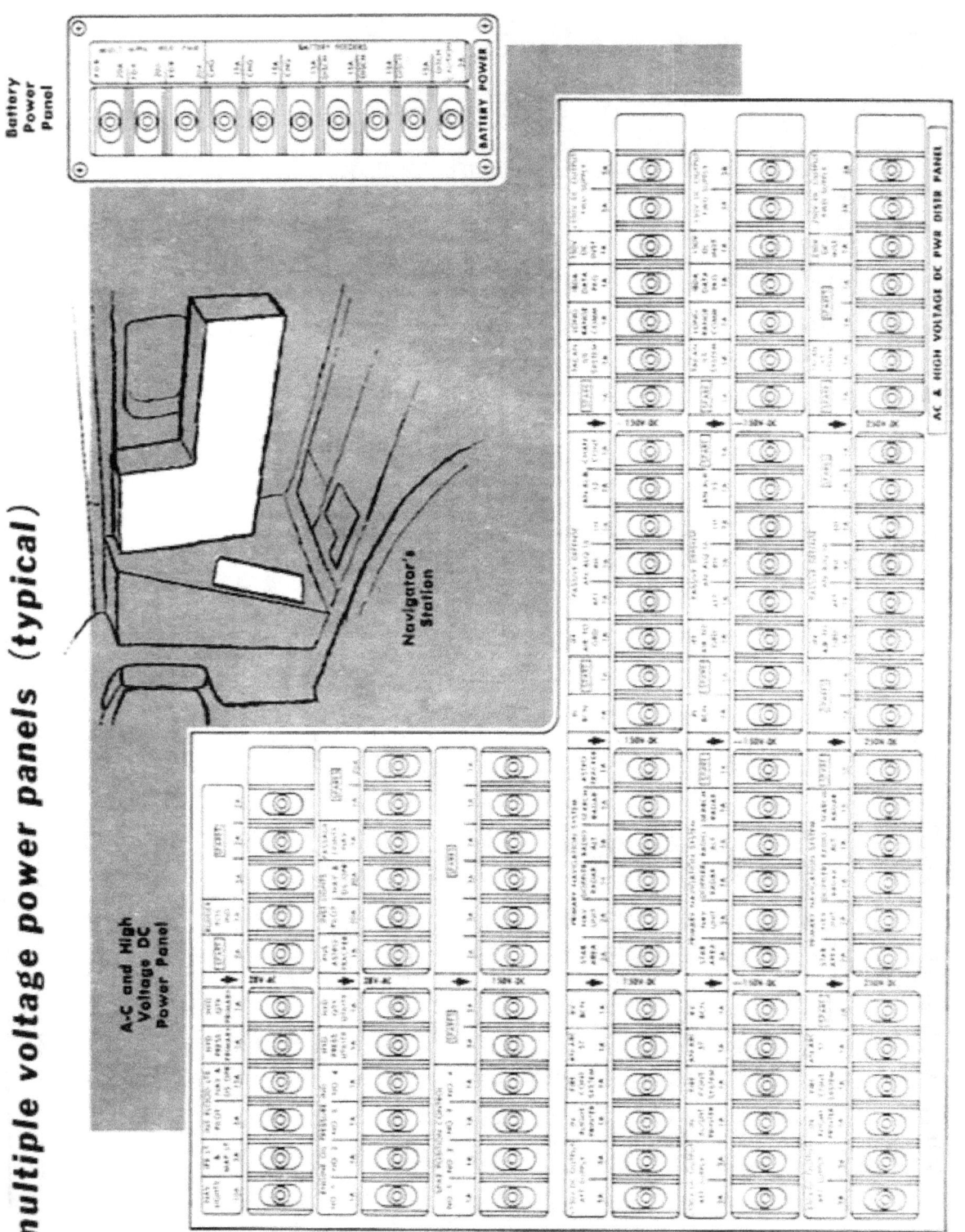

Figure 1-19.

1-42

T.O. 1B-58A-1

Section I
Description

fuse panel and fuse locations

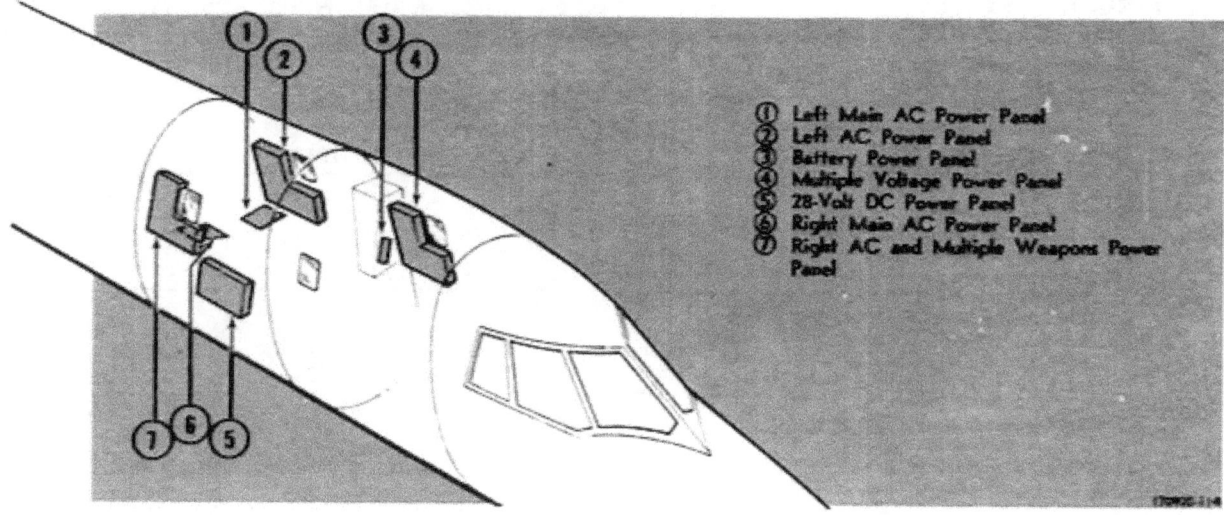

① Left Main AC Power Panel
② Left AC Power Panel
③ Battery Power Panel
④ Multiple Voltage Power Panel
⑤ 28-Volt DC Power Panel
⑥ Right Main AC Power Panel
⑦ Right AC and Multiple Weapons Power Panel

AIRCRAFT SYSTEM	FUSE QTY.	FUSE MARKING	PANEL NO.
ACTIVE DEFENSE SYSTEM (Fire Control)			
Ammo Temperature and Control Indicator	1	AMMO TEMP & CONT IND	③
Computer	1	COMP	④
	1	COMPUTER	③
Control	1	CONTROL	③
FCS Control and Computer	1	FCS CONTROL & COMP	⑥
Fire Access and Gun	1	FIRE ACCESS & GUN	③
Fire Control Computer	1	FCS COMP	④
Fire Control System	3*	FIRE CONT SYSTEM	④
Fire Control Tuning Drives	1	TUNING DRIVES	③
Firing Voltage	1	FIRING VOLTAGE	⑥
Tuning Drive Selector & Round Counter	1	TUNING DR SEL & RD CTR	③
Turret Solenoid and Stowage	1	TUR SOL & STOWAGE	③
AIR CONDITIONING SYSTEM			
Air Conditioning	1	AIR FLOW	③
	1	ENG NO. 2 BLEED AIR	③
	1	ENG NO. 3 BLEED AIR	③
	1	LH PKG CONTROL	③
	1	LOW AIR FLOW	③
	1	PWR SUPPLY GRD COOLING	③
	1	RAIN REMOVAL	③
	1	RAM EJECTOR	③
	1	RH PKG CONTROL	③
Air Flow, Aft Fuselage	1	AIR FLOW, AFT FUS	⑦
Cabin Pressure	1	CABIN PRESS LOW	③
Cabin Temperature	1	TEMP CONT	⑦
	1	CABIN RAM VENT	⑥

*The −250V DC, 1A fuse is inactive (dead ended at fire control system computer).

Figure 1-20. (Sheet 1 of 11)

1-43

Section I
Description

T.O. 1B-58A-1

AIRCRAFT SYSTEM	FUSE QTY.	FUSE MARKING	PANEL NO.
AIR CONDITIONING SYSTEM (Continued)			
Critical Temperature Indicator	1	CRITICAL TEMP IND	②
	1	CRITICAL TEMP IND	③
Ram Air Temperature	1	RAM AIR TEMPERATURE	⑤
AIR DATA SYSTEM			
Air Data Computer	1	AIR DATA COMP	②
Air Data Power	1	AIR DATA POWER	②
AIR NAVIGATION DATA RECORDER	1	INFLIGHT PRINTER	③
	3	INFLIGHT PRINTER	③
	3	INFLIGHT PRINTER	④
ANTI-ICE AND DEFOG SYSTEMS			
Anti-ice Ram Air	1	ANTI-ICE RAM AIR	②
Engine Anti-Ice			
engine no. 1	1	ANTI-ICE	③
engine no. 2	1	ANTI-ICE	③
engine no. 3	1	ANTI-ICE	⑤
engine no. 4	1	ANTI-ICE	⑤
Engine Anti-Ice Control			
engine no. 1	1	NO. 1	⑧
engine no. 2	1	NO. 2	⑧
engine no. 3	1	NO. 3	⑦
engine no. 4	1	NO. 4	⑦
Nacelle Ice Detection	1	NACELLE ICE DETECT	②
	1	NACELLE ICE DETECT	⑦
Windshield Defog	1	DEFOG	③
AUTOPILOT SYSTEM			
Amplifier Computer	3	AMPL COMP	②
Autopilot, Navigator's Station	1	AUTOPILOT NAV STA	③
Control	1	AUTOPILOT CONTROL	②
Elevator	3	ELEV	③
Manual Trims	3	MAN TRIMS	③
PCLA	1	AUTOPILOT PCLA	②
AUXILIARY FLIGHT REFERENCE SYSTEM			
Pilot MM3 Ind. & Attitude Gyro	3	PILOT MM3 IND. & GYRO	②
Auxiliary Attitude Reference	3	J-4 SUBSYSTEM	②③
Control Relay	1	CONTROL RELAY	③
Power	1	POWER	②
BAILOUT WARNING SYSTEM			
Bailout Alert Lamp	1	BAILOUT ALERT	③
Bailout Warning Lamp	1	BAILOUT WARNING	③
Ejection Indicator Lamp	1	EJECTION INDICATOR	③
BEACON SYSTEMS			
PI Beacon	1	PI BEACON	②
	2	PI BCN	④
	3	PI BCN	③

Figure 1-20. (Sheet 2 of 11)

AIRCRAFT SYSTEM	FUSE QTY.	FUSE MARKING	PANEL NO.
BEACON SYSTEMS (Continued)			
RV Beacon	1	RV BEACON	③
	2	RV BCN	④
	3	RV BCN	③
BLANKING PULSE JUNCTION BOX	1	BLANKING PULSE	③
BOMBING SYSTEM			
Cartridge Test and Weapon Release Indicator	1	CTG TEST & WPN REL IND	⑦
Control (Left Forward Weapon)	1	CONT	⑦
Control (Left Aft Weapon)	1	CONT	⑦
Control (Right Forward Weapon)	1	CONT	⑦
Control (Right Aft Weapon)	1	CONT	⑦
Emergency Arm Control Relay 1 & 2	2	EMERG ARM CONT REL 1 & 2	⑦
Jettison Lower Release & Fin Actg 1 & 2	2	JETTISON LWR REL & F ACTG 1 & 2	⑦
Multiple Weapon Emergency Power	3	MULT WPN PWR EMER FDR	③
Multiple Weapon Power Feeder	4	MULT WPN PWR FDR	③
Normal Arm Control Relay 1 & 2	2	NORM ARM CONT REL 1 & 2	⑦
Pod Arm Control	1	ARM CONT	⑦
Pod Lock Indicator	1	POD LOCK IND	⑦
Pod Monitor and Control	1	MONT & CONT	⑦
Power (Left Forward Weapon)	1	PWR	⑦
Power (Left Aft Weapon)	1	PWR	⑦
Power (Right Forward Weapon)	1	PWR	⑦
Power (Right Aft Weapon)	1	PWR	⑦
Release 1 & 2	2	RELEASE 1 & 2	⑦
Unlock Indicator and Control (Left Forward Weapon)	1	UNLOCK IND/CONT	⑦
Unlock Indicator and Control (Left Aft Weapon)	1	UNLOCK IND/CONT	⑦
Unlock Indicator and Control (Right Forward Weapon)	1	UNLOCK IND/CONT	⑦
Unlock Indicator and Control (Right Aft Weapon)	1	UNLOCK IND/CONT	⑦
Weapon and Pod Indicator Arm and Ready	1	WPN/POD IND ARM READY	⑦
Weapon Unlock Indicator	1	WEAPON UNLOCK IND	⑦
BOMB DAMAGE EVALUATION SYSTEM	1	IBDA	③
Bomb Damage Evaluation System Camera Heater	1	IBDA CAMERA HEATER	②
Bomb Damage Evaluation System Data Package	1	IBDA DATA PKG	③
	2	IBDA DATA PKG	④
BRAKE SYSTEM			
Antiskid	1	ANTISKID	⑤
CANOPIES			
Canopy Unlock Indicator	1	CANOPY UNLOCK IND	⑤

Figure 1-20. (Sheet 3 of 11)

Section I
Description

T.O. 1B-58A-1

AIRCRAFT SYSTEM	FUSE QTY.	FUSE MARKING	PANEL NO.
CAPSULE			
Capsule Air Supply	1	CAPSULE AIR SUPPLY	⑤
Capsule Door Closure	1	CAPSULE DOOR CL	⑤
CENTER OF GRAVITY CONTROL SYSTEM (See FUEL SUPPLY SYSTEM)			
COMMUNICATION SYSTEM			
Command Radio (AN/ARC-57)	1	AN/ARC-57	③
	1	AN/ARC-57	③
	3	AN/ARC-57	④
Command Radio Interphone	1	INTERPHONE AN/ARC-57	③
Emergency Communication	1	ARC-74	③
Ground Interphone	1	INTERPHONE AN/AIC-17	③
Interphone Bus	1	CG FAIL & INPH BUS	③
Long Range Communication	1	LONG RANGE COMM	③
	3	LONG RANGE COMM	③
Mayday	1	MAYDAY	③
UHF Command Radio (AN/ARC-34)	3	AN/ARC-34	⑦
DEFENSIVE ELECTRONIC COUNTER MEASURES SYSTEM			
Chaff Dispensing			
chaff control	1	CHAFF CONT.	④
	1	CHAFF CONTROL	③
	1	CHAFF CONTROL	④
chaff counter	1	CHAFF COUNTER	③
chaff valve	1	CHAFF VALVE	③
Radar Trackbreaker	1	AFT AN/ALQ-16	③
	3	AFT AN/ALQ-16	①
	3	AFT AN/ALQ-16	④
	1	LH AN/ALQ-16	③
	3	LH AN/ALQ-16	⑩
	3	LH AN/ALQ-16	④
	1	RH AN/ALQ-16	③
	3	RH AN/ALQ-16	⑩
	3	RH AN/ALQ-16	④
Radar Warning Equipment	1	AN/ALR-12	③
	1	AN/ALR-12	③
	2	AN/ALR-12	④
DRAG CHUTE		DEC CHUTE REL	
	1	DEPLOY	③
	1	JETTISON	⑤
ELECTRICAL POWER SUPPLY SYSTEM			
AC Bus			
bus tie	3	BUS TIE	①

Figure 1-20. (Sheet 4 of 11)

AIRCRAFT SYSTEM	FUSE QTY.	FUSE MARKING	PANEL NO.
ELECTRICAL POWER SUPPLY SYSTEM (Continued)			
	3	BUS TIE	⑥
control	1	AC BUS CONTROL	③
feeder	6	BUS FEEDER	①
	6	BUS FEEDER	⑥
AFT Supply (Input)			
28-volt ac	1	AFT SUPPLY 28V AC	⑨
28-volt dc	3	AFT SUPPLY 28V DC	①
150-volt dc	3	150V DC	⑨
250-volt dc	3	250V DC	⑨
—150-volt dc	3	—150V DC	⑨
AFT Supply (Output)			
28-volt dc output			
No. 1 (2, 3, 4)	4	OUTPUT NO. 1(2,3,4) AFT SUPPLY	⑨
150-volt dc	2	+150V DC OUTPUT AFT SUPPLY	④
250-volt dc	2	+250V DC OUTPUT AFT SUPPLY	④
—150-volt dc	2	—150V DC OUTPUT AFT SUPPLY	④
Battery			
charge	3	BATTERY CHARGER	③
	3	CHG	③
discharge	2	DISCH	③
	1	DISCH RELAY (DISCH)	③
discharge caution lamp	1	DISCH CAUTION (DISCH LIGHT)	③
feeder	3	BATTERY FEEDER NO. 1 (2,3)	③
DC Bus (28 volt dc)			
essential bus			
normal dc feeder	3	ESSENTIAL BUS NO. 1 (2,3)	③
battery feeder	3	BATTERY FEEDER NO. 1 (2,3)	③
bus connectors	3	ESSENTIAL BUS 1-2 (2-3, 3-1)	③
non-essential bus			
bus connectors	8	BUS 1-2 (2-3,3-4,4-5,5-6,6-7,7-8,8-1)	③
External Power	1	EXTERNAL POWER	③
control	1	EXT POWER CONTROL	③
Forward Supply (Input)			
28-volt ac	1	FWD SUPPLY 28V-AC	⑦
28-volt dc	3	FWD SUPPLY 28V-DC	⑥
150-volt dc	3	150V-DC	⑦
250-volt dc	3	250V-DC	⑦
—150-volt dc	3	—150V-DC	⑦
Forward Supply (Output)			
28-volt dc output No. 1 (2,3,4)	4	OUTPUT NO. 1 (2,3,4) FWD SUPPLY	③
150-volt dc	2	+150V DC OUTPUT FWD SUPPLY	④
250-volt dc	2	+250V DC OUTPUT FWD SUPPLY	④
—150-volt dc	2	—150V DC OUTPUT FWD SUPPLY	④
Generator Control No. 1 (2,3)	3	GEN NO. 1 (2,3) CONTROL	③
Generator Control and Decoupler No. 1 (2, 3)	3	GEN CONT NO. 1 (2, 3) & DECOUPLER	③
Isolated Bus	2	ISOLATED BUS	③
Voltage Sensing Relay	1	VOLTAGE SENSING	③

Figure 1-20. (Sheet 5 of 11)

AIRCRAFT SYSTEM	FUSE QTY.	FUSE MARKING	PANEL NO.
EJECTION SEATS			
Seat Position	3	SEAT POS, PILOT (NAV, DSO OPR)	⑦
ENGINES			
Afterburner Control No. 1,2	2	ENGINE AFTERBURNER CONT NO. 1,2	③
Afterburner Control No. 3,4	2	ENGINE AFTERBURNER CONT NO. 3,4	⑦
Exhaust Nozzle Position Indicator No. 1,2	2	EXH NOZZLE POSITION IND NO. 1,2	③
Exhaust Nozzle Position Indicator No. 3,4	2	EXH NOZZLE POSITION IND NO. 3,4	⑦
Exhaust Temperature Indicator No. 1,2	2	ENGINE EXH TEMP IND NO. 1,2	③
Exhaust Temperature Indicator No. 3,4	2	ENGINE EXH TEMP IND NO. 3,4	⑦
Fire Detection No. 1,2,3,4	4	NO. 1,2,3,4 ENGINE FIRE DETECT	③
Fire Detection Test	1	FIRE DETECT TEST	③
Fuel Flow Indicators No. 1,2,3,4	4	ENGINE FUEL FLOW INDICATOR NO. 1,2,3,4	③
Fuel Flow Totalizer	1	ENGINE FUEL FLOW INDICATOR TOTAL RPTR	③
Fuel Valve No. 1,2,3,4	4	NO. 1,2,3,4 ENGINE FUEL VALVE	③
Ignition No. 1,2,3,4	4	NO. 1,2,3,4 ENGINE IGNITION	③
Oil Low Level caution lamps No. 1,2,3,4	4	OIL LOW LEVEL NO. 1,2,3,4	③
Oil Pressure Indicator No. 1,2,3,4	4	ENGINE OIL PRESSURE IND NO. 1,2,3,4	④
Pressure Ratio Indicator No. 1,2	2	ENGINE PRESS RATIO IND NO. 1,2	③
Pressure Ratio Indicator No. 3,4	2	ENGINE PRESS RATIO IND NO. 3,4	⑦
Secondary Nozzle No. 1,2,3,4	4	NO. 1,2,3,4 ENGINE SECONDARY NOZZLE	③
Spike Control No. 1,2	6	ENGINE SPIKE CONTROL NO. 1,2	③
Spike Control No. 3,4	6	ENGINE SPIKE CONTROL NO. 3,4	⑦
Spike Position Control Amplifier	1	SPIKE POS CONT AMP	③
Spike Position Control No. 1,2,3,4	4	SPIKE POSITION CONTROL NO. 1,2,3,4	④
Spike Position No. 1,2,3,4	4	NO. 1,2,3,4 ENGINE SPIKE POSITION	②
Starting Switches No. 1,2,3,4	4	NO. 1,2,3,4 ENGINE START	③
Throttle Retard Control	1	THROTTLE RETARD CONT	③
Throttle Retard	1	THROT RETARD	⑦

Figure 1-20. (Sheet 6 of 11)

AIRCRAFT SYSTEM	FUSE QTY.	FUSE MARKING	PANEL NO.
ESCAPE SYSTEM (See EJECTION SEAT or CAPSULE)			
FLIGHT CONTROL SYSTEM			
Flight Control Ratio Computer	1	FLT CONT RATIO COMP	③
Pitch Damper	1	PITCH DAMPER	⑤
Pitch Damper	3	PITCH DAMPER	③
Rudder Position Indicator	1	RUDDER POS IND	④
Trim Control			
elevator and aileron	1	ELEV & AIR	⑤
rudder	1	RUDDER	⑤
Yaw Damper			
No. 1	1	YAW DAMPER NO. 1	③
No. 2	1	YAW DAMPER NO. 2	③
No. 3	1	YAW DAMPER NO. 3	③
No. 1	1	YAW DAMPER NO. 1	⑦
No. 2	1	YAW DAMPER NO. 2	⑦
No. 3	1	YAW DAMPER NO. 3	⑦
Yaw Damper Warning			
No. 1	1	YAW DMPR WARN NO. 1	③
No. 2	1	YAW DMPR WARN NO. 2	③
FUEL SUPPLY SYSTEM			
Aft Tank Transfer	1	AFT TANK IN-CONNECT	③
Balance Tank Overflow	1	AFT TANK TRANSFER	③
Aft Tank Interconnect	1	BLANCE OVERFLOW	③
Booster Pump Control			
aft tank no. 6	1	AFT NO. 6	③
aft tank no. 7	1	AFT NO. 7	③
aft tank no. 6 & 7	1	AFT NO. 6 & 7	③
aft tank no. 8	1	AFT NO. 8	③
aft tank no. 9	1	AFT NO. 9	③
aft tank no. 8 & 9	1	AFT NO. 8 & 9	③
balance tank no. 10	1	BALANCE NO. 10	③
balance tank no. 11	1	BALANCE NO. 11	③
forward tank no. 1	1	FWD NO. 1	③
forward tank no. 2	1	FWD NO. 2	③
pod aft	1	POD AFT	③
pod forward	1	POD FWD	③
reservoir tank no. 3	1	RES NO. 3	③
reservoir tank no. 4	1	RES NO. 4	③
reservoir tank no. 5	1	RES NO. 5	③
Booster Pumps			
aft pod	3	BSTR PUMP POD AFT	④
aft tank no. 6	3	AFT NO. 6	①
aft tank no. 7	3	AFT NO. 7	④
aft tank no. 8	3	AFT NO. 8	①
aft tank no. 9	3	AFT NO. 9	④
balance tank no. 10	3	BALANCE NO. 10	①
balance tank no. 11	3	BALANCE NO. 11	④

Figure 1-20. (Sheet 7 of 11)

Section I
Description

T.O. 1B-58A-1

AIRCRAFT SYSTEM	FUSE QTY.	FUSE MARKING	PANEL NO.
FUEL SUPPLY SYSTEM (Continued)			
forward pod	3	BSTR PUMP POD FWD	⑦
forward tank no. 1	3	FWD NO. 1	⑥
forward tank no. 2	3	FWD NO. 2	⑦
reservoir tank no. 3	3	RES NO. 3	⑥
reservoir tank no. 4	3	RES NO. 4	⑦
reservoir tank no. 5	3	RES NO. 5	⑥
CG Control	1	CG CONTROL	⑤
CG Failure Detector	1	CG FAIL DETECT	⑤
CG Failed Caution Lamp	1	CG FAIL LIGHT	⑤
Dump Valve	1	DUMP VALVE	⑤
Forward Tank Transfer	1	FWD TANK TRANSFER	⑤
Fuel Manifold			
left low pressure warning	1	LEFT LP WARNING	⑤
left valve	1	LEFT VALVE	⑤
right low pressure warning	1	RIGHT LP WARNING	⑤
right valve	1	RIGHT VALVE	⑤
Fuel Quantity Bus	1	FUEL QTY BUS	⑤
Fuel Quantity Emergency Bus	1	FUEL QTY EMER BUS	⑤
Fuel Quantity Indicators			
Primaries			
aft pod	1	AFT POD	⑦
aft tank	1	AFT	⑦
balance tank	1	BAL	⑦
cg	1	CG	⑦
forward pod	1	FWD POD	⑦
forward tank	1	FWD	⑦
reservoir tank	1	RES	⑦
Repeaters			
aft pod	1	AFT POD	⑦
aft tank	1	AFT	⑦
balance tank	1	BAL	⑦
CG	1	CG	⑦
forward pod	1	FWD POD	⑦
forward tank	1	FWD	⑦
reservoir tank	1	RES	⑦
Totalizer	1	TOT	⑦
Fuel Quantity Transfer Relay	1	FUEL QTY TRANS REL	⑤
Fuel Strainer Bypass Indicator	1	FUEL STR BYPASS IND	⑤
Inflight Refueling Control	1	IFR CONTROL	⑤
Inflight Refueling Emergency	1	IFR EMERGENCY	⑤
Interconnect valve	1	POD IN-CONNECT	⑤
Reservoir Low Level Lamp	1	RES LOW LEVEL LIGHT	⑤
Scavenge No. 12	1	SCAV NO. 12 CONTROL	⑤
	3	SCAV NO. 12	⑤
Scavenge No. 13	1	SCAV NO. 13 CONTROL	⑤
	3	SCAV NO. 13	⑤
Tank Refueling Valve			
aft	1	AFT	⑤
balance	1	BALANCE	⑤
forward	1	FWD	⑤
pod aft	1	POD AFT	⑤
pod forward	1	POD FWD	⑤

Figure 1-20. (Sheet 8 of 11)

AIRCRAFT SYSTEM	FUSE QTY.	FUSE MARKING	PANEL NO.
GROUND TEST POWER	1	GROUND TEST POWER	⑦
HARD LANDING MONITOR	1	HARD LDG MON	③
HYDRAULIC SYSTEM			
Hydraulic Failure 1,2,3,4	4	HYD FAIL	③
Hydraulic Valve 1,2,3,4	4	HYD VALVE	③
Primary Hydraulic Pressure	1	HYD PRESS PRIMARY	④
Primary Hydraulic Quantity	1	HYD QTY PRIMARY	④
Utility Hydraulic Pressure	1	HYD PRESS UTILITY	④
Utility Hydraulic Quantity	1	HYD QTY UTILITY	④
IFF SYSTEM			
Air-to-Ground	2	AIR TO GRD	⑦
	3	AIR TO GRD	④
	1	AIR TO GRD IFF	③
ILS-TACAN SYSTEM			
	1	TACAN	③
	1	TACAN BDH IND	③
	1	TACAN BDH IND	③
	1	TACAN-ILS SYS	③
	3	TACAN	④
INSTRUMENTS			
150 Volt DC Instruments	1	150V DC INST	④
250 Volt DC Instruments	1	250V DC INST	④
—150 Volt DC Instruments	1	—150V DC INST	④
A-C Instruments	1	AC INST	③
	1	AC INST	⑦
Angle-of-Attack Indicator	1	ANGLE-OF-ATTACK IND	③
Attitude Indicator			
Auxiliary	1	PILOT AUX	①
Pilot's MM3	1	PILOT MM3 IND CONT REL	③
	3	PILOT MM3 IND & GYRO	③
Navigator's MM3	1	NAV'S	①
D-C Instruments	1	DC INST	④
Low Altitude Radar Altimeter	1	LOW ALT RADAR	③
	1	LOW ALT RADAR	⑦
Mach Indicator	1	MACH METER	⑨
Pilot's Instrument Vibrator	1	PILOT'S INST VIB	⑦
TACAN BDH Indicator	1	TACAN BDH IND	④
	1	TACAN BDH IND	③
Turn and Slip Indicator	1	TURN & SLIP INDICATOR	③
LANDING GEAR SYSTEM			
Landing Gear Position Indicator	1	LANDING GEAR, POS IND	③
Landing Gear Warning Lamps	1	LANDING GEAR WARNING	①
LIGHTING SYSTEM			
Dimming Relays	1	DIMMING RELAYS	③
Pilot's Emergency Lights	1	LIGHT PILOT	③
Navigator's Emergency Lights	1	LIGHT NAV	③
DSO's Emergency Lights	1	LIGHT DS OPR	③
IFR Light and Map Light	1	IFR LT & MAP LT	④
Instrument Lights	1	PILOT	④
	1	NAV & DS OPR	④

Figure 1-20. (Sheet 9 of 11)

AIRCRAFT SYSTEM	FUSE QTY.	FUSE MARKING	PANEL NO.
LIGHTING SYSTEM (Continued)			
Internal Flood Lights	1	PILOT	④
	1	NAV & DS OPR	④
Landing Lights	1	LANDING LIGHT	⑦
	1	LANDING LIGHT	⑨
Lower Anti-Collision Light	1	LWR ANTI COLL'N LIGHT	⑦
Navigation Lights	1	NAV LIGHTS	④
Passageway Lights	1	PASSAGE LIGHTS NAV	④
Taxi Light	1	TAXI LIGHT	⑨
Upper Anti-Collision Light	1	UP ANTI COLL'N LIGHT	⑨
MALFUNCTION INDICATOR AND WARNING SYSTEM			
Angle-of-Attack Indexer (3)	1	ANGLE-OF-ATTACK IND	③
Master Caution Lamp	1	MASTER CAUTION	⑨
Master Warning Lamp	1	MASTER WARNING	③
Stall Warning Lamp	1	STALL WARN IND	③
Voice Warning	1	VOICE WARNING	⑤
NOSE WHEEL STEERING SYSTEM			
Nose Gear Steering	1	NOSE GEAR STEER	⑦
Nose Wheel Steering	1	NOSE WHEEL STEERING	③
OXYGEN SYSTEM			
Oxygen Low Level	1	OXY LOW LEVEL	⑨
Oxygen Quantity	1	OXY QTY	⑨
PHOTO RECONNAISSANCE SYSTEM			
Camera Power	3	CAMR PWR	⑦
PITOT-STATIC SYSTEM			
Angle-of-Attack Sensor Heater	1	HTR	⑦
Pitot Heater (Primary)	1	PITOT HEATER	⑦
Pitot Heater (Secondary)	1	PITOT NO. 2 HEATER	⑨
POD (See BOMBING SYSTEM)			
PRIMARY NAVIGATION SYSTEM			
Astro Tracker	1	ASTRO-TRACKER	①
	1	ASTRO-TRACKER	③
	1	ASTRO-TRACKER	④
	1	PNS ASTRO-TRACKER	④
Doppler Radar	1	DOPPLER RADAR	③
	3	DOPPLER RADAR	③
	3	DOPPLER RADAR	④

Figure 1-20. (Sheet 10 of 11)

T.O. 1B-58A-1

Section I
Description

AIRCRAFT SYSTEM	FUSE QTY.	FUSE MARKING	PANEL NO.
PRIMARY NAVIGATION SYSTEM (Continued)			
Navigation Unit	1	NAV CONTROL	②
	1	NAV UNIT	②
	3	NAV UNIT	②
	3	NAV UNIT	④
Radio Altimeter	1	RADIO ALT	②
	3	RADIO ALT	④
Search Radar	2	SEARCH RADAR	②
	3	SEARCH RADAR	②
	3	SEARCH RADAR	④
control	1	SEARCH RDR CONT	②
heater	1	SEARCH RDR HTR	①
low voltage power supply	3	PNS S RDR LVPS	②
pressure caution lamps	1	S RDR PRESS LT	②
Stabilization Unit	1	STAB UNIT	②
	3	STAB UNIT	②
	3	STAB AREA	④
heater	1	STAB HEATER	①
SMALL WEAPONS (See BOMBING SYSTEM)			
TACAN (See ILS-TACAN SYSTEM)			
VGH RECORDER	1	VGH RECORDER	②
	1	VGH RECORDER	②

Figure 1-20. (Sheet 11 of 11)

External Power Knob.

The external power knob (2, figure 1-15), located on the electrical control panel, controls electrical power supplied from an external power unit. The four knob positions are marked ALERT, GRD REFUEL, OFF, and GRD MAINT. Placing the knob to GRD MAINT connects the external power supply to the electrical system provided that the generator control switches are positioned to OFF and the air conditioning system is activated. The latter feature prevents possible damage to electronic equipment resulting from inadequate cooling. Placing the knob to GRD REFUEL energizes the ground refueling equipment and isolates the remaining circuits. Placing the knob to ALERT accomplishes the same function as GRD MAINT except that the air conditioning requirement is bypassed.

CAUTION

To prevent possible damage to equipment, units requiring air conditioning should not be turned on unless air conditioning is available for equipment cooling except when following the Scramble procedures in Section II. In this case, the equipment should not be on for more than 90 seconds unless air conditioning is available.

1-53

Section I
Description

T.O. 1B-58A-1

d-c power distribution

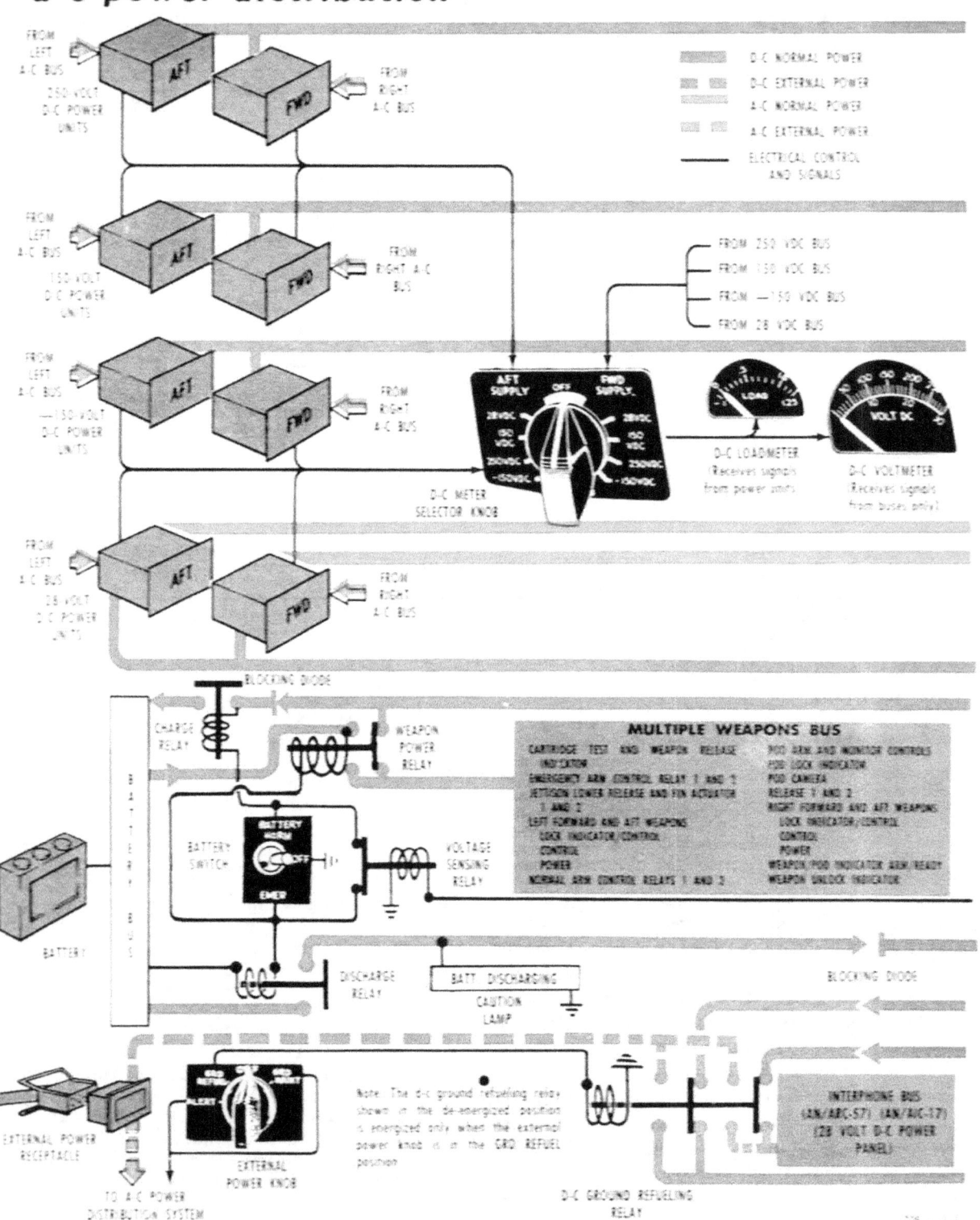

Figure 1-21. (Sheet 1 of 2)

1-54

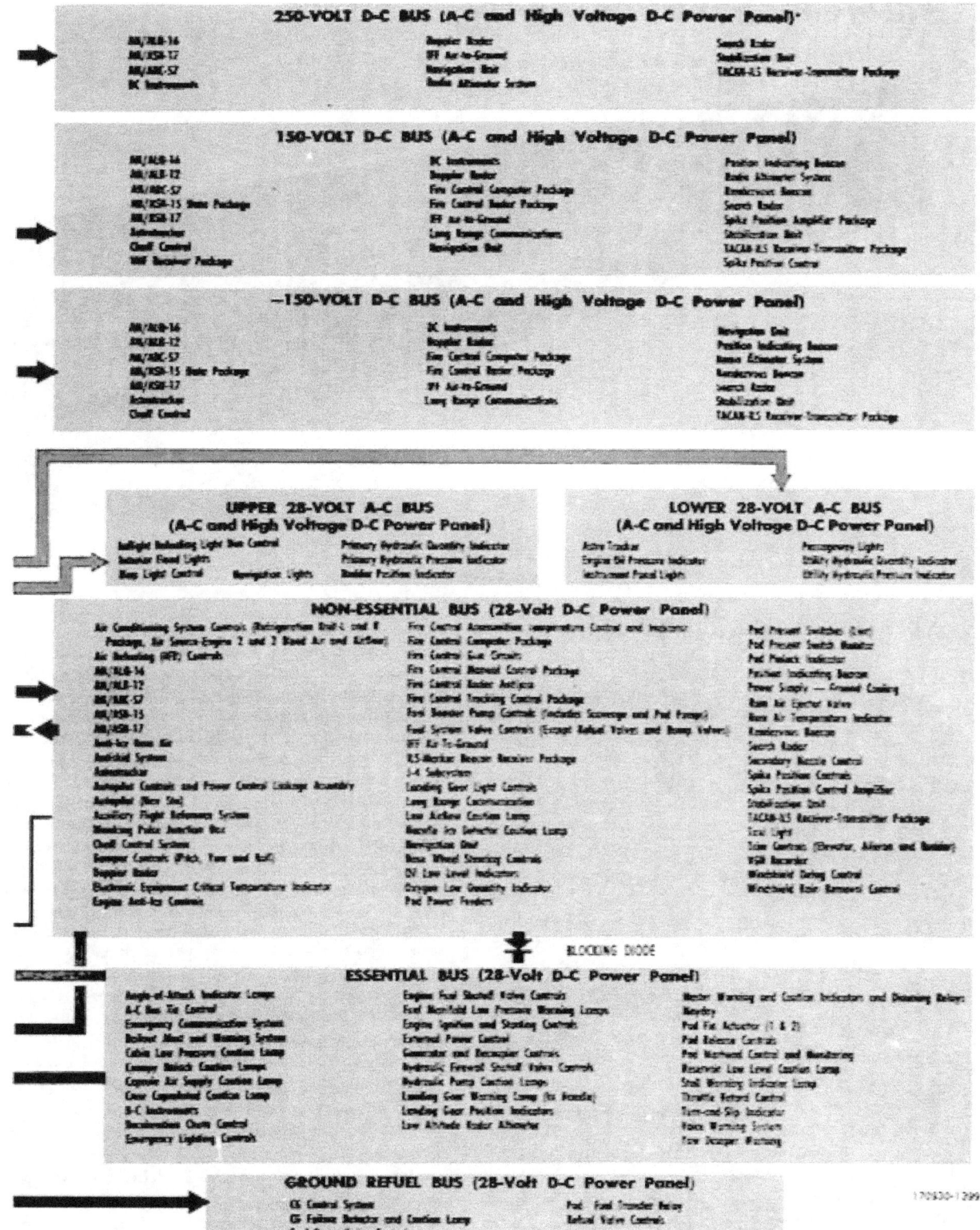

Figure 1-21. (Sheet 2 of 2)

Section I
Description

T.O. 1B-58A-1

d-c system check panel

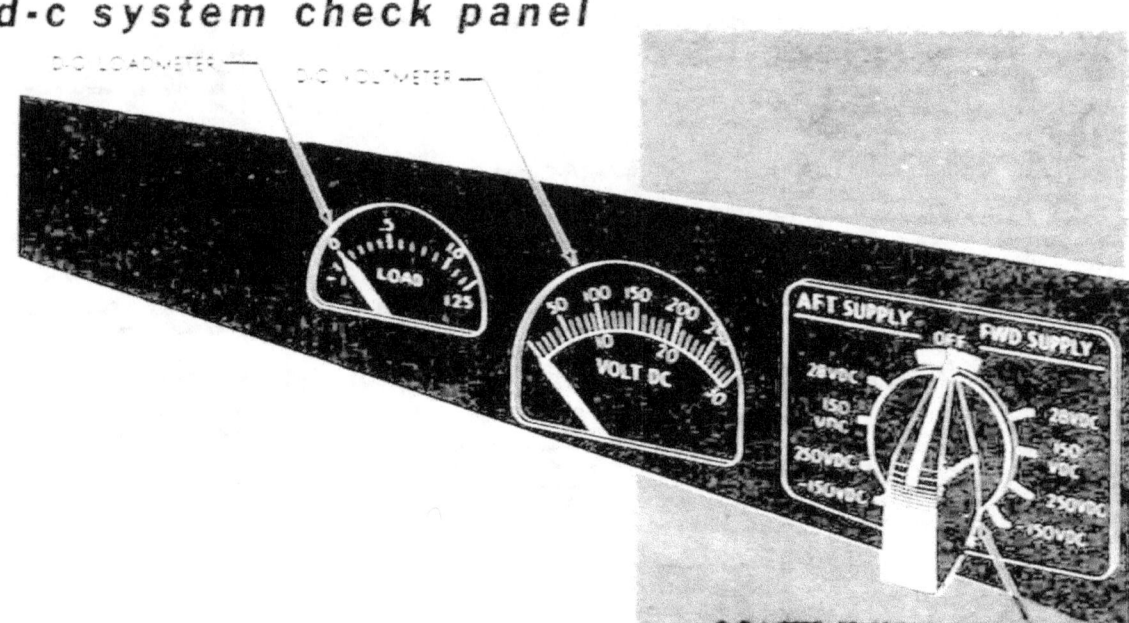

Figure 1-22.

HYDRAULIC POWER SUPPLY SYSTEM.

Two separate, closed, variable delivery, constant-pressure-type hydraulic systems, a utility system (figure 1-24) and a primary system (figure 1-25), supply power for operation of the hydraulic equipment. The two systems are completely independent with no interchange of fluid pressure. The hydraulic power required for operation of the elevon and rudder control surfaces is equally divided between the utility and primary systems, each system being connected to separate actuators. With either system inoperative, the remaining system will assume the entire load of flight control operation. Under such a condition, maximum control surface force output is limited to half that of normal dual system operation. Also, the flow rate is reduced which results in slower response of the control surfaces; however, this will not be appreciably noticeable except when high loads are imposed on the control surfaces. In addition to providing power for the elevon and rudder control surfaces, the utility hydraulic system also supplies power for operating the landing gear, nose wheel steering, wheel brakes, tail turret, search radar, chaff dispensing system, air refueling system, aileron damper servo, elevator damper servo, autopilot servos, and the rudder damper servo. The only additional equipment receiving hydraulic power from the primary system is the rudder damper servo. Each system consists mainly of a pressurized reservoir, two engine-driven pumps, two ram air fluid coolers, two cooler bypass valves, a reservoir bypass valve, two accumulators, two pressure switches, a pressure indicator, a quantity indicator, a spring-loaded surge damper, and two hydraulic shut-off valves. In addition, the utility system includes, landing gear, tail turret, and PCLA filters, a brake accumulator and a brake hand pump. See figure 1-47 for hydraulic fluid specification. Each of the two hyrdaulic systems is independently supplied with fluid from a pressurized reservoir. The reservoirs are located in the main landing gear wheel wells—the utility reservoir in the left wheel well and the primary reservoir in the right wheel well. Each reservoir is pressurized by hydraulic pressure from its respective system. With the systems operating at a normal pressure of 3000 (+200, −125) psi, a pressure of 60 psi will be maintained in the pump suction side of each reservoir. The primary hydraulic system incorporates a pressure regulator valve, accumulator, hand pump, and a pressure gage located in the right wheel well. See figure 1-47 for servicing data. The utility hydraulic system uses a brake accumulator, hand pump, and pressure gage in conjunction with an added pressure regulating valve located in the left wheel well. The reservoir pressurization circuit can be maintained at 3000 psi on the ground by utilizing the hand pump. This will maintain a normal pressure of 60 psi on the remainder of the system which will facilitate maintenance and servicing procedures. The continuous reservoir pressurization system will maintain a positive

1-56

d-c power unit data

Unit Checked	Qty	Fuses Pulled		Voltage Tolerances
		Marking	Location	
250V (FWD)	3 2	AFT SUPPLY 250V-DC AFT SUPPLY 250V-DC OUTPUT	L. a-c pwr. panel AC & H.V. d-c pwr panel	226-277V
250V (AFT)	3 2	FWD SUPPLY 250V-DC FWD SUPPLY 250V-DC OUTPUT	R. a-c pwr panel AC & H.V. d-c pwr panel	226-277V
—150 (FWD)	3 2	AFT SUPPLY —150V-DC AFT SUPPLY —150V-DC OUTPUT	L. a-c pwr. panel AC & H.V. d-c pwr panel	—141-159V
—150 (AFT)	3 2	FWD SUPPLY —150V-DC FWD SUPPLY —150V-DC OUTPUT	R. a-c pwr panel AC & H.V. d-c pwr panel	—141-159V
+150V (FWD)	3 2	AFT SUPPLY +150V-DC AFT SUPPLY +150V-DC OUTPUT	L. a-c pwr. panel AC & H.V. d-c pwr panel	141-159V
+150V (AFT)	3 2	FWD SUPPLY +150V-DC FWD SUPPLY +150V-DC OUTPUT	R. a-c pwr panel AC & H.V. d-c pwr panel	141-159V
28V (FWD)	3 4	AFT SUPPLY 28V-DC AFT SUPPLY OUTPUT NO. 1 (2, 3, 4)	L. main a-c pwr. panel 28-Volt d-c pwr. panel	24.5V-Full scale
28V (AFT)	3 4	FWD SUPPLY 28V-DC FWD SUPPLY OUTPUT NO. 1 (2, 3, 4)	R. main a-c pwr. panel 28-Volt d-c pwr. panel	24.5V-Full scale

Figure 1-23.

pressure and will reduce tendency toward pump cavitation under maximum rate of flight control demand. This will also shorten hydraulic system warmup time during cold weather operations. Pressurization of the reservoirs is necessary because of the remote location from the pumps and by high flow demands. Fluid level in the reservoirs is shown by an integral sliding rod arrangement, visible from the ground, and by the pilot's quantity indicators in the pilot's station. The rod is etched in degrees Fahrenheit to show the quantity of fluid in the reservoir. Fluid level in the reservoir varies with temperature and is serviced according to a placard on the reservoir. The pilot's quantity indicators show actual reservoir level as a percent of its capacity. A placard on the reservoir shows where the level should be with regard to hydraulic system temperature. This temperature can be read on the temperature indicator (dial thermometer) located adjacent to the reservoir. The pilot's quantity indicator reading can be compared to reservoir level reading by a placard mounted on the inside of the main landing gear wheel well door. The system must be pressurized in order to check the fluid level in the reservoir. See figure 1-47 for servicing data. Hydraulic power is supplied to the two systems by four engine-driven pumps, one per engine. Each of the hydraulic systems utilizes two pumps installed in a parallel arrangement—two left wing pumps for the utility system and two right wing pumps for the primary system. In the event of a pump failure in either the utility or the primary hydraulic system, the affected system will continue to function with fluid pressure from the remaining pump. The variable delivery-type pumps are rated to deliver 25 gpm each at 3000 (+200, —125) psi when engine is operated near 100 percent rpm. They are mounted on the aft side of the rear gear case in the lower part of the engine section. A ram air fluid cooler located in the ram air inlet duct of each nacelle provides automatic cooling of the hydraulic fluid during normal operation of the hydraulic systems. The coolers are located in the pump suction supply lines. Each cooler is equipped with an integral thermal bypass arrangement which provides rapid warmup of the fluid during cold starts and prevents supercooling of the fluid in flight. Three piston-type accumulators, two in the primary system and one in

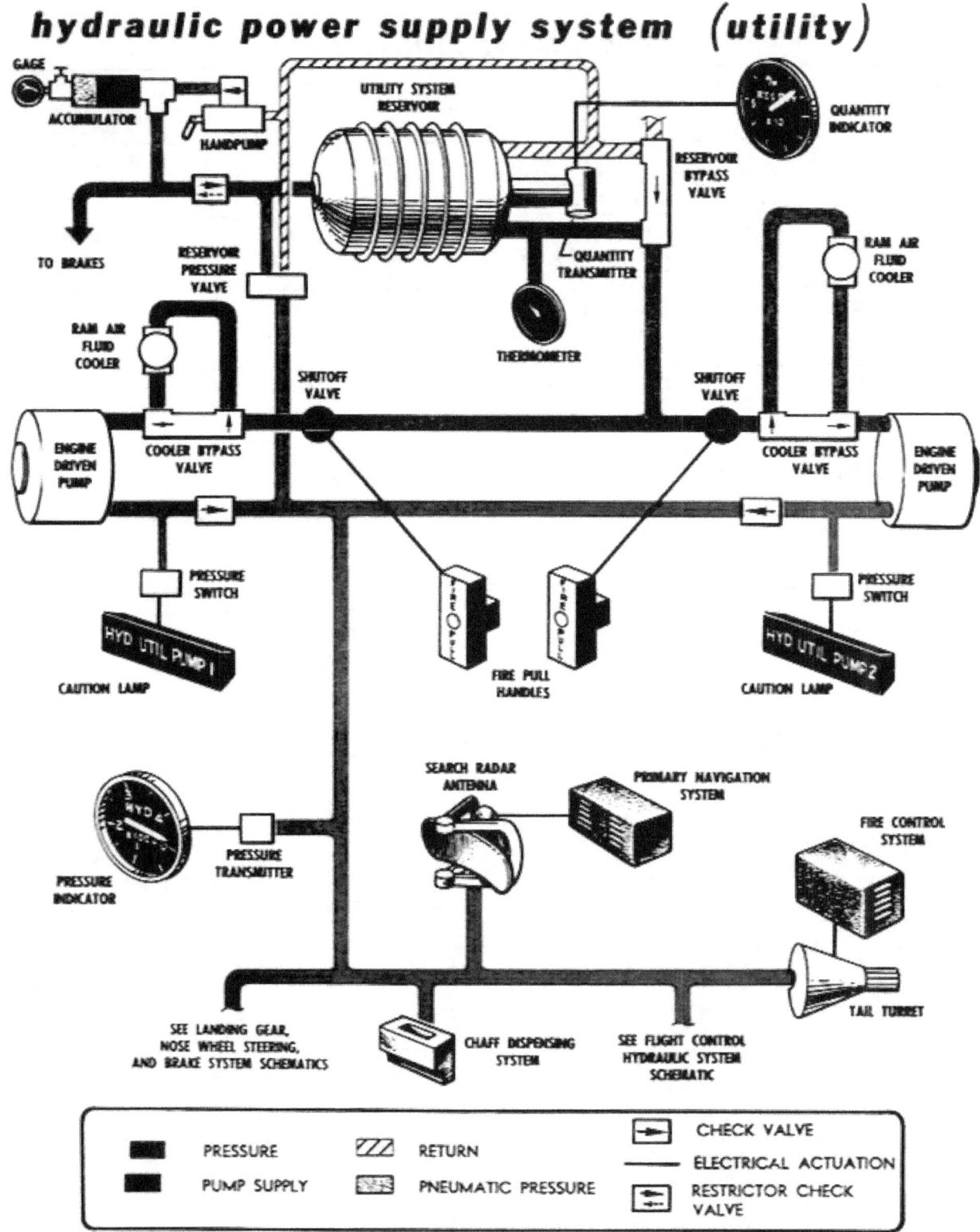

Figure 1-24.

hydraulic power supply system (primary)

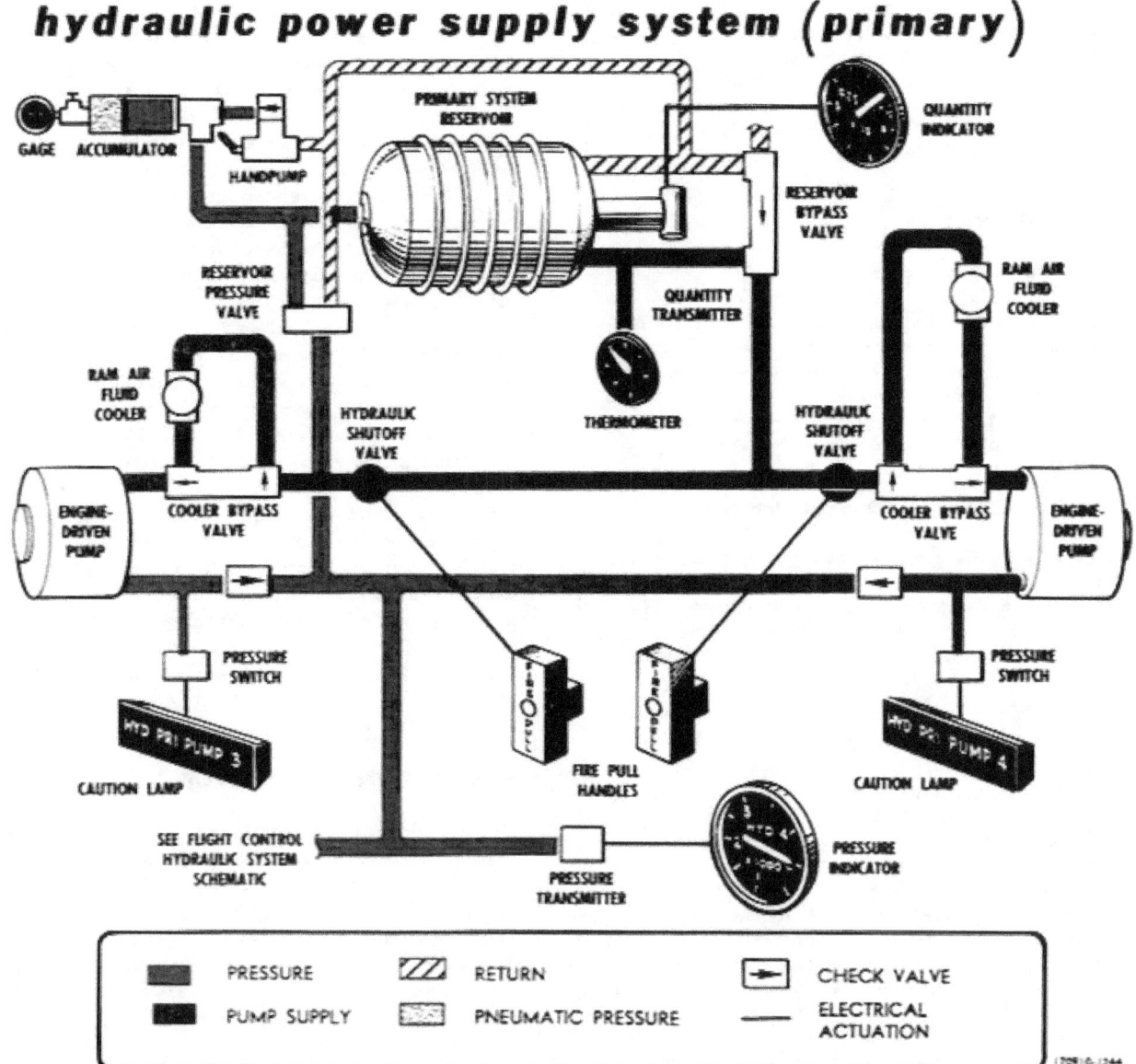

Figure 1-25.

the utility system, provide additional flow to the elevon control surfaces during high rate demands. The utility system includes another piston-type accumulator which supplies flow directly to the PCLA inlet and maintains proper autopilot override function, concurrent with high surface rate demands. Also included in the utility system is a piston-type brake accumulator which supplies pressure for parking brakes. These accumulators are precharged with nitrogen according to the ambient temperature. Placards near the accumulator pressure gages are used to determine the correct precharge pressure. See figure 1-47 for servicing data. A pressure switch located in the hydraulic pressure line downstream from each pump controls a pump failure caution lamp and master caution lamp. The pressure switches, in conjunction with the caution lamps, provide the normal means of determining which hydraulic pump is not functioning in case of pump failure. An electrically actuated hydraulic shutoff valve is incorporated in the fluid suction line of each hydraulic

Section I
Description

T.O. 1B-58A-1

pump and is located above the firewall in the nacelle center section. This valve is utilized to shut off the flow of hydraulic fluid to the nacelle in case of fire in the nacelle area. The hydraulic shutoff valves are controlled with the engine fire pull handles (12, figure 1-5) on the pilot's main instrument panel. Refer to "Emergency Equipment" of this section.

INDICATORS.

Hydraulic Pressure Indicator.

Two hydraulic pressure indicators (2, figure 1-28), one for each hydraulic system, are located on the pilot's lower right console. The indicators are controlled by pressure transmitters and indicate the respective system operating pressure in pounds per square inch. The indicators operate on 28-volt a-c power.

Hydraulic Reservoir Quantity Indicator.

Two hydraulic reservoir quantity indicators (10, figure 1-28), one for each hydraulic system reservoir, are located on the pilot's lower right console. The indicators are actuated by transmitters utilizing 28-volt a-c power and indicate reservoir quantity in percent from 0 to 100.

Hydraulic Pump Caution Lamps.

Four caution lamps (figure 1-13), one for each hydraulic pump, are located on the pilot's caution lamp panel. The caution lamps will go out when pressure increases to 2100 psi maximum. The lamps will light when the pressure drops to 350 psi minimum. The pressure at which a lamp lights should be at least 1000 psi below the pressure at which it went out. When lighted, yellow letters appear on the face of the caution lamp to identify the affected hydraulic system and pump number that is malfunctioning. Since the two pumps in each hydraulic system are manifolded together, these lamps provide the only means of determining the failure of any individual hydraulic pump. The caution lamps will be lighted before the engines are started if electrical power is on the airplane. As the engines are started, the lamps will go out when the hydraulic pressure builds up. The hydraulic pump caution lamps are connected to the master caution lamp circuit and receive power from the 28-volt d-c power panel. For testing and dimming of the lamps, refer to "Malfunction Indicator and Warning System," this section.

PNEUMATIC POWER SUPPLY SYSTEMS.

Power for the pneumatically operated equipment is supplied by independent pneumatic systems and bleed air from the air conditioning system. Power for emergency extension of the landing gear is provided by pneumatic pressure stored in the left main landing gear drag strut. Power for emergency operation of the main landing gear wheel brakes is provided by pneumatic pressure stored in two truss tubes of the left main landing gear linkage assembly. The drag chute receives power from a pressurized pneumatic bottle located in the parachute stowage compartment. The air refueling system has a separate pneumatic pressure storage container for pressurizing the hydraulic fluid in event of utility hydraulic system failure and is located in the nose wheel well. Pressure for opening and closing the canopies is stored in the right main landing gear w-truss. The pneumatic pressure stored in the w-truss is also used for inflating the canopy seals when the canopies are closed from the nose wheel well. A pneumatic container for the chaff dispensing system is located in the right wing. The pressure gage is located in the left wheel well. Each of the independent pneumatic systems uses pressurized nitrogen as the source of pneumatic power. With one or both inboard engines operating, pneumatic power for inflating the canopy seals is supplied by air pressure from the warm air lines of the air conditioning system. For detailed information on these pneumatic systems, refer to "Landing Gear System," "Brake System," "Drag Chute," and "Canopies" of this section.

FLIGHT CONTROL SYSTEM.

The flight control system (figure 1-27) provides control of the airplane by means of three control surfaces—two elevons and a rudder. The control surfaces are controlled by the pilot, the autopilot and by the stability augmentation system (dampers), and utilize hydraulic power for actuation. Hydraulic actuation is essential since the control surface loads become quite high during some flight conditions. Each control surface has two independent sets of hydraulic actuators. One set receives hydraulic power from the utility hydraulic system and the other from the primary hydraulic system. See figure 1-26. With either hydraulic system inoperative, the remaining system will assume the entire load of flight control operation. Under such a condition, maximum control surface load capability is limited to half that of normal dual system operation. Also, the loss of flow in one system results in slower response of the control surfaces; however, this will not be appreciably noticeable except when high loads are imposed on the control surfaces. The elevons perform the combined functions of both ailerons and elevators and are controlled by conventional stick commands. A mixer assembly mechanically converts elevator and aileron commands into right and left elevon commands. The rudder is controlled by

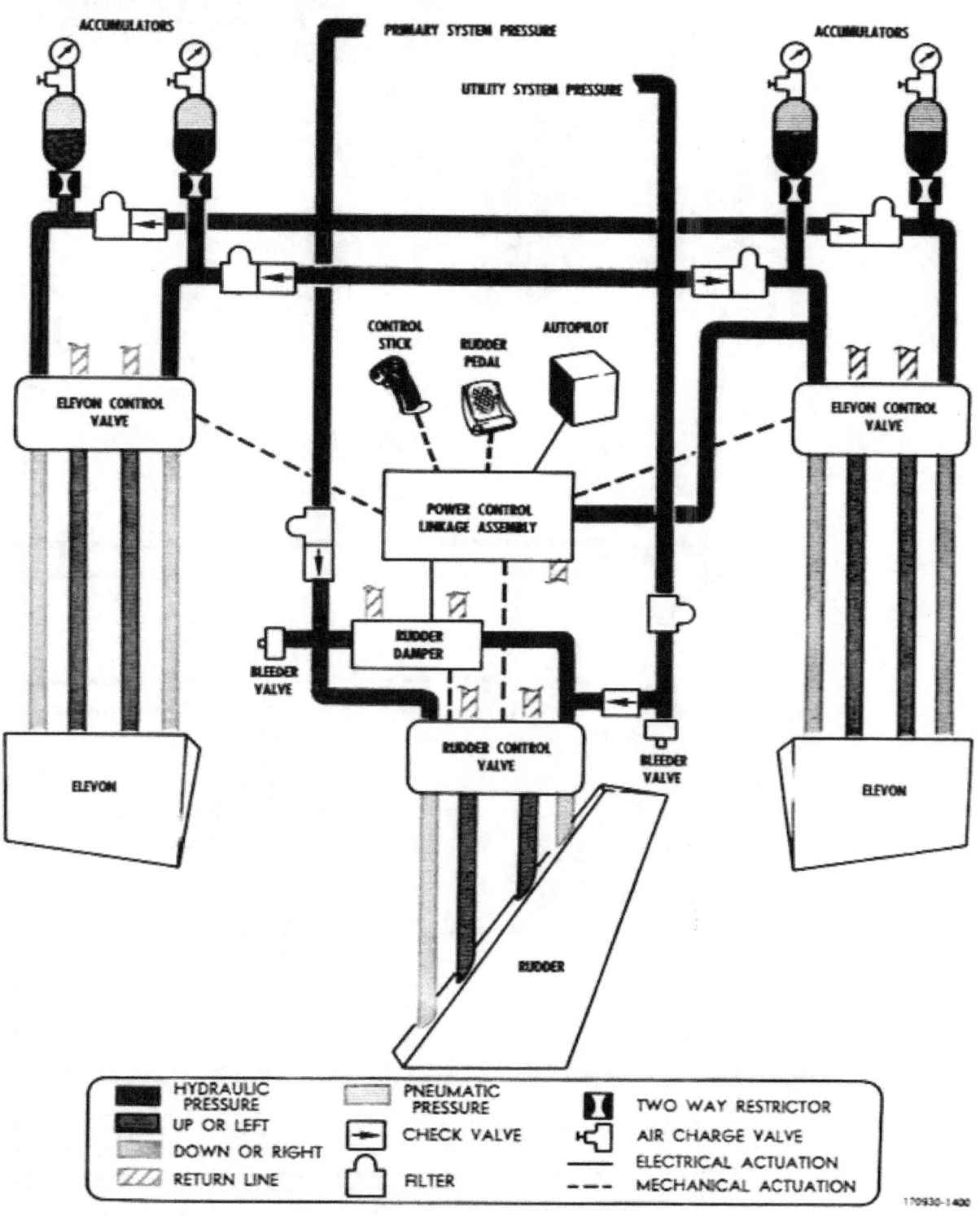

Figure 1-26.

Section I
Description

T.O. 1B-58A-1

flight control system diagram

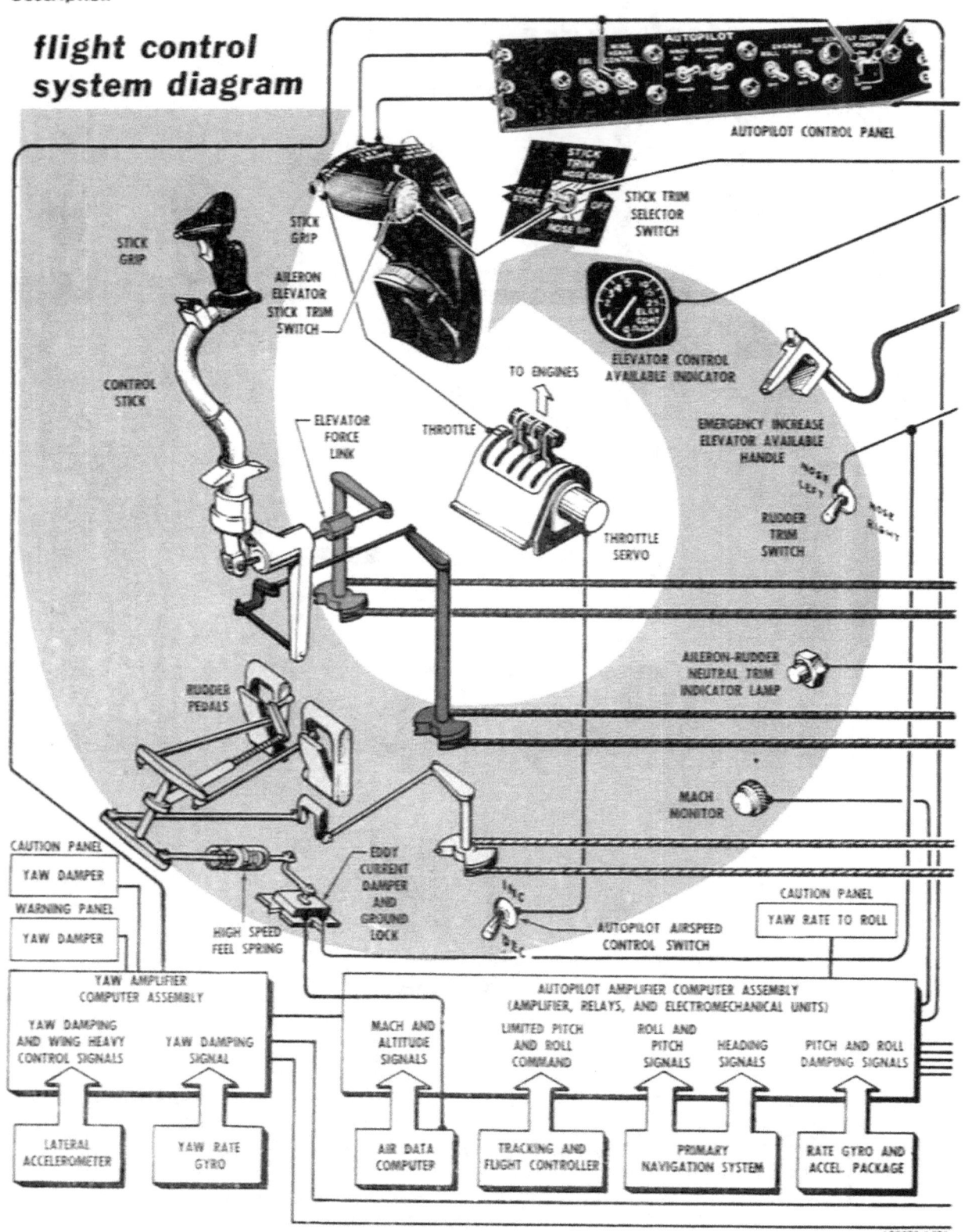

Figure 1-27. (Sheet 1 of 2)

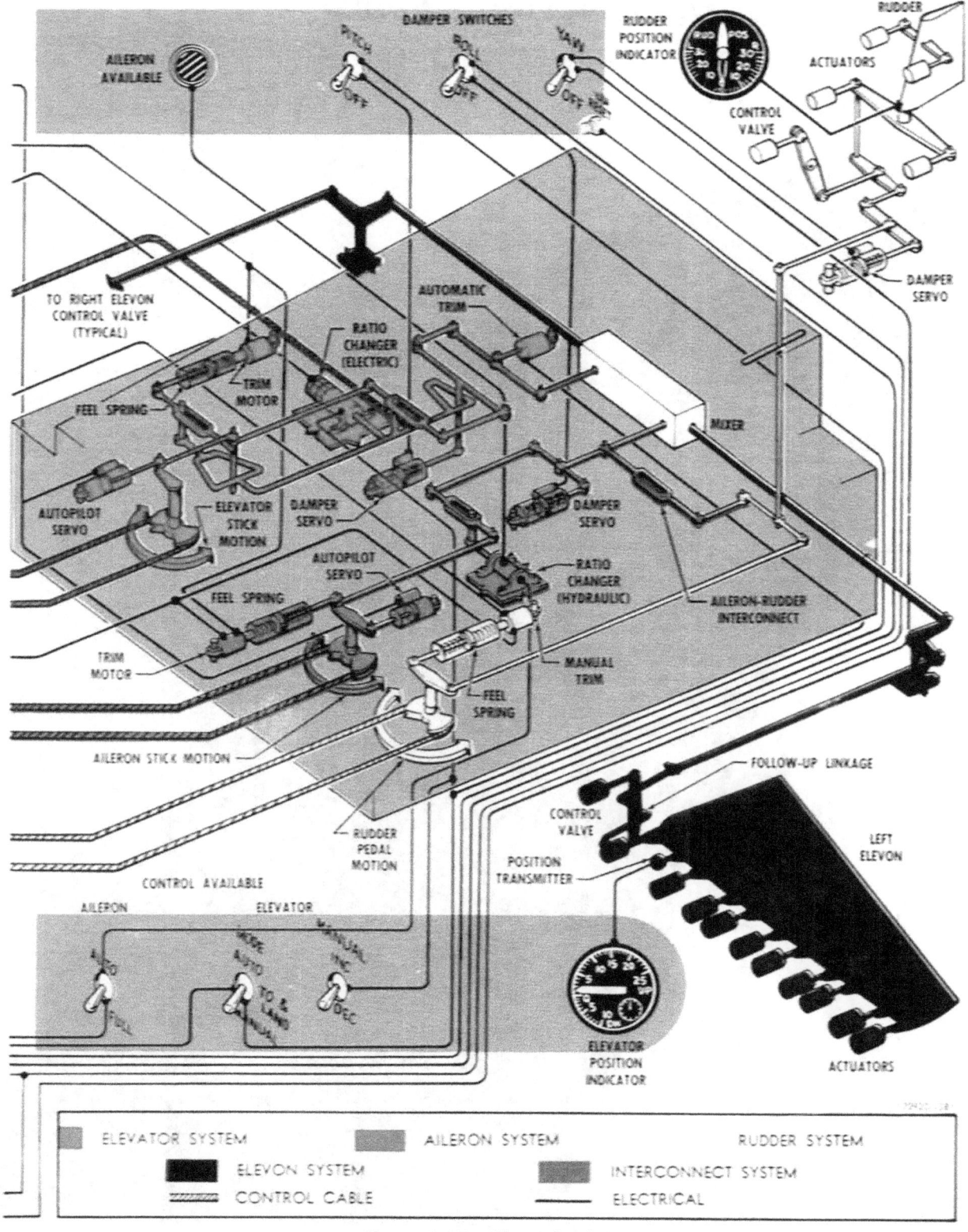

Figure 1-27. (Sheet 2 of 2)

Section I
Description

T.O. 1B-58A-1

pilot's lower right console (typical)

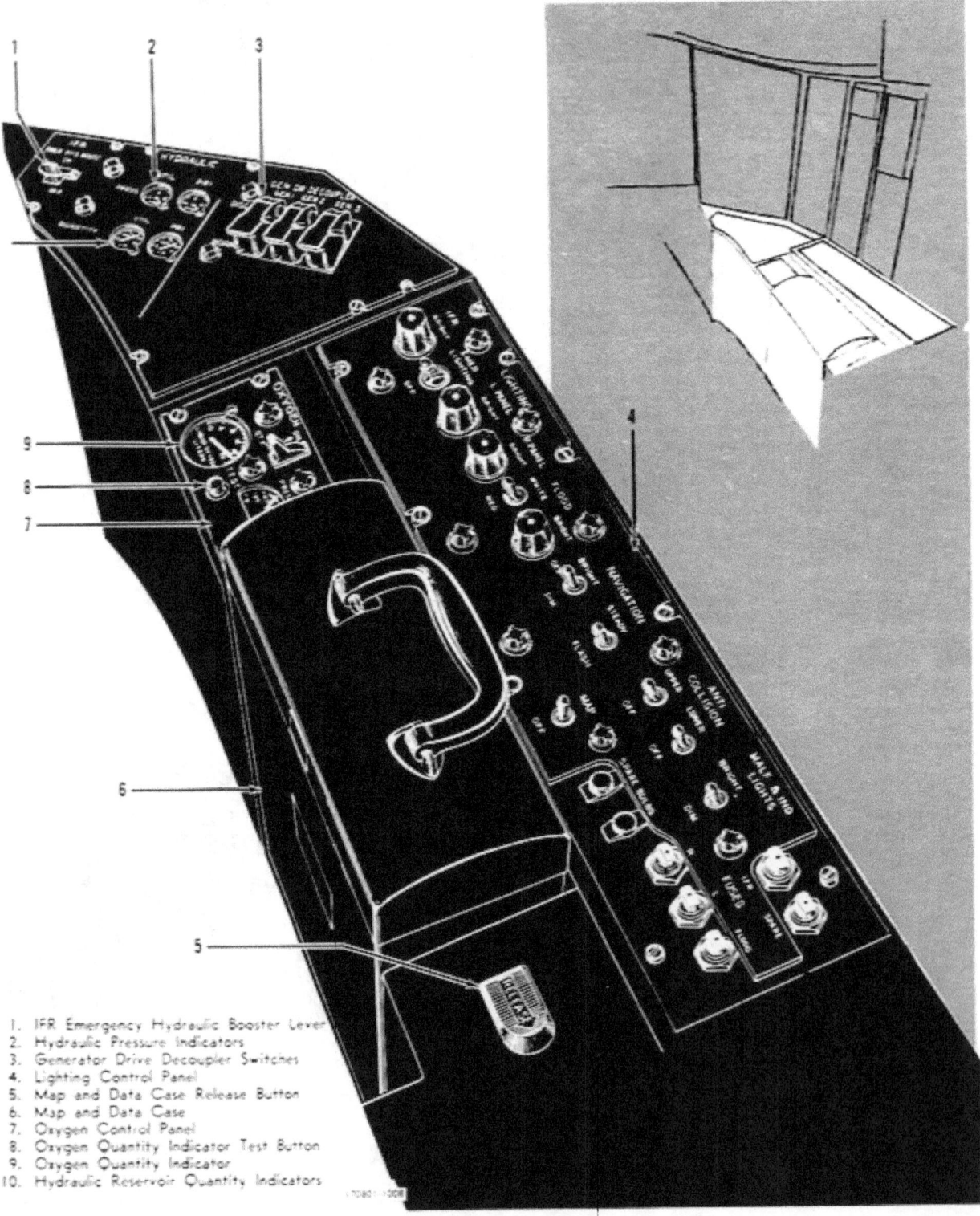

1. IFR Emergency Hydraulic Booster Lever
2. Hydraulic Pressure Indicators
3. Generator Drive Decoupler Switches
4. Lighting Control Panel
5. Map and Data Case Release Button
6. Map and Data Case
7. Oxygen Control Panel
8. Oxygen Quantity Indicator Test Button
9. Oxygen Quantity Indicator
10. Hydraulic Reservoir Quantity Indicators

Figure 1-28.

conventional rudder pedals and yaw damper plus the action of the aileron-rudder interconnect. The elevon and rudder surface hydraulic actuators do not transmit the surface airloads back to the stick or rudder pedals; therefore, artificial feel systems are utilized to provide conventional stick and rudder forces. For the maximum deflections, rates of operation, etc., of the pilot's controls, the control surfaces, and the trim and damper units, refer to "Flight Control System" Section VII. A control valve for each of the control surfaces is mechanically positioned to control the flow of hydraulic fluid to the actuators for surface movement. Mechanical feedback signals, proportional to the surface position, automatically return the control valves to neutral when the surfaces reach the command position, thereby stopping the flow of hydraulic fluid to the actuators. The irreversible surface control hydraulic systems prevent free movement of the surfaces when the hydraulic systems are pressurized. However, the control surfaces will eventually droop if the airplane is parked for an extended period of time without hydraulic pressure on the system. This is normal and should cause no concern, as the control surfaces will return to their normal positions when hydraulic power is applied.

Note

An unusually fast rate of elevon droop indicates an abnormal condition in the system unless the stick has been displaced after shutdown of hydraulic power. Droop to full down position in less than one hour is unusual. Also, one elevon may droop at a faster rate than the other.

Aileron, elevator, and rudder trim switches provide manual control of electrical trim motors for reducing control forces. The trim motors operate directly on the artifical feel systems to relieve control stick and pedal forces. The flying qualities of the airplane are improved by various flight control system features which include an elevator ratio changer, automatic trim, an aileron ratio changer, an aileron-rudder interconnect, a wing heavy control, and roll, pitch, and yaw stability augmentation. Additional description of each of these features is contained in this section. The ratio changers, elevator and aileron autopilot and damper servos, elevon mixer, trim motors, artificial feel systems, and the aileron-rudder mechanical interconnect are grouped together in a power control linkage assembly (PCLA), which is located in the fuselage tail section between the elevons. All pilot command signals are routed through the PCLA to the surface control valves. All other surface commands, with the exception of rudder damper servo commands, are initiated by PCLA components. The flight control system is functionally divided into three subsystems; the elevator control system, the aileron control system, and the rudder control system. For information on operation of the flight control system, refer to Section VII.

Stability Augmentation (Damping).

Stability augmentation is continuously provided in roll, pitch, and yaw during flight. These automatic inputs are introduced through the appropriate damper servo to improve the damping and handling qualities of the airplane. The roll and pitch damping signals are derived from the rate gyro and accelerometer package. The pitch damping signals and the yaw rate input to the roll damper are automatically gain adjusted as a function of mach number and/or altitude by the air data system. The roll damping signals are not automatically gain adjusted; the gain of that channel being fixed. The yaw damping signals are derived from the yaw rate gyro package and the lateral accelerometer package and are automatically gain adjusted as a function of altitude, however, the altitude sensing for this gain function is independent of the air data computer. Refer to figure 7-18. The yaw damper function is provided by a redundant system composed of three separate channels each having its own sensors, gain adjustment, electronics, and servo function. Continuous electronic monitoring of the operation of these three channels is accomplished at several points (monitor blocks) between the sensors and the servos to detect a failure. When the signal in one channel differs from the other two by an amount greater than a predetermined level, the bad channel in that particular monitor block is bypassed and the YAW DAMPER caution lamp in the pilot's station will light, thereby notifying him that an initial failure has occurred. Since two channels remain operable in that monitor block, the system continues to provide yaw damping with no degradation in performance. Similarly, a subsequent failure can occur in any of the other monitor blocks without degrading the yaw damping function, and, since the caution lamp is already lighted as a result of the first failure, no additional notification to the pilot will occur.

Note

The loss of either hydraulic system will cause the yaw damper caution lamp to light. If the primary hydraulic system fails, a slight rudder deflection may occur when the yaw damper transfers to the utility system.

If, however, after an initial failure has occurred in one of the monitor blocks, another failure occurs in one of the two remaining channels of the same monitor block, the system can no longer determine which is the good or bad signal. Therefore, the yaw damper function is automatically disengaged and the yaw damper will return to a neutral position. At the same time the YAW DAMPER warning lamp in the pilot's station will light to notify him that the yaw damper system is inoperative. Occasionally, spurious electrical transients in the monitor circuits can cause the yaw damper caution lamp to light when no malfunction has occurred. For this reason, a yaw reset button has been included to reset the monitor circuit and permit a check to determine whether an actual malfunction has occurred.

WARNING

Do not depress the yaw reset button when the yaw damper warning lamp is lighted. To do so may cause a failed yaw damper channel to engage.

Refer to "Flight Control System Trouble Shooting Procedures", Section VII for reset procedures and malfunction verification. In addition to the yaw damper system, dutch roll stability augmentation is provided at speeds above approximately mach number 0.92 by a dual channel, mach scheduled, yaw rate input to the roll damper. The signals for these yaw rate to roll damper channels are derived from two separate gyros in the rate gyro and accelerometer package and the two signals are summed. A monitor, which is active only when the landing gear is retracted, is provided for these signals and will cause the YAW RATE TO ROLL caution lamp to light anytime the difference between the signals from the two gyros exceeds the normal tolerance. Lighting of this caution lamp indicates that, under the worst conditions, the output of one yaw rate gyro has failed. The roll damper channel will continue to operate on the remaining yaw rate gyro with a slight degradation of performance at airspeeds above mach no. 0.92. Below mach no. 0.92 no degradation of performance will occur. Occasional spurious electrical transients in the monitor circuits can cause the yaw rate to roll caution lamp to light when no malfunction exists. The yaw reset button also resets the yaw rate to roll damper monitor circuits. Refer to "Flight Control System Trouble Shooting Procedures", Section VII for reset procedures and malfunction verification. In the event of failure of the automatic gain adjustment in the pitch channel or the yaw rate to roll damper channel, a switch is provided at the pilot's station to select standby fixed gains. This feature is to be used only in the event of failure of the automatic gain adjustment. Refer to "Mach-Altitude Gain Adjustment Failure", Section VII.

ELEVATOR CONTROL SYSTEM.

The elevator control system consists of the elevator automatic trim system, an elevator ratio changer, the elevator stick trim and feel system, and an elevator damper servo.

Elevator Automatic Trim System.

The elevator automatic trim system contains an electromechanical servo which automatically provides elevator command signals to position the elevator for constant one-"g" flight when the pilot's control stick is in the neutral position. One-"g" flight can occur in a climb or dive as well as level flight. This servo, in addition to the elevator ratio changer, is energized by the elevator control available mode selector switch (9, figure 1-6). Automatic operation of the elevator automatic trim is provided only when the switch is in the AUTO position. When the switch is in either the TO & LAND or MANUAL position, the servo will drive to a position corresponding to 1-1/2 degrees up-elevator and lock in that position until the AUTO position is again selected. However, if elevator available is less than 7 degrees when either TO & LAND or MANUAL is selected, the elevator automatic trim will hold the position it had at the time of selection until elevator available becomes greater than 7 degrees. The output motion of the elevator automatic trim is absorbed by the elevator feel spring and the elevator damper servo and therefore does not move the pilot's control stick. The automatic trim authority in terms of elevator deflection is 10 degrees up and 1.0 degree down regardless of elevator available.

Elevator Ratio Changer.

The elevator ratio changer is an electro-mechanical servo mounted in the PCLA which improves the airplane flying qualities by varying the elevator control stick sensitivity, and which protects the airplane against excessive "g" loading by controlling both elevator available and elevator damper servo authority. The elevator ratio changer mode is controlled by the three-position elevator control available mode selector switch located on the pilot's left sidewall console. The switch positions are marked AUTO, TO & LAND and MANUAL. When AUTO is selected, the elevator ratio changer is automatically controlled. Elevator available is limited to that value required to develop approximate limit load factor. Elevator available is controlled by varying the stick to surface mechanical advantage and by limiting the stick displacement authority. At maximum elevator available (20 degrees), the stick authority is 6 inches aft and 3 inches forward (see figure 7-13). As elevator available decreases, the stick to surface mechanical advantage and the stick displacement authority decreases. At minimum elevator available (1.25 degrees), with the switch in AUTO, and for pilot control of the airplane, the stick displacement authority is 1.5 inches fore or aft, and the minimum elevator is 1.25 degrees for all modes.

The control stick feel sensitivity is also varied by the elevator ratio changer. The feel force at maximum stick displacement is approximately 25 pounds for all values of elevator available. When the elevator control available mode selector switch is placed in the TO & LAND position, the elevator ratio changer drives to the maximum elevator available position and remains in this position until another mode is selected. When the elevator control available mode selector switch is placed in the MANUAL position, control of the elevator ratio changer is transferred to the elevator control available manual adjust switch located on the pilot's left side wall console. When the MANUAL position is selected, elevator available remains fixed until the pilot increases or decreases elevator available with the elevator control available manual adjust switch. The manual mode is used only in case of failure of the automatic mode and during air refueling. The TO & LAND position is used for all take-offs and landings. In the event of failure in the automatic mode, several means are provided to override the elevator ratio changer. First, the elevator control available mode selector switch can be positioned to either TO & LAND or MANUAL. Second, application of approximately 105-120 pounds of force at the top of the stick will trip a force switch in the elevator force link that will automatically return the elevator control available mode selector switch to the TO & LAND position, causing the elevator ratio changer to drive to the maximum elevator available position. When the preceding provisions fail to provide enough elevator available for control of the airplane, an emergency increase elevator available handle (6, figure 1-7), located on the pilot's lower left console, can be used to manually position the elevator ratio changer for an *increase* and/or decrease in elevator control available. The handle provides increased control available in distinct steps. Pulling the handle out to the second detent causes the following switching to occur: the ratio changer actuator electrical circuit is disconnected, the elevator control available mode selector switch is positioned to TO & LAND, and normal electrical power to the automatic trim actuator is disconnected; each subsequent step of the handle provides an increase in elevator available until the maximum is reached. Pushing in the handle reverses the function of the handle and decreases the amount of elevator available to correspond with each position as the handle was pulled out. For the amount of elevator for each position of the handle, see figure 7-16.

Elevator Stick Trim and Feel System.

Airloads on the flight control surfaces are reacted by the hydraulic actuating systems and are not transferred back to the control stick or rudder pedals. Therefore, artificial feel is supplied in each of the three control systems to provide the pilot with synthetic indication of the airloads. The elevator feel spring is located in the PCLA and provides a 5-pound breakout force and feeds back 25 pounds of force to the top of the stick at maximum elevator stick displacements. The elevator stick trim aligns the spring zero-force position with the pilot's stick position, thereby relieving the force at the top of the stick. The elevator trim motor may be manually operated by either the aileron-elevator stick trim switch (7, figure 1-29) located on the control stick grip or by the stick trim selector switch (3, figure 1-30) located on the trim control panel. During autopilot operation the trim motor is automatically and continuously positioned to maintain zero force on the feel spring within the available authority to prevent stick transients at autopilot disengagement. At maximum elevator available the trim motor has ± 10 degrees of authority in terms of elevator surface deflection and can relieve approximately ± 14 pounds of force at the top of the stick. In terms of elevator surface deflection, the trim authority decreases as elevator available decreases. However, discounting system nonlinearities, the elevator trim motor authority is one-half of elevator available for all values of elevator available.

Elevator Damper Servo.

The elevator damper servo is an electrically controlled, hydraulically operated servo that automatically provides elevator commands to damp the rate of pitch of the airplane. This servo is located in the PCLA and is activated by the pitch damper switch located on the pilot's left sidewall console. The output of the elevator damper servo grounds against the elevator feel spring and does not move the pilot's control stick. The authority of the elevator damper servo is controlled by the elevator ratio changer. For values of elevator available greater than 3.33 degrees, the authority limit of the elevator damper servo is ± 2 degrees of elevator. For values of elevator available less than 3.33 degrees, the authority limit of the elevator damper servo is ± 0.6 times the value of elevator available. Hydraulic power for this servo is supplied by the utility hydraulic system. A pitch rate gyro located in the rate gyro and accelerometer package transmits to the servo transfer valve a gain-adjusted electrical signal proportional to the airplane pitch rate. The transfer valve controls, according to the electrical signal, the flow of hydraulic fluid that positions the servo actuator. The output of the actuator, and hence the commanded elevator, is always in a direction to decrease the pitch rate. The elevator damper servo should be energized during all normal flight operations.

Elevator Autopilot Servo.

The elevator autopilot servo is an electrically controlled, hydraulically operated servo mounted in the PCLA. Hydraulic power to the elevator autopilot servo is supplied by the utility hydraulic system through a

Section I
Description

pressure reducer in the power control linkage assembly which reduces the pressure from 3000 psi to 750 psi prior to entering the servo. Actuation of this servo causes the stick to follow the servo motion, and mechanical commands from the servo to the PCLA linkage are very similar to stick commands. For operation of the autopilot, refer to "Autopilot" Section IV.

AILERON CONTROL SYSTEM.

The aileron control system consists of an aileron ratio changer, the aileron manual trim and feel system, and aileron damper servo.

Aileron Ratio Changer.

The aileron ratio changer is a two-position electrically controlled, hydraulically operated servo unit. The servo is controlled by switches at the pilot's station and operates to provide either automatic control of aileron available or full aileron control available. In the automatic mode, the servo provides either full or one-half aileron control available as a function of the position of the elevator control available mode selector switch. Positioning the aileron control available switch to AUTO with the elevator control available mode selector switch in either the AUTO or MANUAL position will cause the aileron control available to drive to HALF. At the pilot's discretion, the servo can be positioned to provide 15 degrees of aileron control available by placing the aileron control available switch to FULL. In the event of loss of either electrical or hydraulic power, the servo will provide automatically 15 degrees of aileron control available. The aileron ratio changer is supplied hydraulic power from the utility system.

Aileron Stick Trim and Feel System.

Artificial feel is also provided in the aileron control system. The feel is supplied by a feel spring located in the PCLA. Due to a non-linear mechanism located between the control stick and the PCLA in the aileron control system, the force gradient at the stick is a function of stick position. With the stick at neutral, the nominal breakout force is 4 pounds at the top of the stick. Also, the force gradient and the stick to surface mechanical advantage is high. As the stick is moved away from neutral, the force gradient increases and the stick to surface mechanical advantage decreases. The maximum aileron stick movement in either direction from neutral is 4.5 inches and the maximum feel force at hardover stick position is approximately 15 pounds. A stick trim motor is provided to align the feel spring zero force position with the stick position; thereby, relieving the forces at the pilot's control stick. The pilot may command force changes with a trim button located on the control stick. Maximum trim authority is ±5 degrees of aileron surface displacement when the aileron ratio changer is in the full position and ±2.5 degrees in the half position.

Aileron Damper Servo.

The aileron damper servo is electrically controlled and hydraulically operated. This servo is activated by a switch at the pilot's station. The output motion of the aileron damper servo grounds against the aileron feel spring and does not move the pilot's control stick. Also, the authority of the servo is not changed by the aileron ratio changer; the authority is always ±3 degrees in terms of aileron surface displacement. The primary function of the aileron damper servo is to damp the airplane roll rate. The airplane roll rate is sensed by the roll rate gyro located in the rate gyro and accelerometer package. Electrical signals proportional to the roll rate are transmitted to the aileron damper servo and cause the servo to command aileron in a direction to decrease the roll rate. The servo receives hydraulic power from the utility system. A secondary function of the servo is to provide yaw damping at airspeeds above approximately mach number 0.92. The yaw rate is sensed by two rate gyros located in the rate gyro and accelerometer package. Electrical signals proportional to the airplane yaw rate are transmitted to the servo and cause the servo to command aileron in a direction to decrease the yaw rate. The aileron damper servo should be operative during all normal flight operations.

Aileron Autopilot Servo.

The aileron autopilot servo is electrically controlled and hydraulically operated. Hydraulic power is supplied by the utility hydraulic system through a pressure reducer in the power control linkage assembly which reduces the pressure from 3000 psi to 750 psi prior to entering the servo. The output signals from the aileron autopilot servo cause the control stick to move with the servo. The authority of this servo is controlled by the aileron ratio changer and is either 15 degrees (full) or 7.5 degrees (half). For operation of the autopilot, refer to "Autopilot" Section IV.

RUDDER CONTROL SYSTEM.

The rudder control system consists of a rudder pedal trim and feel system, a rudder damper servo and an aileron-rudder interconnect. The aileron-rudder interconnect gain is fixed at one degree of rudder per degree of aileron regardless of the flight condition.

Rudder Pedal Trim and Feel System.

The rudder pedal trim and feel system consists of a feel spring and trim motor combination located in the PCLA and a high-speed feel spring assembly located just forward of the pilot's left rudder pedal. This system features a low breakout force and a low force gradient at speeds below mach no. 0.6, a high breakout force and a high force gradient at speeds above mach no. 0.6 for pedal deflections less than 6 degrees of rudder, and a low force gradient for speeds above

1-68

mach no. 0.6 for pedal deflections greater than 6 degrees of rudder. The first feature is provided by the feel spring in the PCLA and the second and third features are provided by the feel spring in the PCLA in combination with the high-speed feel spring assembly. For speeds below mach no. 0.6 the nominal breakout force is 7 pounds and the maximum force at maximum pedal deflection (30 degrees) is approximately 80 pounds at the pedals. This level of force is for ground (nose wheel steering) and takeoff and landing operations. At high speeds the airplane becomes more sensitive to rudder pedal commands. Thus it is desirable to have a high force gradient about the neutral pedal position to control rudder sensitivity during high-speed flight conditions. If the same high spring gradient were maintained throughout the entire rudder authority (30 degrees) it would take 375 pounds of force to command maximum rudder. It is therefore desirable to reduce the spring gradient when rudder commands in excess of a nominal value (6 degrees) are required. For the high-speed conditions the breakout force is approximately 14 pounds. Approximately 75 pounds of force at the pedal is required to command 6 degrees and 170 pounds is required to command maximum authority. The high-speed feel spring assembly is caged by a magnetic brake which is controlled by an electrical signal, proportional to mach number, which is supplied by the air data system. The brake releases and allows the spring ground to float whenever the speed is reduced below mach no. 0.6 or whenever the rudder pedal trim motor is energized. The spring return to the zero force position is restricted by an eddy current damper. The damper acts to slow the rate of return and reduces disengage transients. It will normally take several seconds for the force across the high-speed feel spring assembly to be completely relieved by trim commands. The rudder pedal trim motor is controlled by a switch at the pilot's station. The rudder pedal trim authority is ±10 degrees of rudder. It should be noted that the motor itself only acts directly on the feel spring in the PCLA.

Rudder Damper Servo.

The rudder damper servo is an electrically controlled, hydraulically operated servo located in the vertical tail section. The servo provides rudder command signals proportional to yaw rate and lateral acceleration. The yaw rate signals are generated by the yaw rate gyro package and the lateral acceleration signals are generated by the lateral accelerometer package. These lateral accelerometers are operative at all airspeeds. The rudder damper servo grounds against the rudder and aileron feel springs in the PCLA and therefore does not move the rudder pedals. This servo is activated by the yaw damper power switch located at the pilot's station. The servo should remain activated during all normal flight operations. Hydraulic power for the rudder damper servo is supplied by both the primary and the utility hydraulic systems. The rudder damper servo authority is ± 14.0 degrees.

Wing Heavy Control System.

The wing heavy control system is provided to sense lateral accelerations and provide corrective rudder through the rudder damper servo to prevent lateral fuel shift and subsequent wing heaviness. When the system is engaged it is activated at all times provided that the landing gear is in the retracted position. The system commands a maximum of 3.5 degrees of left or right rudder, and can be overpowered by the pilot.

STANDBY GAINS SYSTEM.

The gains of the pitch autopilot, pitch damper, as well as the yaw rate to roll damper signal, above mach no. 0.92, are automatically adjusted by signals received from the air data computer through the mach altitude repeater. Standby fixed gains are provided to bypass these automatic gains in the event of a malfunction of the air data computer, the mach-altitude repeater, or the automatic gain potentiometers. See figure 7-18. The standby gains have been set approximately equal to the automatic gain values, and within their respective operating regions, will provide damping approximately equal to automatic gain damping. Within the transition corridors, the correct set of standby gains will provide adequate but somewhat degraded damping. The lateral autopilot channels, roll rate to roll damper channel, and the yaw rate to yaw damper channel have fixed gains; consequently no standby gains are provided for these channels. The yaw damping gain is adjusted by an altitude scheduled gain and no standby fixed gains are activated by positioning the gain selector switch to HIGH SPEED or LOW SPEED. For a description of the proper selection of standby gains refer to "Standby Gains System," Section VII and "Gain Selector switch" this section. The use of dampers in standby gains is restricted to the operating regions and transition corridors shown in figure 7-19. Autopilot use in standby gains is restricted to the operating regions shown on figure 7-19 (region A for high speeds and region B for subsonic cruise). Within these operating regions the autopilot may be used in conjunction with standby gains in the following modes: (1) Attitude stabilization; (2) Heading constant; (3) Heading Navigate. Transition between the operating regions or to the landing condition should be made within the transition corridors with switchover from HIGH SPEED to LOW SPEED according to the Instructions in "Flight Control System Trouble Shooting Procedures", Section VII. In the event of automatic gain adjustment failure, landings will be performed with low speed gains. A failure of the mach-altitude adjusted automatic gains is difficult to recognize because it appears to the pilot as a malfunction of the autopilot, the dampers, or the elevator ratio changer. The possible symptoms of an autopilot or damper malfunction (whether the malfunction is caused by a gain adjustment system failure or not) encompass a broad category of abnormal flight control system performance

Section I
Description

T.O. 1B-58A-1

control stick and grip (typical)

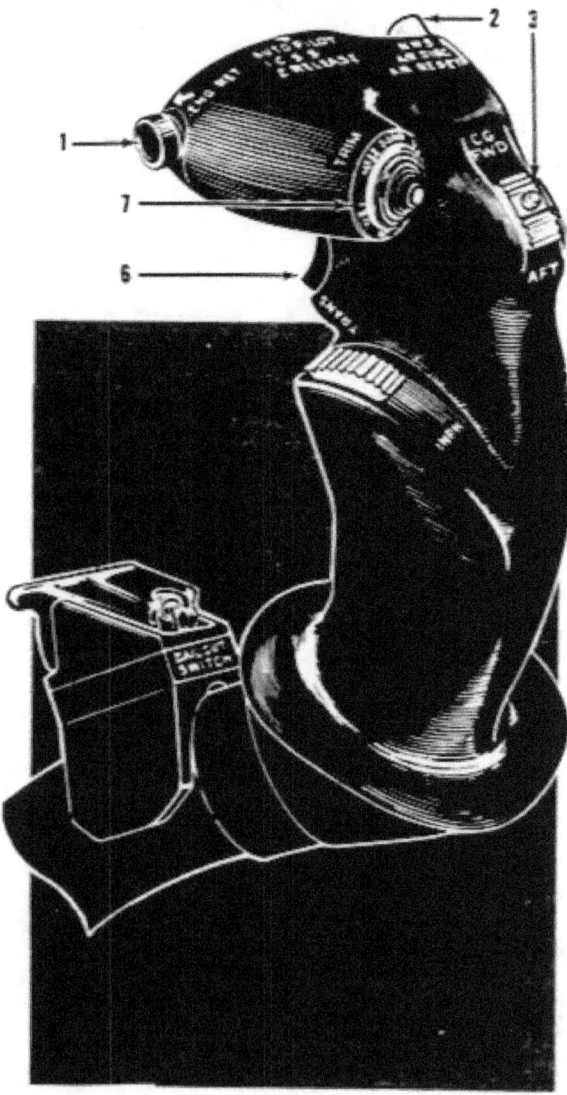

Figure 1-29.

ment between the mach indications of the primary and secondary air speed systems. Since a gain adjustment system malfunction will not necessarily be evidenced by any of these indications, the only positive procedure for diagnosing such a malfunction is trial engagement of the standby gains. The standby gains should not be employed, however, until a preliminary diagnosis of the malfunctioned channel has been made. For example, if system failure is in the nature of an oscillation in pitch, then an attempt should be made to isolate the problems to the pitch damper before engaging the standby gains. If utilization of the standby gains causes the malfunction to disappear, the trouble will have been isolated to the gain adjustment system, and standby gains should be used. If the faulty operation is due to the air data computer, the elevator ratio changer system will be affected. In this instance it is important to search for any improper operation in the elevator ratio changer system, in the automatic mode. The elevator available and elevator position should be monitored in 1-"g" flight while the system is operating in the automatic mode. If these items are maintained at the correct value even with changing flight condition, the elevator control available mode selector switch can be left in the automatic mode during the use of standby gains. For use of the standby gains, refer to "Flight Control System Trouble Shooting Procedures," Section VII.

FLIGHT CONTROLS AND INDICATORS.

Control Stick.

A detachable control stick provides a mechanical means of lateral and longitudinal control of the airplane. The control stick fits into a disconnect fitting at the capsule floor level to provide a separation point in event of capsule ejection. The disconnect fitting also includes quick disconnect of the control stick electrical circuits. Mechanical stops included in the control system linkage limit the envelope of maximum stick displacement attainable. The actual envelope in TO & LAND position will be rectangular in shape with the forward and aft corners chamfered. This limitation is necessary to meet control system requirements for combinations of surface available and is normal. Forward and aft movement of the control stick causes the elevons to move up and down together for elevator control. Left or right movement of the stick causes the elevons to move in opposite directions for aileron control. A mixer assembly mechanically converts elevator and aileron control inputs into elevon commands. Conventional control cables are connected to the control stick and extend aft to the power control linkage assembly (PCLA). Movement of the stick transmits a mechanical signal (motion) to elevator or aileron system linkages located in the PCLA. These linkages act as connections between equipment such as feel springs, trim actuators, ratio changers, damper servos, etc.; therefore, the signal may be altered before reaching

that may range from an overdamped or underdamped airplane to hardover control surface. The pilot should suspect a discrepancy of the gain adjustment system if any of the following conditions are apparent: (1) An irregularity of the mach indicator, such as no change of indicated mach number for a known flight condition change; (2) No changeover of the rudder feel spring gradient at mach no. 0.6, or changeover at an incorrect mach number; (3) Landing gear alarm buzzer operation at incorrect flight condition; (4) A marked disagree-

the mixer assembly. The mixer assembly converts the elevator or aileron signal into elevon motion and mechanically positions the elevon hydraulic control valves for either aileron or elevator action. A followup linkage automatically closes off the flow of hydraulic fluid to the control valves when the desired control surface deflection is obtained. The control stick grip (figure 1-29) incorporates a microphone switch, aileron-elevator stick trim switch, autopilot trigger switch, throttle retard button, cg shift switch and a nose wheel steering, air refueling disconnect, air refueling reset button. A guarded bailout warning switch is located on the forward side of the stick below the grip.

Rudder Pedals.

Conventional rudder pedals provide a mechanical means of directional control of the airplane. Conventional control cables are connected to the rudder pedals and extend aft to the power control linkage assembly (PCLA). Movement of the pedals transmits a mechanical signal (motion) to rudder system linkages located in the PCLA. The resultant movement of the linkages positions the rudder hydraulic control valve for rudder surface action. When the desired rudder deflection is obtained, a followup linkage automatically closes off the flow of hydraulic fluid to the control valve. An artificial feel system, a trim actuator, a damper servo, and a mechanical ARI are incorporated into the rudder linkages. The rudder pedals are collectively adjusted fore and aft by the crank on the lower center edge of the pilot's main instrument panel.

CAUTION

When adjusting pedals, rest feet on pedals but do not apply force. Adjusting the rudder pedals with loads applied can cause a malfunction in the rudder pedal adjust mechanism.

Toe action on the rudder pedals applies wheel brakes. Refer to "Brake System" of this section. With the nose wheel steering system energized, movement of the rudder pedals provides directional control during ground operation. Refer to "Nose Wheel Steering System" of this section.

Flight Control Power Switch.

The flight control power switch (7, figure 4-31) is located on the autopilot control panel and is marked ON and OFF. The OFF position is guarded to prevent moving the switch to OFF inadvertently. The switch controls a-c and d-c power for operation of all automatic features of the flight control system, autopilot, and stability augmentation system. When the switch is positioned to ON, power is supplied to the roll, pitch and yaw damper switches, to the amplifier-computer assembly, and the yaw amplifier-computer assembly. The amplifier-computer assembly in turn supplies power to the autopilot mode switches, controls operation of the aileron and elevator ratio changers in the automatic mode and automatic trim. The yaw damper servo is controlled by the yaw amplifier-computer assembly in conjunction with the yaw damper switch.

Note

The flight control equipment and modes of operation which are not affected by the power switch include manual trims (aileron, elevator and rudder), TO & LAND and MANUAL positions of the elevator available mode selector switch, FULL position of the aileron control available mode switch, aileron control available indicator, elevator position indicator, high-speed rudder feel spring switching, elevator force link switch, elevator control available manual adjust switch, and the rudder position indicator.

The automatic features of the flight control system are normally ready for operation approximately three minutes after the power switch is placed in the ON position.

CAUTION

During ground operations, the air conditioning system must be in operation before the flight control power switch is positioned to ON in order to prevent overheating the amplifier-computer assembly.

Elevator Control Available Mode Selector Switch.

The three-position elevator control available mode selector switch (9, figure 1-6), located on the pilot's

Section I
Description

left sidewall console, supplies 28-volt direct current to relays which direct power to the elevator ratio changer actuator. Also, this switch provides secondary control of the aileron ratio changer. The three positions of the switch are marked AUTO, TO & LAND, and MANUAL. The MANUAL position is guarded to prevent inadvertent positioning of the switch to MANUAL. The switch is cam-held in either MANUAL or AUTO, and is solenoid released to the TO & LAND position. For the elevator ratio changer, when the switch is placed in the AUTO position, the required computed signals drive the ratio changer and automatic trim actuators. This position is normally selected after takeoff and transition to stabilized climb. When the switch is placed in the TO & LAND position, the ratio changer is positioned to provide full elevator control available. The automatic trim actuator will position the elevons to 1-1/2 degrees up-elevator when the control available increases to 7 degrees or more. This switch position is utilized for takeoff and landing. When the switch is placed in the MANUAL position, control of the ratio changer is transferred to the elevator available manual adjust switch. The automatic trim actuator will position the elevons to 1-1/2 degrees up-elevator when the control available is increased to 7 degrees or more. When the elevator control available mode selector switch is positioned to TO & LAND and the aileron control available switch is positioned to AUTO, the aileron ratio changer servo is automatically controlled to provide 15 degrees (full) aileron control available. When the elevator control available mode selector switch is positioned to AUTO or MANUAL, the aileron ratio changer servo is automatically controlled to provide 7-1/2 degrees (half) control available.

CAUTION

The elevator available may drift with the elevator control available mode selector switch in AUTO and the flight control power switch OFF. To prevent drift, place the elevator control available mode selector switch in MANUAL after turning the flight control power switch off.

Elevator Control Available Manual Adjust Switch.

The amount of elevator control available is manually controlled by a three-position switch (10, figure 1-6) located on the pilot's left sidewall console. This switch is utilized only when the elevator control available mode selector switch is placed in the MANUAL position. The manual adjust switch has two momentary positions, marked INC and DEC, which are spring-loaded to an unmarked center (OFF) position. Positioning the switch to either INC or DEC energizes the ratio changer motor which will drive the ratio changer until the desired amount of control available is reached. The ratio changer can be driven through its full range using this switch.

Aileron Control Available Switch.

The two-position aileron control available switch (8, figure 1-6), located on the pilot's left sidewall console, provides automatic control of aileron available or provides full aileron control available. The two positions are marked AUTO and FULL. When the switch is positioned to AUTO, aileron control available is automatically controlled to provide either 7.5 degrees or 15 degrees control available as a function of the elevator control available mode selector switch. Placing the switch to FULL provides 15 degrees control available so that full control stick displacement will result in 15 degrees of aileron deflection. The switch is normally left in the AUTO position. The aileron control available switch requires 28-volt d-c power for operation. Aileron ratio will automatically switch to full when the capsule doors close.

Note

For additional information on control of the aileron ratio changer, refer to "Elevator Control Available Mode Selector Switch," this section.

Rudder Trim Switch.

The three-position rudder trim momentary-type switch (1, figure 1-30) is located on the trim control panel and is used to reposition the rudder feel springs for directional trim. The two switch positions, marked NOSE LEFT and NOSE RIGHT, provide rudder pedal trim action as indicated. When the trim switch is held in the desired position, the electrical trim motor repositions the feel spring in the PCLA and, at airspeeds above mach no. 0.6, the high speed feel spring magnetic brake is released allowing the spring to return to a neutral position. Repositioning of the feel spring in the PCLA deflects the rudder control surface and relieves pedal force.

Note

When the high speed feel spring returns to a neutral position, some of the force is relieved from the pedals. Therefore, due to changes in the feel force on the pedals, care should be exercised when trimming with the pedals deflected in order to avoid inadvertent pedal deflection.

The switch is spring-loaded to the center (OFF) position and controls 28-volt direct current to the trim motor relay.

Aileron-Elevator Stick Trim Switch.

The combination aileron-elevator stick trim switch (7, figure 1-29) is located on the control stick and is used to reposition the aileron or elevator feel spring for lateral and longitudinal trim. This five-position switch has positions marked NOSE UP, NOSE DOWN, LWD (left wing down) RWD (right wing down), and is spring-loaded to an unmarked center (OFF) position. Holding the switch to any one of its positions induces trim as indicated. The switch controls 28-volt d-c electrical power to the aileron and elevator trim motor relay.

Note

The aileron-elevator stick trim switch is inoperative unless the stick trim selector switch, located on the trim control panel, is placed in the CONT STICK position.

Stick Trim Selector Switch.

The four-position stick trim selector switch (3, figure 1-30), located on the trim control panel, is used to control 28-volt d-c electrical power to the aileron-elevator stick trim switch located on the control stick; in event the aileron-elevator stick trim switch malfunctions, it is used as an alternate method of controlling longitudinal trim. The switch positions are marked CONT STICK, NOSE UP, NOSE DOWN, and OFF. Placing the switch to CONT-STICK completes the 28-volt d-c circuit to the aileron-elevator stick trim switch on the control stick so that lateral and longitudinal trim may be controlled from that point. Moving the switch to the center OFF position breaks the electrical circuit to the aileron-elevator stick trim switch and renders that circuit inoperative. The NOSE UP and NOSE DOWN positions are spring-loaded to OFF; therefore, the switch must be held in these positions for the longitudinal trim as indicated.

Note

The stick trim selector switch provides an alternate method for controlling longitudinal trim only. No provision is made for alternate control of lateral trim.

Damper Switches.

Three two-position damper switches (4, 5, 6, figure 1-6) located on the pilot's left sidewall console, are used to control 28-volt d-c electrical power to the roll, pitch, and yaw damper systems. The switches are labeled yaw, pitch, and roll, and have an unmarked ON position. The switches are normally left in the ON position. In the event one of the damper systems becomes inoperative, the respective damper switch should be immediately positioned to OFF. Refer to "Flight Control System Limitations", Section V, for limitations with the dampers inoperative.

Gain Selector Switch.

The gain selector switch (3, figure 1-6), is located on the pilot's left sidewall console. The switch is marked HIGH SPEED, AUTO, and LOW SPEED, and is internally latched in all three positions. It is necessary to pull out on the handle in order to move the switch from one position to another. This switch provides a means of selecting either AUTO, HI SPEED or LOW SPEED gain for the pitch autopilot, the pitch damper, and, at airspeeds above mach number 0.92, the yaw rate to roll damper signal. With the switch in the AUTO position the autopilot and the applicable stability augmentation systems receive correct gain adjustments from the altitude and mach number signals in the air data system. The HIGH SPEED and LOW SPEED positions are used to provide standby fixed gains to the autopilot attitude stabilization mode and the applicable stability augmentation system. HIGH SPEED and LOW SPEED positions should be used only in the event the normal automatic gain adjustment signals malfunction. The switch is normally left in the AUTO position. See figure 7-19 for the standby gain operating regions. The HIGH SPEED position is used to provide standby gains for speeds above mach no. 0.95 and the LOW SPEED position is

Section I
Description

T.O. 1B-58A-1

used to provide standby gains for speeds below mach no. 0.95.

Note

For operation in the operating regions and transition from one region to another using standby fixed gains, refer to "Mach-Altitude Gain Adjustment Failure" Section VII.

Yaw Reset Button.

The yaw reset button (7, figure 1-6) is located on the pilot's left sidewall console. Momentarily depressing this button applies an electrical reset pulse to the yaw damper monitor and to the yaw rate to roll damping monitor; thus, if the yaw damper caution lamp or the yaw rate to roll caution lamp have lighted due to a spurious electrical transient rather than an actual malfunction, the lamp or lamps will go out.

WARNING

Do not depress the yaw reset button when the yaw damper warning lamp is lighted. To do so may cause a failed damper channel to become engaged.

Wing Heavy Control Switch.

A two-position wing heavy control switch (2, figure 4-31), located on the autopilot control panel, controls 28-volt d-c power to the wing heavy control system. The switch is marked OFF with an unmarked ON position. When the switch is placed to ON, power will be furnished to the system any time the landing gear is in the retracted position provided the yaw damper is ON. During flight the wing heavy control switch is normally left in the ON position except for air refueling operations. The roll autopilot cannot be engaged with the wing heavy control switch in the OFF position.

Emergency Increase Elevator Available Handle.

The emergency increase elevator available handle on the pilot's lower left console (6, figure 1-7) is used to

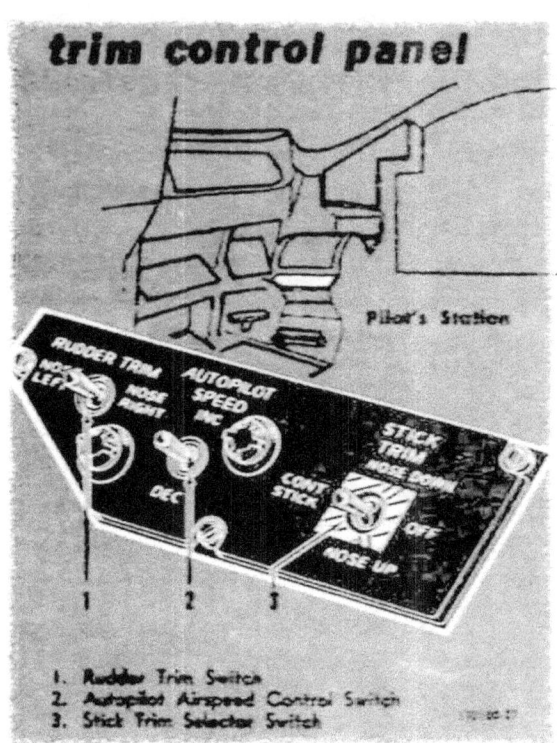

Figure 1-30.

manually position the elevator ratio changer to increase control available in the event of a failure in the normal system. Control available can be increased to 20 degrees with a two-step pull of the handle or it may be increased in distinct steps by selecting any one of 6 detent positions between full in and full out position of the handle (see figure 7-16). The handle contains a release trigger and a thumb trigger. The release trigger on the lower left side of the hand grip is used to unlatch the handle and the thumb trigger on the upper side of the handle grip prevents the operator from obtaining too much control available during the initial movement. To increase control available to the maximum, squeeze the release trigger and pull the handle to the stop position. Move the thumb trigger aft and continue to pull the handle to the full out position (approximately 5 inches). To increase control available to an intermediate value, squeeze the release trigger and pull the handle until the desired control available is obtained; then release the trigger to drop into the desired detent position.

Note

Pulling the handle out to the second detent causes the following switching to occur: the ratio changer actuator electrical circuit is disconnected, and the elevator control available mode selector switch is repositioned to TO & LAND. The automatic trim actuator will position the elevons to 1-1/2 degrees up-elevator when control available is increased to 7 degrees.

Pushing in the handle reverses the function of the handle and decreases the amount of elevator available to correspond with each position as the handle was pulled out. Normal operation of the ratio changer may be re-established by pushing the handle in to the full in position, provided the electrical malfunction has been corrected.

Note

When resetting the emergency increase elevator available handle the elevator available should not be decreased to a value less than the elevator required for trim.

Elevator Position Indicator.

The elevator position indicator (31, figure 1-5) is located on the pilot's main instrument panel and a repeater indicator is located on the DSO's main instrument panel. These indicators are provided to indicate the elevator position of the elevons in degrees. A small vernier scale on the indicator face indicates deflection in tenths of a degree. Aileron action of the elevons has no effect on the indicator since the indicator pointer changes only when the elevons move up or down together. Instrument tolerance is ±0.25 degrees up to 4 degrees elevator deflection, a linear value from 4 degree to 8 degrees of elevator deflection and ±0.4 degree for elevator deflection over 8 degrees. This tolerance should be considered when comparing EPI indication with computed elevator deflection. The elevator position indicator operates on 26-volt a-c power which is stepped down from the 115-volt a-c power source.

Rudder Position Indicator.

The rudder position indicator (28, figure 1-5), located on the pilot's main instrument panel, indicates the rudder position in degrees from neutral. The scale on the face of the indicator indicates rudder deflection from 0 to 30 degrees to the left or right of neutral. The rudder position indicator operates on 28-volt a-c power. Refer to Section V for rudder position limits.

Elevator Control Available Indicator.

The elevator control available indicator (33, figure 1-5) is located on the pilot's main instrument panel and a repeater indicator is located on the DSO's main instrument panel. These indicators are provided to indicate the amount of elevator control available with full control stick movement. For example, if the indicator pointer indicates 5 degrees, a full forward or aft motion of the stick will result in a 5-degree deflection of the control surface from the automatic trim position. The indicator operates on 26-volt a-c power which is stepped down from the 115-volt a-c power source.

Aileron Control Available Indicator.

A three-position indicator (32, figure 1-5) located on the pilot's main instrument panel, indicates the amount of aileron control available with full stick movement. The word FULL or HALF appears in the window of the indicator to correspond with the amount of aileron control available. Parallel white and black diagonal stripes are displayed when there is no electrical power or when the aileron ratio changer is in transit. The indicator operates on 28-volt d-c power.

Aileron-Rudder Neutral Trim Indicator Lamp.

The green aileron-rudder neutral trim indicator lamp (30, figure 1-5) is located on the pilot's main instrument panel. The lamp is used during trimming operations to indicate the neutral position of aileron and/or rudder. The lamp circuit is energized by actuating and holding the rudder trim switch or the aileron-elevator stick trim switch to its respective position for lateral or directional trim; then when the control surface reaches the neutral position the trim motor in the PCLA actuates a limit switch and the lamp will light to indicate that the affected control surface is in neutral position. The lamp will go out as the surface passes through the neutral position. The lamp operates on 28-volt d-c power.

Mach-Monitor Indicator Lamps.

An amber mach-monitor indicator lamp (26, figure 1-5), located on the pilot's and DSO's main instrument panels, provides a means of determining that the mach portion of the mach-altitude repeater corresponds (or does not correspond) to the flight condition of the air-

Section I
Description

plane. If the mach portion of the repeater is functioning normally, the lamp will be lighted in the speed range of Mach No. 1.0 ±0.035 to 1.55 ±0.035. If the lamp lights when speed is below Mach No. 1.0 or above Mach No. 1.55, or does not light when speed is within the range of Mach No. 1.0 to 1.55, a malfunction is indicated and appropriate standby gains should be used. (Refer to standby gain restrictions outlined in Section VII.) The pilot's lamp is checked by depressing the malfunction and indicator lamp test button and is dimmed with the malfunction and indicator lamp dimming switch. The DSO's press-to-test lamp has no provisions for dimming. Both lamps receive power from the 28-volt, d-c power panel through the flight control power switch.

Yaw Damper Caution Lamp.

A yaw damper caution lamp, located on the pilot's caution lamp panel (figure 1-13), will light and display "YAW DAMPER" when the monitor circuit has detected a failure in one of the three yaw damper channels, however the yaw damper system will still function on the two remaining channels with no degradation in performance. The lamp is connected to the master caution lamp circuit and operates on 28-volt d-c power. For testing and dimming the lamp, refer to "Malfunction Indicator and Warning System" this section.

Yaw Damper Warning Lamp.

A yaw damper warning lamp, located on the pilot's warning lamp panel (figure 1-13), will light and display "YAW DAMPER" when the monitor circuit has detected a second failure within the same monitor block in the yaw damper system. The yaw damper will automatically be disengaged when the yaw damper warning lamp is lighted. The lamp is connected to the master warning lamp circuit and operates on 28-volt d-c power. For testing and dimming the lamp refer to "Malfunction Indicator and Warning System" this section.

Yaw Rate to Roll Caution Lamp.

A yaw rate to roll caution lamp, located on the pilot's caution panel (figure 1-13) will light and display "YAW RATE TO ROLL" when the difference between the outputs of the two yaw rate to roll gyros exceeds normal tolerances, provided the landing gear is up and locked. The lamp is connected to the master

T.O. 1B-58A-1

caution lamp circuit and operates on 28-volt d-c power. For testing and dimming the lamp refer to "Malfunction Indicator and Warning System," this section.

LANDING GEAR SYSTEM.

The airplane is equipped with hydraulically operated tricycle landing gear consisting of a two-wheel nose gear and two four-wheel main gears. The eight split-type non-frangible wheels of the main gear are each equipped with two tubeless tires. Each of the two split-type wheels on the nose gear has a single tubeless tire. The non-frangible wheels incorporate a center rolling flange located between the two tires to prevent the inner and outer wheel flanges from contacting the ground if both tires become underinflated. This center flange will resist wheel break-up in case of a multiple tire failure on takeoff. Also the non-frangible wheel incorporates two fusible plugs installed in the inboard wheel half to relieve tire inflation pressure and lessen the possibility of tire blow-out caused by excessive brake energy absorption. For additional information on non-frangible wheels, refer to "Brake System," Section VII. The gear retracts into wheel wells that are enclosed by doors. The nose landing gear door is equipped with an auxiliary pneumatic boost actuator which compensates for heavy airloads created in the nose wheel well area during take-off. See figure 1-4 for servicing data. The doors close, latch, and open mechanically by movement of the gear, but are unlatched and cinched in the latched position hydraulically. The four wheels of each main gear are divided into two sets with a separate axle for each set. The two axles are attached to the forward and aft ends of a horizontal axle beam (7, figure 1-31). The axle beam is attached, at its center, to the bottom of the shock strut (8, figure 1-31) with a trunnion pin. This arrangement permits one set of wheels to pass over an obstacle while the other set remains in contact with the runway. The pivoting feature also permits the wheels and axle beam to be positioned for retraction and extension. As the gear retracts, a pneumatic positioning spring (9, figure 1-31) forces the forward set of wheels down to rotate the axle beam about the center pivot to a position parallel to the shock strut. This permits the wheels to fit into the shallow wheel wells. During landing gear extension, the positioning spring will move the wheels back into the landing position. In the extended position, the landing gear is held down mechanically. The nose gear holddown latch is hydraulically opened for landing gear retraction. In the retracted position, the gear and wheel well doors are secured by hydraulically actuated uplatch mechanisms inside the wheel wells. The main gear wheels rotate independently of each other and are each equipped with

1-76

main landing gear arrangement

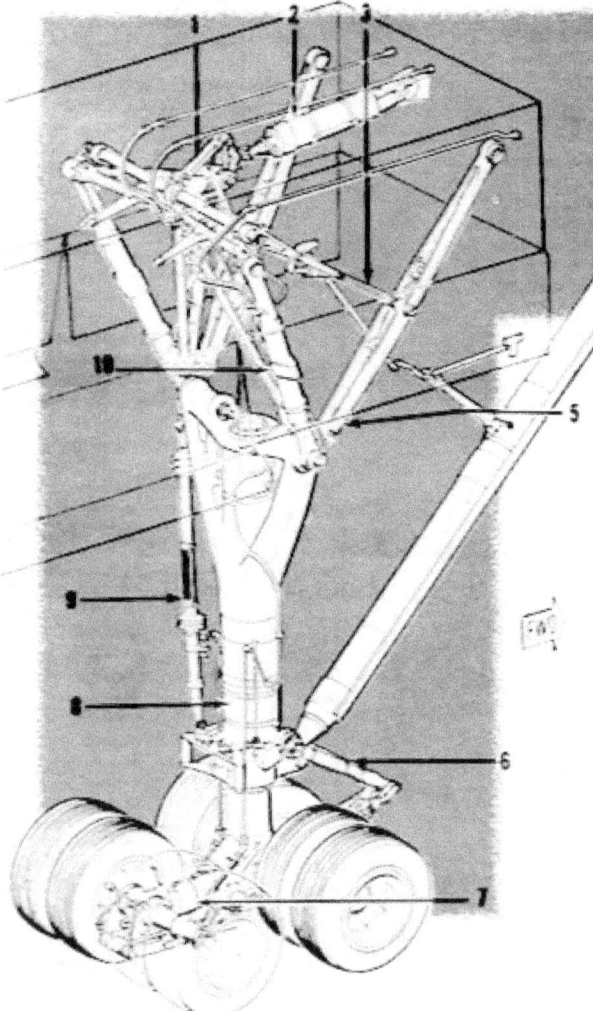

1. Retracting Lever Assembly
2. Gear Actuating Cylinder
3. Downlock Arm
4. Drag Strut
5. Linkage Assembly
6. Torque Arm
7. Axle Beam
8. Shock Strut
9. Positioning Spring
10. Column Assembly (W-Truss)

Figure 1-31.

a multidisc brake assembly. When the weight of the airplane is on the gear, the nose gear strut should be compressed to approximately 8 inches and the main gear strut should be compressed to approximately 4 inches. A nose gear reactance gage is installed on the nose landing gear oleo strut for monitoring the airplane cg as a function of nose gear pressure during refueling. The landing gear operates on hydraulic power supplied by the utility system. (See figure 1-32.) Normally, the time required for retraction or extension is approximately 10 seconds. The landing gear system is provided with an alarm buzzer which is audible through the interphone system when the gear is not down and locked, and certain conditions of airspeed, altitude, and throttle position exist. A landing gear safety switch on the torque arm assembly of the left gear prevents the gear from being retracted when the weight of the airplane is on the gear and de-energizes the brake antiskid system when the weight is off the gear. A pneumatic system is provided for emergency extension of the landing gear in the event the normal hydraulic system fails. Ground safety locks (figure 1-33) are provided; when installed, they prevent unlocking of the gear.

LANDING GEAR CONTROLS AND INDICATORS.

Landing Gear Handle.

The landing gear handle (7, figure 1-34) is located on the pilot's forward left console and has three positions, marked UP, PRES REL, and DOWN. The handle has a wheel-shaped knob which contains a red warning lamp. Placing the handle in either the UP or DOWN position mechanically positions the landing gear selector valve to port hydraulic fluid to the gear-up or gear-down side of the landing gear hydraulic actuators to operate the gear. The landing gear handle is locked in the DOWN position by a spring-loaded electrical solenoid when the weight of the airplane is on the gear. The landing gear safety switch controls 28-volt d-c power to the solenoid. The weight of the airplane compresses the shock strut and opens the limit switch which breaks the electrical circuit to the solenoid. When the solenoid is de-energized, the spring tension extends a mechanical lock which holds the landing gear control handle in the DOWN position. Removing the weight from the landing gear, with electrical power on the airplane, will close the limit switch on the gear and energize the solenoid. The energized solenoid retracts the lock and frees

landing gear system (typical)

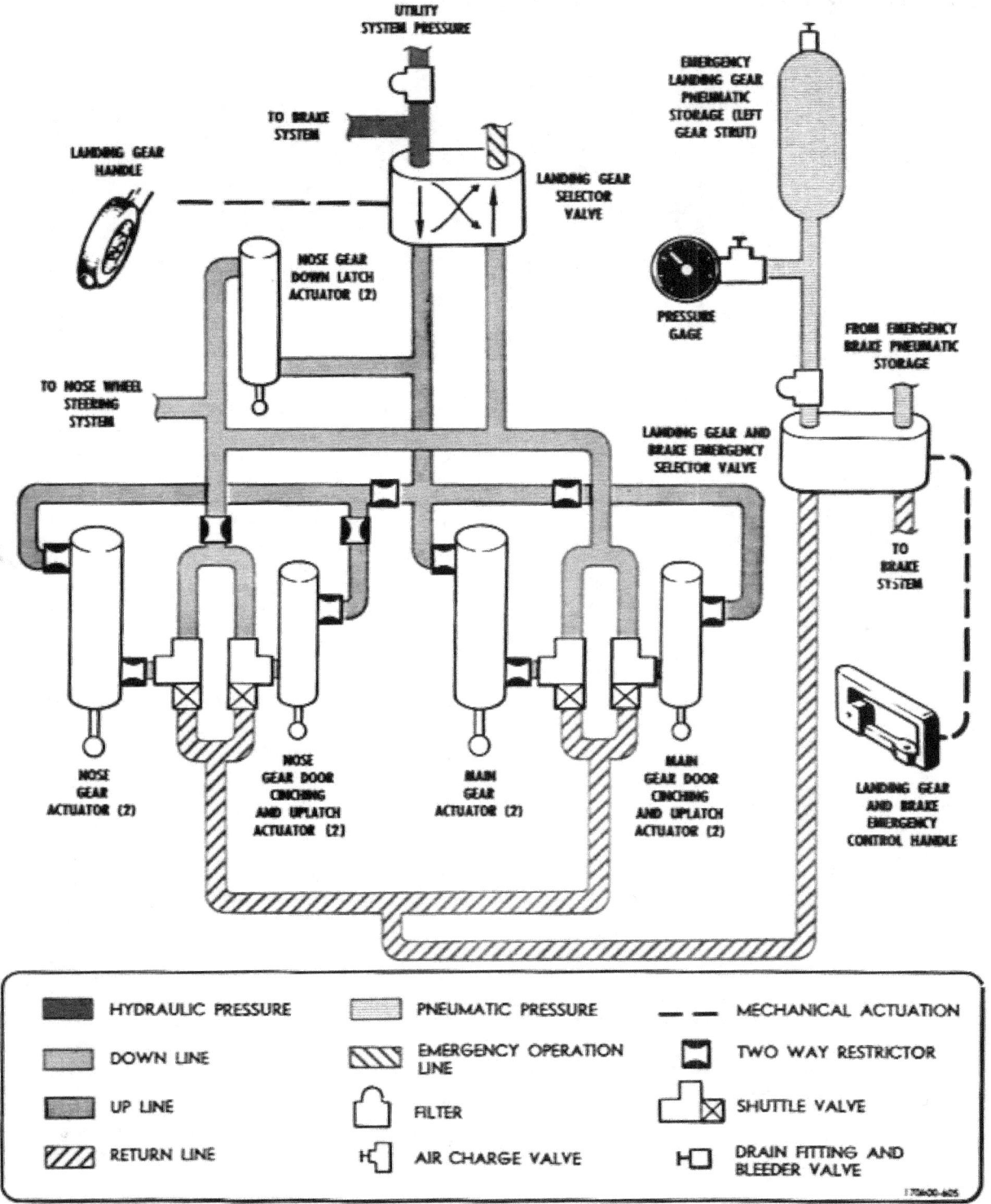

Figure 1-32.

landing gear ground locks

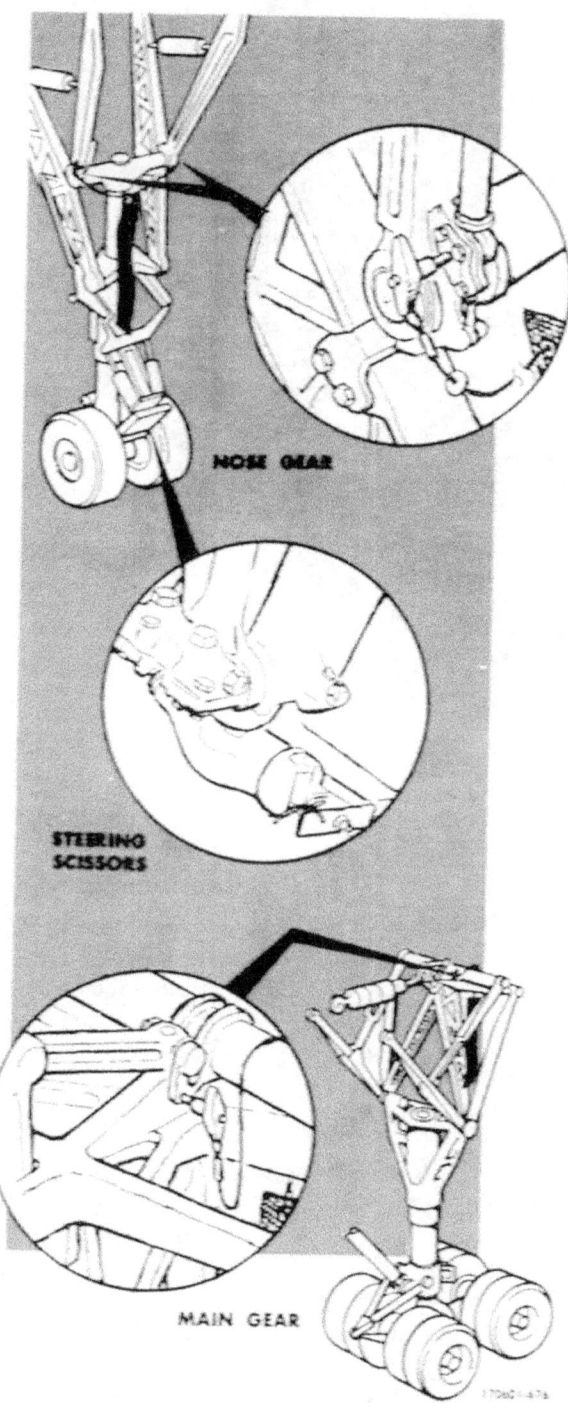

Figure 1-33.

the landing gear control handle. The mechanical lock may be manually released from the handle by depressing the landing gear downlock override button located on the pilot's forward left console. When the landing gear is retracted after takeoff, the landing gear handle will remain in the UP position. In this condition, hydraulic pressure is maintained on the actuators. Placing the handle in the PRES REL position will mechanically position the landing gear selector valve, closing the pressure ports to the actuators and opening a return port to the utility hydraulic reservoir. This action prevents the airplane structure from being subjected to unnecessary stress throughout the flight. The handle must then be pulled out approximately one-half inch to clear a stop before it can be moved to the DOWN position.

Landing Gear Downlock Override Button.

This button (13, figure 1-34), located on the pilot's forward left console is connected to the spring-loaded electrical solenoid which mechanically locks the landing gear control handle in the DOWN position. In event of a malfunction in the electrical circuit of the solenoid, this button may be used to free the landing gear control handle. When the button is depressed, the mechanical lock is released and the handle is free to be moved to the UP position.

Landing Gear Alarm Cutoff Button.

A pushbutton switch (9, figure 1-34), located on the pilot's forward left console provides a means of silencing the alarm buzzer. Depressing the button energizes a relay in the buzzer circuit which cuts off power to the alarm buzzer.

Landing Gear Position Indicator Lamps.

Three green landing gear position indicator lamps (2, figure 1-34) are located on the pilot's forward left console. The lamps are arranged in a triangular relationship corresponding to the landing gear and will light when the corresponding gear is down and locked. The lamps will go out when the gear is in any position other than down and locked. The lamps operate on 28-volt d-c power. For dimming the lamps refer to "Malfunction Indicator and Warning System," this section.

Landing Gear Warning Lamp.

The red landing gear warning lamp (6, figure 1-34) is located in the wheel-shaped knob of the landing gear control handle. When the landing gear handle is moved to either the UP or DOWN position, the warning lamp will light and will remain lighted until the last gear is locked in the selected position. If the landing gear control handle is positioned to DOWN

Section I
Description

T.O. 1B-58A-1

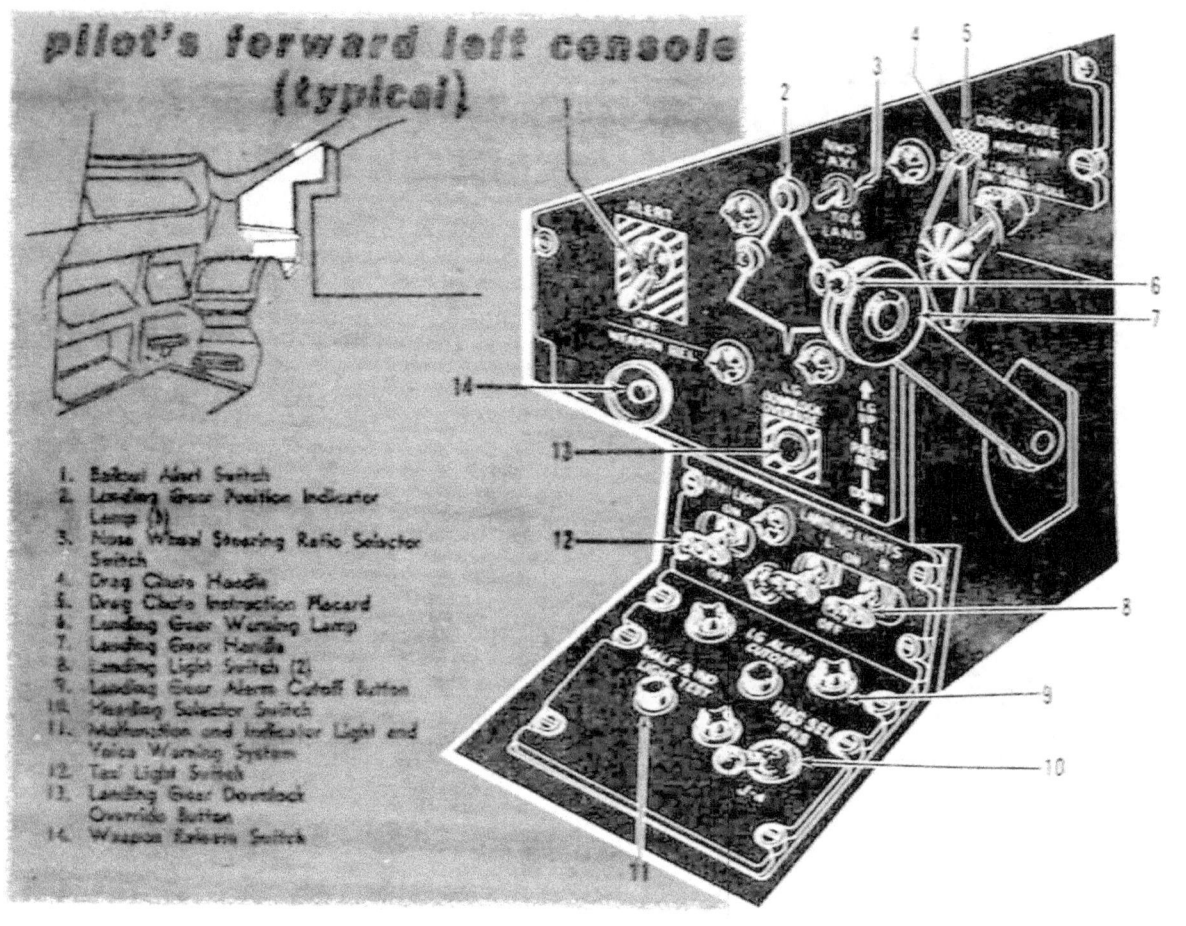

1. Bailout Alert Switch
2. Landing Gear Position Indicator Lamp (3)
3. Nose Wheel Steering Ratio Selector Switch
4. Drag Chute Handle
5. Drag Chute Instruction Placard
6. Landing Gear Warning Lamp
7. Landing Gear Handle
8. Landing Light Switch (2)
9. Landing Gear Alarm Cutoff Button
10. Heading Selector Switch
11. Malfunction and Indicator Light and Voice Warning System
12. Taxi Light Switch
13. Landing Gear Downlock Override Button
14. Weapon Release Switch

Figure 1-34.

and the warning lamp remains lighted, it can be determined which gear is not down and locked by observing the landing gear position indicator lamps. The lamp will also light when the conditions exist which sound the landing gear alarm buzzer. For testing and dimming of the warning lamp refer to "Malfunction Indicator and Warning System," this section.

Landing Gear Alarm Buzzer.

A landing gear alarm buzzer provides an audible warning, through the pilot's interphone system, when certain flight conditions exist and the landing gear is not down and locked. The buzzer will be audible in the pilot's headset when *all* the following conditions exist *simultaneously*:

During takeoff and climb —

1. The airspeed is below mach no. 0.43 (± 0.021).

2. The airplane is below an altitude of 11,000 (± 500) feet.

3. Any one or all four engine throttles retarded below military power setting.

4. Landing gear in any position except down and locked.

During descent from altitude —

1. The airspeed is below mach no. 0.38 (± 0.021).

2. The airplane is below an altitude of 10,000 (± 500) feet.

3. Any one or all four engine throttles retarded below military power setting.

4. Landing gear in any position except down and locked.

The landing gear alarm buzzer operates on 28-volt d-c power.

1-80

LANDING GEAR EMERGENCY PNEUMATIC SYSTEM.

The landing gear emergency pneumatic system (figure 1-32) provides a means of emergency extension of the landing gear in the event the utility hydraulic system fails. The drag strut on the left main gear is charged with nitrogen according to the ambient temperature. A placard near the pressure gage is used to determine the correct pressure. See figure 1-47 for servicing data. The pneumatic system pressure is controlled by the emergency brake and landing gear control handle.

Emergency Brake and Landing Gear Control Handle.

This handle (7, figure 1-7), located on the pilot's lower left console, is mechanically connected to the landing gear and brake emergency selector valve. When the handle is pulled to its full travel, pneumatic pressure (nitrogen) is ported to the landing gear uplatches and the extend side of the actuators to extend the gears. Also, the brake emergency pneumatic system is activated. (Refer to "Brake Emergency Pneumatic System," this section.) The handle may be pushed back to its original position, but the selector valve will remain in an activated position until reset on the ground.

Note

- The emergency brake and landing gear control handle is safety wired with 0.020 inch copper wire and may require a strong pull to release it.

- When the emergency brake and landing gear control handle is pulled, the landing gear control handle should either be in the PRESS REL position or the DOWN position (preferably DOWN).

NOSE WHEEL STEERING SYSTEM.

A steerable nose gear system is provided which allows directional control of the airplane during taxiing. The system is electrically controlled and hydraulically operated. See figure 1-35. The main components of the system are a nose wheel steering button, a control transmitter, a position transmitter, a safety switch, two steering actuators, and an electrically operated hydraulic steering valve. Hydraulic pressure for steering operation is supplied by the utility hydraulic system through the landing gear down line. With the system energized, movement of the rudder pedals will electrically position the steering valve to port hydraulic pressure to the actuators which turn the nose wheel.

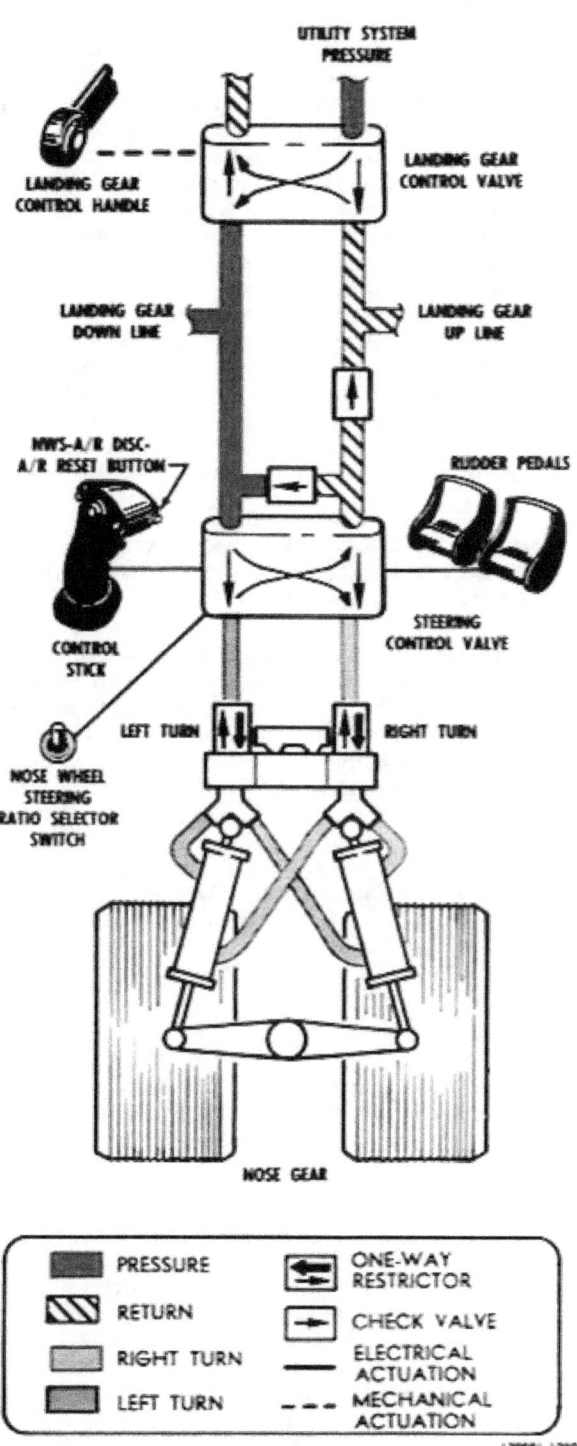

Figure 1-35.

Section I
Description

Nose wheel shimmy is prevented by one-way restrictors which allow a free flow of pressurized fluid into the steering actuators but restrict the flow of return fluid from the actuators. The nose wheel steering system furnishes dual control capability to allow the pilot to select 50 degrees maximum steering control for taxiing or 10 degrees maximum steering control for takeoff and landing. When the airplane is being taxied with the steering system de-energized, the nose wheel is free to caster. When castering, if the nose wheel strut turns to right or left beyond the 50-degree position, a limit switch in the position transmitter will energize the steering valve to port hydraulic pressure to the steering actuators and force the wheel back to the 50-degree position. The nose wheel is kept centered during retraction and extension by centering cams which are engaged by removing the weight from the nose gear. A safety switch in the nose steering electrical control system is also actuated simultaneously with the centering cams to prevent energizing the steering system while the centering cams are engaged.

NWS-A/R DISC-A/R RESET (NOSE WHEEL STEERING – AIR REFUELING DISCONNECT AIR REFUELING-RESET) BUTTON.

A pushbutton switch (2, figure 1-29) on the control stick grip is used to energize the nose wheel steering system, to reset the air refueling system and for air refueling disconnect. The button operates in conjunction with the air refueling system door switch. With the air refueling door switch in the CLOSE position, depressing and holding the button will provide electrical power for operation of the nose wheel steering system. With the system energized, movement of the rudder pedals will turn the nose gear. The system operates on 115-volt a-c power. For information on the inflight refueling reset feature of the button, refer to "Air Refueling System", Section IV.

Note

The nose wheel steering function can be energized only when the air refueling door switch is in the CLOSE position.

The operation of the nose wheel steering system depends on the position of the nose wheel steering ratio selector switch. When the nose wheel steering ratio selector switch is in the TAXI position depressing the nose wheel steering button actuates a hold-down relay to engage the system. The button can then be released and the system will remain engaged until the nose wheel steering button is again depressed and released to open the relay and disengage the system. When the nose wheel steering ratio selector switch is in the TO & LAND position the nose wheel steering button must be depressed and held to engage the system. Releasing the button will disengage the system.

T.O. 1B-58A-1

NOSE WHEEL STEERING (NWS) RATIO SELECTOR SWITCH.

The two position nose wheel steering ratio selector switch (3, figure 1-34), located on the pilot's forward left console is marked TAXI and TO & LAND. The switch functions in conjunction with the pilot's nose wheel steering button to provide 50 degrees of steering control in the TAXI mode or 10 degrees of steering control in the TO & LAND mode.

BRAKE SYSTEM.

Each main landing gear wheel is equipped with a hydraulically operated multidisc brake. The brake system (figure 1-36) is supplied hydraulic power from the utility system and is operated by toe action on the rudder pedals. A metering-type hydraulic brake control valve is equipped with two levers which are actuated by cables connected to the corresponding brake pedals. Each lever controls hydraulic pressure to all wheel brakes of the corresponding main gear. With full application of the brakes, the control valve meters 1000 to 1260 psi hydraulic pressure to the brakes. Hydraulic pressure to the brake control valve is routed through a brake hydraulic pressure shutoff valve. This valve shuts off hydraulic pressure to the brake when the brake emergency pneumatic system is actuated. A brake sequence shutoff valve in the brake line on each main gear prevents brake application when the landing gear is not down and locked. The sequence valves are mechanically closed and opened by movement of the gear during retraction and extension respectively.

CAUTION

Retraction of the landing gear while the wheels are rotating can cause damage to the main landing gear wheel well. To prevent possible damage, the brakes should be applied for a minimum of 2 seconds to stop wheel rotation before positioning the landing gear handle to UP. Brake application after the gear unlocks could result in damage to the retraction mechanism if a brake sequence shutoff valve failed.

The brake system is also equipped with an accumulator which stores pressure for parking brakes and acts as a surge damper during normal operation. The utility system engine-driven hydraulic pumps maintain normal system pressure on the accumulator. The accumulator is precharged with nitrogen according to the ambient temperature. A placard near the accumulator pressure gage in the left wheel well is used to determine the correct precharge pressure. See figure 1-47 for servicing data. The hydraulic pressure charge is retained for parking pressure unless relieved by brake operation. During prolonged periods with no pressure on the utility hydraulic system, the brake accumulator pressure can be maintained with a hand pump which is located in the left wheel well. The accumulator gage should indicate at least 1500 psi to assure adequate pressure for parking brakes. A pneumatic system is provided for emergency brake operation in the event of utility hydraulic system failure. The brake system incorporates an anti-skid system which momentarily releases brake pressure each time the wheels approach a skid condition. For additional information pertaining to the brakes, refer to "Brake System," Section VII.

ANTI-SKID SYSTEM.

The anti-skid system prevents tire skids from occurring by releasing brake pressure before a skidding condition exists. The system consists of a detector unit driven by each main gear wheel, a control unit and an anti-skid valve for each main gear, and an anti-skid control switch located in the pilot's station. The anti-skid system detects an incipient skid condition by sensing the rapid wheel deceleration rate which exists when the brake torque being applied exceeds the frictional force available between the tires and runway. When the anti-skid control switch is positioned to ON and brakes are applied, the detector units supply the control units with electrical voltage signals proportional to the speed of each wheel on the main gear. The control units monitor these signals and sense a skid condition when rotation of the wheels decreases too rapidly. When the wheels approach a skid condition, the control unit energizes the anti-skid valve and brake pressure is released allowing the wheels to accelerate. When the wheels have regained speed, the control unit de-energizes the anti-skid valve and brake pressure is re-applied. The system will cycle in this manner as long as the brake pressure applied is in excess of that which is necessary to achieve maximum braking. The anti-skid system operates independently on each main gear. If a wheel on either gear approaches a skid condition, brake pressure will be released from all wheels on that gear. Pressure will not be released from the wheels of the other gear unless a wheel on that gear approaches a skid condition. The landing gear safety switch de-energizes the anti-skid system when the weight of the airplane is off the gear.

Note

The anti-skid system is inoperative during emergency brake operation.

The anti-skid system receives power from the 28-volt d-c power distribution panel. For additional information pertaining to anti-skid system, refer to "Brake System", Section VII.

ANTI-SKID CONTROL SWITCH.

The anti-skid control switch (4, figure 1-7), located on the pilot's lower left console, controls operation of the anti-skid system. The switch has two positions marked ON and OFF and requires 28-volt d-c power for operation. When the switch is positioned to ON, the anti-skid system is energized if the landing gear safety switch is actuated. However, the anti-skid feature will not begin to function unless the wheels approach a skid condition. Positioning the switch to OFF de-energizes the system, removing the anti-skid feature from the brake system.

Note

When the weight of the airplane is off the gear, the landing gear safety switch will de-energize the anti-skid system. However, if the landing gear safety switch does not function properly the antiskid switch must be placed in the OFF position.

PARKING BRAKE HANDLE.

A parking brake handle (21, figure 1-5), located at the lower center edge of the pilot's main instrument panel, is used to set the brakes for parking the airplane. The parking brakes are set by pulling the parking brake handle out its full length of travel and holding it out while depressing both brake pedals until they catch and remain in the depressed position. When setting the parking brakes, make sure that the parking brake handle is pulled out through its full length of travel and that both pedals remain depressed when force is removed. This will assure that brakes are applied. The brakes are released by depressing the brake pedals.

BRAKE EMERGENCY PNEUMATIC SYSTEM.

The brake pneumatic system (see figure 1-36) is used for emergency brake operation in the event the utility hydraulic system fails. The main components of the system are two nitrogen storage bottles, a selector valve, an emergency brake control valve, brake hydraulic pressure shutoff valve, pneumatic tubing, and the emergency brake and landing gear control handle. The storage bottles (two truss tubes of the left main gear linkage assembly) are charged with nitrogen according to the ambient temperature. A placard near the accumulator pressure gages is used to determine the correct precharge pressure. See figure 1-47 for servicing data. When the emergency brake and landing gear control handle is pulled, pneumatic pressure is routed to the brake shutoff valve and to the metering-type emergency brake control valve. Also, the landing gear emergency pneumatic system is activated. (Refer to "Landing Gear Emergency Pneumatic System," this section.) Actuation of the brake shut-off valve prevents

1-83

Section I
Description

T.O. 1B-58A-1

brake system

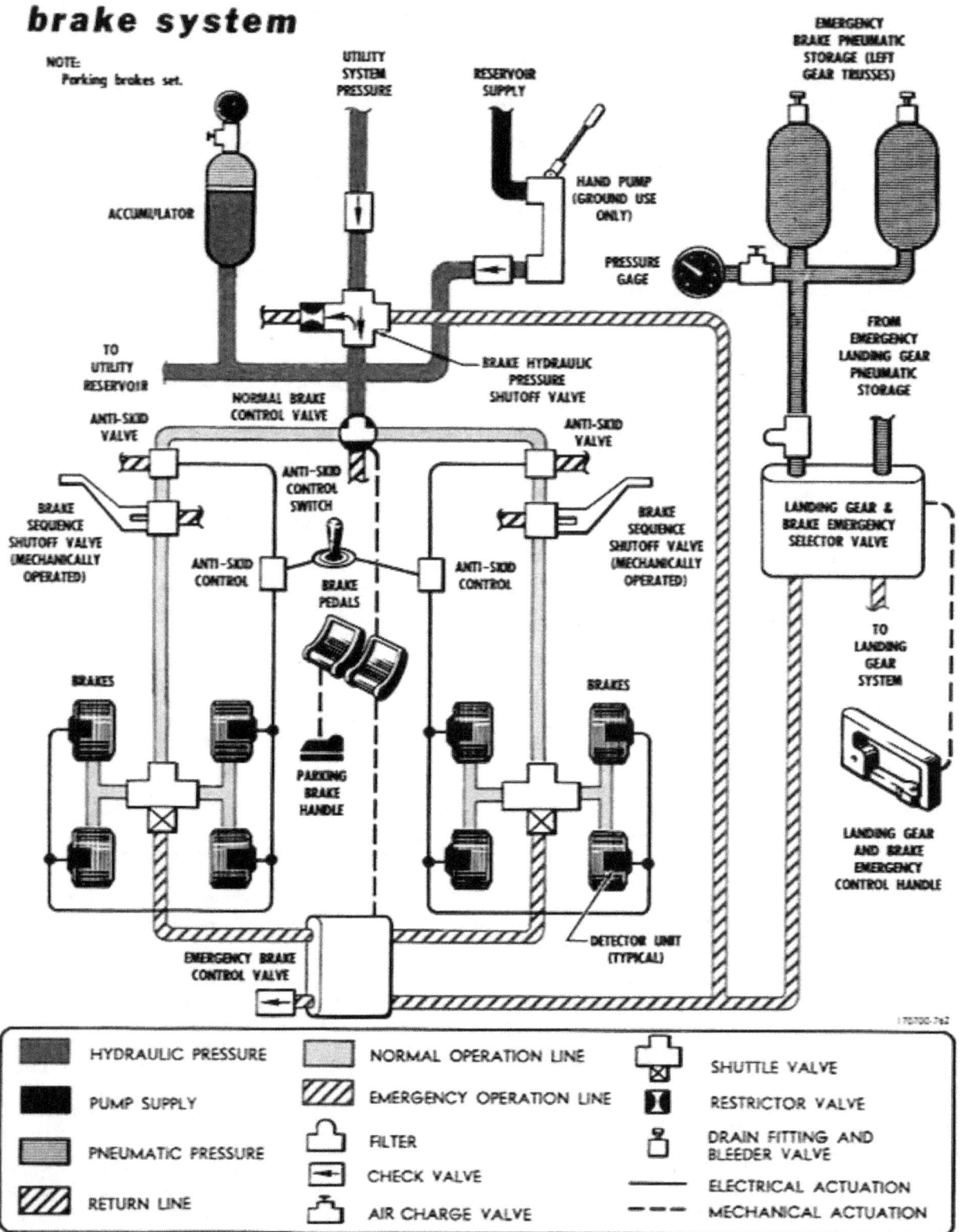

Figure 1-36.

1-84

hydraulic pressure from reaching the normal brake valve by shutting off the supply and dumping the brake accumulator to return. The normal brake control valve is mechanically linked to the emergency control valve so that one set of brake pedal control cables may be utilized for both valves. With pneumatic pressure to the emergency control valve, the action on either brake pedal will direct brake pressure to the respective sets of wheels through the pneumatic tubing. Brakes should be applied with gradual but steady pressure on the pedals. Each time the pedals are released, the pneumatic pressure in the lines is vented overboard; therefore, excessive releasing of the pedals should be avoided. The number of full brake applications that can be obtained depends upon the temperature of the system. If the system temperature is 70°F (21°C), seven to eight full brake applications can be obtained; however, at system temperature of —65°F (—54°C), as little as three full brake applications may be available. After the first full brake application has been released, each subsequent brake application will result in a decreasing amount of pressure being applied to the brakes. If the emergency brake and landing gear control handle is pulled to extend the gear the brake emergency pneumatic system will be activated; therefore, caution should be exercised to prevent inadvertent brake application before the airplane is on the ground.

Note

If sufficient hydraulic pressure is available for gear extension but questionable for brake operation, or in event of hydraulic system failure after gear extension, pulling the emergency brake and landing gear control handle will still provide pneumatic pressure for brake operation.

Emergency Brake and Landing Gear Control Handle.

The emergency brake and landing gear control handle (7, figure 1-7) is used to extend the landing gear and activate the brake pneumatic system in the event of utility hydraulic system failure. Pulling the handle will activate the brake pneumatic system whether the landing gear was extended pneumatically or hydraulically. For further information on this handle refer to "Landing Gear System", this section.

DRAG CHUTE.

The airplane is equipped with a drag chute to supplement the airplane brakes by reducing ground roll during landings and aborted takeoffs. The chute, deployment of which is controlled from the pilot's station, is installed in a compartment located in the bottom of the tail section forward of the tail turret. The compartment is covered by dual clamshell-type doors which are hinged at the outboard edges. The chute installation consists essentially of a main canopy, which is equipped with a pilot chute, and the drag chute doors. The main canopy riser is attached to the aft end of the stowage compartment by a pneumatically actuated hook which engages the chute D-ring. To protect the airplane from excessive drag forces in the event the stowage compartment door should open accidentally and deploy the parachute during flight, the hook remains in a half-open configuration so that the chute assembly will pull free of the airplane. As a further precaution, the D-ring is designed so that it will fail and the chute will be released from the airplane if it is deployed by the control handle at airspeeds above 230 knots IAS. The drag chute system is actuated pneumatically and is controlled electrically. The pneumatic system consists of a filler valve, a pressure gage, a sequence valve and hook actuator assembly, and a door actuator, all located in the parachute stowage compartment, and a nitrogen bottle located in the adjoining compartment. The system is charged with nitrogen according to the ambient temperature. A placard near the pressure gage is used to determine the correct pressure. See figure 1-47 for servicing data.

DRAG CHUTE CONTROL HANDLE.

The drag chute system is controlled by a T-handle (4, figure 1-34) located on the pilot's forward left console. The handle is in its normal position when it is pushed in and the crossbar is vertical. Pulling the handle out to the first stop deploys the chute. Then turning the handle 90 degrees counterclockwise and pulling it out to its full travel will jettison the drag chute. The handle operates the system by supplying 28-volt d-c power to the pneumatic sequence valve through two circuits. Pulling the handle out closes the first circuit, actuating the valve. Actuating the valve closes the hook on the chute D-ring, unlatches the compartment doors, and forces them into the airstream. As the clamshell doors are opened by the airstream, the chute pack is pulled from the stowage compartment. As the pack is forced into the airstream, a ripcord attached to the airplane opens the pilot chute compartment located in the main canopy pack. The pilot chute is then projected into the airstream by a spring which is an integral part of the pilot chute. The opened pilot chute pulls the main canopy from the pack to complete the operation. Turning the handle 90 degrees counterclockwise and pulling the handle out will open the first circuit and close the second, causing the valves to open the D-ring hook, jettisoning the parachute. Returning the handle to its normal position (crossbar vertical) opens the second circuit and allows the D-ring hook to return to its normal half-open position.

secondary pitot-static system deviation from primary system

FLIGHT CONDITION	PRIMARY SYSTEM INDICATED AIRSPEED	SECONDARY SYSTEM DEVIATION	
		NAVIGATOR	DSO
GROUND RUN ATTITUDE (nose wheel on ground)	LESS THAN 100	+19, —8	+19, —8
	100-200	+21, —7	+23, —9
TAKEOFF OR LANDING (with or without pod)	100-160	+20, —7	+22, —9
	170-290	+23, —8	+24, —9
CRUISE (with MB, LA or TCP)	290-340	+17, —11	+21, —15
	341-410	+21, —11	+25, —15
	411-460	+24, —8	+28, —12
	461-510	+26, —6	+31, —11
CRUISE (without pod or with upper pod)	290-340	+21, —8	+25, —12
	341-410	+21, —6	+30, —10
	411-460	+29, —4	+33, —8
	461-510	+32, —1	+37, —6

Note:
1. The primary system airspeed is assumed to be subsonic.
2. Small weapons or pylons will have a negligible effect on the secondary system deviation.

Figure 1-37.

PRESSURE GAGE.

A pressure gage, located in a small compartment adjacent to the forward end of the parachute stowage compartment, indicates drag chute pneumatic pressure in pounds per square inch. The gage is visible through an access door in the compartment.

PITOT-STATIC SYSTEM.

Two complete pitot-static systems, a primary and a secondary, supply the pitot and static pressures necessary to operate various flight instruments and system components. The primary system consists of a pitot-static probe attached to the nose boom and tubing required to connect the probe to the instruments and other components. The secondary system consists of a pitot probe mounted on the left side of the fuselage forward of the pilot's station, separate static pressure ports on each side of the fuselage, and necessary tubing.

The primary system supplies pitot and static pressures to the pilot's airspeed indicator and the air data computer; static pressure only is supplied to the altimeter and vertical velocity indicator. The principle of operation of the secondary system is the same as for the primary; however, only the navigator's and DSO's altimeters and airspeed indicators and the VGH recorder are connected to the secondary system. There is a permanent connection between the primary and secondary system pitot pressure lines to prevent a loss of airspeed indication at the pilot's station if the primary pitot-static probe is damaged or becomes closed due to icing. The probes of both systems contain electrical heating elements to provide protection against icing. Refer to "Anti-icing and Defogging Systems," Section IV. Due to installation differences between the systems, readings on the pitot-static instruments will not be identical at all crew stations; the deviation of the secondary system is shown in figure 1-37. Moisture drains for the systems are located in the nose wheel well and at the pilot's and navigator's stations.

AIR DATA SYSTEM.

The airplane is equipped with an air data system which provides aerodynamic intelligence to various control systems. The air data system consists basically of an electromechanical air data computer which processes raw data from the pitot-static probe and a temperature sensor probe located on the left side of the fuselage above the nose wheel well. The computer utilizes the following raw data: static pressure, pitot pressure, and total temperature. When this data reaches the computer, it is transformed into electrical signal outputs through an arrangement of transducers, mechanical linkage, and servo repeaters. These outputs, when delivered to the various control systems on the airplane, correspond to values of mach number, static pressure, pressure altitude, density ratio, true airspeed, and free stream temperature. The mechanism of the computer operates on 115-volt a-c power. Listed below are the various airplane systems served by the air data system, followed in parentheses by the computer outputs which go to the systems:

1. Flight control (mach number, static pressure).
2. Autopilot (mach number, static pressure).
3. Spike positioning (mach number).
4. Air conditioning (mach number).
5. TACAN (static pressure to marker beacon signal amplifier).
6. Pilot's mach indicator (mach number).
7. Primary navigation (pressure altitude, true airspeed).
8. Bombing (density ratio, pressure altitude, altitude rate of change).
9. Air navigation data recorder (pressure altitude).
10. Fire control (mach number, density ratio).
11. Landing gear warning (mach number, static pressure).

INSTRUMENTS.

The instruments covered here are only those which are not considered to be a part of a complete system. For information on instruments which are an integral part of a particular system, refer to applicable paragraphs in this section and Section IV.

AIRSPEED INDICATOR.

The airspeed indicator (38, figure 1-5), which is on the pilot's main instrument panel, shows indicated airspeed in knots. The instrument should read 40 ±5 KIAS static indication. The indicator is operated by impact and static pressures from the primary pitot-static system. An airspeed indicator is also provided on the right console or the auxiliary flight instrument panel in the navigator's station and is operated from the secondary pitot-static system. Refer to "Pitot-Static System," this section, for further information.

AIRSPEED-MACH INDICATOR.

An airspeed-mach indicator (figure 1-38) is installed just above the radar fire control panel in the DSO's station. The indicator is operated by impact and static pressures from the secondary pitot-static system. The airspeed-mach pointer (solid color pointer) indicates airspeed on the airspeed scale (outer scale) and mach number on the mach scale (inner scale). The maximum allowable airspeed pointer indicates maximum allowable airspeed which is computed by the instrument and requires no inflight adjustment. The airspeed marker set knob in the lower right corner adjusts the airspeed marker position on the outside edge of the airspeed scale. Refer to "Pitot-Static System," this section, for further information.

MACH INDICATOR.

The mach indicator (3, figure 1-5) on the pilot's main instrument panel receives electrical signals from the air data computer and indicates mach number at which the airplane is flying. Mach number is the ratio of true airspeed to the speed of sound. The set knob at the lower right corner of the instrument is used to adjust the two reference pointers. Rotating the knob adjusts the reference pointer on the main dial, and depressing and rotating the knob adjusts the reference pointer on the subdial. In event of a power failure, POWER OFF appears in a window on the face of the main dial.

BAROMETRIC ALTIMETER.

A barometric altimeter (36, figure 1-5), located on the pilot's main instrument panel, indicates altitude in feet.

airspeed - mach indicator

Figure 1-38.

Section I
Description

A low altitude warning symbol in the form of a cross-hatched area appears when the airplane is below 16,666 feet. When at zero feet, the area is fully exposed. The altimeter operates on static pressure from the primary pitot-static system. A barometric pressure set knob located on the lower left corner of the instrument provides a means of adjusting the altimeter to the correct barometric setting.

WARNING

When adjusting the barometric setting check that the 10,000 foot pointer is reading correctly. If the barometric pressure set knob is rotated until the barometric scale goes out of view and then re-appears, the altimeter will read approximately 10,000 feet in error even though the correct setting appears in the barometric scale.

A barometric altimeter is also provided on the auxiliary flight instrument panel in the navigator's station and just above the radar fire control panel in the DSO's station. The navigator's and DSO's altimeters operate on static pressure from the secondary pitot-static system. Altimeter correction cards are provided on all airplanes.

LOW ALTITUDE RADAR ALTIMETER.

Precise altitude indications for absolute altitudes up to 5000 feet are provided by the low altitude radar altimeter set. Altitude indicators associated with this set are located on the pilots main instrument panel (27, figure 1-5) and the navigators right console (5, figure 4-36). These indicators are identical in operation and both receive signals from the same receiver-transmitter unit. Accuracy of the low altitude radar altimeter set is $\pm$ (5 ft. plus 3% of indicated altitude). A fail indicator is provided in the form of a crosshatched area which appears on the face of the altitude indicators when any of the following conditions exist: (1) In the event of a power failure. (2) When airplane altitude exceeds 5000 feet above the terrain. (3) Any time a malfunction of the set occurs. (4) During the warmup period (approximately 2 minutes). Normally the pointer on the indicator will return to 0 when the crosshatch appears, but in any event the indicated altitudes will not be reliable. A control knob, located on the lower left corner of each altitude indicator provides a means of turning the radar altimeter on and is also used to position the minimum altitude index pointer.

Note

Turning the control knob of either altitude indicator to the on position will place the low altitude radar altimeter set in operation and altitudes will be displayed on both indicators.

The push-to-test feature of this knob allows the crew member to check the operation of the low altitude radar altimeter set. When the set is turned on and functioning properly, pressing this knob will cause the instrument pointer to indicate 100 ($\pm$10) feet. An amber warning lamp, which reads "LOW," is located on the lower right corner of each of the altitude indicators. This lamp lights when airplane altitude is below the minimum altitude indexed on the indicator. The minimum altitude index pointers on the two indicators are in no way related to one another. For example, if the index pointer on the pilot's indicator is set at 1000 feet and the index pointer on the navigator's indicator is set at 2000 feet, the amber LOW lamp on the pilot's indicator will be lighted any time the airplane is below 1000 feet absolute altitude and the amber LOW lamp on the navigator's indicator will be lighted any time the airplane is below 2000 feet absolute altitude. The low altitude radar altimeter set operates on 28-volt d-c power from the 28-volt d-c power panel and 115-volt a-c power from the right a-c power distribution panel.

LOW ALTITUDE WARNING LAMPS.

In addition to the amber LOW lamps located on the low altitude radar altimeter indicators, two red low altitude warning lamps are provided; one on the pilot's main instrument panel (37, figure 1-5) and the other on the navigator's auxiliary flight instrument panel (1, figure 4-38). The lamps are marked RADAR ALT LOW and are identical in function. The lamp in either station will light when airplane altitude is below the minimum altitude indexed on the low altitude radar altimeter in that station. The lamps are powered by 28-volt direct current. The RADAR ALT LOW lamp located in the pilot's station may be checked by depressing the malfunction and indicator lamp test button located on the pilot's forward left console.

1-88

VERTICAL VELOCITY INDICATOR.

A vertical velocity indicator (19, figure 1-5), located on the pilot's main instrument panel, measures in feet per minute the rate of climb or descent of the airplane. The indicator operates on static pressure from the primary pitot-static system.

ACCELEROMETER.

The accelerometer (24, figure 1-5) is located on the pilot's main instrument panel. It indicates the vertical load imposed on the airplane in terms of "g" units and enables the pilot to maneuver the airplane within its operational limits. A main pointer gives continuous indication of gravitational load; two auxiliary pointers indicate maximum acceleration—positive and negative —during any maneuver. The two auxiliary pointers maintain their extreme positions until they are reset by depressing the knob on the lower left side of the instrument. The accelerometer is operated by gravitational forces and has no external power source.

MM-3 ATTITUDE INDICATORS.

A visual indication of the flight attitude of the airplane in pitch and roll is provided by two MM-3 attitude indicators, one at the pilot's station (6, figure 1-5), and one at the navigator's station (6, figure 4-38). Both are remote indicating instruments. Changes in airplane attitude are electrically relayed from an attitude reference source to the individual indicator causing displacement of the indicator sphere in relation to a fixed miniature aircraft on the indicator. The amount of displacement is directly proportional to actual airplane attitude deviation from level flight. The indicator displays pitch information by movement of the spherical surface used as a reference background for the fixed miniature aircraft. A line on the sphere represents the horizon and divides the grey portion, which represents the sky from the black portion, which represents the ground. A pitch trim knob, located at the lower right corner of the indicator, is provided for adjusting the horizon line. Both the climb and dive portions of the sphere are graduated in increments of 5 degrees. Roll information is presented by movement of the bank pointer at the top of the instrument in relation to the bank scale along the circumference of the instrument face. The bank scale is marked each 30 degrees, up to 90 degrees; the first 30-degree increment is sub-divided by 10-degree marks. The indicator does not contain gyros; therefore, a caging knob is not provided. An OFF warning is visible in a window at the lower left side of the indicator in the event of power failure. However, a slight reduction in power or a deviation of attitude reference will not cause the warning to appear even though the system is not operating properly. The pilot's indicator receives attitude signals from the Auxiliary Flight Reference System (AFRS) and 115-volt, a-c power from the right a-c bus through the AFRS power switch at the navigator's station.

WARNING

A slight amount of pitch error in the indication of the pilot's MM-3 attitude indicator will result from acceleration or deceleration. It will appear as a slight climb indication after acceleration and as a slight dive indication after deceleration when the airplane is flying straight and level. This error will be most noticeable at the time the airplane leaves the ground during the takeoff run. At this time, a climb indication error of about 2 to 3 degrees will normally be noticed; however, the exact amount of error will depend upon the acceleration and elapsed time of each individual takeoff. The erection system will automatically remove the error after acceleration ceases.

The navigator's indicator receives attitude information from the PNS only and receives 115-volt, a-c power from the left a-c bus. It is used to determine if the stable-table unit in the primary navigation system is erect and is also used when flying the airplane with the tracking and flight control stick. PNS attitude signals are supplied from either the primary or auxiliary stable table, depending on the position of the navigator's vertical reference selector switch, and are limited to 90 degrees of roll and 70 degrees of pitch. AFRS attitude signals are limited to 82 degrees in pitch only. If the limits of either PNS or AFRS are exceeded, the affected instrument will be unreliable and should be cross-checked.

Section I
Description

T.O. 1B-58A-1

WARNING

- A slight reduction in electrical power or failure of certain electrical components within the system will not cause the OFF flag to appear even though the system is not functioning properly.

- A malfunction of either or both MM-3 indicators can be determined by a cross-check between these two instruments or with the auxiliary attitude indicator, turn-and-slip indicator, angle-of-attack indicator, altimeter, vertical velocity indicator, and airspeed indicator.

After a pitch or roll flight maneuver, the AFRS system errors will cancel and the indicator will indicate the correct airplane attitude. However, in maneuvers such as a steep dive followed by a pullout, the system errors will be additive in a manner that makes the prediction of attitude indicator error impossible.

AUXILIARY ATITUDE INDICATOR.

The auxiliary attitude indicator (8, figure 1-5), installed on the pilot's main instrument panel, is identical and performs the same function as the MM-3 attitude indicator except that the indicator receives pitch and roll signals from the primary navigation system (PNS), and 115-volt, a-c power from the left a-c bus.

ANGLE-OF-ATTACK INDICATOR.

The angle-of-attack indicator (figure 1-39), which is located on the pilot's main instrument panel, indicates to the pilot the angular position of the wing chord in relation to the flight path of the airplane. This indicator is used to provide stall warning. It may also be used as an aid in maintaining minimum safe flying and maneuver speeds and in establishing and maintaining approach/flare speed; however, the airspeed indicator is the primary instrument. The indicator receives power from the right 115-volt a-c power panel. The indicator is graduated from zero to twenty degrees with major graduation in increments of five degrees. Immediately above the indicator center, a flag marked OFF is visible when electrical power is removed from the indicator. The indicator is electrically slaved to a transmitter and sensor vane located on the right forward side of the fuselage. In flight, the vane aligns itself with the airflow so that any change in angle of attack will be presented on the indicator. The sensor vane contains electrical heating elements for anti-icing. Refer to "Anti-Icing and Defogging Systems," Section IV. The indicator incorporates a series of cam switches which control power to the angle-of-attack indexer and stall warning indicator lamps. The indexer and stall warning indicator lamps are referenced to the two fixed indices located on the angle-of-attack indicator. The index at 17 degrees is the limit angle of attack. The index at 12½ degrees is the angle of attack at normal approach/flare speeds. The angle-of-attack sensor vane must be moved through its full range to check all functions of the indicator.

ANGLE-OF-ATTACK INDEXER.

The angle-of-attack indexer (figure 1-41) may be used as an aid in maintaining the proper angle of attack for landing approaches; however, airspeed is the primary instrument. The speed symbols on the indexer operate only when the landing gear handle is in the "down" position. The indexer consists of a stall warning lamp and three speed symbols. The low-speed symbol is red, the on-speed symbol green, and the high-speed symbol amber. The low-speed (red) symbol is illuminated when the angle of attack is 13.25 (±0.25) degrees or above. The on-speed (green) symbol is illuminated when the angle of attack is between 11.25 (±0.25) degrees and 13.75 (±0.25) degrees. The high-speed (amber) symbol is illuminated when the angle of attack is 11.75 (±0.25) degrees or less. Within the range of 13.0 to 14.0 degrees angle of attack, both the

angle-of-attack indicator

Figure 1-39.

1-90

low-speed (red) symbol and the on-speed (green) symbol are illuminated simultaneously for at least 0.5 degree angle of attack. Within the range of 11.0 to 12.0 degrees angle of attack, both the high-speed (amber) and the on-speed (green) symbols are illuminated simultaneously for at least 0.5 degree angle of attack. This overlap feature of the speed symbol lights aids in maintaining the desired approach angle of attack. When the low speed (red) symbol only is illuminated the angle of attack is greater than 14.0 degrees. When the on-speed (green) symbol only is illuminated the angle of attack is between 11.5 degrees and 13.5 degrees. When the high-speed (amber) symbol only is illuminated the angle of attack is less than 11.0 degrees.

The symbols receive power from the 28-volt d-c power panel. An indexer rheostat (5, figure 1-41) located at the bottom of the indexer is rotated left to dim the symbols. The angle-of-attack sensor vane must be rotated through its range to check the symbols.

STALL WARNING LAMP.

A stall warning lamp is located on the left side of the angle-of-attack indexer (1, figure 1-41). When the lamp is illuminated, the word STALL in black letters will appear vertically on a background of red. At the same time the lamp is illuminated, a voice warning message will be transmitted. Both the stall warning lamp and the voice warning system are energized when the angle-of-attack exceeds 17 degrees regardless of the landing gear position. The stall warning lamp receives power from the 28-volt d-c power panel and has no provision for dimming.

TURN-AND-SLIP INDICATOR.

A turn-and-slip indicator (5, figure 1-5) is installed at the top of the pilot's main instrument panel. It is operated by 28-volt d-c power.

Note

In the event that the turn-and-slip indicator is misaligned and flight is made with the ball centered, wing heaviness could result due to fuel flowing to the low wing. Refer to "Wing Heaviness", Section VI.

MAGNETIC COMPASS (B-21).

A magnetic compass is installed on the center post of the pilot's windshield. A holder for the compass correction card is on the glare shield below the compass.

ABU-3/A clock

Figure 1-40.

CLOCK.

A mechanical time-of-day, 12 hour elapsed-time clock (figure 1-40) is located on the pilot's main instrument panel. The clock contains a main dial, two subdials, two control knobs, and a control lever. The clock has an eight-day movement and is stem wound. The main dial indicates the time of day and consists of minute, hour, and sweep second hands which are controlled by a winding-set knob located on the lower left corner of the clock. Rotating the knob counterclockwise winds the clock mainspring. Pulling out on the knob stops the clock and zeros the sweep second hand and allows it to be reset as desired. Pushing the knob back in restarts the clock. The upper subdial indicates elapsed time and consists of minute and hour hands which are controlled by a lever located on the upper right corner of the clock. The lever has three positions marked GO, STOP, and 0 (zero). Placing the lever in the corresponding position will start, stop, or zero the minute and hour hands. The lower subdial indicates elapsed time in increments of minutes, and consists of a minute hand which is controlled by a knob located on the lower right corner of the clock. Depressing the knob once starts the minute hand and displays a small white dot on the face of the subdial. A second depression of the knob stops the minute hand and displays a red and white dot. A thrid depression of the knob zeros the minute hand and displays a red dot.

Note

The ABU-3/A clock is being replaced on an attrition basis by the ABU-11/A clock.

Section I
Description

angle of attack indexer

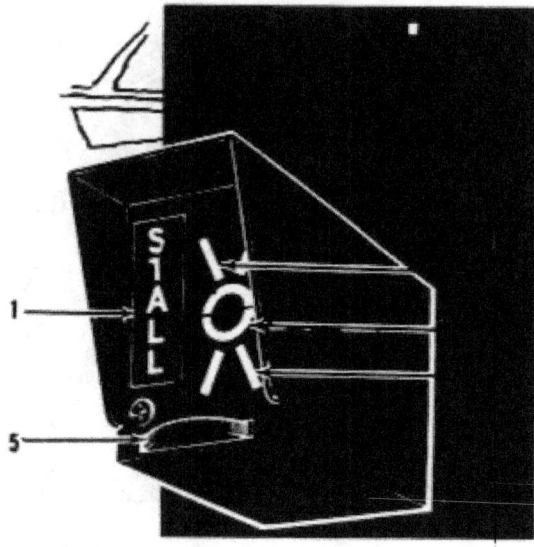

1. Stall Warning Lamp
2. Low-Speed Symbol
3. On-Speed Symbol
4. High-Speed Symbol
5. Indexer Rheostat

Figure 1-41.

MALFUNCTION INDICATOR AND WARNING SYSTEM.

The malfunction indicator and warning system provides both visual and aural warning to the crew of malfunctions or unsafe conditions that require immediate attention. The pilot's indicator lamp system provides visual warning and caution indications for the pilot and works in conjunction with the voice warning system which provides aural messages to all crew members of malfunctions or unsafe conditions.

PILOT'S INDICATOR LAMP SYSTEM.

The pilot's indicator lamp system consists primarily of the lamps on the warning and caution lamp panels (figure 1-13) and the individual lamps located on the pilot's instrument and control panels. All these lamps, except the master warning and caution lamps, are described under the respective systems. The master warning and caution lamps provide visual indications in the event of a system malfunction or unsafe condition requiring immediate attention by the pilot. The system functions in conjunction with the voice warning system.

Warning and Caution Indicator Switch.

The warning and caution indicator switch is located on the pilot's lower left console (12, figure 1-7). Switch positions are marked GROUND CHECK and NORM. The switch permits the warning and caution lamp circuit to be isolated from external electrical power during ground operations; this prevents overheating of the warning and caution lamps. When external power is supplied to the airplane, and the warning and caution indicator switch is in the NORM position, a relay is energized, isolating power from the warning and caution lamp circuit. When the switch is positioned to GROUND CHECK, the relay is de-energized, permitting normal operation of the warning and caution lamps. When airplane power is supplied, the relay is de-energized and the warning and caution lamps are returned to normal operation, regardless of switch position.

Malfunction and Indicator Lamp and Voice Warning System Test Button.

The malfunction and indicator lamp and voice warning system test button (11, figure 1-34) is located on the pilot's forward left console. This button provides a means of simultaneously testing the operation of the master and the individual warning and caution lamps, crew capsulated and emergency air supply lamps, the landing gear warning lamp, the crew ejection, inflight refueling ready, and autopilot second station lamps, the angle-of-attack indicator, stall warning, pilot's low altitude warning, and aileron-rudder neutral trim indicator lamps and the voice warning system.

Note

When using external power, the warning and caution indicator switch must be placed in the GROUND CHECK position to test the warning and caution lamps and voice warning system.

When the test button is depressed, each of these lamps should light and the voice warning system should start to transmit on the highest priority message. Also, when the test button is depressed, the landing gear warning buzzer should sound if the landing gear control handle is in the DOWN position. The button controls 28-volt d-c power for lighting the lamps.

Malfunction and Indicator Lamp Dimming Switch.

The malfunction and indicator lamp dimming switch (11, figure 4-23) is located on the pilot's lighting control panel. The switch has positions marked BRIGHT and DIM and is spring loaded to a neutral position. This switch controls the dimming of the master and the individual warning and caution lamps, the landing gear warning and position indicator lamps, and the inflight refueling ready, autopilot second station, and aileron-rudder neutral trim indicator lamps. When this switch is momentarily positioned to DIM, the intensity of these lamps will be dimmed provided both panel light control knobs on the pilot's lighting panel are rotated approximately 25 degrees from OFF. If either of the knobs are below this setting the warning, caution, and indicator lamps will stay dim only as long as the dimming switch is held in the DIM position. Once these lamps are dimmed they can be brightened by momentarily positioning the switch to BRIGHT. The dimming switch controls 28-volt d-c power to the warning, caution, and indicator lamps.

Master Warning Lamp.

The red master warning lamp (35, figure 1-5) is located at the left side of the pilot's main instrument panel. When the lamp is lighted, MASTER WARNING appears on the face of the lamp. The lamp lights when any individual *warning* lamp on the warning and caution lamp panels becomes lighted as a result of a malfunction or unsafe condition in some system of the airplane. The lamp works in conjunction with the voice warning system. The master lamp remains lighted as long as an individual lamp is lighted. The master lamp can be reset, however, by depressing the face of the lamp. This should be accomplished as soon as possible after the individual warning lamps have been checked to determine the source of trouble. The individual warning lamp will remain lighted as long as the trouble exists and the master warning lamp will remain off until some other source of trouble causes another individual lamp to light. Depressing the lamp will also override the voice warning system message in progress. Dimming of the lamp can be accomplished with the malfunction and indicator lights dimming switch on the pilot's lighting control panel and the lamp can be tested by depressing the malfunction and indicator light test button on the pilot's forward left console. The lamp operates on 28-volt d-c power.

Master Caution Lamp.

The master caution lamp (34, figure 1-5) is located at the left side of the pilot's main instrument panel. When the lamp is lighted, MASTER CAUTION appears on the face of the lamp. The master lamp lights when any individual *caution* lamp on the warning and caution lamps panels become lighted as a result of a malfunction or unsafe condition in some system of the airplane. The lamp works in conjunction with the voice warning system. The master caution lamp remains lighted as long as an individual lamp is lighted or until reset by depressing the face of the lamp. Depressing the lamp will also override the voice warning system message in progress. The control unit for the master caution lamp contains a delay circuit which delays the lighting of the master caution lamp from one to one and one-half seconds after an individual caution lamp has lighted. The master lamp should always be reset as soon as possible after the caution panel has been checked to determine the source of trouble or type of malfunction.

VOICE WARNING SYSTEM.

The voice warning system provides aural warning to alert the crew when malfunctions or unsafe conditions occur during operation of the airplane. The system consists of a signal assembly, a power/reset switch and an override button at the pilot's station, monitoring switches at the navigator's and DSO's stations, sensing switches and necessary wiring and connectors. The system operates in conjunction with the pilot's warning and caution indicator lamp system. When a sensing switch in the system picks up a fault, the switch will light the corresponding lamp on the pilot's warning and caution panel and cause the signal assembly to transmit an appropriate message to the crew over the interphone, alerting them of the malfunction or unsafe condition that exists. The message will be repeated until the condition is corrected or until the pilot silences the system. The pilot can silence the system by depressing the override button or the affected warning or caution lamp. If more than one fault exists when the system is silenced, the next message in order of priority will be transmitted until that message is silenced and so on until all existing faults have been monitored. If a message is being transmitted when a malfunction of higher priority occurs the lower priority message will stop and the higher priority message will start at the beginning of the message. The system provides twenty channels with nineteen pre-recorded messages arranged in priority of importance. (See figure 1-42.) The malfunction and indicator light and voice warning system test button (11, figure 1-34) is used to check the voice warning system. Depressing this button will start the voice warning system transmitting the highest priority message. The override button or the master warning or caution lamp may then be used to check each message in order. Overriding the last message will return the system to normal operation. The system operates on 28 volt d-c power from the main d-c power panel.

Voice Warning System Power/Reset Switch.

The voice warning system power/reset switch (11, figure 1-7) is located on the pilot's lower left console. The switch positions are marked RESET, ON, and OFF. When the switch is placed in the center ON position, 28 volt d-c power is applied to the system. The switch is spring loaded in the ON position from the RESET

Section I
Description

T.O. 1B-58A-1

voice warning system message priority

Priority	Malfunction	Recorded Message
1.	Left fuel manifold pressure low	LEFT MANIFOLD PRESSURE LOW
2.	Right fuel manifold pressure low	RIGHT MANIFOLD PRESSURE LOW
3.	Yaw damper system failure	YAW DAMPER FAILURE
4.	Weapon Unlocked	WEAPON UNLOCKED
5.	Reservoir tank not full	RES TANK NOT FULL
6.	Primary and/or utility hydraulic system failure	HYDRAULIC SYSTEM FAILURE
7.	Oil quantity low on any engine	ENGINE OIL QUANTITY LOW
*8.	Fire on any engine	CHECK FOR ENGINE FIRE
9.	CG is 1% off selected in AUTO	CG OFF
10.	Landing gear unsafe to land	LANDING GEAR UNSAFE
11.	Either utility hydraulic pump inoperative	UTILITY HYDRAULIC PUMP FAILED
12.	Either primary hydraulic pump inoperative	PRIMARY HYDRAULIC PUMP FAILED
13.	Any generator abnormal	GENERATOR ABNORMAL
14.	Any canopy unlocked	CANOPY UNLOCKED
15.	Electronic equipment overheat	LOW AIR FLOW
16.	Oxygen quantity low	OXYGEN QUANTITY LOW
17.	Engine intake ice is forming	ICE FORMING (followed by tone for test purposes and, in a different quality, the tape part number)
18.	Angle-of-attack too high	NOSE HIGH
19.	Spare channel	SPARE CHANNEL NINETEEN
20.	All remaining items on caution panel (except booster pumps)	MONITOR CAUTION PANEL

*The fire detection system is deactivated, however the recorded message is present on the tape and will be heard during ground preflight system check.

Figure 1-42.

position. Momentarily placing the switch to RESET will interrupt any message in progress and reactivate all channels previously silenced that are still present.

Voice Warning System Override Button.

The voice warning system override button (29, figure 1-44) is located on the right leg retraction bar in the pilot's escape capsule. The button is provided to override or silence messages from the voice warning system when the capsule doors are closed. Depressing the button will interrupt a message in progress and either allow the next message of lower priority to be transmitted or silence the system if no other malfunctions are present. The affected master warning or caution lamp will also go out when the override button is depressed.

Voice Warning System Monitoring Switch.

A voice warning system monitoring switch is located on the navigator's and DSO's left console, figures 4-35 and 4-64. The switch is marked VWS and OFF. When the switch is placed in the VWS position, the crew member will monitor any message transmitted by the voice warning system. Placing the switch to OFF will turn off the voice warning system at that station only.

1-94

EMERGENCY EQUIPMENT.

BAILOUT WARNING SYSTEM.

The bailout warning system provides a means for the pilot to alert the crew to a possible inflight emergency and notify them to capsulate or to eject in case of an emergency requiring inflight escape from the airplane. The system also provides the pilot an indication when both crew members have capsulated or ejected. The system consists primarily of bailout alert and warning switches and a crew ejection indicator lamp in the pilot's station, and alert lamps and warning lamps in the navigator's and defensive system operator's (DSO) crew stations.

CONTROLS AND INDICATORS.

Bailout Alert Switch.

A bailout alert switch (1, figure 1-34), located on the pilot's forward left console, is marked ALERT and OFF. The switch is held in the selected position by an internal lock which requires that the switch lever be pulled out before it can be repositioned. When the switch is positioned to ALERT or when the pilot's capsule doors are closed, the amber alert lamps at the navigator's and DSO's station will flash on and off, all crew members will have "hot mike" on interphone and the mayday functions of the communications system are also activated.

Bailout Warning Switch.

A bailout warning switch (4, figure 1-29) is mounted on the front of the control stick below the handgrip. The switch has two positions marked BAILOUT and OFF. The switch is guarded to prevent inadvertent actuation. When the switch is positioned to BAILOUT, or should the pilot eject before warning the crew, the red bailout warning lamps at the navigator's and DSO's station will light to signal the crew to eject. The mayday functions of the communications system are also activated and all crew members will have "hot mike" on interphone when the switch is positioned to BAILOUT or when the pilot ejects.

Bailout Alert Lamps.

The amber bailout alert lamps (7, figure 4-38, 1, figure 4-50, and bailout warning panel, figure 4-63), when flashing on and off, provide a visual signal from pilot to crew members that an emergency exists which may require ejection from the airplane. The crew members should immediately begin to prepare for capsulation and ejection when this lamp begins to flash. A bailout alert lamp is located on the navigator's pod release panel and auxiliary flight instrument panel, and on the defensive system operator's bailout warning panel. The lamps are powered by 28-volt direct current.

Bailout Warning Lamps.

The red bailout warning lamps (2, figure 4-38, 2, figure 4-50, and bailout warning panel, figure 4-63), when lighted, provide a visual signal from pilot to crew members to eject from the airplane using the proper ejection sequence. A bailout warning lamp is located on the navigator's auxiliary flight instrument panel and weapon lock and arm panel, and on the defensive system operator's bailout warning panel. On the capsule, red bailout warning lamps are also located on the left side of the headrest in the navigator's and DSO's capsules. The lamps are energized when the pilot turns his bailout warning switch to BAILOUT. A push-to-test button is provided beside the lamp to check the circuit. The bailout warning lamps are powered by 28-volt direct current.

Note

In case the pilot ejects without placing the bailout switch to BAILOUT, the upward movement of the pilot's capsule will automatically cause all the bailout warning lamps to light.

Crew Ejection Indicator Lamp.

A red lamp (7, figure 1-44) which lights when the crew members have ejected is located to the left of the pilot's headrest. The lamp is controlled by two switches in series arrangement located adjacent to the back of the navigator's and DSO's capsules. Each switch closes when the switch's respective capsule ejects. When both switches have closed a 28-volt d-c circuit is completed causing the lamp to light. The lamp circuit may be checked by depressing the press-to-test button located immediately below the lamp.

Crew Capsulated Indicator Lamp.

An amber crew capsulated indicator lamp (4, figure 1-5) is mounted on the pilot's instrument panel above the attitude indicator. The lamp provides a visual indication from navigator and DSO to pilot that their capsules are closed. The lamp is controlled by two switches (in series) mounted on the navigator's and DSO's capsule door. When both switches are closed a 28-volt direct current circuit is completed to light the lamp. When the lamp is on, the words CREW CAPSULATED appear on the face of the lamp. The lamp circuit may be checked by depressing the malfunction and indicator light test button located on the pilot's forward left console.

Emergency Air Supply Indicator Lamp.

The amber emergency air supply indicator lamp (7, figure 1-5) is located on the pilot's main instrument panel. The lamp provides the pilot with a visual indication that capsule pressurization is being furnished from the self-contained air supply in the capsule. When the lamp lights, indication is that a ten minute supply of air for pressurization remains. The lamp will light when pressure in the right drag strut drops to 270 psi and capsule pressurization is automatically switched from the right drag strut pressure source to the capsule air supply. When the lamp is lighted the words EMER AIR SUPPLY appear on the face of the lamp. The lamp is powered by 28-volt direct current. The lamp circuit may be checked by depressing the malfunction and indicator lamp test button located on the pilot's forward left console.

ENGINE FIRE PULL HANDLES.

Four engine fire pull handles (12, figure 1-5) marked FIRE PULL are located on the top right corner of the pilot's main instrument panel. Warning lamps, which are recessed in the center portion of the pull handles, have been deactivated. The pull handles control the engine fuel shutoff valves and the hydraulic system firewall shutoff valves. Pulling the handles out closes the valves, stopping fuel and hydraulic fluid flow to the applicable nacelles. The valves can be opened again by pushing the handles in.

CAUTION

Pulling a fire pull handle when an engine is operating will cause the hydraulic pump to cavitate, resulting in possible contamination of the hydraulic system with metal particles. For this reason, engines should not be shut down by pulling the fire pull handles, except in an emergency.

ESCAPE ROPES.

An emergency escape rope (10, figure 3-6) is located at each crew station for use during emergency exit from the airplane. Each rope is threaded through a brake mechanism and rolled on a stowage reel inside the side fairing of its respective crew station with the end loop extending through the fairing. The pilot's escape rope is located on the left side of the crew station aft of the window panes. Both the navigator's and defensive system operator's ropes are located forward of the right window in their respective crew stations. Each rope is approximately 29 feet long. To accomplish emergency exit from the airplane on the ground, the crewman grasps the loop of the escape rope and drops over the side of the fuselage (or off the wing).

HAND FIRE EXTINGUISHER.

A type A-20 hand fire extinguisher (17, figure 3-6) is located on the floor at the right side or mounted on the right sidewall of the second crew station. The extinguisher is charged with bromochloromethane and can be used on any type of fire.

WARNING

Prolonged exposure (5 minutes or more) to high concentrations (detected by pronounced irritation of eye and nose) of Bromochloromethane (CB) or its decomposition products should be avoided. CB is an anesthetic agent of moderate intensity. It is safer to use than previous fire extinguishing agents (carbon tetrachloride, methylbromide). However, especially in confined spaces, adequate respiratory and eye protection from excessive exposure, including the use of oxygen when available, should be sought as soon as the primary fire emergency will permit.

Note

Bromochloromethane is highly corrosive to aircraft metal, paint and plexiglass. In the event the fire extinguisher starts to leak, the extinguisher should be inverted and the control valve depressed (cover the nozzle with a cloth or aim into a can, etc. to catch any liquid which may be discharged). This will release the stored charge of pressurizing gas with a minimum discharge of fluid and render the extinguisher harmless. The extinguisher should be returned to its bracket and be reported for replacement in form 781.

FIRST AID EQUIPMENT.

First aid equipment is provided in the survival kits of the escape capsules (see figure 3-6).

CANOPIES.

Each crew station is equipped with a jettisonable clamshell-type canopy which is hinged at the aft end. Each canopy actuator is mechanically connected to a push-rod-bellcrank arrangement which provides automatic latching and unlatching of the canopy in the closed position. The canopies are normally operated by a pneumatic system (figure 1-43) and are controlled from the crew stations and from the nose wheel well. The pneumatic system pressure supply is stored in the right main landing gear w-truss. A filler valve and pressure gage are located in the right wheel well. The system is charged with nitrogen according to the ambient temperature. (A placard located near the filler valve is used to determine the correct precharge pressure.) See figure 1-47 for servicing data. When the system is fully charged, 3 to 10 cycles (opened and closed) are available, depending on temperature. An override control or a bypass tube in the nose wheel provides an alternate method of opening the pilot's canopy in event of system malfunction.

CAUTION

- To prevent canopy seal damage, do not open the canopy with the canopy seal inflated.
- To open canopies, place the applicable canopy control lever (individual crew compartment or nose wheel well) in the CLOSE or DOWN position, hold for a minimum of 5 seconds, then move the applicable control lever to the OPEN or UP position immediately. This procedure will lessen the possibility of shearing the canopy pins. Do not open canopies in headwinds exceeding 60 knots.

A caution lamp and three inspection windows at the pilots' station and latching indicator flags at the other two crew stations indicate when the canopies are locked down. Manual canopy lock release handles are provided on both the interior and exterior of the navigator's canopy for manually opening that canopy. Emergency removal of the canopies is accomplished by individual ballistic-type jettison systems which are a part of the escape provisions but are totally independent of any power system of the airplane. Each jettison system consists primarily of ballistic initiators and the canopy actuator which contains a ballistic charge. The initiators can be fired by controls at each crew station and on the exterior surface of the airplane. Firing a canopy initiator causes a ballistic charge in the actuator to fire which, in turn, jettisons the canopy free of the airplane. Jettisoning of the canopy during an ejection escape results when the trigger in either capsule handgrip is squeezed to initiate capsule ejection. The canopy jettisons a fraction of a second before the capsule. Each canopy is equipped with an inflatable seal to maintain cabin pressurization. Air for inflating the seals is supplied by the canopy pneumatic system or by the air conditioning system. Pressure from the canopy pneumatic system to the seals is controlled from the nose wheel well since this source is normally needed only when the airplane is parked. The pressure from the air conditioning system is available when an inboard engine is operating and is controlled from the navigator's station.

CONTROLS AND INDICATORS.

Canopy Control Levers.

Four canopy control levers, one in the left console of each crew station (figure 1-7, figure 4-35, and figure 4-64) and one in the nose wheel well, control operation of the canopies. The lever in each crew station controls operation of the canopy at that station. These levers are accessible through the hinged canopy control access door in the left console of each station. The levers each have three unmarked positions—OPEN (up), CLOSE (down), and NEUTRAL (center). These levers are mechanically latched in the OPEN position and are spring loaded to NEUTRAL from the CLOSE position. The control levers at crew stations must be left in the OPEN position after exit from the airplane in order for the canopies to be opened or closed from the nose wheel well. The lever in the nose wheel well enables simultaneous operation of the canopies from the ground. The marked lever positions, UP, NEUT, and DOWN, are shown on a decal adjacent to the control valve. The lever is spring loaded to UP from the DOWN and NEUTRAL positions. A lockpin is provided on the control valve to enable the lever to be locked in either the NEUT or UP positions. The pin must be pulled before the lever can be moved from these two positions. Placing the lever in the UP position will open the canopies if the control levers at the crew stations are in OPEN. Leaving the lever in UP supplies pneumatic pressure for operation of canopies from the crew stations. Placing the lever to DOWN will close the cano-

Section I
Description

T.O. 1B-58A-1

canopy pneumatic system (typical)

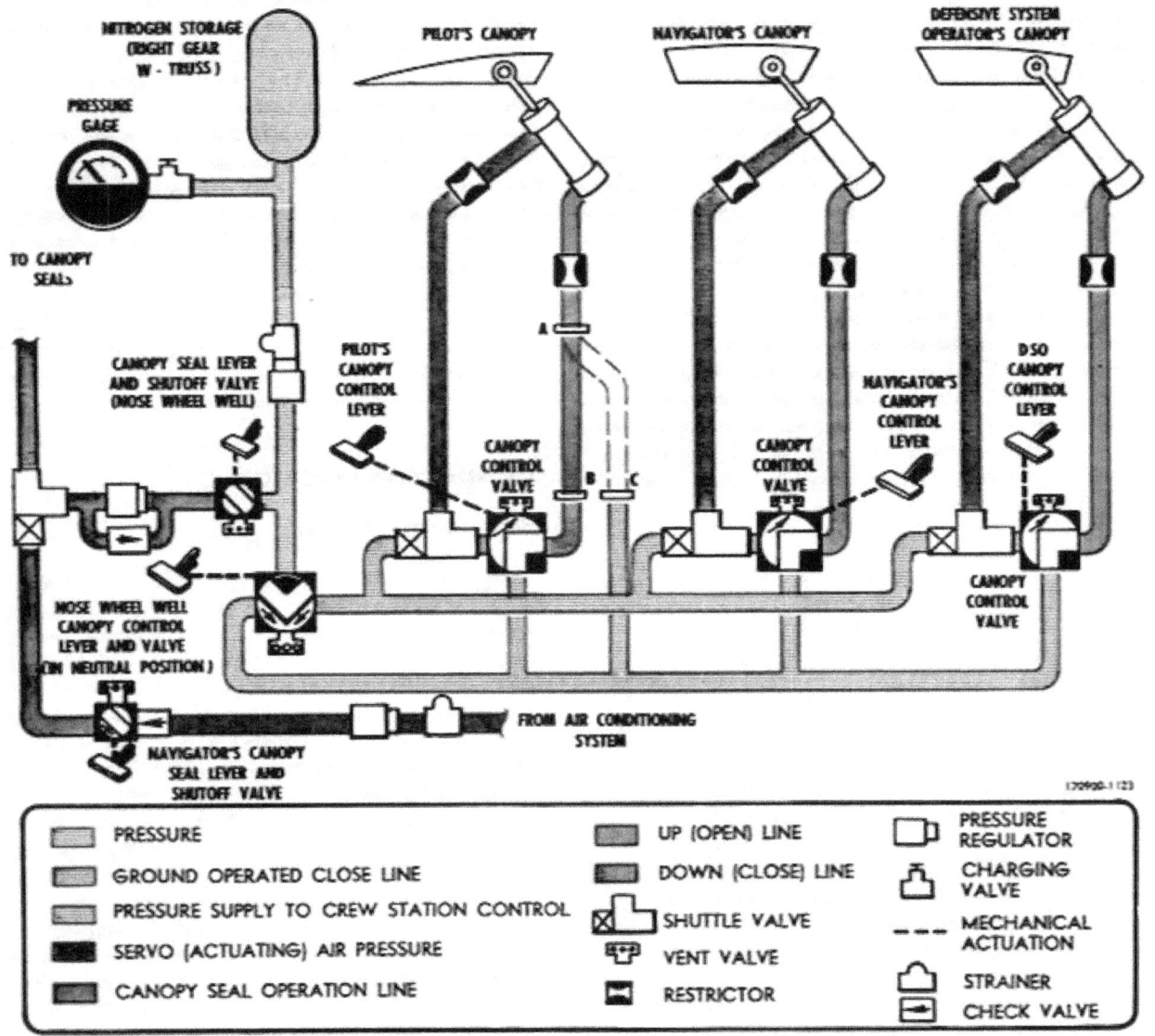

Figure 1-43.

pies. The pressure for canopy operation is shut off when the lever is positioned at NEUTRAL.

WARNING

Be sure the canopy area is clear of personnel when the canopies are operated. Serious injuries could result to anyone struck by a canopy in transit, especially when the canopy is being closed.

Note

The nose wheel well lever must be in the UP position before opening and closing of the canopies can be accomplished from the crew stations.

Pilot's Canopy Override Lever.

The pilot's canopy override lever, located in the nose wheel well, has unmarked ON and OFF positions and is normally safetied to OFF. Placing the lever to ON bypasses pneumatic pressure around the pilot's canopy controls and opens the pilot's canopy. This lever is used in event the pilot's canopy has been inadvertently closed from the nose wheel well while the canopy control lever at pilot's station is in NEUTRAL. On airplanes 22 17 ♦ the pilot's canopy override lever has been replaced by an override bypass tube which accomplishes the same function. The bypass tube located in the aft end of the nose wheel well may be connected between marked points A and B or A and C. To override the pilot's canopy controls and open the canopy the tube must be connected between points A and C. At all other times the tube must be connected between points A and B (as shown on placard located at the bypass tube).

Canopy Seal Control Levers.

Two canopy seal control levers, one in the navigator's station and one in the nose wheel well are provided to inflate and deflate the canopy seals. The navigator's seal control lever has positions marked SEALED and ALL CANOPIES UNSEALED. When the lever is positioned to SEALED, with one or both inboard engines operating, air from the air conditioning system inflates all three canopy seals simultaneously; the seals will remain inflated even if the inboard engines are shut down. The seals deflate when the lever is positioned to ALL CANOPIES UNSEALED. The seal control lever in the nose wheel well functions in the same manner except that this lever controls pressure from the canopy pneumatic system and is for ground use only. This lever has positions marked ON and OFF. The canopy seals can be inflated when the air conditioning system is operating from the ground cart; however, maximum sealing pressure cannot be obtained.

CAUTION

The canopies should not be opened while the canopy seals are inflated; damage to the seals and canopy mechanism will result.

Canopy Jettison Handles.

A canopy jettison handle (16, figure 1-7), located on the left side of each crew station is used to jettison the canopy when escape capsule ejection is not anticipated. Pulling the handle fires the external ballistic charge in the canopy actuator and jettisons the canopy.

Canopy External Jettison Handles.

Three canopy external jettison handles provide a means of jettisoning the canopies from the ground during an emergency. A handle is located below each canopy on the left side of the airplane, in a small compartment which is equipped with an access door. Each handle is attached to a long cable so that the user may stand clear of the airplane to jettison the canopies. The cable unwinds from its stowage when the handle is pulled; when the cable is extended a further pull will fire a ballistic initiator, supplying gas pressure which fires the ballistic charge in the canopy actuator to jettison the canopy.

Section I
Description

T.O. 1B-58A-1

Navigator's Canopy Release Handles.

Two release handles at the navigator's station provide a means of opening the canopy from inside or outside the compartment when pneumatic power is not available. The inside handle is located on the right side of the canopy. Pushing up on the handle unlatches the canopy so that it can be opened and latched open by a canopy actuator brace furnished by the ground crew. The exterior handle is located on the left side of the canopy. It is mounted in a vertical position flush with the canopy skin. The top of the handle pivots out so that it can be grasped and pulled down to unlatch the canopy.

Note

The second station canopy release handles are provided for emergency exit only. The position of these handles should not be used for determining whether or not the canopy is latched.

Canopy Jettison Handle Safety Pins.

A canopy jettison handle safety pin is located in the canopy jettison handle at each crew station to prevent accidental firing of the initiator.

WARNING

The crew member must remove and stow the safety pin prior to flight.

Canopy Actuator Warning Pin.

A warning pin is incorporated in the back portion of the canopy actuator (3, figure 1-44) to show whether the ballistic charge in the actuator has been fired. The pin is a red plunger-type which is normally recessed in the actuator so that it is not visible. When the ballistic charge has been fired, the red plunger will protrude and can be seen by a mirror-type reflector installed on the canopy actuator.

Canopy Layback Lockpins And Stop Pins.

Canopy layback lockpins and stop pins are provided to aid maintenance personnel in removal of the escape capsule. Canopy lockpins and stop pins are installed in the pilot's hinge assembly (figure 2-1), to insure canopy stability and proper jettison in case of ejection. The pilot's canopy lockpins are located in the cutout at the top of the bulkhead. The pilot's canopy stop pins can be seen or felt through the hole in the bulkhead at the aft edge of the canopy. Only lockpins are installed in the navigator's and DSO's canopies and are located on the canopy hinge arm just forward of the canopy frame.

WARNING

These pins must be installed and checked prior to each flight, to insure proper jettison of the canopies in case of ejection.

Pneumatic System Pressure Gage.

A pressure gage for the canopy pneumatic system is installed in the forward left corner of the right wheel well. It indicates pneumatic system supply pressure in pounds per square inch.

Canopy Unlock Caution Lamp.

A canopy unlock caution lamp (figure 1-13) is located on the warning and caution lamp panels in the pilot's station. When lighted, CANOPY UNLOCK appears in yellow letters on the face of the lamp. The caution lamp is actuated by limit switches attached to the canopy mechanism in the canopy. The lamp will light when any one of the canopies unlatches and will remain lighted until the latching mechanism of all canopies is in the overcenter locked position.

The pilot can be assured that his canopy is down and locked by having an unlighted caution lamp and by observing the canopy hook and roller engagement through the canopy hook inspection window. Due to the difference in canopy design, however, an unlighted caution lamp does not constitute a positive indication that the other two canopies are down and locked; the unlighted lamp assures only that the canopies are down and that the latching mechanism of these two canopies are in the overcenter locked position. The latching mechanism indicators for these two canopies must be checked individually to assure that the canopy latching bars are locked in place. The caution lamp is tied into the master caution lamp circuit and receives 28-volt direct current from the d-c power panel. For testing and dimming the canopy caution lamp and for information on the master caution lamp, refer to "Malfunction Indicator and Warning System" of this section.

Canopy Hook Inspection Window.

The pilot's station is equipped with three inspection windows to enable the pilot to see the canopy hook and roller engagement. These windows are installed in the thermal cover just above the windshield. These windows, as well as the caution lamp, give the pilot a positive indication that his canopy is locked.

Canopy Latching Mechanism Indicators.

Red indicator flags incorporated in the forward portion of the right and left latching bar at the navigator's and DSO's stations indicate latching hook position. These flags are mechanically actuated by the latching hooks of their respective canopy and disappear behind shields as the canopy closes.

> **CAUTION**
>
> The flags must be hidden from view before the canopies can be assumed to be locked even when the canopy unlock caution lamp is out.

ESCAPE CAPSULE.

The rocket-type escape capsule (figure 1-44) at each crew station permits safe ejection from the airplane at high speeds and high altitudes and normal descent in event of loss of cabin pressure. The capsule is equipped with three air tight clam shell doors, a window, independent pressurization and oxygen supply systems, seat and back cushions, headrest, restraint equipment, shoulder harness, inertia reel, parachute, stabilization equipment, thermal batteries, chaff dispenser, survival equipment, shock absorbers, flotation equipment, and the necessary controls. All three capsules are basically the same, except the pilot's capsule is equipped with a control stick and the other controls necessary to fly the airplane while capsulated. For a description of the crew ejection indication and bailout warning lamps provided in the pilot's and crew member's capsules, refer to "Emergency Equipment," this section. Normally, the capsule doors remain open throughout the mission to allow the crew member unrestricted movement. The window is located in the center door to provide limited monitoring of the instrument panels. The headrest and back cushion are removable to allow access to capsule oxygen system and survival equipment. Stabilization equipment is incorporated to stabilize the capsule in pitch and yaw during ejection and free fall.

WARNING

- Do not add cushioning material in the seat. To do so could result in spinal injury during ejection. When the added cushion is compressed, it allows the capsule to gain momentum before exerting force on the crew member.

Section I
Description

- A safe stabilized ejection is not assured when capsule weight and balance is upset by the removal of capsule components or survival equipment.

The various functions of the capsule are controlled by compressed air from the right main landing gear drag strut during capsulation and by numerous initiators during and after ejection. See figure 1-45. For the capsule ejection sequence, see figure 1-46. Pulling either handgrip (19, figure 1-44) to the full up position retracts the crew member back in the seat and positions his legs in the capsule before the capsule doors close. Foot guides are provided in the navigator's and DSO's station to guide the feet into the capsule when the leg retracting arms pull the legs into the capsule during capsulation.

WARNING

If only one handgrip is used to capsulate, the crew member must be sure that the other hand is inside the capsule.

A crew capsulated indicator lamp on the pilot's instrument panel will light when both the navigator's and DSO's capsule doors are closed. Refer to "Emergency Equipment," this section. With the doors closed the crew member may continue with the ejection procedure or elect to remain capsulated for descent to a safe altitude. During descent, the inertia reel may be unlocked if desired. When the doors close, the aileron ratio changer is switched to full aileron available, the throttle retard button located on the control stick grip is armed, and the capsule is pressurized with compressed air from the right landing gear drag strut. At altitudes above 37,500 feet, a pressure regulator located behind the seat maintains 37,500 feet ($\pm 2,500$ feet) pressure altitude in the capsule. When the pressure in the drag strut drops to approximately 270 psi, the source of pressure will automatically switch to the emergency air supply within the capsule. An emergency air supply lamp (7, figure 1-5) on the pilot's main instrument panel will light as soon as the system reverts to the emergency air supply. Refer to "Emergency Equipment," this section. When capsulated, the pilot can fly the airplane with the control stick. He can also retard the throttles to approximately 90 percent and shift the center of gravity with switches provided on the control stick grip.

Note

Stick movement may be somewhat restricted by the pilot's legs while capsulated, however, sufficient control movement is available to control the airplane.

When the capsule doors close the "Mayday" functions of the communication system are activated. Refer to "Communication System," Section IV. Should the emergency be corrected or after descent to a safe altitude, the crew member can open the doors. The capsule has the capability of repeated closing and opening cycles. Capsule ejection is accomplished by raising the handgrips; then, squeezing either ejection trigger. This fires three initiators which provide pressure to jettison the canopy, energize the thermal batteries, extend the catapult to start the capsule up the ejection rails and activate the rocket catapult motors. As the capsule moves upward, the control stick is separated from the airplane and quick-disconnects on the back of the capsule disconnect the capsule from the airplane's electrical, pressurization, oxygen, and canopy actuation systems. The upward movement of the capsule actuates (1) the thermal battery rail switch to provide voltage from the thermal batteries to fire ignition elements which rotate the stabilization frame, (2) the ejection signal switch that, on the pilot's capsule, lights crew capsule bailout lamps and activates the communication system to provide a continuous tone transmission for ground station tracking of the pilotless aircraft and, on the navigator's and DSO's capsules, lights a crew ejection indicator lamp in the pilot capsule and also provides the tone transmission for ground tracking, and (3) the trip mechanism to fire an initiator to forcibly eject the stabilization chute. As the stabilization frame extends, the oxygen supply is switched from the airplanes to the capsule, the capsule chaff

T.O. 1B-58A-1

Section I
Description

escape capsule (typical)

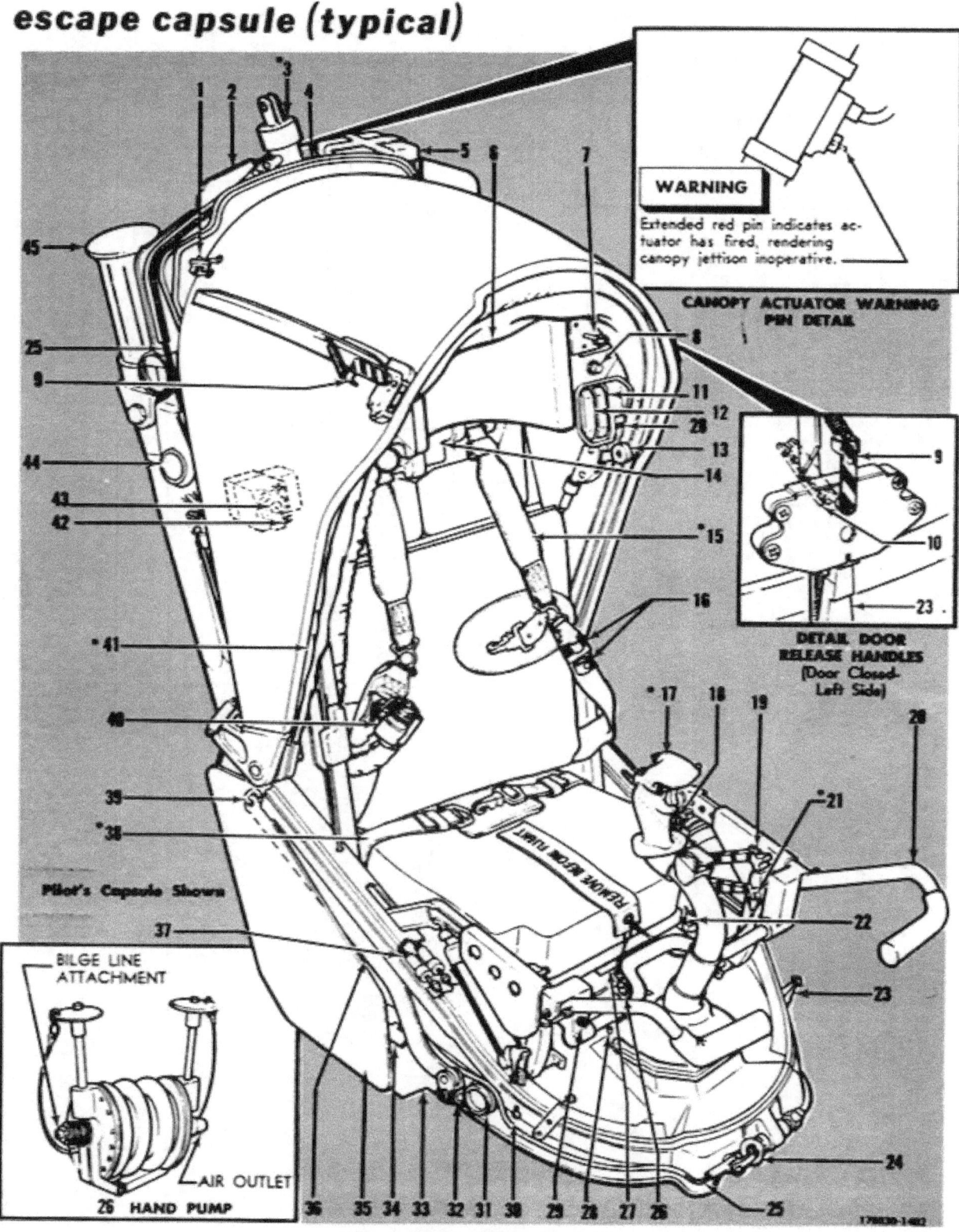

Figure 1-44. (Sheet 1 of 2)

Section I
Description

T.O. 1B-58A-1

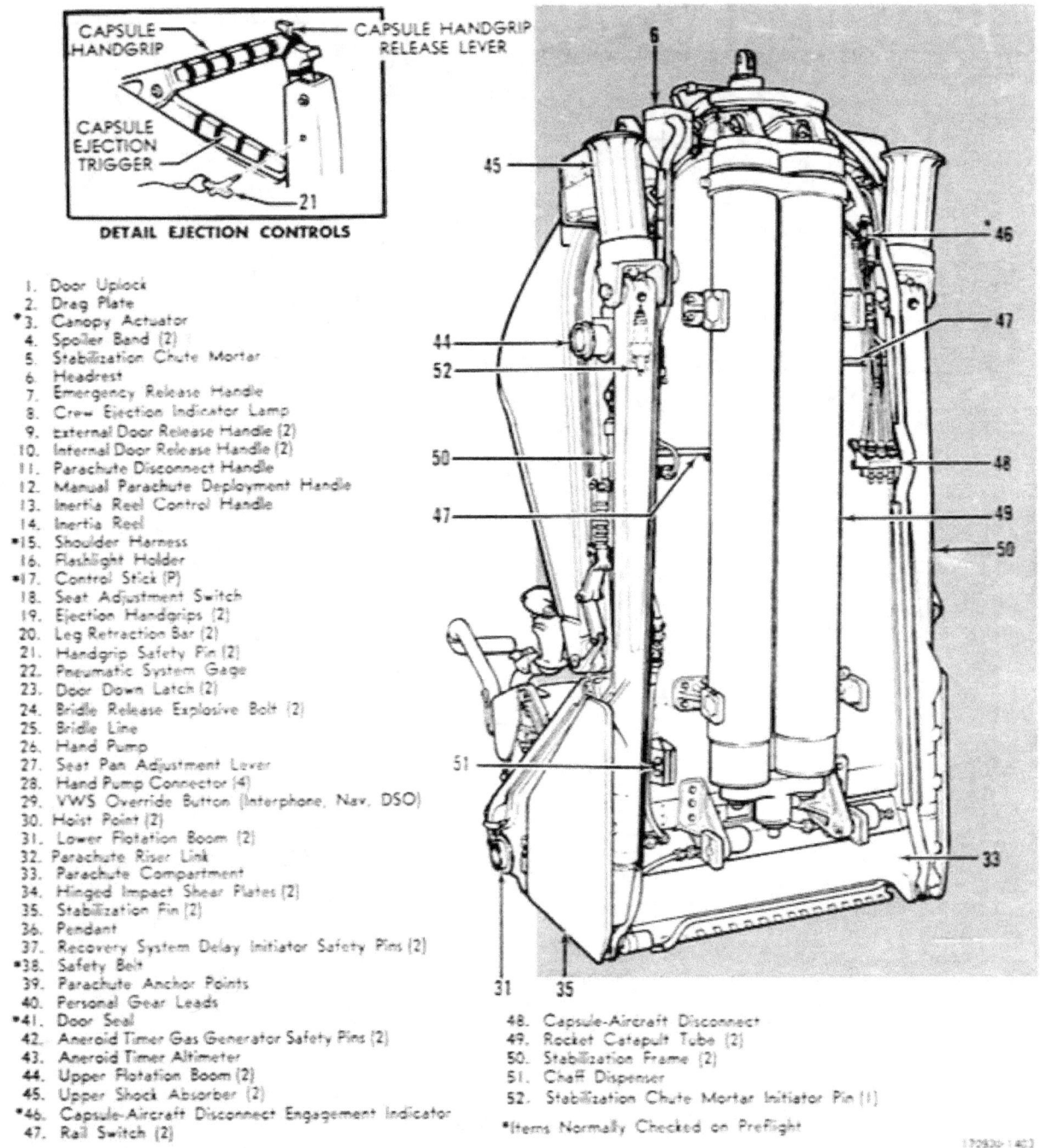

DETAIL EJECTION CONTROLS

1. Door Uplock
2. Drag Plate
*3. Canopy Actuator
4. Spoiler Band (2)
5. Stabilization Chute Mortar
6. Headrest
7. Emergency Release Handle
8. Crew Ejection Indicator Lamp
9. External Door Release Handle (2)
10. Internal Door Release Handle (2)
11. Parachute Disconnect Handle
12. Manual Parachute Deployment Handle
13. Inertia Reel Control Handle
14. Inertia Reel
*15. Shoulder Harness
16. Flashlight Holder
*17. Control Stick (P)
18. Seat Adjustment Switch
19. Ejection Handgrips (2)
20. Leg Retraction Bar (2)
21. Handgrip Safety Pin (2)
22. Pneumatic System Gage
23. Door Down Latch (2)
24. Bridle Release Explosive Bolt (2)
25. Bridle Line
26. Hand Pump
27. Seat Pan Adjustment Lever
28. Hand Pump Connector (4)
29. VWS Override Button (Interphone, Nav, DSO)
30. Hoist Point (2)
31. Lower Flotation Boom (2)
32. Parachute Riser Link
33. Parachute Compartment
34. Hinged Impact Shear Plates (2)
35. Stabilization Fin (2)
36. Pendant
37. Recovery System Delay Initiator Safety Pins (2)
*38. Safety Belt
39. Parachute Anchor Points
40. Personal Gear Leads
*41. Door Seal
42. Aneroid Timer Gas Generator Safety Pins (2)
43. Aneroid Timer Altimeter
44. Upper Flotation Boom (2)
45. Upper Shock Absorber (2)
*46. Capsule-Aircraft Disconnect Engagement Indicator
47. Rail Switch (2)
48. Capsule-Aircraft Disconnect
49. Rocket Catapult Tube (2)
50. Stabilization Frame (2)
51. Chaff Dispenser
52. Stabilization Chute Mortar Initiator Pin (1)

*Items Normally Checked on Preflight

Figure 1-44. (Sheet 2 of 2)

1-104

capsule system schematic

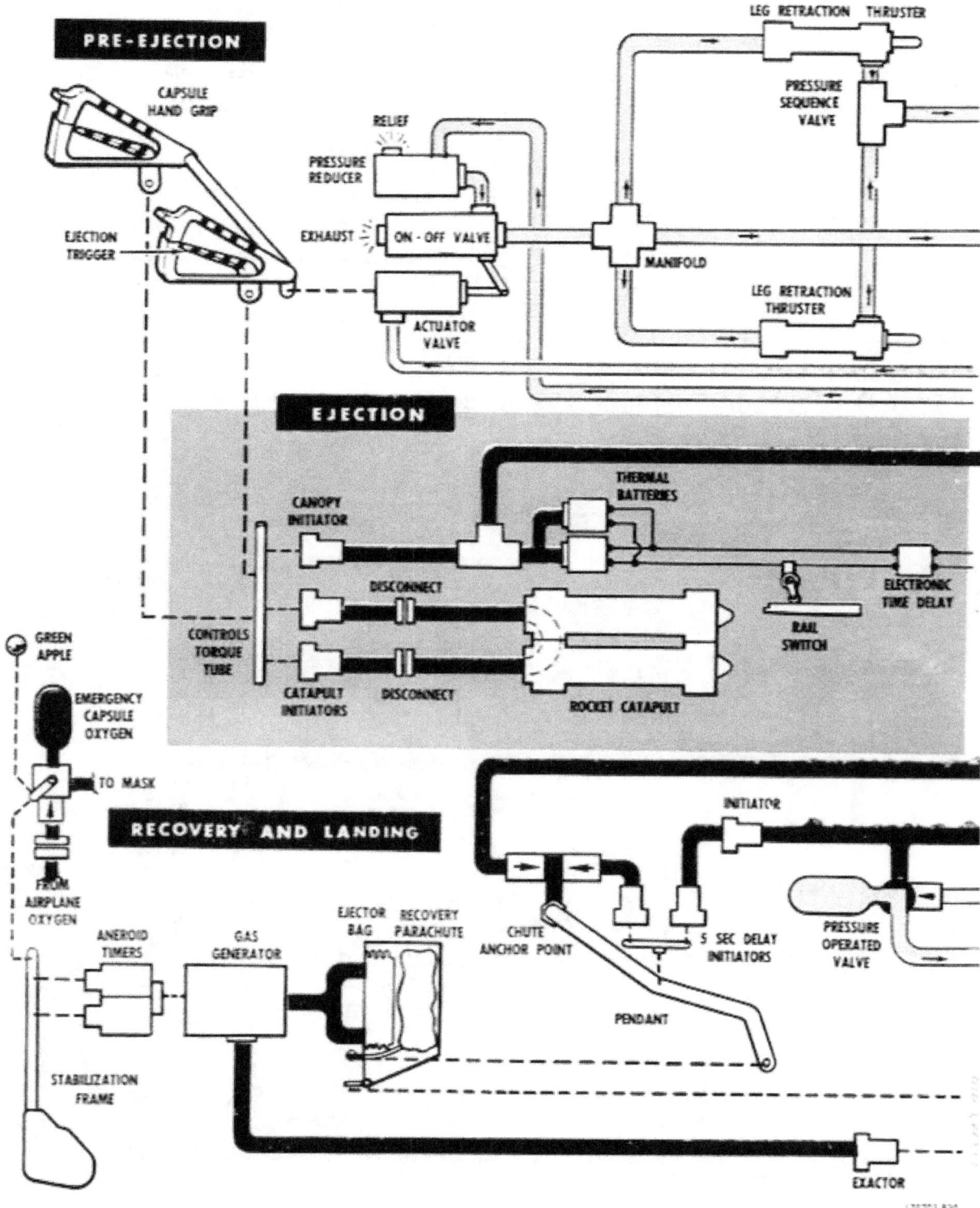

Figure 1-45. (Sheet 1 of 2)

Section I
Description

T.O. 1B-58A-1

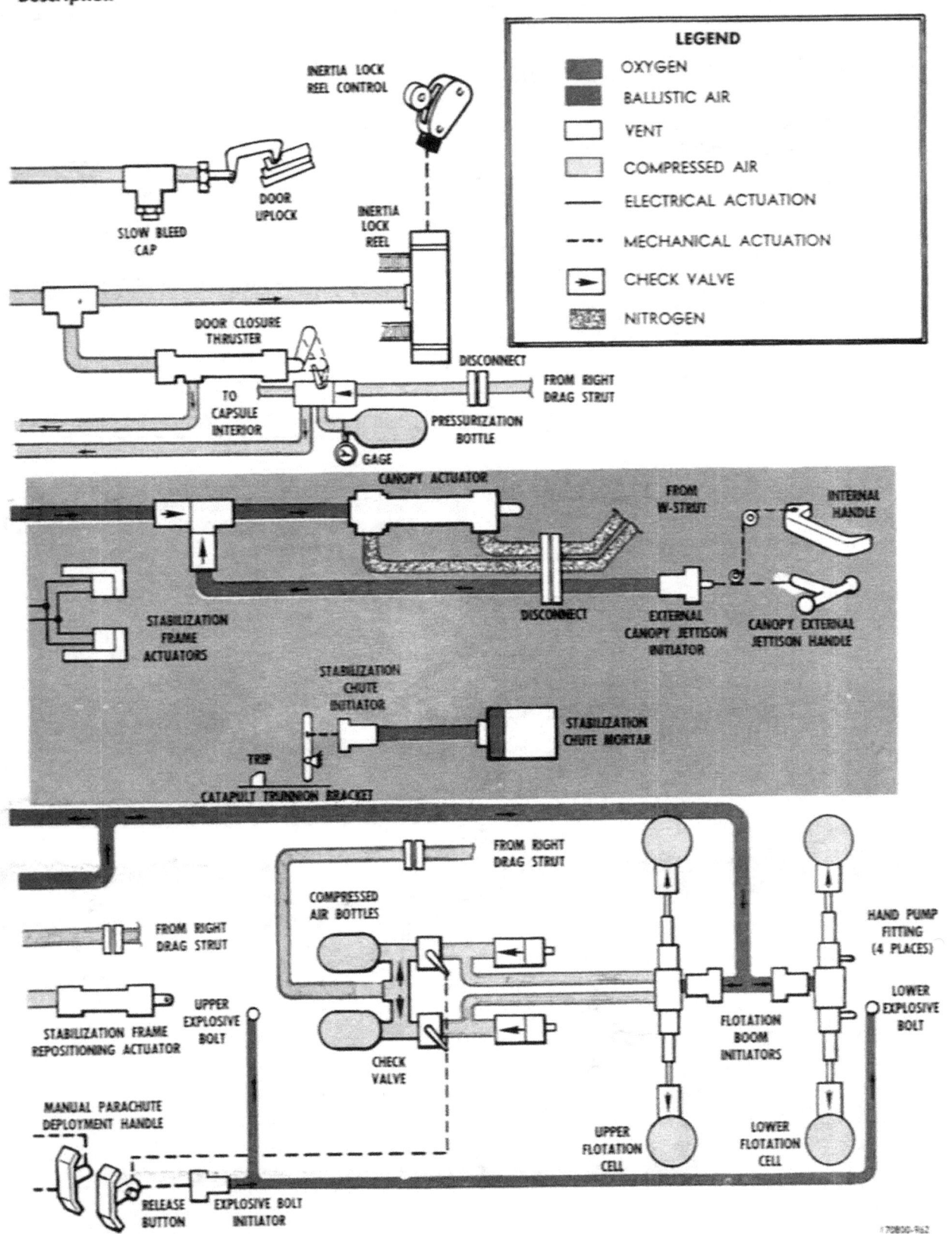

Figure 1-45. (Sheet 2 of 2)

1-106

dispenser opens and an aneroid timer unit controlling the recovery sequence is armed. The slip stream dispenses chaff (if installed) during capsule descent for radar tracking. If ejection is performed at altitudes above 15,000 feet, the capsule will free fall to 15,000 feet pressure altitude before the aneroid timer unit activates the recovery sequence. When the capsule is ejected below 15,000 feet pressure altitude, there is a delay of approximately two seconds before the recovery system is completely deployed. See figure 1-46. Aneroid timer-gas generators supply pressure to automatically deploy the parachute and unlock the manual parachute deployment handle. If the aneroid system fails, the manual deployment handle will not unlock automatically. In this event the deployment handle can be unlocked manually by pulling the emergency release handle (7, figure 1-44).

WARNING

The manual parachute deployment handle will spring out of the recessed position when it is unlocked. If this action is not immediately accompanied by parachute opening shock, the crew member should pull the handle as soon as possible.

The parachute is deployed in a reefed condition to twenty-eight feet to reduce opening shock. Approximately 2 seconds later, the chute opens to its full diameter of forty-one feet. With chute deployment, two delay initiators are mechanically armed. The initiators fire five seconds later to accomplish the following: (1) release the parachute anchor point, allowing the capsule to rotate one quarter turn for landing, (2) open a high pressure air bottle valve to reposition the stabilization frame for landing, and (3) extend the upper and lower flotation booms. If the capsule lands on land, shock absorbers will cushion the landing impact. After landing, the parachute disconnect handle (11, figure 1-44) must be pulled to release the bridle lines and inflate the upper flotation cells. The crew member may then open the doors and evacuate the capsule if on land. If the capsule lands in the water, the flotation cells will provide stabilization. The cells are not necessary to remain afloat unless the capsule is leaking badly.

Note

The crew member must manually inflate the lower flotation cells. A small bellows type hand pump is provided for this purpose.

If the sea state permits, the upper door can be opened for ventilation or to evacuate the capsule by cutting the curtain seal above the window in the designated

capsule ejection sequence

PRE-EJECTION SEQUENCE

WARNING
Make sure that both arms and hands are inside the capsule prior to raising the handgrips.

1. **When either handgrip is raised.**
   a. Torso and legs are positioned.
   b. Capsule doors are closed.
   c. Interphone is switched to hot mike, AN/ARC-57 guard.
   d. Capsule is pressurized from right drag strut.
   e. Aileron available is switched to FULL.
   f. Throttle retard button is armed.

EJECTION SEQUENCE

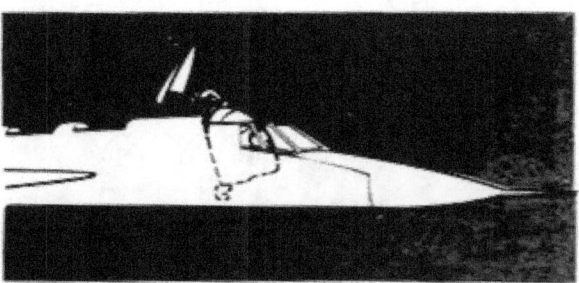

1. **When either ejection trigger is squeezed.**
   a. Canopy is removed.
   b. Catapult is extended.
   c. Control stick and disconnects are separated.
   d. Pressurization is transferred to capsule.
   e. Stabilization chute initiator and frame thrusters are fired by a trip mechanism and a rail switch.
   f. Rocket motors are fired.

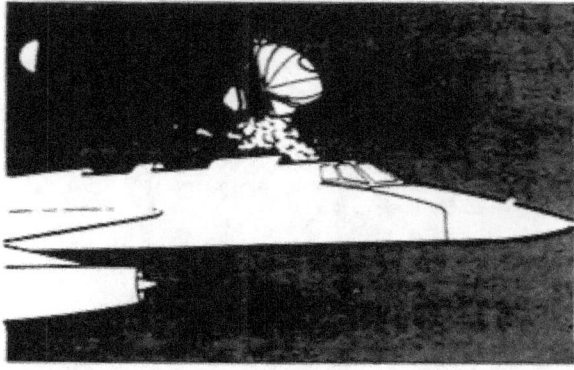

2. **Stabilizer frame is extended.**
   a. Chaff container is opened.
   b. Recovery chute aneroid timers are armed.
   c. Oxygen source is transferred to capsule.
   d. Capsule is stabilized in yaw and pitch.

Figure 1-46. (Sheet 1 of 2)

Section I
Description

T.O. 1B-58A-1

RECOVERY SEQUENCE

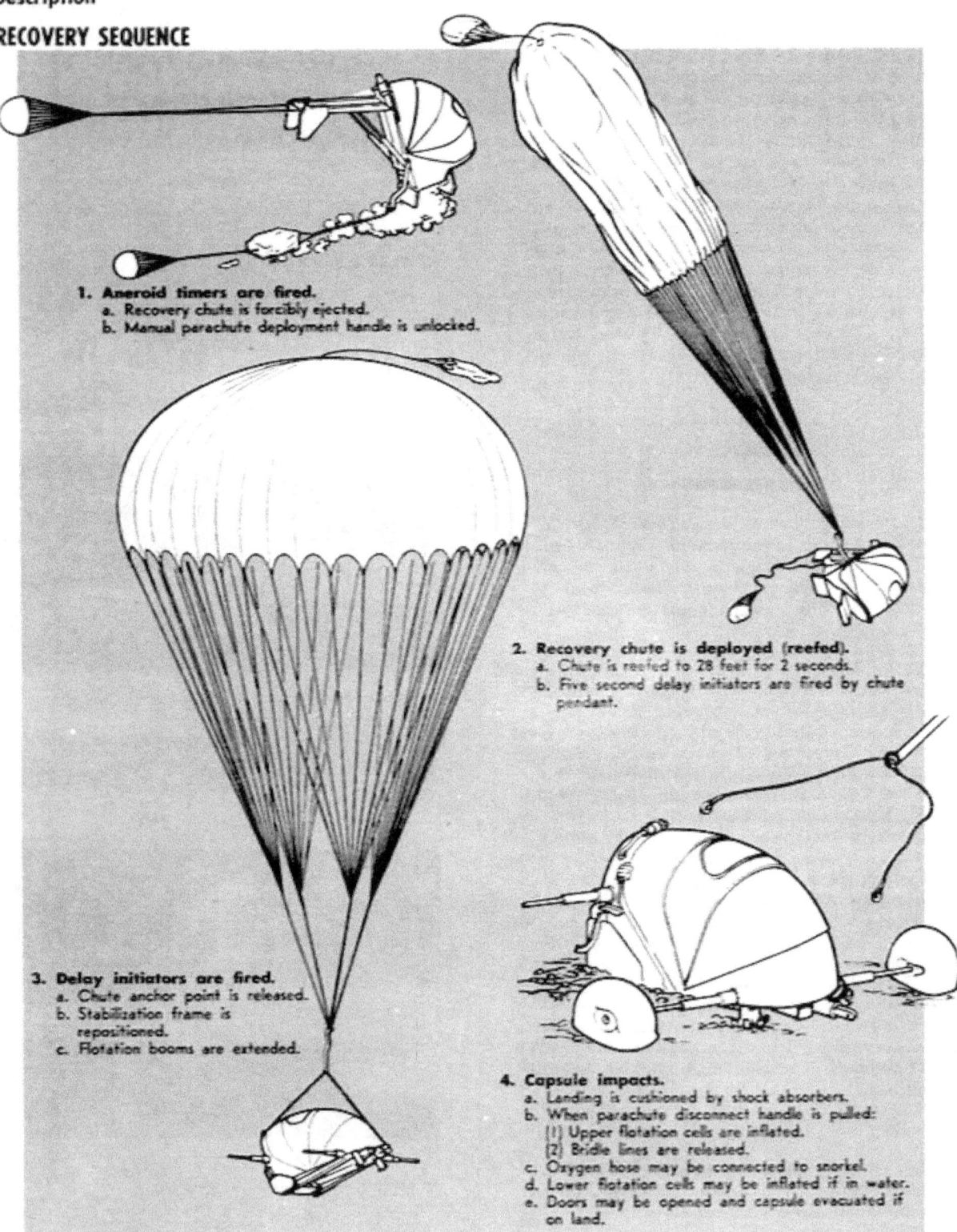

1. **Aneroid timers are fired.**
    a. Recovery chute is forcibly ejected.
    b. Manual parachute deployment handle is unlocked.

2. **Recovery chute is deployed (reefed).**
    a. Chute is reefed to 28 feet for 2 seconds.
    b. Five second delay initiators are fired by chute pendant.

3. **Delay initiators are fired.**
    a. Chute anchor point is released.
    b. Stabilization frame is repositioned.
    c. Flotation booms are extended.

4. **Capsule impacts.**
    a. Landing is cushioned by shock absorbers.
    b. When parachute disconnect handle is pulled:
        (1) Upper flotation cells are inflated.
        (2) Bridle lines are released.
    c. Oxygen hose may be connected to snorkel.
    d. Lower flotation cells may be inflated if in water.
    e. Doors may be opened and capsule evacuated if on land.

Figure 1-46. (Sheet 2 of 2)

area and actuating the upper door release latches provided on either side of the door. A snorkel receptacle located on the right side of the headrest provides outside air for breathing if rough water makes opening of the capsule undesirable. The oxygen hose should be attached to the snorkel to facilitate breathing and alleviate the hazard of carbon dioxide build up in the capsule. A small rubber plug located in the center of the forward edge of the upper door can be removed to provide a hole in the capsule door to extend the survival radio antenna. The plug will be exposed when the curtain seal is out.

Shoulder Harness.

The shoulder harness (15, figure 1-44) is attached to both sides of the seat adjacent to the crew members waist and to the inertia reel behind the seat. The harness is fastened over the crew members chest by a quick release fastener. The harness and fastener are padded for comfort. A wedge shaped manifold block on the lower right strap is provided for attaching the oxygen mask hose to the harness. The pilot's lower left strap has provisions for stowing a small flashlight. When either handgrip is raised, pneumatic pressure actuates the inertia reel (14, figure 1-44) which retracts the crew member back in the seat. When fully retracted, the reel locks, holding the crew member secure during ejection and parachute deployment. The inertia reel also locks automatically under a force of 3 "g's." If the reel is locked automatically by "g" force while the crew member is leaning forward, the harness will retract with him as he straightens up, moving into successive locked positions as he moves back into the seat. An inertia reel control handle (13, figure 1-44), located inside the capsule, provides manual control of the inertia reel lock.

CONTROLS AND INDICATORS.

Capsule Handgrips.

The capsule handgrips (19, figure 1-44) are recessed on either side of the seat when in the stowed position to prevent inadvertent actuation. The handgrips are attached to the seat, which permits them to move up or down with seat adjustment. When either handgrip is raised, both handgrips will come to the full up position, pneumatic pressure actuates the rotating seat pan, leg retraction bars, and shoulder harness inertia reel to position the crew member prior to the door closing. The seat pan rotates upward to position the crew members thighs as the leg retraction bars contact the legs just above the ankle and position them under the seat clear of the doors. Simultaneous with leg retraction, the inertia reel pulls the crew member back in the seat; then, the doors are allowed to close.

WARNING

The crew member should not carry anything in the arm, leg or breast pockets of his flying suit which could interfere with the operation of the restraint system and door closing or cause possible injury to the crew member.

The ejection triggers are exposed when the handgrips are raised. The handgrips are spring-loaded and will return to the stowed position when handgrips are pulled up and the handgrip release levers located on the forward end of the handgrips are pushed forward. Returning the handgrips to the full down position repositions the pneumatic system actuator valve piston for another door closing cycle.

WARNING

The capsule doors will not close in the event it becomes necessary to capsulate again unless the handgrips are in the full down position.

Safety pins, with a red streamer attached, are installed in the handgrips while on the ground.

Capsule Ejection Triggers.

A capsule ejection trigger (figure 1-44) is located in each handgrip and is accessible only after the handgrip is raised to the full up position. Squeezing either trigger mechanically fires three initiators. One initiator removes the canopy and energizes two thermal batteries while the other two initiators provide pressure to extend the rocket catapult and activate the rocket catapult motors.

Inertia Reel Control Handle.

An inertia reel control handle (13, figure 1-44) is located on the left side of the capsule above the crew member's shoulder. The handle positions are marked AUTOMATIC LOCK and MANUAL LOCK. The handle is manually locked by moving the handle to the MANUAL LOCK position. When the handle has been manually locked, unlocking is accomplished by moving the handle up to the AUTOMATIC LOCK position. If the reel has been locked automatically by "g" force, the handle must be moved down to the MANUAL LOCK position and then up to AUTOMATIC LOCK position to unlock the reel. If the inertia reel is locked manually or by "g" force when the crew member is leaning forward in the seat, the reel will retract as he straightens up and lock in any new position he assumes.

Note

The manual control handle must be cycled from MANUAL LOCK to AUTOMATIC LOCK several times to fully relieve the tension (50 pounds maximum) on the straps after a power retraction.

Seat Adjustment Switch.

A three-position seat adjustment switch (18, figure 1-44) located on the left side of the seat on the capsule sill, provides vertical adjustment of the seat. The switch is marked UP and DOWN, and is spring-loaded to an unmarked center off position. Holding the switch in either the UP or DOWN position energizes a 115-volt a-c motor that moves the seat on rails within the capsule enclosure. The leg retraction bars and headrest are attached to the capsule structure and do not move with the seat. The range of adjustment is approximately four and one-half inches.

CAUTION

The escape capsule seat adjustment motor must be allowed to cool for nine minutes after each minute of operation. One complete up and down adjustment cycle takes approximately 40 seconds. Excessive continuous operation will damage the motor.

Seat Pan Adjustment Lever.

The seat pan adjustment lever (27, figure 1-44) is used to raise or lower the forward edge of the seat pan. To operate the lever, place either hand palm down on the front of the seat cushion with the fingers underneath the lever, squeeze and adjust the seat pan vertically, then release the lever. During door closure, the seat pan will be automatically raised to the highest position.

Door Down Lock Release Handles.

Two sets of spring-loaded door down lock release handles (9 and 10, figure 1-44) are located on the left and right sides of the lower door. Each set of handles consists of an internal and external handle splined together by a shaft through the door so that the door down lock can be released from either the inside by the capsule occupant or from the outside should the occupant be incapacitated. To unlock the doors, pull both internal or external handles aft. The handles can be actuated one at a time. When unlocked, the doors can be manually raised to the full-up position.

The pilot's capsule lower door has a single motion emergency release cable which actuates both handles simultaneously and enables the pilot to unlock the capsule doors internally with one hand.

Upper Door Release Latches.

Two upper door release latches, located between the upper and center doors, hold the doors together when they are closed and provide a means for opening the upper door should the capsule land in the water. To actuate the latches, the capsule occupant must cut the curtain seal across the inside of the capsule along the designated marking to expose the inside of the upper door, press against the inside of the upper door with the palms of the hands to move the door forward and loosen the latches, then push outward with the thumbs on the spring clips provided to disengage the latches from the center door. The spring clips will hold the latches open so that the upper door can then be raised.

Manual Parachute Deployment Handle.

A manual parachute deployment handle (12, figure 1-44) is located to the left of the headrest. The handle is provided to manually deploy the parachute in the event the automatic deployment mechanism fails. The handle is locked in a recessed position in order to prevent inadvertent actuation. A ballistic exactor, which is fired by the same gas pressure from the aneroid timer-gas generator that ejects the parachute, unlocks the handle. When unlocked, the handle will spring out of its recessed position.

WARNING

If handle extension is not immediately accompanied by parachute opening shock, the crew member will know that the parachute has not deployed and that he should pull the manual parachute deployment handle.

Emergency Release Handle.

An emergency release handle (7, figure 1-44) located above the manual parachute deployment handle is provided to manually unlock the parachute deployment handle if the aneroid system fails. After pulling the emergency release handle, the manual parachute deployment handle must be pulled to deploy the recovery chute.

WARNING

Do not pull manual parachute deployment handle above 15,000 feet. To do so would result in premature deployment of the chute and could cause structural failure of the recovery system.

Parachute Disconnect Handle.

A parachute disconnect handle (11, figure 1-44) is located in a recess to the left of the headrest. A release button, located beneath the handle, must be depressed to unlock the handle before the handle can be pulled. When the handle is unlocked it will spring out of its recessed position and hang freely by the cable to which it is attached.

WARNING

Do not depress the button or pull the handle until after impact. To do so could result in the capsule being separated from the parachute during decent.

Pulling the handle actuates two separate cables. One cable opens a valve allowing high pressure air to inflate the upper flotation cells. The other cable mechanically fires an initiator which supplies pressure to fire two explosive bolts. The explosive bolts release the parachute bridle lines from the capsule.

Capsule Air Shut-Off Valve Handle.

A capsule air shut-off valve handle is provided in the nose wheel well to control air pressure from the right drag strut to the capsule pressurization system. The handle should be safetied in the open position when all three capsules are installed in the airplane.

Capsule Pneumatic Pressure Gage.

The capsule pneumatic pressure gage (22, figure 1-44), located on the left side of the capsule between the seat and the left arm rest, indicates the pressure contained in the capsule pressurization bottle. The pneumatic air is used to close the capsule doors and pressure the inside of the capsule during capsulation. The green portion of the dial on the gage indicates safe operating pressures; the red portion indicates pressures below safe limits.

Capsule-Airplane Disconnect Engagement Indicator.

The capsule is equipped with a capsule-airplane disconnect engagement indicator (46, figure 1-44), located behind the uplock on the right side of the capsule. The engagement indicator is a round opaque tube equipped with a window that indicates correct and positive connection or faulty connection of the capsule-airplane disconnects.

WARNING

The indicator window must show all white for a positive connection. Any indication of red in the window signifies a faulty or incomplete connection.

Ground Safety Pins.

Ground safety pins (21, figure 1-44) with a red identification streamer attached are installed in each handgrip to prevent inadvertent closure of the capsule. Both ground safety pins must be removed before flight.

WARNING

The absence of a red streamer does not necessarily mean the safety pin has been removed.

Hand Pump

In the event the capsule lands in the water, a small bellows type hand pump is provided to inflate the lower flotation cells or act as a bilge pump should the capsule leak. In the pilot's capsule, the pump (26, figure 1-44) is stowed on the capsule floor behind the control stick boot. In the crew capsule, the hand pump is stowed behind the headrest and the headrest must be removed to gain access to the pump. A length of plastic hose is provided in the hand pump stowage container in the pilot's capsule and beside the hand pump in the crew capsules. To inflate the lower flotation cells, remove the protective caps from the hand pump connectors (28, figure 1-44), attach the hose to the connector and to the exhaust outlet of the pump, then actuate the pump by squeezing the handles together. Approximately 600 actuations are necessary to fully inflate each cell. This will require 5 to 15 minutes pumping operation. Repeat the operation on the opposite flotation cell.

Replace the protective caps on the hand pump connector to prevent dirt entering the system. Hand pump connectors for the upper flotation cells, located each

Section I
Description

T.O. 1B-58A-1

servicing diagram (typical)

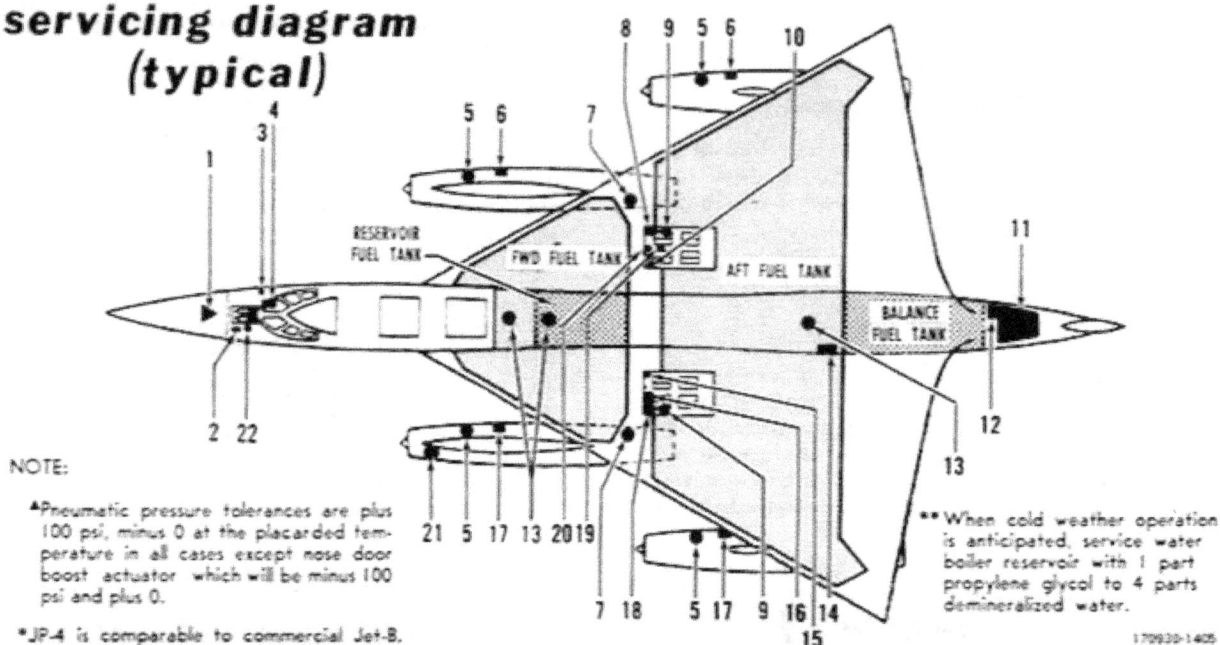

NOTE:

▲ Pneumatic pressure tolerances are plus 100 psi, minus 0 at the placarded temperature in all cases except nose door boost actuator which will be minus 100 psi and plus 0.

* JP-4 is comparable to commercial Jet-B.

** When cold weather operation is anticipated, service water boiler reservoir with 1 part propylene glycol to 4 parts demineralized water.

SERVICING POINTS	UNITS TO BE SERVICED	SERVICING AGENT OR UNIT	SPECIFICATION	NATO SYMBOL	SERVICING LOCATION
1	AIR REFUELING RECEPTACLE	* FUEL JP-4	MIL-J-5624	F-40	UPPER PORTION OF RADOME
2	LIQUID OXYGEN CONTAINERS	LIQUID OXYGEN	MIL-O-27210		LEFT OF NOSE WHEEL DOORS
3	IFR ACCUMULATOR	▲ DRY NITROGEN	MIL-N-6011, GRADE A, TYPE I OR II		NOSE WHEEL WELL
4	FUEL TANKS (SINGLE-POINT GROUND REFUELING)	* FUEL JP-4	MIL-J-5624	F-40	NOSE WHEEL WELL
5	ENGINE OIL TANKS (4)	SYNTHETIC OIL	MIL-L-7808	O-148	RIGHT SIDE NACELLE (EA ENG)
6	PRIMARY HYDRAULIC SYSTEM AND RESERVOIR	HYDRAULIC FLUID	MIL-H-8446		RIGHT SIDE NACELLE NO. 3 OR NO. 4 ENGINE
7	AIR CONDITIONING TURBINE SUMP (2)	SYNTHETIC OIL	MIL-L-7808 FILTERED TO 10 MICRONS OR LESS	O-148	LOWER WING SURFACE, INBOARD OF EACH INBOARD PYLON
8	PRIMARY HYDRAULIC RESERVOIR	HYDRAULIC FLUID	MIL-H-8446		RIGHT MAIN WHEEL WELL
9	WATER BOILER RESERVOIR (2)	** DEMINERALIZED WATER	MIL-D-4024		MAIN WHEEL WELLS
10	CANOPY PNEUMATIC RESERVOIR	▲ DRY NITROGEN	MIL-N-6011, GRADE A, TYPE I OR II		RIGHT MAIN WHEEL WELL
11	DRAG CHUTE COMPARTMENT	DRAG CHUTE PACK	CONVAIR SPEC FZC-4-355		BOTTOM AFT FUSELAGE
12	DRAG CHUTE PNEUMATIC RESERVOIR	▲ DRY NITROGEN	MIL-N-6011, GRADE A, TYPE I OR II		FORWARD OF DRAG CHUTE COMPARTMENT
13	FUEL TANKS (INDIVIDUAL TANK GRAVITY REFUELING (3))	* FUEL JP-4	MIL-J-5624	F-40	TOP FUSELAGE
14	FLIGHT CONTROL ACCUMULATOR (4)	▲ DRY NITROGEN	MIL-N-6011, GRADE A, TYPE I OR II		LOWER AFT FUSELAGE, LEFT SIDE
15	CHAFF DISPENSER ACCUMULATOR	▲ DRY NITROGEN	MIL-N-6011, GRADE A, TYPE I OR II		LEFT MAIN WHEEL WELL
16	BRAKE ACCUMULATOR EMERGENCY BRAKE & GEAR PNEUMATIC RESERVOIRS	▲ DRY NITROGEN	MIL-N-6011, GRADE A, TYPE I OR II		LEFT MAIN WHEEL WELL
17	UTILITY HYDRAULIC SYSTEM AND RESERVOIR	HYDRAULIC FLUID	MIL-H-8446		RIGHT SIDE NACELLE NO. 1 OR NO. 2 ENGINE
18	UTILITY HYDRAULIC RESERVOIR	HYDRAULIC FLUID	MIL-H-8446		LEFT MAIN WHEEL WELL
19	PRIMARY HYDRAULIC SYSTEM ACCUMULATOR	▲ DRY NITROGEN	MIL-N-6011, GRADE A, TYPE I OR II		RIGHT MAIN WHEEL WELL
20	ESCAPE CAPSULE EMERGENCY PRESSURIZATION SYSTEM	MC-1A AIR COMPRESSOR	COMPRESSED DRY AIR		RIGHT MAIN WHEEL WELL
21	STARTER CARTRIDGE	MXU-4A/A CARTRIDGE	FSN 1377-863-9387		NO. 2 ENGINE NACELLE
22	NOSE DOOR BOOST ACTUATOR	▲ DRY NITROGEN	MIL-N-6011, GRADE A, TYPE I OR II		NOSE WHEEL DOORS

Figure 1-47.

side of the seat above the back cushion, are provided to replenish the air supply in the upper cells.

Note

The flotation cells may also be inflated by blowing through the plastic hose.

To use the hand pump as a bilge pump, screw the bilge line located under the right side of the capsule seat to the intake port of the pump (see figure 1-44), attach the plastic hose provided to the exhaust port of the pump and extend the hose outside the capsule, then actuate the pump until the capsule is pumped dry. If the sea state prevents opening the capsule door, the antenna access plug may be removed to provide an opening for the plastic hose.

SAFETY BELT.

Each capsule is equipped with a safety belt (38, figure 1-44) which consists of two straps attached to either side of the seat. The straps are narrow to permit positioning of the crew member's legs prior to door closure and are connected with a quick release fastener. Elastic bands are provided on the belt to retain the loose ends after proper adjustment has been made.

WARNING

The loose ends of the belt may interfere with capsule door closure if not properly stowed.

WINDSHIELD AND WINDOW GLASS PANELS.

The pilot's compartment is equipped with a double section windshield, and two small canopy windows. Each section of the windshield contains three separate glass panels which are divided by metal window framing and form a "V" around the front of the compartment. This wrap-around type windshield provides side viewing as well as forward. The navigator's and DSO's compartments are equipped with a window on each side. All of these glass panels are composed of two plies of tempered plate glass bonded together by a silicone rubber interlayer. Due to high performance capabilities of the airplane, cracks may develop in the interlayer at the outer edges of the glass; therefore the glass should be inspected before flight. Metal retainer strips are installed around the edges of the pilot's windshield glasses to prevent blowout in the event of an interply glass failure.

WARNING

Interlayer cracks, bubbles, and delaminations appearing in certain areas of the glass panels are not acceptable. Failure of these glass panels in flight could result in crew compartment decompression and/or impairment of pilot vision. Refer to "Glass Panel Damage Limitations," Section V.

AUXILIARY EQUIPMENT.

The description and operation of the following auxiliary equipment are contained in Section IV:
Air Conditioning System
Anti-Icing and Defogging Systems
Communication System
Tactical Air Navigation System
Instrument Landing System
Air-to-Ground IFF System
Position Indicating Beacon System (AN/ALQ-136)
Rendezvous Beacon System (AN/APN-135)
Lighting Equipment
Oxygen Systems
Autopilot System
Auxiliary Flight Reference System
Weapons Control System (AN/ASQ-42)
Primary Navigation System
Bombing System
Air Navigation Data Recording System (AN/ASH-17)
Bomb Damage Evaluation (BDE) System (AN/ASH-15)
Bombing Equipment
Photo Reconnaissance System
Defensive Electronic Countermeasure System
Active Defense System
Air Refueling System
Single-Point Refueling System
Miscellaneous Equipment

This is the last page of Section I.

T.O. 1B-58A-1

the B·58A airplane

THIS PAGE INTENTIONALLY LEFT BLANK

Section II
Normal Procedures

TABLE OF CONTENTS.

Preparation for Flight	2-2
Preflight Check	2-4
Before Starting Engines	2-13
Starting Engines	2-15
Engine Ground Operation	2-21
Before Taxiing	2-21
Cocking	2-28
Uncocking	2-30
Scramble/SRP Power-Off Scramble	2-31
Defcon 1/SRP Power-On Cocking Checklist	2-33
Defcon 1/SRP Power-On Scramble Checklist	2-34
Taxiing	2-35
Before Lineup	2-36
Minimum Reaction Cocking Checklist	2-37
Minimum Reaction Scramble Checklist	2-38
Takeoff	2-38
After Takeoff	2-43
Climb	2-44
Leveloff	2-44
Cruise	2-44
Flight Characteristics	2-48
Air Refueling	2-48
Before Acceleration	2-48
During Acceleration	2-49
Deceleration	2-51
Prior to Penetration	2-52
Descent and Before Landing	2-55
Transition Checklist	2-55
Landing	2-56
Go-Around	2-64
After Landing	2-65
Taxi-Back Landing	2-65
Engine Shutdown	2-67
Before Leaving Airplane	2-67
Postflight	2-68
Alert Procedures	2-68
Strange Field Procedure	2-72
Installation of Starter Cartridge	2-78
Aircraft Emergency Movement Checklist	2-79
Functional Check Flights	2-80

Section II
Normal Procedures

T.O. 1B-58A-1

The pilot's and DSO's checklists are presented in two parts, amplified and abbreviated. The pilot's amplified checklist is contained in this section and the DSO's amplified checklist is contained in this section and Section VIII. The abbreviated checklist for both the pilot and DSO is contained in T.O. 1B-58A-1CL-1. An attempt has been made to arrange the checklist items in their most logical sequence so that the preflight and ground checks may be completed in a minimum length of time. The pilot will respond to all uncoded steps read by the DSO. From BEFORE STARTING ENGINES and on, all steps which are coded require response from the applicable crew members indicated as follows: (P) Pilot, (N) Navigator, (DSO) Defense System Operator, (GO) Ground Observer. Items which pertain to a specific pod configuration will be designated by **TC** (two component pod), **MB** (MB-1 pod), or **LA** (LA-331A pod) preceding the line item. On normal training flights, perform each item in the checklist. When it is necessary to operate from an airfield where normal ground support is not available, the flight crew must perform some additional and more detailed checks. The strange field postflight and preflight procedures are outlined in this section. Items of the POWER-OFF and POWER-ON INTERIOR INSPECTIONS which must be performed in addition to the normal procedures are coded **SF**.

PREPARATION FOR FLIGHT.

FLIGHT RESTRICTIONS.

Refer to Section V for information concerning restrictions imposed on the airplane in flight.

FLIGHT PLANNING.

Prior to each mission, prepare takeoff data and a fuel plan. Determine takeoff data, required fuel, speeds, and power settings, using chart data from Appendix I. Fuel management schedules are outlined in "Fuel Supply System," Section VII. Mission planning requirements are outlined in Appendix I. The following items will be accomplished during mission planning.

---

1. Complete clearance form, Form 365F, and flight plan (Form 200 or equivalent).

2. Complete takeoff data.

3. Complete crew briefing:

    a. Review the critical items each crew member will accomplish for the following emergencies:

        (1) Fire and smoke in the pressurized compartment.

        (2) Aborted takeoff.

        (3) Bailout.

    b. Review oxygen procedures.

        All crew members must have mask in place, secured, and be on oxygen during takeoff, climbout, air refueling, supersonic flight, descent and before landing, and landing.

    c. Review the mission, procedures, and duties, as required, for substitute crew member(s) to insure the safe and successful completion of flight.

Section II
Normal Procedures

entrance to the aircraft

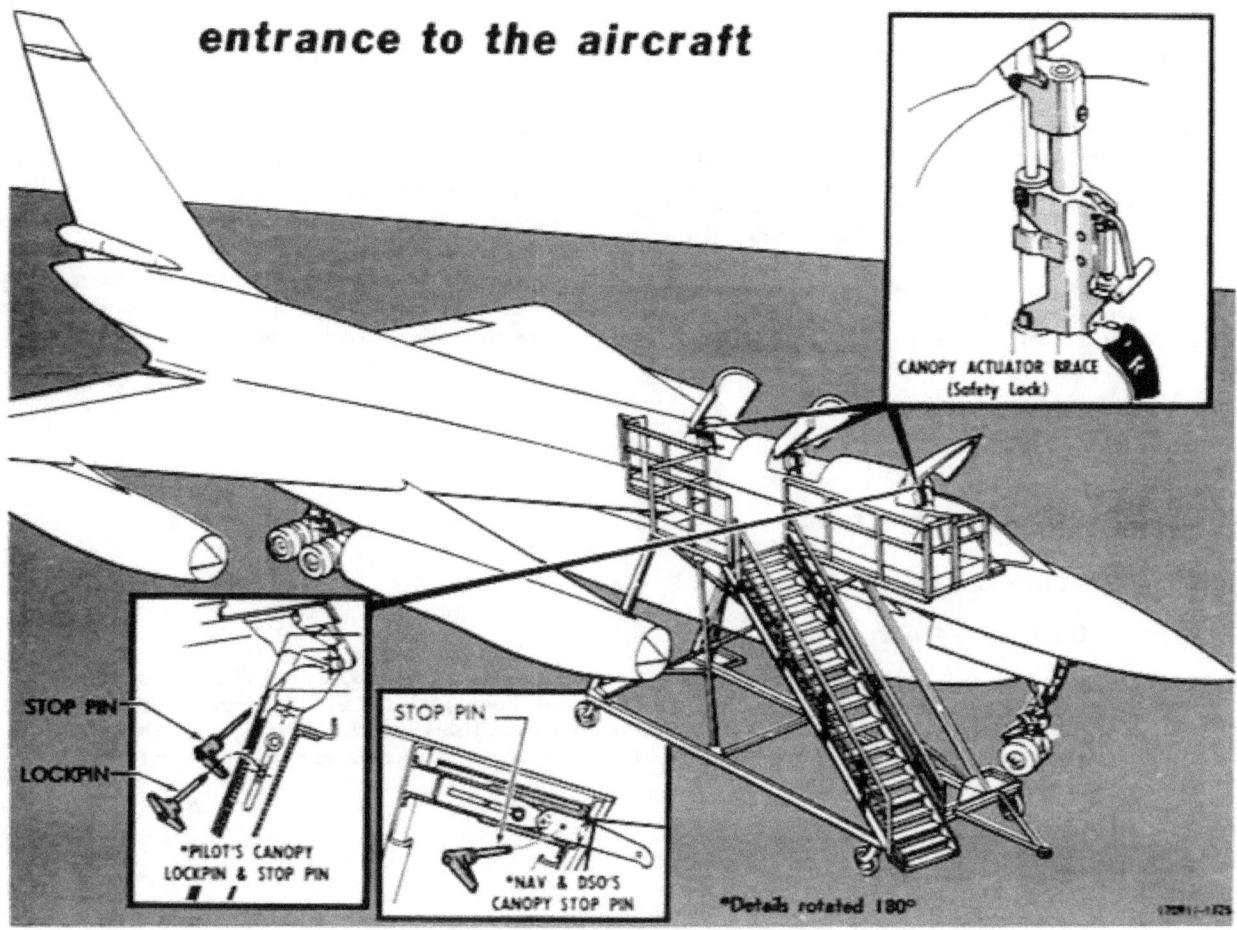

Figure 2-1.

TAKEOFF AND LANDING DATA CARDS.

Compute all takeoff and landing data from Appendix I and complete the Takeoff and Landing Data cards in the Abbreviated Checklist. T.O. 1B-58A-1CL-1. Recheck data just prior to flight to determine the effect of any changes in runway condition or airplane configuration.

WEIGHT AND BALANCE.

Refer to Section V for weight and balance limitations. For loading information, refer to Handbook of Weight and Balance Data, T.O. 1-1B-40. The use of a B-58A balance computer will aid in determining loading and cg data. Before each flight, check the following:

1. Takeoff and anticipated landing gross weights.
2. Weight and balance clearance (Form 365F).
3. Sufficient fuel, oil, oxygen, and special equipment to complete proposed mission.

ENTRANCE TO THE AIRCRAFT.

Entrance to the crew compartment is gained by use of a stand as shown in figure 2-1. The canopy control valve in the nose wheel well is used to open the canopies for initial entry. Prior to opening canopies, check that canopy seal selector is in the OFF position.

CAUTION

If the canopies are opened with the seals inflated, the seals and canopy actuators can be damaged.

To open the canopies, place the canopy control lever in the nose wheel well to the DOWN position and hold for a minimum of 5 seconds; then immediately position the control lever to the UP position. Do not open the canopies in headwinds exceeding 60 knots.

2-3

Section II
Normal Procedures

T.O. 1B-58A-1

PREFLIGHT CHECK.

The following preflight checklists are designed to conduct the preflight and start engines without ground air conditioning and are based on the assumption that maintenance personnel have completed the maintenance preflight in accordance with PRPO Inspection Workcards, 1B-58A-6WC-1PRPO. It is also assumed that the external power and engine starter carts are connected but not supplying service when the flight crew arrives to begin the preflight check. The crew chief will have the Form 781 available to the pilot and the inspection stands will be in place when the flight crew arrives at the airplane (station time). Flight crew station time will normally be an hour and fifteen minutes before scheduled takeoff time. Discrepancies noted during the preflight check will be recorded in Form 781. They will be cleared by authorized personnel prior to takeoff in accordance with 00-20 series T.O.s. The performance of the exterior and interior inspections is the responsibility of the pilot; however, he may designate other crew members to assist with the inspections as desired. If a complete set of ground support equipment is not available, the preflight check may be accomplished by starting number 2 engine using airplane battery power, and an external starter air cart or the cartridge starter; then operate the engine to provide electrical power during the preflight.

BEFORE EXTERIOR INSPECTION.

1. Security guards posted (if required).

2. Check Forms 781.

   Pilot checks Form 781 for engineering status discrepancies and aircraft loading. He also notes fuel loading and distribution for comparison with Form 365F and aircraft gages later during preflight, checks with crew chief that all other required servicing has been accomplished, and that the airplane is ready for flight. Pilot notifies crew of discrepancies that are being carried on the Form 781.

EXTERIOR INSPECTION.

Perform the walk-around exterior inspection for the airplane as shown in figure 2-2. The flight crew should keep in mind that the exterior inspection performed by them is only a flight crew inspection of readily accessible items. Should the pilot wish information on non-accessible items, he should examine the "Preflight Inspection Record". Ground personnel will be at the airplane to discuss the status of the airplane and its systems. The following inspection is based on the assumption that the flight crew is merely accepting the airplane for flight with emphasis on the items that affect safety of flight. In addition to conducting a detailed inspection of items A, B, C and D accomplish the following.

- Check for cuts, scratches, loose rivets, and fluid leaks.
- Check all drain plugs for leakage.
- Check that all vents and ports are clear.
- Check that all access doors, fuel/refuel caps and panels are secure.
- Check ground area around aircraft for cleanliness.

Note

- During bomb preflight, a second nuclear qualified individual will verify switch positions and settings after the steps have been accomplished by the individual having the response.

- During inspections of the airplane weapon combination, if any discrepancy is found that is not specifically covered in the malfunction analysis section of the Nuclear bomb pod/delivery Technical Manual (T.O. 1B-58A-25-2), all physical operations on the airplane/weapons will cease until qualified personnel have determined the necessary reporting and/or corrective action to be taken. The term "qualified personnel" is defined as a qualified Nuclear Weapons officer (Wing Weapons or Munitions Maintenance officer) and a Nuclear Safety officer.

exterior inspection

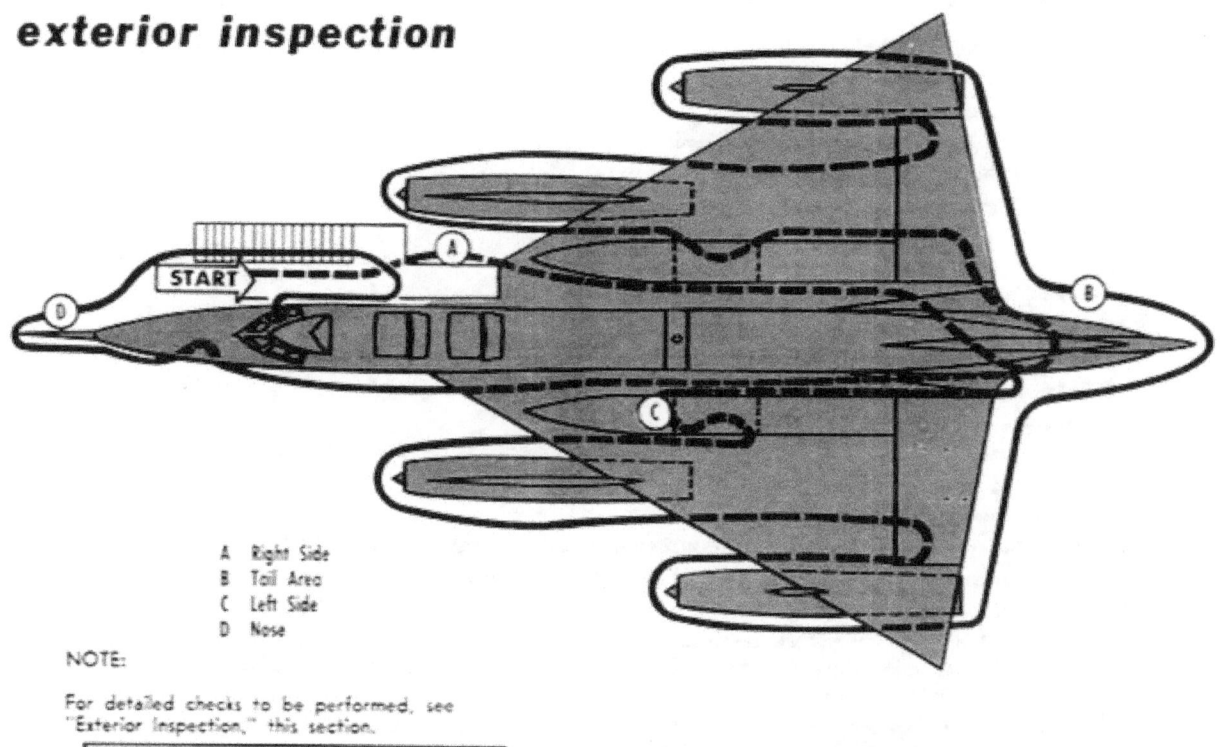

A Right Side
B Tail Area
C Left Side
D Nose

NOTE:

For detailed checks to be performed, see "Exterior Inspection," this section.

SMALL WEAPONS INSPECTION

a. Ground Safety Pin
b. Plenum Block Protectors
c. Antenna Radome Cover
d. Delivery Option Switch
e. Fuzing Option Switch
f. T-Setting
g. Inflight Lock
h. Ready-Safe Switch
i. Fin Protectors
j. Explosive Actuator Safing Assembly

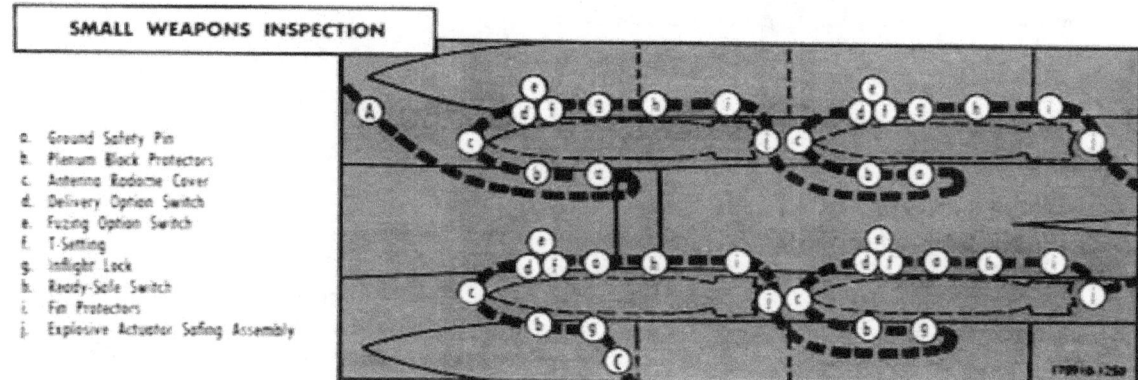

Figure 2-2.

EXTERIOR INSPECTION. (CONT'D)

A. Right Side.

1. Static ports clear.
TC 2. Pod pitot tube cover removed.
MB, LA 3. Right warhead drag pin indicator flush.
4. Small weapons:
    a. Ground safety pin removed.
    b. Plenum block protectors (2) removed.
    c. Antenna radome cover removed.

Section II
Normal Procedures

T.O. 1B-58A-1

EXTERIOR INSPECTION. (CONT'D)

  d. Delivery option switch as briefed.
  e. Fusing option switch as briefed.
  f. T-setting as briefed.
  g. Inflight lock properly positioned.
  h. Ready-safe switch SAFE.
  i. Fin protectors (4) removed.
  j. Explosive actuator safing assembly removed.

B. Tail Area.

1. MD-7 safety pin removed and safety switch flush.

C. Left Side.

1. Small weapons.
   Repeat the same check as for small weapons on right except that steps a and g will be reversed.

MB, LA 2. Pod release safety lockpin checked.
TC 3. Bomb pod ground safety lock removed.
MB, LA 4. Pneumatic release system pressure gages (2) 2550 psi at 70 degrees F.
MB, LA 5. Pneumatic release system pressure gage access panel secure.
TC 6. Arming control valve SAFE.
TC 7. Fuel pod ground safety lock removed.
   Check that inner valve plunger of the lower pod safety lock extends and is seated in the out position under spring tension.
TC 8. Ground safing switch RETARD (W-53).
MB, LA 9. Left warhead drag pin indicator flush.

D. Nose.

1. Secondary pitot tube and static ports.
2. Primary pitot mast tube and static ports.

POWER-OFF INTERIOR INSPECTION.

1. Canopy lock—Installed.
2. Canopy layback lockpins (2) and stop pins (2)—Installed.
3. Handgrip and canopy jettison handle safety pins (3)—Installed.
   Before entering the airplane, check that the two handgrip safety pins are installed. The canopy jettison handle safety pin will be checked immediately upon entering and before any personal equipment is placed in the compartment.
4. Canopy actuator warning pin—Checked.
   Check that canopy actuator warning pin is not visible.

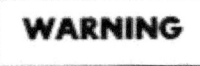

The red pin, when visible, indicates that the canopy actuator ballistics charge has been fired, rendering the associated canopy jettisoning system inoperative.

Note

During some weather conditions, it may be desirable to close the canopies upon entering the crew stations. In this case, insure canopy locks are removed prior to closing canopies.

2-6

POWER-OFF INTERIOR INSPECTION. (CONT'D)

5. Navigation isolation switches—ON.
6. CG adjustment panel.
    a. Pod selector switch—Set.
    b. RC weight and RC moment indicators—Checked.

SF 7. Escape capsule—Checked.
    a. Oxygen supply switch—ON.
    b. Disconnect engagement indicator—Checked.
       Check that the indicator window shows white. If red is showing, the disconnect is not properly seated. Check for no air leakage at the disconnect standpipe.
    c. Door seal condition—Checked.
    d. Emergency oxygen pressure—1800 psi at 70 degrees F.
    e. Control stick—Secure.
       Check that the knurled nut is fully screwed down and the stick mounted securely.

8. Safety belt and shoulder harness (manual and automatic)—Checked.
9. Required publications—Checked.
   Check that current sets of the following FLIP's are in the aircraft; FLIP, Terminal High Altitude; FLIP, Enroute High Altitude and FLIP, Enroute Supplement.
10. External power knob—OFF.
11. Battery switch—OFF.
12. Flight control power switch—OFF.
13. Cartridge start switch—OFF.
14. Engine start switches—OFF.
15. Damper switches—OFF.
16. Elevator control available mode selector switch—TO & LAND.
17. Lower pod ready switch—OFF and safetied.
18. Lower pod release switch—OFF and safetied.
19. Canopy control lever—OPEN.
20. UHF command radio—OFF.
21. TACAN power knob—OFF.
22. Warning and caution indicator switch—GROUND CHECK.
23. Voice warning system power/reset switch—OFF.
24. Small weapon jettison switch—SAFE, safetied.
25. Emergency increase elevator available handle—In.
26. Emergency brake and landing gear handle—In and safetied.
27. Throttles—OFF.
28. Taxi and landing light switches—OFF.
29. Nose wheel steering ratio selector switch—TAXI.
30. Landing gear handle—DOWN.
31. Drag chute handle—In and vertical.
32. Low altitude radar altimeter—OFF.
33. Fire pull handles—In.
34. CG control knob—MANUAL.
35. Manual cg shift knob—OFF.
36. Fuel dump switch—Guarded NORM, and safetied.
37. All other fuel switches—OFF, CLOSE, or NORMAL.
38. IFR emergency hydraulic boost lever—Guarded OFF.
39. Defog switch—DEC.
40. Rain removal switch—OFF.
41. Engine anti-ice switch—OFF.

Section II
Normal Procedures

T.O. 1B-58A-1

POWER-OFF INTERIOR INSPECTION. (CONT'D)

42. Pitot heat—OFF.
43. Air source selector knob—BOTH.
44. Refrigeration unit selector knob—GRD CART.
45. Air conditioning control mode selector knob—OFF.
46. Cabin temperature control knob—Full CCW.
47. Cabin pressure selector knob—NORM.
48. Generator drive decoupler switches—Guarded NORM and safetied.
49. Arm control switch—SAFE and sealed.
50. Arm power switch—NORM.
51. ARC-74—OFF.

DSO'S POWER-OFF INTERIOR INSPECTION.

1. Canopy lock—Installed.
2. Emergency lighting switch—ON.
3. Canopy layback lockpins (2)—Installed.
4. Handgrip and canopy jettison handle safety pins (3)—Installed.
   Before entering the airplane, check that the two handgrip safety pins are installed. The canopy jettison handle safety pin will be checked immediately upon entering and before any personal equipment is placed in the compartment.
5. Canopy actuator warning pin—Checked.
   Check that canopy actuator warning pin is not visible.

WARNING

The red pin, when visible, indicates that the canopy actuator ballistics charge has been fired, rendering the associated canopy jettisoning system inoperative.

Note

During some weather conditions, it may be desirable to close the canopies upon entering the crew stations. In this case, insure canopy locks are removed prior to closing canopies.

SF 6. Escape capsule—Checked.
   a. Oxygen supply switch—ON.
   b. Disconnect engagement indicator—Checked.
      Check that the indicator shows white. If red is showing, the disconnect is not properly seated. Check for leakage at the disconnect standpipe.
   c. Door seal condition—Checked.
   d. Emergency oxygen pressure—1800 psi at 70 degrees F.
7. Safety belt and shoulder harness (manual and automatic)—Checked.
8. Left a-c power panel—Checked.
   Check left a-c power panel for blown fuses and presence of adequate spares.
9. Voice warning system monitoring switch—VWS.
10. Canopy control lever—OPEN.
11. ARC-110 power switch—OFF.
12. MD-7 manual fire control panel:
    a. Master switch—OFF.

2-8

DSO'S POWER-OFF INTERIOR INSPECTION. (CONT'D)

    b. Marker generator switch—OFF.

During ground operation when ammunition is loaded and torqued in, do not place the master switch to STBY or OPR.

13. Pod present monitor switch—OFF.
14. Left ALQ-16 power knob—OFF.
15. ALR-12 power switch—OFF.
16. MD-7 radar fire control panel:
    a. Function controls (4)—CCW.
    b. Safe-fire switch—SAFE and safetied.
17. Chaff dispenser main power switch—OFF.
18. Right ALQ-16 power knob—OFF.
19. D-C power panel—Checked.
    Check the 28V d-c power panel for blown fuses and presence of adequate spares.
20. A/G IFF master control knob—OFF.
21. ARC-57 UHF command radio—OFF.
22. AFT ALQ-16 power knob—OFF.
23. Chaff load switch—Checked.
24. ARC-34 UHF command radio—OFF.
25. Right a-c power panel—Checked (1 amp firing voltage fuse reversed).
    Check right a-c power panel for blown fuses and presence of adequate spares. 1 amp firing voltage fuse reversed.
26. Required publications—Checked.
    Check that current sets of the following FLIP's are in the aircraft: FLIP, Terminal High Altitude; FLIP, Enroute High Altitude; FLIP, Enroute Supplement.

POWER-ON INTERIOR INSPECTION.

On weapon loaded airplanes, battery power shall not be applied until navigator has completed weapon related items in NAVIGATOR'S POWER-OFF INSPECTION.

Note

For explanation of asterisk (*) refer to COCKING, this section.

1. Essential d-c power:
*   a. Battery switch—EMER, battery discharging lamp on.
    b. Power-off inspection—Complete. (N-DSO)
    c. Capsule crew ejection lamp—Checked.
    Press-to-test crew ejection lamp and check that lamp lights.
    d. Bailout alert lamps—Checked. (P-N-DSO)
    Place the bailout alert switch to ALERT; the navigator and DSO's bailout alert lamps should flash on and off. Check the "hot mike" with the function selector knob in INTER.

Section II
Normal Procedures

T.O. 1B-58A-1

POWER-ON INTERIOR INSPECTION. (CONT'D)

    e. Bailout warning lamps—Checked. (P-N-DSO)
        Place the bailout warning switch to BAILOUT; the bailout warning lamps on the panel and in the navigator's and DSO's capsules should light. Check the "hot mike" as in step d, above.

*   f. Battery switch—NORM, battery discharging lamp on.
SF g. Battery voltage—Checked. (DSO)
        Position meter selector knob to either FWD or AFT supply 28-volt d-c and read battery voltage. Minimum acceptable voltage is 23.1 volts.

* 2. External power knob—ALERT and check; battery discharging lamp out.
    Check voltage (115 ±5 volts) and frequency (400 ±6 cycles).

3. Oxygen check (P-DSO):
    Refer to "Oxygen Systems," Section IV for the amplified procedure. Pilot will report oxygen quantity to DSO.

4. Interphone—On call, normal, aux listen, and "hot mike." (P-N-DSO)
    DSO check NORMAL system using right foot microphone button and the AUX listen system using the capsule microphone button.

SF 5. D-C power—Checked. (DSO)
    Check the voltage outputs of the d-c power units (28 ±3.5V; 150 ±9.0V; —150 ±9.0V; 250 +27.0V, —24.0V).

6. Voice warning system power/reset and monitoring switch—ON, checked and OFF (P), Checked. (N-DSO)
    Navigator and DSO will check voice warning system monitor capability. Determine that the voice warning messages are overridden by the following controls.
    a. Master warning lamp override.
    b. Master caution lamp override.
    c. Voice warning system override button.

7. Malfunction indicator lamps—Checked. (P-DSO)
    Press malfunction and indicator lamp and voice warning system test button and check that the master and individual warning and caution lamps are on, plus the following:

Note

The oil low level caution lamps may remain lighted when the test button is released. However, this does not necessarily indicate low oil quantity and the lamps should go out when the engines are started.

    a. Second station control indicator lamp.
    b. Landing gear warning lamp.
    c. Landing gear alarm buzzer will sound. Turn off the buzzer, using the landing gear alarm cutoff button.
    d. Aileron-rudder neutral trim indicator lamp.
    e. Crew capsulated indicator and emergency air supply indicator lamps.
    f. Air refueling ready indicator lamp.
    g. Pod transfer pump low pressure caution lamps.
    h. Angle-of-attack indexer and stall warning lamps.
    i. Mach-monitor indicator lamp. (P-DSO) The DSO's mach-monitor indicator lamp must be pressed to test.
    j. Pilot's low altitude warning lamp. (Amber "LOW" lamp on low altitude radar altimeter indicator will not light.)

8. Landing gear position indicator lamps—On.

POWER-ON INTERIOR INSPECTION. (CONT'D)

9. Fuel quantity indicators, totalizer, and cg failure detector—Cross-checked. (P-DSO)

    The pilot will alert the DSO to monitor the fuel quantity indicators for proper operation during this check. Check the fuel gage power switch in normal and check the cg failed caution lamp out. Press the instrument test button and check the fuel quantity indicators and totalizer for decreasing indications. Check cg indicator for change in indication. Place fuel gage power switch to ALTERNATE, release instrument test button and ascertain that all indicator readings return to the former reading. Place the fuel gage power switch to OFF and check that cg failed caution lamp lights. Return the fuel gage power switch to NORMAL and read to the DSO the fuel quantity gages, totalizer, and cg indicator. The totalizer indication should agree to within 1300 pounds of the sum of the individual fuel quantity gages. The maximum difference between the pilot's and DSO's fuel indicators is ±1.0 percent of the instrument full scale reading. If the DSO's cg indicator disagrees with the pilot's cg indicator by more than ±0.25 percent, or any DSO's fuel gage disagrees with the pilot's gage by more than ±1.0 percent, use the pilot's gages and observe the aft cg limits for airplanes not equipped for monitoring airspeed, fuel or cg by the DSO. The DSO will compute the cg and check the value obtained against that shown on the indicator. The cg check will be made with the gear up index at a deck angle of +2.5 degrees. Ammunition and chaff loaded will not be considered. Indicated and computed cg must agree within ±0.8 percent MAC (or ±0.9 percent MAC with TC or small weapons).

SF10. Fuel system:

WARNING

Advise ground observer to watch for fuel spillage during fuel system check.

a. Reservoir booster pump switch—NORM.
    Check No. 3, 4 and 5 pump caution lamps light momentarily.

Note

On airplanes , No. 5 pump caution lamp will not light.

b. Reservoir to manifold switches—NORMAL.
    Check left and right manifold low pressure warning lamps go out and for reservoir to all engines feed indication. On airplanes , No. 5 pump caution lamp will light momentarily.

Note

If the manifold is pressurized, the manifold lamps may not be lighted.

c. Forward tank to engine supply knob—ON.
    Check No. 1 and 2 pump caution lamps light momentarily, for a forward to all engines feed indications, and reservoir indicator showing no feed.

d. CG selector knob—Set.
    Set selector pointer to coincide with indicated value.

e. CG control knob—AUTO.
    Check that fuel flow indication, if any, ceases before selector pointer is moved more than 0.3 percent beyond indicator pointer.

Section II
Normal Procedures

POWER-ON INTERIOR INSPECTION. (CONT'D)

    f. Aft tank to engine supply knob—ON.

        Check No. 6 and 7 pump caution lamps light momentarily, for a split feed indication, and reservoir indicator showing no feed.

    g. Balance tank refuel-scavenge knob—REFUEL, then OFF.

        Check that fuel does not transfer to the balance tank, then return the balance tank refuel-scavenge knob to OFF.

    h. Control stick cg shift switch—AFT, then OFF.

        Check that cg control knob actuates to MANUAL, that No. 1 pump caution lamp lights momentarily and for a forward to balance tank flow indication. Check No. 6 pump caution lamp lights momentarily when the control stick cg shift switch is returned to OFF.

    i. Control stick cg shift switch—FWD, then OFF.

        Check that No. 10 and 11 (No. 8 also if balance tank fuel is below 1500-2000 pounds) pump caution lamps light momentarily, and for a balance to forward tank flow indication. Check No. 6 pump caution lamp lights momentarily when the manual cg shift knob is returned to OFF.

    j. Forward tank to engine supply knob—OFF.

        Check No. 8 and 9 pump caution lamp light momentarily, for an aft tank to all engines feed indication, and reservoir indicator showing no feed.

    k. Forward tank refuel-scavenge knob—SCAV, then OFF.

        Check No. 1 and 2 pump caution lamps light momentarily, then turn switch OFF. Check No. 6 and 9 pump caution lamps light momentarily.

    l. Balance tank refuel-scavenge knob—SCAV, then OFF.

        Check No. 10 and 11 pump caution lamps light momentarily. Check for aft tank to balance tank flow indication, then turn switch OFF. Check No. 6 and 9 pump caution lamps light momentarily.

    m. Aft tank to engine supply control knob—OFF.

SF11. Angle-of-attack indicator and indexer lamps—Checked.

Note

This check is accomplished with the assistance of a ground observer on a stand near the sensor vane. With the sensor vane at the bottom stop, observe that the indicator pointer is at zero degrees and the high-speed symbol amber lamp is lighted. Instruct ground observer to rotate the sensor vane slowly clockwise from the bottom stop, simultaneously checking the pointer for restrictions or oscillations and the indexer for the following indications:

(1) High-speed (amber) symbol lighted from zero to 11.75 ($\pm$ 0.25) degrees.

(2) Within the range of 11.0 to 12.0 degrees, both the high-speed (amber) and on-speed (green) symbol are lighted simultaneously for at least 0.5 degree.

(3) On-speed (green) symbol lighted from 11.25 ($\pm$0.25) degrees to 13.75 ($\pm$0.25)

(4) Within the range of 13.0 to 14.0 degrees, both the on-speed (green) and low-speed (red) symbols are lighted simultaneously for at least 0.5 degree.

(5) Low-speed (red) symbol lighted from 13.25 ($\pm$ 0.25) degrees to upper stop.

(6) Stall warning lamp and low-speed (red) symbol lighted simultaneously from 17.0 ($\pm$ 0.25) degrees to upper stop.

SF12. Pitot and Angle-of-Attack vane heat—Checked, then OFF.

POWER-ON INTERIOR INSPECTION. (CONT'D)

SF13. Air refueling system:

Note

This check is accomplished with the assistance of a ground observer on a stand located near the receptacle. Hand signals may be used to indicate position of the toggles.

    a. IFR emergency hydraulic boost lever—ON.
    b. Air refueling slipway light control—Full CW.
    c. Air refueling door switch—OPEN, air refueling ready indicator lamp lighted (P), Door open, lamps lighted. (GO)
    d. EBL switch—EBL (P), Toggles engaged. (GO)
    e. IFR disconnect button—Depressed (P), Toggles released. (GO)
    f. IFR disconnect button—Released (P), Toggles engaged. (GO)
    g. EBL switch—OFF (P), Toggles released. (GO)
    h. Air refueling slipway light control—Full CCW (P), Both lamps checked. (GO)
    i. Air refueling door switch—CLOSE (P), Door closed. (GO)
    j. IFR emergency hydraulic boost lever—Guarded OFF.
    k. Air refueling emergency pneumatic system—Repressurized. (GO)
        After air refueling system check is complete, instruct ground observer to reservice the air refueling emergency pneumatic system to 2550 psi at 70°F.

* 14. All weapon related caution lamps—Off.
  15. Interior lights—Checked. (DSO)
  16. Fuse panels—Checked. (DSO)
      Check the left a-c, d-c, and right a-c power panels for blown fuses and the a-c panels for phase indicator lamps on.

BEFORE STARTING ENGINES. (DSO READS)

1. Battery switch and external power—NORMAL and ALERT.
2. Personal gear—Connected and checked. (P-N-DSO)
    Safety belt, shoulder harness, and oxygen hose connected and oxygen check complete.
3. Communication panels—Set. (N-DSO)
    The Navigator and DSO will place their interphone and command mixing switches to ON, to monitor emergency transmissions until after takeoff.
4. Heading selector switch—J-4.
5. Navigation lights—ON.
6. Canopy locks—Removed. (P-N-DSO)

Do not attempt to remove the canopy lock when the weight of the canopy is on the lock. Failure to observe this precaution may allow the canopy to fall on a crew member.

7. ARC-34—ON. (DSO)
8. Parking brakes—Set.
    Check that both pedals remain depressed.

Section II
Normal Procedures

T.O. 1B-58A-1

personal gear connections

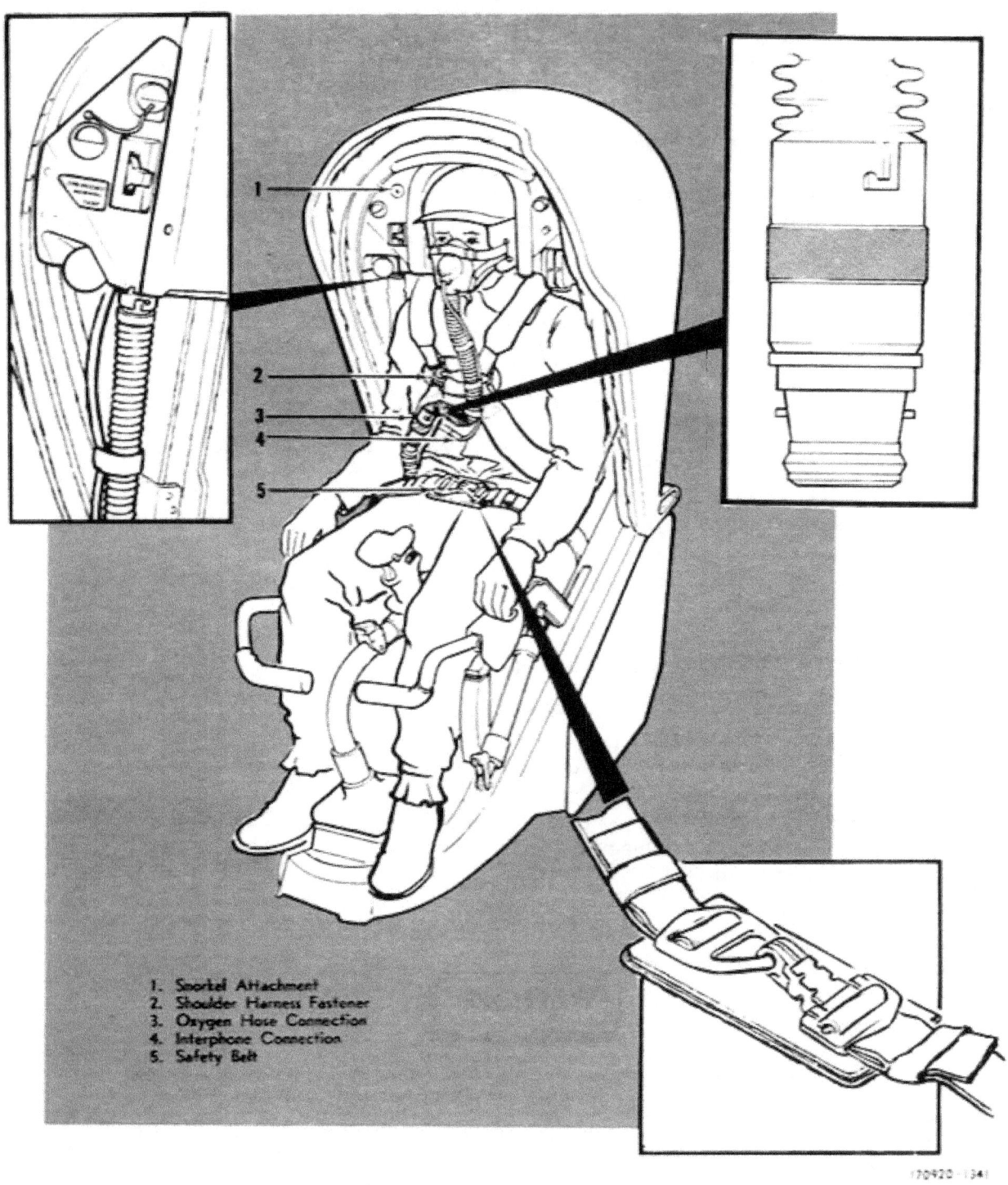

1. Snorkel Attachment
2. Shoulder Harness Fastener
3. Oxygen Hose Connection
4. Interphone Connection
5. Safety Belt

Figure 2-3.

BEFORE STARTING ENGINES. (DSO READS) (CONT'D)

9. Fire pull handles—In.
10. Reservoir booster pump switch—NORM.
11. Aft tank to engine supply control knob—ON.
    Engines will be started on the aft tank.
12. Reservoir to manifold switches—NORMAL.
13. Air conditioning control mode selector knob—MAN.
14. Ground, ready to start: Fire guards posted, chocks in place, external starter air supplied. No. 2 engine starter exhaust door open —Ready. (GO)
15. Tower call—Completed. (DSO)
    DSO will call tower to assure communications prior to starting engines.

STARTING ENGINES. (DSO READS)

During normal engine starting, a qualified ground observer will be in constant communication with the pilot. The pilot will announce his actions at all times during engine starting operations. Action which requires ground personnel to approach an operating engine, such as disconnecting ground service carts, must be performed with caution. Ground fire equipment should be properly manned and standing by. See "Engine Fire on the Ground," Section III, for instructions in combating engine fires. The engine starting sequence is 2, 1, 3, 4. When an external starter air cart is used to start the first engine, the cart is normally used to start all engines. However, as an alternate method, after the number 2 engine is started by a cartridge start or one of the inboard engines is started by an external starter air cart, compressor bleed air from that engine may then be used to start the remaining engines. Refer to "Alternate Engine Starting Procedures," this section. Whenever possible, start the engines with the airplane headed into or at right angles to the wind. Starting with the tail pointed into a strong wind may cause erratic exhaust gas temperature readings.

WARNING

Suction at air inlets is sufficient to kill or seriously injure personnel pulled against or into the inlets. The danger area aft of the airplane is created by high exhaust velocity, temperature, and noise level. See figure 2-4 for danger areas.

1. No. 2 clear—Cleared. (GO)
2. No. 2 engine start switch and throttle—GROUND and IDLE.
   Place the start switch to GROUND and when engine RPM reaches 12 percent place throttle beyond IDLE then back to IDLE. Maximum exhaust gas temperatures during starting are:
   1000°C for 3 seconds
   975°C for 10 seconds
   950°C for 35 seconds
   925°C for 60 seconds.

CAUTION

- The minimum recommended engine rpm for a satisfactory light-off and acceleration is 12 percent. Below this engine speed, severe overtemperature conditions may be expected.
- If the engine fails to light-off within 15 seconds after the throttle is placed at idle, or by the time fuel flow reaches a stable 800 pph, abort the start by returning the throttle to OFF, then start switch to OFF. Light-off failure is indicated by no rise in EGT, no increase in rpm, or abnormally high or low fuel flow. Clear the engine prior to another start attempt. (Refer to "Clearing an Engine," this section.)

Section II
Normal Procedures

T.O. 1B-58A-1

danger areas
engines

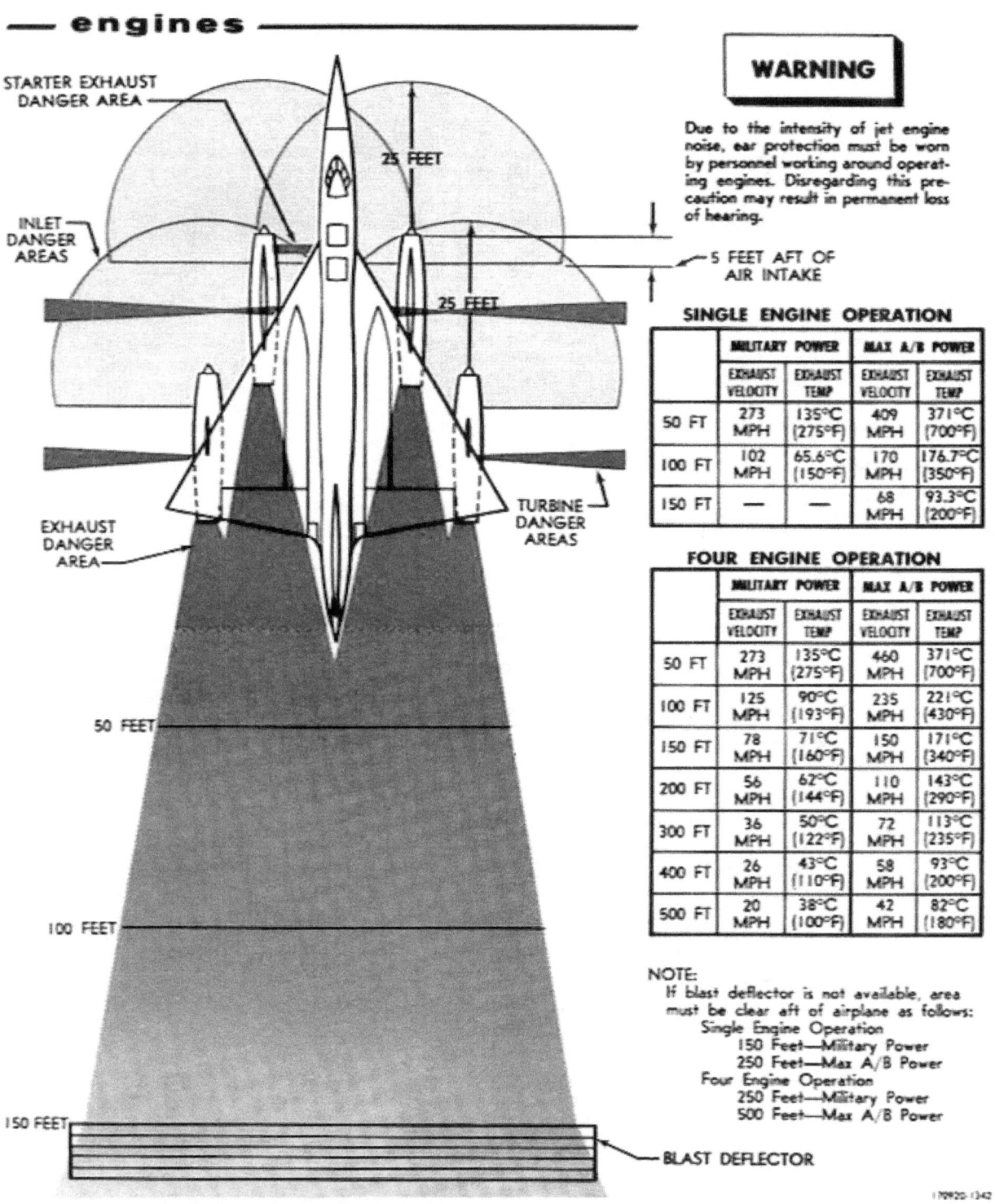

Figure 2-4. (Sheet 1 of 2)

Section II
Normal Procedures

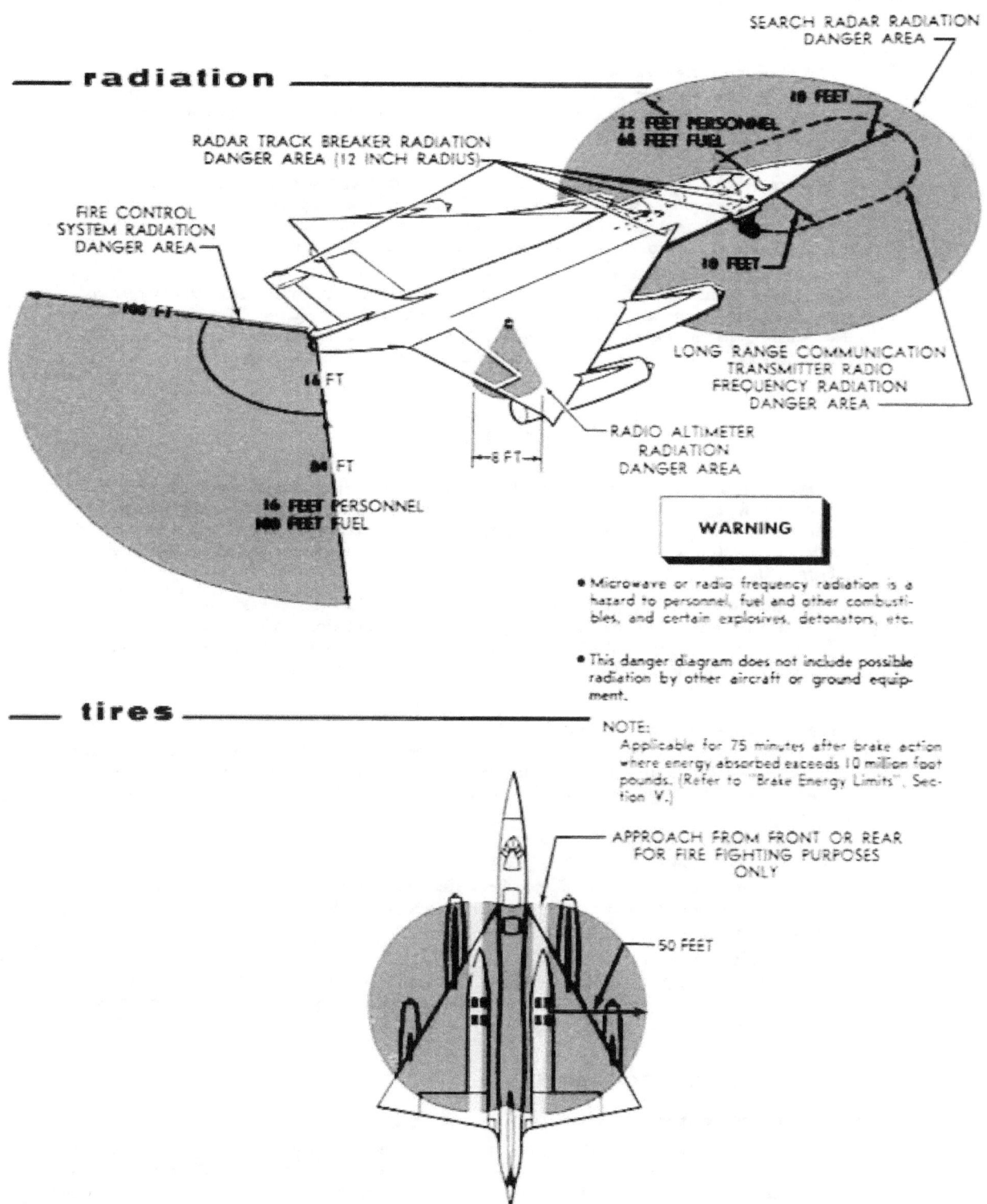

Figure 2-4. (Sheet 2 of 2)

Section II
Normal Procedures

T.O. 1B-58A-1

STARTING ENGINES. (DSO READS) (CONT'D)

Note

The EGT indicators are a-c powered; therefore, in the event of a ground power failure, EGT indication for engines 1, 3, and 4 will not be available until a generator is placed on the line. EGT indication for number 2 engine is available before a generator is placed on the line.

3. Engine start switch—OFF (P), Starter dropout and starter exhaust door closed and latched. (GO) Pilot will place engine start switch in the OFF position at approximately 47 percent rpm. Ground observer will confirm starter dropout and will close and latch number 2 engine starter exhaust door prior to acceleration above idle rpm (67 percent).
4. Engine instruments—Within limits.
    After light-off and during acceleration to idle rpm, check that engine instrument readings do not exceed limitations as set forth in Section V. There may be large fluctuations in fuel flow after starting an engine and during suction feed operation due to air in the fuel lines. When engine has stabilized at idle, check that rpm is approximately 67 percent.

CAUTION

- It is considered a hot start when EGT exceeds starting limits. The seriousness of a hot start depends on the degree of overtemperature and the elapsed time during which engine was subjected to such temperature. Operation that exceeds the time or temperature limits requires a hot section inspection. All hot starts will be logged in Form 781.

- After light-off, if engine rpm does not increase to the idle range but remains at some intermediate speed, and the EGT remains within starting limits, the engine has made a false start. Shut down the engine, allow one minute for fuel drainage, then clear the engine prior to another start attempt.

5. Hydraulic system—Pressure checked.
    Check that No. 2 hydraulic pump caution lamp goes out before hydraulic pressure increases above 2100 psi. Check that utility hydraulic pressure indicator reading is within limits. Refer to "Instrument Markings," Section V. Check utility hydraulic portion of yaw damper servo as follows:
    a. Flight control power switch—ON.
    b. Yaw damper switch—ON, then OFF.
        Turn yaw damper switch on and check that there is no large engage transient (less than 1° on the RPI) then turn yaw damper switch off.
    c. Flight control power switch—OFF.
6. Start engines No. 1, 3, and 4.
    Repeat engine start procedure for engines 1, 3, and 4. Primary hydraulic system will be pressure checked during No. 3 engine start, however, it is not necessary to repeat the yaw damper check.

ALTERNATE ENGINE STARTING PROCEDURES.

Starting Engines With Cartridge Starter.

The number 2 engine may be started utilizing the cartridge starter and airplane battery power thus eliminating the necessity for either the external starter air cart or an external electrical power source. When making a cartridge start, a-c power is supplied to the number 2 EGT indicator only. It is therefore necessary that the number 2 generator be placed on the line as soon as possible in order to obtain other engine instrument readings. It may be advisable to close canopies prior to start to prevent cartridge smoke and fumes from entering cockpit area.

Starting Engines With Cartridge Starter. (Cont'd)

WARNING

- In all cases of malfunction during start, pilot will notify ground crew and ensure that throttle, engine start switch, and cartridge start switch are off prior to cartridge removal.
- Cartridge malfunctions of two types may be encountered during cartridge starts.
    1. Hangfire. An abnormal delay between cartridge actuation and indication of engine RPM. There will be evidence of smoke at the exhaust door. After a period of several seconds, RPM will increase rapidly and will give evidence of near normal operation. If the above indications are observed and start is unsuccessful, the cartridge has been expended. If removal is desired, observe 15 minute waiting period after all evidence of burning has ceased.
    2. Misfire. A cartridge that fails to ignite. There will be no evidence of smoke and no engine rotation. If a misfire occurs, observe the one minute waiting time before cartridge removal.
- Except in an emergency, engine operation is prohibited when a live or misfired cartridge is installed.

1. Cabin temperature control knob—Full CW (warm).
2. No. 2 throttle—IDLE.
   Place throttle beyond idle, then back to idle.
3. Cartridge start switch—START.
4. No. 2 engine start switch—GROUND.
5. Engine start switch—OFF (P), Starter dropout and starter exhaust door closed and latched. (GO)
   Pilot will place engine start switch in the OFF position at approximately 47 percent rpm. Ground observer will confirm starter dropout and will close and latch starter exhaust door prior to acceleration above idle rpm (67 percent).
6. Cartridge start switch—OFF.
7. Generator No. 2—Excited, checked, and ON. Momentarily place the No. 2 generator control switch to RESET and check that abnormal lamp goes out. Place meter selector knob to GEN 2 and check for approximately 115 volts and 400 cycles. Place No. 2 generator switch to ON. Check that power flow indicator shows generator No. 2 supplying power to left and right buses.
8. Engine instruments—Within Limits.
9. Hydraulic system—Pressure checked.
    a. Flight control power switch—ON.
    b. Yaw damper switch—ON, then OFF.
    c. Flight control power switch—OFF.
10. Cabin temperature control knob—Full CCW (cold).
11. Refrigeration unit selector—GRD CART.
12. Engine No. 2—85 percent or higher.
13. Start remaining engines.

Starting Engine Without External Power Cart.

When an external electrical power source is not available, an engine start may be accomplished utilizing airplane battery power and an engine starter air cart. Under these conditions, a-c power will be available to no. 2 engine EGT indicator only, and fuel flow and oil pressure indications will not be available until no. 2 generator is placed on the bus.

1. Cabin temperature control knob—Full CW (warm).
2. No. 2 engine start switch and throttle—GROUND and IDLE.
   Place No. 2 engine start switch to GROUND. After engine RPM stabilizes (12 percent RPM minimum) move throttle beyond IDLE, then back to IDLE.

Section II
Normal Procedures

T.O. 1B-58A-1

Starting Engine Without External Power Cart. (Cont'd)

The minimum recommended engine RPM for a satisfactory light-off and acceleration is 12 percent. Below this engine speed, severe over-temperature conditions may be expected.

3. Engine start switch—OFF (P), Starter dropout and starter exhaust door closed and latched. (GO) Pilot will place engine start switch in the off position at approximately 47 percent rpm. Ground observer will confirm starter dropout and will close and latch starter exhaust door prior to acceleration above idle rpm (67 percent).
4. Generator No. 2—Excited, checked, and ON.
    Momentarily place the No. 2 generator control switch to RESET and check that abnormal lamp goes out. Place meter selector knob to GEN 2 and check for approximately 115 volts and 400 cycles. Place No. 2 generator switch to ON. Check that power flow indicator shows generator No. 2 supplying power to left and right buses.
5. Engine instruments—Within limits.
6. Hydraulic system—Pressure checked.
    a. Flight control power switch—ON.
    b. Yaw damper switch—ON, then OFF.
    c. Flight control power switch—OFF.
7. Cabin temperature control knob—Full CCW (cold).
8. Start remaining engines.

Starting Engine(s) With No. 2 and/or No. 3 Engines Operating.

When it is desired to start one or more engines using compressor bleed air from an inboard engine which is already operating, use the following procedure to start the engine(s) then complete items as necessary in the STARTING ENGINES portion of this checklist. These necessary items will be dictated by events preceding the engine start.

1. No. 2 engine starter exhaust door—Open (if No. 2 engine is to be started).
2. Operating inboard engine(s)—85 percent (or above).
3. Air conditioning control mode selector knob—MAN.
4. Cabin temperature control knob—Full CCW.
5. Refrigeration unit selector—GRD CART.

CAUTION

With the refrigeration unit selector at GRD CART, no airflow is supplied to cool electronic equipment. Do not leave the refrigeration unit selector at GRD CART with electronic equipment operating in excess of 90 seconds. (Refer to figure 4-2.)

6. Start engine(s).
7. Air conditioning panel—BOTH, RESET TO NORMAL, and AUTO.

CLEARING AN ENGINE.

If for any reason it is desired to clear an engine of trapped fuel or vapors prior to starting or after an aborted start, proceed as follows:

1. No. 2 engine starter exhaust door—Open (if No. 2 engine is to be cleared).
2. Throttle—OFF.

Note

If ground starter cart has been removed, advance the inboard engine(s) sufficiently to motor the engine to be cleared to 16 percent rpm.

3. Engine start switch—GROUND.
    Refer to Section V for engine starter limitations.
4. Engine start switch—OFF.

ENGINE GROUND OPERATION.

No warmup period is required for jet engines, except for the oil system when operating under extreme cold weather conditions. Under normal conditions it is desirable that takeoff be accomplished after a minimum of engine ground operation. Check that taxi and runup areas are free of loose debris. During engine ground operation, both before takeoff and after landing, with the refrigeration unit selector knob in BOTH, the air conditioning system may require as much as 75 percent rpm on the inboard engines (85 percent on one engine) to provide sufficient cooling for electronic equipment and maintain normal flow. If, due to the necessity of operating at lower rpm than stated above, the low air flow caution lamp lights, determine that the system goes into reverse flow and the temperature control is at 3 o'clock. (If not, manually select reverse flow operation.) In the event the low airflow caution lamp lights, both inboard engines should be operated at 85 percent rpm as soon as possible. The light should go out within 10 minutes with engines at 85 percent rpm. When the lamp goes out, the system may be reset to normal flow operation. For engine ground operating time limits, refer to Section V.

BEFORE TAXIING. (DSO READS)

1. Aft tank to engine supply control knob—OFF.

    No. 5 booster pump low pressure caution lamp will light momentarily. Check for reservoir tank to all engines feed indication.

2. Reservoir booster pump switch—OFF.

    Left and right manifold low pressure warning lamps will light as the manifold pressure drops due to suction feed. Refer to "Fuel Supply System," Section VII for specific information on operation of the fuel system.

3. Electrical system:

    a. Generators—Excited and checked.
       Momentarily place the generator control switches to reset and check that the abnormal lamps go out. Check generator voltages 115 ($\pm$5) volts and frequencies 400 ($\pm$6) cycles.

    b. No. 1 generator switch—ON.
       Check power flow indicator shows generator No. 1 supplying power to left bus.

    c. External power switch and/or No. 2 generator (as applicable)—OFF.
       If engine start was accomplished using an external electrical power cart, place the external power switch OFF. If engine start was accomplished without external electrical power cart and the No. 2 generator was placed on the line, place generator No. 2 switch OFF. Check bus-tie indicator shows generator No. 1 supplying power to both buses and pod and DECM power caution lamp on.

    d. Pod and DECM power switch—OVERRIDE, AUTO LOAD REDUCTION.
       Check pod and DECM power caution lamp goes out, then select No. 1 generator with a-c meter selector knob and check that load is not excessive. Then return pod and DECM power switch to AUTO LOAD REDUCTION and check caution lamp comes on.

    e. No. 2 generator switch—ON.
       Check power flow indicator and bus-tie indicator (horizontal) show generator No. 1 supplying power to both buses. Check that pod and DECM power caution lamp remains on.

    f. Bus-tie relay—Checked.
       Momentarily depress the bus-tie button and check that the power flow indicator and bus-tie indicator (vertical) show generator No. 1 supplying power to left bus and generator No. 2 supplying power to right bus. Check that pod and DECM power caution lamp goes out.

    g. No. 1 generator switch—OFF.
       Check power flow indicator and bus-tie indicator (vertical) show generator No. 2 supplying power to both buses. The pod and DECM power caution lamp should come on.

    h. No. 3 generator switch—ON.
       Check power flow indicators show generator No. 3 supplying power to right bus and generator No. 2 supplying power to left bus. Check that pod and DECM power caution lamp goes out.

Section II
Normal Procedures

T.O. 1B-58A-1

BEFORE TAXIING. (DSO READS) (CONT'D)

    i. No. 2 generator switch—OFF.

        Check power flow indiactor and bus-tie indicator (horizontal) show generator No. 3 supplying power to both buses and pod and DECM power caution lamp comes on.

    j. No. 1 generator switch—ON.

        Check power flow indicator and bus-tie indicator (horizontal) show generator No. 3 supplying power to both buses. Check that the pod and DECM power caution lamp remains on.

    k. Bus-tie relay—Checked.

        Momentarily depress the bus-tie button and check that the power flow indicator and bus-tie indicator (vertical) show generator No. 1 supplying power to the left bus and generator No. 3 supplying power to right bus. Check that pod and DECM power caution lamp goes out.

    l. No. 2 generator switch—ON.

        Check generator No. 2 goes to standby status.

    m. Voltage and frequencies—Checked.

        Check all generators and both buses for correct voltages (115 ±5) and frequencies (400 ±6 cycles).

    n. D-C power—Checked. (DSO)

        Check the load and voltage of the d-c power units. Loadmeter indications should read from −0.1 to 0.8 for 28V units and −0.1 to 0.7 for all other units. Indications from 28V units must be within 0.85 of its parallel unit and all other units must be within 0.45 of their respective parallel unit. Voltage indications should read: 28 (±3.5)V, 150 (±9.0)V, −150 (±9.0)V, and 250 (+27.0 −24.0)V. If an abnormal indication or load fluctuation is noted, qualified maintenance personnel will be notified.

4. Ground, disconnect starter air and electrical power carts—Disconnected. (GO)

Engine rpm must not exceed 75 percent while ground personnel are around engines.

5. Canopies—Closed and latched. (DSO-N-P)

    The DSO and navigator close their canopies and when the latching mechanism indicator flags are out of sight, report to the pilot. The pilot then closes his canopy and checks hook and roller engagement.

Visual inspection must be made of hook and roller engagement at the pilot's station, and the navigator's and DSO's canopy latching mechanism indicator flags must be out of sight behind their shields to indicate positive locking of the canopy.

6. Canopy unlock caution lamp—Off.
7. Canopy seal lever—SEALED. (N)
8. Air conditioning system:

    a. Refrigeration unit selector knob—BOTH.

        Place this knob in the BOTH position to select airplane air conditioning.

    b. Rain removal switch—REMOVE, then OFF.

        Place the rain removal switch in the REMOVE position momentarily in order to blow out any water that may have backed into the warm air manifold, then return to OFF.

2-22

Section II
Normal Procedures

BEFORE TAXIING. (DSO READS) (CONT'D)

    c. Cabin temperature control knob—3 o'clock.
    d. Flow switch—RESET TO NORMAL.
        Move the flow switch to RESET TO NORMAL momentarily, then release. Check that the reverse airflow caution lamp goes out and that the air conditioning system goes into normal flow.
    e. Control mode selector knob—AUTO.
        Place the knob to AUTO for automatic operation of the air conditioning system.
    f. Engines No. 2 and 3—75 percent rpm.
        Increase power to provide adequate airflow for pressurization.
    g. Cabin altimeter—Checked.
        Check that the cabin altitude does not drop more than 4000 feet below the field altitude. Visually check that the canopy seals are inflated.
    h. Engines No. 2 and 3 throttles—As required.
        If additional cooling will be required during the Before Taxiing check, engines No. 2 and 3 may be left at 75 percent.

9. Electrical power and air conditioning—Normal.
   Notify the navigator and DSO that electrical power and air conditioning are normal.
10. UHF command and TACAN radios—BOTH and T/R (P), T/R (N), BOTH. (DSO)
11. Flight control power switch—ON.
   Check that yaw damper warning and caution lamps light.
12. Reservoir booster pump switch—NORM.
   The left and right manifold low pressure warning lamps will go out.
   If forward tank quantity is over approximately 19,000 pounds, a noticeable drop in the forward tank is normal. If forward tank quantity is less than 19,000 pounds, a noticeable drop in the reservoir tank is normal.
13. Aft tank to engine supply control knob—ON.
   Check for fuel feed indication to all engines.
14. Flight control system:
   Engines will be at idle during flight control system check.
    a. Aileron control available switch—AUTO.
    b. Flight control freedom and position—Checked.
        Ground observer will report all control positions.
        (1) Move control stick in a rectangular pattern such that it is always displaced the maximum distance from the neutral position. Pause momentarily with stick displaced full forward, full left, full aft and full right to permit the ground observer to observe elevator, aileron and rudder positions. The EPI should show approximately 21.5 degrees up with the elevator in the full up position and approximately 10 degrees down with the elevator in the full down position. The RPI should show approximately 15 degrees left with the stick in the full right position and approximately 15 degrees right with the stick in the full left position.

Note

● A momentary decrease in hydraulic pressure is normal with rapid flight control moment during ground operation. This pressure drop may be sufficient to cause a momentary lighting of one or more hydraulic pump caution lamps.

● Stick "talk back" may be expected at the extreme corners of the stick envelope.

        (2) Move rudder full left then full right. RPI should read 30 degrees in both directions.

Section II
Normal Procedures

T.O. 1B-58A-1

elevator available

With Autotrim Full Down: 1.22° ±0.46°

CONFIGURATION	GROSS WEIGHT (1000 LBS)							
	100 & BELOW	105	110	115	120	125	130	135 & ABOVE
MB, LA, or TCP With Small Weapons	5.4±1.1	5.0±1.0	4.6±0.9	4.3±0.9	3.9±0.8	3.5±0.7	3.1±0.6	2.7±0.5
Without Small Weapons	4.4±0.9	4.1±0.8	3.7±0.7	3.4±0.7	3.1±0.6	2.8±0.6	2.5±0.5	2.2±0.4
Upper Pod With Small Weapons	4.0±0.8	3.7±0.7	3.4±0.7	3.1±0.6	2.8±0.6	2.6±0.5	2.3±0.5	2.0±0.4
Without Small Weapons	3.0±0.6	2.7±0.5	2.5±0.5	2.3±0.5	2.1±0.4	1.9±0.4	1.7±0.3	1.5±0.3
Without Pod With Small Weapons	2.2±0.4	2.0±0.4	1.9±0.4	1.7±0.3	1.5±0.3	1.4±0.3	1.2±0.2	1.2±0.2
Without Small Weapons	1.2±0.2	1.2±0.2	1.2±0.2	1.2±0.2	1.2±0.2	1.2±0.2	1.2±0.2	1.2±0.2

Notes:

1. For intermediate gross weights, apply linear interpolation to obtain elevator available.
2. If the values herein do not agree for elevator available for full down autotrim, refer to "Elevator Control Available Check" Section VII.

Figure 2-5.

BEFORE TAXIING. (DSO READS) (CONT'D)

> **CAUTION**
>
> - Prior to moving rudder through full limits move rudder slightly, instruct ground observer to check for nose wheel scrubbing to assure that nose wheel steering is disengaged.
> - Do not operate rudder to full deflection more than necessary to accomplish these checks. To do so will result in shortening the life expectancy of rudder structural parts.

    c. Rudder trim—Checked.

        Hold the rudder trim switch to NOSE LEFT and check for left rudder pedal movement. Hold the switch to NOSE RIGHT and check for right rudder pedal movement. Hold switch to NOSE LEFT and when the aileron-rudder neutral trim indicator lamp lights immediately release the switch. Check that lamp goes out and that the rudder pedals are approximately at neutral. Check that RPI gives proper indication.

    d. Elevator trim—Checked.

        Hold the trim selector switch alternately to NOSE UP and NOSE DOWN and check for correct control stick movements and proper indication on the EPI. Place the trim selector switch to OFF; check that the aileron-elevator stick trim switch is inoperative in all positions. Then place trim selector switch to CONT STICK; now hold the aileron-elevator stick trim switch alternately to NOSE UP and NOSE DOWN and check for correct control stick movement. When check is completed, trim elevators to 1.5 degrees up.

BEFORE TAXIING. (DSO READS) (CONT'D)

e. Aileron trim—Checked.

Hold the aileron-elevator stick trim switch alternately to LWD and RWD and check for correct control stick movement. Then hold the switch to LWD and as the aileron-rudder neutral trim indicator lamp lights release the switch. Check that lamp goes out and that the stick is approximately at neutral aileron. The RPI should now read approximately 0 degrees.

f. Auto trim and elevator available—Checked.

Place elevator control available mode selector switch to AUTO. Push the control stick forward and hold until elevator control available has stopped driving. Elevator available should read within the limits shown in figure 2-5. Release stick pressure and check elevator position. EPI should read 1.22 ($\pm$ 0.46) degrees down. Check that the aileron control available indicator reads HALF.

g. Force link forward—Checked.

Push forward on the control stick and apply sufficient force to actuate the force link. Check that the elevator control available mode selector switch returns to TO & LAND.

h. Elevator control available mode selector switch—MANUAL.

While elevator available is driving following the force link check, switch the elevator control available mode selector switch to MANUAL. Check that the elevator available stops driving.

i. Force link aft—Checked.

Pull back on the control stick and apply sufficient force to actuate the force link. Check that elevator mode selector switch returns to T.O. & LAND and elevator available begins to increase, then release the control stick.

j. Elevator control available mode selector switch—MANUAL.

k. Elevator control available manual adjust switch—INC, then DEC.

Check manual increase momentarily then decrease to minimum available.

l. Emergency increase available handle—Pulled and reset.

Pull handle out to first stop and check that the elevator control available mode selector switch has returned to T.O. & LAND and that aileron control available indicator reads FULL. Pull handle out to full travel and check that the elevator control available increases to at least 20 degrees. Push handle in and LOCK. Elevator available should return to minimum as handle is pushed in and then move toward full elevator available as handle is locked.

Failure to push the emergency increase elevator available handle in so that it locks can cause switching associated with the handle to be actuated by control stick motion.

m. Elevator position and available—Checked.

Check that the elevator available increases to 20 degrees and that elevator position drives to approximately 1.5 degrees up and remains there with the control stick in neutral.

n. Wing heavy control switch—ON.

o. Gain selector switch—AUTO.

p. Damper switches—ON.

Check that yaw damper warning and caution lamps go out.

q. Autopilot—Checked.

(1) Autopilot engage switches—ENGAGE.

Section II
Normal Procedures

T.O. 1B-58A-1

BEFORE TAXIING. (DSO READS) (CONT'D)

      (2) Autopilot poppet valves—Checked.

          (a) Apply a steady left force and check that the aileron autopilot servo can be overpowered; then apply an abrupt left wing down force to actuate the aileron poppet valve. The control stick should be free to move in aileron.

          (b) Apply a steady forward force to actuate the elevator autopilot poppet valve and note that the stick moves only slightly until the poppet valve actuates. The control stick should be free to move in elevator.

          (c) Autopilot trigger switch—CSS (depress to the first detent momentarily). The autopilot servos should re-engage.

          (d) Apply a steady right force and check that the aileron autopilot servo can be overpowered; then apply an abrupt right wing down force to actuate the aileron poppet valve. The control stick should be free to move in aileron.

          (e) Apply a steady force aft to actuate the elevator autopilot poppet valve and note that the stick moves only slightly until the poppet valve actuates. The control stick should be free to move in elevator.

      (3) Autopilot trigger switch—CSS (depress to the first detent).

      (4) Move control stick—Moved.

          Move control stick to check that autopilot has disengaged.

      (5) Release autopilot trigger switch—Released.

          With control stick in a position other than neutral, release autopilot trigger switch. Control stick should remain in that position.

      (6) Autopilot trigger switch—RELEASE (depress to the second detent).

          Depress the trigger switch to the second detent and check that the autopilot engage switches return to OFF.

  r. Yaw, pitch, and roll dampers—Checked.

     Individually turn each damper switch OFF then ON to check that there is no large engage transient or control surface displacement.

  s. Elevator—Checked. Set 1.5 degrees up.

     Move the control stick until the elevator position indicator reads zero with the ground observer reporting the control positions. Then set elevator position indicator 1.5 degrees up.

15. UHF command and TACAN radios—Checked. (P-DSO)

  a. Set function selector to COMM 1 and place the INTER, COMM, and TACAN mixing switches ON.

  b. Perform command radio (ARC-57) check:

     (1) Press radio control transfer button if radio control lamp is not lighted.

     (2) Check that channel indicator on the main instrument panel agrees with the channel indicator on the communication control panel.

     (3) Call tower for radio check and altimeter setting.

  c. Perform command radio (ARC-34) check: (DSO)

     Place function selector knob to COMM 2 position and call for radio check.

  d. Perform TACAN radio check:

     (1) Press ILS—TACAN control transfer button if indicator lamp is not lighted.

     (2) Select and identify TACAN station (if available).

     (3) Check that the course warning flag disappears from CDI. (Glide slope warning flag will remain in view.)

     (4) Check that bearing pointer on the BDH indicator points to appropriate bearing.

     (5) Check that the range warning flag on the BDH indicator disappears and the approximate distance to the station appears in the range indicator.

T.O. 1B-58A-1

**Section II
Normal Procedures**

BEFORE TAXIING. (DSO READS) (CONT'D)

    (6) Rotate the course set knob until the CDI is centered and TO or FROM appears in the TO-FROM indicator. Cross-check indication with bearing pointer for maximum difference of ±3 degrees.

    (7) Slowly rotate the course set knob in either direction from the course that centered the CDI until the CDI has reached full scale deflection. Check that the course in the course selector window has changed 10 ±2 degrees.

    (8) Select and identify ILS station (if available).

    (9) Check that the CDI and GSI warning flags disappear and that deflection of the indicators is correct for location of the ILS transmitters.

16. Instruments—Checked, altimeter set. (P-N-DSO)

   a. Check ram air temperature indicator for correct ambient temperature.
   b. Check mach indicator and turn and slip indicators for proper static condition.
   c. Check that attitude indicator warning flags are retracted and align indices. The miniature airplane should indicate approximately 3 degrees nose down.
   d. Check airspeed indicator at 40 ±5 knots.
   e. Check BDH indicator and J-4 system in coordination with navigator. Cross-check magnetic compass.
   f. Set altimeter to current altimeter setting.

When setting the altimeter, check that the 10,000 foot pointer is reading correctly. If the barometric pressure set knob is rotated until the barometric scale goes out of view and reappears, the altimeter will be approximately 10,000 feet in error even though the correct barometric setting appears on the barometric scale.

   g. Check angle-of-attack indicator warning flag retracted.
   h. Check vertical velocity for proper static condition.
   i. Check clock set and running.
   j. Reset accelerometer.
   k. Low altitude radar altimeter—ON, minimum altitude indexer set (P-N)
      Set minimum altitude index pointer to approximately 50 feet.

Note

- On airplanes prepared for normal training flights, proceed with the remainder of the BEFORE TAXIING checklist.

- On airplanes prepared for alert status, proceed to the COCKING checklist and place airplane on alert. The airplane will be refueled to the proper alert loading.

- On airplanes requiring maintenance, accomplish the AFTER LANDING checklist (starting with item 6), ENGINE SHUTDOWN, BEFORE LEAVING AIRPLANE, and POSTFLIGHT checklists.

17. Landing gear safety lockpins (4)—Removed. (GO)
   Instruct ground observer to remove the 4 landing gear safety lockpins.

18. Handgrip and canopy jettison handle safety pins (3)—Removed and stowed. (P-N-DSO)
   Carefully check safety pins to insure the complete safety pin has been removed from each handgrip.

2-27

Section II
Normal Procedures
T.O. 1B-58A-1

BEFORE TAXIING. (DSO READS) (CONT'D)

19. Hydraulic pressure and quantity—Checked.
    DSO will record quantity.
20. Anti-skid switch—ON.
21. Voice warning system—RESET, then ON (P), VWS. (DSO)
22. Landing gear safety lockpins (4) and canopy locks (3)—In sight.
23. Remove ground static wire, chocks and interphone—Removed. (GO)
24. IFF—STBY. (DSO)
25. Navigator and DSO—Ready to taxi. (N-DSO)

COCKING. (DSO READS)

This checklist prepares the airplane for normal scramble and SRP Power-off scramble.

Note

When the airplane is uncocked for maintenance/defueling, the following checklists will be accomplished prior to performing the COCKING checklist: the pilot's EXTERIOR INSPECTION, the pilot's, navigator's, and DSO's POWER-OFF INTERIOR INSPECTION, and the items flagged with an asterisk (*) in the pilot's and navigator's POWER-ON INTERIOR INSPECTION.

1. Pod fuel transfer—Checked. (Need not be accomplished after bravo or coco alert).
    Transfer a recognizable quantity of fuel from each pod tank to the aft tank to check transfer system.
2. Unnecessary electrical and electronic equipment—OFF. (P-N-DSO)
3. Cabin temperature control knob—Full CCW.
4. No. 1, 2, and 3 generator control switches—OFF.
5. Refrigeration unit selector knob—GRD CART.
6. No. 1, 2, 3, and 4 throttles—OFF.
7. Canopy seal lever—UNSEALED. (N)
8. Canopies—Open. (P-N-DSO)
9. Canopy jettison handle safety pin—Installed. (P-N-DSO)
10. External power switch—OFF.
11. Flight control power switch—ON.
12. Wing heavy control switch—ON.
13. Cartridge start switch—OFF.
14. Engine start switches—OFF.
15. Gain selector switch—AUTO.
16. Damper switches—ON.
17. Aileron control available mode selector switch—AUTO.
18. Elevator control available mode selector switch—TO & LAND.
19. Spike position switches—IN.
20. Anti-skid switch—ON.
21. IFF—STDBY. (DSO)
22. Manual UHF command radio frequencies—Set. (P-DSO)
23. UHF command radios—BOTH, channel selector knob set. (P-DSO)
24. TACAN radio—T/R, channel set, course selector set. (P-N)

2-28

COCKING. (DSO READS) (CONT'D)

25. Small weapon jettison switch—SAFE, safetied.
26. Warning and caution lamp indicator switch—GROUND CHECK.
27. Emergency increase elevator available handle—IN.
28. Stick trim selector switch—CONT STICK.
29. Heading selector switch—J-4.
30. Taxi and landing light switches—OFF.
31. Nose wheel steering ratio selector—TAXI.
32. Drag chute handle—In and vertical.
33. Parking brakes—Set.
34. Fire pull handles—In.
35. CG selector knob—Set.
    Set selector to 27.5 percent.
36. CG control knob—MANUAL.
37. Air refueling door switch—CLOSE.
38. Reservoir booster pump switch—NORM.
39. Aft tank to engine supply knob—ON.
40. Reservoir to manifold switches—NORM.
41. All other fuel switches—OFF, CLOSE or NORMAL.
42. IFR emergency hydraulic boost lever—Guarded OFF.
43. Windshield rain removal switch—OFF.
44. Windshield defog switch—DEC.
45. Engine anti-ice switch—OFF.
46. Pitot heat—OFF.
47. Air source selector knob—BOTH.
48. Air conditioning control mode selector knob—MAN.
49. Cabin pressure selector knob—NORM.
50. Pod and DECM power switch—AUTO LOAD REDUCTION.
51. Generator control switches—OFF.
52. A-C meter selector knob—L BUS.
53. Arm control switch—SAFE and sealed.
54. Arm power switch—NORM.
55. Emergency lighting switch—OFF (P), ON. (N-DSO)
56. Panel and flood lights—Set. (P-N-DSO)
57. Navigation light switches—BRIGHT and STEADY.
58. Map light switch—OFF.
59. Anti-collision light switches—ON.
60. Oxygen regulator—NORMAL and OFF. (P-N-DSO)
61. Auxiliary Flight Reference System power switches—ON. (N)
62. Thermal curtains—Checked, installed (if on alert). (P-N-DSO)
63. Fuse panels—Checked. (N-DSO)
64. Personal gear—Arranged. (P-N-DSO)
65. Battery switch—OFF.
66. CMF—Checked.
67. Canopy control lever—DOWN, then NEUT.
    When all crew members are clear of the canopies, move the canopy control lever in the nose wheel well to DOWN. When all canopies have closed, move the lever to NEUT and insert pin.
68. Canopy seal selector lever—As required.

Section II
Normal Procedures

COCKING. (DSO READS) (CONT'D)

69. Eternal power carts—Off.
70. Wheel chocks—In place.
71. Landing gear safety lock pins (4)—Removed.
72. No. 2 engine starter exhaust door—Open. (GO)

Note

Access to a cocked airplane will be in accordance with command directives.

UNCOCKING.

Each item in this checklist must be performed when the airplane is removed from alert status and will not be flown immediately by the alert crew. Perform this check as applicable before maintenance is performed while the airplane is on the alert line.

1. Canopy seal lever—Unsealed.
2. Canopy control lever—UP.
3. Battery switch—NORM.
4. Flight control power switch—OFF.
5. Damper switches—OFF.
6. Anti-skid switch—OFF.
7. IFF master control knob—OFF. (DSO)
8. UHF command radios mode selector knob—OFF. (P-DSO)
9. Navigation radio—OFF. (P-N)
10. AFRS power switches—OFF. (N)
11. Throttles—OFF.
12. Reservoir booster pump switch—OFF.
13. Aft tank to engine supply knob—OFF.
14. Reservoir to manifold switches—CLOSE.
15. Air conditioning control mode selector knob—OFF.
16. All interior and exterior lights—OFF. (P-N-DSO)
17. Battery switch—OFF.
18. Pod and small weapon inspection—Complete.
    a. Small weapon ready-safe switches (4)—SAFE.
    b. Small weapon ground safety pins—Installed.
- MB c. Pod release safety lockpin—Checked.
- TC d. Bomb pod ground safety lock—Installed.
- TC e. Arming control valve—SAFE.
- TC f. Fuel pod ground safety lock—Installed.
- TC g. Ground safety switch—RETARD (W-53).
19. Canopy locks—Installed.
20. Tail turret safety pin—Installed.
21. Landing gear safety lockpins (4)—Installed.

SCRAMBLE/SRP POWER-OFF SCRAMBLE.

Note

This scramble checklist is to be used for EWO and training launch of aircraft from cocked configuration. All items in the SCRAMBLE/SRP POWER-OFF SCRAMBLE checklist are the minimum requirements for a training scramble. BOLD FACE items are the minimum requirements to be accomplished for an EWO scramble takeoff. When time permits, all items on the SCRAMBLE/SRP POWER-OFF SCRAMBLE checklist should be accomplished.

The scramble procedure is a coordinated effort by all crew members and the ground crew. During these procedures, the pilot must be alert for signals from the ground observer as indicated in the checklist. If assistance is needed, the taxi light will be flashed to signal the ground observer to connect the interphone. The DSO is primarily concerned with communications procedures; however, he will assist the pilot by calling checklist items as soon as communication requirements are completed

Note

- When starting two engines simultaneously, if RPM stabilizes below 12 percent, place one start switch OFF and continue to start one engine at a time.

- If external starter air is not available, refer to "Alternate Engine Starting Procedures" — "Starting Engines With Cartridge Starter" this section.

---

1. **CANOPY COVER—REMOVED. (N-DSO-GO)**
   The DSO and navigator will release the upper hooks while the ground crew releases the lower buckles. All personnel will remove the cover and the ground crew will pull it clear of the airplane.

2. **BATTERY SWITCH AND EXTERNAL POWER—NORM AND ALERT.**

   #### Note

   - If the external power unit fails to operate, engine start can be accomplished using power from the battery for ignition. If external power is not available for engine start, start only one inboard engine and place the generator on the line before starting the other inboard engine and before proceeding with the checklist. Without external power, start cart air is being diverted from the engines to run both air conditioner packs.

   - If external starter air is not available, refer to "Alternate Engine Starting Procedures" —"Starting Engines With Cartridge Starter" this section.

   - When engine start is not required complete double asterisked (**) items of DEFCON 1/SRP POWER-ON COCKING CHECKLIST and continue using Defcon 1 procedures.

3. **ENGINE NO. 2 AND 3 START SWITCHES—GROUND.**

Do not start engines until the ground crew and entrance stand are clear of the inboard engines.

4. Oxygen— NORMAL and ON. (P-DSO)

Section II
Normal Procedures

T.O. 1B-58A-1

SCRAMBLE/SRP POWER-OFF SCRAMBLE. (CONT'D)

5. Personal gear—Connected. (P-DSO)
6. **AT 12 PERCENT RPM, NO. 2 AND 3 THROTTLES—IDLE THEN 85 PERCENT.**
   After EGT has peaked and begins to decrease, advance throttles to 85 percent rpm.
7. **PRIMARY AND UTILITY HYDRAULIC SYSTEMS—PRESSURE CHECKED, NO. 2 AND 3 PUMP CAUTION LAMPS—OFF.**
8. **NO. 2 AND 3 GENERATORS—EXCITED AND ON.**

Note

If the external power unit fails, No. 2 generator must be excited and on before No. 3 generator is placed on. If this is not done, the bus-tie button must be activated before No. 2 generator will supply power to the left bus.

9. **ENGINES NO. 1 AND 4 START SWITCHES—GROUND.**
10. **CANOPY—CLOSED AND LATCHED.**
    The pilot will close his canopy after receiving a visual signal from the ground observer that the navigator and DSO canopies are closed. The ground observer will signal by extending his left arm in front and the right arm over his head and then moving the right arm down to meet the left. This signal will be continued until the pilot closes his canopy. Closing of the pilot's canopy is the signal for the ground observer to remove starter and electrical connections, ground static wires, and chocks.
11. **AT 12 PERCENT RPM, NO. 1 AND 4 THROTTLES IDLE.**
    At 12 percent rpm, place No. 1 and 4 throttles beyond idle, then back to idle.
12. **ENGINE NO. 2 AND 3 THROTTLES—IDLE.**
    Bring No. 2 and 3 engines to idle after engines No. 1 and 4 are at idle rpm. Engines No. 2 and 3 coming to idle is the signal for the ground observer to close and latch No. 2 engine starter exhaust door.
13. **NO. 1 GENERATOR—EXCITED AND ON.**
14. **CANOPY SEAL LEVER—SEALED. (N)**
15. **AIR CONDITIONING PANEL—BOTH, RESET-TO-NORMAL AND AUTO.**
16. Electrical power and air conditioning—Normal.
17. Hydraulic pressure and quantity—Checked.
18. Engine start switches—Off.
19. VWS—Reset and On.
20. Handgrip Safety Pins (2)—Removed and Stowed
    (will not be accomplished for alert exercises). (P-N-DSO)
21. Canopy Jettison Handle Safety Pin—Removed and Stowed. (P-N-DSO)
22. **TAXI LIGHT—ON.**
23. **BRAKES AND STEERING—CHECKED AND ENGAGED.**
24. **TURN AND SLIP, BDHI AND ATTITUDE INDICATORS—CHECKED.**
25. **FLIGHT CONTROLS—CHECKED FREE.**
26. **WARNING AND CAUTION LAMPS—CHECKED.**
27. **ANTI-ICE, DEFOG, RAIN REMOVAL AND PITOT HEAT—AS REQUIRED.**
28. **IFF—NORM. (DSO)**
29. Instruments—Checked and Set.
30. Radio Call—Completed Before Takeoff.
31. **TAKEOFF DATA—REVIEWED. (P-N-DSO)**

Note

Proceed with TAKEOFF checklist.

DEFCON 1/SRP POWER-ON COCKING CHECKLIST. (DSO READS)

This checklist prepares the airplane for scramble from either DEFCON 1 or SRP Power-on posture.
  1. Parking brakes—Set.
  2. Anti-ice, defog, rain removal, and pitot heat—OFF.
  3. No. 1 and 3 generator control switches—OFF.
  4. No. 1, 3, and 4 throttles—OFF.

Note

Flashing the taxi light will be the signal for the ground crew to connect the interphone.

  5. Cabin temperature control knob—Full CCW.
**6. ARC-57 and TACAN radios—OFF. (P-N-DSO)
**7. IFF master control power knob—OFF. (DSO)
**8. Flight control power switch—OFF.
  9. Refrigeration unit selector knob—GRD CART.
  10. Air conditioning control mode selector knob—MAN.
  11. Ground, connect starter and electrical power carts and place electrical power on the line— Connected and on. (GO)
  12. Ground air conditioner/heater—Connected (if required). (GO)
  13. Battery and external power—NORM and ALERT.
  14. No. 2 generator control switch—OFF.
  15. No. 2 throttle—OFF.
  16. No. 2 engine starter exhaust door—Open. (GO)
  17. A-C meter selector knob—L BUS.
  18. Canopy seal lever—UNSEALED. (N)
  19. Canopies—Climatic. (P-N-DSO)
  20. Ground, install wheel chocks—In place. (GO)
  21. Handgrip safety pins (2)—Installed. (P-N-DSO)
  22. Canopy jettison handle safety pin—Installed. (P-N-DSO)
  23. Communications panel—Set. (N-DSO)

Note

Take off data should be revised as indicated by changing runway temperature, field pressure altitude, and surface wind conditions.

**24. Battery switch—OFF.
**25. Reservoir booster pump switch—OFF.
**26. Aft tank to engine supply knob—OFF.
**27. Anticollision and navigation lights—OFF.
**28. Voice warning system—OFF.
**29. Pull following fuses to deactivate equipment. (DSO)
   a. Turn and slip indicator 1 amp fuse.
   b. Spike position control amplifier 1 amp fuse.
   c. Engine fuel flow indicator 1 amp fuses (4).

Section II
Normal Procedures

T.O. 1B-58A-1

DEFCON 1/SRP POWER-ON SCRAMBLE CHECKLIST.

1. BATTERY SWITCH—NORM.
2. RESERVOIR BOOSTER PUMP SWITCH—NORM.
3. AFT TANK TO ENGINE SUPPLY KNOB—ON.
4. ANTICOLLISION AND NAVIGATION LIGHTS—ON AND STEADY.
5. GROUND READY TO START, STARTER AIR SUPPLIED—READY. (GO)

Note

If starter air is not available, refer to "Alternate Engine Starting Procedures"—"Starting Engine With Cartridge Starter" this section.

6. NO. 2 AND 3 START SWITCHES—GROUND.
7. AT 12 PERCENT RPM, NO. 2 AND 3 THROTTLES—IDLE THEN 85 PERCENT.
8. NO. 2 AND 3 GENERATORS—EXCITED AND ON.

Note

If the external power unit fails, No. 2 generator must be excited and on before No. 3 generator is placed on. If this is not done, the bus-tie button must be activated before No. 2 generator will supply power to the left bus.

9. NO. 1 AND 4 START SWITCHES—GROUND.
10. CANOPIES—CLOSED AND LATCHED. (DSO-N-P)
11. GROUND DISCONNECT—DISCONNECTED. (GO)
12. AT 12 PERCENT RPM, NO. 1 AND 4 THROTTLES—IDLE.
    At 12 percent rpm, place No. 1 and 4 throttles beyond idle, then back to idle.
13. ENGINE NO. 2 AND 3 THROTTLES—IDLE.
    Bring No. 2 and 3 engines to idle after engines No. 1 and 4 are at idle rpm. Engines No. 2 and 3 coming to idle is the signal for the ground observer to close and latch No. 2 engine starter exhaust door.
14. NO. 1 GENERATOR—EXCITED AND ON.
15. AIR CONDITIONING PANEL—BOTH, RESET-TO-NORMAL AND AUTO.
16. FLIGHT CONTROL POWER-SWITCH—ON.
17. ARC-57 AND TACAN RADIOS—BOTH AND T/R(P), T/R(N), BOTH. (DSO)
18. IFF—NORM. (DSO)
19. CANOPY SEAL LEVER—SEALED. (N)
20. Engine start switches—OFF.
21. HYDRAULIC PRESSURE AND QUANTITY—CHECKED.
22. Voice warning system—Reset and ON.
23. Handgrip safety pins (2)—Removed and stowed. (P-N-DSO)
24. Canopy jettison handle safety pin—Removed and stowed. (P-N-DSO)
25. BRAKES—CHECKED.
26. NOSE WHEEL STEERING—ENGAGED.
27. BDHI AND ATTITUDE INDICATORS—CHECKED.
28. FLIGHT CONTROLS—CHECKED FREE.
29. WARNING AND CAUTION LAMPS—CHECKED.
30. ANTI-ICE, DEFOG, RAIN REMOVAL, AND PITOT HEAT—AS REQUIRED.
31. Fuses—Installed. (DSO)

Note

Proceed with TAKEOFF checklist.

Section II
Normal Procedures

TAXIING. (DSO READS)

Release the brakes and use engines as necessary for taxiing. If the airplane does not appear to roll free after brake release, investigate for a possible source of the restraint before increasing power above the anticipated normal levels. Care should be exercised to prevent increasing power to the point that the airplane rotates about a restrained main landing gear. Depress the NWS button and utilize the steerable nose wheel to maintain direction control.

> **CAUTION**
>
> - If one main gear is restrained, increased power can develop torsional loads which may cause structural damage.
>
> - Painted areas on runways, taxiways and ramps are significantly more slippery than non-painted areas, particularly when wet. In addition, painted areas sometimes serve as condensation surfaces and it is possible to have wet, frosty, or even icy conditions on these areas when the overall weather condition is dry.
>
> - When conditions of snow or ice exist, the approach ends of the runway are usually more slippery than other areas because of the melting and refreezing of the ice and snow.

minimum turning radius and ground clearance

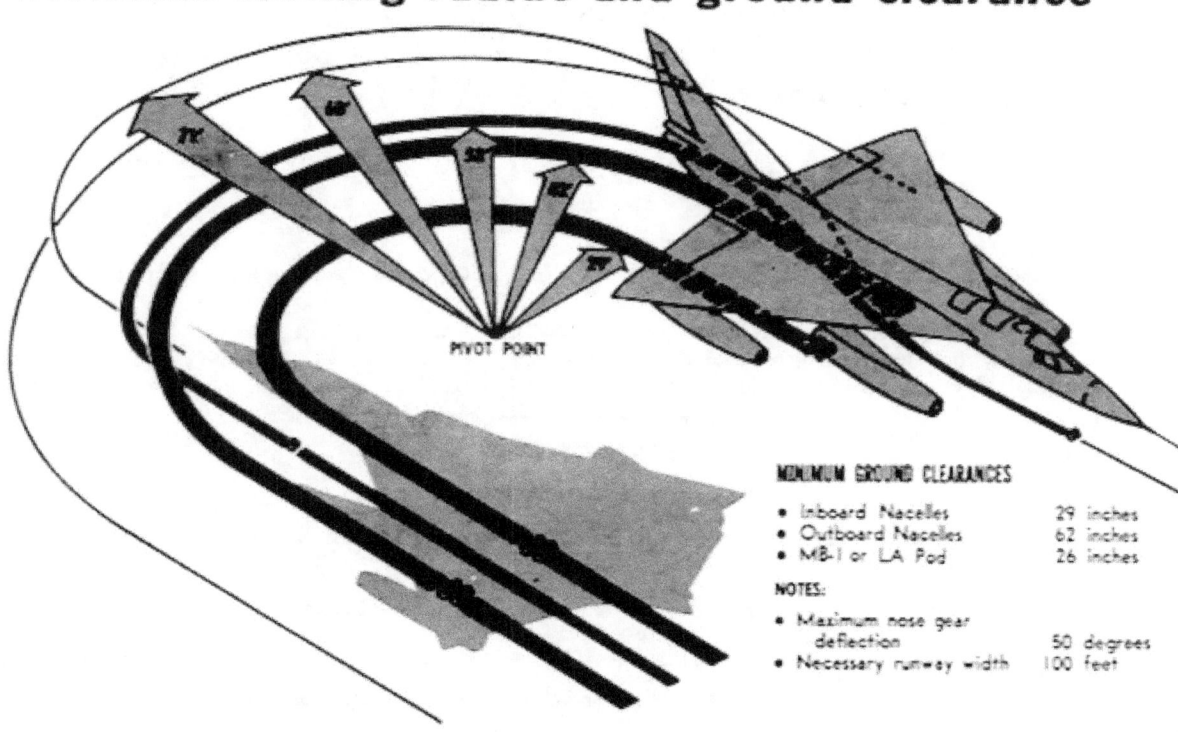

MINIMUM GROUND CLEARANCES

- Inboard Nacelles — 29 inches
- Outboard Nacelles — 62 inches
- MB-1 or LA Pod — 26 inches

NOTES:
- Maximum nose gear deflection — 50 degrees
- Necessary runway width — 100 feet

Figure 2-6.

Section II
Normal Procedures

T.O. 1B-58A-1

TAXIING. (DSO READS) (CONT'D)

Refer to figure 2-6 for minimum turning radius and ground clearances. While taxiing, check the following:

1. Brakes and steering—Checked.
    After initial roll, apply brakes and check operation. Check that steering is engaged.

> **CAUTION**
>
> Braking in turns should be avoided whenever possible to minimize torsional loads on the main landing gear.

2. Hydraulic pressure and quantity—Checked.
    Check utility and primary system hydraulic pressure indicators for normal pressure and quantity at frequent intervals while taxiing. Quantity may change slightly with a change in system temperature. A decrease in quantity indicates a loss of hydraulic fluid and the system should be checked prior to takeoff.

3. Nose wheel steering—Checked.
    Operate rudder pedals to check that nose wheel steering is engaged and operating properly. Straighten path with nose wheel steering, then disengage briefly to check for dragging brakes. Place nose wheel steering (NWS) ratio selector switch to TO & LAND, then engage steering and check for reduced steering authority by moving the rudder pedals. Switch to TAXI mode.

4. Turn-and-slip, BDHI, and attitude indicators—Checked.
    Check the turn-and-slip indicator for proper turn indications while taxiing. Check that BDHI checks closely with the magnetic compass heading and that both attitude indicators have erected.

5. Navigator and DSO fuse panels—Checked. (N-DSO)
6. D-C voltages—Checked. (DSO)

BEFORE LINEUP. (DSO READS)

1. Parking brakes—Set.
2. Gain selector switch—AUTO.
3. Damper switches—ON.
4. Aileron control available—AUTO and FULL.
    Check that aileron control available switch is in AUTO position and that aileron control available indicator reads FULL.
5. Elevator control available mode selector switch—TO & LAND and 20 degrees.
    Check that elevator control available mode selector switch is in TO & LAND position and that elevator available indicator shows 20 degrees available.

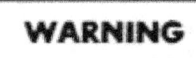

Full elevator deflection may not be available during takeoff unless switch is in the TO & LAND position.

6. Aileron and rudder trim neutral; elevator trim 1.5 degrees up—Checked.
7. Heading selector switch—J-4.
8. Instruments—Checked and set. (P-N-DSO)
    Set altimeter to current altimeter setting and check at a known elevation. The altimeter should read known elevation ±75 feet.
9. Low altitude radar altimeter—Checked and set.
    Push-to-test radar altimeter. Check that indicator reads 100 (±10) feet and that low altitude warning lamps go out. Then set minimum altitude index pointer to desired altitude.
10. Fuel system:
    a. Pod fuel transfer—Checked.
        Transfer a recognizable quantity of fuel from each pod tank to the aft tank to check transfer system

BEFORE LINEUP. (DSO READS) (CONT'D)

    b. Fuel panel—Configuration set and reported.

        Fuel will be adjusted to the desired cg for takeoff. Pilot will set fuel panel to the planned takeoff configuration and report panel settings, fuel quantities, and cg indication to the DSO.

11. Generator configuration—Checked.

    Check that generator No. 1 is supplying the left bus and generator No. 3 is supplying the right bus, with generator No. 2 on standby. Check that generator frequencies are approximately 400 cycles, voltages approximately 115.

12. Anticollision lights—As required.
13. Hydraulic pressures and quantities—Checked.
14. Warning and caution lamps—Off.
15. Takeoff data—Reviewed. (P-DSO)

    Review takeoff data corrected for changes in runway conditions, weather information, and airplane configuration.

16. Anti-ice, defog, rain removal, and pitot heat—As required.

CAUTION

Pitot heat should not be left on for long periods of time during ground operation to prevent overheating.

17. IFF master control knob—NORM or LOW (mode and code as briefed). (DSO)
18. Navigator and DSO—Ready for takeoff, tables stowed. (N-DSO)

    Check that navigator and DSO station checks are completed and that crew members are ready for takeoff.

MINIMUM REACTION COCKING CHECKLIST. (DSO READS)

Note

The SCRAMBLE/SRP POWER-OFF SCRAMBLE checklist will be completed prior to accomplishing the MINIMUM REACTION COCKING CHECKLIST and the MINIMUM REACTION SCRAMBLE CHECKLIST.

1. Parking brakes—Set.
2. Anti-ice, defog, rain removal and pitot heat—OFF.
3. No. 2 throttle—Set.

    During extended periods of operation with only one inboard engine operating, the electronic equipment temperature must be closely monitored to avoid overheat conditions. It may be necessary to increase rpm to prevent overheat.

Note

When operating inboard engines at or above 85 percent rpm in static conditions with the cabin temperature control rheostat set between mid position and full cold, the air conditioning system may vent water from the air-to-water heat exchanger into the engine pylon and spill over the aft engine section.

4. No. 1 and 3 generators—OFF.
5. No. 1, 3, and 4 throttles—OFF.
6. Takeoff data—Revised.

    Takeoff data should be revised as dictated by changing gross weight, runway temperature, field pressure altitude and surface wind conditions.

Section II
Normal Procedures

T.O. 1B-58A-1

MINIMUM REACTION SCRAMBLE CHECKLIST.

1. NO. 2 THROTTLE—85 PERCENT.

> **CAUTION**
>
> Electronic equipment that requires air conditioning is still on. If starting is delayed, do not leave the refrigeration unit selector in GRD CART for more than 90 seconds.

2. AIR CONDITIONING CONTROL MODE SELECTOR KNOB—MAN.
3. CABIN TEMPERATURE CONTROL KNOB—FULL CCW
4. REFRIGERATION UNIT SELECTOR KNOB—GRD CART.
5. NO. 3 START SWITCH—GROUND.
6. AT 12 PERCENT RPM, NO. 3 THROTTLE—IDLE THEN 85 PERCENT.
   After EGT has peaked and begins to decrease, advance throttle to 85 percent.
7. NO. 1 AND 4 STARTER SWITCHES—GROUND.
   Start the outboard engines after No. 3 engine has reached 85 percent rpm.
8. AT 12 PERCENT RPM, NO 1 AND 4 THROTTLES—IDLE.
   At 12 percent rpm, place No. 1 and 4 throttles beyond IDLE, then back to IDLE.
9. PRIMARY AND UTILITY HYDRAULIC SYSTEMS—PRESSURE CHECKED, CAUTION LAMPS—CHECKED.
10. AIR CONDITIONING PANEL—BOTH, RESET-TO-NORMAL, AND AUTO.
11. NO. 1 AND 3 GENERATORS—EXCITED AND ON.
12. Engine start switches—OFF.
13. ANTI-ICE, DEFOG, RAIN REMOVAL AND PITOT HEAT—AS REQUIRED.
14. Takeoff data—Reviewed. (P-N-DSO)

Note

Taxi when cleared and proceed with the TAKEOFF checklist.

TAKEOFF.

The characteristics of the airplane during takeoff are conventional for a tricycle gear, four-engine airplane in the ground run attitude; however, due to the lift characteristics of the delta wing, rotation to a high wing angle of attack (approximately 14 degrees) is required to take off at design takeoff speed. This is a higher angle of attack than that required for takeoff with a conventional airplane. Acceleration during the takeoff roll may be higher than experienced in other airplanes; therefore, timely reaction to abnormal or emergency conditions is essential. Strict adherence to established procedures is required to produce the performance indicated in Appendix I. Refer to Section III for takeoff emergency procedures. Runway available and obstacle clearance are the prime factors to be considered in planning each takeoff. Aircraft gross weight and thrust requirements for takeoff can be determined by using takeoff and climb charts in Appendix I. Takeoffs are accomplished using MAX A/B, MIN A/B or MIL power. The most current runway temperature, field pressure altitude, wind direction and velocity, and runway surface condition must be used in computing these data. Final takeoff data check will be made during the BEFORE LINEUP checklist.

TAKEOFF MONITORING PROCEDURE (S_1/S_2).

The high acceleration of the airplane during takeoff roll reduces the time element to a point where crew coordination and crew reaction time are very critical. Because of the high acceleration rate, conventional instrumentation for monitoring airplane performance has its limitations in that the loss of an afterburner or a dragging brake may not be detected by reference to the airspeed alone. The decision to abort or continue takeoff should normally be based on airplane condition in addition to the indicated airspeed. The takeoff monitoring system is comprised of a single decision speed (S_1) which is based on a fixed value of 132 KIAS. This value is adjusted for wind. Airplane acceleration is timed from brake release to expiration of a precomputed time. The pilot compares the indicated airspeed with the precomputed speed and decides whether to continue or abort the takeoff. Takeoff is committed above S_1 speed/time.

Note

- For rolling takeoffs, four seconds will be subtracted from computed S_1 time.
- When rotation speed is less than S_1 speed use rotation speed as decision speed.

2-38

Section II
Normal Procedures

takeoff typical

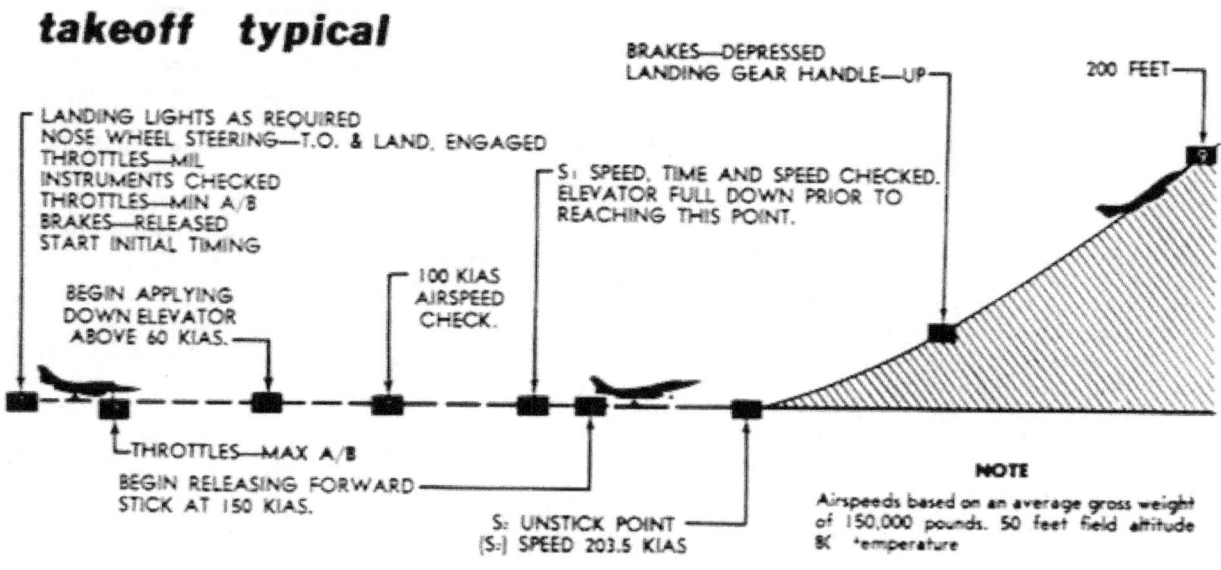

Figure 2-7.

PROCEDURES AND TECHNIQUE.

For takeoff from a static position, after lineup for takeoff the pilot will hold the brakes while performing the takeoff checklist. Place the nose wheel steering in T.O. & LAND and engage steering.

> **CAUTION**
>
> If it is necessary to set the parking brakes after lineup for takeoff, they will be released and the airplane will be allowed to roll forward to insure that brakes released properly. Damage to the landing gear could result if the brakes did not release simultaneously at high power settings.

Advance the throttle to MIL power setting and monitor the engine instruments to check that rpm, EGT, and oil pressure do not exceed limits and that pressure ratio, nozzle position and fuel flow correspond with precomputed data. For use of afterburner on takeoffs, advance throttles to MIN A/B and check for light-off as indicated by an increase in fuel flow and nozzle position. For MIN A/B takeoff, determine highest nozzle position observed on all four engines and advance throttles as required on other engines for equal nozzle position on all four engines. Release the brakes. For MAX A/B takeoff, advance the throttles to MAX A/B and check fuel flow and nozzle position increases to precomputed values. The procedures for rolling takeoffs are the same as for takeoff from a static position except that the throttles are advanced to MIL after the airplane is aligned with the runway. In addition, the MIN A/B step is eliminated to insure a more accurate acceleration check. Above 60 KIAS, gradually apply forward stick in such a manner that full down elevator will be attained prior to S_1 speed. This procedure is not required when rotation speed is below computed S_1 speed.

> **WARNING**
>
> Do not apply abrupt down elevator during takeoff roll to prevent damage to the airplane structure.

The DSO will initiate S_1 timing procedures at brake release for static takeoffs and when throttles are placed in MIL for rolling takeoffs. At 100 knots the pilot and DSO will cross-check the indicated airspeed.

Section II
Normal Procedures

T.O. 1B-58A-1

Note

With a steady headwind, when the DSO's airspeed indicator reads 100 knots, the pilot's airspeed indicator should read between 81 and 109 knots. Excessive variation is reason to abort the takeoff and have a check made of the airspeed system. However, consideration should be given to wind direction and to gusty wind conditions at the time the variation is noted.

Approximately three seconds before the end of the computed S_1 time, the DSO will announce over the interphone "S_1 speed—NOW," with the word "now" being transmitted at the end of the time interval. The pilot will check his airspeed and decide to continue or abort the takeoff, based on time/speed relationship. If the minimum acceptable airspeed has not been reached or an emergency occurs prior to expiration of S_1 time, the takeoff will be aborted. Refer to Section III for aborted takeoff. If the minimum acceptable speed has been attained at the end of the S_1 timing period, the takeoff is committed. Refer to Section III for engine failure during takeoff.

Note

Except under emergency conditions:

- On slippery runways, takeoff will not be attempted when minimum aerodynamic control speed (ground run attitude) is more than 15 knots above S_1 speed.

- On dry runways, takeoffs will not be attempted when minimum control speed is higher than S_1 speed. Minimum control speed will be equal to or below S_1 speed when the following conditions are met:

  1. Crosswind 25 knots or less
  2. Temperature —20°F or greater
  3. Pressure altitude —500 feet or higher.

Refer to Appendix I for minimum control speeds when any of these conditions cannot be met.

At 150 knots gradually release forward stick pressure to attain neutral elevator. The nose wheel will be kept in contact with the runway until 15 knots below computed S_2 speed. At this point, gently apply back stick until the airplane starts to rotate, then smoothly increase back stick to rotate the airplane to the takeoff attitude and allow the airplane to fly off the ground as S_2 speed is reached.

A verbal alert will be given by the DSO that rotation speed is approaching/attained. This alert is intended as a cross-check only. Rotation on DSO indicated airspeed is subject to secondary pitot-static system deviations contained in figure 1-37.

WARNING

- Rotation to the correct angle of attack at the proper speed and rate is important. Premature rotation, rotating late, or rotating to a low angle of attack increases ground roll and may result in exceeding tire limit speed. Refer to Section V for tire limit speed.

- Over rotation can result in an excessive nose high attitude from which recovery may be impossible.

CAUTION

Abrupt application of back stick to rotate the airplane will unnecessarily increase the load on the main landing gear and tires.

The main landing gear will unstick as the wing angle of attack reaches approximately 14 degrees.

TAKEOFF AT LIGHT GROSS WEIGHTS.

When taking off at light gross weights (below 130,000 pounds) with MAX A/B power a pitch-up and reduced nose wheel steering effectiveness may be experienced. This is due to the nose-up moment created by the underslung engines and the aft cg shift due to partially filled fuel tanks. Under these conditions it may be necessary to apply forward stick to minimize the pitch-up and increase nose wheel steering effectiveness. Refer to Section V for down elevator limitations during ground operations.

CROSSWIND TAKEOFFS.

For crosswind takeoff data refer to Appendix I. The weathervaning effect of a crosswind on this airplane in the ground run attitude is similar to that of other tricycle gear airplanes. It is more pronounced for the return component and upper pod configurations than for the TCP and MB or LA configurations. Directional control in a crosswind can normally be maintained by using nose wheel steering. In extreme crosswind conditions at low speed, particularly on slippery runways, the use of asymmetric thrust or braking may be necessary to assist the nose wheel steering. The use of asymmetric thrust or braking should be held to a minimum since the ground roll will be increased.

An increase in rudder deflection will be required when the nose wheel steering becomes ineffective or is disengaged. This will occur above 150 knots when forward stick pressure is reduced and steering becomes ineffective. The speeds shown in figure 2-13 for landing attitude are also applicable to takeoff attitude. Upon rotation to the takeoff attitude, a large amount of aileron deflection is required to maintain wings level during operation in a crosswind. The yawing moment caused by the aileron deflection is in the direction to add to the weather vane effect. Therefore, higher speed is required for directional control in the takeoff attitude than in the ground run attitude where aileron control is not required to maintain wings level. The low roll clearance at high angles of attack should be noted by referring to "Miscellaneous Operational Limitations", Section V.

Note

If S_2 speed is based on minimum aerodynamic control speed due to a crosswind, the three and four engine ground run must be computed for the new speed to insure that sufficient runway is available in event of loss of an engine.

TAKEOFF ON A SLIPPERY RUNWAY.

For takeoff on a slippery runway the reduced stopping capability must be considered in the pre-mission planning phase. Refer to Appendix I, Part 2 to determine the RCR (runway condition reading) "stopping factor" to be applied to the abort distance for takeoff on a slippery runway. For runway conditions other than dry, with runway condition readings greater than 12, an RCR of 12 will be used in computing takeoff. If no RCR is available, use 12 for wet runways and 5 for icy runways.

The procedures for takeoff on a slippery runway are the same as for a dry runway except that in event of an abort, stopping capability is based on reliance of the drag chute.

Note

- If a skid is detected at a higher power setting on initial runup, the brakes should be released and normal takeoff initiated.
- On slippery runways, nose wheel steering effectiveness is considerably reduced and skidding of the nose wheels can easily result from oversteering.

During operations in a crosswind, the airplane may tend to drift to the downwind side of the runway due to the aerodynamic force produced by the crosswind. In this event it may be necessary to induce a slight skid by yawing into the wind so that a frictional force is produced at the wheels to overcome the aerodynamic force effect.

EWO TAKEOFF AND CLIMBOUT.

Special procedures and charts are given for EWO takeoff and climbout to avoid having to off-load fuel and/or reposition the alert force from the optimum end of the runway. These procedures lack the conservatism present in normal training procedures and should not be used except in EWO conditions, and then only if use of normal procedures does not permit takeoff and/or climbout.

Takeoff distances may be shortened by taking off at S_2 speed derived from "Takeoff Distances, EWO ONLY," Appendix I, however, the total distance (from brake release) to clear an obstacle will be greater than when using S_2 speed, Scale B, due to the lower rate of climb at the lower airspeed.

As takeoff distances approach the runway length, proper rotation speed becomes critical. The aerodynamic drag of the airplane is much less in the three point ground run attitude than when the aircraft is rotated to the takeoff attitude.

Climb at these speeds will result in high pitch angles. At cold temperatures pitch angles as high as 25 degrees may occur. Under some conditions climb at liftoff IAS would result in angles of attack greater than 17 degrees. Do not exceed 17 degrees angle of attack. Allow IAS to increase to hold angle of attack at or just below 17 degrees.

Use of these procedures will not ensure minimum aerodynamic control speed or takeoff below tire limit speed. Under EWO conditions, the tire limit speed may be extended to 260 knots ground speed. If the normal 233 knot ground speed limitations is exceeded, tire failure may occur on a subsequent takeoff. Takeoff and climbout at S_2 speed from figure "TAKEOFF DISTANCES—EWO ONLY," will not insure 300 fpm rate of climb on three engines. Refer to Appendix I for EWO takeoff and climbout charts.

TAKEOFF CHECKLIST. (DSO READS)

To perform the takeoff, accomplish the following steps. For MIL power takeoffs, steps 5 and 7 will be omitted. For MIN A/B power takeoffs, step 7 will be omitted. For rolling takeoffs steps 5 and 6 will be omitted.

Note

For rolling takeoffs, the airplane will be aligned with the runway at normal taxi power and speeds.

1. Landing Lights—As required.

Section II
Normal Procedures

TAKEOFF CHECKLIST. (DSO READS) (CONT'D)

2. Nose wheel steering—TO & LAND and Engaged.
    Depress and hold nose wheel steering button until rotation.
3. Throttles—MIL.
    For rolling takeoffs, the pilot response will be given the instant the throttles are placed in MIL to assure accurate S_1 timing. The DSO will initiate S_1 timing upon the pilot's response.

Note

For rolling takeoffs, four seconds will be subtracted from computed S_1 time.

4. Instruments—Checked.
5. Throttles—MIN A/B.
    For MIN A/B takeoff, adjust throttles for equal nozzle position on all four engines.
6. Brakes—Released.
    For takeoffs from a static position, pilot response will be given at instant of brake release to assure accurate S_1 timing. DSO will initiate S_1 timing upon the pilot's response.
7. Throttles—MAX A/B.
    Except under EWO conditions, planned A/B power takeoffs will be aborted if an afterburner fails to light off prior to takeoff roll or goes out prior to S_1 speed/time check.

Note

Above 60 KIAS, gradually apply forward stick in such a manner that full down elevator will be attained prior to S_1 speed.

8. Airspeed checks—Announced as required. (DSO)
    - 100 knots now. (DSO)
        The DSO will give a warning approximately 10 knots before check speed is reached by stating over the interphone "100 knots—now" with word "now" being transmitted at 100 knots IAS. With a steady headwind, when the DSO's airspeed indicator reads 100 knots the pilot's airspeed indicator should read between 81 and 109 knots. Excessive variation is reason to abort the takeoff and have a check made of the airspeed system. However, consideration should be given to wind direction and to gusty wind conditions at the time the variation is noted.
    - S_1 speed now. (DSO)
        Approximately three seconds before the end of the computed time interval, the DSO will announce over the interphone "S_1 speed—now" with the word "now" being transmitted at the end of the time interval. The pilot will check his airspeed and decide to continue or abort the takeoff, based on time/speed relationship and airplane condition.
    - Monitor rotation speed now. (DSO)
        Immediately prior to computed rotation speed, the DSO will announce "Monitor rotation speed—now," with "now" being transmitted at the indicated rotation speed. Decision to rotate will be made by pilot on his airspeed indication.

Note

At 150 knots gradually release forward stick pressure to attain neutral elevator.

AFTER TAKEOFF. (DSO READS)

Note

Only circled items will be accomplished after low altitude tactical operation.

After the airplane is definitely airborne and during transition to climb, accomplish the following:

1. Brakes—Depressed.
   Depress the pedals (minimum 2 seconds) to brake the wheels before retracting the landing gear.
2. Landing gear handle—UP.
   Place the landing gear handle in the UP position; check that the gear position indicator and warning lamps, and the angle-of-attack indexer lamps go out.

WARNING

During takeoff, particularly at heavy gross weight, the aircrew must closely monitor airplane performance to insure normal acceleration and positive rate of climb. Care must be exercised to insure that proper technique is used in aircraft rotation to takeoff attitude. Over-rotation or premature or excessive reduction in power could result in an extremely nose high attitude from which recovery may not be possible.

CAUTION

If it becomes necessary to depress the landing gear downlock override button in order to move the landing gear handle to the UP position, a malfunctioning landing gear safety switch may be the cause. In this case, the anti-skid system will not be automatically de-energized and depressing the brake pedals will not stop wheel rotation. If this condition arises, position the anti-skid switch to OFF and then apply the brakes for at least two seconds prior to retracting the landing gear.

3. Engine instruments—Checked.
   Check that the following engine instrument indications are within operational limits: rpm, EGT, fuel flow, nozzle position, pressure ratio and oil pressure.
4. Landing gear handle—PRESS REL.
   Move the landing gear handle to the PRESS REL position after gear is up and prior to reaching 300 knots.
5. Throttles—MIL.
   Reduce power setting to MIL at 300 to 350 knots IAS.
6. Elevator available mode switch—AUTO.
   The elevator available should not decrease below approximately 1.25 degrees and the aileron control available changes to HALF.
7. Fuel configuration—Set.
8. Hydraulic pressure and quantity—Checked.
   Check that hydraulic pressure indicators show normal pressure, and that hydraulic pump low pressure caution lamps are out. Check hydraulic quantity. Utility system quantity will be slightly lower after landing gear has retracted.
9. Thermal curtains—Closed. (P-DSO) (EWO only)
   Close thermal curtains after climb configuration is established.
10. Oxygen and cabin altimeter—Checked. (P-N-DSO)
11. IFF—Checked. (DSO)

Section II
Normal Procedures

T.O. 1B-58A-1

AFTER TAKEOFF. (DSO READS) (CONT'D)

Note

- After takeoff, the TACAN should be cross-checked with ground radar or airborne radar. When using TACAN for instrument departures, penetrations, or letdowns, utilize airborne radar monitor or ground radar monitor when possible to verify TACAN bearing information.
- As soon after takeoff as flight conditions permit, positive operation of the IFF should be established with an Air Traffic Control Facility if the route of flight will require an operative IFF. Consult appropriate FLIP documents for IFF/SIF traffic control requirements and procedures.

(12) Altimeter—Reset. (P-N-DSO)
Reset altimeter in accordance with appropriate FLIP enroute supplement and/or planning document.

CLIMB.

After takeoff, accelerate to climb airspeed (best climb airspeed is 425 knots IAS). Maintain this speed until mach number 0.9 is reached and continue climb at this mach number. Refer to climb charts in Appendix I for climb performance.

LEVELOFF. (DSO READS)

1. Heading selector switch—J-4.
   Check the heading and attitude indicators for the proper indications.
2. Station check—Completed. (P-N-DSO)
   At leveloff and at hourly intervals the crew will perform a station check.
3. ARC-110—ON. (DSO)
4. MD-7 master switch—STBY, lamps (3) press-to-test. (DSO)
5. ALR-12—ON and Checked. (DSO)
   After the system has been placed in operation, monitor for noise inputs. If excess noise is present that the crew cannot isolate, refer to the ALR-12 Noise Elimination portion of the DSO's CRUISE Checklist, Section VIII.
6. ALQ-16's—ON, confidence checked, STBY. (DSO)
   Turn all ALQ-16's to standby, cam selector on briefed cam. After 3 minutes warmup, turn power knob ON, complete confidence check then return to STBY.

CRUISE.

After transition to cruise follow the mission flight plan, paying particular attention to power settings, IAS/mach altitude, and fuel management. Refer to "Fuel Supply System," Section VII, for fuel management procedures. The pilot and DSO should monitor the mach-monitor indicator lamp for proper indications during subsonic and supersonic cruise.

WARNING

If the lamp lights at speeds below Mach No. 0.95, switch to LOW SPEED standby gains. If the lamp lights at speeds above Mach No. 1.55, switch to HIGH SPEED standby gains. Continue the flight on standby gains observing the restrictions outlined in Section VII.

The wing heavy control system should be on and particular attention should be given to keeping the airplane trimmed with the aileron-rudder neutral trim indicator lamp lighted. When the aileron-rudder neutral trim lamp is lighted, the ball in the turn-and-slip indicator should be centered. Then, rudder displacement induced by operation of the wing heavy control system as a function of lateral acceleration will be indicated to the pilot on the rudder position indicator. If the ball of the turn-and-slip indicator is not centered, the pilot should not attempt to center it using trim unless wing heaviness is noted to build up. A buildup of wing heaviness would be indicated by an increase in aileron to maintain wings level or by an increase in rudder deflection as noted on the rudder position indicator. If the turn-and-slip indicator is misaligned, attempting to keep the ball centered will result in wing heaviness buildup. If wing heaviness is noted to build up while the aileron-rudder neutral trim lamp is lighted, the wing heavy control switch should be turned OFF and the ball maintained in the center. If sideslip is allowed for extended periods of time, fuel will shift in the direction of the slip and will cause wing heaviness. Sideslip may develop as a result of slight thrust variations in the engines during stabilized cruise. Other causes may induce random sideslipping. Reduce all such sideslip as soon as possible using rudder trim. If some fuel shifting does occur due to unnoticed sideslip, maintain wings level using aileron trim if subsonic. Refer to "Wing Heaviness", Section VI for the procedure to be followed when flying at supersonic speeds.

WARNING

Caution must be exercised during turns at supersonic speeds when appreciable aileron trim is required for wings level flight (indicating a heavy wing). During such turns, the increased "g" force acting on the unbalanced fuel load creates a rolling moment on the airplane. This may require large aileron deflections in order to remain in the turn or to roll out. Therefore, use shallow bank angles if it is necessary to turn into a heavy wing at supersonic speeds.

Note

During autopilot flight, the stick trim switch (for aileron trim) is operative only during control stick steering. The rudder trim switch, however, is operative at all times, since the rudder is not controlled by the autopilot.

During subsonic or supersonic cruise, the lighting of either the YAW DAMPER caution lamp or the YAW RATE TO ROLL caution lamp does not constitute an emergency condition, however, corrective action as indicated in "Flight Control System Trouble Shooting Procedures," Section VII, should be promptly initiated. The lighting of the YAW DAMPER warning lamp at supersonic speeds or at speeds above 450 KIAS *does* constitute an emergency condition and immediate corrective action is required. Refer to "Lighting of Yaw Damper Warning Lamp", Section III.

JETTISONING PROCEDURES (POD/SMALL WEAPONS).

Upon jettisoning the pod, the shift of the center of gravity aft due to the release of the pod and the sudden loss of weight causes the airplane to pitch up with a resultant increase in load factor. An additional effect is that the aft center of gravity shift reduces the longitudinal stability of the airplane. The magnitude of the increased load factor and stability change depends upon the location of the airplane-with-pod center of gravity and the pod weight at the time of release. When the pod contains fuel, the weight change and center of gravity shift are larger than for the empty pod; therefore, the airplane center of gravity location before jettisoning a pod with fuel is extremely critical from the standpoint of maintaining control of the airplane and/or preventing structural damage when the pod is jettisoned. Refer to "Pod Drop," Section VI, for additional information on flight characteristics.

Note

Under certain conditions, the required cg for jettisoning a pod with fuel will be forward of the normal forward cg operating limits. In this event, the normal forward cg limits should be ignored. Failure to attain a cg at least as far forward as that specified can result in severe structural damage upon release of the pod.

The forward physical loading limit for the pod in figure 2-8 shows the cg with the airplane forward and reservoir tanks full and the airplane aft and balance tanks empty; with more or less fuel in the airplane tanks the cg cannot be established as far forward. With a large quantity of fuel in the pod tanks it may not be possible to establish a safe cg for jettisoning unless fuel is transferred from the pod tanks. If the cg is determined to be aft of or near the pod jettison aft cg limit, every effort should be made to move the airplane cg forward by dumping or transferring fuel before releasing the pod. The following procedure is applicable for jettisoning the pod under the conditions specified in figure 2-8.

Section II
Normal Procedures

T.O. 1B-58A-1

WARNING

- It is not recommended that the pod be jettisoned immediately after takeoff. Jettisoning the pod at takeoff gross weights will cause the airplane to become extremely unstable with probable catastrophic results.

- Pods and small weapons containing warheads will be jettisoned in accordance with command policy.

aft cg limits for pod and small weapon jettisoning

TWO COMPONENT POD
(GEAR UP OR DOWN NOT TO EXCEED GEAR LIMIT SPEED)

LOWER POD
(BLU-2/B-2 WITH FUEL)

The lower pod can be dropped with any amount of fuel at the conditions given below:

Altitude: Below 20,000 Feet
Airspeed: 250 to 400 Knots
CG After Drop: Forward of 26% MAC

LOWER POD
(BLU-2/B-2 WITHOUT FUEL)
(FAILURE OF THRUSTER TO FIRE)

If a normal release is not accomplished according to Section V, proceed to the conditions given below. Remain in the flight envelope of Figure 5-2 at all times because the pod may separate prior to attaining the conditions below. This is particularly true during maneuvering flight.

Altitude: 500 to 10,000 Feet
Airspeed: 250 to 300 Knots
CG must be at least 1.5% MAC forward of the aft limit for the airplane with upper pod. Refer to "Center of Gravity Limitations" Section V. If the lower pod does not separate, release both upper and lower pods together as required by returning to TCP jettison procedures, this section.

COMPLETE TCP
(BOTH UPPER AND LOWER PODS TOGETHER)

Altitude: All Altitudes
Airspeed: 250 to 350 Knots (not to exceed Mach No. 0.93)
Aft CG Limit for Airplane with Pod: 21.5% MAC.

Jettisoning with fuel not recommended because the airplane response will probably exceed design load factor limits.

UPPER POD
(BLU-2/B-3) (WARHEAD OR BALLAST)

Jettison the upper pod anywhere within the normal flight envelope. The aft CG limit for the airplane without pod must not be exceeded after jettisoning.

LA-331A OR MB-1 POD
(WARHEAD OR BALLAST)
(GEAR UP OR DOWN NOT TO EXCEED GEAR LIMIT SPEED)

LA-331A OR MB-1 WITH NO FUEL

Jettison the LA-331A or MB-1 in the airspeed range of 225 to 325 knots IAS (not to exceed mach No. 0.93). The aft CG limit for the airplane without pod must not be exceeded after jettisoning.

LA-331A OR MB-1 WITH FUEL

Airspeed: 225 to 325 Knots (not to exceed Mach No. 0.93). Pod tank interconnect valve open.

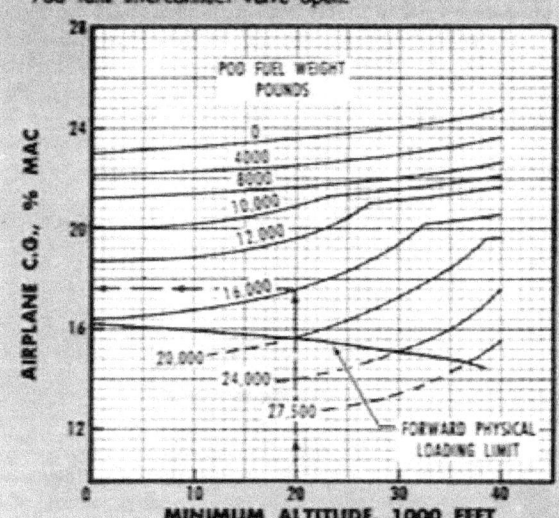

SMALL WEAPONS

The small weapons can be jettisoned anywhere within the normal flight envelope. The CG limit for the airplane without weapons should not be exceeded (see "Center of Gravity Limitations" Section V).

CAUTION

- The MB or LA pod with fins installed should be released prior to release of any small weapon.
- The MB or LA pod with lower fins removed or the lower pod of a TCP should be released prior to release of a forward small weapon.
- If the forward small weapons are jettisoned with either main gear extended, the weapon may hit either the gear or gear doors.

Figure 2-8.

2-46

Lower Pod Jettisoning Procedure.

Note

On EWO missions with a two component pod, the lower pod should be released in accordance with mission planning to reduce drag and increase the range of the airplane. Refer to "Lower Pod Normal Jettison Limits," Section V.

1. Airspeed—Checked. (P-DSO)
   Refer to "Lower Pod Normal Jettison Limits," Section V, for airspeed limits.
2. Center of gravity—Checked. (P-DSO)
   Set cg 1-1/2 percent forward of the aft limit for an aircraft with upper pod.
3. Lower pod ready switch—READY.
4. Lower pod release switch—RELEASE.
   The lower pod should be released only during one-"g" flight.

Before Jettisoning LA, MB, TC, or Upper Pod.

1. Elevator control available mode selector switch to auto (3 degrees minimum)—AUTO or 3 degrees minimum.
   If elevator available in the AUTO mode is less than 3 degrees, select MANUAL and adjust to a minimum of 3 degrees.
2. Airspeed, altitude, and mach no.—Checked. (DSO)
   Check that airspeed, altitude, and mach no. are within safe pod jettison range as shown in figure 2-8.
3. CG—Checked. (DSO)
   Check to be sure center of gravity is within limits established in figure 2-8.

   Example: If it is necessary to jettison MB-1 pod at 20,000 feet altitude with 16,000 pounds of fuel in the pod equally distributed in the forward and aft pod tanks, the pod should be jettisoned between 225 to 325 knots IAS with the airplane cg forward of 17.6 percent MAC.

If cg is determined to be near the established limits, initiate a slight pitch down maneuver concurrent with releasing pod except with the lower pod. Refer to "Pod Drop," Section VI.

Jettisoning LA, MB, TC, or Upper Pod.

Note

Steps 4 and 6 are not applicable to jettisoning the LA pod.

1. Safety lock handle—Pulled. (N)
   Instruct the navigator to rotate and pull the lock handle.
2. Weapon unlock caution lamp—On.
3. Pod lock indicator—UNLOCK. (N)
4. Weapon selector switch—POD. (N)
5. Ball in turn and slip indicator centered and wings level — Ball centered. (P)
6. Electrical release switch—Depressed. (N)

Section II
Normal Procedures

T.O. 1B-58A-1

Jettisoning LA, MB, TC, or Upper Pod. (Cont'd)

Note

In case the release switches are inoperative, the naviagtor can release the pod by rotating the mechanical release handle 90 degrees counterclockwise and then pulling the handle through its full length of travel.

7. Mechanical release handle—Pulled (if required). (N)

Jettisoning Small Weapons.

1. Small weapon lock switches—UNLOCK. (N)
2. Small weapon jettison switch—JETTISON.

Pod Jettisoning With Gear Extended.

If a condition exists that requires jettisoning the pod with gear extended, particular attention should be given to the airplane attitude and cg at the time of release so that the pod will not damage the gear. Transfer all pod tank fuel to the airplane and maintain a stabilized level flight attitude with zero sideslip. The procedure for pod jettisoning with gear extended is the same as with gear retracted.

FLIGHT CHARACTERISTICS.

Refer to Section VI for information concerning flight characteristics of the airplane.

AIR REFUELING.

Refer to Air Refueling Flight Manuals (T.O. 1-1C-1 and T.O. 1-1C-1-6) for procedures and techniques. The pilot's abbreviated checklist contains the checklist items extracted from the amplified checklist in the Air Refueling Flight Manual T.O. 1-1C-1-6.

BEFORE ACCELERATION. (DSO READS)

WARNING

In the event that it is necessary to accelerate to supersonic speed with the elevator control available mode selector switch selected to MANUAL, in emergency manual elevator control, or with the automatic trim system inoperative, increase the elevator available prior to acceleration, to a value at least twice the elevator that will be required to trim in one-"g" flight at low supersonic speed. (For normal cg positions this would be 8 to 12 degrees elevator available.) At subsonic speed the airplane will be very sensitive to longitudinal control with the increased elevator available, but the sensitivity will decrease rapidly during acceleration to supersonic speed. Then as the acceleration continues to progressively higher speeds increase the elevator available as required to maintain a value twice the elevator position in level flight.

BEFORE ACCELERATION. (DSO READS) (CONT'D)

Before accelerating to supersonic speed, accomplish the following checks.

1. Dampers—Checked.

    Side slip airplane a minimum of 1 ball diameter on the turn and slip indicator then abruptly release rudder. Check that there is damping about all axes and that the yaw damper and yaw rate to roll caution lamps do not light. If either of the caution lamps light or there is an absence of damping about any axis, do not accelerate to supersonic speeds.

2. Fuel system configuration—Set.

    Position the knobs and switches on the fuel control panel according to the fuel management schedule for acceleration.

3. CG indicator—Checked.

    Check that the cg is between the supersonic forward limit and the subsonic aft limit. Refer to Section V.

4. Mach and mach-altitude mode switches—OFF.

5. Spike switches—AUTO.

6. Hydraulic pressure and quantity—Checked.

7. Engine anti-ice switch—AUTO or OFF.

8. Throttles—OVSP.

    Set MIL power, MIN A/B, MAX A/B, OVSP, and check for correct EGT, fuel flow, and nozzle position at each setting. With throttles in OVSP, check that rpm increases to approximately 103.5 percent.

> **CAUTION**
>
> If the EGT does not stabilize within the normal limits for MIN A/B operation, but continues to rise, a secondary nozzle may have failed closed. Reduce power to military to prevent overtemperature operation and engine damage.

DURING ACCELERATION. (DSO READS)

During the acceleration, make the following checks:

1. Mach-monitor lamp—Checked. (P-DSO)

    The pilot's and DSO's mach-monitor indicator lamp should light at mach no. 1.0 ($\pm.035$), remain lighted during the acceleration to Mach No. 1.55 ($\pm.035$) at which speed it should go out.

Section II
Normal Procedures

T.O. 1B-58A-1

DURING ACCELERATION. (DSO READS) (CONT'D)

If the mach-monitor indicator lamp does not light at mach no. 1.0, or if the lamp should go out in the speed range between Mach No. 1.0 and 1.55, or if the lamp lights at speeds above Mach No. 1.55, switch to HIGH SPEED standby gains. Continue the flight on standby gains observing the restrictions in Section VII.

2. Elevator control available—Monitoring.

    Monitor the elevator available indicator during the acceleration. Refer to "Longitudinal Flight Characteristics," Section VI, for typical variation of elevator control available with change in mach number.

3. Turn-and-slip indicator—Monitoring.

4. CG selector knob—Set.

    Select desired cg location for supersonic flight using automatic cg control or begin manual shift aft if using manual cg control (if required).

5. Ram air temperature—Monitoring.

CAUTION

To prevent exceeding the maximum ram air temperature limit, monitor the ram air temperature immediately prior to reaching mach no. 2.0 and periodically during mach no. 2.0 flight.

6. Power setting—Stabilized.

    Stabilize power setting when desired mach number is reached.

CAUTION

When power is reduced from manual overspeed, check that rpm remains at approximately 103.5 percent (ram air temperature above 97 degrees C). If rpm decreases, compressor stall margin is reduced and severe compressor stall may occur and EGT must be monitored closely on the engine.

7. CG indicator and fuel system configuration—Checked and set.

    If automatic cg control is used, monitor indicator to insure that cg location shifts to approximate selected value. If manual cg control is used, return manual cg shift knob to OFF when desired cg location is obtained. The fuel panel configuration should be set according to the fuel management schedule for supersonic cruise.

DECELERATION. (DSO READS)

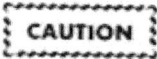

In the event that it is necessary to decelerate to subsonic speed with the elevator control available mode selector switch selected to MANUAL, in emergency manual elevator control, or with the automatic trim system inoperative, decrease the elevator available prior to deceleration to subsonic speed. Pause momentarily between 1.1 and 1.2 mach number and adjust elevator available to a value equal to the elevator (EPI) required to trim in one-"g" flight at low supersonic speeds. This will minimize the sensitivity of the airplane to control upon reaching subsonic speed where the control required to maneuver is much lower than at supersonic speed. Upon attaining subsonic speed adjust the elevator available to a value twice the elevator position in level flight or to three degrees, whichever is greater.

During deceleration to subsonic speed, accomplish the following checks.
1. Mach and mach-altitude mode switches—OFF.
2. Throttles—Set.
   Retard throttles to MIL until mach no. 1.5 is reached, then set as desired.

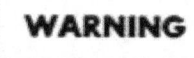

If inlet buzz is encountered when decelerating, retract spikes to eliminate buzz.

3. CG selector knob—Set.
   Select desired cg for deceleration if using automatic cg control or begin manual shift forward if using manual cg control (if required).

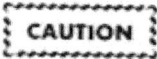

The center of gravity should be moved forward to subsonic position before deceleration below mach no. 1.2.

4. Mach-monitor indicator lamp—Checked. (P-DSO)
   The pilot's and DSO's mach-monitor lamps should light at mach no. 1.55 ($\pm$.035) and remain lighted during the deceleration to mach no. 1.0 ($\pm$.035) at which speed they should go out.

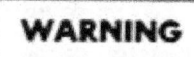

If the mach-monitor lamp lights above mach no. 1.55, or lamp does not light at mach no. 1.55, or if the lamp should go out in the speed range between mach no. 1.55 and 1.0, place the gain selector switch to HIGH SPEED.

Section II
Normal Procedures

T.O. 1B-58A-1

DECELERATION. (DSO READS) (CONT'D)

5. Spike switches—IN.

   Place spike switches IN when below mach no. 1.5 during deceleration.

6. CG indicator—Checked.

   If automatic cg control is used, monitor indicator to insure that cg location shifts to approximate selected value. If manual cg control is used, return manual cg shift knob to OFF when desired cg location is obtained.

7. Fuel system configuration—Checked.

   Position the knobs and switches on the fuel control panel according to the fuel management schedule for deceleration.

8. Elevator control available—Monitoring.

   Monitor the elevator control available indicator during the deceleration. Refer to "Longitudinal Flight Characteristics," Section VI, for typical variation of elevator control available with change in mach number.

9. Altitude—Checked.

   Subsonic optimum altitude should be obtained before decelerating below mach no. 1.2.

PRIOR TO PENETRATION. (DSO READS)

The following procedure is recommended as the best method for accomplishing jet penetrations at most gross weight possibilities. In determining the procedure, consideration was given to stability, fuel availability, environmental control, and range capabilities. Refer to Appendix I for descent time and fuel consumption. A typical normal landing pattern is shown in figure 2-9.

WARNING

Prior to penetration or low level tactical operations, the applicable penetration/entry procedure will be reviewed by the crew. Particular emphasis will be placed on altitudes. During descent for low level tactical operations the DSO will announce altitudes to the pilot every 5000 feet starting with the first multiple of 5000 feet until 5000 feet above any leveloff or minimum altitude, then every 1000 feet down to, and at leveloff or minimum altitude. Subsequent altitude changes will be similarly announced and cross checked. During descent for landing and traffic pattern activity the NAVIGATOR will announce these altitudes. The pilot will acknowledge these calls and indicate awareness of altitude restrictions.

Note

- The low altitude radar altimeter will be used as an aid to prevent the airplane from inadvertently passing through intermediate and/or minimum altitudes. Set the Minimum Altitude Index Pointer (MAIP) at 5000 feet and at 5000 feet above terrain check that the crosshatched (fail) indicator disappears and that the warning lamps light. Reset the MAIP so the warning lamps will light when the airplane descends to less than desired altitude above terrain.

- Only circled items will be accomplished for Low Altitude Tactical Operation.

(1.) Radio call—Completed. (DSO)

   Request from appropriate facility the current weather information.

   a. Destination/alternate: Include altimeter setting, runway temperature, pressure altitude and surface wind.

   b. Low level tactical operation: Include altimeter setting, "D" value, temperature and wind.

2-52

PRIOR TO PENETRATION. (DSO READS) (CONT'D)

2. Review penetration/entry—Reviewed. (P-N-DSO)

    Pilot will insure the crew reviews the penetration or low level entry to be flown, with particular emphasis on any intermediate altitude restrictions and minimum altitude for approach/entry. For penetration, pilot will confirm with crew specific terminal area chart, type of approach, and missed approach procedure.

3. CG—Set.

    Select desired cg for low level tactical operations or landing if using automatic, or begin manual shift if using manual control.

4. Arm control switch—SAFE and sealed.

5. Communication panels—Checked. (N-DSO)

    The navigator and DSO will place their command mixing switches to ON, to monitor emergency transmissions until after engine shutdown.

6. Anti-skid switch—ON.

7. Nose wheel steering ratio selector switch—TO & LAND

8. Fuel system configuration—Checked.

    Position the knobs and switches on the fuel control panel according to the fuel management schedule.

9. Anti-ice, defog, rain removal, and pitot heat switches—As required.

    Position these switches as required for existing weather conditions.

CAUTION

- If rain removal is selected and is followed by a loss of cooling airflow to the crew compartment, position the control mode selector knob to RAM and turn off all unnecessary electronic equipment to prevent damage. Refer to "Air Conditioning System", "Ram Air Operation," Section IV.

- If defog is selected and is followed by a loss of cooling airflow to the crew compartment, position the windshield defog switch to DEC. Crew compartment cooling airflow should start within 30 seconds.

Note

When the ram air mode, the rain removal switch must be ON before the defog system will operate.

10. Warning and caution lamps—Checked.

11. DECM, MD-7, and ARC-110 control switches—OFF. (DSO)

12. Autopilot switches—OFF.

13. Heading selector switch—J-4.

14. Landing data card—Computed; approach/flare speed _____ knots, stopping distance _____ feet. (DSO)

15. Altimeter—Reset. (P-N-DSO)

    Reset altimeters to station pressure immediately prior to initiating penetration or passing through transition altitude.

16. Low altitude radar altimeter—Set.

    Set minimum altitude index pointer to 5000 feet.

2-53

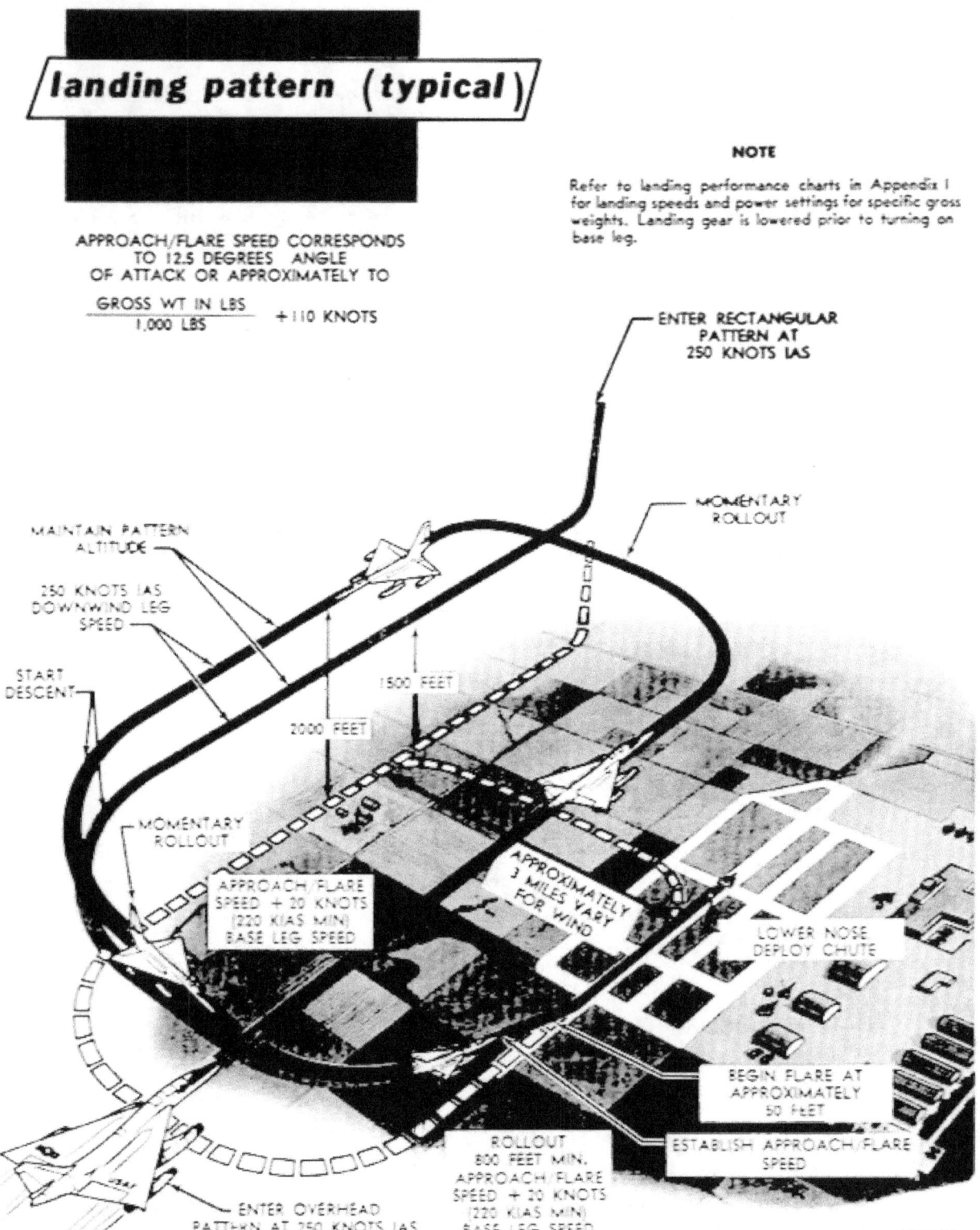

Figure 2-9.

DESCENT AND BEFORE LANDING. (DSO READS)

Note

- This checklist must be completed before the start of final approach. If letdown other than jet penetration is made, all items of this checklist must be accomplished prior to entering, or while in the traffic pattern.
- The pilot may turn off the low altitude radar altimeter for approach and landing.

1. Elevator control available—TO & LAND and 20 degrees.
   Check that the elevator control available mode selector switch is in the TO & LAND position. Check that the elevator control available indicator shows approximately 20 degrees.

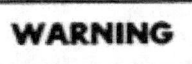

Unless the elevator control available mode selector switch is in the TO & LAND position, maximum elevator control may not be available for landing.

2. Aileron control available—AUTO and FULL.
   Check that aileron control available switch is in the AUTO position and that aileron control available indicator reads FULL.
3. Landing gear handle—DOWN.
   Lower gear below 300 knots.
4. Landing gear indicator lamps—Check.
   Check that landing gear warning lamp goes out, that indicator lamps show the gear down and locked, and that the appropriate angle-of-attack indexer lamp lights.
5. Hydraulic pressure and quantities—Checked.
6. Brake pedals—Depressed.
   Depress pedals one at a time and check for proper brake feel. With each pedal depression, observe utility hydraulic pressure gage for momentary drop in pressure of approximately 100 psi.
7. Work tables—Stowed. (N-DSO)
8. Taxi and landing lights—As required.
   This item may be accomplished after turning on final approach.

Note

The mach monitor warning lamp may blink intermittently while reducing airspeed or flying at low speeds. This is due to system tolerances and inaccuracies in mach measurement at low speeds.

TRANSITION CHECKLIST. (DSO READS)

The following checklist should be used for traffic pattern operation when accomplishing a series of low approaches, touch and go landings or taxi-back landings.

1. Engine instruments—Checked.
2. Hydraulic pressure and quantities—Checked.
3. Landing gear handle—DOWN.
4. Landing gear indicator lamps—Checked.
5. CG—Set.
   Check and set cg within landing limits.
6. Fuel system configuration—Checked.
7. Landing data card—Computed; approach/flare speed _____ knots, stopping distance _____ feet. (DSO)
8. Taxi and landing lights—As required.
9. Review approach—Reviewed. (P-N-DSO) Pilot will confirm with crew specific type of approach, minimum altitude for approach, and missed approach procedures.

Section II
Normal Procedures

T.O. 1B-58A-1

LANDING.

Refer to Section V for maximum landing gross weight limits. The characteristics of the airplane during landing are somewhat different from those with conventional tail design due to the delta wing configuration and the reverse flap effect of the trailing edge elevons. If these characteristics are understood it will be easier to accomplish safe, consistently good landings. The approach and landing speeds of most airplanes are normally determined in relation to the stall speed which is clearly defined by an abrupt loss of lift at a high angle of attack. On a delta wing airplane, however, there is no clearly defined stall within the normal operating range of angles of attack. Refer to "Stalls," Section VI. In addition to considerations of low speed handling qualities and visibility from the cockpit at high angles of attack, approach and landing speeds are based on the variation of the power required to fly the airplane at low speeds. Typical power required curves for approach conditions (free air) and landing conditions (full ground effects) are presented in figure 2-10. At the higher airspeeds, the power required curves are stable; that is, at any particular speed more power is needed for level flight at a higher speed and less power is needed at a lower speed. When speed is reduced to the point at which angle of attack for one "g" flight is approximately 10 to 12 degrees in free air, the power curves become very flat. This flattening indicates that airspeeds within a fairly wide range (30 to 40 knots) can be controlled with little power change. At speeds below the flat region, however, the increasing power required as speed becomes slower indicates the presence of an increasingly unstable situation which characterizes the back side of the power required curve. Flight can be conducted on the back side of the power curve at angles of attack higher than the 17 degrees limit angle of attack because of the large amount of power available. However, the likelihood of experiencing inadvertent slowdown, or the development of high sink rates, or both, would be greatly increased during landing, particularly in instrument conditions or at night. If power corrections are not made, any small increase in angle of attack caused by gusts, flight path angle corrections, or any other factor, will cause a further decrease of airspeed due to the higher drag. This decrease of airspeed will normally be accompanied by a higher sink rate since a larger up elevator deflection is required for trim at the lower speeds. If elevator deflection is then slowly applied to reduce the sink rate without increasing power, airspeed will further decrease due to the additional drag of the elevators as well as that caused by rotation to a higher angle of attack. Thus, if a slow-speed situation develops during the approach, the safest means of reducing sink rate and regaining normal approach airspeeds is to increase power. In free air at normal approach speeds, a one percent change of engine RPM will result in a change of sink rate of approximately 400 feet per minute. The recommended approach speeds of the airplane are the same as the recommended flare speeds and are established as a compromise between low speed handling qualities, visibility from the cockpit at high angles of attack, excessive flare distance, and speeds associated with the back side of the power required curve in free air. In normal conditions the approach/flare speed is given approximately by the formula (Gross Weight divided by 1000) +110 knots and more precisely by the airspeed corresponding to an angle of attack of 12.5 degrees. The angle-of-attack indexer lamps may be used as an aid in establishing and maintaining proper approach/flare speeds; however, airspeed is the primary instrument. The formula: (Gross Weight divided by 1000) +110 knots, is presented only as a check to insure that the approach/flare chart has not been misread and is not to be used to determine exact approach/flare speeds. The angle of attack indexer lamps are programmed such that the approach/flare speed for normal conditions can be maintained within a maximum tolerance of ±10 knots of the correct value on airplanes with an MB, LA or TC pod, independently of gross weight. Normally, the tolerance will be smaller and may be as low as ±4.5 knots.

Note

The maximum and minimum tolerances vary slightly with gross weight and are larger for the heavier gross weights.

GROSS WEIGHT	MAXIMUM TOLERANCE Knots	MINIMUM TOLERANCE Knots
70,000	±9	±4.5
80,000	±10	±5
90,000	±10	±5

Lighting of the on-speed symbol (green) is overlapped by the lighting of both the low-speed (red) and high-speed (amber) symbols so that it is easy to determine the corrections necessary to attain and maintain the approach/flare speed (approximately 12.5 degrees angle of attack). If only the high-speed symbol (amber) is lighted, speed is fast by at least 4.5 to 10 knots (angle of attack is low by at least 0.5 to 1.0 degree). If both the on-speed (green) and high-speed (amber) symbols are lighted, speed is fast by no more than 4.5 to 10 knots (angle of attack is low by no more than 0.5 to 1.0 degree). When only the on-speed symbol (green) is lighted, speed is within a maximum of ±10 knots of the correct value (angle of attack is within a maximum of ±1 degree). If both the on-speed (green) and low-speed (red) symbols are lighted, speed is slow by no more than 4.5 to 10 knots (angle of attack is high

variation of power required during landing

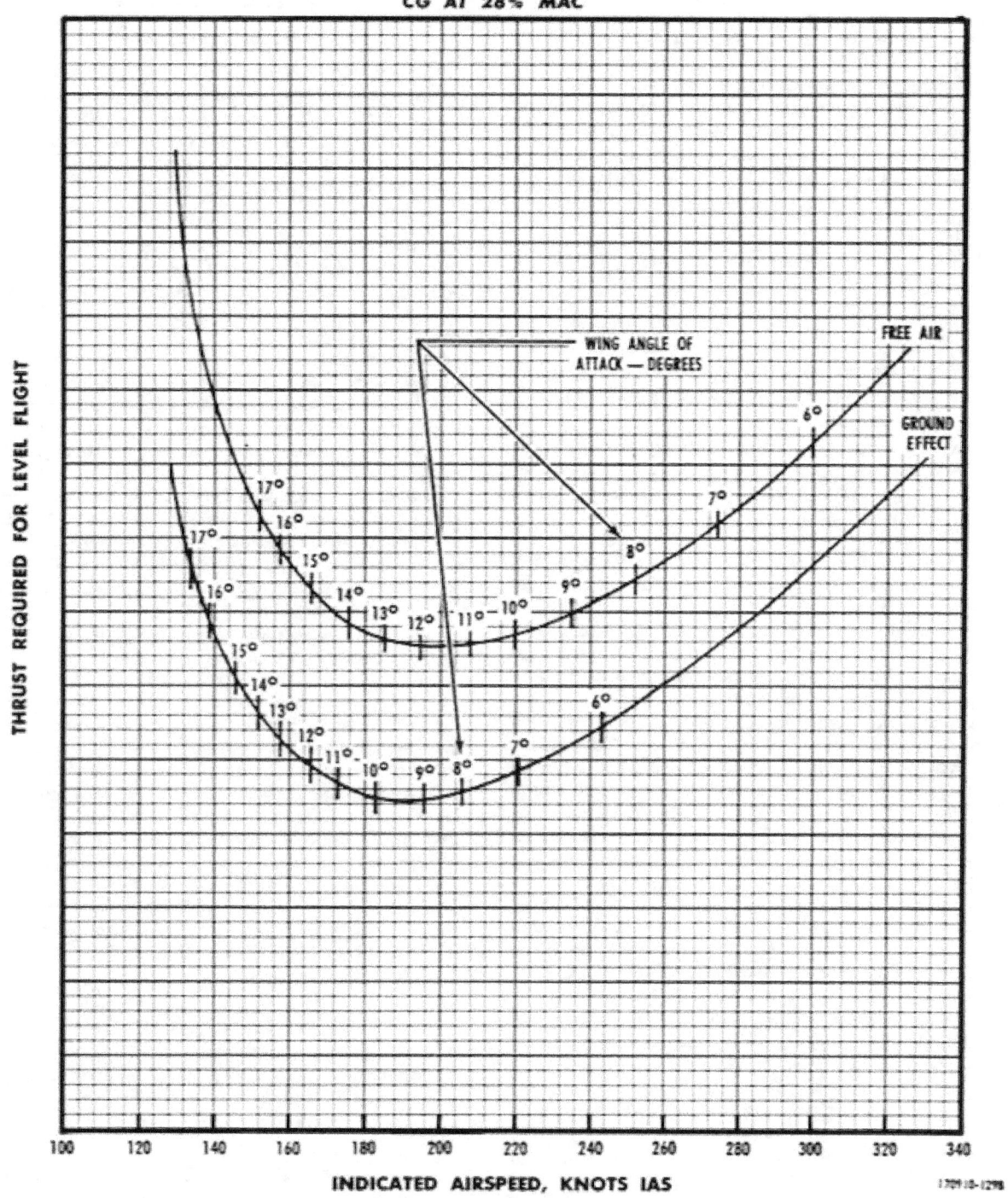

Figure 2-10.

Section II
Normal Procedures

T.O. 1B-58A-1

by no more than 0.5 to 1.0 degree). If only the low speed symbol (red) is lighted, speed is slow by at least 4.5 to 10 knots (angle of attack is high by at least 0.5 to 1.0 degree).

Note

- When the approach/flare speed is increased for landing in a gusty wind or with a cg forward of 26 percent MAC, or decreased for maximum performance landing, having only the green donut lamp lighted does not provide the correct speed. When the correct speed is established using the airspeed indicator, the angle of attack indicator needle can then be used as an aid to maintain the correct angle of attack.

- When landing without a pod or with the upper pod only, the green donut lamp will be lighted at airspeeds approximately 3-1/2 knots lower than the computed approach/flare speed. This is due to the change in air flow at the angle-of-attack sensor vane created by the absence of the MB, LA or lower pod.

During landing approaches in gusty weather, the angle-of-attack indicator lamps and angle of attack indicator needle may oscillate in response to the gusts. In this event the pilot should note only the average indicated angle of attack. The relationship of the power required in free air to that required in full ground effect is of primary importance in accomplishing the landing flare. The normal approach/flare speed in free air can be maintained in ground effect with about 30 percent less power. For this reason, it is necessary to reduce power when flaring to avoid prolonging the flare or contacting the runway at high speeds and increasing the ground roll. However, the power reduction should not be large or abrupt because this will produce a sink rate which most likely cannot be corrected by up elevator in time to prevent a hard landing. The use of abrupt full-up elevator in the flare is not advisable because of the reverse flap effect of the trailing edge elevons. In an airplane with a conventional tail design, up elevator produces an almost immediate increase of lift since the relatively small downward force on the tail produces a large pitching moment to change the wing angle of attack rapidly. In this airplane, however, the downward force caused by up elevator deflection is relatively large in comparison to the resulting pitching moment so that an immediate reduction of lift and a comparatively slow change of angle of attack occurs. For this reason the sink rate increases momentarily until the airplane can rotate to a higher angle of attack. Contact with the runway at a reasonable sink rate is not likely under these circumstances since considerable altitude can be lost before the increased lift is obtained. Figure 2-11 illustrates the results of using abrupt full-up elevator in the flare. Thus, during the landing flare,

if excessive sink rates develop in close proximity to the runway, the best technique to use for recovery is to increase power immediately.

WARNING

Approach power setting should not be reduced until the landing flare is started. Abrupt throttle chop during the flare will cause a rapid sink rate at touchdown and should be avoided. Abrupt up elevator during the flare will also produce a rapid sink rate.

The use of large or abrupt stick movements should be avoided during all phases of landing. Under conditions wherein large control stick commands are being reversed rapidly, there may be an attempt to move the stick at a higher rate than the hydraulic system is capable of moving the control surfaces. When this occurs, stick movement rate will be restricted and it will seem that the control stick will not move. The apparent stick restriction may occur with either an aileron or elevator command but is more likely to occur when these commands are combined. This condition will be aggravated by an inoperative hydraulic system or pump(s). Normal flare should be started at a height of approximately 50 feet above the surface. Reduce power gradually in the flare so as to reach idle RPM at touchdown. Experience indicates that power is difficult to control and sink rate difficult to judge in the flare. A recommended technique is to reduce approximately 50 percent of approach power at the beginning of the flare. Figure 2-12 indicates that 50 percent of approach power is approximately a 5 percent reduction of RPM. An additional power reduction may be necessary to avoid an extended flare, however, some power should be maintained until touchdown at which time the throttles should be retarded to idle. Generally, touchdown will be performed at 12.5 degrees wing angle of attack and a normal rate of descent of 150 feet per minute. Refer to "Maximum Sinking Speed at Touchdown," Section V. Retarding power to idle only after touchdown will more nearly assure that the airplane will remain on the ground and thus reduce the possibility of skipping.

CAUTION

In the event of an excessive bounce or skip on landing, it is recommended that a go-around be accomplished.

Lowering the nose immediately after touchdown to deploy the drag chute will further assure that the airplane is in firm contact with the ground and will

2-58

effect of abrupt full up elevator deflection during flare

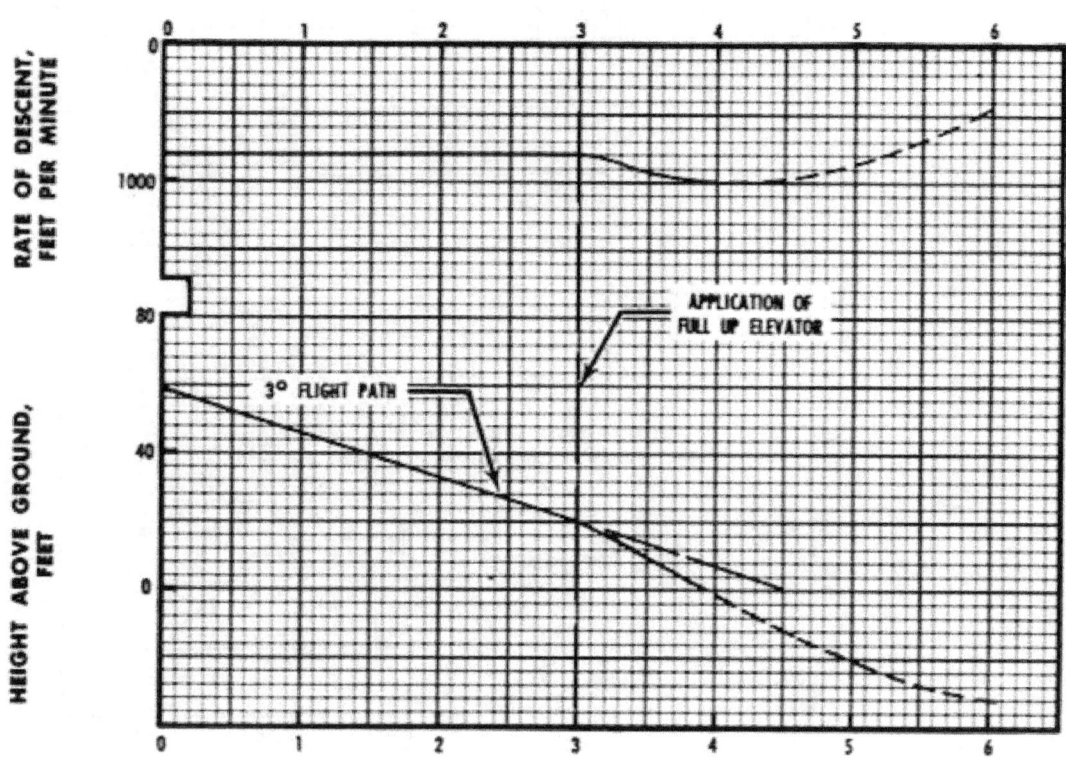

Figure 2-11.

greatly reduce the possibility of rocking from gear to gear, particularly in gusty or crosswind conditions.

WARNING

Do not deploy the drag chute while the airplane is airborne.

Following deployment of the chute, the nose may be raised for maximum aerodynamic braking (15 degrees wing angle of attack is attainable with chute, 17 degrees without chute); however, until the airspeed has decreased to approximately 60 knots below normal approach/flare speed, care should be exercised in rotating to the 17 degree attitude to prevent becoming airborne again. After touchdown, use rudder and aileron for directional control. Landing performance data are obtained from the charts in Part 11 of Appendix I. When computing ground roll, use "Aero Plus Brakes" data to insure that sufficient runway is available in the event of drag chute failure.

APPROACH/FLARE SPEED CORRECTIONS.

The approach/flare speeds can be determined from the charts in Part 11 of Appendix I. For each percent that the cg is forward of 26 percent MAC, increase

thrust variation with engine rpm at landing speeds

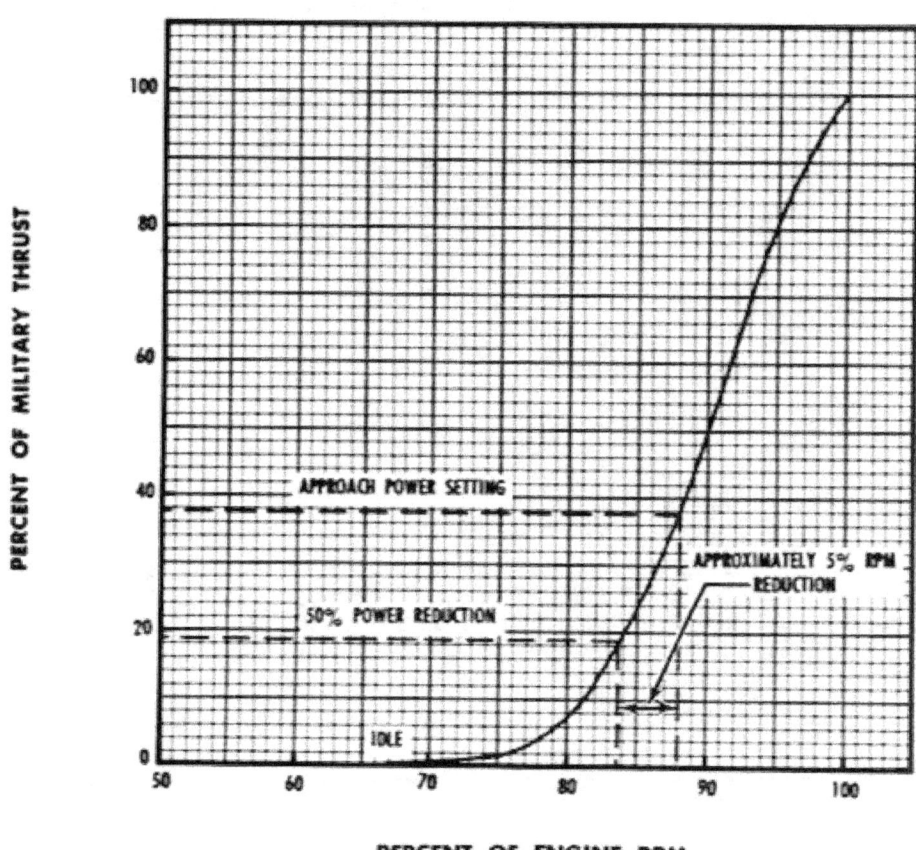

Figure 2-12.

the charted approach/flare and touchdown speeds by four knots. When landing in gusty wind conditions increase the approach/flare speed and touchdown speed by 50 percent of the peak gust velocity above the steady state wind. For example, if wind is 15 knots, gusting to 25 knots, the gust velocity is 10 knots above the steady state wind, therefore 5 knots will be added to the approach/flare and touchdown speeds. This correction will be added whether wind is directly down runway or a crosswind. When a correction is required for a forward cg as well as for gusty winds, the larger of the two corrections should be used.

PROCEDURES AND TECHNIQUES.

There are two basic landing procedures applicable to this airplane; normal landing and maximum perform-

ance landing. For normal landings, approach/flare and touchdown speeds are based on an angle of attack of 12.5 degrees. After touchdown a combination of aerodynamic braking and wheel braking is utilized. This normal procedure is utilized on dry runways when stopping distance is not critical and on slippery runways *under all conditions*. The maximum performance landing procedure is based on approach/flare and touchdown speeds corresponding to an agle of attack of 14 degrees. Immediately after touchdown the nose wheel is lowered to the runway and maximum wheel braking is applied until normal taxi speed is attained. *This procedure (maximum performance) is applicable to landing on dry runways only* because of the hydroplaning effect of tires on slippery runway surfaces. Although some hydroplaning is experienced on a slippery runway when applying brakes from approximately 85

KIAS (normal landing procedure) it is more pronounced when applying wheel brakes from approximately 150 KIAS, (maximum performance landing procedure). The antiskid will be on for all landings except when landing with a blown tire(s). Refer to Section III for procedures when landing with a blown tire(s). The drag chute will not normally be computed in the landing ground roll. This provides a margin of safety in event of drag chute failure; *provided touchdown was made at or short of the computed ground roll distance, and procedures outlined in this section were followed.* In addition, use of the drag chute on all landings will conserve brakes and tires. Refer to Appendix 1 for computation of landing data. In the event the computed ground roll and runway available are not compatible the following alternatives exist:

1. Dry Runway.

    a. If normal landing (aero plus brakes) ground roll is greater than runway available, recompute ground roll utilizing normal landing data (aero plus brakes) at a gross weight reduced to a practical minimum. Plan a normal landing if runway available is greater than recomputed ground roll.

    b. If normal landing (aero plus brakes) ground roll for the reduced gross weight still exceeds the runway available, recompute ground roll utilizing maximum performance landing data (brakes only). Plan a maximum performance landing.

2. Slippery Runway.

    a. If normal landing (aero plus brakes corrected for RCR) ground roll is greater than runway available, recompute ground roll utilizing normal landing data (aero plus brakes corrected for RCR) at a gross weight reduced to a practical minimum. Plan a normal landing (including slippery runway procedures) if runway available is greater than computed ground roll distance.

    b. If normal landing (aero plus brakes corrected for RCR) ground roll distance for the reduced gross weight still exceeds the runway available, commensurate with fuel available, select a suitable alternate for landing.

    c. If it is not possible or practical to proceed to an alternate, recompute ground roll utilizing normal landing data (aero plus brakes *and chute* corrected for RCR). Plan a normal landing (including slippery runway procedures) if runway available is greater than computed ground roll distance.

WARNING

Landing with reliance on the drag chute should be accomplished only in an emergency. The safety of the landing under these conditions is based on strict adherence to procedures outlined in this section.

If the computed ground roll in alternatives 1b and 2c above exceed the runway available and it is not possible to reduce gross weight further or to proceed to a suitable alternate, a safe landing is not assured, however, every attempt should be made to land as close to the approach end of the runway as possible.

NORMAL LANDING.

Initiate the flare approximately 50 feet above the surface, reduce power gradually in the flare so as to reach idle rpm at touchdown, lower the nose approximately half way to the runway, check runway alignment, deploy the drag chute and raise the nose for aerodynamic braking.

WARNING

Following deployment of the chute, the nose may be raised for maximum aerodynamic braking (15 degrees wing angle of attack is attainable with chute, 17 degrees without chute); however, until the airspeed has decreased to approximately 60 knots below normal approach/flare speed, care should be exercised in rotating to the 17 degree attitude to prevent becoming airborne again.

Maintain maximum aerodynamic braking (15 degrees wing angle of attack is attainable with chute, 17 degrees without chute) until 100 knots, then immediately lower nose wheel to the runway. At airspeeds slightly below the touchdown speed, nose-high attitudes cannot be maintained while braking. After the nose wheel is in contact with the runway, apply maximum braking (if required) and full up elevator. At speeds below about 40 knots, full up elevator will provide no additional braking. Except at very low speeds near the end of the ground roll, directional control can be accomplished with rudder and aileron. However, nose wheel steering can be engaged after the nose wheel is in contact with the runway. Do not engage nose wheel steering until the rudder pedals are centered.

WARNING

For each 10 knots above the charted touchdown speed, the ground roll will be increased by approximately 900 feet when using the normal landing technique.

2-61

Note

With the cg forward of 28 percent, aerodynamic braking will be reduced due to the lower attainable angle of attack, and normal landing stopping distances will be greater than those achieved with the cg at or aft of 28 percent.

Refer to Section V for restrictions on brake and drag chute operation.

LANDING ON SLIPPERY RUNWAYS.

When preparing to land on a slippery runway, apply the appropriate runway condition reading (RCR) stopping factor to the normal landing performance (aero plus brakes) data. For wet runways, with runway condition readings greater than 12, an RCR of 12 will be used in computing landing. If no RCR is available, use 12 for wet runways and 5 for icy runways. The approach, flare, touchdown and landing roll procedures are the same as for normal landing except that when stopping distance is marginal, engines 1 and 4 may be retarded to OFF after landing is assured and if not required for electrical or hydraulic power. Refer to Appendix I to determine the "Stopping Factor" to be applied to normal landing performance data for slippery runway operation.

WARNING

After touchdown during operation in a crosswind, the airplane may tend to weathervane into the wind. Be prepared to jettison the drag chute if directional control becomes marginal due to the eeffct of a crosswind on the chute. The airplane may also tend to drift to the downwind side of the runway due to the aerodynamic force produced by the crosswind. In this event, it may be necessary to induce a slight skid by yawing into the wind so that a frictional force is produced at the wheels to overcome the aerodynamic force effect.

Note

The brakes may seem to be ineffective or inoperative; however, if utility hydraulic pressure is normal, maintain brake application. Nose wheel steering effectiveness may be considerably reduced and skidding of the nose wheels may easily result from over-steering.

MAXIMUM PERFORMANCE LANDING (DRY RUNWAY).

The procedures for approach, flare and touchdown for a maximum performance landing are essentially the same as for normal landing, except that approach/flare and touchdown speeds are 10 to 14 knots slower (14 degrees angle of attack). At these speeds the airplane is flying on or approaching the back side of the power curve and power becomes more critical. Avoid large power changes during the approach flare. Initiate the flare approximately 50 feet above the surface, reduce power gradually in the flare so as to reach idle rpm at touchdown, immediately lower the nose wheel to the runway, deploy the drag chute and apply maximum braking (if required) to normal taxi speed.

After the nose wheel is in contact with the runway, the nose wheel steering system may be engaged; however, the rudder pedals must be centered prior to engagement. Refer to Section V for restrictions on brake and drag chute operation.

WARNING

For each 10 knots above charted touchdown speed, the ground roll will be increased by approximately 400 feet when using maximum performance landing technique.

Note

The outboard engines may be shut down after touchdown provided they are not required to furnish hydraulic or electrical power.

HEAVY GROSS WEIGHT LANDING.

In the event that the gross weight cannot be reduced to 95,000 pounds or below, landings at gross weights in excess of 95,000 pounds are permissible provided the sinking speed limitations shown in Section V are observed. Power reduction should be carefully accomplished because of the increased inertia at the higher weights. The landing pattern, approach, and the airplane attitude will be the same as for normal landings. With the increased weight, the approach/flare and touchdown speeds will be higher and the landing distance will be longer. Refer to Appendix I for landing performance. For braking precautions refer to "Brake Energy Limits," Section V.

CROSSWIND LANDING.

When landing in a crosswind, the approach/flare and touchdown speeds derived from Appendix I provide

minimum airspeed for control in a crosswind

DATA BASIS: ESTIMATED
DATE: 7 SEPTEMBER 1962

STANDARD DAY — SEA LEVEL

CROSSWIND 90° TO RUNWAY	WITH GIVEN POD OR WITHOUT POD		WITH MB, LA, OR TC POD	
	GROUND RUN ATTITUDE	LANDING ATTITUDE	GROUND RUN ATTITUDE	LANDING ATTITUDE
KNOTS	RUDDER ONLY	RUDDER PLUS AILERON	RUDDER ONLY	RUDDER PLUS AILERON
10	30 KNOTS	51 KNOTS	17 KNOTS	39 KNOTS
20	62 KNOTS	106 KNOTS	36 KNOTS	83 KNOTS
30	95 KNOTS	163 KNOTS	57 KNOTS	129 KNOTS
40	130 KNOTS	221 KNOTS	79 KNOTS	177 KNOTS

NOTE:
1. Zero nose gear sideload.
2. With or without small weapons.
3. Maximum rudder deflection.
4. No drag chute.
5. Speeds will be greater with drag chute.

CORRECTION FOR NON-STANDARD DAY

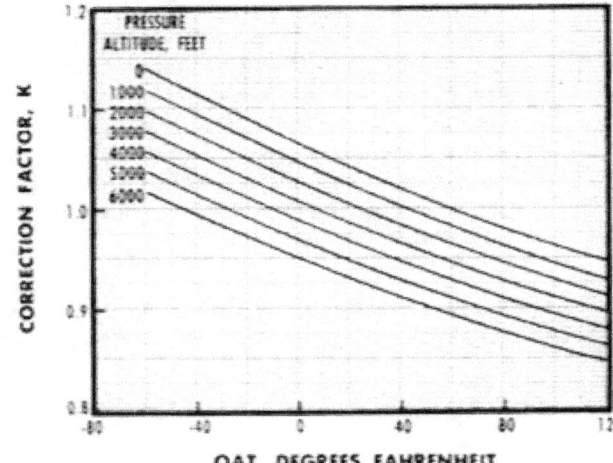

To find the minimum control speed for other than a standard day at sea level, multiply the standard day airspeed by the correction factor from the chart at the left to obtain the correct indicated airspeed for the non-standard conditions.

INDICATED AIRSPEED (KNOTS) FOR NON-STANDARD DAY = K x STANDARD DAY AIRSPEED

Figure 2-13.

sufficient airplane control and engine nacelle clearance for crosswinds up to the maximum recommended for landing. For landing with gusty wind conditions refer to "Approach/Flare Speed Corrections," this section. It is recommended that crosswind landings not be attempted when the 90 degree crosswind component (peak gust) exceeds 25 knots. With engine(s), hydraulic pump(s), yaw and/or roll damper malfunctions, it is recommended that landing not be attempted when the 90 degree crosswind component (peak gust) exceeds 15 knots. For computing the 90 degree crosswind component, refer to the "Landing Crosswind Component" chart in Part 11, Appendix I.

WARNING

When an emergency landing must be made with a crosswind component in excess of the recommended maximum allowable, refer to figure 2-13 for the minimum airspeeds for control in a crosswind. Refer to the applicable landing performance chart, Appendix I, to adjust the approach/flare speed.

Section II
Normal Procedures

T.O. 1B-58A-1

The approach may be made by crabbing into the wind so that the flight path is along the projected centerline of the runway. Immediately before touchdown, the longitudinal axis of the airplane must be aligned with the runway so that large sideloads are not imposed on the main landing gear at touchdown. In a second technique, the approach is made along the projected runway centerline by banking into the wind to compensate for the crosswind component. With this technique, a heading change just prior to touchdown is not required. However, the bank angle at touchdown reduces the clearance between the upwind outboard engine nacelle and the runway. Refer to "Bank Angle Clearance Limits During Takeoff and Landing," Section V. A combination of the crab and wing low techniques can also be used. Sufficient control is available to achieve the necessary wing down sideslip or crab required to maintain a straight ground track. However, the airplane exhibits increased roll due to sideslip or gusts at the higher angles of attack, and larger aileron control inputs are required to correct for rolling motion as speed is decreased. Refer to figure 2-13 for the minimum airspeeds for control in a crosswind. With the roll damper inoperative at high angles of attack, considerable rolling is encountered in response to gusts. Attempt to moderate aileron and elevator commands during the landing so as to avoid the control stick rate restriction due to commands exceeding the hydraulic system capability of moving the control surfaces. In gusty crosswind conditions the airplane may have a tendency to bounce from gear to gear after touchdown. Lowering the nose as soon as possible after touchdown to reduce wing lift will minimize bouncing and prevent sideskip. Deploy the drag chute in a normal manner. The nose may be then raised for aerodynamic braking provided directional control can be maintained with rudder only and excessive sideskipping does not occur. Aileron should be used to maintain wings level.

WARNING

Following deployment of the chute, the nose may be raised for maximum aerodynamic braking (15 degrees wing angle of attack is attainable with chute, 17 degrees without chute); however, until the airspeed has decreased to approximately 60 knots below normal approach/flare speed, care should be exercised in rotating to the 17 degree attitude to prevent becoming airborne again.

If the airplane begins to bounce from one gear to the other, lowering the nose will stop the motion. If directional control becomes marginal due to the effect of the crosswind on the chute, jettison the chute. When the nose is lowered to the runway, do not engage nose wheel steering until the rudder pedals are centered.

TOUCH-AND-GO LANDING.

The procedures for approach, flare and touchdown for touch-and-go landings are the same as for normal landing. After touchdown lower the nose approximately halfway to the runway and check runway alignment. Advance throttles smoothly to MIL and check engine instruments. Liftoff should be accomplished at approximately 45 knots below approach/flare speed. If the brakes are used during touch-and-go landings, allow a minimum of 15 minutes to elapse between landings if the landing gear remains extended or a minimum of 30 minutes if the gear is retracted.

CAUTION

At approximately 45 knots below approach/flare speed sufficient control is available in the event of an outboard engine failure in crosswinds up to ten knots. When crosswind is in excess of ten knots, liftoff should not be accomplished below the approach/flare speed for the approach just completed to insure that sufficient control is available in the event of an outboard engine failure.

The landing gear will normally be left down after a touch-and-go landing to insure adequate tire cooling.

GO-AROUND.

A go-around may be initiated at any point in the approach by advancing the throttles to military power. Regardless of engine rpm at the time go-around is initiated, power is available almost instantaneously because of the rapid acceleration of the engines. Afterburners will ordinarily not be needed for a go-around. If the go-around is initiated when in ground effect, the airplane should not be allowed to climb until the approach-flare speed is reached. Since transition from ground effect and the increased thrust from the engines both tend to raise the nose, use caution to avoid reaching an excessive high angle of attack. The landing gear should normally be left extended for the go-around unless fuel and thrust are critical.

AFTER LANDING. (DSO READS)

WARNING

If energy absorbed during braking exceeded 10 million foot pounds, personnel must not approach the main gear wheels for at least 75 minutes after the airplane is parked. (Refer to figure 2-4.) A serious explosion hazard exists when the brakes, wheels, and tires are hot as a result of braking action during the landing roll.

1. Hydraulic pressure and quantities—Checked.
2. Nose wheel steering ratio selector switch—TAXI.

   Place the nose wheel steering ratio selector switch to TAXI prior to turning off the runway. After clearing active runway, stop aircraft and perform the following:

3. Drag chute—Jettisoned, in and vertical.

CAUTION

The drag chute should be jettisoned with the nose of the airplane into the wind. Under conditions of strong winds, it is possible for the chute to be blown in such a manner as to become ingested into an engine if the airplane is not headed into the wind prior to chute jettison.

4. Parking brakes—Set.
5. Handgrip safety pin(s)—Installed. (P-N-DSO)
6. Damper switches—OFF.
7. Flight control power switch—OFF.
8. IFF master control knob—OFF. (DSO)

   If classified codes have been inserted, they must be removed or properly protected to prevent compromise.

9. TACAN radio—OFF. (P-N)
10. Low altitude radar altimeter—OFF. (P-N)
11. Anti-ice, defog, rain removal, and pitot heat switches—OFF.
12. Anti-collision lights—OFF.
13. No. 1 generator switch—OFF.
14. No. 1 and 4 throttles—OFF.

    After operating engines at idle for 3-5 minutes (part or all of this time may occur while taxiing) shut engines down by retarding throttles to OFF. Monitor engine temperature for possible residual fire during shutdown.

TAXI-BACK LANDING. (DSO READS)

Taxi-back landings may be accomplished provided sufficient time is allowed for brake cooling. Under normal conditions a minimum air time (gear extended) of 15 minutes between takeoff and landing are required. In addition, the following procedures will be utilized.

CAUTION

Energy absorbed by the brakes must be computed after landing (refer to figure 5-11) and precautions for the applicable brake energy zone must be observed.

Section II
Normal Procedures

T.O. 1B-58A-1

TAXI-BACK LANDING. (DSO READS) (CONT'D)

Note

- The normal AFTER LANDING checklist will be utilized; however, the handgrip safety pins need not be installed.
- The ground observer will be on interphone during engine shutdown and start.
- All CG shifts will be accomplished during the BEFORE LINEUP checklist.

1. Parking brakes—Set.
2. ARC—57 radio—OFF.
3. No. 3 generator switch—OFF.
4. No. 3 throttle—OFF.
5. Ground, ready to start: Fire guards posted, chocks in place, engine run area clear. Ready. (GO)
6. No. 2 engine—85 percent.
7. Air conditioning control mode selector knob—MAN.
8. Cabin temperature control knob—Full CCW.
9. Refrigeration unit selector—GRD CART.
10. Start No. 3 engine.
    a. No. 3 clear—Cleared. (GO)
    b. No. 3 engine start switch and throttle—GROUND and IDLE.
    c. Engine start switch—OFF. (P) Starter drop out. (GO)
    d. Engine instruments—Within limits.
    e. Hydraulic system—Pressure checked.
11. No. 3 engine—85 percent.
12. Start engines No. 4 and 1.
    Repeat No. 3 engine start procedure for No. 4 and 1 engines.
13. Inboard engines—75 percent or lower.
14. Electrical system:
    a. Generators—Excited and Checked.
    b. No. 1 generator switch—ON.
    c. No. 3 generator switch—ON.
    d. Bus-tie relay—Checked.
    e. Voltage and frequencies—Checked.
    f. D-C power—Checked. (DSO)
15. Air conditioning systems:
    a. Refrigeration unit selector knob—BOTH.
    b. Rain removal switch—REMOVE then OFF.
    c. Cabin temperature control knob—3 o'clock.
    d. Flow switch—RESET TO NORMAL.
    e. Control mode selector knob—AUTO.
    f. Cabin altimeter—CHECKED.
16. Electrical power and air conditioning—Normal.
17. UHF command and TACAN radios—BOTH and T/R(P), T/R(N), BOTH. (DSO)
18. Flight control power switch—ON.
19. Damper switches—ON.
20. Handgrip safety pins (2)—Removed and stowed. (P-N-DSO)
21. Hydraulic pressure and quantities—Checked.
22. Anti-skid switch—ON.
23. Chocks and interphone—Removed. (GO)
24. NAV and DSO—Ready to taxi. (N-DSO)

CAUTION

Do not start to taxi until cleared by the navigator.

TAXI-BACK LANDING. (DSO READS) (CONT'D)

Note

The normal TAXIING, BEFORE LINE-UP, and TAKEOFF checklists will be utilized. The TRANSITION CHECKLIST will be used following the TAKEOFF checklist for traffic pattern operations. If gear retraction and climb to altitude are desired, accomplish the complete AFTER TAKEOFF, PRIOR TO PENETRATION, and DESCENT AND BEFORE LANDING checklists.

CAUTION

Do not depress the brake pedals or retract the landing gear after takeoff, prior to 15 minutes of air time, to avoid fusing the brakes and possible tire failure and airplane damage.

ENGINE SHUTDOWN. (DSO READS)

1. Parking brakes—Set.
2. Canopy jettison handle safety pin—Installed. (P-N-DSO)
3. UHF command radios—OFF. (P-DSO)
4. No. 2 and 3 generator switches—OFF.
5. Refrigeration unit selector—GRD CART.
6. Air conditioning control mode selector knob—OFF.
7. No. 2 and 3 throttles—OFF.

BEFORE LEAVING AIRPLANE. (DSO READS)

1. Canopy seal lever—UNSEALED. (N)
   Pilot checks that canopy seals are deflated.
2. Fuel system configuration:
   a. CG control knob—MANUAL.
   b. All other fuel switches and controls—OFF, NORM, or CLOSE.
   c. Fuel quantity readings—Recorded. (DSO)
3. Oxygen system—NORMAL and OFF. (P-N-DSO)
4. Canopies—OPEN. (P-N-DSO)
   Place lever to CLOSE and hold for a minimum of 5 seconds; then immediately position lever to OPEN and check that canopy latches up. Do not open canopies in headwinds exceeding 60 knots.
5. Wheel chocks—In place. (GO)
6. Brakes released.
7. Canopy locks installed. (P-N-DSO)
8. All switches OFF or SAFE. (P-N-DSO)
   Check that all switches are OFF, SAFE, or positioned properly before leaving the airplane. All weapon control switches should be safe and sealed if applicable.

POSTFLIGHT.

1. Pod and small weapons inspection—Complete.
   a. Small weapon ready-safe switches (4)—SAFE.
   b. Small weapon ground safety pin(s)—Installed.

   MB, LA   c. Pod release safety lockpin—Checked.
   TC   d. Bomb pod ground safety lock—Installed.
   TC   e. Arming control valve—SAFE.
   TC   f. Fuel pod ground safety lock—Installed.
   SF, TC   g. Ground safing switch—SAFE. (W-53)

2. Tail turret safety pin—Installed.
   Install the tail turret safety pin if ammunition is loaded and torqued in or if the system has been used on a live firing mission.

3. Ground safety lockpins (4)—Installed.
4. Record weapon discrepancies (if required).
5. Complete Form 781.

> **CAUTION**
>
> In addition to the established requirements for reporting any system defects or unusual and excessive operations, the flight crew will also make entries in Form 781 to indicate when any limits in the Flight Manual have been exceeded.

ALERT PROCEDURES.

When tactical organizations are required to maintain standing alert aircraft for minimum time scramble, the alert procedures herein will be utilized in conjunction with the integrated preflight procedures contained in Sections II and VIII of this manual. Use of the checklists prescribed herein will permit preflight of a completely EWO configured airplane, cocking the airplane for scramble, DEFCON 1, SRP, minimum reaction, and subsequent preflight of a "cocked" airplane.

AIRPLANE ACCEPTANCE.

After maintenance personnel have prepared the aircraft in the alert configuration and declared it ready for alert, the flight crew will conduct the acceptance check which will consist of the following:

1. Before Exterior Inspection
2. Exterior Inspection
3. Interior Inspection
4. Before Starting Engines Checklist
5. Starting Engines Checklist
6. Before Taxiing

Note

- Systems which operated satisfactorily during the last flight should not be checked in conjunction with the alert acceptance preflight.
- On airplanes requiring maintenance accomplish the following items:

7. After Landing (Begin with item 6)
8. Engine Shutdown
9. Before Leaving Airplane
10. Postflight (as applicable)

Going On Alert.

When the airplane is placed in the alert line, the airplane will be placed in a "cocked" configuration by the aircrew using the cocking checklists.

Security.

No personnel will be allowed in a "cocked" airplane without approval of the pilot. Personnel will comply with the security concept for access to the airplane/weapon combination in accordance with command directives.

Daily Preflight.

At a predesignated time each 24 hours, the aircrew will accomplish the DAILY ALERT PREFLIGHT CHECKLIST.

Maintenance While On Alert.

At anytime while the airplane is cocked, maintenance may be performed without uncocking provided force timing is not degraded, power is not placed on the aircraft, access to the cockpit is not required and no electrical component is involved. If a requirement exists to defuel, the aircrew will uncock the airplane using the UNCOCKING checklist. When the airplane is uncocked for maintenance/defueling and the work is completed, the following checklists will be accomplished prior to performing the COCKING checklist: the pilot's EXTERIOR INSPECTION, the pilot's, navigator's and DSO's POWER-OFF INTERIOR INSPECTION, and the items flagged with an asterisk (*) on the pilot's and navigator's POWER-ON INTERIOR INSPECTION. Refueling of a cocked airplane may be accomplished only by the pilot. If a person other than the pilot accomplishes the refueling, the airplane will first be uncocked using the UNCOCKING checklist. Normal servicing requirements for water, oxygen, hydraulics or pneumatics, which do not require access to the cockpit, may be accomplished on a cocked airplane.

Crew Changeover Preflight Procedures.

When a new crew accepts an airplane which is already in the alert status and it is desired that the airplane remain in the alert status during the changeover preflight, it will be necessary for the new crew to accomplish the DAILY ALERT PREFLIGHT CHECKLIST.

Scramble.

Aircrews will use the SCRAMBLE/SRP POWER-OFF SCRAMBLE and TAKEOFF checklists when the execution order is given. The checklists may be accomplished while taxiing, however extreme caution will be used to insure safe taxi operations. After takeoff, applicable checklists will be reviewed to insure that all items are complete. After takeoff, normal flight manual procedures will apply. Upon completion of practice scramble, shutdowns will be accomplished using the cocking checklists. The aircraft will be recocked using the COCKING checklist.

DEFCON POSTURE.

If a DEFCON posture or SRP is placed in effect while the aircrew is accomplishing the scramble checklist, the scramble checklist should be terminated and the airplane should be shut down and cocked in accordance with the proper cocking checklist. (DEFCON 1 and SRP Power-on will use DEFCON 1/SRP POWER-ON COCKING CHECKLIST, SRP Power-off will use normal COCKING checklist). The proper scramble and normal TAKEOFF checklists will be used for subsequent alert scrambles while in DEFCON posture or SRP. (DEFCON 1 and SRP Power-on configuration will use DEFCON 1/SRP POWER-ON SCRAMBLE CHECKLIST, SRP Power-off configuration will use SCRAMBLE/SRP POWER-OFF SCRAMBLE checklist).

Note

Navigator will use SCRAMBLE/SRP POWER-OFF SCRAMBLE checklist for scramble from SRP Power-off posture.

MINIMUM REACTION POSTURE.

When notified to assume minimum reaction posture the SCRAMBLE/SRP POWER-OFF SCRAMBLE checklist will be accomplished prior to accomplishing the MINIMUM REACTION COCKING CHECKLIST. The MINIMUM REACTION SCRAMBLE CHECKLIST and the TAKEOFF checklist will be used for subsequent scrambles.

DAILY ALERT PREFLIGHT CHECKLIST. (AIRPLANE ON ALERT LINE)

The DAILY ALERT PREFLIGHT CHECKLIST will be used to perform the daily preflight while the airplane is cocked and in alert status. This is an integrated checklist for the flight crew and the ground crew. There is no separate ground crew checklist for daily preflight and the pilot will direct ground crew actions as necessary. If an alert is sounded while the daily preflight is being performed, the airplane will be completely recocked prior to attempting an alert start and scramble procedure.

Before Interior Inspection.

Before performing the interior inspections, accomplish the following procedures. Inspect the exterior of the airplane using the route as prescribed for normal preflight. This is a generalized visual inspection for overall condition. If either hydraulic system accumulator pressure gage indicates that system pressure has fallen below 700 psi, the system must be checked for correct service and excessive air in the system. The pod and weapon items are listed specifically.

Items 5 through 10 and 13 through 16 need to be accomplished by the new crew only on day of change

Section II
Normal Procedures

T.O. 1B-58A-1

Before Interior Inspection (Cont'd)

over or when uncocked for maintenance when subsequent preflights are conducted on the same aircraft/weapon(s) configuration.

Note

- The bomb(s) preflight need only be accomplished once during the current tour of alert unless there has been a change of aircraft or is required as a result of maintenance except for the items indicated in the DAILY ALERT PREFLIGHT CHECKLIST.
- During bomb preflight, a second nuclear qualified individual will verify switch positions and settings after the steps have been accomplished by the individual having the response.

1. Canopy and engine covers—Removed (if installed). (GO)
2. Nose wheel well canopy seal control lever—OFF. (GO)
3. Nose wheel well canopy control lever—OPEN. (GO)

   Place the lever to CLOSE and hold for a minimum of 5 seconds; then immediately position lever to OPEN and check that all canopies latch up. Care should be exercised to prevent the lever from going to the OPEN position when the lockpin is released as the lever is spring-loaded to the OPEN position.

4. Tires and pneumatic pressures—Checked. (GO)

   Direct the ground crew to check and reservice all tires and pneumatic accumulators.

TC 5. Pod pitot tube cover—Removed.

MB, LA 6. Right warhead drag pin indicator—Flush.

7. Small weapons (right side):
   a. Ground safety pin—Removed.
   b. Plenum block protectors—Removed.
   c. Antenna radome cover—Removed.
   d. Delivery option switch—As briefed.
   e. Fuzing option switch—As briefed.
   f. T-Setting—As briefed.
   g. Inflight lock—Properly positioned.
   h. Ready-safe switch—SAFE.
   i. Fin protectors—Removed.
   j. Explosive actuator safing assembly—Removed.

8. Small weapons (left side):

   Repeat same check as for small weapons on right side except that steps a and g will be reversed.

MB, LA 9. Pod release safety lockpin—Checked.

TC 10. Bomb pod ground safety lock—Removed.

MB, LA 11. Pneumatic release system pressure gages (2)—2550 psi at 70 degrees F.

MB, LA 12. Pneumatic release system pressure gage access panel—Secure.

TC 13. Arming control valve—SAFE.

TC 14. Fuel pod ground safety lock—Removed.

TC 15. Ground safing switch—RETARD (W-53).

MB, LA 16. Left warhead drag pin indicator—Flush.

Interior Inspection.

After pilot and navigator have completed items 1 thru 8 of this checklist, the DSO will read the remainder of the checklist.

1. Pod warhead control selector switch—OFF, OS and sealed. (N)
2. Safety lock handle—In, horizontal and sealed. (N)
3. Small weapon lock switches (4)—LOCK and sealed. (N)
4. Small weapon warhead control selector switches (4)—OFF, OS, and sealed. (N)
5. Auto release switch—OFF. (N)
6. Weapon selector switch—OFF. (N)
7. Arm control switch—SAFE and sealed. (P)
8. Small weapon jettison switch—SAFE, safetied. (P)

WARNING

The above items must be accomplished prior to applying a-c or d-c electrical power to the airplane in order to prevent inadvertent weapon arming or release.

9. Essential d-c power:
    a. Battery switch—EMER, battery discharging lamp on.
    b. Battery switch—NORM, battery discharging lamp on.
    c. Battery voltage—Checked. (DSO)
10. Flight control power switch—OFF.
11. ARC-57 and TACAN—OFF. (P-N-DSO)
12. IFF master control knob—OFF. (DSO)
13. Reservoir booster pump switch—OFF.
14. Aft tank to engine supply knob—OFF.
15. AFRS power switches—OFF. (N)
16. External power knob—ALERT and checked, battery discharging lamp out.
17. Oxygen pressure and quantity—Checked. (P-N-DSO)
    a. Oxygen system ON, check pressure, oxygen system OFF.
    b. Check emergency oxygen pressure (1800 psi at 70°F).
18. D-C power—Checked. (DSO)
19. Fuse panels—Checked. (N-DSO)
20. Fuel system:
    a. Fuel gage power switch—NORMAL.
    b. Fuel quantity indicators and totalizer—Checked. (P-DSO)
    c. Reservoir booster pump switch—NORMAL.
    d. Aft tank to engine supply knob—ON.
21. Parking brakes—Set.
22. Cartridge start switch—OFF.
23. Start switches—OFF.

Section II
Normal Procedures

T.O. 1B-58A-1

Interior Inspection. (Cont'd)

24. ARC-34—Checked. (DSO)
25. Pod warhead control selector switch—SAFE. (N)
26. Small weapon warhead control selector switches (4)—SAFE. (N)
27. Lock indicators (5)—LOCK. (N)
28. Arm indicators (5)—SAFE. (N)
29. Master warning lamp—Off, press-to-test. (N)
30. Weapon selector switch—POD. (N)
31. Pod and weapon released lamps (5)—Out, press-to-test. (N)
32. Weapon selector switch—OFF. (N)
33. Pod warhead control selector switch—OFF. (N)
34. Small weapon warhead control selector switches (4)—OFF. (N)
35. All weapon related warning and caution lamps—Off. (P)
36. External power knob—OFF.

CAUTION

External power must be turned off before proceeding to the next step which begins recocking of the airplane.

37. Flight control power switch—ON.
38. UHF and TACAN radios—BOTH and T/R. (P), T/R. (N), BOTH. (DSO)
39. IFF master control knob—STBY. (DSO)
40. AFRS power switches—ON. (N)
41. Personal gear—Arranged. (P-N-DSO)
42. Battery switch—OFF.
43. CMF containers—Checked secure. (P-N)

Exterior Inspection.

1. Nose wheel well canopy control lever—DOWN, then NEUT. (GO)
2. Nose wheel canopy seal control lever—Climatic. (GO)
3. Starter and electrical power carts—OFF, fuel supply checked. (GO)
4. Canopy and engine covers—Installed (if required). (GO)

STRANGE FIELD PROCEDURE.

If it is necessary to land the airplane at an airfield where normal ground support is not available, there are several items which must be performed by the flight crew after parking the airplane, and prior to takeoff. To assist the flight crew in accomplishing these steps properly, the following checklists are provided.

Note

While performing the postflight and preflight exterior inspection:

- Check for cuts, scratches, loose rivets and fuel leaks.
- Check all drain plugs for leakage.
- Check that all vents and ports are clear.
- Check that all access doors and panels are secure.
- Check ground area around airplane for cleanliness.

Note

During bomb preflight, a second nuclear qualified individual will verify switch positions and settings after the steps have been accomplished by the individual having the response.

strange field exterior inspection

NOTE:
For detailed checks to be performed, see "Strange Field Exterior Inspection," this section.

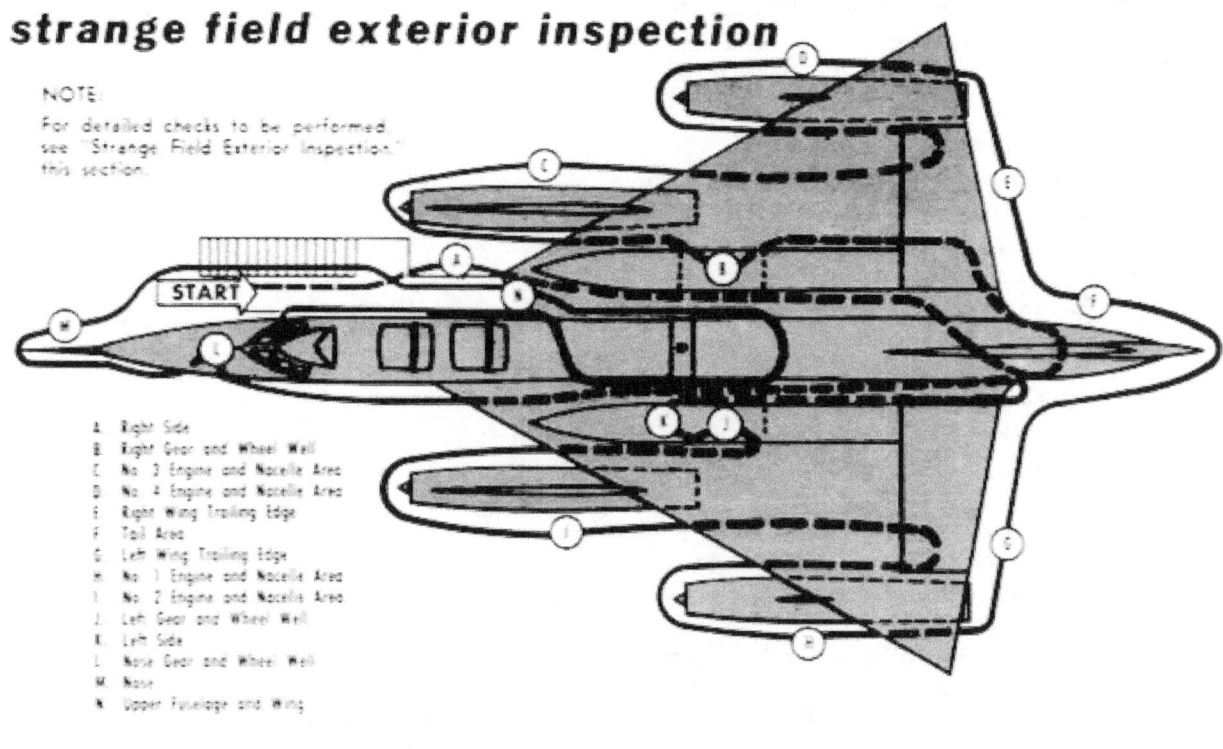

A. Right Side
B. Right Gear and Wheel Well
C. No. 3 Engine and Nacelle Area
D. No. 4 Engine and Nacelle Area
E. Right Wing Trailing Edge
F. Tail Area
G. Left Wing Trailing Edge
H. No. 1 Engine and Nacelle Area
I. No. 2 Engine and Nacelle Area
J. Left Gear and Wheel Well
K. Left Side
L. Nose Gear and Wheel Well
M. Nose
N. Upper Fuselage and Wing

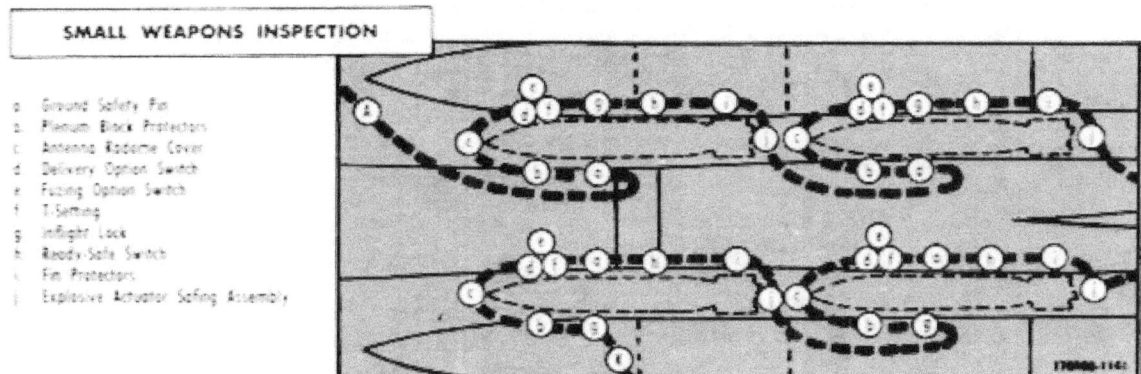

SMALL WEAPONS INSPECTION

a. Ground Safety Pin
b. Plenum Block Protectors
c. Antenna Radome Cover
d. Delivery Option Switch
e. Fuzing Option Switch
f. T-Setting
g. Inflight Lock
h. Ready-Safe Switch
i. Fin Protectors
j. Explosive Actuator Safing Assembly

Figure 2-14.

STRANGE FIELD POSTFLIGHT INSPECTION.

In addition to normal postflight procedures, accomplish the following:
1. Canopies—Closed.
2. Ground locks—Installed (if available).
3. Pitot cover—Installed (if available).
4. Exterior inspection—Complete.
   Follow the route shown in figure 2-14.

Note

If an unscheduled landing has been accomplished and qualified MMS personnel are not available, refer to Section III of T.O. 1B-58A-25-2 for additional weapon safing procedures as needed.

STRANGE FIELD EXTERIOR INSPECTION.

If preflight is delayed beyond 24 hours, it is recommended that the fuel and hydraulic systems be pressurized prior to conducting the exterior inspection. Follow the route shown in figure 2-14 utilizing the following procedures.

Section II
Normal Procedures

T.O. 1B-58A-1

STRANGE FIELD EXTERIOR INSPECTION. (CONT'D)

A. Right Side.

1. Static ports clear.
TC 2. Pod pitot tube cover removed.
MB, LA 3. Right warhead drag pin indicator flush.
4. Small weapons:
   a. Ground safety pin removed.
   b. Plenum block protectors (2) removed.
   c. Antenna radome cover removed.
   d. Delivery option switch as briefed.
   e. Fusing option switch as briefed.
   f. T-Setting as briefed.
   g. Inflight lock properly positioned.
   h. Ready-safe switch SAFE.
   i. Fin protectors (4) removed.
   j. Explosive actuator safing assembly removed.
5. Check general condition of PCLA area:
   a. Check mounts (3) and sway brace for proper installation.
   b. Check fuses and holders for security.
   c. Check hydraulic accumulator pressure (1440 psi at 70 degrees F).
   d. Check hydraulic tubing for leaks, condition, and clearance.
   e. Check push-pull tubes, torque tube and associated linkage, bearings, and lock nuts.
   f. Check control cables and quadrants for security and condition.
6. Drag chute compartment doors secure and over center pin flush.
7. Drag chute pneumatic pressure gage (2550 psi at 70 degrees F).

B. Right Gear and Wheel Well.

1. Wheels and tires for general condition.
   (See figure 2-15 for allowable tire damage.)
2. Strut for condition and proper extension.
3. Landing gear positioning spring pressure gage (1500 psi at 70 degrees F.)
4. Canopy pneumatic system pressure gage (2550 psi at 70 degrees F.)
5. Capsule pressurization system pressure gage (3000 psi at 70 degrees F).
6. Primary hydraulic system pressure and quantity check:
   a. If accumulator pressure is above 700 psi, perform the following:
      (1) Increase pressure to 3000 psi using wheel well hand pump.
      (2) Check for correct reservoir level (20 degrees F below to 40 degrees F above system temperature). Read system temperature on thermometer adjacent to reservoir.
      (3) If fluid is required, connect hand pump ground cart to reservoir pressure regulating valve (located directly below reservoir) and fill to level required for system temperature. Disconnect cart.
   b. If accumulator pressure indicates below 700 psi, perform the following:
      (1) Depressurize the system at reservoir pressure regulating valve (located directly below reservoir), and check accumulator precharge (500 psi at 70 degrees F) per placard instructions.
      (2) Note and record reservoir level.
      (3) Increase pressure to 3000 psi using wheel well hand pump.
      (4) Record reservoir level.

allowable tire damage

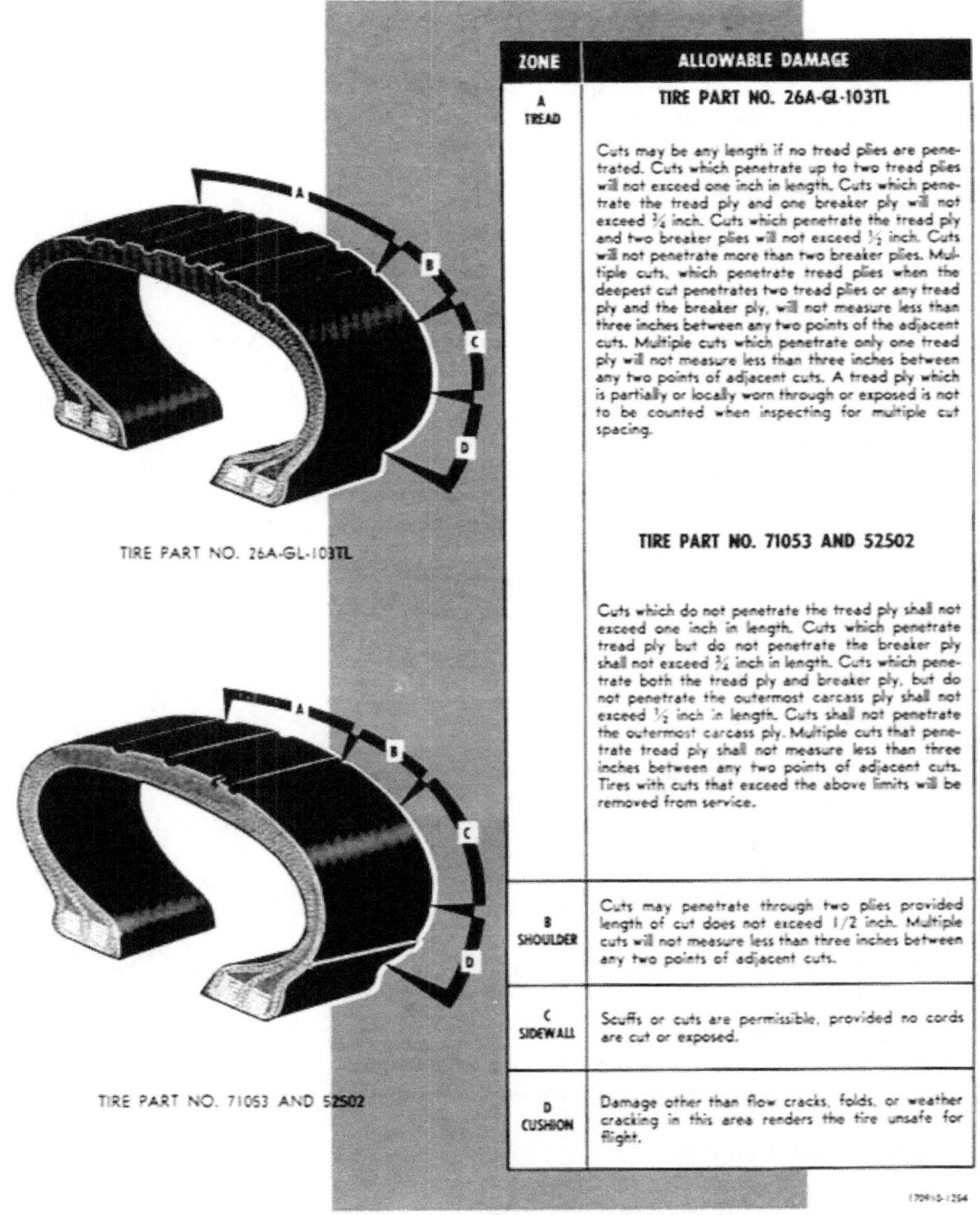

ZONE	ALLOWABLE DAMAGE
A TREAD	**TIRE PART NO. 26A-GL-103TL** Cuts may be any length if no tread plies are penetrated. Cuts which penetrate up to two tread plies will not exceed one inch in length. Cuts which penetrate the tread ply and one breaker ply will not exceed ¾ inch. Cuts which penetrate the tread ply and two breaker plies will not exceed ½ inch. Cuts will not penetrate more than two breaker plies. Multiple cuts, which penetrate tread plies when the deepest cut penetrates two tread plies or any tread ply and the breaker ply, will not measure less than three inches between any two points of the adjacent cuts. Multiple cuts which penetrate only one tread ply will not measure less than three inches between any two points of adjacent cuts. A tread ply which is partially or locally worn through or exposed is not to be counted when inspecting for multiple cut spacing. **TIRE PART NO. 71053 AND 52502** Cuts which do not penetrate the tread ply shall not exceed one inch in length. Cuts which penetrate tread ply but do not penetrate the breaker ply shall not exceed ¾ inch in length. Cuts which penetrate both the tread ply and breaker ply, but do not penetrate the outermost carcass ply shall not exceed ½ inch in length. Cuts shall not penetrate the outermost carcass ply. Multiple cuts that penetrate tread ply shall not measure less than three inches between any two points of adjacent cuts. Tires with cuts that exceed the above limits will be removed from service.
B SHOULDER	Cuts may penetrate through two plies provided length of cut does not exceed 1/2 inch. Multiple cuts will not measure less than three inches between any two points of adjacent cuts.
C SIDEWALL	Scuffs or cuts are permissible, provided no cords are cut or exposed.
D CUSHION	Damage other than flow cracks, folds, or weather cracking in this area renders the tire unsafe for flight.

Figure 2-15.

Section II
Normal Procedures

STRANGE FIELD EXTERIOR INSPECTION. (CONT'D)

      (5) If difference between (2) and (4) exceeds 25 degrees F, excessive air is indicated, and system should be power bled.

      (6) Check level per step a (2). Fill as necessary per step a (3).

7. Primary system pump handle secure.
8. Gear hydraulic actuators for condition.
9. Electrical harness for condition.
10. Landing gear and door mechanism; door lock latch for condition.

C. No. 3 Engine and Nacelle Area.

1. Afterburner nozzle for condition.
2. Pilot burner for condition.
3. Flame holders for cracks.
4. Turbine wheel for condition.
   The turbine wheel may be wet with a small amount of fuel if the engine was motored during the Power-On Inspection but this is not detrimental to engine operation.
5. Fuel strainer bypass indicator plunger retracted.
6. Engine nose cowling and spike for damage.
7. Spike secure and retracted, and anti-ice cone closed.
8. Air inlet opening for foreign material.
9. Inlet guide vanes for condition.
10. Oil tank filler cap access door flush.

D. No 4. Engine and Nacelle Area.

1. Repeat the same check as for No. 3 Engine and Nacelle Area.

E. Right Wing Trailing Edge.

1. Wing tip condition.
2. Wing and elevon trailing edge.

F. Tail Area.

1. Turret and radome checked, safety pin removed, and safety switch flush.
   Check radome and turret for condition and security; check for hydraulic leaks; remove safety pin from barrel housing and check turret safety switch closed.
2. Fuel dump cap flush with fuselage.

G. Left Wing Trailing Edge.

1. Wing and elevon trailing edge.
2. Wing tip condition.

H. No. 1 Engine and Nacelle Area.

1. Repeat the same check as for No. 3 Engine and Nacelle Area.

I. No. 2 Engine and Nacelle Area.

1. Repeat the same check as for No. 3 Engine and Nacelle Area.
   Panel 293 must be removed to view fuel strainer bypass indicator plunger.
2. Starter exhaust door open.

J. Left Gear and Wheel Well.

1. Wheels and tires for general condition.
   (See figure 2-15 for allowable tire damage.)
2. Strut for condition and proper extension (as placarded).
3. Landing gear positioning spring pressure gage (1500 psi at 70 degrees F).

STRANGE FIELD EXTERIOR INSPECTION. (CONT'D)

4. Landing gear emergency pneumatic system pressure gage (2550 psi at 70 degrees F).
5. Brake emergency pneumatic system pressure gage (2550 psi at 70 degrees F).
6. Utility system pressure and quantity check.
   a. If accumulator pressure is above 700 psi, perform the following:
      (1) Increase pressure to 3000 psi using wheel well hand pump.
      (2) Check for correct reservoir level (20 degrees F below to 40 degrees F above system temperature). Read system temperature on thermometer adjacent to reservoir.
      (3) If fluid is required, connect hand pump ground cart to reservoir pressure regulating valve (located directly below reservoir) and fill to level required for system temperature. Disconnect cart.
   b. If accumulator pressure indicates below 700 psi, perform the following:
      (1) Depressurize the system at reservoir pressure regulating valve (located directly below reservoir), and check accumulator precharge (500 psi at 70 degrees F) per placard instructions.
      (2) Note and record reservoir level.
      (3) Increase pressure to 3000 psi using wheel well hand pump.
      (4) Record reservoir level.
      (5) If difference between (2) and (4) exceeds 25 degrees F, excessive air is indicated, and system should be power bled.
      (6) Check level per step a (2). Fill as necessary per step a (3).
7. Chaff dispenser pneumatic accumulator pressure gage (2550 psi at 70 degrees F).
8. Gear hydraulic actuators for condition.
9. Utility system pump handle secure.
10. Electrical harness for condition.
11. Landing gear and door mechanism; doorlock latch for condition.

K. Left Side.

1. Small weapons.
   Repeat the same check as for small weapons on right side except that steps a and g will be reversed.
2. PCLA access panel installed.
3. Landing gear and brake emergency selector valve spring compressed and spring guide extended. No fuel fumes and access door closed.

MB, LA 4. Pod release safety lockpin checked.
TC 5. Bomb pod ground safety lock removed.
MB, LA 6. Pneumatic release system pressure gages (2) 2550 psi at 70 degrees F.
MB, LA 7. Pneumatic release system pressure gage access panel secure.
TC 8. Arming control valve SAFE.
TC 9. Fuel pod ground safety lock removed. Check that inner valve plunger of the lower pod safety lock extends and is seated in the out position under spring tension.

EWO ONLY
TC 10. Ground safing switch RETARD (W-53).

MB, LA 11. Left warhead drag pin indicator flush.

L. Nose Gear and Wheel Well.

1. Tires and wheels for general condition.
   (See figure 2-15 for allowable tire damage.)

Section II
Normal Procedures

STRANGE FIELD EXTERIOR INSPECTION. (CONT'D)

2. Nose strut for proper extension (as placarded).
3. Nose gear steering scissors connected and safety wired.
4. Steering safety switch actuator retainer in place.
5. Gear actuators and lock cylinders for condition.
6. Nose gear door booster pressure gage (2010 psi at 70 degrees F).
7. Single-point refueling adapter cover secure.
8. Capsule air shut-off valve handle safety-wired ON.
9. Pilot's canopy override lever safety-wired OFF (if installed).
10. Inflight refueling emergency pneumatic system pressure gage 2550 psi at 70 degrees F.
11. Canopy control lever latched in UP position.
12. Canopy seal control lever OFF.
13. Electrical harness for condition.

M. Nose.

1. Radome condition.
2. Secondary pitot tube and static ports.
3. Primary pitot tube and static ports.

N. Upper Fuselage and Wing Area.

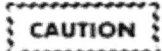

Wear socks over shoes to prevent damage to the wing area when inspecting the upper fuselage and wing area.

1. Fuel system maintenance test buttons (6) flush.
2. Fuel tank caps (3) for security and leakage.
3. Astrodome for cleanliness, cracks, and scratches.
4. Windshield and windows for condition (cleanliness, cracks, etc.)
    Refer to "Glass Panel Damage Limitations," Section V, for permissible damage.

INSTALLATION OF STARTER CARTRIDGE.

The following procedure is for installation of starter cartridge on no. 2 engine. Four spare cartridges are stowed in the crawlway, aft of bulkhead 3.0.

1. Remove nacelle panel 293 to gain access to starter.
2. Remove breech cap by squeezing handle and rotating clockwise.
3. Wipe inside of breech with a dry, lint-free cloth.

Note

Make sure that electrical contact button in the center of cap dome is clean.

4. Remove MXU-4A/A cartridge from its container.
5. Remove grounding clip and bend grounding tabs up to a 45 degree angle between tab and centerline of cartridge to assure good contact with breech cap.

T.O. 1B-58A-1

Section II
Normal Procedures

INSTALLATION OF STARTER CARTRIDGE. (CONT'D)

WARNING

Make sure engine No. 2 cartridge start and engine No. 2 start switches are in the OFF position; otherwise, cartridge will fire during installation.

6. Insert cartridge in breech with ground clip end against cap dome.
7. Install breech cap by rotating counterclockwise until squeeze bar on handle fully releases, indicating breech is locked in position.
8. Install nacelle panel 293.

CAUTION

Do not operate or attempt to start engine pneumatically with unfired cartridge in starter breech.

Note

With exception of steps 4, 5 and 6 the above procedure may also be used for cartridge removal.

AIRCRAFT EMERGENCY MOVEMENT CHECKLIST.

CAUTION

Pilot will ascertain from ground crew that the current aircraft status will allow ground movement.

Note

Ground crew will start and connect external starter air and external power. In event external power is not available, a battery start can be accomplished with external starter air cart only. The number 2 engine may be started using the cartridge starter and battery power.

STARTING ENGINES.

1. CG control knob—MANUAL.
2. Battery switch and external power—NORMAL and ALERT.
3. Parking brakes—Set.
4. Fire pull handles—In.
5. ARC-74—ON.
6. Reservoir booster pump switch—NORM.
7. Aft tank to engine supply control knob—ON.
8. Reservoir to manifold switches—NORMAL.
9. Air conditioning control mode selector—MAN.
10. Refrigeration unit selector—GRD CART.

2-79

Section II
Normal Procedures

STARTING ENGINES. (CONT'D)

Note

Status of engine maintenance will determine the engines to be utilized for aircraft movement. Every effort will be made to utilize one engine from each wing. Engine No. 2 or 1 *must* be started to provide utility hydraulic pressure for brakes and steering.

11. Start No. 2 engine.
    a. No. 2 engine starter exhaust door—Open. (GO)
    b. Engine start switch and throttle—GROUND and IDLE.
    c. Engine start switch—OFF.
    d. Engine instruments—Within Limits.
    e. Hydraulic system—Pressure Checked; lamp out.
    f. Generator—Excited, checked and on.
12. Starter air, electrical power, ground wire, and chocks—Removed. (GO)

Note

Start and stabilization of number 2 engine is the signal for the ground crew to remove external starter air cart, electrical power cart, ground static wires, and chocks.

13. Operating engine—85 percent rpm.
14. Start engine No. 3 or 4—Started.
    Repeat No. 2 engine start procedures.

TAXIING.

1. Brakes—Checked.
2. Nose wheel steering—Checked.
3. Hydraulic pressure and quantity—Monitor.

ENGINE SHUTDOWN.

1. Parking brakes—Set.
2. Unnecessary electrical equipment—OFF.
3. Generators—OFF.
4. Throttles—OFF.

BEFORE LEAVING AIRPLANE.

1. Wheel chocks—In place. (GO)
2. Brakes—Released.
3. All switches—OFF.

FUNCTIONAL CHECKFLIGHTS.

Procedures and criteria for functional checkflights will be accomplished in accordance with T.O. 1-1-300. Flight crew abbreviated checklists, "Functional Checkflight Worksheets", are contained in T.O. 1B-58A-6WS-1CF. The "Emergency Procedures" contained in T.O. 1B-58A-1 will be used. Aircraft requiring functional checkflights are redelivered aircraft, modification maintenance aircraft, and aircraft wherein maintenance performed requires a functional checkflight as specified in T.O. 1B-58A-6. A briefing from the Wing Quality Control Division is required prior to any functional checkflight.

Note

Your normal abbreviated checklist is contained in T.O. 1B-58A-1CL-1.

This is the last page of Section II.

Section III
Emergency Procedures

TABLE OF CONTENTS.

	Page
GROUND EMERGENCIES	3-2
Emergency Ground Egress	3-2
Engine Fire on the Ground	3-2
TAKEOFF EMERGENCIES	3-3
Abort	3-3
Engine Failure	3-4
Engine Fire	3-4
Landing Gear Will Not Retract	3-8
Nose Wheel Uncontrolled Hardover Steering	3-8
Takeoff With One Engine Inoperative	3-8
Tire Failure	3-6
INFLIGHT EMERGENCIES	3-9
Air Conditioning System Emergency Operation	3-35
Air Refueling	See T.O. 1-1C-1-6
Cabin Fire	3-39
Crew Capsulation	3-24
Crew Decapsulation	3-25
Deceleration and Descent, Emergency	3-38
Ejection	3-26
Electrical System Emergency Operation	3-14
Engine Failure	3-9
Engine Fire	3-10

	Page
Flight Control System Emergency Procedures	3-28
Fuel System Malfunction	3-19
Hydraulic System Emergency Procedures	3-18
Inflight Glass Panel Failure	3-38
Landing Gear Malfunction	3-41
Loss of Cabin Pressure	3-37
Loss of Canopy/Glass Panel Blowout	3-37
Oil System Emergency Procedures	3-17
Pitot-Static System Malfunction	3-33
Smoke and Fume Elimination	3-39
Spin Recovery Procedure	3-28
Unlocked Canopy Indication	3-37
LANDING EMERGENCIES	3-41
Brake System Emergency Operation	3-49
Ditching	3-41
Entrance, Emergency	3-52
Go-Around With One or More Engines Inoperative	3-49
Landing Gear Emergency Procedures	3-41
Landing With Blown Tire	3-48
Landing With Broken Positioning Spring	3-47
Landing With One or More Engines Inoperative	3-48
Runway Barrier Engagement	3-50

Section III
Emergency Procedures

T.O. 1B-58A-1

This section contains text and amplified checklists to describe procedures to be followed in emergency situations. The text is divided into primary paragraphs in accordance with the type of emergency and, where applicable, is followed by an amplified checklist for that particular emergency. Each crew member should be thoroughly acquainted with the information covering emergencies which may directly affect his actions. Each descriptive paragraph of the text contains an analysis of some emergency. The amplified checklists describe in detail the actions to be taken. Items which are considered to be critical items are presented in **BOLD FACE** type. Critical items are those actions which must be performed if time and conditions do not permit accomplishment of the complete checklist. These actions must be performed immediately and instinctively to prevent aggravating the emergency condition and to avoid injury or damage. All of the procedures presented in this section are based on the assumption that all crew members will be alerted of the emergency condition as soon as possible while the pilot maintains control of the airplane and initiates critical actions, if applicable.

STOP — THINK — COLLECT YOUR WITS

A thorough evaluation of each emergency should be made prior to initiating corrective action.

GROUND EMERGENCIES

ENGINE FIRE ON THE GROUND.

1. **THROTTLE OFF.**
2. **PULL FIRE PULL HANDLE.**
3. Alert tower. (DSO)
4. Stop airplane.
5. Set brakes.
6. Oxygen ON and EMERGENCY. (P-N-DSO)
   Place oxygen on emergency for protection against possible fire and fumes.
7. Motor engine.
   If No. 2 engine is to be motored, starter exhaust door must be opened. If it can be determined that the fire is confined to the tail pipe, motor the engine to blow out the flames and excess fuel. If ground starter cart has been removed, advance the inboard engine(s) sufficiently to motor the engine to be cleared to 16 percent rpm.
8. Move airplane (if applicable).

WARNING

If raw fuel is running from the affected engine, move the airplane, if possible, to avoid the accumulation of fuel under the wing.

EMERGENCY GROUND EGRESS.

In an emergency requiring ground abandonment, the primary concern should be to leave the immediate area of the airplane as soon as possible. The following procedures are for use in the event of fire, explosion, etc., or expectation of such hazards; salvaging emergency and survival equipment has not been considered. These procedures provide the fastest means of abandoning the airplane; they should be accomplished as soon and as rapidly as possible after the decision to abandon has been made.

Note

The action in this procedure may be initiated while the airplane is in motion, but the safety belt and shoulder harness should remain fastened until the airplane has stopped.

3-2

T.O. 1B-58A-1

Section III
Emergency Procedures

EMERGENCY GROUND EGRESS. (CONT'D)

1. **NOTIFY CREW TO "ABANDON AIRPLANE."**
2. **OPEN OR JETTISON CANOPIES. (P-N-DSO)**

    Use the normal canopy control handle if the airplane is static. If airplane is in motion, the canopies should be jettisoned utilizing the canopy jettison handle. The recommended order of jettisoning the canopies is Pilot, Navigator, and DSO.

3. **UNFASTEN SAFETY BELT AND SHOULDER HARNESS. (P-N-DSO)**

    Unfasten the safety belt and the shoulder harness after the airplane has stopped moving.

WARNING

Be sure that all straps and harnesses are out of the way, leaving a clear path for exit.

4. **DISCONNECT OXYGEN HOSE. (P-N-DSO)**

    Disconnect oxygen hose at the manifold block and retain flight helmet and mask for protection from fire. The mask should be removed only if the hose cannot be disconnected.

5. **ABANDON AIRPLANE. (P-N-DSO)**

    The most expeditious means for safe egress should be used. Exit the aircraft opposite the fire (if applicable) using the emergency escape rope as the primary means. Grasp the loop in the palm of one hand. Do not slip the hand through the loop as this may impair egress if the rope fails to unreel. If the aircraft's attitude at rest provides an alternate means of egress which is more expeditious than the escape rope, the alternate means should be used.

WARNING

Do not egress over the canopies.

Note

If time permits set parking brakes, shut down engines, turn the battery switch OFF and install safety pins in the seat handgrips.

TAKEOFF EMERGENCIES

During takeoff, particularly at heavy gross weights, the aircrew must closely monitor airplane performance to insure normal acceleration and positive rate of climb. Care must be exercised to insure that proper technique is used in airplane rotation to takeoff attitude. Over-rotation or premature or excessive reduction in power could result in an extremely nose high attitude from which recovery may not be possible.

ABORT.

1. **THROTTLES IDLE.**
2. **DEPLOY DRAG CHUTE.**
3. **APPLY BRAKES.**

Note

If a stop can not be made before reaching an obstacle, perform these additional steps.

4. Throttles off—OFF.
5. Fire pull handles—Pulled.

3-3

Section III
Emergency Procedures

ABORT. (CONT'D)

WARNING

If all fire pull handles are pulled, flight controls, nose steering, and hydraulic brakes are inoperative.

6. Pull emergency brake and landing gear control handle—Pulled.
7. Canopy—Open or jettisoned (as required). (P-N-DSO)
   The recommended order of jettisoning canopies is Pilot, Navigator and DSO.

Note

Refer to "Taxi Limitations" or "Brake Energy Limits," as applicable, Section V, for information on further action to be taken.

ENGINE FIRE.

If decision is made to stop:
1. **ABORT.**
   Refer to "Abort" procedures, this section.
2. **THROTTLE OFF.**
3. **PULL FIRE PULL HANDLE.**

If decision is made to continue takeoff:
1. **RETRACT LANDING GEAR.**
2. **MAINTAIN COMPUTED S_2 SPEED OR HIGHER.**
   Maintain takeoff power setting to assure a positive rate of climb and acceleration until reaching a safe altitude and airspeed.
3. Throttle idle—IDLE (on engine indicating fire).
   If indications are normal after retarding the throttle, advance throttle to climb power setting. If there is any evidence of fire proceed with the following steps.
4. Throttle off—OFF.
5. Generator switch off—OFF.
6. Fire pull handle—Pulled.

Do not attempt to restart engine.

ENGINE FAILURE.

Engine failure during the takeoff run can be critical and should be considered and planned for. If an engine failure occurs before S_1 speed/time is reached the takeoff should be aborted. If an engine failure occurs after S_1 speed/time is reached the takeoff is committed. The airplane response to an engine failure is to turn into the failed engine. The deviation from the runway heading will depend on the speed at which the failure occurs, which engine failed (inboard or outboard), the amount and rate of thrust lost and the pilot's reaction to the emergency. After application of rudder and aileron, the airplane may continue along a path at an angle to the runway center line; however, as speed increases sufficient control will become available to resume runway heading. When engine failure occurs above S_1 speed, immediate rudder and aileron should be applied in a direction away from the failed engine to maintain a straight takeoff path and should

directional control of asymmetric thrust

DATA BASIS: ESTIMATED
DATE: 7 FEBRUARY 1964
STANDARD DAY AT SEA LEVEL

ASYMMETRIC THRUST CONDITIONS SEA LEVEL TO 5,000 FEET				MINIMUM AIRSPEED FOR CONTROL WITH CONTROL SURFACES ONLY — ZERO SIDESLIP			
				RUDDER ONLY		RUDDER AND AILERON	
ENGINE NO 1	ENGINE NO 2	ENGINE NO 3	ENGINE NO 4	GROUND RUN ATTITUDE	TAKEOFF ATTITUDE	GROUND RUN ATTITUDE	TAKEOFF ATTITUDE
INOPERATIVE	MAX A/B	MAX A/B	MAX A/B	165	164	135	145
INOPERATIVE	MIN A/B	MIN A/B	MIN A/B	147	146	120	129
INOPERATIVE	MILITARY	MILITARY	MILITARY	132	131	109	116
MILITARY	MAX A/B	MAX A/B	MAX A/B	97	96	80	84
MAX A/B	INOPERATIVE	MAX A/B	MAX A/B	122	121	101	107
MIN A/B	INOPERATIVE	MIN A/B	MIN A/B	110	109	90	96
MILITARY	INOPERATIVE	MILITARY	MILITARY	99	98	81	87
MAX A/B	MILITARY	MAX A/B	MAX A/B	72	71	59	63
INOPERATIVE	INOPERATIVE	MAX A/B	MAX A/B	210	208	172	182
INOPERATIVE	INOPERATIVE	MIN A/B	MIN A/B	183	182	145	154
INOPERATIVE	INOPERATIVE	MILITARY	MILITARY	165	164	137	145
MILITARY	MILITARY	MAX A/B	MAX A/B	122	121	101	107

CORRECTION FOR NON-STANDARD DAY

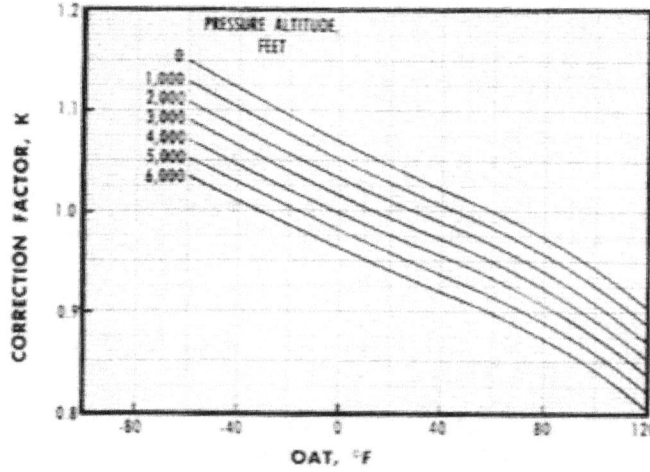

To find the minimum control speed for other than a standard day at sea level, multiply the standard day airspeed by the correction factor from the chart at the left to obtain the correct indicated airspeed for the non standard conditions.

INDICATED AIRSPEED (KNOTS) FOR NON-STANDARD DAY = K × STANDARD DAY AIRSPEED

Figure 3-1.

ENGINE FAILURE. (CONT'D)

be reduced as necessary to maintain control as speed increases. Directional control will be improved with steering engaged and full down elevator for steering effectiveness from S_1 speed to 150 knots.

WARNING

Do not apply full down elevator and full nose wheel steering at speeds above 150 knots to prevent damage to the airplane structure.

Note

On slippery runways although down elevator is applied, nose wheel steering effectiveness is reduced and cannot be relied upon. Aerodynamic control must be used when planning takeoff under these conditions.

Refer to Appendix I for minimum control speed or minimum aerodynamic control speed as applicable. On slippery runways, the minimum aerodynamic control speed may be as much as 15 knots above S_1 speed. If an upwind outboard engine fails during this 15

ENGINE FAILURE. (CONT'D)

knot interval, directional control is not assured using rudder and aileron alone. This is especially true when taking off on narrow runways or near the edge of the runway. Under extreme conditions it may be necessary to reduce thrust on the downwind outboard engine to maintain directional control until aerodynamic control becomes adequate. The effect of the reduced thrust on increasing the ground roll cannot be accurately predicted and the pilot's ability to maintain control may be marginal.

If decision is made to stop:

1. ABORT.

Refer to "Abort" procedures, this section.

If takeoff is continued:

1. RETRACT LANDING GEAR.

Retract the landing gear as soon as airborne. Rate of climb will be improved when gear is retracted.

2. MAINTAIN COMPUTED S_2 SPEED OR HIGHER.

Maintain takeoff power setting to assure a positive rate of climb and acceleration until reaching a safe altitude and airspeed. Do not exceed 17 degrees angle of attack.

3. Throttle off—OFF.

After a safe operating altitude and/or airspeed is attained, retard the throttle of the inoperative engine to OFF.

4. Generator switch off—OFF.

5. Hydraulic valve fuse—Removed. (DSO)

Remove the applicable hydraulic valve 3 amp fuse located on the 28v d-c power distribution panel.

6. Fire pull handle—Pulled.

7. Monitor hydraulic system.

Monitor the applicable hydraulic system quantity for depletion of hydraulic fluid. If evidence of depletion is observed, insert the hydraulic valve 3 amp fuse to isolate the affected engine from the hydraulic system.

TIRE FAILURE.

In the event a tire failure occurs prior to reaching 100 knots, the takeoff should be aborted by using standard abort procedures; however, the anti-skid switch should be turned off before using brakes, particularly at heavy gross weights.

> **CAUTION**
>
> Use brakes only if necessary and then maintain continuous braking. Braking will probably cause the center flange on the wheel to wear flat, resulting in an unbalanced condition which could cause the wheel to disintegrate if the brakes are released above taxi speed.

If a tire failure occurs after reaching 100 knots, tire failure alone should not be considered a significant factor in any decision to abort takeoff. When the tire failure is a nose tire, the nose wheel should be lifted slightly to take the weight off the nose gear; however, the airplane should not be rotated into the takeoff attitude until reaching normal rotation speed. When the tire failure is one or more of the main gear tires and takeoff is continued, the nose steering and rudder controls should give adequate directional control to continue the takeoff. After becoming airborne the landing gear should not be retracted unless climb performance is marginal since fragments of the tires and wheels may have already caused damage to the fuel tanks, hydraulic systems and aircraft structure in the landing gear area. By retracting the landing gear additional damage could be caused from the fragments or from fire or excessive heat from the wheels, brakes and tires. Retracting the landing gear also will increase the possibility of failing to obtain a down and locked landing gear prior to landing. For landing procedures, refer to "Landing With Blown Tire," this section.

T.O. 1B-58A-1

**Section III
Emergency Procedures**

TIRE FAILURE. (CONT'D)

If tire failure occurs below 100 knots on takeoff, perform the following:

1. ABORT.

Refer to "Abort" procedures, this section.

> **CAUTION**
>
> Do not apply brakes before anti-skid is off. Use brakes only if necessary and then maintain continuous braking. Braking will probably cause the center flange on the wheel to wear flat, resulting in an unbalanced condition which could cause the wheel to disintegrate if the brakes are released above taxi speed.

If tire failure occurs above 100 knots on takeoff, perform the following:

1. Do not retract landing gear.

> **WARNING**
>
> After takeoff, at heavier gross weights, with landing gear extended, the aircrew must closely monitor airplane performance to insure normal acceleration and positive rate of climb. Premature or excessive power reduction could result in an extremely nose high attitude from which recovery may not be possible. Attain a safe altitude and airspeed prior to attempting corrective action.

> **CAUTION**
>
> Do not retract landing gear after takeoff unless climb performance is marginal. Fragments of the tires and wheels may have already caused damage to the fuel tanks, hydraulic systems and aircraft structure in the landing gear area. By retracting the landing gear, additional damage could be caused from fire or excessive heat from the wheels, brakes and tires.

2. Check hydraulic pressure and quantity—Checked.

Check hydraulic pressure and quantity to determine if either of the hydraulic systems has sustained damage. After airborne depress the brake pedals and check for a momentary drop in pressure and no loss of fluid from the reservoirs to determine that the brake lines are intact.

3. Visual inspection—Completed.

Prior to landing obtain a visual inspection, if practical, to determine the extent of damage.

Section III
Emergency Procedures

T.O. 1B-58A-1

NOSE WHEEL UNCONTROLLED HARDOVER STEERING.

Nose wheel shimmy or hardover nose wheel steering during landing or takeoff, could result in structural damage to the airplane unless prompt action is initiated. If either of these conditions is encountered on takeoff below S_1 speed, and the nose wheel steering is engaged, disengage steering and abort the takeoff, maintaining directional control with rudder. Up elevator may be applied to reduce the load on the nose wheel. If these conditions are encountered on takeoff above S_1 speed and nose wheel steering is disengaged, engage steering and continue takeoff. If engaging steering does not correct the malfunction, use rudder and aileron to maintain directional control. If nose wheel ground loads and minimum runway requirements are not critical, use up elevator, as necessary, to reduce nose wheel loads. If these conditions are encountered on landing when steering is engaged, disengage steering. If steering is disengaged, engage steering. Use up elevator to maintain reduced nose wheel loads and use brakes for directional control.

LANDING GEAR WILL NOT RETRACT.

If the landing gear does not retract fully when the landing gear handle is positioned UP, attain a safe altitude and airspeed prior to attempting any corrective action.

WARNING

After takeoff, particularly at heavy gross weights, with landing gear failing to retract, the aircrew must closely monitor airplane performance to insure normal acceleration and positive rate of climb. Premature or excessive power reduction could result in an extremely nose high attitude from which recovery may not be possible. Attain a safe altitude and airspeed prior to attempting corrective action.

Reduce airspeed below 300 KIAS and check the utility hydraulic system. If utility system is indicating a possible failure, position gear handle down and refer to "Hydraulic System Emergency Procedures," this section. If utility system appears normal, recycle the handle. If the gear cannot be retracted by recycling, leave the gear extended and maintain airspeeds below 300 knots.

TAKEOFF WITH ONE ENGINE INOPERATIVE. (EMERGENCY EVACUATION)

In cases where emergency evacuation of aircraft becomes necessary, a takeoff with one engine inoperative can be accomplished. Since nose wheel steering must be relied upon for control at low speeds, it is advisable to have the cg at the forward limit to increase the normal load on the nose gear. At brake release, the engine opposite to the inoperative engine should be at idle power. The power can then be increased slowly as long as directional control can be maintained using nose wheel steering and aileron. Above 60 knots, full down elevator can be used if necessary to increase nose wheel steering effectiveness.

WARNING

- Do not apply abrupt down elevator during takeoff roll to prevent damage to the airplane.
- Do not apply full down elevator and full nose wheel steering at speeds above 150 knots to prevent damage to the airplane structure.

Nose wheel steering should be engaged throughout the takeoff roll.

WARNING

On slippery runways, asymmetric thrust is the primary means of maintaining directional control prior to attaining minimum aerodynamic control speed for three engines due to the reduction of nose wheel steering effectiveness.

Refer to Appendix I for take-off distances when taking off with one engine inoperative.

3-8

T.O. 1B-58A-1

Section III
Emergency Procedures

INFLIGHT EMERGENCIES.

ENGINE FAILURE.

An engine failure can usually be determined by observing the engine instruments for a radical change in exhaust gas temperature and a loss in rpm. In case of a malfunction due to material failure (bearing failure, turbine bucket and compressor vane failure, rotor imbalance, stator and rotor friction, etc.) the above indication may be accompanied by noticeable vibration. The yawing maneuver resulting from engine failure may be gradual, moderate, or abrupt depending upon the rate of thrust loss and the number of engines malfunctioning and their location.

ENGINE FAILURE DURING SUBSONIC CRUISE.

Adequate rudder and aileron control are available to maintain straight and level flight throughout the subsonic cruise range with one or two engines inoperative on one side.

ENGINE FAILURE AT SUPERSONIC SPEED.

Without corrective action, instantaneous loss of thrust from an outboard engine will result in large excursions in yaw and roll. This is particularly true at limit speed up to 45,000 feet. The recommended pilot technique in this event is to keep the wings level with aileron, to retard throttles to military power, and apply rudder to moderate yaw excursion and reduce yaw to zero. Although an afterburner failure is not as serious as an engine failure, the instantaneous indications to the pilot will be the same in most cases, and the same pilot technique would apply. After this action has been taken and the affected engine instruments have stabilized, it will then be possible to differentiate between an afterburner failure and an engine failure.

WARNING

If sudden engine failure occurs, the center of gravity must be closely monitored. If engine failure occurs during a turn while operating along the restricted high speed limit with a forward center of gravity, there will be insufficient aileron control available to prevent rolling of the airplane until thrust asymmetry has been reduced, sideslip reduced, or the load factor reduced to one "g". Refer to "Center of Gravity Limitations," Section V.

The aft center of gravity limits are established to provide protection without pilot rudder response or with rudder response expected by inadvertent pilot reaction. Large rudder deflections to reduce initial yaw peaks should not be attempted since they are not required and may increase the tail load developed if applied at or after the initial yaw peak.

WARNING

In the event of sudden engine failure, airplane control and structural integrity are dependent upon roll and yaw damper operation. Observe flight limitations with roll and yaw damper malfunctions. Refer to "Flight Control Limitations", Section V.

Reduction in power on one or two engines will result in loss of airspeed or altitude. Except at the highest speed, a straight ground track can be maintained with wings level. Under high speed conditions, utilize a shallow bank angle to hold a straight ground track during deceleration.

CAUTION

Engine failure or reduction in engine rpm above mach no. 1.6 may result in inlet buzz.

ENGINE FAILURE AT MINIMUM FLYING SPEED.

Engine failure (or hardover damper) at minimum flying speed will cause yaw and roll in the direction of yaw followed by an abrupt nosedown motion and an increase in airspeed. Immediately after the yaw or sideslip is noticed, (1) apply rudder opposite the direction of roll to reduce roll and level the wings, (2) neutralize aileron and use forward stick to neutralize elevators. When airspeed increases to above 240 knots, use aileron to maintain wings-level attitude, then follow normal dive recovery procedure. During recovery do not exceed 17 degrees angle of attack. Spin recovery techniques are presented in this section and Section VI.

Section III
Emergency Procedures

ENGINE NOZZLE FAILURE.

Primary nozzle failure can be detected by variations in nozzle position, exhaust gas temperature, fuel flow and pressure ratio. Secondary nozzle failure in the open position is not detectable in the afterburner power range but may result in a slight thrust reduction at military power and below. Refer to "Engines", Section VII for further information on nozzle malfunctions.

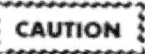

CAUTION

During afterburner operation with the secondary nozzle failed closed the exhaust gas temperature may rise above acceptable limits. Reduce power to military to prevent overtemperature operation and engine damage.

ENGINE FIRE.

1. **SIMULTANEOUSLY RETARD THROTTLE TO IDLE AND OPPOSITE THROTTLE OUT OF AFTERBURNER RANGE.**

   Note
   - If maximum speed is necessary for mission, restore power on opposite engine while trimming airplane.
   - If indications are normal after retarding throttle to IDLE slowly advance throttle to desired power setting. However, if EGT is high, after retarding throttle or if evidence of fire is visible, proceed as follows.

2. Throttle off—OFF.
3. Generator switch off—OFF.
4. Engine spike switch in—IN.
5. Fire pull handle—Pulled.

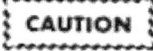

CAUTION

Do not attempt to restart engine.

ENGINE SHUTDOWN.

1. **SIMULTANEOUSLY RETARD THROTTLE TO OFF AND OPPOSITE THROTTLE OUT OF AFTERBURNER RANGE.**

   Note

   If maximum speed is necessary for mission, restore power on opposite engine while trimming airplane.

2. Generator switch off—OFF.
   If the affected engine drives a generator, place the generator control switch OFF to assure a steady power supply to the stable table.

   Note

   By monitoring the EGT, rpm, and fuel flow indicators at time of shutdown, the pilot may be able to determine whether engine malfunction was due to improper fuel scheduling or to material failure. If malfunction was due to material failure, a restart should not be attempted. Shutting off air conditioning bleed air from a malfunctioning inboard engine need not be accomplished unless the engine is contaminating the supply of conditioned air.

ENGINE SHUTDOWN. (CONT'D)

3. Spike switch in—IN.
4. Hydraulic valve fuse—Removed. (DSO)
   Remove the applicable hydraulic valve 3 amp fuse located on the 28v d-c power distribution panel.
5. Fire pull handle—Pulled.
6. Monitor hydraulic system.
   Monitor the applicable hydraulic system quantity for depletion of hydraulic fluid. If evidence of depletion is observed, insert the hydraulic valve 3 amp fuse to isolate the affected engine from the hydraulic system.

ENGINE RESTART.

An engine restart may be performed if the applicable hydraulic valve fuse was removed before the fire pull handle was pulled and the fuse was not reinstalled.

A windmilling airstart can be accomplished successfully with the J79 engine over a wide range of speed and altitudes below 60,000 feet. (See figure 3-2.) If two asymmetrical engines have failed, and it is determined that it is safe to restart both, attempt a restart on the outboard dead engine first.

> **CAUTION**
>
> An engine restart must not be attempted if the engine was shut down by pulling the fire pull handle unless the hydraulic valve fuse was removed prior to pulling the fire pull handle.

1. Throttle off—OFF.
2. Fire pull handle in—IN.
3. Spike switch in—IN.

> **CAUTION**
>
> Do not place spike switch in AUTO position until engine speed is up to 100 percent rpm because of possible engine stall.

4. Engine start switch to air—AIR.
5. Throttle to MIL — MIL.
6. Engine start switch off after light-off — OFF.
7. Generator switch reset—RESET.
8. Check a-c power — Checked.
   Check generator voltage and frequency for proper output.
9. Generator switch on — ON.
10. Hydraulic valve fuse — Installed. (DSO)

Engine Restart After Four-Engine Flameout.

If a four-engine flameout occurs, the best chance for recovery is in getting the engines restarted immediately, before engine rpm drops to the point where the generators de-excite and hydraulic pressure drops to a point below which the primary controls cannot be actuated. De-excitation of all generators results in the loss of a-c power and the subsequent loss of fuel booster pumps. If all airstart attempts are not successful, maintain control of the aircraft until safe ejection altitude is reached. Under no circumstances will a flameout landing be attempted.

Section III
Emergency Procedures

T.O. 1B-58A-1

windmilling airstart speeds

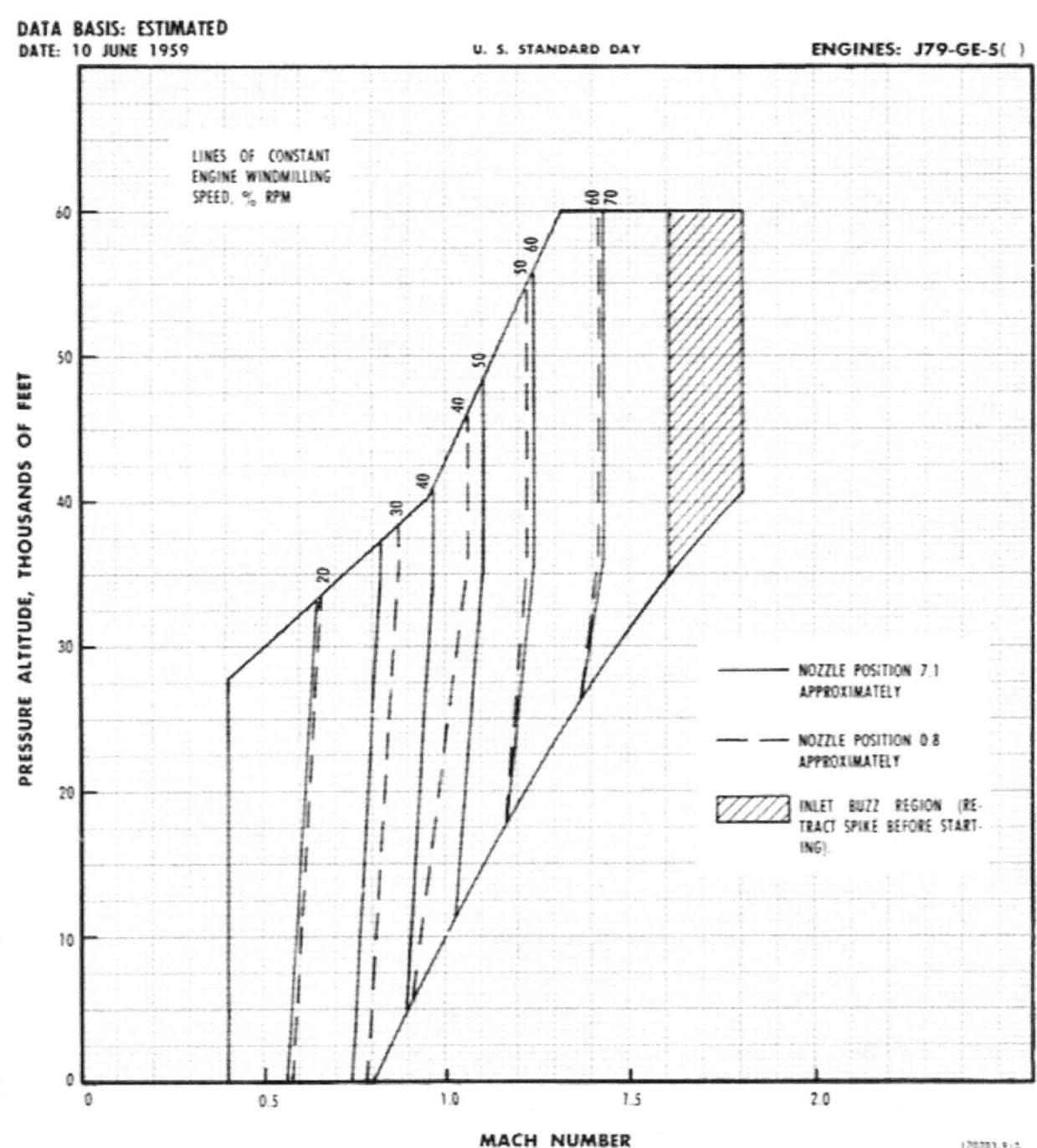

Figure 3-2.

T.O. 1B-58A-1

Section III
Emergency Procedures

Engine Restart After Four-Engine Flameout. (Cont'd)

1. **ENGINE START SWITCHES TO AIR.**
   Place all engine start switches in the AIR position and watch for light-off of all or any engines. If an immediate light-off does not occur, proceed to next step.
2. Throttles MIL—MIL.
3. Check fuel control panel—Checked.
   Reposition the switches on the fuel control panel according to the desired fuel system configuration.
4. If a light-off does not occur within approximately 20 seconds:
   a. Throttles 1 and 4 off—OFF.
      Drain engines 1 and 4 by positioning the throttles to OFF while attempting a light-off on engines 2 and 3.
5. If the inboard engines do not light-off:
   a. Throttles 1 and 4 MIL—MIL.
   b. Throttles 2 and 3 off—Checked.
6. Check electrical control panel—Checked.
   Monitor the electrical control panel for normal power flow configuration and normal voltages, amperages, and frequencies.

Note

If the generators de-excite during restart, place the generator control switches to RESET (momentarily) for re-excitation.

COMPRESSOR STALL CLEARING.

1. Simultaneously retard throttle to idle and opposite throttle out of afterburner range.

Note

If maximum speed is necessary for mission, restore power on opposite engine while trimming airplane.

2. Obtain normal flight attitude.

Note

Steps 1 and 2 are generally sufficient to clear compressor stall; however, if stall continues, proceed with the next five steps.

3. Throttle off—OFF.
4. Spike switch in—IN (if above mach no. 1.42).
5. Generator switch off—OFF.
6. Restart engine (if required).
   Refer to "Engine Restart," this section.
7. Check for compressor stall.
   After engine is started and has accelerated to MIL power, recheck evidence of compressor stall by moving throttle slowly.

If stall is marginal on an engine, it can be prevented by using slow throttle movements and maintaining subsonic flight below maximum altitudes with normal flight attitudes.

> **CAUTION**
>
> If compressor stall occurs when retarding the throttle, the variable stator mechanism is possibly off schedule to the full open position. If this particular malfunction occurs, the engine may be operated normally at power settings near 100 percent but should be shut down before entering the landing pattern.

3-13

Section III
Emergency Procedures

T.O. 1B-58A-1

THREE-ENGINE SUBSONIC FLIGHT.

When three-engine subsonic range is critical, after power setting and airspeed have been stabilized on the operating engines, range may be extended by use of the following procedure, on the inoperative engine, after the engine has been shut down.

1. Extend engine spike—Extended.

    Extend spike on inoperative engine and observe airspeed. As airspeed increases, reduce power on the operating engines to maintain original airspeed.

2. Remove engine spike control, phase A, B, and C fuses — Removed. (DSO)

    Remove engine spike control, phase A, B, and C fuses after spike is extended. (Fuses for engines 1 and 2 are located on left a-c power panel; fuses for engines 3 and 4 are located on right a-c power panel.)

3. Throttle MIL — MIL.

ELECTRICAL SYSTEM EMERGENCY OPERATION.

The loss of one generator does not constitute a flight emergency, since two generators remain to carry the load of the two a-c buses. Normally, with one inoperative, a mission can be completed safely. However, the loss of two generators is considered an emergency, and it is necessary to reduce the electrical load for operation with one generator. (Refer to figure 3-3 for high amperage equipment.) In addition, the airplane must be prepared in case of loss of the last generator.

Note

Refer to T.O. 1B-58A-25-1 for information on the effect of an electrical system emergency on special weapons procedure.

An a-c generator abnormal caution lamp will light if a generator de-excites, is off frequency, or if the supply oil pressure is low. If a slow oil leak occurs which allows a few minutes of operation with the oil level near the top of the standpipe, the abnormal caution lamp will blink on and off. As soon as the oil level drops below the top of the standpipe, the lamp will remain lighted. There is a possibility that a generator-drive can malfunction and, because of failures in the warning circuit, the abnormal lamp will not light. This can be determined from routine monitoring of the generator panel indicators. When a generator de-excites due to generator-drive failure, it is automatically removed from the bus. This condition is indicated by the "power flow" indicators and by voltage and frequency meter readings even though the abnormal lamp does not light. If the "power flow" indicators show an abnormal condition even though the warning lamp is not lighted, the voltage and frequency output should be checked. If the voltage and frequency are normal, attempt to put the generator on the bus. If the generator will not go on the bus, no further action is required unless a second generator is lost. In this event, refer to "Failure of Two Generators," this section. When generator voltages and/or frequencies are outside of the normal operating range and the caution lamp is not lighted, turn off the affected generator and monitor associated engine performance. No further action is required unless a second generator malfunctions. In this event the generator may be placed back on the line.

LIGHTING OF A-C GENERATOR ABNORMAL CAUTION LAMP.

If the generator abnormal lamp blinks on and off or remains lighted, accomplish the following instructions.

1. Check voltage and frequency of affected generator—Checked.

2. Generator switch to reset—RESET. (If generator has de-excited.)

    Place the affected generator control switch to RESET. Then, if generator was No. 1 or No. 3 and it re-excites, the abnormal lamp goes out, and voltage and frequency are normal, attempt to put the generator on the bus. If the generator carries the load, and voltage and frequency remain normal, leave the generator on the bus and continue to monitor the voltage and frequency.

3. If generator will not re-excite, will not carry the load, caution lamp blinks on and off or remains lighted, continue checklist. If caution lamp goes out and voltage and/or frequency are outside the normal operating range, turn off affected generator and monitor associated engine performance.

high amperage a-c loads

SYSTEM	MODE	115 VOLT A-C CURRENT (AMPS)	PHASE Left Bus	PHASE Right Bus
Primary Navigation	Radiate	20.03 16.83 21.43	A B C	
	Standby	18.43 15.93 19.03	A B C	
Search Radar (only)	Radiate	4.35 4.42 7.47	A B C	
	Standby	2.92 3.06 6.46	A B C	
DECM Systems *ALQ-16(T4) left *ALQ-16(T4) aft *ALQ-16(T2) right	Operate Operate Operate	19.08 (each phase) 19.08 " " 12.58 " "	A, B, & C	A, B, & C A, B, & C
Long Range Communication	Transmit Receive	13.58 " " 2.40 " "	A, B, & C A, B, & C	
Active Defense (Fire Control System)	Operate	6.52 8.54 10.35		A B C
	Standby	4.20 6.38 2.31		A B C
Booster Pumps ① ② (Forward Tank) ③ ④ ⑤ (Reservoir Tank) ⑥ ⑦ ⑧ ⑨ (Aft Tank) ⑩ ⑪ (Balance Tank) *⑫ ⑬ (Pod Tanks) Scavenge Pumps ⑭ ⑮		Amps per phase 7.5 (each pump) 8.2 " " 8.2 " " 8.2 " " 8.2 " " 1.05 " "	Even Number Pumps A, B, & C	Odd Number Pumps A, B, & C

*Passive Defense and all pod equipment including fuel pumps will be automatically disconnected from the a-c buses whenever any two generators fail.

Figure 3-3.

LIGHTING OF A-C GENERATOR ABNORMAL CAUTION LAMP. (CONT'D)

a. Generator switch to off—OFF.

b. Generator drive decoupler switch momentarily to disconnect—DISC.

When the generator drive decoupler switch is positioned to DISC, operation of the decoupler can be determined as follows: (1) If the generator is excited, it will de-excite immediately; (2) If the generator is not excited, positioning the generator control switch to RESET two or three times immediately after decoupling the generator. Each attempt to reset the generator will cause a momentary deflection of the voltmeter. Each deflection will be lower in magnitude than the preceding one as generator rotation coasts to a stop.

Note

If the generator drive fails to disconnect, shut the engine down. Refer to "Engine Shutdown," this section.

Section III
Emergency Procedures

T.O. 1B-58A-1

LIGHTING OF A-C GENERATOR ABNORMAL LAMP. (CONT'D)

c. Monitor engine oil pressure.

Monitor engine oil pressure closely after decoupling the generator since loss of generator-drive oil pressure may be due to a leak in the engine oil system.

d. Normal engine operation may be continued.

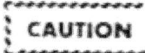

CAUTION

When a generator-drive fails and it is necessary to decouple a generator, care should be exercised to follow the above procedure. Be certain that the correct generator drive decoupler switch is being actuated to prevent disconnecting a good generator which cannot be reconnected after it has been disconnected. After disconnecting a failed generator, there are no restrictions on airplane operation. However, in the event of failure of two generators, the airplane must be landed as soon as possible.

FAILURE OF TWO GENERATORS.

If two generators fail, the remaining generator will automatically power both buses and the a-c load-reducing feature automatically removes electrical power from the pod and DECM equipment. When it is determined that two generators have become inoperative, were de-excited and taken off the bus, accomplish the following:

1. Decelerate and descend (if supersonic).

   After deceleration, flight should be at maximum range altitude and mach number since this requires minimum fuel flow and gives maximum descent range in the event the last generator fails, causing loss of all booster pumps.

2. All nonessential electrical equipment off—Off. (P-N-DSO)

   It may be necessary to deactivate booster pump fuses and/or turn off reservoir booster pump so that no more than four booster pumps are running at one time.

3. Spike switches in—IN.

4. Battery switch on—ON.

5. Check fuel configuration—Checked.

   Maintain as much fuel in forward tank as possible within the cg limits.
   After landing cg is obtained, return reservoir booster pumps to normal and/or replace booster pump fuses if applicable.

6. Land as soon as possible.

Restoring Electrical Power to Pod and DECM Equipment.

If it is desired to override the automatic load-reducing circuits to restore electrical power to the pod and DECM equipment, accomplish the following while closely monitoring the current loads on the good generator:

1. Reduce a-c power load—Reduced.

   Make certain that the restoration of pod and DECM power does not cause power load to exceed single generator capabilities. Normal capacity of one generator is 111 amperes; overload capacity is 166 amperes for 5 minutes. It may be necessary to pull fuses.

2. Pod and DECM power switch reset—RESET or OVERRIDE (as applicable).

   Place the pod and DECM power switch in the RESET or OVERRIDE position to restore electrical power to the pod and DECM equipment.

LIGHTING OF BATTERY DISCHARGING CAUTION LAMP.

Certain malfunctions in the electrical system can cause the battery discharging lamp to light although the battery may not be discharging. To determine the nature of the malfunction, check the left and right a-c buses and the 28-volt d-c power units. If either the forward or aft 28-volt d-c power unit is carrying the load with normal voltage, the lighting of the caution lamp was a false indication; however, the battery switch should be turned OFF until just before the landing approach.

WARNING

If neither 28-volt d-c power unit is carrying the load, reduce electrical load and land as soon as possible. Battery power will drain rapidly under these conditions. Without 28-volt dc power to the booster pumps, only suction feed is available. Air pressure transfer from forward to reservoir tank will be possible.

FAILURE OF ALL GENERATORS.

If all generators become inoperative and the battery switch is in the ON position, the battery automatically assumes the load of the 28-volt d-c essential bus which provides power to all equipment necessary to maintain flight. Flight under these conditions is limited and a landing should be made as soon as possible since only suction fuel feed from the reservoir tank to the engines and air pressure transfer from forward to reservoir tank will be possible.

WARNING

Under a continuous load, battery power will drain rapidly.

Note

In the event of a failure of the automatic transfer circuit, the battery may be connected to the 28-volt d-c essential bus by placing the battery switch in the EMER position.

FAILURE OF A-C BUS.

When an excessive current condition exists, a protection circuit automatically overrides the switch circuits to isolate b... lists the systems connected to each bus. Simultaneous failure of all systems on a bus, lighting of the abnormal caution lamp for the generator that was connected to the bus, normal indications on the power flow indicators, and inability to reset the affected generator are indications of failure of an a-c bus. Check the voltage and frequency of affected bus and if both are zero, proceed with the procedure for "Failure of Two Generators," this section.

OIL SYSTEM EMERGENCY PROCEDURES.

An oil system malfunction (high or low oil pressure) will result in engine seizure within a very short time after actual lubrication deficiency begins, unless the engine is shut down before appreciable bearing damage occurs. The engine will operate at military power for approximately one minute without an oil supply before bearing failure and eventual engine seizure. At 80 to 90 percent rpm, the engine may operate for 4-5 minutes before a complete failure occurs. Since bearing damage can occur before pressure fluctuations begin, it is imperative to shut down the engine as soon as trouble is indicated. Low or fluctuating generator frequency may indicate a loss of oil supply. Pressures outside the limits in Section V, engine vibration, or lighting of a low oil level caution lamp accompanied by associated generator abnormality, should be considered sufficient cause to shut down the affected engine. If pressure fluctuation is greater than ±7.5 psi from the apparent steady state, reduce to cruise power and check the nozzle position and EGT indicator readings. If the nozzle position and EGT readings decrease and then stabilize at cruise power, this indicates that the oil system instrumentation is malfunctioning and normal engine operation can be continued. If the readings do not stabilize at cruise power, this indicates that the oil system is malfunctioning and the affected engine should be shut down. The primary concern is to prevent violent engine seizure, since this can cause loss of one hydraulic system through fluid loss or contamination, fuel system damage, or structural damage. Engine-oil-driven generators may fail prior to engine oil pressure failure, if low oil level is the cause. Complete loss of oil will result in loss of exhaust nozzle control and accompanying loss of thrust may reach 70 percent at 100 percent rpm. If a low oil level caution lamp lights, accompanied by generator abnormality or any other indication of oil starvation, or if any oil pressure limitations are exceeded, shut the engine down. Engine No. 4 will be shut down immediately when the associated oil low level lamp lights. Refer to "Engine Shutdown," this section. When an oil low level caution lamp illuminates and the associated generator indications are normal, continue engine operation and closely monitor oil pressure, nozzle, and generator indications. When an oil low level lamp illuminates during supersonic flight, immediately decelerate to subsonic flight and monitor oil ...dications.

Section III
Emergency Procedures

T.O. 1B-58A-1

HYDRAULIC SYSTEM EMERGENCY PROCEDURES.

PRIMARY OR UTILITY HYDRAULIC SYSTEM FAILURE.

Symptoms of failure will be the same for both the primary and utility hydraulic systems. Impending failure of a hydraulic system can be recognized by abnormally low readings on the pressure or quantity indicators or large, unexplained pressure fluctuations (for example, larger than expected for a flight control command). A steady, abnormal decrease in pressure and/or quantity is probably a forewarning of complete failure of the affected system. Hydraulic pump failure will be indicated by the lighting of the respective pump caution lamp. If one pump in either hydraulic system fails, pressure on that system will fluctuate more than normal as demand on the system varies. Under some flight conditions slower than normal control response may be noted when all hydraulic pumps are not operating normally. Failure of either hydraulic system will cause the yaw damper caution lamp to light.

WARNING

With complete failure of both hydraulic systems the airplane will become uncontrollable; therefore, to increase the chances of a successful ejection, the pilot should attempt to reduce airspeed and attain level flight while the airplane can be controlled. Refer to "Ejection," this section.

Whenever there is a failure of one or more pumps or a confirmed or impending failure of either hydraulic system, demand on both systems should be reduced as much as possible consistent with safe operating requirements by observing the following precautions:

1. Refrain from making abrupt control maneuvers.
2. Discontinue use of nonessential hydraulically operated equipment (tail turret, chaff dispenser, search radar, and autopilot. (P-N-DSO)
3. Decelerate and descend.
4. Avoid flight in turbulence.
5. Land as soon as possible.

CAUTION

Operating a hydraulic system with a failed pump for extended periods may result in contamination of the complete system, thereby causing a possible malfunction of one or more of the hydraulically operated components.

Note

- With failure of the utility hydraulic system the following systems/equipment will be inoperative: Search radar, MD-7 fire control, chaff system, one half of the flight control rams, pitch and roll dampers, landing gear (extension and retraction), wheel brakes and nose wheel steering.
- With failure of the primary hydraulic system, one half of the flight control rams will be inoperative.
- During flight in turbulence or landing in a gusty crosswind, keeping the engine rpm for the good pump in the affected system higher than normal will provide more positive response to flight control demands.

Lower the gear normally unless there is a complete failure of the utility hydraulic system but be prepared to pull the emergency brake and landing gear control handle if airplane control becomes marginal. Refer to "Brake System Emergency Operation," this section.

3-18

HYDRAULIC SYSTEM EMERGENCY PROCEDURES. (CONT'D)

Note

- If one utility system pump has failed, keeping the engine rpm on the remaining pump higher than normal (at about 90 percent) while extending the landing gear will permit the system to more easily satisfy the demand on it.
- If an engine is shut down by using the ENGINE SHUTDOWN checklist, the hydraulic valve will be open and some hydraulic capability will be provided by a windmilling engine.
- If an engine is shut down by using the fire pull handle (hydraulic valve fuse not removed), consider that hydraulic pump failed.

HYDRAULIC PRESSURE OR QUANTITY ABNORMALLY HIGH.

An abnormally high hydraulic pressure indication can be caused by an indicator malfunction or a true increase in system pressure which probably will be accompanied by an increase in quantity indication. An increase in quantity is a result of increased fluid temperature due to aerodynamic heating or the bypassing of fluid due to excessive pressure or other malfunction. If pressure rises above normal or quantity increases rapidly, observe the following procedure:

1. Check hydraulic pressure and quantity indicators—Checked.
   The hydraulic system indicators should be checked frequently, especially during high speed flight. If pressure increases to more than 3350 psi or quantity exceeds 90 percent, perform the next step.
2. Decelerate and descend.
   Reduce airspeed and/or altitude in an attempt to prevent exceeding 90 percent quantity indication. If the quantity increase was due to aerodynamic heating, little advantage will be gained by reducing airspeed below mach no. 0.93 or descending below 40,000 feet.
3. Land as soon as possible (if pressure or quantity cannot be controlled).
   If pressure and quantity cannot be controlled within the limits stated in step 1, land as soon as possible to prevent damage to the system components or complete failure of the affected system.

FUEL SYSTEM MALFUNCTION.

ABNORMAL FUEL DEPLETION.

Abnormal depletion of fuel can occur from a broken fuel supply manifold or from ruptured fuel tanks. These instructions are concerned primarily with the situation resulting from a broken fuel line external to the fuel tanks. Four indications of abnormal fuel depletion are: (1) Excess flow indicated on an engine fuel flow indicator and fuel flow totalizer indicator; (2) Multiple fuel system warning/caution lamp display; (3) Rapid decrease in fuel quantity indicator(s); (4) Mission plan fuel checks.

Note

When any one of the above indications is observed, verify that an abnormal depletion of fuel exists before proceeding with this procedure.

When an abnormal depletion of fuel has been established, an attempt should be made to isolate the area of probable failure to best conserve the remaining fuel supply. In this isolation process, shutting down both engines on the affected side of the airplane may become necessary. When both engines on the right side (engines 3 and 4) are shut down, the primary hydraulic system and number 3 generator will be inoperative. When both engines on the left side (engines 1 and 2) are shut down, the utility hydraulic system, numbers 1 and 2 generators, and the pitch and roll dampers will be inoperative. Other malfunctions which may have occurred prior to noting the abnormal depletion of fuel are not considered in this procedure. However, such previous failures as engine, generator, hydraulic system, and fuel quantity indicating system must be considered when following the instructions below.

WARNING

Closely monitor the cg and elevator position indicators to prevent an unsafe condition from developing due to an unscheduled loss of fuel and deviation from the mission plan.

Section III
Emergency Procedures

T.O. 1B-58A-1

ABNORMAL FUEL DEPLETION. (CONT'D)

In all cases where abnormal fuel depletion is suspected or indicated, the following action should be taken as soon as possible:

1. Throttles MIL or below—Set.
2. Decelerate and descend.
3. CG control knob manual—MANUAL.
   After a safe cg has been obtained select manual cg control.
4. Check fuel dump switch in NORM—Checked.

Engine Fuel Flow Indicator Showing Excessive Flow To One Engine And Abnormal Depletion of Fuel Establishd.

These conditions indicate a failure downstream of the engine fuel flowmeters which are located in the inboard pylon. The following procedures will isolate a failure in these areas.

1. Affected throttle off—OFF.
2. If engine fuel flow indicator continues to show any flow, pull affected engine fire pull handle— Pulled.

Engine Fuel Flow Indicators Showing Normal Flow And Abnormal Fuel Depletion Observed.

A dire emergency exists when depletion of fuel is positively verified, but indications from warning and caution lamps are not decisive, and fuel flow indicators show normal flow to engines.
Perform the following checklist as applicable:

1. Fuel in aft tank. (If aft tank is empty, proceed to step 2.)
   a. Aft tank to engine supply knob on—ON.
   b. Forward tank to engine supply knob off—OFF.
   c. Left and right reservoir to manifold switches closed—CLOSE.
   d. Balance to aft tank interconnect switch closed—CLOSE.
   e. Check balance and aft tank quantity indicators—Checked.
      Balance tank should show no decrease and aft tank should show normal decrease. If these conditions exist, the source of abnormal depletion is a break in a fuel line in the void area between bulkheads 8.0 and 9.0 and it has been effectively isolated. Continue flight in this configuration, see Note below, proceed with steps in "Additional Information for Remainder of Flight," this section, and land as soon as possible.
   (1) If balance tank shows decrease, a break in the refuel manifold in the void area between bulkheads 8.0 and 9.0 is indicated. The following procedure permits gravity feed from balance tank to aft tank, if aft tank level is 28,000 pounds or less, to increase useable quantity in aft tank for remainder of flight.
      (a) Balance to aft tank interconnect switch—INTERCONNECT, then CLOSE. Place switch to INTERCONNECT until fuel is depleted in balance tank then place switch to CLOSE.
      (b) Continue flight in this configuration, proceed with steps in "Additional Information for Remainder of Flight," this section, and land as soon as possible.
   (2) If aft tank shows abnormal depletion and if either manifold low pressure lamp lights, a large break in tee casting in inboard pylon is indicated. The following procedure isolates the break and shuts off fuel.
      (a) Affected throttles off—OFF.
      (b) Remove single d-c booster pump control fuse for the affected aft tank pumps —Removed. (DSO)
      (c) Reservoir to manifold switch for operating engines—NORMAL.
      (d) Continue flight in this configuration, proceed with steps in "Additional Information for Remainder of Flight," this section, and land as soon as possible.
   (3) If aft tank shows abnormal depletion and no manifold low pressure lamp is lighted, perform the following:
      (a) Both reservoir to manifold switches normal—NORMAL.

ABNORMAL FUEL DEPLETION. (CONT'D)

    (b) Check reservoir feed indicator to determine which reservoir manifold is supplying fuel to the engines—Checked.

- If no reservoir feed is indicated there is a structural leak in the aft tank. If the rate of fuel loss and the available fuel from forward tank transfer are such that continuing flight in this configuration is not advisable, proceed to forward tank or reservoir tank feed.

- If the reservoir indicates feed, there is a small break in the tee casting of the inboard pylon. The following procedure isolates break and shuts off fuel.

    (c) Close reservoir to manifold switch on the manifold that indicates flow—CLOSE.

    (d) Affected throttles off—OFF.

    (e) Remove single d-c booster pump control fuse for the affected aft tank pumps—Removed. (DSO)

    (f) Continue flight in this configuration, proceed with steps in "Additional Information for Remainder of Flight," this section, and land as soon as possible.

Note

It may be desired to transfer fuel into the aft tank. If in e(1) above, balance tank quantity indicator showed no decrease and if the source of fuel depletion was definitely established as either the left or right-hand engine supply manifold and that manifold isolated, fuel may be transferred from the forward tank to the aft tank after pulling the forward tank pump fuse on the affected side. If balance tank showed abnormal decrease or if abnormal depletion ceased immediately upon selection of aft tank feed, transfer to the aft tank is not recommended.

2. Fuel in forward tank. Aft tank empty. (If forward and aft tanks are empty, proceed to step 3)

    a. Forward tank to engine supply knob to on—ON.

    b. Right reservoir to manifold switch to close—CLOSE.

    c. Remove d-c booster pump control fuse for pump 1—Removed. (DSO)

    d. Aft tank to engine supply knob off—OFF.

    e. Check the forward and reservoir tank fuel quantity indicators for excessive fuel depletion—Checked.

Note

This fuel configuration should be maintained until a depletion rate is observed in both the forward and reservoir tanks. Under some conditions fuel from the forward tank will air pressure transfer into the reservoir tank.

    f. If excessive fuel depletion is from forward tank with normal depletion from reservoir tank, a break in the right manifold is indicated. Isolate the right manifold as follows:

        (1) Throttles 3 and 4 off—OFF.

        (2) Forward tank to engine supply knob to off—OFF.

        (3) Balance tank refuel-scavenge knob to scavenge—SCAVENGE (if balance tank contains fuel).

        (4) Replace d-c booster pump control fuse for pump 1—Replaced. (DSO)

        (5) Remove d-c booster pump control fuse for pump 2—Removed. (DSO)

Section III
Emergency Procedures

T.O. 1B-58A-1

ABNORMAL FUEL DEPLETION (CONT'D)

      (6) Forward tank to engine supply knob on—ON.
      (7) Continue flight in this configuration, proceed with steps in "Additional Information for Remainder of Flight," this section, and land as soon as possible.

  g. If excessive fuel depletion is from reservoir tank, a break in the left manifold is indicated. Isolate left manifold as follows:
      (1) Throttles 1 and 2 off—OFF.
      (2) Right reservoir to manifold switch to normal—NORMAL.
      (3) Left reservoir to manifold switch close—CLOSE.
      (4) Forward tank to engine supply knob to off—OFF.
      (5) Balance tank refuel-scavenge knob to scavenge—SCAVENGE. (If balance tank contains fuel.)
      (6) Forward tank to engine supply knob on—ON.
      (7) Continue flight in this configuration, proceed with steps in "Additional Information for Remainder of Flight," this section, and land as soon as possible.

Note

If there is fuel remaining in the aft tank which may be desired for engine feed, remove single d-c boost pump control fuse for aft tank pumps on the side of the airplane for which the manifold has been isolated and position aft tank to engine supply knob to on.

3. Fuel in reservoir and balance tanks only:
  a. Reservoir booster pumps switch off—OFF.
  b. Balance tank refuel-scavenge knob to scavenge—SCAVENGE.
  c. If an engine or engines flame out on one side, a break in the manifold on the side is indicated. Retard both throttles on the affected side to off—OFF.
  d. Reservoir to manifold switch for affected side off—OFF.
  e. Reservoir booster pumps switch normal—NORMAL.

Note

If no engine flames out, a small break in either manifold (not large enough to cause the engine to flame out) may exist. Continue flight with reservoir booster pumps OFF to minimize fuel loss.

  f. Continue flight in this configuration, proceed with steps in "Additional Information for Remainder of Flight," this section, and land as soon as possible.

Additional Information For Remainder Of Flight.

1. Position electrical and electronic system switches as indicated below:
  a. Navigation lights—Set.
      Leave in last actuated position.
  b. Anti-collision lights to off—OFF.
  c. Navigation bombing system to off—OFF. (N)
  d. Aft T4-system to off—OFF. (DSO)
  e. Bomb damage evaluation system to off—OFF. (N)
  f. LRC system to off—OFF. (DSO)
  g. Pull VGH recorder fuses—Pulled. (DSO)
      Pull VGH recorder fuse from 28-volt d-c power panel and from left a-c power panel.
  h. Fire control system to off—OFF. (DSO)
  i. Doppler radar to off—OFF. (N)

ABNORMAL FUEL DEPLETION (CONT'D)

j. Radio altimeter to off—OFF. (N)
k. Low altitude radar altimeter—OFF. (P-N)

WARNING

To prevent creating a fire hazard, electrical and electronic system switch positions as indicated above should not again be changed for the remainder of the flight.

2. Closely monitor fuel flow, quantity, and cg for remainder of the flight.

Incorrect information will be displayed by the forward and aft tank fuel flow directional indicators when the d-c booster pump control fuse for pump 1 or the single d-c booster pump control fuse for pumps 8 and 9 are removed. Removal of the d-c booster pump control fuses does not affect the fuel quantity or cg indicating system. If the proper booster pump fuses have been pulled, caution lamps for the affected pumps will not flash or light when switch positions corresponding to the operation of these pumps are selected. Since split feed will not simultaneously feed a single manifold from the forward and aft tanks; split feed should not be selected until a manifold has been isolated. Refer to "Engine Shutdown," "Electrical System Emergency Operation," and "Hydraulic System Emergency Procedures," this section, for other information.

FUEL DUMPING.

Fuel dumping provides a means of rapidly reducing the airplane gross weight in event of an emergency. During the fuel dumping operation the airplane center of gravity moves forward. The cg should be closely monitored during the operation to prevent exceeding the forward center of gravity limit. This is no problem for the airplane without pod because the basic airplane center of gravity is farther aft than that for the airplane with pod and during the dumping operation the center of gravity cannot move forward of the 24 percent MAC limit for the airplane without pod. When fuel is dumped, fuel impinges on the fuselage regardless of the airspeed; however, fuel dumping above mach no. 0.9 or 300 KIAS is not recommended. If fuel is dumped at airspeeds above the maximum recommended airspeeds for fuel dumping, the amount of fuel that impinges on the fuselage will be greater. In either case, some fuel may enter the tail section void areas creating a possible fire hazard.

Note

- If the air conditioning system is in ram air operation, the fuel dump rate will be materially reduced due to lack of fuel tank pressurization.
- The landing gear should be extended prior to starting actual dumping, if conditions permit.

1. Check airspeed—Checked.
   Maintain airspeed below 300 KIAS or mach no. 0.9 whichever is lower, if possible.

Note

After the fuel dumping operation is completed, the airspeed may be increased up to the restricted high speed limit.

2. Switches positioned for dumping—Set.
   Position the following switches as indicated.
   a. Aft T4 power selector knob to off—OFF. (DSO)
   b. ARC-110 power switch to off—OFF. (DSO)
   c. MD-7 master switch to off—OFF. (DSO)

3-23

Section III
Emergency Procedures

T.O. 1B-58A-1

FUEL DUMPING. (CONT'D)

    d. Remove 115V AC Bø radio alt fuse (left main a-c power panel)—Removed. (DSO)
    e. Bomb damage evaluation switch to off—OFF. (N)
    f. Doppler transmitter switch to off—OFF. (N)
    g. Radio altimeter switch to off—OFF. (N)
    h. Remove—150V DC Doppler radar and + 150V DC radio alt fuses (multiple voltage power panel)—Removed. (N)
    i. Low altitude radar altimeter to off—OFF. (P-N)

Note

The above switches should not be repositioned until after aircraft has landed and an inspection completed for presence of fuel in the tail section void areas.

3. Fuel panel—Set.
See Section VII for fuel panel configuration.
4. Fuel dump switch to dump—DUMP.
5. Transfer fuel as required during dumping to maintain proper cg.
6. Fuel dump switch to normal—NORM.
Return the dump switch to NORM when the desired airplane gross weight is obtained.
7. Fuel panel configuration as required—As required.
Upon completion of fuel dumping, return fuel system controls to positions necessary for the remainder of the flight.

CREW CAPSULATION.

The following procedures are for use if it becomes necessary to capsulate during flight and ejection is not anticipated. Remove loose equipment from capsule. The DSO and navigator's altimeter and airspeed indicator are not visible when capsule is closed.

1. **STOW WORK TABLE. (N-DSO)**
2. **RAISE HANDGRIPS. (P-N-DSO)**

- Be sure feet and hands are inside the capsule before raising the handgrips.
- The capsule is ready for ejection when the handgrips are raised. DO NOT TOUCH THE EJECTION TRIGGERS.

3. **LOWER HANDGRIPS. (P-N-DSO)**

Handgrips must be returned to the full down position in order to re-arm the shoulder harness inertial reel lock in event it has been unlocked and slackened.

Note

Higher than normal control stick forces will be required to fly the airplane after capsulation due to loss of cabin pressure. This is caused by the control stick pedestal boot being compressed around the stick by pressure inside the capsule.

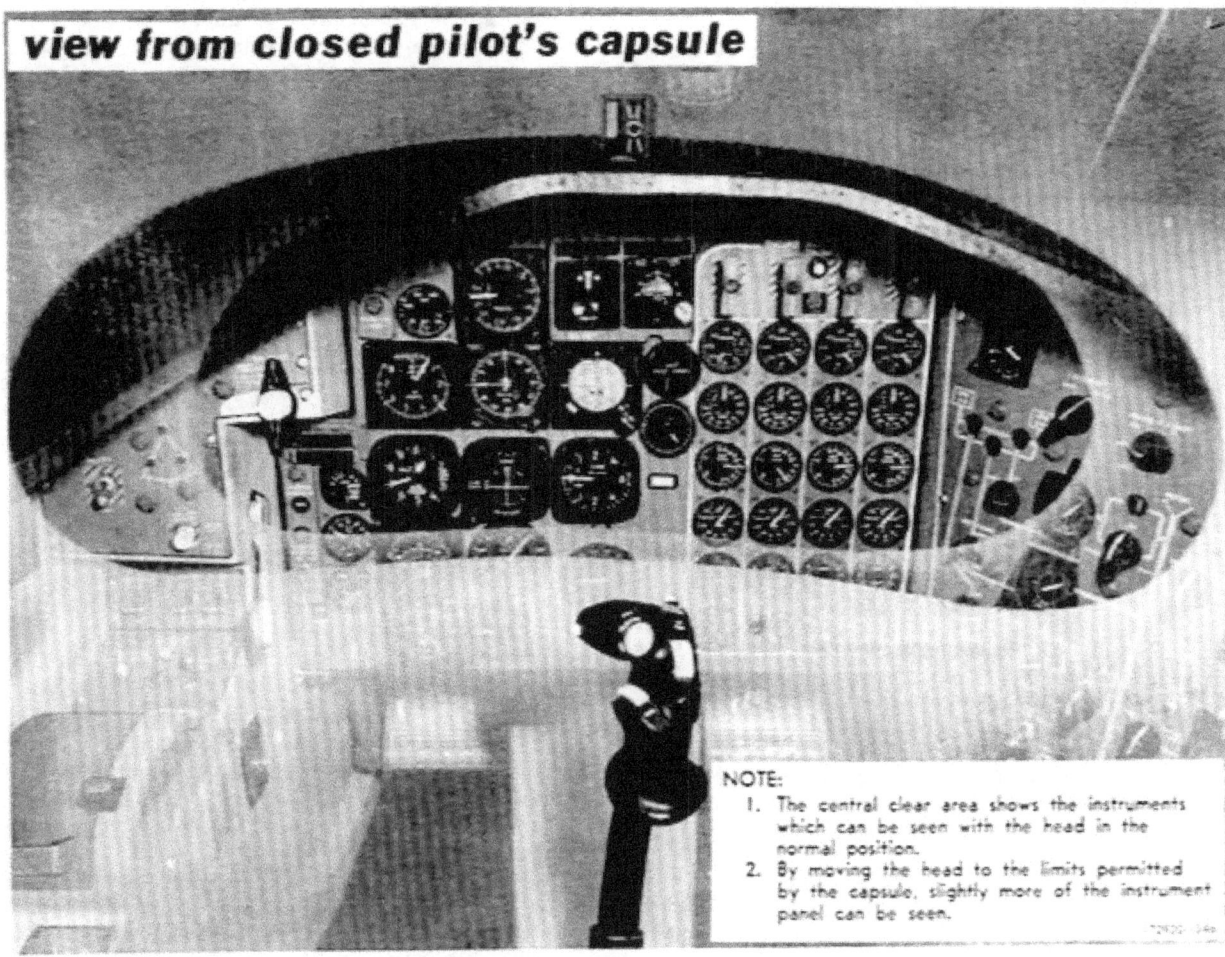

Figure 3-4.

CREW DECAPSULATION.

1. **HANDGRIPS FULL DOWN. (P-N-DSO)**

WARNING

The capsule doors will not close in the event it becomes necessary to capsulate again unless the handgrips are repositioned to the full down position.

2. **INERTIA REEL UNLOCKED. (P-N-DSO)**
3. **UNLOCK AND RAISE CAPSULE DOORS. (P-N-DSO)**
   After doors are raised, lock them in the open position.

CAUTION

To prevent damaging the curtain seal, the internal door release handles must be fully retracted before raising the doors.

EJECTION.

Escape from the airplane in flight should be made in the following sequence: DSO, navigator, and pilot. A crew ejection indicator lamp in the capsule headrest area signals the pilot when both crew members have ejected. See figure 3-5 for ejection procedure. An ejection at low altitudes is facilitated by pulling the nose of the aircraft above the horizon ("zoom-up maneuver"). This maneuver affects the trajectory of the capsule providing a greater increase in altitude than if ejection is performed in a level flight attitude. This gain in altitude will increase the time available for complete actuation of the capsule systems. Refer to "Escape Capsule," Section I, for sequence of events after ejection. When circumstances permit, slow the airplane down as much as possible prior to ejection. Ejection should not be delayed when the aircraft is in a descending attitude and cannot be levelled out.

WARNING

Under level flight conditions, ejection should be accomplished with the envelope shown in figure 3-5. Under spin or dive conditions, ejection should be accomplished above 15,000 feet above the terrain.

The "Emergency Minimum Recovery Height" envelope in figure 3-5 shows only the altitude you must attain in the event of a low altitude emergency. The decision as to when to eject or not eject in an emergency should not be rigidly determined by the fact that the aircraft is in or out of the "Safe" envelope. Every emergency will have its particular set of circumstances involving such factors as aircraft speed, sink rate, attitude and control, as well as altitude.

Ejection with the doors open should be a last resort and if done, the shoulder harness must be tight and locked, the seat pan in its highest position, and the feet tucked tightly into the capsule. The airplane must be slowed to the slowest possible speed before ejecting with the capsule doors open. After ejection, expect the capsule to undergo several unusual gyrations until the parachute has deployed completely.

WARNING

The manual parachute deployment handle will spring out of its recessed position when it is unlocked. If this is not immediately followed by parachute opening shock, pull the handle immediately to deploy the chute. If the manual deployment handle does not spring out at 15,000 ft. or below, pull the emergency release handle. The manual deployment handle then must be pulled to deploy the recovery chute.

Upon landing, depress the parachute disconnect handle release button and pull the handle to release the parachute and to inflate the upper flotation cells.

WARNING

Do not depress the parachute disconnect handle release button prior to landing. The handle should not be accessible during capsule descent. Pulling the parachute disconnect handle before landing will release the parachute causing free-fall of the capsule.

If the landing was made on the ground, actuate both lower door downlatches and rotate doors to stowed position over the hood. Should downlatches be inoperative, cut the curtain above the window at the designated place and make a slit at both spots marking the upper door latches. Since landing impact will tend to cause upper door latches to engage more firmly, it may be necessary to press against the inside of the upper door with the palms of the hands and move the door forward to loosen the latches. Push outward at each latch with the thumbs or any pointed object to release the latches. Raise the upper door and exit from the capsule. If the landing was made on water, cut the curtain above the window at the designated place (cut should be lengthwise rather than crosswise) and make small slits at the spots marking both upper door latches. Move the upper door forward slightly to loosen the latches and press at the designated access holes to release them. Raise the upper door as desired for ventilation or egress. Inflate the lower flotation cells with the hand pump. In event of rough seas, inflate the lower flotation cells prior to opening the upper door. Open the door with caution to avoid shipping water or keep the door closed in rough water and breathe through the oxygen mask with the hose attached to the snorkel fitting. Remove the rubber plug in the center of the forward edge of the upper door and insert the survival radio antenna through the hole when attempting communication in rough water. If the landing was in icy water, open the doors about an inch as soon as possible so that a handhold will be available should a coat of ice form upon the doors.

ejection procedures
ESCAPE CAPSULE

BEFORE EJECTION

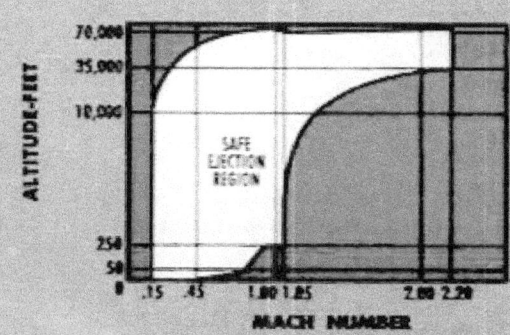
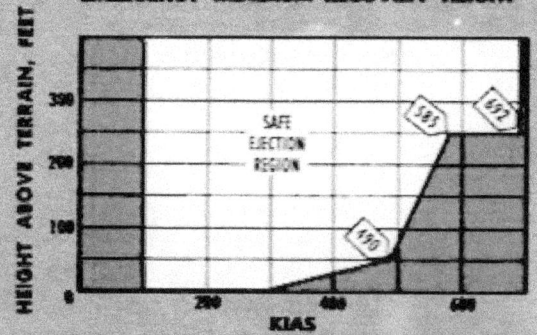

1. Bailout Alert Switch to Alert and alert crew for possible ejection.
2. Reduce airspeed as much as possible.
3. If at low altitude, zoom the aircraft.
4. Remove loose equipment from capsule. (P-N-DSO)
5. Check personal restraint harness—fastened and adjusted properly. (P-N-DSO)

WARNING

- Emergency minimum recovery height presented in this chart was determined through extensive flight tests and is based on distance above terrain on initiation of capsule ejection (i.e., time capsule is fired). These figures do not provide any safety factor for such matters as equipment malfunction, etc. These figures are quoted only to show the minimum altitude you must attain in the event of such low altitude emergencies as fire on takeoff. These minimum altitudes are much higher when the aircraft is losing altitude.
- Under spin or dive conditions, ejection should be accomplished above 15,000 feet above the terrain.

EJECTION

PILOT
1. ORDER CREW TO EJECT.
   Use interphone and/or bailout warning switch.
2. RAISE HANDGRIPS.
3. SQUEEZE TRIGGERS.

NAVIGATOR
1. STOW WORKTABLE.
2. RAISE HANDGRIPS.
3. SQUEEZE TRIGGERS.

DEFENSIVE SYSTEM OPERATOR
1. STOW WORKTABLE.
2. RAISE HANDGRIPS.
3. SQUEEZE TRIGGERS.

DESCENT

1. PULL MANUAL PARACHUTE DEPLOYMENT HANDLE (if necessary). (P-N-DSO)
   Below 15,000 feet pressure altitude, the manual parachute deployment handle will spring out. If parachute opening shock is not felt immediately, pull the handle to deploy the parachute.

WARNING

- Do not depress the parachute disconnect handle release button prior to impact. To do so may result in release of the parachute, causing free-fall of the capsule.
- Do not loosen shoulder harness until after impact and the parachute has been released. Injury could result from impact of the capsule or by wind blowing the parachute with the capsule attached.

AFTER LANDING

1. DEPRESS PARACHUTE DISCONNECT HANDLE RELEASE BUTTON AND PULL PARACHUTE DISCONNECT HANDLE. (P-N-DSO)
   Press the parachute disconnect handle release button, then pull the handle after landing to release the parachute and inflate the upper flotation cell.

2. INFLATE LOWER FLOTATION CELLS (if in the water). (P-N-DSO)

NOTE

Approximately 600 actuations of the hand pump are necessary to fully inflate each cell. Over inflation could result in rupturing the cell.

3. OPEN CAPSULE DOOR. (P-N-DSO)
   Cut the curtain seal and then open the upper door if on the water. Open the lower door if on land.

Figure 3-5.

Section III
Emergency Procedures

SPIN RECOVERY PROCEDURE.

1. **NEUTRALIZE CONTROLS.**
2. **THROTTLES IDLE.**
3. **FULL AILERON IN DIRECTION OF SPIN.**
   Determine spin direction using turn-and-slip indicator.
4. **ELEVATOR CONTROL AVAILABLE TO T.O. & LAND.**

> **CAUTION**
>
> When the elevator available increases to 20 degrees, it will be extremely easy to overcontrol the pitch axis and care should be used in application of elevator control.

5. **START SWITCHES TO AIR.**
6. **NEUTRALIZE AILERONS AS SPIN STOPS AND ESTABLISH NOSE DOWN ATTITUDE.**
7. After spin stops, use angle-of-attack and airspeed to recover from dive attitude.
   Do not let airspeed drop below 240 knots IAS or angle of attack exceed 17 degrees during dive recovery. Reduce angle of attack so that angle of attack will be not more than 6 degrees upon regaining level flight.
8. Start switches to ground—GROUND.
   Placing engine start switch to GROUND will expedite engine starting utilizing compressor bleed air if either inboard engine is operating, and will also rearm the ignition.
9. Start switches off—OFF.
   After normal engine operation is restored, place engine start switches to OFF.

STALL WARNING INDICATION.

If the stall warning lamp lights in flight, immediately cross-check the angle-of-attack, attitude, airspeed, and vertical velocity indicators and the altimeter. If these instruments indicate the desired flight conditions disregard the stall warning lamp. If the flight instruments indicate an excessive nose high flight condition, refer to procedures for slow speed condition under erroneous airspeed indication, this section.

FLIGHT CONTROL SYSTEM EMERGENCY PROCEDURES.

The flight control system emergency procedures presented in this section are the immediate steps required to correct critical abnormal flight characteristics. The sequence of these steps is determined by the degree of emergency. *It may not be necessary to accomplish the complete procedure to correct a particular malfunction.* These procedures are categorized by the abnormal flight characteristic which will be apparent to the pilot. Separate procedures are presented for malfunctions in the elevator control system and aileron and rudder control system. If a malfunction is alleviated by disengaging the autopilot, the airplane may still be operated on one autopilot channel. For example, if the malfunction is pitch oscillation and this is corrected by turning off the autopilot, the airplane may still be operated with the roll autopilot engaged. In the event that any of the following malfunctions are alleviated by turning off the roll or pitch damper, select high speed or low speed standby gains as recommended for the particular flight condition and turn on the damper. If selection of standby gains corrects the malfunction, normal operation may be continued. If this does not correct the problem, turn off the malfunctioning damper and switch back to normal gains. For a hardover damper failure, switching the damper off will normally result in a transient in the opposite direction as the damper servo is recentered. The monitors will automatically disengage a failed yaw damper, thereby preventing the occurrence of a hardover yaw damper servo; however, a slight transient may be felt. With any damper off, observe damper-off operating limits as specified in Section V. For flight control system trouble shooting procedures for less critical malfunctions, refer to "Flight Control System," Section VII. For those procedures where the emergency increase elevator available handle is used, refer to figure 7-16 for the amount of increase in elevator control available with each detent of the handle.

FLIGHT CONTROL SYSTEM EMERGENCY PROCEDURES. (CONT'D)

WARNING

In the event of any situation where control of the airplane cannot be recovered, ejection should be accomplished before descending below 15,000 feet above terrain.

DAMPER HARDOVER AT MINIMUM FLYING SPEED.

If a damper hardover occurs during operation at minimum flying speed, observe the procedure for "Engine Failure at Minimum Flying Speed," this section.

ELEVATOR CONTROL SYSTEM.

Simultaneous Roll With Pitch.

Stick moves diagonally instead of fore and aft on elevator command. This stick motion may be induced as a result of a malfunction.

1. **APPLY FORE AND AFT STICK ONLY.**
   Apply force to move stick fore and aft only. Do not allow lateral stick movement.
2. **APPLY RUDDER.**
   Level airplane using rudder for roll control and stick for pitch control.

WARNING

If malfunction persists, flight to an optimum ejection condition may be attempted but is very hazardous. Do not attempt to land. If control of the airplane cannot be maintained, immediate ejection is recommended.

Elevator Motion Restricted.

Elevator motion is restricted if less than normal stick travel exists, excessive elevator force is required to displace the stick, or the stick is jammed in a fixed position.

1. **AUTOPILOT OFF.**
   Release the autopilot and check that the autopilot switches return to the OFF position. If the autopilot fails to disengage electrically, apply stick force to actuate the autopilot poppets.
2. **CHECK ELEVATOR AVAILABLE.**
   If indicator reads low, increase elevator available by popping the force link. When sufficient elevator available is obtained, switch to MANUAL.
3. Check hydraulic systems.
   With a hydraulic system malfunction, stick motion is restricted aft only if at supersonic speed, at or forward of the forward cg limits. If at supersonic speeds, establish 31.5 percent cg and accomplish procedure for hydraulic system failure. Refer to "Primary or Utility Hydraulic System Failure," this section.

WARNING

If the malfunction persists, elevator control is probably jammed and flight to an optimum ejection condition is very hazardous. Do not attempt to land.

3-29

Section III
Emergency Procedures

T.O. 1B-58A-1

ELEVATOR CONTROL SYSTEM. (CONT'D)

Elevator Free In One Or Both Directions.

Elevator free is when the airplane does not respond to elevator in one or both directions.

1. ENGAGE AUTOPILOT.

Use mach-altitude mode to assist in controlling the airplane.

2. Use trim.

Leave elevator control available mode selector switch in AUTO and move stick to operate automatic trim for airplane control. Use stick trim if more rapid control is desired. If stick is free in one direction, use sufficient manual trim so that stick force is required to maintain level flight.

Note

Landing may be attempted if stick is free in one direction. Prior to landing, adequate control of the airplane should be demonstrated at a safe altitude. If the stick is free in the aft direction, use full manual stick trim in the up direction to insure maximum elevator control for landing.

Pitch Up or Down.

1. AUTOPILOT OFF.

Release the autopilot and check that the autopilot switches return to the OFF position. If the autopilot fails to disengage electrically, apply stick force to actuate the autopilot poppets.

2. INCREASE ELEVATOR AVAILABLE.

Pop the force link to increase elevator available and switch to MANUAL when sufficient elevator available has been obtained.

3. PITCH DAMPER OFF.

Observe pitch damper inoperative restrictions.

Oscillation In Pitch.

1. AUTOPILOT OFF.

Release the autopilot and check that the autopilot switches return to the OFF position. If the autopilot fails to disengage electrically, apply stick force to actuate the autopilot poppets.

2. PITCH DAMPER OFF.

Observe pitch damper inoperative restrictions.

3. CHECK CG. (DSO)

Check that the cg is forward of the aft limit for the flight condition.

4. Increase elevator available—Increased.
5. Flight control power switch to off—Off.
6. Elevator control available mode selector switch to manual—MANUAL.

AILERON AND RUDDER CONTROL SYSTEM.

Aileron Motion Restricted.

Aileron motion is restricted if less than normal stick travel exists, excessive aileron force is required to move the stick, or if the stick is jammed in a fixed position.

1. AUTOPILOT OFF.

Release the autopilot and check that the autopilot switches return to the OFF position. If the autopilot fails to disengage electrically, apply stick force to actuate the autopilot poppets.

2. APPLY RUDDER.

Maintain wings level using rudder to sideslip the airplane. Normal response is for right rudder to raise the left wing and left rudder to raise the right wing.

T.O. 1B-58A-1

Section III
Emergency Procedures

AILERON AND RUDDER CONTROL SYSTEM. (CONT'D)

Note

When flying without a pod at speeds above approximately mach no. 1.9 normal roll response to rudder control is reversed, particularly at the higher altitudes.

3. Check hydraulic systems.

If at supersonic speed with a hydraulic system malfunction, establish 31.5 percent cg and accomplish procedure for hydraulic system failure. Refer to "Primary or Utility Hydraulic System Failure," this section.

Note

Adequate control of the airplane should be demonstrated at a safe altitude prior to landing.

Aileron Free In One Or Both Directions.

The airplane does not respond to aileron commands in one or both directions.

1. **ENGAGE AUTOPILOT.**

   Use heading constant mode to assist in controlling the airplane.

2. **APPLY RUDDER.**

   Level the airplane using rudder for roll control.

3. Manual stick trim—As required.

   Use manual trim to control the airplane. If the stick is free in one direction, aileron control can be obtained by trimming stick in the direction the stick is free so that force is required to maintain wings level.

Note

Landing may be attempted; however, adequate control of the airplane should be demonstrated at a safe altitude.

Lighting of Yaw Damper Warning Lamp.

1. **AUTOPILOT OFF.**

   Release the autopilot and check that the autopilot switches return to the OFF position. If the autopilot fails to disengage electrically, apply stick force to actuate the autopilot poppets.

WARNING

Do not engage the autopilot roll channel when the yaw damper warning lamp is lighted.

2. **DECELERATE AND DESCEND (IF SUPERSONIC).**

3-31

Section III
Emergency Procedures

T.O. 1B-58A-1

AILERON AND RUDDER CONTROL SYSTEM. (CONT'D)

Note

Insure that cg is forward of subsonic aft limit prior to deceleration to subsonic speeds.

3. YAW DAMPER OFF.

Turn yaw damper off and observe damper inoperative restrictions.

Do not depress yaw reset button. To do so may engage a failed yaw damper channel.

Lateral-Directional Oscillation.

1. AUTOPILOT OFF.

Release the autopilot and check that the autopilot switches return to the OFF position. If the autopilot fails to disengage electrically, apply stick force to actuate the autopilot poppets.

2. DECELERATE AND DESCEND (IF SUPERSONIC).

Note

Insure that cg is forward of subsonic aft limit prior to decelerating to subsonic speeds.

3. DAMPER(S) OFF (AS REQUIRED).

- If yaw damper warning lamp is lighted, turn off roll and yaw dampers and observe damper inoperative restrictions.

- If yaw damper warning lamp is not lighted, turn off roll damper; if oscillation does not subside, turn off yaw damper. Observe damper inoperative restrictions.

Use rudder or hold a small amount of side-slip to damp oscillation. When operating with roll and yaw dampers off at supersonic speeds, pilot aileron inputs can cause large lateral-directional oscillations to develop. Aileron control must not be attempted except at a very low rate to maintain bank angle within approximately 10 degrees.

4. Gain selector switch—HIGH or LOW (as required).

Place gain selector switch to the HIGH SPEED or LOW SPEED position, as appropriate for the flight condition.

T.O. 1B-58A-1

Section III
Emergency Procedures

AILERON AND RUDDER CONTROL SYSTEM. (CONT'D)

5. Check damper operation.

    Turn on the roll damper. If the oscillation reoccurs or increases, turn the roll damper off and observe damper inoperative restrictions. If oscillation does not reoccur, continue the flight on standby gains and observe the applicable restrictions for high speed and low speed gain, Section VII, and/or damper inoperative restrictions, Section V.

PITOT-STATIC SYSTEM MALFUNCTION.

The pitot-static system supplies static and impact pressures which are required for proper operation of various systems. Ice may form on the pitot-static probe ports resulting in improper operation; however, previous experience has shown that icing of the static ports on either system is not likely to occur. For the maximum differences between the primary and secondary airspeed indications, refer to "Pitot-Static System," Section I. The following information provides a procedure for operation of the airplane in the event of erroneous airspeed indications.

ERRONEOUS AIRSPEED INDICATION.

Early detection of an airspeed system malfunction is the best means of avoiding a reduction in airspeed. The angle of attack system is a valuable aid in the event of airspeed system malfunctions and can be used to maintain safe airspeeds.

The following instructions will aid in recognizing an airspeed system malfunction and provide a procedure for recovering from an inadvertent slowdown.

1. If any crew members suspects an airspeed system malfunction or sees an unexplained change in airspeed or mach number indication immediately:

    a. Cross-check airspeed. (P-N-DSO)
    b. Check pitot heat On and fuses In. (P-DSO)

    #### Note

    When the pitot heat is turned on, the ammeter on the generator feeding the right bus will flicker.

    c. If pilot's airspeed does not agree with navigator's and DSO's, or if both systems are suspected:

        (1) Disengage autopilot.
        (2) Check attitude on attitude indicators, angle of attack on the angle-of-attack indicator, and vertical velocity indicator.

    d. Slowspeed condition must be assumed to exist if:

        (1) Attitude indicators show five degrees or more above normal cruise attitude and altitude is not increasing or,
        (2) Angle-of-attack indicator shows 10 or more degrees, or,
        (3) Altitude is decreasing in excess of 3000 feet per minute and attitude indicators show normal attitude for cruise.

2. If a slowspeed condition exists:

    a. Lower nose five degrees as read on the attitude indicator.

    #### Note

    It may be necessary to pull the emergency increase elevator available handle to gain sufficient control to lower the nose.

3-33

ERRONEOUS AIRSPEED INDICATION. (CONT'D)

    b. Slowly advance power to military.
    c. Note angle of attack change on the angle-of-attack indicator.
        (1) If angle of attack decreases, establish a speed sufficient to give a maximum of 6 degrees angle of attack.
        (2) If angle of attack remains unchanged (because of frozen or otherwise malfunctioning indicator) descend 5000 feet and stabilize at that altitude.

Note

The airplane should stabilize between mach no. 0.96 and 0.99. The elevator position should rapidly increase at least 2 degrees during acceleration.

3. If slowspeed condition is not identified:
    a. Slowly advance power to military and attempt to maintain cruise altitude using the attitude indicator or maintain cruise angle of attack using the angle-of-attack indicator.
    b. Continue to cross-check airspeed and attitude or angle-of-attack indicator.

Note

If the static ports of both systems are iced (indicated by no change in altimeter or vertical velocity indication) the pilot can dump cabin pressure then use the cabin altimeter for an approximate indication of altitude. To obtain vertical velocity information the pilot can break the glass of his flight altimeter after dumping cabin pressure. Altitude above terrain can also be determined by the radio altimeter. Have the navigator go to altitude malfunction mode and read altitude above terrain on the HSI indicator.

4. Set cg at 29 percent MAC.
5. When airplane has stabilized under the conditions in step 2 or 3:
    a. Set 2.4 EPR, or set power to attain an angle of attack indication of 6 degrees. The airplane should decelerate to mach no. 0.91 to 0.95.
    b. Observe airspeed, altitude, and ground speed from the primary navigation system to determine which airspeed system is good and continue flight on the good system. If the primary system has malfunctioned, the angle-of-attack indicator can be used to maintain essentially a constant airspeed by maintaining the angle of attack noted when airspeed readings are given by N or DSO.
6. If both airspeed systems are malfunctioning the following procedure should be used.
    a. Set 2.4 EPR or set power to attain an angle of attack indication of 6 degrees at cruise altitude.
    b. Advance power when maneuvering and do not allow angle of attack to exceed 12 degrees.
    c. Establish VFR flight conditions as soon as practical.
    d. Descent and landing with angle-of-attack operative.
        (1) Reduce power to attain an angle of attack of 7 degrees.
        (2) Descend to 20,000 feet and stabilize at an angle of attack of 7 degrees.
        (3) Set cg at 27.5 percent MAC.
        (4) Reduce gross weight if necessary to a normal landing gross weight for the airplane configuration.
        (5) When airplane has stabilized, lower landing gear.

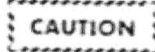

Do not lower landing gear at angles of attack lower than 6 degrees.

T.O. 1B-58A-1

Section III
Emergency Procedures

ERRONEOUS AIRSPEED INDICATION. (CONT'D)

(6) Set power for descent (inboards 85 percent, outboards IDLE). Descend at 8 degrees angle of attack.
(7) Maintain an angle of attack of 9 degrees in the traffic pattern.
(8) Use an angle of attack of 12.5 degrees to execute approach and landing.
(9) The angle-of-attack indexer may be used as an aid in maintaining the proper angle of attack for final approach. The on-speed (green) symbol will light when the angle of attack is between 11.25 and 13.75 degrees. Proper approach/flare speed corresponds to 12.5 degrees angle of attack.

Note

When landing without a pod or with the upper pod only, the on-speed (green) symbol will light at airspeeds approximately 3½ knots lower than the computed approach/flare speed.

e. Descent and landing with angle-of-attack inoperative.
(1) Set inboard engines to 85 percent and outboard engines to idle.
(2) Descend at 4000 feet per minute to 20,000 feet and stabilize at 2.4 EPR.
(3) Set cg at 27 percent MAC.
(4) Reduce gross weight to approximately 80,000 pounds.
(5) Decelerate at the following EPR, maintaining 20,000 feet until the elevator position changes to:

Elevator	EPR	Configuration
2.0 Degrees	1.65	MB Pod
2.0 Degrees	1.65	Upper Pod
3.0 Degrees	1.65	TCP
2.0 Degrees	1.55	Without Pod

(6) After airplane has stabilized, lower landing gear.
(7) Set power for descent (inboards 85 percent, outboards idle) and descend at 5000 feet per minute.
(8) Set power at 1.76 EPR with any pod or 1.66 EPR without pod for level flight in the traffic pattern.
(9) Upon reaching the final approach set power at 1.5 EPR, descend at 800 to 900 feet per minute on a normal glide slope.

AIR CONDITIONING SYSTEM EMERGENCY OPERATION.

CABIN PRESSURIZATION MALFUNCTION.

Cabin Overpressurized.

1. Cabin pressure selector knob to combat—COMBAT.
2. If overpressurized condition still exists, place the cabin pressure selector knob to DUMP.
3. If overpressurized condition still exists, accomplish the following:
   a. Altitude and airspeed within ram air limits—Check.
   b. Control mode selector knob to ram—RAM.
   c. Turn off all unnecessary electronic equipment—OFF. (P-N-DSO)
      Refer to "Air Conditioning System"—"Ram Air Operation," Section IV.

Cabin Underpressurized (Above 8000 Feet).

1. Cabin pressure selector knob to combat or normal (as applicable)—COMBAT or NORM.
2. If underpressurized condition still exists, reduce altitude until low cabin pressure caution lamp goes out or capsulate if necessary. Refer to "Crew Capsulation," this section.

TEMPERATURE CONTROL MALFUNCTIONS.

Low Airflow Caution Lamp Lights.

If the low airflow caution lamp remains lighted with the engine speed at 90 percent or above, observe the following procedure.
1. High airflow to cabin:
   a. Flow switch to reverse—REVERSE (if applicable).
      If the system fails to reverse automatically, the flow switch must be manually placed in REVERSE. The light should go out within five minutes.

Section III
Emergency Procedures

T.O. 1B-58A-1

TEMPERATURE CONTROL MALFUNCTIONS. (CONT'D)

2. Low airflow to cabin:
   a. Flow switch to reverse—REVERSE.
   b. Control mode selector knob to manual—MAN.
   c. Temperature control knob to cool—COOL.
   d. If airflow to the cabin increases, reset to normal when the caution lamp goes out and proceed with flight.
   e. Monitor electronic temperature indicator.
   f. If airflow to cabin does not increase or caution lamps do not go out within ten minutes, perform the following:
      (1) Airspeed and altitude within ram air limit—CHECKED.
         Refer to "Airspeed Limitations," Section V, for ram air mode operating limits.
      (2) Control mode selector knob to ram—RAM.
      (3) Unnecessary electrical and electronic equipment off—OFF. (P-N-DSO)
         Refer to "Air Conditioning System,"—"Ram Air Operation," Section IV.
3. Normal airflow to cabin, electronic temperature indicator reads HOT.
   a. Isolate overheat equipment.
      (1) ARC-57, fire control system and primary navigation system off—OFF then ON.
         Turn all of this equipment OFF then return to the ON position, one at a time. Monitor the temperature indicator to determine which is overheating.

Crew Compartment Overheated.

If the crew compartment becomes overheated and the temperature control is at full cool, perform the following:

1. Refrigeration unit selector knob to L or R (as required)—Set.
   Check the refrigeration unit temperature indicators and select the unit which is not overheating. If, after a reasonable length of time, the condition still exists, proceed with the following steps.
2. Control mode selector knob to manual (if required)—MAN.
3. Windshield defog switch to decrease—DEC.

Note

Allow a reasonable length of time for the cabin temperature to lower before making further adjustments.

4. Flow switch reset to normal (if required)—RESET TO NORMAL.
   If the system is in reverse flow, position the flow switch to RESET TO NORMAL momentarily. If the condition persists, proceed with the next step.
5. Reduce airspeed and altitude (if required)—Reduced.
   Adjust speed to comply with ram air operating limits. Refer to "Airspeed Limitations," Section V.
6. Control mode selector knob to ram—RAM.
7. Electronic equipment off (as required)—Off. (P-N-DSO)
   Turn off all electronic equipment which requires cooling and is not essential to be in operation. Refer to "Air Conditioning System,"—"Ram Air Operation," Section IV.
8. If overheating cannot be controlled, land as soon as practical.

Cabin Too Cold.

1. Cabin temperature control knob to warm (as required)—WARM.

Note

To prevent the loss of cabin pressure when the control mode selector knob is placed to MAN, return the temperature control knob to 12 o'clock before performing the next step.

Section III
Emergency Procedures

TEMPERATURE CONTROL MALFUNCTIONS. (CONT'D)

2. Control mode selector knob to auto or manual (as required)—AUTO or MAN.
3. Refrigeration unit selector knob to L or R (as desired)—L or R.
4. Flow switch to reverse—REVERSE.
   Change system to reverse flow to stop direct flow of cold air on the crew members.
5. Windshield defog switch to increase—INC.

Loss Cabin Cooling Airflow After Selecting Defog and/or Rain Removal Operation.

1. After defog selection, position defog switch to decrease—DEC.
   Cabin cooling airflow should start within 30 seconds.
2. After rain removal selection:
   a. Position control mode selector to ram—RAM.
   b. Turn off all unnecessary electronic equipment—Off. (P-N-DSO)
      Refer to "Air Conditioning System,"—"Ram Air Operation," Section IV.

LOSS OF CABIN PRESSURE.

In case of loss of cabin pressure at high altitude while wearing an oxygen mask it is imperative that the pilot immediately descend to an altitude of 42,000 feet (or less) where cabin pressure is not required. Immediate protection will be afforded by capsulation; however, capsulation is not essential at altitudes of 42,000 feet and below. Refer to "Crew Capsulation," "Crew Decapsulation," and "Cabin Underpressurized (Above 8,000 Feet)," this section.

1. **OXYGEN ON AND EMERGENCY. (P-N-DSO)**
2. **DESCEND IMMEDIATELY.**
   Descend to an altitude where cabin altitude can be maintained at 25,000 feet or less.

UNLOCKED CANOPY INDICATION.

In case the canopy unlock caution lamp comes on during flight, immediately descend (if at high altitude) and reduce speed as much as possible to minimize turbulence in the cabin in the event of canopy loss. Land as soon as practicable.

1. **OXYGEN ON AND EMERGENCY. (P-N-DSO)**
2. **CANOPY CONTROL LEVERS DOWN. (P-N-DSO)**
3. Decelerate and descend.
4. Cabin pressure selector knob to combat—COMBAT (above 25,000 feet).
5. Cabin pressure selector knob to dump—DUMP (below 25,000 feet).

LOSS OF CANOPY/GLASS PANEL BLOWOUT.

In the event of loss of canopy or glass panel blowout during flight at altitudes above 42,000 feet, immediate protection will be provided by capsulation; pressurization will be afforded by the capsule pressurization system. Loss of pilot's canopy or glass panel blowout in flight will cause turbulent airflow and noise levels that may not be tolerable, in regard to pilot's ability to control the airplane. In event of canopy loss or glass panel blowout at altitudes below 42,000 feet, it is not necessary, from a pressurization standpoint, to capsulate. The magnitude and nature of turbulence and noise are not known, however, at high air speeds, it may be necessary for the pilot to capsulate if he can not satisfactorily overcome the effects of turbulence by lowering the capsule seat. Refer to "Crew Capsulation" procedures, this section. When deceleration has been made to low subsonic airspeed, approximately 325 KIAS, the pilot can decapsulate and land as soon as practicable.

3-37

Section III
Emergency Procedures

T.O. 1B-58A-1

LOSS OF CANOPY/GLASS PANEL BLOWOUT. (CONT'D)

1. OXYGEN ON AND EMERGENCY. (P-N-DSO)
2. CAPSULATE (IF REQUIRED). (P-N-DSO)
3. DECELERATE AND DESCEND.
    Decelerate to 325 KIAS or less and descend to 25,000 feet or below.
4. Lower helmet visor (if required). (P-N-DSO)
5. Lower seat (if required). (P-N-DSO)

INFLIGHT GLASS PANEL FAILURE.

The glass panels of the windshield and all crew station windows are constructed of two plies of tempered glass bonded together by a silicone rubber interlayer. A panel failure is readily recognizable, as the tempered plate glass layers will crack (craze) over their entire surface, reducing visibility to zero. Normally a crazed panel will not blow out if the silicone rubber interlayer between the two glass layers is good. Land as soon as practicable.

The following emergency procedures are recommended as an added precaution against complete panel blowout and explosive decompression in case of panel failure.

1. OXYGEN ON AND EMERGENCY. (P-N-DSO)
2. CABIN PRESSURE SELECTOR KNOB TO COMBAT (IF SUPERSONIC)—COMBAT.
    If the cabin pressure selector knob is at NORM when the glass panel failure occurs, immediately reposition the knob to COMBAT.

WARNING

When the cabin pressure schedule is changed from normal to combat, monitor the cabin pressure altimeter for a rapid increase in the cabin altitude. If the cabin altitude does not increase, immediately position the cabin pressure selector knob to DUMP to prevent the possibility of glass panel blowout.

3. DECELERATE AND DESCEND.
4. CABIN PRESSURE SELECTOR KNOB TO DUMP WHEN SUBSONIC—DUMP.

EMERGENCY DECELERATION AND DESCENT.

A rapid descent of approximately 18,500 feet per minute can be achieved at IDLE power using a spiral dive at a bank angle of 60 degrees along the restricted high speed limit. Refer to "Airspeed Limitations," Section V, for the restricted high speed limit. If capsulated, the bank angle should be limited to 30 degrees. Also, the throttles cannot be retarded below approximately 91 percent.

CAUTION

During descent and before entering the transonic region, decrease the load factor to 1.5 "g" to prevent excessive air loads when the transonic pitch up occurs.

Recovery from this descent should be initiated 5,000 feet above level-off altitude. If capsulated, control stick steering should be utilized or the autopilot poppets should be actuated if the autopilot is engaged since it will be very difficult to decapsulate without having the airplane under autopilot control. If the emergency requires capsulation, descend to 25,000 feet or lower and shift cg forward of 30 percent MAC. All necessary instruments and a small portion of the horizon will be visible as shown in figure 3-4.

Note

If descending below 10,000 feet, activate the defog system as soon as possible during the descent to prevent possible fogging of the windshield.

T.O. 1B-58A-1

**Section III
Emergency Procedures**

CABIN FIRE.

In the event that fire is discovered or suspected in any of the crew compartments, immediately alert other crew members. Locate the fire, and using the extinguisher from the second crew compartment, apply a minimum amount of extinguishing agent at the base of the flame.

WARNING

Prolonged exposure (5 minutes or more) to high concentrations (pronounced irritation of eyes and nose) of bromochloromethane (CB) or its decomposition products should be avoided. CB is an anesthetic agent of moderate intensity. It is safer to use than previous fire extinguishing agents (carbon tetrachloride, methylbromide). However, especially in confined spaces, adequate respiratory and eye protection from excessive exposure, including the use of oxygen, when available, should be sought as soon as the primary fire emergency will permit.

1. **OXYGEN ON AND EMERGENCY. (P-N-DSO)**
2. Cabin pressure selector knob to dump—DUMP.

   Dumping cabin pressure may aid in extinguishing the fire. Also, this will help in eliminating smoke and fumes.

3. Nonessential electrical equipment off—Off. (P-N-DSO)

   Turn off all nonessential electrical equipment, especially those components located in the compartment area. Pull fuses if necessary.

4. Air conditioning control mode selector knob to manual—MAN.
5. When normal operations can be resumed, return equipment and systems to original operation. (P-N-DSO)

SMOKE AND FUME ELIMINATION.

A light concentration of smoke and fumes can usually be cleared by positioning the temperature control knob to full cool. A heavy concentration of smoke should be cleared by dumping cabin pressure and adjusting cabin temperatures to full cool. The source of the smoke may be determined by checking the frequency of the No. 2 and 3 generators, refrigeration unit indicators and electronic temperature indicator.

1. **OXYGEN ON AND EMERGENCY. (P-N-DSO)**
2. Temperature control knob ccw—CCW (if required).
3. Check No. 2 and 3 generator frequencies—Checked.

   If either No. 2 or 3 generator frequencies is abnormal, select the opposite engine on the air source selector knob.

4. Check refrigeration unit indicators—Checked.

   If a refrigeration unit overheat condition is present, select the opposite unit. If an electronic equipment overheat condition exists, turn off equipment served by it. Place equipment, which has been turned off, back on progressively to locate the malfunctioning equipment. Refer to "Air Conditioning System," Section IV to identify equipment served by the electronic overheat indicator.

5. Cabin pressure selector knob to dump—DUMP (if required).

WARNING

If it is necessary to dump cabin pressure make sure that maximum altitude for unpressurized cabin is not exceeded (42,000).

3-39

miscellaneous emergency equipment

1. Upper Right Container (N, DSO)
   - Fishing Kit
   - Utility Containers (2)
   - Ski Goggles
   - First Aid Kit
2. Radio, Battery and Radiac Meter (3)
3. Left Headrest Container (N, DSO)
   - Wool Pile Socks
   - Wool Ski Socks
   - Wool Knit Hood
   - Trousers
   - Parka
4. Upper Left Container (N, DSO)
   - Drinking Water
5. Lower Left Container (N, DSO)
   - Rations (2)
   - Rifle
   - Heat Tabs & Stove
   - 5 Qt Container
   - Poncho
   - Knife, Pocket
   - Desalting Kit
   - Lensatic Compass
   - Utility Containers (2)
   - Soap Tissue
   - Salt Tablets
   - Handle
   - Razor
   - Seasoning
   - Survival Manual
   - Spoon
6. Foot Container (N, DSO)
   - Overcoat
   - Down Overboots
   - Mittens
7. Center Headrest Container (Pilot)
   - Down Overboot
   - Mittens
   - Poncho
   - Wool Ski Socks
   - Plastic Overboot
   - Trousers
   - Parka
   - Heat Tabs & Stove
8. Left Headrest Container (Pilot)
   - Overcoat
   - Down Overboot
   - 5 Qt Container
9. Upper Left Container (Pilot)
   - Ski Goggles
   - Matches
   - Wire Saw
   - Heat Tabs & Stove
   - Razor
   - 22 Hornet Cartridges
   - Gill Net
   - Monocular
   - Salt Tablets
   - Compass
   - First Aid Kit
   - Utility Containers (4)
10. Escape Rope (3)
11. Lower Left Container (Pilot)
    - Knife, Pocket
    - Signal Mirror
    - Survival Manual
    - Rations (4)
    - Combination Tool
    - Plastic Overboot
    - Mosquito Head Net
    - Wool Socks
    - Rifle
    - Wire Snare
    - Spoon
    - Seasoning
12. Lower Right Container (Pilot)
    - Desalter Kit
    - Lensatic Compass
    - Rations (2)
    - Fishing Kit
    - Wool Knit Hood
    - Foot Sack
    - Candle
    - Whetstone
    - Soap Tissues
    - 6" Flat File
    - 3 Pt Container
    - Seasoning
    - Drinking Water (Canned)
13. Upper Right Container (Pilot)
    - Drinking Water
14. Left External Container (N, DSO)
    - Plastic Overboots
    - Wire Saw
    - Rations
15. Right External Container (N, DSO)
    - 6" Flat File
    - Wire Snare
    - Foot Sack
    - Compass
    - Spade
16. Lower Right Container (N, DSO)
    - Heat Tabs & Stove
    - Axe
    - Signal Mirror
    - Matches
    - Mosquito Head Net
    - 22 Hornet Cartridges
    - Rations (4)
    - Whetstone
    - Candle
    - Monocular
    - Gill Net
    - 3 Pt Container
17. Fire Extinguisher

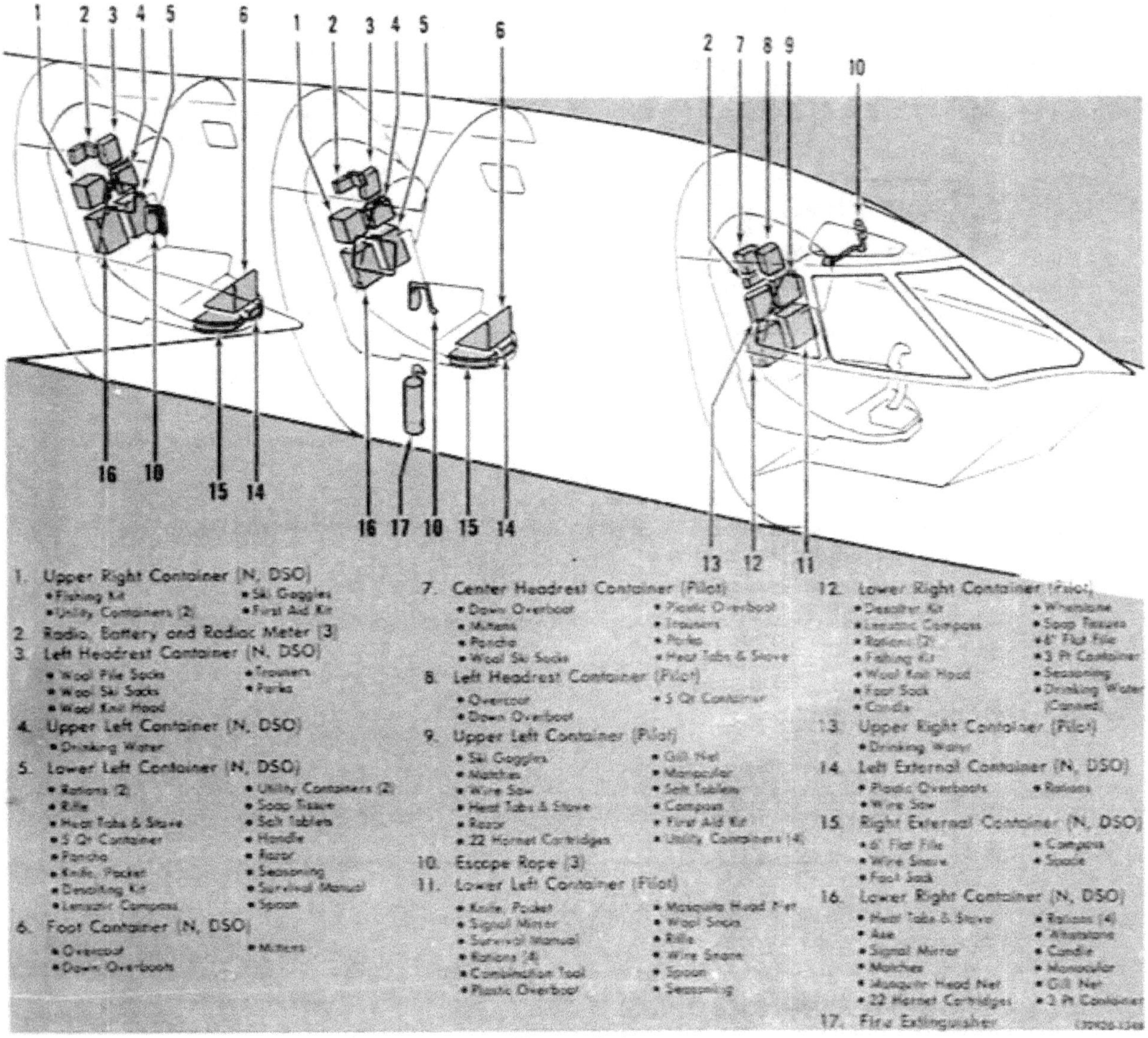

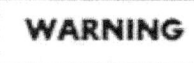

Figure 3-6.

SMOKE AND FUME ELIMINATION. (CONT'D)

6. Check d-c power units—Checked. (DSO)

   When smoke is observed coming from the vent holes of a d-c power unit, the input fuses will normally blow; however, if the smoke becomes excessive before the fuses blow, the unit may be deactivated by pulling the input fuses.

WARNING

If it cannot be determined which unit is smoking, no input fuses should be removed. When a unit is malfunctioning, pulling the fuse to its parallel unit will remove all power from the associated bus.

T.O. 1B-58A-1

Section III
Emergency Procedures

SMOKE AND FUME ELIMINATION. (CONT'D)

Note

If the smoking unit is a +150V DC, −150V DC, or 250V DC unit and the input fuses in the DSO station have been pulled, then the output fuses in the navigator's station should also be removed. For location of all electrical equipment fuses, refer to "Electrical Power Supply System," Section I.

7. Control mode selector to ram—RAM (if required).

If emergency ram operation is necessary, adjust airspeed and altitude within limits. Refer to "Airspeed Limitations"-"Ram Air Mode Limit Speed," Section V. Nonessential electronic equipment should be turned off. Refer to "Air Conditioning System,"-"Ram Air Operation," Section IV. If any of the steps above correct the situation, repressurize the cabin and proceed with mission within scope of existing equipment.

LANDING GEAR MALFUNCTION.

LANDING GEAR EXTENDS INVOLUNTARILY.

If the landing gear extends involuntarily at speeds above 300 Knots IAS, do not retract the landing gear. Land as soon as practical.

> **CAUTION**
>
> If the landing gear extends at speeds above 300 Knots IAS, do not retract the landing gear as damage to the system could have resulted.

LIGHTING OF LANDING GEAR WARNING LAMP.

If the landing gear warning lamp lights in flight, prompt action is necessary to prevent damage to the airplane.

1. Landing gear handle up—UP.
   Move the landing gear handle to UP so that hydraulic pressure will hold the gear up. After the warning lamp goes out, leave the landing gear handle in UP and normal flight may be continued; however, the utility hydraulic system pressure and quantity should be monitored for indications of system failure.

   If the warning lamp remains lighted or there is evidence of utility hydraulic system failure, proceed with the following steps:

2. Decelerate.
   Immediately decelerate to gear limit speed of 300 knots IAS.
3. Land as soon as practical.

LANDING EMERGENCIES

DITCHING.

Do not attempt to ditch this airplane except as a last resort. Ditching should be performed only if lack of altitude or ejection system failure would prevent successful bailout. Specific ditching procedures have not been established.

LANDING GEAR EMERGENCY PROCEDURES.

LANDING GEAR UNSAFE OR HANDLE STUCK IN THE PRESS REL POSITION.

In the event that the gear will not extend or lock down when the landing gear handle is positioned to DOWN, reduce airspeed as low as practical, consistent with other requirements, to minimize air loads on the landing gear. If gear still will not extend or lock down, or the landing gear warning lamp

3-41

Section III
Emergency Procedures

LANDING GEAR UNSAFE OR HANDLE STUCK IN THE PRESS REL POSITION. (CONT'D)

remains lighted and/or the warning buzzer is heard while the landing gear position indicators are lighted, use the procedures shown below to extend the landing gear.

If the landing gear handle is stuck in the PRESS REL position, it may be due to a malfunction of the landing gear handle mechanism. When this occurs, insert a finger or pencil through the hole in the panel (at the base of the landing gear handle) and manually raise the guide (see figure 3-7) while placing the landing gear handle into the down position. If the landing gear handle remains stuck in the PRESS REL position, use the following procedure to extend the landing gear.

1. Pull emergency brake and landing gear control handle—Pulled.

> **CAUTION**
>
> Do not exceed airspeed limits for landing gear extension and do not attempt to retract gear after an emergency gear extension. For landing gear extension limitations refer to "Airspeed Limitations," Section V.

Note

- If the emergency system is used to extend the gear, only emergency pneumatic pressure will be available for brake operation.
- Under conditions of extremely low atmospheric temperature and/or where high pneumatic leakage has occurred, the emergency pneumatic system pressure will be less than that normally available. Such conditions will result in slower landing gear extension (approximately 15 seconds). Extension of landing gear will be completed when the available pneumatic pressure exceeds the opposing landing gear loads.

The taxi light is operative if either nose gear downlatch is hooked. If there is an indication that the nose gear is not down and locked, turn on the taxi light switch. Illumination of the taxi light will verify that at least one hook is latched, and a normal landing should be made. The nose gear down lock latches are painted red-orange to provide a visual method of determining that the gear is down and locked. When the latches are properly engaged the orange-red portion will not be visible. After accomplishing the above procedure, if there is still an indication that the nose gear is not down and locked, it is recommended that a chase plane be requested to verify the nose gear latch position.

landing gear control guide

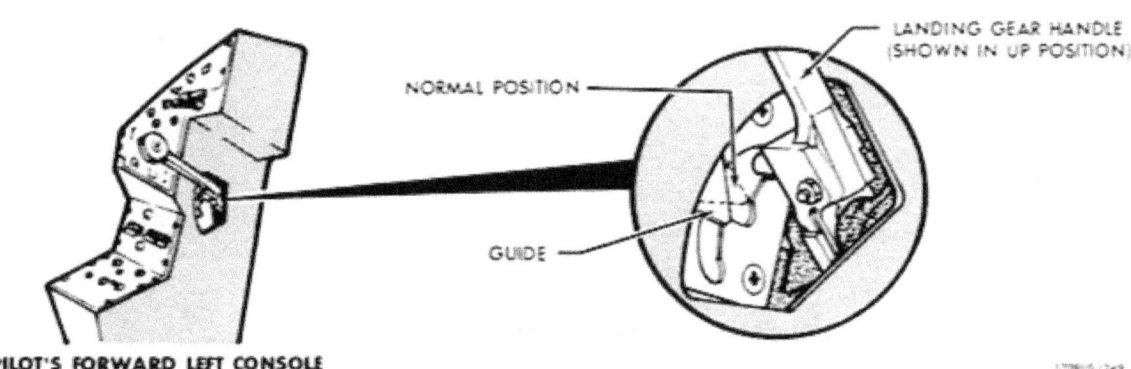

PILOT'S FORWARD LEFT CONSOLE

Figure 3-7.

3-42

LANDING GEAR HANDLE STUCK IN THE UP POSITION.

> **CAUTION**
>
> This procedure results in loss of the utility hydraulic system. It should be executed just prior to landing and *only* if the landing gear handle is stuck in the UP position.

1. Remove 28-volt d-c engine No. 1 and 2 fuel shutoff valve fuses—Removed. (DSO)

2. Pull engine No. 1 and 2 fire pull handles—Pulled.

    Pull engine No. 1 and 2 fire pull handles to close hydraulic shutoff valves. The resulting effect should be as follows:

    a. Operation of engines No. 1 and 2 should not be affected.

    b. Hydraulic pump No. 1 and 2 low pressure caution lamps should come on.

    c. Utility hydraulic system pressure indicator will decrease to zero psi.

    d. Engine No. 1 and 2 fuel flow indicators will decrease to zero flow.

3. Reduce airspeed—Reduced.

    Reduce airspeed to as low as practical, consistent with other requirements, to minimize air loads on landing gear.

4. Pull emergency brake and landing gear control handle—Pulled.

    Landing gear should extend and lock down in approximately 40 ($\pm$20) seconds. Moderate control surface cycling will achieve shorter extend time.

5. Remove engine No. 1 and 2 hydraulic valve fuses—Removed. (DSO)

> **WARNING**
>
> Utility hydraulic system must remain off until system can be ground serviced; otherwise, the landing gear will assume a partially retracted position.

Note

When the emergency system is used to extend the gear, only emergency pneumatic pressure will be available for brake operation.

6. Engine No. 1 and 2 fire pull handles—Reset (in).

    Engine No. 1 and 2 fuel flow indicators will return to normal.

7. Replace 28-volt d-c engine No. 1 and 2 fuel shutoff valve fuses—Replaced. (DSO)

Section III
Emergency Procedures

LANDING WITH LANDING GEAR MALFUNCTON.

If time and conditions permit, reduce the gross weight to the minimum practical for landing.

WARNING

It is recommended that the crew eject rather than attempting an emergency landing on an unprepared surface or where the terrain is unknown. Recent studies indicate that an emergency landing under these conditions is extremely critical from the standpoint of crew safety and damage to the aircraft.

For any main landing gear emergency, the navigator and DSO are given the option of ejection since this presents less hazard to these crew members. Approach and landing speeds will vary depending upon the type of landing emergency, the airplane gross weight, the cg location, and the angle of attack. Generally, however, a normal approach and touchdown should be made with a minimum sink rate at touchdown.

Note

For the maximum sinking speed at touchdown for landings at gross weights above 95,000 pounds, refer to "Miscellaneous Operational Limitations," Section V.

Under certain conditions, an emergency landing can be accomplished with a malfunction of the landing gear. A landing gear malfunction may result in any one of six gear configurations: nose gear up or unlocked, one main gear up or unlocked, both main gear up or unlocked, nose gear and one main gear up or unlocked, all gear up or unlocked (belly landing), or one or more gear damaged (alone or with any combination outlined above). An emergency landing attempt is not recommended under any of these circumstances unless all conditions (landing surface, airplane control, weather, visibility, etc.) indicate a reasonably good chance that the landing can be safely accomplished.

WARNING

- Do not attempt an emergency landing with one main gear down and the other two gear up or unlocked, or, with a pod attached to the airplane.
- A belly landing is recommended only under ideal landing conditions. The pilot must consider the safety of his crew with respect to ejection versus gear-up landing. Wind direction and velocity, terrain or runway conditions, availability of rescue facilities, fire fighting capability, and runway foaming equipment are all very important factors in the making of such a decision.
- If the emergency brake and landing gear control handle is pulled in an attempt to lower the landing gear, the only braking available will be pneumatic and the anti-skid system will be inoperative.

The following procedures are recommended in case it is considered reasonably safe to attempt an emergency landing with malfunctioning landing gear.

Preparation For Emergency Landing.

The preparatory actions in all cases are the same and after these procedures have been accomplished use the applicable specific procedure.

1. Jettison pod—Jettisoned.
   Refer to "Jettisoning Procedures (Pod/Small Weapons)," Section II, for procedures.
2. Complete DESCENT AND BEFORE LANDING checklist—Complete.
   Accomplish all applicable steps in the normal checklist.
3. ARC-74 on—ON.
   Prior to final approach turn the ARC-74 switch ON, and perform a radio check.
4. Nonessential electrical and electronic equipment off—OFF. (P-N-DSO)
5. Check cg—Checked.
   Check that fuel distribution provides the required cg for landing.

Note

With a "Nose Gear Up, Unlocked or Damaged" gear configuration, obtain a cg of 31.0 percent MAC prior to landing.

6. Lock shoulds

Section III
Emergency Procedures

LANDING WITH LANDING GEAR MALFUNCTION. (CONT'D)

Nose Gear Up, Unlocked Or Damaged.

Before landing with the nose gear up, unlocked or damaged, a cg of 31.0 percent MAC should be obtained. Immediately after touchdown, the cg should be shifted aft at maximum rate. This will aid in maintaining a tail down attitude until the aircraft comes to a complete stop with the aft portion of the fuselage and nacelles contacting the runway.

1. CG selector and control knobs—35 percent and MANUAL.
2. Make normal flare and touchdown.
3. Deploy drag chute—Deployed.
4. No. 1 and 4 throttles off—OFF.
5. CG control knob—AUTO.
    Position cg control knob to AUTO immediately after touchdown. Control stick cg shift switch may be used in lieu of cg control knob.
6. Canopies jettisoned. (P-N-DSO)
    The canopies should be jettisoned utilizing the canopy jettison handle while the airplane is in motion. The recommended order of jettisoning the canopies is pilot, navigator and DSO. Refer to "Emergency Ground Egress", this section, for canopy procedures when the airplane is static.
7. Brakes—As required.
    Braking may be used as long as the nose does not tend to pitch down. Light braking may be used to maintain directional control after rudder becomes ineffective. Near end of landing roll, the tail should slowly settle to the runway.

WARNING

Excessive braking or angle of attack less than 13 degrees should be avoided at speeds below 100 knots. Excessive use of brakes or low deck angles after elevators have become ineffective may cause the aircraft to pitch forward on the nose.

8. No. 2 and 3 throttles off—OFF.
    When airplane stops, shut down the engines.
9. Abandon the airplane.
    Refer to "Emergency Ground Egress," this section.

One Main Gear Up, Unlocked, Or Damaged.

In order to minimize damage to the airplane, the weight should be reduced to a minimum prior to landing. Fuel dump and pod jettisoning should be accomplished as indicated in "Fuel Dumping," this section, and "Jettisoning Procedures (Pod/Small Weapons)," Section II. However, sufficient fuel should be retained to provide a cg of 29 percent MAC at landing. A normal approach and touchdown should be made while maintaining a slight bank angle to raise the malfunctioning main gear. The landing should be made near the edge of the runway opposite the malfunctioning main gear. After touchdown, lower the nose slightly to check alignment with the runway and deploy the drag chute using aileron to maintain wings level. After the drag chute has deployed, raise the nose to at least the touchdown attitude. This action provides wing lift which can be effectively used to hold a wings-level attitude to a lower speed than with aileron alone. As speed decreases, maintain the nose-high attitude with elevator deflection and use aileron deflection to maintain wings level. As long as a wings-level attitude can be maintained, directional control can be maintained with the rudder. As airspeed approaches about 120 knots, wing lift and full aileron deflection will no longer be sufficient to maintain wings level. If the malfunctioning main gear collapses, the wing will drop and the outboard engine nacelle will contact the runway. At this time, the nose wheels will drop to the runway and can then be used in conjunction with braking to maintain directional control. If the malfunctioning main gear does not collapse, lower nose to the runway at 100 knots. Use brakes on the operative main gear for stopping and nose wheel steering for

3-45

Section III
Emergency Procedures

T.O. 1B-58A-1

LANDING WITH LANDING GEAR MALFUNCTION. (CONT'D)

One Main Gear Up, Unlocked, Or Damaged.

1. Make normal flare and touchdown slightly wing low.
2. Lower nose slightly to check alignment with runway and deploy drag chute.
3. Canopies jettisoned. (P-N-DSO)
   The canopies should be jettisoned utilizing the canopy jettison handle while the airplane is in motion. The recommended order of jettisoning the canopies is pilot, navigator and DSO. Refer to "Emergency Ground Egress," this section, for canopy procedures when the airplane is static.
4. Raise nose to touchdown attitude.
5. Rudder and aileron—As required.
   Use rudder for directional control and aileron to maintain wings level.
6. Maintain nose high attitude with elevator until outboard nacelle contacts runway or speed is reduced to 100 knots.
7. Brakes and nose wheel steering—As required.
   Use brakes on the operative main gear for stopping and utilize nose wheel steering for directional control.
8. Throttles off—OFF (when brakes and nose wheel steering are no longer effective).
9. Abandon the airplane.
   Refer to "Emergency Ground Egress," this section.

Both Main Gear Up, Unlocked, Or Damaged.

A landing with both main gear up, unlocked or damaged should be accomplished in much the same manner as a normal landing. A normal approach will be made. Touchdown should be made with an angle of attack not exceeding 12.5 degrees. The sinking speed at touchdown should not exceed 120 feet per minute. Maintain directional control with the rudder or nose wheel steering as long as possible.

1. Make normal flare then touchdown with a maximum of 12.5 degrees angle of attack.

WARNING

- Landing with an angle of attack greater than 12.5 degrees is likely to result in an extreme pitchdown at the time of initial contact with the runway.
- Do not exceed a sink rate of 120 feet per minute at time of touchdown.

2. Throttles off—OFF (immediately after touchdown).
3. Canopies jettisoned. (P-N-DSO)
   The canopies should be jettisoned utilizing the canopy jettison handle while the airplane is in motion. The recommended order of jettisoning the canopies is pilot, navigator and DSO. Refer to "Emergency Ground Egress," this section, for canopy procedures when the airplane is static.
4. Deploy drag chute after nose wheel is on runway.
5. Abandon the airplane.
   Refer to "Emergency Ground Egress," this section.

All Gear Up Or Unlocked (Belly Landing).

Recent studies indicate that landing with all gear up or unlocked (belly landing) is feasible provided ideal conditions exist. If all effort to extend the gear has failed, utilize the following procedure:

3-46

Section III
Emergency Procedures

LANDING WITH LANDING GEAR MALFUNCTION. (CONT'D)

All Gear Up Or Unlocked (Belly Landing). (Cont'd)

1. Make normal flare then touchdown with a maximum of 12.5 degrees angle of attack.

WARNING

- Landing with an angle of attack greater than 12.5 degrees is likely to result in an extreme pitchdown at the time of initial contact with the runway.
- Do not exceed a sink rate of 120 feet per minute at time of touchdown.

2. Throttles off—OFF (immediately after touchdown).
3. Canopies jettisoned. (P-N-DSO)
   The canopies should be jettisoned utilizing the canopy jettison handle. The recommended order of jettisoning is Pilot, Navigator and DSO. Refer to "Emergency Ground Egress," this section, for canopy procedures when the airplane is static.
4. Deploy drag chute after touchdown.
5. Abandon the airplane.
   Refer to "Emergency Ground Egress," this section.

LANDING WITH BROKEN POSITIONING SPRING.

A positioning spring may break during landing gear extension. With this condition the main gear wheels will align parallel, or nearly parallel, to the strut with the forward wheels down as indicated in figure 3-8. This condition cannot be detected by the pilot and all cockpit indications will be normal. Observation by a ground observer and/or a chase plane can give positive indications of a broken positioning spring. After confirmation that a broken spring is the *only* abnormal gear condition existing (including verification by flight crew of normal cockpit indications and utility hydraulic system operation), a normal approach and touchdown should be made. For other abnormal main landing gear conditions, refer to "Landing With Landing Gear Malfunction", this section.

extended main landing gear

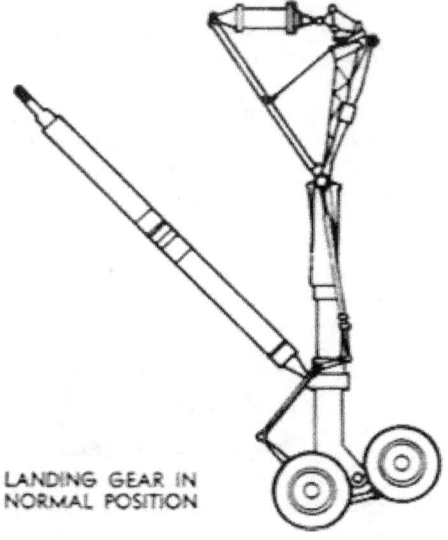

LANDING GEAR IN NORMAL POSITION

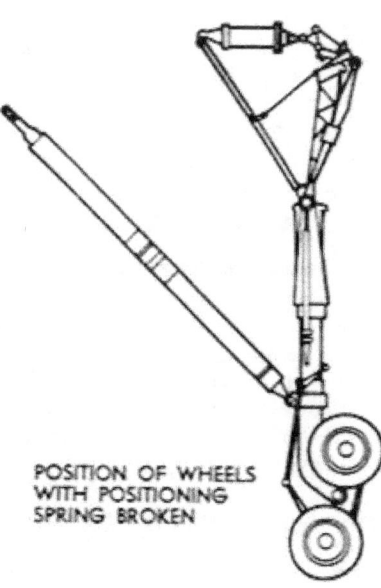

POSITION OF WHEELS WITH POSITIONING SPRING BROKEN

Section III
Emergency Procedures

T.O. 1B-58A-1

LANDING WITH BLOWN TIRE.

1. Jettison pod—Jettisoned (if necessary).
   The pod should be jettisoned only if there is damage to the landing gear other than blown tire. Refer to "Jettisoning Procedures (Pod/Small Weapons)," Section II.

   #### Note
   Foaming the runway is unnecessary unless the wheels are damaged to the extent that a hazardous landing condition exists.

2. Reduce gross weight—Reduced.
   Reduce gross weight to the minimum practical.
3. Anti-skid switch off—OFF.
   Turn anti-skid switch OFF if main gear tire(s) are blown.
4. Pull emergency brake and landing gear handle (if required)—Pulled.
   If utility system has failed, actuate brake and landing gear emergency pneumatic system. (Anti-skid will be inoperative.)
5. Deploy drag chute—Deployed.
   Deploy drag chute and use aerodynamic braking as much as possible.

   #### CAUTION
   Use brakes only if necessary and then maintain continuous braking. Braking will probably cause the center flange on the wheel to wear flat, resulting in an unbalanced condition which could cause the wheel to disintegrate if the brakes are released above taxi speed.

6. Open or jettison canopies (if required). (P-N-DSO)
   Use normal canopy control lever if airplane is static. If airplane is in motion, the canopies should be jettisoned utilizing the canopy jettison handle. The recommended order of jettisoning the canopies is Pilot, Navigator, and DSO.

LANDING WITH ONE OR MORE ENGINES INOPERATIVE.

Landing with one or two engines inoperative may be accomplished without undue difficulty up to maximum landing gross weights. Landing with three engines inoperative is not recommended. Procedures and techniques for a partial-engine landing are essentially the same as for a normal landing. When landing in a crosswind with one or more engine(s) inoperative, the recommended maximum cross wind component is 15 knots.

WARNING
When an emergency landing must be made with a crosswind component in excess of the recommended maximum allowable, refer to figure 2-13 for the minimum airspeeds for control in a crosswind. Refer to the applicable landing performance chart, Appendix I, to adjust the approach/flare speed.

For landing with gusty wind conditions refer to "Approach/Flare Speed Corrections," Section II. If minimum drag is desired in the pattern, do not extend the landing gear until completing the turn on final approach. Do not allow the airspeed to drop below the normal pattern and approach/flare speeds. When landing with two engines inoperative on the same side, plan carefully in order to avoid a go-around.

Note
If both left engines are inoperative, the utility hydraulic system will be inoperative. If both right engines are inoperative, the primary hydraulic system will be inoperative. Refer to "Primary or Utility Hydraulic System Failure," this section, for systems and equipment affected by an inoperative hydraulic system.

Full thrust with such an asymmetric power configuration may cause excessive yawing. Refer to figure 3-1 for minimum rudder control speeds at various asymmetric power configurations.

WARNING
Do not attempt a dead-stick landing. With all engines flamed out, the windmilling rpm of the engines at any safe landing speed is not sufficient to support the engine-driven hydraulic pumps.

T.O. 1B-58A-1

Section III
Emergency Procedures

GO-AROUND WITH ONE OR MORE ENGINES INOPERATIVE.

The decision to go around with one or more engines inoperative should be made as early as possible and without hesitation. If the airspeed is too low for the gross weight, an excessive sink rate may develop which can be difficult to detect and correct with partial thrust. Full engine power may be applied, even on an engine with the spike extended. If thrust is critical retract the landing gear as soon as it becomes evident that the airplane will not sink onto the runway.

Note

If gear has been extended pneumatically, it can not be retracted.

The normal approach/flare speeds provide sufficient speed for control with two engines inoperative on one side and the other two engines at MIL power, however, if go around is attempted after initiating the landing flare and touchdown, sufficient speed for control may not be available. Prior to initiating an approach with one or more engines inoperative, the minimum aerodynamic control speed for rudder and aileron in the takeoff attitude must be determined from figure 3-1 based on operating engines at MIL power.

WARNING

If gear is in contact with the runway, do not attempt lift off below the speed computed in accordance with the preceding instructions. The data derived from figure 3-1 does not include crosswind effect. Therefore, where possible avoid landing when crosswind is from the direction of the inoperative engine(s). If go-around is attempted in a crosswind from the direction of the inoperative engine(s) at speed derived from figure 3-1, sufficient speed for control is available, however, it will not be possible to maintain a straight flight path until speed increases.

BRAKE SYSTEM EMERGENCY OPERATION.

Note

In the event of a malfunction in the anti-skid system, positioning the anti-skid switch to OFF will return the brake system to normal operation without the anti-skid feature. The anti-skid feature will also be inoperative when the emergency brake and landing gear system is activated.

1. Pull emergency brake and landing gear control handle (if required).

    If the emergency brake and landing gear control handle is not already pulled as a result of emergency gear extension, pull the handle out through its full length of travel to pressurize emergency brake system.

2. Apply brakes as required.

    Operate brake pedals as required for stopping airplane. The anti-skid feature is inoperative under this condition.

CAUTION

With extremely cold temperatures, a minimum of three full brake applications can be obtained with normal pressure in the emergency system. The pilot must, therefore, apply the brakes with a gradual steady pressure and avoid releasing them until the desired braking action has been accomplished.

3-49

Section III
Emergency Procedures

RUNWAY BARRIER ENGAGEMENT.

The BAK-11/BAK-9 or the BAK-11/BAK-12 combination runway barrier provides an effective means of stopping the airplane on the runway after an aborted takeoff run or in an emergency landing situation. Engagement tests with the airplane carrying the MB-1 or BLU-2 pods have been conducted. Test data indicate that at 90,000 pounds the airplane is capable of engaging the barrier at approximately 150 knots and that at 145,000 pounds, it can engage at 125 knots. These limits represent an aircraft structural limitation and are also close to the barrier capacity. The airplane should enter the barrier at a 90 degree angle, as near the runway centerline as possible; however, it is better to engage offcenter than to attempt drastic corrections which could jeopardize control of the airplane. The unbalanced arresting force caused by offcenter barrier engagements will steer the airplane away from the runway centerline. The steering tendency can easily be overcome by the use of nosewheel steering or differential braking, if available; however, corrective action should not be taken unless the airplane is in danger of leaving the paved surface. Power should be reduced to minimum; however, engine No. 2 or 1 should be operating at idle speed to provide adequate nosewheel steering and wheel brake operation. There is no minimum speed for barrier engagement. Excessive braking prior to engagement should be avoided to reduce the possibility of tire blowouts, which could cause loss of directional control and possibly prevent barrier engagement. During arrestment, airplane behavior is satisfactory, with a possible yawing action during offcenter engagements due to unbalanced arresting loads. The yawing action can result in violent reactions in the cockpit and the shoulder harness should not be released until the airplane has stopped. Due to the energy limitations of some barrier installations, moderate airplane braking should be used, if available, following the engagement. As the barrier brings the airplane to a stop, the airplane will probably be pulled backward slightly. If this occurs, there is a possibility of damaging the nosewheel; therefore, it is advisable to apply the wheel brakes and engage nosewheel steering prior to the airplane coming to a stop to prevent the nosewheel from castering. The barrier tension will relax gradually within a 20-second period after the aircraft has stopped. If only one main landing gear is engaged, the airplane will veer in the direction of the engaged gear. This tendency increases as the engagement speed increases, but will also occur further out in the runout due to the increased inertia of the aircraft. Directional control should be maintained with nosewheel steering and differential braking, if available, but only if the aircraft is in danger of leaving the paved surface.

1. Steer the airplane toward the center of the runway.
    Airplane may be steered using nose wheel steering, differential wheel braking, elevons, or combination of all three methods.
2. Attempt to engage perpendicular to the cable.
3. Disengage nose wheel steering prior to reaching the cable.
4. Avoid excessive wheel braking prior to engagement and use moderate braking following engagement.
5. Be prepared to correct for yaw after engagement.
6. Engage nose wheel steering and apply wheel brakes as the aircraft comes to a stop.
    Barrier tape tension will be released gradually within a 20-second period.
7. Abandon the airplane.
    Refer to "Emergency Ground Egress," this section.

emergency entrance

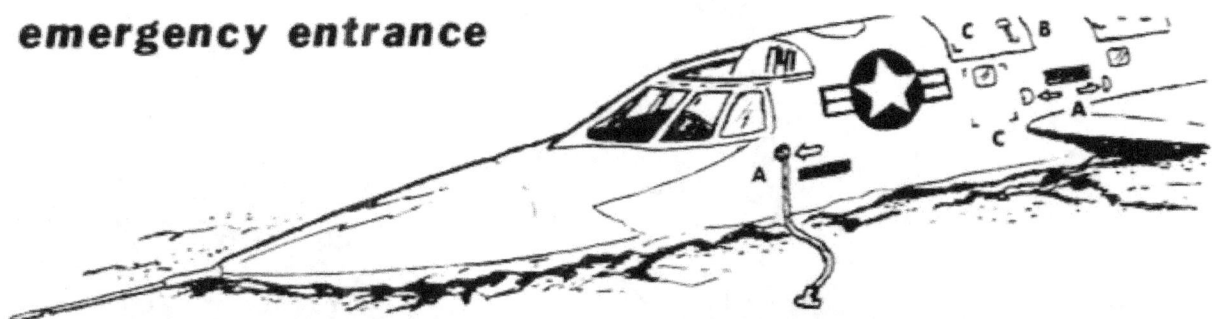

1 JETTISON CANOPIES

A Extend cable to limit; then pull hard on handle (typical of all three canopies).

WARNING

Stay clear of canopy path when canopies are jettisoned.

B

IF CANOPIES CANNOT BE JETTISONED

Open navigator's station canopy with handle located on left side of canopy.

C

AS A LAST RESORT

Chop hole through left side of fuselage or canopy in designated space.

Figure 3-9. (Sheet 1 of 2)

Section III
Emergency Procedures

T.O. 1B-58A-1

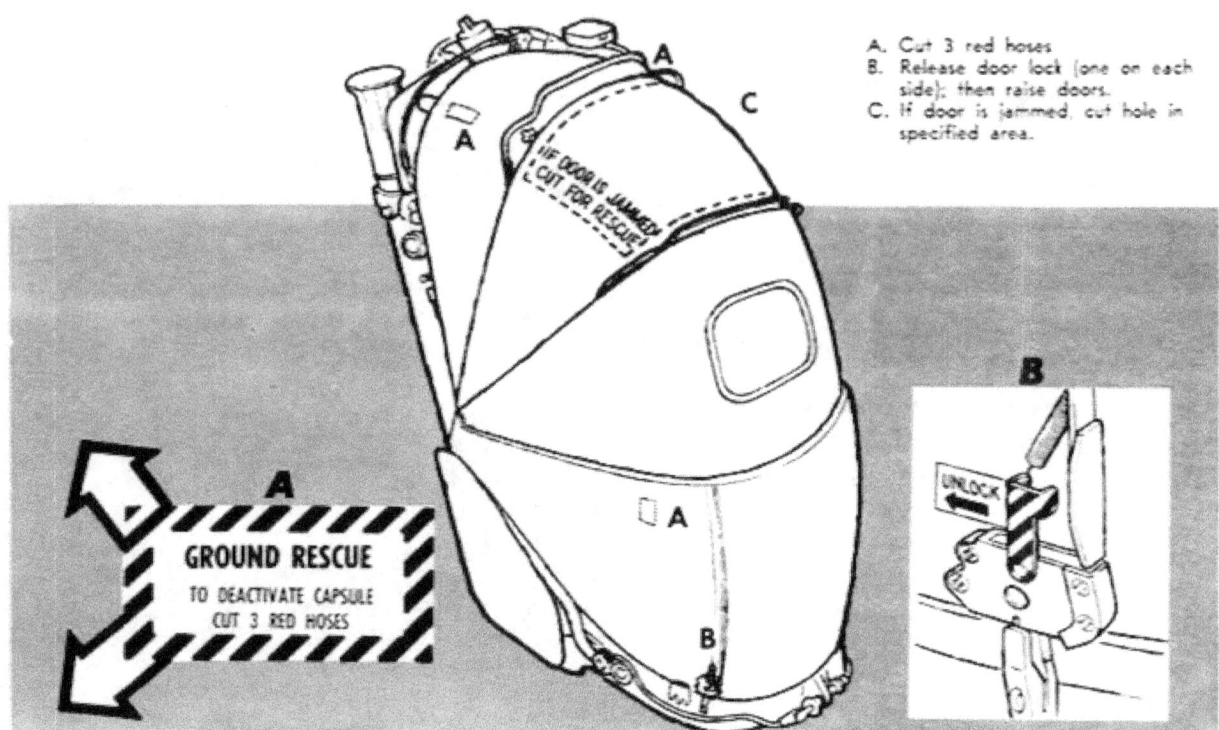

Figure 3-9. (Sheet 2 of 2)

EMERGENCY ENTRANCE.

See figure 3-9 for emergency entrance.

Note

Your emergency abbreviated checklist is contained in T.O. 1B-58A-1CL-1.

This is the last page of Section III.

Section IV
Auxiliary Equipment

TABLE OF CONTENTS.

	Page
Air Conditioning System	4-1
Anti-Icing and Defogging Systems	4-12
Communication System	4-16
Tactical Air Navagation System	4-31
Instrument Landing System	4-34
Air-to-Ground IFF System	4-34
Position Indicating Beacon System (AN/APN-136)	4-36
Rendezvous Beacon System (AN/APN-135)	4-38
Lighting Equipment	4-39
Oxygen Systems	4-43
Autopilot System	4-47
Auxiliary Flight Reference System	4-53
Weapons Control System (AN/ASQ-42)	4-56
Primary Navigation System	4-56
Bombing System	4-79
Air Navigation Data Recording System (AN/ASH-17)	4-88
Bomb Damage Evaluation (BDE) System (AN/ASH-15)	4-92
Bombing Equipment	4-94
Photo Reconnaissance System	4-103
Defensive Electronic Countermeasure System	4-105
Active Defense System	4-106
Air Refueling System	4-112
Air Refueling Procedures and Techniques	Refer to Air Refueling Flight Manuals T.O. 1-1C-1 and T.O. 1-1C-1-6.
Single-Point Refueling System	4-114
Miscellaneous Equipment	4-116

AIR CONDITIONING SYSTEM.

The air conditioning system (figure 4-1) utilizes bleed air from the 17th stage compressor discharge of the inboard (No. 2 and No. 3) engines to provide conditioned air for the following purposes:

1. Crew compartment and electronic equipment cooling, heating, pressurization, and ventilation.
2. Windshield rain removal and defog.
3. Fuel tank pressurization.

In general, operation of the system is fully automatic throughout normal flight. The cool air and warm air furnished by the system enables the pilot to select the desired cabin temperature and at the same time prevent overheating of electronic equipment. This same air automatically furnishes cabin pressurization according to the cabin pressurization schedule selected by the pilot.

REFRIGERATION AND COLD AIR DISTRIBUTION.

Cooling of engine bleed air is accomplished by two separate refrigeration units, each of which consists of a two-stage (primary and secondary) air-to-air heat exchanger, an air-to-water heat exchanger, a throttle valve, a refrigeration compressor-turbine, and a water separator. The left refrigeration unit is located in the nacelle pylon of the No. 2 engine pylon and wing area and normally cools the bleed air furnished by that same engine; the right unit is in the No. 3 engine pylon and wing area and normally cools the bleed air from that engine. This cooling arrangement can be modified, however, so that both units will cool the bleed air from either inboard engine, or, so that either unit will cool the bleed air from both engines. This cross-feed feature is possible since the engine bleed air inlet ducts join in a single warm air manifold duct. The hot bleed air which is to be cooled flows from each inboard engine through a flow limiting nozzle, a bleed air check-and-shutoff valve, and then through the primary stage

Section IV
Auxiliary Equipment

T.O. 1B-58A-1

air conditioning system (typical)

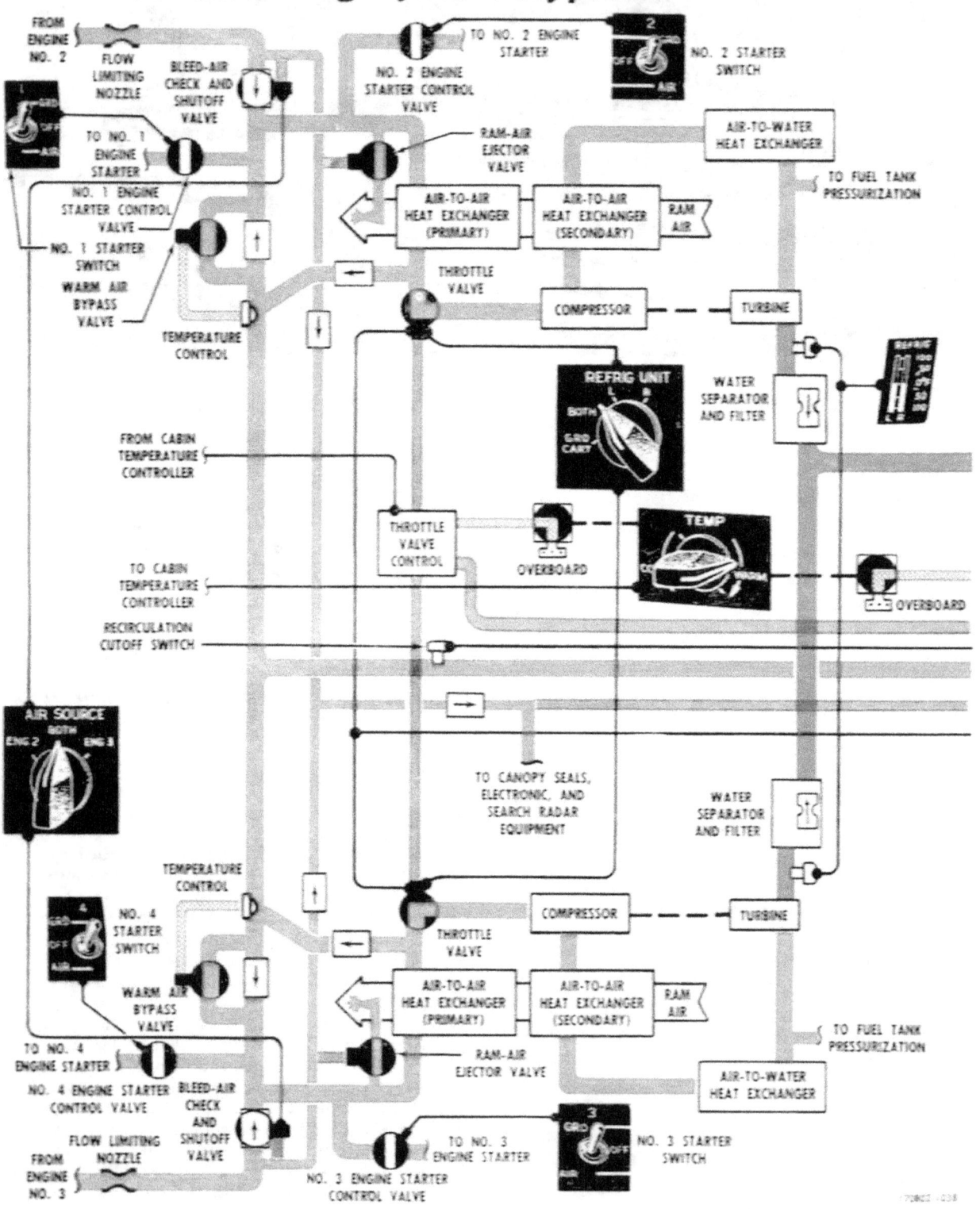

Figure 4-1. (Sheet 1 of 2)

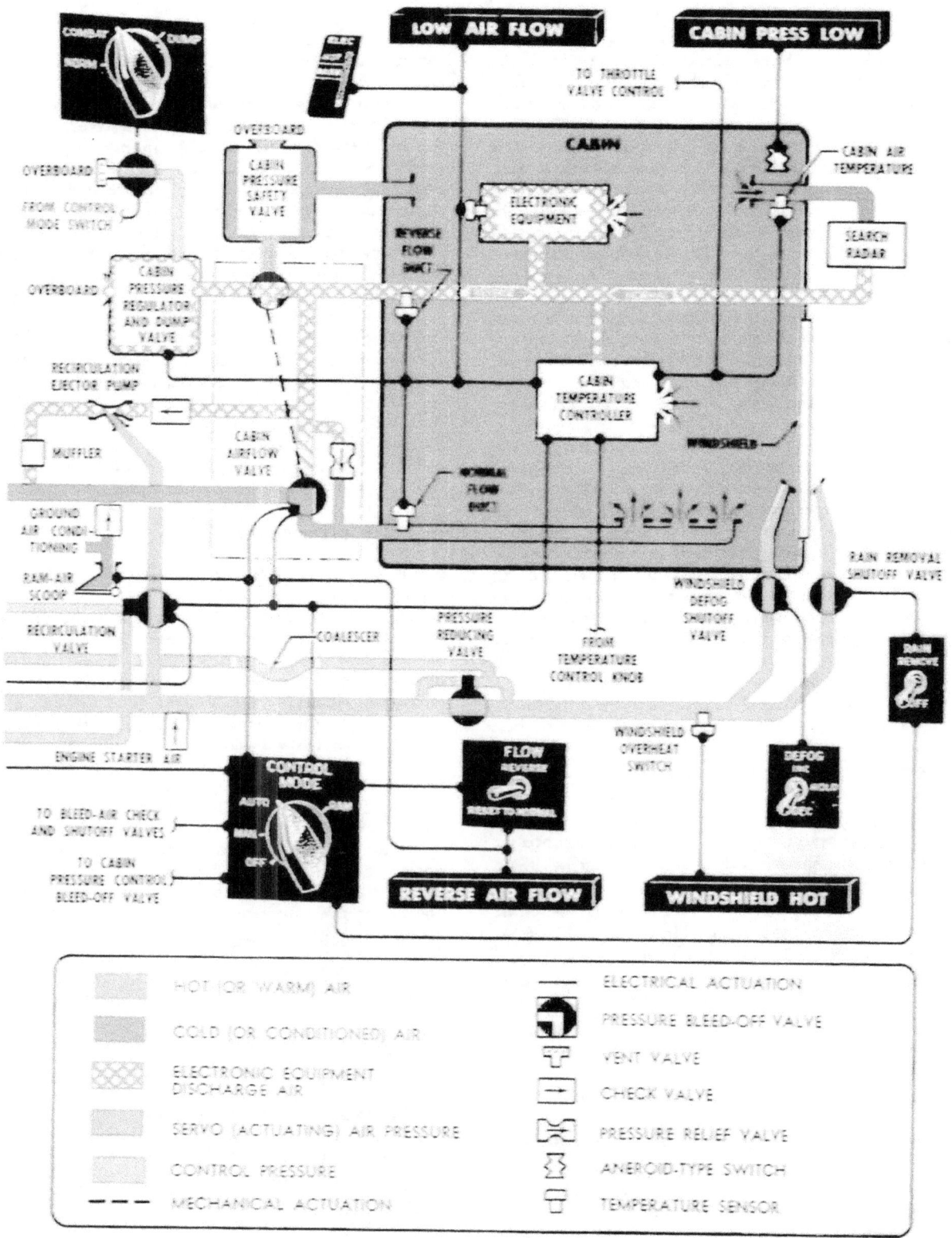

Figure 4-1. (Sheet 2 of 2)

Section IV
Auxiliary Equipment

T.O. 1B-58A-1

of the air-to-air heat exchanger. The nozzle limits the maximum amount of air which can enter the air conditioning system. When electrically energized, the bleed air check and shutoff valve stops the entire flow of bleed air from its respective engine into the system. The valve also prevents any back flow of bleed air through the valve from the opposite engine. The primary stage of the air-to-air heat exchanger in each unit accomplishes partial cooling of the hot bleed air. The air is then routed to the throttle valve which controls the pressure of the air entering the refrigeration compressor. Both throttle valves are regulated by servo air from a common throttle valve control. Either throttle valve can be closed to completely shut off the supply of cold air from its respective refrigeration unit. The throttle valve of each unit, together with the common throttle valve control, is the primary controller of cooling airflow. The air which is admitted past this valve passes through the compressor, the secondary stage of the air-to-air heat exchanger, the air-to-water heat exchanger and finally through the refrigeration turbine. The compressor increases the temperature and pressure of the air. Both stages of each air-to-air heat exchanger utilize outside ram air for cooling. At speeds below mach no. 0.6 ram air ejector pumps automatically increase the flow of outside ram air through the heat exchangers to increase their cooling capacity. Air from the secondary heat exchanger passes through the air-to-water heat exchanger where it is cooled to approximately the boiling point of water. An air-to-water heat exchanger tank is located in each main landing gear wheel well and is serviced according to an instruction placard located near the filler neck. See figure 1-47 for servicing data. This air then passes through the turbine where it is expanded and its heat energy is transformed into mechanical energy and used to drive the compressor. If the air entering the turbine-compressor becomes excessively hot, thermal switches upstream of the turbine-compressor unit causes the throttle valve to close, shutting down that refrigeration unit. The cold air is then filtered and dehumidified and the cold air from both units is joined in a single cold air supply duct. In the event the filter and dehumidifier becomes clogged, the air will bypass the water separator through a pressure relief valve. The valve opens at approximately 30 to 40 psi. The majority of the air is then routed to the crew compartments, but a portion is ducted aft to cool remote electronic equipment. The air from the supply duct normally enters the compartments through inlet diffusers in the crew stations, circulates throughout the cabin, exits through the electronic packages, and collects in an exhaust manifold from where it is dumped overboard through the cabin pressure regulator. In the event additional heating is required in the cabin, a portion of the air in the exhaust manifold (having been warmed when passing over the electronic equipment) is ducted through a recirculation ejector pump and is mixed with the cold air in the supply duct for recirculation in the cabin. In the event that the quantity of cabin discharge air is insufficient to maintain the cabin electronic equipment within their safe temperature ranges, reverse flow operation will automatically occur or can be manually selected by the pilot. In reverse flow, the air in the supply duct enters the cabin first through the exhaust duct, passes across the electronic packages and is then circulated through the cabin and dumped overboard through the pressure regulator. An emergency ram air scoop on the lower right side of the airplane can be extended into the airstream to supply the airplane with cooling and ventilating air if both refrigeration systems fail. The air will flow directly into the cold air ducts, bypassing the refrigeration systems. A portion of the air will go forward into the cabin areas, through the electronic equipment, and overboard through the cabin pressure regulator in the normal flow manner of cabin circulation. The remaining portion of the air will go aft to the remote electronic equipment. For a list of the electronic equipment requiring cooling air and the control switch for that equipment, see figure 4-2.

HOT AIR DISTRIBUTION.

Air is supplied to the warm air ducts from the compressor section of each inboard engine through the warm air manifold valves. Air temperature in the ducts is regulated by temperature sensors which control the opening and closing of these valves. When the valves move toward the closed position, partially cooled air from the primary heat exchanger flows through a by-pass duct and mixes with hot air just downstream of the warm air by-pass and check valve. The warm air by-pass and check valve, and warm air temperature control work in conjunction with each other to prevent the warm air from increasing above approximately 149° ±33°C (300° ±60°F). The partially cooled air from both engines is then joined in a single warm air manifold duct. This air, plus hot air bleed routed directly from the bleed air inlet lines, is furnished for the following purposes:

1. Windshield rain removal and defog.

2. Pumping action in the recirculation ejector pump.

3. Canopy seal and electronic equipment pressurization.

4. For use as servo and control pressure in positioning various valves and controls of the system.

TEMPERATURE CONTROL SYSTEM.

The temperature control system can be operated in either the automatic or the manual modes to maintain comfortable cabin temperatures and to assure adequate cooling for the protection of electronic equipment. Control of the system is accomplished by the cabin temperature controller and the cabin temperature control knob during the automatic mode of system opera-

electronic equipment requiring cooling air

Pilot's Station	Control Switch
ILS TACAN	Power Knob
UHF Communication (AN/ARC-57)	Command Mode Selector Knob
Flight Controls	Power Switch
Air Conditioning System	Control Mode Selector Knob (In Auto only)
Low Altitude Radar Altimeter	Control Knob

Navigator's Station	Control Switch
Air Navigation Data Recording System (AN/ASH-17)	Power Switch
ILS-TACAN	Power Knob
Search Radar System	Power Switch
Doppler System	Transmitter Switch
Radio Altimeter	Radio Altimeter ON, OFF, Calibrate Switch
Bombing Navigation System	Function Selector Knob
RV Beacon	Power Switch
PI Beacon	Power Switch
Bomb Damage Evaluation System (AN/ASH-15)	Power Switch
Auxiliary Flight Reference	Power Switch
Pod Camera (KA-56)	Pod Air Conditioning Control Switch
Low Altitude Radar Altimeter	Control Knob

DSO's Station	Control Switch
AN/ALQ-16, AFT T-4, left T-4, right T-2	Power Selector Knob (3)
Chaff Dispensing System	Main Power Switch
Long Range Communication System	Power Switch
UHF Communication (AN/ARC-57)	Command Selector Knob
Fire Control System	Master Switch
AN/ALR-12	Power Switch
Air-to-Ground IFF	Master Control Knob

Figure 4-2.

tion and by the temperature control knob alone during the manual mode of operation. Both of these controlling devices utilize the throttle valve control and the recirculation valve in exercising control of the system. When the automatic mode of system operation is selected, the controller operates to maintain a steady temperature in the cabin and to select adequate cooling for electronic equipment. Normally, once the temperature control knob is positioned and a comfortable temperature is attained in the cabin, the same temperature will be maintained throughout the flight. Should a condition arise where the system is incapable of providing sufficient cooling for electronic equipment, the system will automatically change to reverse flow. In this configuration, it may be necessary to adjust the control knob from time-to-time since cabin temperature control is not completely automatic in reverse flow. In the event the controller malfunctions, the manual mode of system operation should be selected. In the manual mode, the controller is de-energized and the cabin temperature control knob has complete control of the system. In this mode, the temperature control knob is pneumatically coupled to both throttle valves and the recirculation valve. Rotating the knob for warmer temperatures causes the recirculation valve to move toward open and the throttle valve to reposition toward closed. Since the electronic protective features of the controller are inactive during manual operation, the electronic equipment temperature indicator and caution lamp should be closely monitored. In case the temperature begins to rise it may be necessary to rotate the knob towards cool for protection of electronic equipment at the expense of lower than desirable temperatures in the cabin. If electronic temperatures cannot be maintained within limits during normal flow and manual (or automatic) operation, it will be necessary for the pilot to select reverse flow. Once the system is in reverse flow during either automatic or manual operation, the system will remain in reverse until the pilot resets to normal flow. Cabin temperature is controlled in the same manner during reverse flow as during normal flow.

Note

A reverse flow caution lamp on the pilot's caution lamp panel remains lighted when the system is in the reverse flow configuration. An electronic overheat caution lamp on the same panel will light, indicating "Low Flow," when the system reverses but should go out within approximately 10 minutes if adequate cooling is available. If the overheat lamp comes on and the system fails to reverse automatically, the caution lamp will remain on requiring that the pilot manually select reverse flow.

Reverse flow will automatically occur in either the manual or automatic mode of operation when an overheat condition exists.

Section IV
Auxiliary Equipment

T.O. 1B-58A-1

cabin pressure schedule

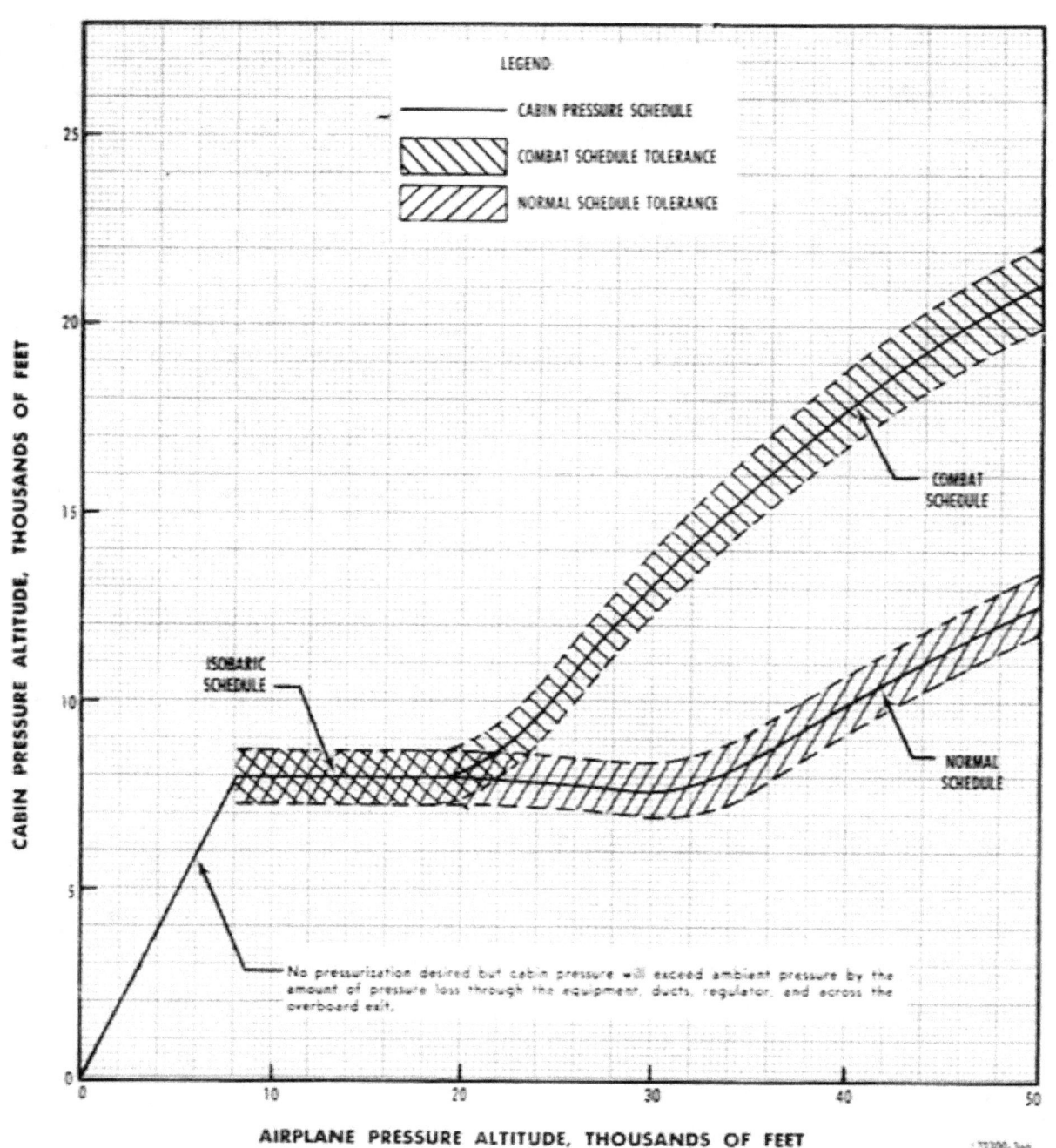

Figure 4-3.

PRESSURIZATION CONTROL.

Cabin pressure is regulated automatically by a cabin pressure regulator which controls the flow of air being vented from the cabin. The regulator is controlled by the cabin pressure selector knob located on the air conditioning control panel. The pressure selector knob is manually positioned to select one of three pressure schedules provided. NORMAL schedule is selected for normal flight when sudden depressurization is unlikely to occur. COMBAT schedule is selected when there is a possibility of sudden depressurization of the cabin. DUMP schedule is selected when emergency depressurization of the cabin is necessary. Regardless of the schedule selected, when the airplane is below 8000 feet, the cabin pressure regulator automatically maintains an unpressurized condition in the cabin. At altitudes above 8000 feet the cabin is automatically pressurized in accordance with the schedule selected. When the normal schedule is used and the airplane is in the 8000 to 35,000-foot range, cabin pressure altitude remains constant at approximately 8000 feet (for exact tolerances, see figure 4-3). As airplane altitude increases, the differential between cabin pressure and ambient pressure increases until at 35,000 feet the differential is approximately 7.45 psi. Above 35,000 feet the 7.45 psi differential remains constant and cabin pressure varies with altitude. When the combat schedule is used and the airplane is in the 8000 to approximately 20,000-foot range, cabin pressure remains constant at a pressure altitude of approximately 8000 feet. At altitudes above approximately 20,000 feet a constant differential of approximately 4.75 psi between cabin pressure and ambient pressure is maintained. A minimum flow sensor in the pressure regulator will cause an increase in cold air output (if required) to maintain pressurization. If the cabin pressure regulator should fail in the closed position, an 8-psi pressure differential is maintained by the cabin pressure safety valve. When a sudden transition from high altitude to lower altitude results in a cabin pressure lower than ambient pressure, both the cabin pressure regulator and the cabin pressure safety valve allow outside air to enter until the pressure is equalized. Pressure inside the cabin is indicated in feet of equivalent altitude by the cabin pressure altimeter located on the air conditioning control panel (figure 4-4). If the equivalent cabin altitude rises above 27,000 feet, a caution lamp lights on the pilot's warning and caution lamp panel.

CONTROLS AND INDICATORS.

Control Mode Selector Knob.

A four-position control mode selector knob (10, figure 4-4) on the pilot's air conditioning control panel is used for selecting the mode of system operation. The knob positions are marked AUTO, MAN, RAM, and OFF. When the selector knob is in either the AUTO or MAN position, a close signal is removed from both bleed air check and shutoff valves. Then the air source selector knob can be positioned to select the engine compressor discharge bleed air source for the system. In the AUTO position, the cabin temperature controller is energized and automatically controls the opening of the refrigeration throttle valves and the recirculation valve. The controller also evaluates electrical signals from temperature sensors throughout the system and automatically selects the amount of air flow necessary to prevent electronic equipment overheating. In the MAN position, the controller is de-energized requiring that the pilot control the system temperature by means of the cabin temperature control knob. When the knob is placed in the RAM position, the recirculation valve, both throttle valves, and both bleed air check and shutoff valves will close, preventing engine bleed-air from entering the system. The ram air scoop and the cabin pressure regulator will open allowing outside ram air to flow through the cabin and out through the wide open regulator in the normal flow circulation pattern. The cabin air flow valve locks in the normal flow position during ram operation.

Note

- In the event that the rain removal switch is at REMOVE when the control mode knob is placed to RAM, both bleed air check and shutoff valves will remain open to supply warm air for rain removal but the air cannot flow through the refrigeration units to the cabin since the throttle valves will close.
- Refer to "Ram Air Operation," this section for operation of electronic equipment during ram air cooling.

When the control mode knob is at OFF, the bleed air check and shutoff valves, throttle valves, recirculation valve, and ram air scoop are each maintained in a closed position and the temperature controller is de-energized. The knob should not be positioned to OFF during flight since this will result in stopping the circulation of air. The control mode selector knob controls 28-volt direct current and 115-volt alternating current for operating the system.

Refrigeration Unit Selector Knob.

A four-position refrigeration unit selector knob (6, figure 4-4) is provided on the air conditioning control panel for use in selecting the source of air conditioning cold air. The knob positions are marked BOTH, L, R, and GRD CART. When the knob is placed in the BOTH position, refrigerated air is supplied from both units according to the amount of throttle valve opening selected by the throttle valve control. In the L position, a close solenoid is energized on the right throttle valve to shut down that unit and cold air is supplied

4-7

Section IV
Auxiliary Equipment

T.O. 1B-58A-1

air conditioning control panel (typical)

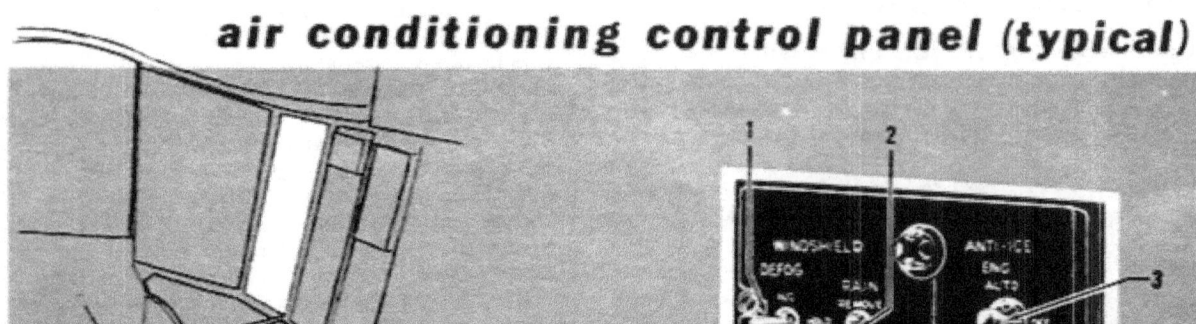

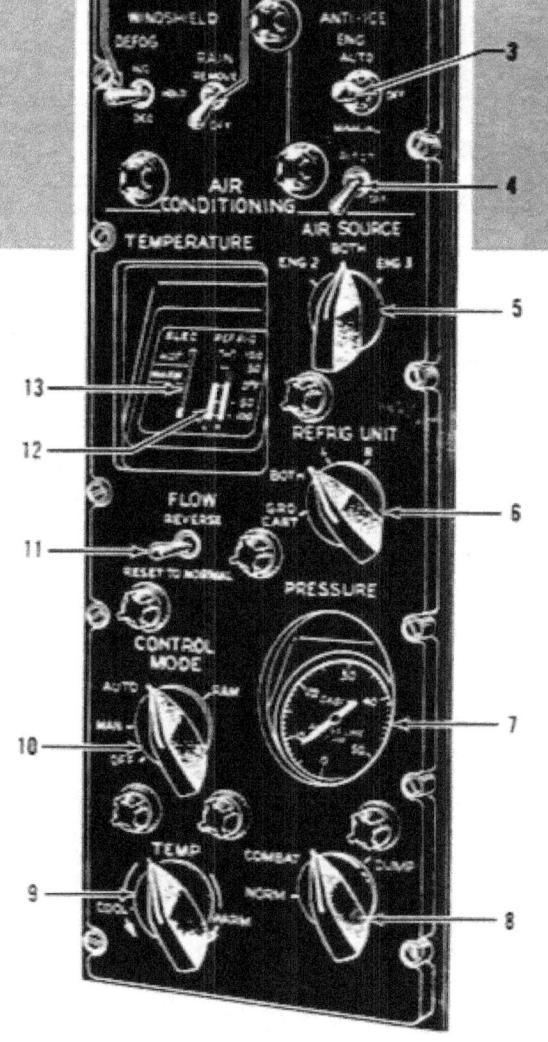

from the left unit. With the knob placed to R, the right unit supplies cold air since the left unit is shut down in the same manner. Placing the knob to the GRD CART position energizes the close solenoid on both refrigeration unit throttle valves so that cold air can be supplied from the air conditioning ground cart only. In this position, the system is locked in reverse flow so that normal flow is not possible. When starting engines on compressor bleed air from an operating inboard engine, the selector knob must be in GRD CART position to prevent an engine hot start condition. The knob controls 28-volt direct current for selecting the source of cold air. The supply of ground cart air can be continued during the transition to air conditioning system supplied air.

Air Source Selector Knob.

A three-position air source selector knob (5, figure 4-4) is located on the air conditioning control panel and is used in selecting the source of engine bleed air for the air conditioning system. The knob positions are marked BOTH, ENG 2, and ENG 3. When the knob is placed in the BOTH position, bleed air from both inboard engines enters the system through their respective bleed air check and shutoff valves. With the knob in the ENG 2 position, bleed air is supplied from the left inboard engine only, since the No. 3 engine bleed air check and shutoff valve is closed. Placing the switch in the ENG 3 position shuts off the supply of bleed air from No. 2 engine and allows the right inboard engine to furnish bleed air. The selector knob controls 28-volt direct current for selecting the source of bleed air.

Cabin Pressure Selector Knob.

The three-position cabin pressure selector knob (8, figure 4-4) located on the air conditioning control panel is

1. Windshield Defog Switch
2. Windshield Rain Removal Switch
3. Engine Anti-Ice Switch
4. Pitot Anti-Ice Switch
5. Air Source Selector Knob
6. Refrigeration Unit Selector Knob
7. Cabin Pressure Altimeter
8. Cabin Pressure Selector Knob
9. Cabin Temperature Control Knob
10. Control Mode Selector Knob
11. Flow Switch
12. Refrigeration Temperature Indicator
13. Electronic Equipment Temperature Indicator

Figure 4-4.

4-8

Section IV
Auxiliary Equipment

used to select the desired cabin pressure schedule (see figure 4-3), which is maintained during either normal or reverse flow. The knob has positions marked NORM, COMBAT, and DUMP and is used to position a rotary selector which is pneumatically coupled to the cabin pressure regulator. In the DUMP position, the knob mechanically bleeds off control pressure in the cabin pressure regulator so that the regulator is wide open and pressure is dumped. In the COMBAT position, the knob mechanically bleeds off a portion of the control pressure causing the regulator to maintain the combat pressure schedule. In the NORM position, the regulator automatically maintains the normal schedule since the knob has no effect on the regulator control pressure. The cabin pressure selector knob is independent of any power system of the airplane. In the event of malfunction of the pressure regulator, the cabin pressure safety valve maintains a pre-selected 8.0 psi pressure differential.

Flow Switch.

A three-position airflow switch (11, figure 4-4) is located on the air conditioning control panel and is used to manually select reverse or normal flow operation of the system. The switch is marked REVERSE and RESET TO NORMAL and is spring-loaded from each of these positions to a center unmarked NEUTRAL position. Momentarily placing the switch to the REVERSE position energizes a relay in the cabin temperature controller to reposition the cabin air flow valve which, in turn, routes the conditioned air across the electronic equipment before the air is circulated through the cabin. Momentarily positioning the switch to RESET TO NORMAL energizes a solenoid which shuts off servo air pressure causing the cabin air flow valve to reposition to the normal flow configuration. The switch controls 28-volt direct current for selecting normal or reverse flow. The system can be either in normal or reverse flow with the air flow switch in the NEUTRAL center position. The direction of flow can be determined by observing the reverse air flow caution lamp.

Cabin Temperature Control Knob.

The cabin temperature control knob (9, figure 4-4) is located on the air conditioning control panel for use in adjusting temperature in the cabin. The control knob can be positioned at any setting between the marked COOL and WARM positions. When the control mode selector knob is in the AUTO position, the temperature control knob sends electrical signals to the cabin temperature controller which, in turn, electrically controls the volume of cold air output and the amount of recirculation to maintain the desired cabin temperature. Clockwise rotation of the knob results in warmer cabin temperatures. When the control mode knob is in the MAN position, the knob is pneumatically coupled to the recirculation valve and to the throttle valves. Rotation of the temperature knob mechanically controls bleed-off of control pressure for proportioning the cold air output and cabin recirculation. If a large knob adjustment is made, the air conditioning system may go into reverse flow.

> **CAUTION**
>
> In the event that electronic equipment overheats during manual operation, rotating the temperature control knob towards COOL may be necessary to accomplish an increase of cold air output for the protection of electronic components. Knob adjustments should be minimized, especially during automatic system operation, since the system responds gradually for changes in temperature and air flow. A sufficient time interval between knob adjustments must be allowed for reaction to the selected change.

Refrigeration Temperature Indicators.

Two refrigeration temperature indicators (12, figure 4-4) are located on the air conditioning control panel, one indicator marked L for the left refrigeration unit and the other marked R for the right unit. With both refrigeration units in operation, a difference in the temperature reading on the two indicators of more than 20°F is an indication of a malfunction or failure of that unit which shows the highest reading. However, the malfunctioning unit should not be shut down as long as the cabin temperature remains satisfactory and there is no evidence of overheating or loss of equipment. The refrigeration temperature indicators operate on 115-volt alternating current.

Electronic Equipment Temperature Indicator.

An electronic equipment air temperature indicator (13, figure 4-4) on the air conditioning control panel provides a continuous indication of electronic equipment temperatures, by means of an air temperature sensor unit located in the AN/ARC-57 receiver-transmitter unit, radar package control indicator, and navigation servo unit. The indicator has increments marked HOT and WARM. In automatic operation of the system the indicator serves as a reference in monitoring system operation. In manual operation of the system, the indicator aids the pilot in adjusting cabin air temperature to satisfy the electronic cooling requirements. The indicator should be considered a secondary means of evaluating the air conditioning system operation, the primary indication being the low airflow caution lamp with the system operating in AUTO mode. In the event any of these electronic units become overheated,

Section IV
Auxiliary Equipment

T.O. 1B-58A-1

the temperature indicator will register HOT and the "LOW AIR FLOW" caution lamp (figure 1-13) will light. The indicator operates on 28-volt direct current.

Cabin Pressure Altimeter.

The cabin pressure altimeter (7, figure 4-4), located on the air conditioning control panel, is a barometric-type instrument which indicates cabin air pressure in feet of equivalent altitude.

Low Cabin Pressure Caution Lamp.

The low cabin pressure lamp (figure 1-13), located on the pilot's caution lamp panel, lights when cabin pressure drops to 5 psia (pressure altitude above 27,000 feet). When lighted, CABIN PRESS LOW appears on the face of the lamp in yellow illuminated letters. The lamp is powered by 28-volt direct current and is tied-in to the master caution lamp. (For testing and dimming the cabin pressure caution lamp and for information on the master caution lamp, refer to "Malfunction Indicator and Warning System," Section I.)

Low Air Flow Caution Lamp.

The electronic overheat caution lamp (figure 1-13), located on the pilot's caution lamp panel, lights in the event of inadequate cooling airflow to the electronic equipment. When lighted, LOW AIR FLOW appears on the face of the lamp in yellow illuminated letters. The lamp should light when the air conditioning system automatically changes from normal flow to reverse flow. During ground operation, both inboard engines should be operated at 85 percent where possible until the lamp goes out. If this does not occur within 10 minutes, malfunction is indicated. The air conditioning system must be operated in the AUTO mode for the low airflow caution lamp to indicate anything of significance. (An exception to this is when the electronic equipment temperature indicator reads HOT in which case the lamp would be lighted in normal flow MAN mode of air conditioning operation.) The lamp will light to indicate that the air conditioning system has automatically switched to reverse flow whether the system is operating in the automatic or manual mode. The lamp operates on 28-volt d-c power and is connected to the master caution lamp panel. For dimming and testing the low airflow caution lamp and for information on the master caution lamp, refer to "Malfunction Indicator and Warning System," Section I.

Warning Horn.

A warning horn is installed to indicate insufficient cooling air and consequent overheating of electronic equipment. The warning horn is intended to warn maintenance crews of electronic equipment overheating, and will operate only when the external power

cart is connected to the airplane. When the external power knob is in the GRD MAINT position, the horn will sound continuously until sufficient cooling air is supplied to the airplane, except the horn will not sound when the control mode selector knob is in MAN position and the refrigeration unit selector knob is in the GRD CART position, even if an overheat condition exists.

Reverse Flow Caution Lamp.

The reverse flow caution lamp (figure 1-13), located on the pilot's caution lamp panel, lights when the air conditioning system is in reverse flow. When lighted, REVERSE AIR FLOW appears in yellow illuminated letters on the face of the lamp. The lamp operates on 28-volt direct current and is tied-in to the master caution lamp. (For dimming and testing the reverse flow lamp and for information on the master caution lamp, refer to "Malfunction Indicator and Warning System," Section I.)

NORMAL OPERATION.

For normal system operation, the air conditioning control panel should be set up as follows:

1. Air source selector knob—BOTH
2. Refrigeration unit selector knob—BOTH
3. Control mode selector knob—AUTO

Note

Refer to Section V, 1B-58A-1A for the air conditioning water boil-off rate.

CAUTION

Do not place control mode selector knob in AUTO position except when system is operating and cold air is being supplied. When the control mode selector knob is placed in the AUTO position, power is directed to the electronic simulator. Overheating for approximately 3 minutes will damage the unit.

4. Cabin pressure selector knob—NORMAL
5. Cabin temperature control knob—Between unmarked 3 o'clock and 4 o'clock position.

Allow the system time to respond to any changes in knob adjustment.

6. Flow switch—RESET TO NORMAL (if required)

Momentarily position flow switch to RESET TO NORMAL if it is desired to change system from reverse to normal flow.

7. Reverse flow caution lamp—Out.

The reverse flow caution lamp should immediately go out when the air flow switch is positioned to RESET TO NORMAL.

Note

- During any operation with only one inboard engine supplying cooling air to both refrigeration units, maintain at least 85 per cent rpm on that engine to assure normal airflow operation.

- At altitudes below 20,000 feet, with the inboard engines at idle power, the air conditioning system may switch to reverse flow. This characteristic is not a malfunction of the system. Both inboard engines should be operated at 80 percent rpm if flight conditions permit in order to put the light out within 5 minutes and then the system reset to normal flow if desired. Do not select MAN to put the light out.

8. Electronic equipment temperature indicator—Below WARM.

9. Refrigeration temperature indicators—Same on both.

Both indicators should have approximately the same reading.

Extended Range Operation.

For extended range, air refueling, high speed missions, the quantity of water in the water boilers may be conserved by operating the air conditioning system in a cross feed configuration as follows:

1. Air source selector knob—ENG. 3 (or ENG. 2).
2. Refrigeration unit selector knob—L (or R).
3. Control mode selector knob—MAN.
4. Cabin pressure selector knob—NORMAL.
5. Flow switch—RESET TO NORMAL.

Monitor the electronic equipment temperature indicator while adjusting the cabin temperature control knob as required to maintain adequate electronic equipment cooling and approximately a 90°F cabin temperature. For extended range sub-sonic missions, operate the air conditioning system in the normal manner.

Manual Cabin Temperature Control Operation.

Manual Operation should only be used in the event of a cabin temperature controller malfunction. In manual operation, the controller is de-energized and the temperature of both the cabin and the electronic equipment must be controlled by means of the cabin temperature control knob. This deactivates the overheat indicator provided by the controller (through the low airflow caution lamp) and forces reliance upon the electronic equipment temperature indicator which is a less accurate indication, in addition to its being of no use in reverse flow. There is no reliable indication of an overheat condition while operating the system in MAN and reverse flow. With the control mode selector in MAN position, the cabin temperature control knob is pneumatically coupled to the recirculation air valve and to the throttle valves of the refrigeration units. Rotation of the knob to the COOL position opens the throttle valve. Rotation of the knob to the WARM position opens the recirculation valve and closes the throttle valve to a set minimum position. For this reason, more cooling air is usually available in the AUTO mode since both recirculation and throttle valves can be full open to satisfy the demands of the cabin temperature controller. A substantial amount of cooling effect is obtained by recirculation air. During ram air cooling, adequate cooling air is marginal in some flight conditions. This will result in higher operating temperatures for all force-cooled electronic equipment.

Reverse Flow Operation.

Reverse flow operation is used primarily for cooling electronic equipment with the ground cooling cart when the airplane is on the ground and the canopies are open. This arrangement permits checking of electronic equipment without operating the refrigeration system. Normally operate the system in normal flow, except when the electronic overheat lamp is lighted. If reverse flow operation occurs during flight without a cabin blowout, cabin pressure will be maintained according to the selected pressure schedule.

Note

During reverse flow operation, the electronic equipment temperature indicator does not indicate a true reading. Resetting to normal flow will be necessary to obtain a true temperature reading from the electronic equipment temperature indicator.

RAM AIR OPERATION.

During ram air operation, adequate cooling air is marginal at some flight conditions resulting in higher operating temperatures for all force-cooled electronic equipment. For ram air operation, accomplish the following steps:

1. Airspeed and altitude within ram air limit—Checked. Refer to "Airspeed Limitations", Section V for ram air mode operating limits.
2. Control mode selector knob—RAM.
3. The following equipment should not be operated:
   a. AN/ALQ-16, Aft T4.
   b. Fire Control System.

Section IV
Auxiliary Equipment

T.O. 1B-58A-1

c. Bomb-Navigation System (Function Selector Knob to GYRO).

Note

Placing the Function Selector Knob to the GYRO position will de-activate the Doppler, Radio Altimeter and Astrotracker.

4. The following equipment should not be operated unless essential to flight, due to degraded performance and/or damage from overheating.

   a. Search Radar.
   b. AN/ALQ-16 Left T4.
   c. AN/ALQ-16, Right T2.
   d. AN/ARC-57.
   e. ILS.
   f. TACAN.
   g. Long Range Communication System.
   h. Low Altitude Radar Altimeter.

5. The following equipment should be operated only if required. These units receive ram air cooling; however, cooling requirements are not critical:

   a. Air-to-ground IFF.
   b. Bomb Damage Evaluation System (AN/ASH-15).
   c. PI Beacon.
   d. RV Beacon.
   e. Chaff Dispensing System.
   f. AN/ALR-12.
   g. Auxiliary Flight Reference System.
   h. Flight Control System.
   i. Air Navigation Data Recording System (AN/ASH-17).
   j. Pod Camera (KA-56).

6. Land as soon as practical.

Note

If fuel dumping is necessary, the fuel dump rate will be materially reduced due to lack of fuel tank pressurization.

ANTI-ICING AND DEFOGGING SYSTEMS.

WINDSHIELD RAIN REMOVAL AND DEFOG SYSTEM.

The airplane is provided with a system for removing rain from the windshield during takeoff and landing and for removing condensate when fogging conditions exist inside the airplane. A rain removal duct provides a stream of warm air across the outside surface of the left front pane of the pilot's windshield. A defog duct directs air across the inside surface of the front four panes. Air is taken from the warm air lines in the air conditioning system. It is routed forward under the cabin floor, over a thermal switch connected to a caution lamp, and then to discharge nozzles installed at the windshield. The rain removal airstream flows over the windshield from two flush mounted nozzles located at the upper left and bottom left corners of the pane. The airstream for fog removal passes through an ejector where cabin air is mixed with the hot air before being distributed over the windshield through four nozzles located along the lower edge of the front four panes. The defog and rain removal system is controlled by means of two switches on the air conditioning control panel. A windshield overheat caution lamp on the pilot's caution lamp panel warns the pilot when the temperature of the air is high enough to damage the windshield when using the rain removal system.

Note

Rain removal is operative during ram air operation. Windshield defog is also operative during ram air operation if the rain removal system is on.

Windshield Rain Removal Switch.

The windshield rain removal switch (2, figure 4-4) is located on the air conditioning control panel and has positions marked REMOVE and OFF. Placing the switch in the REMOVE position routes 28-volt d-c power to open the solenoid on the rain removal shutoff valve. Opening of this solenoid permits servo (actuating) air pressure to open the shutoff valve and allow warm air to flow across the left front pane of the pilot's windshield.

Windshield Defog Switch

The windshield defog switch (1, figure 4-4) is a three-position switch located on the air conditioning control panel. The switch controls 28-volt d-c power to the shutoff valve in the defog duct. The switch is marked DEC, HOLD, and INC. It is spring-loaded from the INC position to HOLD. Holding the switch in INC moves the valve toward the open position. Releasing it to HOLD stops the valve travel. Placing the switch in the DEC position moves the valve toward the closed position. The valve will travel from one extreme position to the other in approximately 15 seconds.

Windshield Overheat Caution Lamp.

The windshield overheat caution lamp (figure 1-13) on the pilot's caution lamp panel lights when the air temperature in the defog and rain removal warm air supply duct rises to the extent that the air could cause damage to the windshield. When lighted, WINDSHIELD HOT appears on the face of the lamp in yellow illuminated letters. Rain removal and defog should be kept to a minimum when the lamp is lit. The lamp is controlled by a thermal switch in the warm air duct upstream from the defog and rain removal shutoff valves. The lamp operates on 28-volt direct current and is tied-in to the master caution lamp. (For testing and dimming the overheat lamp and for information on the master caution lamp, refer to "Malfunction Indicator and Warning System," Section I.)

Normal Operation.

Windshield Defogging. The windshield defog system should be put into operation at the first evidence of fog forming on any windshield surface. The system is inoperative during ram air operation except when the rain removal switch is in the REMOVE position.

Note

Under high relative humidity atmospheric conditions, fog can be expected to form on inside windshield surfaces.

Rain Removal. Do not operate the rain removal system on the ground, except when necessary for visibility. Extensive ground operation may result in damage to the windshield. The rain removal system is inoperative on the ground except with one (or both) inboard engines operating or with the engine starter cart connected and operating. The system is operative during ram air operation.

Emergency Operation.

If the windshield overheat caution lamp lights, place the windshield rain removal switch in the OFF position and the defog switch in the DEC position.

Turn the switches off only if flight safety will not be endangered by restricting the pilot's vision.

PITOT ANTI-ICING SYSTEM.

The primary pitot-static probe and the secondary probe are anti-iced by heating elements located in each probe. The secondary static ports are not heated. The primary and secondary pitot pressure systems are manifolded together. If either the primary or secondary pitot pressure system becomes blocked by ice, the ice free system will provide pitot pressure to the pilot's, navigator's and DSO's airspeed indicator. The primary and secondary static systems are not manifolded together. The pitot anti-icing system should be placed in operation when icing conditions are anticipated.

Pitot Anti-Ice Switch.

The pitot anti-ice switch is a two-position switch located on the air conditioning control panel (4, figure 4-4). The switch is marked PITOT and OFF. Placing the switch to PITOT, 115-volt a-c power is applied to the primary pitot-static probe heater from the right a-c power distribution panel and 115-volt a-c power is applied to the secondary pitot-static probe heater from the left a-c power distribution panel. The angle-of-attack anti-icing system is connected through the pitot anti-ice switch. When the pitot anti-ice switch is placed in the PITOT position, 115-volt a-c power is applied to the angle-of-attack sensor vane heater from the right a-c power distribution panel.

ENGINE AND SPIKE ANTI-ICING SYSTEMS.

The engine and spike anti-icing systems utilize hot air to prevent icing of the frontal areas (see figure 4-6). These systems are designed primarily for use during takeoff, low altitude flights, landing, and when aerodynamic heating cannot be relied upon to prevent icing. Although the two systems are separate, they share the same controls and caution lamps, and operate as a single system. The engine anti-icing system provides anti-icing for the inlet guide vanes and the compressor front frame strut. The system components consist primarily of air supply ducts, an engine anti-icing valve, anti-icing caution lamp, ice detector, icing caution lamp, and a front frame overtemperature sensor. The hot air for anti-icing is supplied from the engine's compressor. When the system is turned on, the solenoid operated anti-icing valve opens, allowing hot air to flow through the supply ducts. The air is then circulated inside the compressor front frame struts and hub, the inlet guide vanes, and is discharged into the inlet air stream. The air flow inside the duct is regulated by the anti-icing valve which senses downstream pressure. This pressure signals the anti-icing valve to open or close as required to maintain a constant air pressure in the system. The system provides either manual or automatic operation. When manual operation is selected, the system is in constant operation until turned off. When automatic operation is selected, the ice detector relay controls the system, turning the system on and off as required. The spike anti-icing system principal components consist of air supply ducts, a spike anti-icing valve and a temperature sensor. The spike anti-icing system is controlled by the engine anti-icing system switch and operates simultaneously with the engine anti-icing system in both manual and automatic selections. When the system is turned on (either manually or by the ice detector relay) the spike retracts to the anti-icing position, the air outlet at the spike lip opens, and the spike anti-icing valve opens. The compressor bleed air then flows through the spike anti-icing valve to the ejector nozzle where it is mixed with cold air drawn from the ram air duct. The mixed air then passes through the

4-13

Section IV
Auxiliary Equipment

engine and spike anti-icing systems (typical)

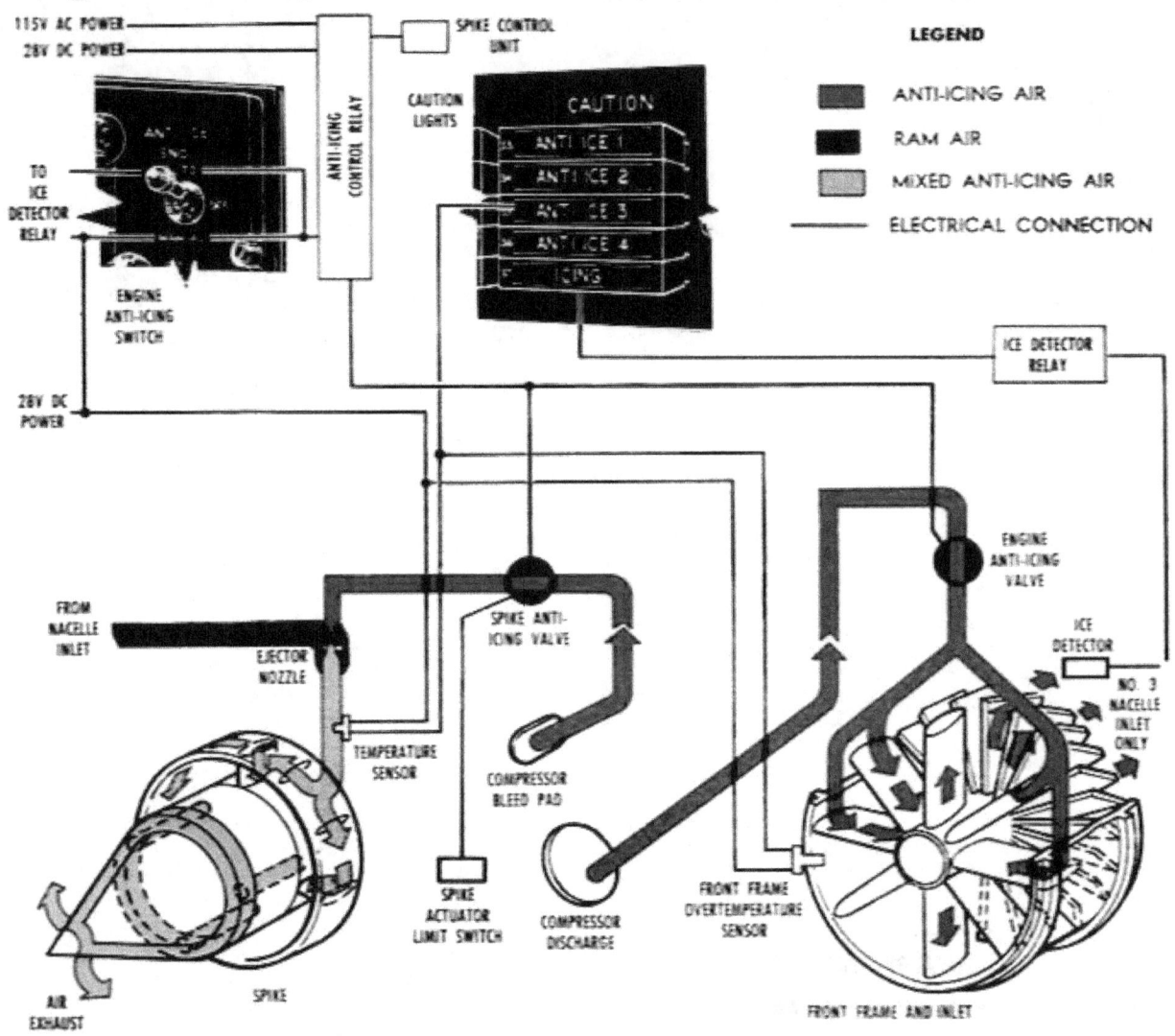

Figure 4-5.

spike strut to the annular passages around the spike and out through the opening in the spike tip. In the event of an electrical failure, both the engine and spike anti-icing valves will automatically close, shutting off the anti-icing air flow.

Engine Anti-Ice Switch.

The engine anti-ice switch (3, figure 4-4) is located on the air conditioning control panel and has positions marked AUTO, MANUAL and OFF. When the switch is placed in the MANUAL position, a 28-volt d-c relay is energized directing 115-volt a-c power to the anti-icing valve in each engine causing warm air to flow to the iced areas. The system works automatically if ice is encountered when the switch is placed in the AUTO position. The spike anti-icing system operates simultaneously with the engine anti-icing system.

Anti-Ice Caution Lamps.

The anti-ice caution lamp for each engine is located on the pilot's warning and caution panel (see figure

1-13). The anti-ice caution lamps are controlled by the engine front frame overheat temperature sensor, located in the front frame strut, and the spike overheat temperature sensor located in the spike duct. The anti-ice caution lamps will not light until the spike has retracted to the anti-icing position. A lighted caution lamp indicates a malfunction of the engine and spike anti-icing shutoff valve, causing an overheat condition to exist.

Icing Caution Lamp.

The icing caution lamp is located on the pilot's warning and caution lamp panel (see figure 1-13). When ice has formed on the ice detector probe, located in No. 3 engine air inlet, an electrical signal from the ice detector interpreter relay will light the icing caution lamp. The lamp will remain lighted as long as icing exists. The icing caution lamp operates independently from the anti-icing system and is not affected when the anti-icing system is turned on or off. The lamp is connected to the master caution lamp circuit and operates on 28-volt direct current.

Engine And Spike Anti-Icing System Operation.

Operate the engine and spike anti-icing system as follows:

WARNING

Do not operate the anti-icing system when ram air temperature exceeds 15°C (59°F). This may cause structural damage or failure of the compressor front frame bearing seals and spike structure.

1. Engine anti-ice switch—AUTO when icing conditions are anticipated or when icing caution lamp is lighted.

Note

- If the system became inoperative in AUTO position, place the anti-icing switch to MANUAL position.
- When utilizing the anti-icing system during takeoff at low ambient temperatures, the airplane accelerates rapidly and thrust loss due to anti-icing system operation is negligible.

2. Engine anti-ice switch—OFF. The anti-ice switch should be turned OFF when icing is no longer anticipated or exists, because operation of the anti-icing system will increase fuel consumption and reduce engine thrust.

Extended periods of operations at low speeds in icing conditions should be avoided to prevent the possibility of excessive ice buildup on the nacelle inlet lips and other airplane surfaces which are not provided with anti-icing.

Note

Icing of the inlet guide vanes may be indicated by low ram air temperature accompanied by a loss of power. This may be accompanied by an increase in nozzle opening and an increase in fuel flow.

Anti-Icing Caution Lamp Lighted.

When one or more anti-ice caution lamp(s) light(s), the indication is that the engine or spike anti-icing air temperature is too high. A high anti-icing air temperature may be due to the engine or spike anti-icing valve failed in the open position or anti-icing operation at altitudes above 15,000 feet at high power setting. If the anti-ice caution lamp(s) remains lighted after the anti-icing system is turned off, the indication is that the engine or spike anti-icing system is operating at an overheated condition or the engine or spike anti-icing valve has failed in the open position. This malfunction becomes critical only at supersonic speed or if the ram air temperatures go above 15°C (59°F). When detecting a malfunction in the anti-icing system, immediately accomplish the following steps:

1. During supersonic flight with the anti-icing system off and one or more anti-ice caution lamps lighted, immediately decelerate to subsonic speed.

2. Attempt to close the malfunctioning anti-icing valve(s) by momentarily placing the engine anti-ice switch to MANUAL and OFF.

3. If the lamp(s) remains lighted, decrease power on the affected engine(s) until the lamp(s) goes out.

4. If the lamp(s) remains lighted, shut down the affected engine(s), if feasible. When the lamp(s) goes out, restart the engine(s). If the lamp(s) remains out, resume normal flight. If the lamp(s) lights again, shut down the engine(s) again. If engine shutdown is inadvisable, or if the engine(s) is restarted because safety of flight becomes marginal, observe the following restrictions:

   a. Reduce power to 85 percent or less on the affected engine(s).

   b. Remain subsonic and maintain an altitude above 15,000 feet, where practical.

4-15

Section IV
Auxiliary Equipment

T.O. 1B-58A-1

c. If flight below 15,000 feet is required, maintain an airspeed as near Mach No. 0.6 as feasible.

d. Land as soon as possible.

Note

These limitations are based on a full-open anti-icing valve. The engine front frame structure will not be damaged with a full-open valve if this operation does not exceed twenty cumulative hours.

COMMUNICATION SYSTEM.

The communication system provides a means of crew intercommunication, plus normal and emergency air-to-air and air-to-ground communication. The complete system is composed of an interphone and a UHF command radio system (AN/ARC-57), a secondary UHF command radio system (AN/ARC-34), an emergency communication system (AN/ARC-74), and a long range communication system (LRC). The communication system is equipped with mayday capability which provides a means of expediting communication in the event of an emergency. When the Bailout Warning System is actuated a series of relays is energized which accomplish the following:

● "Hot Mike" communication between crew members.

● Command radio (AN/ARC-57) energized and tuned to the guard frequency. The guard receiver will be turned on regardless of the position of the command mode selector knob. It will remain OFF if the preset channel selector knob is in the G position. When a-c power is not available the emergency communication system (AN/ARC-74) is turned on and tuned to the guard frequency. If the AN/ARC-74 system is in operation when the mayday relays are energized, the system will continue to operate on the selected channel.

● Long range communication (LRC) system activated and tuned to the last selected frequency and mode of operation.

● Simultaneous reception and simultaneous push-to-talk transmission on the above systems. Any other audio selected by mixing switches will also be available to the headsets.

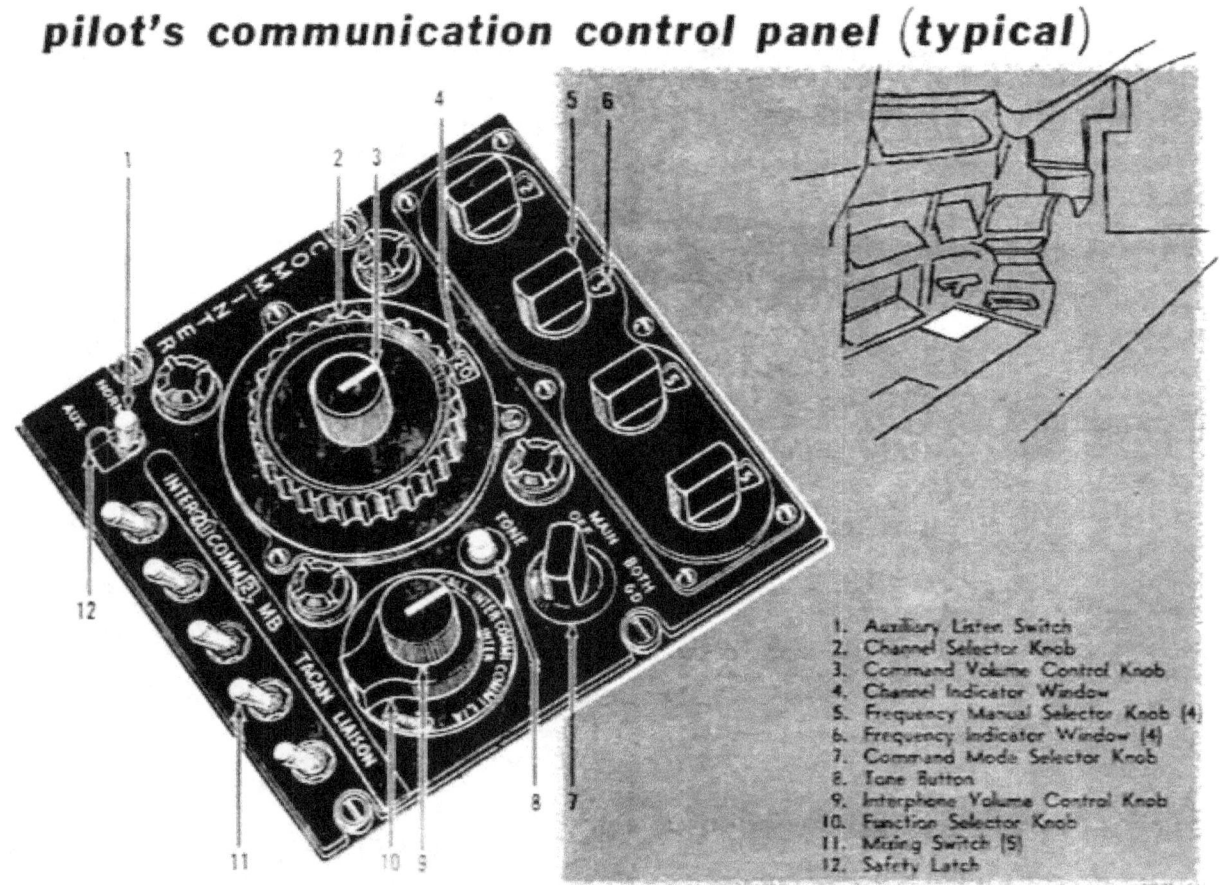

pilot's communication control panel (typical)

1. Auxiliary Listen Switch
2. Channel Selector Knob
3. Command Volume Control Knob
4. Channel Indicator Window
5. Frequency Manual Selector Knob (4)
6. Frequency Indicator Window (4)
7. Command Mode Selector Knob
8. Tone Button
9. Interphone Volume Control Knob
10. Function Selector Knob
11. Mixing Switch (5)
12. Safety Latch

Figure 4-6.

Section IV
Auxiliary Equipment

dso's communication control panel (typical)

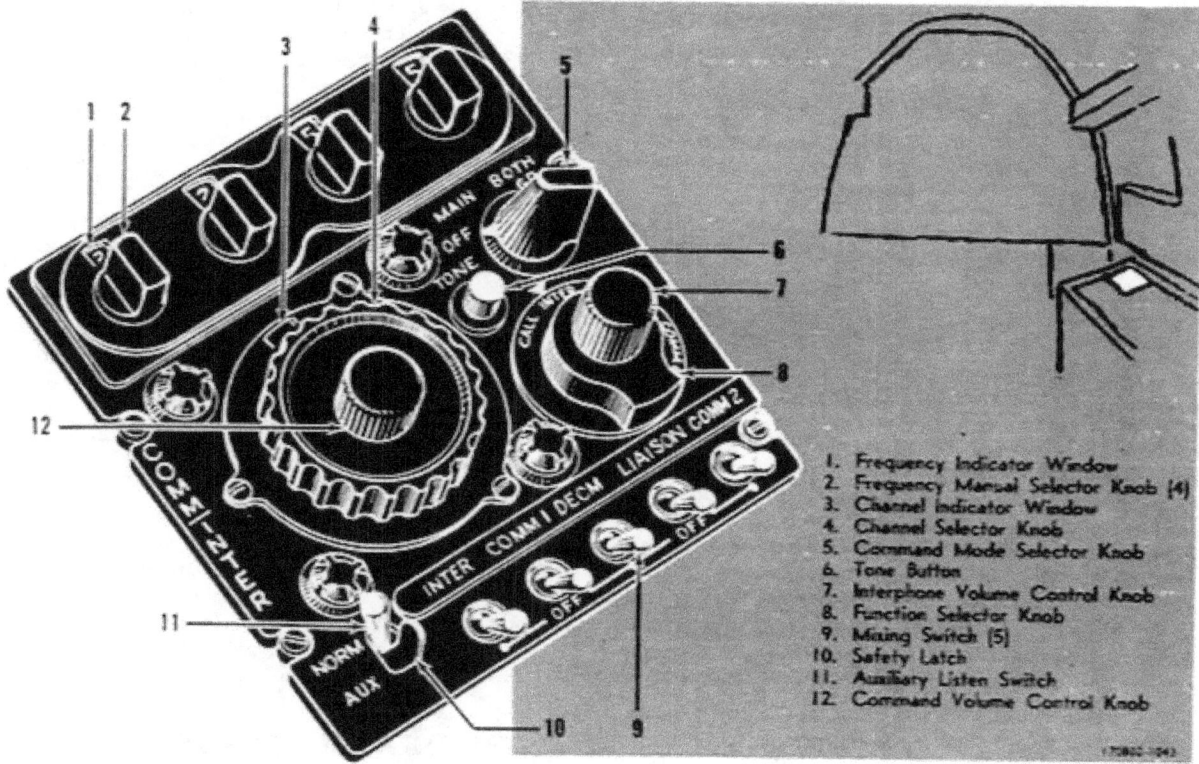

1. Frequency Indicator Window
2. Frequency Manual Selector Knob (4)
3. Channel Indicator Window
4. Channel Selector Knob
5. Command Mode Selector Knob
6. Tone Button
7. Interphone Volume Control Knob
8. Function Selector Knob
9. Mixing Switch (5)
10. Safety Latch
11. Auxiliary Listen Switch
12. Command Volume Control Knob

Figure 4-7.

● The crew member has no reception capability on the LRC system, unless his LIAISON mixing switch is on, when in MAYDAY mode.

● A control panel in AUX (AUX LISTEN) during MAYDAY operation has the following listening functions:

1. With all mixer switches off, the UHF systems (either ARC-57 or ARC-74) will be heard. Interphone audio will not be available.
2. With the interphone mixer switch on, only interphone audio will be heard. No other audio signal will be available.
3. The individual COMM or LIAISON mixer switches must be on in order to receive LRC and UHF. Interphone will not be available.
4. If any mixer switch other than INTER, COMM, or LIAISON is on with all others switches OFF, the audio associated with that mixer will be the only one heard. LRC, UHF, and interphone will not be available.

● A control panel with function selector knob at CALL has transmission capability on the LRC and UHF (either AN/ARC-57 or AN/ARC-74) systems. However, other crew members will be unable to hear the transmission.

● Air-to-Ground IFF energized and set up to respond in an emergency code to mode 1 and mode 3 interrogation.

When the bailout warning system is turned off, the relays are released and all systems affected will return to normal operation. If the pilot ejects, a switch on his ejection rail will be actuated. Actuation of this switch energizes the mayday relays, keys the transmitters, and grounds the audio tone of the AN/ARC-57 to modulate the transmitted carrier, thus providing additional time for ground stations to obtain a "fix" on the pilotless aircraft. For the table of communication and associated electronic equipment, refer to figure 4-15.

INTERPHONE AND UHF COMMAND RADIO SYSTEM (AN/ARC-57).

The AN/ARC-57 communication system provides a means of crew intercommunication, plus air-to-air and air-to-ground communication. The complete system is composed of an interphone system and a UHF command radio.

4-17

Section IV
Auxiliary Equipment

T.O. 1B-58A-1

The interphone system provides the crew with the following capabilities:

• Either push-to-talk or "hot mike" communication between crew members.

• Command radio reception and transmission for each crew member.

• Emergency communication between crew members, regardless of control settings.

• Landing gear audio warning to the pilot. (Refer to "Landing Gear System," Section 1.)

• Communication with the ground crew by means of external receptacles, and an AN/AIC-17 ground interphone set.

The interphone system consists mainly of controls located on a communication or interphone control panel at each crew station, microphone buttons or switches at each crew station, and external interphone receptacles (figure 1-1) located on the fuselage near the leading edge of the right wing and in the nose wheel well. The controls and indicators for the interphone system, some of which are common to the command radio, are discussed under the UHF command radio. The interphone system operates on 28-volt direct current through fuses on the 28-volt d-c power panel. The

UHF command radio provides plane-to-plane and plane-to-ground line-of-sight voice communication. The radio also provides for transmitting a continuous tone signal. The frequency range of the radio is 225.0 to 399.9 megacycles in increments of one-tenth megacycle, thus permitting manual selection of any one of 1750 frequencies. Twenty-three of these frequencies, including a guard frequency, may be preset and selected by channel number. When operating the AN/ARC-57 in conjunction with the AN/ARC-34, crosstalk can be expected when the frequencies on the respective radios are less than one megacycle apart. A separate guard receiver, with a frequency range of 238.0 to 248.0 megacycles, allows the crew to monitor a preset guard channel and receive on another command channel simultaneously. Channel selection and mode of operation of the command radio must be determined by the pilot or DSO. However, once the set is placed in operation, other crew members may transmit and receive through their interphone controls. The command radio system includes a transceiver, (transmitter, main receiver, guard receiver) a flush-mounted antenna, and controls on the pilot's and DSO's communication control panel. The command radio operates on 28-volt d-c power from the 28-volt d-c power panel, 115-volt, 400-cycle, a-c power from the left a-c power panel; and 150-volt, minus 150-volt, and 250-volt direct current from the a-c and high voltage d-c power panel.

navigator's interphone control panel (typical)

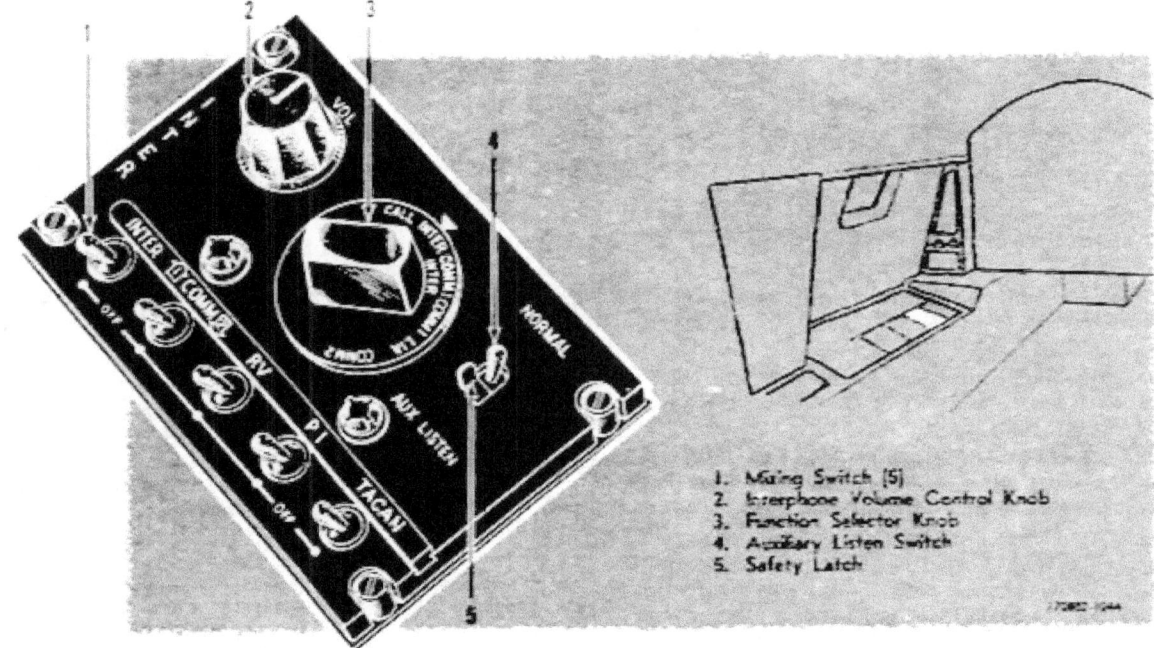

1. Mixing Switch (5)
2. Interphone Volume Control Knob
3. Function Selector Knob
4. Auxiliary Listen Switch
5. Safety Latch

Figure 4-8.

4-18

Function Selector Knob.

The function selector knob (10, figure 4-6, 8, figure 4-7, 3, figure 4-8) is located on the pilot's and DSO's communication control panels and on the navigator's interphone control panel. At each crew station the function selector knob selects the operating function of the communication system. The knob has six positions: CALL, INTER, COMM 1 INTER, COMM 1, LIA, and COMM 2. The CALL position, which is spring-loaded to INTER, is for emergency use. With the knob in the CALL position, the crew member at the calling station interrupts all normal interphone functions at all stations and may contact other crew members at high volume level without depressing his microphone button. With the function selector knob at the INTER position, normal interphone transmission is accomplished by depressing the microphone button. With the knob at the COMM 1 INTER position, the crew member has a "hot mike" capability on interphone plus a receiving-transmitting capability on the selected command channel. With the "hot mike" function selected at any station, the interphone transmitting and receiving circuits at that station are live at all times, permitting the crew member to contact any other crew member without depressing his microphone button or manipulating any other controls; he must depress his microphone button to transmit on the command channel. With the function selector knob at the COMM 1 or COMM 2 position, the navigator and DSO may receive and transmit on the AN/ARC-57 or AN/ARC-34 utilizing his microphone button. The pilot may transmit on the AN/ARC-57 or AN/ARC-34 or interphone by using the control stick microphone switch. The interphone mixing switch must be in the up position to receive any transmission on the interphone from the other stations or to monitor sidetone. The COMM 1 position will also be used to receive and transmit on the AN/ARC-74.

Note

Although each crew member has the capability of receiving and transmitting on the command radio, only the pilot (or DSO) can place the radio in operation and select frequencies.

Positioning the selector knob to LIA gives the crew member push-to-talk capability on the long range communication system. Although all crew members can receive and transmit on the system, only the DSO can place the unit into operation and select the channel frequencies and mode of operation.

Radio Control Transfer Buttons.

Two radio control transfer buttons (1, figure 4-9 and 3, figure 4-10) marked TAKE, located on the pilot's comm-nav transfer panel and the DSO's comm-inter transfer panel, are used to transfer control of UHF command radio between the pilot and DSO stations. The crew member desiring control takes control by pushing the button and notes that his radio control indicator lamp (2, figure 4-9, and 2, figure 4-10) lights, indicating that control has been transferred.

Control Stick Microphone Switch.

The control stick microphone switch (5, figure 1-29) is located on the pilot's control stick grip. The switch has two marked positions, TRANS and INPH, which are spring-loaded to an unmarked OFF position. When the switch is held in the TRANS position, transmission is available through the respective facility selected by the pilot's function selector knob. Holding the switch to INPH enables the pilot to transmit on interphone for all positions of the function selector knob except the CALL and COMM INTER "hot mike" positions. Actuation of the switch to INPH when the function selector knob is at CALL will prevent transmission of the call signal. Actuating the switch to INPH in the other "hot mike" position will not affect the transmitting capability. When capsule doors are closed, the pilot will be automatically switched to "hot mike" interphone. The stick mounted microphone switch must be utilized to transmit on UHF command radio and LRC systems.

Foot-Operated Microphone Buttons.

Two foot-operated microphone buttons (figure 4-33 and 4-63), located in the floor ahead of the capsule at both the navigator's and DSO's stations, are marked INTERPHONE and TRANSMIT for identification. The interphone button is on the left and the transmit button is on the right at the navigator's station. The buttons are reversed at the DSO's station. Depressing the transmit button allows the crew member to transmit on the facility selected by the function selector knob, except CALL and the interphone "hot mike" function of COMM 1 INTER. Depressing the interphone button allows interphone communications only.

Capsule Microphone Button.

Capsule microphone buttons (29, figure 1-44), are located on the right leg retraction arm in the navigator's and DSO's capsules. During operation, with the capsule doors open the button serves the same function as the TRANSMIT button at the navigator's station and DSO's station.

Section IV
Auxiliary Equipment

T.O. 1B-58A-1

comm-nav transfer panel

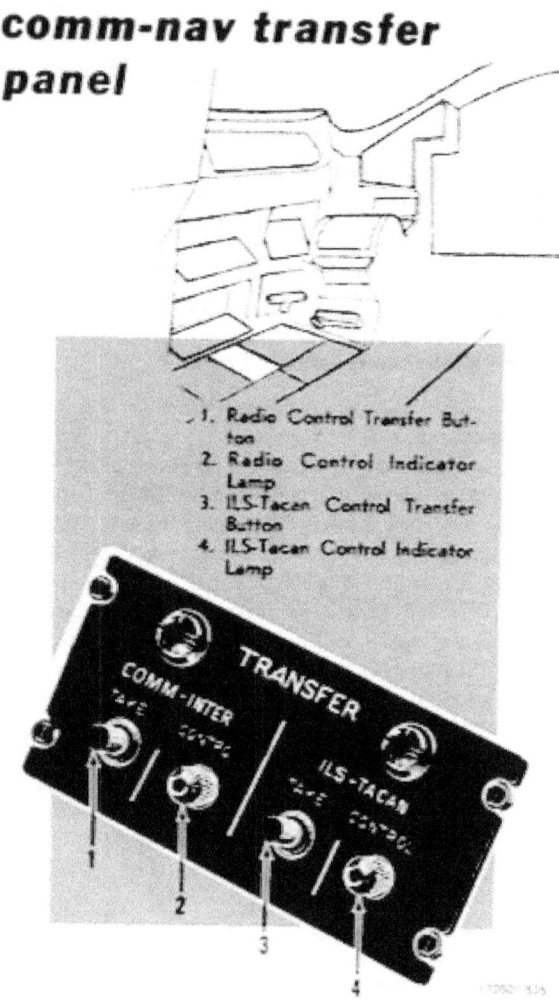

1. Radio Control Transfer Button
2. Radio Control Indicator Lamp
3. ILS-Tacan Control Transfer Button
4. ILS-Tacan Control Indicator Lamp

Figure 4-9.

Interphone Volume Control Knob.

An interphone volume control knob (9, figure 4-6; 7, figure 4-7, and 2, figure 4-8), is located on the pilot's and DSO's communication control panels and on the navigator's interphone control panel. At each crew station this knob provides a means of adjusting the volume of the audio signal received at the headset. The knob is inoperative when the auxiliary listen switch is at AUX (AUX LISTEN) or when the function selector knob is held at CALL.

Mixing Switches.

Five mixing switches (11, figure 4-6; 9, figure 4-7 and 1, figure 4-8) are located on the pilot's and DSO's communications control panels and the navigator's interphone panel. The switches on the pilot's communications control panel are marked INTER, 1 COMM 2, MB (marker beacon), TACAN and LIAISON. All the switches except the 1 COMM 2 switch are two position switches with an unmarked off position. The switches on the navigator's interphone control panel are marked INTER, 1 COMM 2, RV (rendezvous beacon), PI (position indicating beacon) and TACAN. All the switches except the 1 COMM 2 switch are two position switches with a marked OFF position. The 1 COMM 2 switches on the pilot's and navigator's panels are three position switches with a center unmarked off position. Arrows indicate up for 1 COMM and down for COMM 2 to monitor AN/ARC-57 or AN/ARC-34 respectively. The switches on the DSO's communications control panel are marked INTER, COMM 1, DECM (defensive electronic counter measures), LIAISON and COMM 2. All the switches are two position switches with a marked OFF position. The crew member can monitor any facility desired by selecting the respective marked switch.

Auxiliary Listen Switch.

The two-position auxiliary listen switch (1, figure 4-6, 11, figure 4-7, and 4, figure 4-8), is located on the pilot's and DSO's communication control panels and on the navigator's interphone control panel. The positions are marked NORMAL and AUX (or AUX LISTEN). With the switch in the NORMAL position, interphone facilities at that station will operate normally. With the switch in the AUX (or AUX LISTEN) position, the interphone circuitry at that station bypasses the listen amplifier in the control panel and provides the crew member with reception of only one mixing switch facility at a fixed volume level. If more than one mixing switch on the control panel is on, the facility associated with the switch farthest to the left will be heard. The AN/ARC-34 and AN/ARC-57 cannot be monitored with the 1 COMM 2 mixing switch. If it is desired to monitor one of these radios, all mixing switches must be turned OFF and desired command radio selected on the function selector knob. If all mixing switches on the panel are off, the facility selected by the function selector knob will be heard. The auxiliary listen switch should be placed in the auxiliary position only when the listen amplifier at that control panel is malfunctioning or inoperative. When in AUX (AUX LISTEN) position, the presence of a side tone indicates proper operation of this function. A safety latch on the switch prevents it from being moved inadvertently to the auxiliary position.

Command Mode Selector Knob.

The four-position mode selector knob (7, figure 4-6 and 5, figure 4-7), located on the pilot's and DSO's communication control panels, enables the pilot or DSO

4-20

to select the operating mode of the AN/ARC-57 command radio. The knob positions are marked OFF, MAIN, BOTH, and GD. With the knob in the MAIN position, the command transmitter and main receiver are operative on the same selected frequency. With the knob in the BOTH position, the transmitter and main receiver are again operative on the same selected frequency and in addition, the guard receiver is receiving on the preset guard frequency. With the knob in the GD position, the transmitter and both receivers are tuned to the preset guard frequency as a back up in lieu of the normal tuning circuit. The backup tuning circuit does not function as well as the normal tuning circuit, therefore, the GD position should be selected only when the command tuning system malfunctions or becomes inoperative. Placing the mode selector knob in the OFF position de-energizes the entire command radio system.

Note

The AN/ARC-74 power switch is connected in series with the command mode selector knob and must be placed to OFF before power is available to the command radio.

Channel Selector Knob.

The channel selector knob (2, figure 4-6 and 4, figure 4-7), located on the pilot's and DSO's communication control panels, permits the pilot or DSO to select the desired channel or frequency for command radio tranmission and reception. The knob has 24 positions marked 1 through 22, G, and M. The selected position appears in a channel indicator window (4, figure 4-6) located immediately above the knob. Placing the knob at one of the 22 numbered channel positions allows transmission and reception on a preset frequency. Placing the knob at the G position allows transmission and reception on the preset guard frequency. Placing the knob at the M position allows transmission and reception on the frequency selected by the frequency manual selector knobs.

Frequency Manual Selector Knobs.

Four frequency manual selector knobs (5, figure 4-6 and 2, figure 4-7), are located on the pilot's and DSO's communication control panels. Each knob selects a frequency digit, which appears in a window (6, figure 4-6 and 1, figure 4-7), above the knob. The frequency manual selector knobs may be manipulated to select any one of the 1750 frequencies available within the 225.0 to 399.9 megacycle range of the command radio.

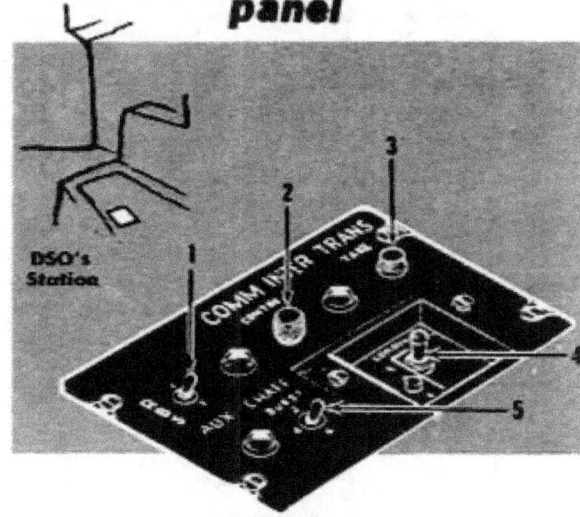

comm-inter transfer and auxiliary chaff control panel

1. RBS Tone Selector Switch
2. Radio Control Indicator Lamp
3. Radio Control Transfer Button
4. Chaff Dispenser Loading Switch
5. Chaff Burst Switch

Figure 4-10.

Command Volume Control Knob.

The command volume control knob (3, figure 4-6 and 12, figure 4-7) on the pilot's and DSO's communication panels permits the pilot or DSO to standardize the command radio audio volume with volume level of other signals received by the interphone system. The DSO command radio volume control knob regulates the navigator's command radio volume. The DSO's volume control knob should be set for normal listening level with the respective COMM 1 or COMM 2 mixer in the OFF position.

Tone Button.

The tone button (8, figure 4-6 and 6, figure 4-7), is located on the pilot's and DSO's communication control panels. With the command radio in operation, depressing the tone button interrupts reception and transmits a continuous tone signal on the selected frequency.

RBS Tone Selector Switch.

The RBS tone selector switch (1, figure 4-10) is located on the comm-inter transfer and auxiliary chaff control panel on the DSO's right console. The switch has two positions marked 1 and 2. With the switch in the number 1 position, an RBS tone signal can be transmitted by the navigator on the AN/ARC-57 com-

Section IV
Auxiliary Equipment

T.O. 1B-58A-1

antenna locations (typical)

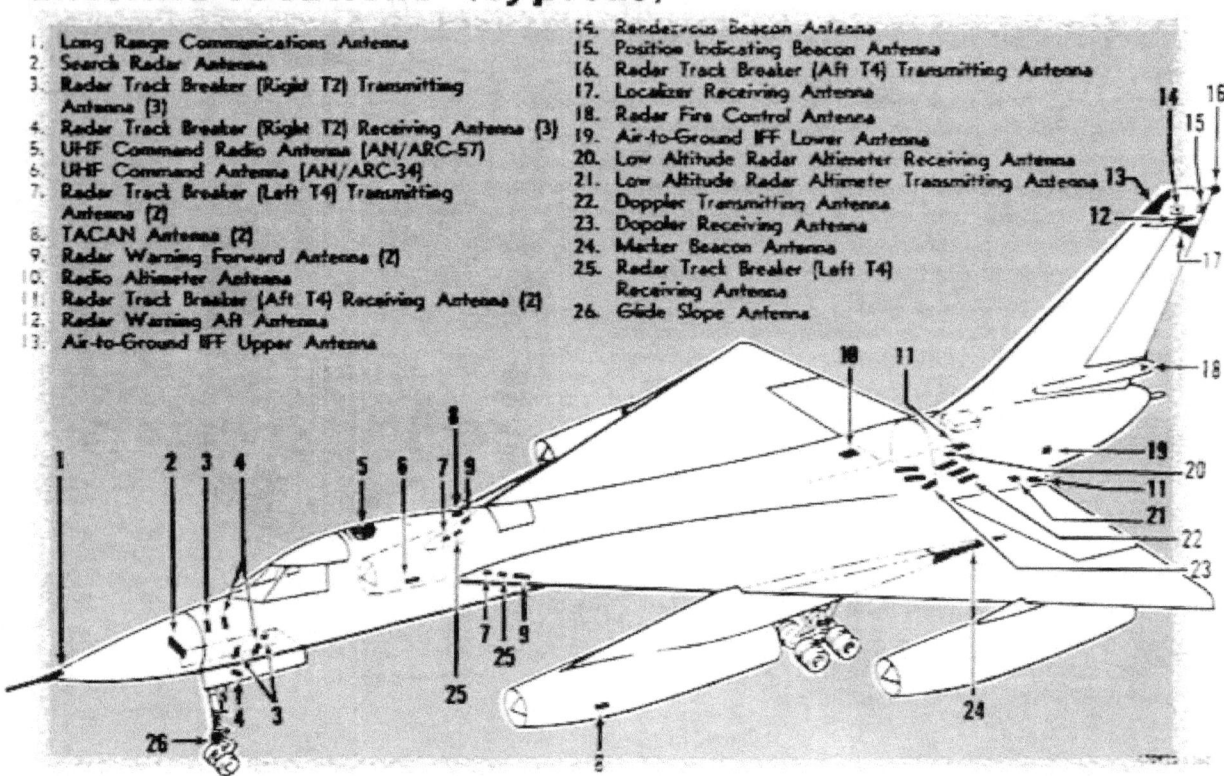

1. Long Range Communications Antenna
2. Search Radar Antenna
3. Radar Track Breaker (Right T2) Transmitting Antenna (3)
4. Radar Track Breaker (Right T2) Receiving Antenna (3)
5. UHF Command Radio Antenna (AN/ARC-57)
6. UHF Command Antenna (AN/ARC-34)
7. Radar Track Breaker (Left T4) Transmitting Antenna (2)
8. TACAN Antenna (2)
9. Radar Warning Forward Antenna (2)
10. Radio Altimeter Antenna
11. Radar Track Breaker (Aft T4) Receiving Antenna (2)
12. Radar Warning Aft Antenna
13. Air-to-Ground IFF Upper Antenna
14. Rendezvous Beacon Antenna
15. Position Indicating Beacon Antenna
16. Radar Track Breaker (Aft T4) Transmitting Antenna
17. Localizer Receiving Antenna
18. Radar Fire Control Antenna
19. Air-to-Ground IFF Lower Antenna
20. Low Altitude Radar Altimeter Receiving Antenna
21. Low Altitude Radar Altimeter Transmitting Antenna
22. Doppler Transmitting Antenna
23. Doppler Receiving Antenna
24. Marker Beacon Antenna
25. Radar Track Breaker (Left T4) Receiving Antenna
26. Glide Slope Antenna

Figure 4-11.

munication system. Number 2 position will allow an RBS tone transmission by the navigator on the AN/ARC-34 communication system.

Remote Channel Indicator.

The remote channel indicator (9, figure 1-5) is located on the pilot's main instrument panel. The indicator, which displays the position selected by the channel selector knob, permits the pilot to switch channels on the command radio without taking his eyes from the main instrument panel. The indicator shows the channel selected by the station in control.

Note

The remote channel indicator is covered when the command mode selector knob is in the OFF position or when the AN/ARC-74 radio is on. With the AN/ARC-74 radio off, all other positions expose the indicator.

Normal Operation of AN/ARC-57 Communication System.

Normal operation of the AN/ARC-57 communication system is accomplished for the various crew members as follows:

Note

The interphone system is energized whenever d-c power is applied to the 28-volt d-c power panel.

Pilot and DSO Operation. The interphone and command radio functions are operated from the pilot's and DSO's station according to the following procedures:

1. Check that auxiliary listen switch is at NORMAL.
2. Check that the AN/ARC-74 power switch is in the OFF position. (P)
3. Place function selector knob at COMM 1 INTER.
4. Press radio control transfer button if radio control indicator lamp is not lighted.
5. Adjust interphone volume control knob to obtain a comfortable volume level.
6. Place command mode selector knob at BOTH. Time-delay relays will prevent command radio operation for approximately one minute while equipment warms up and completes a tuning cycle.
7. Select desired channel or frequency using the channel selector knob or the frequency manual selector knobs. If a frequency is selected using the manual

selector knobs, set channel selector knob at M (manual).

Note

Crosstalk between AN/ARC-57 and AN/ARC-34 can be expected when the frequencies on the respective radios are less than one megacycle apart.

8. Adjust command volume control knob to obtain a comfortable volume level.

9. Place desired mixing switches in the on position.

With the AN/ARC-57 system set up at the pilot's station as outlined above, the pilot has "hot mike" interphone capability; transmission is possible on the selected command channel by holding the control stick microphone switch in the TRANS position; reception is possible on the selected command channel through the main receiver and on the guard frequency through the guard receiver; and simultaneous reception is possible from all facilities associated with the selected mixing switches. A continuous tone transmission can be made on the selected command channel by depressing and holding the tone button. This information is true for the DSO's station except that the foot-operated TRANSMIT button or capsule microphone button is used for transmission on the selected command channel. With the function selector knob at the INTER position, the pilot may transmit on interphone by holding the control stick microphone swith either in the INPH or the TRANS position; he cannot transmit on command radio. With the function selector knob at the COMM 1 or COMM 2 position, the pilot may transmit on interphone by holding the control stick microphone switch to INPH; he may transmit on the selected command channel by holding the microphone switch to TRANS.

Note

Holding the control stick microphone switch to INPH when the CALL function is selected will prevent transmission of the call signal.

All transmitting switches must be released on the AN/ARC-57 radio before a new channel or frequency is selected. This is to allow the tuning mechanism to drive to the new frequency. After approximately ten seconds the tuning cycle is complete and communication may be resumed. The command radio is turned off by moving the command mode selector knob to OFF.

Navigator Operation. The interphone and command radio functions are operated from the navigator's station according to the following procedures.

1. Check that auxiliary listen switch is at NORMAL.
2. Place function selector knob at COMM 1 INTER.
3. Adjust interphone volume control knob to obtain a comfortable volume level.
4. Place desired mixing switches in the on position.

With the AN/ARC-57 system set up at the navigator's station as outlined above, the navigator has "hot mike" interphone capability; transmission is possible on the selected command channel by depressing and holding the foot-operated TRANSMIT or capsule microphone button; command radio reception is possible according to the mode selected by the pilot; and simultaneous reception is possible from all facilities associated with the selected mixing switches. A tone transmission cannot be made from the navigator's station except through the RBS tone switch. With the function selector knob at the INTER position, the crew member may communicate on interphone by depressing the foot-operated TRANSMIT or capsule microphone buttons; he cannot transmit on command radio. With the function selector knob at the COMM 1 or COMM 2 position, the crew member may transmit on the selected command channel by depressing the TRANSMIT or capsule microphone button; he cannot transmit on interphone. Transmission on interphone is possible by use of the INTEPHONE foot operated microphone button or by "hot mike" on COMM INTER position.

Operation with Ground Interphone Set. An AN/AIC-17 ground interphone set may be plugged into the airplane interphone system at the external interphone receptacles. This enables any crew member to communicate with ground personnel. Follow normal interphone procedures for operation with the ground interphone set.

Emergency Operation of AN/ARC-57 Communication System.

Procedures for various abnormal and emergency conditions of the AN/ARC-57 system are outlined in the following paragraphs.

Section IV
Auxiliary Equipment

T.O. 1B-58A-1

Reception Garbled or Headset Silent. If all audio signals at any station become garbled or if headset becomes totally silent, it is possible that the listen amplifier at that control panel is malfunctioning. After checking to make sure that the personal interphone lead is securely connected, proceed as follows:

1. Select one mixing switch facility if desired. Place all other mixing switches in the off position.
2. Move safety latch and place auxiliary listen switch at AUX (or AUX LISTEN).

Note

- With the auxiliary listen switch in the AUX (AUX LISTEN) position, it is possible to receive only one mixing switch facility. If all mixing switches are off, the facility selected by the function selector knob will be heard. If more than one mixing switch is on, the facility associated with the switch farthest to the left will be heard.

- The AN/ARC-34 and AN/ARC-57 cannot be monitored through use of the 1 COMM 2 mixing switch function. If it is desired to monitor one of these radios, all mixing switches must be turned OFF and desired command radio selected on the function selector knob.

Command Radio Does Not Tune Selected Channel. If it becomes apparent that the command radio is not tuning the selected channel, it is possible that the tuning system is malfunctioning. A time-delay relay may render the system temporarily inoperative if it fails to tune within 20 seconds. Should this occur, proceed as follows:

1. Place Command mode selector knob to OFF.
2. After a one-minute cooling period, place mode selector knob to MAIN or BOTH, as desired.
3. Select desired channel with channel selector knob. After waiting approximately one minute to allow for stabilization and completion of the tuning cycle, communication may be attempted.
4. If the desired channel cannot be obtained, place the channel selector knob at M and manually select the desired frequency using the frequency manual selector knob. If this procedure fails, try a different frequency.

CAUTION

If a frequency below 225 megacycles is selected manually, the tuning system will be rendered inoperative. This condition will be evidenced by a lack of sidetone during attempted transmission. To clear the condition, repeat steps 1 through 4 above.

Note

The ARC-57 UHF radio will not channelize, transmit or receive whenever the UHF channelization access door in the crawlway is open.

5. If all attempts to tune a desired frequency fail, place the command mode selector knob to GD. This bypasses the normal tuning system and allows transmission and reception on the fixed guard frequency.

Crew Emergencies. If it becomes necessary to contact other crew members immediately, hold the function selector knob to the CALL position. This interrupts all functions at all stations and allows immediate transmission to other crew members.

UHF COMMAND RADIO SYSTEM (AN/ARC-34).

The AN/ARC-34 command radio system provides backup air-to-air and air-to-ground voice line of sight communications. The radio also has provisions for transmitting a continuous tone signal. There are 1750 frequencies available in steps of one-tenth of a megacycle within the operating frequency range of 220 to 339.9 megacycles. Twenty of these frequencies may be preset at one time and in any order. If desired, a frequency other than one that has been preset may be set manually without disturbing any of the preset channels. Both a main receiver and a preset guard receiver are provided to permit the selected frequency and the guard frequency to be received simultaneously. The system includes a transceiver, (transmitter, main receiver, guard receiver) and an antenna mounted on number three engine nacelle. The control panel is located at the DSO's station, with controls on the pilot's and DSO's communication control panels and navigator's interphone control panel. The AN/ARC-34 radio operates on 400 cps, 3 phase a-c power from the right a-c bus.

Note

When operating the AN/ARC-34 command radio in conjunction with the AN/ARC-57 command radio, cross-talk can be expected when the frequencies on the respective radios are less than one megacycle apart.

Section IV
Auxiliary Equipment

AN/ARC-34 command radio control panel

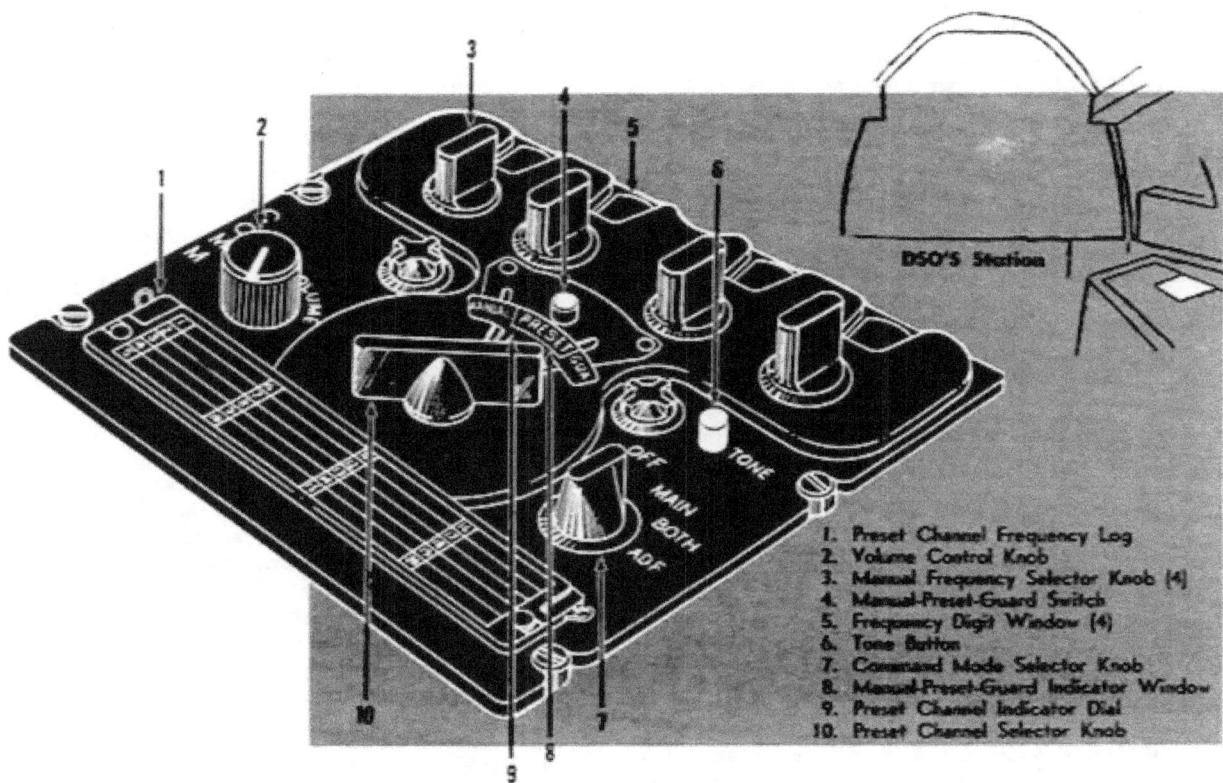

1. Preset Channel Frequency Log
2. Volume Control Knob
3. Manual Frequency Selector Knob (4)
4. Manual-Preset-Guard Switch
5. Frequency Digit Window (4)
6. Tone Button
7. Command Mode Selector Knob
8. Manual-Preset-Guard Indicator Window
9. Preset Channel Indicator Dial
10. Preset Channel Selector Knob

Figure 4-12.

Manual Frequency Selector Knobs.

Four manual frequency selector knobs (3, figure 4-12), located on the AN/ARC-34 command radio control panel, are used to manually select any operating frequency other than those available on the preset channels. Adjustment of these knobs does not disturb the settings on the preset channels. The manual frequency selector knob must be in the MANUAL position before the numbers above the control knobs will become visible. Each knob is turned until the desired frequency digit appears in the window.

Tone Button.

The tone button (6, figure 4-12), located on the AN/ARC-34 command radio control panel, energizes the transmitter and an audio oscillator when depressed. A continuous 1000 CPS tone is transmitted until the button is released. The tone can be transmitted with the command mode selector knob in either the MAIN or BOTH position.

Command Mode Selector Knob.

A four position command mode selector knob (7, figure 4-12), located on the AN/ARC-34 command radio control panel, enables the DSO to select the operating mode of the command radio. The knob positions are marked OFF, MAIN, BOTH, and ADF. With the knob in the MAIN position, the command transmitter and main receiver are operative on the same frequency. With the knob in the BOTH position, the transmitter and main receiver are operative on the same frequency and in addition the guard receiver is receiving on the preset guard frequency. The ADF position is inoperative. Placing the mode selector to OFF de-energizes the entire system.

Preset Channel Selector Knob.

The rotary type preset channel selector knob (10, figure 4-12), located on the AN/ARC-34 command radio control panel, enables the DSO to select any one of the 20 preset frequencies. The channel number selected is visible in a window above the switch when the manual-preset-guard switch is in the PRESET position.

4-25

Section IV
Auxiliary Equipment

T.O. 1B-58A-1

Command Volume Control Knob.

The command volume control knob (2, figure 4-12), located on the AN/ARC-34 command radio control panel, enables the DSO to adjust the volume of both main and guard receivers. It will be necessary for the DSO to adjust the volume control to a level desirable for the pilot and navigator. Receiver output cannot be reduced below a fixed audible level.

Manual-Preset-Guard Switch.

The manual-preset-guard switch (4, figure 4-12), located on the AN/ARC-34 command radio control panel, enables the DSO to determine the method of frequency selection. The switch has three positions marked MANUAL, PRESET, and GUARD. With the switch in the MANUAL position, the covers over the frequency indicator windows are retracted, exposing the manual frequency numbers. The desired frequency can then be set using the manual frequency selector knobs. Preset channels can be checked or changed without disturbing the MANUAL operating frequency. The preset channel number is covered when the switch is in the MANUAL position, and the PRESET and GUARD markings are visible through a green window. With the switch in the PRESET position, the preset channel selector switch may be used to select any one of the 20 preset frequencies. In this position, the markings MANUAL and GUARD are visible through a green window. With the switch in the GUARD position, the main receiver and transmitter are operative on the guard frequency with the command mode selector knob in the main position.

Note

With the manual-preset-guard switch in the GUARD position and with the command mode selector in the BOTH position, both the main and guard receivers will be receiving guard channel transmissions. The noise from both receivers may make the incoming signal unintelligible.

In the GUARD position, the windows over the preset channel number and the manual frequency numbers are closed. The markings MANUAL and PRESET are visible through a green window.

Normal Operation of AN/ARC-34 Command Radio System.

The AN/ARC-34 command radio system can be operated from all three crew stations, with the respective crew members function selector knob in the COMM 2 position, after the DSO has accomplished the following procedures.
Preset Channel Operation.
 1. Check that the manual-preset-guard switch is at PRESET.
 2. Place the preset channel selector switch to desired channel.
 3. Place the command mode selector knob at BOTH.

Note

A minimum warmup time of one minute including a four-second tuning cycle is required before operating the AN/ARC-34 command radio.

 4. Turn the volume control knob to desired volume level.

Manual Frequency Operation.

 1. Check that the manual-preset-guard switch is at MANUAL.
 2. Place the command mode selector knob at MAIN or BOTH.
 3. Set the manual frequency selector knobs to the desired frequency.

CAUTION

It is possible to select a frequency below the design range of the equipment. Selection of any frequency below 220 megacycles can cause serious damage by continuous cycling.

Note

Approximately four seconds should be allowed for completion of the tuning cycle before operating the AN/ARC-34 command radio.

 4. Turn the volume control knob to the desired volume level.

Guard Channel Operation.

 1. Check that the manual-preset-guard switch is at GUARD.
 2. Place the operating mode selector knob at MAIN.
 3. Turn the volume control knob to the desired volume level.

EMERGENCY COMMUNICATION SYSTEM (AN/ARC-74).

This system provides emergency communication facilities in the event of failure or malfunction of the command radio. Operating from the essential bus, the system is capable of operation even if all other power fails. When the AN/ARC-74 is energized, the command radio antenna input is connected to the emergency communication system. The microphone inputs are connected to the communications system when the function selector knob is in COMM 1 position or the communication system is in MAYDAY mode. Turning the AN/ARC-74 on turns power off to the AN/ARC-57 since both systems use the same antenna. The AN/ARC-74 operates on either of two predetermined channels, main and guard, at frequencies of 243.5 and 243.0, respectively. Aural monitoring of the transmitted signal is available to the operator, whenever the unit is energized. Primary system equipment consists of a receiver-transmitter and a control panel. The AN/ARC-74 must be placed into operation by the pilot; however, once the system is operating other crew members may transmit and receive through their interphone controls. Current is supplied to the system through a fuse located on the 28-volt d-c power panel.

Power Switch.

The three-position power switch (figure 4-13), located on the emergency communication panel, is marked MAIN, GUARD, and OFF. Placing the switch to MAIN selects the main channel, breaks the command radio power circuit, and energizes the system. This channel is not usually monitored by control towers or radio stations. Therefore the guard channel will normally be used in flight. Placing the switch to GUARD accomplishes the same functions as the MAIN position except the guard channel is selected. Placing the switch to OFF de-energizes the system and completes the command radio power circuit.

Volume Control Knob.

The volume control knob (figure 4-13), marked VOL, is located on the emergency communication panel. Turning the knob clockwise increases the volume of the audio output to the headset.

Normal Operation of Emergency Communication System.

Pilot Operation.

1. Function selector knob — COMM 1.
2. Interphone and AN/ARC-74 volume controls—Midposition.

Note

The MAIN channel is not monitored by control towers or radio stations. However after coordination with the receiving facility on the GUARD channel, the MAIN channel may be utilized.

With the emergency communication system set up at the pilot's station as outlined above, the pilot may transmit on the selected channel by holding the control stick microphone switch to TRANS. Reception is possible on the same channel.

Navigator and DSO Operation. After the equipment has been placed into operation by the pilot the other crew members may operate the system as follows:

1. Interphone function selector knob—COMM 1.
2. Interphone volume control—Midposition
3. Interphone auxiliary listen switch—NORMAL

With the emergency communication system set up as outlined above, the crew member may transmit on the channel selected by the pilot by depressing the foot-operated TRANSMIT or capsule microphone buttons.

emergency communication panel

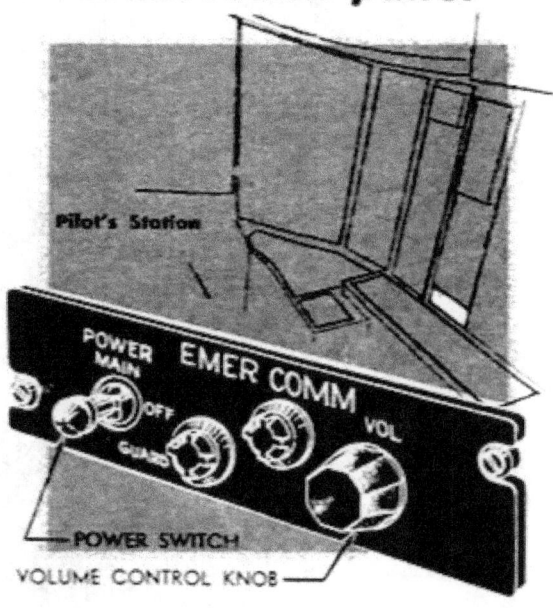

Figure 4-13.

LONG RANGE COMMUNICATION SYSTEM (AN/ARC-110).

The long range communication (LRC) system (AN/ARC-110) provides high frequency long range single side band, air to air and air to ground communications for the aircrew. The system operates in three modes: USB, upper side band; LSB, lower side band, and AM, upper side band with amplitude-modulated carrier for receivers without single side band reception capability. There are 28,000 channels available in 1 kilocycle increments within the frequency range of 2.000 through 29.999 megacycles. Components of the system include an antenna, an antenna coupler, antenna coupler control, receiver-transmitter and HF communication panel. The antenna (figure 4-11) is impedance matched to the receiver-transmitter by the pressurized antenna coupler. The HF communication panel (figure 4-14) is located at the DSO's station. When the DSO places the system in operation the pilot and navigator can transmit and receive through their respective interphone communications panels. The system operates on 28 volt d-c power from the 28 volt d-c power panel and 115 volt a-c three phase power from the left a-c power panel at the DSO's station.

Frequency Selector Knobs.

Four rotary type frequency selector knobs (1, figure 4-14) are located on the HF communications panel.

4-27

Section IV
Auxiliary Equipment

T.O. 1B-58A-1

dso's hf communication panel (an/arc-110)

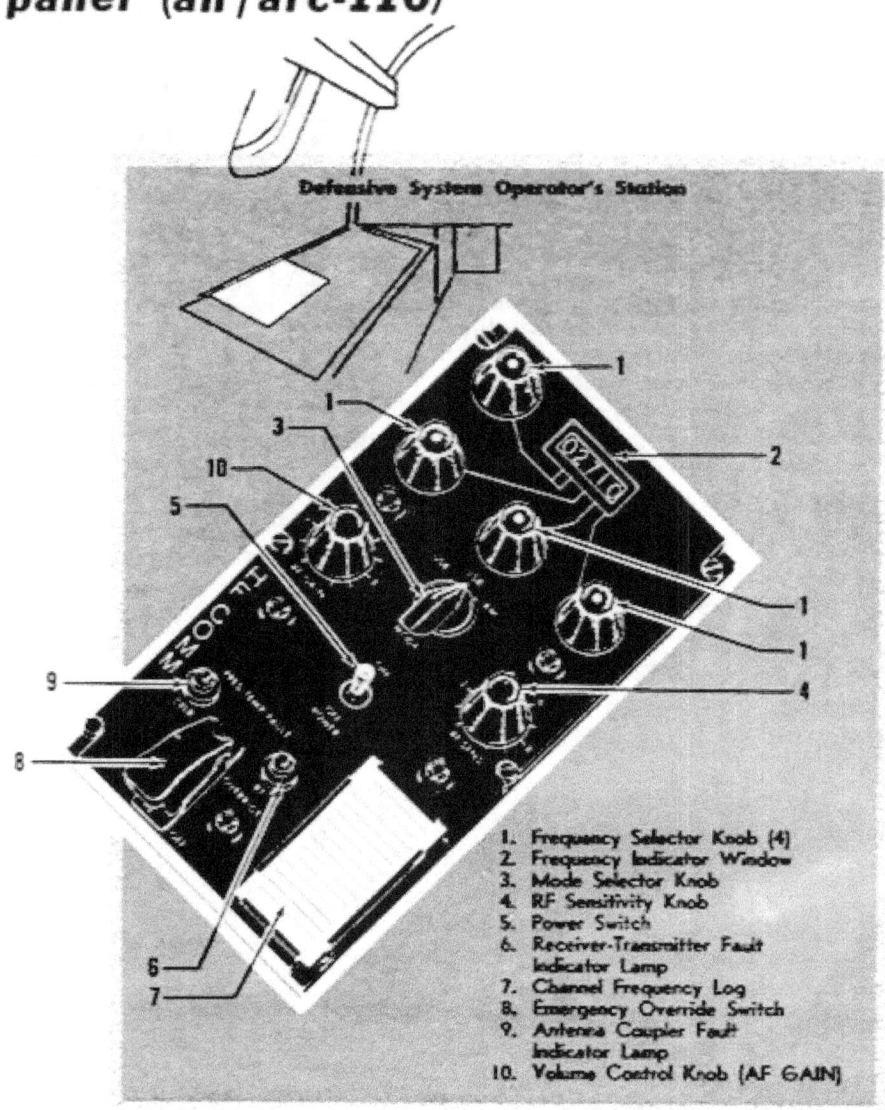

Figure 4-14.

The three knobs located below the frequency indicator window are for setting 1, 10, and 100 kilocycles from right to left respectively. The fourth knob, located on the left side of the frequency indicator window, is used to set megacycles.

Frequency Indicator Window.

The frequency indicator window (2, figure 4-14) located on the HF communications panel indicates the frequency selected for transmission or receiving. The indicator has five digits, the first two digits are set by the frequency selector knob to the left of the window. Each of the remaining three digits has an individual frequency selector knob.

Mode Selector Knob.

The mode selector knob (3, figure 4-14) located on the HF communications panel, has three positions marked USB, LSB and AM. Placing the knob to USB or LSB provides upper or lower side band transmission and reception. The AM position provides upper side band transmission with an amplitude-modulated car-

T.O. 1B-58A-1

Section IV
Auxiliary Equipment

communication and electronic equipment

TYPE	DESIGNATION	USE	OPERATOR	RANGE (APPROX)	LOCATION OF CONTROLS
A/G IFF	AN/APX-47	IDENTIFICATION TO GROUND STATION	DSO	LINE OF SIGHT	DSO'S STATION
PI BEACON	AN/APN-136	INTER-AIRCRAFT POSITION INDICATION	NAVIGATOR	200 MILES	NAVIGATOR'S STATION
RV BEACON	AN/APN-135	TRANSMIT RANGE, BEARING, AND IDENTITY INFORMATION FOR RENDEZVOUS OPERATIONS	NAVIGATOR	200 MILES	NAVIGATOR'S STATION
INTERPHONE	AN/ARC-57	CREW COMMUNICATION	ALL CREW MEMBERS		EACH CREW STATION
UHF COMMAND RADIO		PLANE-TO-PLANE OR PLANE-TO-GROUND COMMUNICATION	ALL CREW MEMBERS	200 MILES AT 20,000 FEET OR LINE OF SIGHT	PILOT'S AND DSO'S STATION
UHF COMMAND RADIO	AN/ARC-34	PLANE-TO-PLANE OR PLANE-TO-GROUND COMMUNICATION	ALL CREW MEMBERS	200 MILES AT 20,000 FEET OR LINE OF SIGHT	DSO'S STATION
EMERGENCY COMMUNICATION SYSTEM	AN/ARC-74	PLANE-TO-PLANE OR PLANE-TO-GROUND COMMUNICATION IN EVENT OF COMMAND RADIO FAILURE	PILOT	200 MILES AT 20,000 FEET OR LINE OF SIGHT	PILOT'S STATION
LONG RANGE COMMUNICATION SYSTEM	AN/ARC-110	PLANE-TO-PLANE OR PLANE-TO-GROUND LONG RANGE COMMUNICATION	DSO	5000 MILES	DSO'S STATION
TACAN OR INSTRUMENT LANDING SYSTEM (ILS)	TACAN — AN/ARN-65	UHF NAVIGATION	PILOT AND NAVIGATOR	195 MILES	PILOT'S AND NAVIGATOR'S STATION
	LOCALIZER — AN/ARN-69	INSTRUMENT APPROACH	PILOT	45 MILES	PILOT'S STATION
	MARKER BEACON — AN/ARN-69	LOCATION OF MARKER SIGNAL ON NAVIGATION BEAM	PILOT	LOCAL	PILOT'S STATION
	GLIDE SLOPE — AN/ARN-69	GLIDE ANGLE INFORMATION FOR INSTRUMENT APPROACH	PILOT	25 MILES	PILOT'S STATION
AIR NAVIGATION RECORDING SYSTEM	AN/ASH-17	RECORDS NAVIGATION DATA	NAVIGATOR		NAVIGATOR'S STATION
BOMB DAMAGE EVALUATION SYSTEM	AN/ASH-15	BOMB DAMAGE EVALUATION	NAVIGATOR		NAVIGATOR'S STATION

NOTE: REFER TO T.O. 1B-58A-1A FOR DATA ON THE FOLLOWING SYSTEMS: RADAR WARNING, RADAR TRACK BREAKER, CHAFF DISPENSING, FIRE CONTROL RADAR, AND WEAPONS CONTROL SYSTEM.

Figure 4-15.

rier for reception by receivers without single side band capability.

Power Switch.

The power switch (5, figure 4-14), located on the HF communications panel, is a two position switch marked ON and OFF. Placing the switch to ON applies power to the system.

Note

Power is supplied to the crystal oven in the receiver-transmitter whenever d-c power is available on the airplane regardless of the position of the power switch.

Volume Control Knob (AF GAIN).

The volume control knob (10, figure 4-14) located on the HF communications panel, is a rotary type knob labeled AF GAIN. Turning the knob clockwise increases the audio output of the radio.

RF Sensitivity Knob (RF SENS).

The RF sensitivity knob (4, figure 4-14), located on the HF communications panel, is a rotary knob labeled RF SENS. The knob provides a means of adjusting receiver sensitivity.

Section IV
Auxiliary Equipment

Channel Frequency Log.

The channel frequency log (7, figure 4-14) located on the HF communication panel provides a log of commonly used frequencies.

Emergency Override Switch.

The emergency override switch (8, figure 4-14) located on the HF communications panel is a two position switch marked OVERRIDE and OFF. The switch is guarded in the OFF position. Placing the switch to OVERRIDE, overrides pressure and temperature sensitive switches in the antenna coupler and receiver-transmitter unit to allow emergency operation of the system.

Receiver-Transmitter Fault Indicator Lamp (RT).

The amber press-to-test receiver-transmitter fault indicator lamp (6, figure 4-14), located on the HF communications panel, will light when cabin pressure altitude exceeds 30,000 feet or when the temperature in the receiver-transmitter unit exceeds 100 degrees centigrade.

Antenna Coupler Fault Indicator Lamp (CPLR).

The amber press-to-test antenna coupler fault indicator lamp (9, figure 4-14), located on the HF communications panel, will light when air pressure in the coupler drops below 16 PSIA or when the temperature exceeds 150 degrees centigrade.

Normal Operating Procedures (AN/ARC-110).

The following precautions must be observed during ground operation of the LRC transmitter:

- When a TC pod with a nuclear warhead is installed on the airplane, the LRC transmitter is restricted from tune-up below four megacycles and between six and twenty-five megacycles. This is to reduce the electromagnetic radiation environment of the loaded weapon.

- Do not energize the transmitter for at least one-half hour after any transfer of fuel within, to, or from the aircraft. (Excluding engine feed.)

- All fuel carts, fuel containers, and liquid oxygen carts must be moved away from the vicinity of the airplane.

- Personnel should not enter the region within ten feet of the nose probe and radome because of high voltage and radio frequency radiation.

- Ground personnel should avoid making or breaking contact with the fuselage in order to prevent radio frequency burns.

DSO's Operating Procedure.

1. Place the interphone function selector knob to LIA.
2. Place liaison mixing switch in the on position if aural monitoring is desired.
3. Place the POWER switch to ON.
4. Set the desired frequency in the frequncy indicator window.

Note

- When a frequency change is made a mute period will indicate the receiver-transmitter setting to the new frequency. The system should not be keyed during this period.

- If the frequency select knobs were already set to the desired frequency when the POWER switch was set to ON, rotate the 1-kilocycle select knob one digit off frequency and then back to the desired frequency. This will allow the receiver-transmitter to retune to the desired frequency.

5. Set the MODE selector switch to the desired mode of operation.
6. Adjust the RF SENS control high enough to receive signals which are just above the noise level, then adjust the AF GAIN control for a comfortable listening level. Proper balance is indicated when background noise (antenna "white" noise) is just audible and a weak signal is raised to a comfortable level.
7. Depress the foot-operated TRANSMIT or capsule microphone button in standard manner.

Note

- After a frequency change, a 1000-cps tone will be heard when the button is first depressed. This indicates that the receiver-transmitter and antenna coupler are tuning. When the tone ceases, the tuning cycle is completed. A side tone will be heard when transmitting.

- If tuning requires as much as 30 seconds (1000-cps tone present) and is followed by the absence of sidetone when transmission is attempted, rechannel. If tuning fails again, tune to a second authorized frequency.

Pilot's and Navigator's Operating Procedure.

After the system has been placed into operation by the DSO the pilot or navigator can receive and transmit as follows:

1. Place the function selector switch to LIA.

2. Place the liaison mixing switch in the on position if aural monitoring is desired. (Pilot only)

3. Operate "mike" button in standard manner. (P)

4. Depress the foot-operated TRANSMIT or capsule microphone button in standard manner. (N)

TACTICAL AIR NAVIGATION SYSTEM.

The tactical air navigation (TACAN) system provides continuous indications of bearing and slant distance to a selected surface beacon. The system transmits interrogation pulses which trigger responding pulses from the ground station. Slant distance to the station is then computed from the elapsed time. Both bearing and distance are visually displayed on the bearing-distance-heading (BDH) indicator. Deviation of the airplane course from the selected course is shown on the course indicator. The system is capable of operation on any one of 126 channels and has a range of about 195 nautical miles. The unit operates on the following UHF frequency ranges: receiver—926 to 1024 megacycles and 1151 to 1213 megacycles; transmitter—1025 to 1150 megacycles. TACAN and ILS utilize common controls located on the ILS-TACAN control panel at the pilot's station. A duplicate ILS-TACAN control panel is located in the navigator's station. Provisions are also provided for transferring control of ILS and TACAN between the pilot and navigator. A mixing switch located on the pilot's communication and navigator's interphone panels provides aural monitoring of the TACAN system. For antenna locations, see figure 4-11. Power is supplied to the system through fuses located on the following panels: a-c and high voltage d-c power panel, 28-volt d-c power panel, and left a-c power panel.

CONTROLS AND INDICATORS.

Channel Selector Knobs.

Two coaxial rotary type channel selector knobs (2, figure 4-16), located on the ILS-TACAN control panel, are used to select a channel (frequency in ILS mode) for system operation. In the TACAN mode, rotating the large knob varies the first two digits in the channel number. Turning the small knob varies the last digit. In the ILS mode, turning the large knob adjusts the first three digits of the localizer frequency. Rotating the small knob varies the last (tenth-megacycle) digit.

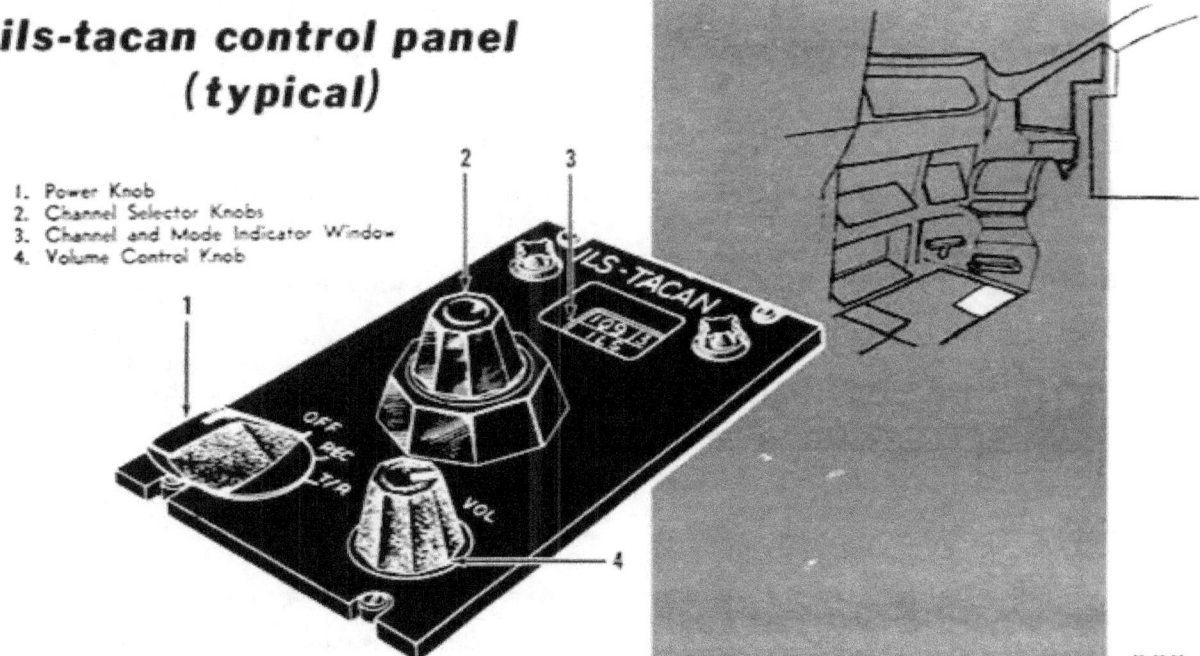

ils-tacan control panel (typical)

1. Power Knob
2. Channel Selector Knobs
3. Channel and Mode Indicator Window
4. Volume Control Knob

Figure 4-16.

With the knobs in the extreme counterclockwise position, the panel will be in ILS mode at a frequency of 108.1 megacycles. As the knobs are rotated clockwise from this position the localizer frequency will vary from 108.1 megacycles to 111.9 megacycles. Further rotation will change the mode to TACAN and vary the TACAN channels from 0 through 129.

Note

Although TACAN channels 0 to 129 may be selected on the panel, only channels 1 to 126 are operational.

Power Knob.

The rotary type power knob (1, figure 4-16), located on the ILS-TACAN control panel, is marked OFF, REC, and T/R. With the knob in the REC position, no pulses are transmitted by the TACAN system. Only bearing information is received and displayed. When the knob is placed to T/R, both bearing and distance information are available. The ILS receivers are energized in either the REC or T/R position.

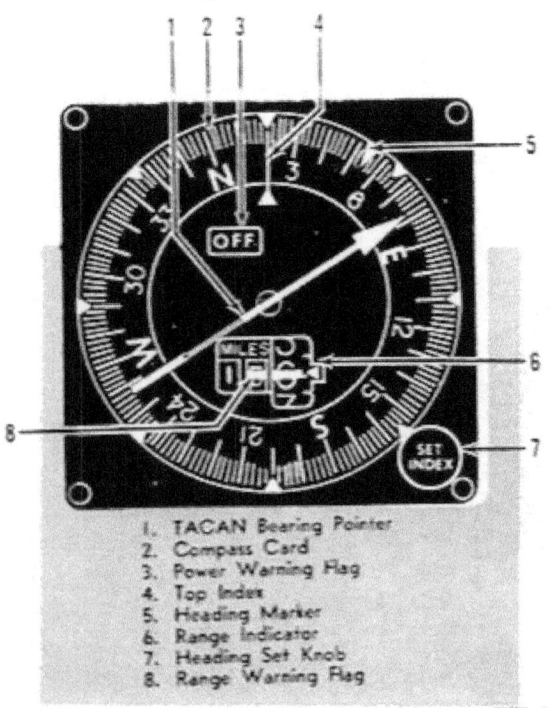

bearing-distance-heading indicator

1. TACAN Bearing Pointer
2. Compass Card
3. Power Warning Flag
4. Top Index
5. Heading Marker
6. Range Indicator
7. Heading Set Knob
8. Range Warning Flag

Figure 4-17.

Volume Control Knob.

The octagonal-shaped volume control knob (4, figure 4-16), located on the ILS-TACAN control panel, adjusts the audio signal strength of the surface beacon identification signal. Rotating the knob clockwise increases the output.

TACAN Mixing Switch.

The two position lever type TACAN mixing switch (11, Figure 4-6), located on the pilot's communication panel and (1, figure 4-8), on the Navigator's interphone control panel allows the pilot and navigator to monitor the TACAN station identification signals when the switch is placed to the TACAN position.

Channel and Mode Indicator Windows.

The channel and mode indicator window (3, figure 4-16), located on the ILS-TACAN control panel, indicates the channel (frequency in ILS mode) to which the system is tuned, and also indicates either TACAN or ILS mode. When in the TACAN mode, the last (tenth-megacycle) digit is covered.

ILS-TACAN Control Transfer Buttons.

The ILS-TACAN control transfer buttons provide a means of transferring control of the ILS and TACAN systems between the pilot and navigator. The pilot's ILS-TACAN control transfer button, marked TAKE, is located on the Comm-Nav transfer panel (3, figure 4-9). Depressing the button assumes control of the ILS-TACAN control panel. The navigator's ILS-TACAN control transfer button is located on the navigator's right console (figure 4-36). Marking and operation of the navigator's button is identical to that of the pilot's.

ILS-TACAN Control Indicator Lamps.

The pilot and navigator each are provided with an ILS-TACAN control indicator lamp. When either the pilot or navigator depress the ILS-TACAN control transfer button, the respective control indicator lamp will light indicating that control has been assumed. The pilot's lamp is located on the Comm-Nav transfer panel (4, figure 4-9) and the navigator's lamp is located on the navigator's right console (figure 4-36).

Bearing-Distance-Heading Indicator.

The bearing, distance, and heading (BDH) indicator (figure 4-17) is located on the pilot's main instrument panel. A duplicate indicator is located on the navigator's right console (figure 4-36). Magnetic heading of the airplane is shown by the index at the top of the instrument and a compass card. The heading function of both the BDH indicators is controlled by the pilot's heading selector switch (10, figure 1-34). Slant distance to a selected surface beacon is presented on digital type drums. When the indicator is searching for the correct range or when the power knob is in the REC position, the range warning flag is out and warns the pilot that the distance reading is unreliable. The BDH indicator has a bearing pointer which indicates the magnetic bearing of the airplane to the TACAN surface beacon. The system is so designed that when correct bearing information cannot be determined or the equipment is not operating properly, the bearing pointer will rotate rapidly (search), preventing the pilot from deriving unreliable information. The range warning flag partially obscures the range indicator digital drums whenever the distance information is unreliable. In addition, a window is provided in the upper face of the instrument to indicate various types of instrument power failure. The appearance of OFF in the window indicates that the BDH indicator is not energized or that power is not available to the compass card. The appearance of PTR in the window indicates that power is not available to the TACAN bearing pointer.

Note

Blind spots (weak signal areas) from 3 to 12 miles wide sometime exist in surface beacon antenna patterns. When entering such an area the BDH indicator may "search" until the airplane is clear of the weak signal zone. One or two of these weak signal zones may be encountered within the 200 mile distance inbound or outbound from the station.

The set index knob located on the lower right side of the indicator is used to set the heading index to a desired magnetic heading. Once set, the index rotates with the compass card.

Course Indicator.

A course indicator (figure 4-18) is installed on the pilot's main instrument panel. This instrument gives the pilot glide slope, marker beacon, localizer, and TACAN surface beacon course indications. A course selector window located at the top of the indicator can be set to the desired course of a TACAN or ILS facility. The course is set in the course selector window with the course set knob located on the lower left corner of the instrument. The pilot controls the course selection regardless of which station has control of TACAN. When in the TACAN mode, deviation of the airplane from the selected course will be indicated by

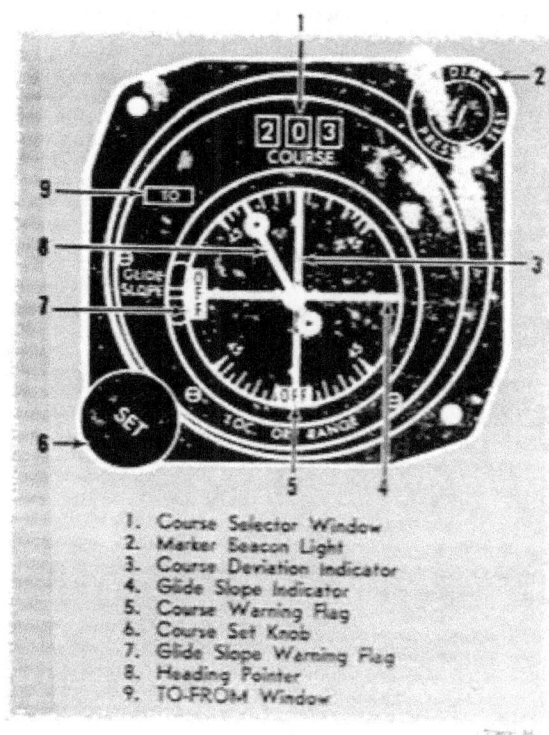

1. Course Selector Window
2. Marker Beacon Light
3. Course Deviation Indicator
4. Glide Slope Indicator
5. Course Warning Flag
6. Course Set Knob
7. Glide Slope Warning Flag
8. Heading Pointer
9. TO-FROM Window

Figure 4-18.

displacement of the course deviation indicator (CDI) on the face of the instrument.

Note

When tuned to ILS mode, the CDI displays airplane position relative to the localizer course regardless of the course set in the course selector window. However, the ILS front course should be set in the course selector window when flying ILS front or back courses. The CDI will then be directional in relation to the heading pointer.

The TO-FROM indicator indicates whether the course selected, if intercepted and flown, will take the airplane to or from the station. The glide slope indicator indicates airplane position relative to the glide slope beam. Airplane heading with respect to the course set in the course window is shown by the heading pointer. The pointer receives magnetic heading signals from the flight reference system. The marker beacon light located on the upper right side of the course indicator signifies when lighted that the airplane is crossing a marker beacon signal. Two warning flags, one for the CDI and one for the glide slope indicator, signify when in view that the signal level is insufficient to provide reliable operation of the associated indicator.

4-33

Section IV
Auxiliary Equipment

T.O. 1B-58A-1

NORMAL OPERATION OF THE TACAN SYSTEM.

1. Power knob—Turn to T/R. Allow pointer to start counter-clockwise rotation and range counters to rotate for warmup.

2. Channel selector knobs—Rotate channel knobs to the desired channel.

Note

When turning the TACAN on or when switching channels, the system may lock-on a false bearing which will be 40 degrees or a multiple of 40 degrees in error.

Cross check the BDH indicator for a false lock-on with ground radar, airborne radar, dead reckoning or other means. If a false lock-on is suspected switch to another channel, check for correct bearing and then switch back to the desired channel. If the false lock-on is still suspected, turn the equipment OFF and then on. Re-check for false lock-on. If false lock-on is still suspected, do not use the equipment except in an emergency.

3. Volume control—As desired.

4. Course set knob—Set the desired course in the course selector window of the course indicator.

Note

- Check to see that warning flags disappear.
- Range information will not be available in the REC position.
- If reliable signals are not available, the BDH indicator will "search" constantly and the course warning flags will be visible.

INSTRUMENT LANDING SYSTEM.

The instrument landing system (ILS) consists of localizer, glide slope, and marker beacon receivers; associated antennas; and control panel. Information from the ILS receivers is displayed on the course indicator to give vertical and horizontal guidance to a pilot making an instrument landing system approach. For antenna positions see figure 4-11. Localizer and glide slope receivers operate on 20 fixed, separate frequency channels. Localizer frequencies range from 108.1 to 111.9 megacycles and glide slope frequencies from 329.3 to 335 megacycles. The proper glide slope frequency is selected automatically when the localizer frequency is selected at the ILS-TACAN control panel. The marker beacon receiver operates on a fixed frequency of 75 megacycles. All controls located on the ILS-TACAN control panel are common to the ILS

and TACAN systems. An additional control for aural monitoring of the marker beacon receiver is located at the pilots' station. Power for the ILS unit is supplied through a fuse, marked TACAN-ILS system, located on the 28 volt d-c power panel. The glide slope indicator is inoperative when landing gear is in up position.

MARKER BEACON (MB) MIXING SWITCH.

The two position lever type marker beacon mixing switch (11, figure 4-6) is located on the pilot's communication control panel. The switch positions ON (up) and OFF (down) are unmarked. Placing the switch to MB (on) allows the pilot to monitor marker beacon audio signals.

Note

All other ILS controls and indicators which are common to TACAN are discussed under the TACAN system in this section.

NORMAL OPERATION OF THE ILS SYSTEM.

1. Power knob—to the REC or T/R. Allow approximately 90 seconds warm-up.

2. Channel selector knobs—Set to desired localizer frequency.

3. Course set knob—Set the localizer front course in the course selector window.

4. Marker beacon mixing switch—MB.

Note

Check to see that warning flags disappear. If reliable signals are not available the course indicator warning flags will be visible.

AIR-TO-GROUND IFF SYSTEM. (AN/APX-47)

The air-to-ground IFF system provides the airplane with an automatic means of selective identification to ground, shipboard, or airborne IFF recognition installations operating in the L-band frequency range. The equipment replies to proper interrogations from Mark X IFF systems and SIF (selective identification feature) stations. Operation is possible in three modes, plus I/P (identification of position) and emergency identification. The modes of operation have the following significance at ground recognition stations:

Mode 1—Security Identity
Mode 2—Personal Identity
Mode 3—Traffic Identity

The equipment consists of an air-to-ground IFF control panel, an air-to-ground SIF control panel, a transmitter-receiver, a decoder-coder, an antenna lobing

4-34

switch, and two radiator-type antennas. The controls are located on the DSO's right console. The equipment does not perform interrogation but only transmits coded replies to correctly coded interrogation. The two radiator-type antennas are arranged to provide an upper and lower antenna. (Refer to figure 4-11 for antenna locations.) The motor-driven lobing switch rapidly transfers contact of the transmitter-receiver from one radiator to the other. This constant alternation eliminates blind spots in the antenna pattern caused by airplane structure. The transmitter-receiver package is located in the aft fuselage unpressurized area and incorporates a duplexer which permits use of the same antennas for receiving and transmitting. The receiver is sensitive to all signals within its frequency range; however, only those signals meeting the complete predetermined requirements of the code being used will be recognized and answered. This is a function of the decoder-coder, as directed and modified by switch settings within the decoder-coder and on the two control panels. The decoder-coder is located below the navigator's left console. Two recessed push-to-test buttons located on the lower front panel of the decoder-coder are for test purposes only. Mode 2 code settings are screwdriver adjustments, made by means of slotted-shaft switches reached through openings in the front panel of the decoder-coder. All other codes are set up at the control panels. Mode 1 is always on whenever the equipment is operating. All other modes can be turned on or off at the IFF control panel. The equipment replies to mode 1 interrogations at all times, even while replying to other modes. Replies to modes 1, 2, and 3, as well as to I/P and emergency interrogations, are shown on the ground station radar scope. In the case of the more complicated SIF codes, ground stations will use a plan position indicator (PPI) and letter symbol indicator to decode and indicate supplementary information such as specific identification and location, and flight or aircraft conditions. Mode 1 has 32 possible code combinations. Mode 2 has 4,096 though only a portion of these are usable with existing ground facilities. Mode 3 has 64 combinations. Code numbers to be used at any given time will be assigned by area commanders. An optional low-power setting provision restricts sensitivity so that replies are made only to local interrogations. The transmitter-receiver package is cooled by the airplane air conditioning system. Five thermostatically controlled electric heaters provide warmup heat as required. The heaters operate automatically when the airplane electrical system is energized. The heaters operate on 115 volt A-C power through the right A-C distribution bus.

MASTER CONTROL KNOB.

The five-position master control knob (5, figure 4-19), located on the air-to-ground IFF control panel, controls operation of the air-to-ground IFF equipment. The knob positions are marked OFF, STDBY, LOW,

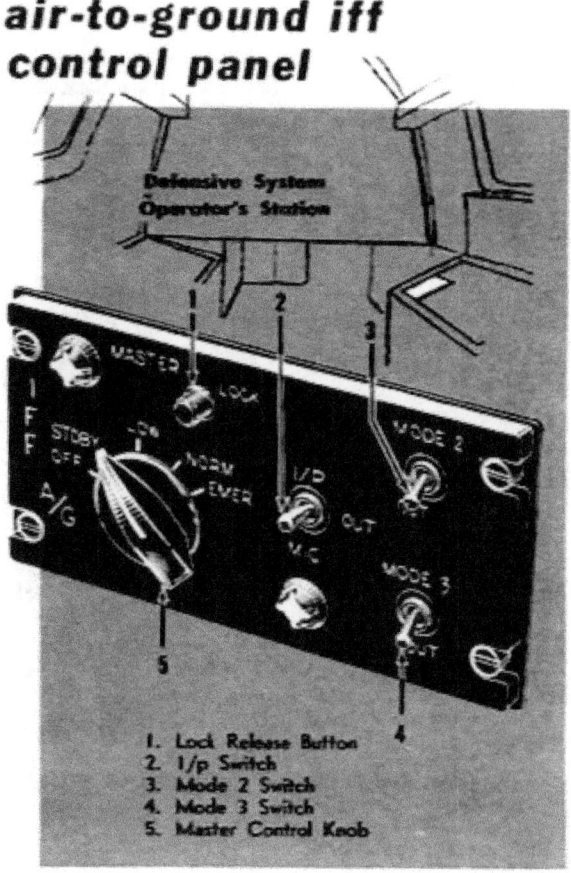

air-to-ground iff control panel

1. Lock Release Button
2. I/p Switch
3. Mode 2 Switch
4. Mode 3 Switch
5. Master Control Knob

Figure 4-19.

NORM, and EMER. When the knob is turned to the STDBY position, the equipment is placed and maintained in a ready state, but it will not transmit. When the knob is turned to LOW, only local (strong) interrogations are recognized and answered. With the knob in the NORM position, full range recognition and replies occur. When the knob is placed in the EMER position, an emergency-indicating pulse group is transmitted each time a mode 1 or mode 3 interrogation is recognized. The emergency pulse group will also be transmitted whenever the bailout warning system is activated, regardless of the master control knob setting.

Note

The master control knob is prevented from being inadvertently moved to the EMER position by an internal lock. A lock release button (1, figure 4-19), when depressed and held, allows the knob to be placed in the EMER position. The knob can be moved out of the EMER position without pressing the lock release button.

Section IV
Auxiliary Equipment

T.O. 1B-58A-1

MODE SWITCHES.

Two two-position mode switches (3, and 4, figure 4-19), one for mode 2 and one for mode 3, are located on the air-to-ground IFF control panel to control transmission of mode 2 and 3 replies. When a mode switch is in the up position, its corresponding selected code will be transmitted to answer correctly coded interrogating reception. When a switch is in the OUT position, its corresponding code is not transmitted.

IDENTIFICATION-OF-POSITION (I/P) SWITCH.

The identification-of-position (I/P) switch (2, figure 4-19), located on the air-to-ground IFF control panel, is used to control transmission of I/P pulse groups. The switch has three positions—a MIC position, an OUT position, and a spring-loaded I/P position. When the switch is momentarily held in the I/P position, the I/P timer is energized for 30 seconds. If a mode 1 or mode 3 interrogation is recognized within this 30-second period, I/P replies will be made. When the switch is placed in the MIC position, the circuit is set up so that when the command radio is operating and either of the foot-operated TRANSMIT or capsule microphone buttons are depressed or the control stick microphone switch is placed to TRANS, the I/P timer is energized for 30 seconds. If a mode 1 or mode 3 interrogation is recognized within this 30-second period, I/P replies will be made. When the buttons or switch are open, transmission of the I/P pulse groups will be withheld.

CODE SELECTOR KNOBS.

Two code selector knobs (figure 4-20), one for mode 1 and one for mode 3, are located on the air-to-ground SIF panel. Each selector knob consists of an inner and outer selector ring. The outer selector ring of the mode 1 knob is marked 0, 1, 2, and 3; the inner selector ring is marked 0, 1, 2, 3, 4, 5, 6, and 7. Each selector ring of the mode 3 knob is marked 0, 1, 2, 3, 4, 5, 6, 7. Code numbers are read from left to right. For example, code 32 is selected by setting the 3 of the inner selector ring and the 2 of the outer selector ring at the index marker.

NORMAL OPERATION OF THE AIR-TO-GROUND IFF SYSTEM.

Under extreme conditions (cold soaked at —65°F) transmitter-receiver package may require up to 15 minutes warmup time before the frequency is fully stabilized. Of course, at higher temperatures the warm up time will be proportionally less. Place the IFF equipment in operation as follows:

1. Code selector knobs—As required.
2. Mode switches—As required.

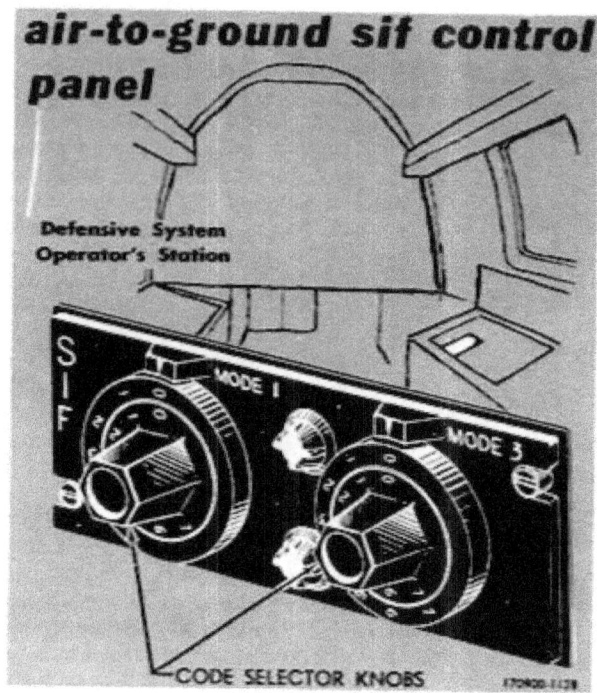

Figure 4-20.

3. I/P switch—OUT or MIC.
4. Master control knob—LOW or NORM.

Note

In the event that the A/G IFF must be placed into immediate operation, a thermal time delay will prevent damage to the equipment.

POSITION INDICATING BEACON SYSTEM (AN/APN-136).

The position indicating (PI) beacon is a J-band airborne beacon system which, when used in conjunction with the airplane search radar unit provides a means of inter-aircraft position indication. In response to appropriate interrogation from a bomber search radar system, operating in beacon mode, the beacon automatically transmits a coded reply which results in a PPI presentation on the interrogating radar scope. This presentation indicates the range, bearing, and identity of the interrogated airplane. Pulse width discrimination prevents the beacon equipment from responding to radars operating in modes other than the beacon interrogation mode. System equipment consists of a receiver-transmitter, control panel, and antenna. See figure 4-11 for antenna location. The receiver-transmitter unit is cooled by the airplane air conditioning system. PI beacon equipment is controlled from the navigator's station. System fuses are located on the 28-volt d-c power panel, left a-c power panel, and the a-c and high voltage d-c power panel.

PI BEACON POWER KNOB.

The PI beacon power knob (4, figure 4-21), located on the PI beacon control panel is marked OFF, STBY, and POWER. Placing the knob to the STBY position energizes the receiver-transmitter low voltage circuits; enables the unit to receive but not reply; and maintains the equipment in a ready state. The POWER position energizes the system for normal operation. The OFF position removes all power from the unit.

PI BEACON CODE ELEMENT KNOBS.

Eight PI beacon code element knobs (2, figure 4-21), located on the PI beacon control panel, are used to set up code combinations for beacon response. The code element corresponding to an individual knob can be included in the reply by pulling out on the knob and lifting upward to the unmarked ON position.

Note

Normally, a code should contain a maximum of six elements. The first element is stationary and included in all codes, therefore, under normal conditions the operator is not required to select more than five elements.

PI BEACON COMMON CODE ELEMENT KNOB.

The PI beacon common code element knob (1, figure 4-21), located on the PI beacon control panel, is stationary and corresponds to the first code element. The first element is preset and automatically included in every code combination.

PI MIXING SWITCH.

The PI mixing switch (1, figure 4-8), located on the navigator's interphone control panel, provides aural monitoring of beacon interrogation and reply when in the unmarked ON position.

PI BEACON CODE ELEMENT INDICATOR LAMPS.

Nine code element indicator lamps (3, figure 4-21), located on the PI beacon control panel, indicate when lighted that the associated code element is included in the beacon response.

NORMAL OPERATION OF THE PI BEACON SYSTEM.

1. PI beacon code element knobs—As required.
2. PI beacon power knob—STBY for approximately fifteen minutes, then POWER.

Note

Placing the beacon power knob in the POWER position prior to the fifteen minute warm-up period will not damage the equipment. However, temporary degraded performance will result.

3. PI mixing Switch—ON.
4. Search radar—As required.

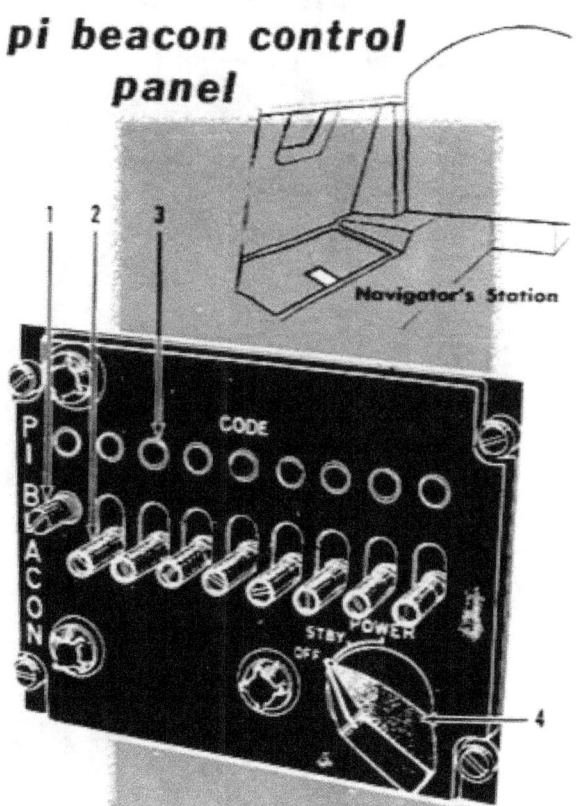

1. PI Beacon Common Code Element Knob
2. PI Beacon Code Element Knob (8)
3. PI Beacon Code Element Indicator Lamp (9)
4. PI Beacon Power Knob

Figure 4-21.

Section IV
Auxiliary Equipment

T.O. 1B-58A-1

EMERGENCY OPERATION OF THE PI BEACON SYSTEM.

If the system fails to operate in a selected code, the operator may switch to an alternate code after coordination with the aircraft commander and interrogating aircraft. If the system still fails to function, turn the PI beacon power knob to OFF. Inflight maintenance cannot be performed on this equipment.

RENDEZVOUS BEACON SYSTEM (AN/APN-135).

The rendezvous (RV) beacon is an L-band airborne navigational aid system which enables a rendezvous between bomber and compatibly equipped tanker aircraft for air refueling. When interrogated by a tanker radar the beacon automatically transmits a coded reply. This response results in a presentation on the tanker radar scope which indicates the range, bearing, and identity of the bomber. If the tanker is equipped with J-band beacon equipment the bomber can obtain a similar presentation of the tanker by utilizing the search radar (in beacon mode) to interrogate the tanker beacon. With the tanker thus equipped, rendezvous operations can be conducted without requiring the use of the command radio. However, the bomber command radio must be used to facilitate rendezvous operations if the tanker is not equipped with a J-band beacon unit. System equipment consists of a receiver-transmitter, control panel, and an antenna. For the antenna location see figure 4-11. The receiver-transmitter unit is cooled by the airplane air-conditioning system. RV beacon operating controls are on the RV beacon control panel at the navigator's station. An additional control for aural monitoring of beacon interrogation and reply is on the navigator's interphone panel. System fuses are located on the 28-volt d-c power panel, left a-c power panel, and the a-c and high voltage d-c power panel.

RV BEACON POWER KNOB.

The RV beacon power knob (4, figure 4-22), located on the RV beacon control panel, is marked OFF, STBY, and POWER. Positioning the knob to STBY energizes the receiver-transmitter low voltage circuits; enables the unit to receive but not reply; and maintains the equipment in a ready state. Positioning the knob to POWER energizes the system for normal operation. The OFF position removes all power from the unit.

RV BEACON CODE ELEMENT KNOBS.

Eight RV beacon code element knobs (2, figure 4-22), located on the RV beacon control panel, are used to set up a code combination for the beacon response. The code element corresponding to an individual knob can be included in the reply by pulling out on the knob and lifting upward to the unmarked ON position.

Note

Normally, a code should contain a maximum of six elements. The first element is stationary and included in all codes, therefore, under normal conditions the operator is not required to select more than five elements.

RV BEACON COMMON CODE ELEMENT KNOB.

The RV beacon common code element knob (1, figure 4-22), located on the RV beacon control panel, is stationary and corresponds to the first code element. The first element is preset and automatically included in every code combination.

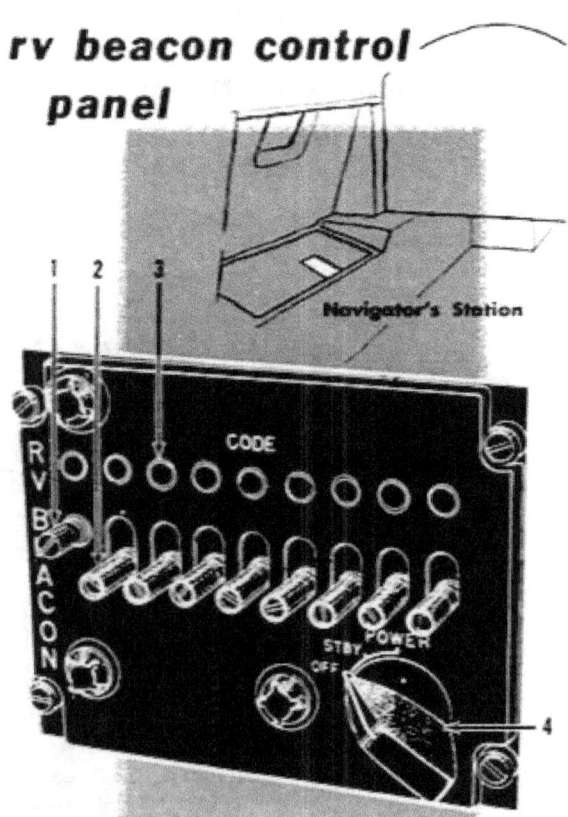

1. RV Beacon Common Code Element Knob
2. RV Beacon Code Element Knob (8)
3. RV Beacon Code Element Indicator Lamp (9)
4. RV Beacon Power Knob

Figure 4-22.

RV MIXING SWITCH.

The RV mixing switch (1, figure 4-8), located on the navigator's interphone control panel, provides aural monitoring of beacon interrogation and reply when in the unmarked ON position.

RV BEACON CODE ELEMENT INDICATOR LAMPS.

Nine of these lamps (3, figure 4-22), on the RV beacon control panel, indicate when lighted that the associated code element is included in the beacon response.

NORMAL OPERATION OF THE RV BEACON SYSTEM.

1. RV beacon code element knobs—As required.
2. RV beacon power knob—STBY for approximately fifteen minutes then POWER.

Note

Placing the beacon power knob in the POWER position prior to the fifteen minute warm-up period will not damage the equipment. However, temporary degraded performance will result.

3. RV mixing switch—ON.
4. Command radio—As required.
5. Search radar—Beacon mode. (If tanker has compatible beacon equipment)

EMERGENCY OPERATION OF THE RV BEACON.

If the system fails to operate in a selected code, the operator may switch to an alternate code after coordination with the pilot and interrogating aircraft. If the system still fails to function, turn the RV beacon power knob to OFF. Inflight maintenance can not be performed on this equipment.

LIGHTING EQUIPMENT.

The airplane lighting equipment is divided into two groups: exterior lighting and interior lighting. The exterior group includes landing lights, taxi lights, navigation lights, anticollision lights, air refueling slipway lights, and a light for ground refueling. The interior group consists of various instrument, panel, flood, and tunnel area lights necessary to provide adequate lighting in the crew compartments.

EXTERIOR LIGHTS.

Two sealed-beam landing lights are mounted on the nose landing gear, one on each drag strut. The lights are ground-adjustable and retract with the nose gear. A switch is provided for each light. One sealed-beam taxi light is mounted on the left drag strut of the nose landing gear above the left landing light. A microswitch on the landing gear prevents the taxi and landing lights from being energized when the landing gear is in the retracted position. The landing lights receive 115-volt alternating current supplied from the left and right a-c power panels; the 115-volt a-c power is reduced to 28-volts by a transformer located on each light. The taxi light operates on 28-volt direct current supplied from the main d-c power panel. The navigation lighting system, which is used to indicate position and direction of the airplane, consists of five lights. A wing light is located just forward of each wing tip on the leading edge. The left wing light is red and the right wing light is green. A white light is located on top of the fuselage between the navigator's and DSO's canopies. Two white tail lights are mounted side-by-side between transparent glass fairings in the rudder tip just forward of the trailing edge. All of the navigation lights operate on 28-volt alternating current. The wing and tail lights will burn steady or can be made to flash alternately through control of a switch in the pilot's compartment. These lights can be made to burn bright or dim in either the steady or flashing mode of operation. The white fuselage light does not flash, but it can be made bright or dim. Two red, rotating, high-intensity anticollision lights are located on the vertical stabilizer. The upper anticollision light is located on the leading edge near the top. The lower light is located on the trailing edge between the fuselage and the fire control system radome. Together, the anticollision lights provide 360 degree coverage. The lights receive 115-volt a-c power from the left and right a-c power panels. A white light is located in the air-refueling slipway. This light, which has two separate bulbs, comes on when the slipway door is open and the slipway light control knob is out of the full CCW position, and provides a target for the tanker boom operator during night refueling operations. The slipway light has a variable intensity and receives 28-volt a-c power from the 28-volt a-c and high-voltage d-c power panel. An additional light is installed in the slipway to provide more adequate lighting. This light also comes on when the slipway doors are open, however, a dimming control for this light is not provided. Two floodlights are installed in the nose wheel well adjacent to the single point refueling adapter to provide lighting for ground refueling operations. The lights are powered by 28-volt d-c power from the 28-volt d-c power panel.

Landing Light Switches.

Two on-off switches (8, figure 1-34), marked L and R and located on the pilot's forward left console, control the left and right landing lights. Placing the switches in the ON position closes a 28-volt d-c relay

Section IV
Auxiliary Equipment

T.O. 1B-58A-1

pilot's lighting control panel

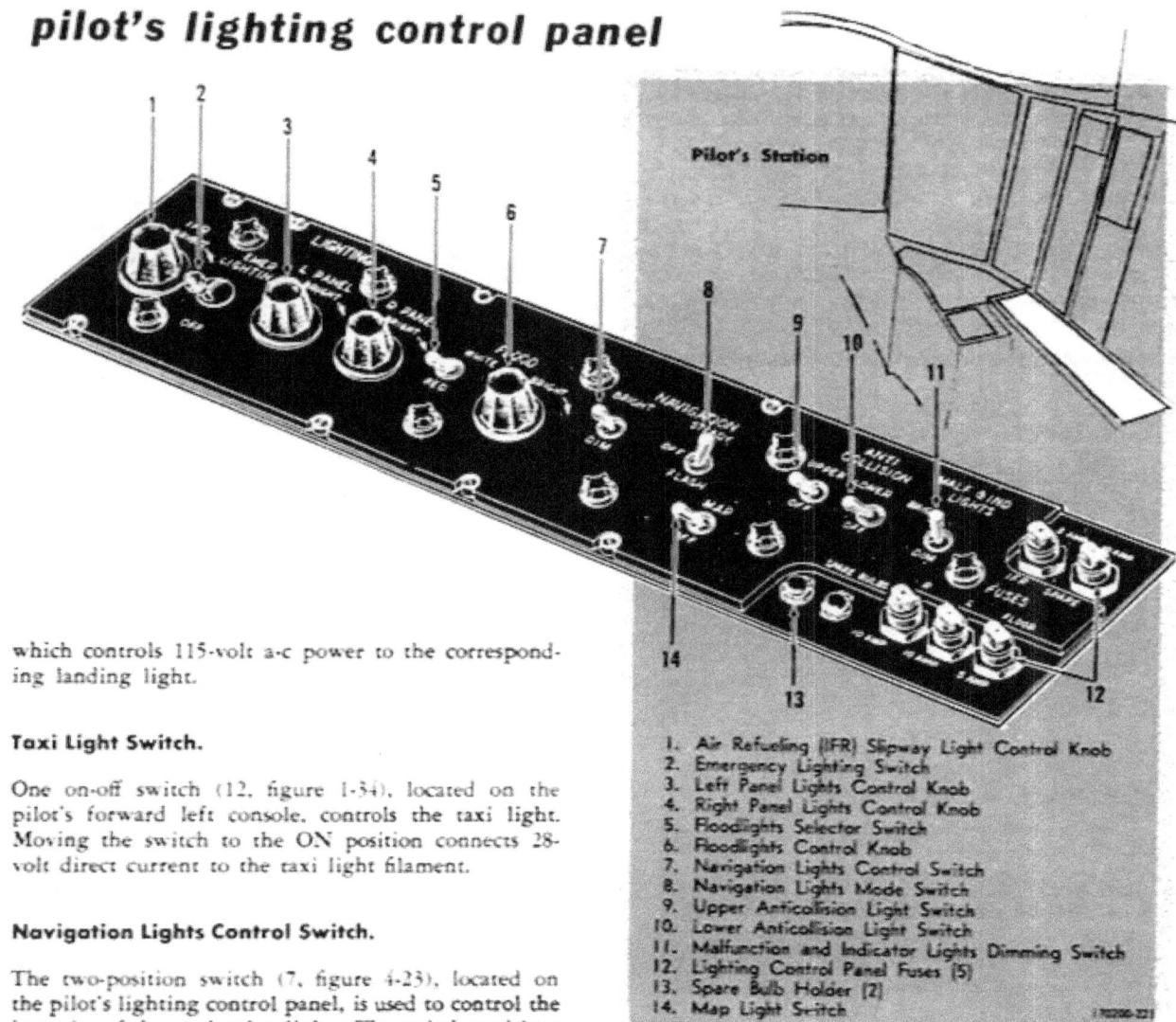

1. Air Refueling (IFR) Slipway Light Control Knob
2. Emergency Lighting Switch
3. Left Panel Lights Control Knob
4. Right Panel Lights Control Knob
5. Floodlights Selector Switch
6. Floodlights Control Knob
7. Navigation Lights Control Switch
8. Navigation Lights Mode Switch
9. Upper Anticollision Light Switch
10. Lower Anticollision Light Switch
11. Malfunction and Indicator Lights Dimming Switch
12. Lighting Control Panel Fuses (5)
13. Spare Bulb Holder (2)
14. Map Light Switch

Figure 4-23.

which controls 115-volt a-c power to the corresponding landing light.

Taxi Light Switch.

One on-off switch (12, figure 1-34), located on the pilot's forward left console, controls the taxi light. Moving the switch to the ON position connects 28-volt direct current to the taxi light filament.

Navigation Lights Control Switch.

The two-position switch (7, figure 4-23), located on the pilot's lighting control panel, is used to control the intensity of the navigation lights. The switch positions are marked BRIGHT and DIM.

Navigation Lights Mode Switch.

The three-position switch (8, figure 4-23), located on the pilot's lighting control panel, is used to turn the navigation lights on or off and to select either the steady or the flashing mode of operation. The switch positions are marked STEADY, FLASH and OFF.

Anticollision Light Switches.

Two anticollision light switches (9 and 10, figure 4-23), located on the pilot's lighting control panel, control power to the anticollision lights. Each switch has two positions. One switch is marked UPPER and OFF; the other is marked LOWER and OFF. When a switch is placed in the up (ON) position the respective anticollision light will light and rotate.

Air Refueling (IFR) Slipway Light Control Knob.

The air refueling slipway light control knob (1, figure 4-23), located on the pilot's lighting control panel, is used to regulate the intensity of the air refueling slipway light. The light will be brightest with the knob at the fully clockwise position and will be out with the knob in the full counterclockwise position or with the door control switch in the closed position.

Single Point Refueling Floodlight Switch.

The single point refueling floodlight switch is located beside the single point refueling adapter in the nose wheel well. The switch positions are marked REFUEL LIGHT and OFF.

INTERIOR LIGHTS.

The interior lighting equipment consists of instrument lights, panel edge lights, indirect and direct floodlights, a map light, emergency lights, and tunnel area lights. All instruments are lighted either internally or by post-mounted lights on the instrument. The instrument lights at the pilot's station are red; those at the other stations are white. Edge lighting of the panels at the pilot's station is accomplished by small red lights set into the acrylic panels. The other stations have white edge lights. Floodlights are provided at all stations to provide overall lighting. The pilot's floodlights consist of small red and white lamps located under the glare shield and in the control panel wells along the left side of the station. In addition, a large red floodlight and a white storm light are mounted on the aft wall of the compartment to the right of the seat headrest. The navigator's floodlights consist of white lamps located in two long baffled fixtures, one on each side of the station near the canopy ledge. The DSO's floodlights are identical to those of the navigator's station. A white overhead map light mounted in the canopy at the pilot's station, is equipped with a red filter and columnator to reduce glare. A white flood light is mounted in the canopy liner at the navigator's and DSO's station for emergency lighting. The tunnel area between the pilot's and navigator's stations has two white dome lights. The interior lights are controlled entirely from the lighting control panels at each station and receive 28-volts a-c power from the 28-volt a-c and high-voltage d-c power panel. For some instrument lights, the 28-volt a-c power is reduced to 5 volts by transformers.

Pilot's Panel Light Control Knobs.

Two control knobs on the pilot's lighting control panel regulate the instrument and panel lights at the pilot's station. The knob marked L PANEL (3, figure 4-23) regulates the lights on the left side of the station up to but not including the engine instruments. The knob marked R PANEL (4, figure 4-23) regulates the lights on the right side of the station and the engine instrument lights.

Navigator's and DSO's Panel Light Control Knobs.

Panel light control knobs marked MAIN INST PANEL (5, figure 4-24, 3, figure 4-25) and AUXILIARY PANEL (3, figure 4-24, and 2, figure 4-25) are located on the navigator's and DSO's lighting control panels. The main instrument panel control knobs regulate the instrument and panel edge lights on the main forward panels at the respective stations. The auxiliary panel control knobs regulate the lights on the left and right consoles at the respective stations.

navigator's lighting control panel (typical)

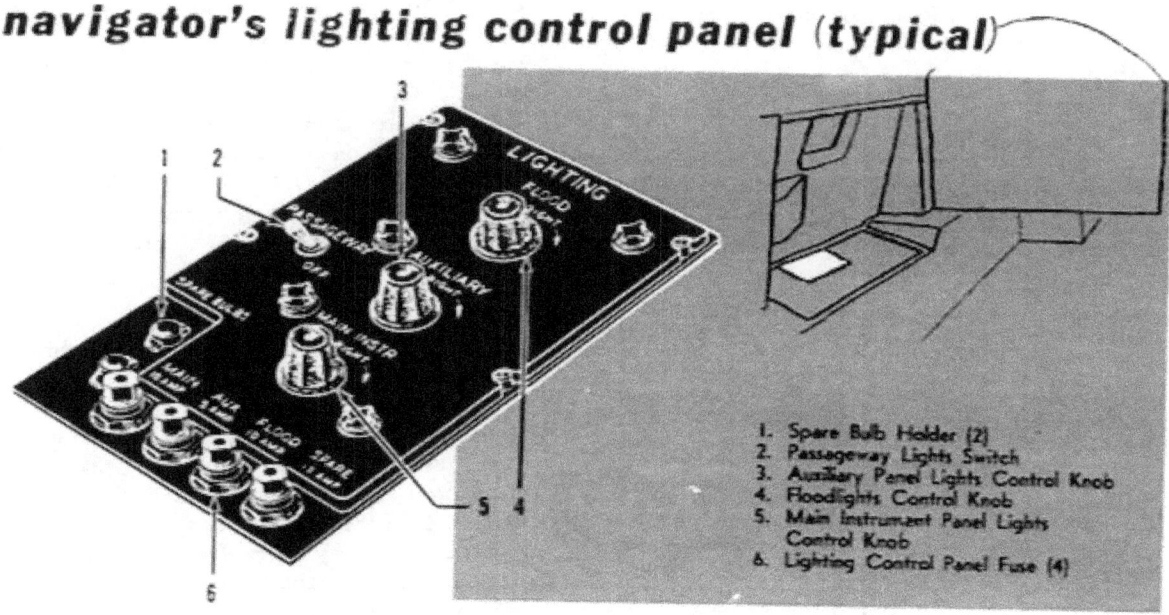

1. Spare Bulb Holder (2)
2. Passageway Lights Switch
3. Auxiliary Panel Lights Control Knob
4. Floodlights Control Knob
5. Main Instrument Panel Lights Control Knob
6. Lighting Control Panel Fuse (4)

Figure 4-24.

Section IV
Auxiliary Equipment

T.O. 1B-58A-1

dso's lighting control panel (typical)

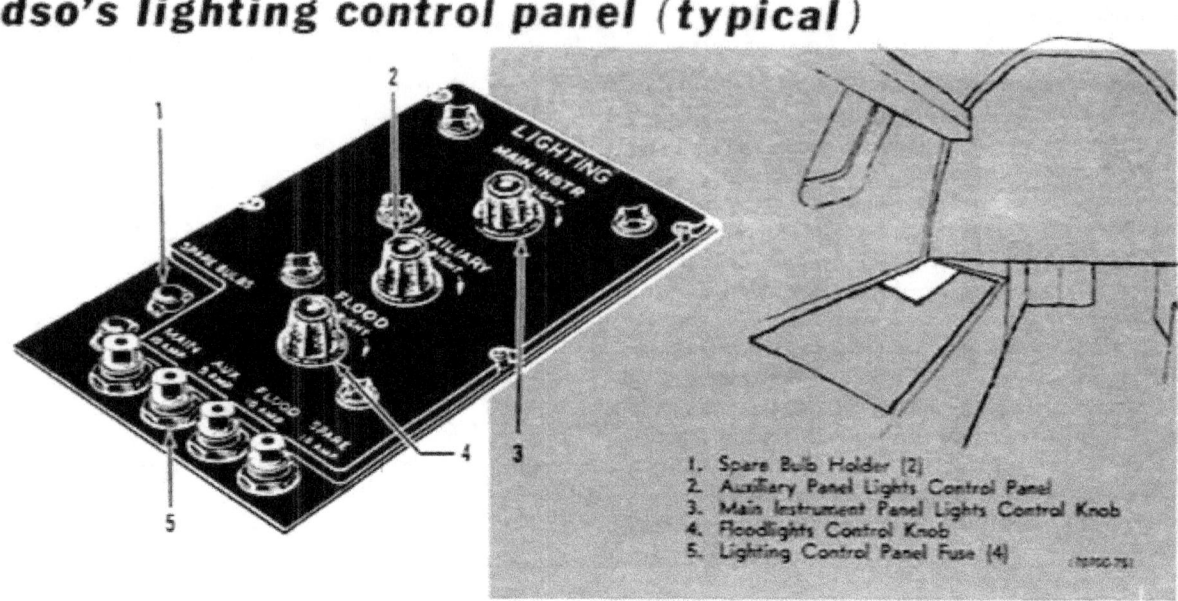

1. Spare Bulb Holder (2)
2. Auxiliary Panel Lights Control Panel
3. Main Instrument Panel Lights Control Knob
4. Floodlights Control Knob
5. Lighting Control Panel Fuse (4)

Figure 4-25.

Floodlight Control Knobs.

Floodlight control knobs (6, figure 4-23, 4, figure 4-24, and 4, figure 4-25) are located on each lighting control panel. The knobs regulate the floodlights of the respective stations. At the pilot's station, the storm light is turned on when the floodlight control knob is rotated fully clockwise and the floodlight selector switch is at WHITE.

Pilot's Floodlight Selector Switch.

The two-position selector switch (5, figure 4-23), located on the pilot's lighting control panel, is marked WHITE and RED and permits the pilot to select either white or red floodlights at his station.

Map Light Switch.

The two-position map light switch (14, figure 4-23), located on the pilot's lighting control panel, is marked MAP and OFF. Placing the switch in the MAP position turns on the overhead map light at the pilot's station.

Passageway Light Switches.

The dome lights, located in the tunnel area between the pilot's and navigator's stations, are turned on and off by a switch marked PASSAGEWAY LIGHT (2, figure 4-24) on the navigator's lighting control panel.

Pilot's Emergency Lighting Switch.

An internally guarded, two-position emergency lighting switch (2, figure 4-23) is located on the pilot's lighting control panel. The switch is marked EMER LIGHTING and OFF. When the switch handle is pulled outward and placed in the EMER LIGHTING position, the pilot's white floodlights are lighted by power from the 28-volt d-c essential bus in the 28-volt d-c power panel. This feature assures lighting at the pilot's station in case of a-c power failure. When the switch is in the OFF position, the white floodlights can be connected to their normal 28-volt a-c power source through the floodlight controls on the panel.

Navigator's and DSO's Emergency Lighting Switches.

The two-position emergency lighting switches are located on the emergency floodlight brackets in the navigator's and DSO's stations. The ON-OFF switches control power to the white floodlights mounted overhead in the canopy liners. The floodlights, which provide emergency lighting in the event of a-c power failure, are lighted by power from the 28-volt d-c essential bus when the respective switch is placed to ON. The floodlights are fused on the 28-volt d-c power panel.

Fuses and Spare Bulb Holders.

Each lighting control panel has fuses (12, figure 4-23, 6, figure 4-24, and 5, figure 4-25), for each lighting control knob. Amperages are marked under each fuse. Each panel also has a spare fuse and two spare bulb holders.

OXYGEN SYSTEMS.

Oxygen systems are provided for both normal and emergency use. Each system is designed for use with a pressure demand oxygen mask.

NORMAL SYSTEM.

The normal liquid oxygen system consists essentially of two 10-liter vacuum-insulated liquid oxygen containers, a quantity indicating system, and diluter-demand regulators. The containers, located in the forward portion of the nose wheel well, maintain a system operating pressure of approximately 70 to 110 psi until the oxygen supply is virtually depleted. This pressure remains constant until the oxygen supply is virtually depleted. Relief valves prevent excessive pressure buildup. The liquid oxygen is converted to a gas as it passes through lines from each container to the crew stations. At each station, the lines converge into a single tube for delivery to the escape capsule oxygen system. Check valves assure continued oxygen supply in the event that one of the containers or its plumbing should fail. A conditioning coil warms the gaseous oxygen at the pilot's station to a comfortable breathing temperature; at the navigator's and DSO's stations, the plumbing distance from the containers is sufficient to adequately warm the gas. The quantity indicating system incorporates a capacitance-type quantity indicator and a probe in each container to electrically measure total liquid oxygen quantity. The indicating system, which operates on 115-volt single-phase a-c power from the left a-c power panel, also provides a low level warning. The oxygen system is serviced through two automatic filler-buildup and vent valves one for each container, located on the outside of the nose wheel well. See figure 1-17 for servicing information. Each valve automatically positions to vent for filling when the servicing cart hose is connected. When the hose is removed, the valve repositions to the buildup position. This feature insures correct valve position at all times.

oxygen duration - normal system
TWO TEN-LITER LIQUID OXYGEN CONTAINERS

☐ 100% OXYGEN
▨ NORMAL OXYGEN

CABIN ALTITUDE FEET	HOURS REMAINING FOR THREE CREW MEMBERS QUANTITY INDICATOR READING--LITERS										BELOW 2
	20	18	16	14	12	10	8	6	4	2	
35,000 AND UP	38.6	34.8	30.9	27.0	23.1	19.3	15.4	11.6	7.7	3.8	EMERGENCY
	38.6	34.8	30.9	27.0	23.1	19.3	15.4	11.6	7.7	3.8	
30,000	27.8	25.1	22.3	19.5	16.7	13.9	11.1	8.3	5.5	2.7	
	28.6	25.8	22.9	20.0	17.2	14.3	11.4	8.6	5.7	2.8	
25,000	21.6	19.3	17.2	15.6	12.9	10.7	8.5	6.7	4.3	2.1	DESCEND TO ALTITUDE NOT REQUIRING OXYGEN
	27.0	24.3	21.6	18.9	16.2	13.5	10.8	8.1	5.4	2.7	
20,000	16.3	14.7	13.1	11.4	9.8	8.2	6.5	4.9	3.2	1.6	
	30.6	27.5	24.4	21.3	18.3	15.3	12.2	9.2	6.1	3.0	
15,000	13.1	11.8	10.5	9.2	7.8	6.5	5.2	3.9	2.6	1.3	
	37.0	33.4	29.8	25.9	22.2	18.5	14.8	11.1	7.4	3.7	
10,000	10.5	9.5	8.4	7.4	6.3	5.3	4.2	3.2	2.1	1.0	
	37.0	33.4	29.8	25.9	22.2	18.5	14.8	11.1	7.4	3.7	
5,000	8.7	7.9	7.0	6.1	5.3	4.4	3.5	2.6	1.7	0.8	
	37.0	33.4	29.8	25.9	22.2	18.5	14.8	11.1	7.4	3.7	

Figure 4-26.

Section IV
Auxiliary Equipment

T.O. 1B-58A-1

The oxygen system is ready for use immediately after filling the last container. Total oxygen duration for a fully serviced system varies from 38.6 hours under optimum conditions to 8.7 hours for the most demanding conditions. See figure 4-26 for oxygen duration. With the airplane on the ground and with no oxygen demand, a fully serviced system will completely boil off in approximately 16 days.

EMERGENCY SYSTEM.

The emergency oxygen system with the escape capsule consists of a high pressure oxygen bottle (H-2 type), pressure reducer, snorkel air inlet assembly, stabilization frame trip cable, pressure gage, emergency actuator (green apple), an outlet hose. The emergency oxygen system is normally actuated automatically when the capsule stabilization frame extends. However, the system can be activated by pulling the "green apple". When this occurs, oxygen is provided to the oxygen regulator from the high pressure oxygen bottle through a pressure reducer. When ejected, ambient air is drawn through the snorkel air inlet. The emergency oxygen supply duration is dependent upon ejection altitude and control lever position. In an ejection at maximum altitude, the descent time to 10,000 feet is 4 minutes (approx.). With the oxygen control lever

oxygen duration — capsule system

One 25 cubic inch bottle per capsule

Altitude (ft.) Ambient	Minutes available for each crew member	
	Emergency Position	Normal Position
Sea Level	3.8	20.7
5,000	4.7	20.7
10,000	5.9	20.7
15,000	7.4	20.7
20,000	9.2	17
25,000	12.1	15.1
30,000	15.8	15.9
35,000 & up	21.6	21.6

Figure 4-27.

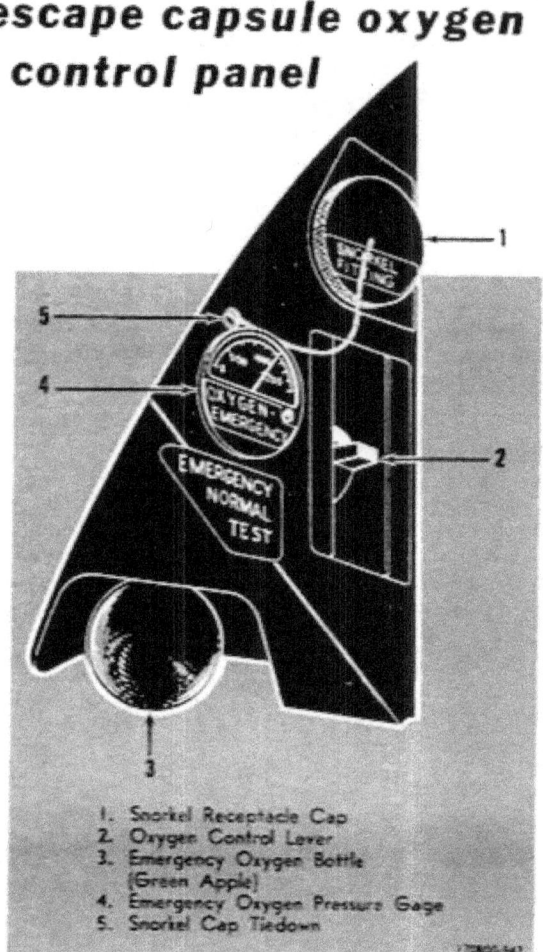

escape capsule oxygen control panel

1. Snorkel Receptacle Cap
2. Oxygen Control Lever
3. Emergency Oxygen Bottle (Green Apple)
4. Emergency Oxygen Pressure Gage
5. Snorkel Cap Tiedown

Figure 4-28.

in NORMAL, the oxygen consumption during this period is approximately 20% of oxygen available. With the oxygen control lever in EMERGENCY, the oxygen consumption during this period is approximately 40% of oxygen available. When the emergency oxygen supply has been exhausted, the crew member can breathe ambient air through the regulator and snorkel inlet. For easier breathing, remove the snorkel cap (1, figure 4-28), disconnect the oxygen hose from the regulator outlet, and connect the hose to the snorkel receptacle. This allows ambient air to by-pass the diluter valve in the regulator. The emergency oxygen pressure gage (4, figure 4-28) is located on the capsule oxygen control panel. The gage should indicate from 1800 to 2200 psi when the system is fully serviced. In event the airplane normal system becomes inoperable, actuation of the "green apple" will provide capsule oxygen as shown in figure 4-27.

4-44

pilot's oxygen control panel

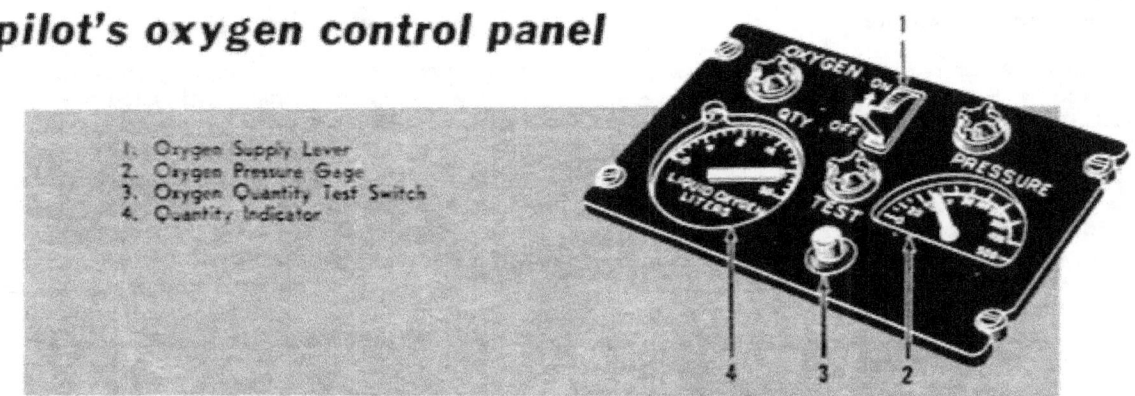

1. Oxygen Supply Lever
2. Oxygen Pressure Gage
3. Oxygen Quantity Test Switch
4. Quantity Indicator

Figure 4-29.

OXYGEN REGULATOR.

The automatic pressure-breathing, diluter-demand oxygen regulator, which is an integral part of the escape capsule oxygen control panel, is located on the right side of each capsule headrest (figure 4-28). From sea level to 32,000 feet cabin altitude, the regulator mixes air with oxygen in varying amounts and delivers a quantity of the mixture with each inhalation. Between 32,000 and 40,000 feet cabin altitude, the regulator provides 100% oxygen at positive pressure. At 40,000 feet cabin altitude, the pressure increases sharply until the regulator delivers maximum pressure of approximately .55 psi at 47,000 feet. In emergencies or for ground testing, the regulator can be set to deliver positive pressure, continuous flow, and 100% oxygen at all altitudes.

OXYGEN CONTROLS AND INDICATORS.

Supply Lever.

The green on-off supply lever, which is an integral part of the oxygen control panel, is located on the pilot's lower right console (1, figure 4-29) and on the navigator's and DSO's left consoles (1, figure 4-30). Placing the supply lever in the ON position opens a shutoff valve to permit a flow of oxygen to the regulator.

WARNING

In an unmanned position the oxygen supply lever should be in the OFF position. This is to prevent depletion of the supply in case the regulator is inadvertently left in the continuous-flow EMERGENCY setting.

Oxygen Control Lever.

An oxygen control lever (2, figure 4-28) is located on the capsule oxygen control panel to the right of the headrest. The lever has three positions marked EMERGENCY, NORMAL, and TEST, and is spring-loaded from TEST to NORMAL. Placing the lever in the EMERGENCY position delivers a continuous flow of 100% oxygen to the mask. With the lever positioned in NORMAL, the regulator controls the percent of oxygen mixed with air at each inhalation. From sea level to 32,000 feet, oxygen is mixed with air in increasing amounts. At 32,000 feet and above, the crew member will receive 100% oxygen. The TEST position is used for the purpose of checking the mask for leaks.

WARNING

When positive pressure and continuous flow is required, it is important that the oxygen mask be well fitted to the face. Unless special precautions are taken to prevent leakage, continued use of positive pressure may result in the rapid depletion of the oxygen supply.

Pressure Gage.

The pressure gage (2, figure 4-29 and 2, figure 4-30), is located on the oxygen control panel at each crew station. The gage, which is marked from 0 to 500 psi, indicates oxygen system pressure at the control valve inlet. Normal system pressure is approximately 70 to 110 psi. During pulsating demands on the system, the pressure may be as low as 65 psi. The gage will indicate system pressure whether the supply lever is ON or OFF. For the range markings of the pressure gage, see figure 5-1.

4-45

Section IV
Auxiliary Equipment

T.O. 1B-58A-1

Oxygen Quantity Indicator.

The oxygen quantity indicator is located on the pilot's oxygen control panel (4, figure 4-29). The indicator, marked from 0 to 20 liters, indicates the total quantity of liquid oxygen in the containers. When the containers are full after normal servicing, the indicator needle will read between 18 and 20 liters (approximately). In the event of electrical power failure to the quantity indicating system, the needle will remain in the position it held at the time of failure. When testing the indicator, the quantity indicator test button is pressed. If the indicator needle does not go down scale toward zero, the fuse may be defective. If not, and the indicator continues to malfunction, hold the test button down for approximately 15 seconds. If the oxygen quantity caution lamp comes on, the needle is slipping on the shaft. Remaining oxygen can be determined by noting the time between pressing the button and the actuation of the caution lamp. Approximate remaining quantities are as follows:

    20 liters—13 seconds
    15 liters—10 seconds
     9 liters— 5 seconds
     5 liters— 2 seconds

Quantity Indicator Test Button.

The press-to-test button is located on the pilot's oxygen control panel (3, figure 4-29). When the button is pressed, the quantity indicator needle will move toward zero if the indicating system is operating properly. The oxygen quantity caution lamp will light when the needle shows less than two liters. When the button is released, the indicator needle should move back to the proper reading.

navigator's and dso's oxygen control panel

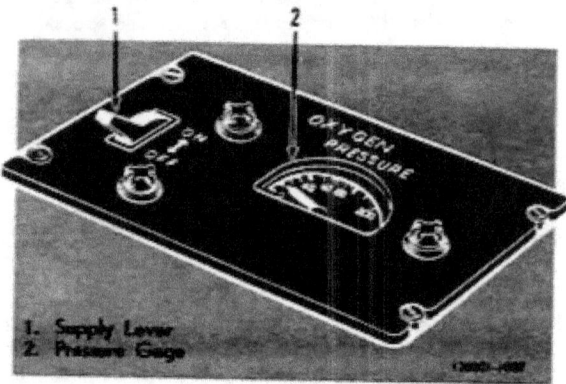

1. Supply Lever
2. Pressure Gage

Figure 4-30.

Oxygen Quantity Caution Lamp.

The oxygen quantity caution lamp (figure 1-13) is located on the caution lamp panel at the pilot's station. The lamp lights when the oxygen quantity indicator shows less than two liters remaining. When lighted, OXYGEN LOW appears on the face of the lamp in yellow illuminated letters. The caution lamp is tied into the master caution lamp circuit and receives 28-volt direct current from the 28-volt d-c power panel. (For testing and dimming the oxygen quantity caution lamp and for information on the master caution lamp, refer to "Malfunction Indicator and Warning System", Section I.)

NORMAL OPERATION OF OXYGEN SYSTEM.

The oxygen system is put into normal operation for any crew member by accomplishing the following at the respective crew station:
1. Oxygen supply lever—ON.
2. Capsule oxygen control panel lever—NORMAL.

EMERGENCY OPERATION OF OXYGEN SYSTEM.

Regulator Failure.

If the oxygen regulator is not delivering the desired oxygen or hypoxia is suspected, the emergency lever on the oxygen control panel should be placed to EMERGENCY position. If the oxygen regulator becomes inoperative when oxygen is required, pull the "green apple" on the escape capsule oxygen control panel and notify the pilot to descend to an altitude not requiring oxygen.

Oxygen System Leakage.

If the oxygen quantity indicator shows oxygen depletion at an abnormal rate, observe the following precautions:

1. Place the supply lever to OFF. If the oxygen supply stops depleting, the leak is probably in the hoses or face equipment. Return the lever to ON and see that the hoses between the capsule oxygen panel and the mask are securely fastened.

2. Position the emergency lever to EMERGENCY and note a slight increase in mask pressure. Return the lever to NORMAL.

3. If the oxygen continues to deplete with the supply lever at OFF, determine if the quantity indicator is at fault. If the indicator shows no malfunction, descend to a safe altitude, since the leak is probably upstream from the regulator.

OXYGEN SYSTEM PREFLIGHT CHECK.

System Hook-Up.

Before takeoff, each crew member completes the oxygen hook-up (figure 2-3) for mask and oxygen hose as follows:

4-46

Note

The CRU-60/P connector is normally attached to the bayonet fitting on the face mask.

1. Check CRU-60/P connector and mask bayonet fitting for security.

2. Plug the CRU-60/P quick disconnect into the capsule hose and listen for click. Check that the connector is firmly attached and that the lockpin is locked.

3. Check oxygen hose bayonet fitting at the regulator for security and mounting.

Operational Check.

The crew members should complete the following oxygen checks during preflight inspection:

1. Quantity Indicator and Caution Lamp—Check.

  a. Pilot check liquid oxygen indicator for required quantity. Refer to "Oxygen Duration Chart," figure 4-26.

  b. Press test button until quantity indication decreases below 2 liters and check oxygen quantity caution lamp lights. Then release test button and check for return of oxygen quantity needle to former reading.

2. Oxygen pressure—70 to 110 psi.

Note

During pulsating demands, the pressure may be as low as 65 psi.

3. Oxygen supply lever—ON.

4. System flow and mask leakage—Check.

With the mask snugly fitted to the face, breathe normally and accomplish the following checks:

  a. Place oxygen control lever to NORMAL and check for normal breathing.

  b. Place oxygen control lever to EMERGENCY and note a continuous flow with noticeable pressure increase in the mask.

  c. Place oxygen control lever to TEST and hold. A continuous flow and positive pressure increase should be felt in the mask. Hold breath to insure there is no oxygen leakage around oxygen mask. Release the control lever and note that positive pressure ceases.

  d. Check that oxygen pressure reads 70 to 110 psi after the previous check.

  e. Check that emergency oxygen pressure gage reads 1800 psi @ 70°F.

AUTOPILOT SYSTEM.

The autopilot system consists of electronic, mechanical, and hydraulic components which control the airplane during various selected modes of autopilot flight. These modes, several of which may be in operation simultaneously, are: attitude stabilization, constant mach, constant mach-altitude, navigation ground track, and constant ground track. Attitude stabilization is the basic mode and is in effect at all times when the autopilot is engaged. The other modes, when selected, merely modify the basic mode references to accomplish specific tasks. The autopilot (attitude stabilization) may be engaged with the airplane in any desired pitch and roll attitude within the limits of the primary navigation system stable table. Pitch and bank synchronizers assure that the autopilot servos are constantly synchronized with actual attitude in order to prevent transient maneuvers during engagement. Attitude stabilization will then hold the airplane at the reference pitch and roll attitude until selection of another autopilot control mode or until the pilot initiates control stick steering. The pilot can manually maneuver the airplane at any time with the control stick through the use of control stick steering without disengaging the autopilot. This feature replaces the turn and pitch knobs common to other types of autopilot systems. During normal operation of the autopilot, the control stick reflects the position of the flight control surfaces and automatic trim functions to keep the airplane automatically trimmed for one-"g" flight the same as for manual flight with the elevator control available mode selector switch in the AUTO position. Manual stick trim follow up is provided to trim the stick at any elevator position commanded by the autopilot, within the 10 degree limit of trim authority. This prevents large transients should the autopilot be disengaged with the stick out of the neutral position. The pilot can disengage the autopilot electrically by turning the autopilot engage switches off or by squeezing the control stick grip trigger switch to the RELEASE position or mechanically by actuating the autopilot servo poppets with stick force. If the autopilot poppets are actuated by stick force, the electrical functions of the system will remain active and manual stick trim follow up will be effective so that the pilot will have to return the stick to neutral after making pitch corrections and hold it there momentarily until the elevator is trimmed to the new airplane attitude. When on autopilot control, the airplane is damped in the same manner as when flying the airplane manually. Autopilot control of the airplane may be transferred to the navigator for bomb runs or for emergency operation. The autopilot servos are electrically controlled and hydraulically operated and receive hydraulic pressure from the utility hydraulic system. The servos and other autopilot components are powered by 28-volt d-c and 115-volt a-c electrical power from the 28-volt d-c power panel and the left a-c power panel.

ATTITUDE STABILIZATION (BASIC AUTOPILOT) MODE.

The attitude stabilization mode is the basic control mode upon which all other modes act to accomplish specific tasks. When engaged, the autopilot servos receive attitude error signals through the amplifier-computer assembly from the primary navigation system stable tables (PNSU or ARU as selected by the navigator). These signals are used to hold the airplane at the reference pitch and roll attitude existing at the time of autopilot engagement. Required control surface changes are made by the autopilot servos through the elevator and aileron channels. The mode requirements (type of control provided by the autopilot servos in a particular surface control system) change when any other control mode is selected, and the servos will control the airplane according to the new requirements. However, when the new mode is discontinued, the autopilot reverts back to attitude stabilization in the affected surface control system and will maintain the pitch or roll attitude that existed at the time of disengagement. For example, if the autopilot is engaged with the airplane in a twenty-degree bank, this bank angle will be held constant. If the heading constant mode is then selected, the airplane will respond by holding constant ground track; the original pitch angle will continue to be controlled by attitude stabilization and will remain unchanged. If the constant ground track mode is subsequently discontinued, the autopilot will revert back to attitude stabilization in the aileron control system, again holding a constant bank angle at the new reference wings-level attitude. The pilot may change the attitude stabilization pitch and bank references at any time by using control stick steering.

CONSTANT MACH MODE.

The constant mach mode provides cruise control for optimum range performance. When operating in this mode, the autopilot receives actual mach signals originating in the air data system. These signals are compared to a constant reference mach signal equal to the mach number existing at the time of mode selection. The resulting error signal controls pitch through the elevator control system. Airplane velocity is held at the reference mach number by varying altitude. The aileron control system remains unaffected by this mode. The pilot may increase or decrease the reference mach number in small increments by means of the autopilot airspeed control switch.

CONSTANT MACH—ALTITUDE MODE.

The constant mach-altitude mode provides for the constant mach number and constant altitude performance required by stabilized bomb runs and by air traffic control (ATC) procedures. When operating in this mode, the autopilot receives mach and barometric altitude signals originating in the air data system. These signals are compared to the reference mach and altitude signals equal to the altitude and mach number existing at the time of mode selection. The resulting mach error signals are applied to a throttle servo to maintain the reference mach number by varying engine thrust. Likewise, the resulting altitude error signals control pitch through the elevator control system to maintain the reference altitude. The aileron channel remains unaffected by this mode. The pilot may change the reference mach number in small increments by means of the autopilot airspeed control switch; he may change the reference altitude by using control stick steering. If desired, the throttle servo may be left disconnected by leaving the throttle lock lever unlocked, thus controlling mach number with manual throttle control. When operating the autopilot in this manner, only the altitude control portion of the mach-altitude mode is utilized.

Note

Since the autopilot is not specifically designed to provide a constant altitude mode, certain restrictions to its operation should be observed.

- Do not accelerate or decelerate through the transonic region using constant altitude control in the mach-altitude mode since altitude pressure errors in the air data computer could cause a slight pitch up or pitch down condition.

- Do not resume normal mach-altitude mode operation after changing mach number without first either disengaging the mach-altitude switch or depressing the control stick steering switch to the first detent, releasing the trigger, allowing 10 seconds for the throttle servo to reset; then locking the throttle lever. This is to prevent throttle transients upon relocking the throttle.

- Do not use constant mach-altitude mode when air turbulence is encountered.

HEADING NAVIGATION MODE.

When operating in this mode, the autopilot receives steering error signals from the primary navigation system. With the primary navigation system in the navigation mode (navigator's function selector knob at NAVIGATION and the navigator's auto steering switch ON) these signals will steer the airplane to follow a computed great circle ground track. In the bomb mode (navigator's function selector knob at BOMB) the airplane is steered on a computed aim-point ground track to the target by the navigation system. Required heading changes are made through the aileron control system. The elevator control system remains unaffected by this mode.

HEADING CONSTANT MODE.

In this mode (with the navigator's auto steering switch ON) the autopilot receives primary navigation

Section IV
Auxiliary Equipment

autopilot control panel

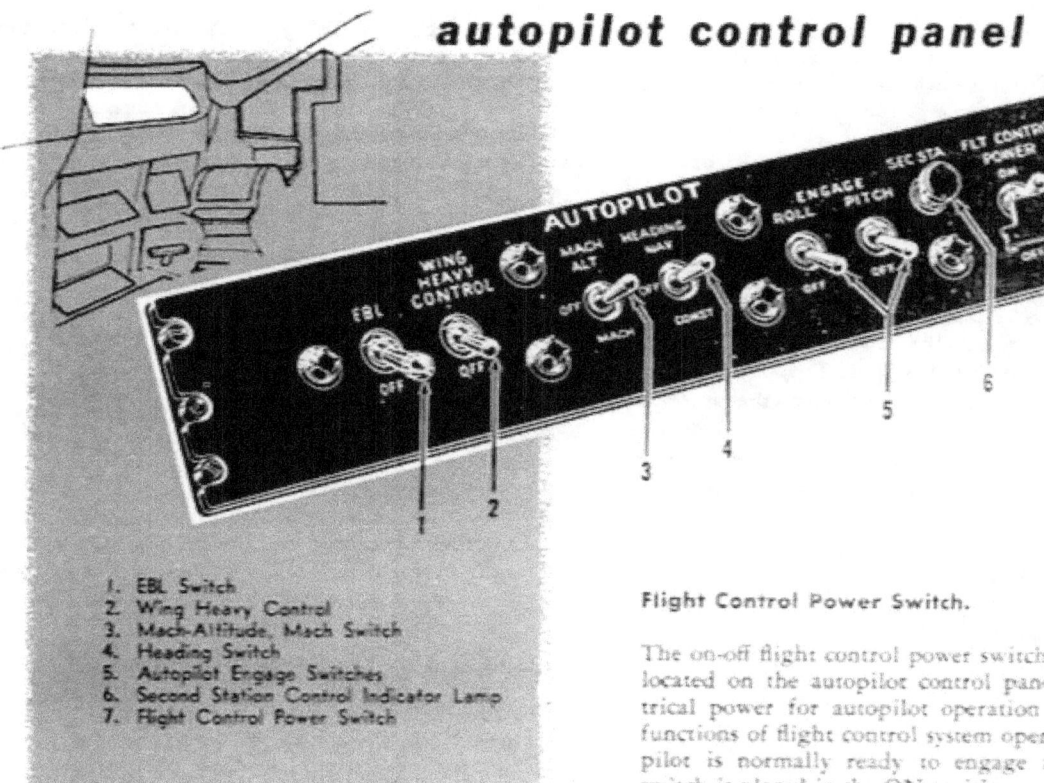

1. EBL Switch
2. Wing Heavy Control
3. Mach-Altitude, Mach Switch
4. Heading Switch
5. Autopilot Engage Switches
6. Second Station Control Indicator Lamp
7. Flight Control Power Switch

Figure 4-31.

system steering error signals which are derived from the ground track reference existing at the instant of mode selection. These signals are used to steer the airplane to follow a rhumb line constant ground track. Required heading changes are made through the aileron control system. The elevator control system remains unaffected by this mode. The pilot may change the ground track (heading) reference by using control stick steering.

CONTROLS AND INDICATORS.

Autopilot controls and indicators are located at the pilot's station. The engage and control mode switches, all located on the autopilot control panel, are spring-loaded, solenoid-held toggle switches. The entire autopilot switching circuit is electrically interlocked to prevent incompatible control modes from being energized at the same time, and to drop out all modes when the autopilot is disengaged. When a change in the panel switching combination causes power to be removed from the solenoid of a switch, the switch handle physically moves to the OFF position, thereby deactivating the associated autopilot function. A switch will not remain in the ON position until the panel switching combination allows a closed circuit to the switch solenoid.

Flight Control Power Switch.

The on-off flight control power switch (7, figure 4-31), located on the autopilot control panel, controls electrical power for autopilot operation and for certain functions of flight control system operation. The autopilot is normally ready to engage after the power switch is placed in the ON position and the navigation system stable table is properly erected. A guard must be raised in order to position the switch to OFF.

Note

Since the flight control power switch also controls electrical power to certain functions of the manual flight control system, this switch should normally remain in the ON position throughout all flights. For additional information, refer to "Flight Control System", Section I, and VII.

Autopilot Engage Switches.

Two autopilot engage switches (5, figure 4-31), are located on the autopilot control panel. One switch is marked ROLL and OFF and the other is marked PITCH and OFF. The switches operate independently of each other and may be separately engaged without affecting the other. When the switches are engaged in the ROLL and PITCH positions, the autopilot servos will engage and maintain constant roll and pitch attitude. The circuitry also allows selection of other autopilot modes. The switches will not engage unless the flight control power switch and the damper switches are ON, and the autopilot servos are synchronized with airplane attitude. The pitch autopilot channel cannot be engaged with the pitch damper

Section IV
Auxiliary Equipment

T.O. 1B-58A-1

switch OFF. The roll autopilot channel cannot be engaged with the roll or yaw damper switch or the wing heavy control switch OFF. When the engage switches are placed to OFF, the autopilot servos will disengage, all mode switches will move to OFF, and the airplane will revert to pilot-controlled flight.

Mach-Altitude, Mach Switch.

The three-position mach-altitude, mach switch (3, figure 4-31), located on the autopilot control panel, is marked MACH ALT, OFF, and MACH. When the switch is placed in the MACH ALT position and the throttle lock lever is pushed forward, the autopilot will control the airplane in the constant mach-altitude mode. If the autopilot is engaged in this mode with the throttles unlocked, the autopilot will maintain constant altitude but throttle control must be accomplished manually. When the switch is positioned to MACH, the autopilot will control the airplane in the constant mach mode. The switch will not latch in either position if the autopilot pitch engage switch is OFF.

Heading Switch.

The three-position heading switch (4, figure 4-31), located on the autopilot control panel, is marked HEADING NAV, OFF, and CONST. When the switch is placed in the NAV position, the autopilot will control the airplane in the navigation ground track mode. With the switch in the CONST position, the autopilot will control the airplane in the constant ground track mode. The heading switch will not latch in the NAV or CONST positions if the roll axis engage switch is at OFF or if the navigator's auto steering switch is at OFF. When the heading switch is placed in the OFF position, the autopilot will discontinue controlling the airplane in a ground track mode, reverting to attitude stabilization in the aileron control system.

Autopilot Trigger Switch.

The autopilot trigger switch (6, figure 1-29), located on the control stick grip, permits the pilot to disengage the autopilot without removing his hand from the stick, or to utilize control stick steering without fully disengaging the autopilot. The trigger switch has two detent positions, marked CSS (control stick steering) and RELEASE. These positions are spring-loaded to an unmarked OFF position. When the switch is squeezed to the first-detent CSS position and held, the aileron and elevator autopilot servos are deactivated, thus allowing the pilot to manually maneuver the airplane. When the switch is released from the CSS position, the autopilot will regain control and

maintain flight according to the corrected or new references. Squeezing the trigger switch all the way to the second-detent RELEASE position de-energizes the holding solenoid of the autopilot engage switches, allowing it (them) to return to OFF. This disengages all autopilot functions and places the airplane under pilot control.

Autopilot Airspeed Control Switch.

The autopilot airspeed control switch (2, figure 1-30), located on the trim control panel, is marked INC or DEC. These positions are spring-loaded to a center unmarked OFF position. Holding the switch to the INC or DEC position causes the reference mach number to increase or decrease accordingly within a range of mach no. ±0.12 at a constant rate of mach no. 0.0054 per second. In the constant mach-altitude modes, this change is accomplished through a throttle servo which drives the throttles to vary engine thrust. In the constant mach mode, the change is accomplished by pitch control through the elevator control system.

Second Station Control Indicator Lamp.

The amber second station control indicator lamp (6, figure 4-31), marked SEC STA, is located on the autopilot control panel. The lamp lights when the navigator places the tracking and flight controller selector switch in AUTOPILOT position. The lighted lamp informs the pilot that the navigator has selected AUTOPILOT and will be in control should he engage autopilot. The lamp goes out when autopilot control is returned to the pilot's station by the navigator or when the pilot depresses the autopilot trigger switch to its first detent (CSS). If the pilot causes the lamp to go out by use of the autopilot trigger switch, the navigator cannot again obtain control (light the pilot's lamp) without positioning the tracking and flight controller selector switch to some position other than AUTOPILOT, and then returning it to the AUTOPILOT position.

Manual Steering Indicator Lamp.

The amber press-to-test lamp (5, figure 4-38), marked MANUAL STEERING, is located on the navigator's auxiliary flight instrument panel. The lamp lights when the autopilot is engaged and the navigator places the tracking and flight controller selector switch in the AUTOPILOT position. The lamp goes out when autopilot control is returned to the pilot's station.

NORMAL OPERATION OF AUTOPILOT.

Refer to "Airspeed Limitations" and "Minimum Altitude Limitations," Section V, for limitations on autopilot operations.

Engaging the Autopilot.

1. Attain a safe altitude and trim the airplane to the desired attitude.

4-50

2. Check the attitude indicator for normal indications to make certain that primary navigation system is functioning properly.

3. Check that elevator control available mode switch is in the AUTO position.

4. Check that flight control power switch is ON with guard closed.

5. Check that all damper switches are ON and that dampers are operating properly.

Note

If damping in any axis is erratic or inoperative, the associated damper switch should be placed OFF. With the pitch damper switch OFF, the pitch autopilot axis cannot be engaged. With the roll or yaw damper switch OFF, the roll autopilot axis cannot be engaged. Refer to "Flight Control System," Section VII.

6. Wing heavy control switch—ON.

7. Gain selector switch—AUTO.
Check that gain selector switch is in the AUTO position.

Note

If it is desired to engage the autopilot using the standby gains (gain selector switch at either HIGH SPEED or LOW SPEED), check first that airplane is operating within the correct speed and altitude range. Refer to "Flight Control System", Section I for a description of the gain selector switch. Refer to "Flight Control System", Section VII, for specific procedures to follow in case of mach-altitude gain adjustment failure.

8. Place the engage switches to ROLL and PITCH positions.

Note

- If an engage switch does not remain engaged, while the flight control power switch and damper switches are ON, it is possible that the autopilot servos are not fully synchronized with airplane attitude. Fly a steady attitude while holding the engage switch up for several seconds. This should be sufficient time to allow the servos to synchronize, permitting the engage switch to latch in the engaged position.

- Mild low amplitude stick jitter may be noted when the autopilot is engaged and the LRC system is transmitting in the 11 to 14 megacycle frequency range.

Selecting Autopilot Control Modes.

After the autopilot is initially engaged in attitude stabilization, the pilot may select a single control mode or a combination of comparable modes by means of the mode switches on the autopilot control panel. A mode affecting the elevator control system (constant mach or constant mach-altitude) may be selected simultaneously with a mode affecting the aileron control system (constant ground track or navigation ground track). However, two elevator control modes or two aileron control modes cannot be selected simultaneously. If an attempt is made to do so, one of the incompatible mode switches will automatically return to OFF. The following procedures are for selecting each control mode after the autopilot is initially engaged.

Selecting the Constant Mach Mode. Manually maneuver the airplane to achieve the desired mach number and altitude for optimum range. Then place the mach-altitude, mach switch to MACH. If it is desired to increase or decrease the reference mach number while operating in this mode, hold the autopilot airspeed control switch to INC or DEC, as applicable. The reference mach number can be increased or decreased within a range of ± mach no. 0.12 at a constant rate of mach no. 0.0054 per second with the autopilot airspeed control switch.

WARNING

Do not use constant mach mode below 2000 feet absolute altitude. Sudden loss of thrust or malfunction of the autopilot and/or flight control system when using constant mach could result in a sudden pitch down of the airplane with rapid loss of altitude.

This mode of autopilot operation may be used for cruise-climb to obtain optimum performance. During operation in the constant mach mode for cruise-climb, the altitude should be closely monitored and compared with optimum altitude obtained from the charts in Appendix I, Part 4.

Section IV
Auxiliary Equipment

T.O. 1B-58A-1

Selecting the Constant Mach-Altitude Mode. Manually maneuver the airplane to the desired altitude, using control stick steering, and trim for level flight at the desired mach number. Then place the mach-altitude, mach switch in the MACH ALT position. Adjust the throttles to achieve symmetric thrust and lock the throttle lock lever. If it is desired to increase or decrease the reference mach number while oeprating in this mode, hold the autopilot airspeed control switch to INC or DEC, as applicable. If asymmetric power conditions develop as a result of changing the reference mach number, thrust may be equalized by unlocking the throttle lock lever, readjusting the throttles, and relocking the lever. Constant altitude control may be selected by placing the mach-altitude, mach switch in the MACH ALT position and leaving the throttle lock lever unlocked, or by unlocking the throttles if in the constant mach-altitude mode.

Note

When using the mach-altitude mode, do not accelerate or decelerate through the transonic region since altitude pressure errors in the air data computer could cause a slight pitch up or pitch down condition.

If constant mach-altitude mode operation is to be resumed after changing mach number by manual throttle control, depress the control stick steering switch to the first detent, allow 10 seconds for the throttle servo to reset, release the triggrs, then lock the throttle lever. This is to prevent large amplitude throttle transients upon relocking the throttle. If the throttle lock is applied without first using control stick steering or disengaging the mode, transients may result. This applies only to resuming normal mach-altitude operation after utilizing the constant altitude feature of the autopilot.

Selecting the Heading Navigation Mode. Check with navigator that the primary navigation system is in auto steering. Then place the heading switch to NAV.

Note

If the steering error needle on the pilot's data indicator is not centered the airplane will immediately bank towards the steering error needle. Though the initial rate of roll is higher than normally used while manually maneuvering the airplane, the bank limiter will not allow the stabilized bank angle to exceed 30 degrees. If the heading switch is selected to NAV while the airplane is in a bank toward the steering error, the airplane may momentarily increase bank angle beyond 30 degrees but will then return to a stabilized bank angle of 30 degrees or less.

Selecting the Heading Constant Mode. Manually maneuver the airplane to the desired heading and level the wings, using control stick steering. Check with navigator that the primary navigation system is in auto steering. Then place the heading switch to CONST.

Control Stick Steering Operation.

If it is desired to change the autopilot attitude, heading, or altitude references while operating in any control mode, squeeze and hold the autopilot trigger switch to the first detent CSS position and maneuver the airplane with the control stick as in manual flight. When the desired conditions are attained, release the trigger switch. The autopilot will resume control according to the newly selected references. While the pilot is using control stick steering, the switches on the autopilot control panel will remain in their selected positions. The use of control stick steering also will remove autopilot control from the navigator's station.

Navigator's Station Control Operation.

After the autopilot is initially engaged by the pilot, control may be transferred to the navigator's station by placing the navigator's tracking and flight controller selector switch to AUTOPILOT. The autopilot will revert to attitude stabilization mode when control goes to second station. Check that the manual steering lamp lights. The second station control indicator lamp at the pilot's station should light also. All mode switches will turn OFF. Bank angle limiting will be effective and will restrict the bank angle to 30 degrees. Maneuver the airplane by means of the navigator's tracking and flight control stick. If the pilot initiates control stick steering, autopilot control is transferred back to the pilot. Control may be regained at the second station only after the pilot releases the trigger switch and the tracking and flight controller selector switch is moved out of, then back to the AUTOPILOT position. Autopilot control is also transferred back to the pilot when the navigator moves the controller selector switch out of the AUTOPILOT position. Since the navigator does not have control of engine throttles or pitch attitude authority limits, pitch commands using the flight controller handle should be restricted to small changes in pitch attitude.

4-52

Disengaging the Autopilot.

To disengage all autopilot functions and place the airplane under pilot control, either squeeze the autopilot trigger switch all the way back to the second detent RELEASE position or place the autopilot engage switches to OFF. In either case, all mode switches will move to OFF.

EMERGENCY OPERATION OF AUTOPILOT.

When an autopilot malfunction occurs, the autopilot may be disengaged electrically by squeezing the autopilot trigger switch to the second detent RELEASE position. If the autopilot fails to disengage electrically or in the event of a hardover malfunction, stick force may be applied to actuate the autopilot servo poppets. An abrupt force of 15 to 25 pounds is required to actuate the aileron servo poppets. An abrupt or steady force of 45 to 70 pounds is required to actuate the elevator servo poppets.

Note

Actuating the autopilot servo poppets by stick force disengages the autopilot servos only; therefore, manual trim follow-up will remain effective until the autopilot engage switches are placed in the OFF position. The pilot will be able to manually maneuver the airplane after the poppets have been actuated; however, after making pitch corrections, the stick will have to be returned to neutral and held there until manual trim follow-up trims the elevator to the new attitude.

CAUTION

If a force of 105 to 120 pounds is inadvertently exerted on the stick while actuating the elevator servo poppet, the force link will actuate, causing the elevator ratio changer to drive to maximum elevator available position and the structural protection that is normally provided in automatic mode of operation of the flight control system will no longer exist.

If the autopilot poppets have been actuated, the autopilot servos may be reset by squeezing the trigger switch to the CSS position and then releasing it or by placing the engage switches to OFF. The autopilot can then be re-engaged in the normal manner. Refer to Normal Operation of Autopilot, this Section. If the malfunction is not severe, the gain selector switch may be placed in the appropriate position. Refer to "Flight Control System," Section VII, for specific procedures to follow for mach-altitude gain adjustment failure. If the malfunction is still present upon autopilot re-engagement, disengage the autopilot and do not attempt further autopilot emergency procedures.

AUXILIARY FLIGHT REFERENCE SYSTEM.

An auxiliary flight reference system (AFRS) provides attitude and heading information for pilot reference. The system can operate independently, or in conjunction with the primary navigation system (PNS). The system consists of a number of electronic packages which receive, compute and transmit gyroscopic attitude and heading reference signals for pilot and navigator reference. Basic components of the auxiliary flight reference system consist of an MD-1 vertical gyro, a rate switching gyro, a directional gyro, a servo amplifier, and a remote compass transmitter (flux valve). Controls for the system are on the auxiliary flight reference system control panel, located on the navigator's right console. A control for selection of reference signals is provided in the pilot's station. The MD-1 vertical gyro establishes the vertical reference line from which pitch and roll deviation is measured. The gyro is unlimited in roll indication but is limited to ± 82 degrees in pitch. Any change in airplane attitude with respect to the vertical reference line is detected by the vertical gyro and electrically transmitted to the pilot's MM-3 attitude indicator. For further information, refer to "Instruments," Section I. The directional gyro, servo amplifier, and flux valve operate together as the J-4 compass system to provide heading reference for the pilot's and navigator's BDH indicators and pilot's course indicator. This system operates either as a gyro-stabilized magnetic compass (MAG mode) or as a directional gyro (DG mode). The two modes, MAG and DG, provide accurate heading reference for all latitudes. In the magnetic mode, the system is basically a directional gyro slaved to the remote compass transmitter. This mode is designed for use at latitudes up to 70 degrees. In the area of the magnetic poles, the direction of the earth's magnetic field becomes vertical rather than horizontal to such an extent that the MAG mode is no longer reliable and the directional gyro mode should be used. In the DG mode, the system is freed from the remote compass transmitter and operates as a free directional gyro indicating an arbitrary gyro heading, and is corrected for apparent gyro drift due to the earth's rotation. The random drift (precession rate) of the gyro

Section IV
Auxiliary Equipment

T.O. 1B-58A-1

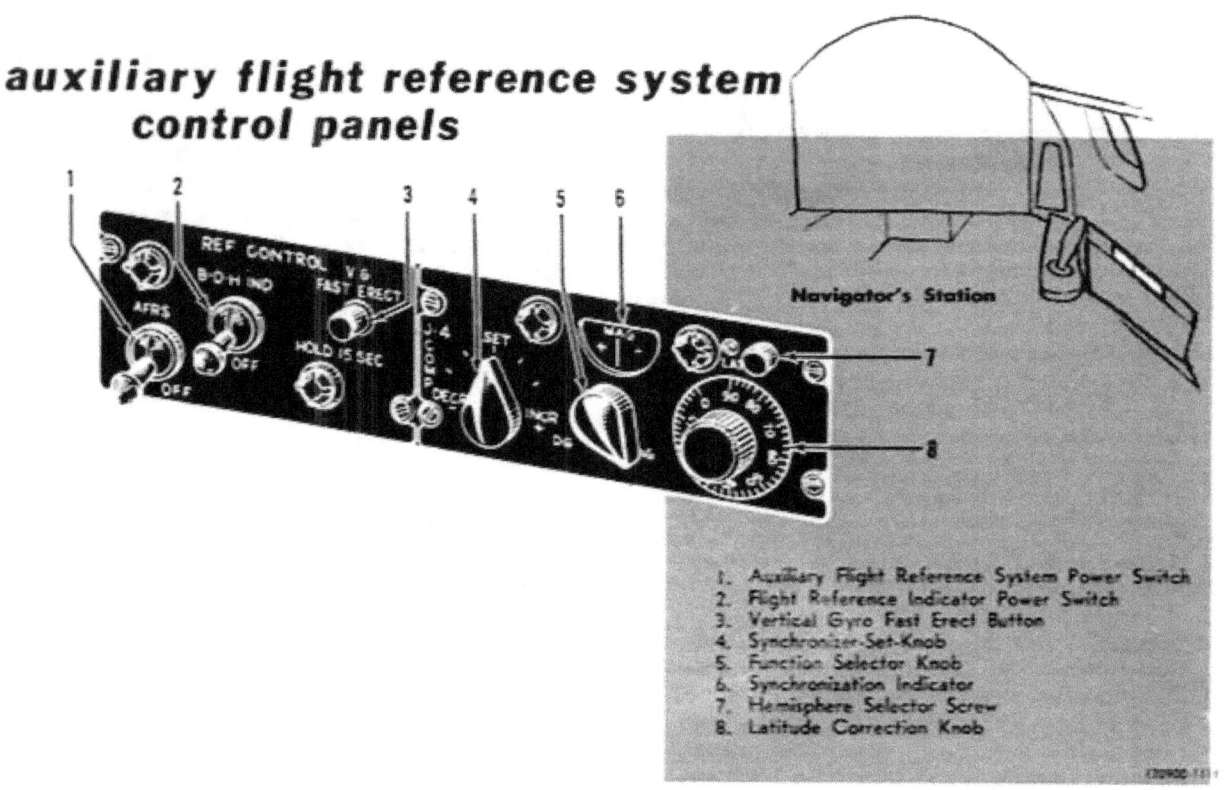

Figure 4-32.

in this mode of operation should not exceed (≡) 3 degrees per hour. This mode may be used at all latitudes but is most useful when operating in the polar region or when the magnetic field is weak or distorted. Compensation of the MD-1 gyro and J-4 compass for inherent errors due to turning the airplane is accomplished by the rate switching gyro. The AFRS provides heading information for the pilot's and navigator's BDH indicators and the pilot's course indicator when the pilot's heading selector switch is in the J-4 position. Attitude information is furnished directly to the pilot's MM-3 attitude indicator. The auxiliary flight reference system operates on 115-volt, three-phase, 400 cycle, alternating current and 28-volt direct current.

CONTROLS AND INDICATORS.

Heading Selector Switch.

The heading selector switch (10, figure 1-34) located on the pilot's forward left console, has two positions marked PNS and J-4. Placing the switch in the PNS position provides heading signals to the pilot's and navigator's BDH indicators and the pilot's course indicator from the primary navigation system. In the J-4 position, the pilot's and navigator's BDH indicators and the pilot's course indicator receives heading signals from the J-4 compass components.

4-54

Auxiliary Flight Reference System Power Switch.

The auxiliary flight reference system (AFRS) power switch (1, figure 4-32) located on the auxiliary flight reference system control panel is marked AFRS and OFF. Placing the switch in the AFRS position supplies power to the auxiliary flight reference system and to the pilot's MM-3 attitude indicator.

Flight Reference Indicator Power Switch.

The flight reference indicator power switch (2, figure 4-32) located on the auxiliary flight reference system control panel is marked BDH-IND and OFF. Placing the switch in the BDH-IND position supplies power to the pilot's and navigator's BDH indicators. The switch must be in BDH-IND position for either mode of operation selected by the heading selector switch.

Vertical Gyro Fast Erect Button

The vertical gyro fast erect button (3, figure 4-32), located on the auxiliary flight reference system control panel, provides a means of fast erecting the MD-1 vertical gyro. The button is marked VG FAST ERECT. Normally, the vertical gyro takes approximately 1.5 minutes to erect after power is supplied to the system. However, in the event a fast erection is desired, the fast erect button may be depressed and held approximately 15 seconds after an initial warmup of 45 seconds. The attitude warning flag on the pilot's attitude indicator will appear when the VG fast erect button is depressed if the reference selector switch is in AFRS.

Function Selector Knob.

The function selector knob (5, figure 4-32), located on the auxiliary flight reference system control panel, is used to select the mode of operation for the J-4 compass. The knob is marked MAG and DG. Placing the knob to MAG position selects the magnetic mode of operation. Automatic fast sychronizing takes place within 10 seconds after the selector knob is placed to MAG or each time the selector knob is turned from MAG to DG, then back to MAG. Placing the selector knob to the DG position selects the directional gyro mode and covers the sychronization indicator.

Hemisphere Selector Screw.

The hemisphere selector screw (7, figure 4-32), located on the auxiliary flight reference system control panel, has a small window beside the knob which displays N or S to indicate the hemisphere selected. The position determines the direction of drift correction for the directional gyro; therefore, the position selected must correspond with the hemisphere designation of the area in which the airplane is operating.

Latitude Correction Knob.

The latitude correction knob (8, figure 4-32), located on the auxiliary flight reference system control panel, is marked with latitudes from 0 to 90 degrees. Setting the knob to the latitude at which flight is being made determines the rate of gyro drift correction when the function selector knob is in the DG position.

Synchronizer-Set Knob.

The synchronizer-set knob (4, figure 4-32), located on the auxiliary flight reference system control panel, provides a means of manually synchronizing the directional gyro with the remote compass when the function selector knob is in MAG mode, and to set in desired heading on the BDH indicator when the knob is in the DG mode. The knob is marked DECR— (decrease minus) in the full left position, INCR+ (increase plus) in the full right position, and SET in the center position. The knob is spring-loaded to the SET position from both left and right positions. Rotating the knob in clockwise direction, toward the INCR— position, will cause a clockwise heading change on the BDH indicator. The opposite will occur if the knob is moved to the DECR— position. Rate of sychronization with the directional gyro rotation can be governed by moving the knob either direction to the first white marker (3 degrees per second) or to the second white marker (approximately 42 degrees per second). When in the DG mode of operation, the direction of movement of the knob is determined by whether an increased or decreased heading is desired. When in the MAG mode, the direction of rotation of the knob is determined by the synchronization indicator needle.

Synchronization Indicator.

The synchronization indicator (6, figure 4-32) is a window indicator on the auxiliary flight reference system control panel that indicates whether or not the directional gyro and remote compass are synchronized. With the J-4 compass operating in the MAG mode, the top center portion of the window is marked MAG, the left side of the window is marked + (plus) and the right side is marked — (minus). A needle in the center of the window will deflect either left (+) or right (—) if the directional gyro is not synchronized with the remote compass. If the needle is deflected to the plus side of the window, the synchronizer-set knob must be rotated toward the INCR+ mark to return the needle to center (null). With the needle centered, synchronization is complete. In the DG mode of operation, the indicator window is covered with a flag marked DG. Synchronization is not possible until the mode of operation is returned to MAG. In normal operation the needle will fluctuate slightly, except during turns.

NORMAL OPERATION OF THE AUXILIARY FLIGHT REFERENCE SYSTEM.

Put the AFRS into operation as follows:
 1. Flight reference indicator power switch—BDH-IND.
 2. Auxiliary flight reference system power switch—AFRS.

A period of approximately 1.5 minutes is normally required for erection of the MD-1 vertical gyro. The directional gyro requires 2 minutes warmup time. After 2 minutes have been allowed for warmup, select the mode of operation (MAG or DG) for the J-4 compass as follows:

Magnetic Mode.

 1. Function selector knob—MAG.
Automatic fast synchronizing takes place within 10 seconds after the selector knob is placed to MAG, or each time the selector knob is turned from MAG to DG, then back to MAG.

CAUTION

When turning the function selector knob from DG to MAG, allow at least 10 seconds for the thermal delay relay in the amplifier to cool, before recycling through another DG to MAG.

 2. Synchronization indicator—check.
Check the synchronization indicator to see if the system is synchronized. The indicator needle should align itself closely with the center index showing no synchronizing error. If a synchronizing error is indicated, to align the indicator needle closely with the center index of the indicator, use the synchronizer set knob for manual synchronization or recycle the function selector knob for fast synchronization.

Directional Gyro Mode.

 1. Hemisphere selector screw—Select desired hemisphere.
Select the desired hemisphere with selector screw and check the N or S indication in the hemisphere selector window.
 2. Latitude correction knob—Select local latitude.
Select knob to present latitude and reset as changes occur during flight.
 3. Function selector knob—DG.
 4. Synchronizer knob—Set.
Set or verify desired heading on BDH indicator by use of synchronizer knob.

WEAPONS CONTROL SYSTEM (AN/ASQ-42).

The airplane is equipped with an AN/ASQ-42 integrated navigation-bombing system. The system consists of the following subsystems: an AN/APN-113 Doppler radar, an AN/APN-110 radio altimeter, an astrotracker, a computation and stabilization system, a search radar, a ballistics computer, and malfunction detection and switching equipment. Information on this equipment can be found under "Primary Navigation System" and "Bombing System" of this section.

PRIMARY NAVIGATION SYSTEM.

The primary navigation system, controlled from the navigator's station, guides the airplane over a great circle course to any desired destination without visual references and with a minimum of radio-radar transmission. It is assisted by the bombing system during bomb run, which enables it to maintain a correct bombing course and to accomplish automatic weapon release. Two modes of operation are provided: navigation and bombing. The navigation and bombing modes are used for navigation missions. For bombing missions, the bombing mode is used during the bomb run, the navigation mode being used for guidance to and from the target area. Automatic radar photography can be accomplished whenever the system search radar is not being used for navigation checks. The primary navigation system is basically a Doppler-inertial system using an astrotracker for a standard heading reference. Aircraft course and position are continuously computed by a precise dead reckoning operation, which may be checked and corrected by periodic search radar sightings. Altitude above terrain is obtained by a radio al-

Section IV
Auxiliary Equipment

navigator's station (typical)

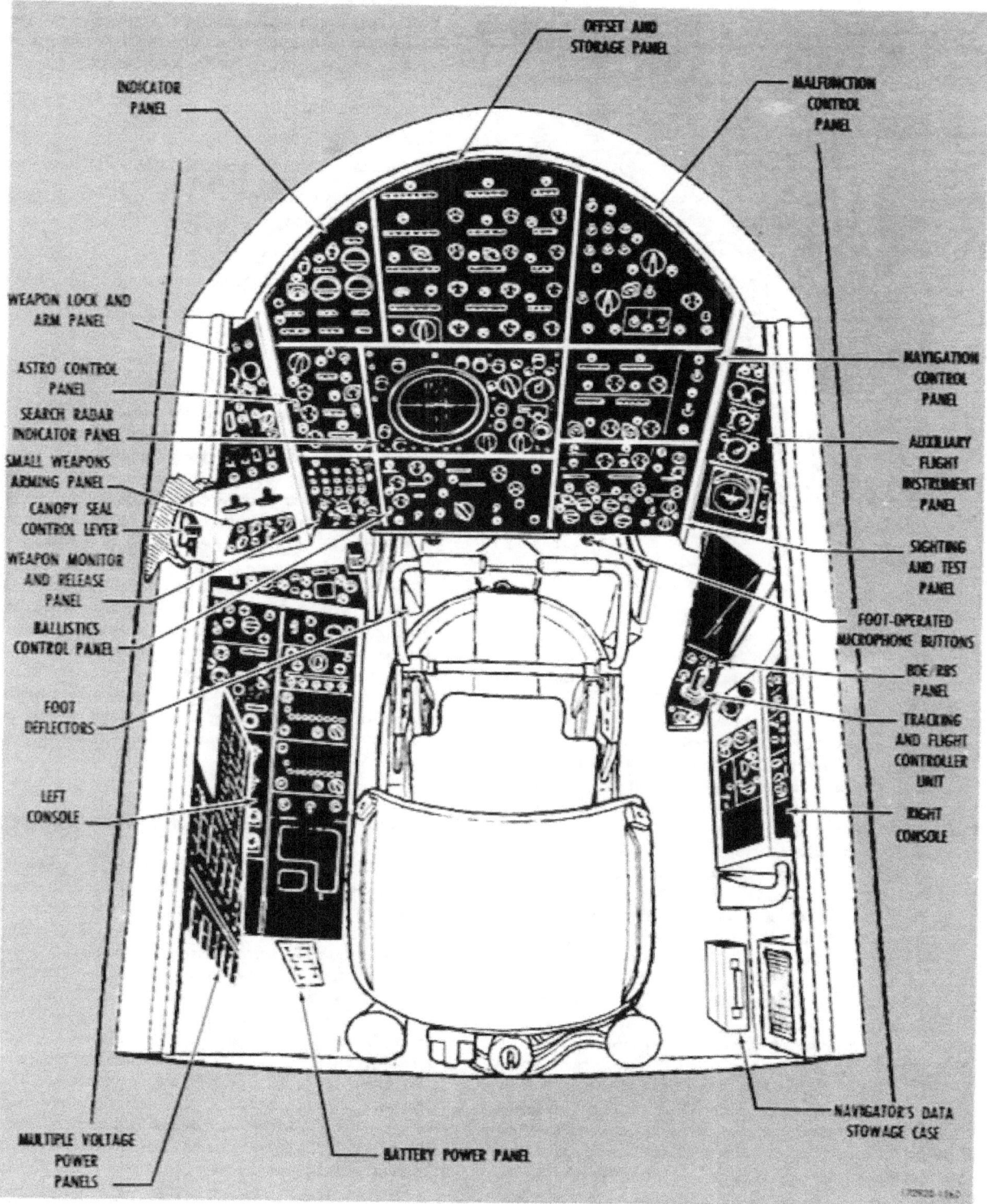

Figure 4-33.

pilot's data indicator

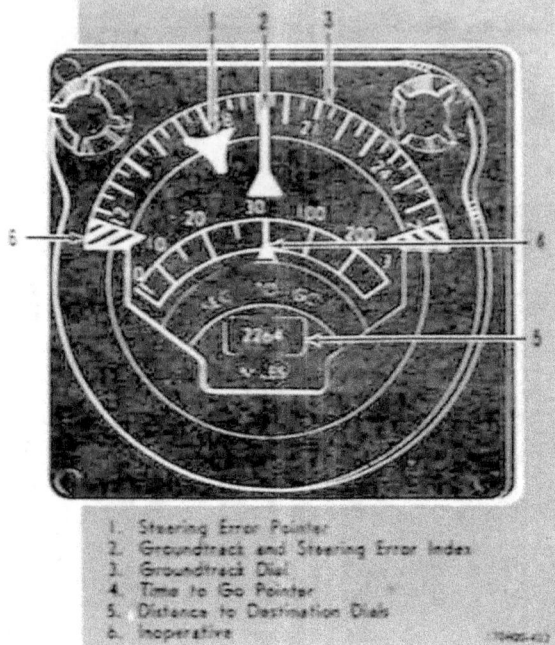

Figure 4-34.

timeter. All radiating equipment may be operated intermittently if desired, without seriously degrading system accuracy. Automatic great circle steering is performed in the navigation mode. In the bomb mode, rhumb line steering is performed, suitably altered to allow for wind drift and Coriolis effects on the pod after release. Evasive action may be taken in the target area. Transverse coordinate operation is provided for accurate polar navigation. A pilot's data indicator (figure 4-34) at the pilot's station indicates groundtrack, steering error (navigation mode), steering error for weapon release (bomb mode), time-to-go and distance to destination or target. The navigator is supplied distance to destination, a radar view of the terrain ahead, present latitude and longitude, true heading, barometric altitude, radio altitude, terrain elevation, groundspeed, true airspeed, star data, and malfunction indications. The heart of the system is the primary stable table, (PNSU) which supplies attitude, heading, and velocity data to other portions of the system. This table is described as being erect when at plumb-bob vertical. While this is a necessary condition, it is not the only critical one. The table must also be kept positioned properly in azimuth so that the accelerometers are correctly oriented and a true heading indication may be supplied for the DR process. Once erect, the table is kept stable by the properties of, and signals from, the gyros, accelerometers, earth rate computer, and astrotracker or flux valve. The auxiliary stable table (ARU) is an alternate source of attitude, heading, and velocity, though somewhat less accurate than the primary, and is normally kept in a standby condition. The system must accomplish and maintain a plumb-bob vertical for one of the stable tables before any of the following functions can begin, or continue once begun.

1. Attitude indication (PNS reference)
2. Astrotracker operation
3. Automatic dead reckoning (Present Position)
4. Autopilot operation
5. Auto radar photography
6. Course computing
7. Steering error (PDI and autopilot)
8. Time to go
9. Groundtrack
10. Auto ballistic release.

Many of the control knobs are associated with motor driven indicator-potentiometer linkages (powered only in STANDBY or beyond) that are set at low speed by applying a slight rotary pressure on the knob, in the direction rotation is desired. Additional pressure increases the speed. Braking devices give immediate stops without overrun when the knob is released. All latitude and longitude knobs, plus sidereal hour angle and star declination knobs, have this feature. Manual setting is accomplished by pushing the knob in and turning in the desired direction. The knobs cannot be pushed in during the slewing process. The primary navigation system is divided functionally into the following subsystems: computation and stabilization (inertial), Doppler radar, astrotracker, search radar, radio altimeter, and malfunction detection and switching.

COMPUTATION AND STABILIZATION SYSTEM.

The computation and stabilization system provides the airplane with inertial guidance facilities and computer functions necessary for normal navigation system operation. The system consists of an analog computer, coupled with a continuously compensated gyro stabilized stable table with accelerometers, and interconnected with the Doppler radar, search radar, astrotracker, radio altimeter, air data, and flux valve systems. Using a combination of preset values, inertial sensing, Doppler data, air data signals, search radar and astro fixes, and flux valve information, the system derives true heading, groundspeed, groundtrack, true airspeed, distance to destination, great circle steering signals, navigation error, and present position in both true and transverse coordinates. In the bomb mode, the system works with the bombing system ballistics computer to derive steering signals for the bomb runs and compute and deliver a release point signal.

navigator's left console (typical)

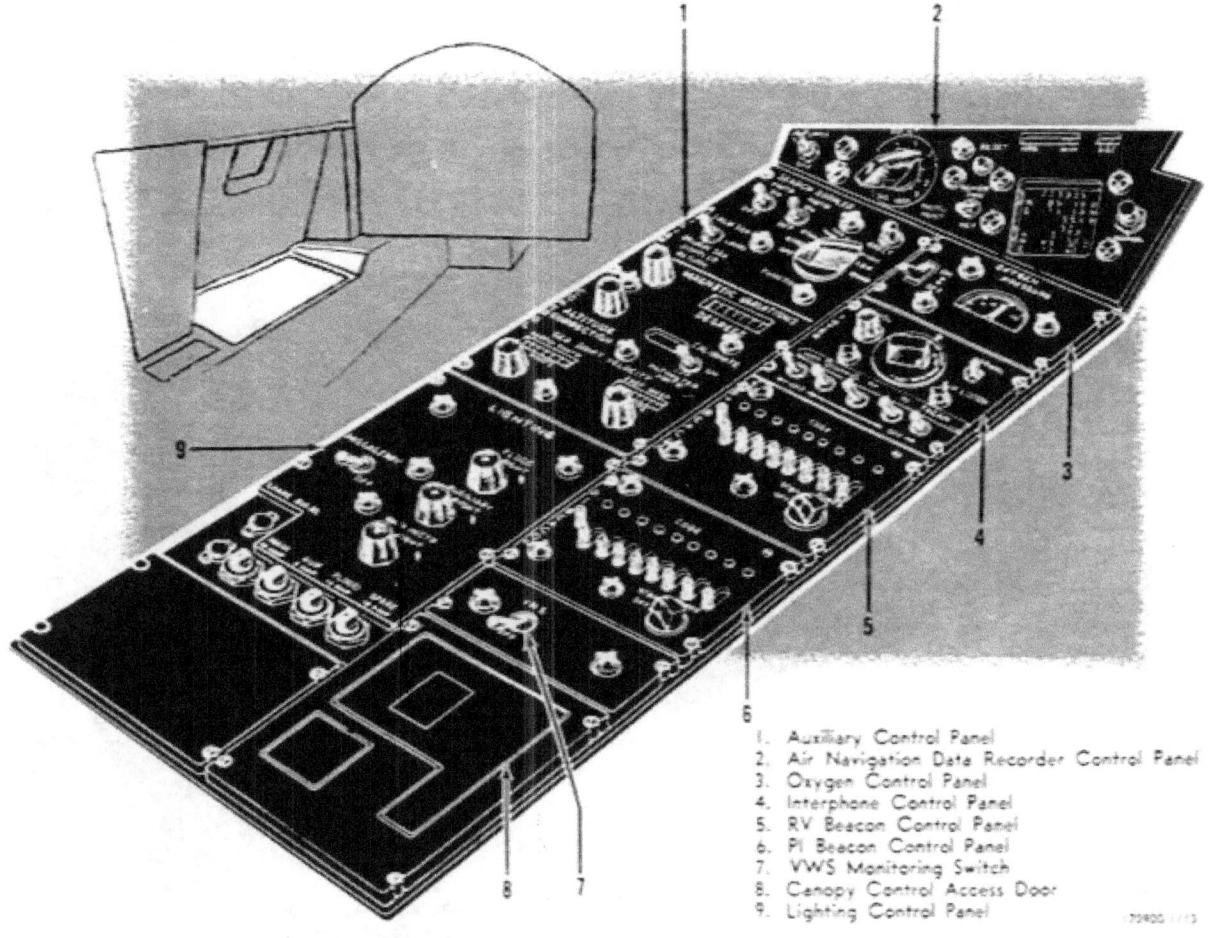

1. Auxiliary Control Panel
2. Air Navigation Data Recorder Control Panel
3. Oxygen Control Panel
4. Interphone Control Panel
5. RV Beacon Control Panel
6. PI Beacon Control Panel
7. VWS Monitoring Switch
8. Canopy Control Access Door
9. Lighting Control Panel

Figure 4-35.

ASTROTRACKER (KS-39).

The astrotracker provides a drift-free heading reference for the navigation system (PNS stable tables supply attitude reference for tracker operation). The equipment consists of a telescope-type star and sun tracker capable of the search and tracking of celestial bodies within a range of —4 to +78 degrees in altitude and 360 degrees in azimuth. The photo sensitivity response of the astrotracker is of an S-4 magnitude. The astrotracker provides automatic heading information by tracking the sun or a star whenever weather conditions permit celestial observation. Present position data must be correct within 120 minutes, and true heading must be correct within 2 degrees, in order to obtain a lock. A series of interchangeable filters provide compensation for the different optical conditions required for sun tracking, star tracking, and star tracking through an aurora display. Greatest accuracy is attained by tracking stars below 50 degrees in altitude.

Note

The reliability of present position monitoring from astrotracker data varies widely dependent on the quality of the particular system in use. Periodic oscillations in computer system vertical reference, velocity, stabilization and/or astrotracker malfunctions may yield highly erroneous celestial data.

Section IV
Auxiliary Equipment

T.O. 1B-58A-1

navigator's right console

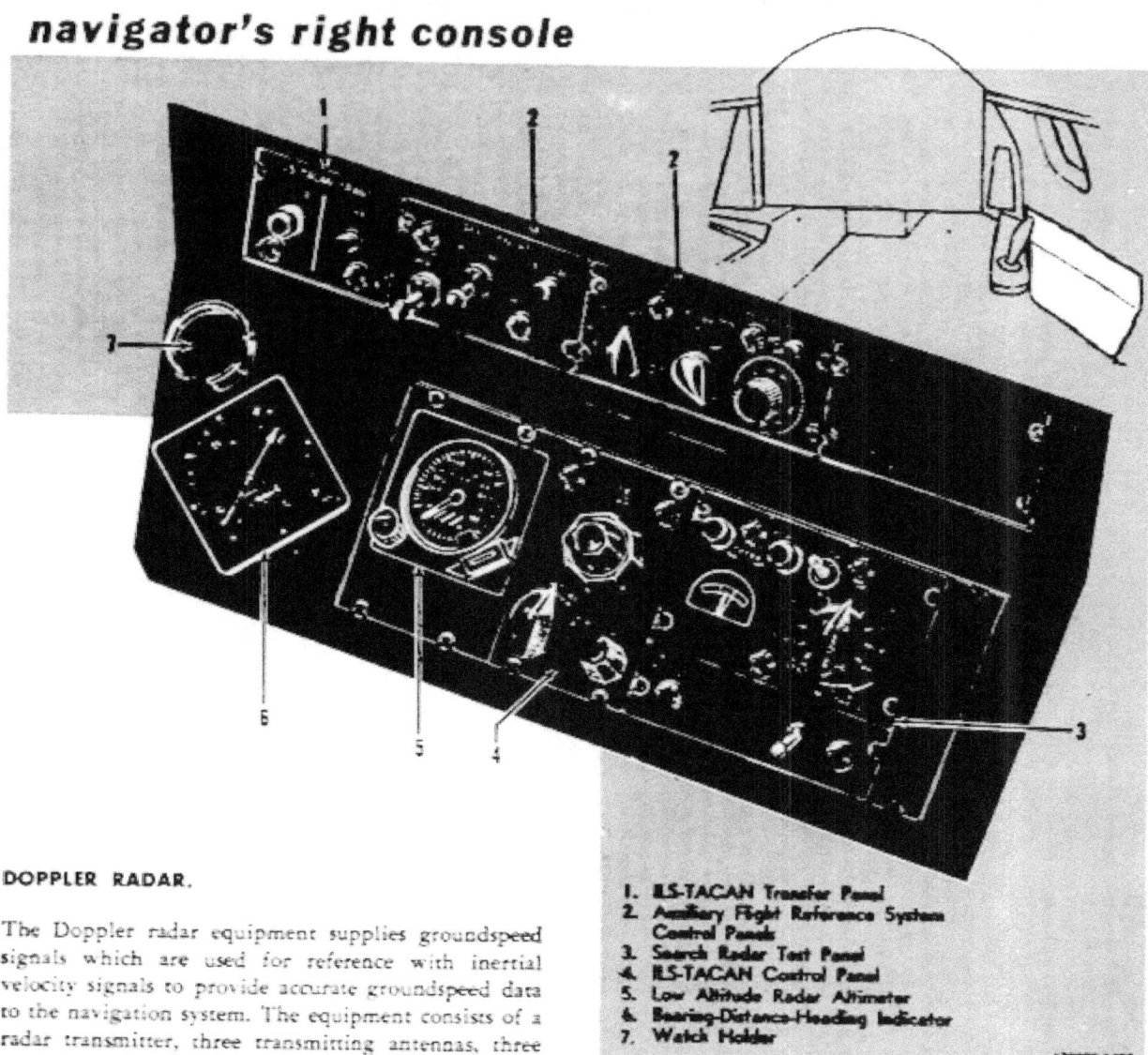

1. ILS-TACAN Transfer Panel
2. Auxiliary Flight Reference System Control Panels
3. Search Radar Test Panel
4. ILS-TACAN Control Panel
5. Low Altitude Radar Altimeter
6. Bearing-Distance-Heading Indicator
7. Watch Holder

Figure 4-36.

DOPPLER RADAR.

The Doppler radar equipment supplies groundspeed signals which are used for reference with inertial velocity signals to provide accurate groundspeed data to the navigation system. The equipment consists of a radar transmitter, three transmitting antennas, three receiving antennas, a radar receiver, and a velocity computer. Provision is made for surface feature variation by compensating circuits selectable for calm sea, rough sea, or land returns. Sea returns may be further corrected by the sea drift velocity knobs.

SEARCH RADAR.

The search radar, operable in both automatic and manual (independent of computer functions) modes, provides a correction to the computed aircraft present position based on a radar observation of a known point on the earth (a fixpoint or target). It also has provisions for manual radar bombing and aiding tanker rendezvous operations. The equipment consists of a radar transmitter, antenna, receiver, indicator console, and radar photo unit. The equipment can provide a continuous view of the terrain ahead, if desired, and at the same time furnish accurate fixpoints for position correction. If non-radiating flight is desired the transmitter may be kept in STBY position until near the fixpoint since the crosshair distance is shown on the crosshair distance indicator. Unknown or previously unmapped landmarks in the flight path may be radar photographed, and the latitude and longitude recorded. A single radar photo may be made at any time, or continuous striptype radar photographs may be made, with controllable overlap, range, and threshold.

4-60

RADIO ALTIMETER.

The radio altimeter provides altitude above terrain information which is used to calibrate altitude above sea level when flying over terrain of known elevation. The equipment consists of a transmitter, antenna, receiver, and control unit. Automatic self-calibration (internal circuitry only), which requires 4 seconds, is accomplished each time the transmitter is turned on, and occurs once every 15 minutes while operating. The calibration is made known to the operator by means of the calibration and malfunction warning lamps located in the dial of the altitude above terrain indicator, which is lighted while calibration is in progress. A continuous light indicates a radio altimeter malfunction. The accuracy tolerance of the radio altimeter is ±250 feet from 500 feet above the terrain up to the maximum altitude capability of the airplane.

WARNING

- The radio altimeter may be erroneous below 750 feet above the terrain. When below this altitude it may oscillate rapidly or indicate a multiple of the actual altitude, therefore, the system should not be relied upon below 750 feet above the terrain.

- Terrain clearance greater than actually exists may be indicated by the radio altimeter when flying over great depths of ice and snow. This is due to the fact that radio and radar waves tend to penetrate the surface of snow and ice fields.

MALFUNCTION DETECTION AND SWITCHING.

A malfunction may become evident through readings of the various indicators on the navigation system panels. The malfunction detection and switching equipment provides a means of tracing the cause of a malfunction to some particular part of the primary navigation system and to initiate switching that will enable the system to operate despite the malfunction. The equipment is designed either to bypass a malfunctioning unit by using an alternate mode of operation, or to switch in an auxiliary unit. The equipment consists of five malfunction test knobs, a test good lamp, a test bad lamp, various circuits, and switches for comparison, substitution and bypassing, and spare servos.

AUXILIARY CONTROL PANEL.

Function Selector Knob.

The function selector knob (9, figure 4-37) located on the auxiliary control panel, turns the entire navigation system on or off, and selects the mode of operation. The knob has seven positions, marked OFF, GYRO, STANDBY, TAXI & TAKEOFF, NAVIGATION, CBP, and BOMB. When the knob is in the GYRO position, heater power is routed to the gyros and accelerometers, with the remaining system power off. Manual search radar may be operated in GYRO if the search power switch is in the XMTG position. When the knob is advanced to the STANDBY position, system power is turned on, and gyro (table) erection begins. The erect indicator lamp will light in 20±6 seconds, indicating start of the rapid erect cycle. In 27±6 seconds, the attitude indicator may assume a dumped position, indicating application of plate power. In 42±5 seconds the various odometer-type indicators (true heading, etc.) will begin to function. Standby self test inputs are inserted when the function selector knob is at STANDBY and the malfunction test selector knobs are not zeroed. The groundspeed indicator will be driven to between 218 and 258 knots, groundtrack to TH plus 45° ±2°, and altitude above sea level to between 35,000 and 37,000 feet, with the altitude correction knob centered, returning to normal at end of rapid erect if all test selector knobs are zeroed. During the rapid erect cycle the tables are restrained by the reduction or removal of certain voltages required in full system operation. At the end of approximately 6 minutes the rapid erect cycle ends, and if any of the five malfunction test knobs are off zero, the erect indicator lamp will go out at this time. By zeroing these knobs after this lamp goes out, the lamp may be used to monitor accelerometer—Zero output (lamp out at approximately 10 knots or less). For warmup time required to erect to a usable vertical refer to T.O. 1B-58A-1-2. When the function selector knob is advanced to the TAXI & TAKEOFF position, the system operates in the pure inertial mode, prior to Doppler lock. While in this position actual heading, groundspeed, groundtrack, and present position should be indicated. When the knob is advanced to the NAVIGATION position, the entire system is operative, with continuous great circle computing and great circle steering signals. When the knob is advanced to the BOMB position, great circle operation ceases, and the navigation system, coupled with the free-fall bombing equipment, sets up and maintains a rhumb line course which will bring the airplane to the proper point for automatic bomb release. The knob must be raised slightly in order to turn it back to TAXI & TAKE-OFF (or lower positions) from NAVIGATION. The CBP position is inoperative.

4-61

Section IV
Auxiliary Equipment

T.O. 1B-58A-1

auxiliary control panel

1. Sea Drift Velocity Knob (2)
2. Sea Drift Velocity Indicator (2)
3. Altitude Correction Knob
4. Magnetic Variation Knob
5. Doppler Return Switch
6. Search Power Switch
7. Doppler Transmitter Switch
8. Erect Indicator Lamp
9. Function Selector Knob
10. Magnetic Variation Indicator
11. Radio Altimeter Switch

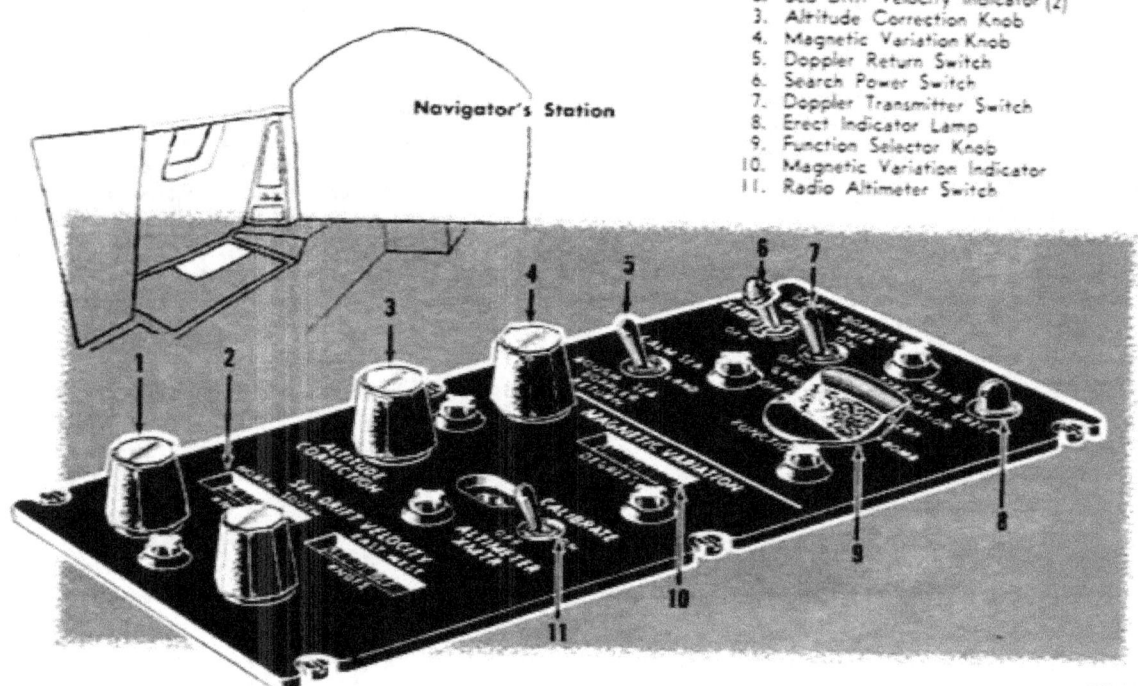

Figure 4-37.

Seach Power Switch.

The search power switch (6, figure 4-37), located on the auxiliary control panel, is marked OFF, STBY, and XMTG. When the search power switch is OFF all hydraulic system demands by the search radar antenna are eliminated. When the switch is in STBY, and the function selector knob is in GYRO or beyond, the search radar is kept in a ready state, but will not transmit. In the XMTG position, transmission will occur if the function selector knob is in GYRO or beyond. The switch is a mechanically latched type switch which must be pulled to actuate.

Doppler Transmitter Switch.

The Doppler transmitter switch (7, figure 4-37), located on the auxiliary control panel, and marked ON and OFF, is used to turn the Doppler radar transmitter on or off. This switch has no effect on the Doppler receiver. Maximum Doppler turn-off without de-fusing can only be done with the Doppler isolation switch or the function selector knob (OFF or GYRO). De-fusing is necessary to remove all power.

Radio Altimeter Switch.

The radio altimeter switch (11, figure 4-37), located on the auxiliary control panel, is used to turn the radio altimeter transmitter on or off. The switch positions are marked OFF, ON, and CALIBRATE. When the switch is in the ON or CALIBRATE position, radio altitude is displayed on the altitude above terrain indicator. When flying over known terrain, the CALIBRATE position is used to calibrate altitude above sea level. This is accomplished by manually adjusting the altitude correction knob so that the fixpoint elevation indicator reads the altitude of a known point being passed over, with the switch in the CALIBRATE position. The radio altimeter switch must be in the ON or CALIBRATE position before automatic crosshair laying is possible. Both the radio altimeter power and isolation switches must be OFF to remove power from the radio altimeter.

Magnetic Variation Knob.

The magnetic variation (MAG VAR) knob (4, figure 4-37), located on the auxiliary control panel, is used to correct the flux valve information for local variation. The correction value set in at any time is shown on the magnetic variation indicator next to the knob. This correction should be kept current to insure proper BDH indication during ASTRO or FREE GYRO heading reference, and, when using FLUX VALVE, for proper true heading indication. This is a manual function. There is no automatic compensation for latitude or position.

Doppler Return Switch.

The Doppler return switch (5, figure 4-37), located on the auxiliary control panel, is used to select compensating circuits for varying surface conditions. The switch is marked CALM SEA, LAND, and ROUGH SEA.

Sea Drift Velocity Knobs.

The sea drift velocity knobs (1, figure 4-37), located on the auxiliary control panel, are used to set in compensations for known ocean currents, so as to minimize Doppler return errors when operating over ocean areas having consistent or predictable current. Values set in are shown on the sea drift velocity indicators above the knobs. If necessary, these knobs may be used, over land or water, to vary groundspeed and groundtrack computation. Maximum setting is ±99 knots.

Altitude Correction Knob.

The altitude correction knob (3, figure 4-37), located on the auxiliary control panel, is used to correct the altitude above sea level indicator.

Erect Indicator Lamp.

The erect indicator lamp (8, figure 4-37), located on the auxiliary control panel, when lighted indicates that table erection is in progress, but not complete. When this indicator lamp goes out, it indicates that primary table erection is complete, if the following conditions exist: (a) function selector knob at STANDBY, (b) malfunction test knob "A" at some position other than zero during timing cycle, then turned to zero. When using the ARU, the erect lamp will light when there is a PNSU and ARU velocity difference of approximately 11 knots or more. When using the PNSU, the erect lamp will light whenever the primary table accelerometer output (difference from Doppler) is approximately 11 knots or more. The erect lamp monitors ARU rapid erection when malfunction test knob "A" is at 12. When at "A-12" the erect lamp and the test good lamp cannot both light at the same time.

AUXILIARY FLIGHT INSTRUMENT PANEL.

Airspeed-Inertial Switch.

The two-position airspeed-inertial switch (9, figure 4-38) is located on the auxiliary flight instrument

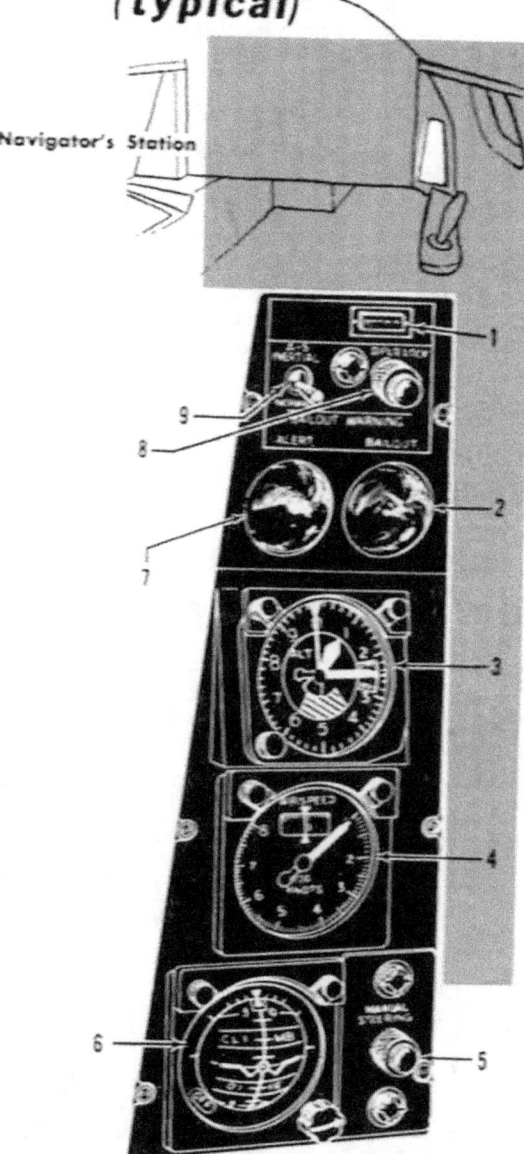

auxiliary flight instrument panel (typical)

1. Low Altitude Warning Lamp
2. Bailout Warning Lamp
3. Barometric Altimeter
4. Airspeed Indicator
5. Manual Steering Indicator Lamp
6. Attitude Indicator
7. Bailout Alert Lamp
8. Doppler Lock Indicator Lamp
9. Airspeed Inertial Switch

Figure 4-38.

Section IV
Auxiliary Equipment

T.O. 1B-58A-1

panel. The switch is marked NORMAL and AIRSPEED INERTIAL and allows the navigator to substitute airspeed signals for Doppler data when necessary or desirable. Placing the switch to NORMAL, with Doppler operating and locked, supplies Doppler data to the navigation system. When the switch is in the AIRSPEED INERTIAL position the navigation system is supplied airspeed signals and Doppler is withheld (Doppler timer indicator lighted yellow).

Note

Do not use AIRSPEED INERTIAL position below 250 knots. To do so may cause the connected table to dump.

Doppler Lock Lamp.

The green Doppler lock lamp (8, figure 4-38) indicates when the Doppler is locked in either mode (NORMAL or INERTIAL) of the airspeed-inertial switch. The press-to-test feature of this lamp tests operation of the bulb. The lamp operates on 28-volt d-c power.

INDICATOR PANEL.

Time to Go Indicator.

The time to go indicator (7, figure 4-39), located on the indicator panel, indicates the time in seconds before pod release. This timing sequence begins 300 seconds before release, and is operative in the bomb mode only. The indicator has a zero to 300 upper scale with a pointer which begins moving to zero when time to go reaches 300 seconds. The zero to 30 lower scale has a pointer which begins moving to zero when time to go reaches 30 seconds. The expanding lower scale provides an easier reading reference during the critical period of the bomb run.

Altitude Above Terrain Indicator.

The altitude above terrain indicator (4, figure 4-39), located on the indicator panel, is used to display aircraft altitude above terrain when the radio altimeter transmitter is operating. The amber calibration malfunction caution lamps are lighted when the radio altimeter is not operating properly. During altitude malfunction mode operation with the radio altimeter off, the indicator displays altitude above sea level.

True Heading Indicator.

The true heading indicator (2, figure 4-39), located on the indicator panel, indicates aircraft heading measured clockwise from the north pole of the coordinate system in use.

indicator panel

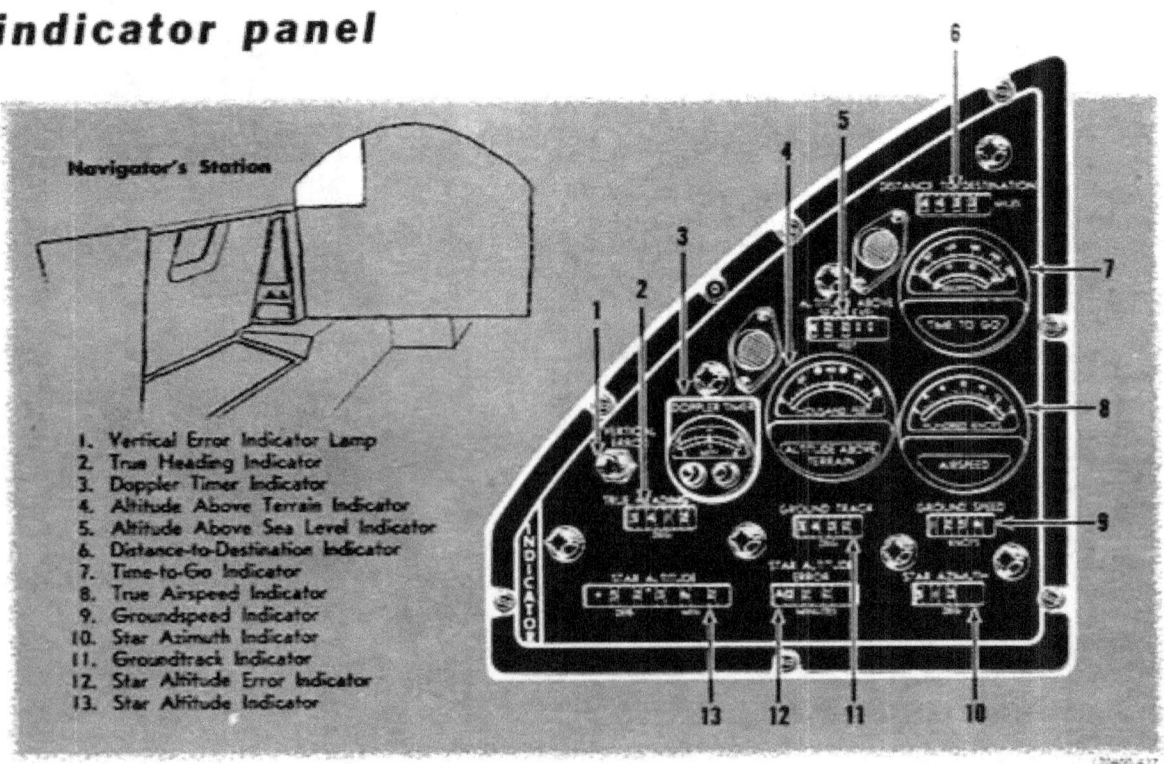

Figure 4-39.

4-64

Altitude Above Sea Level Indicator.

The altitude above sea level indicator (5, figure 4-39), located on the indicator panel, normally indicates aircraft altitude above sea level. This indicator displays altitude above terrain during altitude malfunction mode operation if the radio altimeter is operating.

Doppler Timer Indicator.

The Doppler timer indicator (3, figure 4-39), located on the indicator panel, is used to indicate Doppler radar activity. When the Doppler radar is unlocked, airspeed inertial is being utilized, or the malfunction test selector knob is in A-3, A-4, A-5, B-3 or B-4, the lower scale of the indicator is lighted by an amber lamp and the indicator pointer moves in a clockwise direction. When the Doppler radar is locked on all three channels, and Doppler velocities are being fed to the system, the upper scale of the timer indicator is lighted by a white lamp and the pointer moves in a counterclockwise direction.

Note

LRC transmissions at frequencies below 2.7 megacycles may affect Doppler signals to the extent of causing unlock or false lock, resulting in erroneous Doppler information.

Vertical Error Indicator Lamp.

The vertical error indicator lamp (1, figure 4-39), located on the indicator panel, is lighted whenever the inertial groundspeed data (PNSU only) and the Doppler groundspeed or airspeed data differ more than approximately 50 knots.

Groundspeed Indicator.

The groundspeed indicator (9, figure 4-39), located on the indicator panel, indicates system groundspeed in knots. The groundspeed value shown here is used in the automatic dead reckoning process. The indicator displays airspeed when operating in T_G malfunction mode.

True Airspeed Indicator.

The true airspeed indicator (8, figure 4-39), located on the indicator panel, indicates system true airspeed in knots.

Distance to Destination Indicator.

The distance to destination indicator (6, figure 4-39), located on the indicator panel, displays nautical miles to destination. In the navigation mode this represents the spatial difference between present position and destination position. In the bomb mode, fixpoint position is substituted for destination position.

Groundtrack Indicator.

The groundtrack indicator (11, figure 4-39), located on the indicator panel, indicates the angle (measured clockwise) between aircraft groundtrack and the north pole of the coordinate system in use.

Star Altitude Indicator.

The star altitude indicator (13, figure 4-39), located on the indicator panel, indicates measured star altitude. Indication is in degrees, minutes, and tenths of minutes. Some oscillation of minutes and tenths of minutes may occur in normal operation.

Star Azimuth Indicator.

The star azimuth indicator (10, figure 4-39), located on the indicator panel, displays computed star azimuth. Indication is in degrees, of the coordinate system in use.

Star Altitude Error Indicator.

The star altitude error indicator (12, figure 4-39), located on the indicator panel, displays in minutes the difference between computed and measured star altitude, which can serve as a monitor of the accuracy of present position and table attitude. Indication is in minutes, preceded by a T or A, indicating error toward star or error away from star, and has limits of 0-128 minutes.

ASTRO CONTROL PANEL.

Heading Reference Selector Knob.

The heading reference selector knob (1, figure 4-40), located on the astro control panel, is a five-position selector knob, marked as follows: ASTRO, FREE GYRO, FLUX VALVE, MAN SLEW +, and MAN SLEW —. When the knob is in ASTRO position and the astro tracker is locked on a star, the astro tracker is supplying heading correction. If a lock-on is not obtained the system will revert to free gyro. When the knob is in FREE GYRO, system heading utilizes gyro reference previously compensated for drift in ASTRO or FLUX VALVE. When the knob is in FLUX VALVE, the remote compass transmitter supplies the system heading correction. Placing the knob in MAN SLEW + or MAN SLEW — will cause the true heading indicator to slew at approximately 36 degrees per minute to any desired position. ASTRO

Section IV
Auxiliary Equipment

T.O. 1B-58A-1

astro control panel

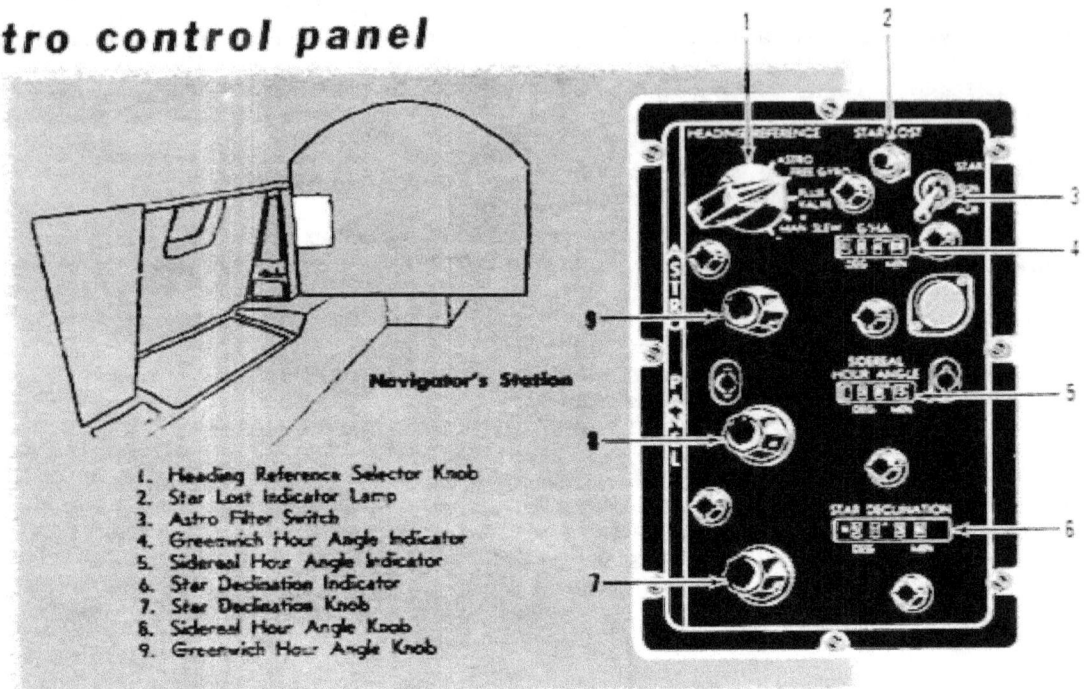

Figure 4-40.

is the normal position used, if weather permits. FREE GYRO is used when switching stars, or when other modes are inoperative or undesirable.

Note

Although it is possible to obtain an astro lock in the FLUX VALVE position, the flux valve remains the system heading reference. It is necessary to use the ASTRO position to initiate an astro search pattern.

Astro Filter Switch.

The astro filter switch (3, figure 4-40), located on the astro control panel, is used to select the proper filter for various viewing conditions. The switch is marked STAR, SUN, and AUR. Current atmospheric conditions will determine the selection of switch positions. The filters are spring-loaded to the SUN position when no power is applied.

Greenwich Hour Angle Knob.

The Greenwich hour angle (GHA) knob (9, figure 4-40), located on the astro control panel, is used to set (manual only) the Greenwich hour angle of Aries or the Greenwich hour angle of a body into the astro computer. This set-in value is shown on the Greenwich hour angle indicator near the knob. This indicator drives at a sidereal rate. On some airplanes this knob is replaced with a spring-loaded crank type handle.

Star Declination Knob.

The star declination knob (7, figure 4-40), located on the astro control panel, is used to set the declination of a celestial body into the astro computer. The value set in is displayed on the star declination indicator near the knob. The indicator can be slewed to the proper value by rotating the knob in the desired direction. The degree of rotation determines the slewing speed. The value may be manually set in by pushing in on the knob and turning in the desired direction.

Sidereal Hour Angle Knob.

The sidereal hour angle (SHA) knob (8, figure 4-40), located on the astro control panel, is used to set the sidereal hour angle of a body into the astro computer. The value set in is displayed on the SHA indicator near the knob. The indicator can be slewed to the proper value by rotating the knob in the desired direction. The degree of rotation determines the slewing speed. The value may be manually set in by pushing in on the knob and turning in the desired direction.

**Section IV
Auxiliary Equipment**

Star Lost Indicator Lamp.

The star lost indicator lamp (2, figure 4-40), located on the astro control panel, indicates loss of a body being tracked. The lamp lights when this occurs. When a body is lost, an automatic switchover to free gyro heading occurs if the heading reference selector knob is at ASTRO.

Note

In the event the astrotracker locks on a false signal, the star lost indicator lamp may not light, however, the heading will drive in error.

NAVIGATION CONTROL PANEL.

True Present Position Knobs.

The true present position knobs (2, figure 4-41), located on the navigation control panel, are used to set in present position latitude and longitude and to make adjustments, if needed, after enroute fixtaking. Latitude and longitude settings are displayed on indicators above the knobs. Each lined mark on the knobs (8 per knob), when turned past the index, adds or subtracts 0.5 minute from the previous setting whether the indicators are driving or not driving. It is from the point determined by these settings that the system determines course and distance to destination. The indicator can be slewed to the proper value by rotating the knob in the desired direction. The degree of rotation determines the slewing speed. The value may be manually set in by pushing in on the knob and turning in the desired direction.

Note

Depressing either knob will slew out, at approximately 36 degrees per minute, any existing heading error whenever the system is utilizing flux valve or astro heading reference.

Transverse Present Position Knobs.

The transverse present position knobs (6, figure 4-41), located on the navigation control panel, are used to set in transverse present position latitude and longitude. Each lined mark on the knobs (8 per knob), when turned past the index, adds or subtracts 0.5 minute from the previous setting whether the indicators are driving or not driving. When the polar/non-polar switch is in the POLAR position, these values will be used and indicated as such in the transverse position indicators above the knobs. When the polar/non-polar

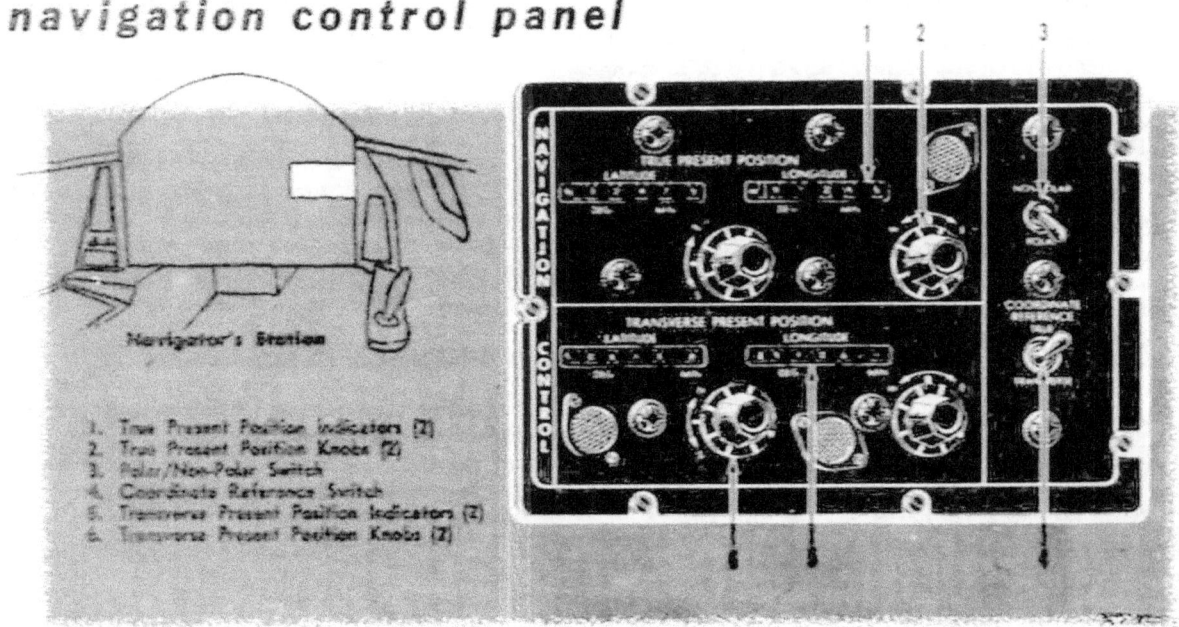

Figure 4-41.

Section IV
Auxiliary Equipment

T.O. 1B-58A-1

switch is in the NON-POLAR position, these indicators will show true latitude and longitude. The indicators can be slewed to the proper value by rotating the knob in the desired direction. The degree of rotation determines the slewing speed. The value may be manually set in by pushing in on the knob and turning in the desired direction.

Note

Although the transverse indicators will show either true or transverse coordinates, the correct initial setting must be made in each case before selecting the rate of indicator drive with the polar/non-polar switch. Position corrections made in the true mode are not automatically made in the transverse indicators. This includes sea drift effects.

Polar/Non-Polar Switch.

The polar/non-polar switch (3, figure 4-41), located on the navigation control panel, and marked POLAR and NON-POLAR, is used to select either true or transverse driving rate for the transverse present position indicators. The transverse rate is established in the POLAR position, the true rate in the NON-POLAR position. This allows the use of the transverse indicators as a standby true function in the event of failure of the normal true coordinate indicators.

Coordinate Reference Switch.

The coordinate reference switch (4, figure 4-41), located on the navigation control panel, is used to change coordinate reference systems when entering or leaving polar areas. The switch has two positions marked TRANSVERSE and TRUE. The switch is placed in the TRANSVERSE position for polar operation and in the TRUE position for non-polar operation. In the TRUE position the standard north pole is the reference point. In the TRANSVERSE position the polar reference is shifted to the point on the equator where the 180° meridian intersects. The meridians converge and meet at this transverse pole in the same manner as the true system, hence the TRANSVERSE position cannot be used within approximately 20° of the transverse pole. The transverse system is not compatible with the USAF grid system.

Note

When switching to TRANSVERSE, all indicators using coordinate references are re-oriented (true heading, ground track, star azimuth, PDI (groundtrack), and radar scope). The offset aimpoint, ballistic winds, and sea drift settings must be manually reset to transverse reference. The polar position should be selected prior to switching to transverse.

OFFSET AND STORAGE PANEL.

Aimpoint Selector Knob.

The aimpoint selector knob (9, figure 4-42), located on the offset and storage panel, is marked FIX, 1, and 2, and is used to select a fixpoint or either of two offset aimpoints for display on the search radar indicator. When the knob is in the FIX position, the search radar indicator displays crosshairs at the coordinates set in the fixpoint position indicators. When position 1 or 2 is selected, the offset value is applied to the fixpoint position indicators.

Storage Fixpoint Knobs.

The storage fixpoint knobs (7, figure 4-42), located on the offset and storage control panel, are used to set storage fixpoint latitude and longitude into the system for eventual transfer to the fixpoint position indicators. Values set are displayed on the storage fixpoint indicators (8, figure 4-42). The indicators can be slewed to the proper value by rotating the knob in the desired direction. The degree of rotation determines the slewing speed. The value may be manually set in by pushing in on the knob and turning in the desired direction.

Storage Fixpoint Elevation Knobs.

The storage fixpoint elevation knobs, (6, figure 4-42), located on the offset and storage control panel, are used to set storage fixpoint elevation. Values set are displayed on the storage fixpoint elevation indicators (5, figure 4-42).

Offset Aimpoint Knobs.

The offset aimpoint knobs (2, figure 4-42), located on the offset and storage control panel, are used to set into the system the rectangular offset distances from target or fixpoint to two offset aimpoints. Values set are shown on the offset aimpoint indicators (1, figure 4-42).

Offset Aimpoint Elevation Knobs.

The offset aimpoint elevation knobs (4, figure 4-42), located on the offset and storage control panel, are used to set offset aimpoint elevation into the system. Values set are shown on the offset aimpoint elevation indicators (3, figure 4-42).

SIGHTING AND TEST PANEL.

Destination Position Knobs.

The destination position knobs (2, figure 4-43), located on the sighting and test panel, are used to set in destination latitude and longitude in degrees and minutes.

4-68

offset and storage panel

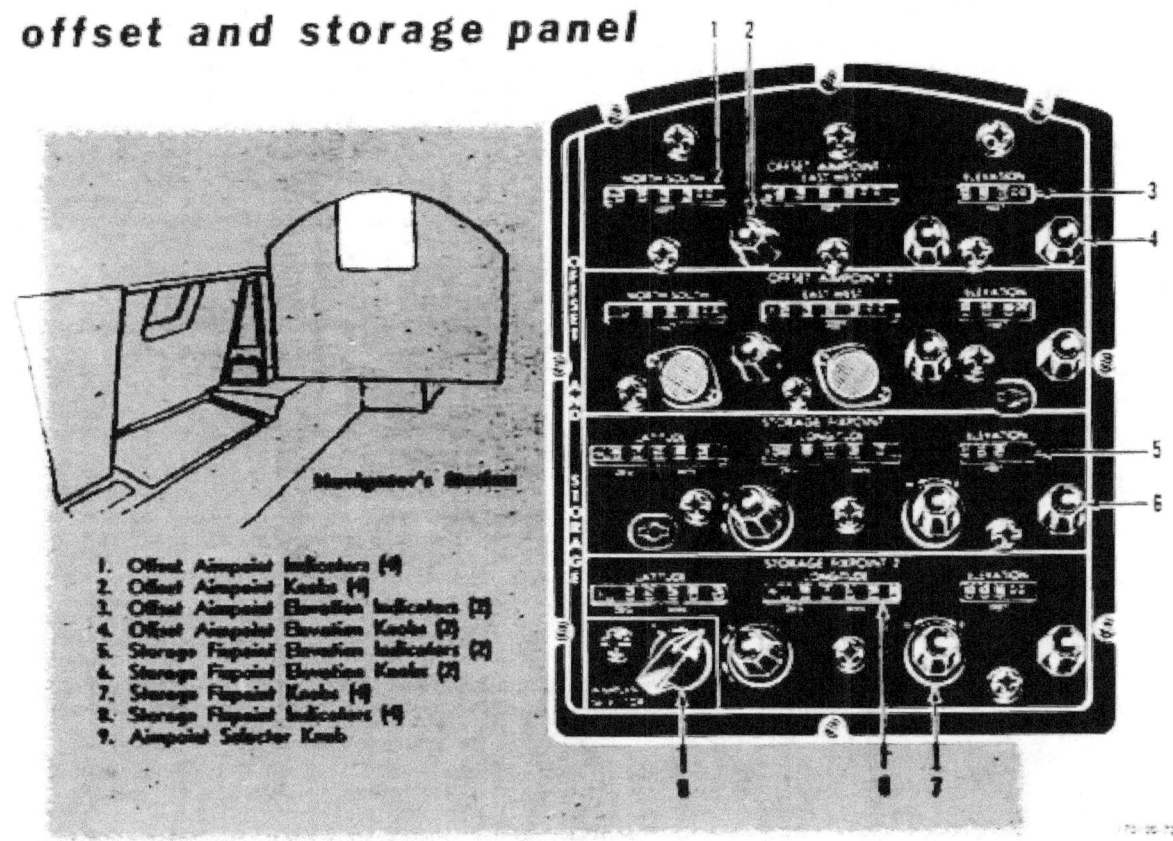

1. Offset Aimpoint Indicators (4)
2. Offset Aimpoint Knobs (4)
3. Offset Aimpoint Elevation Indicators (2)
4. Offset Aimpoint Elevation Knobs (2)
5. Storage Fixpoint Elevation Indicators (2)
6. Storage Fixpoint Elevation Knobs (2)
7. Storage Fixpoint Knobs (4)
8. Storage Fixpoint Indicators (4)
9. Aimpoint Selector Knob

Figure 4-42.

These data are displayed on the destination position indicators (1, figure 4-43). These settings establish the end point for computation of great circle course and steering, and distance to destination. In normal use only degrees and minutes are visible on the indicators. In sight malfunction mode, the tenths of minutes indicator becomes visible. Whenever a minute digit is fully visible, the tenths of minutes reads .5, due to the continuous gearing. Thus, in setting the indicators in this malfunction mode, bear in mind that an initial setting will be .5 minute high, and must be refined accordingly. The indicators can be slewed to the proper value by rotating the knob in the desired direction. The degree of rotation determines the slewing speed. The value may be manually set in by pushing in on the knob and turning in the desired direction.

Fixpoint Selector Knob.

The fixpoint selector knob (3, figure 4-43), located on the sighting and test panel, is used to insert fixpoint data into the fixpoint position indicators. The switch is marked PRESENT POSITION, MANUAL, 1, and 2. The MANUAL position is used when manually setting fixpoint data. Position 1 or 2 is used for automatic data transfer from fixpoint storage. The PRESENT POSITION is used to slave the fixpoint position indicators to the true present position indicators.

Note

The tracking and flight control selector knob must not be in the FIX PT POS CORR position to transfer stored data.

Fixpoint Position Knobs.

The fixpoint position knobs (12, figure 4-43), located on the sighting and test panel, are used to set fixpoint latitude and longitude into the system. The values being used are shown on the fixpoint position indicators (13, figure 4-43). The indicator can be slewed to the proper value by rotating the knob in the desired direction. The degree of rotation determines the slewing speed. The value may be manually set in by pushing in on the knob and turning in the desired direction.

4-69

Fixpoint Position Elevation Knob.

The fixpoint position elevation knob (5, figure 4-43), located on the sighting and test panel, is used to set fixpoint position elevation into the system. The elevation value being used is shown on the fixpoint position elevation indicator (4, figure 4-43).

Automatic Radar Photography Switch.

The automatic radar photography switch (8, figure 4-43), located on the sighting and test panel, is used to control the automatic radar photography functions. The switch is marked OFF, ON, and RECORD. The equipment is in standby condition when the switch is in the ON position, and will not photograph unless the manual button on the inflight printer is depressed, at which time a single exposure is made. Automatic crosshair laying is operative in the ON and RECORD positions with the function selector switch in the NAVIGATION position and with the radio altimeter switch at either ON or CALIBRATE. When the switch is in the RECORD position, a regular series of radar photographs will be taken automatically, subject to settings of the percent overlap selector knob and minimum range selector knob. See figure 4-43. In the BOMB mode, and RECORD position, pictures are taken each 3.5 seconds.

Minimum Range Selector Knob.

The minimum range selector knob (7, figure 4-43), located on the sighting and test panel, is used to select the range at which radar photographs will be taken, in the ARP mode. When the range to the point being photographed equals the range set by the knob, the camera is triggered to take a picture.

Percent Overlap Selector Knob.

The percent overlap selector knob (6, figure 4-43), located on the sighting and test panel, is used to select the desired overlap between successive sets of radar photographs taken in the ARP mode (RECORD position only).

sighting and test panel

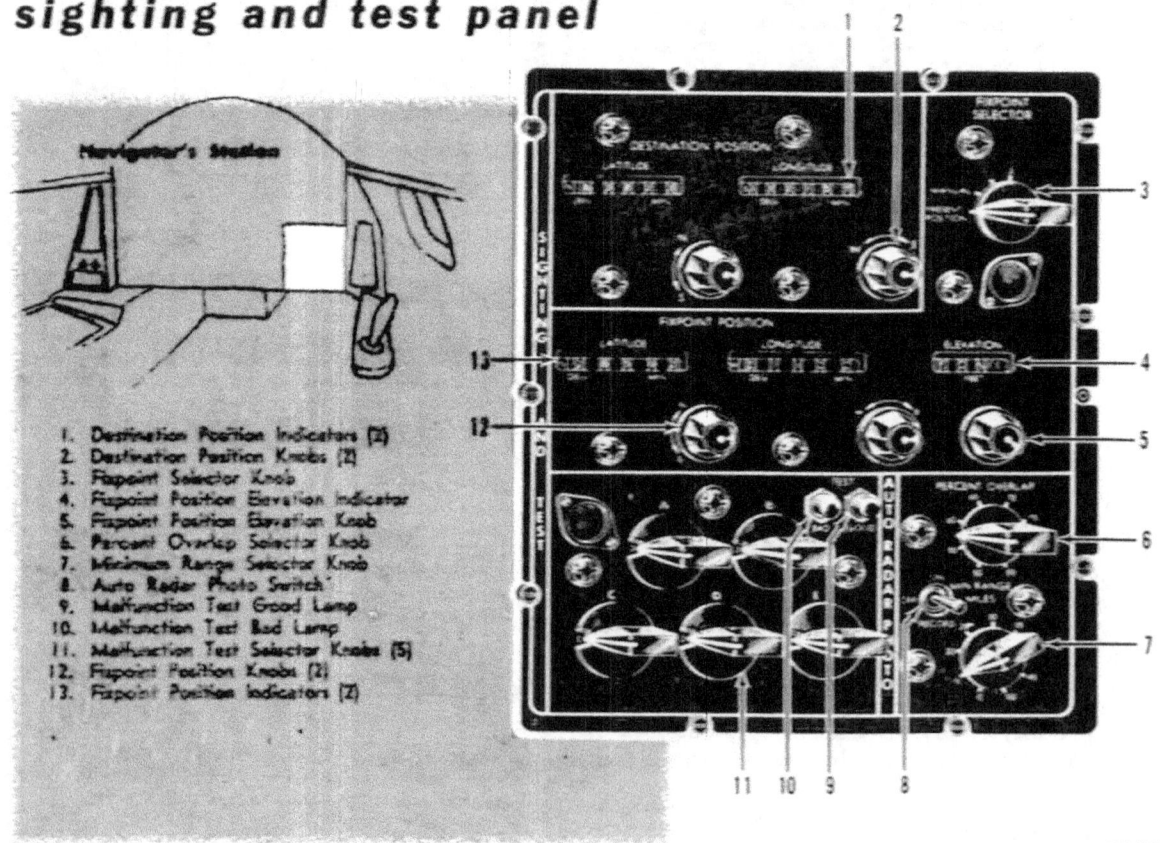

1. Destination Position Indicators (2)
2. Destination Position Knobs (2)
3. Fixpoint Selector Knob
4. Fixpoint Position Elevation Indicator
5. Fixpoint Position Elevation Knob
6. Percent Overlap Selector Knob
7. Minimum Range Selector Knob
8. Auto Radar Photo Switch
9. Malfunction Test Good Lamp
10. Malfunction Test Bad Lamp
11. Malfunction Test Selector Knobs (5)
12. Fixpoint Position Knobs (2)
13. Fixpoint Position Indicators (2)

Figure 4-43.

Malfunction Test Selector Knobs.

The malfunction test selector knobs (11, figure 4-43), located on the sighting and test panel, are used to perform inflight troubleshooting of the various portions of the navigation system. The knobs are identified by letter, A, B, C, D, and E. The knob positions are identified by number, each having zero through 13. Only one knob may be used at any one time. The other knobs not in use must be set to ZERO position. The ballistic malfunction test knob must be in the OFF position prior to making the tests. Each knob position initiates a different system test. Tests results are indicated by the lighting of either of two lamps, the test bad lamp (10, figure 4-43), or the test good lamp (9, figure 4-43), located just above the knobs. The knob letter and position number may be used as an index to provide corrective information.

Note

Test bad indications of either A1 or A2 self test invalidates other test results.

TRACKING AND FLIGHT CONTROLLER UNIT.

Tracking and Flight Controller Selector Knob.

The tracking and flight controller selector knob (3, figure 4-45), located on the tracking and flight controller unit, is used to select the function of the tracking and flight control stick. The knob positions are marked OFF, FIX PT POS CORR, PRES POS CORR, and AUTOPILOT. When the knob is in FIX PT POS CORR, (Search power switch at STBY or XMTG) the tracking and flight control stick corrects the fixpoint position indicators or sets the position of an unknown point into the fixpoint position indicators. When the knob is in PRES POS CORR, the tracking and flight control stick corrects the true present position indicators. When the knob is in AUTOPILOT, the tracking and flight control stick sends coordinated flight control signals (pitch and roll independent of PNS) to the autopilot. The amber manual steering indicator lamp (5, figure 4-38) will light when this flight condition exists. The knob must be raised to turn to or from the AUTOPILOT position.

Note

If the pilot takes control of the autopilot from the navigator, the tracking and flight controller knob must be rotated out of the AUTOPILOT position and then returned before control can be regained at the second station.

Tracking and Flight Control Stick.

The tracking and flight control stick (2, figure 4-45), located on the tracking and flight controller, is used to make tracking corrections and aircraft heading changes, in conjunction with the tracking and flight controller selector knob. An engaging switch (1, figure 4-45) is embedded in the handgrip, which must be depressed to correct system data. Depressing the engaging switch when operating in either the fixpoint position correction or present position correction modes will cause a photo identification lamp (figure 4-44) in the photo recorder to light and remain on to identify the first photo exposure taken after the correction is made. When the tracking and flight controller selector knob is in PRES POS CORR and flux valve or astro heading reference is utilized, depressing the engaging switch will slew out any existing heading error. The engaging switch is inoperative when the tracking and flight controller selector knob is in the AUTOPILOT position. Operation of the stick is similar to an aircraft control stick when the controller selector knob is in autopilot.

SEARCH RADAR INDICATOR PANEL.

Search Radar Mode Selector (SRCH) Knob.

The search radar mode selector knob (17, figure 4-46), located on the search radar indicator panel, is used to select several different radar functions. It has one beacon position, marked BCN, and two search positions, marked GRD and SL. In the GRD position the sweep is delayed in proportion to the altitude set into the system. In the SL position there is no altitude delay. The BCN position is used for tanker rendezvous and PI beacon operation, with K-band equipped airplanes.

Range and Magnification Selector (RNG MI MGNF MI/DIA) Knob.

The range and magnification selector knob (20, figure 4-46), located on the search radar indicator panel, is used to select five combinations of range, in nautical miles, and magnification, in nautical miles per indicator diameter. Appropriate range markers appear as each combination is selected. Combinations are arranged for optimum viewing.

Antenna Tilt (TILT) Knob.

The antenna tilt knob (4, figure 4-46), located on the search radar indicator panel, is used to increase or decrease the amount of search radar antenna tilt from that provided by automatic control. The normal position is marked β. When the beta switch is in the MAN

Section IV
Auxiliary Equipment

T.O. 1B-58A-1

photo recorder coding (typical)

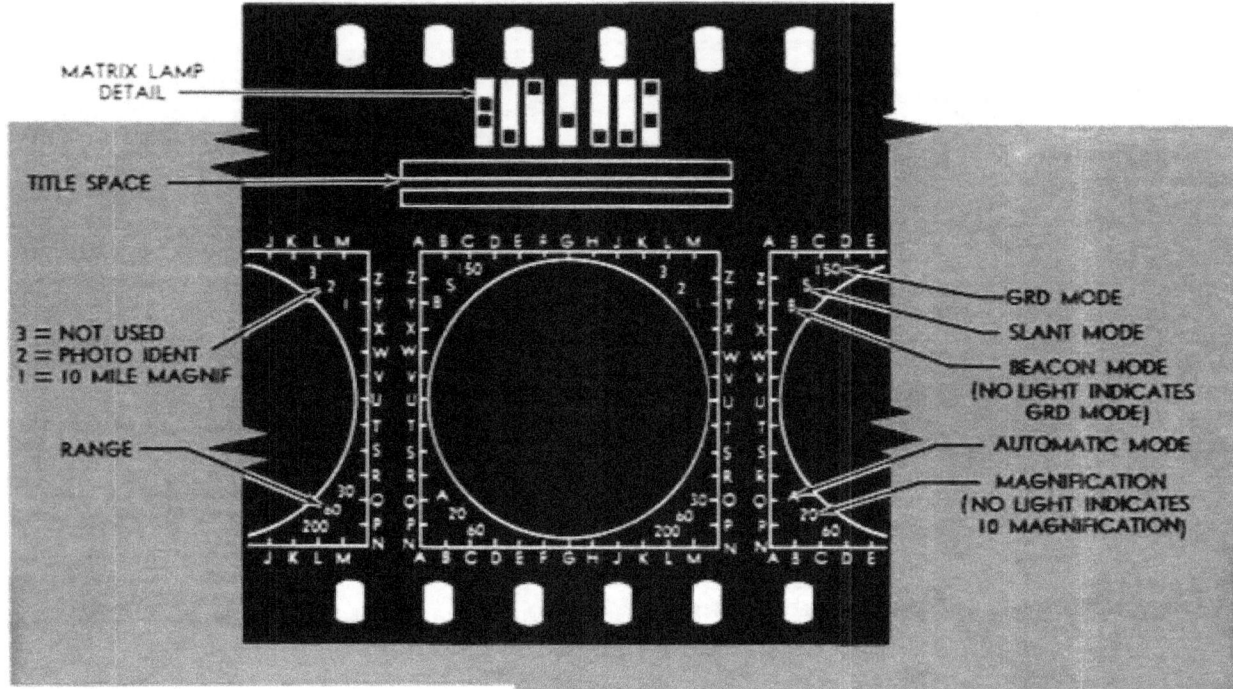

INSTRUCTIONS

1. Always ignore column 1.
2. Columns 2 through 7 have a constant base of 10 or 6 as indicated in the example.
3. Dark blocks indicate lighted lamps. White blocks indicate unlighted lamps. Read lamps from top to bottom.

   a. Determine lighted and unlighted lamps in column 2 (3 lighted — 1 unlighted) of the EXAMPLE then find the same lamp pattern in the CODE opposite BASE 10. Always read to the right of EVEN to determine the first time digit. This is number 1.

   b. Determine lighted and unlighted lamps in column 3 of the EXAMPLE then find same lamp pattern in the CODE opposite BASE 10 and read to the right of ODD, since first time digit was odd, to find the second time digit (number 2).

   c. Determine lighted and unlighted lamps in column 4 of the EXAMPLE then find same lamp pattern in the CODE opposite BASE 6 and read to the right of EVEN, since second time digit was even, to find the third digit (number 3).

   d. Find remaining digits in this manner.

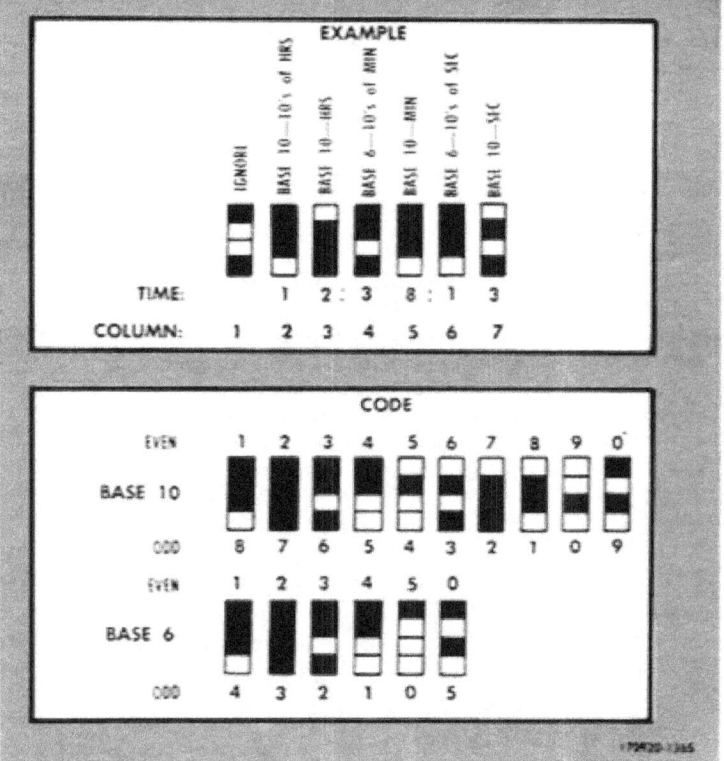

Figure 4-44.

4-72

position, a biased —3° control is set up, in detent, and the antenna tilt knob will then have command of the antenna thru its full mechanical range of travel.

Sector Knob.

The sector knob (6, figure 4-46), located on the search radar indicator panel, is used to select any one of four sector sweeps. These are marked 30°, 60°, 180° FWD, and 360°, and are operative in both manual and automatic modes.

Receiver Frequency Tuning (MAN TUN) Knob.

The receiver frequency tuning knob (10, figure 4-46), located on the search radar indicator panel, is used for receiver frequency control when the manual/automatic receiver tuning switch is in the MFC position.

Transmitter Frequency Tuning (FREQ) Knob.

The transmitter frequency tuning knob (7, figure 4-46), located on the search radar indicator panel, is used to tune the transmitter frequency, except when in beacon mode. Turning the knob clockwise increases the frequency.

Manual/Automatic Receiver Tuning (MFC/AFC) Knob.

The manual/automatic receiver tuning switch (8, figure 4-46), located on the search radar indicator panel, and marked MFC and AFC, is used to select automatic receiver frequency control or manual receiver frequency control, as desired. When the switch is in MFC, tuning is accomplished with the receiver frequency tuning knob except in beacon mode. In beacon mode receiver tuning is accomplished with the transmitter frequency tuning knob.

Cursor Rotation (CRSR) Knob.

The cursor rotation knob (3, figure 4-46), located on the search radar indicator panel, controls the mechanical rotation of the cursor grid-lines on the indicator.

Variable Range Marker (VRM) Knob.

The variable range marker knob (13, figure 4-46), located on the search radar indicator panel, is used to make smooth variations in intensity of the range crosshair display.

Fixed Range Marker (FRM) Knob.

The fixed range marker knob (19, figure 4-46), located on the search radar indicator panel, is used to make smooth variations in intensity of the range marks display.

tracking and flight controller unit

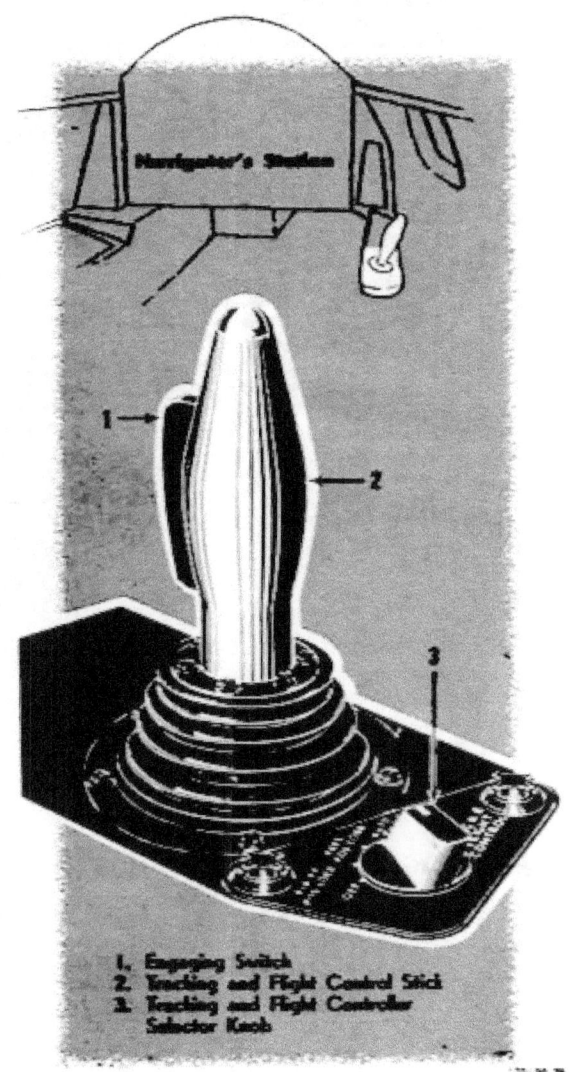

1. Engaging Switch
2. Tracking and Flight Control Stick
3. Tracking and Flight Controller Selector Knob

Figure 4-45.

Azimuth Mark Intensity (AZ MK) Knob.

The azimuth mark intensity knob (18, figure 4-46), located on the search radar indicator panel, is used to make smooth variations in intensity of the azimuth crosshair display.

Bearing Illumination (BRG ILLUM) Knob.

The bearing illumination knob (16, figure 4-46), located on the search radar indicator panel, is used to control the cursor illumination on the search radar indicator.

4-73

Section IV
Auxiliary Equipment

T.O. 1B-58A-1

search radar indicator panel

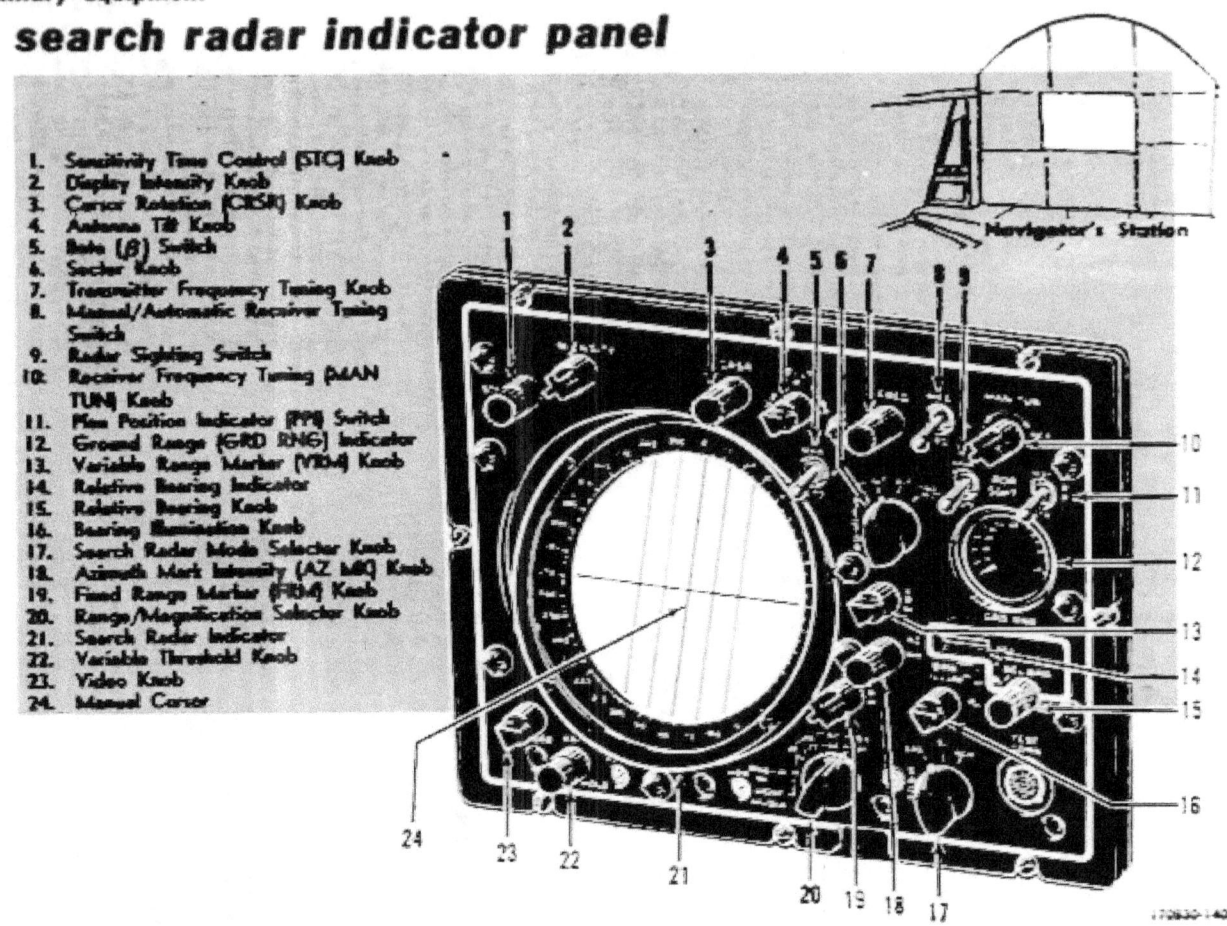

1. Sensitivity Time Control (STC) Knob
2. Display Intensity Knob
3. Cursor Rotation (CRSR) Knob
4. Antenna Tilt Knob
5. Beta (β) Switch
6. Sector Knob
7. Transmitter Frequency Tuning Knob
8. Manual/Automatic Receiver Tuning Switch
9. Radar Sighting Switch
10. Receiver Frequency Tuning (MAN TUN) Knob
11. Plan Position Indicator (PPI) Switch
12. Ground Range (GRD RNG) Indicator
13. Variable Range Marker (VRM) Knob
14. Relative Bearing Indicator
15. Relative Bearing Knob
16. Bearing Illumination Knob
17. Search Radar Mode Selector Knob
18. Azimuth Mark Intensity (AZ MK) Knob
19. Fixed Range Marker (FRM) Knob
20. Range/Magnification Selector Knob
21. Search Radar Indicator
22. Variable Threshold Knob
23. Video Knob
24. Manual Cursor

Figure 4-46.

Variable Threshold (VAR THRESHOLD) Knob.

The variable threshold knob (22, figure 4-46) is located on the search radar indicator panel. It is used to vary the level that the received signal must exceed in order to appear on the search indicator.

Display Intensity (INTENSITY) Knob.

The display intensity knob (2, figure 4-46), located on the search radar indicator panel, is used to adjust sweep intensity of the search radar indicator display.

Video Knob.

The video knob (23, figure 4-46), located on the search radar indicator panel, is used to vary video gain to suit viewing conditions. It is functional in both manual and automatic radar modes.

Sensitivity Time Control (STC) Knob.

The STC knob (1, figure 4-46) located on the search radar indicator panel is used to control the slope of the automatic increase in receiver sensitivity with increasing target distance. By avoiding excessive receiver gain with close targets, saturation of the search radar receiver is minimized. Maximum sensitivity of the STC control is in the CCW position.

Plan Position Indicator (PPI) Switch.

The two-position plan position indicator switch (11, figure 4-46), located on the search radar indicator panel, is used to control sweep vertex position. Placing the switch to CTR places the vertex at the indicator center. Moving the switch to OFST places the vertex at the indicator edge. The switch is inoperative except in manual sighting mode.

Beta (β) Switch.

The beta (β) switch (5, figure 4-46), located on the search radar indicator panel, is used to select automatic or manual antenna tilt control. Positions are marked MAN and AUTO. Manual control may be selected at any time by placing the switch to MAN,

4-74

turning the fixpoints selector knob to PRESENT POSITION, or placing the radar sighting switch to MANUAL. Automatic control may be selected by moving the switch to AUTO, provided the radar sighting switch is in the AUTO position, and the function selector knob is at STANDBY or beyond.

Radar Sighting (RDR SGHT) Switch.

The two-position radar sighting switch (9, figure 4-46), located on the search radar indicator panel, is used to select automatic or manual search radar control. Positions are marked MAN and AUTO. The automatic mode may be selected by placing the switch to the AUTO position, provided the function selector knob is at STANDBY or beyond. The manual mode may be selected by placing the switch in the MAN position, provided the function selector knob is at GYRO or beyond.

Ground Range (GRD RNG) Indicator.

The ground range indicator (12, figure 4-46), located on the search radar indicator panel displays the crosshair distance in nautical miles.

Relative Bearing (REL BRG) Knob.

The relative bearing knob (15, figure 4-46), located on the search radar indicator panel, is used to vary the indicator azimuth mark to any bearing. The bearing of the azimuth mark with respect to aircraft heading is displayed on the relative bearing indicator (14, figure 4-46). Relative bearing (0-360) is operative only in the manual sighting mode.

Search Radar Indicator.

The search radar indicator (21, figure 4-46) in AUTO mode presents a north-oriented, displaced-center plan position indicator display with electronically generated crosshairs and range markers. Re-orientation to the transverse pole occurs when changing to transverse coordinate navigation mode. In manual radar use, the top of the indicator represents airplane heading. A hood is provided to shield the face of the indicator from glare.

Note

- LRC transmission may cause interference with the search radar presentation. This interference may appear as an increase in intensity of the scope display.

- Simultaneous operation of the search radar and fire control system on the same frequency may result in interference with the search radar presentation. Interference may appear as a symmetrical dot pattern on the search radar scope. Changing the frequency of either system should eliminate the interference.

SEARCH RADAR TEST PANEL.

Indicator Console Unit (ICU) Switch.

The indicator console unit (ICU) switch (5, figure 4-47), located on the search radar test panel, is used to disable the ICU when the search power switch, located on the auxiliary control panel, is placed in the STBY position. If the search radar is in the STBY mode and the ICU switch is in the NORM position, the search radar display is blanked by removing ICU B+ voltages. If the search radar is in STBY mode and the ICU switch is in TEST position, the search radar display is present without video signal returns. This function provides the ability to perform maintenance and preflight checks on the radar without transmitting radio frequency energy (radiation). With the ICU switch in either the NORM or TEST position, the normal display will be present on the ICU when the search power switch is in the XMTG position.

Monitor Meter Selector Knob.

The 12-position monitor meter knob (4, figure 4-47), located on the search radar test panel, is used to select any one of 11 search radar circuits for monitoring by the monitor meter (6, figure 4-47), located left of the knob. Markings are as follows: OFF, IF DET, TRIG, +300, MAG I, RDR and BCN (RCVR AFC SWEEP), BCN XTAL, AFC XTALS, MOD I, SIG XTALS, and LVPS. System operation, within allowable limits, is indicated by a reading on the test panel meter falling between the green lines.

4-75

Section IV
Auxiliary Equipment

T.O. 1B-58A-1

search radar test panel (typical)

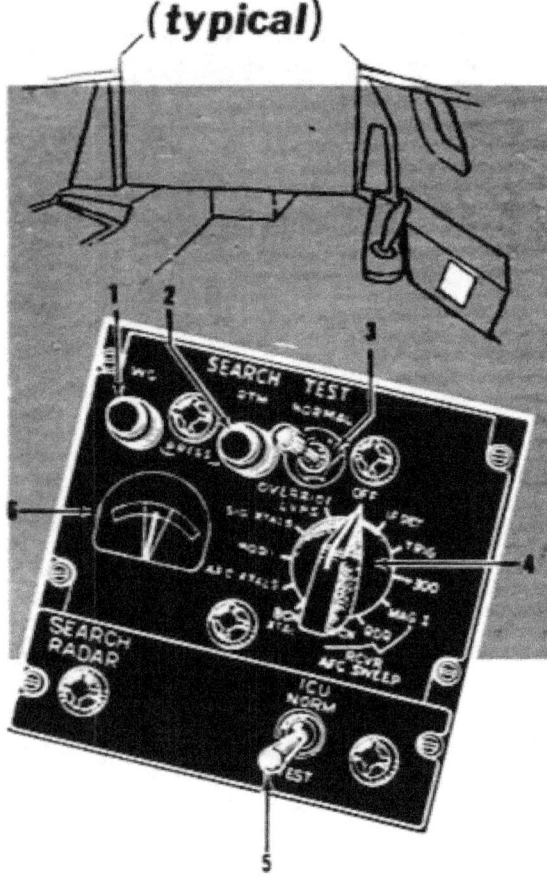

1. Waveguide Pressure Loss Lamp
2. RTM Pressure Caution Lamp
3. Search Test Normal/Override Switch
4. Monitor Meter Selector Knob
5. Indicator Console Unit (ICU) Switch
6. Monitor Meter

Figure 4-47.

Waveguide Pressure Loss Lamp (WG PRESS).

The amber waveguide pressure loss lamp (1, figure 4-47), located on the search radar test panel, indicates to the navigator that a loss of waveguide pressure has occurred. When this occurs the search radar RTM is automatically shut down.

RTM Pressure Caution Lamp (RTM PRESS).

The amber RTM pressure caution lamp (2, figure 4-47), on the search radar test panel, lights to indicate that RTM pressure is too low for safe operation of search radar.

> **CAUTION**
>
> Whenever the RTM caution lamp lights, indicating that pressure is too low for safe operation, turn the search radar off immediately.

Search Test Normal/Override Switch.

The search test normal/override switch (3, figure 4-47), located on the search radar test panel, is a two-position switch marked NORMAL and OVERRIDE. The switch is normally left in the NORMAL position. Placing the switch in the OVERRIDE position overrides the automatic shutdown of the search radar RTM.

> **CAUTION**
>
> Operation of the search radar with low waveguide pressure, is possible only at altitudes of 10,000 feet, or less. If mechanical damage exists in the search radar waveguide, overriding the automatic shutdown of the RTM will, in most cases, cause extensive damage to search radar RTM components.

MALFUNCTION CONTROL PANEL.

Auto Steering Switch.

The auto steering switch (9, figure 4-48), located on the malfunction control panel, and marked ON and OFF, is used to control automatic steering signals to the autopilot and the PDI. When the switch is OFF, autopilot heading modes cannot be engaged.

Vertical Reference Selector Switch.

The vertical reference selector switch (17, figure 4-48), located on the malfunction control panel, is used to select either the primary stable table or the auxiliary stable table as the source of inertial data. The switch is marked NORMAL, AIR ERECT, and MALF. In the NORMAL position, the primary stable table is used, and the auxiliary stable table is kept in a standby condition. When the switch is placed in the AIR ERECT position, the auxiliary stable table is used, and the primary stable table is kept in a standby condition. When the switch is placed to the MALF position, the auxiliary table is used, and the primary table is disconnected and de-energized. The AIR ERECT position should normally be used when the PNSU rapid erect switch is ON if the ARU vertical and heading are reliable. Gyro heaters remain energized in all positions.

WARNING

Do not actuate this switch without first going to manual flight control. Check condition of the table selected with the attitude indicators before restoring autopilot. If neither stable table is satisfactory, autopilot operation must not be attempted.

Primary Rapid Erect Switch (PNSU R.E.).

The two-position primary rapid erect switch (1, figure 4-48), located on the malfunction control panel, is marked ON and OFF. The switch is used to hold the primary stable table in rapid erection (ON), or to allow normal erection (OFF). On some airplanes this switch is a mechanically latched type switch which must be pulled to actuate. Vertical reference selector switch should normally be in AIR ERECT when this switch is ON if the ARU vertical and heading are reliable. If the ARU output is not reliable the PNSU should be rapid erected with the vertical reference switch in NORMAL. However, heading error will be introduced as the result of the PNSU relative heading being driven to zero. This error should be manually corrected with the heading reference selector knob.

WARNING

Actuation of the primary rapid erect switch to ON when the vertical reference selector knob is in NORMAL will result in loss of the PNSU vertical reference. Autopilot operation must be discontinued until alternate reference source is selected or the PNSU is re-erected.

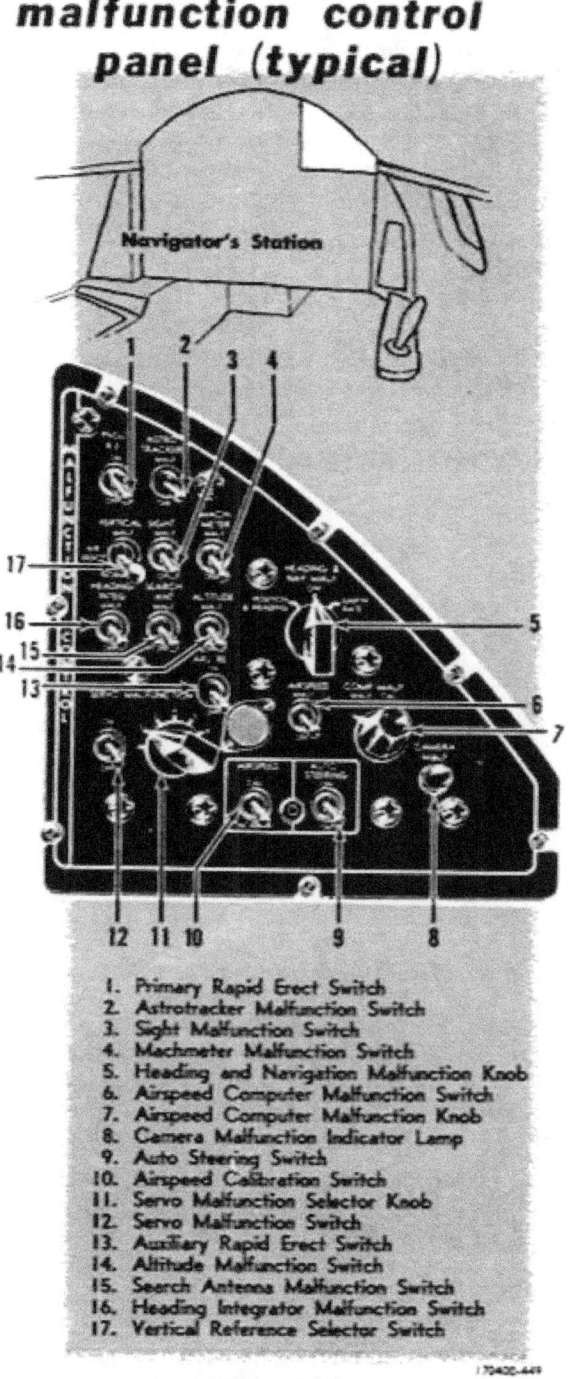

malfunction control panel (typical)

1. Primary Rapid Erect Switch
2. Astrotracker Malfunction Switch
3. Sight Malfunction Switch
4. Machmeter Malfunction Switch
5. Heading and Navigation Malfunction Knob
6. Airspeed Computer Malfunction Switch
7. Airspeed Computer Malfunction Knob
8. Camera Malfunction Indicator Lamp
9. Auto Steering Switch
10. Airspeed Calibration Switch
11. Servo Malfunction Selector Knob
12. Servo Malfunction Switch
13. Auxiliary Rapid Erect Switch
14. Altitude Malfunction Switch
15. Search Antenna Malfunction Switch
16. Heading Integrator Malfunction Switch
17. Vertical Reference Selector Switch

Figure 4-48.

Auxiliary Rapid Erect Switch (ARU RE).

The two-position auxiliary rapid erect switch (13, figure 4-48), located on the malfunction control panel, is marked ON and OFF. The switch is used to manually initiate auxiliary stable table rapid erection. The

Section IV
Auxiliary Equipment

switch is spring-loaded to the OFF position, and must be held to ON for 5 seconds of relatively level and unaccelerated flight. The ARU erect cycle is monitored by the A-12 test position. When the erect lamp goes out and the test good lamp comes on, the ARU has erected properly. The duration of the rapid cycle is determined by the time the switch is held to ON.

Airspeed Calibration Switch.

The airspeed calibration switch (10, figure 4-48), located on the malfunction control panel, and marked CAL and NORMAL, is used to calibrate airspeed by placing the switch in the CAL position.

Astrotracker Malfunction Switch.

The astrotracker malfunction switch (2, figure 4-48), located on the malfunction control panel, is used to energize and substitute a standby amplifier and photo tube. The switch is marked MALF and OFF.

Airspeed Computer Malfunction Calibrate Knob.

The airspeed computer malfunction knob (7, figure 4-48), located on the malfunction control panel, is used with the airspeed computer malfunction switch to correct airspeed in the event of a malfunction of the airspeed computer circuits. It may also be used with the machmeter malfunction switch, to set airspeed during machmeter malfunctions.

Airspeed Computer Malfunction Switch.

The airspeed computer malfunction switch (6, figure 4-48), located on the malfunction control panel, and marked OFF and MALF, is used to energize the potentiometer controlled by the airspeed computer malfunction knob. This is accomplished by placing the switch to MALF.

Mach Indicator Malfunction Switch.

The mach indicator malfunction switch (4, figure 4-48), located on the malfunction control panel, and marked MALF and OFF, is used to substitute the malfunction calibration potentiometer for the autopilot airspeed potentiometer. After placing the switch in MALF, best known airspeed is set, using airspeed computer malfunction knob. Airspeed calibration may be performed when operating in mach indicator malfunction mode.

Altitude Malfunction Switch.

The altitude malfunction switch (14, figure 4-48), located on the malfunction control panel, and marked MALF and OFF, is used to substitute the north ground range servo for the altitude above sea level assembly. If the radio altimeter is off, altitude above sea level will be shown on the altitude above terrain meter at this time.

Sight Malfunction Switch.

The sight malfunction switch (3, figure 4-48), located on the malfunction control panel, and marked MALF and OFF, is used to substitute the destination latitude and longitude assemblies and north and east ground range assemblies for the fixpoint latitude and longitude assemblies and circuits. While this switch is in the MALF position, great circle computation is not possible, since some of the transferred units are portions of the great circle computer. Also, in MALF, stored data cannot be transferred, and the tracking and flight control stick is inoperative in FIX PT POS CORR.

WARNING

Autopilot heading switch must be OFF when switching the sight malfunction switch to MALF.

Heading and Navigation Malfunction Knob.

The heading and navigation malfunction knob (5, figure 4-48), located on the malfunction control panel, and marked EARTH RATE, OFF, and POSITION & HEADING, is used to correct a malfunction in the present position and heading circuits when placed in the POSITION & HEADING position, or to correct a malfunction in the earth rate computation when placed in the EARTH RATE position. When in POSITION & HEADING, the θ_D synchros and resolvers are replaced with similar θ_{DT} components, and the true and transverse position indicators are interchanged.

Heading Integrator Malfunction Switch.

The heading integrator malfunction switch (16, figure 4-48), located on the malfunction control panel, is used to substitute a spare amplifier for the θ_D integrator pre-amplifier. The switch is marked MALF and OFF.

Search Antenna Malfunction Switch.

The search antenna malfunction switch (15, figure 4-48), located on the malfunction control panel, is marked MALF and OFF. When the switch is placed in the MALF position the antenna is stabilized about the airplane attitude.

Servo Malfunction Selector Knob.

The servo malfunction selector knob (11, figure 4-48), located on the malfunction control panel, and marked 1, 2, 3, 4, 5, and 6, is used to substitute a spare servo for any one of six servos in the system. The servo malfunction switch (12, figure 4-48), next to the servo malfunction selector knob, is used to energize the substitute servo after the proper selector position is made.

Camera Malfunction Indicator Lamp.

The camera malfunction indicator lamp (8, figure 4-48), located on the malfunction control panel, is used to indicate the presence of a malfunction in the photo recorder camera. There is no provision for inflight malfunction correction of this camera unit. The lamp will blink during film transport.

PRIMARY NAVIGATION SYSTEM ISOLATION SWITCHES.

Four guarded primary navigation system isolation switches (figure 4-49), located in the tunnel area between the pilot's and navigator's stations, provide a means of isolating the computation and stabilization system, astrotracker, Doppler radar, and radio altimeter. The switches are marked ON and OFF and are labeled COMP, ASTR, DOPP and ALT. The search radar has no isolation switch, this function being performed by the OFF position of the search power switch. Placing the COMP switch to OFF will disable all navigation and bombing equipment except manual search radar. The ASTR, DOPP, and ALT switches affect only the indicated equipment.

PRIMARY NAVIGATION SYSTEM OPERATION.

Refer to Navigator's Checklist, Section VIII, for operating instructions.

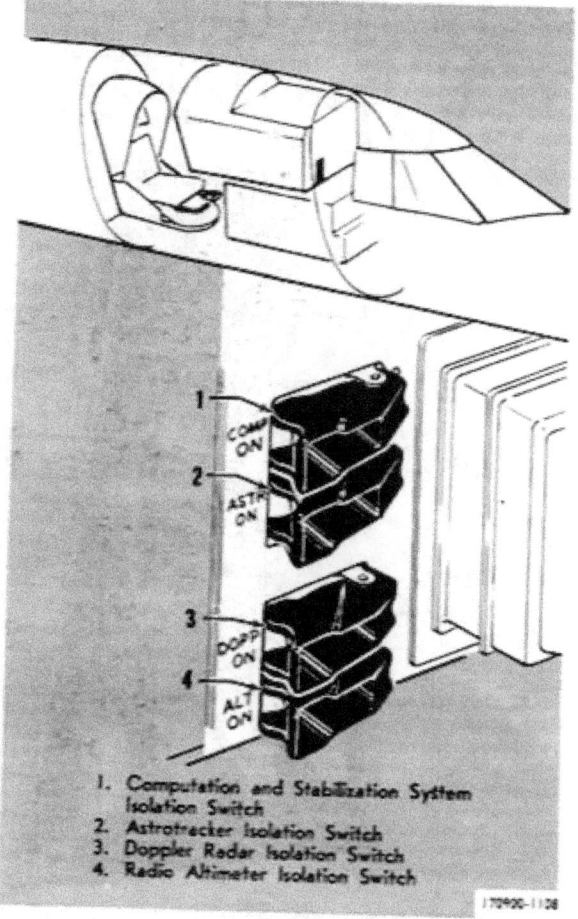

1. Computation and Stabilization System Isolation Switch
2. Astrotracker Isolation Switch
3. Doppler Radar Isolation Switch
4. Radio Altimeter Isolation Switch

Figure 4-49.

BOMBING SYSTEM.

The airplane is equipped with a bombing system which is used in conjunction with the primary navigation system to steer the airplane on the bomb run and to automatically drop a weapon(s) at a time calculated to provide burst at a predetermined point. The weapons controlled by the bombing system consist of a pod, and four small weapons (B-43 bombs) mounted in tandem, two on each side of the pod. All the weapons may be dropped free-fall. Pods with -53 warheads and the small weapons also have retarded drop capability. The bombing system consists essentially of a ballistics computer and the necessary controls. The ballistics unit and the weapon monitor and release panel, located at

Section IV
Auxiliary Equipment

T.O. 18-58A-1

weapon lock and arm panel

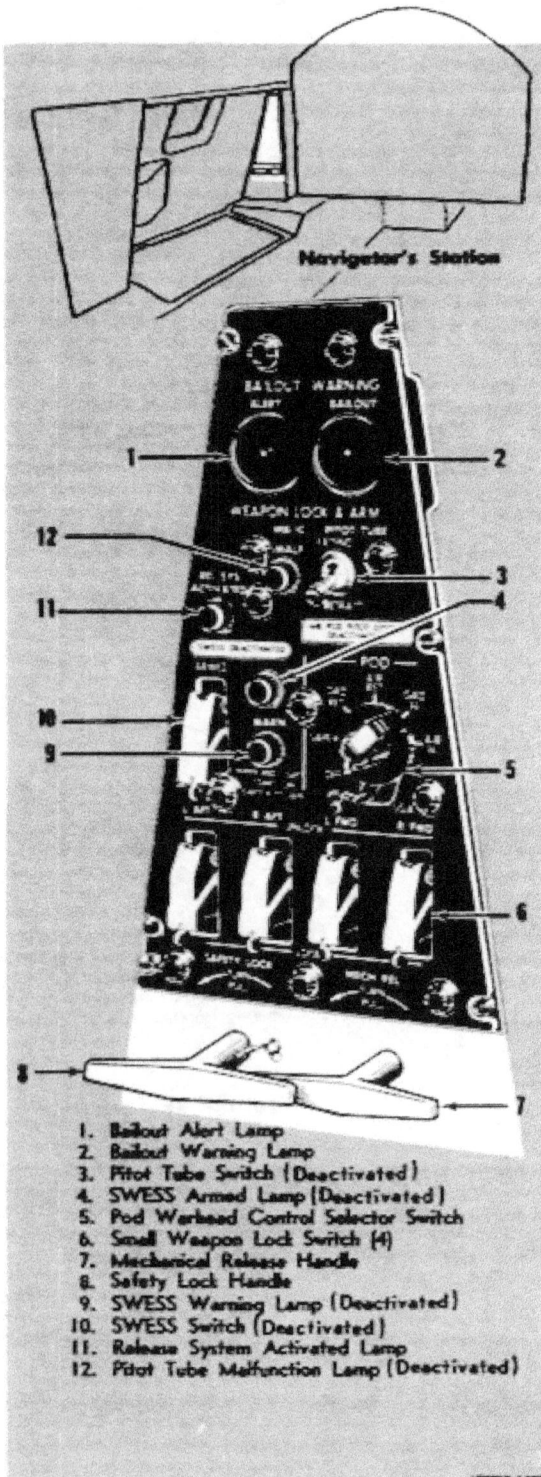

1. Bailout Alert Lamp
2. Bailout Warning Lamp
3. Pitot Tube Switch (Deactivated)
4. SWESS Armed Lamp (Deactivated)
5. Pod Warhead Control Selector Switch
6. Small Weapon Lock Switch (4)
7. Mechanical Release Handle
8. Safety Lock Handle
9. SWESS Warning Lamp (Deactivated)
10. SWESS Switch (Deactivated)
11. Release System Activated Lamp
12. Pitot Tube Malfunction Lamp (Deactivated)

Figure 4-50.

the navigator's station as an interchangeable unit can be replaced by other units, or omitted, if ballistic bombing is not planned. The ballistics unit is an analog computer which supplies trail and time-of-fall signals to the primary navigation system. The ballistic unit and weapon must be compatible or the computed values of trail and time-of-fall will be erroneous. A marking on the lower right corner of the ballistic control panel (figure 4-53) indicates the type unit installed.

Note

If the panel is unmarked or is marked MB-1C, the unit is compatible with MB pods. If the panel is marked BLU MK, the unit is compatible with bomb pods with -53 warheads and small weapons (B43 bombs).

Manually set-in values of trail and time-of-fall should be substituted for the computed values if an incompatible configuration is installed or a retarded drop is planned. The primary navigation system uses the trail and time-of-fall information in computing steering error signals and an automatic release signal. The ballistics computer receives signals for its computations from the primary navigation system, the air data computer, and data set into the control panel on ballistic winds and desired burst altitude. Controls are provided for performing inflight malfunction checks and for substituting circuits if malfunctioning circuits are detected. Other controls allow the selection of an air burst, a ground burst, or a safe condition of each warhead. The warhead is armed automatically on release. Although normally released automatically, any weapon can be released by means of a release switch at the pilot's or navigator's station if the automatic circuit malfunctions. A mechanical release handle at the navigator's station is provided for release of the pod if a malfunction exists in the electrical release system. Safety lockpins are provided which, when inserted, prevent inadvertent weapon release. The lockpin position is controlled by a handle at the navigator's station. The small weapon lockpins are controlled by switches at the navigator's station. A radio tone signal is incorporated to simulate bomb release for RBS runs. This signal is controlled by a switch at the navigator's station.

CONTROLS AND INDICATORS.

Safety Lock Handle.

The safety lock handle (8, figure 4-50), located at the lower edge of the weapon lock and arm panel, is provided to remove the pod safety pin from the release mechanism. Turning the handle counterclockwise and pulling to full length of travel unlocks the mechanical release handle and removes the safety lockpin from the pod release actuator rod. The lockpin may be reinserted at any time by pushing in the handle. The safety lockpin must be removed before any type of pod release can be made. Normal handle travel is 2.25 inches. Lockpin position is indicated on the weapon unlock caution lamp on the pilot's warning and caution lamp panel (figure 1-13) and the pod lock indicator (1, figure 4-55), on the navigator's weapon monitor and release panel.

Small Weapon Lock Switches.

Four guarded small weapon lock switches (6, figure 4-50), located on the weapon lock and arm panel, control the unlock solenoids in the respective weapon rack. Placing a switch in LOCK breaks the power circuit to the respective unlock solenoid. Placing a switch to UNLOCK applies power to actuate the solenoid and unlock the weapon rack. The position of the small weapon safety lock is indicated on the weapon unlock caution lamp located on the pilot's warning and caution lamp panel (figure 1-13), and on the four small weapon lock indicators (2, figure 4-55), located on the navigator's weapon monitor and release panel.

Mechanical Release Handle.

The mechanical release handle (7, figure 4-50), is located at the lower edge of the weapon lock and arm panel. The handle provides a means of releasing the pod, in the event of a malfunction of the electrical release system, by mechanically actuating the pod release pneumatic system. The handle must be turned 90 degrees counterclockwise and pulled aft to full length of travel for actuation of the release system. Operation is mechanically blocked until the pod safety lockpin release handle has been turned and pulled. A fail-safe feature prevents the handle from being pulled before being rotated. Normal handle travel is 2.25 inches.

Electrical Release Switch.

The electrical release switch (6, figure 4-55), located on the weapon monitor and release panel, is used for emergency release of the pod and small weapons. This pushbutton switch is in parallel with and functionally identical to the pilot's weapon release switch.

Weapon Release Switch.

The weapon release switch (14, figure 1-34), located on the pilot's forward left console, is used for emergency release of the pod and small weapons. This

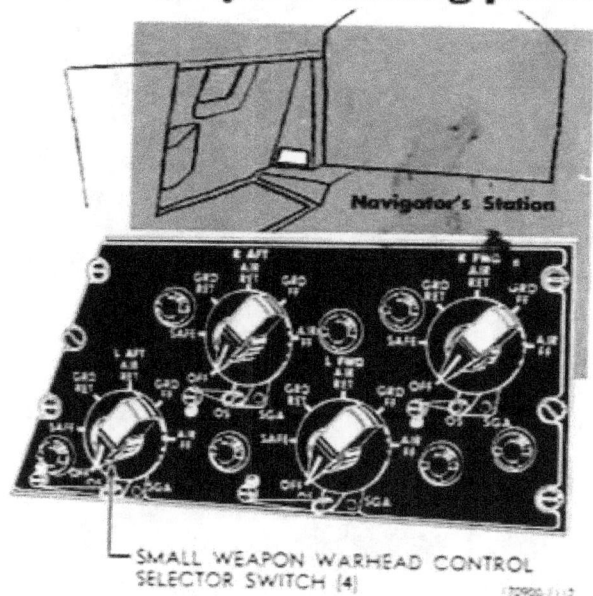

small weapons arming panel

SMALL WEAPON WARHEAD CONTROL SELECTOR SWITCH (4)

Figure 4-51.

pushbutton switch is connected in parallel with the navigator's electrical release switch and is functionally identical. When the weapon release switch is depressed, a release signal is sent to the weapon selected by the weapon selector switch. Depressing the switch causes the release signal present caution lamps in the first and second station to light. Each time the switch is released, the weapon selector switch will step clockwise to the next weapon position (if that position is unlocked) until the last pod position is reached.

Auto Release Switch.

The auto release switch (10, figure 4-55) is located on the weapon monitor and release panel and is used to control automatic release of the pod and small weapons. The switch is a three-position switch marked RELEASE and OFF and has an unmarked center position. The switch is spring-loaded from RELEASE to the center position. When the switch is momentarily placed to RELEASE, the auto release ready lamp will light and the system is prepared for an automatic release of the weapon selected by the weapon selector switch. The auto release switch must be momentarily placed to RELEASE after each release if more than one weapon is to be automatically released. In the event release of a locked weapon is attempted, the weapon cannot be released until the auto release switch is placed to OFF, the weapon unlocked, the auto release switch is momentarily placed to RELEASE, and an automatic release signal is again present.

4-81

pilot's bomb panel (typical)

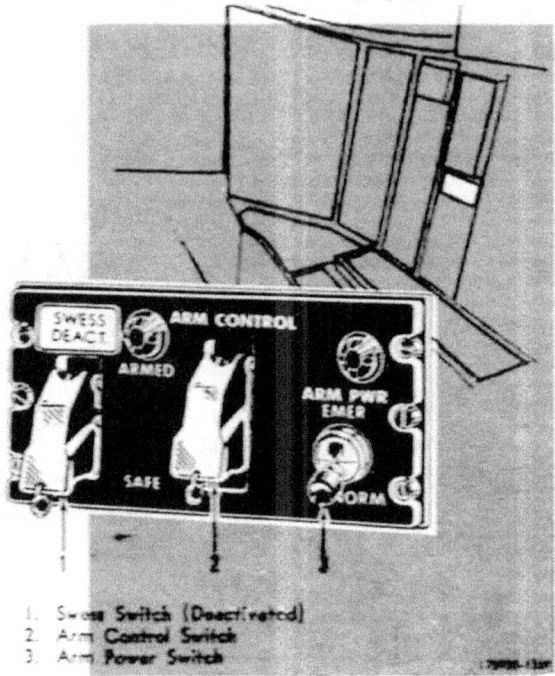

1. Swess Switch (Deactivated)
2. Arm Control Switch
3. Arm Power Switch

Figure 4-52.

lease of a selected weapon unless the last POD position was selected or release power remains present at the selector switch. A time delay of approximately 1.5 seconds is required for the switch to step to the next position upon automatic release of a weapon.

WARNING

Manually repositioning the selector switch when the release signal present lamp is lighted will result in immediate release of the selected weapon.

CAUTION

- The MB or LA pod with fins installed should be released prior to release of any small weapon.
- The MB or LA pod with lower fins removed or the lower pod of a TCP should be released prior to release of a forward small weapon.

Small Weapon Jettison Switch.

The small weapon jettison switch (9, figure 1-7), located on the pilot's lower left console, provides a means of releasing all four weapons simultaneously. The switch has two positions, marked SAFE and JETTISON. A guard covers the switch to prevent accidental actuation. Placing the switch to JETTISON electrically fires gas generators in all four racks to release all weapons simultaneously. The small weapons must be unlocked before they can be jettisoned.

Weapon Selector Switch.

The weapon selector switch (8, figure 4-55), located on the weapon monitor and release panel, is used to complete the release circuit to the desired weapon and to select the correct function of the auto ballistic computer. TCP with —53 warhead ballistics are available when the selector switch is in the OFF position. This rotary type switch is marked OFF, POD, L AFT, R AFT, L FWD, R FWD, and POD. The release circuit is incomplete when the OFF position is selected. The two pod positions are identical. The switch may be manually positioned, however, the switch will automatically step clockwise to the next position upon re-

Arming Power Switch.

The arming power switch (3, figure 4-52), located on the pilot's bomb panel, is a two-position switch used to provide power for small weapon arming in the event of loss of normal 28-volt d-c power. The switch is marked NORM and EMER. The switch is normally positioned to NORM. When in the NORM position arming power is supplied from the 28-volt d-c non essential bus. Placing the switch to EMER provides limited arming power from the 28-volt d-c battery bus if normal power is not available.

WARNING

Arming power is very limited when the arming power switch is in EMER and the airplane battery is supplying power.

Arm Control Switch.

The guarded arm control switch (2, figure 4-52), located on the pilot's bomb panel, is a two-position switch marked ARMED and SAFE. The switch is used to control the position of the ready-safe switch or arming control valve in the MB and TC pods and also enables the small weapons to be armed. For further information, refer to T.O. 1B-58A-25-1.

Pod Warhead Control Selector Switch.

The pod warhead control selector switch (5, figure 4-50), located on the weapon lock and arm panel, is a six-position switch marked OFF, SAFE, GRD RET, AIR RET, GRD FF, and AIR FF. The switch is equipped with a control lever marked OS (off-safe) and SGA (safe-ground-air). The selector switch can only be rotated to those positions selected by the control lever. The control lever can be re-positioned only when the selector switch is in SAFE. Positioning the switch to SAFE closes the circuit to the arming control switch, pod arm indicator, and the pod arm and ready lamp. For information concerning the burst option positions (GRD RET, AIR RET, GRD FF, and AIR FF), refer to T.O. 1B-58A-25.

Small Weapon Warhead Control Selector Switches.

The small weapon warhead control selector switches (figure 4-51), located on the small weapon arming panel, are six-position switches marked OFF, SAFE, GRD RET, AIR RET, GRD FF, and AIR FF. All four switches are identical in function and appearance except each controls a separate weapon (L AFT, R AFT, L FWD, and R FWD). The switch is equipped with a control lever which is functionally identical to the pod warhead control selector switch control lever. Placing the switch to SAFE closes the circuit to the small weapon arm indicator and to the arm and ready lamp of the respective weapon. For information concerning the burst option positions (GRD RET, AIR RET, GRD FF, and AIR FF), refer to T.O. 1B-58A-25.

Radar Bomb Scoring (RBS) Tone Switch.

The radar bomb scoring tone switch (3, figure 4-54), located on the bomb damage evaluation/radar bomb scoring system panel, is provided to control a RBS tone (CW) signal used to score practice bomb runs.

Note

To insure that the RBS tone signal is transmitted to the ground RBS site, the radar bomb scoring tone selector switch (1, figure 4-10), located on the comm-inter transfer and auxiliary chaff control panel at the DSO's station, must be positioned to the command radio (AN/ARC-34 or AN/ARC-57) being used to communicate with the RBS site.

The switch is marked ON and OFF and is spring-loaded to an unmarked center position. When the switch is placed to the ON position, a hold-in relay is closed to initiate the tone signal. An automatic ballistic computer release signal from the bombing system will turn the tone off to simulate actual bomb release for RBS scoring. The auto release switch must be OFF before the computer release signal can turn off the tone. The tone may be manually turned off by placing the switch to the OFF position.

Radar Bomb Scoring (RBS) Tone Indicator Lamp.

The amber press-to-test radar bomb scoring tone indicator lamp (2, figure 4-54), located on the bomb damage evaluation/radar bomb scoring systems panel, is provided to indicate when the RBS tone signal is on. The lamp will light when the RBS tone switch is placed to ON, and the tone signal is being transmitted.

Ballistic Malfunction Test Knob.

The ballistic malfunction test knob (8, figure 4-53) on the ballistics control panel allows the navigator to perform a malfunction test of the bombing equipment before making the bomb run. The knob has eight positions marked OFF, L-TF, L RES, TG-REL OFF, REL ON, VERT VEL, COR, and L-TF MALF. When the knob is placed in one of the test positions, the operator can check for malfunctioning in the equipment being selected by observing the test good and test bad lamps located on the navigation sighting and test panel. Tests should not be conducted with the system in BOMB mode. Positioning the knob at L-TF checks the trail and time-of-fall computer circuits. The L RES position checks the trail resolver circuits. The L-RES test is also valid in the L-TF, Coriolis, and servo 6 malfunction modes. The time-to-go circuit and the release relay are checked by moving the test switch to TG REL OFF and REL ON. The VERT VEL position

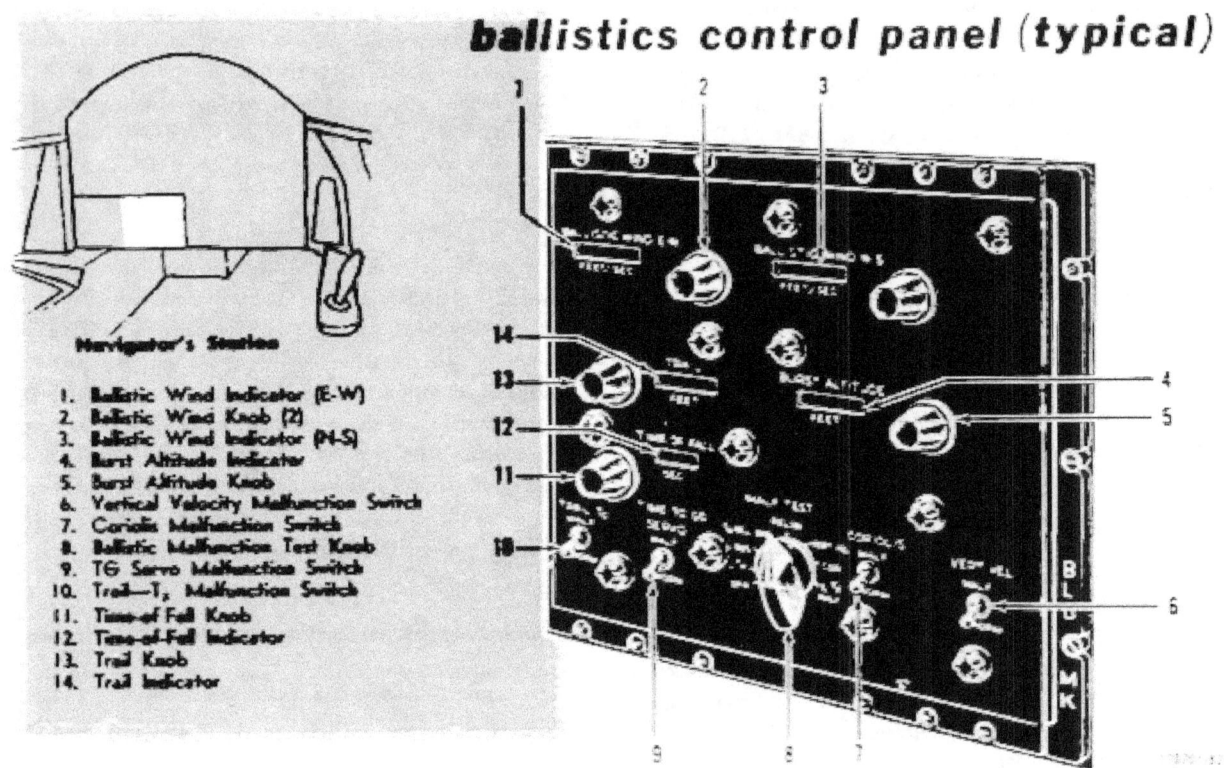

Figure 4-53.

checks the vertical acceleration circuits, and the COR position, the circuits for Coriolis correction. The L-TF MALF position is utilized to test the trail and time-of-fall malfunction circuits in the event a test bad indication was observed during the L-TF check. To perform the L-TF MALF check, the following values should be preset into the applicable indicators on the ballistics panel: time-of-fall — 38.2 seconds and trail — 76,000 feet.

Vertical Velocity Malfunction Switch.

A vertical velocity malfunction switch (6, figure 4-53) marked NORM and MALF is located on the ballistics control panel. When the switch is positioned at NORM, the vertical velocity correction circuit in the ballistics computer receives signals from a vertical accelerometer. Placing the switch to MALF replaces the circuit from the accelerometer with a signal from the air data computer.

Coriolis Malfunction Switch.

The Coriolis malfunction switch (7, figure 4-53) on the ballistics control panel has two positions marked MALF and NORM. The NORM position allows normal operation of the Coriolis corrective circuits; the MALF position substitutes alternate circuits which supply a Coriolis correction based on fixed latitude.

Time-to-Go Servo Malfunction Switch.

The time-to-go servo malfunction switch (9, figure 4-53) on the ballistic control panel provides for the substitution of alternate circuits for the generation of time-to-go and automatic release signals. The switch is marked NORM and MALF. The NORM position allows normal operation of the time-to-go circuit and release relay. Placing the switch in the MALF position automatically substitutes a spare release relay for a malfunctioning time-to-go circuit. This circuit has priority over SIGHT MALF and ALT MALF.

Trail and Time-of-Fall Malfunction Switch.

A two-position trail and time-of-fall malfunction switch (10, figure 4-53) on the ballistics control panel supplies alternate trail and time-of-fall values to the primary navigation system. The switch is marked NORM and MALF. When the switch is positioned at NORM, computer circuits in the ballistics unit supply signals to the primary navigation system for use in solving the bombing problem. When the switch is placed to MALF, the set-in values of trail and time-of-fall shown on the indicators are substituted for the computed values. Ballistic wind and coriolis are still effective in MALF.

Pod Lock Indicator.

The pod lock indicator (1, figure 4-55) located on the weapon monitor and release panel, provides the navigator with an indication of the position of the pod safety lockpin. The indicator shows LOCK (lighted green) or UNLOCK (lighted amber) as applicable. Diagonal stripes appear in the indicator when no power is available or after the pod has been released.

Weapon Unlock Caution Lamp.

The weapon unlock caution lamp (figure 1-13), located on the pilot's caution lamp panel, indicates when lighted that the pod and/or one or more small weapons are unlocked.

Small Weapon Lock Indicators.

The small weapon lock indicators (2, figure 4-55), located on the weapon monitor and release panel, provide a visual indication of the position of the locking solenoid in each weapon rack. LOCK appears in an indicator when the solenoid is de-energized. UNLOCK appears in an indicator when the solenoid is energized. Diagonal stripes appear in an indicator when no power is available.

Pod Arm Indicator.

The pod arm indicator (11, figure 4-55), located on the weapon monitor and release panel, displays the condition (SAFE, ARM, or malfunction) of the warhead whenever warhead control power is on. The indicator shows SAFE (lighted green) whenever the pod warhead selector switch is positioned to SAFE, the warhead monitor circuit is continuous, and all related components are properly positioned. The indicator displays ARM (lighted amber) when any burst position is selected, the pilot's arming control switch is in ARM, the warhead monitor circuit is continuous, and all related components are properly positioned. The indi-

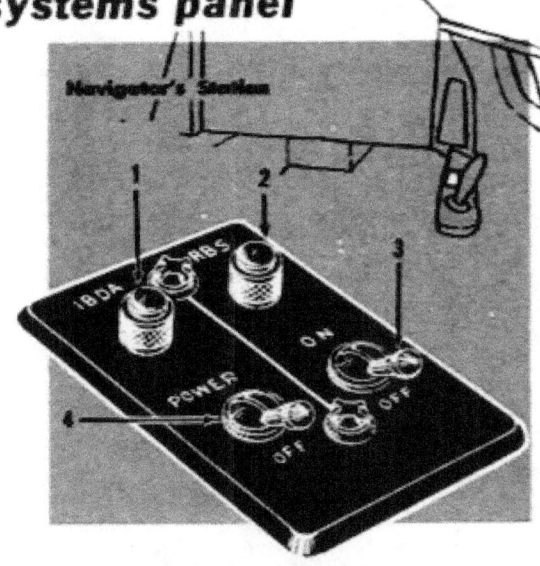

bomb damage evaluation/ radar bomb scoring systems panel

1. Bomb Damage Evaluation System Lamp
2. Radar Bomb Scoring (RBS) Tone Lamp
3. Radar Bomb Scoring (RBS) Tone Switch
4. Bomb Damage Evaluation System Switch

Figure 4-54.

cator shows red lighted diagonal stripes whenever a malfunction is present, there are improperly positioned controls, and/or the warhead monitor circuit is broken.

Small Weapon Arm Indicators.

The small weapon arm indicators (4, figure 4-55), located on the weapon monitor and release panel, display the condition (SAFE, ARM, or malfunction) of the small weapon warheads, whenever warhead control power is ON. An indicator is provided for each of the small weapons (L AFT, R AFT, L FWD and R FWD). The indicator shows SAFE (lighted green) when the respective small weapon warhead control selector switch is in SAFE, the ready-safe switch in the warhead is safe, the warhead monitor circuit is continuous, and all related components are properly positioned. The indicator displays ARM (lighted amber) when the warhead control selector switch is positioned to a burst option, the pilot's arming control switch is in ARMED, the ready-safe switch is in R (ready) and the warhead monitor circuit is continuous and all related components are properly positioned. The indicator will show red lighted diagonal stripes if a mal-

Section IV
Auxiliary Equipment

T.O. 1B-58A-1

function is present, there are improperly positioned controls, or the warhead monitor circuit is broken.

Master Warn Lamp.

The red master warn lamp (3, figure 4-55), located on the weapon monitor and release panel, comes on and remains on whenever a malfunction exists in any of the warhead control circuits. At least one arm indicator should show red lighted diagonal stripes when this lamp is lighted.

Pod Arm and Ready Caution Lamp.

The pod arm and ready caution lamp (figure 1-13), located on the pilot's caution lamp panel, indicates when lighted that the pod is present, unlocked, and armed.

Small Weapon Arm and Ready Caution Lamps.

Four small weapon arm and ready caution lamps (figure 1-13), located on the pilot's caution panel, indicate when lighted that the respective weapon (L AFT, R AFT, L FWD, and R FWD) is present, unlocked, and armed.

Release System Activated Caution Lamp (MB).

The amber release system activated caution lamp (11, figure 4-50), located on the weapon lock and arm panel, will light when pneumatic pressure is attempting to release the MB pod with the lockpin inserted. The release system must be restored to a non-release configuration before the lamp will go out and before the lockpin can be pulled. The lamp will blink momentarily when the pod is released.

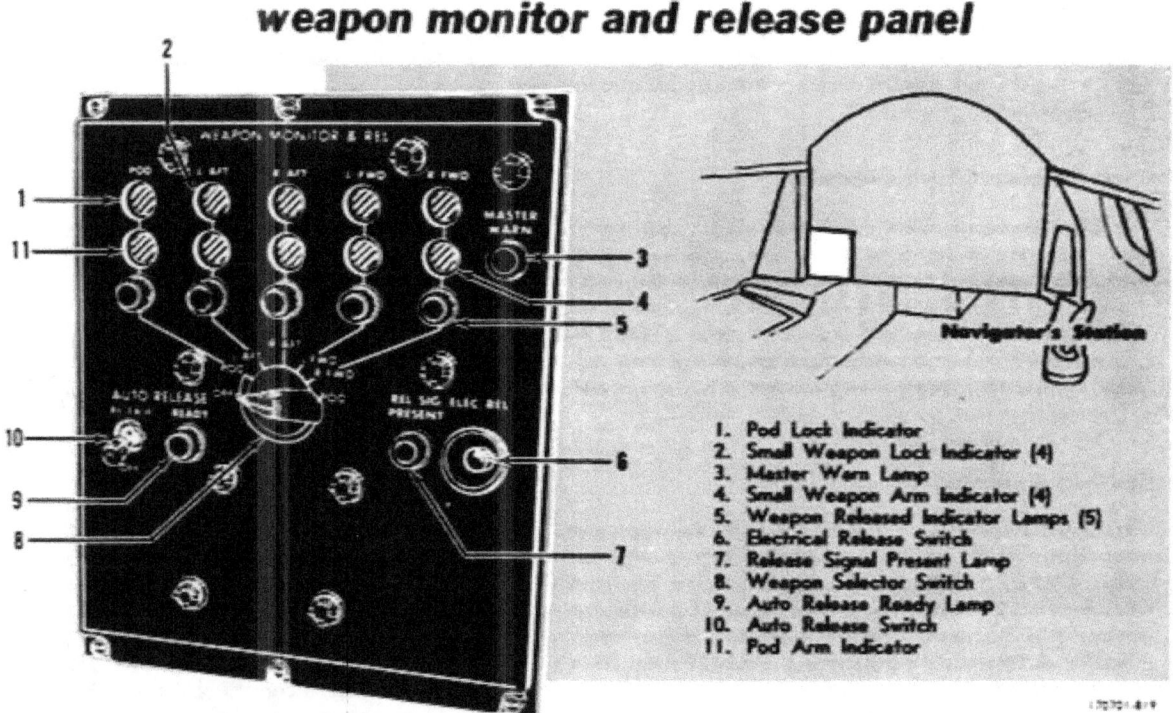

weapon monitor and release panel

1. Pod Lock Indicator
2. Small Weapon Lock Indicator (4)
3. Master Warn Lamp
4. Small Weapon Arm Indicator (4)
5. Weapon Released Indicator Lamps (5)
6. Electrical Release Switch
7. Release Signal Present Lamp
8. Weapon Selector Switch
9. Auto Release Ready Lamp
10. Auto Release Switch
11. Pod Arm Indicator

Figure 4-55

Auto Release Ready Lamp.

The amber press-to-test auto release ready lamp (9, figure 4-55), located on the weapon monitor and release panel, indicates that the release circuit is prepared for an automatic release signal.

Release Signal Present Caution Lamps.

The amber release signal present caution lamps located on the pilot's warning and caution lamp panel (figure 1-13) and on the navigator's weapon monitor and release panel (7, figure 4-55) provide a visual indication that a release signal(s) is present in the release system.

WARNING

Manually positioning the weapon selector switch when this lamp is on will result in immediate release of the selected weapon.

Weapon Released Indicator Lamps.

Five green weapon released indicator lamps (5, figure 4-55), located on the weapon monitor and release panel, provide visual indications of weapon release. The lamps, one for the pod and each small weapon, light when the respective weapon is released from the airplane. The press-to-test function of the lamps provides a cartridge test circuit for the cartridge actuated devices of the TC pod and each small weapon. The press-to-test function of the pod released indicator lamp is inoperative when carrying an MB or LA pod. The lamps are inoperative, except for press-to-test, when the weapon selector switch is OFF.

Ballistic Wind Indicators.

Two ballistic wind indicators (1 and 3, figure 4-53), one for east and west and one for north and south, are located on the ballistics control panel. The indicators (except at zero) show in feet per second the partial ballistic wind components set into the ballistic computer circuits as correction factors to be used in the computation (manual and auto) of trail. When set at zero, 0.4 wind is fed into the ballistics computer. The wind components are set in by means of a knob (2, figure 4-53) adjacent to each indicator.

Time-of-Fall Indicator.

A time-of-fall indicator (manual) (12, figure 4-53) on the left side of the ballistic control panel shows an alternate time-of-fall value (estimated time lapse between pod or small weapons release and burst) for the pod or small weapons. This value is set into the ballistics computer circuits for use during the malfunction check. In the event the ballistics computer malfunctions, it is used in solving the bombing problem. The time-of-fall information is set in with a knob (11, figure 4-53) adjacent to the indicator.

Trail Indicator.

A trail indicator (manual) (14, figure 4-53) on the ballistics control panel shows in feet an alternate ballistic trail of the pod or small weapons. This value is set into the ballistics computer circuit for use in the malfunction check. It is also used by the primary navigation system, in the event of ballistics computer malfunction, in solving the bombing problem. The trail information is set in with a knob (13, figure 4-53) adjacent to the indicator.

Burst Altitude Indicator.

The burst altitude indicator (4, figure 4-53) on the right side of the ballistics control panel shows the desired burst altitude of the bomb in feet above sea level. The burst altitude shown on the indicator is set into the ballistics computer circuits to be used in the computation of trail and time-of-fall in the automatic mode. The burst altitude is set in with a knob (5, figure 4-53) adjacent to the indicator.

BOMBING SYSTEM OPERATION.

For bombing system operating procedures, refer to "Navigator's Checklist," Section VIII.

Section IV
Auxiliary Equipment

T.O. 1B-58A-1

AIR NAVIGATION DATA RECORDING SYSTEM (AN/ASH-17).

The air navigation data recording system is an automatic, electronically operated, data handling system which records flight information for inflight reference and for post flight evaluation. The system also supplies digitized time to other intelligence-gathering systems of the airplane. The system is composed of an air navigation data recorder and a recorder control unit (RCU), both of which are located at the navigator's station. Flight data from the primary navigation system and from the air data computer is received and decoded by the RCU and printed by the recorder. In addition to its normal use, the data recorded by the system, especially when supported by data from the Bomb Damage Evaluation System, provides a valuable aid in postflight analysis of certain abnormal and/or emergency flight conditions. For further information on use of the system during inflight emergencies, refer to "Operation of Air Navigation Data Recording System During Emergencies" this section. The system is controlled from the navigator's station. Direct current for the system is supplied from the a-c and high voltage d-c power panel. Alternating current for the system is supplied from the left a-c power panel.

AIR NAVIGATION DATA RECORDER.

The air navigation data recorder is a high speed, general purpose type recorder located at the forward end of navigator's left console. The recorder receives flight data from various systems of the airplane and records this data on paper tape. The printed flight data provides information for routine inflight decisions; provides a permanent log of the flight; provides the crew with sufficient data to begin manual navigation in the event of failure of the primary navigation system; and provides information for postflight bomb damage evaluation. Basic components of the recorder include the printing mechanism, the timing mechanism, the paper advance and reverse mechanism, and the recorder control panel (figure 4-58). All of these recorder components are in the recorder cabinet except for the recorder control panel which is located on the upper aft corner of the cabinet. Normal operation of the recorder is virtually automatic after the recorder timing mechanism has been set to the correct Greenwich mean time and the recorder has been regulated to print at the desired time intervals. The recorder will record flight data at regular intervals depending upon the position of the intervalometer selector switch. Printed flight data can be obtained any time between the regular printing intervals by depressing

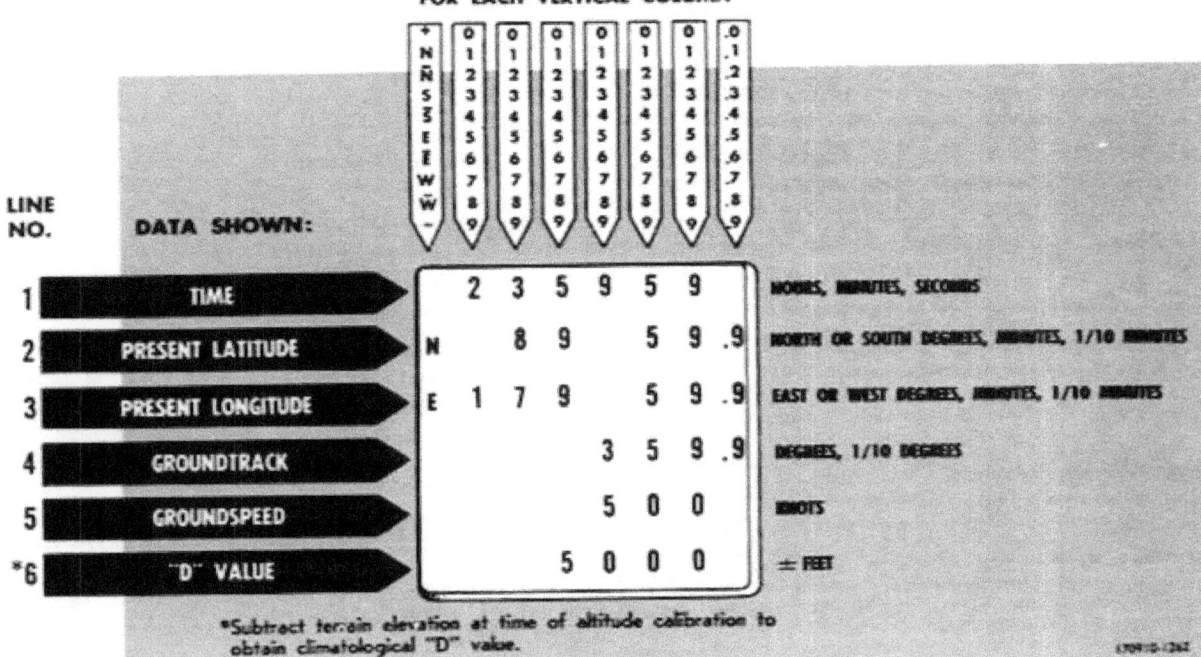

4-88

T.O. 1B-58A-1

Section IV
Auxiliary Equipment

air navigation data recorder format (typical)

RADAR CAMERA DATA REQUEST

LINE NO.	DATA SHOWN:									
1	TIME		2	3	5	9	5	9		HOURS, MINUTES, SECONDS
2	PRESENT LATITUDE	N		8	9		5	9	.9	NORTH OR SOUTH DEGREES, MINUTES, 1/10 MINUTES
3	PRESENT LONGITUDE	E	1	7	9		5	9	.9	EAST OR WEST DEGREES, MINUTES, 1/10 MINUTES
4	GROUND TRACK					3	5	9	.9	DEGREES, 1/10 DEGREES
5	GROUND SPEED					5	0	0		KNOTS
*6	"D" VALUE	+		5	0	0	0			± FEET
7	FIX LATITUDE	N		8	9		3	0	0	NORTH OR SOUTH DEGREES, MINUTES, 1/10 MINUTES
8	FIX LONGITUDE	E	1	7	9		4	0	0	EAST OR WEST DEGREES, MINUTES, 1/10 MINUTES

*Subtract terrain elevation at time of altitude calibration to obtain climatological "D" value.

Figure 4-57.

the manual data request button. Whenever the manual request button is depressed, and the search power switch is in XMTG position, a single photo is taken. Previously printed information can be reviewed by means of the data review switch. The recorder records flight information a block at a time with each block consisting of from six to nine lines of printed data. In the normal printing mode, a block of flight data is recorded each time the recorder receives a data request from the intervalometer, the manual data request switch, or the primary navigation system radar camera. The number of lines of data printed in each block depends upon what type of data request has been received in the recorder. An intervalometer data request results in the printing of a format (figure 4-56) of data containing six lines. These lines consist of Greenwich mean time, present latitude, present longitude, ground track, groundspeed, and Bomb Nav System "D" value (the difference between air data pressure altitude and radio altitude). A radar camera data request can be initiated either automatically by the primary navigation system or manually by the manual data request button when the automatic radar photography switch is in any position (OFF, ON or RECORD) if a photograph is not in progress and the search power is in the XMTG position. Either of these data requests results in the printing of an eight line block of data (figure 4-57) which consists of fix latitude and fix longitude in addition to the same six lines of data which result from an intervalometer data request. In the bomb damage evaluation (BDE) mode, a block of flight data is printed once every second throughout the BDE recording cycle. Refer to "Bomb Damage Evaluation (BDE) System," this section.

RECORDER CONTROL UNIT.

The recorder control unit (RCU) is an electronic controlling unit located at the navigator's station beneath the air navigation data recorder. The RCU receives digital and analog data from the primary navigation system and from the air data computer. This data is stored until needed and then transmitted to the recorder upon receipt of a data request. The RCU also initiates printing cycles for the recorder, and receives and handles the radar camera, intervalometer, and manual data requests as often as once per second. The functional subsystems of the RCU consist of the timing pulse generator, radar time index read-out, multiplexer, multiplexer control, data request register, storage read-in circuits, servo digitalizers, central recorder

Section IV
Auxiliary Equipment

T.O. 1B-58A-1

air navigation data recorder control panel (typical)

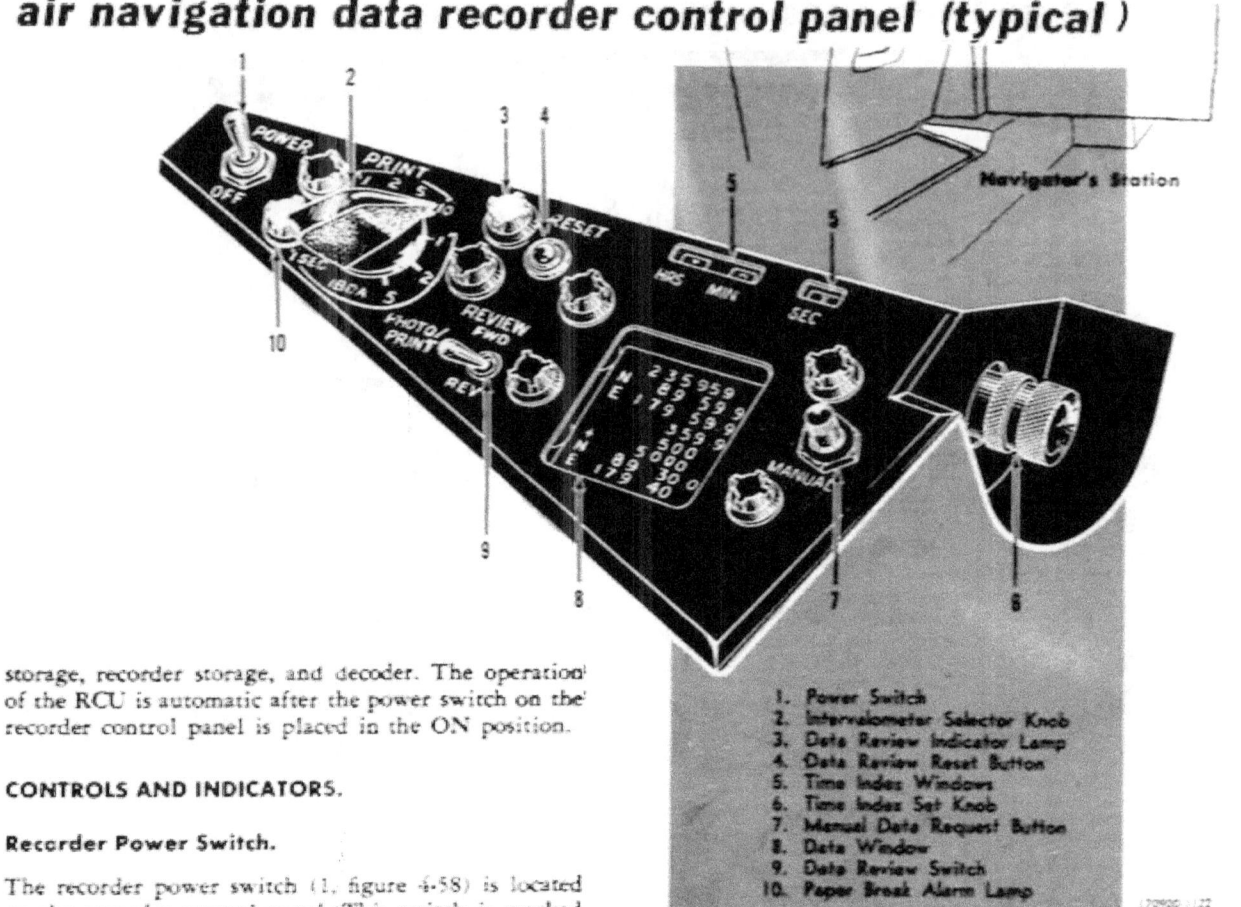

Figure 4-58.

1. Power Switch
2. Intervalometer Selector Knob
3. Data Review Indicator Lamp
4. Data Review Reset Button
5. Time Index Windows
6. Time Index Set Knob
7. Manual Data Request Button
8. Data Window
9. Data Review Switch
10. Paper Break Alarm Lamp

storage, recorder storage, and decoder. The operation of the RCU is automatic after the power switch on the recorder control panel is placed in the ON position.

CONTROLS AND INDICATORS.

Recorder Power Switch.

The recorder power switch (1, figure 4-58) is located on the recorder control panel. This switch is marked POWER and OFF. When placed in the POWER position, the switch energizes the recorder and the recorder control unit. The switch controls 28-volt d-c power from the main d-c power panel. There is approximately 1 minute minimum delay after power ON before printing capability exists. Under extreme conditions (—65°F) a warmup period of up to 15 minutes may be required before normal operation is realized. Of course, at higher temperatures the warmup time will be proportionally less.

Intervalometer Selector Knob.

The intervalometer selector knob (2, figure 4-58), located on the air navigation data recorder control panel, has nine positions arranged in a clockwise sequence. The positions are marked 1, 2, 5, and 10 on the left upper scale and 1, 2, 5, IBDA, and 1 SEC on the right lower scale. The four positions marked 1, 2, 5 and 10 on the upper left scale control the interval of data requests to the air navigation data recorder for printing of flight data every 1, 2, 5 or 10 minutes respectively. The 1, 2, and 5 positions on the right lower scale, will provide data at 1, 2 and 5-minute intervals for both the air navigation data recorder and the radar camera. Placing the knob to the IBDA (bomb damage evaluation) position, with the bomb damage evaluation power switch in the POWER position, will provide the following automatic control of the air navigation data recorder and BDE and radar cameras:

- From 15 seconds prior to weapon release up to weapon release; one data block printout by the air navigation data recorder and one exposure on the BDE camera each second.

- From weapon release through switchover one data block printout by air navigation data recorder each four seconds; one BDE camera exposure each two seconds; and one radar camera exposure each second.

- For 95 seconds following switchover one data block printout by air navigation data recorder each four seconds and one BDE camera exposure each two seconds.

Placing the intervalometer selector knob to 1 SEC position at any time will provide one radar camera exposure and one data block print out by the air navigation data recorder per second. Complete photo iden-

4-90

tification of weapon or simulated release within one second after release will be provided by switching off the units-of-hours row of the time index matrix lights in the PRU if the bomb damage evaluation power switch is in the POWER position. Selecting a normal setting as soon as possible after weapon release will conserve paper and radar camera film.

Data Review Switch.

The data review switch (9, figure 4-58), located on the recorder control panel, has positions marked FWD and REV. These positions are spring-loaded to a center unmarked OFF position. When the switch is held in the FWD position, the paper tape in the data window (8, figure 4-58) will move forward. To move the tape in reverse, the switch must be momentarily placed to FWD and then held to REV. The tape will move in reverse until the switch is released. By means of this switch the operator may review previously printed data. The recorder will not accept data requests while the tape is being reviewed.

Data Review Reset Button.

The data review reset button (4, figure 4-58) is a pushbutton-type switch located on the recorder control panel. The button is marked RESET and must be pressed after each review of the printed tape, in order that the recorder will again accept standard data requests. Overprint will occur if tape is not run to clear area before pressing reset button.

Manual Data Request Button.

The manual data request button (7, figure 4-58) is a pushbutton-type switch located on the recorder control panel. By momentarily depressing the manual button, a data request is initiated which results in the immediate printing of a block of flight data consisting of time, present latitude, present longitude, groundtrack, groundspeed, "D" value (the difference between air data pressure altitude and radio altitudes), and when the search power switch is in XMTG, fix longitude and fix latitude, and a single photo is taken. Holding this button down will result in continuous data requests.

Time Index Set Knob.

The time index set knob (6, figure 4-58) is used to set the odometer-type digit indicators of the time index indicator digitalizer (TIID), which are visible on the recorder control panel. The TIID can be set at the beginning of or during a mission in which the recorder is to be utilized. The set knob is located in a recess on the inboard side of the recorder cabinet. To set the second, tens of seconds, and the minute indicators, the set knob must be pushed in; to set the tens of minutes, hours, and tens of hours indicators, the set knob must be pulled out. When pushed in and rotated, the set knob adjusts the digit indicators in increments of 1 second. When pulled out and rotated, the set knob adjusts the digit indicators in increments of 10 minutes. The set knob is spring-loaded to return to a neutral disengaged position when not in use. When setting the TIID, the marking on the minute indicator must agree with the marking on the tens-of-minutes indicator. If a red vertical mark is visible on one, a red mark should be visible on the other, or else no markings should be visible on either. The significance of the red marks is discussed in this section under "Time Index Indicator Digitalizer."

Time Index Indicator Digitalizer.

The time index indicator digitalizer (TIID) is essentially an elapsed time indicator synchronized by one per second pulses from the primary navigation system. The TIID displays the current Greenwich mean time on cylindrical odometer-type digit indicators in two time index windows (5, figure 4-58) at the right upper edge of the recorder control panel. Time is shown in increments of hours, minutes, and seconds with the maximum possible reading being 23 hours, 59 minutes, and 59 seconds. The odd numbers on the tens-of-minutes indicator have red vertical lines at the right of the numerals. The minute indicator has two complete sets of digits, one set which has red vertical marks adjacent to the numerals. When setting the indicators to correct time, the minute indicator must be set to agree with the tens-of-minutes indicator. If a red mark appears on the tens-of-minutes indicator, a similar mark must appear on the minute indicator; conversely, if no marking appears on one, no mark should appear on the other. Aligning the indicators in this manner synchronizes the mechanical linkage to assure an accurate read-out. When a maximum time reading is attained by the time indicators, all the digits revert to zero and begin another cycle. A set knob located in a recess on the inboard side of the recorder cabinet is used to set the TIID digit indicators to the correct time either before or during flight. The same time reading as displayed by the TIID is printed on the first line of each new block of flight data. The TIID also converts time to a binary-coded form and transmits this coded time to the PRU and the BDE system for the correlation of data. The TIID operates on 28-volt d-c power furnished from the main d-c power panel.

> **CAUTION**
>
> If the TIID stops stepping, turn off the air navigation data recorder at once.

Section IV
Auxiliary Equipment

T.O. 1B-58A-1

Paper Break Alarm Lamp.

The paper break alarm lamp (10, figure 4-58) is an amber lamp located on the recorder control panel. When lighted, the lamp indicates the roll of paper tape in the printer is broken or that the roll of tape has been exhausted. A continuous red line on the paper tape indicates the amount of tape remaining by its proximity to the edge. Supply is depleted as the line runs from left to right. A roll lasts 12 hours at 1-minute setting. However, during the BDE cycle, the tape is depleted at approximately four inches per second. The recorder discontinues printing when the alarm lamp is lighted and remains inoperative until the roll of paper is repaired. The alarm lamp receives 28-volt d-c power from the main d-c power panel.

Data Review Indicator Lamp.

The unmarked data review indicator lamp (3, figure 4-58) is located on the recorder control panel. The lamp lights whenever the data review switch is held to the FWD or REV position, and remains lighted until the reset button is pressed. The lighted lamp thus indicates that the recorder cannot accept data requests until the reset button is pressed.

OPERATION OF AIR NAVIGATION DATA RECORDING SYSTEM DURING EMERGENCIES.

For operation of the system during inflight emergencies, place the bomb damage evaluation (IBDA) power switch to POWER. This will place the system in standby. Then, when a special format is desired, place the radar bomb scoring (RBS) switch to ON then to OFF. The BDE format will be printed and the BDE camera will take radar pictures for approximately 120 seconds or until the bomb damage evaluation (IBDA) power switch is returned to OFF, whichever is first. Since recorder tape and IBDA film will be consumed at a rapid rate, the power switch should be returned to OFF as soon as sufficient record is accumulated rather than permit the complete 120-second cycle to expire. For operation of the system other than during inflight emergencies, refer to Navigator's Checklist, Section VIII.

BOMB DAMAGE EVALUATION (BDE) SYSTEM (AN/ASH-15).

The bomb damage evaluation (BDE) system, in conjunction with the recorder and the primary navigation system records inflight information from which weapon ground zero may be derived. Using this information, trained ground personnel may evaluate target damage without requiring post-strike reconnaissance. In addition to its normal use, the data recorded by the system, especially when supported by data from the Air Navigation Data Recording System, provides a valuable aid in post-flight analysis of certain abnormal

and/or emergency flight conditions. The system consists of a camera and a data package. The camera is located in a compartment on the underside of the fuselage just forward of the drag chute doors. Operating automatically, the camera makes one exposure every 2 seconds and printed information is recorded every 4 seconds from weapon release to BDE OFF. The camera carries 50 feet of 35-mm film which is ample film for five complete BDE cycles. The camera is mounted in a fixed position looking aft and down 25 degrees from the aircraft centerline. The viewing field of the lens is large enough to get adequate coverage of either a ground or air burst with the aircraft tail-on to the burst. Lens opening, shutter speed, film type and filter must be selected on the ground prior to flight. The BDE data package is located in the cabin area. It contains the components necessary to program the BDE recording cycle and to effect the proper interrelated operations of the primary navigation system, the recording system, and the BDE camera. A preflight test switch located on the package prints a single block of flight data (see figure 4-59) whenever the switch is depressed and held for approximately 4 seconds. The data package is cooled by cabin air conditioning. Controls for the BDE system are located at the navigator's station. The BDE system receives positive and negative 150-volt d-c power from the a-c and high-voltage d-c power panel, 115-volt a-c power from the left a-c power panel, and 28-volt d-c power from the 28-volt d-c power panel.

BOMB DAMAGE EVALUATION (BDE) RECORDING CYCLE.

The bomb damage evaluation (BDE) recording cycle is an electronically controlled schedule during which the BDE system, the primary navigation system, and the recording system function together to produce and record the information necessary to evaluate nuclear bomb damage or radar bomb scoring accuracy. The recording cycle is initiated and programmed by the BDE data package. The cycle begins 15 seconds prior to weapon release and continues for approximately 125 seconds. During the 15 seconds prior to weapon release the BDE camera and the air navigation data recorder record information at a rate of one photo and readout per second. During the period from weapon release to switchover the air navigation data recorder records information at the rate of one readout every four seconds; the BDE camera records information at the rate of one exposure every two seconds; and the radar camera records information at the rate of one exposure each second. During the period from switchover to BDE OFF the air navigation data recorder records information at the rate of one readout every four seconds, and the BDE camera records information at the rate of one exposure every two seconds. If no weapon or simulated release signal is initiated, the BDE cycle will terminate after 30 seconds have elapsed. The flight data blocks printed during the BDE recording cycle (figure 4-59) consist of nine lines

air navigation data recorder format (typical)

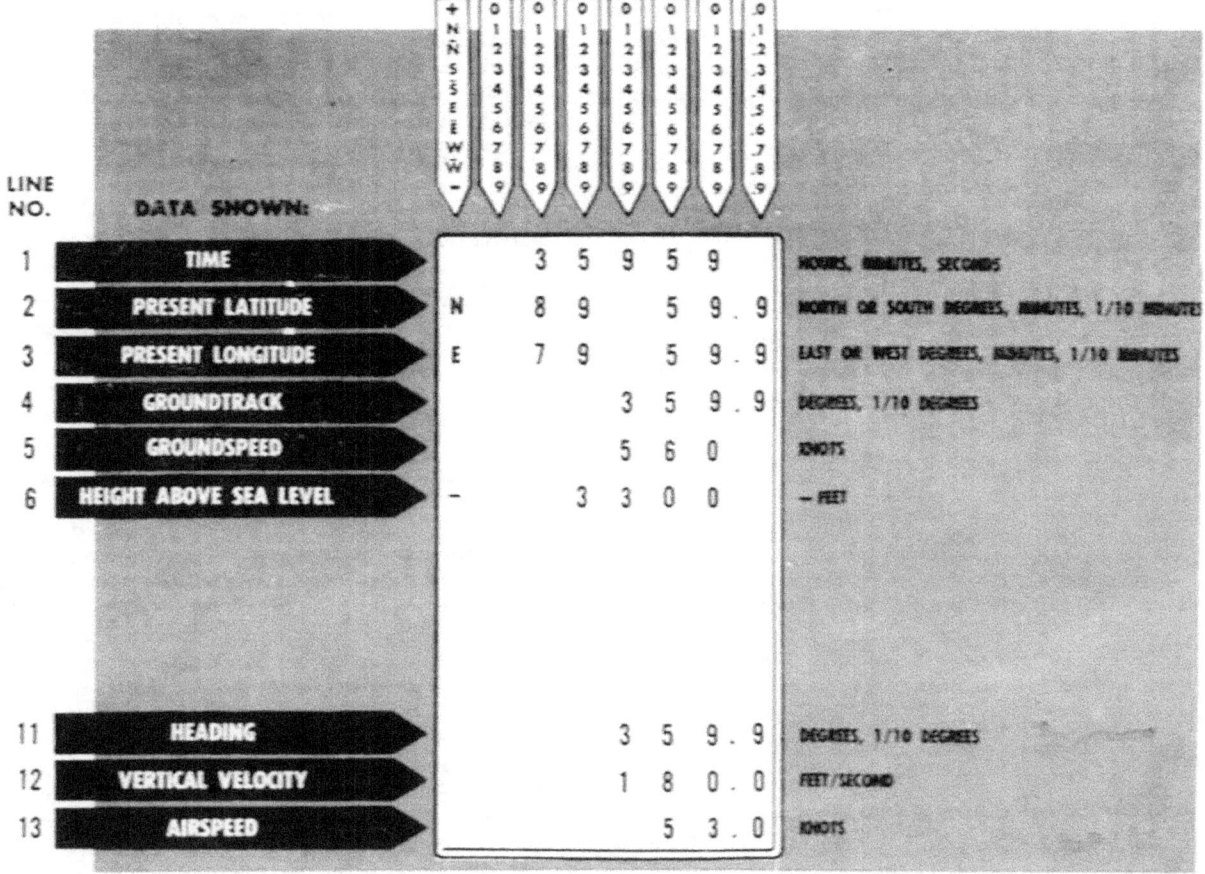

Figure 4-59.

of data. The lines printed during the first portion of the cycle are time, present latitude, present longitude, groundtrack, groundspeed, height above sea level, heading, vertical velocity, and airspeed. Airspeed is printed until weapon release at which time relative air density is printed for fifteen seconds. Pitch is then printed for the remainder of the recording cycle. Much of the data printed during BDE mode can be read directly from the tape. However, the following cannot:

Time—The tens-of-hours digit is not printed. Therefore, it is necessary to refer to a pre-BDE mode block of data to determine what this digit should be.

Present longitude—The hundreds of degrees digit is not printed. For example: A printout of E 75 00.0 could indicate a longitude of either East 75 degrees or East 175 degrees. Therefore, it is necessary to refer to a pre-BDE mode block of data to determine the correct present longitude.

Height above sea level and airspeed—The printed value must be multiplied by ten.

Vertical velocity—The value 050.0 represents zero reference. For each two feet per second of vertical velocity this value is increased or decreased by an increment of one. Upward vertical velocity increases the value, downward vertical velocity decreases the value. For example, an upward velocity of ten feet per second would be printed as 055.0.

Relative air density—Relative air density is equal to minus 0.012780 times the value printed on the tape in degrees plus 1.7572.

Roll and pitch—The value 180.0 represents zero reference. Pitch or roll in degrees is either added to or subtracted from this value. Roll to the right or pitch upward is added to the value. Roll or pitch in the opposite direction is subtracted. For example: A pitch upward or roll to the right of 3 degrees would be printed as 183.0.

CONTROLS AND INDICATORS.

Bomb Damage Evaluation (BDE) Power Switch.

The two-position bomb damage evaluation (BDE) power switch (4, figure 4-54), is located on the bomb damage evaluation/radar bomb scoring systems panel. The switch has positions marked POWER and OFF. With the switch in the POWER position, the BDE system is energized and placed in a standby condition, ready to begin the automatic recording cycle. Placing the switch in the OFF position de-energizes the entire system.

Note

The BDE cycle may be interrupted and a new cycle started by placing the power switch to OFF, placing the weapon selector switch to another weapon position and then placing the power switch to POWER.

Bomb Damage Evaluation (BDE) Indicator Lamp.

The amber press-to-test bomb damage evaluation (BDE) indicator lamp (1, figure 4-54) is located on the bomb damage evaluation/radar bomb scoring systems panel. The lamp lights when electrical power is applied to the system; it goes out when power is removed.

NORMAL OPERATION OF BOMB DAMAGE EVALUATION (BDE) SYSTEM.

The bomb damage evaluation (BDE) system is put into operation by placing the BDE power switch in the POWER position at least one minute prior to weapon release. At the end of the recording cycle, the system will automatically return to a standby condition, allowing the recorder to return to the normal mode of printing. The power switch may be returned to the OFF position approximately three minutes after weapon release.

BOMBING EQUIPMENT.

The bombing equipment consists of a two component pod (TC) (figure 4-62) and four small weapons (B43 bombs) (figure 4-60).

SMALL WEAPONS (B43 BOMB).

The airplane is equipped to carry four small weapons mounted under the wing between the fuselage and the main landing gear. Two weapons are carried on either side of the fuselage in tandem. Each weapon is attached to a rack by cartridge actuated hooks (one forward and one aft) which latch on lugs attached to the top of the weapon. The racks contain the release mechanism and electrical disconnects for monitoring and are enclosed in streamlined pylons. Main components of the weapon are a jettisonable nose cone which covers the impact spike, a center section sub-assembly which houses the warhead, and a tail section which houses the retardation parachute and supports four tail fins. An inspection window located on the lower right side of the center section allows visual check of the ready-safe switch. The weapon weighs approximately 2100 pounds.

- Overall Length   12 feet
- Maximum Diameter   1.5 feet

Warhead Arming and Fuzing System.

Each small weapon is equipped with a ready-safe switch which functions as a part of the warhead arming and fuzing system. The ready-safe switch (figure 4-60), located inside the weapon on the right side, is a rotary-type switch with four small windows on the cover which exposes the letter "R" when the switch is in the ready position or "S" when it is in the safe position. The position of the switch can be visually checked through a window in the side of the weapon. Placing the pilot's arm control switch to ARMED completes a circuit to the navigator's small weapon warhead control selector switches. Then, when the

T.O. 1B-58A-1

Section IV
Auxiliary Equipment

small weapon b 43

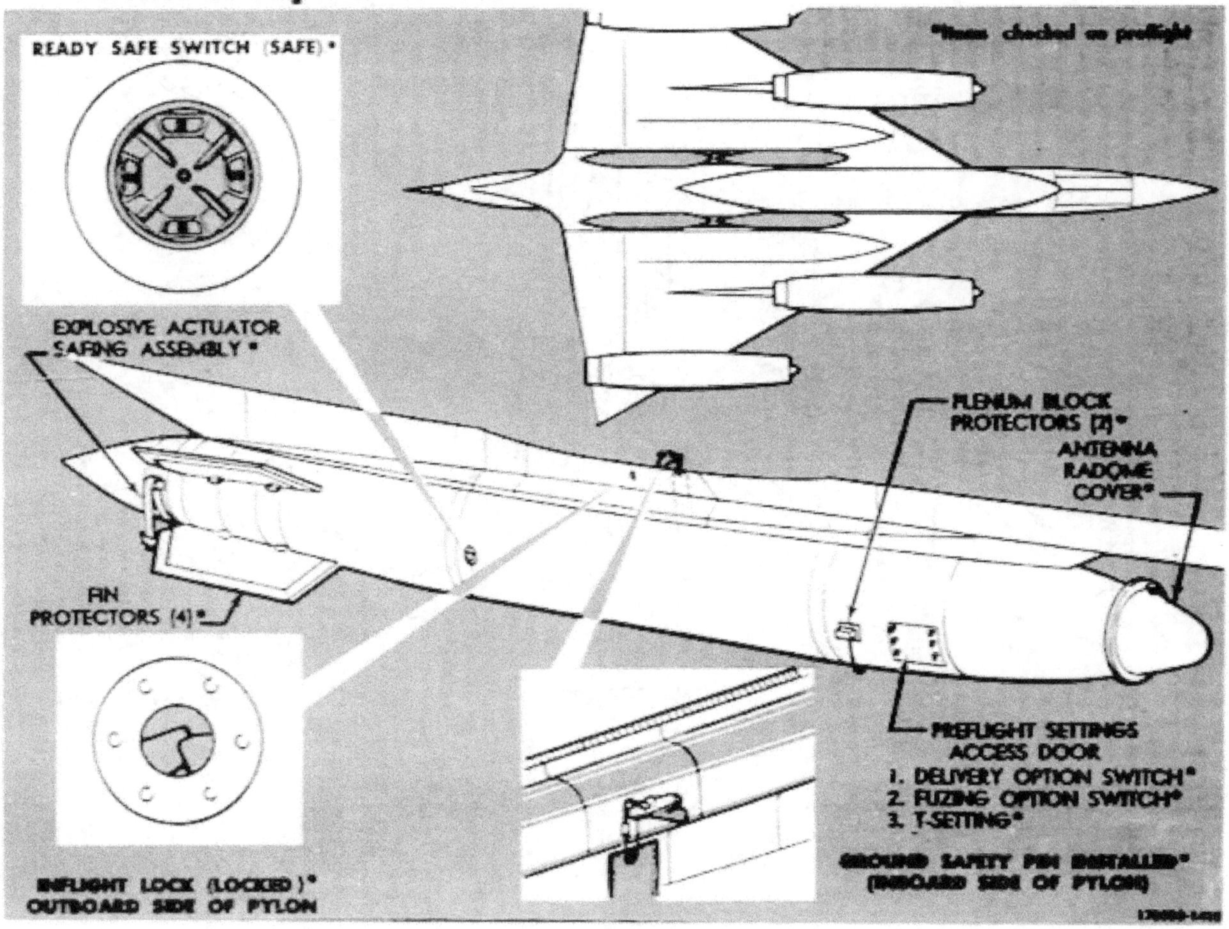

*Items checked on preflight

- READY SAFE SWITCH (SAFE)*
- EXPLOSIVE ACTUATOR SAFING ASSEMBLY*
- FIN PROTECTORS (4)*
- INFLIGHT LOCK (LOCKED)* OUTBOARD SIDE OF PYLON
- PLENUM BLOCK PROTECTORS (2)*
- ANTENNA RADOME COVER*
- PREFLIGHT SETTINGS ACCESS DOOR
  1. DELIVERY OPTION SWITCH*
  2. FUZING OPTION SWITCH*
  3. T-SETTING*
- GROUND SAFETY PIN INSTALLED* (INBOARD SIDE OF PYLON)

Figure 4-60.

warhead control selector switches are individually placed to any position other than SAFE or OFF, the corresponding ready-safe switch will electrically step to the ready position. With the circuits set up in this manner, a momentary impulse of airplane electrical power will initiate the arming and fuzing sequence for each weapon as it is released. Positioning each warhead control selector switch to SAFE or OFF will step the corresponding ready-safe switch to the "S" safe position. Placing the arm control switch to SAFE will step all ready-safe switches to the "S" safe position. For additional information on the small weapon warhead arming and fuzing system, refer to T.O. 1B-58A-25-1.

Release System.

The small weapon is released by electrically firing a gas generator which supplies high pressure gas to mechanically actuate a release actuator. The release actuator rotates a pivot arm to simultaneously retract two hooks that hold the weapon on the rack. Automatic release is initiated by an electrical impulse from the primary navigation system. Emergency release is accomplished electrically by positioning the weapon selector switch to the desired weapon position and actuating either the weapon release switch at the pilot's station or the electrical release switch at the navigator's station. An inflight safety lock is provided on each small weapon rack. When engaged, the locks prevent rotation of the pivot arms and thereby locks the hooks so that the weapons cannot be released. The locks are controlled by use of the small weapon lock switches located on the weapon lock and arm panel at the navigator's station. Inspection windows, located on the outboard side of the pylons above each weapon, allow a visual check of the inflight safety locks. Holes, provided in the inboard side of the pylons opposite the windows, allow insertion of ground safety pins to prevent inadvertent actuation of the release hooks. For release procedures, refer to Section VIII. For jettison procedures, refer to Section II.

4-95

Section IV
Auxiliary Equipment

T.O. 1B-58A-1

mb and la pod

*Items checked on preflight.

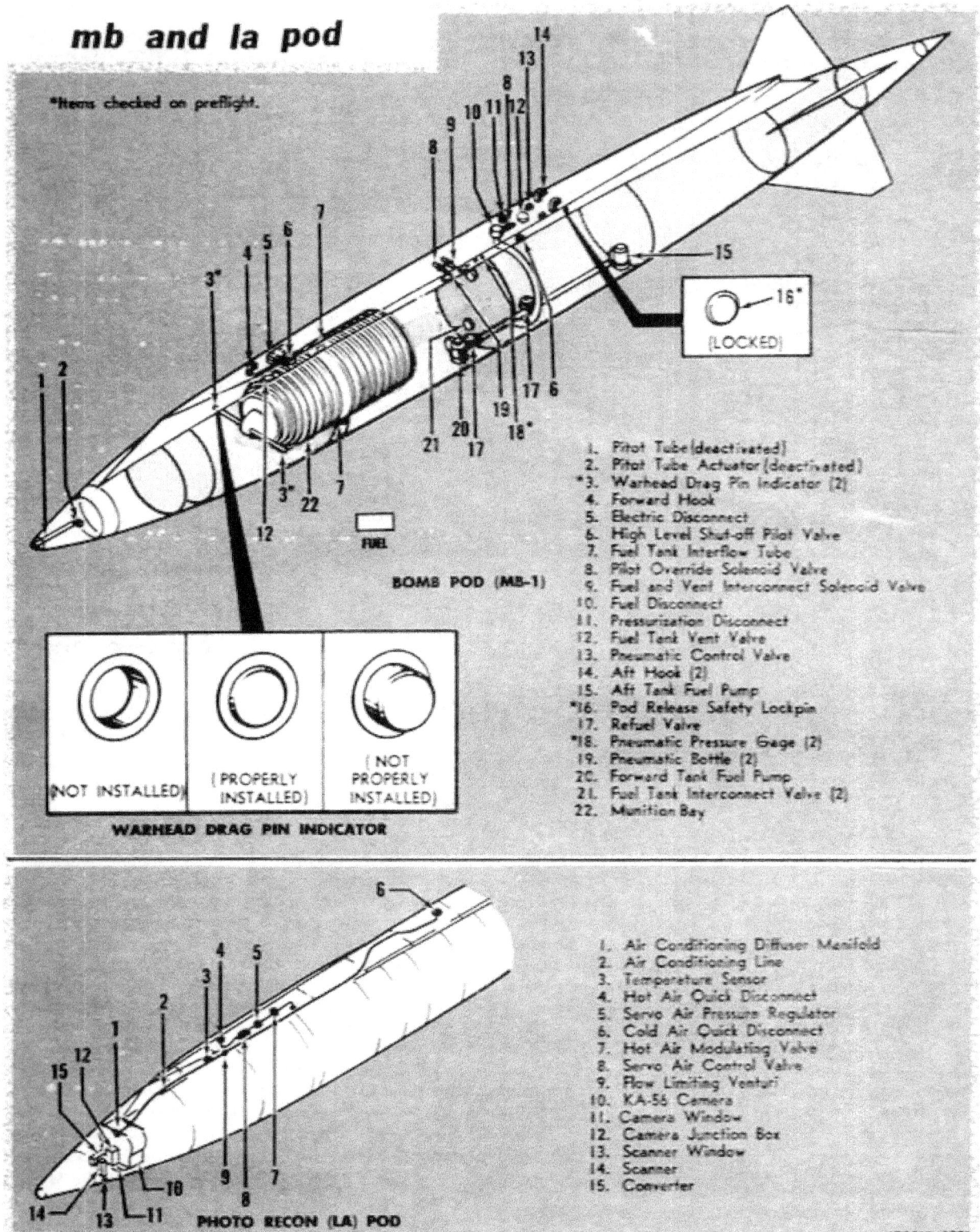

BOMB POD (MB-1)

1. Pitot Tube (deactivated)
2. Pitot Tube Actuator (deactivated)
*3. Warhead Drag Pin Indicator (2)
4. Forward Hook
5. Electric Disconnect
6. High Level Shut-off Pilot Valve
7. Fuel Tank Interflow Tube
8. Pilot Override Solenoid Valve
9. Fuel and Vent Interconnect Solenoid Valve
10. Fuel Disconnect
11. Pressurization Disconnect
12. Fuel Tank Vent Valve
13. Pneumatic Control Valve
14. Aft Hook (2)
15. Aft Tank Fuel Pump
*16. Pod Release Safety Lockpin
17. Refuel Valve
*18. Pneumatic Pressure Gage (2)
19. Pneumatic Bottle (2)
20. Forward Tank Fuel Pump
21. Fuel Tank Interconnect Valve (2)
22. Munition Bay

WARHEAD DRAG PIN INDICATOR
(NOT INSTALLED) (PROPERLY INSTALLED) (NOT PROPERLY INSTALLED)

PHOTO RECON (LA) POD

1. Air Conditioning Diffuser Manifold
2. Air Conditioning Line
3. Temperature Sensor
4. Hot Air Quick Disconnect
5. Servo Air Pressure Regulator
6. Cold Air Quick Disconnect
7. Hot Air Modulating Valve
8. Servo Air Control Valve
9. Flow Limiting Venturi
10. KA-56 Camera
11. Camera Window
12. Camera Junction Box
13. Scanner Window
14. Scanner
15. Converter

Figure 4-61.

MB POD.

The MB pod is carried beneath the fuselage of the airplane by three pneumatically actuated hooks (one forward and two aft) which are mounted to the pod. The pod consists of an equipment bay, a forward fuel tank and munitions bay, an aft fuel tank, a tail cone and fins, and a pylon. The equipment bay extends from the nose of the pod to the forward fuel tank bulkhead. The forward fuel tank and munitions bay is divided into two sections by the munitions loading splice. The loading splice is necessary for installing ballast in the munitions bay. The pylon encloses the release system and components of other pod systems installed on the upper surface of the pod. An electrical disconnect mechanically connects electrical circuits of the pod to the airplane. Fuel and fuel pressurization disconnects engage matching components on the airplane. These disconnects allow the pod fuel system and the airplane fuel system to be connected, and pressurized air to enter the pod fuel system from the airplane. All disconnects release and close instantly when the pod is released. Pod stabilization after release is achieved by means of fins mounted on the tail cone.

MB or LA Pod Principal Dimensions:

- Overall Length   57 feet
- Maximum Diameter   5 feet

MB or LA Pod Gross Weights:

- With maximum fuel load   36,087 pounds
- Dry weight (including ballast)   8,550 pounds

MB or LA Pod Drag Pins.

The MB or LA pod incorporates two drag pin indicators which provide an external indication of whether or not the ballast is installed in the pod. The pins indicate ballast not installed when pins are recessed; ballast installed and drag pins properly engaged when pins are flush with pod skin; and drag pins not properly engaged when the pins are protruding from the pod skin. (3, figure 4-61).

TC POD (BLU-2B).

The BLU-2B pod is a two-component pod (TC) consisting of an upper (BLU-2B-3) pod and a lower (BLU-2B-2) pod. The purpose of the two component pod is to allow jettison of the lower pod after fuel carried in the pod is expended on an EWO mission, to reduce drag and thus increase the range or speed of the airplane.

Upper Pod.

The upper pod consists of a forward fuel tank, a munitions bay, an aft fuel tank, a tail cone, parachute retardation system, pylon, and three fins.

Note

When the munitions bay does not contain a warhead, a ballast assembly will be installed before flight.

The upper pod is carried beneath the airplane by three pneumatically actuated hooks (one forward and two aft) which are mounted to the pod. The two aft hooks are mechanically connected to each other and to the hook actuator by a torque tube. The forward hook is linked to the torque tube by the pod release actuator tube. The pod electrical circuit is connected to the airplane electrical circuit through the pod electrical disconnect located aft of the forward hook. Upper pod stabilization after release is achieved by the three fins. Two of the fins are mounted to the sides of the pod at thirty degrees to and above the pod horizontal center line. The third (lower) fin is located on the pod lower vertical center line and is retracted within the upper pod when the lower pod is attached. The pylon contains the release system and various components of other pod systems installed on the upper surface of the upper pod. All disconnects release and close simultaneously when the pod is released.

Upper Pod Principal Dimensions:

- Overall Length   35 feet
- Maximum Diameter   3½ feet

Upper Pod Gross Weights:

- With Maximum Fuel Load & -53 Warhead   11,970 pounds
- Dry Weight (Including -53 Warhead or Ballast)   9,540 pounds

Section IV
Auxiliary Equipment

T.O. 1B-58A-1

two component pod (blu-2b)

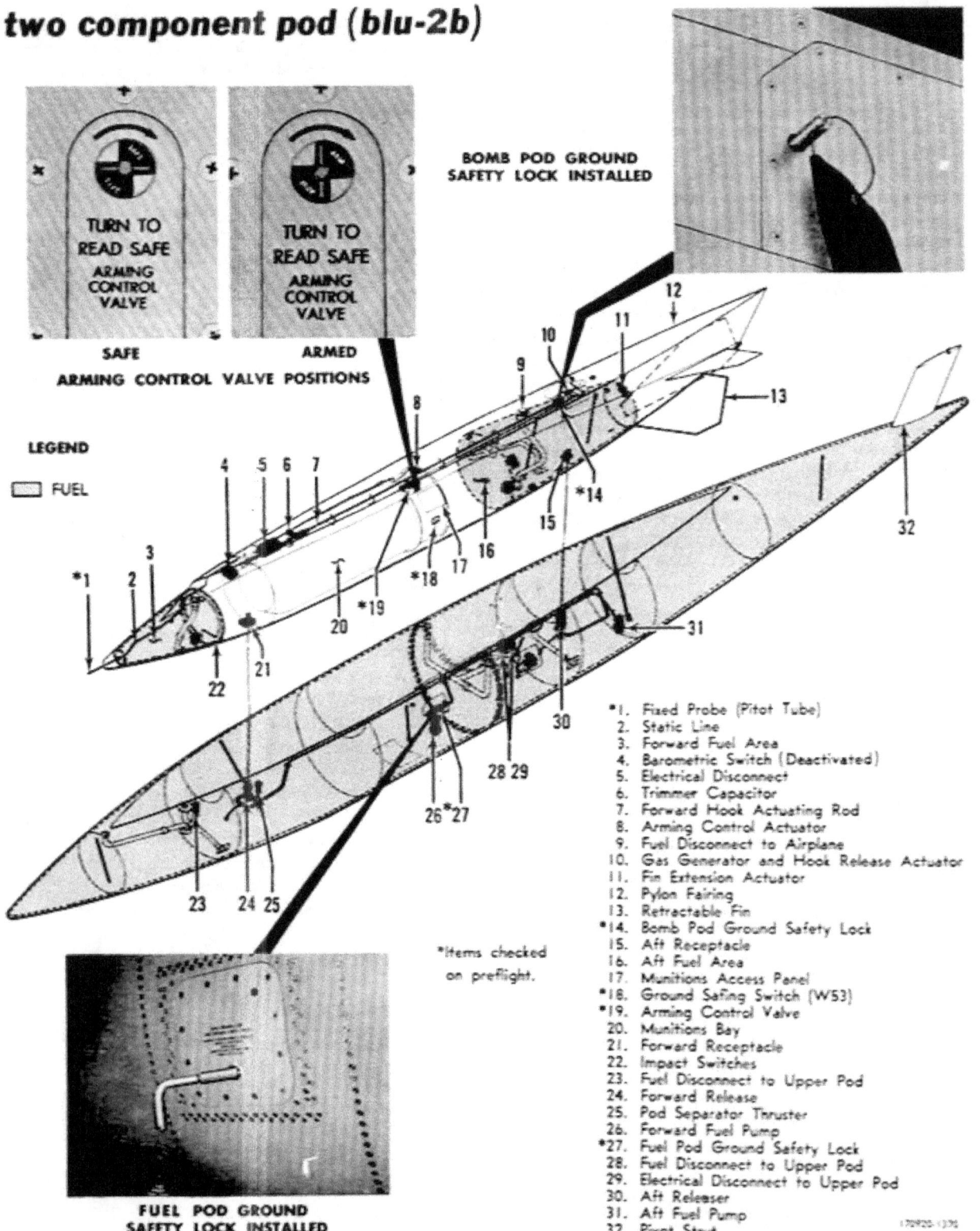

Figure 4-62.

Lower Pod.

The lower pod is carried beneath the upper pod by one forward and one aft releaser. The lower pod consists of a forward fuel area and an aft fuel area (the upper portions of which are concaved to receive the upper pod). A pivot strut is mounted on the aft end of the pod to facilitate proper separation between lower pod and upper pod. Fuel and fuel tank pressurization disconnects engage matching components on the upper pod and airplane. All disconnects release and close instantly when the pod is released.

Lower Pod Principal Dimensions:

- Overall Length   54 feet
- Maximum Diameter   5 feet

Lower Pod Gross Weights:

- Load with Maximum Fuel   26,000 pounds
- Dry Weight   1,900 pounds

WARHEAD ARMING AND FUZING SYSTEM.

Upper Pod.

The upper pod incorporates a fixed pitot tube and an arming control valve as a part of the arming and fuzing system of the warhead. The pitot tube serves as a pressure source for the differential pressure switch, and arming and firing switches. The pitot tube switch located on the navigator's weapon lock and arm panel is inoperative for the upper pod because the pitot tube is fixed in the extended position. The arming control valve is used to connect or interrupt release system gas pressure to the arming control actuator mounted at the aft end of the warhead. When the arming control valve is in ARM, release system gas pressure is ported from the release system hook actuator through the arming control valve to the arming control actuator cylinder. When the arming control valve is in SAFE, release system gas pressure is ported from the release system hook actuator through the arming control valve to the atmosphere. For additional information on the warhead arming and fuzing system refer to T.O. 1B-58A-25-1.

POD FUEL SYSTEM.

The MB, LA and TC pods are designed to carry a fuel supply which supplements the airplane fuel supply. For a complete description and fuel system schematic on the pod fuel system refer to "Fuel Supply System," Section I.

POD RELEASE SYSTEM.

MB Pod.

The MB pod is released by pneumatically unlatching the three pod hooks from the airplane. The forward hook is connected to the two aft hooks and pod release actuator by an actuator tube and operates simultaneously with the aft hooks. The release actuator pneumatically actuates the hooks by receiving high pressure nitrogen from pneumatic bottles through the pneumatic control valves. Two pneumatic pressure gages are used to check the pressure in the bottles. The gages can be visually checked through an inspection window in the pylon. The release actuator is locked with a pod release safety lock pin to prevent accidental operation of the pod release mechanism.

Note

The lock pin must be removed before the pod can be released.

The lock pin is visible from the exterior of the pod, and the pin indicates whether the release actuator is locked or unlocked. The actuator is locked when the pin is flush with the pylon skin and unlocked when the pin is protruding approximately one inch from the pylon skin. A safety lock handle located below the weapon lock and arm panel in the navigator's station will unlock the release actuator and mechanical release handle. The safety lock handle is safetied and sealed to show if the handle has been tampered with. The handle must be rotated 90° counterclockwise before being pulled aft, and must remain aft in order to mechanically release the pod with the mechanical release handle. Rotating the handle will break the safety wire and unlock the pod mechanical release handle. Returning the handle to the full in position and rotating it 90° clockwise will re-insert the lockpin and lock the mechanical release handle. Normal inflight pod release is controlled by automatic or manual switches which route electrical current to the solenoids of the pneumatic control valves. When the weapon selector switch is positioned to the POD position and the auto release switch is positioned to RELEASE, the pod will be released automatically by the bombing navigation system. In the event of malfunction in the automatic circuit, release can be accomplished by positioning the weapon selector switch to the POD position and manually depressing the electrical release switch located on the navigator's weapon monitor and release panel, or with the weapon release switch on the pilot's forward left console. If there is an electrical system failure, release can be accomplished manually with the mechanical release handle located below the weapon lock and arm panel in the navigator's station. For release procedures, refer to "Normal Bombing," Section VIII, and "Jettisoning Procedures," Section II.

Two Component Pod.

Lower Pod. The lower pod is released by firing the release system gas generators which supply a high pres-

Section IV
Auxiliary Equipment

T.O. 1B-58A-1

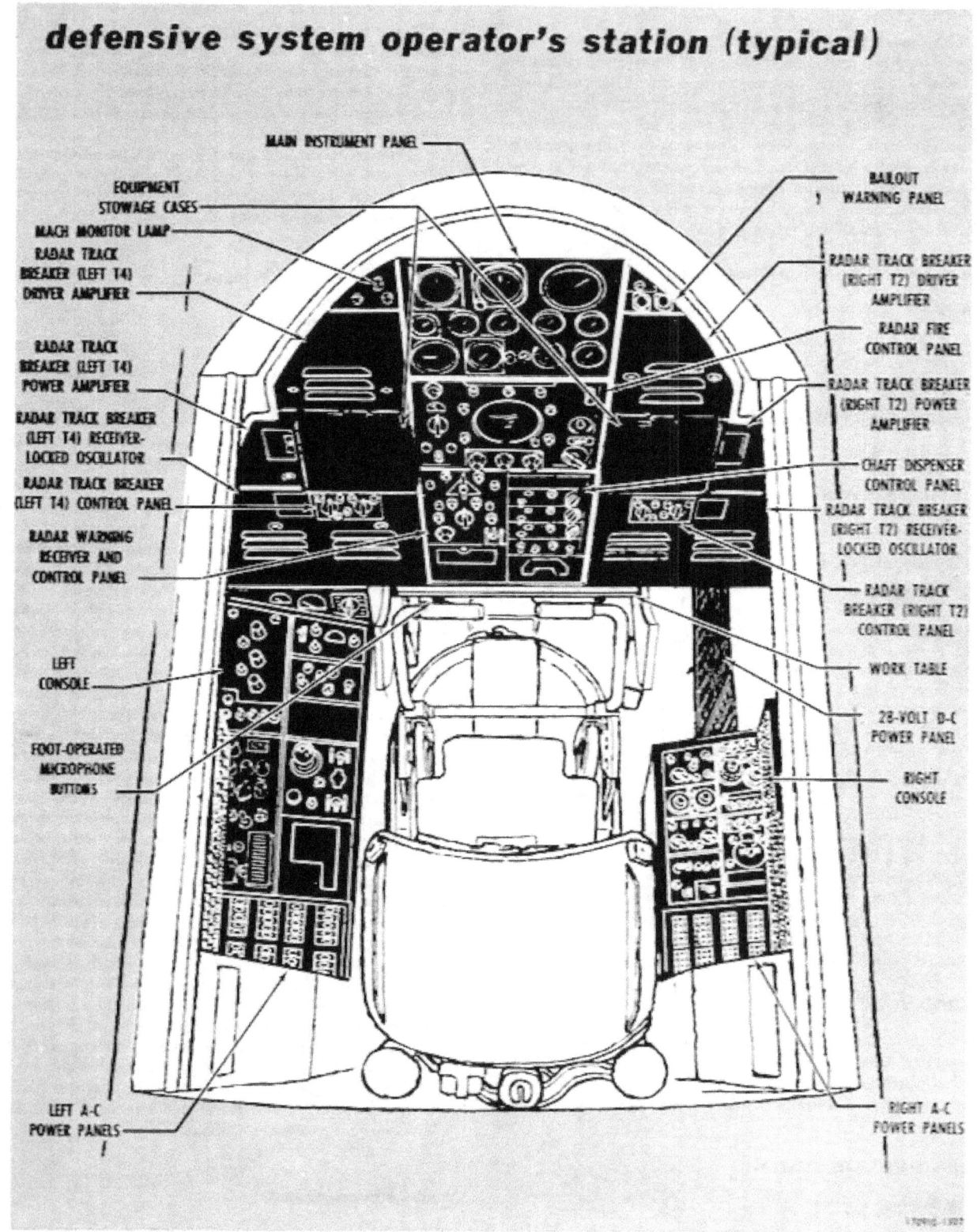

Figure 4-63.

dso's left console

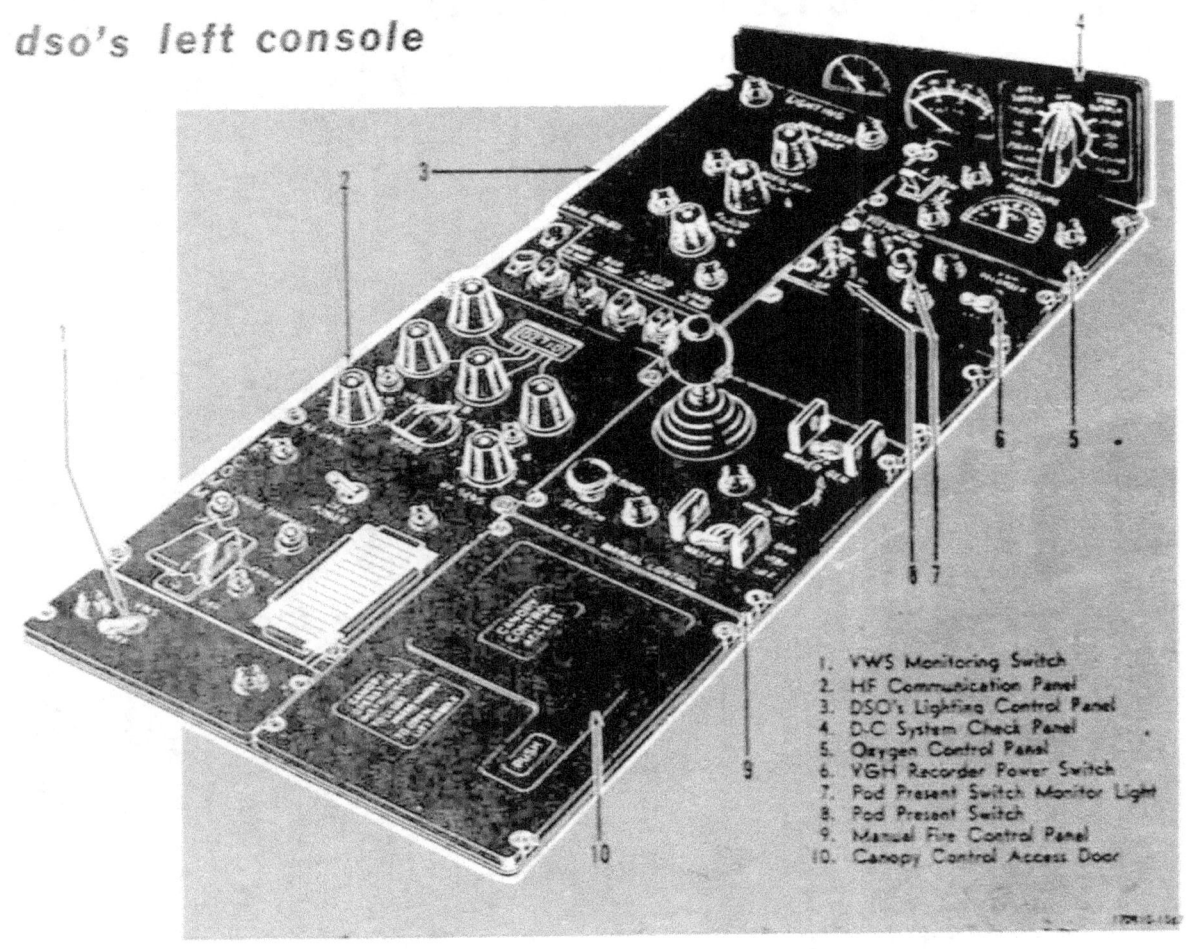

1. VWS Monitoring Switch
2. HF Communication Panel
3. DSO's Lighting Control Panel
4. D-C System Check Panel
5. Oxygen Control Panel
6. VGH Recorder Power Switch
7. Pod Present Switch Monitor Light
8. Pod Present Switch
9. Manual Fire Control Panel
10. Canopy Control Access Door

Figure 4-64.

sure gas to actuate the lower pod releasers. After the pod fuel is transferred to the airplane and if refueling is not planned, lower pod release can be initiated by the pilot. Upon actuating the switches an electrical pulse fires the lower pod release system gas generator sending high pressure gas to the lower pod releasers. For release procedures, refer to "Jettisoning Procedures," Section II.

Upper Pod. The upper pod is released by retracting the three pod hooks. The release actuator actuates the hooks by receiving gas pressure from the gas generator. Normal release is initiated by an electrical pulse from the bombing navigation system. Emergency release is initiated electrically by positioning the pilot's or navigator's pod release switch to RELEASE. Emergency release is initiated by mechanically firing the gas generator with the mechanical release handle located on the navigator's weapon lock and arm panel. The pod release actuator is locked by a pod release mechanism.

Note

The lock pin must be disengaged before the pod can be released.

The lock pin, located in the upper pod pylon, mechanically prevents operation of the release actuator. After the lower pod has been dropped, the upper pod lower fin gas generator is fired when the pod release lock pin is disengaged.

Section IV
Auxiliary Equipment

T.O. 1B-58A-1

dso's right console (typical)

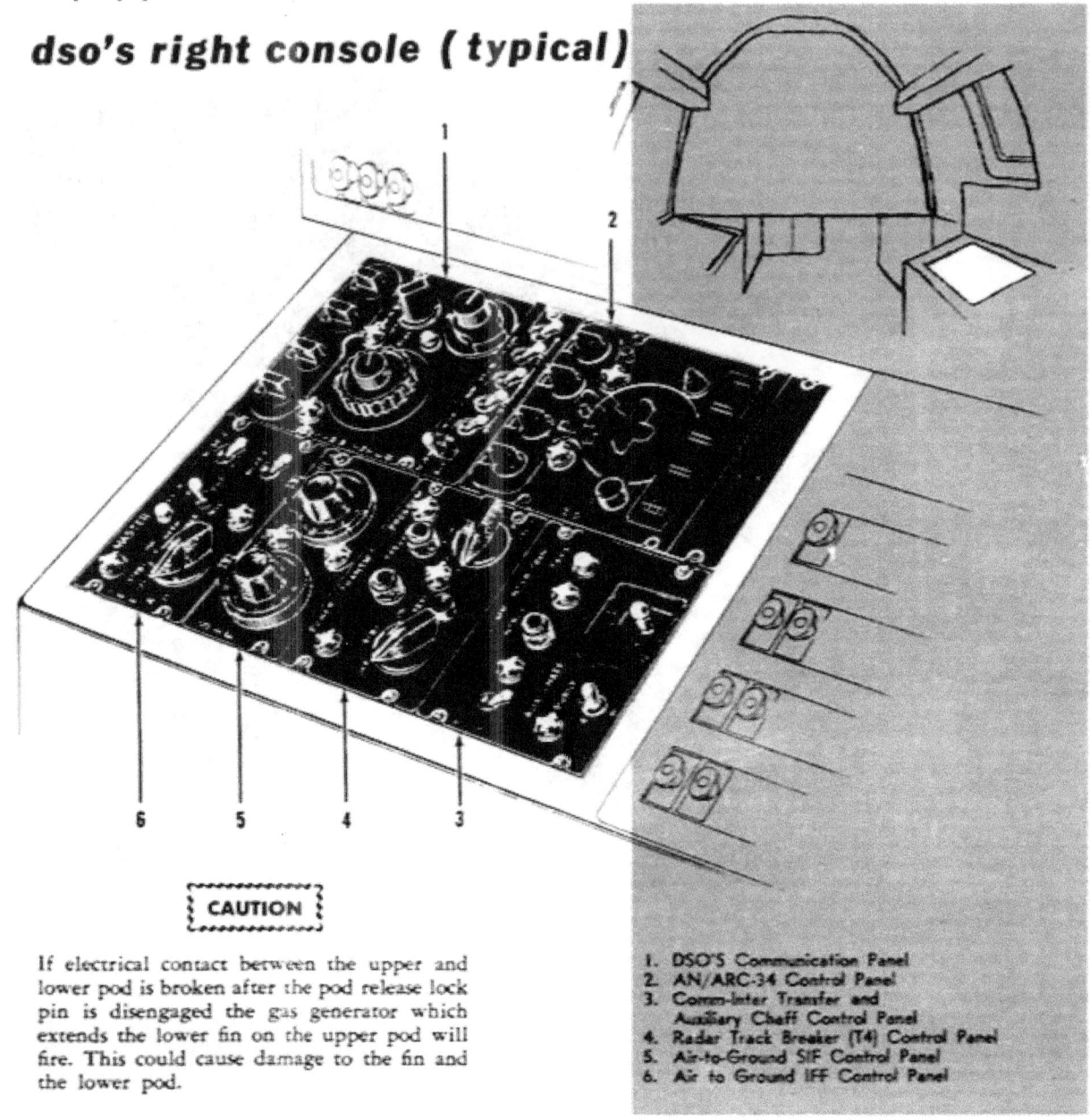

> **CAUTION**
>
> If electrical contact between the upper and lower pod is broken after the pod release lock pin is disengaged the gas generator which extends the lower fin on the upper pod will fire. This could cause damage to the fin and the lower pod.

For release and jettisoning procedures, refer to "Normal Bombing," Section VIII, and "Jettisoning Procedures," Section II, respectively.

POD PRESENT SWITCH MONITOR.

The pod present switch monitor (figure 4-64), located on the DSO's left console, provides a means of ground checking the pod present switches for the presence of redundant grounds to the autopilot ACA (amplifier computer assembly) during preflight. The monitor switch is marked TCP, OFF, and MB-1. When the switch is positioned for the applicable pod the mal-

1. DSO'S Communication Panel
2. AN/ARC-34 Control Panel
3. Comm-Inter Transfer and Auxiliary Chaff Control Panel
4. Radar Track Breaker (T4) Control Panel
5. Air-to-Ground SIF Control Panel
6. Air to Ground IFF Control Panel

Figure 4-65.

function lamp will remain off if the pod present switches are correctly positioned and the pod is attached. The TCP position of the switch should be used for either the complete TCP or upper pod. When monitoring the pod present switches, the malfunction lamp will light when a malfunction exists in the switches or if the pod present monitor switch is not properly positioned. A malfunction indication merely reflects the possibility of an ACA ground loss since the monitor circuit checks only the position of the pod presence switches and not the pod disconnect grounds. However, if a malfunction indication is obtained during preflight with the monitor switch correctly positioned the pod present switches should be checked for correct position prior to flight to insure the presence of electrical grounds to the flight control system. The normal position for the switch is OFF.

FUEL POD READY SWITCH.

The lower (fuel) pod ready switch (2, figure 1-7), located on the pilot's lower left console, is marked READY and OFF. When the switch is placed in READY, the lower pod release system electrical circuit is completed to the fuel pod release switch. The switch is guarded in the OFF position.

FUEL POD RELEASE SWITCH.

The lower (fuel) pod release switch (3, figure 1-7), located next to the fuel pod ready switch on the pilot's lower left console, is marked REL and OFF. When the switch is placed in the REL position, the electrical circuit is completed to the lower pod release system gas generators which actuate the lower pod releasers. The switch is guarded in the OFF position.

For the description and operation of weapon controls and indicators, refer to "Bombing System" in this section.

PHOTO RECONNAISSANCE SYSTEM.

Airplanes equipped to carry the photo recon pod (LA) (figure 4-61) have the capability of performing daylight photographic reconnaissance missions. The photo recon pod is an MB pod modified to carry a KA-56 camera in the space previously provided for warhead related equipment in the nose of the pod. The system consists of the KA-56 camera and magazine, a scanner and converter, a pod camera control panel and an air conditioning and electrical system. The KA-56 camera is a panoramic type camera capable of horizon-to-horizon scanning with automatic exposure control and image motion compensation. The camera magazine is automatically driven by the camera drive mechanism. The magazine holds up to 1000 feet of film and must be removed from the pod for loading. The scanner and converter furnishes data to the camera for image motion control. The pod camera control panel (figure 4-67) located at the navigator's station replaces the weapon monitor and release panel when the photo recon pod is installed. The panel provides the necessary controls and indicators to operate the system. Air conditioning from the airplane's system is supplied to the pod through quick disconnects in the fuselage to control the temperature environment of the camera and defog the camera and scanner windows. Air from the camera compartment exhausts overboard through a vent just forward of the camera window.

dso's main instrument panel (typical)

1. Airspeed Mach Indicator
2. Barometric Altimeter
3. Fuel Flow Totalizer Indicator
4. Airplane Fuel Quantity Repeater Indicator (4)
5. Pod Fuel Quantity Repeater Indicator (2)
6. Automatic CG Off Caution Lamp
7. CG Repeater Indicator
8. Elevator Position Indicator
9. Elevator Available Indicator

Figure 4-66.

The system operates on 28 volt d-c and 115 volt a-c power from the right a-c and multiple weapons 28 volt d-c power panel.

PHOTO RECON POD RELEASE SYSTEM.

The release system for the photo recon pod is identical to the mechanical release system for the MB pod. No means for electrical release is provided. For emergency release procedures refer to the EMERGENCY JETTISON procedures applicable to the MB pod in Section III.

Section IV
Auxiliary Equipment

CONTROLS AND INDICATORS.

Manual V/H Input Knobs.

Two manual V/H input knobs (1, figure 4-67), located on the navigator's pod camera control panel, are used to manually set altitude above terrain and ground speed for operation of the camera in the event automatic image motion compensation malfunctions. An indicator beside each knob facilitates setting the proper values. Altitude may be set from 200 to 10,000 feet. The altitude indicator scale is colored red from 1000 feet through 10,000 feet to prevent misinterpretation of the scale. Ground speed may be set from 200 to 1100 knots.

V/H Control Converter Power Switch.

The V/H control converter power switch (2, figure 4-67), located on the navigator's pod camera control panel, is a two position switch marked OFF and labeled CONV POWER in the ON position. Placing the switch to the CONV POWER position provides power to the scanner and converter which in turn furnishes altitude above terrain and ground speed information for image motion compensation. The switch should be placed in the CONV POWER position at least five minutes before camera operation to allow the system to warmup.

V/H Control Selector Switch.

The V/H control selector switch (3, figure 4-67), located on the navigator's pod camera control panel, is a two position switch marked AUTO and MANUAL. The switch controls the mode of altitude above terrain and ground speed inputs to the camera. When the switch is in the AUTO position altitude above terrain and ground speed information from the scanner and converter are automatically fed to the image motion compensation mechanism of the camera. With the switch in MANUAL the navigator must use the manual input knobs to set altitude above terrain and ground speed into the system. The switch should normally be in AUTO position. The MANUAL position is used when the scanner or converter malfunctions.

V/H Control Auto Hold Lamp.

The amber press-to-test V/H control auto hold lamp (4, figure 4-67), located on the navigator's pod camera control panel, provides an indication that automatic altitude above terrain and ground speed information to the camera has been interrupted. This may be caused by a sudden change in altitude such as passing over a sharp ridge or depression or by cloud cover below the airplane. When the lamp comes on the system will hold the last setting before the interruption. If the interruption lasts longer than 750 milliseconds the system will adjust to the new values and the lamp will go out. If the lamp remains on a malfunction of the scanner or converter is indicated and the navigator should place the V/H control selector switch in MANUAL and manually set the input indicators to the existing altitude above terrain and ground speed values. The lamp may stay on when flying over highly reflective surfaces such as water, however, this does not indicate a malfunction.

Film Remaining Counter.

The film remaining counter (5, figure 4-67), located on the navigator's pod camera control panel, provides an indication in feet of the amount of unexposed film remaining in the camera magazine. The counter has three digit windows and will read between 999 and 000 indicating the amount of film remaining. When the camera is turned on the counter will provide an indication that the camera is functioning as the amount of film remaining is reduced.

Film Failure Indicator Lamp.

The amber press-to-test film failure indicator lamp (6, figure 4-67), is located on the navigator's pod camera control panel. The lamp is labeled FAIL and will light if the film breaks or when all film is expended. When the lamp lights camera operation should be discontinued. An indication of film remaining on the film remaining counters will indicate the film has broken or jammed.

Camera Power Switch.

The camera power switch (9, figure 4-67), located on the navigator's pod camera control panel, is a two position switch marked OFF and labeled POWER in the ON position. When the switch is placed in the POWER position a red press-to-test camera power lamp (7, figure 4-67), located above the switch, will light to indicate 28 volt d-c power is being furnished to the camera system.

pod camera control panel

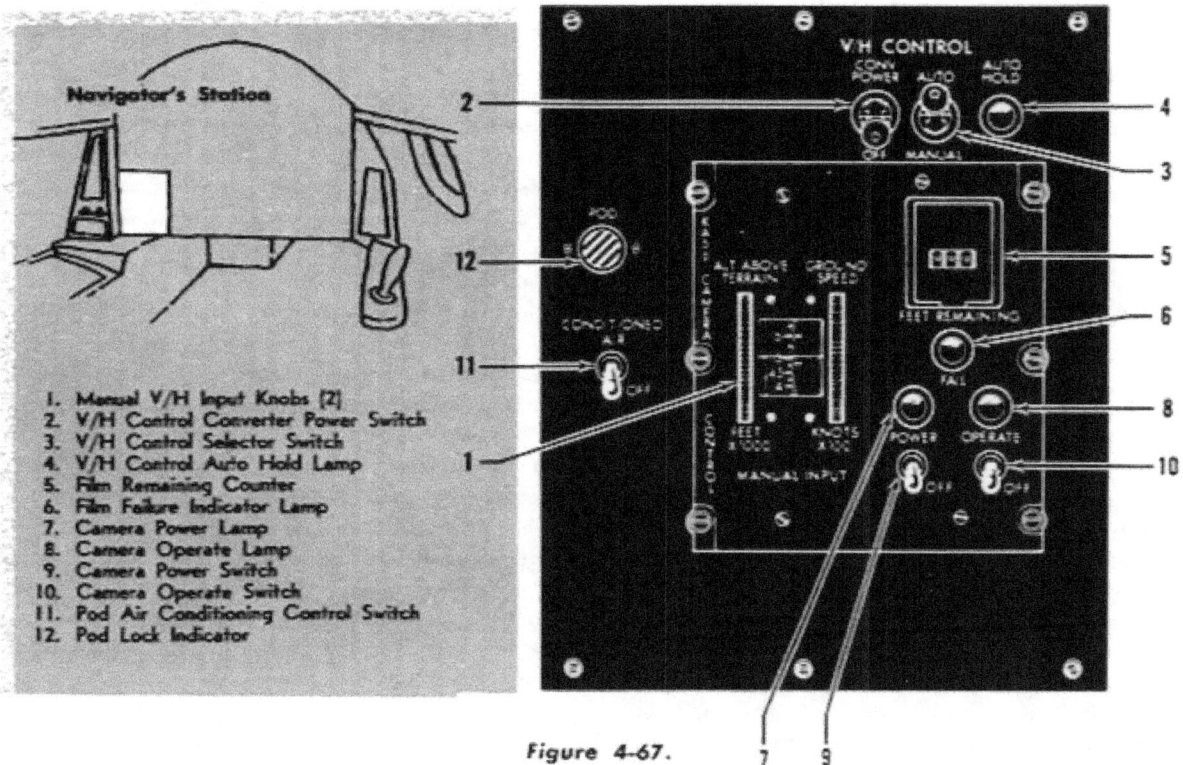

1. Manual V/H Input Knobs (2)
2. V/H Control Converter Power Switch
3. V/H Control Selector Switch
4. V/H Control Auto Hold Lamp
5. Film Remaining Counter
6. Film Failure Indicator Lamp
7. Camera Power Lamp
8. Camera Operate Lamp
9. Camera Power Switch
10. Camera Operate Switch
11. Pod Air Conditioning Control Switch
12. Pod Lock Indicator

Figure 4-67.

Camera Operate Switch.

The camera operate switch (10, figure 4-67), located on the navigator's pod camera control panel, is a two position switch marked OFF and labeled OPERATE in the ON position. When the switch is placed to the OPERATE position a green press-to-test camera operate lamp (8, figure 4-67), located above the switch, will light to indicate that the camera is operating.

Pod Air Conditioning Control Switch.

The pod air conditioning control switch (11, figure 4-67), located on the navigator's pod camera control panel, is a two position switch marked OFF and labeled CONDITIONED AIR in the ON position. When the switch is placed in the CONDITIONED AIR position a servo air control valve in the pod will control the flow of air from the airplane air conditioning system to the camera compartment in the pod where it is used to defog the scanner and camera windows and maintain the proper temperature (70°F) environment for the camera.

Pod Lock Indicator.

The pod lock indicator (12, figure 4-67), located on navigator's pod camera control panel, provides an indication of the position of the pod safety lockpin. The indicator shows LOCK (lighted green) or UNLOCK (lighted amber) as applicable. Diagonal red stripes appear in the indicator when no power is available or when the pod is not installed.

PHOTO RECONNAISSANCE SYSTEM OPERATION.

For photo reconnassance system operation procedures, refer to Navigator's Checklist, Section VIII.

DEFENSIVE ELECTRONIC COUNTER-MEASURE SYSTEM.

For information pertaining to the defensive electronic countermeasure (DECM) system, refer to the Confidential Supplement, T.O. 1B-58A-1A.

Section IV
Auxiliary Equipment

T.O. 1B-58A-1

ACTIVE DEFENSE SYSTEM.

The airplane is equipped with an active defense system consisting of an electronically directed and hydraulically driven tail turret and a radar fire control system with controls at the DSO's station. The system is designed primarily for defense against gun and rocket-firing fighters flying aerodynamic lead pursuit courses. Limited defense against unconventional attacks of interceptors and missiles is provided.

TAIL TURRET.

The tail turret is equipped with a six-barrel 20mm Gatling-type gun which has an extremely high rate of fire. The gun is aimed remotely by the fire control system and fired by means of a firing button. Ammunition, which is drawn from a box in the fuselage just forward of the turret, is pushed through a flexible chute to the gun by a booster motor. For the total number of rounds carried in the ammunition box and chute, refer to this section in confidential supplement T.O. 1B-58A-1A. In case of emergency, the DSO may jettison all unexpended ammunition by means of the ammo jettison button. Cartridge cases, belt links, and jettisoned live rounds are automatically ejected overboard through an ejection hatch located in the turret structure below the gun. The turret, gun, ammunition booster, and ejection hatch are hydraulically operated and receive hydraulic pressure from the utility hydraulic system. The gun receives 28-volt d-c power from the 28-volt d-c power panel.

FIRE CONTROL SYSTEM (MD-7).

The radar fire control system, consists of a group of electronic packages which search, acquire, and track targets; compute the fire control problem; and aim the gun at the tracked predicted position. For areas searched by the fire control system and covered by the gun, refer to Section IV in the confidential supplement T.O. 1B-58A-1A. The FCS antenna is located in the upper tail turret assembly at the root of the vertical stabilizer. A radar fire control panel (figure 4-68) and a manual fire control panel (figure 4-69) are located at the DSO's station. The fire control system has four methods of operation; search, automatic target acquisi-

tion (ATA), manual target acquisition (MTA), and track. During search the FCS automatically searches a set pattern to the rear of the aircraft, and displays target range and azimuth position data on the radar scope. Automatic target acquisition (ATA) begins when a certain number of pulses are received by the radar from a target within the ATA range. After the acquisition period, a maximum time duration or 1 second, the gun will be moved to the computed firing position, the firing circuits will be automatically armed, and the DSO will be given an indication of time to fire. In manual target acquisition (MTA) the DSO manually selects the desired target, through an extended lock-on range; all other functions of MTA are identical to those performed after ATA. In track operation all fire control system electronic units are in operation to keep the radar cone on the target, the gun continually positioned to the predicted firing position, and to give the DSO an indication when to fire by the future range meter indication. Mach number and relative air density information is continually supplied to the FCS computer by the aircraft air data computer. Gross weight information is continually supplied to the FCS computer by the autopilot amplifier-computer assembly. The fire control system uses plus and minus 150 volts d-c from the aircraft multiple voltage power supply, through the a-c and high voltage d-c power panel; 28 volts d-c from the 28-volt d-c power panel; and 115/200 volts, three phase a-c power from the aircraft alternators through the right a-c power panel.

CONTROLS AND INDICATORS.

Master Switch.

The three-position guarded master switch (6, figure 4-69), located on the manual fire control panel, is marked STBY, OPR, and OFF. Placing the switch to the STBY position supplies power to the heater circuits in the fire control system to warm up the system, to the electronic circuits which require long stabilizing periods, and to the gun circuits so that the guns may be fired. A fifteen minute warmup period is recommended. Placing the switch to STBY also enables utility hydraulic pressure to be applied to the system. Placing the switch directly to the OPR position provides automatic switch-in to full fire control system

Section IV
Auxiliary Equipment

operation after a time delay of 8 to 15 minutes (the length of this time-out is determined by the amount of time the gyros require to reach operating temperature, which will vary with outside temperature). After the time delay is completed the trace on the radar scope will automatically begin its horizontal sweep.

Safe-Fire Switch.

The two-position guarded safe-fire switch (5, figure 4-68), located on the radar fire control panel, is marked SAFE and FIRE. Placing the switch in the SAFE position opens the firing button circuit and closes the circuit to the ammo jettison button when the master switch is at STBY. Placing the switch in the FIRE position closes the circuit to the firing button and energizes the gun control circuit. The safe-fire switch guard should be safetied in the down position to prevent inadvertently placing the switch to the FIRE position.

Firing Button.

The red firing button (8, figure 4-68) is located on the radar fire control panel. With the safe-fire switch at FIRE and the ready-fire light on, depressing the button will fire the gun. Then electrical power is routed to the ejection door control solenoid and the door opens to eject the empty cartridge cases.

WARNING

Do not press firing button with ammunition aboard, unless over a designated firing area.

Automatic Target Acquisition (ATA) Range Control Knob.

The ATA (automatic target acquisition) range control knob (1, figure 4-68) is located on the radar fire control panel. The knob positions are unmarked. The fully counterclockwise position is OFF. Turning the knob clockwise varies the range at which the system will lock on a target in the ATA mode of operation. Refer to Section IV in the confidential supplement T. O. 1B-58A-1A, for ATA lock-on range limits.

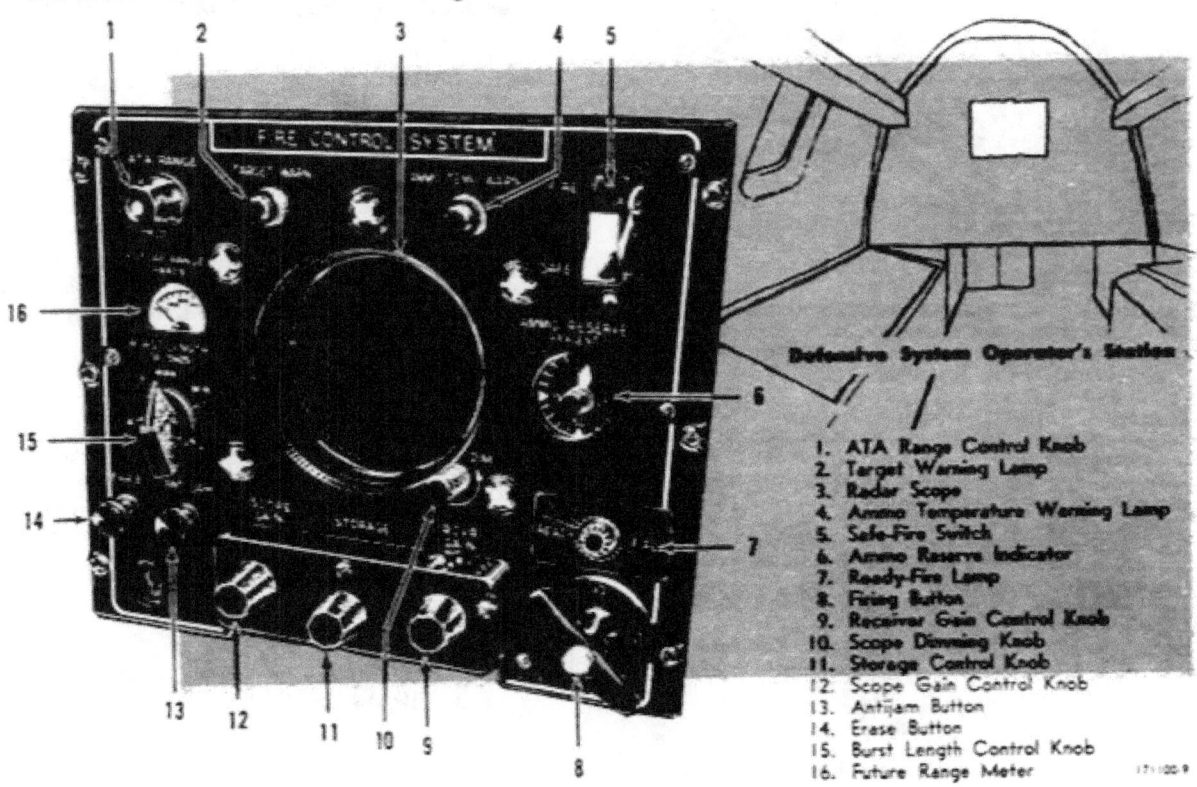

Figure 4-68.

manual fire control panel

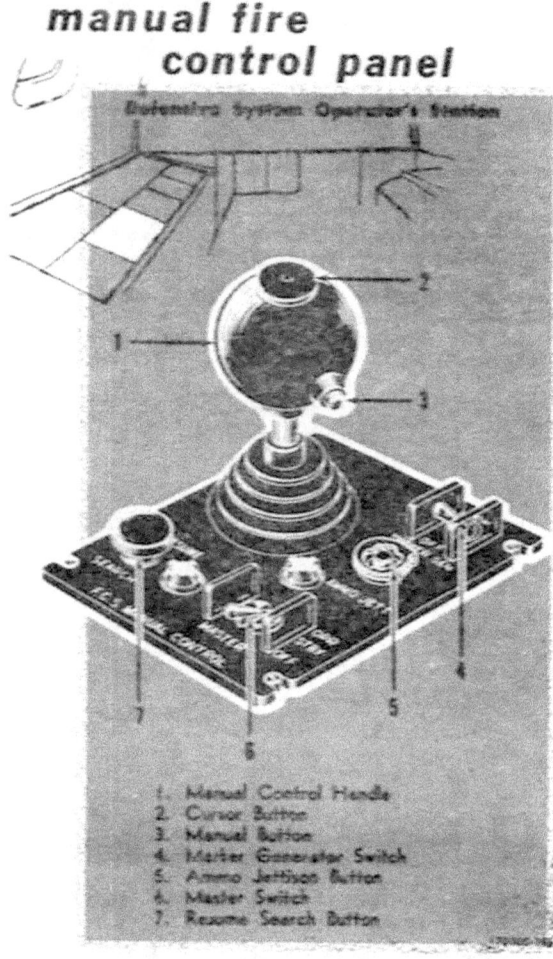

Figure 4-69.

Note

The maximum ATA range is variable and is determined by an internal adjustment of the system.

Receiver Gain Control Knob.

The receiver gain control knob (9, figure 4-68) located on the radar fire control panel is used to adjust the sensitivity of the system to receive targets by varying the gain of the receiver. Turning the knob clockwise increases the sensitivity.

Note

Do not adjust receiver gain control knob to achieve desired scope display. The receiver gain control knob is adjusted to determine maximum lock-on sensitivity.

Scope Gain Control Knob.

The scope gain control knob (12, figure 4-68) is located on the radar fire control panel. Turning the knob clockwise increases the intensity of the writing beam on the radar scope screen. The scope gain control knob should be adjusted alternately with the storage control knob.

Scope Dimming Knob.

The scope dimming knob (10, figure 4-68), located on the right side of the radar scope, varies the degree of brightness of the radar scope through a polaroid adjustment. The knob can be turned clockwise and counterclockwise to locate position of optimum scope and grid brilliance.

Manual Control Handle.

The manual control handle (1, figure 4-69) is located on the manual fire control panel. With the cursor button depressed, the control handle is moved laterally to position the cursor in azimuth and fore and aft to position the cursor in range. With the manual button depressed (MTA operation), the handle controls the antenna position in azimuth and the antenna will automatically nod from limit to limit in elevation.

Cursor Button.

The cursor button (2, figure 4-69) is located on the top of the manual control handle. When the button is depressed and held, a cursor (a short vertical line) is displayed on the radar scope whenever the antenna azimuth position is coincident with the hand control azimuth position as the antenna moves in its search pattern. The cursor represents the manual acquisition gate range and hand control azimuth position.

Manual Button.

The manual button (3, figure 4-69), located on the right side of the manual control handle, is used to place the fire control system in the MTA operation. When the button is depressed, the antenna stops searching, aligns itself with the position of manual control handle in azimuth, and nods in elevation.

Note

The fire control system will not lock on a target while the manual button is depressed.

Marker Generator Switch.

The two-position guarded marker generator switch (4, figure 4-69), located on the manual fire control panel, is marked ON and OFF. When the switch is placed to the ON position, the range marker generator circuit is energized to generate range markers at 1000 yard intervals with the first marker occurring at 500 yards. These markers are used for test purposes. However, intermediate markers appearing between the major markers may be observed at some scope gain setting. Decreasing the scope gain to prevent saturation or eliminating the intermediate marker display may be necessary.

Burst Length Control Knob.

The burst length control knob (15, figure 4-68) is located on the radar fire control panel. The knob has positions marked MIN, MAN and 5 numbered variable positions. Turning the knob clockwise increases the burst length from 0.6 to 5 seconds. In the MAN (detent) position, the burst limiter circuit is shorted out and permits the operator to fire the gun at whatever length he desires.

Antijam Button.

The antijam pushbutton (13, figure 4-68), located at the left side of the radar fire control panel, changes the frequency of the radar in the event of radar jamming or other interference. When the scope display is obscured momentarily press the button to clear the video. The scope display will momentarily blank out while the frequency is changing and stabilizing.

Storage Control Knob.

The storage control knob (11, figure 4-68) is located on the radar fire control panel. Turning the knob regulates the persistence of the radar scope during search (until angle lock-on occurs) from a fraction of a second to 12 seconds. Optimum setting should be approximately 4 seconds.

Erase Button.

The erase button (14, figure 4-68) is located on the radar fire control panel. When the button is depressed, the radar scope display is blanked out.

Resume Search Button.

The resume search button (7, figure 4-69) is located on the left side of the manual fire control panel. The system will search as long as the button is depressed. When the button is momentarily depressed, the system will automatically unlock from a target and return to the search mode. If the target is within the selected maximum ATA range the system will automatically re-acquire the target upon receipt of an ample number of return pulses.

Ammo Jettison Button.

The covered ammo jettison button (5, figure 4-69) is located on the manual fire control panel. When the button is depressed, the unexpended ammunition is jettisoned through the gun chamber without being fired. The ammo cannot be jettisoned unless the master switch is in STBY or OPR and the safe-fire switch is in the SAFE position.

Radar Scope.

The radar scope (3, figure 4-68), located in the center of the radar fire control panel, is used to present target displays to the operator. The B-scope display indicates azimuth and range of the target. Illumination of the etched azimuth and range grid lines is controlled by the main instrument panel control knob on the DSO's lighting control panel. The normal search display (1, figure 4-70) should appear on the radar scope when no targets are present. When the airplane is on the ground or when the airplane is flying below approximately 30,000 feet, ground clutter will normally appear at the top of the scope at random ranges (2, figure 4-70). In the event no other targets are available these ground return signals may be used to indicate the system is searching. Depress the cursor button and move the hand control to see that the cursor on the radar scope is positioned accordingly in range and azimuth. A split cursor is permissible if separation between the display is 1/8 inch or less. The cursor should appear as a short vertical trace; targets normally appear as horizontal traces in the display (2, figure 4-70).

Target Warning Lamp.

The red target warning push-to-test lamp (2, figure 4-68), located on the radar fire control panel, warns the operator that a target is within the range of the fire control system. The target warning lamp will light for one second each time the antenna passes over a target within the maximum range of the fire control system, producing a flashing effect until angle lock-on occurs. When the angle lock-on occurs, the lamp goes out. The lamp lights again when range lock-on occurs and remains lighted as long as the system remains locked on the target.

Ready-Fire Lamp.

The red ready-fire press-to-test lamp (7, figure 4-68), located on the radar fire control panel, indicates (when lighted) the system is locked on a target and the gun is ready to fire. In addition the lamp will also light when the master switch is in the STBY position and the safe-fire switch is in the FIRE position indicating that the gun is capable of being fired.

Section IV
Auxiliary Equipment

T.O. 1B-58A-1

md-7 scope presentations

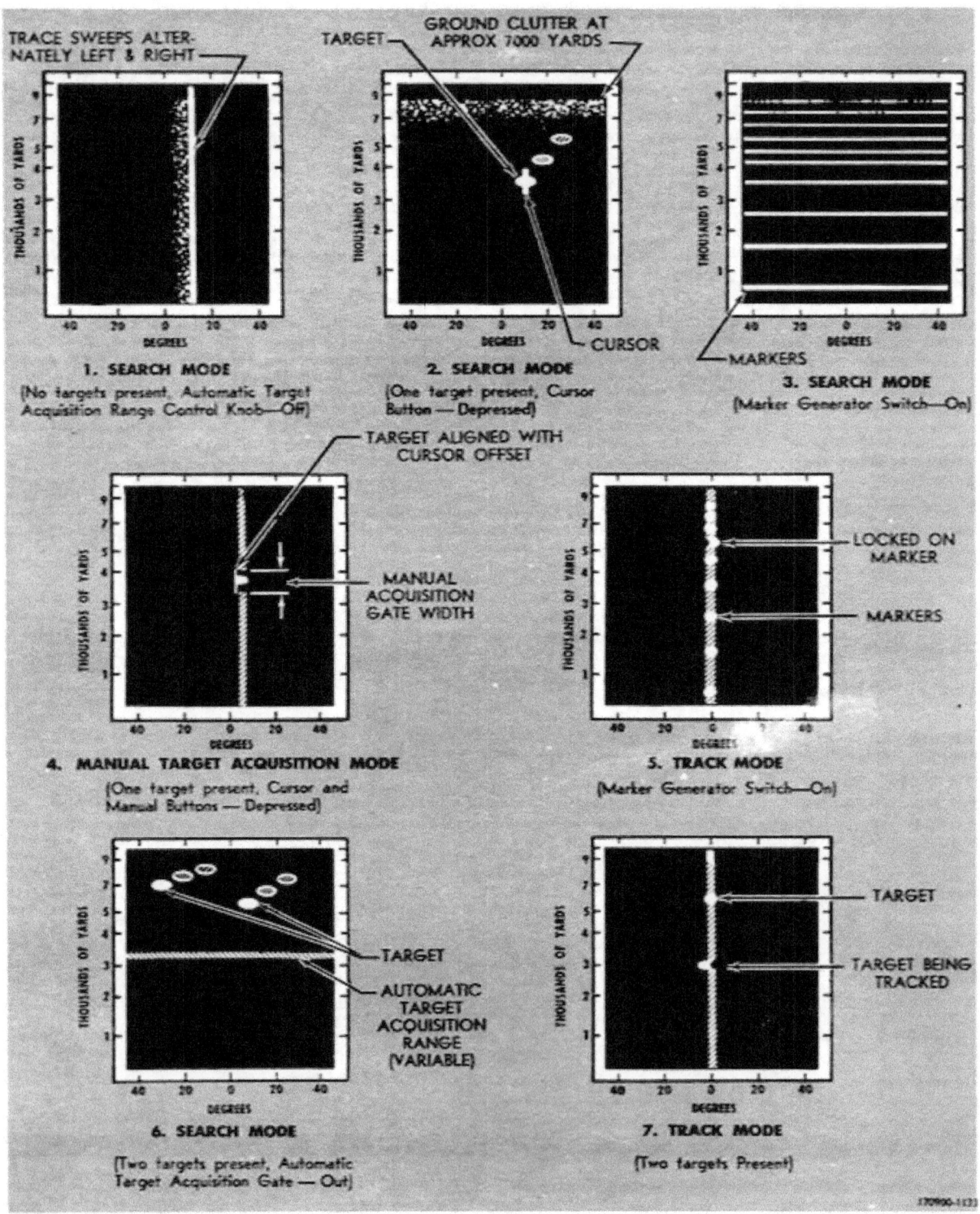

Figure 4-70.

4-110

Future Range Meter.

The future range meter (16, figure 4-68), located on the radar fire control panel, indicates the predicted range of the target in yards, with the system locked on. When the indicator needle begins to move toward the red segment on the meter, the target is within range and the gun may be fired. However, the fire may be inaccurate. When the indicator needle reaches the red segment on the meter, the target is within effective range and the gun can be fired with maximum accuracy. The indicator needle always hangs up at 1250 (± 100) yards when in the unlocked operate mode.

Ammo Temperature Warning Lamp.

The red ammunition temperature warning lamp (4, figure 4-68), located on the radar fire control panel, indicates (when lighted) that the temperature in the ammunition box has become excessive. Firing the gun while the press-to-test warning lamp is lighted may result in inaccurate fire and decreased life of gun components due to increased chamber pressure.

Note

Firing can be continued without endangering the airplane if the lamp lights during a tactical mission. However, firing should be discontinued if the lamp lights during a training mission to avoid exposing the gun unnecessarily to increased chamber pressures. Once the lamp comes on during flight it will not extinguish as it is operated by a welding type bimetallic sensor located on the ammo chute.

Ammo Reserve Indicator.

The ammunition reserve indicator (6, figure 4-68), located on the radar fire control panel, indicates in percent the number of rounds of ammunition in reserve. The small reset control knob projecting from the center of the instrument is used for resetting the indicator when ammunition boxes are reloaded.

NORMAL OPERATION OF ACTIVE DEFENSE SYSTEM.

Refer to DSO's Checklist Section VIII for operating procedures.

Automatic Target Acquisition (ATA) Test.

After the system has been placed in operation rotate the ATA range control knob clockwise until the leading edge of the ATA gate is at the same range of the desired target. Lock on should occur. If the target drops back out of range or moves out of the angular limits of the system the system will automatically return to the search mode. Depressing and holding the resume search button will return the system to the search mode regardless of the target position.

Test-Firing the Gun.
Place the master switch to the STBY position and place the safe-fire switch to the FIRE position. Fire as short a burst as possible by momentarily pressing the firing button. The ammunition reserve indicator should show that rounds have been fired. To safety the gun, return the safe-fire switch to the SAFE position.

WARNING

Do not fire the gun or jettison ammo unless over a designated firing area.

Multiple Targets and High Noise.

If the target warning lamp flashes more often than every four seconds and no jamming is present, multiple targets may be indicated. This condition can be overcome by either of two methods: (1) use MTA to its maximum capability, or (2) set ATA to the desired maximum tactical range and when a target crosses this line and is acquired and tracked, depress and hold the resume search button to scan the radar field of view for other targets. When the target reaches minimum tactical range, release the resume search button and allow ATA lock-on to occur. When the system shows a tendency to continually lock-on false targets, and this tendency cannot be eliminated by reducing receiver gain, or when normal search cannot be maintained unless the ATA RANGE control is positioned to OFF, a high-noise condition is indicated. High noise conditions may possibly be eliminated by pressing the ANTI-JAM button (but not more often than once every 20 seconds). The other alternative in a high-noise condition is to use MTA.

Manual Target Acquisition.

After the system has been placed in operation depress the cursor button and align the cursor display on the desired target. Move the control handle fore and aft to move the cursor display in range and laterally to move the cursor display in azimuth. Momentarily depress and release the manual button to lock-on the target. After lock-on has been completed release the cursor button. If the target drops back out of range or moves out of the angular limits of the system, the system will automatically return to the search mode. Depressing the resume search button will return the system to the search mode regardless of the target position.

EMERGENCY OPERATION OF ACTIVE DEFENSE SYSTEM.

Most of the equipment is inaccessible during flight and no emergency repair is possible.

Section IV
Auxiliary Equipment

T.O. 1B-58A-1

Radar Jamming.

Depress the anti-jam button whenever the indicator display is obscured by radar jamming.

Note

During routine training mission a 20 second time delay should be observed between each actuation of the anti-jam button to prolong the service life of the tuning drives.

CAUTION

During tactical missions, a time delay of at least two seconds should be observed between depressions to prevent freeze-up of relay contacts in the tuning drives.

System Failure.

Should the computer equipment become inoperative, some protection would be afforded by placing the master switch to the STBY position, the safe-fire switch to the FIRE position, and firing the gun.

AIR REFUELING SYSTEM.

The airplane is equipped with an air refueling system capable of receiving fuel from a KC-135 boom-type tanker aircraft. The system, consisting of a flying boom receptacle, slipway door, hydraulic valves and actuators, a hydraulic pressure transfer cylinder, and a signal amplifier, is controlled from the pilot's station. The system hydraulic power is supplied from the utility hydraulic system; the electrical power is supplied from the 28-volt d-c power panel. Pneumatic pressure supplied to pressurize the air refueling system hydraulic pressure transfer cylinder for emergency operation is furnished from an independent emergency pneumatic system located in the nose wheel well. The receptacle and slipway door are located in the upper portion of the radome forward of the pilot's station. When the slipway door is open, it forms a guide for the flying boom. The door is flush with the contour of the radome when closed. A lamp, equipped with two bulbs, is located in the receptacle slipway to aid the tanker boom operator during night refueling. The lamp operates on 28-volt d-c power and lights when the air refuel door switch (5, figure 1-11) is placed in the OPEN position. For dimming control of the slipway lamp, refer to "Lighting Equipment," this section. An additional lamp is installed in the forward right section of the receptacle slipway and has no brightness control. This lamp also operates on 28-volt d-c power and lights when the air refuel door switch is placed in the OPEN position. During normal operation, electrical power is supplied to the ready lamp and the nozzle latch controls through the signal amplifier. In the event of failure of the signal amplifier and limit switches in the receptacle, electrical power can be supplied to the nozzle latch controls through an emergency boom latch switch and a disconnect switch. The fuel panel configuration for air refueling must be established prior to making contact with the tanker boom. When contact is made and the refueling operation started, fuel enters the refueling manifold and flows into the reservoir tank, and the forward main, aft main, forward pod, and aft pod simultaneously if they have been selected. When the aft tank becomes full, a float-type switch in the aft tank allows the balance tank refuel valve to open permitting fuel to flow into the balance tank. When the tanks are full, a float-type shutoff valve in each tank closes the corresponding tank refuel valve. The pilot of the receiver airplane and the boom operator are provided a control for initiating a disconnect at any time during the refueling operation. An automatic disconnect will occur if the receiver refueling manifold pressure exceeds 67 (± 3) psig or when the boom extension force exceeds 5400 pounds. An automatic disconnect will also occur if the air refueling boom envelope limits are exceeded. This is a feature of the tanker boom assembly and may be made inoperable by the boom operator if for some reason the automatic disconnect provision is not desired.

CAUTION

If the automatic disconnect feature malfunctions or is made inoperable by the boom operator, the receiver airplane can foul the boom under some flight conditions.

If the receiver airplane is disconnected from the tanker boom after the initial hookup, a reset button located on the control stick grip must be momentarily depressed before another contact can be made. Information relative to area, altitude, and airspeed for air refueling operations is predetermined during preflight planning. For air refueling performance data, refer to Part 5 of Appendix I and for flight characteristics of the aircraft during air refueling, refer to "Air Refueling," Section VI.

CONTROLS AND INDICATORS.

Air Refueling Door Switch.

The air refueling door switch (5, figure 1-11), located on the fuel control panel, is marked OPEN and CLOSE. The switch is mechanically latched in both positions; it is necessary to pull out on the switch handle to move the switch out of either position. Placing the switch in the OPEN position accomplishes the following: hydraulically opens the slipway door, lights two lamps in the receptacle slipway, energizes the signal amplifier, lights the ready lamp, closes the balance tank refuel valve if the aft tank is not approximately full, and deactivates nose wheel steering. Placing the switch to the CLOSE position hydraulically closes the door flush with the contour of the radome. The switch requires 28-volt d-c power.

Nose Wheel Steering — Air Refueling Disconnect — Air Refueling Reset (NWS-A/R DISC — A/R RESET) Button.

The pushbutton-type switch (2, figure 1-29) is located on the control stick grip and is marked NWS-A/R DISC—A/R RESET. The disconnect function of the switch provides a means of disconnecting from the tanker boom any time during the refueling operation. During normal refueling operation, momentarily depressing the button will cause an immediate disconnect from the tanker boom. Also, a disconnect signal is transmitted to the tanker through the boom signal coil to indicate a disconnect. In addition the button is used in conjunction with the emergency boom latch switch to open and close the boom latch toggles during emergency boom latching and disconnecting. The A/R RESET function is operative only when the air refueling door switch (5, figure 1-11) is in the OPEN position. After a boom operator or an automatic disconnect has been accomplished, momentarily depressing the A/R RESET button resets the automatic control circuits of the signal amplifier and lights the ready lamp. After resetting, the air refueling system is ready for another contact. A pilot initiated disconnect will automatically reset the air refueling system for another contact. The button requires 28-volt d-c power. For information on the nose wheel steering feature of the button, refer to "Nose Wheel Steering System," Section I.

Emergency Boom Latch. (EBL) Switch.

The emergency boom latch (EBL) switch (1, figure 4-31), located on the autopilot control panel, has positions marked EBL and OFF. Placing the switch in the EBL position supplies electrical power directly to the nozzle latch controls and bypasses the signal amplifier, the limit switches in the receptacle, and the door limit switch. This position is used in conjunction with A/R DISC (IFR disconnect) button during manual boom latching and/or disconnecting operations. The nozzle latches move to the latched position when the emergency boom latch switch is placed to EBL. Therefore, the IFR disconnect button must be held in the depressed position while making contact with the tanker airplane in order to hold the nozzle latches in the open position. Releasing the IFR disconnect button when the boom nozzle bottoms in the receptacle, allows the latches to close, locking the nozzle in place.

Note

When the EBL switch is in the EBL position, the air refueling ready lamp will not light.

Air Refueling (IFR) Slipway Lamp Control Knob.

The air refueling (IFR) slipway lamp control knob (1, figure 4-23), located on the pilot's lighting control panel, varies the brightness of the two night refueling lamps located in the receptacle slipway. Turning the knob clockwise increases the brightness of the two lamps. An additional lamp is installed in the forward right section of the receptacle slipway and has no brightness control.

IFR Emergency Hydraulic Boost Lever.

Note

The IFR emergency boost lever is to remain in the OFF position until needed. This will conserve the limited volume of hydraulic fluid by preventing long term, accumulative, fluid leakage loss.

The IFR emergency hydraulic boost lever (1, figure 1-28), located on the pilot's lower right console, provides a means of pressurizing the air refueling system hydraulic fluid in the event of failure of the utility hydraulic system upstream of the air refueling system check valves. The lever is marked ON and OFF, and is guarded in the OFF position. Placing the lever in the ON position allows pneumatic pressure to pressurize the air refueling system hydraulic pressure transfer cylinder. Pneumatic pressure is supplied to pressurize

Section IV
Auxiliary Equipment

T.O. 1B-58A-1

the air refueling system hydraulic pressure transfer cylinder for emergency operation. The air refueling system has an independent emergency pneumatic system located in the nose wheel well. This provides sufficient hydraulic fluid to open the door and to operate the nozzle latches through two complete latching cycles. Placing the lever in the OFF position shuts off the supply of pneumatic pressure and relieves the pneumatic pressure in the hydraulic pressure transfer cylinder.

Air Refueling Ready Indicator Lamp.

A green air refueling ready indicator lamp (4, figure 1-11), located on the fuel control panel, will light when the slipway door is open and the air refueling system is electrically ready for contact with the tanker boom. The lamp will go out when the boom is latched into the receptacle or when the A/R RESET (NWS-IFR reset) button is depressed. Also the lamp will not light when the emergency boom latch switch is in the EBL position. For dimming and testing of the lamp, refer to the "Malfunction Indicator and Warning System," Section I. The lamp operates on 28-volt d-c power.

> **CAUTION**
>
> Except under emergency conditions, a hookup should not be attempted whenever the ready indicator lamp does not light after the air refueling door has been opened. Failure of the lamp to light may indicate that the door is not fully open and could cause the boom to hang up on the door.

AIR REFUELING PROCEDURES AND TECHNIQUES.

Refer to Air Refueling Flight Manuals, T.O. 1-1C-1 and 1-1C-1-6 for this information.

SINGLE-POINT REFUELING SYSTEM.

The airplane and pod fuel tanks are normally serviced on the ground by means of a single-point pressure refueling system. The single-point refueling adapter is located in the right side of the nose wheel well. Two lights are installed in the nose landing gear wheel well to provide illumination for night refueling. The switch is located in the nose wheel well aft of the single-point refueling adapter. The lights operate on 28-volt d-c power. Fuel is routed from the adapter to the reservoir, aft, and balance tanks of the airplane and the tanks of the pod through refuel valves located in each tank.

> **Note**
>
> Up to 77 pounds of unusable fuel may be trapped if single point refuel line is not drained at close of refueling operation.

The forward tank refuel valve is located in the reservoir tank. Fuel routed to the forward tank flows through the forward tank refuel valve and into the reservoir tank. If the reservoir tank is full, fuel will flow through the reservoir tank overflow line and into the forward tank. The reservoir tank refuel valve is automatically controlled by a float-type pilot valve in the reservoir tank. When fuel drops below the level of the float-type pilot valve, the valve opens and allows refuel manifold pressure to bleed through it from the back side of the refuel valve. This creates a differential pressure across the refuel valve, allowing the higher pressure on the front side of the valve to overcome spring tension and open the valve. The tank will fill until fuel again closes the float valve. Closing the float valve causes fuel pressure to equalize across the refuel valve and the valve is then closed by spring tension. The refuel valves of the forward, aft, and balance tanks are controlled by solenoid valves as well as high level shutoff float-type valves. Each solenoid valve is located in a line between the refuel valve and its respective float valve and is energized open or closed by manual selector knobs on the fuel control panel. When the solenoid valve is open, operation of the refuel valves is similar to that of the reservoir refuel valve. However, closing the solenoid valve performs the same function as closing of the high level shutoff float valve by blocking the flow of fuel from the back side of the refuel valve, allowing it to be closed. Four fuel system maintenance test buttons, located on the upper exterior surface of the reservoir and aft tanks, provide a means of checking the operation of the individual tank high level shutoff valves during refueling. Depressing the buttons allows fuel from the refuel manifold to enter and flood the respective high level shutoff float-type valve, thereby closing it and allowing the respective refuel valve to close. The refuel valves are also used to direct fuel during fuel transfer operations.

> **Note**
>
> The fuel quantity indicators at the pilot's station must be closely monitored during the refueling operation. The refuel valves must be closed by the control switches if they do not operate automatically.

On airplanes with or without a pod attached, prior to refueling transfer fuel to the reservoir, forward, and if necessary, the aft tank. After fuel is transferred forward, the tanks are refueled simultaneously. A nose gear reactance pressure gage is provided to indicate the load induced on the nose landing gear during refueling. Maintaining certain pressure levels ensures

4-114

protection against dangerous cg conditions. Refer to "Center-of-Gravity Limitations," Section V, for the landing gear design loading.

> **CAUTION**
>
> Failure to maintain the nose gear reactance pressure gage between 150 and 950 psi will give a dangerous cg condition which may upset the airplane or damage the nose landing gear.

If pressure refueling equipment is not available, the reservoir, forward, and aft tanks of the airplane can be serviced in the order listed through three fillers located on the top of the fuselage. Also the tanks of the pod may be fueled through the negative relief valves.

SINGLE-POINT REFUELING SYSTEM CONTROLS.

Forward Tank Refuel-Scavenge Knob.

The forward tank refuel-scavange knob (6, figure 1-11), located on the fuel control panel, has three positions marked REFUEL, SCAV, and OFF. Placing the knob in the REFUEL position opens the forward tank refuel solenoid valve. The refuel valve is then opened by manifold pressure. For information on the other functions of this switch refer to "Fuel Supply System," Section I.

Balance Tank Refuel-Scavenge Knob.

The balance tank refuel-scavenge knob (16, figure 1-11), located on the fuel control panel, has three positions marked REFUEL, SCAV, and OFF. Placing the knob in the REFUEL position opens the balance tank refuel solenoid valve, allowing the refuel valve to be opened by manifold pressure. However, during air refueling, a float type switch in the aft tank prevents the balance tank refuel solenoid valve from opening before the aft tank becomes full. For information on the other functions of this switch refer to "Fuel Supply System," Section I.

Aft Tank Refuel Valve Knob.

The aft tank refuel valve knob (18, figure 1-11), located on the fuel control panel, has positions marked REFUEL and OFF. Placing the knob in the REFUEL position opens the aft tank refuel solenoid valve. The refuel valve is then opened by manifold pressure.

Pod Tank Transfer-Refuel Knobs.

Two pod tank transfer-refuel knobs (8, figure 1-11), one for the forward tank of the pod and one for the aft tank of the pod, are located on the fuel control panel. The knobs have three positions marked TRANS, OFF and REFUEL ONLY. Placing either knob in the REFUEL ONLY position, opens the respective pod refuel solenoid valve which allows manifold pressure to open the refuel valve and permits the tank to be refilled through the airplane refuel manifold. For information on the other function of this switch refer to "Fuel Supply System," Section I.

SINGLE-POINT REFUELING OPERATION.

1. External power switch—GROUND REFUEL (or GRD REFUEL).

2. Fuel Nozzle—Connected.

Instruct observer to connect the fuel nozzle to the single-point refueling adapter.

3. External power—Connected.

Instruct observer to connect external power.

4. CG control switch—MANUAL.

5. Instruct observer to start the fuel truck and open the fuel nozzle.

> **CAUTION**
>
> During refueling, do not exceed 60 psi on the refueling unit gage. When refueling the pod tanks, check the pod tank vent valves for proper operation before exceeding 12 psig. Failure to observe these pressure limitations may result in damage to the fuel lines, fittings, or pod fuel tanks.

6. Position the refueling control knob to REFUEL as applicable for the tanks scheduled to receive fuel.

> **CAUTION**
>
> While refueling, the airplane cg must be kept within safe limits. Maintain the nose gear reactance gage reading between 150 and 950 psi. If nose strut pressure approaches 150 psi, close the balance and aft tank refuel valves. With a nose gear reactance gage reading above 150 psi, the airplane cg remains forward of the upset limit. If nose strut pressure approaches 950 psi, close the forward tank and forward pod tank refuel valves. For the upset limit refer to "Center of Gravity Limitations," Section V.

Section IV
Auxiliary Equipment

T.O. 1B-58A-1

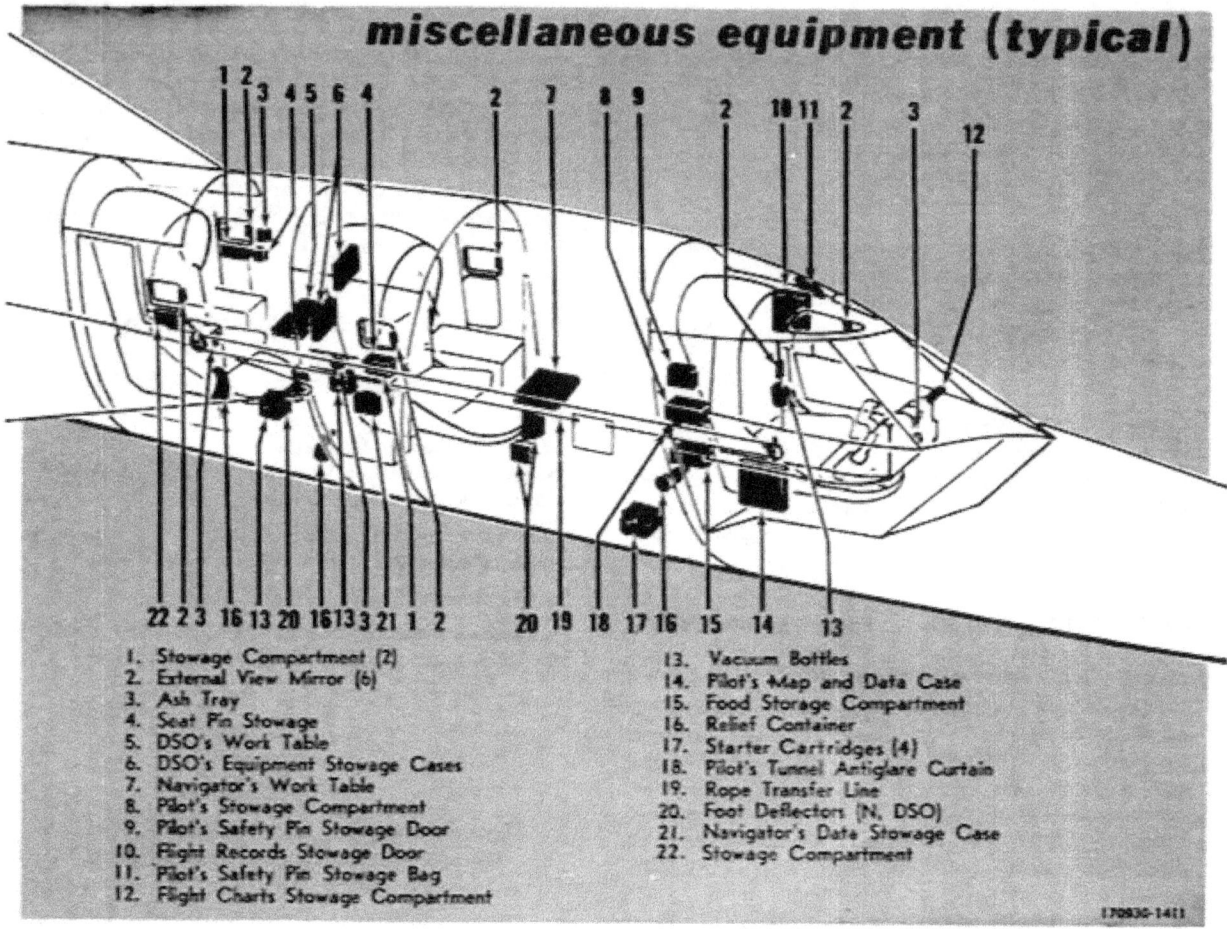

Figure 4-71.

7. Fuel quantity indicator—Check.

Monitor fuel quantity indicator to make sure tank is receiving fuel.

8. When the tank fuel quantity reaches the desired level, position the knob of the respective tank refuel valve to OFF.

MISCELLANEOUS EQUIPMENT.

FOOD STORAGE COMPARTMENTS.

Each station is provided with food storage compartments (15, figure 4-71) for storing Air Force cold-sandwich type snack packs. The storage compartment at the pilot's station stores two food packs and is located in the right sidewall aft of the sidewall control panels. The navigator's station has two food storage compartments located beneath the bombing and navigation system control panels. The storage compartment at the DSO's station stores two food packs located on the underside of the DECM control panels.

RELIEF CONTAINERS.

Each station is equipped with a portable relief container (16, figure 4-71). The pilots' relief container is stowed on the floor aft of the right console. The navigator's container is stowed on the floor outboard of the tunnel area at the bulkhead. The DSO's container is stowed on the floor near the forward end of the right console. The relief containers do not drain overboard but must be emptied after flight.

ASH TRAYS.

Each station is equipped with an ashtray (3, figure 4-71) which can be recessed flush with the mounting when not in use. The pilot's ashtray is located on the side of the left forward console just forward of the throttle quadrant. The navigator's ashtray is located on the right sidewall aft of the right window. The DSO's ashtray is located forward of the left window.

4-116

THERMAL CURTAINS.

Thermal curtains are made of thermal material which is coated on one side with vacuum deposited aluminum particles and on the other side with a gray silicone rubber emulsion. Each station is equipped with thermal curtains. The pilot's canopy curtains (eyebrow) fasten to the canopy liner with snaps. The windshield curtain fastens to the glare shield with "velcro" tape and to the upper window frame with snaps. A zipper flap on the windshield curtain enables the pilot to see out without unsnapping the curtain. When not installed the curtains are removed from the airplane and stowed in accordance with applicable procedures. The effectiveness of the curtains is sharply reduced by dirt or stains on the reflective surface.

WARNING

The thermal curtains must be kept free from grease, dirt and mold as this will seriously affect the value of the curtain.

SEAT PIN STOWAGE PROVISIONS.

Each station is equipped with provisions for stowing the seat pin assembly during flight. The pilot's station has two safety pin stowage provisions: A stowage bag (11, figure 4-71) located on the glare shield above the autopilot control panel, and a safety pin stowage door (9, figure 4-71) located in the right sidewall aft of the window. Navigator's seat pins (4, figure 4-71), are stowed in the thermal curtains stowage compartment located under the right window. The DSO's seat pins are stowed in a compartment (4, figure 4-71) located beside the left window.

FLIGHT RECORDS STOWAGE DOOR.

A flight records stowage door (10, figure 4-71) is located at the pilot's station in the left sidewall aft of the window. A compartment inside the door provides for stowing the Form 781 and other aircraft records.

FLIGHT CHARTS STOWAGE COMPARTMENT.

A flight charts stowage compartment (12, figure 4-71) is located on top of the pilot's anti-glare shield.

PILOT'S MAP AND DATA CASE.

A map and data case (14, figure 4-71) is stowed in the pilot's lower right console. The case lid is spring-loaded so as to remain open when unlatched. A release button (5, figure 1-29) permits removal of the case from the console.

WARNING

The pilot's map and data case should always be installed so that the lid opens away from the capsule door, otherwise the lid may interfere with closing the capsule door in event of ejection.

PILOT'S TUNNEL ANTIGLARE CURTAIN.

An antiglare curtain (18, figure 4-71) is installed at the pilot's entrance to the tunnel area. The curtain, which is provided to exclude light coming from the navigator's station, is attached to the forward side of the bulkhead and hangs across the tunnel opening. The curtain may be rolled up and fastened in a stowed position when not in use.

FOOT DEFLECTOR AND GUIDE-STOWAGE ASSEMBLY.

A foot deflector and guide-stowage assembly (20, figure 4-71) is located in the floor of the navigator and DSO station. The purpose of the assembly is to act as a guide for the crew members' feet during capsulation. The guide on the right may be used as a stowage compartment.

WARNING

To prevent possible injury these guides will be properly installed for each flight.

NAVIGATOR'S AND DSO'S EQUIPMENT STORAGE CASES.

There are provisions for installing an equipment storage case (21, figure 4-71) on the right side of the navigator's station and for installing two equipment cases (6, figure 4-71) on the right and left sides of the DECM package in the DSO's station.

NAVIGATOR'S AND DSO'S WORK TABLE.

A navigator's work table (7, figure 4-71) is located below the ballistic control panel. A DSO's work table

(5, figure 4-71) is located below the DECM package. The tables are held in the storage position by a storage compartment. To unstow the table pull up, out and down until the table locks in place. To gain access to the table storage compartment lift up on the hinged table top. To stow the table rotate the table up approximately 40 degrees until the table is released from the pivot lock pin; then slide the table into the storage compartment. The navigator's and DSO's tables are interchangeable.

WARNING

The work table should be stowed before capsulation to prevent possible injury to the crew member.

MIRRORS.

Two mirrors (2, figure 4-71) are installed at each crew station (one on each side window frame) to permit crew members to view external parts of the airplane without moving from a normal sitting position. The convex mirror face permits the pilot to view both engine nacelles on each side; other crew members have a corresponding viewing angle. A ball and socket joint with a knurled locking cap behind the mirror permits quick adjustment throughout a wide range of positions.

VGH RECORDER.

The airplane is equipped so that a VGH recorder can be mounted on the floor of the pilot's station at the tunnel opening. The VGH recorder receives velocity and normal acceleration signals from a remotely located transmitter and pressure altitude from the pitot-static system. It records these signals on a magnetic tape for postflight inspection. The tape record is used by ground personnel in maintaining a structural fatigue history of the airplane. Once the VGH recorder is turned on prior to flight by means of a switch (6, figure 4-64) on the DSO's left console, it requires no further attention by the crew.

ROPE TRANSFER LINE.

A rope transfer line (19, figure 4-71), located in the crawlway between the three crew stations provides a means for passing mission forms, flight data, etc. between crew stations. The line consists of pulleys mounted at the pilot's and DSO's station with a nylon bag attached to a rope running between the pulleys. A small clip attached to the bag may be used for transfer of small items. The rope passes through the second station under the navigator's right console.

LIQUID CONTAINERS.

Each station is provided with stowage provisions for two pint size vacuum bottles (liquid containers) (13, figure 4-71). The bottle stowage holder in the pilot's station is located on the bulkhead aft and above the lower left console. The navigator's station has a bottle stowage holder on the right console. The bottle stowage holder for the DSO's station is located on the floor on the right side.

HARD LANDING INDICATOR.

A hard landing indicator, located on the forward end of the navigator's right console, provides a visual indication that vertical loads in excess of 2.5 g's (absolute) have occured during landing. The unit includes two red press-to-test lamps, one of which will light when vertical loads exceed 2.5 g's and the other when loads exceed 3.0 g's. When the lamp or lamps are lighted as a result of a hard landing, they will remain on as long as there is electrical power on the airplane, and if power is interrupted they will come on again when power is restored. The only way the light or lights may be turned off is by inserting and turning a key in the RESET slot on the side of the unit. The indicator senses g-loads only with the landing gear handle in the DOWN position. The primary purpose of the indicator is to inform ground personnel of the occurrence of a hard landing; however, it may be useful to the flight crew during taxiing and for touch-and-go or taxi-back landings. The indicator is operated by 115V a-c power.

This is the **last** page of Section IV.

T.O. 1B-58A-1

Section V
Operating Limitations

Section V
OPERATING LIMITATIONS

TABLE OF CONTENTS.

Introduction	5-1
Minimum Crew Requirements	5-1
Engine Limitations	5-1
Airspeed Limitations	5-6
Prohibited Maneuvers	5-8
Acceleration Limitations	5-9
Center of Gravity Limitations	5-9
Taxi Limitations	5-22
Hydraulic System Limitations	5-23
Flight Control System Limitations	5-23
Brake Energy Limits	5-24
Canopy Operation Limitations	5-29
Escape Systems	5-29
Minimum Altitude Limitations	5-29
Miscellaneous Operational Limitations	5-29
Weight Limitations	5-33

INTRODUCTION.

This section includes all important *unclassified* limitations that must be observed during normal operation of the airplane. For information on the classified limitations refer to Section V, T.O. 1B-58A-1A. Special attention should be given to the instrument marking illustration (figure 5-1), since these limitations are not necessarily repeated under their respective sections. When necessary, an additional explanation of instrument markings covered under appropriate headings.

CAUTION

The flight crew will make all necessary entries in Form 781 to indicate when any limitations have been exceeded.

MINIMUM CREW REQUIREMENTS.

The minimum crew for normal, safe, nontactical flights consists of two crew members. A third crew member will be added as required, at the discretion of the Commander.

ENGINE LIMITATIONS.

Engine operating limitations are shown in figure 5-1. Additional information is given in the following paragraphs and is applicable to the J79-5 series engines.

OVERSPEED.

T_2 Reset or Manual Selected Overspeed.

Normal engine speed for T_2 reset or pilot selected overspeed is 103.5 ($\pm$0.5) percent rpm.

Maximum Allowable Overspeed.

Maximum allowable overspeed is 105 percent rpm. Any time this limit is exceeded, the rpm and time over the limit must be recorded on Form 781. Operation in the 105 to 107 percent rpm range for periods of 5 seconds or less is permissible.

5-1

Section V
Operating Limitations

T.O. 1B-58A-1

instrument markings

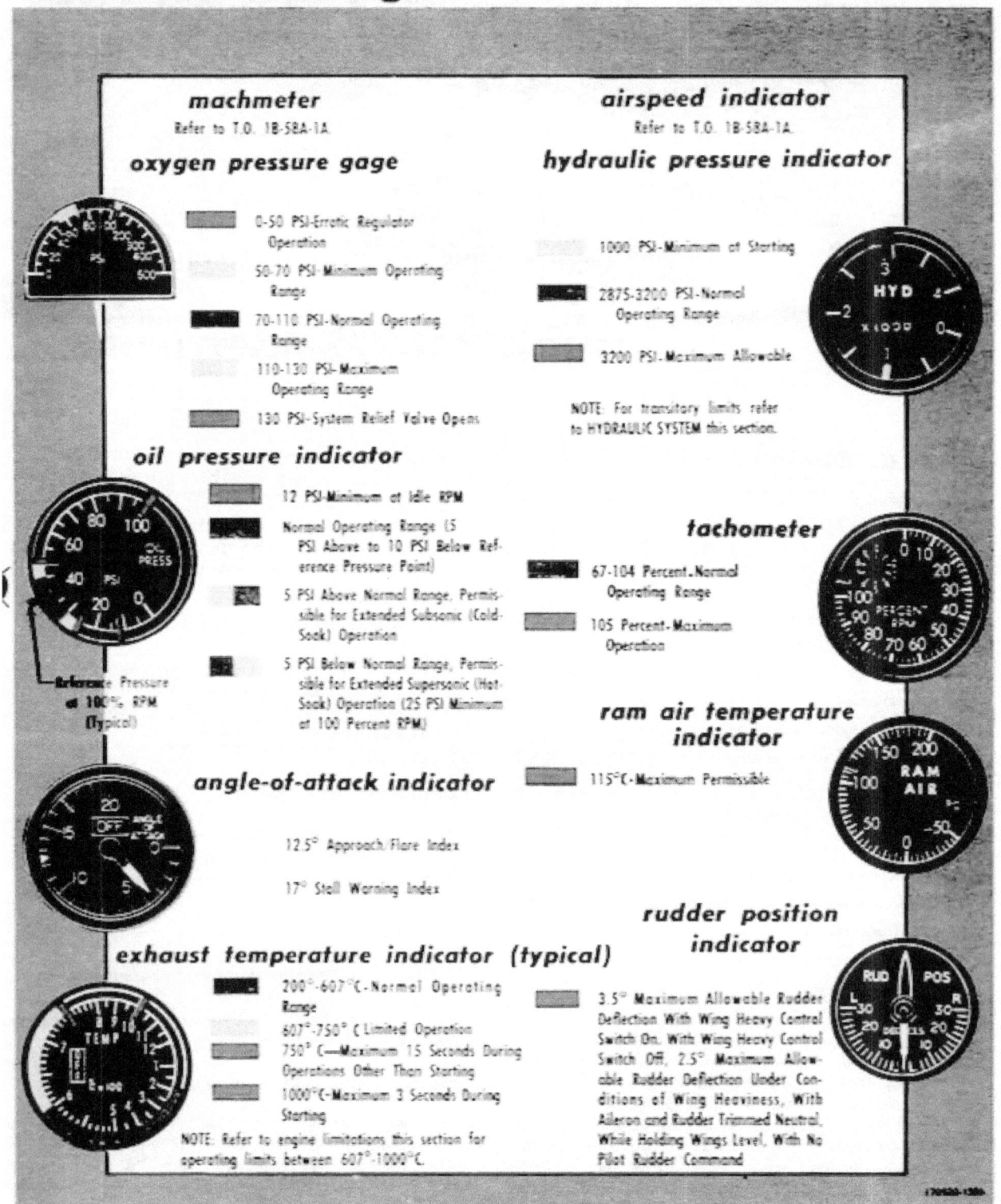

Figure 5-1.

T.O. 1B-58A-1

Section V
Operating Limitations

NORMAL SPEED.

The engine rpm at military and afterburner should be 100 ($\pm$1)% rpm with ram-air temperature above −11.7°C (11°F). At low ram air temperatures the T_2 cutback feature limits engine rpm. Refer to "T_2 Cutback," Section VII. Some overspeed may occur with the throttle at MAX A/B. This overspeed is permissible provided it does not increase more than 2.5% above military rpm of that particular engine, however, it must never exceed 102.5% rpm. This overspeed results from the main fuel control cam approaching overspeed position.

IDLE SPEED.

Engine idle speed is 67 ($\pm$1) percent rpm at sea level.

GROUND OPERATING TIME LIMITS.

To prevent overheating of the nacelles, wing and engine nozzle actuators, the following ground operating time limits must be observed.

Military	30 minutes
Afterburner:	
Inboard engines (with elevons in neutral)	30 seconds
Outboard engines	1 minute

CAUTION

Engines must be returned to idle for two minutes after operating for the maximum time in order to allow the nacelles and wing to cool before setting another power.

FLIGHT OPERATING TIME LIMITS.

The following time limits for continuous flight operation must be observed.

Below 35,000 feet altitude:	
Afterburner Operation and pilot selected overspeed	30 minutes
Military Power	30 minutes
Above 35,000 feet altitude:	
Afterburner Operation and pilot selected overspeed	2 Hours
Military Power	No Limit

Refer to "Airspeed Limitation," Section V, T.O. 1B-58A-1A for operating time limits based on airspeed.

EXHAUST GAS TEMPERATURE LIMITS.

In reading the EGT indicator, a maximum fluctuation of $\pm$5°C is permissible. Exceeding the time limits placed on engine operation at any of the following temperatures constitutes an exhaust gas overtemperature condition:

Operation for any period at temperatures over the following values requires trouble shooting and correction of engine or EGT indicating discrepancy prior to next flight to prevent recurrance, and must be recorded in Form 781.

  800°C for 6 seconds (during starting)
  730°C for 10 seconds (during starting)
  710°C for 90 seconds (during starting)
  607°C (other than starting, except no limit during A/B lightoff for 3 seconds)

Operation for any period over the following values requires engine removal for a hot section inspection.

Maximum during starting:

  1000°C for 3 seconds
  975°C for 10 seconds
  950°C for 35 seconds
  925°C for 60 seconds
  916°C for 70 seconds
  732°C for 90 seconds

Maximum other than starting:

  No limit during A/B lightoff for 3 seconds
  750°C for 15 seconds
  720°C for 1 minute
  680°C for 3 minutes
  650°C for 5 minutes
  607°C for more than 5 minutes

The EGT should stabilize at 596° $\pm$11°C at military power and above unless engine is in T_2 cutback (refer to "T_2 Cutback," Section VII). The minimum EGT for takeoff is 585°C at military power or above unless in T_2 cutback. When engine is operating in T_2 cutback, minimum acceptable EGT for takeoff is:

  555°C at 97% rpm
  515°C at 93.5% rpm

RAM AIR TEMPERATURE LIMITS.

The maximum ram air temperature for all flight conditions is 115°C. Exceeding this limit requires an entry in Form 781.

ENGINE OIL PRESSURE.

Typical oil pressure indicator markings are shown in figure 5-1. A reference oil pressure of 40 psi is used in the example; however, the reference oil pressure is determined during engine installation by operating the engine at 100% RPM and is different for each engine. It can be expected to vary widely among engines on the same airplane. Pressure indications during changing engine operating conditions, particularly when the nozzles are changing position, are not valid. The higher temperatures produced by extended supersonic flight will cause lower oil pressures due to lowered oil viscosity.

Note

● In addition to the limits shown in figure 5-1, a fluctuation no greater than $\pm$7.5 psi from the apparent steady pressure with the engine operating at a constant speed is permissible. The average of the fluctuation shall be used to determine whether the limits in figure 5-1 have been exceeded.

5-3

Section V
Operating Limitations

T.O. 1B-58A-1

lower pod normal jettison limits

DATA BASIS: FLIGHT TEST
DATE: 7 SEPTEMBER 1962

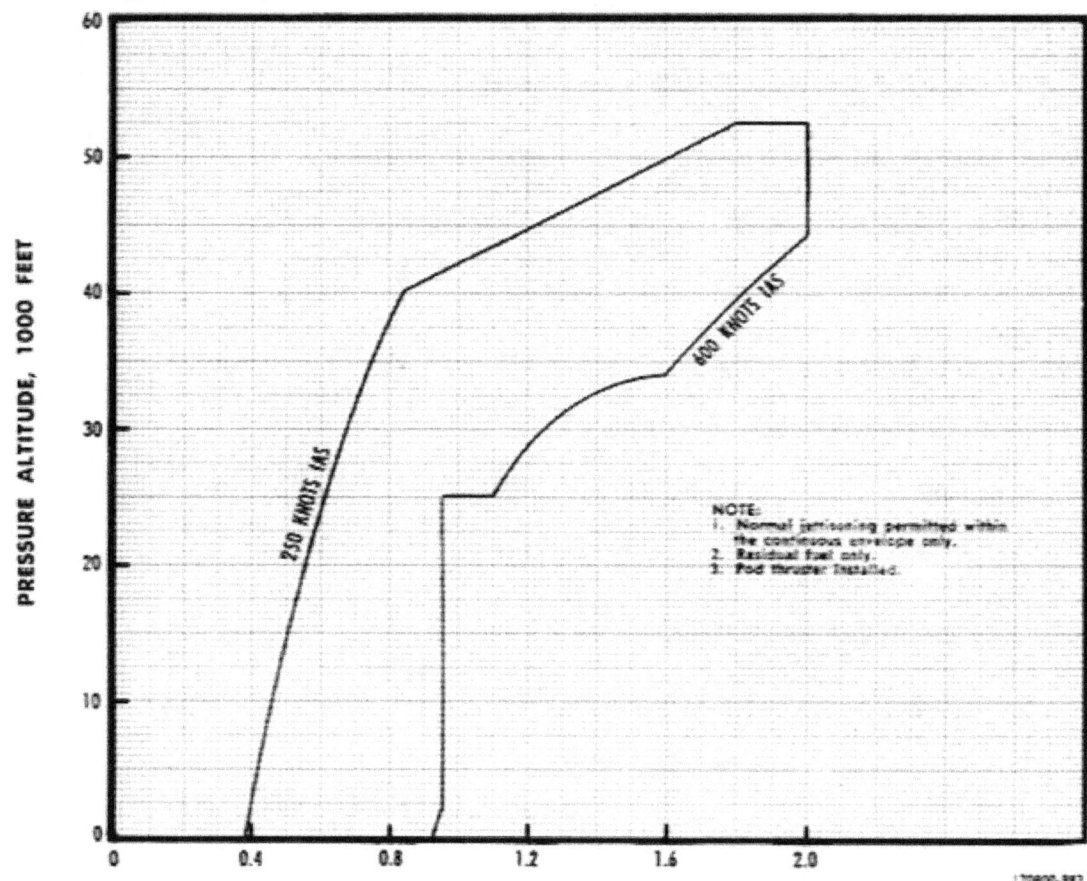

Figure 5-2. MACH NUMBER

- Upon engine start, allow at least 10 minutes of engine operation to stabilize oil temperatures.
- During starts in extreme cold weather, gage may peg at 100 psi. If practical, idle rpm should not be exceeded until pressure reduces to normal. (Pressure should come off peg within 5 minutes.)

STARTER LIMITS.

Pneumatic starts have the following limitations:

1. Maximum operation	1 minute (cumulative within any 3 minute period)
2. Minimum cooling after 1-minute operation	3 minutes
3. Minimum cooling after two 1-minute cycles	10 minutes

Cartridge starts on Engine #2 have the following limitations:

1. Not more than two cartridge starts will be made in any 60-minute period.
2. Minimum elapsed time between starts is 5 minutes.
3. Minimum elapsed time before removing a cartridge is as follows:

Spent cartridge	5 minutes
Misfired cartridge	1 minute
Hang-fire cartridge	5 minutes (after all evidence of burning has ceased)

Cartridge malfunctions are defined as:

a. Misfire. A cartridge that fails to ignite. There will be no evidence of smoke and no engine rotation.

b. Hangfire. An abnormal delay between cartridge actuations and indication of engine

5-4

tire limit speed

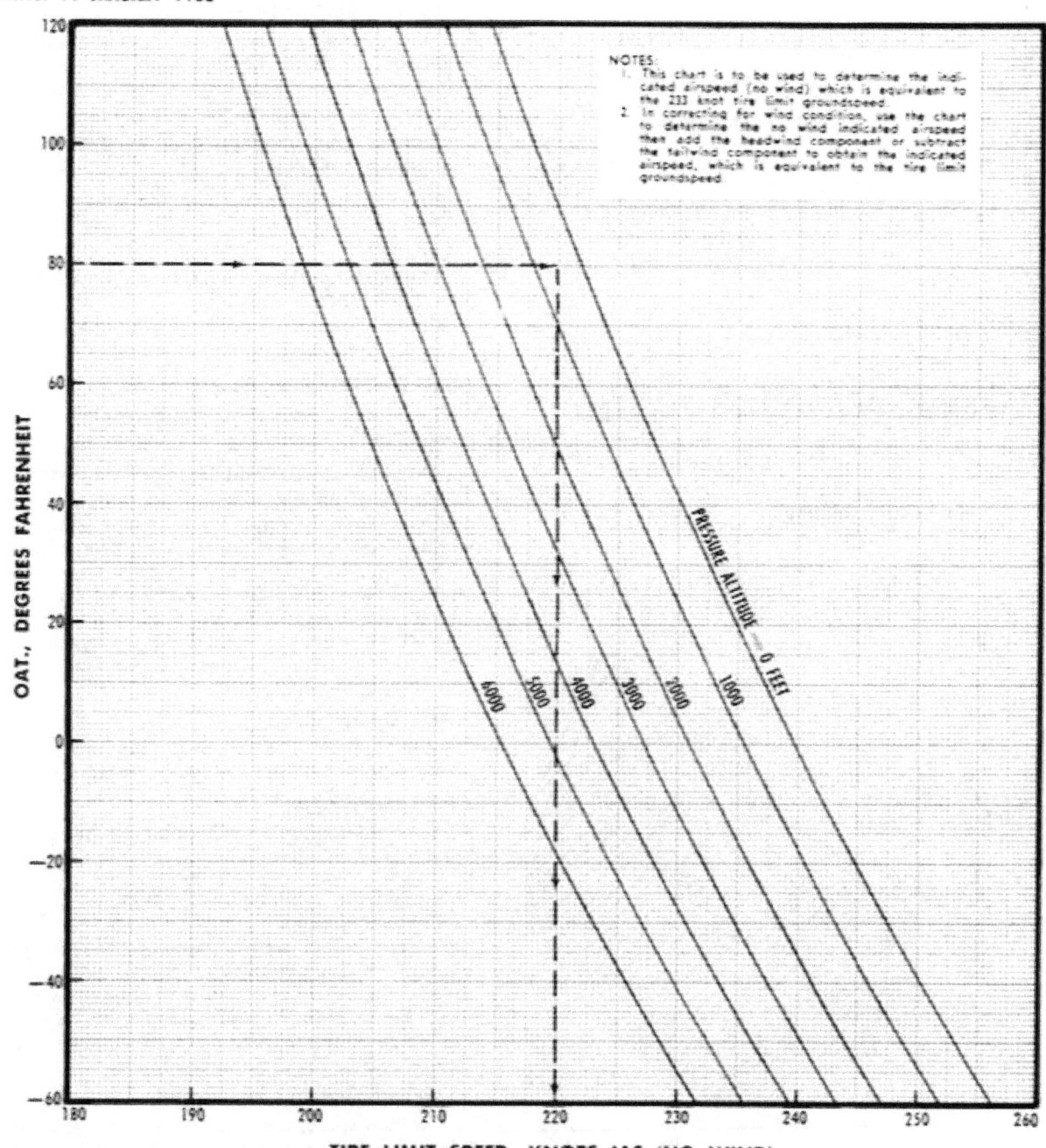

Figure 5-3.

Section V
Operating Limitations

T.O. 1B-58A-1

RPM. There will be evidence of smoke at the exhaust door. After a period of several seconds, RPM will increase rapidly and will give evidence of near normal operation. If the above indications are observed and start is unsuccessful, the cartridge has been expended.

WARNING

- Do not remove cartridge that has fired normally, hangfired or misfired until there is no evidence of smoke at the exhaust door, and appropriate above time limitations have elapsed. Wear asbestos gloves when removing the cartridge.
- Except in an emergency, engine operation is prohibited when a live or misfired cartridge is installed.

ram air mode limits

U.S. STANDARD DAY

DATA BASIS: ESTIMATED
DATE: 22 JULY 1960

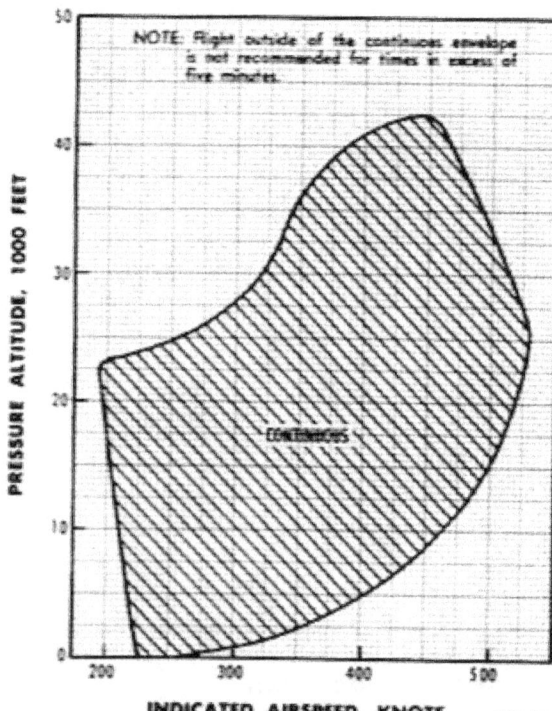

Figure 5-4.

AFTERBURNER LIGHT-OFF LIMITS.

Successful afterburner light-off can be accomplished throughout the normal flight envelope.

AIRSPEED LIMITATIONS.

FLUTTER RESTRICTION.

Do not exceed 515 knots IAS below 9000 feet until at least half of the fuel has been used from either the forward or aft pod tank. When either of the pod tanks is half full or less, the flutter restriction is removed.

LANDING GEAR EXTENSION AND RETRACTION MAXIMUM SPEED.

Landing gear extension and retraction is limited to speeds below 300 knots IAS or mach no. 0.9, whichever is less.

MAXIMUM AIRSPEED LIMIT WITH DRAG CHUTE DOORS OPEN.

With the drag chute doors open, do not exceed 450 knots IAS or mach no. 0.90, whichever is less.

DRAG CHUTE DEPLOYMENT SPEED.

The maximum drag chute deployment speed is 218 knots IAS.

LOWER POD NORMAL JETTISON LIMITS.

The speed limits for normal jettisoning of the lower pod are shown in figure 5-2. The cg must be moved to 1.5% MAC forward of the aft limit for the airplane with upper pod before normal jettisoning of the lower pod. Refer to "Pod Drop," Section VI for flight characteristics during jettisoning. If a normal release is not obtained, refer to figure 2-8 for the airspeed and altitude limits that will insure pod separation if the pod thruster fails to fire.

FUEL DUMP SPEED.

For the recommended airspeed for fuel dumping operations, refer to "Fuel Dumping" Section III.

TIRE LIMIT SPEED.

The tires are limited to 233 knots groundspeed.

Note

This value may be exceeded in an emergency.

See figure 5-3 to determine the indicated airspeed (no wind) which is equivalent to the 233 knot ground speed. Figure 5-3 also provides instructions for applying the headwind or tailwind component corrections to the indicated airspeed (no wind) obtained from the chart.

RAM AIR MODE LIMIT SPEED.

Maximum speeds for ram air operation at various altitudes are shown in figure 5-4. Operation outside the continuous envelope for more than 5 minutes is not recommended because there is inadequate airflow for cooling at the lower airspeeds and cabin temperature will be too cold at the higher altitudes.

minimum flying and maneuver speed

DATA BASIS: ESTIMATED
DATE: 7 FEBRUARY 1964

(BASED ON 17° WING ANGLE OF ATTACK)

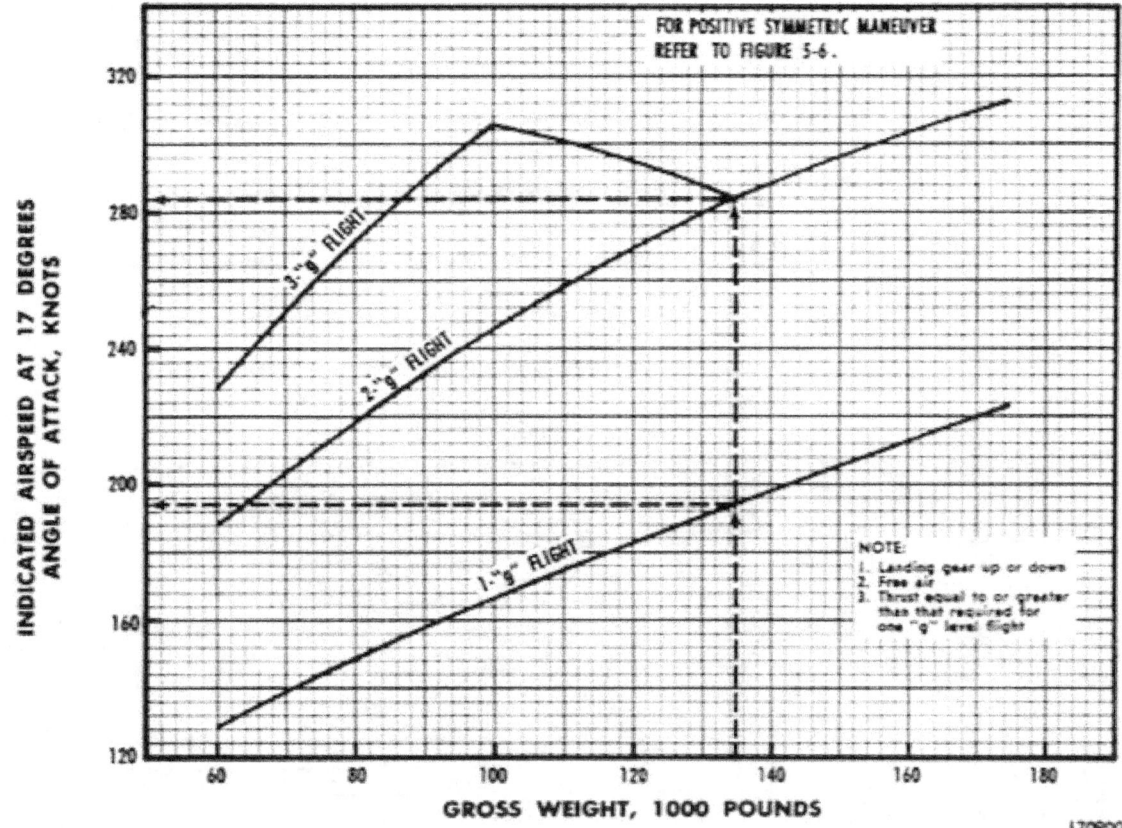

Figure 5-5.

During ram air operation, adequate cooling air is marginal at some flight conditions resulting in higher operating temperatures for all force-cooled electronic equipment. For recommended electronic equipment operation during ram air cooling, refer to "Ram Air Operation," Section IV.

MINIMUM FLYING AND MANEUVER SPEEDS.

Minimum safe-flying and maneuver speeds at 17 degrees angle of attack will be determined from figures 5-5 and 6-3. The angle-of-attack indicator may be used as an aid in maintaining minimum safe flying and maneuver speeds by observing the 17 degrees angle of attack limit however, the airspeed indicator is the primary instrument. Figure 5-5 provides minimum safe-flying and maneuver speeds corresponding to an angle of attack of 17 degrees.

Note

As a general rule, 310 knots may be used as the minimum flying speed to assure that 17 degrees angle of attack will not be exceeded regardless of gross weight for maneuvers up to limit load factor. If a lower, more precise speed is desired, it may be obtained from the curves at the particular gross weight for operation.

Large deflections of aileron or rudder at high angles of attack with resultant large yawing and rolling moments can precipitate a sharp pitch up and spin entry. As there is no necessity for operation of the airplane at angles of attack above 17 degrees this value should not be exceeded. Following the example line on figure 5-5, the minimum flying and maneuver speed for 1"-g" flight at a gross weight of 135,000 pounds is 194 knots IAS. At this same gross weight the limit maneuver load factor speed is 284 knots IAS.

Section V
Operating Limitations

T.O. 1B-58A-1

limit maneuver load factors

DATA BASIS: ESTIMATED
DATE: 18 SEPTEMBER 1964

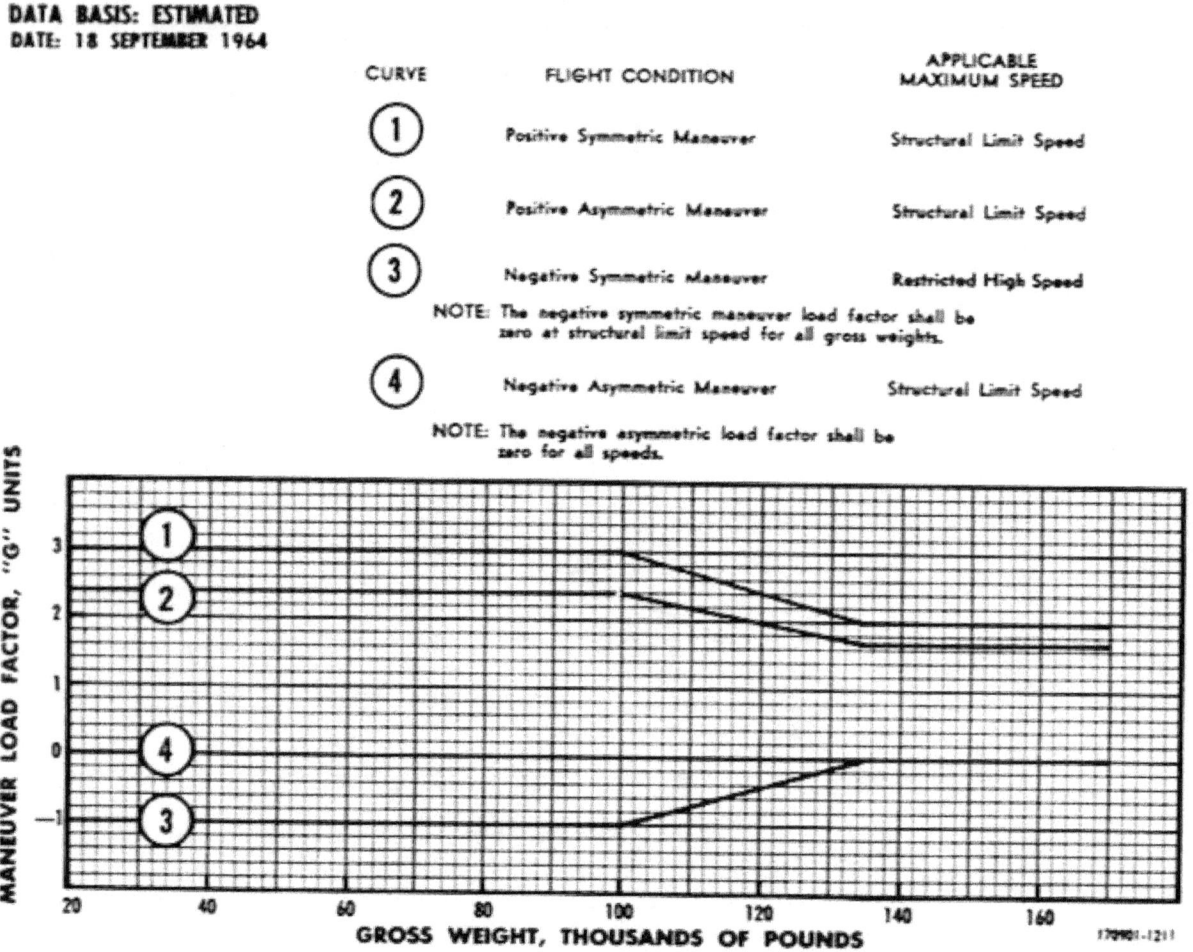

Figure 5-6.

To prevent the possibility of spin entry the following precautions should be observed:

1. The minimum flying and maneuver speeds in figure 5-5 should be closely observed.

2. Large aileron or rudder deflections at or near the minimum speeds indicated should be avoided.

3. Control movements should be coordinated to prevent sideslip.

4. Do not operate in buffet of more than moderate intensity, ±0.1 incremental normal load factor, or develop limit load factor at speeds lower than 310 knots IAS to insure that the 17-degree angle of attack is not exceeded.

RESTRICTED HIGH SPEED.

Refer to T.O. 1B-58A-1A.

STRUCTURAL LIMIT SPEED.

Refer to T.O. 1B-58A-1A.

PROHIBITED MANEUVERS.

All acrobatics, including spins, stalls, and inverted flight, are prohibited.

ACCELERATION LIMITATIONS.

Design limit maneuver load factors are shown in figure 5-6.

CAUTION

- When operating along the restricted high speed line at gross weights below 100,000 pounds, a maneuver load factor of minus 0.8 "g" can cause distortion of the inlet airflow to such an extent that engine flameout may occur.

- Airframe structural damage or failure may result if these limits are exceeded. The symmetric maneuver limits apply to maneuvers in which small changes in bank angle are experienced or aileron inputs are small. Rolling maneuvers cause wing loads to be greater than those developed during symmetric flight at the same maneuver load factor, therefore, the limit maneuver load factor must be reduced. Asymmetric maneuver limits apply when performing pull-up maneuvers involving large changes of bank angle or large aileron inputs.

CENTER OF GRAVITY LIMITATIONS.

The aft center of gravity limitations in the subsonic and transonic regions are established as the most aft loading for which minimum acceptable longitudinal stability is available. These limits are as specified in figure 5-7.

WARNING

Operation of the airplane aft of these limits is hazardous.

Acceptable minimum longitudinal stability is measured by the distance between the center of lift (aerodynamic center), and center of gravity. The minimum acceptable longitudinal stability occurs when the center of lift is at 3% MAC aft of the center of gravity.

WARNING

As the longitudinal stability is reduced the characteristics of the airplane are such as to require less and less up elevator to trim and less elevator available for maneuver. If the cg moves aft of the aerodynamic center, the airplane will not nose back after a nose up gust but will increase in angle of attack. Thus for conditions of negative stability the airplane could pitch up to an attitude beyond which the small amount of elevator available could provide control; resulting in an uncontrolled divergence in either the nose up or nose down direction.

The aft cg limit is variable with mach number as shown in figure 5-7. At the cruise flight condition of mach no. 0.92, the aft limit is considerably further aft than at lower mach numbers.

WARNING

As speed is reduced and the aerodynamic center is moved forward, there will be a marked and dangerous reduction of longitudinal stability.

Airspeed and center of gravity must be monitored frequently when operating near the aft cg limits.

OPERATIONAL CENTER OF GRAVITY LIMITS CHART.

The subsonic longitudinal limits on the center of gravity chart (figure 5-7) represent a minimum static margin of 3 percent MAC. This is the minimum allowable static margin for acceptable longitudinal stability. For a discussion of static stability refer to "Longitudinal Flight Characteristics", Section VI. To reduce the possibility of inadvertent operation at neutral or negative static margins it is recommended that the following procedures be followed for operation between 30 and 33 percent MAC. The DSO should closely monitor his instruments to insure that the center of gravity is maintained within the limits for 3 percent static margin. Fuel management procedures should be observed so that it is always possible to shift fuel forward of a 30 percent cg when a 30 to 33 percent cruise cg is programmed. In the event a cg of 30 percent MAC cannot be attained by shifting fuel forward and a situation is encountered where increased

Section V
Operating Limitations

T.O. 1B-58A-1

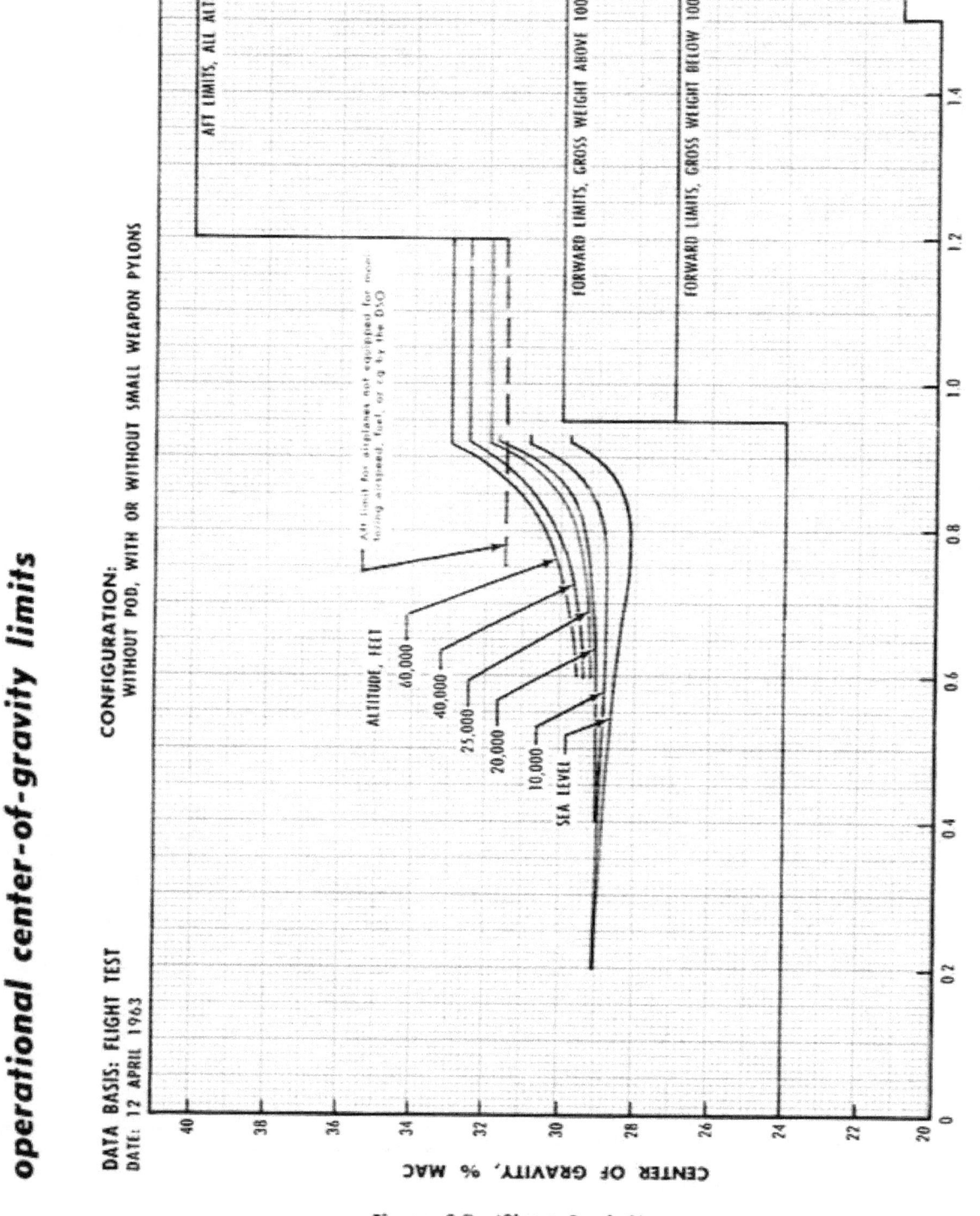

Figure 5-7. (Sheet 1 of 3)

operational center-of-gravity limits

DATA BASIS: FLIGHT TEST
DATE: 20 MAY 1968

CONFIGURATION:
1. WITH MB-1 POD
2. WITH TCP, WITH OR WITHOUT SMALL WEAPONS OR PYLONS

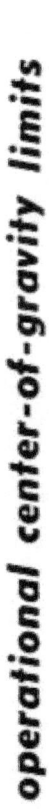

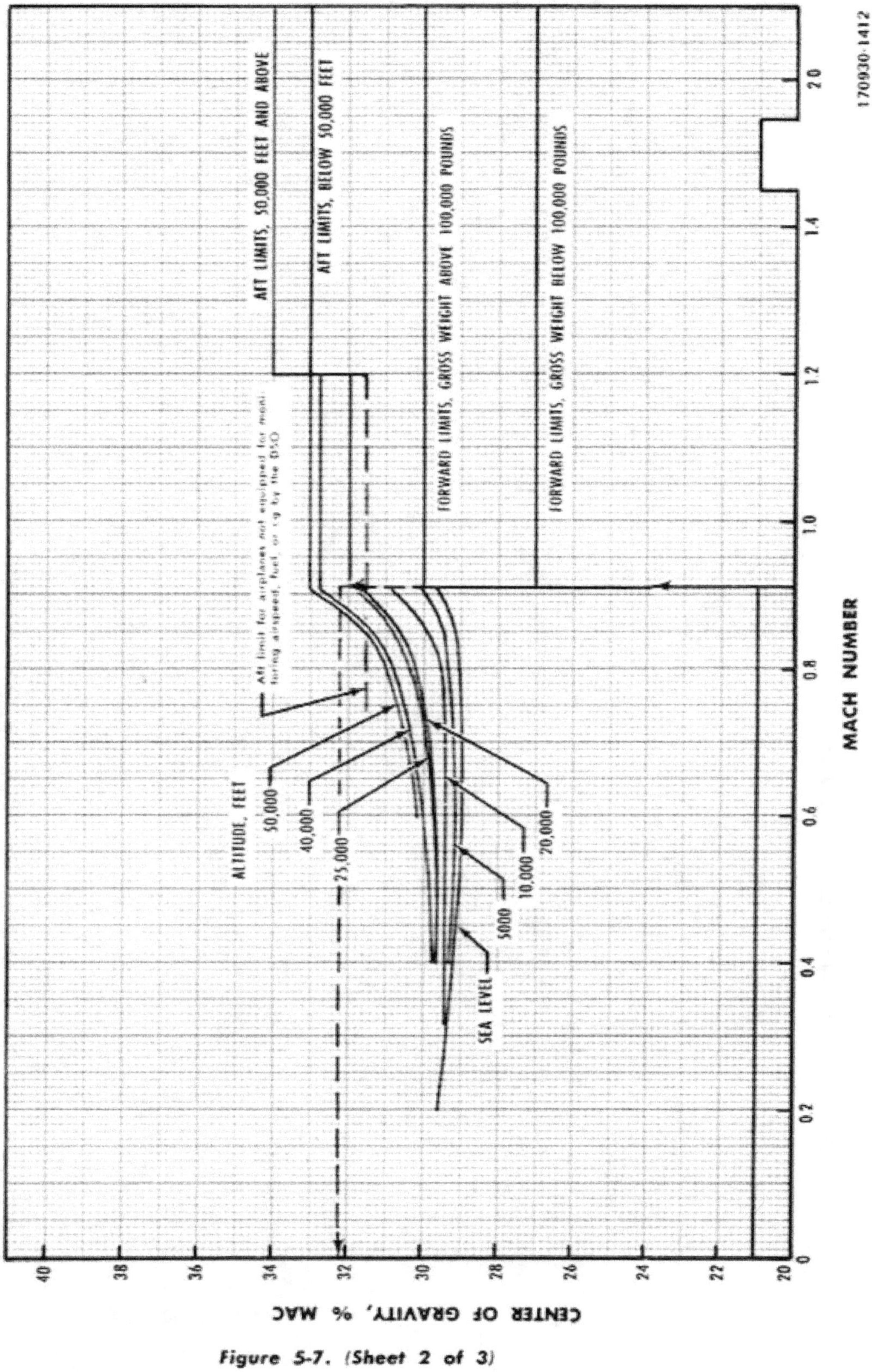

Figure 5-7. (Sheet 2 of 3)

Section V
Operating Limitations

T.O. 1B-58A-1

operational center-of-gravity limits

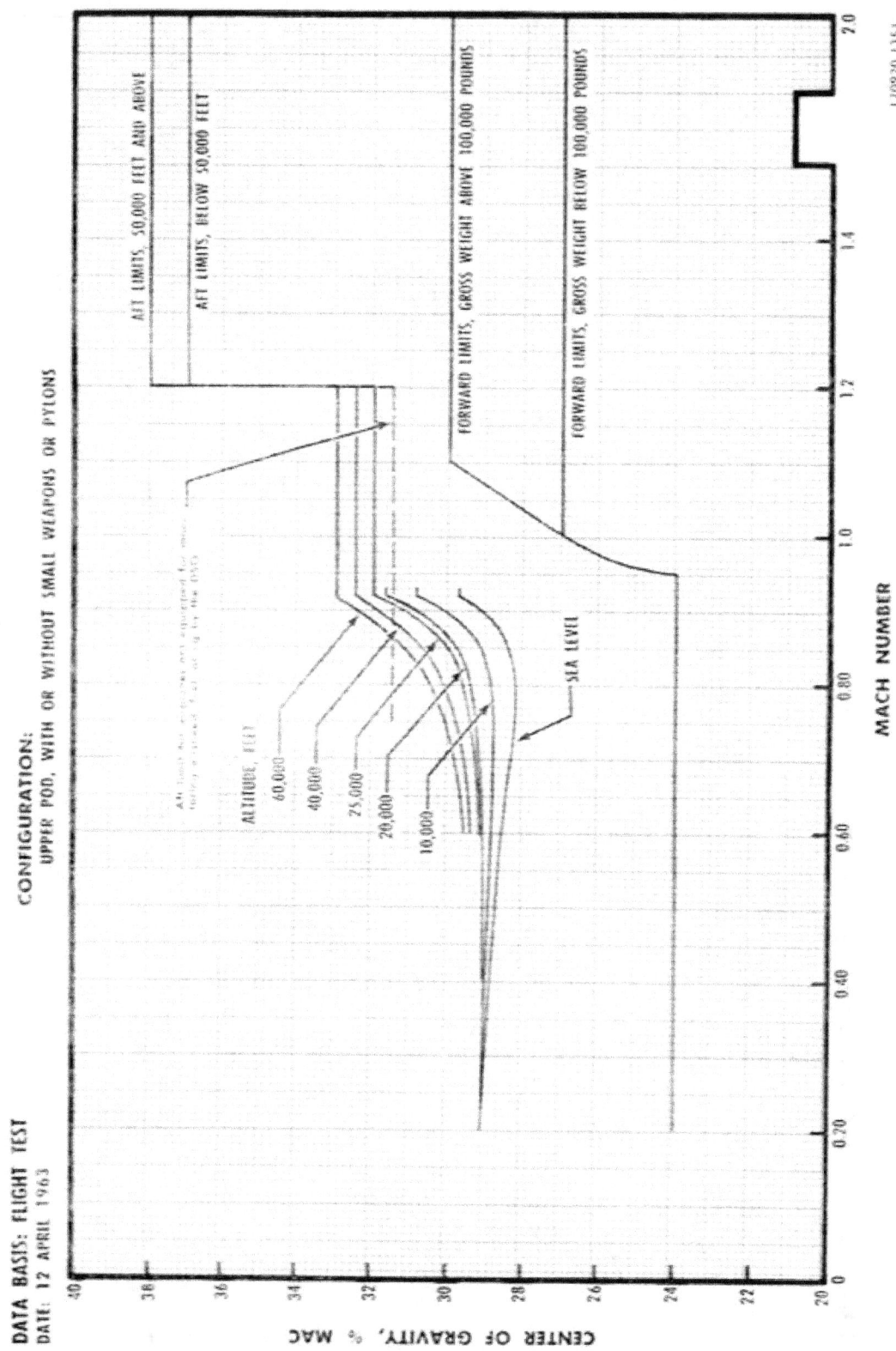

Figure 5-7. (Sheet 3 of 3)

static margin or reduction in airspeed is desired, sufficient fuel must be burned from the aft tank prior to decelerating to move the cg forward to prevent exceeding operational limits during deceleration. If the situation is critical and time does not permit burning off fuel, then fuel dumping must be employed at subsonic cruise to remedy the condition. (Refer to "Fuel Dumping," Section III.)

WARNING

In decreasing speed from supersonic flight, the pilot must not enter the transonic region until subsonic centers of gravity have been obtained. If the center of gravity is too far aft when subsonic speeds are achieved, the airplane might possess insufficient or negative stability, resulting in critical or catastrophic flight conditions. This is particularly important for the airplane without the pod because of the more aft allowable supersonic limits.

The aft center of gravity limits at supersonic speed represent those to which sudden engine failure tests have been performed at mach no. 2.0 to demonstrate the airplane stability and structural integrity of the airframe. Because of the rapid response of the airplane, this limit is set such that the pilot need not assist in controlling the maneuver beyond holding the wing level with the ailerons during the initial resulting motion. Refer to "Inflight Emergencies" — "Engine Failure," Section III for recommended emergency procedures in the event of engine failure.

Note

The supersonic aft center of gravity limits for the airplane with pod are more forward than for the airplane without pod because addition of the pod, with most of its volume forward of the airplane center of gravity, has a destabilizing effect resulting in lower directional stability of the airplane. Hence the response of the airplane with pod is larger than that of the airplane without pod in the event of a sudden engine failure when the center of gravity location is the same for both.

The subsonic forward limit for the airplane, with and without the pod installed, defines the most forward center of gravity position which is compatible with nose gear unstick, landing, and low speed maneuver requirements. It is to be noted that the forward limit of 24 percent MAC for the airplane without pod is outside of the physical loading capability of the airplane except for the range between 80,000 and 84,000 pounds gross weight, and then can be attained only with the fuel located as far forward as possible. The supersonic forward center of gravity limits provide that the hinge moment required to trim in one "g" flight with power on will not be greater than the rated capacity of either of the independent dual hydraulic systems, provided that not more than one degree of aileron is needed to counteract wing heaviness, along the restricted high speed boundary of the aircraft. It is to be noted that the forward hinge moment limits, for airplanes with MB or TC pods, apply for all speeds above mach no. 0.91. Refer to Section VI for a discussion of wing heaviness. The hinge moment limits are somewhat conservative at flight conditions inside of the restricted high speed boundaries and at low gross weights.

CAUTION

During automatic center of gravity control, the accuracy to which the automatic controller can maintain center of gravity must be considered and allowance for center of gravity tolerance must be made in making up the flight plan. The center of gravity limits defined here are for very precise manual control of center of gravity location. For a discussion of the accuracy to which center of gravity may be controlled automatically, refer to "Fuel Management", Section VII.

Following the example line on figure 5-7, sheet 2 the operational center of gravity limits at 30,000 feet altitude at mach no. 0.91 are 21 percent MAC forward to 32.2 percent MAC aft.

CENTER OF GRAVITY LOADING LIMITATIONS AND CAPABILITIES.

See figure 5-8 for the airplane loading limitations for ground handling, takeoff, and landing compared to the available loading range of the airplane. Figure 5-8 shows extremities of fuel loading capability for two deck angles, −2.3 degrees and +10 degrees. Three aft limits for upset are included for planning of ground conditions.

1. Airplane upset limit (zero thrust).
2. Military thrust upset limit.
3. Maximum A/B thrust upset limit.

Section V
Operating Limitations

T.O. 1B-58A-1

center-of-gravity loading limitations

CONFIGURATION: WITHOUT POD

DATA BASIS: ESTIMATED
DATE: 12 APRIL 1963

GROUND HANDLING, TAKEOFF AND LANDING CONDITIONS

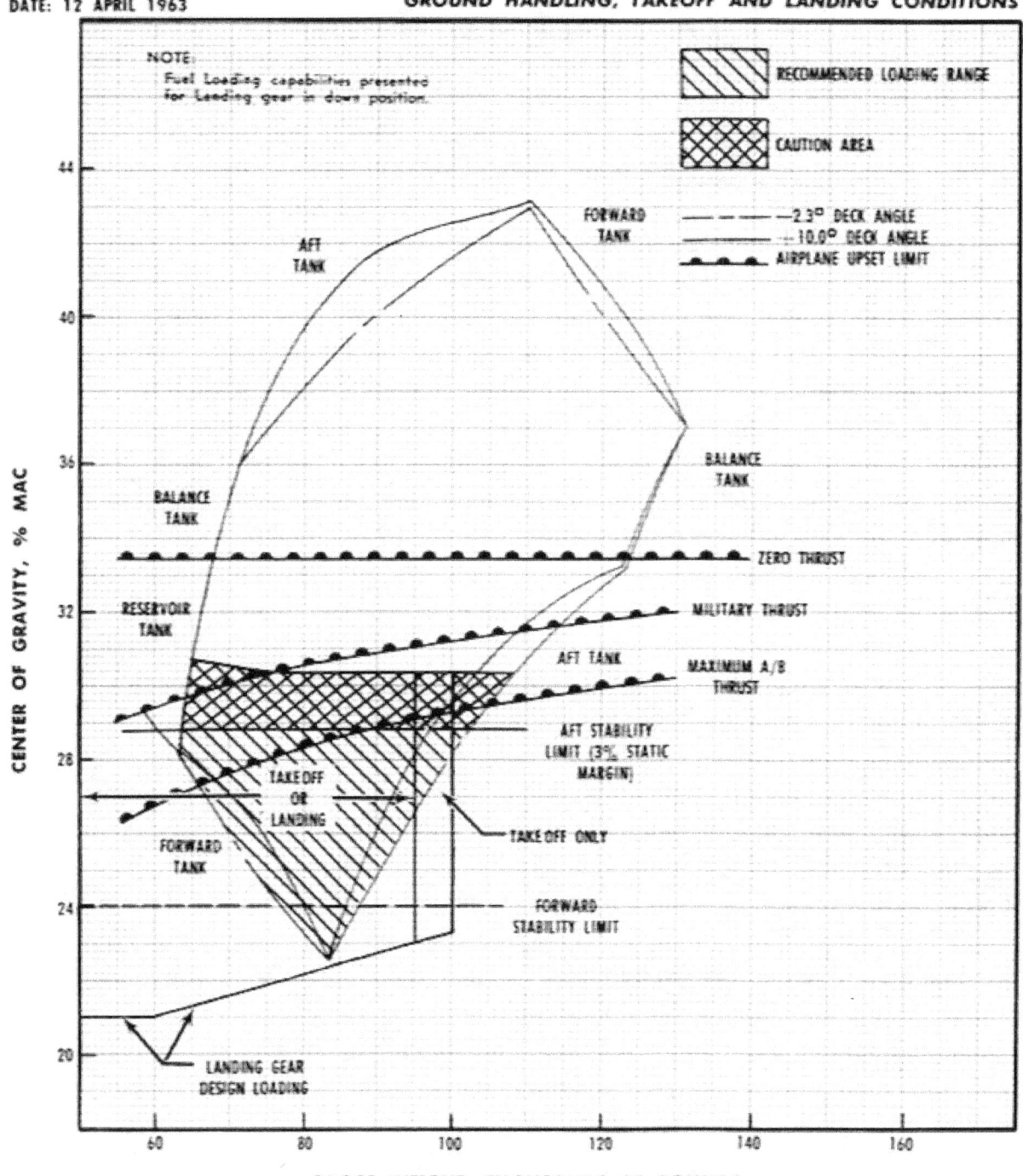

Figure 5-8. (Sheet 1 of 7)

5-14

center-of-gravity loading limitations

CONFIGURATION: WITH MB OR LA POD

DATA BASIS: ESTIMATED
DATE: 2 JULY 1965

GROUND HANDLING, TAKEOFF AND LANDING CONDITIONS

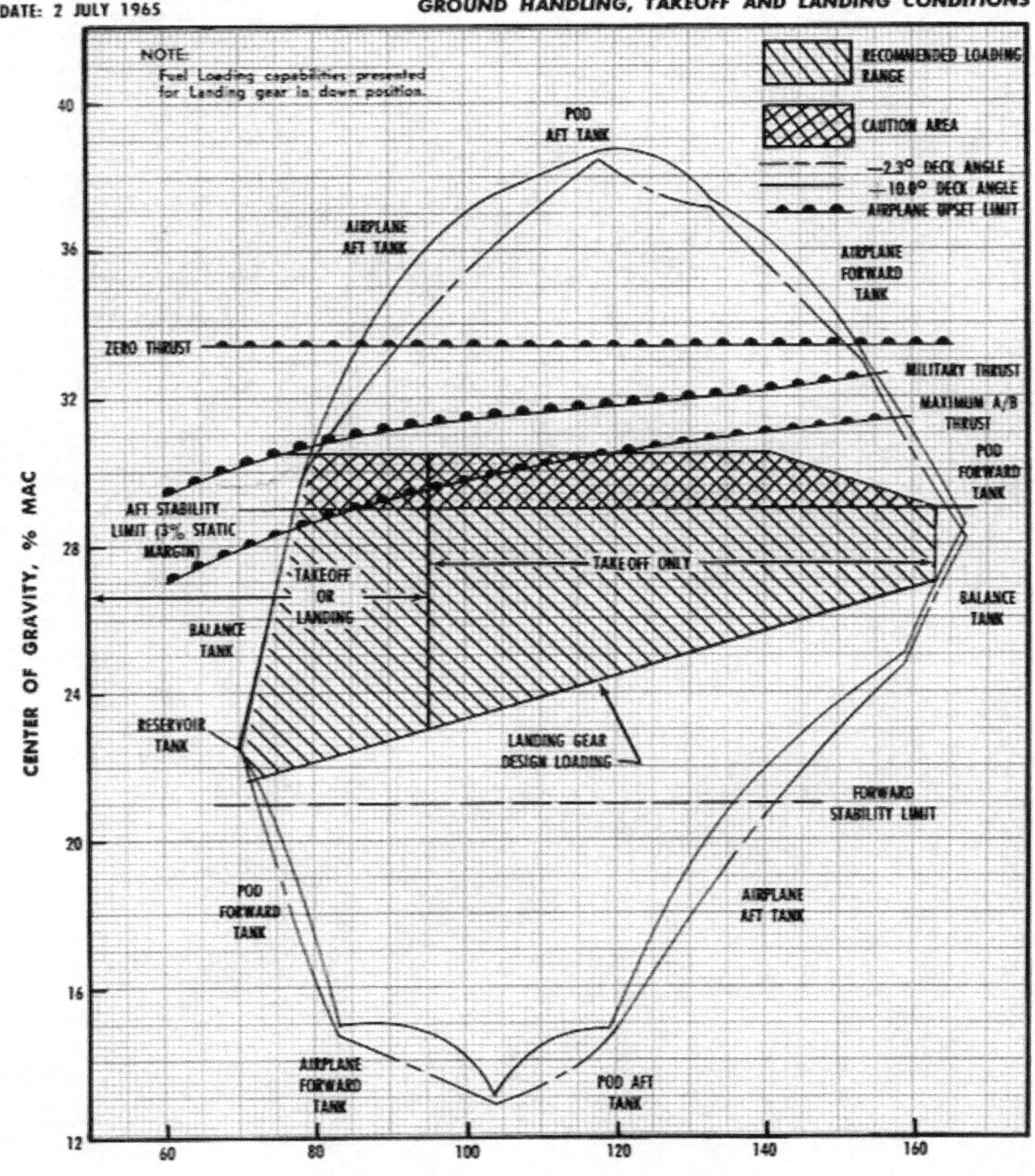

Figure 5-8. (Sheet 2 of 7)

Section V
Operating Limitations

T.O. 1B-58A-1

center-of-gravity loading limitations

CONFIGURATION:
WITH TCP

DATA BASIS: ESTIMATED
DATE: 12 APRIL 1963

GROUND HANDLING, TAKEOFF AND LANDING CONDITIONS

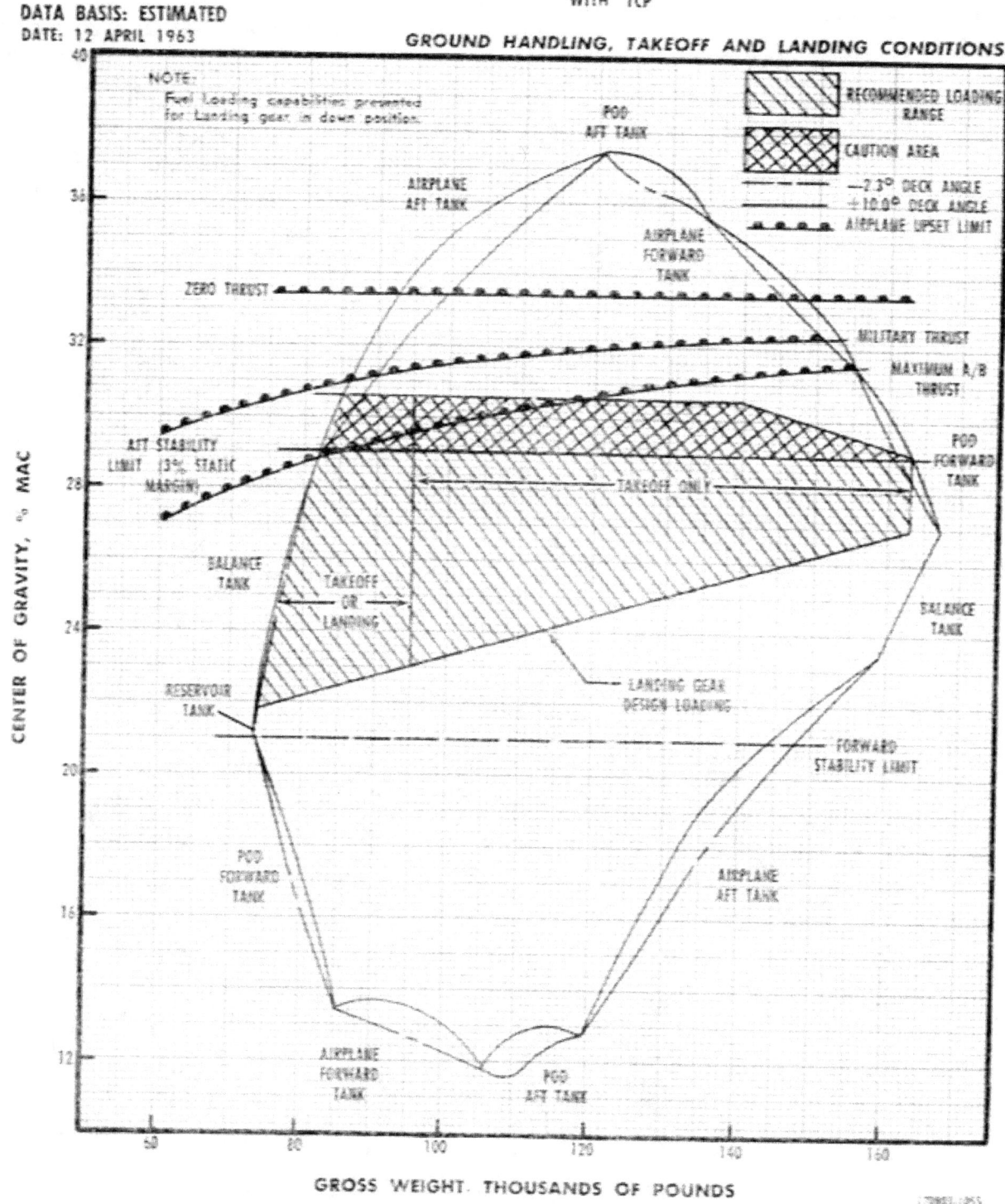

Figure 5-8. (Sheet 3 of 7)

center-of-gravity loading limitations

CONFIGURATION: WITH UPPER POD

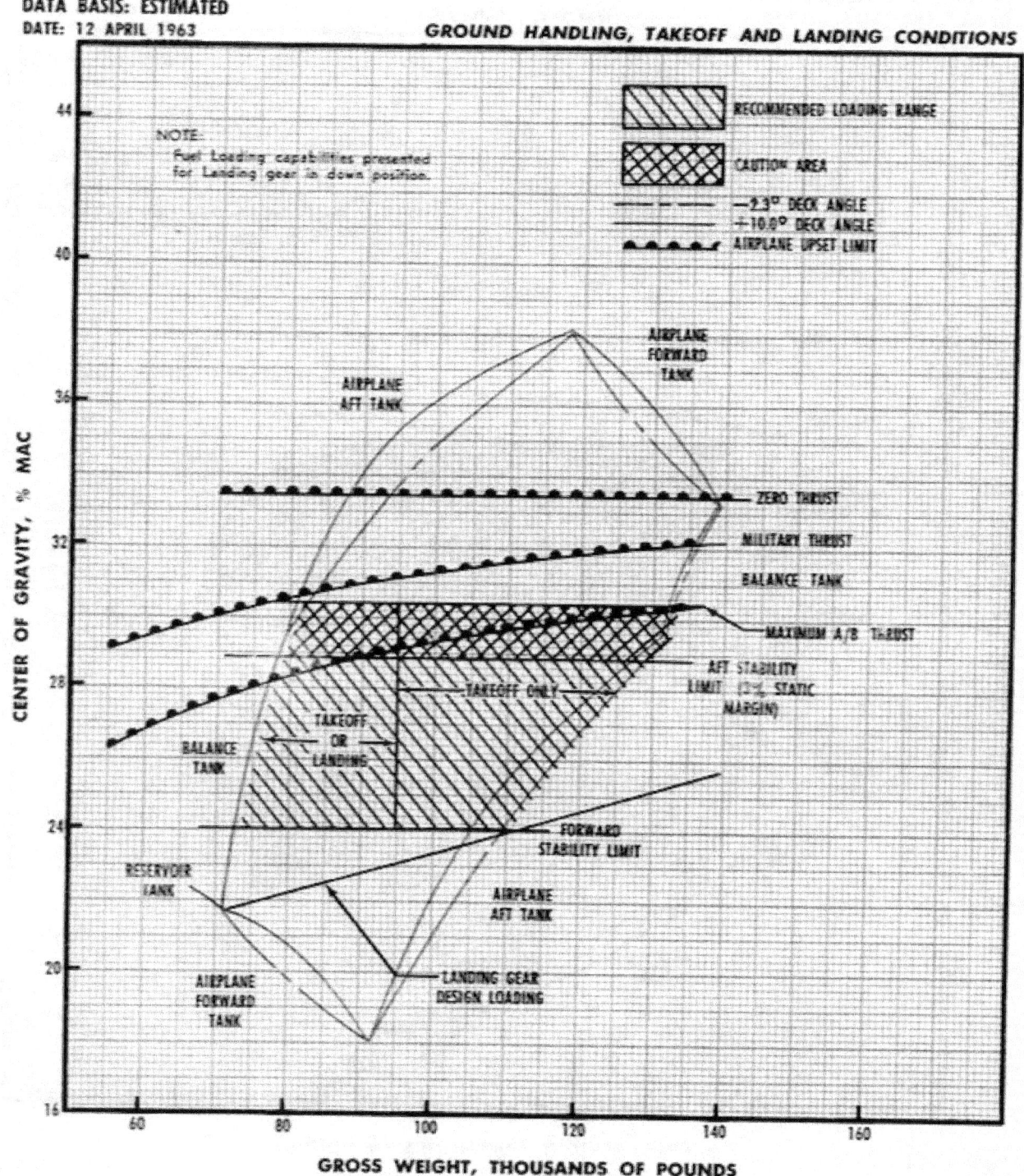

Figure 5-8. (Sheet 4 of 7)

Section V
Operating Limitations

T.O. 1B-58A-1

center-of-gravity loading limitations

CONFIGURATION:
MB, LA OR TCP WITH 4 SMALL WEAPONS

DATA BASIS: ESTIMATED
DATE: 2 JULY 1965

GROUND HANDLING, TAKEOFF AND LANDING CONDITIONS

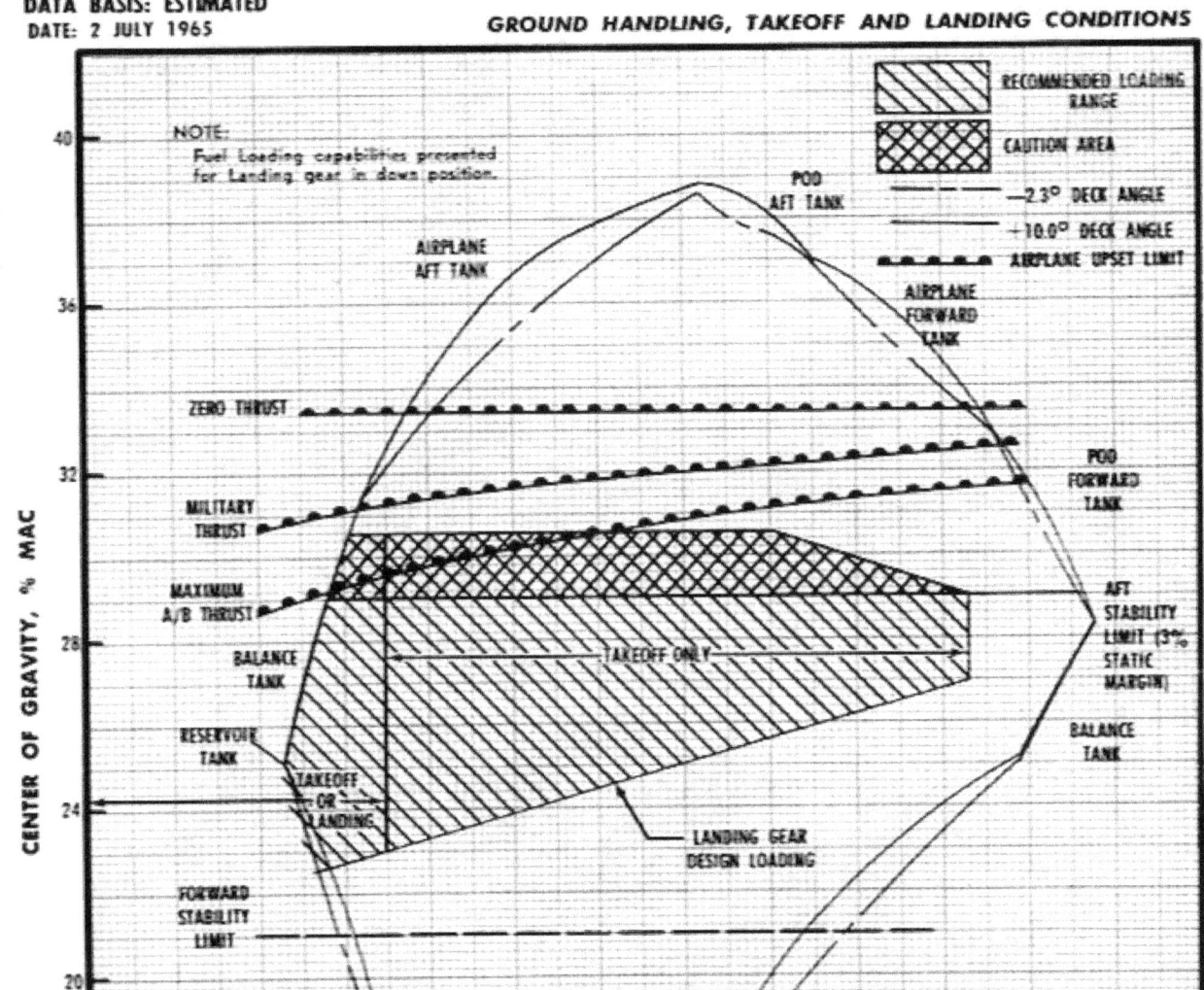

Figure 5-8. (Sheet 5 of 7)

5-18

center-of-gravity loading limitations

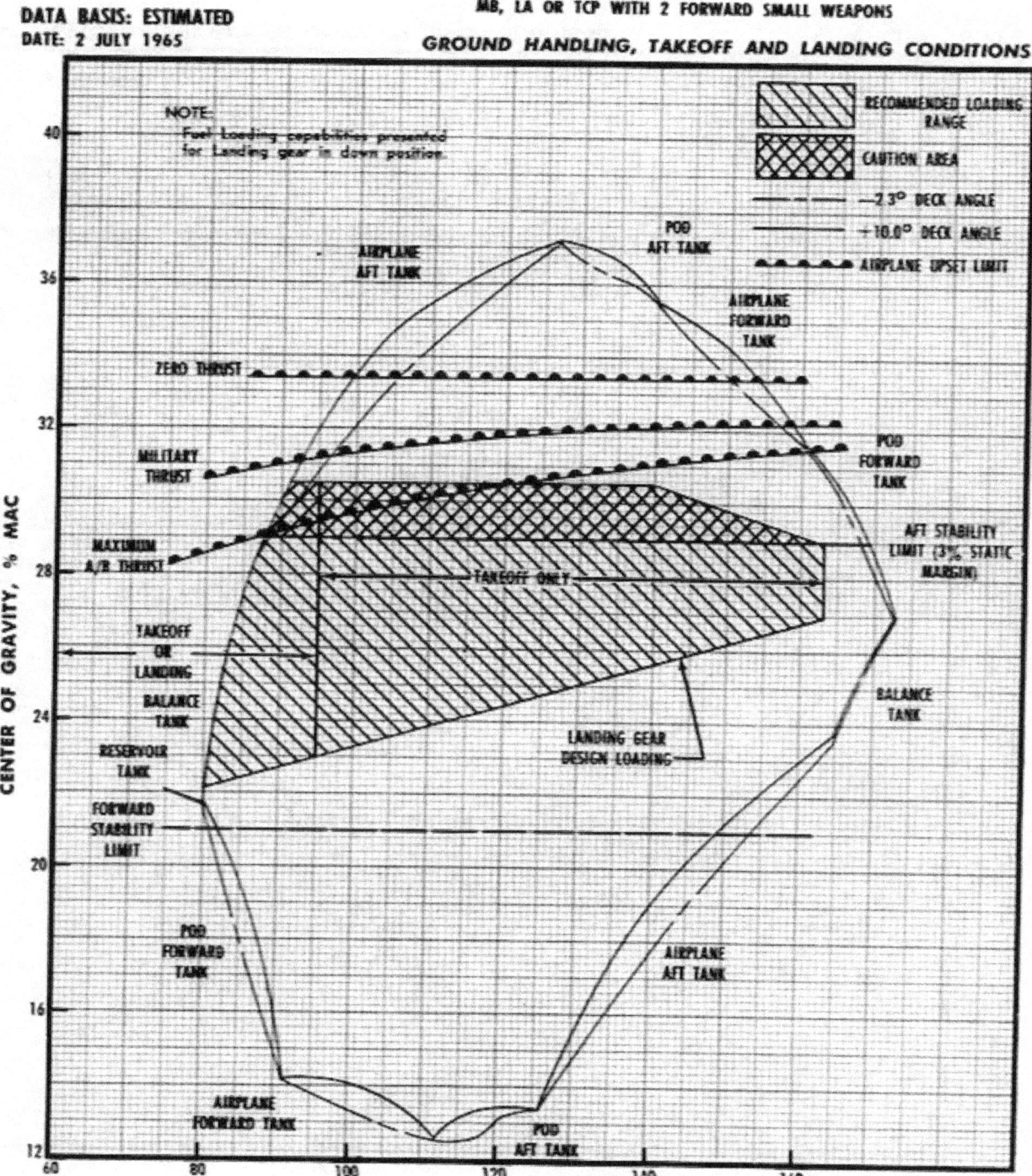

Figure 5-8. (Sheet 6 of 7)

Section V
Operating Limitations

T.O. 1B-58A-1

center-of-gravity loading limitations

CONFIGURATION:
MB, LA OR TCP WITH 2 AFT SMALL WEAPONS

DATA BASIS: ESTIMATED
DATE: 2 JULY 1965

GROUND HANDLING, TAKEOFF AND LANDING CONDITIONS

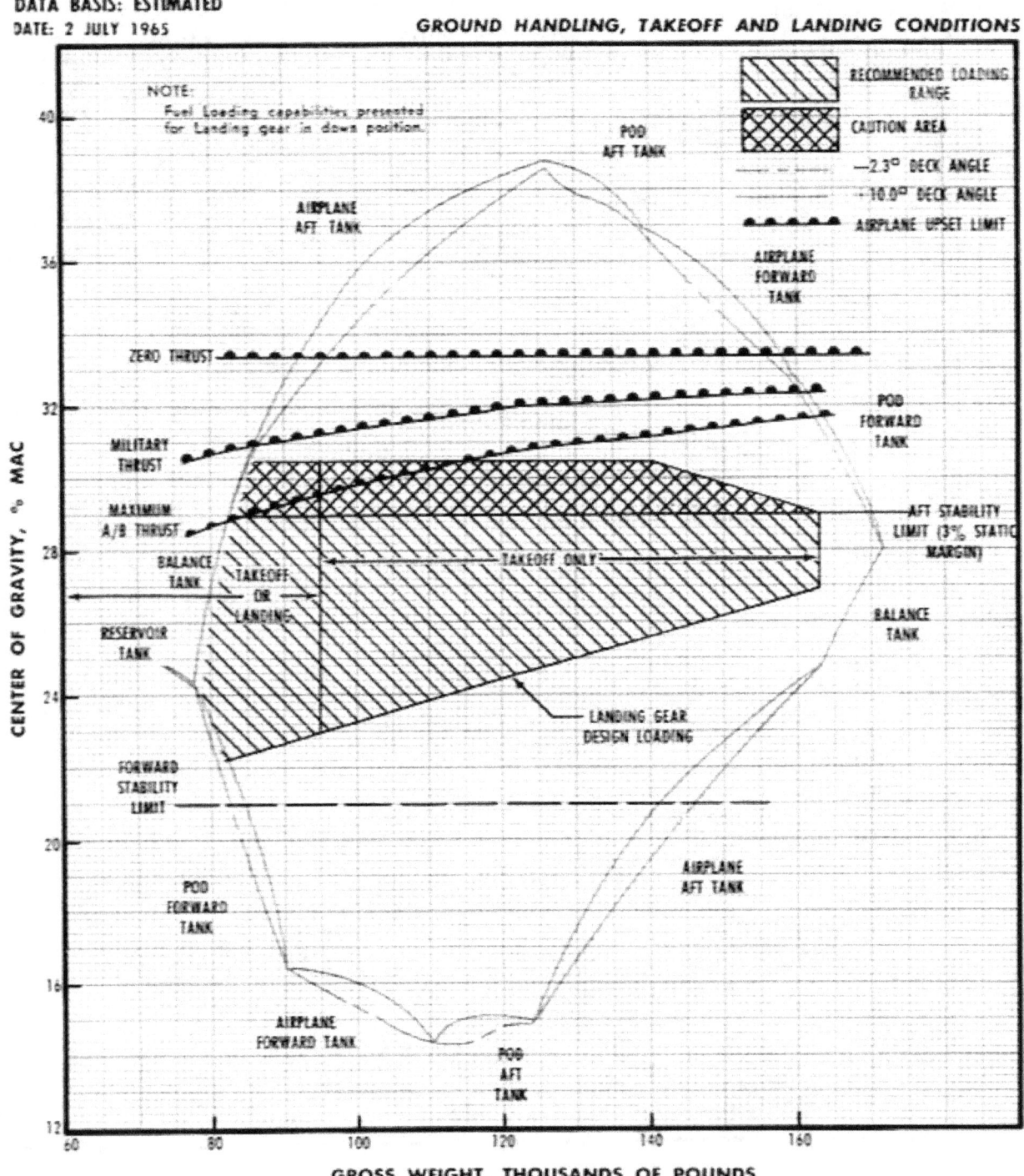

Figure 5-8. (Sheet 7 of 7)

maximum taxi distance

DATA BASIS: ESTIMATED
DATE: 26 NOVEMBER 1963

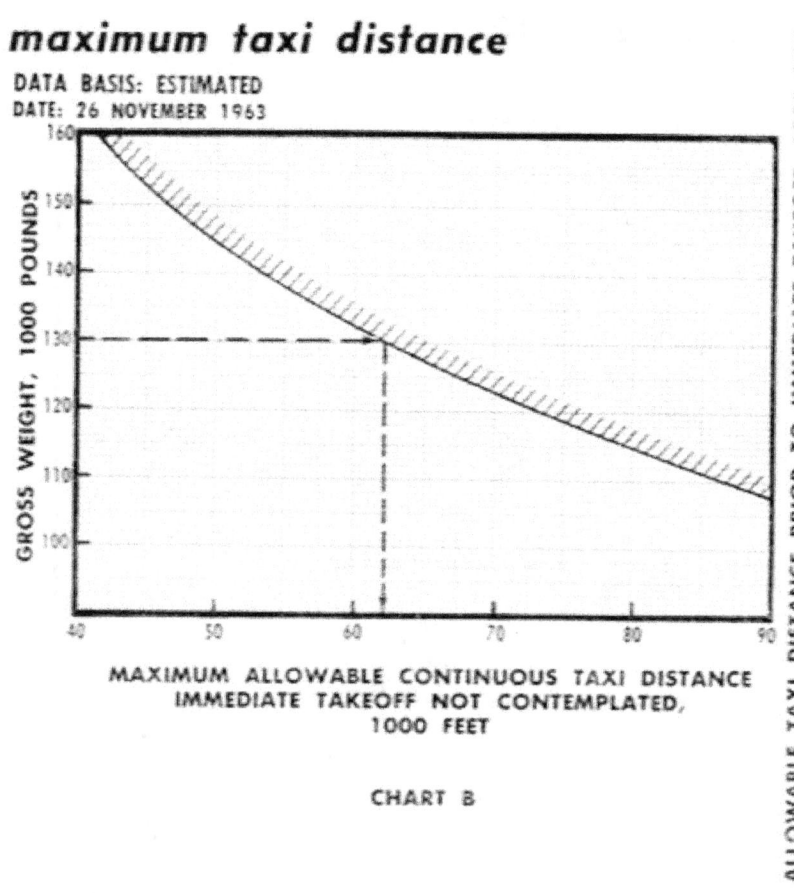

CHART B

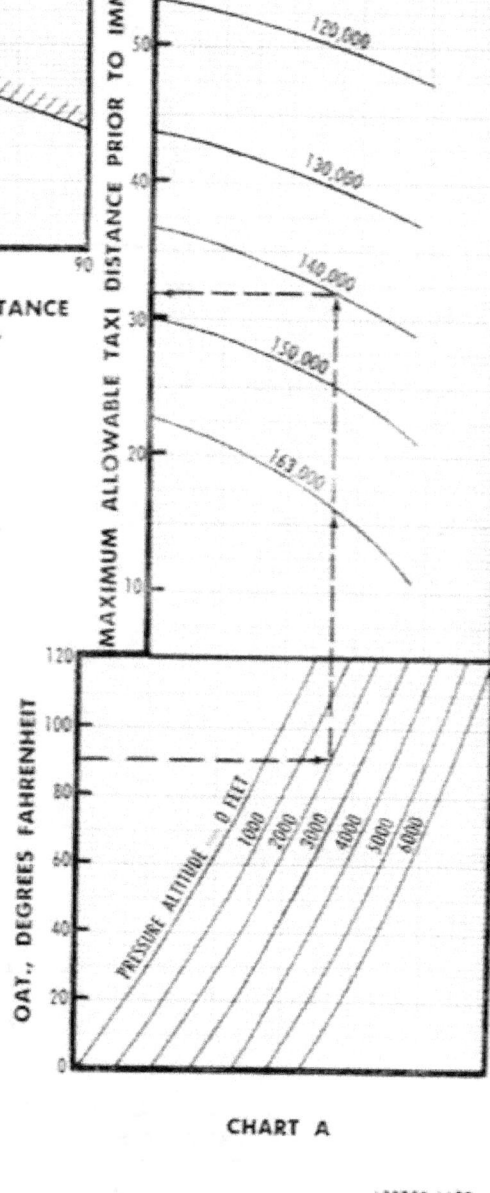

CHART A

The cg of the airplane should at all times be maintained forward of the zero thrust upset limit. For movement of the airplane under its own power, the military thrust and maximum A/B thrust limits should be considered. Operation at or near these cg's and power settings could result in upset or reduced steerability resulting in damage to the airplane. The usable ranges for takeoff and landing are shown in figure 5-8. The caution area should be avoided if practicable. Increasing caution should be observed as the center of gravity approaches the aft limit of the caution area since this limit represents a static margin less than 3 percent. The forward and aft stability limits are also included. The forward loading limitations for all airplane configurations is the forward stability limits or the landing gear design loading limits, whichever is the most restrictive. These limits are more fully defined under "Center of Gravity Limitations" of this section.

Note

All aft center of gravity limits shown in figure 5-8 are based on a deck angle of —10 except for the zero thrust upset limit which is based on —2.3 deck angle.

Figure 5-9.

Section V
Operating Limitations

T.O. 1B-58A-1

nose wheel ground turning limits

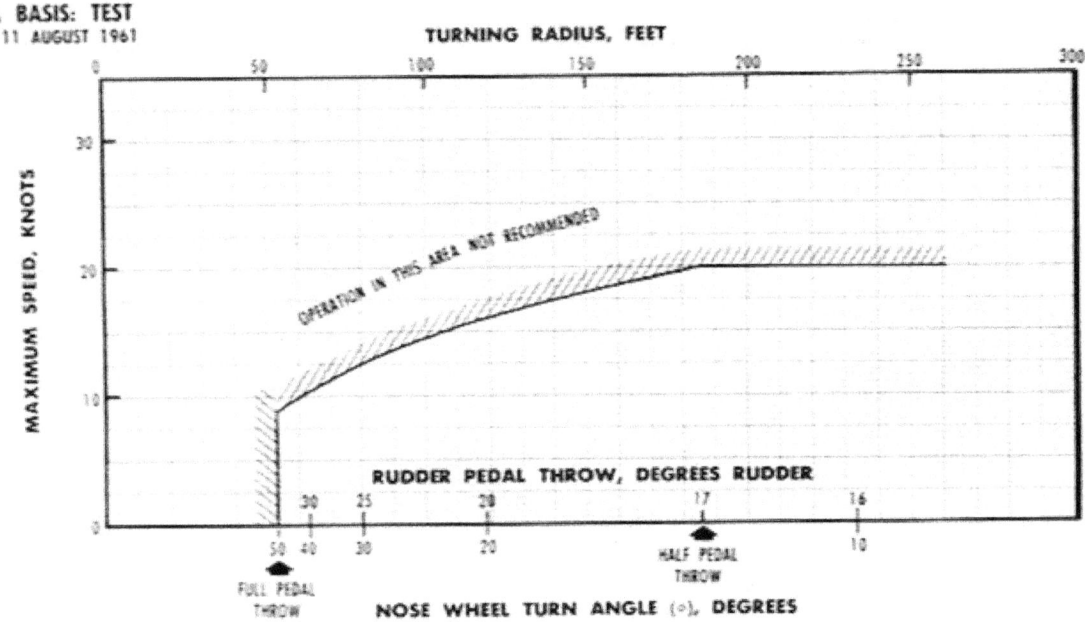

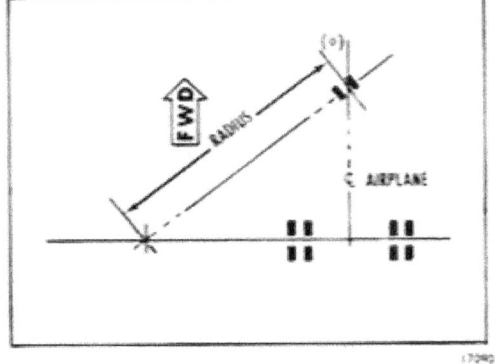

Figure 5-10.

TAXI LIMITATIONS.

TAXI SPEEDS.

To prevent excessive heat buildup in the tires, the airplane is limited to a maximum taxi speed of 30 knots. The limitations shown in figure 5-10 must be observed when turning.

> **CAUTION**
>
> In order to prevent damage to the canopies, the airplane should not be taxied with any canopy open.

MAXIMUM TAXI DISTANCE.

Maximum taxi distance limits have been established to prevent excessive heat buildup in the tires. Figure 5-9 should be used for taxiing and aborted takeoff runs where braking was not sufficient to use the brake energy limit chart. Use figure 5-9, Chart A to determine the maximum taxi distance preceding an immediate takeoff.

> **CAUTION**
>
> If the distance limit in Chart A is exceeded, the tires must be allowed to cool to 100°F (cool when touched with bare hands) or less before takeoff.

Note

The maximum taxi distance is not accumulative but applies to one continuous operation.

Chart B of figure 5-9 is used to determine the maximum continuous taxi distance when an immediate takeoff is not contemplated. Tires must cool to 100°F or less before takeoff.

CAUTION

Exceeding the distance limit in Chart B requires that all tires be replaced.

Example No. 1: Immediate take-off after taxiing.

Given: Outside Air Temperature = 90°F
Pressure Altitude = 2000 feet
Gross Weight = 140,000 pounds

Find: Maximum allowable taxi distance.

Solution:
Following the example line in Chart A, the maximum allowable taxi distance is 31,700 feet.

Example No. 2: Immediate Take-off Not Contemplated.

Given: Gross Weight = 130,000 pounds
Find: Maximum continuous taxi distance

Solution:
Follow the example line in Chart B, the maximum continuous taxi distance is 62,200 feet.

MINIMUM TURNING RADIUS.

The minimum turning radius is 53 feet measured from the nose gear strut. This value corresponds to a 50-degree nose gear steering angle.

MAXIMUM TURNING SPEED.

The maximum turning speed is shown in figure 5-10.

HYDRAULIC SYSTEM LIMITATIONS.

In addition to the normal operating range of 2875-3200 psi, a pressure range of 2800-3200 psi is permissible for transitory and special conditions; such as single engine operating, engine rpm changes, engine speeds below idle, and during the first five minutes of engine operation. At some engine rpm's periodic or cyclic hydraulic pressure swing may exist. The fluctuation must be within the transitory limits of 2800-3200 psi and must be of a character indicating it to be simple momentary pressure and flow compensation. A normal indicator variation is approximately one cps. The cyclic indicator swings should not exceed 150 psi in any one cycle.

FLIGHT CONTROL SYSTEM LIMITATIONS.

FLIGHT LIMITATIONS WITH STABILITY AUGMENTATION MALFUNCTION.

Yaw Damper Warning Lamp Lighted.

If the yaw damper warning lamp lights during ground operations, do not attempt takeoff. If the yaw damper warning lamp lights during flight, observe yaw damper inoperative restrictions.

WARNING

Do not depress the yaw reset button when the yaw damper warning lamp is lighted. To do so may cause a failed damper channel to become engaged.

Yaw Damper Caution Lamp Lighted.

If the yaw damper caution lamp lights during ground operation and cannot be reset using procedures set forth in "Flight Control System Trouble Shooting Procedures", Section VII, do not attempt takeoff. If the yaw damper caution lamp lights during flight and cannot be reset using the procedures set forth in "Flight Control System Trouble Shooting Procedures", Section VII, do not exceed mach no. 0.91.

Yaw Rate To Roll Caution Lamp Lighted.

If the yaw rate to roll caution lamp lights and cannot be reset using the procedures set forth in "Flight Control System Trouble Shooting Procedures", Section VII, do not exceed mach no. 0.91.

Damper Inoperative Restrictions.

Adherence to these restrictions will assure safe flying qualities and structural integrity of all airplane configurations for non-maneuvering flight operations only.

WARNING

Avoid making abrupt and/or full control deflections with any damper inoperative. The damper system affords the airplane structural protection; therefore, abrupt and/or full control deflections could result in exceeding structural design limits with the possibility of causing structural failure.

Section V
Operating Limitations

Pitch Damper. With pitch damper inoperative, do not exceed 450 knots IAS at altitudes between 5000 and 40,000 feet.

Yaw Damper. With yaw damper inoperative, do not attempt takeoff. If yaw damper becomes inoperative in flight, position the yaw damper switch to OFF and do not exceed 450 knots IAS or mach no. 0.91, whichever is less.

Roll Damper. With roll damper inoperative, do not exceed 450 knots IAS or mach no. 0.91, whichever is less.

Roll and Yaw Damper. With the roll and yaw dampers inoperative, do not exceed 450 knots IAS or mach no. 0.91 (whichever is less), or 40,000 feet altitude. Landing at gross weights greater than 80,000 pounds without small weapons, or 90,000 pounds with small weapons, should not be attempted.

ELEVATOR CONTROL AVAILABLE MODE RESTRICTIONS.

Automatic Mode.

1. Do not use automatic mode for takeoff.

2. Do not use automatic mode for landing, for flight with landing gear down, or for flight at airspeeds below 300 knots IAS at altitudes below 20,000 feet except during emergency jettisoning of a pod.

3. Do not make abrupt and/or full up elevator control deflections, especially in the transonic speed range.

WARNING

Closely monitor accelerometer during maneuvering flight to prevent exceeding limit load factor.

Takeoff and Land Mode.

1. Do not use takeoff and land mode at airspeeds above 400 knots IAS except in emergencies.

2. Do not operate autopilot in takeoff and land mode.

Manual Mode.

1. Do not select manual mode without first increasing elevator control available to a sufficient value.

2. Do not use manual mode for takeoff.

3. Do not use manual mode except during air refueling or in the event of malfunction of the automatic mode.

4. Do not engage the pitch autopilot channel in manual mode.

ALLOWABLE AILERON COMMAND.

For normal flight full stick throw may be used at any mach number and altitude within the normal flight envelope without exceeding the maximum roll rate.

WARNING

In certain emergency situations, full aileron (15°) may be required (for example, during high speed turn with excessive wing heaviness). Under these conditions, with the aileron control available switch positioned to FULL, 15 degrees aileron may be used by displacing the stick slowly and avoiding large roll rates. Large abrupt aileron commands under these conditions can result in excessive roll rates.

MAXIMUM ROLL RATE.

The maximum allowable roll rate is 100 degrees per second.

BRAKE ENERGY LIMITS.

Wheel brakes absorb a large portion of the airplane's kinetic energy in the form of heat during a stop and then dissipate this heat into the surrounding air during a cooling period after the stop. A four-hour cooling period is required to restore the brakes to their full energy absorbing capacity. If the brakes are used before the four-hour cooling period has elapsed, the energy added will be cumulative to that retained from

Section V
Operating Limitations

the previous stop. This will degrade braking capability for future stops by the amount shown in figure 5-12. The degree of tire damage and the likelihood of tire failure is determined by tire temperature. Since a portion of the heat dissipated by the brakes is temporarily absorbed by the tires, the tire temperature after a braked stop is proportional to the amount of energy absorbed in the brake during the stop. Therefore, it is necessary to determine the amount of energy absorbed in the brakes during a stop so that any hazard which exists due to possible tire failure is known, and so that proper precautions can be taken to prevent injury to personnel and to minimize possible damage to the airplane. Taxiing the airplane after a braked stop will not cool the tires but will cause them to be subjected to the heat generated by flexing in addition to that received from the brakes. If a takeoff is to be made before a full four-hour brake cooling period has elapsed, two very significant factors must be considered:

1. The brake energy absorbing capacity available for use in the event that takeoff is aborted will be reduced by the amount retained from previous braking operations, including any braking during the taxi roll.

2. The heat generated within the tires during taxi and takeoff will cause tire temperature build up cumulative to that existing from previous braking operations.

When a subsequent takeoff is to be made before a full four-hour cooling period has elapsed after a previous braked stop, the brake energy absorbing capacity available for use in the event that takeoff is aborted can be determined from the brake cooling rate chart (figure 5-12). The value of brake energy absorbing capacity available can then be used to determine the maximum brake application speed.

WARNING

In some cases the airplane may accelerate above maximum brake application speed during the three second reaction time. Coast down to maximum brake application speed is required prior to brake application to prevent exceeding brake energy limits.

Using the example lines shown in figure 5-11 the following examples explain how to find the amount of energy absorbed by the brakes during a stop and how to find the maximum brake application speed for reduced brake energy absorbing capacity.

Note

Subtract 40 percent of the headwind component measured by the tower from the IAS. A tailwind component must be added to the IAS.

Example No. 1: Full stop landing.
   Given: Gross Weight — 82,000 lbs.
          Airspeed when brakes applied
          — 150 knots IAS
          Tower Reported Wind Velocity
          — 5 knot tail wind
          Pressure Altitude — 1,000 ft.
          Outside air temperature — 70° F
   Find: Brake Energy Absorbed.

Solution:
   a. With drag chute deployed.

Following example line on figure 5-11 (Sheet 1 of 2), the brake energy absorbed is 8 million foot-pounds per brake. Observe precaution for normal zone. Since a cooling period of 20 minutes per million foot-pounds in excess of 4 million is required prior to subsequent takeoff, takeoff must be delayed 80 minutes.

   b. Without drag chute deployed.

Following example line on figure 5-11 (Sheet 2 of 2), the brake energy absorbed is 11.0 million foot-pounds per brake. Observe precautions for caution zone.

Example No. 2: Takeoff subsequent to braked stop described in example 1a.
   Given: Gross Weight — 140,000 lbs.
          Outside Air Temp — 70° F
          Pressure Altitude — 1,000 ft.
          Brake cooling time — 80 minutes
          Runway measured headwind velocity —
          10 knots
   Find: Brake energy capacity available and maximum brake application speed.

Solution:

Following example line on figure 5-12, the brake energy capacity available for an aborted takeoff is 15.6 million foot-pounds per brake. Enter figure 5-11 (Sheet 2 of 2) with the available energy of 15.6 million foot-pounds per brake, follow example line and find that maximum brake application speed is 139 knots IAS

5-25

Section V
Operating Limitations

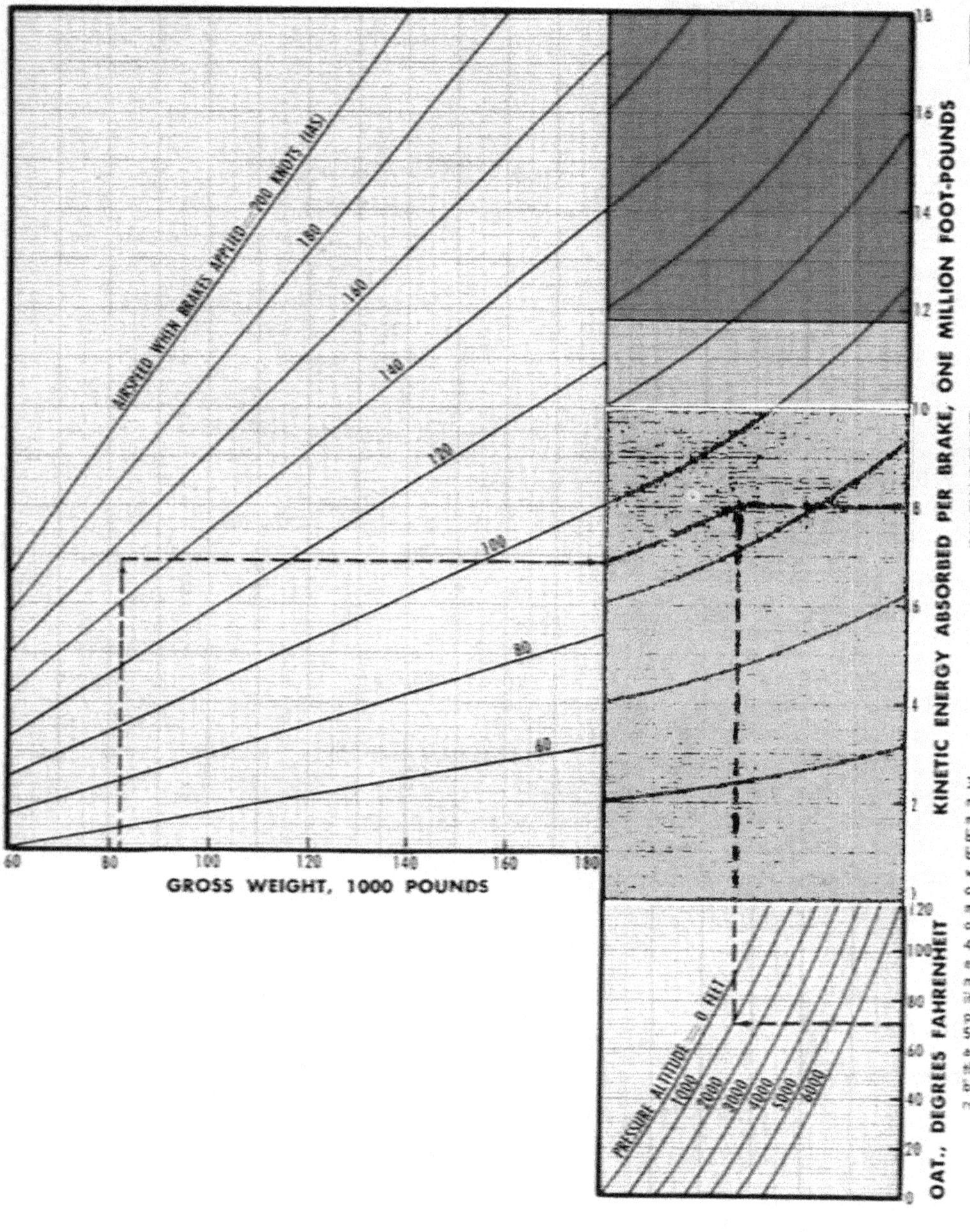

T.O. 1B-58A-1

brake energy limits

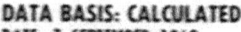
WITH DRAG CHUTE

Figure 5-11. (Sheet 1 of 2)

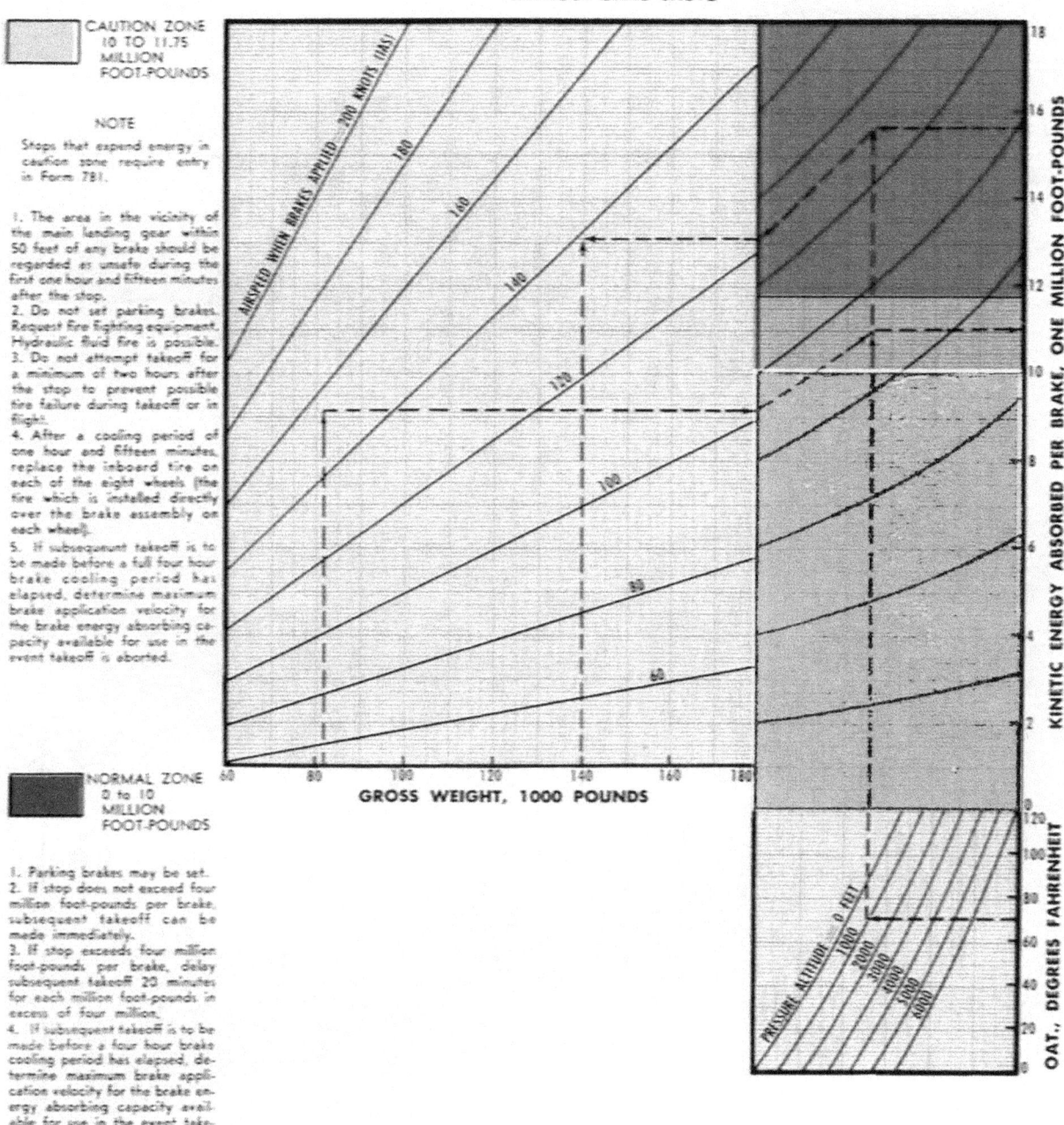

Figure 5-11. (Sheet 2 of 2)

Section V
Operating Limitations

T.O. 1B-58A-1

brake cooling rate

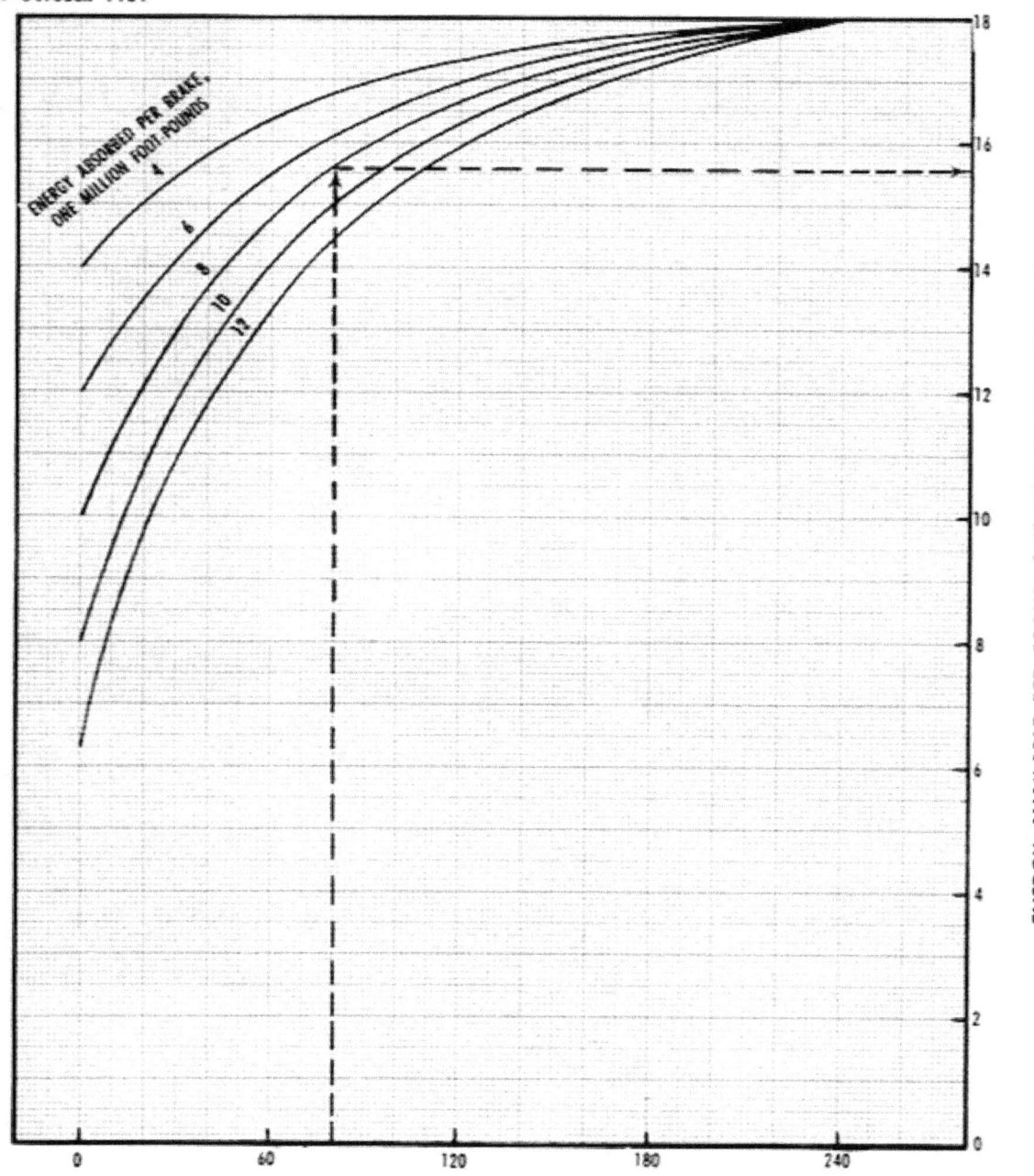

Figure 5-12.

for no wind. Add 80 percent of runway measured headwind for a corrected maximum brake application speed of 147 knots.

Note

When figure 5-11 is used to determine values of brake energy absorbed and maximum brake application speed, it is assumed that the airplane is brought to a complete stop with a single continuous application of the brakes.

BRAKE ENERGY ZONES.

Upon completion of any braked stop during which brakes are applied at a speed of 60 knots IAS or greater, the amount of brake energy absorbed can be determined by using the appropriate chart in figure 5-11. When the amount of energy absorbed is determined, the precautions for the applicable brake energy zone should be observed.

CAUTION

To prevent tire skidding and the possibility of a blowout, do not use maximum braking below 25 knots except in an emergency. Maximum braking below this speed can cause an increase in torque of 200 to 300 percent. This increase in torque can damage the brake linkage and/or shuttle valves and create a fire hazard from leaking hydraulic fluid.

Brake energy values determined from figure 5-11 are the average of all brakes. If there is any reason to suspect that this energy is not equally distributed among all brakes, the precautions for the next higher brake energy zone should be observed. Two conditions which will cause an unequal brake energy distribution are:

a. A braking operation during which rudder and/or nose steering are used to maintain directional control of the airplane during landing.

b. A prolonged application of light brake pedal force during taxi or landing.

CANOPY OPERATION LIMITATIONS.

To open canopies place the applicable canopy control lever (individual crew compartment or nose wheel well) in the CLOSE or DOWN position, hold for a minimum of 5 seconds, then move the applicable control lever to the OPEN or UP position immediately. This procedure will lessen the possibility of shearing the canopy pins. Do not open canopies in headwinds exceeding 60 knots.

CAUTION

Except during emergencies the canopies must never be opened while the canopy seals are inflated; damage to the seals and canopy mechanism will result.

ESCAPE SYSTEMS.

ESCAPE CAPSULE.

The escape capsule seat adjustment motor must be allowed to cool for nine minutes after each minute of operation. One complete up and down adjustment cycle takes approximately 40 seconds.

MINIMUM ALTITUDE LIMITATIONS.

Sudden malfunction of the autopilot and/or flight control system could result in a hazardous flight condition when flying at low altitudes. Therefore, except under EWO conditions, or during takeoff and landing, the following limitations must be observed:

- When flying under VFR conditions, do not operate below 800 feet absolute altitude with any channel of the autopilot engaged.

- When flying under IFR or night conditions, do not operate below 1000 feet absolute altitude while flying manually or with the roll channel of the autopilot engaged.

- When flying under IFR or night conditions, do not operate below 1500 feet absolute altitude with the pitch channel of the autopilot engaged.

MISCELLANEOUS OPERATIONAL LIMITATIONS.

MAXIMUM SINKING SPEED AT TOUCHDOWN.

The maximum sinking speeds at touchdown are as follows:

Less than 25 knots crosswind component.

Less than 95,000 pounds	540 feet per minute
Over 95,000 pounds	300 feet per minute

Section V
Operating Limitations

T.O. 1B-58A-1

bank angle limits during takeoff and landing

DATA BASIS: CALCULATED
DATE: 12 JUNE 1959

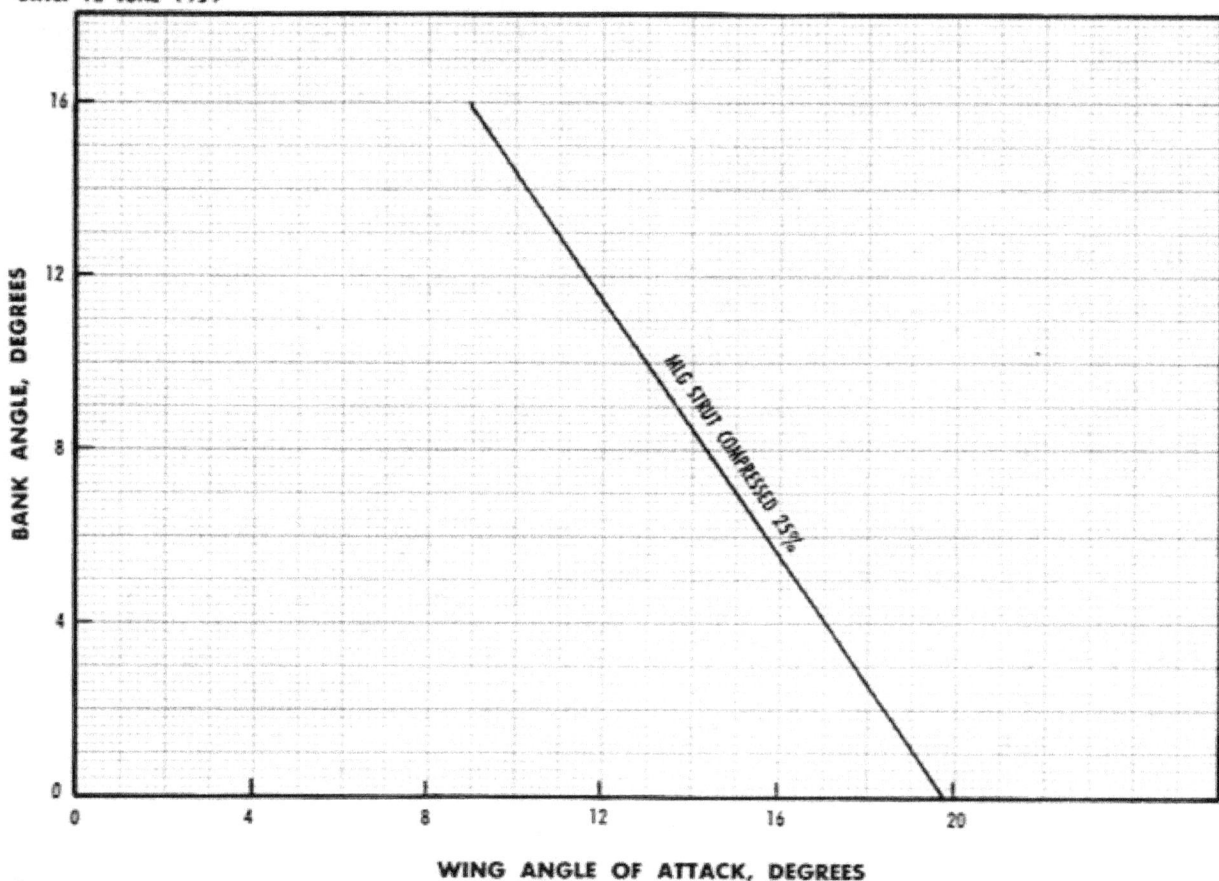

Figure 5-13.

Over 25 knots crosswind component.

Less than 95,000 pounds	300 feet per minute
Over 95,000 pounds	150 feet per minute

The airplane center of gravity should be between 26% and 29% MAC when landing at gross weights higher than 95,000 pounds.

WARNING

High brake energy absorption can be expected during stops following landing of gross weights greater than 95,000 pounds. Observe appropriate precautions listed in "Brake Energy Limits," Section V.

BANK ANGLE CLEARANCE LIMITS DURING TAKEOFF AND LANDING.

Bank angle clearance during takeoff and landing is shown in figure 5-13. This chart shows the bank angle limit beyond which the outboard engine nozzle leaves will drag the runway if the main landing gear is compressed 25%. Simulated tests show the strut is compressed approximately 25% for takeoff and landings, whether the landings are normal or hard.

WING ANGLE OF ATTACK.

The maximum wing angle of attack that assures adequate ground clearance for takeoff and landing and protection against the possibility of spin entry, which may occur at higher angles of attack, is 17 degrees.

T.O. 1B-58A-1

Section V
Operating Limitations

down-elevon deflection limits (ground operations)

CONDITION		THRUST	TIME LIMIT FOR CONTINUOUS RUN	MAX ELEVON DOWN POSITION LIMITATIONS
TAKEOFF OPERATION	*STATIC BEFORE START OF ROLL	IDLE TO MILITARY	(NO LIMITATIONS)	5° DOWN
		AFTERBURNER	30 SEC	3° DOWN
	ROLL 0-60 KNOTS	UP TO MILITARY	ACTUAL REQUIRED UP TO 60 SEC	(NO LIMITATIONS)
		AFTERBURNER	ACTUAL REQUIRED UP TO 60 SEC	3° DOWN
	ROLL 60-180 KNOTS	UP TO MILITARY	ACTUAL REQUIRED UP TO 30 SEC	(NO LIMITATIONS)
		AFTERBURNER	ACTUAL REQUIRED UP TO 30 SEC	10° DOWN

*AT IDLE RPM, FULL ELEVATOR AND AILERON DEFLECTION CAN BE UTILIZED MOMENTARILY DURING CONTROL SYSTEM CHECKOUT.

Figure 5-14.

DOWN-ELEVON DEFLECTION.

The down-elevon deflection limitations for ground operations are given in figure 5-14.

ALLOWABLE AIRPLANE FUEL IN POD TANKS.

In Flight: The pod tanks shall be empty of airplane fuel for gross weights of 100,000 pounds and under.

pod fuel tank loading limits

AIRPLANE GROSS WT. POUNDS	MB or LA POD FUEL, POUNDS		TCP POD FUEL, POUNDS	
	FWD TANK	AFT TANK	FWD TANK	AFT TANK
135,000	13,055	14,991	12,154	13,601
130,000	11,200	12,855	10,424	11,667
125,000	9,345	10,719	8,695	9,733
120,000	7,490	8,583	6,965	7,798
115,000	5,635	6,448	5,236	5,864
110,000	3,780	4,312	3,506	3,930
105,000	1,925	2,176	1,776	1,966
100,000	70 (scavenged)	40 (scavenged)	47 (scavenged)	62 (scavenged)

NOTE:

If unable to remove airplane fuel such that the above limits must be exceeded, a speed limit of 450 knots IAS should be observed and large maneuver and landing load factors should be avoided. While landing, the maximum allowable sink speed at touchdown is 300 feet per minute and airplane center of gravity should be between 26% and 29% MAC. The landing gross weight should be minimum attainable within center of gravity limits of 26% to 29% MAC.

Figure 5-15.

Section V
Operating Limitations

glass panel damage limitations

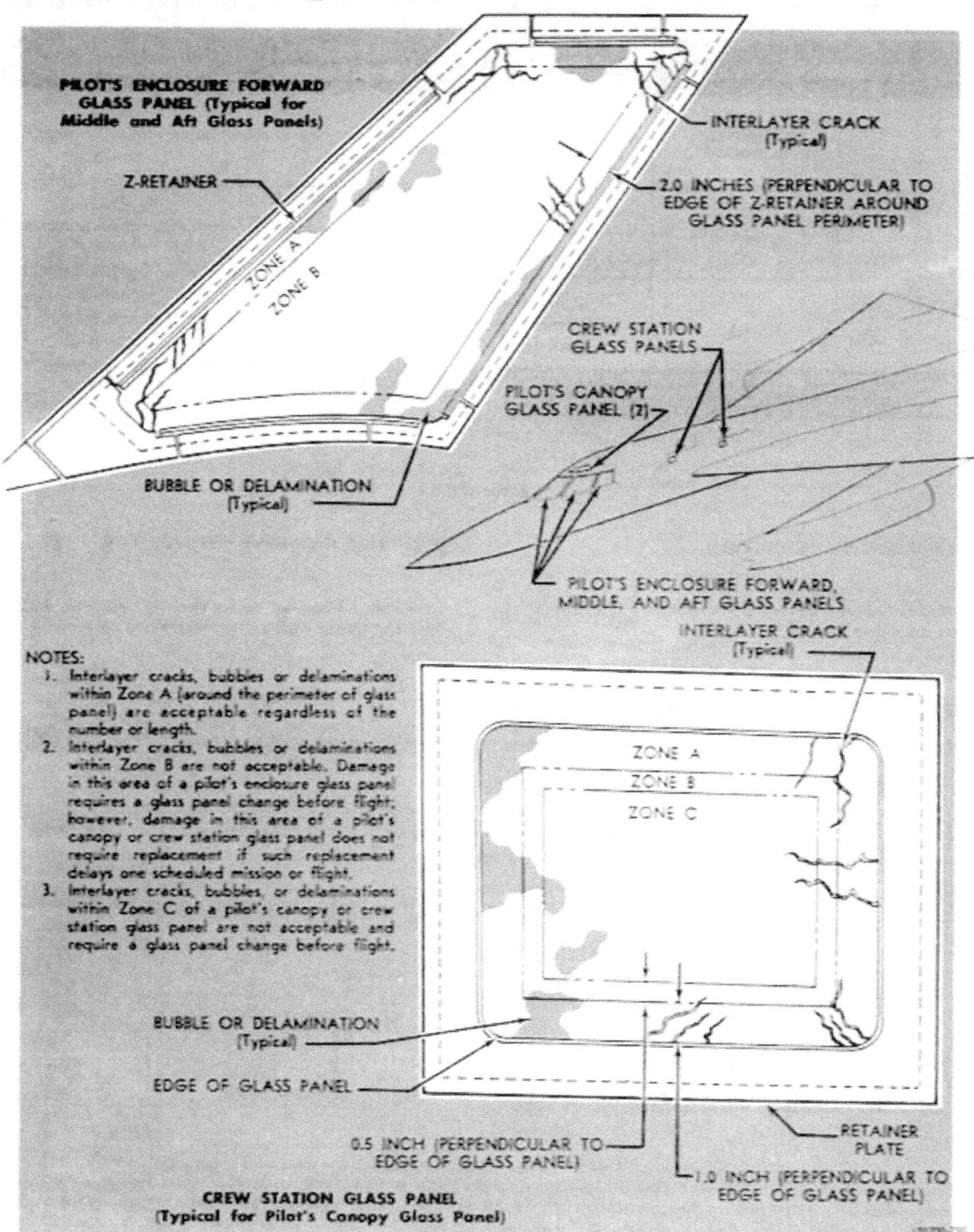

Figure 5-16.

The maximum amount of airplane fuel allowed in each pod tank varies linearly with airplane gross weight from empty tanks at a gross weight of 100,000 pounds to full tanks at a gross weight of 135,000 pounds. See figure 5-15 for pod fuel tank loading limits. These limits are based on the structural load capacity for maximum gust or maneuver load factors.

WARNING

If while in flight, the pod tanks contain usable airplane fuel that cannot be removed, and the amount exceeds the values shown in figure 5-15, allowable gust and maneuver load factors are reduced. A maximum speed limit of 450 knots IAS and a maximum positive symmetric limit load factor of 2.0 g's shall apply to all gross weights.

During Air Refueling: It is permissible to begin refueling pod tanks at gross weights less than 100,000 pounds provided the limitation on allowable airplane fuel in pod tanks is not exceeded when air refueling is completed. This does not change the permissible amounts of fuel in the pod tanks for flight other than air refueling. (Refer to Air Refueling Flight Manuals, T.O. 1-1C-1 and 1-1C-1-6 for air refueling procedures.) Each pod tank may be full of fuel for gross weights of 135,000 pounds and above.

While Landing: If the pod tanks contain normally usable airplane fuel that cannot be removed, the maximum allowable sink speed at landing gear touchdown is 300 feet per minute, and the airplane center of gravity should be between 26% and 29% MAC. Landing gross weight should be minimum attainable within center of gravity limits of 26% to 29% MAC.

WARNING

Landing with the center of gravity forward of 26% MAC can result in nose gear damage, loss of ground control; and pod damage may result if fuel is present in the forward pod tank.

GLASS PANEL DAMAGE LIMITATIONS.

Permissible windshield and window glass panel damage is shown in figure 5-16.

WEIGHT LIMITATIONS.

MAXIMUM GROSS WEIGHT.

Static, Taxi, and Takeoff
 (all configurations) .... 163,000 pounds

Note

This weight is the maximum landing gear design load.

Inflight (without small
 weapons) .... Physical Loading Limit
Inflight (with small
 weapons) .... Physical Loading Limit
Landing .... 95,000 pounds

MINIMUM GROSS WEIGHT.

Takeoff (all configurations
 with MAX A/B) .... 115,000 pounds

This is the last page of Section V.

the B·58A airplane

THIS PAGE INTENTIONALLY LEFT BLANK

T.O. 1B-58A-1

Section VI
Flight Characteristics

TABLE OF CONTENTS.

	Page
Introduction	6-1
Angle of Attack	6-2
Stalls	6-2
Spins	6-6
Flight Controls	6-7
Longitudinal Flight Characteristics	6-9
Lateral-Directional Flight Characteristics	6-16
Maneuvering Flight	6-18
Buffet	6-18
Diving	6-20
Pod Drop	6-20
Air Refueling	6-22

INTRODUCTION.

Emphasis has been directed toward providing satisfactory flight characteristics from low subsonic to high supersonic speeds over the wide range of altitude and loading capabilities of the airplane with and without pod and with or without small weapons. Flight characteristics throughout these wide ranges have been greatly improved by use of the following control system features: automatic trim control; elevator and aileron ratio changers; and stability augmentation about the three airplane axes.

DEFINITION OF AIRPLANE ANGLES AND RELATIVE WIND.

The following definitions are presented to avoid any misunderstanding of terminology used in the discussion of airplane flight characteristics.

Flight path angle. The angle determined by the airplane rate of climb or descent and true airspeed. See figure 6-1.

Deck angle or pitch angle. The angle between the airplane body reference line and the horizontal. See figure 6-1. The attitude indicator would indicate true pitch angle in flight if:

- The indicator was set at 2 degrees 18 minutes nose down with the airplane perfectly level on the ground.

- There was no precession error in the attitude indicating system.

- The indicator was not reset in flight.

Angle of incidence. The angle between the airplane body reference line and the wing chord plane through the mean aerodynamic chord (MAC). The angle of incidence of the airplane is 3 degrees with leading edge of the MAC up relative to the body line. See figure 6-1.

Angle of attack. The angle between the wing chord plane at the MAC and the relative wind. This angle is equal to the airplane flight path angle plus the pitch angle plus the angle of incidence. See figure 6-1. Angle of attack is indicated to the pilot by an angle of attack indicator and the angle of attack indexer. Refer to "Angle of Attack Indicator," Section I and "Angle of Attack," this Section.

Relative wind. The wind relative to the airplane along the airplane flight path. The velocity of the relative wind is the airplane's true airspeed.

6-1

longitudinal reference angles

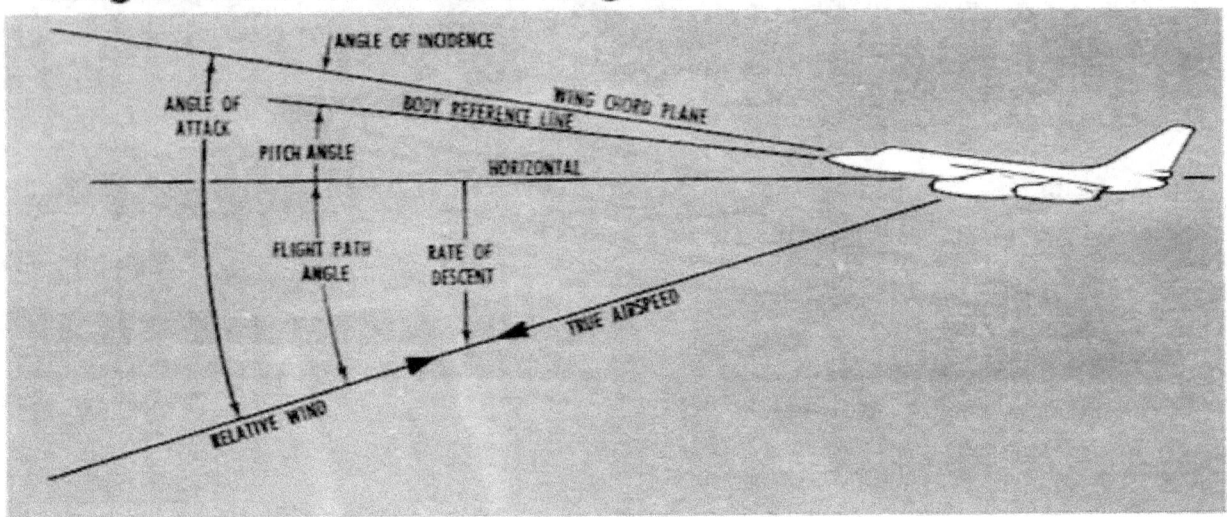

Figure 6-1.

ANGLE OF ATTACK.

Angle of attack is of primary importance since, for a given airplane weight and airspeed, sufficient lift can be generated to maintain one-g flight only at a particular angle of attack. That is, lift is a function of airspeed and angle of attack. Thus, at one-g flight if airspeed is held constant, angle of attack will remain constant. If airspeed decreases, angle of attack must increase if one-g flight is to be maintained. Conversely, if airspeed increases, angle of attack must decrease to maintain one-g flight. This direct relationship of angle of attack and airspeed with lift allows angle of attack to be used in place of airspeed, if necessary. Should the airspeed system malfunction, angle of attack can be held constant and calibrated airspeed will remain relatively constant varying in proportion to gross weight but remaining essentially independent of altitude. Further, rate of descent or ascent can be controlled by power changes and airspeed will remain constant as long as angle of attack remains constant. Typical angles of attack for one-g flight are shown in figure 6-2 for low altitude and high altitude at subsonic speeds at representative c.g.'s and heavy and light gross weight. Linear interpolations can be made for intermediate gross weights or altitudes. Information is not presented for angle of attack at supersonic speed since excessive angle of attack will not be encountered at supersonic speed during normal operation. Speeds defined for takeoff in Part 2 of Appendix 1 are based on an angle of attack of 14 degrees at liftoff. Thus, the angle of attack indicator may be used to prevent overrotation during takeoff, with consequent increased drag and longer takeoff run. After takeoff, angle of attack decreases rapidly as speed is increased. During cruise flight at optimum altitude, the angle of attack, regardless of gross weight is approximately 6 degrees. During normal landings, the recommended approach/flare speeds correspond to 12.5 ($\pm$0.5 to 1.0) degrees angle of attack regardless of gross weight. The angle-of-attack indexer is programmed so that in the range of 12.5 ($\pm$0.5 to 1.0) degrees only the on-speed symbol is lighted to result in approach/flare speed $\pm$4.5 to 10.0 knots. During landing approach in gusty conditions the angle of attack indicator will oscillate as the airplane responds to the gusts. By using average indicated angle of attack, the angle-of-attack indicator system may be used as an aid in maintaining proper approach/flare speed under these conditions; however, the airspeed indicator is the primary instrument.

STALLS.

The airplane does not exhibit normal stall characteristics up to the maximum allowable angle of attack of 17 degrees. Minimum flying speeds are provided as a substitute for stalling speeds. These speeds are defined by maximum available ground clearance for takeoff and landing and to reduce susceptibility to spin entry which might occur at angles of attack in excess of 17 degrees. During flight at angles of attack of less than 17 degrees, spin entry is not likely to occur as a result of sudden asymmetrical thrust, hardover damper failures, or amount or rate of control application. Minimum flying speeds are shown in figures 5-5 and 6-3. Good handling characteristics and control response exist at air speeds down to these minimum speeds.

angle of attack for one-"g" flight

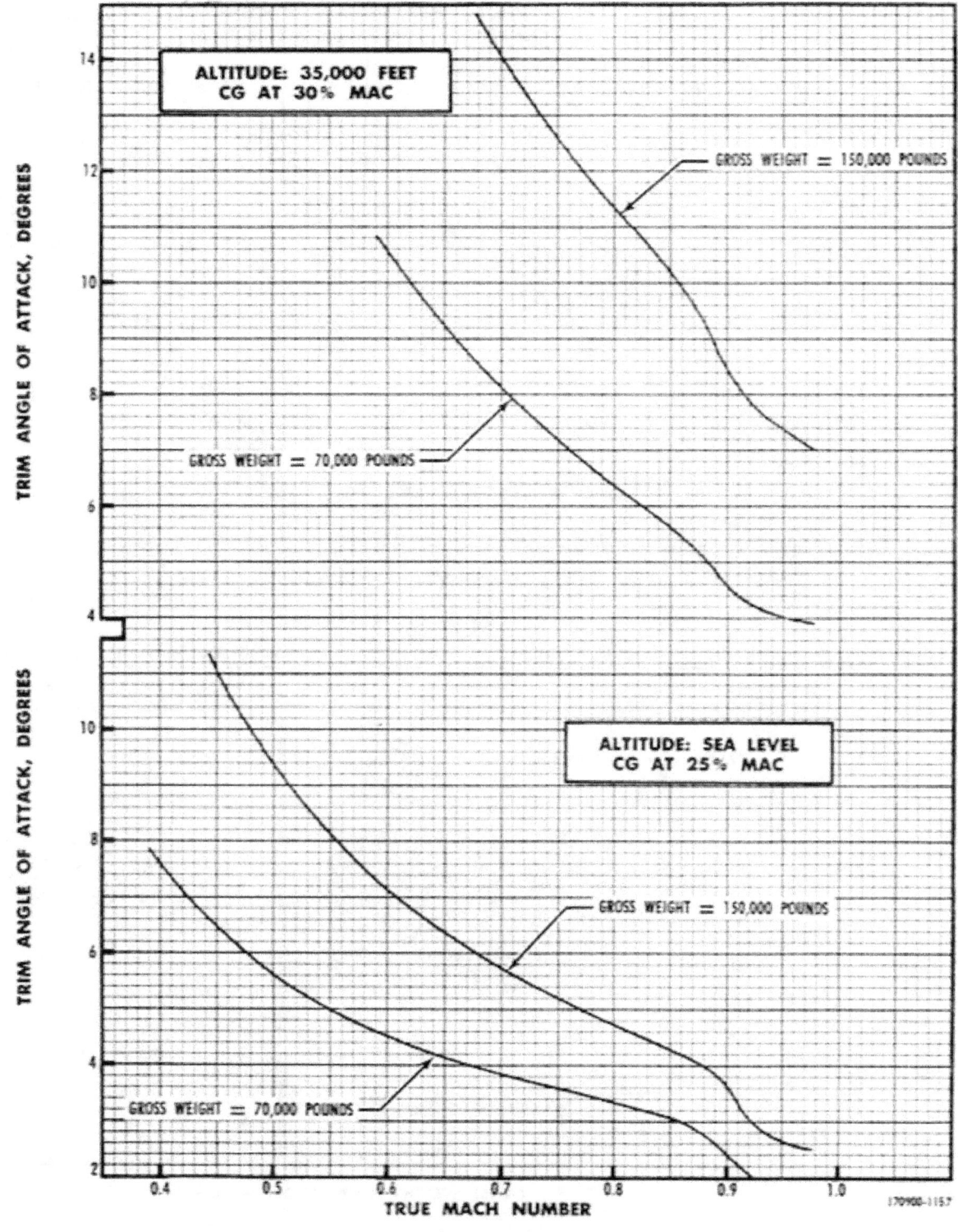

Figure 6-2.

Section VI
Flight Characteristics

T.O. 1B-58A-1

minimum flying speed

DATA BASIS: ESTIMATED
DATE: 7 SEPTEMBER 1962

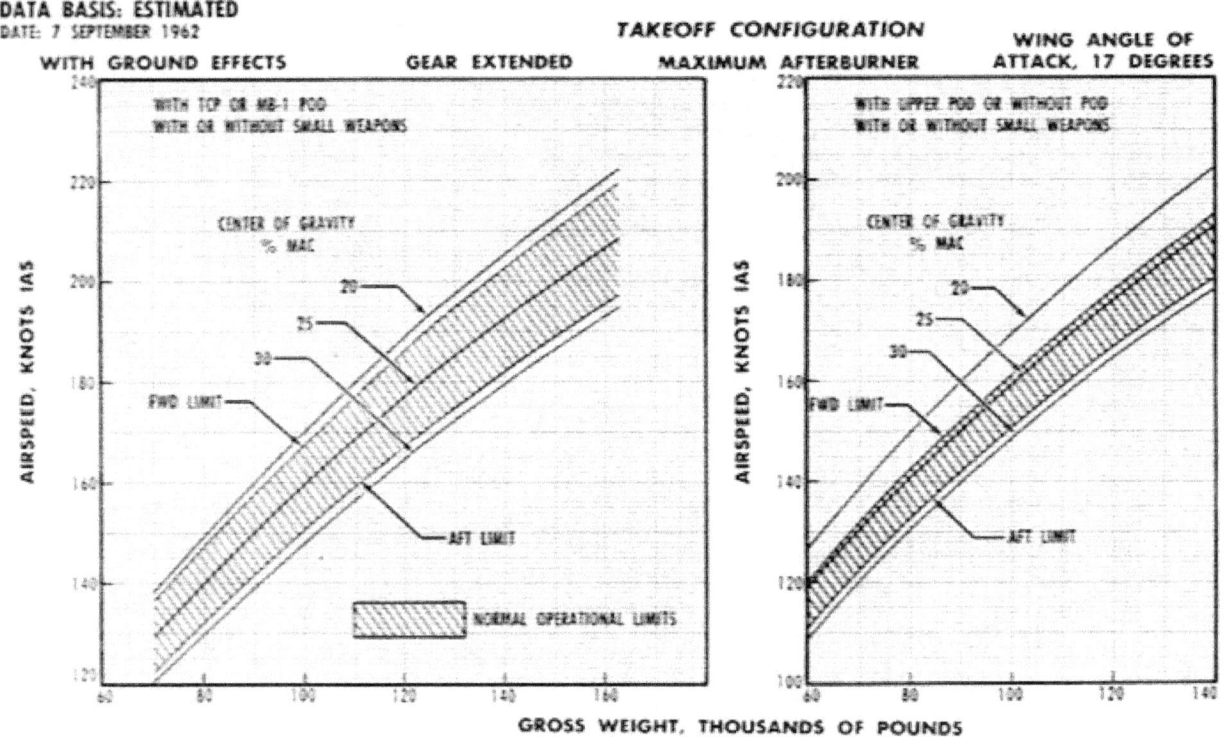

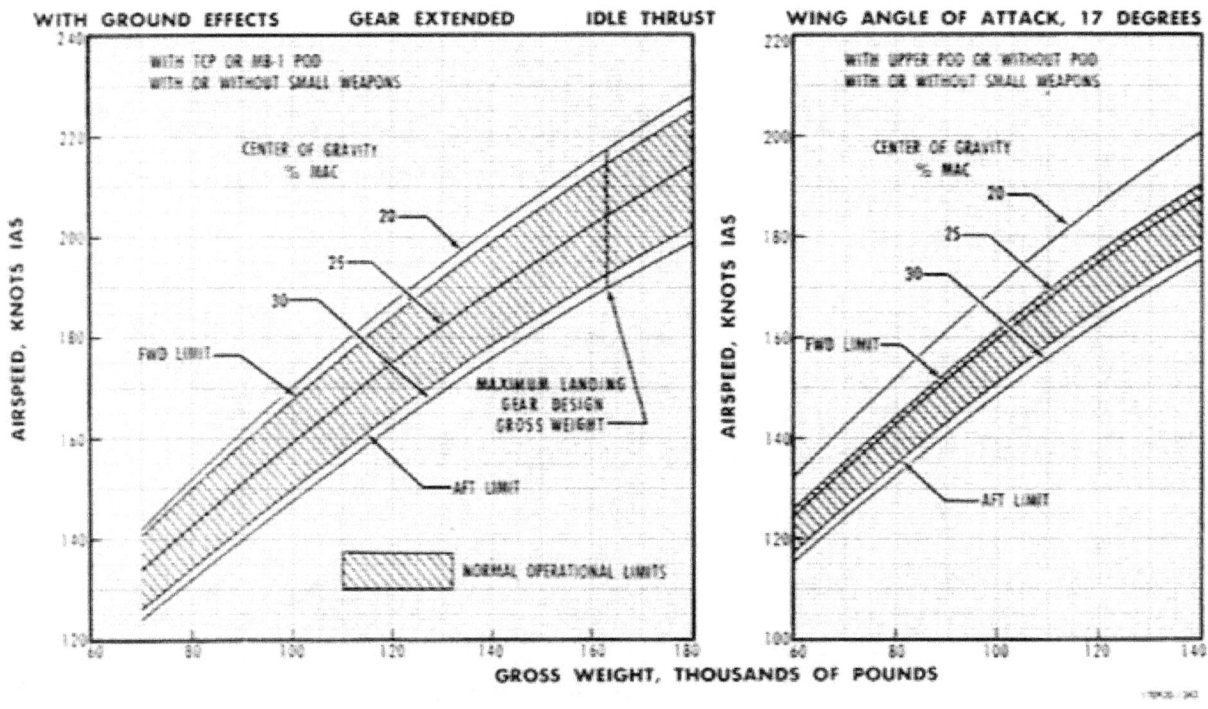

Figure 6-3. (Sheet 1 of 2)

minimum flying speed

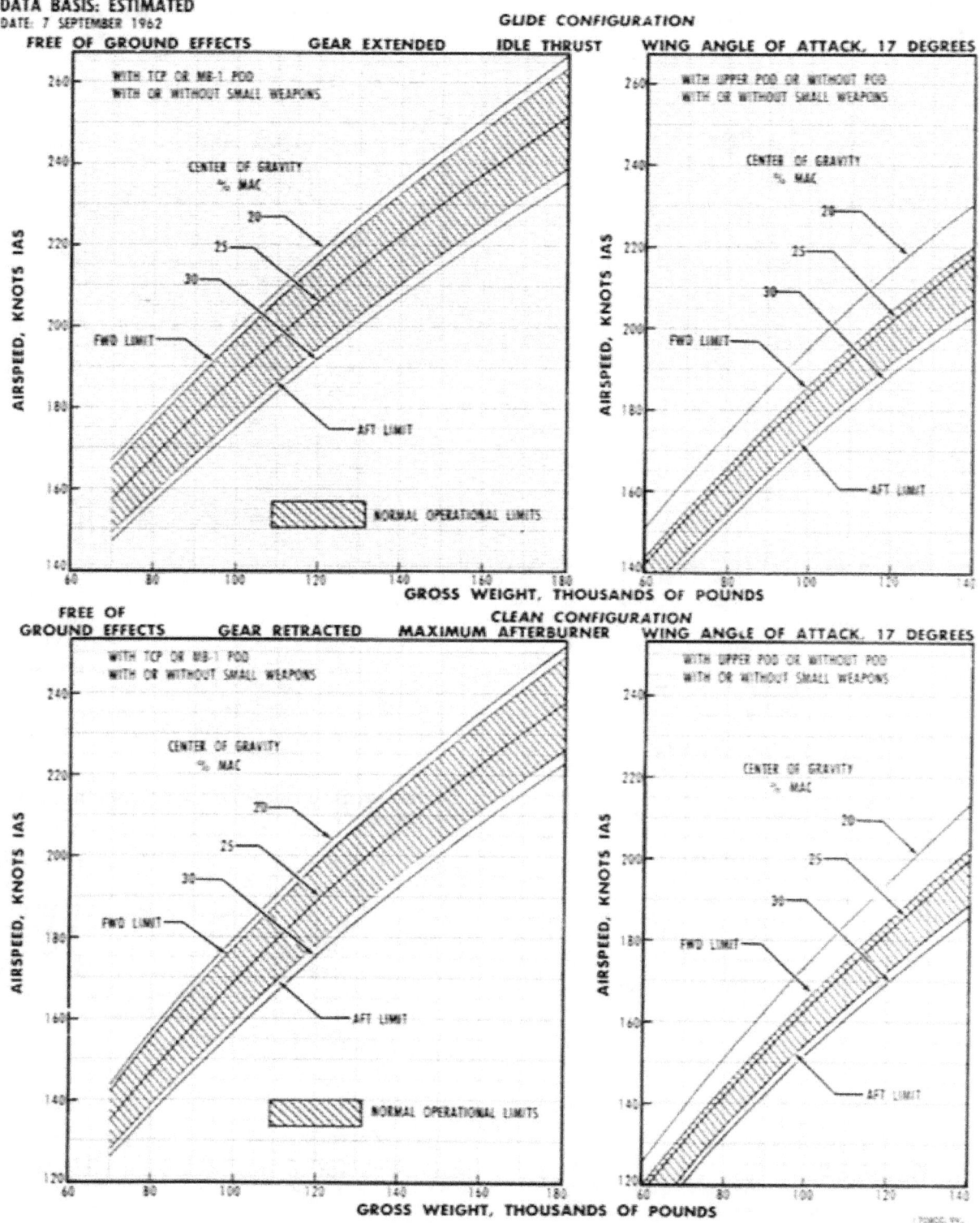

Figure 6-3. (Sheet 2 of 2)

Section VI
Flight Characteristics

T.O. 1B-58A-1

The following angle of attack indicating equipment has been installed on the airplane: an angle of attack indicator graduated in degrees, a red stall warning light that comes on at 17 degrees indicated angle of attack, and a voice warning of "nose too high" that is given at 17 degrees angle of attack.

Note

Do not operate in buffet of more than moderate intensity, ±0.1 "g" or develop limit load factor at speeds lower than 310 knots IAS. This will insure that the angle of attack limit of 17 degrees is not exceeded regardless of gross weight.

During simulated landings and low speed flight, caution must be observed so that an excessive rate of sink is not inadvertently developed. In the speed range between 200 and 300 knots, thrust required to maintain altitude varies only slightly, therefore chances of an excessive rate of sink being developed due to small changes in velocity are small. Flying at speeds below 200 knots IAS is known as flying on the back side of the power required curve. Care must be observed in flying below 200 knots IAS as in this region a small decrease in speed will cause a great increase in thrust required to maintain level flight. If a sudden decrease in power occurs in this region, intentional or otherwise, an excessive rate of sink and further decrease in speed will result. This could lead to spin entry.

WARNING

Operation at extremely low speeds and high angles of attack during approach and landing should be avoided because of the possibility of excessive rates of sink due to the inherent high thrust required as speed decreases.

If the airplane inadvertently enters a slow speed region, use the following procedures to recover:

1. Add power by gradually increasing the throttles to military power. Do not use afterburner power unless absolutely essential to provide a safe margin of terrain clearance.

CAUTION

At medium and high altitudes, failure of one or more afterburners to light if selected is very likely. Operation at extreme angles of attack at high altitude will cause engine inlet flow distortion and can result in compressor stall which may be followed by spin entry.

Note

In the event asymmetric thrust occurs use rudder to minimize sideslip, hold wings level, and reduce power on the corresponding opposite engine(s).

2. If altitude permits, lower the nose straight ahead to regain flying speed. If sufficient elevator control is not immediately available, use the emergency increase elevator available handle to gain full control. Do not pull back on the stick since this will only accentuate the rate of sink. Spin entry may result if one or more engines fail to respond when power is applied at angles of attack greater than 17 degrees unless adequate corrective rudder is applied immediately. Application of very large aileron action, such as that used to roll out of a turn, even with symmetric thrust, can also result in spin entry.

3. Monitor the angle-of-attack indicator and decrease angle of attack to not more than 6 degrees for normal cruise flight.

For safety purposes, simulated landings and slow speed flight must be conducted at altitudes of at least 20,000 feet above the terrain.

SPINS.

Intentional spins are strictly prohibited. The possibility of inadvertently entering a spin is remote if the minimum flying speeds and control techniques (flight and thrust) outlined under stalls above are observed. In the event a spin is encountered, the following recovery procedure is recommended.

SPIN ENTRY CHARACTERISTICS AND RECOVERY PROCEDURES.

Spin entry may occur at an angle of attack greater than 17 degrees as a result of large yawing moments due to engine asymmetry (especially afterburner) or large aileron or rudder deflection. Identical action results from rapid rolling which generates sideslip as a result of uncoordinated rudder action. Entry to a spin can be identified by a progressively increasing yawing motion. During this early yawing stage, use the following procedure to recover.

1. Apply rudder to stop the yawing motion.

2. Retard throttles to a point of symmetric thrust.

3. Avoid use of ailerons.

4. Apply forward stick to reduce the angle of attack and allow airspeed to increase.

If rudder is ineffective in stopping the yawing motion, use the procedure for recovery from a developed spin.

DEVELOPED SPIN CHARACTERISTICS AND RECOVERY PROCEDURES.

The developed spin occurs if recovery from the spin entry is not effected. The developed spin is characterized by highly oscillatory motion in pitch, roll and sideslip. Pitch angle oscillates between zero and minus 45 degrees nose down. The airplane descends vertically at a rate of approximately 18,000 feet per minute. The indicated airspeed oscillates between zero and 120 knots. The yaw rate corresponds to approximately 60 degrees per second (10 revolutions per minute).

Note

Because of the highly oscillatory nature of the developed spin, distinguishing between the rolling and yawing motion and ascertaining the direction of the spin may be difficult unless the turn-and-slip indicator is used. The turn needle is deflected in the direction of the spin.

Spin Recovery Procedure.

The following procedures are recommended for developed spin recovery:

1. Neutralize all controls.

2. Retard throttle to IDLE.

3. Apply full aileron in the direction of spin (right stick for spin to the right). Use turn-and-slip indicator to determine direction of spin.

4. Elevator control available mode selector switch— T.O. & LAND.

CAUTION

When the elevator available increases to 20 degrees, it will be extremely easy to overcontrol the pitch axis and care should be used in application of elevator control.

5. Engine start switches to AIR.

6. Neutralize ailerons as the spinning motion stops and, establish a nose down attitude.

7. After spinning stops, use angle-of-attack and airspeed to recover from dive attitude. Do not let airspeed drop below 240 knots IAS or angle of attack exceed 17 degrees during dive recovery. Reduce angle of attack so that angle of attack will be not more than 6 degrees upon regaining level flight.

8. Engine start switches to GROUND.

Placing the engine start switches to GROUND will expedite engine starting by utilizing compressor bleed air if either inboard engine is operating, and will also rearm the ignition.

9. Engine start switches to OFF.

After normal engine operation is restored, place the engine start switches to OFF.

WARNING

- If aileron control is applied against the spin (stick left for right spin), then spin recovery cannot be executed.

- If spinning motion has not been stopped before reaching an altitude of 15,000 feet above the terrain, EJECT.

Spin recovery is characterized by halting of the spinning motion together with a sharp drop of the nose into a diving attitude. When an airspeed of 240 knots is attained, the pilot can then safely exercise control to recover from the dive. Minimum flying and maneuvering speeds should be observed during dive recovery. After the spinning motion has stopped, dive recovery may be executed within an additional 8,000 to 10,000 feet loss in altitude. Refer to "Dive Recovery", Section VI, T.O. 1B-58A-1A. The number of turns and the altitude required to effect spin recovery when the prescribed spin recovery techniques are followed depends upon the loading condition of the airplane. Complete recovery with the center of gravity aft of the aft limit is doubtful. Failure to neutralize ailerons and to initiate dive as the yawing motion stops may result in a spin in the opposite direction. Application of large down elevator during spin recovery may result in transition from an erect to an inverted spin. Rudder control opposite to the direction of the spin (as shown by the turn-and-slip indicator) should be utilized for recovery from developed inverted spins. Rudder is not effective during developed erect spins.

FLIGHT CONTROLS.

A description of the flight control system can be found in Sections I and VII. A review of certain features in the control system is presented here to provide a functional understanding of the system with respect to the resulting flight characteristics. The operation of the automatic trim system and the elevator ratio changer system should be particularly noted.

Section VI
Flight Characteristics

LONGITUDINAL CONTROL.

The automatic trim and elevator ratio changer in the longitudinal control system accomplish the following:

1. Mask the trim instability in the transonic region from the pilot's controls.

2. Automatically provide the elevator deflection required for one-"g" flight.

3. Minimize variation in elevator sensitivity.

4. Provide a measure of structural protection.

Elevator Ratio Changer.

Three modes of operation are available for the elevator ratio changer: takeoff and land, automatic, and manual.

Takeoff And Land Mode. The takeoff and land mode is normally used only for takeoff and landing of the airplane. In this mode the automatic trim is fixed in the 1-1/2 degree up-elevator position. Full elevator position, within the limits of the mixer, can be controlled by the stick. Pitch damper operation is incorporated so that it is not felt at the stick. Stick trim is utilized in the takeoff and land mode.

Automatic Mode. The other normal operational mode of the elevator ratio changer is the automatic mode. In this mode the automatic trim is operable to provide the elevator required for one-"g" flight, and any stick displacement is a "g" maneuver command. Stick trim should be in neutral for one-"g" flight in the automatic mode, and any stick motion will therefore maneuver the airplane. For level flight a pilot must return the stick to neutral (have zero stick displacement signal). The output of the automatic trim (elevator required for one-"g" flight) is corrected by function of mach and altitude which accounts for the small difference between elevator per additional load factor and elevator for one-"g" flight. The elevator per unit load factor is essentially the same as elevator position for one-"g" flight in most flight regions, except at minimum altitude in the transonic region. Thus the functions from the ratio changer computer have only a small effect on the elevator per unit load factor. This means that the elevator available should follow a direct relationship with elevator position in level flight, the primary difference between them being the allowable incremental load factor that can be commanded.

Manual Mode. The manual mode of the elevator ratio changer is available as an alternate mode for use if the computer operating the automatic position of the ratio changer or automatic trim malfunctions. Variations in elevator available are obtainable in the manual mode by pilot operation of the elevator control available manual adjust switch.

T.O. 1B-58A-1

| CAUTION |

The manual mode does not incorporate automatic trim or continuous automatic variation of elevator control available; therefore, "g" protection and control sensitivity must be adjusted by the pilot.

It is desirable to adjust the elevator available to a value that will provide a measure of structural protection and will provide adequate elevator control in both the aft and forward stick direction. The automatic trim actuator is locked at the value it was in prior to switching to the manual mode until elevator available is increased to 7 degrees or greater. The actuator is then positioned at 1.5 degrees up elevator deflection for all subsequent operation in the manual mode. As a result, the elevator deflection that can be commanded is not the same for full aft as for full forward stick command from the trim position (position of the stick for one-"g" flight) unless the elevator to trim in one-"g" flight is the same as the automatic trim actuator position. In the manual mode the pitch damper and stick trim operate in the same manner as in the automatic mode. The extent of pitch damper authority restrictions and the adjustment of stick feel force gradients are dependent upon the elevator ratio changer position selected by the pilot. If the elevator available is adjusted to the value desired for structural protection, these features will be the same as when operating in the automatic mode.

LATERAL CONTROL.

The description of the aileron control system is presented in Section I. The roll damping of the airplane is augmented through operation of an electrohydraulic servo which performs two functions:

1. Provides desired damping in roll by positioning aileron deflection proportional to roll rate.

2. Provides additional yaw damping at airspeeds above approximately mach no. 0.92, by positioning aileron deflection proportional to yaw rate.

DIRECTIONAL CONTROL.

The various features of the rudder control system used for directional control are described in Section I. The rudder damper servo which operates to incorporate the signals from the stability augmentation system has three functions:

1. Provides desired Dutch roll damping.

2. Improves static directional stability at high mach numbers.

3. Refines coordination during aileron rolls through an aileron-to-rudder interconnect.

LONGITUDINAL FLIGHT CHARACTERISTICS.

Sufficient elevator control is provided to unstick the nose gear at 80 percent takeoff speed for all allowable loadings. However, it is recommended that the airplane be maintained at a low attitude until just prior to lift-off in order to obtain the best acceleration performance. Generally, airplane lift-offs will be performed at 14 degrees wing angle of attack. After takeoff, longitudinal trim change with gear retraction is insignificant. Transition of the elevator ratio changer from the takeoff and land mode to the automatic mode is smooth and should be accomplished as soon as convenient after climb-out conditions are established. Figure 6-4 illustrates the effect of center of gravity on the elevator required for one-"g" flight and on the variation of stick force required to maintain one-"g" flight as a function of mach number up to mach no. 1.0 for a typical gross weight and altitude condition in the MANUAL mode. This is presented so that the difference in flight characteristics between MANUAL and AUTOMATIC mode of operation may be fully understood. The centers of gravity illustrated correspond to the aft cg limit; 32.4 percent MAC, at mach no. 0.91 at 35,000 feet, an intermediate forward cg; 25 percent MAC, below mach no. 0.93 and the forward limit; 29 percent MAC from mach no. 0.93 to mach no. 1.0. The stick force is that which would result during acceleration or deceleration from a cruise speed of mach no. 0.91, with the elevator available adjusted by following the instructions under "Elevator Control System" in Section VII for operation in the MANUAL mode and with the stick force manually trimmed to zero at mach no. 0.91. In addition, a breakout force of 5 pounds is assumed. This is the reason for the abrupt changes in stick force, shown in figure 6-4, where the stick force goes through zero. Note that for the 29 percent cg condition, it is assumed that the center of gravity is shifted at mach no. 0.91 and the elevator available and manual trim readjusted at this time. The effect on elevator position and stick force of adjusting thrust during the slowdown or acceleration to maintain speed and altitude at each different mach number as compared to maintaining throttle lever at the position required to maintain speed and altitude at mach no. 0.91 without changing throttle position as speed varies is also illustrated. At the altitude and weight used for illustration, operation is on the backside of the power required curve below approximately mach no. 0.92. Below this speed, thrust has to be increased to maintain speed. The curves of figure 6-4 illustrate that during operation in the MANUAL mode, if a slowdown is begun with the center of gravity forward at 25 percent MAC the elevator for one-"g" flight and consequently back stick force will increase as the slowdown progresses. Thus, if the slowdown is unintentional, the pilot will be made aware of the slowdown by the change in stick force required to maintain the airplane attitude even if he is not monitoring airspeed. If the center of gravity is just slightly forward of the aft cg limit, there will be no change in trim or stick force as the airplane decelerates and consequently no warning to the pilot. With the center of gravity at or aft of the aft operational limit, the pilot will have to apply some forward stick force to keep the nose from rising during deceleration. During acceleration with any center of gravity location, the pilot must apply back stick force to prevent the nose dropping with increase in speed. In the AUTOMATIC mode the stick force for one-"g" flight is zero at any stabilized speed. During a rapid acceleration or deceleration through the transonic range, approximately mach no. 0.95 to 1.0, some back stick force or forward stick force is necessary to prevent the airplane nosing down or pitching up. This occurs because the elevator required for one-"g" flight changes very rapidly in this region and the automatic trim does not drive fast enough to keep up during very rapid acceleration or deceleration through this region. In the AUTOMATIC mode, the airplane tends to fly a straight flight path in level flight and in climb and dives; but does not tend to maintain a constant airspeed and lift coefficient unless the thrust is correct for the flight condition. In other words, the automatic trim system automatically positions the elevator for one-"g" flight with the stick in the neutral position. During operation on the back side of the power required curve, at speeds below approximately mach no. 0.6 to 0.9 at normal cruise altitudes dependent upon gross weight and altitude, if any disturbance of the airplane causes it to begin slowing down, speed will then continue to decrease more and more rapidly until the pilot takes corrective action by increasing thrust or nosing the airplane down to regain speed. If the pilot concentrates on maintaining altitude and does not monitor airspeed closely, the change in airspeed may easily go unnoticed since there is no change in stick force required to maintain attitude during operation in the AUTOMATIC mode.

> **CAUTION**
>
> During normal subsonic cruise operation in the AUTOMATIC mode or during operation in the MANUAL mode with the center of gravity near the aft limit, the pilot must monitor airspeed very closely to avoid a slowdown-stall-spin situation because of the tendency to continue to slow down during operation on the back side of the power required curve.

Section VI
Flight Characteristics

T.O. 1B-58A-1

typical elevator position and stick force for one "g" flight

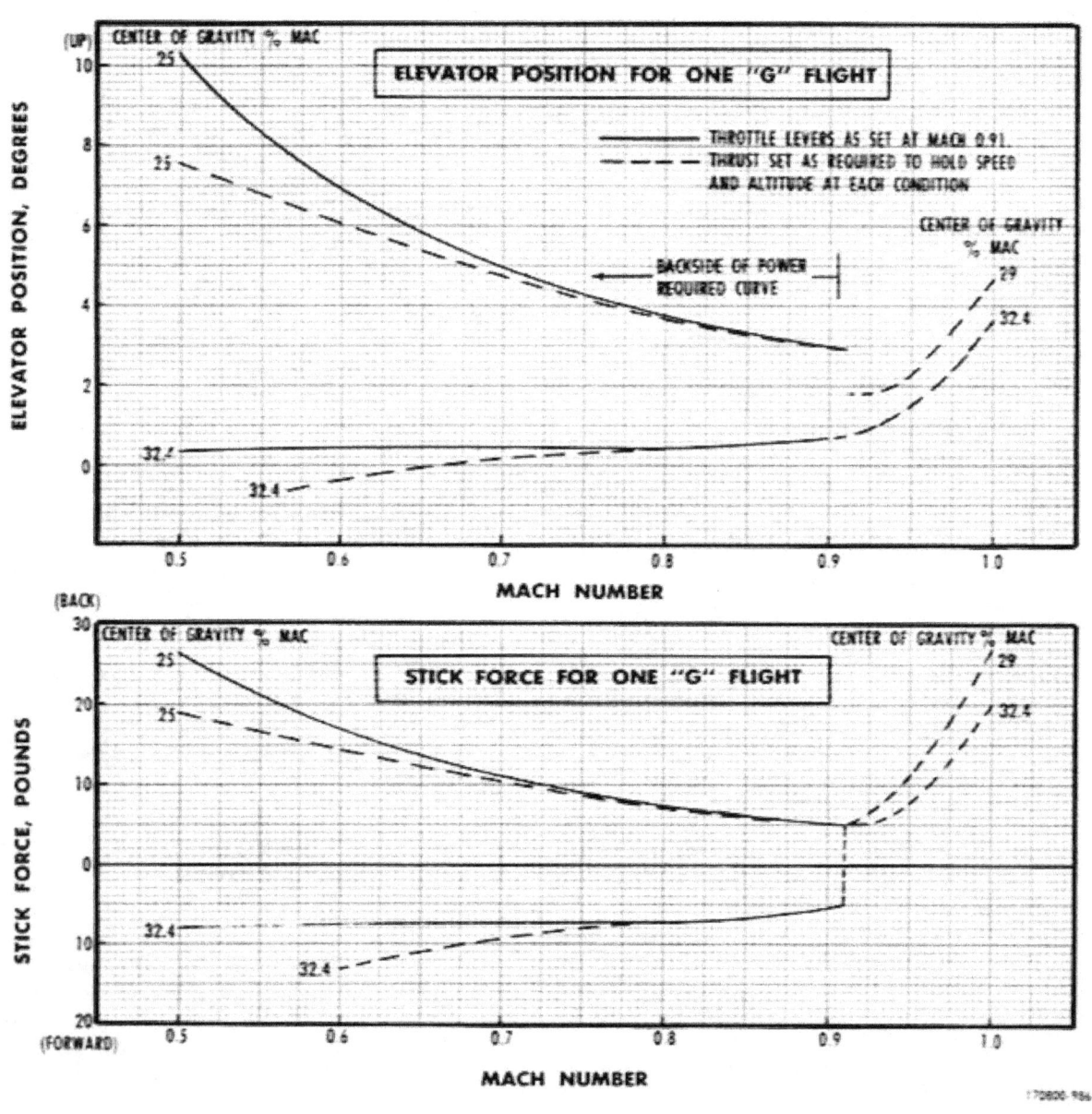

Figure 6-4.

During turning flight, also, the automatic trim functions to supply the proper trim for one-"g" flight and the ratio changer maintains constant stick-force-per-"g" so that there is no control stick force change with changing speed. Hence, during turns, the pilot must pay particular attention to the airspeed indicator or mach meter and adjust thrust to maintain speed. Elevator position for one-"g" flight is automatically supplied and stick trim will not be necessary. Any stick displacement by the pilot changes the flight path direction and the stick force encountered can be trimmed out. When one-"g" flight is resumed, any stick force trimmed out for the maneuver should be removed, as with conventional control systems.

Note

In order to facilitate operation of automatic trim, it is recommended that stick forces during the maneuver not be trimmed out.

The automatic operation of the elevator ratio changer provides for relatively constant stick force per "g" over the complete flight range. When in the automatic mode, the elevator ratio changer provides a large measure of structural protection. The elevator ratio changer provides symmetrical "g" protection, under most flight conditions, either up or down from one-"g" flight within the limits of maximum elevator deflection. This "g" protection was designed for maneuvers initiated from a trimmed flight condition; therefore, high rates of acceleration or deceleration, particularly through the transonic region, causes this protection to be changed. During acceleration to supersonic speed, sufficient elevator may not be available to develop limit load factor; and during deceleration from supersonic speed, greater than limit load factor can be developed with the elevator available.

WARNING

- Elevator required to trim is larger than predicted under some flight conditions. Since elevator available is proportional to elevator required to trim, the structural protection normally provided by the automatic mode of the elevator ratio changer does not exist under certain flight conditions, especially in the transonic speed range, and the structural limits of the airplane can be exceeded by an abrupt and/or full up elevator deflection.

- Closely monitor accelerometer during maneuvering flight to prevent exceeding limit load factor.

During a maximum performance trimmed maneuver, the elevator position indicator will read the sum of the elevator for one-"g" flight and the elevator control available, if this sum is equal to or less than 23 degrees up or 10 degrees down-elevator. Elevator deflection introduced by the pitch damper will be reflected by the elevator position indicator and small control surface movements with no pilot command will be normal when operating in turbulence. For flight conditions which require greater than 10 degrees up-elevator deflection (limit of automatic trim authority), the automatic trim system will not function and the elevator ratio changer will not be set at the proper value. The elevator available to the stick will remain at the value associated with 10 degrees up-elevator deflection. When this condition is encountered, stick trim should be used to remove the stick force required to maintain one-"g" flight. Structural protection is no problem, but maximum maneuverability may be reduced. Normally, elevator control available should be at least as much as the elevator position for one-"g" flight. When operating at high altitude, light gross weight, and forward center-of-gravity location, the elevator control available will be approximately twice the elevator for one-"g". During flight in the automatic mode, the control stick sensitivity matches the airplane response. That is, stick deflections are small where the short-period pitching oscillation frequencies are high, and stick deflections are relatively large where the pitch frequencies are low. The longitudinal short-period dynamic characteristics are satisfactory over most of the flight envelope with pitch damper on or off. At flight and loading conditions where the pitch oscillation frequencies are low (high altitude), however, the dynamic characteristics are considerably degraded with the pitch damper off.

EFFECTS OF CENTER-OF-GRAVITY LOCATION.

To fully understand the effects of center of gravity location on longitudinal flight characteristics, familiarization with the terms "static stability", "static margin" and "dynamic stability" is necessary. These terms may be defined as follows:

1. Static stability: The characteristic of an airplane in flight to tend to return to one-"g" flight after being disturbed from its trimmed attitude. An example of a statically stable system is shown in figure 6-5. In the example, if the angle of attack is increased by an upward gust or outside disturbance, the increased lift

Section VI
Flight Characteristics

T.O. 1B-58A-1

created will cause a nose down moment about the center of gravity tending to return the airplane to its trimmed attitude.

2. Static margin: The distance, measured in percent of MAC, between the aerodynamic center of the airfoil and the center of gravity of the airplane. The degree of static stability of an airplane is determined by static margin. Static margin can be changed by shifting the center of gravity or by varying the air speed to shift the aerodynamic center. As static margin is increased, small disturbances from the trimmed attitude of the airplane will result in larger restoring moments. As static margin is decreased, stability of the airplane will decrease accordingly to a point where an outside disturbance could cause a divergence, either up or down, past the point where control can be effected by the pilot.

3. Dynamic Stability: The characteristic of an airplane in flight that causes the oscillation resulting from a disturbance from its trimmed condition to dampen out and return the airplane to its original attitude. Examples of a statically stable system depicting dynamic stability, dynamic neutral stability and dynamic instability are shown in figure 6-6 along with a statically unstable system showing pure divergence or loss of control.

That the relation of center of gravity to aerodynamic center has a definite effect on the static stability of the airplane is evident from the above definitions. If the center of gravity is forward of the aerodynamic center, changes in angle of attack will result in the creation of restoring moments and the airplane may be said to have static stability. The further forward the cg is moved, the larger the restoring moment will be. Movement of the center of gravity aft to decrease static margin, will decrease static stability accordingly. The pilot can control a small degree of static instability by proper use of the elevator control. If the center of gravity is allowed to move aft of the aerodynamic center, a disturbance of the airplane could result in causing the airplane to continue to nose up or down from the trim condition. If the airplane is allowed to diverge beyond the point which the pilot can control with full stick application complete loss of control will result.

statically stable system

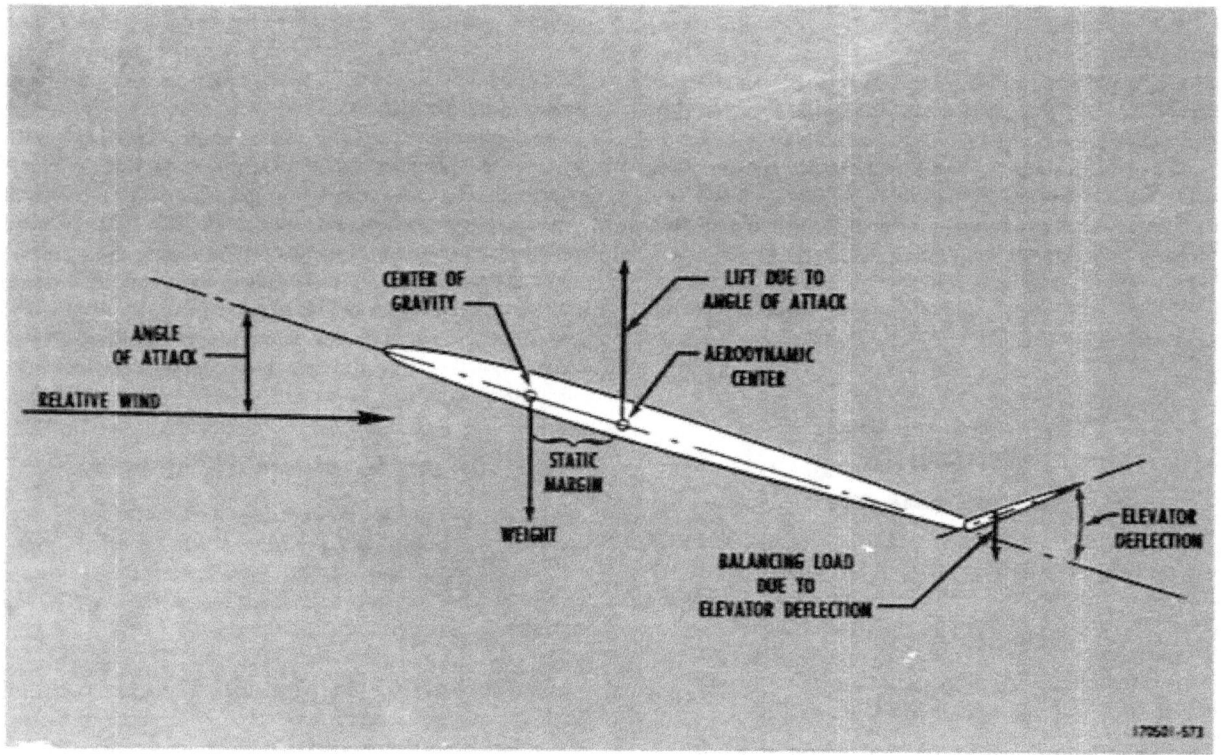

Figure 6-5.

6-12

Note

As the center of gravity is moved aft, and static margin is decreased, less elevator deflection is required to maneuver. As the aft cg limit is exceeded in the subsonic region and neutral stability is approached, the elevator ratio changer drives to minimum elevator available. This condition will restrict the pilot's capability of controlling the airplane if the cg is moved too far aft or if speed is reduced in the subsonic region with an aft cg condition.

The aft subsonic center of gravity limits of 3 percent positive static margin shown in Section V have been selected to insure acceptable static stability and handling qualities. At forward center of gravity locations, large elevator deflections are required to trim and maneuver the airplane. If range is a consideration, the center of gravity should be maintained as near the aft center of gravity limit as practical to require minimum elevator deflection and reduce drag. Figure 6-7 illustrates the effect of center of gravity on the elevator position for one-"g" flight as a function of mach number for a representative gross weight and altitude. The "short period longitudinal oscillation" is the terminology used to describe the relatively short-time pitching motion of an airplane resulting from a gust or other disturbance. During normal operation with the pitch damper on the longitudinal short period motion is so heavily damped that the pilot is not aware of any oscillatory motion. During operation at very high altitude or near mach no. 2.0 with the pitch damper turned off however, a disturbance of the aircraft will result in oscillatory motion (nose up—nose down—nose up) that will persist for several cycles before the motion subsides (damps out). The effect of pitch damper operation and center of gravity on this motion is illustrated by figure 6-8. Note that moving the center of gravity forward shortens the time required for each cycle of motion and moving the center of gravity aft increases the time for each cycle. If the center of gravity is moved progressively farther aft, as the static margin approaches zero the time per cycle for the short period oscillation will become increasingly longer. At zero static margin (center of gravity behind the aft limit), there will no longer be any oscillation. If the center of gravity is moved still farther aft, to a negative static margin, the airplane will exhibit a pure divergence. That is, the airplane will continue to pitch in the same direction at an increasing rate upon being disturbed from trim. The pilot can correct for the pitching motion using elevator control if the amount of instability, negative static margin, is small and if he applies corrective control as soon as he recognizes any pitching motion and does not allow the airplane rotational motions to become

dynamic stability variations

STATICALLY STABLE

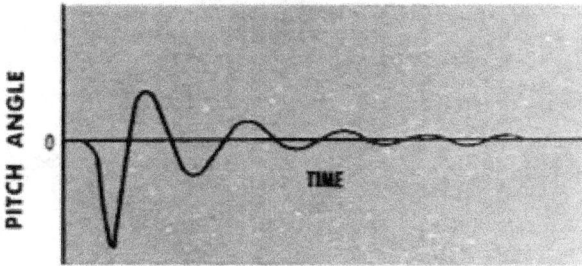

a. Dynamically stable

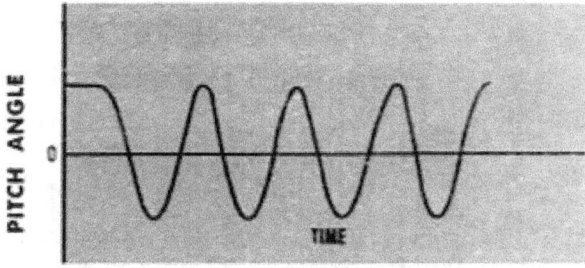

b. Dynamically neutrally stable

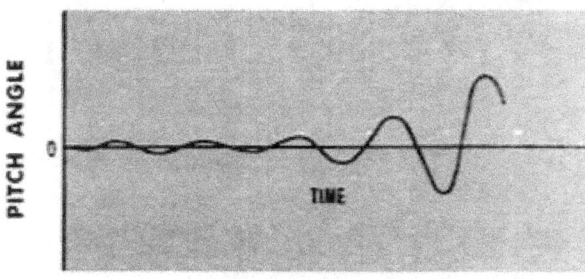

c. Dynamically unstable

STATICALLY UNSTABLE

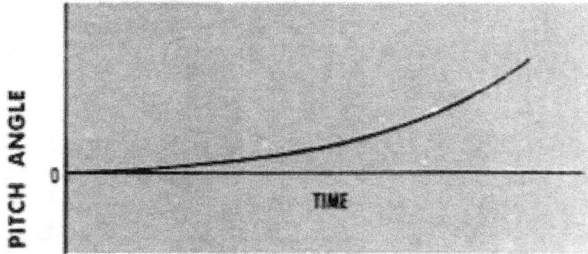

d. Pure divergence

Figure 6-6.

Section VI
Flight Characteristics

T.O. 1B-58A-1

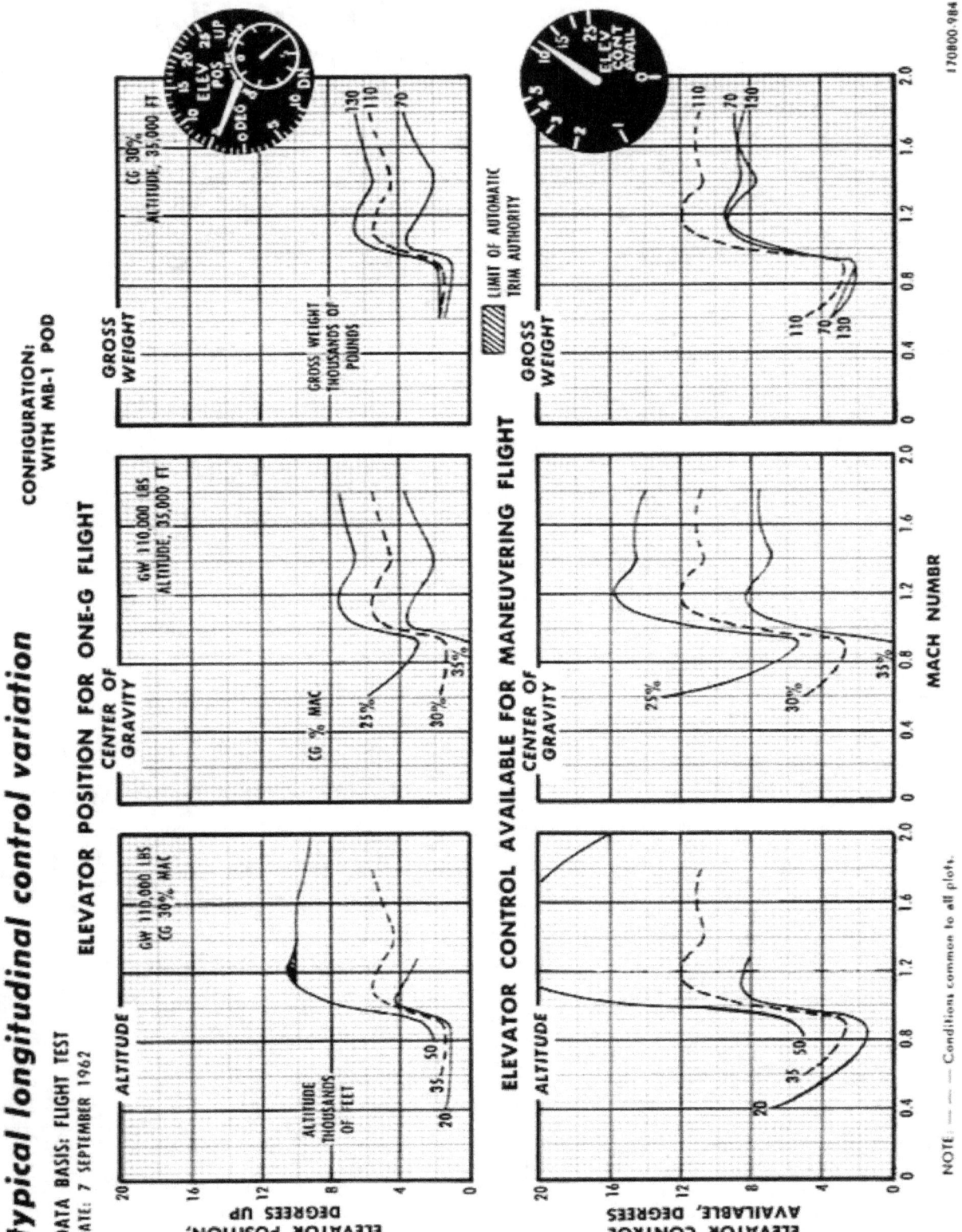

Figure 6-7.

large. If he allows the motions to become large, however, the pitching moment due to angle of attack will exceed the corrective moment that he can supply with elevator and loss of control will result.

WARNING

Maintaining the center of gravity within the prescribed limits is imperative, particularly at subsonic cruise conditions, to prevent the possibility of attaining negative static margin with consequent loss of control. Static margin should immediately be increased by increasing speed or by transferring fuel to move the center of gravity forward if:

- The elevator deflection required to trim is significantly smaller than predicted for the flight condition.

- Longitudinal oscillations are of a very long period.

- The airplane tends to continue to nose up in response to gusts.

Continuous long period correction of pitch attitude by the autopilot may also indicate that the center of gravity is aft of the normal limits at subsonic speed. This stick motion may go unnoticed and a dangerous condition will exist if the autopilot is disengaged.

During operation within the center of gravity limits, the period of the short period oscillation will not be less than one second per cycle nor, except for very low speeds or extremely high altitudes, longer than four seconds per cycle. Since the airplane motions are heavily damped and subside rapidly upon disturbance, there is no tendency for the pilot to attempt to damp the motion with the controls. Location of the aerodynamic center is a function of mach number and (because of the variation of aircraft flexibility with changes in dynamic pressure at constant mach number) altitude. The aerodynamic center moves forward very rapidly with decreasing speed in the transonic region.

CAUTION

Closely monitoring the mach number and altitude and avoiding slowing down and/or descending during cruise at transonic speeds

effects of pitch damper and center of gravity on longitudinal short period characteristics

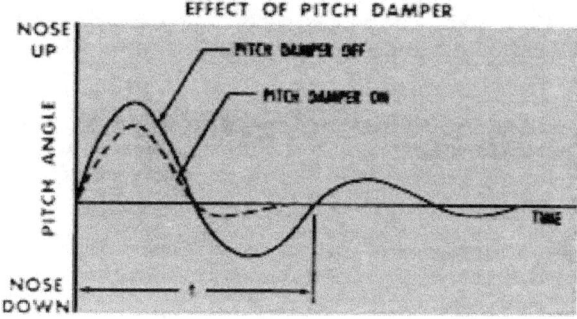

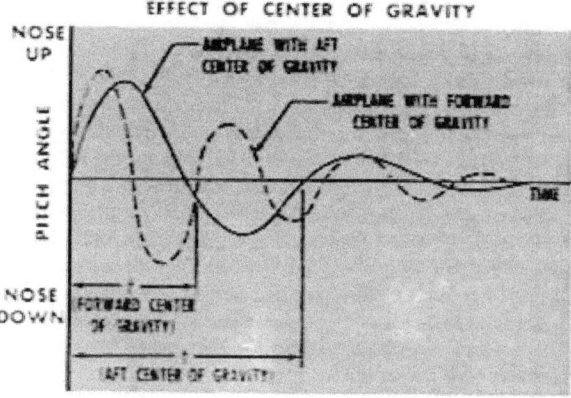

Figure 6-8.

with the center of gravity at the aft limit is extremely important. Loss of airspeed and/or altitude could result in a dangerous reduction in stability.

In the event of slowdown and/or loss of altitude or inadvertent aft center of gravity shift, increased stability (larger static margin) can be most rapidly attained by nosing over and increasing power to gain airspeed.

WARNING

If the airplane attitude change cannot be controlled, immediately utilize the emergency increase elevator available handle to obtain at least 6 degrees of elevator available.

Section VI
Flight Characteristics

With a nose high attitude and low airspeed, nose the airplane down with elevator to pick up airspeed. If large or rapid aileron and/or rudder is used at high angle of attack and low airspeed, the possibility of entering a spin is imminent.

LATERAL-DIRECTIONAL FLIGHT CHARACTERISTICS.

The lateral-directional flight characteristics during takeoff and landing are discussed in Section II.

Adequate lateral-directional stability and control are available to assure safety of flight during emergencies such as engine failure, stability augmentation malfunction, etc., within allowable operational center-of-gravity limits.

The airplane exhibits relatively good coordination during aileron rolling (banking) maneuvers in all flight conditions.

During supersonic flight at the lower altitudes, full aileron control of 15 degrees becomes sensitive and a two-position aileron ratio changer is incorporated in the aileron control system to reduce this sensitivity. For normal operation, the AUTO position of the aileron ratio changer is selected which provides sufficient roll for all normal operations. During extreme maneuvering flight at the higher altitudes or for certain control system malfunctions more aileron control may be desired than is available in the AUTO position. Refer to "Flight Control System Trouble Shooting Procedures," Section VII. For these conditions, it is recommended that the pilot select the FULL position which allows full aileron available (15 degrees) for full stick throw. Without corrective action, instantaneous loss of thrust from an outboard engine will result in large excursions in yaw and roll. This is particularly true at limit speed up to 45,000 feet. The recommended technique in this event is to keep the wings level with aileron, reduce thrust to military power, and apply corrective rudder to moderate the yaw excursions and to return the airplane to zero yaw.

WARNING

In the event of sudden engine failure, airplane control and structural integrity are dependent upon roll and yaw damper operation. Observe flight limitations with roll and yaw damper malfunction.

Note

The aft center-of-gravity limits are established to provide protection without pilot rudder response or with the rudder response expected by inadvertent reaction of the pilot. Large rudder deflections to reduce initial yaw peaks should not be attempted since they are not required and may increase the tail load developed if applied at the wrong time.

Asymmetric thrust on the outboard engines results in relatively large yawing moments acting on the airplane. In the extreme case of an outboard engine shutdown with the other outboard engine at maximum afterburner power as much as 10-12 degrees rudder deflection may be required to trim the airplane at supersonic speed. When the airplane is trimmed in level flight with the ball centered, the aileron required to maintain wings level is very small, on the order of 1 degree. Asymmetric thrust on the inboard engines during operation at supersonic speed results in appreciably smaller yawing moments acting on the airplane than with asymmetric thrust on the outboard engines but causes larger rolling moments. The inboard engine exhaust nozzles are relatively far ahead of the trailing edge of the wing, consequently, thrust changes on an inboard engine greatly affect pressure distribution beneath the wing. Reduction of thrust on an inboard engine reduces the pressure beneath the wing at speeds above approximately mach no. 0.91. This results in a decrease in lift and therefore a rolling moment in the direction of the reduced thrust. Aileron deflections of as much as 4 to 6 degrees can be required to maintain wings level with thrust reduced on an inboard engine at supersonic speeds. This is particularly significant in the event of failure of an inboard engine at supersonic speed as the airplane will roll rapidly in the direction of the failed engine and the pilot will have to apply a large aileron deflection to return the airplane to the wings-level attitude. Large thrust unbalance can significantly affect the maneuver capability of the airplane, particularly for forward center of gravity loadings because of the large hinge moments required to maintain wings-level one-"g" flight. In the event of loss of one hydraulic system at supersonic speed during operation with reduced thrust on an inboard engine, there may be insufficient hydraulic system capacity to prevent rolling of the aircraft unless thrust is reduced on the opposite inboard engine. The aileron deflection required to maintain wings level at subsonic speeds with unbalanced thrust on the inboard engines is quite small compared to that required at supersonic speed.

Note

The pilot should attempt to maintain symmetric thrust on the engines at all times, particularly during supersonic flight.

If one hydraulic system is lost during operation with the center of gravity near the forward limit and with significant wing heaviness present, reduction of thrust on the inboard engine opposite to the heavy wing can be used to reduce the amount of aileron deflection required. For example, if the airplane is left wing heavy reduction of thrust on the number 3 engine will reduce the aileron required thereby increasing the margin of control available for longitudinal control. Care should be exercised when retrimming the rudder from a trimmed asymmetric thrust condition. Actuation of the rudder trim switch abruptly relieves the load on the high speed rudder feel spring. Therefore, retrimming with the pedals deflected can cause an inadvertent transient. Satisfactory lateral-directional oscillatory characteristics are realized under all flight conditions with the stability augmentation features operating. Extremely short periods (2 seconds) of lateral-directional oscillations will be experienced with the airplane without the pod at low supersonic speeds at low altitudes, particulary with the forward center-of-gravity locations. The oscillations may be bothersome if the yaw or roll damper becomes inoperative. The airplane is dynamically stable in all flight conditions when the dampers are either on or off. That is, airplane oscillations resulting from atmospheric gust disturbances or pilot control actions, etc., damp out (subside) of their own accord. Damping of the oscillations is rapid when the dampers are on, whereas it is moderate to slow when the damepers are off. In supersonic flight when yaw and roll dampers are off, the airplane exhibits a combined yawing-rolling oscillation (Dutch-Roll) which is slow to damp out. When flying in this condition, the pilot's aileron inputs tend to "couple-in-phase" with the yawing rolling oscillation, thereby, causing the oscillation to build-up rapidly rather than damp out. This is particularly true in the mach no. 1.4 to 1.6 range but is characteristic of the complete supersonic range. When this occurs, the resulting side forces and accelerations acting on the aircraft can become disturbing to the crew members as well as hazardous to the aircraft.

WARNING

When the yaw or roll damper is inoperative, do not exceed 450 knots IAS or mach no. 0.91, whichever is less. With the yaw and roll dampers both inoperative, do not exceed 40,000 feet altitude.

If it is suspected that either the roll or yaw damper is inoperative or if any of the roll/yaw damper caution or warning lamps light, observe the restrictions set forth in "Flight Control System Limitations," Section V, and follow the procedures outlined in "Flight Control System Trouble Shooting Procedures", Section VII.

When operating with roll and yaw dampers off, at supersonic speeds, pilot aileron inputs can cause large yaw-roll oscillations to develop. Therefore, minimize use of the ailerons except as needed in slowly approximating the desired bank angle, and if necessary, utilize pilot-applied rudder action to reduce severity of the oscillations. To accomplish this damping action when flying on instruments, carefully apply small and momentary rudder inputs in opposition to the displacements of the turn needle of the turn and slip instrument. That is, when the needle displaces to the right, apply momentary left rudder. When the needle displaces to the left, apply momentary right rudder. During deceleration from high supersonic speed with roll and yaw dampers inoperative, pilot capability to minimize lateral-directional oscillations may be improved by holding the airplane in a sideslip which displaces the ball 1/2 ball diameter. Flight experience has indicated that this tends to damp the oscillation and will improve controllability.

WARNING

In utilizing pilot-applied rudder for yaw damping, put in small rudder pedal displacements initially so that the effect can be confirmed before additional rudder is considered. The rudder inputs must be phased in opposition to yaw in order to be beneficial. The rudder is very effective at high subsonic speeds at low altitude and abrupt rudder commands under these conditions should be avoided.

WING HEAVINESS.

In supersonic flight the airplane may become wing heavy when fuel in the aft tank is shifted spanwise to an unbalanced condition. Spanwise shifting of the fuel is caused principally by the side acceleration force acting on the fuel as a result of sideslip of the aircraft. This occurs even with small sideslip angles of less than one degree since significant side acceleration is produced when operating at high dynamic pressures that are encountered at supersonic speeds. The rate at which the wing heaviness increases is related to the magnitude of the side acceleration acting on the airplane and fuel as a result of the sideslip. An indication of the side acceleration acting on the fuel is displayed to the pilot by the displacement of the ball of the turn and slip indicator. The fuel in the aft tank shifts laterally with time in the same direction as displacement of the ball. The wing heaviness occurs predominantly to the left.

Note

The most severe wing heaviness attainable by sideslip occurs when the aft tank is about half full.

A wing heavy control system is incorporated in the yaw damper system to sense lateral acceleration and apply corrective rudder to reduce lateral fuel shift and subsequent wing heaviness. Refer to "Wing Heavy Control System," Section I. The wing heavy control system has a sufficient rate and authority to adequately correct for wing heaviness and under normal circumstances the pilot will not need to make additional corrections. The most effective method of avoiding wing heaviness buildup is to maintain zero sideslip for all flight operations and to keep the ball in the center of the turn-and-slip indicator by the use of rudder and maintaining symmetrical engine thrust. It is not recommended that manual rudder trim be used to correct for wing heaviness. In the event of a malfunction, or if an asymmetric condition has been allowed to exist, wing heaviness can develop. The onset of wing heaviness can be detected by the fact that an aileron stick force is required in order to keep the wings level. Wing heaviness can build up rapidly since the aileron required to keep the wings level produces an unfavorable yaw and lateral acceleration which causes the fuel to become more unbalanced. To correct for the additional unbalance more aileron is required and the process repeats itself. If significant wing heaviness is encountered, operate near the aft cg limit and decelerate to mach no. 1.4, or below, to rebalance fuel. The proper procedure to correct for wing heaviness by rebalancing fuel is to apply rudder toward the heavy wing with enough deflection to displace the turn-and-slip indicator one half ball diameter toward the light wing. Maintain this displacement for about ten seconds and then remove the rudder input. If wing heaviness is still present, repeat the process using discretion as to the duration and direction of the correction. There are several reasons why aileron inputs to control wing heaviness should be minimized: (1) The aileron deflections required for trim of severe wing heaviness can exceed half stick deflection in level flight because of the reduced aileron effectiveness which exists during supersonic flight. In turning flight, or during a pull-up, the aileron required for trim of the unbalanced fuel increases with the incremental load factor and can exceed the aileron available in severe cases. The pilot should roll out of a turn if more than half aileron stick is required to maintain bank angle. (2) Large aileron deflections produce especially large hinge moments with the center of gravity near the forward limit at medium to high supersonic speeds. With these large hinge moments present a failure of one hydraulic system could seriously degrade airplane control due to the reduced aileron control available.

MANEUVERING FLIGHT.

As indicated in the preceding paragraphs on longitudinal flight characteristics, operation of the automatic trim and elevator ratio changer systems provide a large measure of structural protection. Except for the transonic region, any wing buffeting which may occur during performance of routine maneuvers will be light to moderate and will not be severe enough to impose limits on maneuverability. In the transonic region, particularly at the higher altitudes, moderate to heavy buffeting will be encountered at near the limit load factor that will restrict the airplane maneuverability in this flight region. Maneuvering flight should be avoided when normal operations of either the stability augmentation system or the "g" limiting feature of the elevator control system is not available. When decelerating from supersonic speeds below mach no. 1.2, the load factor should not exceed 1.5-"g's". A nose-up tendency, which is aggravated in accelerated (more than one-"g") flight, occurs during rapid deceleration through the transonic region. Sufficient thrust is not always available to maintain airspeed during sustained maneuvers; therefore, deceleration can be expected.

> **CAUTION**
>
> Aerobatics are strictly prohibited. Caution must be exercised when maneuvering to near limit load factor with minimum elevator control available.

BUFFET.

Aerodynamic buffeting of the airplane is caused by the oscillatory separation and re-attachment of the airflow over some portion of the airplane surface, usually the wing. Buffeting is evident to the crew and appears as a shudder similar to early stall warnings on conventional airplanes. Buffet is encountered at moderate to high altitudes in the subsonic to low supersonic speed region. The onset of buffet is a function of altitude, mach number, gross weight, and load factor. The buffet boundary is based on a buffet intensity of about ± 0.03 g's incremental which is felt as an airframe vibration. (Refer to "Miscellaneous Data", Appendix I, T.O. 1B-58A-1-1 for the buffet bundary at a particular flight condition.) Specific reasons for avoiding buffet are as follows:

1. The altitudes at which 1-"g" buffet occurs are higher than those for maximum range and therefore, should be avoided as much as possible because of the lower miles per pound.

2. The increase in drag which occurs during buffet causes a significant increase in thrust required. This reduces range.

3. Any constant altitude turns in or near the buffet region result in increased buffet and thus increased power required.

4. The longitudinal disturbance degrades the quality of the ride and is disconcerting to the crew.

5. The intensity of the disturbance can increase to ±0.3 to ±0.5 "g's" incremental if the buffet boundary is penetrated as far as the airplane's ceiling with maximum afterburner power.

It is possible that the airplane can enter the buffet region during subsonic climb without experiencing buffet. This can occur during subsonic climb with afterburner power which provides an increment of lift resulting in the pilot not noticing any buffet until thrust is reduced for cruise flight. Flying above optimum altitude to get above the tops of clouds is the usual cause for being in the buffet region. Buffet phenomena is characterized in two regions of flight: subsonic, up to about mach no. 0.9; and, high subsonic to low supersonic, from mach no. 0.9 to about 1.1.

SUBSONIC BUFFET REGION.

Factors affecting the airplane operation in or near the subsonic buffet region are as follows:

1. Buffet boundary is defined as a function of mach number and altitude and is essentially a function of angle of attack. (Refer to "Miscellaneous Data", Appendix I, T.O. 1B-58A-1-1.)

2. Buffet intensity increases gradually as the airspeed is decreased or as the normal load is increased. There is no marked transition from light to heavy buffet. The airplane remains fully controllable in this region as well as in the transonic region. Light buffet may sometimes be experienced in the terminal period of a heavy gross weight air refueling operation at a marginally high altitude. The buffet will increase drag noticeably but will not significantly affect handling qualities of the airplane.

3. If buffet is encountered in the subsonic region and if weather is not a prohibiting factor, it is recommended that the altitude be reduced as required in avoiding the condition.

Note

Considerable flight experience in the subsonic buffet region has been obtained during flight tests without encountering operational difficulty.

HIGH SUBSONIC TO LOW SUPERSONIC BUFFET REGION.

Factors affecting the airplane operation in or near the high subsonic to low supersonic buffet region are as follows:

1. The buffet boundary in this region is characterized by a sharp dip in the altitude for onset of buffet at about mach no. 0.97. (Refer to "Miscellaneous Data," Appendix I, T.O. 1B-58A-1-1.)

2. Buffet can be encountered by acceleration into this region or by deceleration from supersonic speed at a high altitude.

3. During deceleration from supersonic speed at high altitudes and heavy gross weights, buffet can be encountered at transonic speeds at an altitude which would be buffet free at supersonic speeds.

4. During acceleration to supersonic speed, an aft shift in the center of lift causes the up elevator position required for level flight trim to be increased. This is noticeable from mach no. 0.9 to 1.1. If the acceleration is slow, the automatic trim will continuously supply the required elevator position. However, for more rapid acceleration, some momentary up elevator control must be applied in order to prevent a slight nose down tendency of the airplane in passing through this region. The opposite effect occurs during deceleration through the transonic region. This transitory characteristic of elevator position required for trim makes stabilization at a constant mach-altitude condition very difficult between mach no. 0.96 and 1.02. This characteristic, coupled with the buffet makes it necessary for the pilot and the automatic features of the flight control system to be continuously correcting small pitching motions.

5. There is a noticeable change in pitch and buffet intensity when the secondary nozzles open as the throttle levers are moved from MIL to MIN A/B. This is most noticeable with the outboard engines, with which there is a small nose down pitch and a reduction in buffet intensity as the secondary nozzles open. Less effect is noted with the inboard engines. Retarding the throttles from MIL to where the secondary nozzles open also causes a small nose down pitch change.

6. If buffet is encountered in this region, it is recommended that altitude be decreased. If altitude cannot be reduced because of weather or other considerations, airspeed may be increased to mach no. 1.2 in order to accelerate through the buffet region.

7. The airplane carrying an upper pod (BLU-2B-3) and small weapons or small weapon pylons will encounter buffet of light to moderate intensity at all altitudes in the high subsonic speed range. The onset of buffet will be detected at approximately mach no. 0.95 and will be more pronounced with small weapons than with the pylons only. However, in either case this intensity will be well within the established boundary

Section VI
Flight Characteristics

T.O. 1B-58A-1

and, therefore, should be no cause for alarm. The mach number at which buffet onset occurs varies with altitude and airplane external store configuration. Above mach no. 1.1 to 1.2, this buffet disappears.

OPERATION IN TURBULENCE.

> **CAUTION**
>
> Intentional flight through areas of extreme turbulence is not recommended since airplane structural limits may be exceeded. Refer to Section IX if operational commitments dictate flight through areas of extreme turbulence.

Estimated data on the effects of turbulence on the hydraulic system operations have been evaluated at specific flight conditions utilizing the hydraulic system test stand mockup. These tests indicate that under certain flight and loading conditions where there are large loads on the elevon the effect of damper operation during turbulence may result in stick talk back. Stick talk back is a result of up elevon reaching the maximum capability of the hydraulic system during damper operation. When the control surface reaches the upper limit the controlling damper movement is fed back to the control stick causing a pulsating or kicking movement in the pilot's hand. With both hydraulic systems functioning properly this condition will only occur at lower altitudes at supersonic speeds at very heavy gross weights and/or extreme forward center of gravity loading. The pilot can maintain level flight by firmly deflecting the stick against these forces to override the dampers. Maneuvering capability will be limited to capability of the hydraulic system. If stick talk back should suddenly appear during flight it may be an indication that one of the two hydraulic systems is failing or is not developing full pressure. Under any condition in which stick talk back occurs, the center of gravity should be moved to within 2% MAC of the aft limit as soon as possible. If the condition persists the airplane should be decelerated to subsonic speed.

DIVING.

Dives must be executed with care to avoid speeds (even in shallow dives) in excess of the structural limit speed. (Refer to "Airspeed Limitations," Section V.) Steep and rapid descents, as outlined under normal descent in Appendix I, can be accomplished by extending the landing gear and decreasing thrust to idle. A controllable nose-up transient may occur when the gear is extended at the higher airspeeds. During recovery from dives, it is recommended that the pilot's accelerometer be monitored closely to insure that allowable load factors are not exceeded. Refer to Section VI, T.O. 1B-58A-1A for dive recovery information.

POD DROP.

Caution should be exercised to establish proper center-of-gravity location prior to pod drop to insure satisfactory airplane response characteristics after release of the pod. The center-of-gravity after release must not exceed the airplane-without-pod normal operating aft limits. At the instant of pod release, an immediate rearward shift of the airplane center of gravity occurs. The center-of-gravity shift should be precomputed utilizing the load adjuster as all Pod Drop situations are not the same in relation to weight, speed and altitude. As a general rule approximate shifts of 1.5% mac for lower Pods and 5.5% mac for MB, LA and upper pods may be expected. The weight loss due to releasing a pod combined with the shift in center of gravity and certain aerodynamic changes cause the airplane to experience a nose-up transient at release. In normal operation, pod drop is to be accomplished on autopilot which will minimize the transient at release; however, there are no restrictions on drops with pilot control instead of autopilot. After release, the airplane can fly any escape trajectory within the allowable maneuver capability of the airplane. Pod jettisoning procedures are contained in Section II.

MB, LA OR UPPER POD DROP.

The appreciable loss in weight (8400 to 9600 lbs) and large center-of-gravity shift (approximately 5.5% MAC) due to dropping an MB, LA or upper pod gives a moderate airplane response with an initial peak of 1.6 to 2.5 "g's." The airplane response is largest at the highest indicated airspeed and smallest at the lowest indicated airspeed. Analytical predictions of aircraft response to MB, LA or upper pod drops indicate that airplane structural load limits may be exceeded during drops with the airplane center of gravity at the normal aft limits if the pitch damper is inoperative. If dropping a pod with the pitch damper inoperative is necessary, observe the speed restrictions for operation with the pitch damper inoperative, and move the airplane (with pod) center of gravity at least 3 percent forward of the cg precomputed for normal drops.

aft cg limit after upper pod drop (EWO only)

CONFIGURATION:
WITH OR WITHOUT SMALL WEAPONS

GROSS WEIGHT > 100,000 LBS

DATA BASIS: ESTIMATED MODEL: B-58A
DATE: 13 MAY 1966 ENGINES: J79-GE-5( )

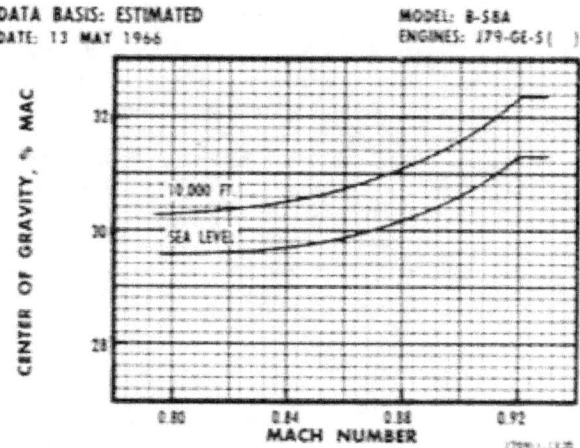

Figure 6-9.

UPPER POD DROP (EWO ONLY)

Due to the forward CG loading limitations at heavier gross weights of the airplane with upper pod, it is normally necessary to plan subsonic drops of the upper pod at intermediate gross weights so that the normal airplane aft center of gravity limits are not exceeded after the drop. If, under EWO conditions, it is desirable to drop the upper pod at somewhat heavier gross weights, the normal aft center of gravity limits of the airplane may be exceeded temporarily. Figure 6-9 contains the aft CG limits for the airplane without pod which may be used for EWO only. When these center of gravity limits are used, the airplane response following pod drop will be larger than normal. The drop should be made with the complete autopilot engaged but can be made with only the pitch channel engaged. With the autopilot engaged, limit load factor will not be exceeded. If the autopilot is not engaged at drop, limit load factor will be exceeded and the airplane structure may be damaged unless the pilot applies the proper corrective action. Immediately after drop, forward stick should be applied to moderate the upward motion; however, care must be exercised during the subsequent motion to avoid overcontrolling. Fuel should be transferred forward as soon as possible after the drop so as to move the center of gravity to be within the normal limits. If the drop is made above mach number 0.85, care must be exercised not to reduce speed until the center of gravity is shifted forward.

WARNING

Failure to move the center of gravity to within the normal limits before slowing down can result in a longitudinally unstable airplane which the pilot may not be able to control.

LOWER POD DROP.

Dropping the lower pod results in an aft center-of-gravity shift of approximately 1.5% MAC and a weight loss of 1800 lbs. At subsonic mach numbers this results in a mild airplane response at indicated airspeeds less than 450 knots and moderate airplane response at indicated airspeeds greater than 450 knots. The airplane response due to dropping a lower pod at subsonic mach numbers is similar to the airplane response for dropping an MB, LA or upper pod except that the magnitude is smaller at indicated airspeeds less than 450 knots and about the same magnitude at indicated airspeeds greater than 450 knots. At supersonic speeds, however, the airplane response after release of the lower pod is different in character from that after release of the upper, LA or MB pod. The lower pod pitches down rapidly at release, rotating downward about the pivot strut. The airstream deflected upward from the top of the pod results in a large increase in lift acting on the airplane coupled with a nosedown pitching moment. This causes an increase in airplane load factor initially with very little airplane rotation followed immediately by a rapid nosedown pitching motion of the airplane. The use of autopilot for supersonic lower pod drops is recommended. There are no restrictions on dropping the pod under pilot control. When dropping the pod under pilot control, corrective stick must not be applied until after initial drop transients have subsided. At supersonic speeds these transients will reach an initial peak of approximately 2.0 to 2.7 "g's" positive load factor and will approach a peak of minus 1 "g" negative load factor.

WARNING

Pilot elevator control inputs before initial drop transients subside could result in a peak negative load factor considerably in excess of one "g", thereby exceeding the limit maneuver load factor for the airplane. To avoid structural damage to the airplane, the pilot must not attempt to control the initial transients. If the drop cannot be made on autopilot, it is recommended that the airplane be trimmed out and the drop be performed with hands off the stick until the initial transient response has subsided, to prevent involuntary pilot stick input.

Section VI
Flight Characteristics

T.O. 1B-58A-1

The recommended spectrum for normal lower pod drops is illustrated by figure 5-2.

SMALL WEAPON DROP.

Airplane response upon dropping the small weapon is small as the weight of the weapon is low compared to that of the MB, LA or upper pods and the center of gravity shift will be small. Dropping the aft weapons individually will result in a forward center of gravity shift on the order of 0.5 percent MAC and dropping the forward weapons will result in approximately 0.25 percent MAC shift aft.

CAUTION

- The MB or LA pod with fins installed should be released prior to release of any small weapon.

- The MB or LA pod with lower fins removed or the lower pod of a TCP should be released prior to release of a forward small weapon.

AIR REFUELING.

The airplane is very stable at all gross weights during refueling. No "dishing" (side-to-side motion) is evident while in the refueling position.

Note

Air refueling can be accomplished with any damper or combination of dampers inoperative using normal techniques. However, refueling with the roll damper inoperative will normally be the most difficult. With both roll and yaw dampers inoperative, the airplane will be very sensitive to pilot control inputs, therefore, large or rapid control inputs should be avoided.

This is the last page of Section VI.

TABLE OF CONTENTS.

	Page
Engines	7-1
Fuel Supply System	7-5
Brake System	7-29
Flight Control System	7-30

ENGINES.

VARIABLE INLET GUIDE AND STATOR VANE SYSTEM.

The purpose of the inlet guide and variable stator vane system is to meter the weight flow of air into the engine and thus provide satisfactory compressor performance over a wide range of engine operating conditions. A conventional, fixed-vane-angle, axial flow compressor can be designed to operate at high efficiency only within a very limited range, usually at or near 100 percent engine speed. Moving out of this range results in aerodynamic mismatching of the successive stages and reduced compressor efficiency. An increase in engine speed would effectively lower the blade angle of attack, and conversely a decrease in engine speed would result in an effective increase in blade angle leading to a stall whenever the critical angle of attack is exceeded. However, by varying the angle of the variable vanes relative to the compressor rotors, the system will aerodynamically re-align the succeeding stages of compression within the design limits of the system. The IGV and variable stator system provides this efficient compressor operation at all engine speeds by automatically positioning the vanes to the proper angle of attack for all engine speeds and inlet temperatures. In this manner, the airflow is always directed against the compressor blades at an angle below critical. This decreases the load on the aft stages of the compressor at lower engine speeds, thus preventing compressor stall. Stall free, efficient compressor operation over a wide rpm range, plus fast engine acceleration and deceleration is characteristic of the variable stator type compressor. Estimated acceleration times for the engine at a ram air temperature of 15.6°C for airspeeds up to 150 knots at runway altitude from sea level to 6000 feet are: 5 seconds from IDLE to MIL thrust, and 10 seconds from IDLE to MAX A/B. The vanes are full closed during start and idle. At sea level static standard day conditions, the vanes begin to open as engine speed is increased from idle, and are fully open at approximately 93.5 percent engine speed. These opening and closing points change as the inlet temperature varies. The IGV vary 35 degrees from the open position to the closed position.

ENGINE COMPRESSOR STALL.

Engine compressor stall is a result of compressor blade airfoils stalling due to an excessive angle of attack of the blades relative to the airflow. It can be induced by various factors such as: main fuel control malfunction, IGV and variable stators being off schedule, CIT sensor cold shift, and poor inlet air pressure distribution caused by high airplane angles of attack or yaw. These conditions can result in air striking the compressor blades at too high an angle of attack and producing a stalled condition. Stall reduces airflow and can result in reversed flow through the engine, or loss of combustion. The severity of the stall will vary, depending on the number of stages that are involved. Some stalls are accompanied by loud banging and chugging sounds which are definitely noticeable in the cockpit, while others may be inaudible to the crew and characterized only by engine roughness and a rumbling sensation, plus a noticeable loss of thrust. A drop in RPM and/or

Section VII
Systems Operation

T.O. 1B-58A-1

excessive EGT is characteristic of a compressor stall. RPM "hang-up" may be encountered during engine acceleration and is usually accompanied by an increase in EGT. This is usually the result of a compressor stall, and the RPM "hangs up" at a value considerably lower than that scheduled by the throttle. Further advancing the throttle may result in an increase in severity of the stall. For stall clearing procedures, refer to "Compressor Stall Clearing," Section III.

T_2 RESET.

The automatic T_2 reset feature of the J79-5B/C engine fuel control system permits engine speed to increase beyond rated speed (7460 rpm—100 percent rpm) at high ram air (compressor inlet) temperatures. This increase in engine speed is necessary to obtain the airflow and thrust required for design speed. At a ram air temperature above 97°C as shown on figure 7-1, idle speed and rated speed become equal and remain equal as the temperature increases. In this region engine speed is independent of throttle position. However, retarding the throttles from the afterburner position reduces thrust resulting in a decrease in airspeed and ram air temperature. Then, as the temperature drops below 97°C, the T_2 reset feature is cutout and normal throttle control is re-established. The manual overspeed feature permits an immediate increase in engine speed up to 103.5 percent rpm by advancing the throttles beyond the MAX A/B position to the OVSP

t_2 reset and cutback versus engine speed

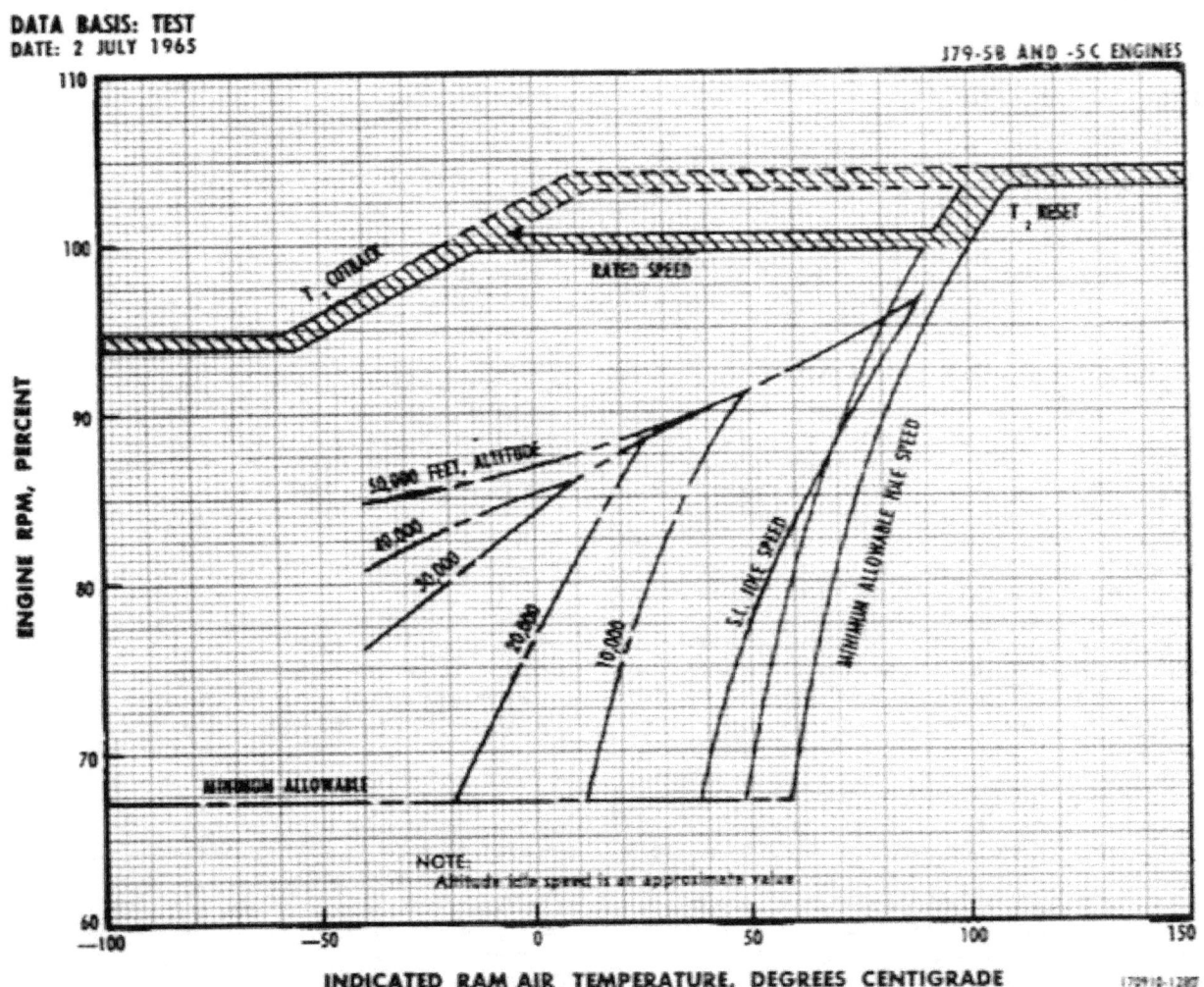

Figure 7-1.

T_2 cutback-rpm vs exhaust gas temperature

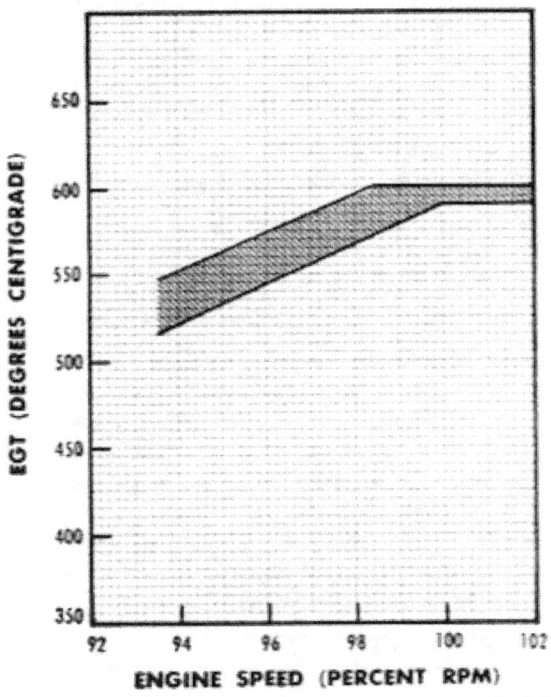

Figure 7-2.

position providing the ram air temperature is above 10-16 degrees centigrade. However, this does not provide additional thrust to the engines until a higher ram air temperature is obtained.

T_2 CUTBACK.

At low ram air (compressor inlet) temperatures, the T_2 cutback feature of the fuel control system prevents high corrected engine speed compressor stalls by decreasing the rated engine speed from 100 to 94.2 percent as shown on figure 7-1. EGT is also reduced when in T_2 cutback as shown in figure 7-2. When operating in the T_2 cutback region, advancing the throttles will have no effect on engine rpm until a higher ram air temperature is obtained.

ENGINE NOZZLE FAILURE.

Primary Nozzle Failed Open.

A primary nozzle failure in the open position can cause a maximum of approximately 60% loss in thrust and 70% decrease in fuel flow at military power with a resultant decrease in exhaust gas temperature of approximately 48%. Also, interference between the primary and secondary nozzles may be encountered when the secondary nozzle is in the closed position. Afterburner light-off may be possible up to an altitude of 5,000 feet and if lighted, may remain operable up to 20,000 feet. A decrease in airspeed will occur when a primary nozzle fails open if power is not increased on the remaining good engines. If failure occurs during subsonic flight, the airspeed at the time of failure can be maintained by increasing power on the remaining good engines or by utilizing all available thrust up to 100% on the malfunctioning engine. Maintaining some supersonic airspeeds may not be possible when afterburner operation on the affected engine cannot be sustained.

Primary Nozzle Failed Closed.

A primary nozzle failure in the closed position will constitute approximately 9% increase in thrust and 17% increase in fuel flow at military power with a resultant increase in exhaust gas temperature of approximately 10%. Engine power should be retarded to a value less than military power in order not to exceed the exhaust gas temperature limit. Should failure occur while in afterburner operation, compressor stall and engine flameout may result. Refer to "Engine Restart," Section III. If engine flameout does not occur, decrease power immediately on malfunctioning engine to keep within the exhaust gas temperature limits.

Secondary Nozzle Failed Open.

A secondary nozzle failure in the open position will not cause interference between the primary and secondary nozzles. At military power, a secondary nozzle failing open will constitute approximately 16% loss in thrust with no change in fuel flow or exhaust gas temperature.

Note

There is no loss in engine performance during afterburner operation. All thrust available may be utilized on the malfunctioning engine.

Secondary Nozzle Failed Closed.

Operation during subsonic flight requiring from 85% rpm to military power will not be affected by this type of nozzle failure. Therefore, all subsonic missions can be performed under these conditions. Interference between the primary and secondary nozzles can be encountered below 85% rpm.

CAUTION

During afterburner operation with the secondary nozzle failed closed, the exhaust gas temperature may rise above acceptable limits. Reduce power to military to prevent overtemperature operation and engine damage.

fuel system operation

OFF DE-ENERGIZED COMPONENT
ON ENERGIZED COMPONENT
CL COMPONENT CLOSED
OP COMPONENT OPEN
● COMPONENT ENERGIZED CLOSED BUT MAY BE OPENED MANUALLY
X PUMP ON STANDBY AND WILL AUTOMATICALLY ACTUATE WHEN MANIFOLD PRESSURE DROPS BELOW 19(±1) PSIG
■ AS REQUIRED
★ OPEN IF BALANCE TANK HAS DECREASED TO APPROXIMATELY 1500 TO 2000 POUNDS

NOTE:
Automatic operation differs from manual operation only in the case of forward fuel transfer. During automatic operation aft tank boost pumps 7 and 8 are actuated by the balance tank quantity gages for a forward transfer. These pumps are turned on immediately when transferring forward while in manual operation. During normal operation, the reservoir pumps are ON and the reservoir-to-manifold shutoff valves are open

• From FWD tank to BAL and AFT tanks.
•• From BAL and AFT tanks to FWD tank.

OPERATION	COMPONENT																									
	FWD TANK PUMPS		RES PUMPS			AFT TANK PUMPS				BAL TANK PUMPS		SCAVENGE PUMPS		POD PUMPS		FWD REFUEL VALVE	AFT REFUEL VALVE	BAL REFUEL VALVE	BAL TANK OVERFLOW SOLENOID VALVE	RES MANIFOLD SHUTOFF VALVES	FWD TRANS CONTROL VALVE	AFT TRANS CONTROL VALVE	DUMP VALVE	POD REFUEL VALVES		BAL AND AFT TANK INTERCONNECT VALVE
	1	2	3	4	5	6	7	8	9	10	11	12	13	14	15									FWD	AFT	
Reservoir Engine Supply	OFF	OFF	ON	ON	ON	OFF	OFF	OFF	OFF	OFF	OFF	OFF	OFF	OFF	OFF	●	●	●	CL	OP	CL	CL	CL	●	●	CL
Fwd Tank Engine Supply	ON	ON	ON	ON	X	OFF	OFF	OFF	OFF	OFF	OFF	OFF	OFF	OFF	OFF	●	●	●	CL	OP	CL	CL	CL	●	●	CL
Aft Tank Engine Supply	OFF	OFF	ON	ON	X	ON	ON	ON	ON	OFF	OFF	OFF	OFF	OFF	OFF	●	●	●	CL	OP	CL	CL	CL	●	●	CL
Split Feed Engine Supply	OFF	ON	ON	ON	X	ON	ON	OFF	OFF	OFF	OFF	OFF	OFF	OFF	OFF	●	●	●	CL	OP	CL	CL	CL	●	●	CL
• Fwd Tank Engine Supply With Trans Aft	ON	ON	ON	ON	X	OFF	OFF	OFF	OFF	OFF	OFF	OFF	OFF	OFF	OFF	CL	●	OP	OP	OP	OP	CL	CL	●	●	CL
•• Fwd Tank Engine Supply With Trans Fwd	ON	ON	ON	ON	X	OFF	ON	ON	OFF	ON	ON	OFF	OFF	OFF	OFF	OP	●	CL	CL	OP	CL	★	CL	●	●	■
•• Aft Tank Engine Supply With Trans Fwd	OFF	OFF	ON	ON	X	OFF	ON	ON	OFF	ON	ON	OFF	OFF	OFF	OFF	OP	●	CL	CL	OP	CL	★	CL	●	●	■
• Aft Tank Engine Supply With Trans Aft	ON	ON	ON	ON	X	OFF	ON	ON	OFF	OFF	OFF	OFF	OFF	OFF	OFF	CL	●	OP	OP	OP	OP	CL	CL	●	●	CL
•• Split Feed With Trans Fwd	OFF	ON	ON	ON	X	OFF	ON	ON	OFF	ON	ON	OFF	OFF	OFF	OFF	OP	●	CL	CL	OP	CL	★	CL	●	●	■
• Split Feed With Trans Aft	ON	ON	ON	ON	X	OFF	ON	OFF	OFF	OFF	OFF	OFF	OFF	OFF	OFF	CL	●	OP	OP	OP	OP	CL	CL	●	●	CL
Fwd Tank Scavenge	ON	ON	ON	ON	X	OFF	OFF	OFF	OFF	OFF	OFF	ON	OFF	OFF	OFF	CL	●	●	CL	OP	OP	CL	CL	●	●	CL
Aft & Bal Tank Scavenge	■	■	ON	ON	X	OFF	■	■	OFF	ON	ON	OFF	ON	OFF	OFF	●	●	CL	CL	OP	CL	CL	CL	●	●	■
Trans From Bal Tank to Aft Tank (Fwd Tank Full)	■	■	ON	ON	X	OFF	ON	ON	OFF	ON	ON	OFF	OFF	OFF	OFF	OP	OP	CL	CL	OP	CL	★	CL	●	●	■
Trans From Bal Tank to Aft Tank (Fwd Tank Not Full)	■	■	ON	ON	X	OFF	■	■	OFF	ON	ON	OFF	OFF	OFF	OFF	CL	OP	CL	CL	OP	CL	CL	CL	●	●	■
Trans from Fwd Tank to Aft Tank (No Fuel Desired in Bal Tank)	ON	ON	ON	ON	X	OFF	■	■	OFF	OFF	OFF	OFF	OFF	OFF	OFF	CL	OP	●	CL	OP	OP	CL	CL	●	●	CL
Trans From Pod Tanks to Airplane Tanks	■	■	ON	ON	X	■	■	■	■	OFF	OFF	OFF	OFF	■	■	■	■	■	CL	OP	CL	CL	CL	CL	CL	CL
Trans From Pod Aft Tank to Pod Fwd Tank	■	■	ON	ON	X	■	■	■	■	OFF	OFF	OFF	OFF	OFF	ON	●	●	●	CL	OP	CL	CL	CL	OP	CL	CL
Trans From Pod Fwd Tank to Pod Aft Tank	■	■	ON	ON	X	■	■	■	■	OFF	OFF	OFF	OFF	ON	OFF	●	●	●	CL	OP	CL	CL	CL	CL	OP	CL
Fuel Dump	ON	ON	ON	ON	X	OFF	OFF	OFF	OFF	■	■	OFF	OFF	■	■	●	●	●	CL	OP	●	CL	OP	●	●	■

Figure 7-3.

INLET SPIKE SYSTEM FAILURE.

An unscheduled position of an inlet spike will probably be indicated to the pilot by a loss of thrust on the affected engine. In case of a system malfunction, attempt to retract the defective spike by placing the spike position switch to IN. If the spike cannot be retracted, exceeding mach no 1.5 or a nacelle angle of attack of 6 degrees is not recommended. Attempt to retract the spike at a low mach number before landing. Full engine power is permissible if a go-around is necessary.

CAUTION

Care should be exercised in the event it is necessary to land with the spikes not fully retracted. Large thrust losses may result due to reduction in the inlet throat area.

Note

In case of electrical power failure to the system the spikes will remain in the position they were in at the time of failure.

Failure of a spike to extend is not considered an emergency. However, penalties from a spike failing to extend would probably be inability to attain design speed, thereby resulting in a change in flight plan to a lower mach number.

ENGINE INLET BUZZ.

Engine inlet buzz is a phenomenon associated with supersonic flight where a high frequency inlet duct pressure fluctuation occurs. Engine inlet buzz can occur above mach number 1.6 under certain conditions. The frequency of the pressure fluctuations is approximately 25 cycles per second and can vary in intensity from light to moderate. The inlet components have been designed to withstand these pressure fluctuations for short periods; however, if buzz is encountered, immediate corrective action should be taken. Engine instruments will not indicate buzz, but it can be felt as a vibration in the airframe and may possibly be heard as a low rumble.

Note

If inlet buzz is encountered it will be recorded on Form 781 so that an appropriate inspection will be made by the maintenance crews.

In the event that the T_2 reset mechanism in the main fuel control fails to increase engine speed when ram air temperature is above 97 degrees ± 5 degrees Centigrade, buzz may be encountered. However, with such a control failure, the engine is operating off schedule and this would be indicated by a comparison of the engine instruments with those of the other engines. Windmilling operation of the engine with the spike in automatic operation above mach no. 1.6 might also cause buzz to occur. It is possible for light buzz to occur under extreme maneuvers if an inlet spike is off schedule. However, buzz will cease when the airplane is returned to normal flight attitude.

The following procedure is recommended for elimination of engine inlet buzz.

CAUTION

Prolonged operation during inlet buzz should be avoided to prevent excessive structural loads on the nacelle.

1. Obtain normal flight attitude.
   Obtain a normal flight attitude by minimizing bank angle, sideslip and angle of attack.
2. If buzz continues, accomplish the following:
   a. Check engine rpm—Checked.
      Check to see if low rpm exists on one or more engines.
   b. Spike position switch in—IN (if low engine rpm exists).
      Retract spike on affected engine by moving spike switch to the IN position. Buzz should stop within 15 seconds.
   c. Throttle—OVSP (if buzz stops).
      If buzz stops, attempt to correct low rpm by advancing the throttle to the manual overspeed position.
   d. Spike position switch auto—AUTO (if engine rpm increases).
      If RPM can be increased by advancing the throttle to OVSP, place the spike switch to AUTO.
   e. Spike position switch in—IN (if buzz reoccurs).
      If buzz reoccurs continue airplane operation with spike retracted.

Note

It should be recognized that high speed flight with spike retracted will have some adverse effect on range.

3. Reduce airspeed—Reduced (if buzz continues).
   If buzz continues, decelerate to below mach no. 1.7 by retarding throttles to military power. When buzz stops, the affected engine throttle can then be advanced to A/B if desired.

FUEL SUPPLY SYSTEM.

Inflight management of the fuel system varies with the airplane configuration and the desired cg for the par-

Section VII
Systems Operation

T.O. 1B-58A-1

fuel panel configurations

OPERATION	PANEL CONFIGURATION FOR OPERATION LISTED	
	SWITCH NAME	POSITION
RESERVOIR ENGINE SUPPLY	Reservoir Tank Booster Pumps Reservoir to Manifold	NORM NORMAL
FORWARD TANK ENGINE SUPPLY	Forward Tank to Engine Supply Aft Tank to Engine Supply	ON OFF
AFT TANK ENGINE SUPPLY	Forward Tank to Engine Supply Aft Tank to Engine Supply	OFF ON
SPLIT FEED ENGINE SUPPLY	Forward Tank to Engine Supply Aft Tank to Engine Supply	ON ON

FORWARD TANK ENGINE SUPPLY WITH TRANSFER AFT (FROM FORWARD TANK TO BALANCE AND AFT TANKS)	Forward Tank to Engine Supply
	Aft Tank to Engine Supply
	MANUAL CG CONTROL:
	  CG Control
	  Manual CG Shift
	AUTOMATIC CG CONTROL:
	  CG Selector
	  Manual CG Shift
	  CG Control
		ON
		OFF
		
		MANUAL
		AFT
		
		Select aft cg
		OFF
		AUTO

FORWARD TANK ENGINE SUPPLY WITH TRANSFER FORWARD (FROM BALANCE AND AFT TANKS TO FORWARD TANK)	Forward Tank to Engine Supply
	Aft Tank to Engine Supply
	MANUAL CG CONTROL:
	  CG Control
	  Manual CG Shift
	AUTOMATIC CG CONTROL:
	  CG Selector
	  Manual CG Shift
	  CG Control
		ON
		OFF
		
		MANUAL
		FWD
		
		Select fwd cg
		OFF
		AUTO

AFT TANK ENGINE SUPPLY WITH TRANSFER FORWARD (FROM BALANCE AND AFT TANKS TO FORWARD TANK)	Forward Tank to Engine Supply
	Aft Tank to Engine Supply
	MANUAL CG CONTROL:
	  CG Control
	  Manual CG Shift
	AUTOMATIC CG CONTROL:
	  CG Selector
	  Manual CG Shift
	  CG Control
		OFF
		ON
		
		MANUAL
		FWD
		
		Select fwd cg
		OFF
		AUTO

AFT TANK ENGINE SUPPLY WITH TRANSFER AFT (FROM FORWARD TANK TO BALANCE AND AFT TANKS)	Forward Tank to Engine Supply
	Aft Tank to Engine Supply
	MANUAL CG CONTROL:
	  CG Control
	  Manual CG Shift
	AUTOMATIC CG CONTROL:
	  CG Selector
	  Manual CG Shift
	  CG Control
		OFF
		ON
		
		MANUAL
		AFT
		
		Select aft cg
		OFF
		AUTO

SPLIT FEED WITH TRANSFER FORWARD (FROM BALANCE AND AFT TANKS TO FORWARD TANK)	Forward Tank to Engine Supply
	Aft Tank to Engine Supply
	MANUAL CG CONTROL:
	  CG Control
	  Manual CG Shift
	AUTOMATIC CG CONTROL:
	  CG Selector
	  Manual CG Shift
	  CG Control
		ON
		ON
		
		MANUAL
		FWD
		
		Select fwd cg
		OFF
		AUTO

Figure 7-4. (Sheet 1 of 3)

OPERATION	PANEL CONFIGURATION FOR OPERATION LISTED	
	SWITCH NAME	POSITION

SPLIT FEED WITH TRANSFER AFT (FROM FORWARD TANK TO BALANCE AND AFT TANKS)	Forward Tank to Engine Supply
	Aft Tank to Engine Supply
	MANUAL CG CONTROL:
	  CG Control
	  Manual CG Shift
	AUTOMATIC CG CONTROL:
	  CG Selector
	  Manual CG Shift
	  CG Control
		ON
		ON
		
		MANUAL
		AFT
		
		Select aft cg
		OFF
		AUTO

FORWARD TANK SCAVENGE	CG Control Manual CG Shift Forward Tank Refuel—Scavenge	MANUAL OFF SCAV
AFT AND BALANCE TANK SCAVENGE (ENGINE SUPPLY AS REQUIRED)	CG Control Manual CG Shift Balance Tank Refuel—Scavenge	MANUAL OFF SCAV
TRANSFER FROM BALANCE TANK TO AFT TANK (FORWARD TANK FULL) (ENGINE SUPPLY OPTIONAL)	CG Control Manual CG Shift Aft Tank Refuel Valve	MANUAL FWD REFUEL
TRANSFER FROM BALANCE TANK TO AFT TANK (FORWARD TANK NOT FULL) (ENGINE SUPPLY OPTIONAL)	CG Control Manual CG Shift Balance Tank Refuel—Scavenge Aft Tank Refuel Valve Forward Tank Refuel—Scavenge	MANUAL OFF SCAV REFUEL OFF
TRANSFER FROM FORWARD TANK TO AFT TANK (NO FUEL DESIRED IN BALANCE TANK) (ENGINE SUPPLY OPTIONAL)	CG Control Manual CG Shift Balance Tank Refuel—Scavenge Forward Tank Refuel—Scavenge Aft Tank Refuel Valve	MANUAL OFF OFF SCAV REFUEL

TRANSFER FROM POD TANKS TO AIRPLANE TANKS (ENGINE SUPPLY OPTIONAL)	CG Control
	Manual CG Shift
	Forward Tank Refuel—Scavenge
	  Select REFUEL, if fuel is scheduled
	  to enter forward tank
	Balance Tank Refuel—Scavenge
	  Select REFUEL, if fuel is scheduled
	  to enter balance tank
	Aft Tank Refuel Valve
	  Select REFUEL, if fuel is scheduled
	  to enter aft tank
	Forward Pod Tank Transfer—Refuel
	  Select TRANS, if fuel is to be transferred
	  from forward pod tank
	Aft Pod Tank Transfer—Refuel
	  Select TRANS, if fuel is to be transferred
	  from aft pod tank
		MANUAL
		OFF
		As Required
		
		As Required
		
		As Required
		
		As Required
		
		As Required

TRANSFER FROM POD AFT TANK TO POD FORWARD TANK (ENGINE SUPPLY OPTIONAL)	CG Control Manual CG Shift Forward Pod Tank Transfer—Refuel Aft Pod Tank Transfer—Refuel	MANUAL OFF REFUEL ONLY TRANS
TRANSFER FROM POD FORWARD TANK TO POD AFT TANK (ENGINE SUPPLY OPTIONAL)	CG Control Manual CG Shift Aft Pod Tank Transfer—Refuel Forward Pod Tank Transfer—Refuel	MANUAL OFF REFUEL ONLY TRANS

Figure 7-4. (Sheet 2 of 3)

Section VII
Systems Operation

T.O. 1B-58A-1

OPERATION	PANEL CONFIGURATION FOR OPERATION LISTED	
	SWITCH NAME	POSITION
FUEL DUMP IN MANUAL CG CONTROL (TRANSFER FUEL AS REQUIRED TO MAINTAIN CG)	Forward Tank to Engine Supply Aft Tank to Engine Supply CG Control Manual CG Shift Fuel Dump Aft Tank Refuel Valve Pod Transfer Pumps	ON OFF MANUAL OFF DUMP REFUEL TRANSFER
FUEL DUMP IN AUTOMATIC CG CONTROL (AUTO 27.5 PERCENT MAC CG CONTROL)	Forward Tank to Engine Supply Aft Tank to Engine Supply CG Control CG Selector Fuel Dump Aft Tank Refuel Valve Pod Transfer Pumps	ON OFF AUTO Set to Obtain 27.5 Percent MAC DUMP REFUEL TRANSFER

Figure 7-4. (Sheet 3 of 3)

ticular flight condition. It requires understanding of the fuel and center of gravity systems. Refer to "Fuel Supply Systems," Section I for information on the fuel system and its controls. For fuel system trouble shooting procedures refer to figure 7-11.

FUEL MANAGEMENT.

Inflight management of the fuel for cg control can be accomplished either automatically or manually. The automatic cg control system may be used for all flight conditions except takeoff, landing, initial climb, transfer of fuel from the pod, and aerial refueling. In the event some malfunction precludes the automatic cg control system from maintaining proper cg, manual cg is to utilized. Manual cg control should be used when insufficient fuel is available to attain a desired cg. This condition will be noted during an aft shift by the lighting of the booster pump low pressure caution lamps for pumps 1 and 2, low fuel quantity reading on the forward tank indicator, and if on auto cg control subsequent lighting of the automatic cg off caution lamp. No minimum fuel quantity is required in the forward or aft tanks for engine supply.

WARNING

When in manual cg control, do not position the cg selector pointer aft of the cg limit for the given flight condition. To do so can result in exceeding the aft cg limit in the event the cg control is placed in the automatic position.

For operation of the fuel system see figure 7-3, and for the fuel panel configurations see figure 7-4.

CG DETERMINATION.

Three means of determining airplane center of gravity during flight are:

1. The weight and balance computer (refer to T.O. 1-1B-40),
2. The cg indicator,
3. The elevator position indicator.

Since all three methods are dependent upon other inputs, some discussion of normal discrepancies between them is in order.

1. The normal weight and balance computer errors may accumulate as a result of:
   a. Readability of the fuel gages.
   b. The accuracy with which the slide-rule computation can be made.

These factors are considered to contribute 0.3 percent MAC error, when all other factors are precisely correct. Since the computation is dependent upon fuel gage indications for inputs, erroneous indications may contribute additional error to the determination of the actual cg.

2. The cg indicating system computes the cg, electrically, in much the same manner as the balance computer except that no compensation is made for airplane attitudes other than 2.5 degrees nose up. When comparing this system to the balance computer, differences in cg determination may accumulate as a result of:

   a. The 0.3 percent MAC computer calculation errors noted above.

   b. The normal cg control system tolerance of 0.5 percent MAC (0.6 percent MAC with TCP or small weapons attached to the airplane), when calculation is based on an airplane attitude of 2.5 degrees nose up and the fuel gages read directly.

These factors represent 0.8 percent MAC (or 0.9 percent with TCP or small weapons) as an allowable discrepancy between indicated and computed cg. Therefore, when stabilized at normal cruise attitude (2.5 degrees nose up), the accuracy of the cg indicator system has been demonstrated to be within plus or minus 0.8 percent MAC (or 0.9 percent with TCP or small weapons) of actual. During other stable cruise conditions, (eg refueling, etc.) at various attitudes from plus 0.5 degrees to plus 6.5 degrees, the cg indicator accuracy has been demonstrated to be within plus or minus 1.5 percent MAC of actual.

Note

An additional error of plus or minus 0.2 percent MAC may occur at attitudes between 0.0 and plus 0.5 degrees.

3. The elevator position indicator method of determining cg is subject to errors as noted in Part 13 of Appendix 1. In addition, errors in gross weight, mach number or altitude will adversely affect the accuracy of the computation. One means of determination then may conceivably show that the cg is at or near the extreme allowable deviation from normal in one direction while another shows the cg to be at the other extreme. If this should be the case, the more conservative of the two should be relied upon. For example, if EPI appears normal and the cg indicator is forward of predicted, use the EPI. If EPI is high and the cg system is indicating near the aft limit, use the cg indicator. If the cg indication is near the aft limit and EPI is reading lower than predicted, transfer fuel forward until EPI reads the predicted value.

WARNING

If EPI differs from calculated by more than 1.0 degree (which may, at some flight configurations, represent approximately five percent MAC) and cg indication differs by more than 1.5 percent MAC from cg calculated at current flight attitude, use recommended procedures in "Fuel Quantity Measuring System Failure," this section and figure 7-10. Careful monitoring of the fuel consumption and distribution should enable the crew to continue use of the balance computer to determine the approximate airplane center of gravity.

PROCEDURES.

The following fuel management procedures are recommended for the various flight conditions and operations. Under all conditions the cg should be monitored frequently by comparing the elevator position indicator, the cg indicator, and the computation made using the balance computer. Any discrepancy should be corrected or resolved immediately. See "CG Determination" this section. Figure 7-10 lists elevator deflections for one-g flight for safe cg locations if the fuel quantity measuring system malfunctions.

WARNING

If the cg system is in error, the system should not be relied upon to hold that error constant. Under no circumstances should automatic cg be used when the cg system error is in excess of 0.8 percent MAC (or 0.9 percent MAC with TCP or small weapons).

Takeoff.

For afterburner takeoff use aft tank supply with manual cg control. Split feed may be used for MIL power takeoffs. Center of gravity must be within allowable limits of Section V. With this configuration, the cg will move forward during takeoff and initial acceleration.

Climb.

Continue manual cg control but switch to split feed engine supply. Pod fuel should not normally be transferred until initial cruise altitude has been reached.

Level Off.

Since the cg has moved forward during takeoff and initial acceleration, the cg should be moved aft to obtain cruise condition. The balance tank fuel quantity indicator should be monitored during all fuel transfer operations in order to detect any undesired increase in fuel quantity. If air refueling is planned, refueling time may be shortened by having the maximum allowable fuel in the pod tanks at time of hookup. Therefore, cruise cg should be corrected by transferring fuel to the balance tank from the forward tank, plus only that amount from the pod tanks necessary to prevent exceeding structural limitations. Refer to "Miscellaneous Operational Limitations", Section V. If no air refueling is planned or after air refueling, it is recommended that the pods be emptied as quickly as possible consistent with cg requirements. Transfer of pod fuel to the aft tank can be used for correcting cg. Various aft cg shift rates are available: the fastest is forward pod tank to aft tank; the slowest is aft pod tank to aft

fuel transfer rates

DATA BASIS: TEST
DATE: 4 JANUARY 1960

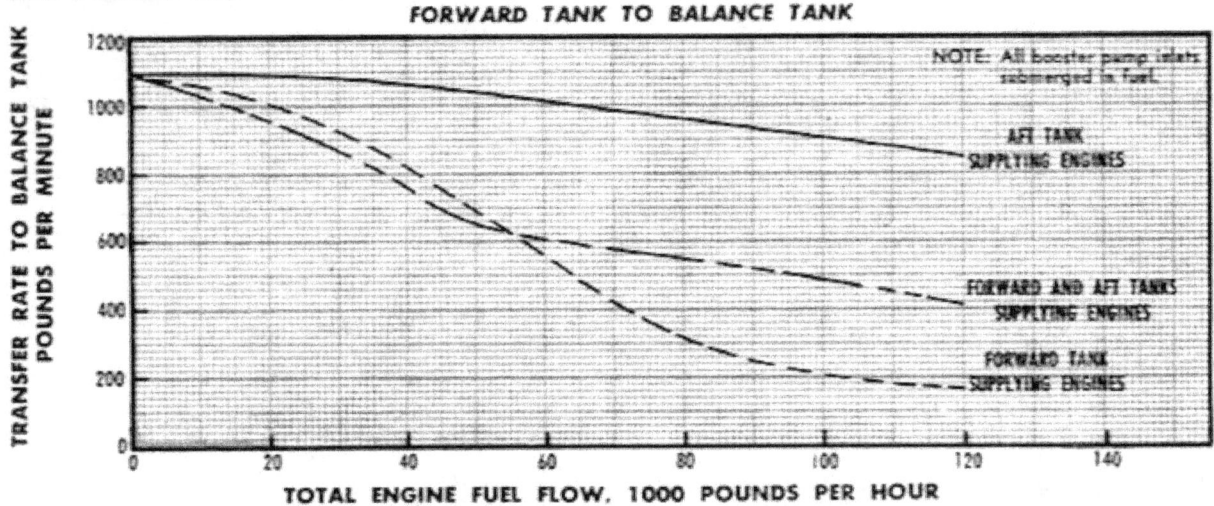

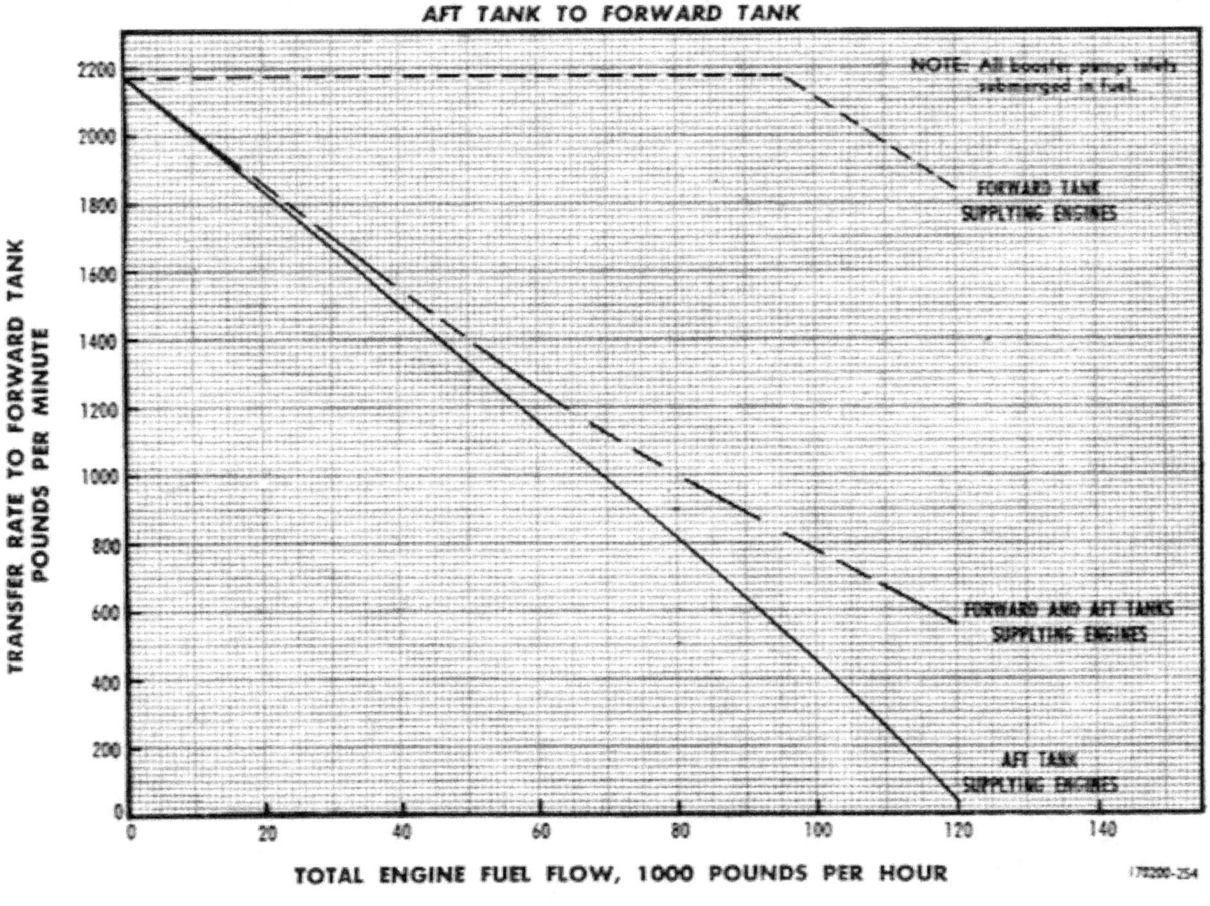

Figure 7-5.

tank. Regardless of the method used, an attempt should be made to keep the quantity of fuel in the pod tanks approximately equal.

Note

Although fuel may be transferred from the pod tanks to the airplane tanks during automatic cg control, fuel delivery from the pods may be delayed momentarily when forward fuel shifts are dictated by the automatic cg control system. This delay occurs during a forward cg shift due to the pod pumps being electrically locked out.

Subsonic Cruise.

Subsonic cruise is normally accomplished on split feed. During the cruise portion of the flight, cg control is necessary to attain planned range. Use of the aft cg limit positions is essential for range. CG's for maximum range shown in part 4 of Appendix I should be used. If range is not critical, a cg of 29 percent can be used for all airplane configurations. Cruise legs should be accomplished with automatic cg control after pod fuel has been transferred.

Low Level Cruise.

Low level cruise is normally accomplished on split feed. Care must be exercised in observing the aft cg limits in Section V. When flying below 9000 feet altitude with an IAS of 515 knots or higher, the fuel quantity in at least one of the pod tanks must be less than one half of its capacity. If this fuel transfer is not possible, an IAS of 515 knots must not be exceeded.

Acceleration.

Acceleration is accomplished with aft tank supply. When the decision is made to continue acceleration, attain mach no. 1.2 prior to moving the cg aft of the subsonic aft limit.

Supersonic Cruise.

For total fuel flows above 90,000 pph use aft tank supply. For total engine fuel flows less than 90,000 pph use aft tank supply or split feed. If range is not critical, a cg of 31.5 percent can be used for all airplane configurations. This CG is safe for all altitudes and mach numbers within the supersonic range.

Deceleration.

The center of gravity should be moved forward to subsonic position before deceleration below mach no. 1.2. The shift is small for the airplane with pod but can amount to an 11 percent forward shift for the airplane without pod. Since the deceleration time to mach no. 1.2 is of short duration the cg can be shifted only about 3 percent forward during this time. Therefore, on an airplane without a pod, the cg should be shifted forward to 35 percent MAC before deceleration is started. If the cg is not in proper position at mach no. 1.2, speed should be stabilized until the cg is correct. Descent to at least subsonic optimum altitude should be obtained before decelerating below mach no. 1.2.

Descent.

Descent is accomplished with same fuel management procedures as subsonic cruise.

Landing.

Use manual cg control for landing. Normally, because of fuel distribution, the forward tank supply must be used landing the airplane at light gross weights without the pod. If sufficient fuel is available, the landing can be accomplished with aft tank supply or on split feed. Center of gravity must be within allowable limits in Section V. For fuel panel configuration, refer to Section II.

FUEL TRANSFER.

The airplane cg is controlled either automatically or manually by transferring fuel as necessary for the various flight conditions. The method in which fuel is to be transferred depends upon the airplane configuration, the flight condition, and the rate at which fuel is to be transferred. The rate of transfer from the airplane forward and aft tanks varies with the engine supply configuration and total engine fuel flow. For the fuel transfer rates from the airplane forward and aft tanks, see figure 7-5. The transfer rate from the balance tank to the forward tank is approximately 2000 pounds per minute with both inlets of each booster pump submerged. At a deck angle of 2.5 degrees, the upper inlet of the pumps will be uncovered when the fuel quantity in the balance tank decreases to approximately 2200 pounds. For this condition, the transfer rate is approximately 700 pounds per minute.

WARNING

It should be noted that all pod fuel must be transferred to the airplane before the airplane gross weight decreases to 100,000 pounds. This limitation on pod fuel can be exceeded only during air refueling. Refer to "Allowable Airplane Fuel in Pod Tanks", Section V.

TANK SCAVENGING.

Fuel in the forward and aft tanks should be scavenged when the booster pump low pressure caution lamps remain lighted. At this fuel level, booster pump delivery pressure is so erratic that they will not maintain sufficient manifold pressure.

FUEL DUMPING.

Fuel dumping is used to reduce the airplane gross weight as rapidly as possible or as an emergency means for moving the center of gravity forward. Fuel dump rate from the aft tank is approximately 4000 pounds per minute when at maximum aft tank pressure. If air conditioning system is in ram air operation, a reduced dump rate may be expected. Refer to "Fuel Dumping," Section III. For fuel panel configuration see figure 7-4.

Negative Gravity Operation.

The reservoir tank is the only tank with provisions for supplying the engines during negative gravity operation. While the airplane is experiencing negative "g" loads, the inlets to the booster pumps in the forward, aft, and balance tanks will tend to become uncovered. Therefore, the engines will be supplied automatically from the reservoir tank during this operation.

WARNING

A negative gravity operation must not be initiated when the reservoir tank not full caution lamp is lighted.

Partial Booster Pump Operation.

If either the right or left a-c bus should fail, part of the booster pumps will be inoperative since the right a-c bus supplies electrical power to pumps No. 1 in the forward tank, 3 and 5 in the reservoir tank, 7 and 9 in the aft tank and 11 in the balance tank, and the left a-c bus supplies power to pumps No. 2 in the forward tank, 4 in the reservoir tank, 6 and 8 in the aft tank and 10 in the balance tank. If failure of either a-c bus occurs while flying supersonically, the cg should be moved forward and a deceleration to subsonic flight should be initiated as soon as possible.

Note

Transfer of pod fuel to the aircraft may be accomplished with one pod pump operating, by opening the pod tank interconnect.

Fuel transfer rate will be considerably decreased, since one-half of the booster pumps in the aft and balance tanks are inoperative. After deceleration, flight should be at maximum range altitude and mach number since this requires minimum fuel flow and gives maximum descent range in the event a progressive failure of the remaining a-c bus should occur.

transfer rates into aft tank for dumping

DATA BASIS: PREDICTED

Tank from which transferring	Actual tank rate (pounds per minute)	Total rate into aft tank (pounds per minute)
FORWARD	1660	1660
BALANCE	1800	1800
FORWARD POD	1010	1010
AFT POD	950	950
FORWARD POD / AFT POD	940 / 910	1850
FORWARD POD / FORWARD	890 / 1560	2450
FORWARD POD / BALANCE	950 / 1730	2680
AFT POD / FORWARD	820 / 1560	2380
AFT POD / BALANCE	890 / 1750	2640
FORWARD / BALANCE	1500 / 1560	3060
FORWARD POD / AFT POD / BALANCE	840 / 780 / 1510	3130
FORWARD / FORWARD POD / AFT POD	1400 / 750 / 720	2870

NOTE:
1. All booster pump inlets submerged in fuel.
2. Transfer rate from forward tank assumes no engine supply from this tank.

Figure 7-6.

Note

The reservoir tank is the only tank that has suction feed provisions and is capable of sustaining MAX A/B operation at altitudes below 6,000 feet. However, successful suction feed has been demonstrated at high altitudes at reduced power.

The reservoir to manifold switches must be in the guarded NORMAL position to allow fuel to flow by suction to the engines. The flight should be terminated as soon as possible since there is a limited amount of fuel available in the reservoir tank. Considering descent from 40,000 feet altitude, only about 70 nautical miles descent range and 75 nautical miles range at sea level is available before fuel starvation. Any increase in range above this will come from cruising at as high an altitude as possible with suction feed. This altitude can be found by allowing altitude to stabilize where fuel flow required can be sustained by suction.

Inoperative Engines.

The possibility of all engines flaming out simultaneously is very remote. If engines 1, 2, and 3 should flame out, a-c power will probably be maintained until the engine windmilling speed drops below 40 percent rpm. If the engines cannot be restarted before the windmilling speed drops below 40 percent rpm, the booster pumps will be inoperative. The reservoir to manifold switches must be in the NORMAL position to allow fuel to flow by suction from the reservoir tank for restarting the engines.

Minimum Pumps for Afterburner Operation.

Only the aft tank has sufficient pumping capacity for single tank supply during takeoff and acceleration conditions when the total engine fuel flow exceeds approximately 90,000 pounds per hour. The reservoir will begin to supply the engines if higher flow rates are experienced when engine supply is from the forward tank.

Unusable Fuel.

For unusable fuel quantities in the forward, aft, and balance tanks, see figure 7-7. In addition, the approximate fuel quantity at which the forward and aft tank booster pump low pressure caution lamps come on is shown. The unusable fuel quantity in the pod tanks at a normal flight attitude of 2.5 degrees is approximately 70 pounds in the forward tank and 40 pounds in the aft tank.

Forward and Aft Tank Fuel Quantities at High Level Shutoff.

The forward and aft tank fuel quantities at high level shutoff versus deck angle are shown in figure 7-8. For other fuel tank quantities at deck angles of −2.3 degrees, 2.5 degrees and 6.5 degrees, refer to "Fuel Supply System," Section I.

Minimum Forward Tank Fuel Quantity For Transfer To Reservoir Tank By Air Pressure.

When the reservoir tank is the only tank supplying the engines, fuel is automatically transferred into the reservoir tank by air pressure. This transfer takes place only if the fuel level in the forward tank is sufficient to cover the outlet of the vent and overflow pipe from the reservoir tank. Figure 7-9 shows the minimum forward tank fuel quantity for transfer to the reservoir tank by air pressure.

Fuel Quantity Measuring System Failure.

The pilot should be able to recognize a failure of the cg control system by cross-checking with the elevator position indicator. At this time, the cg control switch should be placed to MANUAL to prevent the system from pumping the fuel into an unsafe condition. The rest of the flight must be flown using the elevator position indicator as a cg indicator. Fuel should be shifted to maintain the required elevator position. A forward fuel shift will increase elevator position and an aft shift will decrease elevator position. The most probable cause of failure of the cg control system is a failure of a fuel quantity indicator or tank gaging system. The fuel quantities used by the cg computer come from the indicator; therefore, any indication error will cause a cg error. One type of indicator or gaging system malfunction can be recognized by the constant reading of the indicator while feeding engines or transferring from the tank. Also, a failure of an individual tank unit may cause a partial deflection of the indicator gage. These types of failures, of course, would take time to recognize from the indicator. Other types of malfunctions will show zero fuel or full fuel at all times and therefore are quite obvious. The failure of a tank gaging system does not preclude use of that tank for feeding engines or for transferring fuel. The pump low pressure caution light is an indication that the tank is empty. In case the flight plan is abandoned and range is not critical, it may be desired to shift the airplane cg to a position which is safe at all altitudes and speeds. Figure 7-10 is a table presenting elevator deflections for a cg at 29 percent MAC for subsonic operation (except pattern speed) and 30 percent (or

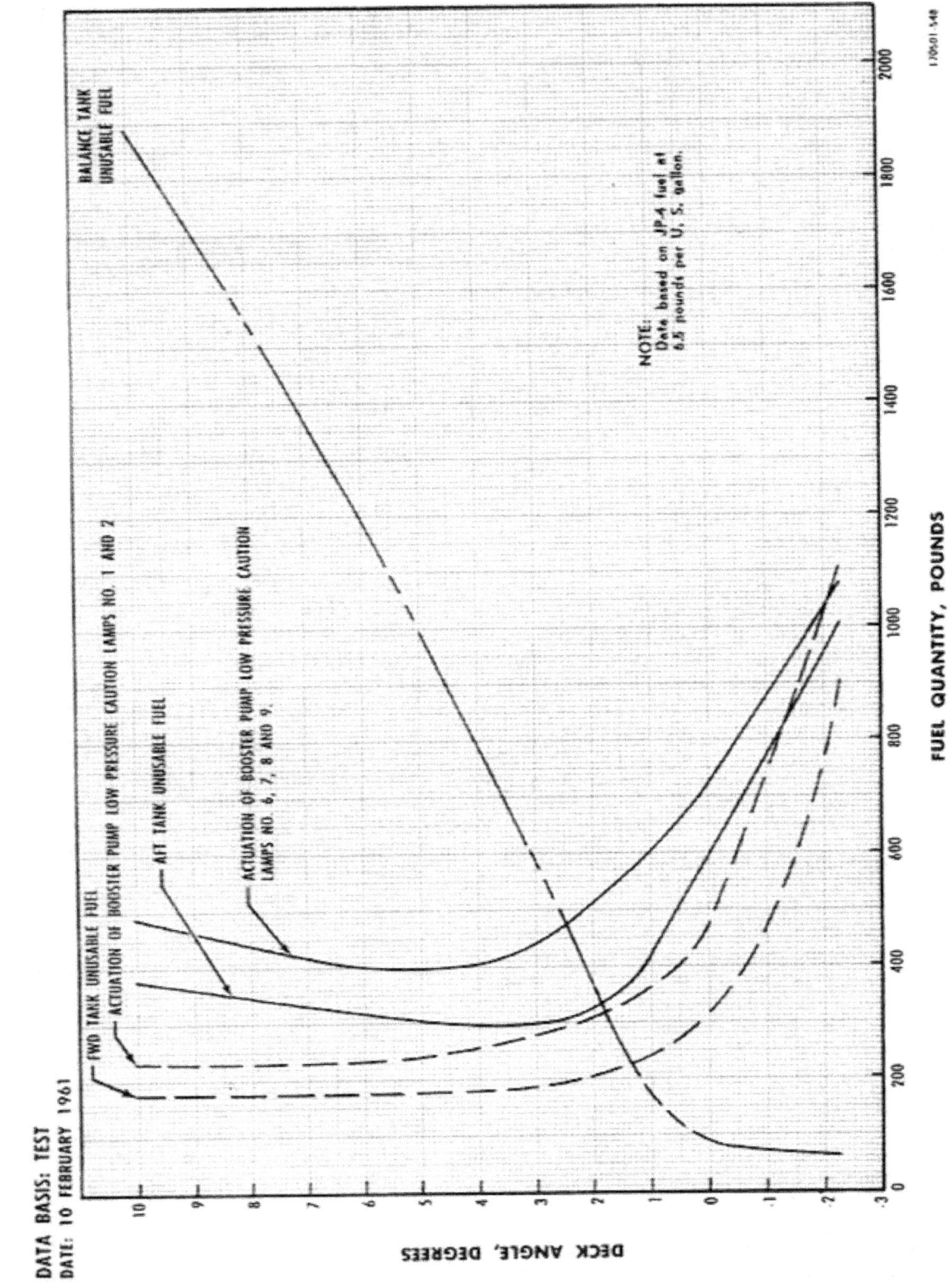

Figure 7-7.

T.O. 1B-58A-1

Section VII
Systems Operation

fwd and aft tank fuel quantities at high level shutoff versus deck angle

DATA BASIS: ESTIMATED AND CALIBRATED
DATE: 21 DECEMBER 1962

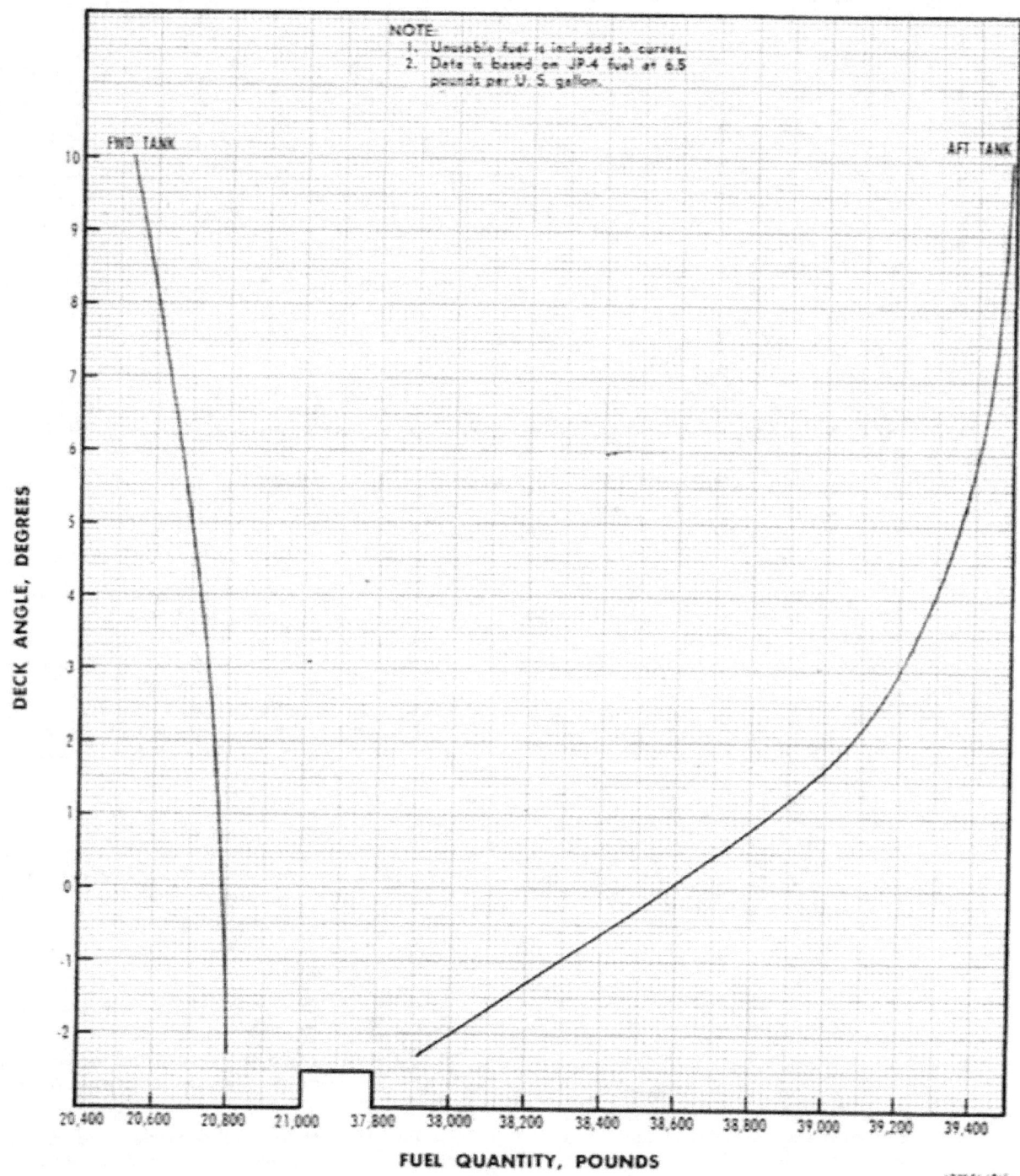

Figure 7-8.

7-15

Section VII
Systems Operation

T.O. 1B-58A-1

minimum forward tank fuel quantity for air pressure transfer to reservoir tank

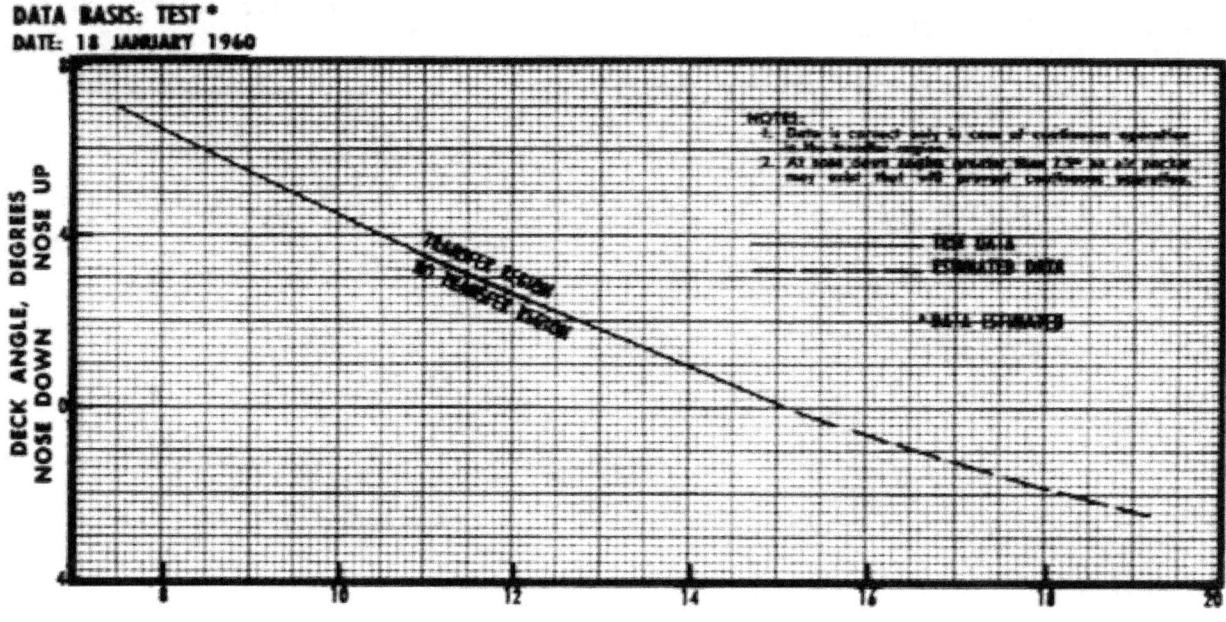

Figure 7-9.

the forward limit if aft of 30 percent) for supersonic operation. The following instructions apply to the use of these "safe" cg's.

1. Airplane Without Pod With or Without Small Weapons.

   a. If failure of the fuel measuring system occurs while supersonic, position the cg control switch to MANUAL.

   b. Transfer fuel forward as necessary to obtain an elevator position indicator reading corresponding to that in figure 7-10 at the flight mach number and altitude. When an aft tank booster pump low pressure caution lamp lights, start feeding engines from the forward tank and decelerate to subsonic speed.

   CAUTION

   At gross weights above approximately 102,000 pounds, the cg is aft of 30 percent MAC without pod. For this condition transfer fuel forward to maintain the center of gravity as far forward as possible. Do not decelerate below mach no. 1.2 at a gross weight estimated to be above 115,000 pounds, at which

condition the center of gravity will be at approximately 33 percent MAC. Do not decelerate below mach no. 0.92 until the elevator position indicator reading coincides with the values in figure 7-10 for mach no. 0.92 at 95,000 pounds gross weight. This will result in a center of gravity location of approximately 29 percent MAC with all fuel forward.

   c. If failure occurs at subsonic speed position the cg control knob to manual and feed the engines from the aft tank, and transfer fuel aft intermittently to maintain, as closely as possible, the elevator positions in figure 7-10. Split feed can also be used.

   d. Prior to landing transfer all aft and balance tank fuel to the forward tank.

2. Airplane With Any Pod With or Without Small Weapons (No Fuel in Pod).

   a. If failure of the fuel measuring system occurs during supersonic flight, position the cg control switch to MANUAL.

   b. Transfer fuel forward as necessary to obtain an elevator position indicator reading corresponding to that in figure 7-10 at the flight mach number and altitude.

T.O. 1B-58A-1

Section VII
Systems Operation

elevator deflection for one-g flight for safe cg location if fuel quantity measuring system malfunctions

AIRPLANE WITHOUT POD
65,000 and 95,000 Pounds Gross Weights*

Mach Number	Elevator Position, Degrees UP — Altitude, thousands of feet							
	S.L.	10	20	30	40	50	60
2.0					6.8 8.2	7.3 9.5	10.4 13.7
1.2			2.0 3.1	1.8 3.2	2.9 4.9	5.4 8.3	
0.92	0.8 0.9	0.5 0.7	0.4 0.6	0.3 0.6	0.5 1.0		
0.60	1.0 1.1	1.1 1.3	1.4 1.7				

Pattern Speed (Downwind leg speed): Transfer all fuel to forward tank

AIRPLANE WITH MB OR LA POD
70,000 and 150,000 Pounds Gross Weights*

Mach Number	Elevator Position, Degrees UP — Altitude, thousands of feet							
	S.L.	10	20	30	40	50	60
2.0					4.9 8.9	6.2 12.3	9.8 18.2
1.2			1.9 5.1	2.3 6.5	3.6 9.3	6.4 14.4	
0.92	2.2 2.7	1.4 2.0	1.2 1.9	1.1 2.2	1.1 2.6		
0.60	0.6 1.1	0.8 1.5	1.2 2.2				

Pattern Speed (Downwind leg speed): Minimum 2.0 degrees, Maximum 4.0 degrees (regardless of gross weight)

AIRPLANE WITH UPPER POD
70,000 and 100,000 Pounds Gross Weights*

Mach Number	Elevator Position, Degrees UP — Altitude, thousands of feet							
	S.L.	10	20	30	40	50	60
2.0					5.8 7.4	7.4 9.7	10.4 13.7
1.2			4.4 5.5	4.0 5.4	4.7 6.7	6.9 9.8	
0.92	1.7 1.9	1.3 1.5	1.1 1.4	0.8 1.2	1.0 1.5		
0.60	0.9 1.0	1.0 1.2	1.3 1.6				

Pattern Speed (Downwind leg speed): Minimum 1.7 degrees, Maximum 3.0 degrees (regardless of gross weight)

AIRPLANE WITH TCP
70,000 and 150,000 Pounds Gross Weights*

Mach Number	Elevator Position, Degrees UP — Altitude, thousands of feet							
	S.L.	10	20	30	40	50	60
2.0					5.3 9.2	7.0 13.1	10.4 18.9
1.2			3.9 7.0	4.0 8.1	5.4 10.9	8.0 15.8	
0.92	2.8 3.3	1.8 2.4	1.5 2.2	1.4 2.5	1.5 2.9		
0.60	1.7 2.3	2.0 2.7	2.3 3.3				

Pattern Speed (Downwind leg speed): Minimum 3.0 degrees, Maximum 5.0 degrees (regardless of gross weight)

*(1) Upper number in each block is the lighter weight and the lower number is the heavier weight of the weights called out under the aircraft configuration.

(2) Interpolate or extrapolate linearly for gross weights different from those called out for the respective aircraft configuration.

(3) These elevator deflections indicate that the center of gravity location is as follows: Subsonic speeds—29% MAC for all indicated configurations (except for pattern speed); Supersonic speeds—30% MAC for airplane without pod, 31.5% MAC for airplane with upper pod, and 30% MAC for airplane with MB or LA pod or TCP.

Figure 7-10. (Sheet 1 of 6)

Section VII
Systems Operation

T.O. 1B-58A-1

elevator deflection for one-g flight for safe cg location if fuel quantity measuring system malfunctions

Mach Number	AIRPLANE WITHOUT POD PLUS PYLONS 65,000 and 95,000 Pounds Gross Weights*							AIRPLANE WITH MB OR LA PLUS PYLONS 70,000 and 150,000 Pounds Gross Weights*						
	Elevator Position, Degrees UP							Elevator Position, Degrees UP						
	Altitude, thousands of feet							Altitude, thousands of feet						
	S.L.	10	20	30	40	50	60	S.L.	10	20	30	40	50	60
2.0					6.8 8.2	7.3 9.5	10.4 13.7					4.9 8.9	6.2 12.3	9.8 18.2
1.2			1.0 2.1	1.6 3.0	2.9 4.9	5.4 8.3				1.4 4.6	2.2 6.4	3.6 9.3	6.4 14.4	
0.92	0.8 0.9	0.5 0.7	0.4 0.6	0.3 0.6	0.5 1.0			2.1 2.6	1.4 2.0	1.2 1.9	1.1 2.2	1.1 2.6		
0.60	0.8 1.0	1.0 1.2	1.3 1.6					0.0 0.5	0.2 0.9	0.6 1.6				
Pattern Speed (Downwind leg speed)	Transfer all fuel to forward tank							Minimum 1.4 degrees Maximum 3.4 degrees (regardless of gross weight)						
Mach Number	AIRPLANE WITH UPPER POD PLUS PYLONS 70,000 and 100,000 Pounds Gross Weights*							AIRPLANE WITH TCP PLUS PYLONS 70,000 and 150,000 Pounds Gross Weights*						
	Elevator Position, Degrees UP							Elevator Position, Degrees UP						
	Altitude, thousands of feet							Altitude, thousands of feet						
	S.L.	10	20	30	40	50	60	S.L.	10	20	30	40	50	60
2.0					5.8 7.4	7.4 9.7	10.4 13.7					5.3 9.2	7.0 13.1	10.4 18.9
1.2			4.4 5.5	4.0 5.4	4.7 6.7	6.9 9.8				3.4 6.5	3.9 8.0	5.4 10.9	8.0 15.8	
0.92	1.7 1.9	1.3 1.5	1.1 0.9	0.8 1.1	1.0 1.4			2.8 3.3	1.8 2.4	1.5 2.2	1.4 2.5	1.5 2.9		
0.60	0.7 0.8	0.8 1.0	1.1 1.4					1.1 1.7	1.4 2.1	1.7 2.7				
Pattern Speed (Downwind leg speed)	Minimum 1.5 degrees Maximum 2.8 degrees (regardless of gross weight)							Minimum 2.4 degrees maximum 4.4 degrees (regardless of gross weight)						

*(1) Upper number in each block is the lighter weight and the lower number is the heavier weight of the weights called out under the aircraft configuration.

(2) Interpolate or extrapolate linearly for gross weights different from those called out for the respective aircraft configuration.

(3) These elevator deflections indicate that the center of gravity location is as follows: Subsonic speeds—29% MAC for all indicated configurations (except for pattern speed); Supersonic speeds—30% MAC for airplane without pod plus pylons, 31.5% MAC for airplane with upper pod plus pylons, and 30% for airplane with MB or LA or TCP plus pylons.

Figure 7-10. (Sheet 2 of 6)

T.O. 1B-58A-1

Section VII
Systems Operation

elevator deflection for one-g flight for safe cg location if fuel quantity measuring system malfunctions

Gross Weights* 65,000 and 95,000 Pounds
Note: Plus sign preceding elevator deflection indicate degrees down deflection

Mach Number	AIRPLANE WITHOUT POD PLUS 1 STORE							AIRPLANE WITHOUT POD PLUS 2 STORES						
	Elevator Position, Degrees UP							Elevator Position, Degrees UP						
	Altitude, thousands of feet							Altitude, thousands of feet						
	S.L.	10	20	30	40	50	60	S.L.	10	20	30	40	50	60
2.0					6.2 / 7.6	7.7 / 9.9	11.0 / 14.2					6.2 / 7.6	7.7 / 9.9	11.0 / 14.2
1.2			0.8 / 1.9	1.3 / 2.7	2.8 / 4.9	5.4 / 8.3				0.4 / 1.5	1.0 / 2.4	2.5 / 4.6	5.1 / 8.0	
0.92	0.5 / 0.6	0.3 / 0.5	0.3 / 0.6	0.3 / 0.7	0.5 / 1.0			0.2 / 0.4	0.2 / 0.4	0.2 / 0.4	0.2 / 0.6	0.4 / 0.9		
0.60	0.8 / 0.9	1.0 / 1.2	1.3 / 1.6					0.7 / 0.8	0.9 / 1.1	1.2 / 1.5				
Pattern Speed (Downwind leg speed)	Transfer all fuel to forward tank							Transfer all fuel to forward tank						

Mach Number	AIRPLANE WITHOUT POD PLUS 3 STORES							AIRPLANE WITHOUT POD PLUS 4 STORES						
	Elevator Position, Degrees UP							Elevator Position, Degrees UP						
	Altitude, thousands of feet							Altitude, thousands of feet						
	S.L.	10	20	30	40	50	60	S.L.	10	20	30	40	50	60
2.0					5.9 / 7.3	6.4 / 8.6	9.6 / 12.9					5.9 / 7.3	6.4 / 8.6	9.6 / 12.9
1.2			0.2 / 1.3	0.3 / 1.8	1.7 / 3.7	4.3 / 7.2				+0.3 / 0.8	0.0 / 1.4	1.4 / 3.4	4.0 / 6.9	
0.92	0.0 / 0.1	0.0 / 0.2	0.0 / 0.2	0.0 / 0.3	0.2 / 0.7			+0.5 / +0.4	+0.4 / +0.2	+0.3 / 0.0	+0.3 / 0.1	0.0 / 0.5		
0.60	0.7 / 0.9	0.9 / 1.1	1.2 / 1.5					0.6 / 0.7	0.7 / 0.9	1.0 / 1.4				
Pattern Speed (Downwind leg speed)	Transfer all fuel to forward tank							Transfer all fuel to forward tank						

*(1) Upper number in each block is the lighter weight and the lower number is the heavier weight of the weights called out under the aircraft configuration.

(2) Interpolate or extrapolate linearly for gross weights different from those called out for the respective aircraft configuration.

(3) These elevator deflections indicate that the center of gravity location is approximately 29.0% MAC at subsonic speeds (except for pattern speed); and 30% MAC at supersonic speed.

Figure 7-10. (Sheet 3 of 6)

7-19

Section VII
Systems Operation

T.O. 1B-58A-1

elevator deflection for one-g flight for safe cg location if fuel quantity measuring system malfunctions

Gross Weights* 70,000 and 100,000 Pounds
Note: Plus sign preceding elevator deflection indicate degrees down deflection

Mach Number	AIRPLANE WITH UPPER POD PLUS 1 STORE – Elevator Position, Degrees UP – Altitude, thousands of feet							AIRPLANE WITH UPPER POD PLUS 2 STORES – Elevator Position, Degrees UP – Altitude, thousands of feet						
	S.L.	10	20	30	40	50	60	S.L.	10	20	30	40	50	60
2.0					4.4 / 6.0	5.7 / 8.0	9.2 / 12.6					4.4 / 6.0	5.7 / 8.0	9.2 / 12.6
1.2			3.5 / 4.7	3.2 / 4.7	4.4 / 6.4	6.7 / 9.5				3.1 / 4.3	2.9 / 4.4	4.1 / 6.1	6.4 / 9.3	
0.92	1.7 / 1.9	1.2 / 1.4	0.6 / 0.9	0.8 / 1.1	0.9 / 1.4			1.5 / 1.7	1.0 / 1.2	0.5 / 0.7	0.7 / 1.0	0.8 / 1.3		
0.60	0.6 / 0.7	0.7 / 1.0	1.0 / 1.4					0.5 / 0.6	0.6 / 0.9	1.0 / 1.3				
Pattern Speed (Downwind leg speed)	Minimum 1.5 degrees / Maximum 3.0 degrees (regardless of gross weight)							Minimum 1.4 degrees / Maximum 2.7 degrees (regardless of gross weight)						

Mach Number	AIRPLANE WITH UPPER POD PLUS 3 STORES – Elevator Position, Degrees UP – Altitude, thousands of feet							AIRPLANE WITH UPPER POD PLUS 4 STORES – Elevator Position, Degrees UP – Altitude, thousands of feet						
	S.L.	10	20	30	40	50	60	S.L.	10	20	30	40	50	60
2.0					4.4 / 6.0	6.0 / 8.3	9.2 / 12.6					4.4 / 6.0	6.0 / 8.3	9.2 / 12.6
1.2			1.5 / 2.7	1.8 / 3.3	3.2 / 5.2	5.6 / 8.4				1.1 / 2.3	1.4 / 3.0	2.9 / 4.9	5.3 / 8.1	
0.92	0.4 / 0.6	0.3 / 0.5	0.3 / 0.6	0.4 / 0.7	0.5 / 1.0			+0.1 / 0.1	0.0 / 0.2	0.1 / 0.3	0.2 / 0.5	0.3 / 0.9		
0.60	0.9 / 1.1	1.1 / 1.3	1.4 / 1.8					0.7 / 0.9	0.9 / 1.2	1.3 / 1.6				
Pattern Speed (Downwind leg speed)	Minimum 1.8 degrees / Maximum 3.1 degrees (regardless of gross weight)							Minimum 1.7 degrees / Maximum 3.0 degrees (regardless of gross weight)						

*(1) Upper number in each block is the lighter weight and the lower number is the heavier weight of the weights called out under the title.

(2) Interpolate or extrapolate linearly for gross weights different from those called out for the respective aircraft configuration.

(3) These elevator deflections indicate that the center of gravity location is approximately 29.0% MAC at subsonic speeds (except for pattern speed); and 31.5% MAC at supersonic speeds.

Figure 7-10. (Sheet 4 of 6)

elevator deflection for one-g flight for safe cg location if fuel quantity measuring system malfunctions

Gross Weights* 70,000 and 150,000 Pounds

Mach Number	AIRPLANE WITH TCP PLUS 1 STORE							AIRPLANE WITH TCP PLUS 2 STORES						
	Elevator Position, Degrees UP							Elevator Position, Degrees UP						
	Altitude, thousands of feet							Altitude, thousands of feet						
	S.L.	10	20	30	40	50	60	S.L.	10	20	30	40	50	60
2.0					4.3 / 8.3	5.8 / 11.9	9.6 / 18.2					4.3 / 8.3	5.8 / 11.9	9.6 / 18.2
1.2			4.2 / 7.3	4.0 / 8.1	5.3 / 10.9	8.5 / 15.9				3.8 / 7.0	3.7 / 7.8	5.1 / 10.7	7.8 / 15.7	
0.92	3.3 / 3.9	2.1 / 2.7	1.3 / 2.0	1.4 / 2.5	1.5 / 3.0			3.1 / 3.6	1.9 / 2.5	1.1 / 1.9	1.3 / 2.4	1.4 / 2.9		
0.60	1.1 / 1.6	1.3 / 2.0	1.7 / 2.7					1.0 / 1.5	1.2 / 1.9	1.6 / 2.6				
Pattern Speed (Downwind leg speed)	Minimum 2.8 degrees Maximum 4.5 degrees (regardless of gross weight)							Minimum 2.7 degrees Maximum 4.4 degrees (regardless of gross weight)						

Mach Number	AIRPLANE WITH TCP PLUS 3 STORES							AIRPLANE WITH TCP PLUS 4 STORES						
	Elevator Position, Degrees UP							Elevator Position, Degrees UP						
	Altitude, thousands of feet							Altitude, thousands of feet						
	S.L.	10	20	30	40	50	60	S.L.	10	20	30	40	50	60
2.0					4.3 / 8.3	6.2 / 12.2	9.6 / 18.2					4.4 / 8.3	6.2 / 12.3	9.6 / 18.2
1.2				2.2 / 5.4	2.6 / 6.7	4.2 / 9.8	6.9 / 14.8				1.7 / 4.9	2.2 / 6.4	3.9 / 9.5	6.6 / 14.6
0.92	1.9 / 2.4	1.2 / 1.8	1.0 / 1.8	1.0 / 2.1	1.1 / 2.6			1.3 / 1.9	0.9 / 1.5	0.8 / 1.5	0.8 / 1.9	0.9 / 2.4		
0.60	1.5 / 2.0	1.7 / 2.4	2.0 / 3.0					1.3 / 1.8	1.5 / 2.2	1.9 / 2.9				
Pattern Speed (Downwind leg speed)	Minimum 3.1 degrees Maximum 4.8 degrees (regardless of gross weight)							Minimum 2.9 degrees Maximum 4.6 degrees (regardless of gross weight)						

*(1) Upper number in each block is the lighter weight and the lower number is the heavier weight of the weights called out under the title.

(2) Interpolate or extrapolate linearly for gross weights different from those called out for the respective aircraft configuration.

(3) These elevator deflections indicate that the center of gravity location is approximately 29.0% MAC at subsonic speeds (except for pattern speed); and 30.0% MAC for supersonic speeds.

Figure 7-10. (Sheet 5 of 6)

elevator deflection for one-g flight for safe cg location if fuel quantity measuring system malfunctions

Gross Weights* 70,000 and 150,000 pounds

Note: Plus sign preceding elevator deflection indicates degrees down deflection

Mach Number	AIRPLANE WITH MB OR LA PLUS 2 STORES							
	Elevator Position, Degrees UP							
	Altitude, thousands of feet							
	S.L.	10	20	30	40	50	60
2.0					4.0 8.0	5.0 11.0	9.0 17.4
1.2			1.9 5.1	2.1 6.3	3.4 9.1	6.2 14.2	
0.92	2.2 2.7	1.4 2.0	1.2 1.9	1.1 2.2	1.1 2.6		
0.60	+0.1 0.4	0.1 0.8	0.5 1.5				
Pattern Speed (Downwind leg speed)	Minimum 1.3 degrees Maximum 3.3 degrees (regardless of gross weight)						

*(1) Upper number in each block is the lighter weight and the lower number is the heavier weight of the weights called out under the title.

(2) Interpolate or extrapolate linearly for gross weights different from those called out for the respective aircraft configuration.

(3) These elevator deflections indicate that the center of gravity location is as follows: Subsonic speeds—29% MAC for all indicated configurations (except for pattern speeds); Supersonic speeds—30% MAC for airplane with MB or LA plus pylons.

Figure 7-10. (Sheet 6 of 6)

c. Upon deceleration to subsonic speed, or if failure occurs at subsonic speed, position the cg control knobs to manual and supply the engines from the forward and aft tanks (split feed) and transfer fuel *as required* to maintain, as closely as possible, the elevator positions in figure 7-10.

d. Complete the flight while supplying engines from the forward and aft tanks.

e. Elevator positions between those tabulated for "pattern speed" in figure 7-10 will result in a safe center of gravity for landing at any gross weight. Fuel should be transferred forward to maintain an elevator deflection between the values tabulated in the charts, figure 7-10, at normal pattern, downwind leg, speed regardless of the gross weight of the aircraft.

3. Airplane With Any Pod With or Without Small Weapons (Fuel in Pod).

a. Follow the instructions in item 2 until sufficient fuel has been used from the airplane fuel tanks to allow transferring the pod fuel to the airplane.

b. Transfer pod fuel in predetermined amounts to the forward or aft tank; engine feed is optional but should be considered in determining fuel transfer plans. Monitor the elevator position indicator during the transfer to maintain elevator position indicator reading corresponding to those in figure 7-10.

c. Upon completion of transfer of fuel from the pod, follow the instructions in item 2.

fuel system trouble shooting procedures

Note

- Check the appropriate fuse on the 28V DC panel before assuming valve is malfunctioned. There is no electrical connection to the reservoir refuel valve.

- When DC power is interrupted to the control solenoid portion of the appropriate valve system, the valve will remain in the position it was in at the time of the malfunction.

- Foreign objects may cause a valve to fail in the full closed, full open or partially opened condition. When this happens that valve will not function normally.

- The high level cutoff function of all fuel tank refuel valves is a fluid and pressure function; therefore, an electrical failure will not affect the high level cutoff function.

- In order to positively identify the malfunctioning valve it must be established which tanks do or do not take fuel and from which tanks the fuel is coming. If a particular valve is suspected refer to it in the following procedure. The corrective action should assist in bypassing the malfunction.

Failure	Symptom	Corrective Action
FORWARD TANK REFUEL VALVE FAILED CLOSED	1. Unable to transfer fuel into forward tank. 2. The reservoir tank will fill to only 3900 pounds through reservoir refuel valve when refuel manifold is pressurized from other tanks or during air refueling. 3. CG shift aft will be at normal rate. 4. CG shift forward will be impossible by normal procedures. 5. Engine feeds will be normal.	1. Shift CG forward as follows: a. Scavenge balance tank and open aft tank refuel valve. b. Open balance tank to aft tank interconnect. Fuel will seek common level as follows: AFT TANK BALANCE TANK 38,000 lbs. 8,000 lbs. 31,000 lbs. 4,000 lbs. 24,000 lbs. 2,000 lbs. 17,000 lbs. 1,000 lbs. c. Use aft feed. 2. Forward tank can be emptied by either forward feed, split feed or CG shift aft.

Figure 7-11. (Sheet 1 of 6)

Section VII
Systems Operation

T.O. 1B-58A-1

fuel system trouble shooting procedures

Failure	Symptom	Corrective Action
FORWARD TANK REFUEL VALVE FAILED CLOSED (Cont'd)		3. Transfer fuel from pod to aft tank as needed to preclude exceeding pod tank loading limits and/or CG limits. **CAUTION** Air refueling must be done with extreme caution to keep from exceeding CG limits for flight condition.
FORWARD TANK REFUEL VALVE FAILED OPEN	1. When the refuel manifold is pressurized either by CG shift or refueling, the reservoir tank will fill to 4100 to 4200 pounds and overflow into the forward tank. If the valve has mechanically failed the forward tank will fill up and vent fuel overboard (approximately 5200 pounds per minute) since high level cutoff of forward refuel valve can not function. If the valve has electrically failed, high level cutoff will function normally. 2. CG shift forward will be normal. 3. CG shift aft will be slow since some fuel recycles through open forward refuel valve back into forward tank. 4. Engine feeds will be normal.	**WARNING** Extreme care must be exercised to never completely fill forward tank since fuel will vent overboard. **CAUTION** Air refueling should be done with extreme caution never allowing forward tank to completely fill. 1. Pod fuel should be brought up into internal tanks slowly. Do not allow forward tank to fill up.
FORWARD TRANSFER CONTROL VALVE FAILED CLOSED	1. No CG shift aft either manual or automatic, or by scavenging forward tank. 2. CG shift forward, air refueling, pod fuel transfer and engine feeds will be normal.	1. Forward tank can be emptied by forward or split engine feed. 2. Shift CG aft by transferring pod fuel into aft or balance tank or by forward engine feed.
FORWARD TRANSFER CONTROL VALVE FAILED OPEN	1. When boost pumps 1 or 2 are operating the refuel manifold will be pressurized and fuel will flow from the forward tank into any open tank. 2. CG shift aft will be normal. 3. CG shift forward on aft feed will be normal. 4. The transfer rate on split or forward feed will be slow since some fuel from forward tank will recycle to forward tank. 5. Engine feeds will be normal.	1. Go to aft feed during CG shift forward, air refueling or pod fuel transfer. 2. Forward or split feed may be used at all other times.

Figure 7-11. (Sheet 2 of 6)

7-24

fuel system trouble shooting procedures

Failure	Symptom	Corrective Action
RESERVOIR REFUEL VALVE FAILED CLOSED	1. No symptoms unless reservoir tank is feeding engines and forward tank is below air pressure transfer level. 2. CG shifts, pod fuel transfer, air refueling and engine feeds will be normal.	1. Reservoir tank can be kept full by: a. Air pressure from forward tank. b. CG shift forward through forward refuel valve. c. Pressurizing refuel manifold by balance tank scavenging and opening forward refuel valve.
RESERVOIR REFUEL VALVE FAILED OPEN	1. When the refuel manifold is pressurized either by CG shift or refueling, the reservoir tank will fill to 4100 to 4200 pounds and overflow into the forward tank. The forward tank will fill up and vent overboard, (approx. 5200 pounds per minute). 2. CG shift forward will appear normal. 3. CG shift aft will be slow since some fuel recycles through open reservoir refuel valve back into forward tank.	**WARNING** Extreme care must be exercised so as to never completely fill forward tank as fuel will vent overboard. **CAUTION** Air refueling should be done with extreme caution never allowing forward tank to completely fill. 1. Pod fuel should be brought up into internal tanks and closely monitored. Do not allow forward tank to completely fill.
AUTO TRANSFER VALVE FAILED CLOSED	1. No symptoms unless reservoir tank is feeding engines then reservoir tank will not be kept filled automatically to 3600 pounds level when forward tank is below air pressure transfer level. 2. CG shifts, refueling, pod fuel transfer, and engine feeds will be normal.	1. Reservoir tank may be kept full by forward CG shift, balance tank scavenging, pod fuel transfer, or forward tank scavenging.
AUTO TRANSFER VALVE FAILED OPEN	1. The refuel manifold will be constantly pressurized. Every time a refuel valve is opened fuel will flow into that tank. 2. CG shifts forward and aft will be abnormal. 3. Engine feeds will be normal.	1. For CG shift aft go to forward feed and shift CG aft manually or automatically. 2. For CG shift forward go to aft feed and shift CG forward manually or automatically, fuel will flow from aft and balance tank into forward tank. The rate will be abnormal. 3. Transfer pod fuel as follows: a. To bring pod fuel to aft tank, go to split or aft feed and open aft refuel valve. Place pods to transfer. Pod fuel will enter aft tank along with recycled fuel from aft tank. The rate will be abnormal.

Figure 7-11. (Sheet 3 of 6)

Section VII
Systems Operation

T.O. 1B-58A-1

fuel system trouble shooting procedures

Failure	Symptom	Corrective Action
AUTO TRANSFER VALVE FAILED OPEN (Cont'd)		b. To bring pod fuel to forward tank, go to forward feed and open forward refuel valve. Place pods to transfer. Pod fuel will enter forward tank along with recycled fuel from forward tank. The rate will be abnormal. 4. For air refueling use aft feed and monitor CG and individual tank indications during refueling since some recycling and shifting of fuel may occur.
AFT TANK REFUEL VALVE FAILED CLOSED	1. There will be no fuel quantity increase in the aft tank when the refuel manifold is pressurized and the aft tank refuel valve is positioned to refuel. 2. CG shifts and engine feeds will be normal.	1. Transfer pod fuel as follows: a. Bring pod fuel to forward tank normally. b. Bring pod fuel to aft tank as follows: (1) Place balance tank refuel valve to refuel. (2) Open balance to aft tank interconnect and transfer fuel. Monitor CG closely. 2. For air refueling, with air refueling door not yet opened, proceed as follows: a. Place balance tank refuel valve to refuel. b. Remove 28v d-c balance tank refuel valve fuse. c. While refueling open balance to aft tank interconnect and transfer fuel through balance to aft tank. Monitor CG closely. d. Replace 28v d-c balance tank refuel valve fuse to close balance tank refuel valve. 3. To air refuel with air refueling door open proceed as follows: a. Shift CG aft. b. Remove 28v d-c balance tank refuel valve fuse and stop CG shift. c. Open balance to aft tank interconnect. d. Transfer fuel through balance tank to aft tank. Monitor CG closely. e. Replace 28v d-c balance tank refuel valve fuse to close balance tank refuel valve. f. Close balance to aft tank interconnect.
AFT TANK REFUEL VALVE FAILED OPEN	1. When the refuel manifold is pressurized either by CG shift or air refueling or pod tank transfer the aft tank will receive fuel. If the valve has failed mechanically, high level cutoff of the aft tank will not function and if aft tank is completely filled fuel will vent overboard (approx 5200 pounds per minute). If the valve has failed electrically high level cutoff will function normally.	**WARNING** Do not allow aft tank to completely fill as fuel will vent overboard. 1. Transfer pod fuel into internal tanks as required. Monitor CG and tank quantities closely.

Figure 7-11. (Sheet 4 of 6)

fuel system trouble shooting procedures

Failure	Symptom	Corrective Action
AFT TANK REFUEL VALVE FAILED OPEN (Cont'd)	2. CG shift aft will be slow and abnormal since fuel will enter aft tank as well as balance tank. 3. CG shift forward will be slow and abnormal since fuel will enter aft tank from balance tank as well as enter desired forward tank.	**WARNING** During air refueling do not allow aft tank to completely fill. 2. Monitor CG and internal tank quantities closely during CG shifts.

AFT TANK TRANSFER CONTROL VALVE FAILED CLOSED	1. CG shift forward will be normal until balance tank is empty. Then no more fuel can be shifted forward by CG shift.
	2. CG shift aft, refueling, pod fuel transfer and engine feeds will be normal.
		1. Accomplish CG shift forward when balance is empty as follows:
		  a. Place balance tank refuel-scavenge knob to scavenge.
		  b. Place forward tank refuel scavenge knob to refuel.
		  c. Scavenge pump 13 will place 6000 pounds per hour into balance tank to be used for CG shifts.

AFT TANK TRANSFER CONTROL VALVE FAILED OPEN	1. When boost pump 6, 7, 8 or 9 is operating, the refuel manifold will be pressurized and fuel will enter any open tank. 2. During CG shift forward fuel will flow from both the balance and aft tanks if boost pump 6, 7, 8 or 9 is operating. 3. CG shift aft will be slow if boost pump 6, 7, 8 or 9 is operating since fuel will flow from both the forward and aft tanks into balance tank. Engine feeds will be normal.	1. During CG shifts, air refueling and pod fuel transfer go to forward feed. Fuel movement will be normal. 2. Aft or split feed may be used except during CG shifts, air refueling and pod fuel transfer.
BALANCE TANK REFUEL VALVE FAILED CLOSED	1. CG shift forward, pod fuel transfer and engine feeds will be normal. 2. CG shift aft will be impossible by normal means.	1. To shift CG aft either call for CG shift aft, scavenge forward tank, or transfer pod fuel, then place aft tank refuel knob to refuel or transfer fuel into aft tank. **Note** CG movement will be slower since fuel will enter aft instead of balance tank. 2. During air refueling if fuel space is needed in balance tank, open balance to aft tank interconnect and the two tanks will seek a common level.

Figure 7-11. (Sheet 5 of 6)

Section VII
Systems Operation

T.O. 1B-58A-1

fuel system trouble shooting procedures

Failure	Symptom	Corrective Action
BALANCE TANK REFUEL VALVE FAILED OPEN	1. When refuel manifold is pressurized either by CG shifts, air refueling or pod tank transfer, fuel will enter balance tank. 2. CG shift aft and engine feeds will be normal. 3. CG shift forward will be slower than normal since balance tank fuel will recycle into balance tank through open balance refuel valve.	**WARNING** Extreme care must be exercised to keep CG within limits during all fuel movements. 1. CG shift forward may be assisted by using aft feed. 2. Transfer pod fuel into internal tank carefully. Monitor CG and individual tank quantities during transfer. 3. During air refueling open balance to aft tank interconnect to allow fuel to flow from balance to aft tank to assist in keeping CG within limits for refueling. Tanks will seek common level.
POD REFUEL VALVE FAILED CLOSED (EITHER AFT OR FORWARD)	1. Air refueling of affected pod will be impossible by normal means. 2. Fuel may be transferred from pods to internal tanks normally. 3. CG shifts and engine feeds will be normal.	1. If fuel space is required affected pod can be filled by opening pod interconnect and allow both pods to seek common level. This will be a very slow process.
POD REFUEL VALVE FAILED OPEN (EITHER FORWARD OR AFT)	1. Transfer of pod fuel to internal tanks will be slow since fuel will recycle through open refuel valve into affected pod tank. 2. High level cutoff of affected pod tank may be inoperative in which case fuel will vent overboard if tank is filled completely. 3. CG shifts and engine feeds will be normal.	**WARNING** During air refueling do not fill affected pod completely full as fuel will vent overboard.

Figure 7-11. (Sheet 6 of 6)

BRAKE SYSTEM.

During a stop, the brakes convert a large portion of the airplane's kinetic energy into heat. This energy which is absorbed in the brakes during the stop is dissipated into the surrounding air after the stop. Indiscriminate use of the brakes can cause tire damage due to the resultant heat generated within the brakes. Under normal landing conditions, the brakes should not be used to stop the airplane with the shortest possible ground roll. Since the brake energy capacity is reduced by whatever energy is absorbed while taxiing, braking before takeoff should be held to a minimum to insure that the maximum energy capacity is available in the event that takeoff is aborted. The brakes should not be used to facilitate ground turns. If a reduction in speed is necessary, it should be accomplished before entering the turn. The stopping force which can be produced is limited by either the brake drag capability or by the frictional force which can be developed between the tires and runway surface. At low airplane gross weights, the capability of the brakes may be greater than the frictional force which can be developed if maximum brake pressure is applied. The anti-skid system will prevent tire skids at ground speed above approximately 25 knots. To achieve maximum brake system efficiency, the following procedures are recommended:

1. Applying brakes on a non-frangible wheel with both tires flat will probably cause the wheel to skid, even though the anti-skid system is on. If possible, brake application should be avoided on a gear where both tires on a single wheel are known to have failed. When brakes are applied and wheel skidding occurs, wear is extremely rapid and the skidding wheel will develop a flat spot on the center rolling flange. A "flat-spotted" wheel is not likely to start rolling again, even though the brakes are released. However, it is better for a "flat-spotted" wheel not to resume rolling. To prevent the possibility of the wheel rolling, maintain brake pressure after initial application. Skidding wheel has very little effect on stopping distance. However, a prolonged skid will probably damage the lower landing gear components. Refer to "Landing With Blown Tire" Section III.

2. Take advantage of all possible aerodynamic braking; use the drag chute during all landings and aborted takeoffs, use the full length of the runway; and, utilize wheel braking as required. Intermittent application of medium brake pedal force is recommended rather than a prolonged application of light brake pedal force.

> **CAUTION**
>
> When light brake pedal force is applied, the amount of energy absorbed may not be equally distributed among all brakes. Therefore, prolonged light brake pedal force will greatly increase the possibility of tire blowout.

3. For maximum brake effort stops, apply full brake application until the forward speed has been decreased to approximately 25 knots. Use moderate braking below 25 knots. Refer to "Brake Energy Limits," Section V.

> **WARNING**
>
> Do not taxi the airplane into a crowded parking area or set the parking brakes after the brakes have been used excessively. Peak temperatures occur in the wheel and brake assembly approximately 15 minutes after maximum braking operations. Therefore, danger from brake fire and/or tire explosion exists for approximately 1 hour and 15 minutes.

4. If the brakes are used during touch-and-go landings, allow a minimum of 15 minutes to elapse between landings if the landing gear remains extended or a minimum of 30 minutes if the gear is retracted. A takeoff is not recommended until a sufficient brake cooling period is allowed because the additional tire temperature build-up during takeoff could cause tire failure in the wheel well resulting in serious damage to the airplane. Also, in the event a takeoff must be aborted, the brake energy available will be reduced by the amount retained from the previous stop, and the likelihood of brake failure will be greatly increased. (Refer to "Brake Energy Limits," Section V to determine the amount of energy absorbed during a braked stop and to determine the cooling period required to sufficiently restore the brake capability in the event that takeoff is aborted.) After a new set of brakes has been installed, available static brake torque may not be sufficient to maintain the airplane static when all engines are operating at military power. In order to develop the static torque capabilities of the brakes at an early point in their service life, it is recommended that a brake "burn-in" be accomplished (at gross weights up to 95,000 pounds) during the initial landing after the new brakes are installed. This is accomplished during landing roll by maintaining constant medium braking from 110 knots IAS until the airplane is almost stopped. After this is accomplished, the brakes will hold the airplane static with all engines operating at minimum afterburner.

ANTISKID SYSTEM.

During brake operation with the antiskid switch positioned to ON, the brakes should be applied with a gradual increase in pressure. If the brakes begin to cycle, pressure should be gradually reduced until the cycling ceases. The system should not be forced to cycle anymore than necessary to determine the amount of force on the brake pedals that causes cycling. For most normal landing conditions, when the brake system is operating according to the recommended procedure, the antiskid system will not cycle even though the antiskid switch is positioned to ON.

WARNING

The antiskid system will not prevent tire skids prior to initial wheel spin-up; therefore, landings should not be attempted with brakes applied at touchdown.

Note

Heavy braking with resulting antiskid cycling may cause tire damage below 25 knots. However, slight relaxation of brake pressure will prevent this.

FLIGHT CONTROL SYSTEM.

A description of the flight control system can be found in Section I. An amplification of particular features is presented here to more readily provide an operational understanding of the system. Figure 7-12 shows the maximum deflection of the control surfaces, rates of operation, etc., of the pilot's controls and the trim and damper units. Stick movement limits and surface deflection authority of the elevator control system are shown in figure 7-13.

ELEVATOR CONTROL SYSTEM.

In the elevator control system, the operation of the automatic trim system and the elevator ratio changer in the automatic mode should be particularly noted. The basic computing circuit for automatic elevator trim is indicated in the lower portion of figure 7-14.

flight control system data
WITH MAXIMUM ELEVATOR AND AILERON CONTROL AVAILABLE

		ELEVATOR		AILERON		RUDDER	
PILOT'S CONTROLS	MAXIMUM DISPLACEMENT (INCHES)	6.0 ▼	3.45 ▼	4.5	4.5	3.64	3.64
	MAXIMUM BREAKOUT FORCE (POUNDS)	5		4		7 (Below Mach No. 0.6) 14 (Above Mach No. 0.6)	
	NOMINAL FORCE FOR FULL DISPLACEMENT (POUNDS) ◆	25	19	15		80 (Below Mach No. 0.6) 170 (Above Mach No. 0.6)	
	STICK AND PEDAL TRIM RATE (POUNDS/SECOND)	2.1		0.66		2.0	
CONTROL SURFACE	TOTAL DEFLECTION (DEGREES) FOR ELEVATORS FROM 20° UP TO 23.0° UP FOR ELEVATORS FROM 5° DOWN TO 10° DOWN	23.0 ▼	10 ▼	15 ● 12 Min 10 Min	15 ● 12 Min 10 Min	30	30
	STICK AND PEDAL TRIM AUTHORITY (DEGREES)	10 ▼	10 ▼	5	5	10	10
	AUTOMATIC TRIM AUTHORITY (DEGREES)	10	1.0				
	DAMPER AUTHORITY (DEGREES)	2 ▼	2 ▼	3	3	14.0	14.0
	MAXIMUM AUTOMATIC TRIM RATE (DEGREES/SECOND)	0.2					
	RATE OF DEFLECTION AT 1/2 MAX HINGE MOMENT (DEGREES/SECOND)	20		20		35	

▼ MAXIMUM VALUE (VARIES WITH ELEVATOR AVAILABLE)
● EXCEPT FOR EXTREME ELEVATOR DEFLECTIONS
◆ INCLUDES BREAKOUT FORCE

Figure 7-12.

elevator control system
Stick Movement Limits and Surface Deflection Authority

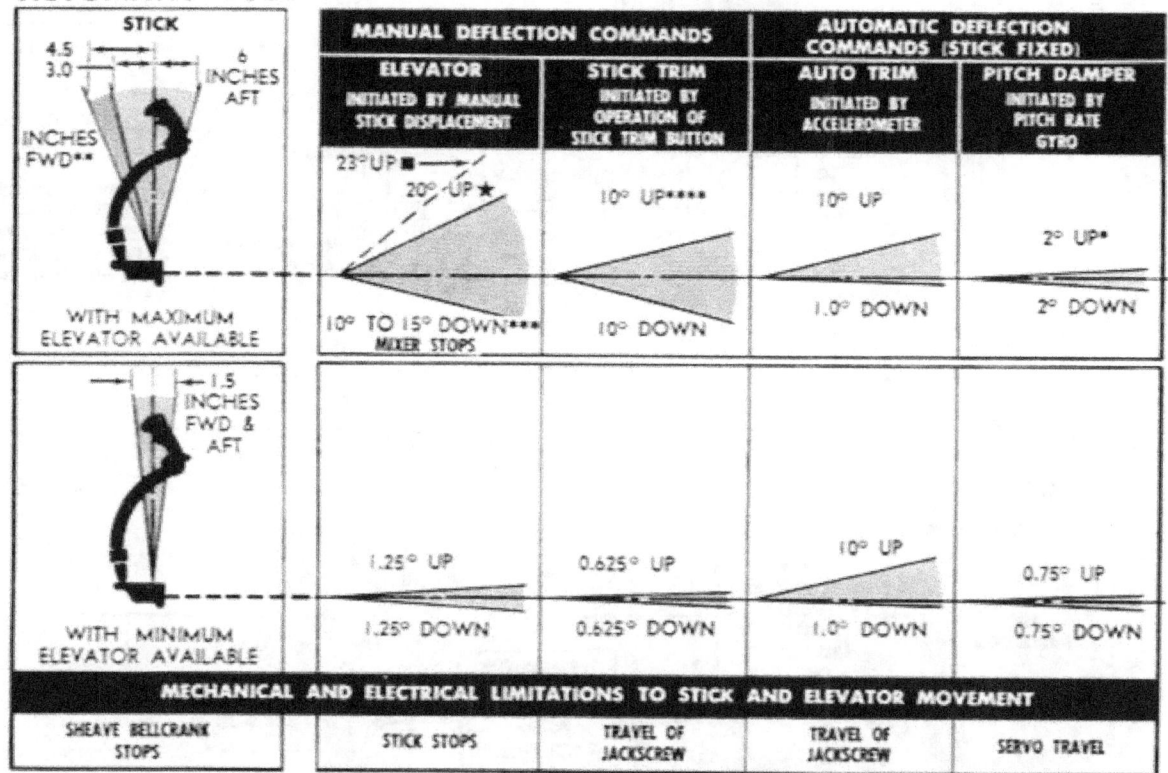

Figure 7-13.

Section VII
Systems Operation

T.O. 1B-58A-1

operation of automatic trim and elevator ratio changer computers

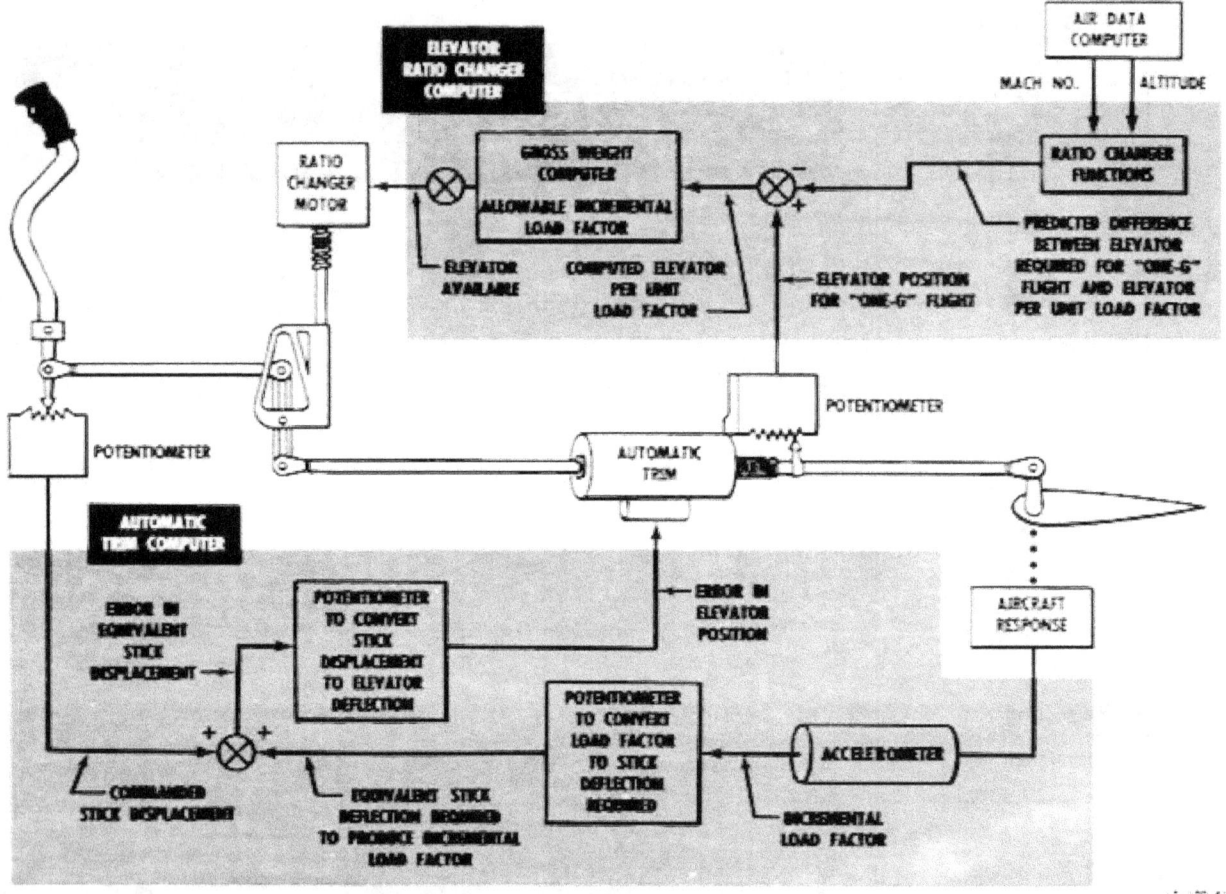

figure 7-14.

The upper portion of figure 7-14 summarizes the computation of the required elevator per unit load factor. The elevator available follows a direct relationship with elevator position in level flight. The primary difference between them is the allowable incremental load factor that can be commanded. Example: If elevator for one-"g" flight is 3 degrees and the airplane gross weight is below 100,000 pounds, for which an incremental 2"g" can be developed, the elevator available will be of the order of magnitude of 2 times 3 degrees, or 6 degrees. Actual relationships between elevator automatic trim position, elevator available, pitch damper authority, and stick trim authority, for a typical supersonic and subsonic cruise, are illustrated in figure 7-15. In the manual mode of the elevator ratio changer, variations in elevator available must be manually adjusted by pilot operation of the elevator control availa-

ble manual adjust switch. It is desirable to adjust the elevator available to a value providing structural protection and adequate elevator control in both forward and aft stick motion. The recommended procedure for determining the elevator available required in the manual mode is as follows:

1. For less than 1.5 degrees elevator required to trim in one-"g" flight:

   a. Read the value of elevator required to trim, from the EPI, with the airplane at a constant altitude in constant speed flight. Determine the elevator available for normal operation in the automatic mode at the particular flight condition using the elevator available nomograms in Part 13, Appendix 1, T.O. 1B-58A-1-1.

   b. Add 1.5 degrees to the elevator available obtained in Step a and set this value with the elevator control available manual adjust switch. Monitor EPI, MACH

7-32

T.O. 1B-58A-1

Section VII
Systems Operation

elevator control system-automatic mode-
Typical Cruise Conditions for Airplanes with MB or LA Pod

Subsonic Cruise

MACH NO.	0.93	CG	29% MAC
ALTITUDE	30,000 FT	ALLOWABLE INCREMENTAL	
GROSS WEIGHT	110,000 LBS	LOAD FACTOR	1.71 G

STICK TRAVEL	ELEVATOR DEFLECTION	PITCH DAMPER AUTHORITY	STICK TRIM AUTHORITY	ELEVATOR AVAILABLE
1.61 INCHES FWD / 1.61 INCHES AFT	For "One-G" Flight (Automatic Trim Position)	±1.72° From Automatic Trim Position	±1.43° From Automatic Trim Position	±2.86° From Automatic Trim Position
	1.5° UP	3.22° UP / 0.22° DOWN	2.93° UP / 0.07° UP	4.36° UP / 1.36° DOWN

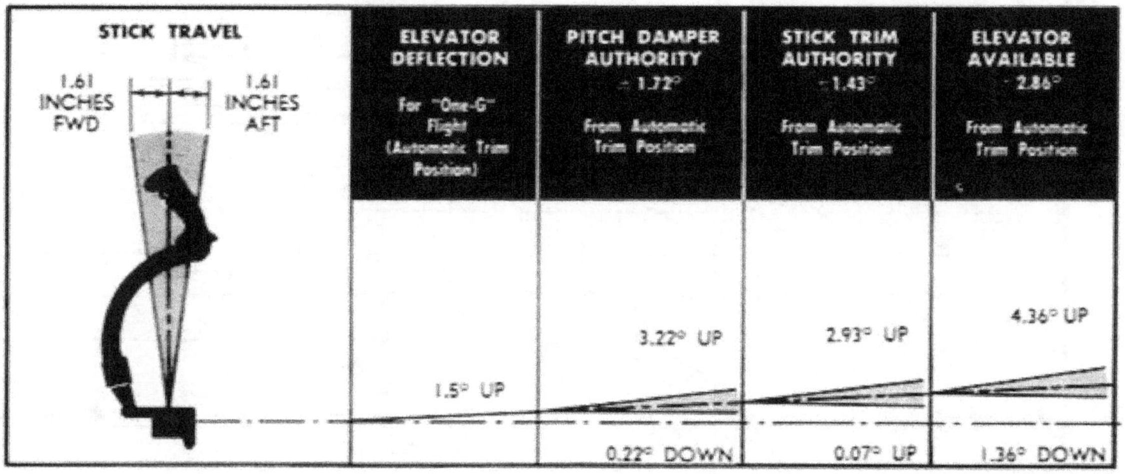

Supersonic Cruise

MACH NO.	2.0	CG	33% MAC
ALTITUDE	45,000 FT	ALLOWABLE INCREMENTAL	
GROSS WEIGHT	110,000 LBS	LOAD FACTOR	1.71 G

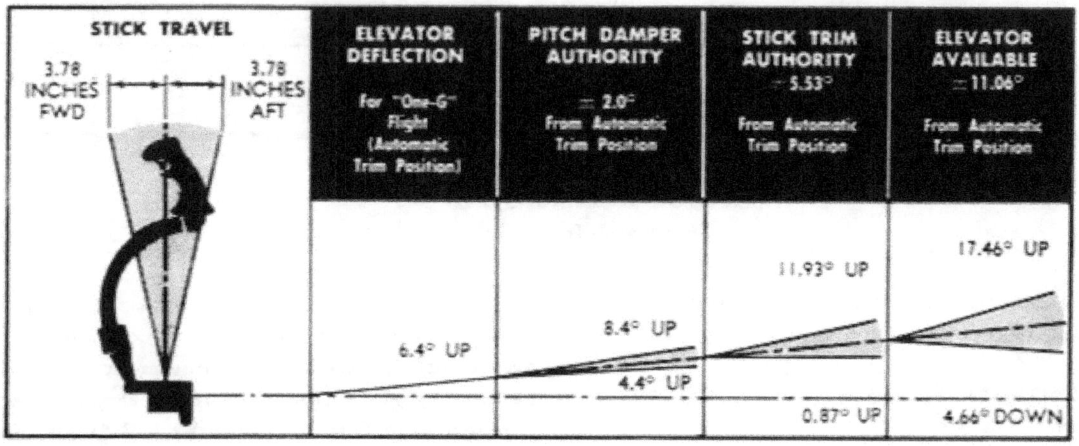 STICK TRAVEL	ELEVATOR DEFLECTION	PITCH DAMPER AUTHORITY	STICK TRIM AUTHORITY	ELEVATOR AVAILABLE
3.78 INCHES FWD / 3.78 INCHES AFT	For "One-G" Flight (Automatic Trim Position)	±2.0° From Automatic Trim Position	±5.53° From Automatic Trim Position	±11.06° From Automatic Trim Position
	6.4° UP	8.4° UP / 4.4° UP	11.93° UP / 0.87° UP	17.46° UP / 4.66° DOWN

Figure 7-15.

Section VII
Systems Operation

T.O. 1B-58A-1

elevator available versus travel of emergency increase elevator available handle

DATA BASIS: ESTIMATED
DATE: 19 MAY 1961

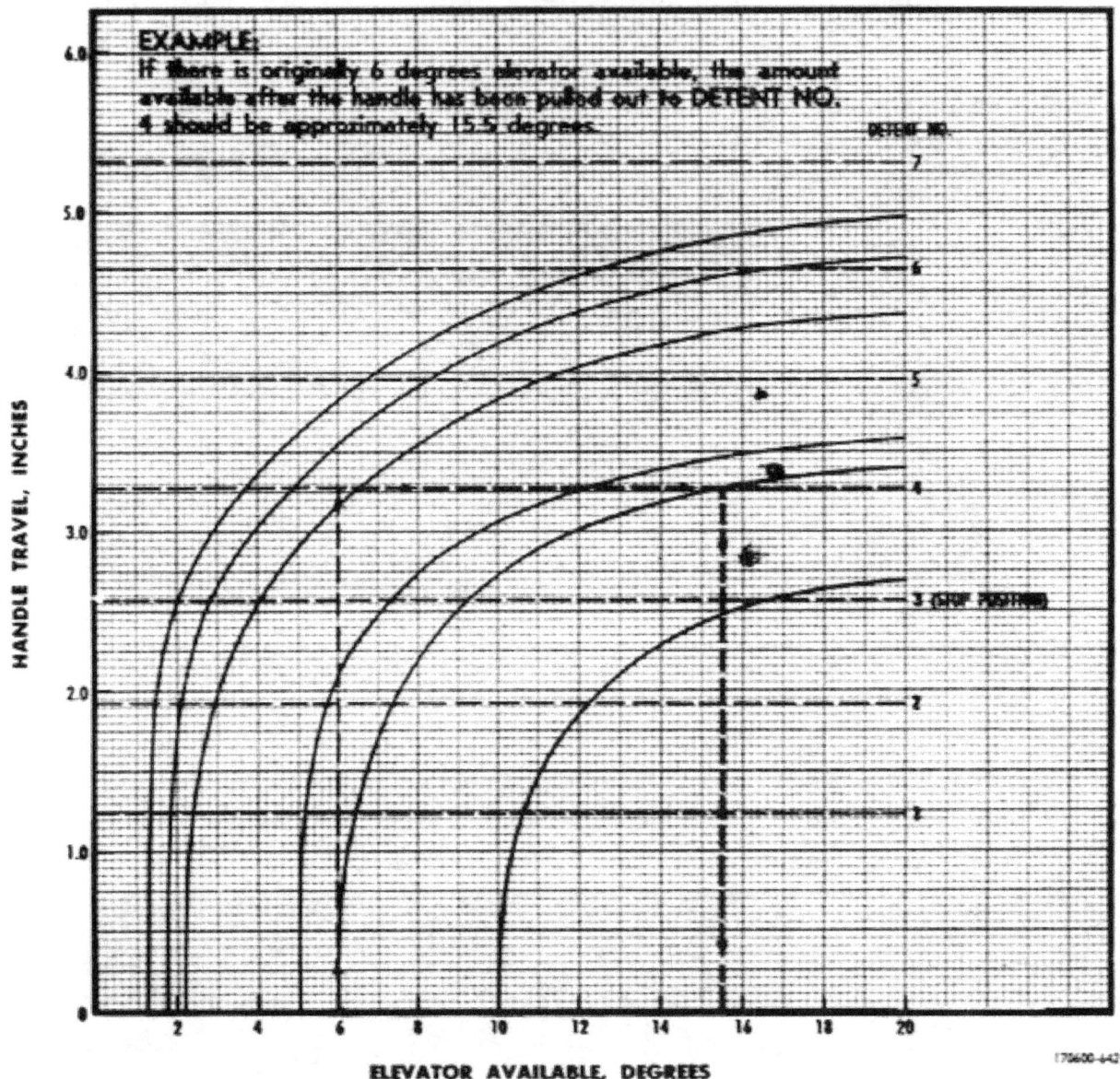

Figure 7-16.

number, and altitude; and readjust the elevator available as required.

2. For greater than 1.5 degrees elevator required to trim in one-"g" flight:

a. Read the value of elevator required to trim, from the EPI, with the airplane at a constant altitude in constant speed flight. Determine the elevator available for normal operation in the automatic mode at the particular flight condition using the elevator available nomograms in Part 13, Appendix I, T.O. 1B-58A-1-1.

b. Add to this the elevator required to trim in one-

elevator available versus gross weight

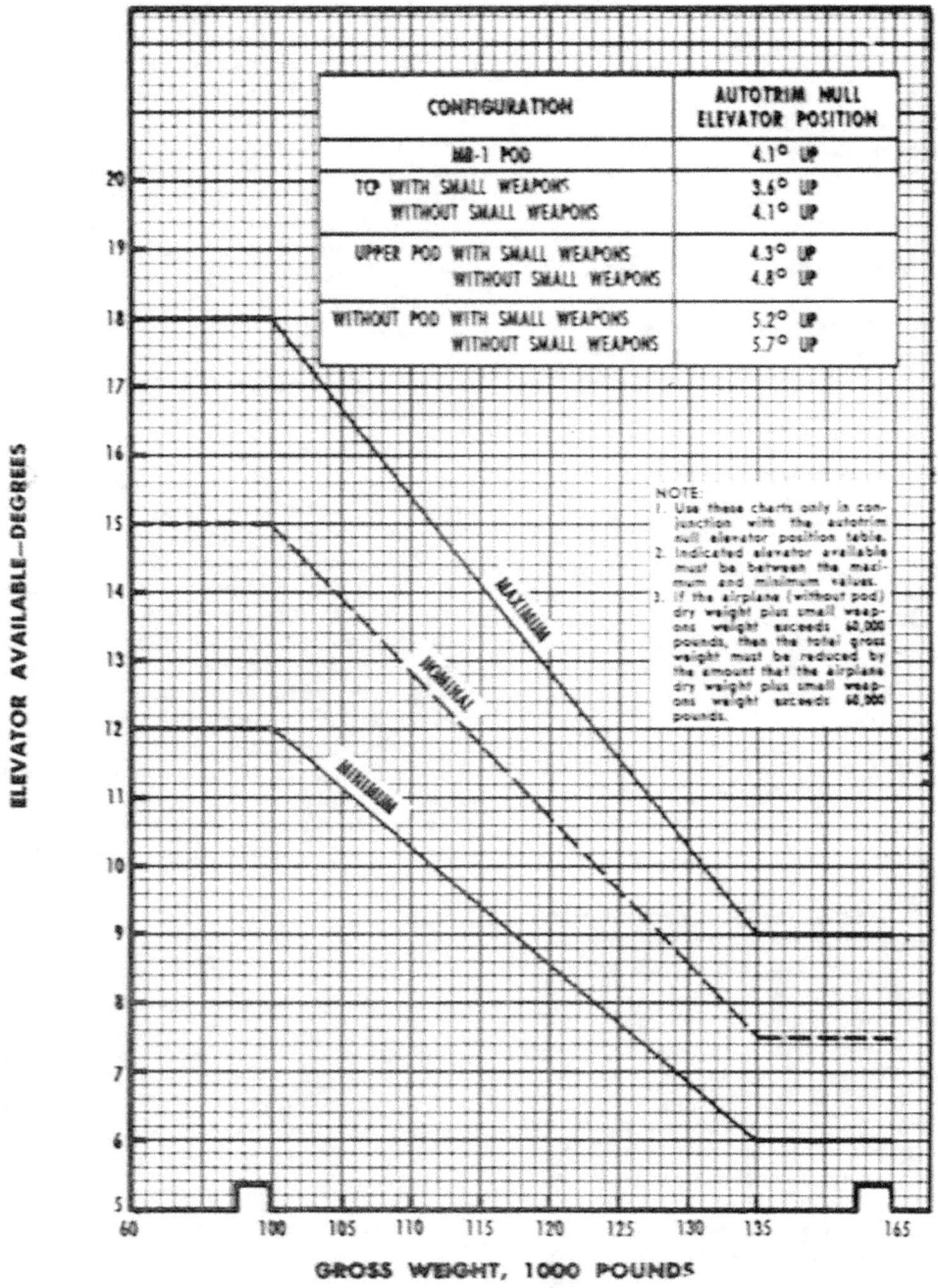

Figure 7-17.

"g" flight as read from the elevator position indicator and set in the sum with the elevator control available manual adjust switch. Monitor EPI, MACH number, and altitude; and readjust the elevator available as required.

3. For operation when the values of elevator available for normal operation are not known, use manual adjust switch to set elevator available equal to twice the elevator position for level flight as shown on the elevator position indicator or 3 degrees, whichever is greater.

Section VII
Systems Operation

> **CAUTION**
>
> These methods provide the minimum values of elevator available that will insure adequate control, but they do not necessarily provide structural protection. Therefore, the pilot should monitor normal acceleration carefully and avoid large or abrupt longitudinal control motion.

EMERGENCY INCREASE ELEVATOR AVAILABLE.

The function of the emergency increase elevator available handle is described in Section I. See figure 7-16 for elevator available versus travel of emergency increase elevator available handle.

ELEVATOR CONTROL AVAILABLE CHECK.

Elevator control available may be checked as follows:

1. Place elevator control available mode switch in AUTO.

2. By means of slight forward or aft stick movements, position autotrim to the elevator position shown in figure 7-17. Use manual trim to relieve all stick pressure (stick free).

3. The elevator available should read within limits shown in figure 7-17 as a function of gross weight.

CONTROL STICK.

During ground operation of the flight controls, when no air loads are imposed on the control surfaces, only a small percentage of the hydraulic system pressure capability is required to move the controls. If the control surfaces are moved at a rapid rate, so that full hydraulic system flow capacity is utilized, system pressure will drop momentarily and may cause a momentary lighting of the hydraulic pump caution lamps. When checking control stick movement on the ground a pulsating kick, known as stick talk back, may be felt at the extreme corners of the control stick limit envelope. This is normal and is caused by the momentary action of hydraulic fluid decompression in the system as the control stick is moved off the extreme limit of its travel. Stick talk back may also be encountered in flight when switching damper channels or under unusually high damper demands such as recovery from severe disturbances. Use of additional stick force makes stick talk back more noticeable. This is caused by control valve bottoming when damper demands are in excess of hydraulic system capacity. Stick talk back has no adverse effect other than on feel at the controls. For further discussion of stick talk back, refer to "Operation in Turbulence", Section VI.

STANDBY GAINS SYSTEM.

The manner by which the standby gains bypass the air data computer, mach-altitude repeater and automatic gain potentiometer is shown in figure 7-18. When the standby gain selector switch is positioned to either HIGH SPEED or LOW SPEED, all signals from the rate gyro and accelerometer package bypass the automatic gain potentiometer and are routed to the dampers through fixed gain resistors. Refer to "Flight Control System" Section I for a description of the standby gains and compatible autopilot modes of operation, and to "Flight Control System Trouble Shooting Procedures," this Section for engagement and use of the standby gains.

FLIGHT CONTROL SYSTEM TROUBLE SHOOTING PROCEDURES.

The flight control system trouble shooting procedures (other than mach-altitude gain adjustment failure) are presented in table-form in figure 7-20. Because of the difficulty in determining component malfunctions of the flight control system, these procedures are presented as corrective actions to be taken when abnormal flight characteristics are experienced by the pilot. For each abnormal symptom, the table also indicates which component could have possibly failed, the characteristics of flight which are peculiar to these component failures, and the corrective action necessary for a safe return flight. Separate procedures are provided for malfunctions in the elevator control system and in the aileron and rudder control systems. In those procedures where the emergency increase elevator available handle should be used, see figure 7-16 for the amount of increase in control available with each detent of the handle.

Note

- For any malfunction listed in the table, if disengagement of the autopilot alleviates the problem, the airplane may still be operated on autopilot in one channel. For example, if the problem is oscillation about the pitch axis and this is corrected by turning off the autopilot, the airplane may still be operated with the roll autopilot engaged.

- The sequence of steps in figure 7-20 is determined by the degree of emergency. Accomplishing the complete procedure to correct a particular malfunction may not be necessary.

MACH-ALTITUDE GAIN ADJUSTMENT FAILURE.

In the event of abnormal flight control system performance, the pilot should take corrective action as outlined in figure 7-20. After control is restored, standby gains should be selected if recommended in the Corrective Action column.

standby gains and gain adjustment system

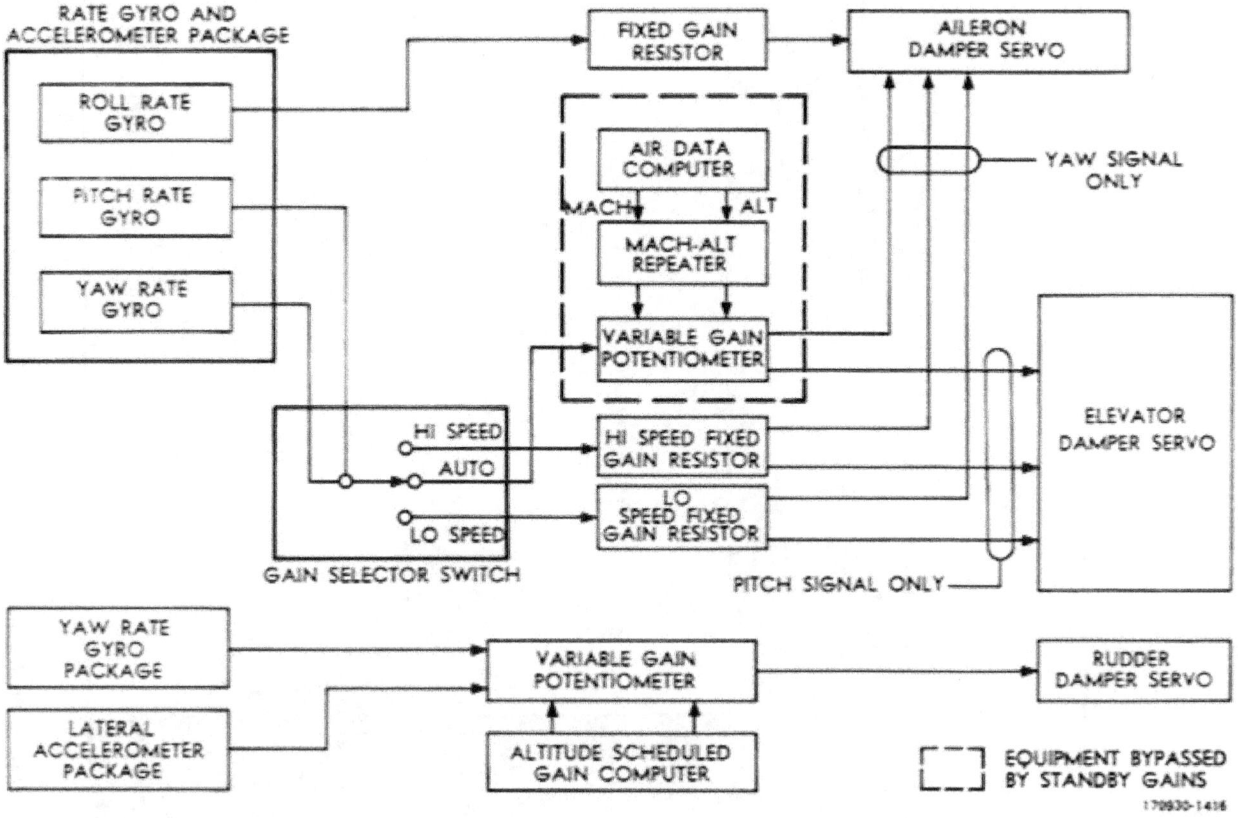

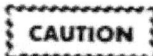

Figure 7-18.

Note

The autopilot and damper switches must be assumed to be in the positions required by the flight control system trouble shooting procedures for the particular condition experienced. Assumption must also be made that a preliminary diagnosis has at least led to isolation of the problem to the roll or yaw channel if the problem is lateral-directional in nature. To avoid significant transients, turn the autopilot OFF prior to selecting standby gains.

The procedure for engagement and use of standby gains is as follows:

1. Check flight condition—Checked.

Do not select standby gains outside of the operating regions or transition corridors. See figure 7-19.

2. Gain selector switch—As required.

CAUTION

Remain within the operating regions or transition corridors.

3. Roll and pitch dampers and autopilot switches—As required.

The damper and/or autopilot switches should be re-engaged to determine if the malfunction still exists.

4. If the malfunction reappears when the damper and/or autopilot are re-engaged, the malfunction is not due to the automatic gain adjustment system. Then automatic gains should be selected with appropriate

Section VII
Systems Operation

T.O. 1B-58A-1

standby gain operating regions

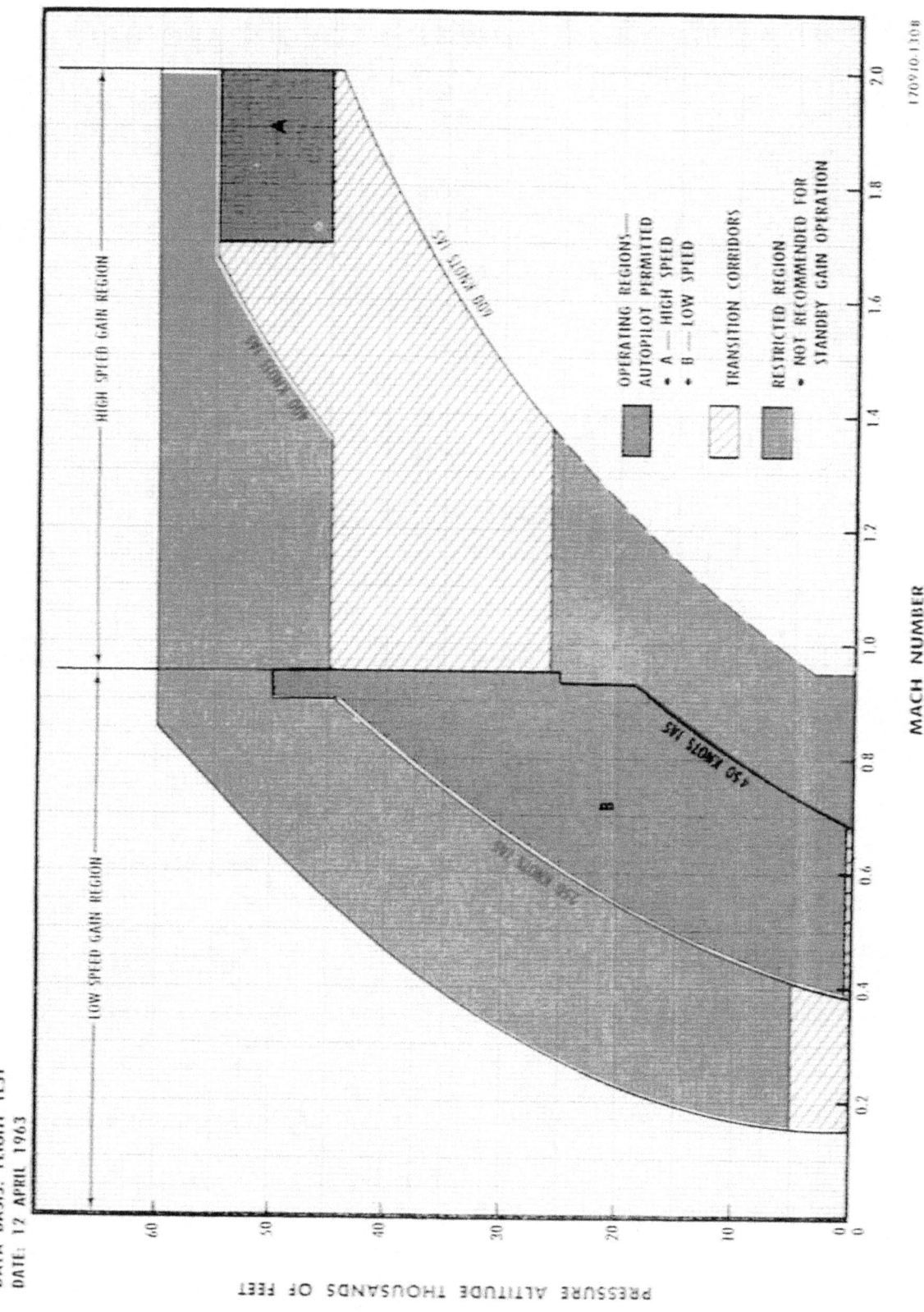

DATA BASIS: FLIGHT TEST
DATE: 12 APRIL 1963

Figure 7-19

damper and/or autopilot turned OFF and the flight restrictions for a damper-off condition should be observed if applicable.

5. Elevator control available mode selector switch—As required.

Monitor elevator available and elevator position for one "g" flight during operation in the automatic mode. If the elevator control available does not maintain itself at the correct value, then position the elevator control available mode selector switch to T.O. & LAND until the elevator control available indicator shows the desired reading, then switch to MANUAL.

6. Elevator control available manual adjust switch—INC or DEC (if required).

Hold the switch to INC or DEC as necessary to obtain the desired elevator available.

WARNING

Structural protection is not assured during operation in the manual mode. However, selecting a level of elevator control available appropriate to flight conditions with the elevator control available manual adjust switch will provide some measure of protection. The control available should be readjusted as the flight conditions change. Refer to "Flight Control System," this section, for the procedure to be followed in selecting elevator available in the manual mode.

Note

Selection of high speed or low speed gains as recommended in the Corrective Action column of figure 7-20 should be based upon the flight conditions defined in figure 7-19.

flight control system trouble shooting procedures

ELEVATOR CONTROL SYSTEM

SIMULTANEOUS ROLL WITH PITCH

Symptom	Failure	Corrective Action
1. Stick moves diagonally instead of fore and aft on elevator command. This stick motion may be induced as a result of a malfunction. 2. Fore and aft stick movement causes roll as well as pitch. 3. Airplane pitches up or down and rolls.	1. One elevon linkage, control valve, or surface actuator jammed. 2. One elevon linkage broken. 3. One elevon linkage broken with elevon hardover action.	**1. APPLY FORE AND AFT STICK ONLY.** Apply force to move stick fore and aft only. Do not allow lateral stick movement. The force required to unstick a valve is a function of elevator and/or aileron available and should not exceed 150 pounds. **2. APPLY RUDDER.** Level airplane using rudder for roll control and stick for pitch control. **WARNING** If malfunction persists, flight to an optimum ejection condition may be attempted but is very hazardous. Do not attempt to land. If control of the airplane can not be maintained immediate ejection is recommended.

Figure 7-20. (Sheet 1 of 14)

Section VII
Systems Operation

T.O. 1B-58A-1

flight control system trouble shooting procedures

SIMULTANEOUS ROLL WITH PITCH (CONT'D)

Symptom	Failure	Corrective Action
		3. Flight to an optimum ejection condition may be attempted as follows: 　a. If too low, climb by slowly transferring the cg aft and slowly increasing thrust. 　b. If too fast, slow down by switching to full aileron available and carefully rolling into a turn to initially lose altitude. As altitude and speed is lost, bank angle can be varied to control load factor and/or altitude. Upon reaching subsonic speed, reduce thrust and level the airplane.

ELEVATOR MOTION RESTRICTED

Symptom	Failure	Corrective Action
1. Stick motion is restricted if less than normal stick travel exists, excessive elevator force is required to displace the stick, or the stick is jammed in a fixed position. 2. Airplane maneuverability is reduced. 3. Stick can be pushed forward but cannot be pulled back. Pilot will not be able to produce positive load factors. Hydraulic system caution lamps will indicate a malfunction. 4. Stick cannot be moved. Auto trim may not operate. Stick may also be restricted in aileron.	1. Autopilot engaged or failed to disengage. 2. Elevator ratio changer runaway to minimum or jammed at low value. 3. One hydraulic system inoperative. 4. Jammed linkage.	**1. AUTOPILOT OFF.** Release the autopilot and check that the autopilot switches return to the OFF position. If the autopilot fails to disengage electrically, apply stick force to actuate the autopilot poppets. **2. CHECK ELEVATOR AVAILABLE.** If elevator available reads low, pop the force link to increase elevator and switch to MANUAL when sufficient elevator available has been obtained. Maintain appropriate value with manual adjust switch. If elevator fails to increase, return to AUTO for subsonic cruise. Decelerate slowly to assure that automatic trim will keep up during transition through transonic region. Prior to landing, use emergency increase elevator available handle. If elevator available cannot be increased by this method, do not attempt to land. 3. Check hydraulic systems. With a hydraulic system malfunction, stick motion is restricted aft only. If at supersonic speed, establish 31.5 percent cg and accomplish procedure for hydraulic system failure. Refer to "Primary or Utility Hydraulic System Failure," Section III. **WARNING** Do not attempt to land.

Figure 7-20. (Sheet 2 of 14)

7-40

flight control system trouble shooting procedures

ELEVATOR MOTION RESTRICTED (CONT'D)

Symptom	Failure	Corrective Action
		4. Flight to an optimum ejection condition is very hazardous but may be attempted. Procedure as follows:
		a. If too low, climb by slowly transferring the cg aft and slowly increasing power.
		b. If at supersonic speed, decelerate slightly with power to determine if auto trim is operative.
		(1) If auto trim is operative, use the throttles to slowly decelerate. Decelerate through the transonic range in a turn to prevent an excessive noseup attitude as the airplane goes subsonic.
		(2) If auto trim is inoperative, start forward fuel transfer. Maintain cg at position for one-"g" flight. Decelerate slowly to subsonic speed using the throttles to control speed and avoid rapid thrust changes. Prior to deceleration to subsonic speed, move the cg as far forward as possible without gaining speed.
		WARNING
		Deceleration to subsonic speed with elevator control jammed and with an aft cg can result in a pitch up to load factors in excess of limit structural load factor in the transonic range.
		Note
		As the cg is moved forward, the airplane will settle to progressively lower altitudes.
		If aileron control is available, decelerate through the transonic range in a turn to prevent attaining an excessively nose-high attitude as the airplanes goes subsonic. If aileron control is not available and airplane starts to roll, maintain wings level by sideslipping the airplane to pick up the low

Figure 7-20. (Sheet 3 of 14)

Section VII
Systems Operation

T.O. 1B-58A-1

flight control system trouble shooting procedures

ELEVATOR MOTION RESTRICTED (CONT'D)

Symptom	Failure	Corrective Action
		wing. The airplane may trim in one-"g" flight again at low subsonic speed. **WARNING** Spin may result from nose high attitude in subsonic speed region. Eject when favorable conditions have been established.

ELEVATOR FREE IN ONE OR BOTH DIRECTIONS

1. Stick free is when the airplane does not respond to elevator in one or both directions. If stick is free in both directions, automatic trim may keep the airplane level if the stick is held in neutral.	1. Cable or linkage failure.	**1. ENGAGE AUTOPILOT.** Use mach-altitude mode to assist in controlling the airplane. 2. Use trim. Leave elevator control available mode selector switch in AUTO and move stick to operate automatic trim for airplane control. Use stick trim if more rapid control is desired. If stick is free in one direction, use sufficient manual trim so that stick force is required to maintain level flight. Note ● Landing may be attempted if stick is free in one direction. Prior to landing, adequate control of the airplane should be demonstrated at a safe altitude. If the stick is free in the aft direction use full manual stick trim in the up direction to insure maximum elevator control for landing. ● Do not attempt to land if stick is free in both directions. Flight to an optimum ejection condition may be attempted. If at supersonic speed, decelerate slowly through transonic speed region and avoid rapid power changes. Do not operate near aft cg limits in the subsonic speed region.

Figure 7-20. (Sheet 4 of 14)

flight control system trouble shooting procedures

PITCH UP OR DOWN

Symptom	Failure	Corrective Action
1. Airplane will pitch up or down either gradual or abrupt. 2. Nose up or down will be gradual and associated with change in flight condition. Push or pull stick force will be required for level flight with changes in flight condition. Elevator available will not change automatically with elevator position for level flight. 3. Airplane will nose-up or down at a moderately rapid rate. For nose up, elevator available will increase to near full available. For nose down, elevator available will move toward minimum. 4. Airplane will nose down if rapid acceleration from cruise speed is made with this malfunction. Elevator available will go to 1.25. 5. Airplane will nose up or down with rapid acceleration or deceleration from cruise speed with this malfunction. 6. Airplane will abruptly nose up or down. Pitch damping will be light and may not be recognized. Turning pitch damper off will normally cause opposite pitch transient. If this transient does not occur, the pitch damper is stuck hardover. Automatic trim, in correcting for this, will provide more than normal elevator available for nose down runaway and less than normal elevator available for nose up runaway. 7. Airplane nose up or down will be moderately rapid. Approximately 12.5 pounds of stick force will be required to maintain level flight. Stick will be neutral for level flight.	1. Autopilot malfunction. 2. Automatic trim failure (not runaway) 3. Automatic trim runaway. 4. Elevator ratio changer runaway to minimum. 5. Electrical failure of ratio changer. 6. Pitch damper hardover. 7. Stick trim runaway.	**1. AUTOPILOT OFF.** Release the autopilot and check that the autopilot switches return to the OFF position. If the autopilot fails to disengage electrically, apply stick force to actuate the autopilot poppets. **2. INCREASE ELEVATOR AVAILABLE.** a. Pop the force link to increase elevator available and switch to MANUAL when sufficient elevator available is obtained. **Note** A controllable pitch transient will occur when elevator available reaches 7 degrees. Use stick trim to reduce stick forces. b. Use emergency increase elevator available handle to increase elevator available to desired value. **Note** A controllable pitch transient will occur when elevator available reaches 7 degrees. Use stick trim to reduce stick forces. If at supersonic speed, use a forward cg for deceleration. **3. PITCH DAMPER OFF.** Observe pitch damper inoperative restrictions. Check standby gains. 4. Autopilot can be used to help release stick force. **Note** Large transient will occur when autopilot is disengaged if stick is not held in trim position.

Figure 7-20. (Sheet 5 of 14)

Section VII
Systems Operation

T.O. 1B-58A-1

flight control system trouble shooting procedures

PITCH UP OR DOWN (CONT'D)

Symptom	Failure	Corrective Action
		For nose up only, switch to **MANUAL** with elevator available greater than 7 degrees. Reduction in elevator available will provide further reduction in stick force. **Note** Do not reduce elevator available less than value of elevator position for level flight. For nose up only, forward cg position will also relieve forces.

OSCILLATION IN PITCH

1. Airplane will oscillate up and down. The oscillation may be lightly damped, sustained or divergent. Stick will follow oscillation. 2. Airplane oscillation probably will be fairly divergent. Stick will move with oscillation while on autopilot. Turning pitch damper off may cause nose up or nose down transient. See information on pitch damper runaway (nose up or down) to determine effect on elevator ratio changer setting. 3. Airplane oscillation may be large. The stick will not follow the oscillation. 4. Airplane appears to oscillate because of pilot overcontrol. 5. Airplane oscillation will be slow. When airplane noses up, elevator available will increase; when airplane noses down, elevator available will decrease.	1. Autopilot malfunction. 2. Pitch damper failure (or hardover) while on autopilot. 3. Pitch damper malfunction. 4. Center of gravity too far aft (in subsonic speed range). 5. Automatic trim malfunction.	**1. AUTOPILOT OFF.** Release the autopilot and check that the autopilot switches return to the OFF position. If the autopilot fails disengage electrically, apply stick force to actuate the autopilot poppets. **2. PITCH DAMPER OFF.** Observe pitch damper inoperative restrictions. Check standby gains. **3. CHECK CG.** Check that the cg is forward of the aft limit for the flight condition. 4. Increase elevator available. 5. Flight control power switch to off. If the preceding corrective action did not turn off the offending equipment turn off the flight control power switch. 6. Elevator control available mode selector switch to manual.

Figure 7-20. (Sheet 6 of 14)

T.O. 1B-58A-1

Section VII
Systems Operation

flight control system trouble shooting procedures

OVER-SENSITIVE CONTROL WITH LOW ELEVATOR CONTROL AVAILABLE

Symptom	Failure	Corrective Action
1. Airplane becomes increasingly sensitive to stick control even though elevator available is minimum. This is normally the result of a slowdown from supersonic or high subsonic speed with the cg position too far aft. This may be the result of inadvertent fuel transfer aft. If gyrations get large, additional control may be needed to keep the aircraft from becoming uncontrollable.	1. Center of gravity too far aft (in subsonic region)	1. Engage autopilot. 2. Move cg forward. 3. Increase airspeed (dive or thrust).

OVER-SENSITIVE CONTROL WITH HIGH ELEVATOR CONTROL AVAILABLE

Symptom	Failure	Corrective Action
1. Airplane is very sensitive to stick motion. Level flight is maintained by automatic trim. Elevator available indicator reads larger than normal.	1. Elevator ratio changer runaway to high available.	1. Elevator control available mode selector switch to manual. 2. Elevator control available manual adjust switch to DEC until appropriate value of elevator available is obtained. **Note** If elevator available cannot be reduced establish cg at 24 percent for subsonic flight. Use stick trim to reduce forces. Maintain adequate elevator available by using elevator control available manual adjust switch.

STICK BUZZ

Symptom	Failure	Corrective Action
1. High frequency stick oscillation which is not followed by airplane response. Normal pilot controlled flight will be available after corrective action is accomplished. 2. Small, high frequency stick oscillation which is not followed by airplane. May not be noticed by pilot.	1. Autopilot malfunction. 2. Pitch damper malfunction.	1. Autopilot off. Re-engage autopilot and use only attitude stabilization mode. Check standby gains. Refrain from using pitch autopilot if problem recurs. 2. Turn off pitch damper. Check standby gains. 3. Flight control power switch off. If the preceding corrective action did not turn off the offending equipment, turn off the flight control power switch.

Figure 7-20. (Sheet 7 of 14)

Section VII
Systems Operation

T.O. 1B-58A-1

flight control system trouble shooting procedures

CONTINUOUS LONG PERIOD PITCH CORRECTION BY AUTOPILOT

Symptom	Failure	Corrective Action
1. Continuous small motion of stick will occur with long period oscillation. **WARNING** This stick motion may not be noticed; a dangerous condition will exist if autopilot is disengaged. This condition may result from slowdown from supersonic or high subsonic speed with the cg position too far aft. It may also be due to inadvertent fuel transfer aft.	1. Center of gravity too far aft (in subsonic region.)	1. Do not release autopilot. 2. Increase airspeed (dive or thrust). 3. Re-establish proper cg position.

FORWARD STICK MOVEMENT WITHOUT AIRPLANE RESPONSE WHILE ON AUTOPILOT

Symptom	Failure	Corrective Action
1. Stick motion will be moderately rapid. Stick may move nearly full forward. Elevator control available indicator will read approximately 20 degrees available. Autopilot operation may be more abrupt and tend toward oscillation more than normal.	1. Nose up automatic trim runaway while on autopilot.	1. If elevator required to trim is less than 1.5 degrees up, transfer fuel to move cg forward. 2. Release autopilot. 3. Elevator available to manual. A moderately rapid nose down transient may occur, indicating automatic trim ran down to the 1.5 degrees index position. After transient, adjust elevator available to sufficient value, using the elevator control available manual adjust switch. 4. Use stick trim to reduce forces.

LOSS OF STICK FEEL

Symptom	Failure	Corrective Action
1. Airplane will appear very sensitive. Airplane control is maintained but there is no sense of feel. Also, there is no increase in force for stick motion; however, the airplane will respond.	1. Failure of stick feel spring.	1. Use autopilot. 2. Refrain from large pitch maneuvers. 3. Leave elevator available mode selector switch in AUTO until normal switchover to TO & LAND.

Figure 7-20. (Sheet 8 of 14)

Section VII
Systems Operation

flight control system trouble shooting procedures

AILERON MOTION RESTRICTED.

Symptom	Failure	Corrective Action
1. Stick motion is restricted if less than normal stick travel exists, excessive aileron force is required to move the stick, or if the stick is jammed in a fixed position. 2. Both stick and rudder will be restricted. Hydraulic system caution lamps will indicate a malfunction.	1. Auto pilot engaged or failed to disengage or aileron control jammed. 2. One hydraulic system inoperative.	**1. AUTOPILOT OFF.** Release the autopilot and check that the autopilot switches return to the OFF position. If the autopilot fails to disengage electrically, apply stick to actuate the autopilot poppets. **2. APPLY RUDDER.** Maintain wings level using rudder to sideslip the airplane. Normal response is for right rudder to raise the left wing and left rudder to raise the right wing. **Note** When flying without a pod at speeds above approximately mach no. 1.9, normal roll response to rudder will be reversed, particularly at the higher altitudes. 3. Check hydraulic systems. If at supersonic speed with a hydraulic system malfunction, establish 31.5 percent cg and accomplish procedure for hydraulic system failure. Refer to "Primary or Utility Hydraulic System Failure," Section III. **Note** Adequate control of the airplane should be demonstrated at a safe altitude prior to landing.

AILERON FREE IN ONE OR BOTH DIRECTIONS

1. Airplane does not respond to aileron commands in one or both directions.	1. Cable or linkage failure.	**1. ENGAGE AUTOPILOT.** Use heading constant mode to assist in controlling the airplane. Use stick trim. **2. APPLY RUDDER.** Level the airplane using rudder for roll control. 3. Manual stick trim as required. Use manual trim to control the airplane. If the stick is free in one direction, aileron control can be obtained by trimming stick in the direction the stick is free so that force is required to maintain wings level. Switch aileron control available to FULL. **Note** Landing may be attempted; however, adequate control of the airplane should be demonstrated at a safe altitude.

Figure 7-20. (Sheet 9 of 14)

Section VII
Systems Operation

T.O. 1B-58A-1

flight control system trouble shooting procedures

LATERAL-DIRECTIONAL OSCILLATION

Symptom	Failure	Corrective Action
1. The airplane will oscillate with a combined yaw and roll motion (dutch roll). The stick will follow the oscillation. Oscillation may be lightly damped, sustained, or divergent.	1. Autopilot malfunction or roll and/or yaw damper malfunction.	**1. AUTOPILOT OFF.** Release the autopilot and check that the autopilot switches return to the OFF position. If the autopilot fails to disengage electrically, apply stick force to actuate the autopilot poppets. **2. DECELERATE.** If supersonic, retard power to decelerate. **Note** Insure that cg is forward of subsonic aft limit prior to decelerating to subsonic speeds. **3. DAMPER(S) OFF (AS REQUIRED).** • If yaw damper warning lamp is lighted, turn off roll and yaw dampers and observe damper inoperative restrictions. • If yaw damper warning lamp is not lighted, turn off roll damper; if oscillation does not subside turn off yaw damper. Observe damper inoperative restrictions. **WARNING** Use rudder or hold a small amount of side-slip to damp oscillation. When operating with roll and yaw dampers off at supersonic speeds, pilot aileron inputs can cause large lateral-directional oscillations to develop. Aileron control must not be attempted except at a very low rate to maintain bank angle within approximately 10 degrees. **4. Gain selector switch—HIGH or LOW** (as required). Place gain selector switch to the HIGH SPEED or LOW SPEED position, as appropriate for the flight condition.

Figure 7-20. (Sheet 10 of 14)

flight control system trouble shooting procedures

LATERAL-DIRECTIONAL OSCILLATION (CONT'D)

Symptom	Failure	Corrective Action
		5. Check damper operation. Turn on the roll damper. If the oscillation reoccurs or increases, turn the roll damper off and observe damper inoperative restrictions. If the oscillation does not reoccur continue the flight on standby gains and observe the applicable restrictions for high speed and low speed gains and/or damper off operation.

ROLL OFF

Symptom	Failure	Corrective Action
1. Airplane roll off may be either abrupt or gradual. The stick will follow the movement. 2. Airplane roll off will be abrupt. The stick will not follow the roll and will be displaced off center to hold wings level. Opposite abrupt roll will occur when damper is turned off. 3. Roll off will be moderately rapid. 4. Gradual roll off (wing heaviness) may be noticed after sideslips or after several uncoordinated turns in one direction.	1. Autopilot malfunction. 2. Roll damper hardover. 3. Stick trim runaway. 4. Asymmetrical fuel loading.	1. Autopilot off. Release the autopilot and check that the autopilot switches return to the off position. If the autopilot fails to disengage electrically, apply stick force to actuate the autopilot poppets. 2. Re-engage the autopilot. Do not use heading mode. 3. Turn off roll damper. A transient in the opposite direction will occur as damper centers. Observe damper inoperative restrictions. Use full aileron available. Refrain from large roll maneuvers Check standby gains. 4. Use stick trim. Autopilot may be used to relieve stick forces. **Note** Large transients will occur at disengagement if stick is not held neutral. 5. Fly straight and level for about 5 minutes. Position wing heavy control switch OFF.

YAW

Symptom	Failure	Corrective Action
1. Airplane will yaw at a gradual, moderate, or abrupt rate depending on engine position and rate of thrust loss.	1. Loss of thrust on one engine. 2. Pedal trim runaway.	1. Maintain wings level with ailerons (except at airspeeds of 240 knots or below). 2. Reduce thrust to military (if in afterburner at other than takeoff).

Figure 7-20. (Sheet 11 of 14)

flight control system trouble shooting procedures

YAW (CONT'D)

Symptom	Failure	Corrective Action
2. Yaw will be moderately abrupt. About 35 pounds of force must be held to maintain zero sideslip. Rudder pedals will be in neutral for zero sideslip flight.		3. Apply rudder gradually to reduce sideslip to zero. 4. Above mach no. 0.6 do not use rudder trim until rudder is neutralized with rudder pedals. Relief of rudder pedal trim force can be obtained above mach no. 0.6 by deflecting rudder pedals against the force (beyond neutral) actuating the rudder trim switch and then returning the pedals to neutral. Extent of force relief is limited by maneuver commanded by pedal deflection. If this proves unsuccessful, pilot must hold force. Autopilot operation will not alleviate the need for pilot to hold forces. Flight at speeds below mach no. 0.6 will reduce the force to be held. 5. Use asymmetric thrust to reduce pedal force required.

PEDAL MOTION RESTRICTED

Symptom	Failure	Corrective Action
1. Rudder pedals restricted in movement or jammed in fixed position. 2. Hydraulic system caution lamps will indicate a malfunction.	1. Jammed rudder channel. 2. One hydraulic system inoperative.	1. Control yaw with asymmetric thrust. Decelerate to subsonic speed. Avoid large or abrupt rolls at subsonic speed. Do not turn yaw damper off. 2. Check hydraulic system. Shut down all unnecessary hydraulic equipment. If supersonic, establish 31.5 percent cg and accomplish procedure for hydraulic system failure. Refer to "Primary or Utility Hydraulic System Failure," Section III.

PEDALS FREE IN ONE OR BOTH DIRECTIONS

Symptom	Failure	Corrective Action
1. Airplane does not respond to rudder in one direction. 2. Rudder will be free in both directions.	1. Cable failure. 2. Linkage failure.	1. Use rudder trim to maintain straight flight. Directional control can be obtained by trimming rudder in the direction the pedal is free so that force is required to maintain straight flight. 2. Use asymmetric thrust to obtain additional control. 3. Decelerate to subsonic speed. 4. Avoid large or abrupt rolls at low speed. 5. Leave roll or yaw dampers on.

Figure 7-20. (Sheet 12 of 14)

flight control system trouble shooting procedures

YAW DAMPER WARNING LAMP LIGHTED

Symptom	Failure	Corrective Action
1. Yaw Damper warning lamp lights (before takeoff or during flight).	1. A malfunction of like components in any two of the three yaw damper channels. (Yaw damper servo automatically disengages and centers.)	● If lamp lights before takeoff: 1. Verify that yaw damper is ON. If it is on, do not take off. ● If lamp lights during flight: **1. AUTOPILOT OFF.** Release the autopilot and check that the autopilot switches return to the OFF position. If the autopilot fails to disengage electrically, apply stick force to actuate the autopilot poppets. **2. DECELERATE AND DESCEND (IF SUPERSONIC).** *Note* Insure that cg is forward of subsonic aft limit prior to decelerating to subsonic speeds. **3. YAW DAMPER OFF.** Turn yaw damper off and observe damper inoperative restrictions. **WARNING** Do not depress yaw reset button. To do so may engage a failed yaw damper channel.

YAW DAMPER CAUTION LAMP LIGHTED

Symptom	Failure	Corrective Action
1. Yaw Damper caution lamp lights (before takeoff, during subsonic flight, or during supersonic flight).	1. A malfunction of a component in any of the three yaw damper channels.	● If lamp lights before takeoff (after engine start): 1. Press yaw reset button. If lamp resets, perform a taxi turn in each direction. If lamp does not relight, proceed with takeoff. As soon after takeoff as practical, perform test given below for "lamp lights during subsonic flight". If lamp does not reset or relights while performing taxi turns, do not take off. ● If lamp lights during subsonic flight: 1. Press yaw reset button. If lamp resets, sideslip airplane at least one

Figure 7-20. (Sheet 13 of 14)

Section VII
Systems Operation

T.O. 1B-58A-1

flight control system trouble shooting procedures

YAW DAMPER CAUTION LAMP LIGHTED (CONT'D)

Symptom	Failure	Corrective Action
		ball width on the turn-and-slip indicator and abruptly release rudder. If lamp does not relight proceed with the flight. If the lamp fails to reset or relights after sideslip, do not exceed mach no. 0.91. ● If lamp lights during supersonic flight: 1. Decelerate and descend. When subsonic, repeat corrective action described for subsonic flight above.
	Note During generator checks, or when bus power is transferred from one generator to another, the yaw damper and/or yaw rate to roll caution lamps may light. If this occurs, press the yaw reset button. If the lamp resets, proceed with the mission. If the lamp does not reset, do not exceed mach no. 0.91.	

YAW RATE TO ROLL CAUTION LAMP LIGHTED

Symptom	Failure	Corrective Action
1. Yaw rate to roll caution lamp lights before takeoff. 2. Yaw rate to roll caution lamp lights during subsonic flight or supersonic flight.	1. Malfunction of landing gear uplock switch. 2. A malfunction of a component in one of the two yaw rate to roll damper channels.	● If lamp lights before takeoff: 1. Do not takeoff. ● If lamp lights during subsonic flight: 1. Press the yaw reset button. If the lamp resets, sideslip the airplane at least one ball width on the turn-and-slip indicator and abruptly release rudder. If the lamp does not relight, proceed with the flight. If the lamp fails to reset or relights after sideslip, do not exceed mach no. 0.91. ● If lamp lights during supersonic flight: 1. Press the yaw reset button. If the lamp resets, continue the flight. If the lamp does not reset, decelerate to mach no. 0.91 or less.

Figure 7-20. (Sheet 14 of 14)

This is the last page of Section VII.

Section VIII
Crew Duties

TABLE OF CONTENTS.

	Page
Crew Coordination	8-1
Navigator's Checklist	8-13
Manual Groundspeed Correction Procedure	8-50
Multiple Drift Procedure	8-50
Radar Position Fix Procedure	8-50
Ground Bombing Computer Check	8-51
Altitude Calibration and Radar Ranging Check	8-51
Defensive System Operator's Checklist	8-52
Ground Crew Alert Checklist	8-57

The purpose of this section is to provide a compact collection of material wherein each crew member can readily determine his duties in relation to the accomplishment of the over-all mission. Instructions relating to crew duties do not include information which is already covered in other sections.

CREW COORDINATION

Coordination of actions within a crew is of prime importance to insure the optimum degree of mission success and safety during all phases of operation. This coordination is not necessarily limited to actions alone. Complete familiarity with one's crew position, the responsibilities thereof and a working knowledge of the other crew members' duties will contribute immeasurably toward crew coordination. Each crew member must be constantly on the alert and should notify the responsible crew member of any deviation or discrepancy which will affect successful accomplishment of the mission. Liaison between individuals concerned must be established prior to initiating any action or procedure which will alter aircraft configuration or require correlation of activities between crew members. Prior to flight the pilot must insure that all crew members are thoroughly familiar with all aspects of the assigned mission as pertains to their crew specialty to include:

1. Applicable instructions in the flight information publications.
2. Departure routes, altitudes, obstructions and traffic procedures.
3. Route of flight.

Section VIII
Crew Duties

T.O. 1B-58A-1

CREW COORDINATION. (CONT'D)

4. Navigation.
5. Air refueling information.
6. Bombing.
7. DECM activities.
8. Gunnery.
9. Normal and emergency communications procedures.
10. Penetration, approach, missed approach, landing patterns, altitudes, and obstructions at both destination and alternate airfields. Available aids such as current FLIP, Terminal and approach charts must be studied. A complete set of current approach charts must be available for in-flight use of each crew member.
11. Any special instructions or procedures pertaining to the mission.

Prior to accomplishment of any of the following, verbal coordination between applicable crew members will be required when:

1. Changing fuel control settings or cg control mode.
2. A crew member goes off interphone or airplane oxygen system.
3. Autopilot is being engaged or disengaged.
4. Autopilot control of airplane is transferred between the navigator and pilot, or vertical reference (stable table) is changed.
5. Any electrical power source is changed.
6. The position of the navigation system function selector knob is changed.
7. A primary navigation system malfunction mode affecting aircraft heading on attitude reference is switched.
8. The facility being monitored on any radio is changed.

COMMUNICATIONS.

The pilot will make the necessary calls for taxi instructions and will receive and acknowledge the ARTC clearance. He will also normally make the necessary calls to departure and approach control. The pilot or DSO will normally make the radio calls. The navigator will monitor communications at all times, and assist with communications when required. The DSO will normally make the necessary calls on the high frequency radio. During takeoff and other critical phases of flight, the navigator and DSO will set the interphone control panel function selector knobs to COMM 1 or COMM 2. The navigator will place the COMM mixing switch to radio not selected by function selector knob and DSO will place both COMM mixing switches ON.

LOW ALTITUDE NAVIGATION.

During low altitude tactical operations, special emphasis by all crew members will be directed to maintain route corridor, proper airspeed and prescribed altitudes. Crew coordination is extremely essential for each change of heading, airspeed and/or altitude. The DSO will notify the crew when altitude or airspeed deviates significantly from that planned. The navigator will announce the new heading, altitude, and ETA/ETE to next turn point. This information will be crosschecked by the pilot and DSO. The pilot will monitor airplane position and take necessary action to insure corridor limits are not exceeded.

PILOT.

The pilot is the crew commander and is responsible for the airplane and crew. The successful accomplishment of the mission is of prime importance; in no instance, however, will the safety of the airplane or crew be compromised. The pilot is responsible for the issuance of instructions governing all phases of flight operation. In addition to his regular function, the pilot will perform the following:

Mission Preparation.

1. Attend general briefing.
2. Coordinate with other crew members on route charts, targets, items pertinent to individual crew procedures, and supervise the completion of required forms.

T.O. 1B-58A-1

**Section VIII
Crew Duties**

Mission Preparation. (Cont'd)

3. Complete Form 175.
4. Coordinate with other crew members to establish position reporting points and cruising altitudes.
5. Prepare Form 70 (or equivalent) or obtain a copy of the flight plan for inflight use.
6. Attend specialized briefing.

Preflight And Operating Procedures To Level-off.

Accomplish the checklists and procedures as outlined in Section II. The DSO will read checklists as required or at the pilot's request.

Cruise.

1. Level off at predetermined altitude and establish appropriate power setting.
2. Monitor navigation to insure knowledge of airplane position at all times.
3. Check with DSO at regular intervals concerning aircraft performance, fuel transfer, gross weight and cg, and actual fuel consumption versus predicted.
4. Analyze incidents or discrepancies which necessitate change of flight plan and make appropriate decisions.
5. Monitor all engine and systems instruments periodically.
6. Insure that position reports and the required GCI, RBS and HF radio contacts are completed.
7. Accomplish oxygen, station, and periodic weapon checks at appropriate intervals.

Air Refueling.

Perform air refueling checks as outlined in Air Refueling Flight Manual, T.O. 1-1C-1-6 and complete the refueling operation as briefed.

Photo Run.

Pilot will inform navigator when to turn camera operate switch on and off during target run.

Bomb Run.

1. Establish and maintain bomb run Mach number and altitude.
2. Coordinate with the navigator to accomplish bomb run procedures.
3. Call time-to-go at 200, 100, 30, 20 and 0 second intervals. Request tone ON at approximately 10 seconds time-to-go.
4. After bomb release, disengage the heading switch, perform escape maneuver, if applicable, and at appropriate time, zero steering error on PDI for next destination and re-engage the heading NAV mode.

Descent, Landing And Afterflight Procedures.

Accomplish the check lists and procedures outlined in Section II.

NAVIGATOR.

The navigator must work continuously with the pilot and DSO to insure successful completion of the mission. During all critical phases of flight, the navigator will monitor indicated airspeed, altimeters, and attitude indicator to insure immediate recognition of a dangerous condition and so advise the pilot.

Section VIII
Crew Duties

T.O. 1B-58A-1

Mission Preparation.

1. The general mission planning should be accomplished with the cooperation of the other crew members.

2. Attend general briefing.

3. Obtain necessary metro data for route and target area to include:

   a. Wind and temperature data for all phases of the flight.

   b. Location of jet streams and unusual weather phenomena.

   c. Pressure pattern information, if required.

   d. Navigation and fuel planning may be completed using climatic data. The low altitude portion (high penetration fix to high exit fix) of the flight plan may be completed using a no wind condition and standard day temperatures. An operational forecast will be reviewed prior to takeoff. If the forecast weather data will adversely affect the mission or mission timing, the necessary replanning will be accomplished prior to takeoff. For subsonic climb and supersonic acceleration, climb and cruise, the forecast temperature should be considered. The amount of fuel used may vary substantially as the temperature departs from standard.

4. Select maps and charts of suitable scale and projection as dictated by the requirements of the mission. Polar navigation will require charts gridded with a transverse coordinate overlay. Additional charts should be available to provide coverage for emergency changes in the flight plan.

5. The complete route will be plotted on charts.

   a. Turns and overruns past targets will be considered when drawing the mission route on maps.

   b. Turns will be computed for the turn point prior to the target on low level navigation legs to roll out on the planned/briefed axis of attack (started short of turning point).

   c. All other turns will be started when over the briefed turning point and/or target.

6. The Jet Mission Flight Plan (Form 200) will be completed in accordance with the following instructions. (See figure 8-1 for typical example).

   a. Show all times and date in Zulu. Enter duration of flight as logged in Form 781.

   b. Each line of the flight plan provides for the navigation/performance plan for one leg or flight condition. Off-load and on-load lines will be provided to facilitate fuel and cg computations associated with air refueling, gunnery, chaff drop, and weapon release. Entries for variable or changing conditions not of navigation or performance significance will be entered as VAR (variable). A check mark (✓) may be used to indicate no change from the preceding entry. Blocks not requiring specific entry may be left blank.

      (1) ROUTE—The route may be entered in coordinates, in relation to a radio aid or as a geographic description. The first line will be used to record the total predicted fuel used to start, taxi, and stabilize. The second line will be used to record the total predicted fuel, time and distance for takeoff, acceleration to climb speed, and climb to the jet departure fix or level-off position.

      (2) FLT COND—Optional. May be used to indicate significant points such as ARIP, ARCP, etc.

      (3) TC—Enter intended true course in three digits. For transverse operation, enter both true and transverse course.

      (4) W/V—Enter sea drift values or flight planning W/V (climatology or forecast).

Mission Preparation. (Cont'd)

(5) DC—Enter drift correction.

(6) TH, VAR, MH—Self explanatory.

(7) TEMP AND ALT—For cruise legs, enter standard day or forecast temperature and altitude for end of leg. For descent/climb legs enter average temperature and the altitude for the end of leg. For high altitude cruise legs, where altitude is changed over a small portion of the leg, enter temperature for major portion of leg and altitude for end of leg.

(8) IND MACH AND TAS—For cruise legs, enter Mach No. or IAS for end of leg as applicable. For legs involving changing mach numbers, VAR may be entered. Enter TAS as computed from mach and temperature or an average TAS for legs involving changing flight conditions. Average TAS for climb/descent/acceleration and deceleration can be determined by time and air distance from the performance charts.

(9) TWC AND GS—Enter TWC if desired. Enter ground speed for leg.

(10) GRD DIS AND ACC GRD DIS—Enter ground distance for leg. For timing delays enter zero ground distance. For supersonic releases, which require a breakaway, enter the ground distance from level off to bomb release point. Enter accumulated total ground distance to the end of the leg.

(11) TIME AND ACC TIME—Enter time required for the leg. Enter accumulated total time to the end of the leg. Time for descent to low level will be determined from available performance charts or by dividing altitude changed by desired descent rate.

(12) AIR DIS AND ACC AIR DIS—Optional.

(13) ETA—Enter ETA to the end of each leg.

(14) ATA—May be utilized for recording time of arrival if IFP/recorder is inoperative.

c. Use of the back side of Form 200 is optional.

7. The navigation chart(s) and/or flight plan will contain the following annotations:

a. Restricted, warning, danger, alert and prohibited areas within 50 NM of the planned route and within the planned FLIP altitude structure will be clearly marked as to time and altitude limitations.

b. Geographical coordinates for all turn points and for fix points spaced at intervals no greater than 300 NM for high altitude navigation and 100 NM for low altitude navigation.

c. Climb, descent, level off, acceleration and deceleration points for low level and supersonic activity.

d. Air refueling control point (ARCP), receiver IP, AR descent point, and end air refueling.

e. HHCL and PCTAP.

f. True to transverse correction angle (B angle) for entry and any turn points exceeding 20 degrees.

g. For low level navigation, add the following:

(1) Obstructions within 20 nautical miles of track if not already appearing on chart.

(2) IFR/VFR altitudes for each segment of the route, including penetration and withdrawal.

(3) Magnetic course/heading and estimated time between points of planned heading and altitude changes.

(4) IFR/VFR route corridors.

(5) Timing points for emergency bombing.

h. Position reporting points when other than turning points.

8. Accomplish target study for normal and emergency bombing on each target as applicable.

Section VIII
Crew Duties
T.O. 1B-58A-1

navigators mission flight plan — form 200 (typical)

MISSION FLIGHT PLAN

PILOT	COPILOT	NAVIGATOR	RADAR NAVIGATOR	EW OFFICER	GUNNER OR BOOM OPR	SQ	WING	CREW NO	ACFT TYPE	ACFT SERIAL NO
BOTT, MAJ.		SMITH, CAPT.		FOX, CAPT.		068	300	S-99	B-58A	61-2000

ENGINE START 0020 | TAXI 0749 | TAKEOFF 0100 | DURATION OF FLT 6:50 | DATE OF TAKEOFF 1 JAN 68

FROM / ROUTE	COND PTS	T.C.	W/V / DC	T.H.	VAR	M.H.	ALT / TEMP	IAS / MACH	TAS / T.W.C.	GS	ACC. GRD DIS / GRD DIS	ACC. TIME / TIME	ACC. AIR DIS / AIR DIS	ETA	ATA	REMARKS
BUNKER HILL AFB																
START–																
TAXI-STAB																
SID #3																
BATTLEGROUND		009	250/50 / -5	004	-1	003	29.0 / -42	.91 M	537	560	70 / 260	:09 / :28		0109		
GRB 089/84											330	:37		0137		
TIME PAD									:01½			0138½	C.T.				
4710N SAW	HI ENT	330	↓ / -5	325	0	325	20.0 / -42	↓ M	537	525	184 / 514	:20½ / :59		0159		
5829W 319/68																
4710N-8913W		270	290/30 / +1	271	0	271	11.0 / -16A	435 KIAS	534A	505	30 / 544	:03½ / 1:02½		0202½		
4740N-8920W	LO ENT	360	288/15 / -2	358	0	358	2.4 / +1A	.752A M	486A	480	35 / 579	:04.4 / 1:06.9		0206.9		
4745N-8920W	TP #1	360	L/V / 0	360	0	360	2.4 / +1	.701 M	458	458	5 / 584	:00.6 / 1:07.5		0207.5		
REMAINDER OF LOW ALTITUDE ROUTE			288/15								257 / 841	:33.5 / 1:41		0241		
4510N-8547W	S/C	255	+1	256	+2	258	10.0 / +2A	425 KIAS	483	469	29 / 870	:04 / 1:45		0245		
4510N-8633W		255	290/25 / +2	257	+1	258	12.0 / (-7)	↓ M	500A	480	34 / 904	:04 / 1:49		0249		
4443N-8607W		097	290/40 / -1	096	↓	097	21.0 / -18A	↓ M	542A	581	40 / 944	:04 / 1:53		0253		
GRB 088/114	HI EXIT	097	290/40 / -1	096	↓	097	25.0 / -31A	.904 M	546A	586	24 / 968	:02½ / 1:55½		0255½	C.T.	
4640N-8533W																
DLH 089/100		314	250/50 / -5	307	-1	308	31.0 / -46	.91 M	532	505	232 / 1200	:28½ / 2:24		0324		
DLH 059/112		360	↓ / -5	352	-1	354	31.0 / -46	↓ M	↓	550	58 / 1258	:06 / 2:30		0330		
OFFLOAD AMMO – CHAFF																
4553N-9104W	ST	200	↓ / +4	204	-2	202	↓ / -50	↓ M	500	500	128 / 1386	:15 / 2:45		0345		
4511N-9019W	ACC	142	+4	146	-2	144	33.0 M	↓	527	540	55 / 1441	:06 / 2:51		0351		

Figure 8-1. (Sheet 1 of 2)

T.O. 1B-58A-1

Section VIII
Crew Duties

FROM ROUTE	LGHT COND FLT	T.C.	W/V DC	T.H.	VAR	M.H.	TEMP ALT	IAS MACH	TAS T.W.C.	GS	GRD DIS ACC. GRD DIS	TIME ACC. TIME	AIR DIS ACC. AIR DIS	ETA	ATA	REMARKS
4511N-9019W			250/50				-50				50	:04				
4431N GRB	S/C	143	↓4	147	-2	145	33.0 M	VAR	725A	738A	1491	2:55		0355		
8936W 268/59		↓	245/65	147	-2	145	VAR	M VAR	945A		57	:03				
4347N GRB	L/O		↓4				49.0 M			958A	1548	2:58		0358		
8847W 208/52			↓	146	↓	144	49.0 M	2.0	1150	1164	50 1598	:02½ 3:00½		0400½		
VORTAC MKE 096/08	BRL	143	↓3					↓	↓		25	:01.3				
RIGHT TURN		VAR	↓					M			1623	3:01.8		0401.8		
BREAKAWAY			↓	140	-2	138	VAR 37.0 M	.91	828 ±20	1150 848	63 1686	:04.5 3:06		0406		
5NM EAST WOODSTOCK, ILL.	L/O	135	±5					M								
REMAINDER OF ROUTE								M								
ARIP	SD	099	270-60 ±1	100	-2	098	-58 37.0 M	.91	522	582	40 2798	:04 5:14		0614		
4039N-8609W	ARCP	↓	↓	↓			VAR	M VAR	535	595	100 2898	:10 5:24		C.T. 0624		
4023N-8358W	END A/B	100	↓	101	±2	099 103	24.0 M 25.0 M	↓ .80A	482	542	115 3013	:13 5:37		0637		
4004N-8130W							M									
ON LOAD FUEL							M									
3937N-7846W		101	↓	102	±4	106	-42 29.0 M	.91	538	598	130 3143	:13 5:50		0650		
SPRINGFIELD, OH		279	↓ -2	277	±4	281	-40 28.0 M	↓	540	498	231 3374	:28 6:18		0718		
BRL 219/40		276	↓	274	0	274	↓	↓	↓	↓	134 3508	:16 6:34		0734		
PENT AND LAND							M					:15 6:49		0749		

Figure 8-1. (Sheet 2 of 2)

8-7

Section VIII
Crew Duties

Mission Preparation. (Cont'd)

9. Complete the Bombing Data Form, SAC Form 298, in accordance with instructions in T.O. 1B-58A-25-3 and SACM 55-10 with the following exceptions:

   a. Bombing Data Form: Pre-Flight Computations

   (1) GEOGRAPHIC DATA: For successive runs on the same target, only the target need be entered if the remainder of the data is the same.

   (a) TGT, WEAP, LOC—Enter RBS/NIKE site and target designator, type weapon ballistics used (if desired), weapon selector position (if desired) to simulate a specific sequence of weapon release.

   (b) OAP DESCRIPTION—Enter OAP description and elevation for planned synchronous runs.

   (2) PREFLIGHT BALLISTICS: (Left-hand column) Compute prior to flight. For *High Altitude* computations use climatological or latest metro data. For *Low Altitude* computations use either standard day information or metro data from the final weather briefing. For successive runs on the same target, when the same altitude is planned, preflight ballistics need not be recomputed. Only the ATF and TRAIL to set in the computers need be entered.

   (a) IND PRES ALT, HSL—Enter planned indicated pressure/pressure altitude for the run. For *Low Altitude* computations: Indicated pressure altitude is the term for FAA assigned altitude corrected for altimeter setting and is to be used for low altitude ballistics computations. It is not to be confused with the altitude the pilot actually reads on his altimeter. The pilot will set the current altimeter setting in the Kollsman window and fly the assigned FAA altitude corrected for the B-58 altimeter position error. Compute the indicated pressure altitude IAW SACM 55-10 using the space provided at the lower left-hand corner of the bombing form. Subtract 29.92 from predicted ground level altimeter setting. Reverse the sign and convert to feet by multiplying the value shown in PAV line by a *minus* 1000. Apply the PAV in feet to the FAA assigned bomb run MSL altitude to obtain indicated pressure altitude. (For multiple releases, this value need only be entered in the first column.)

   (b) TAB TF, TAB L—Enter tabulated values of TF and L.

   When making high altitude RBS runs with HSL less than 25,000 feet, use TF and L values for 25,000 feet HSL and subtract "A factor" corrections for the appropriate computed HSL.

   (c) HB COR—When making high altitude RBS runs, apply HB correction without interpolation. If HB is half-way or more between the two tabulated height of burst altitudes, go to the higher altitude; if less than halfway, go to the lower altitude.

   (3) TIMING INITIATION POINT: (Left-hand column) Compute prior to flight. Items necessary to compute MH and GS are mandatory (i.e. TC, W/V, DCA, GS, TH, VAR and MH values).

   High Altitude: For high altitude computations use climatological or latest metro data. The following items (D-TGT, L, D-VIP, TIME TO VIP, TF, and TIME TO RELEASE) are optional for high altitude bombing because a suitable high altitude timing initiation point is not always available. They will be computed when possible to provide timing information.

   Low Altitude: Low altitude computations will be based on the planned aircraft position, abeam or over the TIP or in relation to the RB/FRM to the target for single/first releases and from bomb release point to the next target for multiple releases.

   (a) TC, D/V—Enter true course to target; enter wind used.

Mission Preparation. (Cont'd)

        (b) DCA, GS—Enter drift correction angle; enter ground speed.

    (4) EMERGENCY TIMING POINT: (left-hand column) Compute prior to flight. This will normally be the information used to establish the time of bomb release when accomplishing an emergency run. The radar return to be used may be either the target itself, a return other than the target, or a return used to establish the bomb release point. If desired, timing may be computed from more than one return. For successive runs on the same target(s), when the same timing point, altitude, true course, and groundspeed are planned, only the planned T-REL need be entered.

  b. Bombing Data Form: Inflight Computations

    (1) INFLIGHT BALLISTICS: (right-hand column) If *High Altitude* inflight HSL and TAS differ from preflight, recompute ballistics in accordance with the instructions for preflight ballistics. When inflight HSL and TAS are the same as preflight, only the TF and L values need be entered. When auto ballistics are used, enter AUTO in the inflight TF and L Columns. *Low Altitude:* If standard day information was used to compute preflight ballistics, then metro from final weather briefing or inflight metro must be used to compute inflight ballistics. When inflight HSL and TAS are the same as preflight, only TF and L values need be entered.

    (2) TIMING INITIATION POINT: (right-hand column) Information will be computed when there has been a significant change in HSL, TAS or GS. If timing information is included on a separate bombing form, timing sheet, or chart, only time to release and computations necessary to determine magnetic heading and ground speed need be entered.

    (3) EMERGENCY TIMING POINT: (right-hand column) Information will be recomputed when there has been a significant change in HSL, TAS or GS. If timing information is included on a separate bombing form, timing sheet, or chart, only time to release need be entered.

    (4) RELEASE DATA:

        (a) SCHED TIME, REL TIME—Enter planned and actual bomb release times.

        (b) θH, θT, DCA—Enter actual true heading and true course read from the panel and compute the value of Drift Correction Angle.

        (c) HSL, VG, VA—Enter height above sea level, groundspeed and true airspeed at time of release.

        (d) RBS SCORE, TYPE, SEA DRIFT—Enter encoded RBS score, type of release accomplished, and sea drift values set in the equipment.

10. Celestial data planning for flight will be accomplished on celestial data form (figure 8-2) in accordance with the following instructions:

  a. Preflight.

    (1) PLANNED TIME—Enter the approximate time that an astro lock will be initially attempted. If flight is a day/night flight, enter initial time for each period.

    (2) BODY—Enter the name of the body selected.

    (3) GHA—Enter GHA of the Sun/Planet for the planned time. This entry is required only once.

    (4) +360—Self explanatory.

    (5) TOTAL—Self explanatory.

    (6) −GHA—Enter the GHA of Aries for the planned time.

Note

Items (4), (5), (6) will be utilized to compute SHA of the Sun/Planets if desired.

Section VIII
Crew Duties

T.O. 1B-58A-1

celestial data form (typical)

CELESTIAL DATA						
NAME Smith	DATE 10 May 68	ACFT. NO. 011	WING 43		SQDN. 64	
PLANNED TIME	1430	1655				
BODY	Sun	Procyon				
GHA BODY	034-15	062-20				
+ 360 (IF NEC)	360					
TOTAL	394-15					
— GHA γ	073-10					
SHA BODY	321-05	245-40				
DEC	S 8-45	N 5-19				
TIME	1500	1530	1600	1655		
PRES. POS. LAT.	70-18N	68-18N	60-28N	52-40N		
PRES. POS. LONG.	010-36W	035-40W	040-38W	040-38W		
INTERCEPT	2 T		15A	14 T		
ZN	180		185	199		
θT		273	266			
VG		560	551			
TAS		534	538			
TRUE TRANS HDG	270	270	262	180		
÷ B ANGLE	270	268	250			
TOTAL	540	538	512			
—360 (IF NEC)	360	360	360			
TRUE HDG	180	178	152	180		
VAR	—30	—40	—42	—20		
MAG HDG (COMPUTED)	150	138	110	160		
B-16 OR J-4 MAG HDG	152 271	140 272	120 262	162		
DIFF	2 1	2 2	10 0	2		
ADJ. POS. LAT.						
ADJ. POS. LONG.						
W/V - SEA DRIFT		S10 W23		270/39		

Figure 8-2.

Mission Preparation. (Cont'd)

    (7) SHA—Enter tabulated SHA. Enter computed SHA of the Sun/Planets if desired.

    (8) DEC—Enter declination of the body selected.

  b. Inflight.

    (1) TIME—Enter time of observation.

    (2) PRES POS LAT—Enter latitude.

    (3) PRES POS LONG—Enter longitude.

    (4) INTERCEPT—Enter star altitude error.

    (5) ZN—Enter azimuth of the body.

    (6) TRACK, VG, TAS—To be completed at the navigator's discretion.

    (7) TRANS HDG—Enter PNS transverse heading.

    (8) +B—Enter measured B at time of observation.

    (9) TOTAL—Self explanatory.

    (10) −360—Self explanatory.

    (11) TRUE HDG—Enter computed true heading or PNS true heading as applicable.

    (12) VAR—Enter variation at time of observation.

    (13) MAG HDG—Enter computed Mag Heading.

    (14) B-21 or J-4 MAG HDG—Enter heading from B-21 or J-4 compass system. If operating with J-4 compass system in transverse, this column will be divided and both B-21 and J-4 compass readings entered.

    (15) DIFF—Enter the difference between computed Mag Heading and B-21 or J-4 compass reading. If operating with J-4 in transverse, enter the difference between computed Mag Hdg and B-21 compass and the difference (precession) between transverse heading and J-4 compass reading.

    (16) ADJ POS LAT—Enter the adjusted latitude if present position latitude counter is reset on celestial data.

    (17) ADJ POS LONG—Enter the adjusted longitude if present position longitude counter is reset on celestial data.

    (18) W/V SEA DRIVE—Enter W/V used or computed or sea drift set if doppler is inoperative.

Note

Minimum navigation information requirements for operation with an IFP malfunction and/or manual navigation are: time, track and groundspeed or time, true heading, true airspeed and wind.

11. Programming Navigation Leg forms, manual navigation leg forms and the inflight portion of celestial data sheets may be used in lieu of map station circles for recording inflight data obtained while flying programming navigation legs, manual navigation legs or integrated systems navigation legs, as appropriate. If desired, any of these forms may be used to record general navigation data in event the inflight printer is inoperative.

12. Airborne radar approach planning will be accomplished, using current patterns in FLIP terminal high altitude charts.

Section VIII
Crew Duties

T.O. 1B-58A-1

Mission Preparation. (Cont'd)

13. Record briefed PI beacon code, if applicable.
14. Attend specialized briefing.
15. Determine maintenance history and condition of the navigation system from A&E personnel.

Preflight And Operating Procedures To Level-off.

1. Accomplish the checklist and procedures as outlined in this section.
2. Respond to the command response items on the pilot's checklist when appropriate.
3. Monitor airplane attitude, heading and airspeed during takeoff and departure.

Cruise.

1. Perform cruise procedures as outlined in this section.
2. Coordinate with the pilot periodically on airplane position, heading and ground speed. Compute or revise ETA's as necessary and advise crew.
3. Monitor penetration, low level headings, altitudes, and withdrawal procedures.
4. Request airspeed calibration runs and steering changes when necessary.
5. Coordinate on communications procedures as necessary.
6. Accomplish station checks as follows:
   a. Fuse panels—Checked.
   b. Oxygen system—Pressure checked.
   c. Instrument cross check—Altimeter, airspeed, attitude, and J-4 compass.

Air Refueling.

1. Conduct rendezvous using all available equipment.
2. Monitor airplane position during air refueling by use of the primary navigation system.

Bomb Run.

1. Perform required checklists and procedures as outlined in this section.
2. Coordinate with the pilot in completion of the checklist.

Descent, Landing And Afterflight Procedure.

Accomplish the checklists and procedures as outlined in this section. Monitor penetration, low approach and missed approach procedures with particular emphasis on altitude restrictions.

DEFENSIVE SYSTEM OPERATOR.

The primary responsibility of the DSO is the utilization of defensive systems to provide electronic defense against ground based and airborne electronic devices and active fire control against airborne interceptors. The secondary responsibilities of the DSO are:

1. To assist (as directed by the pilot) with the pilot's "Exterior Inspection."
2. To read checklists as required.
3. To monitor airplane performance and advise pilot as necessary on fuel management, fuel consumption, optimum altitude and cg.
4. During all phases of flight, the DSO will monitor the mach-airspeed indicator and altimeter to insure immediate recognition of a dangerous condition and so advise the pilot.

Mission Preparation.

1. Attend general briefing.
2. Accomplish study of all intelligence data necessary for the accomplishment of the DECM and fire control portion of the mission.
3. Accomplish flight planning in coordination with other crew members.
4. Accomplish weight and balance and fuel management portion of mission planning with pilot.
5. Attend specialized briefing.
6. Coordinate with A & E personnel to determine history and status of DECM and MD-7 equipment.

Preflight And Operating Procedures To Level-off.

1. Accomplish the checklists and procedures as outlined in this section and in Section II.

Cruise.

1. Perform Cruise procedures as outlined in this section.
2. Maintain inflight log. Complete a station check at least each hour during subsonic flight and each 15 minutes during supersonic cruise to include a full column recording on the inflight log.
3. Advise pilot as necessary concerning fuel configuration, cg and fuel consumption.
4. Coordinate on communications procedures as necessary.
5. Monitor the mach-airspeed indicator to insure that the airspeed is compatible with the Mach number.
6. Coordinate with crew during penetrations, low altitude flight, approaches and missed approaches with particular emphasis on altitude restrictions.
7. Accomplish oxygen and station check.

Air Refueling.

1. Record fuel tank readings and then advise the pilot concerning fuel loading, configuration, fuel on-loaded, gross weight and cg. Complete fuel tank readings and cg computations will be obtained prior to and after refueling.

Descent, Landing And Afterflight Procedures.

1. Accomplish the checklists and procedures as outlined in Section II.
   Compute flare speed and stopping distance.

NAVIGATOR'S CHECKLIST

The navigator will respond to all uncoded items read by the DSO. All items which are coded require response from the applicable crew members indicated as follows: (P) Pilot, (N) Navigator, (DSO) Defensive System Operator, (GO) Ground Observer. Those procedures contained within blocks entitled "EWO ONLY" are to be accomplished only in the event an actual pod or small weapon release is desired. For training missions the items within the blocked in area will be simulated. For supplementary information concerning pods, special weapons, and associated equipment refer to T.O. 1B-58A-25-1. All items in **BOLD FACE** beginning with the SCRAMBLE/SRP POWER-OFF SCRAMBLE checklist are the minimum requirements for a training or EWO scramble takeoff if time prohibits accomplishing the entire checklist. Bold face items which are not required to be accomplished during EWO operations, if they would delay takeoff, are so noted in the amplification of the line item. See alert procedures, Section II, for additional information and checklists concerning alert line operation. Checklist titles followed by (NAVIGATOR READS) will be read by the navigator over interphone. On airplanes equipped with the pod camera control panel in place of the weapon monitor and release panel the items flagged with ▶ and the items contained in the EWO ONLY blocks in the Navigator's Checklist need not be accomplished. When a checklist title is flagged ▶, the flag applies to that entire checklist. Items coded **SF** (strange field) need only to be accomplished when operating from an airfield where maintenance personnel are not familiar with the airplane.

8-13

Section VIII
Crew Duties

T.O. 1B-58A-1

PREFLIGHT CHECK.

BEFORE EXTERIOR INSPECTION.

1. Form 781—Checked.

EXTERIOR INSPECTION.

There is no specified exterior inspection for the navigator. The items of equipment peculiar to navigator functions are checked visually by the pilot as part of his Exterior Inspection.

POWER-OFF INTERIOR INSPECTION.

CAUTION

To prevent damage to equipment due to overheating, ac power should not be applied to the airplane until step 26 is completed.

Note

During inspection of the airplane/weapon combination, if any discrepancy is found that is not specifically covered in the malfunction analysis section of the Nuclear bomb pod/bomb delivery technical manual (T.O. 1B-58A-25-2), all physical operations on the airplane/weapons will cease until qualified personnel have determined the necessary reporting and/or corrective action to be taken. The term "Qualified Personnel" is defined as a qualified nuclear weapons officer (wing weapons or munitions maintenance officer) and a nuclear safety officer.

1. Canopy lock—Installed.
2. Emergency lighting switch—ON.
3. Canopy layback lockpins (2)—Installed.
4. Handgrip safety pins (2)—Installed.
    Before entering the airplane, check that safety pins are installed in both handgrips.
5. Canopy actuator warning pin—Check.
    Check that the canopy actuator warning pin is not visible.

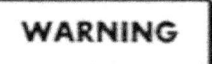

The red pin, when visible, indicates that the canopy actuator ballistics charge has been fired rendering the associated canopy jettisoning system inoperative.

Note

During some weather conditions, it may be desirable to close the canopies upon entering the crew stations. In this case, insure canopy locks are removed prior to closing canopies.

6. Canopy jettison handle safety pin—Installed.
    Upon entering the airplane, and before any personal equipment is placed in the compartment, check that canopy jettison handle safety pin is installed.
SF 7. Escape capsule—Checked.
   a. Oxygen supply lever—ON.
   b. Disconnect engagement indicator—Checked.
      Check that the indicator window shows white. If red is showing, the disconnect is not properly seated. Check for no air leakage at the disconnect standpipe.

POWER-OFF INTERIOR INSPECTION. (CONT'D)

    c. Door seal condition—Checked.
8. Safety belt and shoulder harness (manual and automatic)—Checked.
9. Oxygen—Checked.
    a. Adapter connector and mask bayonet fitting—Checked and connected.
    b. Regulator bayonet fitting—Checked.
    c. Oxygen pressure—Checked (70-110 PSI).
    d. Oxygen supply lever—ON.
    e. Oxygen flow and mask leakage—Checked.
    f. Oxygen pressure—Checked (70-110 PSI).
    g. Emergency oxygen pressure—Checked (1800 PSI at 70°F).
10. Canopy seal control lever—UNSEALED.
11. Weapon lock and arm panel:
  ▶ a. Pod warhead control selector switch—OFF, OS, and sealed.
  ▶ b. Small weapon lock switches (4)—LOCK and sealed.
    c. Safety lock handle—In, horizontal and sealed.
    d. Mechanical release handle—In, horizontal.
▶ 12. Small weapon warhead control selector switches (4)—OFF, OS, and sealed.
13. Weapon monitor and release panel:
  ▶ a. Auto release switch—OFF.
        Check full down detent.
  ▶ b. Weapon selector switch—OFF.
14. Pod camera control panel: (if installed)
    a. Pod air conditioning control switch—OFF.
    b. V/H control converter power switch—OFF.
    c. V/H control selector switch—MANUAL.
    d. Camera power switch—OFF.
    e. Camera operate switch—OFF.
15. Recorder power switch—OFF.
16. Auxiliary control panel:
    a. Search power switch—OFF.
    b. Doppler transmitter switch—OFF.
    c. Function selector knob—GYRO.
    d. Doppler return switch—LAND.
    e. Magnetic variation knob—Local value.
    f. Radio altimeter switch—OFF.
    g. Sea drift indicators—Zero.
17. RV Beacon power knob—OFF.
18. PI beacon power knob—OFF.
19. Voice warning system monitoring switch—VWS.
20. Canopy control—OPEN.
21. Airspeed inertial switch—NORMAL.
22. Bomb damage evaluation (BDE) power switch—OFF.
23. Tracking and flight controller selector knob—OFF.
24. Auxiliary flight reference system power switches—OFF.
    Place flight reference indicator power switch and auxiliary flight reference system power switch to OFF.
25. Low altitude radar altimeter—OFF.
26. TACAN power knob—OFF.

Section VIII
Crew Duties

POWER-OFF INTERIOR INSPECTION. (CONT'D)

27. J4 compass controls—Set.
    Set J-4 compass function selector knob to MAG, hemisphere selector to applicable hemisphere, and latitude correction knob to local latitude.
28. ICU switch—NORMAL.
29. Search test normal/override switch—NORMAL.
30. Aimpoint selector knob—FIX.
31. Malfunction control panel switches—As required.
    a. Auto steering switch—ON.
    b. All other switches—OFF or NORMAL.
32. Astro control panel:
    a. Heading reference selector knob—FLUX VALVE.
    b. Astro filter switch—As required.
33. Search radar indicator panel:
    a. STC knob—CCW.
    b. Display intensity knob—Centered.
    c. Antenna tilt knob—β (Beta) detent.
    d. Manual/auto receiver tuning switch—AFC.
    e. PPI switch—OFST.
    f. Radar sighting switch—MAN.
    g. Sector knob—60 degrees.
    h. Beta (β) switch—AUTO.
    i. VRM knob—As required.
    j. AZ MK knob—As required.
    k. FRM knob—As required.
    l. Relative bearing knob—Zero degrees.
    m. Search radar mode selector knob—GRD.
    n. Range/magnification selector knob—30/10.
    o. Variable threshold knob—As required.
    p. Video knob—Centered.
34. Navigation control panel:
    a. Polar/non-polar switch—As required.
    b. Coordinate reference switch—As required.
35. Ballistics control panel:
    a. All malfunction controls—OFF or NORM.
    b. Ballistics—Set for ballistics check.
        (1) Set Tf—38.2 seconds.
        (2) Trail—76,000 feet.
        (3) Ballistic wind indicators—Zero.
36. Sighting and Test Panel:
    a. Fixpoint selector knob—PRESENT POSITION.
    b. Malfunction test selector knobs—Zeroed and in detent.
    c. Auto radar photo switch—OFF.
37. Required publications—Checked.
    Appropriate FLIP terminal high altitude charts (4 for ZI flights) and enroute supplement.

BEFORE TARGET AREA (CONT'D.)

Note

The first action by the pilot on his POWER-ON INTERIOR INSPECTION will be a check of the interphone and bailout warning system. This will be the signal to the Navigator to prepare to respond to checklist items.

POWER-ON INTERIOR INSPECTION.

Note

For explanation of asterisk (*) refer to COCKING checklist.

1. "Power-off Inspection"—Complete. (N-DSO)
2. Bailout alert lamps (2)—Checked. (N)
   When the alert lamps flash on and off check the "hot mike" with the interphone function selector knob in INTER.
3. Bailout warning lamps (3)—Checked. (N)
   When the warning lamps light check the "hot mike" as in step 2, above.
4. Interphone—On call, normal (2), aux listen, hot mike. (N)
   For normal interphone check, check both floor microphone buttons. For aux listen interphone check, use capsule microphone button.
5. Voice Warning System—Checked. (N-DSO)
   Check for voice warning system monitoring capability.
6. Weapon lock and arm panel:
   * ► a. Pod warhead control selector switch—SAFE.
   * ► b. Release system activated lamp—Off, press-to-test.
*► 7. Small weapon warhead control selector switches (4)—SAFE.
8. Weapon monitor and release panel:
   * ► a. Lock indicators (5)—LOCK.
   * ► b. Arm indicators (5)—SAFE.
   * ► c. Navigator's master warning lamp—Off, press-to-test.
   * ► d. Weapon selector switch—POD.
   * ► e. Pod and weapon released lamps (5)—Off, press-to-test.

Note

The pod released lamp will not press-to-test if an MB pod is installed.

   * ► f. Weapon selector switch—OFF.
   * ► g. Auto release ready lamp—Off, press-to-test.
   * ► h. Release signal present lamp—Off, press-to-test.
*► 9. Pod warhead control selector switch—OFF.
*► 10. Small weapon warhead control selector switches (4)—OFF.
11. Camera pod lock indicator—LOCK (if installed).
12. Interior lights (5)—Check.
    Turn on and check all interior lights, and adjust. Check for spare bulbs and fuses.

8-17

Section VIII
Crew Duties

POWER-ON INTERIOR INSPECTION. (CONT'D)

13. All remaining warning and press-to-test lamps (10)—Checked.
    Check by press-to-test the following: PNS erect lamp, BDE indicator lamp, RBS lamp, manual steering indicator lamp, ILS-TACAN control indicator lamp, waveguide pressure lamp, RTM pressure caution lamp, doppler lock indicator lamp, and hard landing indicator lamps (2).
* 14. High voltage d-c power panel and battery power panel fuses—Checked.
    Check for blown, poorly seated, and adequate spare fuses.
15. Report to pilot—"Power-On Inspection" complete.

BEFORE STARTING ENGINES.

1. Personal gear—Connected and checked. (P-N-DSO)
   Safety belt, shoulder harness, oxygen hose connected and oxygen check complete.
2. Communications panel—Set. (N-DSO)
3. Canopy lock—Removed. (P-N-DSO)

Do not attempt to remove the canopy lock when the weight of the canopy is on the lock. Failure to observe this precaution may allow the canopy to fall on a crew member.

▶4. Weapon lock indicators (5)—LOCK.
5. Camera pod lock indicator—LOCK (if installed).

BEFORE TAXIING.

The navigator's BEFORE TAXIING checklist contains those items necessary to effect coordination with the pilot, and DSO during their BEFORE TAXIING checklist. In addition, it contains those items necessary to place the radar and PNS in operation. In the event the navigator has not completed his BEFORE TAXIING checklist by the time the pilot is ready to taxi, taxiing need not be delayed to complete the navigator's BEFORE TAXIING checklist except for items 37 and 38. Taxiing prior to completion of the BEFORE TAXIING checklist may increase the time required for the stabilization tables to fully erect or PNS heading to orient itself depending upon length of time system has been in operation prior to taxiing, outside air temperature, etc.

Note

For hot weather operation, PNS and radar turn-on may be delayed until such time as is deemed necessary to have an operational system by takeoff time.

1. Canopies—Closed and latched. (DSO-N-P)
   Close canopy when instructed and report when the latching mechanism indicator flags are out of sight. Sequence: DSO, navigator, pilot.

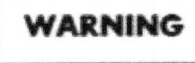

Each canopy latching mechanism indicator flag must be out of sight behind its shield to indicate positive locking of the canopy.

8-18

BEFORE TAXIING. (CONT'D)

2. Canopy seal lever—SEALED. (N) (When requested).
3. Electrical power and air conditioning—NORMAL. (P)

CAUTION

Do not proceed to STANDBY with the function selector knob or search power switch until notified that the electrical system is stabilized on aircraft power. The system cannot be erected unless normal voltages and frequencies are present.

4. Function selector knob—STANDBY.
   For minimum PNSU gyro warmup time in GYRO prior to switching to STANDBY subtract six minutes from the value obtained from T.O. 1B-58A-1-2.
5. Search power switch—STBY.

Note

If the indicator console unit (ICU) switch, located on the search radar test panel, is in the NORM position, the ICU display will not be present until the search radar is transmitting. There is a 5 minute delay before the transmitter can be energized. If, after the 5 minute delay, it is desired to view the ICU display (minus video returns) without transmitting RF energy, the ICU switch should be placed in the TEST position.

6. TACAN—T/R. (P-N)
7. AFRS switch—AFRS.
8. BDH-IND switch—BDH-IND.
9. Pod camera control panel: (if installed)
   a. Pod air conditioning control switch—ON.
   b. V/H control converter power switch—ON.
   c. V/H control auto hold lamp—Checked, press-to-test.

Note

Lamp indication may be erratic during warmup but should go out after two minutes.

   d. All indicator lamps—Check, press-to-test.
   e. Camera power switch—ON.
   f. Camera power lamp—ON.

Note

To conserve film, the following steps are to be accomplished as rapidly as possible.

   g. Camera operate switch—ON.
   h. Camera operate lamp—ON.
      Film remaining counter should reduce. Film failure indicator lamp should not come on.
   i. Camera operate switch—OFF.
   j. Camera power switch—OFF.
   k. V/H control converter power switch—OFF.
10. Erect indicator lamp—Lighted, "A" malfunction test selector knob to 1.
    Check that erect indicator lamp lights in approximately 20 ±6 seconds, indicating table erection in progress.

Section VIII
Crew Duties

T.O. 1B-58A-1

BEFORE TAXIING. (CONT'D)

11. Plate power—Checked.

    Check presence of plate power, approximately 27 (± 6) seconds after going to STANDBY, by movement of attitude indicator to dumped position. In 42 (± 5) seconds, check drive of the true heading indicator.

12. "A" Malfunction test selector knob—A-2, A-1.

    Check both A-1 and A-2 positions for a "good" indication to verify tester status and return test selector knob to A-1.

13. PNS indicator lamps (6)—Press-to-test.

    Press-to-test PNS indicator lamps to check status of lamps and 28-volt DC power and switching circuits: Erect lamp, star lost lamp, vertical error lamp, camera malfunction lamp, test good lamp, and test bad lamp.

14. Magnetic variation—Checked and set.

    Rotate magnetic variation knob alternately left and right to check proper movement of true heading indicator and reset to local variation. This check should be completed during the rapid erect cycle.

15. Storage fixpoint and elevation—Set.

16. True present position indicators—Set.

17. Transverse present position indicators—Set as required.

18. Destination position indicators—Set.

19. Recorder, TIID, and intervalometer—On and set.

20. GHA indicator—Set.

21. SHA indicator—Set, as required.

22. Star declination indicator—Set.

23. Heading reference selector Knob—ASTRO, if applicable; if not, FLUX VALVE.

24. True heading—Checked with alternate compass.

25. Erect indicator lamp—Out, "A" malfunction test selector knob to zero.

    After function selector knob is in STANDBY for 5 to 7 minutes, the lamp should go out. Before the erect lamp goes out check that the ground speed indicator reads 218 to 258 knots, groundtrack indicator reads true heading plus 45 (± 2) degrees, and altitude above sea level reads 35,000 to 37,000 feet with the altitude correction knob centered. When the lamp goes out, turn the "A" malfunction test selector knob to zero.

Note

The erect lamp should light when the "A" malfunction test knob is reset to zero if the PNSU accelerometer output is 11 knots or greater.

26. Vertical error indicator lamp—Off.

    The vertical error lamp will remain lighted when the velocity difference between the accelerometer outputs and zero velocity reference is 50 knots or greater. This velocity difference must be eliminated (lamp out) before using the pure inertial mode (TAXI-TAKEOFF position).

27. Waveguide and RTM pressure caution lamps—Off, press-to-test.

28. Ballistic malfunction test—Completed, test knob OFF.

    Check test positions 3, 4, 6, 7, 8 for test good indication. Check position 5 as follows:
    a. Turn T_F pot to maximum.
    b. Place switch in REL-ON position.
    c. TEST BAD lamp should light.
    d. Turn T_F pot down until TEST GOOD lamp lights. This should occur at a T_f of 62.2 (± 3) seconds.

BEFORE TAXIING. (CONT'D)

    e. If the TEST GOOD lamp lights above 65.2 seconds, this is an indication of a malfunction in the T_G normal mode and T_G MALF should be used for operation.

Note

This test provides a calibration of the T_G computations within ± 0.15 seconds. The 0.15 seconds is due to operator errors when reading the T_F counter and determining the precise moment that the test good lamp lights. A reading which deviates from the nominal 62.2 seconds is a measure of the error in the T_G computation. This includes the V_G servo, T_G servo, T_F pot and bomb release closure. The difference between a nominal 62.2 seconds and the T_F counter reading when the test good lamp lights, is a measure of the T_G computation error. Thus, if a reading of 63.2 seconds is obtained, one second should be added to the nominal T_F value for a particular mission. This test is valid in STANDBY and NAVIGATE only.

Turn ballistic malfunction test knob to off at completion of check. Reset T_F pot to required setting.

29. Altitude above sea level indicator—Set.

    Set so that readout equals the field elevation.

30. Airspeed—Set. (if desired)

    Place the TG servo malfunction switch to MALF, airspeed computer malfunction switch to MALF and set the airspeed in the ground speed indicator to 250 knots by rotating the airspeed computer malfunction knob. Return the TG servo malfunction switch to NORM.

31. RTM Timing Cycle—Checked.

    Check timing cycle complete by checking TRIG current on search radar monitor unit. Sweep and marks will appear 90 seconds after going to standby and will drop out approximately 4-1/2 minutes later. Sweep and marks will not reappear until search power switch is placed to XMTG.

32. Search power switch—XMTG.

    Check scope for sweep, marks, centering and video returns.

WARNING

To insure that personnel and equipment are not exposed to dangerous radiation, clear the area of all personnel and equipment. Refer to "DANGER AREAS", Section II.

- Turn the search radar off immediately whenever the RTM pressure caution lamp lights indicating that the pressure is too low for safe operation.

- Lighting of the waveguide (WG) pressure loss lamp indicates that a loss of waveguide pressure has occurred and caused a shutdown of the search radar RTM. Placing the normal/override switch in the OVERRIDE position overrides the automatic shutdown of the RTM. Operation of the search radar with low waveguide pressure is possible only if the airplane altitude is under 10,000 feet. If mechanical damage exists in the search radar waveguide, overriding the automatic shutdown of RTM will, in most cases, cause extensive damage to search radar RTM components.

Section VIII
Crew Duties

T.O. 1B-58A-1

BEFORE TAXIING. (CONT'D)

33. Manual data request button—Depress.
    Check camera operation and recorder tape readout versus panel indicators.
34. Search power switch—STBY (OFF for cocking).
35. PNSU and ARU—Checked.
    a. Astro heading and astro lock—Checked. (if possible)
    b. Velocities—Checked.
    c. Attitude indicator—Checked.

36. Instruments—Checked, altimeter set. (P-N-DSO) (When requested)
    a. Barometric altimeter—Set and checked.
       Set altimeter to current altimeter setting.

WARNING

When setting the altimeter, check that the 10,000 foot pointer is reading correctly. If the barometric pressure set knob is rotated until the barometric scale goes out of view and reappears, the altimeter will be approximately 10,000 feet in error even though the correct barometric setting appears on the barometric scale.

   b. Attitude indicator—Set and checked.
      Set pitch trim knob on index and check that the attitude indicator shows approximately 3° nose down.
   c. Airspeed indicator—Checked.
      Static airspeed should indicate 40 ($\pm$ 5) knots.
   d. J-4 compass—Checked.
      (1) J-4 compass function knob—DG. Slew heading a minimum of 45 degrees with synchronizer—set knob and check both indicators for heading agreement.
      (2) Rotate J-4 compass function knob to MAG. Check that both BDH indicators slew to the correct magnetic heading $\pm$2 degrees with the synchronization indicator needle centered.
   e. Low altitude radar altimeter—On, minimum altitude indexer set.
      Set minimum altitude index pointer to approximately 50 feet.

Note

- On airplanes requiring maintenance accomplish items 2, 4, and 5 of the AFTER LANDING checklist, the ENGINE SHUTDOWN checklist and the BEFORE LEAVING AIRPLANE checklist.
- On airplanes prepared for alert status, proceed to the COCKING Checklist and place airplane on alert.

37. Handgrip and canopy jettison handle safety pins (3)—Removed and stowed. (P-N-DSO)
38. Report to pilot—Ready to taxi. (N-DSO) (when requested)

T.O. 1B-58A-1

Section VIII
Crew Duties

COCKING.

This checklist prepares the airplane for normal scramble and SRP Power-off scramble.

Note

When the airplane is uncocked for maintenance/defueling and the work is completed, the following checklists will be accomplished prior to performing the COCKING checklist: the navigator's POWER-OFF INTERIOR INSPECTION checklist and the asterisked (*) items on the navigator's POWER-ON INTERIOR INSPECTION checklist.

1. Malfunction test selector knobs—All positions checked.
   Check all tester positions of malfunction test selector knobs A thru E that are applicable to standby mode. Return all test selector knobs to zero detent after test.
2. Search power switch—OFF.
3. True and transverse present position indicators—Reset.
4. Recorder power switch—OFF.
5. Function selector knob—GYRO.

CAUTION

To reduce residual heat, all components of the primary navigation system should be turned off at least five minutes before engine shutdown.

6. Vertical reference selector switch—AIR ERECT.
7. Primary rapid erect switch—ON.
8. Unnecessary electrical and electronic equipment—Off. (P-N-DSO)
9. Heading reference selector—FLUX VALVE.
10. Canopy seal lever—UNSEALED (when directed). (N)
11. Canopy—OPEN. (P-N-DSO)
    At completion of COCKING checklist crew member will not install canopy locks, but will monitor canopy closure by ground crew.
12. Canopy jettison handle safety pin—Installed. (P-N-DSO)

CAUTION

Do not proceed with the following items until the Pilot and DSO call for the next item. To do so may result in equipment requiring air conditioning being turned on without cooling air.

13. TACAN—T/R, channel selector knob set. (P-N)
14. Emergency lighting switch—ON. (N-DSO)
15. Panel and flood lights—Set. (P-N-DSO)
16. Oxygen regulator—NORMAL and OFF. (P-N-DSO)
17. Auxiliary flight reference system power switches—ON. (N)
    Place flight reference indicator power switch to BDH-IND and auxiliary flight reference system power switch to AFRS.
18. Thermal curtains—Checked, installed (if on alert). (P-N-DSO)
    Check for cleanliness, general condition, proper fit, and installation.

8-23

Section VIII
Crew Duties

T.O. 1B-58A-1

COCKING. (CONT'D)

19. Fuse panels—Checked. (N-DSO)
20. Personal gear—Arranged. (P-N-DSO)

DAILY ALERT PREFLIGHT.

The daily alert preflight checklist will be used to perform the daily preflight when the airplane is cocked and in alert status. If an alert is sounded while the daily preflight is being performed, the airplane will be completely recocked prior to proceeding to the scramble checklist.

1. Pod warhead control selector switch—OFF, OS and sealed.
2. Safety lock handle—IN, horizontal and sealed.
3. Small weapon lock switches (4)—Locked and sealed.
4. Small weapon warhead control selector switches (4)—OFF, OS, and sealed.
5. Auto release switch—OFF.
6. Weapon selector switch—OFF.

WARNING

The above items must be accomplished prior to applying a-c or d-c electrical power to the airplane in order to prevent inadvertent weapon arming or release.

7. TACAN—OFF.
8. AFRS power switches—OFF.
9. Oxygen pressure—Checked.
   a. Oxygen supply lever ON, check pressure, oxygen supply lever OFF.
   b. Emergency oxygen pressure, 1800 psi at 70°F.
10. Fuse panels—Checked.
11. Pod warhead control selector switch—SAFE.
12. Small weapon warhead control selector switches (4)—SAFE.
13. Lock indicators (5)—LOCK.
14. Arm indicators (5)—SAFE.
15. Navigator's master warning lamp—Off, press-to-test.
16. Weapon selector switch—POD.
17. Pod and weapon released lamps (5)—Off, press-to-test.
18. Weapon selector switch—OFF.
19. Pod warhead control selector switch—OFF.
20. Small weapon warhead control selector switches (4)—OFF.

CAUTION

External power must be turned off before proceeding to the next step which begins recocking of the airplane.

21. TACAN—T/R.
22. AFRS power switches—ON.
23. Personal gear—Arranged.
24. CMF container—Checked secure.

UNCOCKING.

There is no separate UNCOCKING checklist for the navigator. The UNCOCKING checklist in Section II is an integrated crew checklist and contains all items to be accomplished by the navigator for uncocking the airplane. Refer to UNCOCKING, Section II for checklist description and specific items.

T.O. 1B-58A-1

Section VIII
Crew Duties

SCRAMBLE/SRP POWER-OFF SCRAMBLE.

Note

This checklist is to be used for EWO and training launch of aircraft from a cocked configuration.

Scramble procedure is a coordinated procedure by all crew members and the ground crew. In the event MRP is directed, the SCRAMBLE/SRP POWER-OFF SCRAMBLE checklist will be completed. This checklist will be used for normal scramble and SRP Power-off scramble.

1. **CANOPY COVER—REMOVED.**
    The DSO and navigator will release the upper hooks while the ground crew releases the lower buckles. All personnel will remove the cover and the ground crew will pull it clear of the airplane.
2. **ASTRODOME COVER—REMOVED.**
3. **CANOPY—CLOSED AND LATCHED.**
4. **HELMET ON—NAV ON INTERPHONE, CANOPY CLOSED. (N)**

Note

When engine start is not required, complete the double asterisked (**) items of the navigator's DEFCON 1/SRP POWER-ON COCKING CHECKLIST after completing items 1 thru 4 above. If scramble is then accomplished, use the navigator's DEFCON 1/SRP POWER-ON SCRAMBLE checklist.

5. **CANOPY SEALS—SEALED, when directed.**
6. **FUSE PANEL—CHECKED.**
    Takeoff will not be delayed during EWO alert operations to accomplish this item.
7. **OXYGEN—NORMAL AND ON.**
    Takeoff will not be delayed during EWO alert operations to accomplish this item.
8. **PERSONAL GEAR—CONNECTED.**
    Takeoff will not be delayed during EWO alert operations to accomplish this item.
9. **HANDGRIP SAFETY PINS (2) REMOVED AND STOWED. (will not be accomplished for bravo or coco alert) (P-N-DSO)**
    Takeoff will not be delayed during EWO alert operations to accomplish this item.
10. **CANOPY JETTISON HANDLE SAFETY PIN—REMOVED AND STOWED. (P-N-DSO)**
    Takeoff will not be delayed during EWO alert operations to accomplish this item.
11. Function selector knob—STANDBY.
    Function selector knob will not be placed to STANDBY until pilot indicates that electrical power and air conditioning are normal.

Note

- When a scramble and launch is directed, but, prior to takeoff, a DEFCON 1 is initiated, the navigator will request that power and air conditioning be maintained until he notifies the crew that the timing cycle has been completed, at which time, the DEFCON 1/SRP POWER-ON COCKING CHECKLIST can be started.

- Takeoff should be made in STANDBY, going directly to NAVIGATION from STANDBY upon reaching 250 knots. If the timing cycle is completed prior to takeoff and if the heading and attitude are good, TAXI & TAKEOFF may be used for takeoff, however, ground speed may be erroneous until going to NAVIGATION at 250 knots.

8-25

Section VIII
Crew Duties

T.O. 1B-58A-1

SCRAMBLE/SRP POWER-OFF SCRAMBLE. (CONT'D)

12. Search power switch—STBY.

    If the indicator console unit (ICU) switch, located on the search radar test panel, is in the NORM position, the ICU display will not be present until the search radar is transmitting. There is a 5 minute delay before the transmitter can be energized. If, after the 5 minute delay, it is desired to view the ICU display (minus video returns) without transmitting RF energy, the ICU switch should be placed in the TEST position.

13. Recorder power switch—ON.
14. True heading—Checked, slew to correct heading if necessary.
15. Altimeter—Set. (P-N-DSO)
▶16. Auto release switch—OFF.
▶17. Pod and small weapon lock indicators (5)—LOCK.
18. Warhead control selector switches (5)—OFF.
19. Camera pod lock indicator—LOCK. (if installed)
20. P.I. Beacon—ON and set.
21. Malfunction test selector—A-5.
22. Doppler transmitter—ON.

Note

If SCRAMBLE/SRP POWER-OFF SCRAMBLE checklist is completed, proceed to the AFTER TAKEOFF checklist. Following an alert practice exercise, accomplish the COCKING checklist.

DEFCON 1/SRP POWER-ON COCKING CHECKLIST.

Note

Double asterisked (**) items are those items to be completed after completing item 4 of the SCRAMBLE/SRP POWER-OFF SCRAMBLE checklist when engine start is not required. If a scramble is then accomplished use the navigator's DEFCON 1/SRP POWER-ON SCRAMBLE CHECKLIST.

**1. Auxiliary flight reference system power switches—OFF.

   Turn off the flight reference indicator power switch and the auxiliary flight reference system power switch.

2. Function selector knob—GYRO, after monitoring the rapid erect lamp on the auxiliary control panel.
3. Search power switch—OFF.
4. Recorder power switch—OFF.
**5. TACAN—OFF. (P-N)
6. Doppler transmitter switch—OFF.
7. P.I. Beacon—OFF.
8. Canopy seal lever—Unsealed. (when directed)
9. Canopies—Climatic. (P-N-DSO)
10. Handgrip safety pins (2)—Installed. (P-N-DSO)
11. Canopy jettison handle safety pin—Installed. (P-N-DSO)
12. Communications panel—Set. (N-DSO)

DEFCON 1/SRP POWER-ON SCRAMBLE CHECKLIST.

1. **CANOPIES—CLOSED AND LATCHED. (DSO-N-P)**

> **CAUTION**
>
> Electronic equipment that requires air conditioning is being turned on without air conditioning. If starting is delayed, do not leave equipment on for more than 90 seconds.

2. **AUXILIARY FLIGHT REFERENCE SYSTEM POWER SWITCHES—ON.**
   Place flight reference indicator power switch to BDH-IND and auxiliary flight reference system power switch to AFRS.
3. **CANOPY SEAL LEVER—SEALED. (N)**
4. TACAN—T/R. (P-N)
5. **FUSE PANELS—CHECKED. (N-DSO)**
6. Personal gear—Connected. (P-N-DSO)
   Connecting personal gear will not delay takeoff.
7. **HANDGRIP SAFETY PINS (2)—REMOVED AND STOWED. (will not be accomplished for bravo or coco alert). (P-N-DSO)**
   Takeoff will not be delayed during EWO alert operations to accomplish this item.
8. **CANOPY JETTISON HANDLE SAFETY PIN—REMOVED AND STOWED. (P-N-DSO)**
   Takeoff will not be delayed during EWO alert operations to accomplish this item.

> **CAUTION**
>
> Do not proceed with further checklist items until pilot indicates that electric power and air conditioning are normal.

9. Function selector knob—STANDBY.

Note

Take off should be made in STANDBY, going directly to NAVIGATION from STANDBY upon reaching 250 knots. If the timing cycle is completed prior to takeoff and if the heading and attitude are good, TAXI & TAKEOFF may be used for take off, however, ground speed may be erroneous until going to NAVIGATION at 250 knots.

10. Search power switch—STBY.

Note

If the indicator console unit (ICU) switch, located on the search radar test panel, is in the NORM position, the ICU display will not be present until the search radar is transmitting. There is a 5 minute delay before the transmitter can be energized. If, after the 5 minute delay, it is desired to view the ICU display (minus video returns) without transmitting RF energy, the ICU switch should be placed in the TEST position.

Section VIII
Crew Duties

DEFCON 1/SRP POWER-ON SCRAMBLE CHECKLIST. (CONT'D)

11. Recorder power switch—ON.
12. True heading—Checked, slew to correct value if necessary.
13. Altimeter—Set. (P-N-DSO)
▶14. Auto release switch—OFF.
▶15. Pod and small weapon lock indicators (5)—LOCK.
16. Warhead control selector switches (5)—OFF.
17. Camera pod lock indicator—LOCK. (if installed)
18. P.I. Beacon—ON and set.
19. Malfunction test selector—A-5.
20. Doppler transmitter switch—ON.

TAXIING.

1. Low altitude radar altimeter—Checked and set.
   Push-to-test radar altimeter. Check that indicator reads 100 ($\pm$10) feet and that low altitude warning lamps go out. Then set minimum altitude index pointer to desired altitude.
2. Fixpoint position and elevation indicators—Set.
   If first fixpoint is within 200 minutes of latitude and 300 minutes of longitude of base, it may be set in with fixpoint selector knob in MANUAL; otherwise, leave fixpoint selector knob at PRESENT POSITION.
3. Fuse panels—Checked. (N-DSO)
4. RV Beacon—As required.
5. P.I. Beacon—As required.
6. Primary navigation system—Monitored.
   While taxiing, the navigator will monitor the bomb-nav system. No specific checks are necessary, however, monitoring the front panel readouts will indicate system condition. A check of both stabilization units will determine which unit is the most reliable for initial use.
7. Malfunction test selector—A-5.
8. Doppler transmitter switch—ON.

LINEUP.

Note

In the event a rolling takeoff is to be made, accomplish this checklist in the runup area just prior to start of takeoff roll.

1. Barometric altimeter—Checked and set.
   Set altimeter to current altimeter setting and check at a known elevation. The altimeter should read known elevation $\pm$75 feet.
2. True and transverse present position—Checked.
3. True heading—Checked.
4. Function selector knob—TAXI & TAKEOFF.
5. Report to pilot—Ready for takeoff, table stowed. (N)

Note

Monitor airplane attitude, heading and airspeed during takeoff and departure. Notify pilot immediately of any dangerous situation or deviation from the planned departure.

AFTER TAKEOFF.

WARNING

- The navigator will delay AFTER TAKEOFF checklist until the airplane has attained a safe attitude, airspeed, and altitude. The navigator will notify the pilot immediately of any dangerous situation or deviation from planned departure.

- Any indication of a release system activated or weapons unlocked will preclude any exercise of the computer bomb function except for actual release. Check that the auto release switch is OFF. During EWO operations, after weapon preparation for release, the computer bomb function may be used.

1. Function selector knob—NAVIGATION or BOMB.
   Set function selector knob to NAVIGATION or BOMB when airspeed is in excess of 250 knots.
2. Radio altimeter—ON.
3. Doppler lock—Checked.
   Check A-5, A-4, and A-3 positions for "Test Good" and then return to zero. Check Doppler timer upper scale illuminated, time indicator decreasing, and doppler lock indicator lamp on. Check groundspeed readout for reasonable value. If test bad indication is noted, continue monitoring for good Doppler.
4. Oxygen check—Completed. (P-N-DSO)
5. TIID—Reset. (if necessary)
6. GHA—Reset. (if necessary)
7. Altimeter—Reset. (P-N-DSO)
8. RV Beacon—As required.

LEVELOFF.

1. Station check—Completed. (P-N-DSO)
   At level-off the crew will accomplish a station check: Fuse panels, oxygen pressure, altimeter, airspeed, attitude indicator, and J-4 compass. During cruise, the crew will accomplish station checks at hourly intervals. Sequence for check will be pilot, navigator and DSO.
2. AFRS heading—Cross-checked, J-4 vs PNS.
   Cross check J-4 heading from BDH indicator with PNS heading plus local variation.

   Note

   The BDH indicator may have a random error of plus or minus 10 degrees, due to an overloaded heading synchro driver, when operating in the primary navigation mode. Operation in the auxiliary flight reference mode should be within the normal plus or minus two degree accuracy limits.

3. Primary rapid erect switch—OFF (if applicable).
   Place the primary rapid erect switch to OFF after five minutes of straight and level unaccelerated flight.
4. Altitude calibration—Completed.
   While over terrain of known elevation, turn altimeter transmitter switch to CALIBRATE (this switch must have been in the ON position for at least 4 seconds) while setting terrain elevation on fixpoint position elevation indicator with altitude correction knob. An altitude calibration should be accomplished: (1) after each airspeed change of more than 300 knots; (2) after an altitude change of more than 5000 feet.

LEVELOFF. (CONT'D)

Note

If the warning lamp in the altitude above terrain indicator lights during this procedure, indicating periodic automatic self-calibration of the radio altimeter, the procedure must be repeated. Self calibration of the radio altimeter must be accomplished by placing transmitter switch to OFF for 20 seconds and returning to ON. The self calibration cycle is over when the calibration warning lights of the altitude-above-terrain indicator have gone out.

5. Airspeed—Calibrated or set.
    a. With Doppler lock:
        Proceed with following steps or compute and set TAS as described under airspeed-inertial mode.

Note

Airspeed cannot be calibrated automatically with the airspeed computer malfunction switch in the MALF position.

   (1) Place airspeed calibration switch to CAL.
   (2) Request the pilot to make a 20 degree minimum turn.
   (3) After flying a minimum of 45 seconds on new heading, return airspeed calibration switch to NORMAL.
   (4) Resume heading.
   (5) Cross check accuracy of TAS system by noting the readout of the Vg indicator with the time-to-go servo malfunction switch in the MALF position. Compute TAS using pilot's IAS corrected to CAS, RAT and corrected pressure altitude or RAT and mach.

Note

If re-calibration is necessary, allow at least 45 seconds for the θH shaft to zero before returning the airspeed calibration switch to CAL.

   b. Airspeed-inertial mode (Doppler inoperative).
   (1) Compute true airspeed using pilot's indicated airspeed corrected to calibrated airspeed, ram air temperature and corrected pressure altitude or RAT and mach.
   (2) Select airspeed computer malfunction mode and with airspeed computer malfunction knob set on index mark, read system VA on groundspeed indicator by placing the TG servo malfunction switch to the MALF position.
   (3) Compare computed TAS with system VA and, if not in close agreement, set computed value by use of the airspeed computer malfunction knob.

6. Heading reference selector knob—ASTRO.

Note

- If unable to obtain a lock-on, check sun filter position by switching the astro filter switch to SUN and then to STAR. When a flight involves passing through evening or morning twilight, it is probable that there will be a period of time where an immediate change from sun track to star track (or vice versa) cannot be made. This period will vary with altitude, heading, latitude, and groundspeed. Do not fly in the ASTRO mode during this time, but use FREE GYRO or FLUX VALVE mode. If in ASTRO at this time, one or more false astro locks may drive the azimuth drift assembly off, precess the stable table, and steer the airplane off course before the condition is discovered.

LEVELOFF. (CONT'D)

7. Autopilot heading switch—NAV. (P) (if desired)
8. PNSU or ARU—Checked. (as applicable)

If takeoff was performed on the ARU crosscheck heading, attitude, velocity and intercepts after one-hour operation. If PNSU has not stabilized, initiate PNSU rapid erect cycle (if applicable). If takeoff was performed on PNSU, check A-12. If A-12 tests bad, initiate ARU rapid erect cycle. Evaluate and select better table.

▶ LEVELOFF AND PERIODIC INFLIGHT. (NAVIGATOR READS)

This check will be completed at leveloff and periodically while inflight.

In the even any weapon lock indicator shows crosshatch or unlock, discontinue use of computer bomb function, and check auto release switch OFF. Return to briefed base avoiding populated areas. During EWO operations follow command policy.

1. Pilot's small weapon jettison switch—SAFE, safetied. (P)
2. Pilot's arm control switch—SAFE, sealed. (P)
3. Weapon lock and arm panel:
    a. Pod warhead control selector switch—SAFE, OS, and sealed.
    b. Release system activated lamp—Off, press-to-test.
4. Small weapon warhead control selector switches—SAFE, OS, and sealed.
5. Weapon monitor and release panel:
    a. Lock indicators (5)—LOCK.
    b. Arm indicators (5)—SAFE.
    c. Auto release switch—OFF.
    d. Weapon selector switch—POD.
    e. Pod and weapon released lamps (5)—Off, press-to-test.

Note

The pod released lamp will not press-to-test if an MB pod is installed.

   f. All other warning and indicator lamps (3)—Off, press-to-test.
6. Pod and small weapon warhead control selector switches—OFF.

PHOTO RUN.

BEFORE TARGET AREA.

To provide adequate warmup of system, accomplish the following procedures at least five minutes before reaching target area.

1. V/H control converter power switch—ON.

Section VIII
Crew Duties

BEFORE TARGET AREA. (CONT'D)

2. V/H control selector switch—AUTO.
3. V/H control auto hold lamp—Monitored.
   Lamp indication may be erratic during initial warmup but should go out within two minutes.
4. Manual V/H input knobs—Set.
   Set altitude above target and ground speed for use in case manual operation should be required.
5. Camera power switch—ON.
6. Camera power lamp—ON.

TARGET RUN.

1. Camera operate switch on (P)—ON. (N)
2. Camera operate lamp—ON.
3. Film remaining counter—Monitored.
   Check that counter digits reduce, indicating that camera is operating.
4. Film failure indicator lamp—Monitored.
   If the film failure indicator lamp comes on, the film is broken, jammed or exhausted. Discontinue camera operation.
5. V/H control auto hold lamp—Monitored.
   If the V/H control auto hold lamp comes on, check for cause (such as a cloud or ground ridge). If V/H controls auto hold lamp remains on for no apparent reason, shift V/H control selector switch to MANUAL and continue the target run in manual mode, adjusting manual input knobs as necessary.

AFTER TARGET RUN.

1. Camera operate switch off (P)—OFF. (N)
2. Camera power switch—OFF.
3. V/H control converter power switch—OFF.

TRANSVERSE ENTRY.

1. Polar/non-polar switch—POLAR.
2. Transverse present position indicators—Set.
   Set the transverse indicator counters to the approximate transverse coordinates of the present position.
3. Autopilot heading switch—OFF (P).
4. Fixpoint selector knob—PRESENT POSITION.
5. Coordinate reference switch—TRANSVERSE.
   Observe fixpoint counters driving to agree with transverse present position; ground track to transverse track; astro computer star azimuth realigns to transverse star azimuth. Check that ground track settles out on predetermined value. If sea drift is being utilized, reset in relation to transverse north.
6. Destination position indicators—Set to transverse.
7. Transverse present position—Corrected.
8. Heading check—Complete.
   Check PNS transverse heading against J-4 compass heading by applying B angle and magnetic variation.

TRANSVERSE ENTRY. (CONT'D)

9. Autopilot heading switch—NAV. (P)
10. J-4 compass—Set.
    Set mid-latitude, correct hemisphere, switch to DG mode, set correct transverse heading. Periodically reset data.

TRANSVERSE EXIT.

1. True present position indicators—Set.
   Set the true present position indicators to the approximate true coordinates of the present position.
2. Autopilot heading switch—OFF (P).
3. Fixpoint selector knob—PRESENT POSITION.
4. Coordinate reference switch—TRUE.
   Observe ground track driving to true track; astro computer star azimuth realigns to true star azimuth. Check that ground track settles out on predetermined value. If sea drift is being utilized, reset in relation to true north.
5. Destination position indicators—Set to true.
6. True present position—Corrected.
7. Autopilot heading switch—NAV. (P)
8. J-4 compass—Set.
   Switch to MAG mode and synchronize indicator to correct magnetic heading.

Note

If back-up true present position indicator capability is desired, place polar/non-polar switch to NON-POLAR and reset transverse present position indicators to true data.

9. Heading check—Complete.
   Check 6H against J-4.

NORMAL BOMBING.

BOMBING EQUIPMENT CHECK.

1. Safety check. (Navigator Reads).
   a. Pilot's weapon unlock caution lamp—Off. (P)
   ▶ b. Auto release switch—OFF.
      Check that the auto release switch on the weapon monitor and release panel is OFF and that the auto release ready lamp is out.
   c. Lock indicators (5)—LOCK.
   ▶ d. Weapon selector switch—OFF.

Any indication of a release system activated or weapon unlocked will preclude any exercise of the computer bomb function except for actual release. Check that the auto release switch is off. During EWO operations, after weapon preparation for release, the computer bomb function may be used.

Section VIII
Crew Duties

T.O. 1B-58A-1

BOMBING EQUIPMENT CHECK. (CONT'D)

2. Offset and elevation indicators—Set.
    Set desired offset and elevation values.

3. Storage fixpoint counters and elevations—Set.
    Set aimpoint coordinates and elevations in storage fixpoints 1 and 2.

4. Altitude calibration—Completed.

5. Ballistics—Set.
    Set HB, TRAIL and TF as required for next run to be accomplished.

6. Trail-TF malfunction switch—MALF.

7. Fixpoint position indicators—Set.
    Check that fixpoint storage and elevations 1 and 2 transfer correctly.

8. Function selector knob—BOMB.

9. Bomb damage evaluation switch—POWER, lamp lighted.

10. Auto radar photo switch—RECORD.

11. Intervalometer selector knob—1 PHOTO/PRINT.

12. Center PDI—Centered. (P)

13. Autopilot heading switch—HEADING NAV. (P)

14. Velocity check—Completed. (if desired).
    Time from 50-30 mile fixed range marks, compute groundspeed and crosscheck BNS groundspeed.

15. Offset aiming points—Checked.
    Check crosshairs move in the proper direction of offset components. Return aimpoint selector knob to FIX position.

16. Steering check—Completed.
    a. Radar sighting switch—MANUAL.
        Set drift angle into relative bearing indicator. Check that aizmuth mark goes through aiming point.
    b. Radar sighting switch—AUTO.
        Reposition crosshairs on aiming point if necessary.

17. TG—Crosschecked.
    Check that TG meters are driving and read the same values (± 5 sec) after TG reads less 180 seconds.

18. RBS tone selector switch—Checked. (DSO)
    The RBS tone selector switch must be in the correct position for the UHF radio being used to transmit the RBS tone.

BOMBING EQUIPMENT CHECK. (CONT'D)

19. Radar sighting switch—MANUAL.

    Switch to manual sighting with RNG/MAG 30/20 prior to 10 miles on ground range indicator. (RNG/MAG 30/10 and 5 miles for low level).

20. TG hack—Initiated. (N-DSO)

    As aiming point reaches the 10 mile fixed range mark (5 mile fixed range mark for low level), navigator and DSO start stop-watches.

21. Pilot calls TG:

    a. 30 seconds (P)

    b. 20 seconds (P)

    c. 10 seconds (P), RBS Tone—ON. (N)

22. TG hack—Terminated. (N-DSO)

    a. At tone off, stop stopwatches.

    b. Compute time-to-go to release from the applicable FRM (TI-ATF=TG).

    c. Compare computed time-to-go with actual time from the TG hack initiation to tone off.

23. Bomb damage evaluation switch—OFF.

24. Auto radar photo switch—OFF.

25. Intervalometer selector knob—As desired.

26. Function selector knob—As desired.

▶ 27. Weapon selector switch—POD.

28. Auto ballistics bomb accuracy check—Completed.

    This check is required when auto ballistics are to be used.

    a. Tracking selector knob—FIX PT POS CORR.

    b. Ballistic data—Set.

        Set weapon ballistic data for present aircraft Hsl and Va. Set height-of-burst dial to value used to compute ballistics.

    c. Autopilot heading switch—OFF. (P)

    d. Function selector knob—BOMB.

    e. Auto ballistics—Checked.

        Hold TAS and altitude corresponding to ballistic data set, position crosshairs to the extent that TG is approximately 60 seconds and decreasing. Switch trail-Tf switch from malfunction to normal observing that TG does not dip or fluctuate in excess of two seconds when TG reads 30 seconds or less.

    f. Tracking selector knob—PRES POS CORR.

Section VIII
Crew Duties

T.O. 1B-58A-1

▶ **WEAPON PREPARATION FOR RELEASE. (NAVIGATOR READS)**

Perform within 15 minutes prior to HHCL or within 15 minutes prior to descent for low-altitude mission, whichever is reached first, and only after the "GO" code has been received and authenticated.

— EWO ONLY —

WARNING

Checklist items contained within the block titled "EWO ONLY" will be called out on all missions, training and EWO. For training missions, all switch positions, safety lock and mechanical release handle positions within the blocked-in area will be simulated.

1. Thermal curtains—Closed and fastened. (P-N-DSO)
2. Auto release switch—OFF.
3. Release signal present lamp—Off, press-to-test.
4. Safety lock handle—Out.
   Rotate safety lock handle counterclockwise and pull handle full length of travel. (approximately 2.25 inches.)

Note

Forceful overrotation of the safety lock handle may cause mechanism binding. If an unlocked indication is not obtained, recycle the safety lock handle.

5. Small weapon jettison switch—SAFE, safetied. (P)
6. All small weapon lock switches (4)—Unlock.

Note

Place all small weapon lock switches to UNLOCK position regardless of the number of weapons loaded.

7. Lock indicators (5)—Unlock.
8. Released lamps (5)—Off, press-to-test.
9. Pilot's weapon unlocked caution lamp—On. (P)
10. Pilot's arm control switch—ARMED. (P)
11. Warhead control selector switches (5)—As briefed.
12. Navigator's master warn lamp—Off, press-to-test.
13. Arm indicators (5)—ARM.
14. Pilot's arm/ready caution lamps for appropriate weapons—ON. (P)
15. Weapon selector switch—Appropriate position.

CAUTION

- The MB or LA pod with fins installed should be released prior to release of any small weapon.
- The MB or LA pod with lower fins removed or the lower pod of a TCP should be released prior to release of a forward small weapon.

16. Cabin pressure selector knob—COMBAT. (P)

8-36

T.O. 1B-58A-1

Section VIII
Crew Duties

PREDESCENT AND DESCENT. (LOW ALTITUDE TACTICAL OPERATION)

1. Barometric altimeter reset to current setting—Completed. (P-N-DSO)
    Reset altimeters to station pressure immediately prior to initiating penetration or passing through transition altitude.
2. Altitude calibration—Completed.
    a. Level off at a barometric altitude of terrain elevation plus approximately 5000 feet and calibrate HSL using either the radio altimeter or the search radar.
    b. Compare HSL with barometric altitude and (EWO only) notify crew to reset altimeters.
3. Low altitude radar altimeter—Checked (if installed). (P-N)
    Set the minimum altitude index pointer at 5000 feet and at 5000 feet above terrain check that the crosshatched (fail) indicator disappears and that the warning lamps light.
4. Low altitude radar altimeter—Set (if installed). (P-N)
    Position the minimum altitude index pointer so the warning lamps light when airplane descends to less than desired altitude above terrain.

PRIOR TO BOMB RUN. (HIGH/LOW ALTITUDE) (NAVIGATOR READS)

Accomplish the following checklist in the vicinity of the PRE-IP and prior to reaching the IP. In the event PRE-IP's and IP's are not designated, accomplish this checklist in sufficient time to prepare for the bomb run.

▶ 1. Weapon selector switch—Appropriate position.

> **CAUTION**
>
> - The MB or LA pod with fins installed should be released prior to release of any small weapon.
> - The MB or LA pod with lower fins removed or the lower pod of a TCP should be released prior to release of a forward small weapon.

2. CG—Checked and set. (P-DSO)
    Check cg and adjust as necessary for the weapon to be released.
3. Offset and elevation indicator—Checked against preflight data.
4. Storage and Fixpoint counters and elevations—Set.
    Set aimpoint coordinates and elevations in storage fixpoints 1 and 2.
5. Destination indicators set—Set target coordinates in destination indicators, if not previously set.
6. Variation set—Set target variation.
7. Altitude above sea level—Adjusted.
    Calibrate altitude over terrain of known elevation and apply "D" value difference between measurement point and target, and set HSL. If unable to calibrate altitude, compute and set HSL using pressure altitude and "D" value.
8. Ballistics—Set.
    Set Hb, Dbw, trail, and Tf as required.
9. Trail-Tf malf switch—Checked.
    Position trail-Tf switch to NORM for auto ballistics run, to malfunction position for fixed ballistics run.
10. Release ETE/ETA, Heading and Timing—Established, crew advised.
    The navigator will inform the crew of the ETE or ETA to the first release and magnetic heading and time between minimum interval releases.

BOMB RUN. (HIGH/LOW ALTITUDE)

This checklist should commence in the vicinity of the IP. If no IP is designated, commence this checklist in time to complete all items up to the pilot's 200 second TG call prior to reaching 200 seconds TG.

1. Fixpoint position indicators—Set, target coordinates and elevation.
2. Function selector knob—BOMB.

Section III
Crew Duties

T.O. 1B-58A-1

BOMB RUN. (HIGH/LOW ALTITUDE) (CONT'D)

3. Bomb damage evaluation switch—POWER, lamp lighted.
4. Auto radar photo switch—RECORD.
5. Intervalometer selector knob—1 PHOTO/PRINT.
6. Center PDI—Centered. (P)
   Heading navigate mode of autopilot may be used when applicable.
7. RBS tone selector switch—Checked. (DSO)
   The RBS tone selector switch must be in the correct position for the UHF radio being used to transmit the RBS tone.
8. Pilot calls TG:
   a. 200 seconds. (P)
   b. 100 seconds. (P)
   c. 30 seconds. (P)
   d. 20 seconds. (P)
   e. 10 seconds, RBS tone—ON. (N) (RBS only)

EWO ONLY

WARNING

Checklist items contained within the block titled "EWO ONLY" will be called out on all missions, training and EWO. For training missions, all switch positions, safety lock and mechanical release handle positions within the blocked-in area will be simulated.

   f. 10 seconds, auto release switch—RELEASE, momentarily, ready lamp lighted.
      The switch will return to the intermediate position.

WARNING

Do not change position of any malfunction switch, malfunction selector knob, malfunction test knob, or the malfunction test selector knob after placing the auto release switch to the RELEASE position. To do so may cause inadvertent release of selected weapon.

---

   g. TG zero (P)—Tone off, lamp off. (N) (RBS only)

EWO ONLY

   h. TG zero (P)—Bombs away. (N)
      The navigator monitors the automatic release system by observing the applicable weapon released lamp coming ON and/or the applicable arm-safe indicator going to cross-hatch at TG zero.
      (1) If automatic release of the pod does not occur at TG zero, turn the auto release switch off and depress the electrical release switch. If the pod still fails to release, pull the mechanical release handle.
      (2) If automatic release of a small weapon did not occur at TG zero, turn the auto release switch off and depress the electrical release switch.

Note

Activating the navigator's electric release switch or the pilot's weapon release switch after the weapon selector switch steps to the next weapon position will result in an inadvertent release of a second weapon.

BOMB RUN. (HIGH/LOW ALTITUDE) (CONT'D)

9. Timing/heading change—Initiated. (P-N-DSO)

    For high altitude release navigator will monitor time and heading change of escape maneuver. For subsequent release navigator and DSO will start timing. Pilot will turn to new target heading and navigator will cross-check.

MINIMUM INTERVAL RELEASE.

▶10. Release signal present lamp—Off, press-to-test. (N)

EWO ONLY

11. Weapon selector switch—Appropriate position. (N)

    Check to see that the weapon selector switch is positioned to the weapon to be released.

Note

If the release point is to be determined by the BNS, continue with steps 12 through 20. Otherwise proceed to step 18.

▶12. Auto release ready lamp—Off, press-to-test. (N)

13. Target coordinates and elevation—Set. (N)

    Set/transfer target cordinates and elevation in the fixpoint indicators. If transferring, check to insure that correct coordinates and elevation transfer to the fixpoint indicators.

14. Center PDI—Centered. (P)

    Heading navigate mode of autopilot may be used when applicable.

15. Offset and elevation indicators—Set. (N) (if applicable)

16. Ballistic data—Reset. (N) (if applicable)

EWO ONLY

17. Auto release switch—Release momentarily, ready lamp lighted. (N)

---

18. RBS tone—ON. (N) (RBS only)

    Navigator turns tone on at approximately 10 seconds TG.

19. TG zero/timing expiration, RBS tone—OFF. (N) (RBS only)

Section VIII
Crew Duties

T.O. 1B-58A-1

MINIMUM INTERVAL RELEASE. (CONT'D)

--- EWO ONLY ---

20. TG zero/timing expiration—Bombs away. (N)
    a. Auto release.
       The navigator monitors the automatic release system by observing the applicable weapon released lamp coming ON and/or the applicable arm-safe indicator going to cross-hatch at TG zero.
       (1) If automatic release of the pod does not occur at TG zero, turn the auto release switch OFF and depress the electrical release switch. If pod fails to release, pull the mechanical release handle.
       (2) If automatic release of a small weapon did not occur at TG zero, turn the auto release switch OFF and depress the electrical release switch.
    b. Timing release.
       (1) For pod release the navigator will depress the electrical release switch at timing expiration. If the pod fails to release, pull the mechanical release handle.
       (2) For a small weapon release depress the electrical release switch at timing expiration.

Note

Activating the navigator's electrical release switch or the pilot's weapon release switch after the weapon selector switch steps to the next weapon position will result in an inadvertent release of a second weapon.

Note

For subsequent release or escape maneuver return to step 9 of the BOMB RUN checklist.

POST RELEASE CHECK.

When minimum interval releases are being accomplished, this checklist, except for necessary release data, will be completed after the last release only.

1. Release data—Recorded.
► 2. Released lamp—ON.
► 3. Auto release ready lamp—Off.
► 4. Release signal present lamp—Off, press-to-test.
► 5. Weapon selector switch—Steps clockwise to the next position. Step manually, if required.
6. Bomb damage evaluation switch—OFF.
7. Auto radar photo switch—OFF.
8. Intervalometer selector knob—As desired.
9. Aimpoint selector knob—Fix.
10. Destination indicators—Set.

Note

For each successive weapon release, repeat NORMAL BOMBING procedures beginning with PRIOR TO BOMB RUN through POST RELEASE CHECK.

WEAPON ABORT PROCEDURE. (NAVIGATOR READS)

Note

Accomplish only if weapon preparation for release has been performed.

1. Pilot's arm control switch—SAFE. (P)
2. Small weapon lock switches (4)—LOCK.
3. Safety lock handle—In and horizontal.
4. Pod warhead control selector switch—SAFE.
5. Small weapon warhead control selector switches (4)—SAFE.
6. Lock indicators (5)—LOCK, pod indicator diagonal stripes if pod has been released.
7. Arm indicators (5)—SAFE, diagonal stripes if weapon has been released.
8. Auto release switch—OFF.
9. Weapon selector switch—POD.
10. Pod and small weapon released lamps (5)—Off, press-to-test, on, if weapon has been released.
11. All small weapon warhead control selector switches—OS.
12. Pod warhead control selector switch—OS.
13. Weapon unlock caution lamp—Off. (P)
14. Armed and ready caution lamp(s)—Off. (P)

ALTERNATE BOMBING.

Note

Perform these checklists when using manual radar emergency timing procedures at both low and high altitudes. The aiming point may be the target which should track down the electronic azimuth marker; or it may be a return other than the target which should track parallel to a cursor line.

BOMBING EQUIPMENT CHECK.

Perform to the extent possible consistent with equipment malfunction.

WEAPON PREPARATION FOR RELEASE.

Same as normal procedure.

PRIOR TO BOMB RUN.

Accomplish this checklist in sufficient time to prepare for the bomb run.

▶ 1. Weapon selector switch—Appropriate position.

CAUTION

- The MB or LA pod with fins installed should be released prior to release of any small weapons.
- The MB or LA pod with lower fins removed or the lower pod of a TCP should be released prior to release of a forward small weapon.

Section VIII
Crew Duties

T.O. 1B-58A-1

PRIOR TO BOMB RUN. (CONT'D)

2. CG—Checked and Set. (P-DSO)
   Check cg and adjust as necessary for the weapon to be released.

3. Bomb run heading—Determined.
   Establish bomb run heading using best known information. Use computer heading, track, and groundspeed, if available.

4. TG—Determined.
   Determine TG from applicable fixed range marker using best known ground speed and bombing altitude. Refer to EMERGENCY BOMBING PROCEDURES in T.O. 1B-58A-25-3 or adjust precomputed data as required. Navigator will furnish the DSO with the appropriate time to go information.

BOMB RUN.

Commence this checklist in time to accomplish initial lineup at maximum aiming point range.

1. Fixpoint position indicators—Set.
   Set coordinates in vicinity of IP.

2. Function selector knob—BOMB.

3. BDE switch—POWER, lamp lighted.

4. Auto radar photo switch—RECORD.

5. Intervalometer selector knob—1 PHOTO/PRINT.

6. Radar sighting switch—MANUAL.

7. Range magnification selector knob—Appropriate range selected.

8. PPI switch—OFST.

9. Search radar mode selector knob—SL.

10. RBS tone selector switch—Checked. (DSO)
    The RBS tone selector switch must be in the correct position for the UHF radio being used to transmit the RBS tone.

11. Autopilot heading switch—OFF. (P)

12. Set relative bearing indicator and align heading—Accomplished.
    a. When the aiming point is the target:
       (1) Set relative bearing indicator to predetermined drift angle for briefed axis of attack; that is, if a 6° left drift has been determined, set relative bearing to 354°.
       (2) Correct airplane heading so that aiming point appears under the azimuth mark.
       (3) Observe that the aiming point tracks down the azimuth mark.
       (4) If aiming point drifts to one side of the azimuth mark, correct relative bearing indicator (in opposite direction of target drift) by amount of apparent drift, *or* accomplish multiple drift correction and set relative bearing indicator.
       (5) Turn airplane to re-align aiming point under the azimuth mark.
       (6) Repeat steps (4) and (5) as necessary until aiming point tracks down the azimuth mark.
    b. When the aiming point is a return other than the target:
       (1) Set relative bearing indicator to precomputed relative bearing (±DCA) for the

BOMB RUN. (CONT'D)

first range magnification setting to be used.

Example: Precomputed relative bearing is 344° and DCA is minus 4°, set relative bearing dial to 348°.

(2) With airplane on desired heading, observe that the aiming point tracks down the cursor line.

(3) If aiming point does not track down cursor line, make course corrections by "S" turning in the direction of apparent drift, insuring that the airplane returns to original desired heading.

(4) Repeat course corrections as needed until aiming point tracks down the cursor line.

(5) If range magnification is changed adjust relative bearing indicator.

13. TG hack—Initiated. (N-DSO)

As aiming point reaches the selected fixed range mark, navigator and DSO start stopwatches. Navigator may continue to monitor airplane track/heading and make necessary corrections.

14. RBS tone—ON. (N) (RBS Only)

Navigator turns tone ON at approximately 10 seconds TG. In some cases, this may be prior to the TG hack.

15. Timing expiration, RBS tone—OFF. (N) (RBS Only)

EWO ONLY

WARNING

Checklist items contained within the blocks titled "EWO ONLY" will be called out on all missions, training and EWO. For trainning missions, all switch positions, safety lock and mechanical release handle positions within the blocked-in area will be simulated.

16. Timing expiration—Bombs away. (N)

   a. For pod release the navigator will depress the electrical release switch at timing expiration. If the pod fails to release, pull the mechanical release handle.

   b. For a small weapon release depress the electrical release switch at timing expiration.

Note

Activating the navigator's electrical release switch or the pilot's weapon release switch after the weapon selector switch steps to the next weapon will result in an inadvertent release of a second weapon.

8-43

Section VIII
Crew Duties

BOMB RUN. (CONT'D)

17. Timing/heading change—Initiated. (P-N-DSO)

   For high altitude release navigator will monitor time and heading change of escape maneuver. For subsequent releases navigator and DSO will continue timing. Pilot will turn to new target heading and navigator will crosscheck.

MINIMUM INTERVAL RELEASE.

▶18. Release signal present lamp—Off, press-to-test. (N)

EWO ONLY

19. Weapon selector switch—Appropriate position. (N)

   Check to see that the weapon selector switch is positioned to the weapon to be released.

---

20. RBS tone—ON. (N) (RBS only)

   Navigator turns tone on at approximately 10 seconds TG.

21. Timing expiration, RBS tone—OFF. (N) (RBS only)

EWO ONLY

22. Timing expiration—Bombs away. (N)

   a. For pod release the navigator will depress the electrical release switch at timing expiration. If the pod fails to release, pull the mechanical release handle.

   b. For a small weapon release depress the electrical release switch at timing expiration.

Note

For subsequent release or escape maneuver return to step 17 of the BOMB RUN checklist.

POST RELEASE CHECK.

When minimum interval releases are being accomplished, this checklist, except for necessary release data, will be completed after the last release only.

1. Release data—Recorded.
2. Released lamp—On.
3. Release signal present lamp—Off, press-to-test.
▶ 4. Weapon selector switch—Steps clockwise to next position. Step manually, if required.

POST RELEASE CHECK. (CONT'D)

5. Bomb damage evaluation switch—OFF.
6. Auto radar photo switch—OFF.
7. Intervalometer selector knob—As desired.
8. Aimpoint selector knob—FIX.
9. Destination indicators—Set.
10. Search radar mode selector knob—GRD.

Note

Repeat ALTERNATE BOMBING checklist, as required, for each successive weapon release.

PRIOR TO PENETRATION.

WARNING

The navigator will confirm penetration procedures for penetration, low approach, or low altitude tactical operations with particular emphasis on altitude restrictions.

Note

For explanation of asterisked(*) items refer to "Taxi-Back Landing Procedures", this section.

1. Communication panel—Checked. (N-DSO)
   Place command mixer switch to ON to monitor emergency transmissions until after engine shutdown.
2. Fixpoint indicators—Set.
   Set coordinates and elevation of HI ALT FIX in the fixpoint indicators. Set coordinates and elevation of upwind end of runway in storage fixpoint indicators.
3. MAG VAR—Set.
4. Ballistics—Set.
   TF set for approach, trail and BW zeroed. (ATF computed from AFT for Airborne Approach chart, figure 8-3).
5. Trail-TF malfunction switch—MALF.
6. Safety check—Complete.
   a. Pilot's arm control switch—SAFE. (P)
   b. Pod warhead control selector switch—SAFE.
   c. Small weapon lock switches (4)—LOCK.
   d. Safety lock handle—In, horizontal.
   e. Small weapon warhead control selector switches (4)—SAFE.
   f. Lock indicators (5)—LOCK.
      Pod lock indicator will show diagonal stripes if pod has been released.
   g. Arm indicators (5)—SAFE.
      Diagonal stripes will show if weapon has been released.
   ▶h. Weapon selector switch—OFF.

Section VIII
Crew Duties

T.O. 1B-58A-1

PRIOR TO PENETRATION. (CONT'D)

► i. Auto release switch—OFF.
  j. Pod warhead control selector switch—OFF.
  k. Small weapon warhead control selector switches (4)—OFF.
7. Function selector knob—BOMB.
   Direct or monitor aircraft to the high altitude fix or radio facility.
* 8. Barometric altimeter—Reset. (P-N-DSO)
   Reset altimeters to station pressure immediately prior to initiating penetration or passing through transition altitude.

atf for airborne approach

Trail Set to O

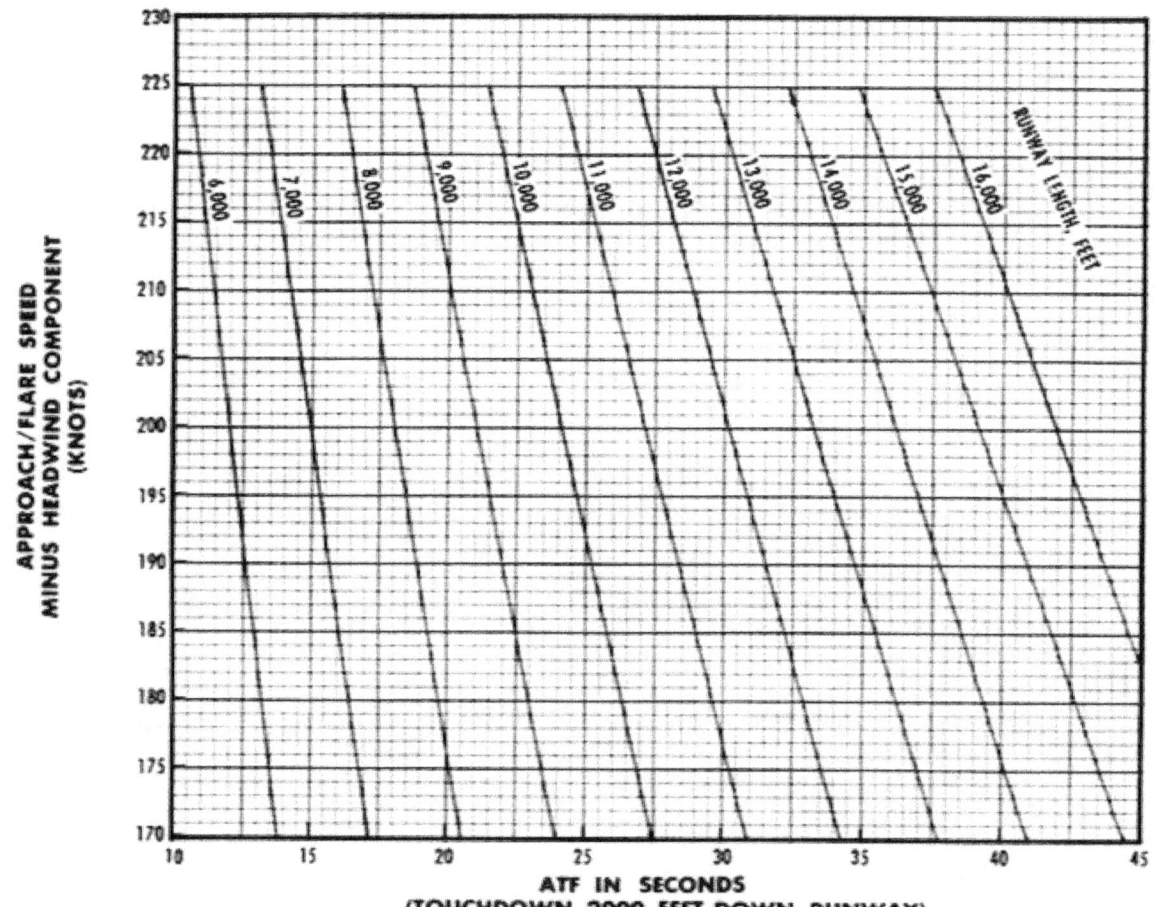

ENTER AT LEFT WITH APPROACH/FLARE SPEED MINUS HEADWIND COMPONENT, GO HORIZONTALLY RIGHT TO RUNWAY LENGTH, VERTICALLY DOWN AND READ ATF FROM THE ATF SCALE.

Figure 8-3.

PENETRATION.

> **WARNING**
>
> The navigator will monitor airplane altitudes and position during penetration, approach, and missed approach. Reference will be made to the applicable FLIP chart to ascertain that the airplane is following the established pattern. The pilot will be notified of any significant deviation from the penetration, approach or missed approach pattern.

Note

- As a cross check of airplane position, utilize manual search radar occasionally during holding or penetration legs on which the course is divergent from the PDI indication. This will insure that the navigator has radar coverage of the terrain along and adjacent to the aircraft's ground track.

- For explanation of asterisked (*) items refer to "Taxi-Back Landing Procedures", this section.

1. Penetration fix—Start penetration.
    a. Use present position counters or TG zero plus TF to determine when airplane is over the penetration fix.
    b. Fixpoint position indicators—Set.
2. Descent altitude calls—Accomplish.
    The navigator will announce altitudes to the pilot every 5000 feet starting with the first multiple of 5000 feet until 5000 feet above any leveloff or minimum altitude, then every 1000 feet down to, and at leveloff or minimum altitude.
3. Aircraft descent and altitude—Directed or monitored.
    PDI centered on inbound leg to the station.
* 4. Work table—Stowed. (N-DSO).
5. Low altitude radar altimeter—Checked.
    Set the minimum altitude index pointer at 5000 feet and at 5000 feet above terrain check that the crosshatched (fail) indicator disappears and that the warning lamps light.
6. Low altitude radar altimeter—Set.
    Position the minimum altitude index pointer so the warning lamps will light when airplane descends to less than desired altitude above terrain.

APPROACH.

Note

Navigator calls TG and corresponding MSL altitudes to adjust rate of descent. Altitude referenced to TG in checklist represent altitudes above field elevation. Slant ranges reference to altitude in checklist represent distance to near end of the runway based on a 2.5 degree glide path and are to be used to cross check aircraft position using manual radar.

1. TG 100 seconds, 1350 feet   MSL (Start Descent)   5 NM
2. TG 60 seconds, 800 feet   MSL   3 NM
3. TG 30 seconds, 400 feet   MSL   1.5 NM
4. TG 15 seconds, 200 feet   MSL   0.75 NM
5. TG 0 seconds, 0 feet   MSL (Touchdown).

Section VIII
Crew Duties

T.O. 1B-58A-1

APPROACH. (CONT'D)

Note

- At TG zero the aircraft will be at touchdown point, which is 2000 feet down the runway.
- If a practice radar directed approach is being made, it will be discontinued at the established SAC minimum approach altitude.
- For hot weather operation or an air conditioning malfunction, the BNS and search radar may be turned off in the traffic pattern during VFR conditions.

6. Function selector knob—TAXI & TAKEOFF.

AFTER LANDING.

1. Manual request—Performed, cycle camera 5 times to prevent film fogging.
   When the search power switch is in STBY, the ICU switch must be placed to TEST before the camera will advance film.
2. Unnecessary electrical equipment—OFF.
   To reduce the air conditioning requirements and residual heat of the primary navigation system, de-energize all electrical and electronic equipment not required immediately upon touchdown and during the landing roll.

CAUTION

To reduce residual heat, all components of the primary navigation system should be turned off at least five minutes before engine shutdown.

   a. Recorder power switch—OFF.
   b. Search power switch—OFF.
   c. Doppler transmitter switch—OFF.
   d. Function selector knob—OFF.
   e. Radio altimeter switch—OFF.
   f. PI beacon power knob—OFF.
   g. RV beacon power knob—OFF.
   h. AFRS power switch(es)—OFF.
3. Handgrip safety pins (2)—Installed. (P-N-DSO)
4. TACAN—OFF. (P-N)
5. Low altitude radar altimeter—OFF. (P-N)

TAXI-BACK LANDING.

Note

The normal AFTER LANDING checklist will be utilized, however, the Function Selector knob will be placed to GYRO and the handgrip safety pins need not be installed. After the drag chute installation is complete, continue with the following checklist.

Prior to Taxi.

1. Electrical power and air conditioning—Normal. (P)
2. Function selector knob—Standby.

8-48

TAXI-BACK LANDING. (CONT'D)

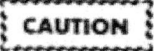

Do not clear pilot to taxi until one minute after function selector knob is advanced to standby, in order to prevent damage to BNS stabilization tables.

3. Search power switch—Standby.
4. ICU switch—Normal.
5. AFRS switch—AFRS.
6. BDH-IND switch—BDH-IND.
7. TACAN—T/R. (P-N)
8. Fuse Panels—Checked. (N-DSO)
9. Handgrip safety pins (2)—Removed and stowed.

Note

- Continue with the normal LINE-UP checklist. If a climbout to altitude is to be made, accomplish the complete AFTER TAKEOFF checklist.

- If traffic pattern altitude is to be maintained, accomplish the asterisked (*) items of the PRIOR TO PENETRATION and PENETRATION checklists prior to landing and proceed with the AFTER LANDING checklist after the final landing.

ENGINE SHUTDOWN.

1. Canopy jettison handle safety pin—Installed. (P-N-DSO)
2. Pod air conditioning control switch—OFF (if installed).

BEFORE LEAVING AIRPLANE.

1. Canopy seal control lever—UNSEALED. (when requested).
2. Oxygen system—NORMAL and OFF. (P-N-DSO)
3. Canopies—Open. (P-N-DSO)
   Place lever to CLOSE and hold for a minimum of 5 seconds; then immediately position lever to OPEN. Do not open canopies in headwinds exceeding 60 knots.
4. Canopy lock—Installed. (P-N-DSO)
5. All switches—OFF or SAFE. (P-N-DSO)
   Check that all switches are off, safe or positioned properly before leaving airplane. All weapon control switches should be safe and sealed, if applicable.

Note

Your normal and emergency abbreviated checklists are contained in T.O. 1B-58A-1CL-2.

Section VIII
Crew Duties

T.O. 1B-58A-1

MANUAL GROUNDSPEED CORRECTION PROCEDURE.

1. Select a radar target of known or determinable elevation.
2. Turn fixpoint selector knob to MANUAL.
3. Turn aimpoint selector knob to FIX.
4. Set elevation of selected target on fixpoint position elevation indicator.
5. Turn tracking and flight controller selector knob to FIX PT POS CORR.
6. Turn search transmitter switch to ON, and adjust for optimum indicator presentation.
7. Depress engaging switch, center image under crosshairs with tracking and flight stick, and release engaging switch.
8. If crosshairs drift, adjust sea drift velocity knobs to cancel drift. (Adjust sea drift component values in the direction of X-hair drift, i.e., X-hair drift N.E., sea drift values must be N. & E.).
9. Turn fixpoint selector knob to PRESENT POSITION.
10. Turn search transmitter switch to OFF.
11. Turn tracking and flight controller selector knob to OFF.

MULTIPLE DRIFT PROCEDURE.

1. After initial lineup, with azimuth mark through target area, note or record relative bearing indication when target passes through the nearest fixed range marker.
2. Repeat this procedure when target passes through the next range marker. The azimuth difference times range ratio will be the drift difference required. Example: Initial relative bearing was 354° at the 80 NM fixed range marker. The next bearing was 358° at the 60 NM fixed range marker, the azimuth change was 4° right, the range ratio 80 NM to 20 NM; or 4; therefore, multiply 4 x 4 to obtain 16°R drift correction.
3. Correct relative bearing indicator (in opposite direction of target drift) by the amount computed (16°L).
4. Correct aircraft heading until the azimuth marker is through the target.
5. Repeat the multiple drift correction as needed.

RADAR POSITION FIX PROCEDURE.

1. Turn aimpoint selector knob to FIX.
2. Set fixpoint altitude above sea level on fixpoint position elevation indicator.
3. Monitor present position indicators. When present latitude is within 200 minutes of fixpoint latitude and present longitude is within 300 minutes of fixpoint longitude, turn fixpoint selector knob to MANUAL.
4. Place radar sighting switch to AUTO.
5. Set fixpoint latitude and longitude on fixpoint position indicators.
6. Place search power switch to XMTG and adjust for optimum indicator presentation.
7. Monitor crosshair distance indication, and as airplane closes on fixpoint, turn range and magnification selector knob progressively to decrease range and increase magnification.
8. If crosshairs do not coincide with fixpoint, turn tracking and flight controller selector knob to PRES POS CORR, depress engaging switch, center crosshairs with tracking and flight control stick, and release engaging switch. True present position indicators now show corrected latitude and longitude.

GROUND BOMBING COMPUTER CHECK.

1. RBS tone selector switch—Checked. (DSO)
   Set radio on unused channel.
2. Function selector knob—STANDBY.
3. Search power switch—STBY.
4. Vertical reference selector switch—AIR ERECT.
5. Airspeed inertial switch—A-S INERTIAL.
6. Function selector knob—BOMB.
7. TG servo malfunction switch—MALF.
8. Machmeter malfunction switch—MALF.
   With the airspeed computer malfunction knob, set 600 knots TAS in the groundspeed indicator.
9. TG servo malfunction switch—NORMAL.
   Check that the groundspeed indicator still reads 600 knots.
10. ICU switch—TEST.
11. Radar sighting switch—AUTO.
12. Range/magnification selector knob—60/60.
13. Ballistics—Set.
    Set Tf to a value of 4.0 seconds and trail to a value of zero feet. Check Trail-TF switch in MALF.
14. Heading reference selector knob—Slew TH and TC to 360°.
15. Heading reference selector knob—FREE GYRO.
16. True present position indicators—Set.
    Set latitude and longitude to present position.
17. Fixpoint position indicators—Set.
    a. Set fixpoint longitude to present position longitude.
    b. Set fixpoint latitude to present position latitude, plus 30 nautical miles north.
18. PDI—Checked. (P)
    Check that the PDI is centered and the ground track dial reads 360°.
19. Computer release check—Accomplished.
    a. When the 10 mile FRM and the VRM coincide, start stopwatch.
    b. Stop timing at release—Tone off.
    c. The BNS computer release should be 56 (± 3) seconds.

CAUTION

To reduce residual heat, all components of the primary navigation system should be turned off at least five minutes before engine shutdown.

ALTITUDE CALIBRATION AND RADAR RANGING CHECK.

Note

For manual altitude calibration, set fixpoint elevation counter to local terrain elevation, turn radio altimeter switch to other than calibrate position and perform steps 4 through 10 and step 13 below.

Section VIII
Crew Duties

T.O. 1B-58A-1

ALTITUDE CALIBRATION AND RADAR RANGING CHECK. (CONT'D)

1. Radio altimeter switch—CALIBRATE.
2. Calibrate altitude normally. Note Hsl in Hsl indicator.
3. Radio altimeter switch—ON.
4. Radar sighting switch—AUTO.
5. Range magnification—30/10.
6. Fixpoint selector switch—PRESENT POSITION.
7. Antenna tilt—Full down.
8. Search mode selector knob—SL.
9. Search power switch—XMTG.
10. Altitude correction knob—Adjusted.

    Adjust altitude correction knob until range crosshair and first ground return coincide, note Hsl. Compare corrected Hsl with Hsl noted in step 2. If Hsl difference exceeds 500 feet, proceed with step 11.

Note

If Hsl difference exceeds 500 feet, an error exists in either radar ranging or radio altimeter calibration circuit.

11. Correct pressure altitude for instrument error and apply D value. Compare reading with Hsl determined in steps 2 and 10. Determine correct Hsl.
12. Remedial action:
    a. If error exists in radio altitude calibration circuit, apply correction factor for future radio altitude calibrations.
    b. Utilize fixed angle bombing technique.
13. Reposition switches for normal operation—Reset.

    Antenna tilt detent; Range magnification as desired; Radar sighting switch manual; Search mode selector ground; Search power switch as desired; Fixpoint selector knob as desired.

DEFENSIVE SYSTEM OPERATOR'S CHECKLIST

CRUISE.

1. MD-7 Operational Check:
   a. Scope dimming knob—As desired.
      Check for proper edge lighting.
   b. Receiver gain—Adjust to 3/4 clockwise.
   c. Scope gain—Adjust clockwise for vertical trace.
   d. Master switch—OPR.
      Observe a horizontal sweep of the vertical trace, within the azimuth limits of the scope after the system has timed in.

Note

● In an emergency, the fifteen minute warm-up period may be omitted. If the master switch is turned from the OFF position directly to the OPR position, the system will become operative after a time delay of 8 to 15 minutes after which the system may be fired accurately.

CRUISE. (CONT'D)

- Simultaneous operation of the search radar and fire control system on the same frequency may result in interference with the search radar presentation. Interference may appear as a symmetrical dot pattern on the search radar scope. Changing the frequency of either system should eliminate the interference.

- When switching the trackbreaker systems from STANDBY to ON positions, the transient signal may cause the fire control system to get a false lock-on. When this lock-on occurs, the system will automatically return to search after approximately one second. If the system does not return to search, depress the resume search button.

 e. ATA range knob—Full CW.

 f. Receiver gain—Adjust.

  Adjust clockwise until system locks on noise. Decrease (CCW) until just below lock-on level. If noise lock-on cannot be eliminated by reducing receiver gain, select another frequency with the anti-jam button.

 g. ATA range control—OFF.

 h. Marker generator—ON.

 i. Scope gain—Adjust.

  Adjust the scope gain control until range markers appear at the desired intensity without saturation. Observe that range markers appear at odd multiples of 500 yards.

 j. Storage control—Adjust.

  Adjust alternately with scope gain control for desired persistence. Receiver gain adjustments should not be used to achieve a desired scope display.

 k. Marker generator—OFF.

  Turn the marker generator off and observe that the marker presentation fades from the scope in approximately four seconds. If the fade time is greatly different from 4 seconds, adjust the storage control for desired persistence.

 l. Erase button—Depress.

  Depress the erase button and note that the video is blanked from the scope.

 m. Cursor button—Checked.

  Depress the cursor button on the manual control handle and move the handle in all quadrants noting that the cursor marker is positioned accordingly in azimuth and range.

 n. Marker generator—ON.

 o. Manual target lock-on—Completed.

  Depress the cursor button and position the cursor on the 1500 yard marker; depress the manual button, allowing time for the antenna to position in azimuth; release the manual button first, then release the cursor button. The system should remain locked on the marker and future range meter should indicate 1500 yards. Note that the target warning lamp remains lighted.

 p. Resume search button—Depress.

  Depress the resume search button momentarily and release. The system should return to search.

 q. Anti-jam button—Checked.

  (1) Manually lock on 6500 yard range marker.

  (2) Depress resume search button.

  (3) Depress anti-jam button.

  (4) Repeat above three steps on all 10 channels and observe the following.

   The range markers will fade from the scope and reappear as system finds new frequency. Allow a minimum of 20 seconds between each actuation of the anti-jam button during training missions. For tactical missions, allow a minimum of two seconds between actuations.

Section VIII
Crew Duties

T.O. 1B-58A-1

CRUISE. (CONT'D)

Note

- A slight difference may be noted between intensity of range markers which would not indicate a malfunction. With some scope adjustment, it may be difficult to see all ten range markers. The target warning lamp may be disregarded during the above check.
- If acquisition at 6500 yards is not possible on any channel, a malfunction exists on that channel.

r. ATA range knob—Full CW.

Turn ATA range knob fully clockwise. Automatic acquisition of one of the markers should occur, as indicated by a change in presentation to a vertical row of dots, one of which is offset by the tracking gate. Observe that the target warning lamp is lighted.

Note

Azimuth position has no meaning when locked on markers, and a slow drift to an azimuth limit is not abnormal. The vertical row of dots may not extend the full range of the scope due to track level automatic gain control action.

s. Marker generator—OFF.
t. Resume search button—Depress.

Check that the leading edge of the ATA gate is at the maximum range.

u. ATA range knob—As required.
v. Burst length control knob—SET.

For training missions set burst length control knob to the 2-second position. For EWO set as briefed.

──────────── EWO ONLY ────────────

w. Firing voltage amp fuse—Inserted.

At briefed point during EWO mission insert 1 amp firing voltage fuse.

x. Safe-Firing Switch—FIRE.
y. Scope (MD-7)—Monitor for fighters.

────────────────────────────────────

2. MD-7 Live Fire Training Procedures.
   a. Range Clearance—Obtained.
   b. MD-7 System—ON—Operational Check Complete.
   c. Firing voltage 1 amp fuse—Inserted.
   d. Safe-Fire Switch—FIRE.
   e. Scope (MD-7)—Observe To Clear Area.

WARNING

Scope vigilance must be maintained throughout training firing by depressing the resume search button for at least six seconds after each firing burst. Cease firing if MD-7 fire control radar becomes inoperative.

   f. Lock on—Accomplished.

The MD-7 must be locked on noise or a range marker to fire when the master switch is in the operate position.

CRUISE. (CONT'D)

    g. Fire out—Completed.

        Press the firing button to fire 2-second bursts with a minimum of 10 seconds between bursts.

    h. Safe-Fire switch—SAFE.

    i. Firing voltage 1 amp fuse—Removed and inverted.

    j. MD-7 master switch—OFF.

    k. Safety check—Reported.

        Reported to crew that the safe-fire switch is safe, firing voltage fuse is removed, and MD-7 master switch is OFF prior to departing the gunnery range or firing area.

3. Fighter Interceptor Training Procedures:

    a. MD-7 System—ON and operational check complete.

    b. Safety Procedures:

        (1) Firing voltage 1 amp fuse—Removed and inverted.

        (2) Safe-Fire switch—SAFE and safetied.

        (3) Ammo-jettison button—Guarded down.

        (4) Report Safety check complete—Reported.

            Report to crew and controller that safety check is complete.

    c. UHF mixer switch—ON.

        DSO will monitor GCI frequency during fighter attacks.

    d. GCI clearance—Obtained.

        Clearance must be obtained from GCI to activated ECM equipment and to drop chaff.

Do not depress firing button.

    e. Accomplishments—Logged.

        At completion, confirm accomplishments with GCI controller.

4. Chaff Dispenser (when chaff is to be dispensed).

    a. Chaff clearance—Obtained (training only).

    b. Trackbreak, deception, and delayed opening channel power switch—OFF.

    c. Mode switch—As required.

    d. Burst switch—As required.

    e. Main power switch—STBY 10 sec., then ON.

    f. Power interrupt light—OFF.

        When the power interrupt light is ON, the system will not dispense chaff.

    g. Trackbreak, deception, and delayed opening channel power switches—As required.

    h. Chaff drop—Completed.

    i. Main power switch—OFF.

5. ALR-12 Noise Elimination.

Note

An abnormal voltage or frequency may cause interference.

Position equipment switches as indicated while monitoring the ALR-12. If a system is not causing interference it may be returned to the desired mode of operation immediately while continuing the remainder of the check.

    a. MD-7—STBY.

Section VIII
Crew Duties

T.O. 1B-58A-1

CRUISE. (CONT'D)

    b. ALQ-16s—STBY.
    c. Chaff Dispenser Power Switch—OFF.
    d. Chaff Control Fuse, Right AC Panel—Reversed.
    e. IFF—STBY.
    f. ARC-110—Transmit briefly.
    g. ARC-110—OFF.
    h. ALR-12—OFF then ON.
    i. TACAN—REC. (P)
    j. Anti Collision lights—OFF. (P)
    k. Navigation lights—OFF. (P)
    l. PI Beacon (APN-136)—OFF. (N)
    m. RV Beacon (APN-135)—OFF. (N)
    n. Radio Altimeter (APN-110)—OFF. (N)
    o. Doppler Radar—OFF. (N)
    p. Search Radar (RTM)—STBY. (N)

DECM SYSTEM OPERATIONAL GROUND CHECK.

This check should be accomplished by the DSO whenever the aircraft is being placed on Alert, when requested by A&E, or when the DSO deems it necessary.

> **CAUTION**
>
> DECM equipment must not be operated without air conditioning.

1. ALQ-16 power knobs (3)—STBY, lamps press-to-test.
2. ALQ-16 program selector knobs (3)—CAM 1.
3. Chaff dispenser power interrupt lamp—Press-to-test.
4. ALR-12 power switch—POWER, lamps press-to-test, then OFF. Place ALR-12 power switch to power and after 30 seconds warmup, press-to-test lamps. Place DECM mixer switch ON and check for signals in each Quadrant with the audio selector knob. Signal reception will depend on Radar Equipment in the area. Turn Power Switch OFF.
5. ALQ-16 Operational Check.
    After a 3 minute warmup period each ALQ-16 will be checked individually as follows:
    a. Programmer—Checked.
        Select CAM 2 with the program selector knob. After the program change lamp goes out (approximately 6 seconds), return program selector knob to CAM 1. Program change lamp should go out in approximately 2 minutes.

Note

If lamp does not go out, the programmer is most likely stuck. (Refer to T.O. 1B-58A-1A for further action.)

    b. Program selector knob—CYCLIC.
    c. Power knob—ON (T-4); Mode I or Mode II (T-2).

DECM SYSTEM OPERATIONAL GROUND CHECK. (CONT'D)

   d. Test button—Checked.

      Momentarily depress test button and check that transmitter warning lamp lights and that the green program change lamp lights momentarily to indicate program change. A momentary flicker of the program change lamp is an indication of operation.

> **CAUTION**
>
> It may be necessary to hold the test button depressed up to 10 seconds to allow warm-up before transmitter warning lamp lights; but to prevent test oscillator damage, do not hold the test button depressed with the transmitter warning lamp on for extended periods of time.

   e. Power knob—OFF.

> **Note**
>
> Your normal abbreviated checklist is contained in T.O. 1B-58A-1CL-1.

GROUND CREW ALERT CHECKLIST.

When the airplane is moved to the alert line, the ground crew will refuel the airplane as necessary, then complete the "Alert Line Preparation" checklist after the flight crew has cocked the airplane.

Access to a cocked airplane will be in accordance with command directives.

When the order to scramble is given, the ground crew shall immediately complete the ground crew scramble checklist and assist the flight crew as indicated. Two ground crew men will be required. If local conditions or the weather require additional personnel, the extra personnel will assist the normal ground crew in expediting the launch. After a practice alert, the airplane will be refueled if necessary and the "Alert Line Preparation" checklist will be completed after the flight crew has re-cocked the airplane.

ALERT LINE PREPARATION.

1. Install engine inlet and exhaust covers as required.
2. Open No. 2 engine starter exhaust door (if installed).
3. Install canopy cover as required.
4. Install astrodome cover as required.
5. Install static ground wires on right and left main gear so that they will pull off when the airplane moves forward.
6. Install wheel chocks in front of nose gear and behind each main gear.
7. Install wheel covers as required.
8. Position two fire bottles: one between the starter and electrical power carts, and one by the outboard engine farthest from the power cart.

Section VIII
Crew Duties

T.O. 1B-58A-1

GROUND CREW ALERT CHECKLIST. (CONT'D)

9. Position crew entrance stand with back wheels locked straight, the front wheels cocked and the brakes set.
10. Position floodlights and ladder as required.
11. Position ground heater for cold weather operation. Keep the heater running at all times to preheat the ground power units using a two-way air duct outlet: one outlet to the starter cart and the other to the electrical power car.
12. Position ground power equipment well outboard of the wing tip with the starter cart hose and, if possible, the electric power lead routed behind the main gear to allow for immediate safe taxiing of the airplane.
13. Position the ground interphone cord for ready access and easy installation in event it is required during the start.
14. Reservice canopy pneumatic system pressure.

SCRAMBLE.

Crew Chief (GO =1)   **Assistant (GO =2)**

1. **REMOVE NO. 3 AND 4 ENGINE COVERS AND RIGHT MAIN TIRE COVERS.**

   REMOVE NO. 1 AND 2 ENGINE COVERS AND LEFT MAIN TIRE COVERS.

2. **REMOVE NOSE GEAR TIRE COVERS.**

   RELEASE CANOPY COVER BUCKLES AND PULL COVER CLEAR OF AIRPLANE.

   #### Note
   The Navigator and DSO will release the upper hooks and push the cover off.

3. **START ENGINE STARTER CART AND OPEN AIR OUTPUT SWITCH; THEN, START ELECTRICAL POWER CART AND TURN ON GENERATORS.**

   UNSEAL AND OPEN CANOPIES.

4. ———

   REMOVE 3 PITOT TUBE COVERS.
   Remove cover from pitot boom, secondary pitot tube and pod pitot tube.

5. **HELP REMOVE CREW ENTRANCE STAND (REAR).**

   REMOVE CREW ENTRANCE STAND (FRONT).
   Release brakes and push stand clear of the airplane and reset the brakes.

6. **STAND FIRE GUARD ON ENGINE NO. 3 AND 4.**

   STAND FIRE GUARD ON ENGINE NO. 1 AND 2.

   Monitor engine starts as fire guard while accomplishing other necessary items. In the event that trouble develops, contact the crew using the ground interphone as soon as possible.

7. **SIGNAL PILOT WHEN NAVIGATOR AND DSO CANOPIES ARE CLOSED.**
   Signal by extending the left arm in front and the right arm over the head and then moving the right arm down to meet the left. This signal will be continued until the pilot closes his canopy.

8-58

T.O. 1B-58A-1

**Section VIII
Crew Duties**

SCRAMBLE. (CONT'D)

Crew Chief (GO =1)   Assistant (GO =2)

Note

Closing of the pilot's canopy is the signal for the ground crew to continue with the remainder of the checklist items.

8. **CLOSE STARTER CART AIR OUTPUT SWITCH AND TURN OFF ELECTRICAL POWER CART GENERATORS.**

   REMOVE START CART AND ELECTRICAL POWER CART LEADS AND SECURE COVER PLATES.

   WARNING

   Be sure that GO =1 has turned off the carts before removing the leads.

9. **CLOSE AND LATCH NO. 2 ENGINE STARTER EXHAUST DOOR (IF INSTALLED) WHEN ENGINES ARE AT IDLE.**

   REMOVE CHOCKS AND STATIC WIRES.

   WARNING

   Be sure that all engines are at idle before entering engine inlet danger area.

10. **SIGNAL PILOT WHEN CLEAR TO TAXI.**

    SHUT DOWN STARTER AND ELECTRICAL POWER CARTS AND GROUND HEATER.

Note

Pilot will flash taxi light as signal for ground observer to connect interphone. Proceed as directed by pilot.

GROUND CREW SCRAMBLE CHECKLIST FROM POWER-ON STANDBY POSITION.

Crew Chief (GO =1)   Assistant (GO =2)

1. **START ENGINE STARTER CART AND OPEN AIR OUTPUT SWICH WHEN ADVISED BY THE AIRCREW.**

2. **STAND FIRE GUARD ON ENGINES NO. 3 AND 4.**

   STAND FIRE GUARD ON ENGINES NO. 1 AND 2.

8-59

Section VIII
Crew Duties

T.O. 1B-58A-1

GROUND CREW SCRAMBLE CHECKLIST FROM POWER-ON STANDBY POSITION. (CONT'D)

Crew Chief (GO =1)   **Assistant (GO =2)**

Monitor engine starts as fire guard while accomplishing other necessary items. In the event that trouble develops, contact the crew using the ground interphone as soon as possible.

3. CLOSE STARTER CART AIR OUTPUT SWITCH AND TURN OFF ELECTRICAL POWER CART GENERATORS WHEN ADVISED BY THE AIRCREW.

REMOVE START CART AND ELECTRICAL POWER CART LEADS AND SECURE COVER PLATES.

WARNING

Be sure that GO =1 has turned off the carts before removing the leads.

4. CLOSE AND LATCH NO. 2 ENGINE STARTER EXHAUST DOOR (IF INSTALLED) WHEN ENGINES ARE AT IDLE.

WARNING

Be sure that all engines are at idle before entering engine inlet danger area.

5. REMOVE INTERPHONE CORD.

6. SIGNAL PILOT WHEN CLEAR TO TAXI.

REMOVE CHOCKS AND STATIC WIRE.

SHUT DOWN STARTER AND ELECTRICAL POWER CARTS AND GROUND HEATER.

Note

The abbreviated ground crew checklist is contained in the "Navigator's Abbreviated Flight Crew Checklist," T.O. 1B-58A-1CL-2. It is the responsibility of each unit to ascertain that the ground crew portion of that checklist is routed to the appropriate personnel.

This is the last page in Section VIII.

Section IX
All Weather Operation

TABLE OF CONTENTS.

	Page		Page
Instrument Flight Procedures	9-1	Night Flying	9-12
Ice and Rain	9-9	Cold Weather Procedures	9-12
Turbulence and Thunderstorms	9-11	Hot Weather and Desert Operation	9-17

Note

- In general this section consists of procedures and information which differ from, or are supplementary to, the normal operating instructions of Sections II and IV. In some cases, however, repetition has been necessary for emphasis, clarity, or continuity of thought.

- For the purpose of instrument approaches the B-58 is classified as a category E aircraft.

Instrument Flight Procedures

The airplane, designed for supersonic flight, demands a high degree of instrument flying proficiency and conscientious preflight mission planning. Proficient instrument flying is aided by a sound knowledge of the automatic trim feature of the flight control system and the aerodynamic characteristics of flying in the transonic region.

The airplane is essentially "G" stable when flying in the automatic mode of flight control operation, whereas conventional subsonic bomber aircraft are "speed stable". Once trimmed (control stick in the null position), the automatic trim will reposition the elevator, tending to maintain one "G" flight regardless of airspeed changes or thrust changes.

9-1

Section IX
All Weather Operation

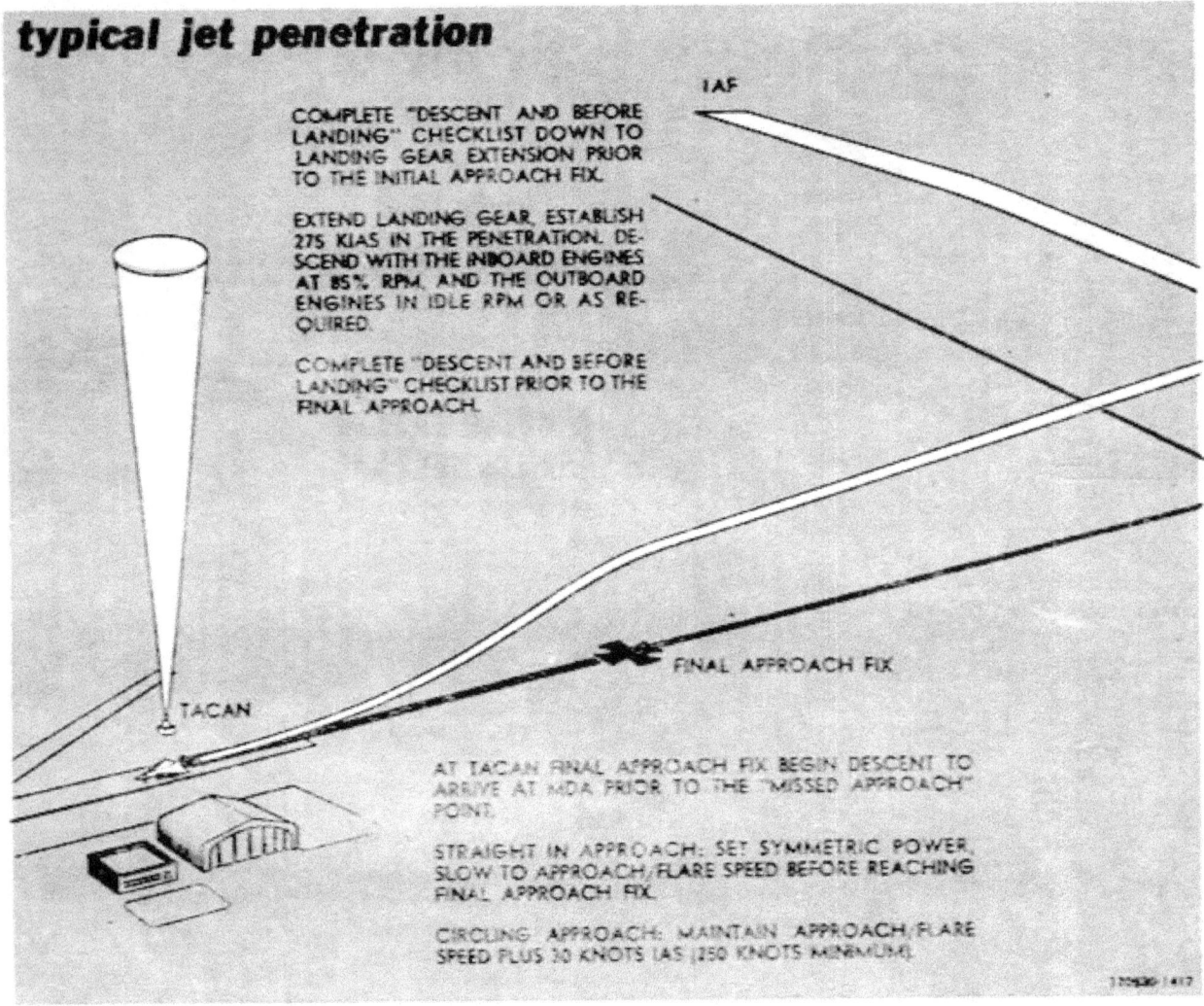

Figure 9-1. (Sheet 1 of 2)

The following procedures and techniques are provided only for supplementing normal procedures during instrument flight conditions. Due to the variations in facilities and terrain from one base to another, this information should serve only as a guide to commanders in setting up standard instrument procedures. In planning instrument flights, fuel requirements for completion of jet penetration, low approach and missed approach procedures and possible diversion to an alternate base, plus reserve fuel requirements must be included in preflight planning. Complex ATC departure clearances should be avoided. A minimum of channel changes, reporting points, airspeed and/or altitude changes is not only desirable but mandatory during this critical phase of instrument flight. Crew coordination and check list procedures should be accomplished in a manner that will not distract the pilot. The value of preplanning and crew coordination cannot be over-emphasized during instrument flight conditions.

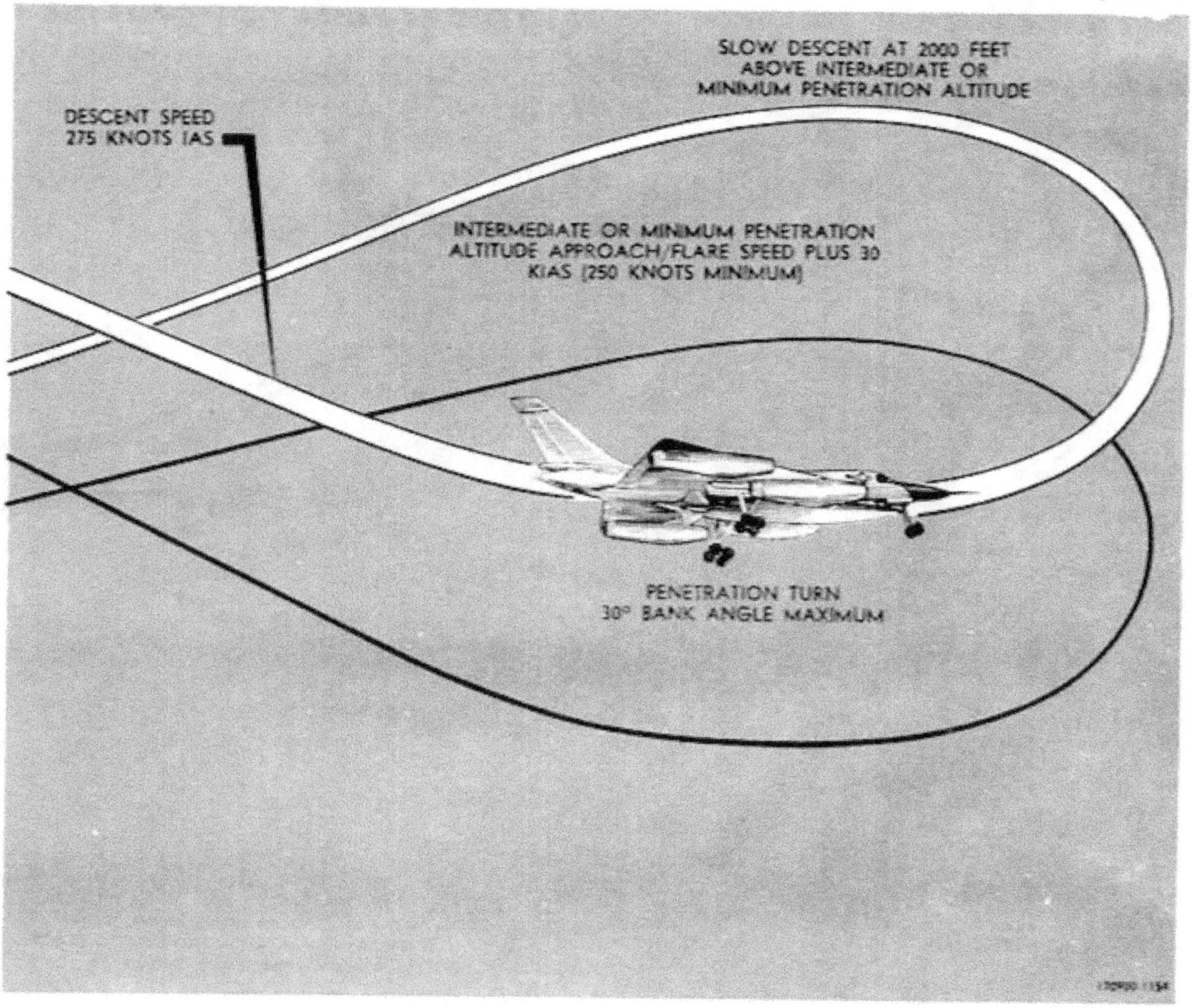

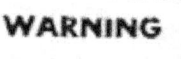

Figure 9-1. (Sheet 2 of 2)

INSTRUMENT TAKEOFF.

Particular emphasis should be given to pitot heat, rain removal system, defog system, all radio equipment and IFF. The pilot's heading selector switch should be positioned to J-4 position for takeoff and climb. If both the PNS and AFRS fail, heading can be read from the magnetic compass. In taxi attitude, with the index mark on the pitch trim knob aligned with the reference mark on the MM-3 indicator, the attitude should show approximately 3 degrees nose down. Rotation to a takeoff attitude of 10 degrees nose up will approximate the optimum takeoff attitude at takeoff speed.

WARNING

An acceleration error of 2 or 3 degrees on the pilot's MM-3 attitude indicator should be taken into consideration.

With the airplane aligned on the runway and ready for takeoff, check the indications of the BDHI and the magnetic compass against known runway heading. Takeoff procedures during an instrument takeoff are essentially the same as for a visual takeoff. The BDHI

Section IX
All Weather Operation

T.O. 1B-58A-1

typical radar approach

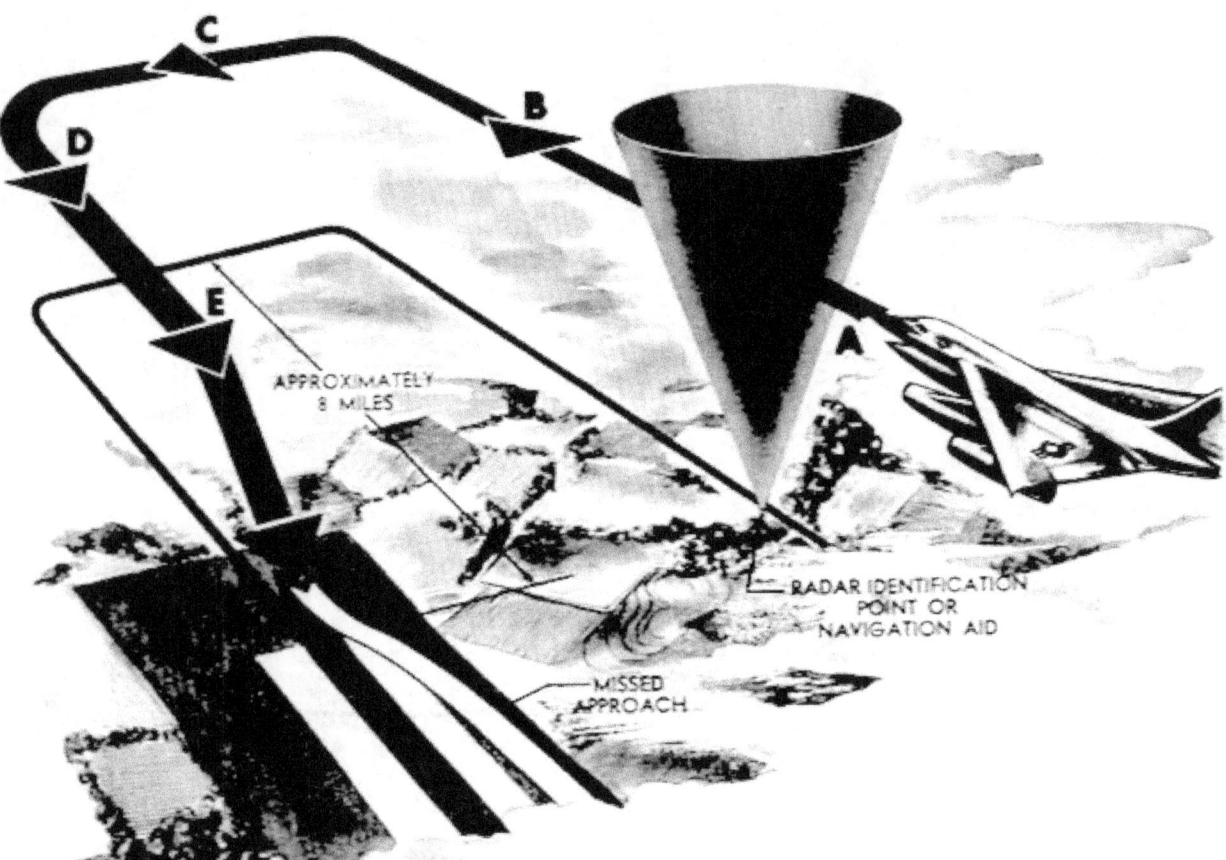

A The "Descent and Before Landing" check list should be completed prior to reaching radar identification point or as soon as possible after release to the radar controller. Comply with all radar instructions throughout the pattern.

B Set symmetric power. Maintain straight and level flight on downwind leg. Establish or maintain approach/flare speed plus 30 knots IAS (250 knots minimum).

C Prior to turning on final approach, slow to approach/flare speed plus 20 knots IAS (220 knots minimum).

D After completing turn to final approach, continue straight and level flight and slow down to approach/flare speed.

E Upon reaching glide path, gradually reduce power and begin a constant rate of descent to stabilize the airplane on the glide path. Maintain approach/flare speed.

F Maintain approach/flare speed.

NOTE

In the event a straight-in approach is made, accomplish steps A, B, C, and D before reaching the glide path.

Figure 9-2.

should be closely monitored for maintaining airplane heading on the runway, but reference should also be made to the runway centerline or the runway lights. Use of rain removal system may be required to improve forward visibility during precipitation.

Takeoff attitude should be approximately 10 degrees nose up on the MM-3 attitude indicator which will give an angle of attack of approximately 14 degrees. As the aircraft leaves the ground the MM-3 attitude indicator is used for both pitch and bank control. Both the altimeter and vertical velocity indicator will give negative indications during the takeoff roll and for approximately the first 150 feet of climb. After a definite climb indication is noted on the vertical velocity indicator and a positive increase in altitude is noted on the altimeter, brake wheels and then retract landing gear.

INSTRUMENT CLIMB.

Maintain a definite rate of climb on the vertical velocity indicator throughout the initial climb.

WARNING

Do not allow the vertical velocity to decrease below 500 feet per minute climb.

Airspeed will increase with the aircraft maintained at takeoff attitude and there is no noticeable pitch change as the gear retracts. Accelerate until climb speed of 350 or 425 KIAS is reached. Maintain climb speed schedule to level-off. Maximum bank angles of 30 degrees are normally used during climbing turns. When level-off is accomplished at intermediate altitudes, excessive speed will be avoided by reducing power to approximately 85 percent rpm. Power must then be readjusted to maintain between 350 and 425 knots IAS.

Note

The navigator should monitor the attitude indicator and notify the pilot of any unreliable indication.

INSTRUMENT CRUISING FLIGHT.

The flight characteristics of the airplane permit supersonic flight during instrument cruise conditions. In general, instrument cruise procedures do not differ from normal flight procedures. Refer to Section VI for cruising characteristics at high speed. For normal operation, limit maximum angle of bank to 30 degrees in all turns.

DESCENT.

Instrument descent to initial penetration altitudes may be made without difficulty with landing gear either up or down. However, for maximum ease of handling, a gear up, constant mach airspeed let down utilizing the automatic mode of elevator control is recommended. Maintain mach no. 0.9 or 300 knots IAS to initial penetration altitude. Normally the elevator control available mode selector switch is changed to T.O. & LAND before the landing gear is extended. However, at normal cruising altitudes and airspeeds the flight controls are overly sensitive and "G" protection is forfeited if T.O. & LAND is selected. The recommended gear up descent should be used until departing the initial penetration altitude at the initial approach fix. If a penetration is initiated from cruise (optimum) altitude, or any altitude appreciably above the normal 20,000 foot initial penetration altitude, the flight control system should remain in the AUTO mode. The recommended procedure is to reduce power and descend at mach no. 0.9 or 300 knots IAS. When passing through 20,000 feet, place the elevator control available mode selector switch to T.O. & LAND and check for an increase to 20 degrees available.

HOLDING.

Holding should be accomplished at the altitude directed with landing gear retracted, at an IAS of 300 knots. Maximum bank angles of 30 degrees are normally used while holding.

JET PENETRATION.

Prior to beginning penetration ascertain the weather conditions and the availability of radar or ILS if the weather is below TACAN approach minimums. If ceiling or visibility is below published minimums, make the decision to proceed to alternate while still at altitude. Jet penetrations should be accomplished in accordance with the JAL (jet approach and landing charts) as shown in the latest FLIP, Terminal (High Altitude). Accomplish the "Descent and Before Landing" check list down to Landing Gear Extension prior to the initial approach fix or while in holding pattern.

Note

When penetrating from very high altitude or whenever the possibility exists that fogging will occur during penetration, activate windshield defog prior to penetration. Isolated cases have occurred where pilot's windshield has completely frosted over when power was applied at minimum penetration altitude and the pilot had failed to select defog prior to descent. Three to five minutes of maximum windshield defog may be required to clear a minimum area to maintain visual flight.

Section IX
All Weather Operation

T.O. 1B-58A-1

typical ils approach

A
Set symmetric power and complete "Descent and Before Landing" Checklist. Establish or maintain approach/flare speed plus 30 knots IAS (250 knots minimum) from initial fix to ILS system. Set inbound ILS course in course selector window. Intercept localizer course at an angle of 45° or less and at the specified altitude.

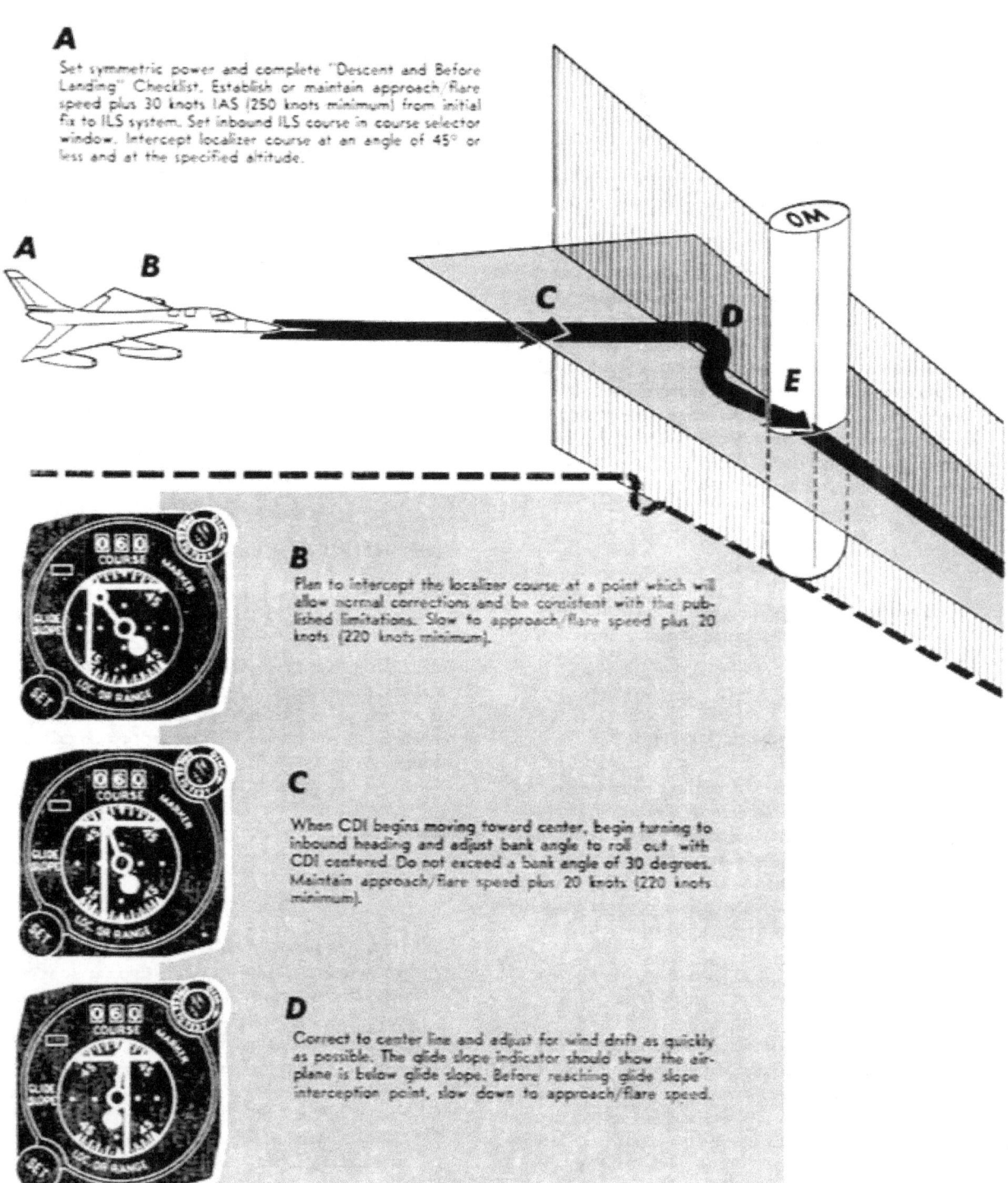

B
Plan to intercept the localizer course at a point which will allow normal corrections and be consistent with the published limitations. Slow to approach/flare speed plus 20 knots (220 knots minimum).

C
When CDI begins moving toward center, begin turning to inbound heading and adjust bank angle to roll out with CDI centered. Do not exceed a bank angle of 30 degrees. Maintain approach/flare speed plus 20 knots (220 knots minimum).

D
Correct to center line and adjust for wind drift as quickly as possible. The glide slope indicator should show the airplane is below glide slope. Before reaching glide slope interception point, slow down to approach/flare speed.

Figure 9-3. (Sheet 1 of 2)

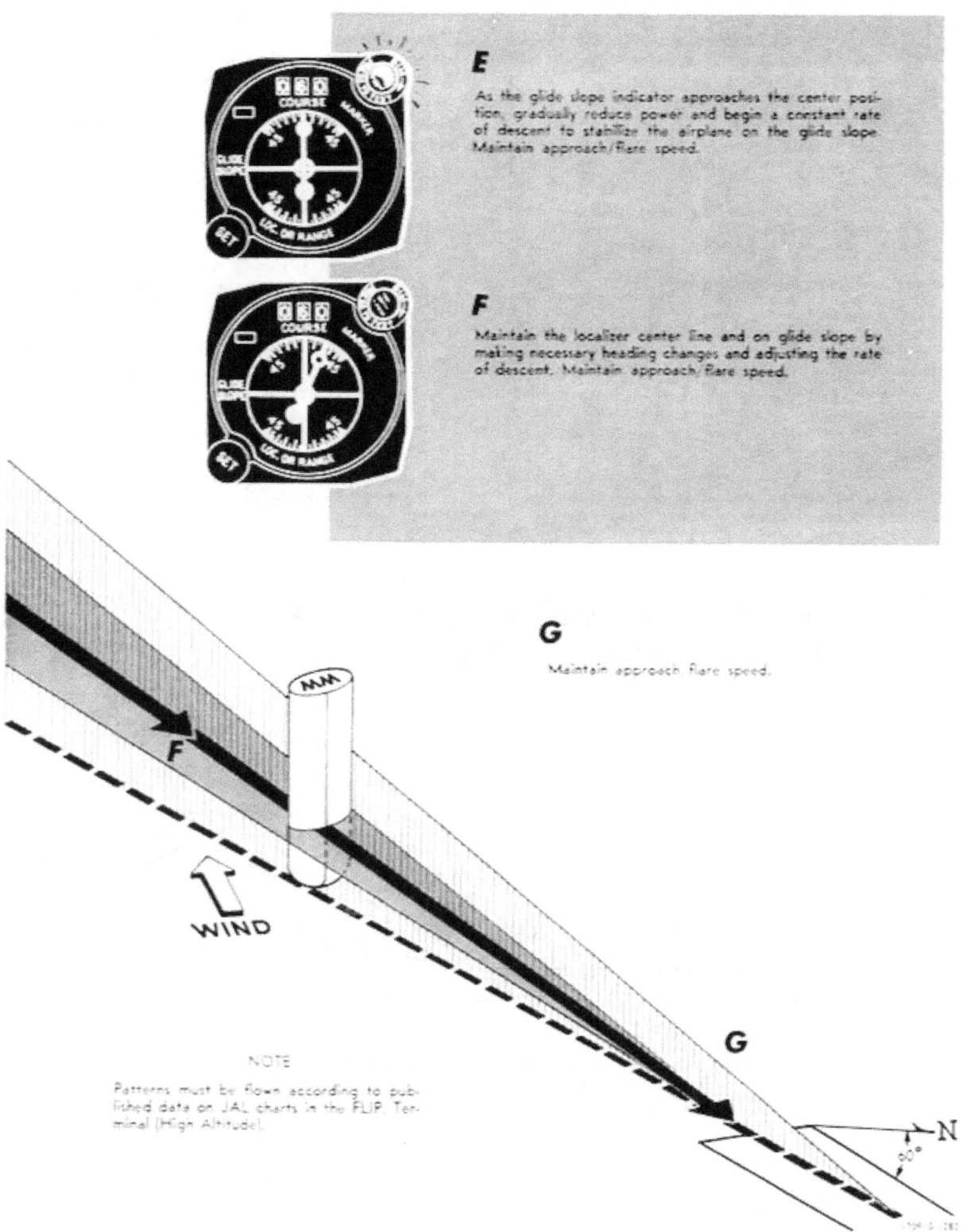

Figure 9-3. (Sheet 2 of 2)

Section IX
All Weather Operation

T.O. 1B-58A-1

Extend landing gear, establish 275 KIAS in the penetration. Descend with the inboard engines at 85% rpm, and the outboard engines in idle rpm or as required. Complete the DESCENT AND BEFORE LANDING checklist prior to starting final approach. Prior to penetration, the pilot will notify the crew of the initial or minimum penetration altitude for level off. The navigator will announce altitudes to the pilot every 5000 feet starting with the first multiple of 5000 feet until 5000 feet above any leveloff or minimum altitude, then 1000 feet down to and at leveloff or minimum altitude.

INSTRUMENT APPROACHES.

TACAN, radar, and ILS approaches are readily accomplished using standard procedures. Flight characteristics during instrument approaches do not differ from those encountered during normal visual flight. For those letdowns which allow only a small area for maneuvering, close attention and prior planning is required to prevent exceeding published limitations, particularly during the penetration phase. No problems should be encountered executing any published penetration procedure. Figure 9-1 illustrates a typical TACAN approach procedure. Landing lights should be turned on for all instrument approaches when not in contact with the tower. Caution should be exercised in the use of landing lights during night low approaches with reduced visibility due to precipitation, haze or fog. The angle at which the lights are aimed causes a glare to be reflected into the pilot's cockpit during reduced visibility.

CAUTION

If touchdown must be accomplished within the first 3000 feet of runway in order to stop in the runway remaining, a change in flight path angle must be made after establishing visual contact in order to flare the airplane properly. See figure 9-4. This flight path angle change is critical. Normal pilot reaction is to reduce power to accomplish this maneuver. Inadvertent high sink may develop and/or airspeed may be reduced significantly. When performing this maneuver, avoid large power reductions, maintain approach/flare speed until reaching the desired flare point, and execute a normal landing flare.

visual phase of instrument approach (stopping distance critical)

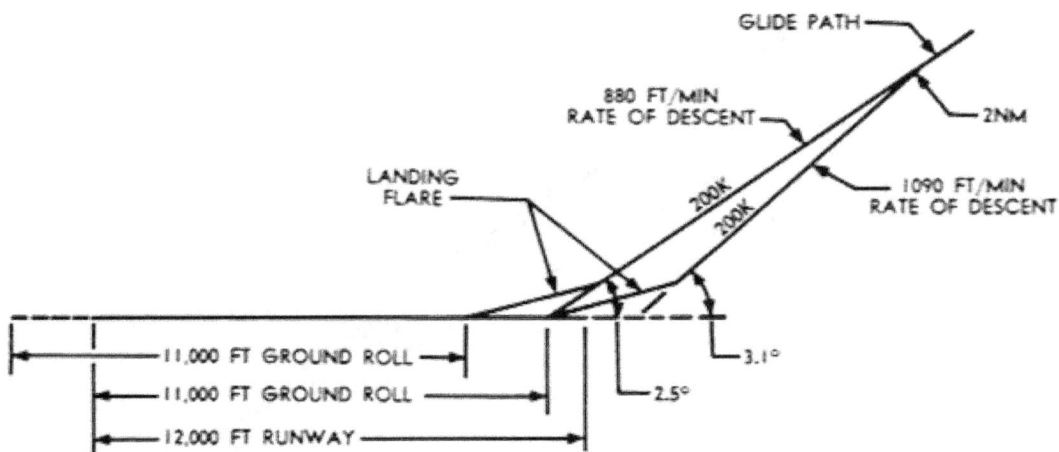

Figure 9-4

9-8

MISSED APPROACH PROCEDURES.

Executing a missed approach, even with an outboard engine shut down, offers no problems as there is sufficient thrust available without use of afterburners. The recommended procedure for executing a missed approach is to advance throttles to military power, establish an instrument climb attitude and allow the airplane to accelerate. When a definite rate of climb and increase in altitude has been established, adjust power as may be required to limit airspeed to 250 knots IAS. Follow published missed approach procedure or as instructed by controlling agency. Do not retract the landing gear until the decision has been made to climb to altitude or establish low altitude endurance. If thrust is critical retract the landing gear as soon as it becomes evident that the airplane will not sink onto the runway.

RADAR APPROACH.

The time and fuel required for a radar approach will vary at different bases depending upon local procedures and type of pattern in use. The pattern requiring minimum time and fuel would be a radar pickup affected during penetration and utilizing a straight-in-final approach. Figure 9-2 illustrates a typical radar approach.

INSTRUMENT LANDING SYSTEM (ILS).

ILS Procedures.

ILS approaches may be accomplished using the ILS equipment and standard ILS ground equipment. ILS equipment is described in Section IV. ILS approaches should be accomplished in accordance with applicable JAL charts in the latest FLIP, Terminal (High Altitude). Figure 9-3 shows a typical ILS approach.

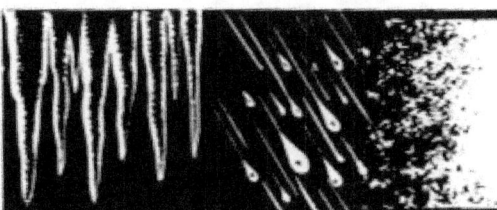

Ice and Rain

Ice and rain may be encountered both in flight and on the ground during instrument and contact flight, especially during takeoff and initial climb or during approach and landing.

AIRPLANE ICING.

The airplane is equipped with engine anti-icing, spike anti-icing, pitot heat, and windshield rain removal provisions. Refer to "Anti-Icing and Defogging Systems," Section IV. The windshield rain removal system is also effective for windshield anti-icing. The air conditioning system includes a windshield defog system to aid in keeping the windshield unobstructed. There are no provisions for surface anti-icing. Flight through areas of sustained heavy icing is not recommended. The high performance capabilities of the airplane should be utilized to avoid extreme icing conditions. When moderate to heavy icing is encountered, a change in altitude, course, or an increase in airspeed should be made quickly to prevent ice accumulation on the wings, vertical fin and nacelles. If operation in icing conditions cannot be avoided maintain high enough speed to keep the ram air temperature above freezing for as long as possible. If ice accumulates to a thickness of 1.25 inches on the engine spikes, engine speeds above 88% can cause flameout or ice ingestion damage. Therefore, when flight through icing conditions is unavoidable and ice accumulates to approximately one inch thickness on any portion of the airplane, maintain the minimum engine rpm necessary for safe flight. After leaving icing conditions maintain the minimum engine rpm necessary for safe flight until the ice on the airplane has melted.

WARNING

In the event of the pitot tube icing, the airspeed and mach indicators may drop to zero or remain fixed and all systems that receive intelligence based on pitot pressure through the air data computer will be affected. The loss of airspeed indication during climb or descent is an extremely dangerous safety of flight hazard. The attitude indicator, angle-of-attack indicator, vertical velocity indicator, altimeter and power setting can be used during the emergency flight condition. Refer to "Pitot-Static System Malfunction," Section III for additional information.

Section IX
All Weather Operation

Substantial ice buildups can necessitate increased power setting for maintaining airspeed and could cause distortions in the shape of airfoil surfaces, thus affecting the lift and handling characteristics of the airplane. Either of these conditions tend to reduce total range. Flight can be safely accomplished during light to moderate icing by using normal flight procedures. Rain has little or no appreciable effect on the flight characteristics.

ENGINE ICING.

The frontal areas of the engines are anti-iced and the system should be operated any time icing is present or suspected. The engine anti-ice switch should be positioned to AUTO prior to entering areas of known icing. Thrust loss due to icing can be reduced by employing the following throttle burst technique. After the engines have been exposed to actual icing conditions for five minutes, they should be operated at military power for 10 seconds to provide adequate heat for anti-icing. This procedure should be repeated for each five-minute period of exposure. For additional information refer to "Engine and Spike Anti-Icing System," Section IV.

OPERATION IN RAIN OR ICING CONDITIONS.

GROUND OPERATION.

Operate the airplane and systems as indicated in the "Cold Weather Procedures" in this section. Rain removal should be used when needed to improve visibility.

CRUISE.

Operate the airplane as necessary to avoid icing conditions whenever possible. When ice is encountered, pitot heat and engine anti-icing should be used. Do not operate in rain, sleet or hail longer than absolutely necessary. If it becomes necessary to fly in these conditions, constantly check the aircraft leading edges, including radomes, for indications of peeling or other structural deterioration on the airplane surfaces. In the event structural deterioration is observed, maintain airspeed as low as practicable and land at the nearest suitable airfield as soon as possible. If heavy precipitation conditions of the above type are encountered at any speed or light to moderate conditions exist at high speeds, an entry must be made in form 781.

WARNING

When operating in polar regions radio and radar measurements of terrain clearance are unreliable since these areas are usually covered by large depths of snow and ice. Radar and radio waves can penetrate the surface of snow and ice fields; therefore, when this equipment is used for measuring terrain clearance, it may indicate a greater clearance than actually exists.

CAUTION

To minimize impact damage from rain, sleet or hail, do not exceed 350 knots IAS below 15,000 feet pressure altitude. At pressure altitudes above 15,000 feet fly at minimum airspeeds consistent with safe airplane controllability.

DESCENT.

During descent into icing conditions, monitor the ram air temperature for indications of icing temperatures. Turn rain removal switch ON to prevent rain or ice from forming on the windshield. For information relative to operation in rain, sleet or hail and operational limits to be observed during these operations, refer to "Cruise," this section. If an abnormal rise in EGT is noted during descent through icing conditions, ice may have formed on the engine frontal areas, spike and spike struts; therefore, use the following procedures to eliminate the ice: Advance the throttle(s) (singly or together) to military power at five-minute intervals and hold for 10 seconds. This will provide enough heat to anti-ice the engines and supply residual heat for five minutes of additional exposure to icing conditions.

Note

This throttle burst technique will generally be employed only once during a descent because of the high rate of descent used and the relatively thin vertical extent of icing conditions to which jet engines are most susceptible. The throttle burst technique should be avoided at low airspeeds to prevent suction injection of ice chunks into the compressor.

LANDING.

In the event visibility is restricted because of ice, snow, rain or fog on the windshield, the rain removal system should be used and necessary power maintained on inboard engines to provide enough airflow through the system. For information relative to operation in rain, sleet or hail and operational limits to be observed during these operations, refer to "Cruise," this section.

Note

Rain removal is ineffective above approximately 250 knots IAS but increases in effectiveness as airspeed is decreased and pitch attitude is increased. The degree of effectiveness is directly dependent on the amount of airflow through the system. In light to moderate rain the visibility should be materially improved.

For landing procedures, refer to "Landing on Slippery Runways," Section II.

Turbulence and Thunderstorms

WARNING

Flight through thunderstorm activity or known severe turbulence is not recommended and should be avoided if at all possible. Careful judgment must be exercised by the pilot in determining capability to safely enter or circumnavigate areas of such weather activity. The appropriate corrective action to be taken if moderate or greater turbulence is forecast will be preplanned with assistance of the weather forecaster during the weather briefing for all flights.

In case it becomes necessary to fly through a thunderstorm, the navigator should establish a course (by means of search radar) which will avoid the areas of most intense turbulence and possible hail. Heavy turbulence can be penetrated safely at mach no. 0.9; however, penetration speed should not exceed 350 knots IAS for ease of handling. When in moderate to severe turbulence, the mach indicator fluctuates and the same inputs affect the air data computer but the resulting transients are too rapid to materially affect the ratio changer. During flight in turbulent air, primary consideration should be given to maintaining a constant attitude at the expense of altitude as this will help to prevent overcontrolling and the resulting trim changes in the transonic speed range.

If turbulence is encountered, observe the following procedure:

1. Mach, mach-altitude mode switch—OFF.
2. Course—Correct for minimum turbulence.
3. CG—Adjust.

CG should be set approximately 2 percent forward of the normal aft limit to provide a safe CG in case of an inadvertent slow down.

4. Airspeed—Adjust to mach no. 0.9 but not to exceed 350 knots IAS.
5. Altitude—Reduce altitude to avoid turbulence or fly 4000 feet below optimum for greater stability.

Before entering a storm, the pilot should accomplish the following steps:

1. Autopilot—Disengaged.
2. Heading selector switch—J-4.
3. Course—Correct for minimum turbulence and exposure.
4. CG—Adjust.

CG should be set approximately 2 percent forward of the normal aft limit to provide a safe CG in case of an inadvertent slow down.

5. Airspeed—Adjust to mach no. 0.9 (not to exceed 350 knots IAS).
6. Altitude—Adjust altitude to fly 4000 feet below optimum in order to achieve greater stability.
7. Pitot heat—ON.
8. Engine anti-ice switch—AUTO.
9. Windshield rain removal switch—As required.
10. Windshield defog switch—As required.
11. Left and right panel light knobs—Fully clockwise.
12. Malfunction and indicator light dimming switch—BRIGHT (momentarily).
13. Flood light selector switch—Set.
14. Flood light control knob—Fully clockwise.

Night Flying

Flight procedures at night differ very little from instrument procedures. Instrument proficiency is extremely important during night flying since the reduced visibility will require dependence on the instruments and visual reference to the horizon may be impossible. The red interior lighting should be selected for the instrument panels and flood lights so that glare from the light will not impair night vision. The exterior lights are normally operated with the navigation lights in the STEADY and BRIGHT positions and the anti-collision lights ON. The taxi light and both landing lights may be used for takeoff. The taxi light and both landing lights should be turned ON while on the final approach for landing. The landing lights should be used as necessary during taxiing to provide adequate lighting.

Cold Weather Procedures

The majority of cold weather operating difficulties are encountered on the ground. Flight and maintenance crews must cooperate closely in exercising constant vigilance to overcome the cold weather hazards during preparation for flight. Flight itself is relatively unaffected by cold weather, because, at the operating altitudes of the airplane, temperatures are fairly consistent regardless of geographical location. Some phases of flight, such as takeoff and landing, are enhanced in the artic regions by virtue of cold, dense air which increases thrust and shortens ground runs. Icing conditions during flight will not be considered here as they have been covered under "Ice and Rain," this section. No fuel system problems should be expected providing the airplane is serviced with cold fuel properly filtered to remove water and ice particles. Operation of seals, actuators, electronic components and mechanical accessories is degraded at sub-zero temperatures. Additional time should be allowed for the flight crew preflight during cold temperature operation. Even though preflight has been accomplished by the ground crew, the flight crew should insure that items outlined in the following paragraphs, in addition to the procedures in Section II are checked.

BEFORE STATIONS INSPECTION.

1. Engines—Check for internal ice.

Check bottom section of front stator blades for evidence of ice and see that the turbine wheel rotates freely.

> **CAUTION**
>
> Engine heat on shutdown melts ice accumulated during flight and the resulting moisture will freeze in the lower sections of the front stator and rotor blades. An attempted engine start may result in starter failure. If ice is suspected, external heat should be applied to forward engine sections just prior to engine start.

EXTERIOR INSPECTION.

1. Airplane exterior surface—Check for frost, ice and snow.

Takeoffs with light coatings of frost (approximately 1/8 inch) or powdery snow can be safely performed. Heavier coatings of frost and/or wet snow must be removed by sweeping the areas and applying a light coat of de-icing fluid. Ice can be removed by a direct flow of heated air from portable ground heaters. Check to insure that water resulting from ice removal by this method does not refreeze on the airplane surfaces, especially on the control surface hinge lines.

> **CAUTION**
>
> Chipping or scraping ice will likely cause damage to the airplane skin and radome. Check the two drain holes just forward of the vertical stabilizer for evidence of ice accumulation. If ice is encountered, the panel should be removed and rudder torque arm deck inspected for ice accumulation.

Note

- Remove snow from top of fuselage as heating the cabin may result in melting of snow and causing it to refreeze on the lower portion of the fuselage. As a result ice may form in the vicinity of the unheated secondary airspeed system static ports which can block the static holes or deform the air flow and lead to inaccurate indications.
- Light coatings of deicing fluid applied within an hour before takeoff will keep surfaces clear if all excessive snow and frost is first brushed off.
- Panels removed during maintenance and stored in a heated shelter may not fit securely when reinstalled on a cold airplane.

2. Tank Vents—Check.

Check all accessible oil and fuel tank vents for clear openings; have any traces of ice or frost removed.

3. Shock struts, actuating rods and limit switches—Checked.

Check free of ice and dirt and the exposed portion of actuating rods wiped with lubriacting oil.

4. Hydraulic actuators and rams—Check.

BEFORE STARTING ENGINE.

If the outside air temperature is −30°F or below, motor each engine prior to engine start to reduce excessive hydraulic, engine and generator oil pressures.

1. Parking brakes—Set.

Have ground observer check brake pistons for proper operation during actuation of brakes and then set parking brakes.

STARTING ENGINES.

1. Engine pre-heat—As required.

Heating of jet engines is seldom required. However, portable ground heaters should be available in the event it becomes necessary to apply heat to engine starter valves and fuel control units.

Section IX
All Weather Operation

T.O. 1B-58A-1

2. Start engines—Normal manner.

Throttle should be moved from OFF to a position well above IDLE and then retarded. Force required to move throttles will be high at low temperatures until the engine is started. Engine oil pressure will indicate maximum during start at low temperature. Engines should be operated at idle rpm until oil pressure stabilizes in the operating range. If there is no oil pressure after 30 seconds or if pressure drops below minimum after start, shut down and check for ruptured oil lines. A sudden loss of oil pressure is usually due to broken oil line or sheared main engine lubricating pump shaft. If engine will not start or fails to continue operating, ground heat should be applied through the nacelle cooling door for approximately five minutes to warm the starter, fuel control unit and throttle torque booster unit.

SYSTEMS CHECK.

1. Generators—Excited and checked.

The frequency meter will read high after exposure to cold temperatures and generator frequency will normally be high until the fluid in the constant speed drive unit has warmed up.

CAUTION

Do not place the generator on the bus until frequency has stabilized at accepted values.

2. Hydraulic System Warmup—As required.

When the airplane has been cold soaked in ambient temperatures below 0°F (−18°C), the hydraulic systems must be allowed to warm up before satisfactory operation of flight controls and other hydraulically operated equipment can be obtained. Warmup time for system is as follows:

Initial Temperature	Estimated Warmup Time
0°F (−18°C)	0 minutes
−20°F (−29°C)	2.5 minutes
−40°F (−40°C)	7 minutes
−60°F (−51°C)	14.5 minutes

Note

The warmup times shown in this table are estimated and are to be used only as a guide. Acceptance of hydraulic system warmup prior to takeoff will be based on obtaining normal operation, not on time required.

After warmup, hydraulic system will remain operational as long as operating pressure is maintained. Before starting the engines or ground hydraulic unit, the fire control system master switch and the chaff dispenser power control switch must be positioned to OFF and remain there until warmup has been completed. Initial control movement will be sluggish and hydraulic pressure sensitivity more pronounced than normal. Therefore, stick movement should be made slowly and smoothly at a rate which does not cause more than 500 psi drop in hydraulic pressure indication. For convenience, the controls may be cycled by means of the elevator and rudder trim switches. They should be actuated through one complete cycle for every 10°F below 0°F.

Note

The tendency of the pressure to collapse rather than reduce in proportion to movement is an indication that rate is too fast. If pressure collapses, stop control stick movement until pressure fully recovers.

During warmup, systems should be checked periodically by deliberately moving the control stick at a rate which will cause pressure drop indication to exceed 500 psi. Adequate warmup is indicated by the capability of the systems to receive control demands with proportionate drops in pressure of the magnitude normally experienced with the systems known to be warm. When the hydraulic systems are adequately warmed, the control surface actuators should be purged of residual cold fluid by moving the control stick in a rectangular pattern such that it is always displaced the maximum distance from neutral and alternately fully depressing rudder pedals. Verify normal response by performing maximum rate elevator or aileron command and checking for normal stick feel and pressure response.

Note

For scramble operation, control rate capability equivalent to that customarily required during takeoff, should be considered satisfactory operational capability. System warmup to attain this capability can be accomplished during taxi out.

If the primary navigation system is to be operated on takeoff, the hydraulic supply to the radar antenna requires additional warmup. This may be performed during taxi, through azimuth sweep operation of the antenna (with the primary navigation function selector knob positioned at standby). Operation of the radar antenna is permissible prior to any warmup of the utility hydraulic system and results only in degraded antenna performance until fluid supply is warmed.

> **CAUTION**
>
> Do not operate nose wheel steering with the airplane static, with or without brakes applied, to prevent tire wear and/or possible fuselage structural damage.

TAXIING INSTRUCTIONS.

Caution must be exercised to avoid loss of control when taxiing on ice or snow covered areas, particularly during windy conditions. Taxi speeds should be reduced to the minimum practicable and when following other aircraft the normal distance between the aircraft should be increased accordingly. If possible, the taxi route should be planned so as to avoid sharp turns.

> **CAUTION**
>
> - Painted areas on runways, taxiways and ramps are significantly more slippery than non-painted areas, particularly when wet. In addition, painted areas sometimes serve as condensation surfaces and it is possible to have wet, frosty or even icy conditions on these areas when the overall weather condition is dry.
>
> - When conditions of snow or ice exist, the approach ends of the runways are usually more slippery than other areas because of the melting and refreezing of the ice and snow at this point.

Avoid taxiing in deep snow or slush as steering control will be more difficult and brakes and gear may accumulate moisture and freeze after takeoff. Be especially careful in maneuvering when following the path of other aircraft as the exhaust of the engines can melt snow and slush which may then freeze into glazed ice. If it is necessary to taxi behind and across the path of nearby aircraft which have engines running, turns should not be attempted until clear of the aircraft's slipstream. The use of nose wheel steering is the most desirable method of directional control for all surface conditions. When taxiing on slippery surfaces, however, the turning performance capability is reduced and care must be exercised to avoid loss of control. Asymmetric braking or thrust may be used to maintain directional control, but these techniques are less desirable than the use of nose wheel steering. Asymmetric braking or thrust must be accompanied by the use of nose wheel steering so as not to impair turning performance due to dragging the nose wheels through the turn. The recommended procedure for taxiing on slippery surfaces is as follows:

- Use minimum symmetric power to initiate rolling and to maintain a minimum practicable speed.

- Use nose wheel steering as the primary directional control.

- If a sharp turn is to be made, stop the airplane before entering the turn. Initiate the turn from a standstill using minimum symmetric power.

- If nose wheel steering is lost during a turn and maneuvering room is available, slow the airplane by reducing power, if above idle, and using gentle, symmetric braking until control is regained. Regain steering effectiveness by centering the rudder pedals and gradually reapplying steering.

> **CAUTION**
>
> Increasing the steering angle after control is lost will further reduce steering effectiveness.

- If nose wheel steering is lost during a turn and the turn must be continued, use asymmetric braking in conjunction with nose wheel steering. The steering angle should be reduced slightly from the position at which control was lost and braking used to complete the turn or until nose wheel steering again becomes effective.

> **CAUTION**
>
> Care must be exercised in using brakes to avoid locking the wheels since the anti-skid system is ineffective at low speeds.

- Turning capability with the brakes can be considerably reduced if not used in conjunction with nose wheel steering since the nose wheels may be dragged through the turn.

It is recommended that asymmetric power not be used for turning except as a last resort, and then only in small amounts, in order to avoid inducing or aggravating dangerous skids.

Section IX
All Weather Operation

BEFORE LINE UP.

In the event that the runway is ice or snow covered it would be advisable to perform engine performance checks in a cleared area prior to taking the runway. At low ram air (compressor inlet) temperatures, lower engine RPM and EGT may be expected. Refer to "T_2 Cutback" Section VII.

TAKEOFF.

Apply brakes and advance throttles to military power. If airplane starts to slide on ice or snow before military power is reached, release brakes and begin take off run. Continue advancing power during takeoff run and check engine instruments for proper indication. Rudder control will become effective at approximately 70 knots and afford additional control on icy surfaces.

> **CAUTION**
>
> During takeoff on icy runways, lack of nose wheel steering effectiveness should be anticipated.

Utilize engine anti-icing as required. During takeoff at low ambient temperatures the airplane accelerates rapidly and thrust losses due to engine anti-icing operation are negligible.

AFTER TAKEOFF.

If takeoff was made with slush on the runway, the gear should be cycled up and down several times, weather permitting, prior to continuing the climb. Cycling the gear will reduce the possibility of the limit switches, actuator uplatch mechanisms and wheel brake assemblies freezing.

CLIMB.

Follow normal procedures for climb.

CRUISE.

Follow normal procedures for cruise. Temperatures at cruise altitude are essentially the same regardless of geographical location.

DESCENT.

If descent is made into precipitation turn rain removal ON. Rain removal is effective in preventing ice formation on a portion of the windshield as well as clearing rain. Maintain a minimum of 85% rpm on inboard engines to insure adequate air flow to rain removal nozzle.

APPROACH.

Follow normal procedures for approach.

> **CAUTION**
>
> Long flat unbroken stretches of snow make depth perception difficult. The tendency is to flare late. For this reason it is recommended that radar or ILS be utilized to aid in monitoring the final approach under this condition.

LANDING.

If snow or slush covered runways are encountered, make a practice visual approach to landing runway if weather permits, observing surface conditions, overruns and obstacles. Request runway condition reading (RCR). To perform a minimum landing roll without using brakes, cross the runway threshold at approach/flare speed. Excessive speed at this point, in addition to the higher than normal engine thrust at low temperatures, will cause the airplane to float. For landing procedures, refer to Landing on Slippery Runways, Section II.

> **CAUTION**
>
> If the runway is slick and landing is made in a crosswind, the aircraft may have a tendency to slide and nose into the wind. Be prepared to jettison the drag chute if this should occur.

AFTER LANDING.

While taxiing to the ramp on ice or snow covered surfaces observe the same cautions as when taxiing for takeoff. With the airplane at a light grossweight and with the excess thrust at idle under cold temperatures, extreme caution must be observed.

POST FLIGHT INSPECTION.

Follow normal procedures.

Hot Weather and Desert Operation

Hot weather and desert operation requires that added precautions be taken against damage from dust, sand, and high temperatures. Particular attention should be given to those components and systems (engine, fuel, oil, hydraulic, pitot-static, etc.) which are most susceptible to contamination, malfunction, or damage from sand and dust. All of the filters on the airplane should be checked more frequently than is normally required. Components containing plastic or rubber parts should be protected as much as possible from blowing sand and extreme temperatures. The canopies should be closed and sealed and all protective covers should be installed when the airplane is not in use during conditions of blowing sand and dust.

BEFORE STATIONS INSPECTION.

Check engine inlet ducts for dust or sand accumulations.

INTERIOR INSPECTIONS.

Inspect the crew compartments for excessive dust accumulation.

EXTERIOR INSPECTION.

Inspect the exposed areas of the shock strut and actuator pistons on the landing gear and have them cleaned as required. Check tires for signs of blistering and check for over-inflation of tires and struts due to high ambient temperatures. Check for fuel or hydraulic leakage due to thermal expansion of sealing materials. Inspect the area aft of the airplane to make sure that engine exhaust will not cause sand or dust to be blown onto personnel or equipment when engines are started.

STARTING THE ENGINE.

Normal starting procedures are used in hot weather. Canopies may be left open during starting however, they must be closed prior to beginning the air conditioning system check.

BEFORE TAXIING.

Ground testing should be complete but accomplished as expeditiously as possible.

TAXIING.

Follow normal procedures.

TAKEOFF.

Allow for longer takeoff distances in hot weather. Refer to Appendix for recommended takeoff speeds and required takeoff distances. Manual overspeed will provide a small amount of additional thrust when ambient temperature is above 80°F.

CAUTION

It is imperative that takeoff not be made at lower than recommended speeds. When outside air temperature is high, do not rotate too soon, as more than usual takeoff distance will be required to obtain takeoff speed.

DESCENT.

Check that the windshield and canopy defog system is on at least four minutes before any rapid descent from altitude to prevent fogging and frosting of the windshield and canopy.

Section IX
All Weather Operation

APPROACH AND LANDING.

Maintain recommended approach and landing speeds as shown in the Appendix. Allow for longer landing rolls resulting from increased true airspeeds. Avoid the use of braking as much as possible to prevent tire failure and utilize all possible runway distance for stopping. Deploy drag chute as usual during initial landing roll.

CAUTION

Hot weather operation requires the pilot to be cautious of gusts and wind shifts near the ground.

ENGINE SHUTDOWN.

Prior to engine shutdown, run inboard engines to 85% for five minutes with air conditioning system in REVERSE FLOW and all unnecessary electrical equipment OFF. This will reduce residual heat in electronic equipment after all airplane systems are shut down.

POSTFLIGHT.

Follow normal procedures.

This is the last page in Section IX.

> **NOTE**
>
> For Appendix I, refer to Supplement, T.O. 1B-58A-1-1.

the B·58A airplane

THIS PAGE INTENTIONALLY LEFT BLANK

Alphabetical Index

A

	Page
Abort Procedure, Weapon	8-41
Aborted Takeoff	3-3
A-C Ammeter	1-35
A-C Power Distribution	1-34*
A-C Power Panel (Typical), Left	1-37*
A-C Power Panel Right	1-38*
A-C Power System	1-32
A-C Voltmeter	1-35
Acceleration	2-49
Acceleration, Fuel Management	7-11
Acceleration Limitations	5-9
Accelerometer	1-89
Active Defense System	4-106
Controls	4-106
Emergency Operation	4-111
Fire Control System	4-106
Indicators	4-106
Normal Operation	4-111
Tail Turret	4-106
Aft CG Limit After Upper Pod Drop (EWO Only)	6-21*
Aft CG Limits for Pod and Small Weapon Jettisoning	2-46*
After Landing	2-67, 8-48
After Landing, Cold Weather Procedures	9-16
After Takeoff	2-43, 8-29
After Takeoff, Cold Weather Procedures	9-16
Afterburner Fuel Control System	1-14
Afterburner Ignition System	1-14
Afterburner Lightoff Limits	5-6
Afterburner Operation, Minimum Pumps for	7-13
Afterburner System, Engine	1-14
Aileron Control System	1-68, 3-30
Autopilot Servo	1-68
Damper Servo	1-68
Ratio Changer	1-68
Stick Trim and Feel System	1-68
Air Conditioning System	4-1, 4-2*
Cabin Pressurization Malfunction	3-35
Control Panel	4-8*
Controls	4-7
Emergency Operation	3-35
Extended Range Operation	4-11
Hot Air Distribution	4-4

	Page
Indicators	4-7
Manual Cabin Temperature Control Operation	4-11
Normal Operation	4-10
Pressurization Control	4-7
Refrigeration and Cold Air Distribution	4-1
Ram Air Operation	4-11
Reverse Flow Operation	4-11
Temperature Control System	4-4
Temperature Control Malfunctions	3-35
Aircraft Emergency Movement Checklist	2-79
Air Data System	1-87
Air Navigation Data Recording System	4-88
Control Panel	4-90*
Controls	4-90
Data Recorder	4-88
Emergency Operation	4-92
Format	4-88*, 4-89*, 4-93*
Indicators	4-90
Recorder Control Unit	4-89
Air Navigation System, Tactical	4-31
Air Refueling System	4-112
Controls	4-113
Flight Characteristics	6-22
Indicators	4-113
Air-to-Ground IFF Control Panel	4-35*
Air-to-Ground IFF System	4-34
Control Knobs	4-35
Switches	4-36
Normal Operation	4-36
Air-to-Ground SIF Control Panel	4-36*
Airplane Acceptance	2-68
Airplane Dimensions	1-1
Airplane Icing	9-9
Airspeed, Erroneous Indication	3-33
Airspeed Indicator	1-87
Airspeed Mach Indicator	1-87, 1-87*
Airspeed Limitations	5-6
Alarm Lamp, Paper Break	4-92
Alert Procedures	2-68, 8-24
Allowable Aileron Command	5-24
Allowable Tire Damage	2-75*
Altimeter, Barometric	1-87
Altimeter, Cabin Pressure	4-10
Altimeter, Low Altitude Radar	1-88
Altimeter, Radio	4-61
Altitude Calibration and Radar Ranging Check	8-51

*Denotes Illustration

Index
Ammeter, A-C
Brake Energy Zones

T.O. 1B-58A-1

	Page
Ammeter, A-C	1-35
Ammo Jettison Button	4-109
Ammo Reserve Indicator	4-111
AN/ARC-74 Normal Operating Procedures	4-27
AN/ARC-110 Normal Operating Procedure	4-30
Angle of Attack	6-2
Angle of Attack for One-G Flight	6-3*
Angle-of-Attack Indexer	1-90
Angle-of-Attack Indicator	1-90, 1-90*
Antenna Locations	4-22*
Anti-Icing Caution Lamp Lighted	4-15
Anti-Icing and Defogging System, Normal Operation	4-13
Anti-Icing System	4-12
Engine and Spike	4-13
Pitot	4-13
Anti-Jam Button	4-109
Anti-Skid Control Switch	1-83
Anti-Skid System	1-83, 7-29
Approach and Landing, Hot Weather Operation	9-18
Approach Check	8-47
Approach, Cold Weather Procedures	9-16
Approach/Flare Speed Corrections	2-59
Ashtrays	4-116
Astro Control Panel	4-65, 4-66*
Astrotracker	4-59
ATF for Airborne Approach	8-47*
Attitude Indicators	1-89, 1-90
Auxiliary	1-90
Automatic Trim System, Elevator	1-66
Autopilot	4-47
Control Panel	4-49*
Controls	4-49
Disengaging	4-53
Emergency Operation	4-53
Engaging	4-50
Indicators	4-49
Indicator Lamps	4-50
Modes	4-48, 4-51
Navigator's Station Control Operations	4-52
Normal Operation	4-50
Servo, Aileron	1-68
Servo, Elevator	1-67
Switches	4-49, 4-50
Auxiliary Attitude Indicator	1-90
Auxiliary Control Panel	4-61, 4-62*
Auxiliary Equipment	1-113
Auxiliary Flight Instrument Panel	4-63, 4-63*
Auxiliary Flight Reference System	4-53
Control Panels	4-54*
Controls	4-54
Indicators	4-54
Normal Operation	4-56

B

	Page
Bailout Warning System	1-95
Ballistic Wind Indicators	4-87
Ballistics Control Panel	4-84*
Bank Angle Limits During Takeoff and Landing	5-30, 5-30*
Barometric Altimeter	1-87
Barrier, Runway, Engagement	3-50
BDE Recording Cycle	4-92
Bearing-Distance-Heading Indicator, TACAN	4-31, 4-32*
Before Acceleration	2-48
Before Exterior Inspection	2-4, 8-14
Before Landing	2-55
Before Leaving Airplane	2-67, 2-80, 8-49
Before Lineup	2-36, 9-16
Before Starting Engines	2-13, 8-18
Before Starting Engines, Cold Weather Procedures	9-13
Before Stations Inspection	9-13, 9-17
Before Taxiing	2-21, 8-18
Belts, Safety	1-113
Bomb Damage Evaluation System	4-92
Controls	4-94
Indicators	4-94
Normal Operation	4-94
Radar Bomb Scoring Panel	4-85*
Recording Cycle	4-92
Bomb Run	8-37, 8-42
Bombing Check	
Alternate Bombing	8-41
Normal	8-33
Bombing Equipment	4-94
Fuel Pod Ready Switch	4-103
Fuel Pod Release Switch	4-103
Pod Present Switch Monitor	4-102
Pod Release System	4-99
Small Weapons	4-94
Two Component Pod	4-99
Warhead Arming and Fuzing System	4-99
Bombing System	4-79
Controls and Indicators	4-80
Operation	4-87
Pilot's Bomb Panel	4-82*
Booster Pump Operation, Partial	7-12
Brake Cooling Rate	5-28*
Brake Emergency Control Handle, Landing Gear and	1-81, 1-85
Brake Emergency Pneumatic System	1-83
Brake Energy Limits	5-24, 5-26*
Brake Energy Zones	5-29

*Denotes Illustration

	Page
Brake System	1-82, 1-84*, 7-29
Antiskid Control Switch	1-83
Antiskid System	1-83, 7-29
Emergency Operation	3-49
Parking Brake Handle	1-83
Buffet	6-18
Burst Altitude Indicator	4-87
Bus-Tie Button	1-35
Bus-Tie Indicator	1-36

C

	Page
Cabin Fire	3-39
Cabin Pressure, Loss of	3-37
Cabin Pressure Schedule	4-6*
Cabin Pressurization Malfunction	3-35
Cabin Temperature, Manual Control	4-11
Canopies	1-97
Actuator Warning Pin	1-100
Control Levers	1-97
Controls	1-97
External Jettison Handles	1-99
Hook Inspection Window	1-101
Indicators	1-97
Jettison Handles	1-99
Latching Mechanism Indicators	1-101
Layback Lockpins and Stop Pins	1-100
Loss of During Flight	3-37
Override Lever, Pilot's	1-99
Operation Limitations	5-29
Pneumatic System	1-98*
Pneumatic System Pressure Gage	1-100
Release Handle, Navigator's	1-100
Safety Pins	1-100
Seal Control Levers	1-99
Unlock Caution Lamp	1-100
Unlocked Indication During Flight	3-37
Capsulation, Crew	3-24
Capsule, Escape	1-101, 1-103*
Controls	1-109
Ejection	3-26
Ejection Sequence	1-107*
Indicators	1-109
System Schematic	1-105*
Caution Lamps	
A-C Generator, Abnormal	1-36
Anti-Icing	4-14
Automatic CG Off	1-30
Battery Discharging	1-40, 3-17
Booster Pump Low Pressure	1-31
Canopy Unlock	1-100
CG Failed	1-30
Engine Anti-Icing	4-14
Hydraulic Pump	1-60
Icing	4-15

	Page
Low Air Flow	4-10
Low Cabin Pressure	4-10
Master	1-93
Oil Low Level	1-14
Oxygen Quantity	4-46
Pod and DECM Power	1-39
Pod Arm and Ready	4-86
Pod Transfer Pump Low Pressure	1-32
Release Signal Present	4-87
Release System Activated	4-86
Reservoir Tank Not Full	1-32
Reverse Flow, Air-Conditioning	4-10
RTM Pressure	4-76
Small Weapon Arm and Ready	4-86
Weapon Unlock	4-85
Windshield Overheat	4-12
Yaw Damper	1-76
Yaw Rate to Roll	1-76
Celestial Data Form	8-10*
Center of Gravity Indicating and Control System	1-21*, 1-23
Center of Gravity Limitations	5-9
Center of Gravity Loading Limitations	5-13, 5-14*
Center of Gravity Location, Effects of	6-11
CG Determination	7-8
CG System Adjustment Panel	1-28*
Channel and Mode Indicator Window	4-32
Channel Frequency Log	4-30
Characteristics and Features	1-1
Check, Preflight	8-14
Clearing an Engine	2-20
Climb	2-44
Climb, Cold Weather Procedures	9-16
Climb, Fuel Management During	7-8
Climb, Instrument	9-5
Climbout, EWO	2-41
Clock, ABU-3/A	1-91, 1-91*
Cocking	2-28, 8-23
Cold Weather Procedures	9-12
Comm-Inter Transfer and Auxiliary Chaff Control Panel	4-21*
Comm-Nav Transfer Panel	4-20*
Command Radio Control Panel (AN/ARC-34)	4-25*
Command Radio, Interphone and UHF (AN/ARC-57)	4-17
Command Radio System UHF (AN/ARC-34)	4-24
Communications and Electronic Equipment	4-29*
Communication System	4-16
AN/ARC-34	4-24
AN/ARC-57	4-17
AN/ARC-57, Emergency Operation	4-23
AN/ARC-74 Emergency	4-26
Long Range	4-27
Normal Operation	4-22

*Denotes Illustration

Index
Communications, Crew Duties
Effect of Abrupt Full Up Elevator
Deflection During Flare

	Page
Communications, Crew Duties	8-2
Compass, Magnetic	1-91
Compressor Stall Clearing	3-13
Computation and Stabilization System	4-58
Containers, Liquid	4-118
Control Stick, Flight	1-70, 1-70*, 7-36
Controls	
Active Defense System	4-106
Air Conditioning	4-7
Air Navigation Data Recording System	4-88
Air Refueling System	4-113
Autopilot	4-49
Auxiliary Flight Reference System	4-54
Bailout Warning System	1-96
BDE System	4-94
Canopy	1-97
Escape Capsule	1-101
Flight	1-70
Fuel System	1-26
Landing Gear System	1-77
Manual CG	1-24
Oxygen	4-45
Recording System	4-90
Single-Point Refueling System	4-115
TACAN	4-31
Course Indicator	4-33, 4-33*
Crew Coordination	8-1
Crew Capsulation	3-24
Crew Decapsulation	3-25
Crew, Flight	1-1
Crosswind Landing	2-62
Crosswind Takeoff	2-40
Cruise	2-44, 8-52
Cruise, Cold Weather Procedures	9-16
Cruise, Fuel Management During	7-11
Cruise, Ice and Rain	9-10
Cruising Flight, Instrument	9-5
Cursor Button	4-108
Curtains, Thermal	4-117

D

	Page
Daily Alert Preflight Checklist	2-69, 8-24
Damper Hardover at Minimum Flying Speed	3-29
Damper Inoperative Restrictions	5-23
Danger Areas	2-16*
Data Review Reset Button	4-91
D-C Loadmeter	1-40
D-C Meter Selector Knob	1-40
D-C Power Distribution	1-54*
D-C Power Panel, Multiple Weapon	1-38*
D-C Power Panel (Typical), 28-Volt	1-41*
D-C Power System	1-39
D-C Power Unit Data	1-57*
D-C System Check Panel	1-56*
D-C Voltmeter	1-40

	Page
Decapsulation, Crew	3-25
Deceleration	2-51
Deceleration, Emergency	3-38
Deceleration, Fuel Management During	7-11
Defcon Posture	2-69
Defcon 1/SRP Power-on Cocking Checklist	2-33, 8-26
Defcon 1/SRP Power-on Scramble Checklist	2-34, 8-27
Defensive Electronic Countermeasure System	4-105
Defensive System Operator's Check List	8-52
Defensive System Operator's Duties	8-12
Defensive System Operator's Station	4-100*
Definition of Airplane Angles and Relative Wind	6-1
Defogging System	4-12
Defogging System, Normal Operation	4-13
Descent	8-37, 9-5, 9-10, 9-16, 9-17
Descent and Before Landing	2-55
Descent Cold Weather Procedures	9-16
Descent, Emergency	3-38
Descent, Fuel Management During	7-11
Descent, Hot Weather Procedures	9-17
Descent, Ice and Rain	9-10
Desert Operation	9-17
Dimensions, Airplane	1-1
Directional Control	6-8
Directional Control of Asymmetric Thrust	3-5*
Directional Gyro Mode	4-56
Ditching	3-41
Diving	6-20
Door Down Lock Release Handles	1-110
Doppler Radar	4-60
Down Elevon Deflection	5-31
Down Elevon Deflection Limits	5-31*
Drag Chute	1-85
Control Handle	1-85
Deployment Speed	5-6
Pressure Gage	1-86
DSO's Communication Control Panel	4-17*
DSO's HF Communication Panel	4-28*
DSO's Left Console	4-101*
DSO's Lighting Control Panel	4-42*
DSO's Main Instrument Panel	4-103*
DSO's Power-Off Interior Inspection	2-8
DSO's Right Console	4-102*
DSO's Station	4-100*
DSO's Work Table	4-117
During Acceleration	2-49
Dynamic Stability Variations	6-13*

E

	Page
Effect of Abrupt Full Up Elevator Deflection During Flare	2-59*

*Denotes Illustration

Effects of Pitch Damper and Center of Gravity on Longitudinal Short Period Characteristics	6-15*
Egress, Ground Emergency	3-2
Ejection	3-26
Ejection Procedures	3-27*
Ejection Triggers, Capsule	1-109
Electrical Control Panel	1-36*
Electrical Power Supply System	1-32
Electrical System Emergency Operation	3-14
Electrically Operated Equipment	1-40
Electronic Equipment Requiring Cooling Air	4-5*
Electronic Equipment Temperature Indicator	4-9
Elevator	
Automatic Trim System	1-66
Autopilot Servo	1-67
Available	2-24*
Available Versus Gross Weight	7-35*
Available Versus Travel of Emergency Increase Elevator Available Handle	7-34*
Control Available Check	7-36
Control Available Mode Restrictions	5-24
Control System	1-66, 3-29, 7-30, 7-31*
Control System—Automatic Mode	7-33*
Damper Servo	1-67
Deflection for One-g Flight for Safe CG Location if Fuel Quantity Measuring System Malfunctions	7-17*
Position and Stick Force for One "g" Flight	6-10*
Ratio Changer	1-66, 6-8
Stick Trim and Feel System	1-67
Emergencies	
Ground	3-2
Inflight	3-9
Landing	3-41
Takeoff	3-3
Emergency Brake and Landing Gear Control Handle	1-81, 1-85
Emergency Communication Panel	4-27*
Emergency Communication System	4-26
Emergency Deceleration	3-38
Emergency Descent	3-38
Emergency Entrance	3-51*, 3-52
Emergency Equipment	1-95, 3-40*
Bailout Warning System	1-95
Bailout Warning System Controls	1-95
Bailout Warning System Indicators	1-95
Engine Fire Pull Handles	1-96
Escape Ropes	1-96
First Aid Equipment	1-96
Hand Fire Extinguisher	1-96
Oxygen System	4-43
Emergency Hydraulic Boost Lever (IFR)	4-113
Emergency Increase Elevator Available Handle	1-74
Emergency Lighting Switch	4-42

Emergency Movement Checklist	2-79
Emergency Operation	
Active Defense System	4-111
Air Conditioning System	3-35
Air Refueling System	4-112
Anti-Icing System	4-13
Autopilot	4-53
Brake System	3-49
Communication System	4-23
Defogging System	4-13
Electrical System	3-14
Landing Gear System	3-8, 3-41
Oxygen System	4-46
PI Beacon System	4-38
Pitot-Static System Malfunction	3-33
RV Beacon Equipment	4-39
Windshield Rain Removal	4-13
Emergency Pneumatic System, Brake	1-83
Emergency Pneumatic System, Landing Gear	1-81
Emergency Release Handle	1-110
Engine and Spike Anti-Icing Systems	4-14*
Engines	1-5, 7-1
Afterburner System	1-14
Alternate Starting Procedures	2-18
Anti-Icing System	4-13
Before Starting	2-13, 8-18, 9-13
Clearing	2-20
Compressor Stall	7-1
Compressor Stall Clearing	3-13
Failure	3-4, 3-9
Failure During Flight	3-9
Failure During Takeoff	3-4
Fire During Flight	3-10
Fire During Takeoff	3-4
Fire on the Ground	3-4
Fire Pull Handles	1-96
Fuel Control and Variable Exhaust Nozzle System	1-6*
Fuel Control System	1-5
Fuel Supply System	1-17
Ground Operation	2-21
Icing	9-10
Inlet Buzz	7-5
Inoperative	7-13
Instruments	1-13
Limitations	5-1
Nacelle Cooling System	1-13
Main Ignition System	1-12
Nozzle Failure	3-10, 7-3
Oil Pressure	5-3
Operation	7-1
Restart During Flight	3-11
Shutdown	2-67, 2-80, 8-49, 9-18
Shutdown During Flight	3-10
Starter System	1-12

Index

Engines (Cont'd)
Fuel Tank Scavenging

T.O. 1B-58A-1

	Page
Engines (Cont'd)	
Starting	2-15, 2-79, 9-13, 9-17
Starting, Emergency Movement	2-79
T₂ Cutback	7-3
T₂ Reset	7-2
Variable Exhaust Nozzle System	1-10
Variable Inlet Guide and Stator Vane System	1-10, 7-1
Entrance, Emergency	3-51*, 3-52
Entrance to the Aircraft	2-3, 2-3*
Erase Button, Radar	4-109
Escape Capsule	1-101, 1-103*
Controls	1-109
Indicators	1-109
Limitations	5-29
Oxygen Control Panel	4-44*
Shoulder Harness	1-109
Escape Ropes	1-96
Escape System Limitations	5-29
EWO Takeoff and Climbout	2-41
Exhaust Gas Temperature Limits	5-3
Exterior Inspection	2-4, 2-5*, 2-73
Exterior Inspection, Cold Weather Procedures	9-13
Exterior Inspection, Hot Weather Procedures	9-17
Exterior Inspection, Strange Field	2-73
Exterior Lights	4-39
Control Knobs	4-40
Switches	4-39, 4-40
External Power Source	1-40

F

	Page
Failure	
A-C Bus	3-17
Engine	3-4, 3-9
Engine Nozzle	3-10, 7-3
Fuel Quantity Measuring System	7-13
Generators	3-16, 3-17
Glass Panel	3-37, 3-38
Inlet Spike System	7-5
Tire, During Takeoff	3-6
Film Remaining Counter	4-104
Fire, Cabin	3-39
Fire Control System (MD-7)	4-106
Fire, Engine	3-2, 3-4, 3-10
Fire, Extinguisher, Hand	1-96
Fire Pull Handles	1-96
Firing Button	4-107
First Aid Equipment	1-96
Flight Characteristics	6-1, 6-16
Flight Charts Stowage Compartment	4-117
Flight Control Emergency Procedures	3-28
Flight Control Hydraulic System	1-61*
Flight Control System	1-60
Aileron Control System	1-68
Controls and Indicators	1-70

	Page
Data	7-30*
Diagram	1-62*
Elevator Control System	1-66
Emergency Procedures	3-28
Limitations	5-23
Rudder Control System	1-68
Standby Gains System	1-69
Trouble Shooting Procedures	7-36, 7-39*
Flight Controls	6-7
Flight Crew	1-1
Flight Limitations with Stability Augmentation Malfunction	5-23
Flight Operating Time Limits	5-3
Flight Planning	2-2
Flight, Preparation for	2-2
Flight Procedures, Instrument	9-1
Flight Records Stowage Door	4-117
Flight Restrictions	2-2
Flutter Restriction	5-6
Food Storage Compartment	4-116
Foot Deflector and Guide-Stowage Assembly	4-117
Forward and Aft Tank Fuel Quantities at High Level Shutoff, Fuel Management	7-13
Forward and Aft Tank Fuel Quantities at High Level Shutoff Versus Deck Angle	7-15*
Frequency Indicator Windows	4-28
Frequency Meter	1-35
Frequency Operation, Manual	4-26
Frequency Selector Knobs, Manual	4-25
Fuel	
Abnormal Depletion	3-19
Control System, Afterburner	1-14
Control System, Engine	1-5
Controls and Indicators	1-26
Dump Speed	5-6
Dump System	1-25
Dumping	3-23, 7-12
Flow Indicators	1-13
Flow Totalizer Indicator	1-13
Management	7-8
Pod Tank Allowable	5-31
Quantity Measuring System	1-26
Quantity Measuring System Failure	7-13
Supply System	1-17, 1-18*, 7-5
System Malfunction	3-19
Transfer System	1-20, 7-11
Unusable	7-13
Vent and Pressurization System	1-25
Fuel Control Panel	1-24*
Fuel Panel Configurations	7-6*
Fuel Quantity Data	1-22*
Fuel System Operation	7-4*
Fuel System, Pod	4-99
Fuel System Trouble Shooting Procedures	7-23*
Fuel Tank Scavenging	7-12

*Denotes Illustration

6

	Page
Fuel Transfer Rates	7-10*
Fume Elimination	3-39
Functional Checkflights	2-80
Fuse Panel and Fuse Location	1-43*
Fuse and Spare Bulb Holders	4-43
Future Range Meter	4-111

G

	Page
General Arrangement Diagram	1-2*
Generators, Failure	3-16, 3-17
Glass Panel Damage Limitations	5-32*, 5-33
Glass Panel Blowout	3-37
Glass Panel Failure, Inflight	3-38
Glass Panels, Windshield and Window	1-113
Go-Around	2-64
Go-Around With One or More Engines Inoperative	3-49
Gross Weight, Airplane	1-1
Gross Weights, Pods	4-97, 4-99
Ground Bombing Computer Check	8-51
Ground Crew Alert Checklist	8-57
Ground Crew Scramble from Power-On Standby Position	8-59
Ground Egress Emergency	3-2
Ground Emergencies	3-2
Emergency Ground Egress	3-2
Engine Fire on the Ground	3-2
Ground Operation, Engine	2-21
Ground Operating Time Limits	5-3
Ground Safety Pins	1-111
Groundspeed Correction Procedures, Manual	8-50
Guard Channel Operation	4-26

H

	Page
Hand Fire Extinguisher	1-94
Handgrips, Capsule	1-109
Hand Pump, Capsule	1-111
Handle, Capsule Air Shutoff Valve	1-111
Hard Landing Indicator	4-118
Harness, Shoulder	1-109
Heavy Gross Weight Landing	2-62
Hemisphere Selector Screw	4-55
High Amperage A-C Loads	3-15*
Holding	9-5
Hot Weather and Desert Operation	9-17
Hydraulic	
Power Supply System	1-56, 1-58*, 1-59*
Power Supply System Indicators	1-60
Pressure or Quantity Abnormally High	3-19
System Emergency Procedures	3-18
System, Operating Limitations	5-23

I

	Page
Ice and Rain	9-9
Icing, Airplane	9-9
Icing, Engine	9-10
Idle Speed	5-3
IFR Emergency Hydraulic Boost Lever	4-113
Ignition System, Afterburner	1-14
Ignition System, Main	1-12
ILS Approach, Typical	9-6*
ILS-TACAN Control Panel	4-31*
ILS-TACAN Control Transfer Buttons	4-32
Indexer, Angle-of-Attack	1-90
Indicator Lamps System, Pilot's	1-92
Indicator Lamps	
Aileron-Rudder Neutral Trim	1-75
Air Refueling Ready	4-114
Antenna Coupler Fault	4-30
BDE	4-94
Camera Malfunction	4-79
Code Element, PI Beacon	4-37
Code Element, RV Beacon	4-39
Crew Capsulated	1-95
Crew Ejection	1-95
Data Review	4-92
Emergency Air Supply	1-96
Erect	4-63
Film Failure	4-104
ILS-TACAN Control	4-32
Landing Gear Position	1-79
Mach Monitor	1-75
Manual Steering, Autopilot	4-50
RBS Tone	4-83
Receiver-Transmitter Fault	4-30
Second Station Control, Autopilot	4-50
Star Lost	4-67
Vertical Error	4-65
Weapon Released	4-87
Indicator Panel	4-64, 4-64*
Indicators	
Active Defense System	4-106
Aileron Control Available	1-75
Air Conditioning	4-7
Air Navigation Data Recording System	4-88
Air Refueling System	4-112
Airspeed	1-87
Airspeed Mach	1-87
Altitude Above Sea Level	4-65
Altitude Above Terrain	4-64
Ammo Reserve	4-111
Angle-of-Attack	1-90, 1-90*
Attitude	1-89, 1-90
Autopilot	4-49
Auxiliary Attitude	1-90
Auxiliary Flight Reference System	4-54
Bailout Warning System	1-95
Ballistic Wind	4-88
BDE System	4-95

*Denotes Illustration

Index

Indicators (Cont'd)

	Page
Bearing-Distance-Heading	4-32
Bombing System	4-81
Burst Altitude	4-88
Bus-Tie	1-36
Canopy	1-98
Capsule-Airplane Disconnect Engagement	1-111
CG	1-30
CG Repeater	1-30
Course	4-33
Distance to Destination	4-65
Doppler Time	4-65
Electronic Equipment Temperature	4-9
Elevator Control Available	1-75
Elevator Position	1-75
Exhaust Temperature	1-14
Flight Control	1-70
Fuel Flow	1-13
Fuel Flow Direction	1-30
Fuel Flow Totalizer	1-13
Fuel Quantity	1-29
Fuel Quantity Repeater	1-29
Fuel Quantity Totalizer	1-29
Fuel System	1-26
Ground Range	4-75
Groundspeed	4-65
Groundtrack	4-65
Hard Landing	4-118
Hydraulic Pressure	1-60
Hydraulic Reservoir Quantity	1-60
Landing Gear System	1-77
Latching Mechanism, Canopy	1-101
Mach	1-87
MM3 Attitude	1-89
Nozzle Position	1-10
Oil Pressure	1-14
Oxygen	4-45
Oxygen Quantity	4-46
Pod Arm	4-85
Pod Lock	4-85, 4-105
Power Flow	1-35
Pressure Ratio	1-13
Ram Air Temperature	1-14
Recording System	4-90
Refrigeration Temperature	4-9
Remote Channel	4-22
Rudder Position	1-75
Search Radar	4-75
Small Weapon Arm	4-85
Small Weapon Lock	4-85
Star Altitude	4-65
Star Altitude Error	4-65
Star Azimuth	4-65
Synchronization	4-55
TACAN	4-31
Time Index Indicator Digitalizer	4-91
Time of Fall	4-87
Time to Go	4-64
Trail	4-87
True Airspeed	4-65
True Heading	4-64
Turn and Slip	1-91
Vertical Velocity	1-89
Inertia Reel Control Handle	1-109
Inflight Emergencies	3-9
Air Conditioning System	3-35
Cabin Fire	3-39
Crew Capsulation	3-24
Crew Decapsulation	3-25
Deceleration and Descent	3-38
Ejection	3-26
Electrical System	3-14
Engine Failure	3-9
Engine Fire	3-10
Flight Control System	3-28
Fuel System	3-19
Glass Panel Failure	3-37, 3-38
Hydraulic System	3-18
Landing Gear	3-41
Loss of Cabin Pressure	3-37
Loss of Canopy	3-37
Oil System	3-17
Pitot Static System	3-33
Spin Recovery	3-28
Unlocked Canopy Indication	3-37
Inflight Glass Panel Failure	3-38
Inlet Spike System	1-15
Inlet Spike System Failure	7-5
Inspection, Exterior	2-4, 2-5*, 2-73, 8-14, 9-13, 9-17
Inspection, Power-Off Interior	2-6, 8-14
Inspection, Power-On Interior	2-9, 8-17
Inspection Windows, Canopy Hook	1-101
Installation of Starter Cartridge	2-78
Instrument Approaches	9-8
Instrument Climb	9-5
Instrument Cruising Flight	9-5
Instrument Flight Procedures	9-1
Instrument Landing System	4-34, 9-9
Instrument Markings	5-2*
Instrument Takeoff	9-3
Instrument Test Button	1-29
Instruments	1-87
Instruments, Engine	1-13
Interior Inspection, Hot Weather	9-17
Interior Inspection, Power Off	2-6, 8-14
Interior Inspection, Power-On	2-9, 8-17
Interior Lights	4-41
Control Knobs	4-41
Switches	4-42
Fuses and Spare Bulb Holders	4-43

*Denotes Illustration

	Page
Interphone and UHF Command Radio System (AN/ARC-57)	4-17

J

	Page
Jet Penetration	9-2*, 9-5
Jettison Handles, Canopy External	1-99
Jettison Limits, Lower Pod Normal	5-6, 5-4*
Jettisoning, Lower Pod	2-47
Jettisoning, Pod	2-45
Jettisoning, Small Weapons	2-45

K

	Page
Knobs	
A-C Meter Selector	1-33
Aft Tank Refuel Valve	1-28, 4-115
Aimpoint Selector	4-68
Air Refueling (IFR) Slipway Lamp Control	4-40, 4-113
Air Source Selector	4-8
Airspeed Computer Malfunction	4-78
Altitude Correction	4-63
Antenna Tilt	4-71
ATA Range Control	4-107
Azimuth Mark Intensity	4-73
Balance Tank Refuel Scavenge	1-28, 4-115
Ballistic Malfunction Test	4-83
Bearing Illumination	4-73
Burst Length Control	4-109
Cabin Pressure Selector	4-8
Cabin Temperature Control	4-9
CG Control	1-26
Channel Selector, TACAN	4-31
Channel Selector, UHF	4-21
Code Element, Position Indicating Beacon Equipment	4-37
Code Element, Rendezvous Beacon Equipment	4-38
Code Selector, Air-to-Ground IFF Equipment	4-36
Command Mode Selector, UHF	4-20, 4-25
Command Volume Control, UHF	4-21, 4-26
Common Code Element, PI Beacon	4-37
Common Code Element, RV Beacon	4-38
Control Mode Selector	4-7
Cursor Rotation	4-73
D-C Meter Selector	1-40
Destination Position	4-68
Display Intensity	4-74
External Power	1-53
Fixed Range Marker	4-73
Fixpoint Position	4-69
Fixpoint Position Elevation	4-70
Fixpoint Selector	4-69
Floodlight Control	4-42
Forward Tank Refuel-Scavenge	1-28, 4-115
Frequency Manual Selector	4-21
Frequency Selector, LRC System	4-27
Function Selector, Auxiliary Flight	4-55
Function Selector, Interphone	4-19
Function Selector, Primary Navigation	4-61
Greenwich Hour Angle	4-66
Heading and Navigation Malfunction	4-78
Heading Reference Selector	4-65
Intervalometer Selector	4-90
Latitude Correction	4-55
Magnetic Variation	4-62
Malfunction Test Selector	4-71
Manual CG Shift	1-26
Manual Frequency Selector	4-25
Manual VH Input	4-104
Master Control, Air-to-Ground IFF Equipment	4-35
Minimum Range Selector	4-70
Mode Selector, LRC	4-28
Monitor Meter Selector	4-75
Navigator's and DSO's Panel Light Control	4-41
Offset Aimpoint	4-68
Offset Aimpoint Elevation	4-68
Percent Overlap Selector	4-70
Pilot's Panel Light Control	4-41
Pod Selector	1-27
Pod Tank Transfer Refuel	1-29, 4-115
Power, PI Beacon Equipment	4-37
Power, RV Beacon Equipment	4-38
Power, TACAN	4-32
Preset Channel Selector	4-25
Range and Magnification Selector	4-71
Receiver Frequency Tuning	4-73
Receiver Gain Control	4-108
Refrigeration Unit Selector	4-7
Relative Bearing	4-75
RF Sensitivity	4-29
Scope Dimming	4-108
Scope Gain Control	4-108
Sea Drift Velocity	4-63
Search Radar Mode Selector	4-71
Sector	4-73
Sensitivity Time Control	4-74
Servo Malfunction Selector	4-79
Sidereal Hour Angle	4-66
Slipway Light Control, Air Refueling	4-40, 4-113
Star Declination	4-66

*Denotes Illustration

Knobs (Cont'd)	Page
Storage Control	4-109
Storage Fixpoint	4-68
Storage Fixpoint Elevation	4-68
Synchronization-Set	4-55
Tank-to-Engine Supply	1-26
Time Index Set	4-91
Tracking and Flight Controller Selector	4-71
Transmitter Frequency Tuning	4-73
Transverse Present Position	4-67
True Present Position	4-67
Variable Range Marker	4-73
Variable Threshold	4-74
Video	4-74
Volume Control, AN/ARC-74	4-27
Volume Control, Interphone	4-20
Volume Control, LRC	4-29
Volume Control, TACAN	4-32
Volume Control, UHF	4-27

L

	Page
Lamps	
Auto Release Ready	4-87
Bailout Alert	1-95
Doppler Lock	4-64
Master Warn	4-86
Paper Break Alarm	4-92
Ready-Fire	4-109
V/H Control Auto Hold	4-104
Waveguide Pressure Loss	4-76
Landing	2-56
After	2-65
Approach/Flare Speed Correction	2-59
Before	2-55
Cold Weather	9-16
Crosswind	2-62
Data Card	2-3
Fuel Management During	7-11
Heavy Gross Weight	2-62
Hot Weather	9-18
Ice and Rain	9-11
Maximum Performance	2-62
Normal	2-61
On Slippery Runways	2-62
Procedures and Techniques	2-60
Taxi-back	2-65, 8-48
Touch-and-Go	2-64
With Blown Tire	3-48
With Broken Positioning Spring	3-47
With Landing Gear Malfunction	3-44
With One or More Engines Inoperative	3-48
Landing Emergencies	3-41
Brake System Emergency Operation	3-49
Ditching	3-41
Emergency Entrance	3-52
Go-Around With One Engines Inoperative	3-49
Landing Gear	3-41
Landing With Blown Tire	3-48
Landing With Broken Positioning Spring	3-47
Landing With One or More Engines Inoperative	3-48
Runway Barrier Engagement	3-50
Landing Gear System	1-76, 1-78*
Alarm Buzzer	1-80
Alarm Cutoff Button	1-79
Control Guide	3-42*
Controls	1-77
Downlock Override Button	1-79
Emergency Control Handle, Landing Gear and Brake	1-81, 1-85
Emergencies	3-8, 3-41
Emergency Pneumatic System	1-81
Extension and Retraction Maximum Speed	5-6
Ground Locks	1-79*
Handle	1-77
Indicators	1-77
Position Indicator Lamps	1-79
Warning Lamp	1-79
Landing Pattern (Typical)	2-54*
Lateral Control	6-8
Lateral Directional Flight Characteristics	6-16
Level-Off	2-44, 8-29
Level-Off and Periodic Inflight	8-31
Lighting Equipment	4-39
Lighting of A-C Generator Abnormal Caution Lamp	3-14
Lighting of Battery Discharging Caution Lamp	3-17
Lighting of Landing Gear Warning Lamp in Flight	3-41
Lighting of Yaw Damper Warning Lamp	3-31
Lights, Exterior	4-39
Lights, Interior	4-41
Limit Maneuver Load Factors	5-8*
Limitations	
Acceleration	5-9
Airspeed	5-6
Altitude	5-29
Brake Energy	5-24
Canopy Operation	5-29
Center of Gravity	5-9
Center of Gravity Loading	5-13
Engine	5-1
Flight Control System	5-23
Hydraulic System	5-23
Miscellaneous Operational	5-29
Taxi	5-22
Weight	5-33
Line-Up	8-28
Lineup, Before	2-36, 9-16
Liquid Containers	4-118
Loadmeter, D-C	1-40
Long Range Communication (LRC) System	4-27

*Denotes Illustration

	Page
Longitudinal Control	6-8
Longitudinal Control Variation	6-14*
Longitudinal Flight Characteristics	6-9
Longitudinal Reference Angles	6-2*
Loss of Cabin Pressure	3-37
Loss of Canopy During Flight	3-37
Low Altitude Navigation	8-2
Low Altitude Radar Altimeter	1-88
Low Altitude Warning Lamp	1-88

M

	Page
Mach-Altitude Gain Adjustment Failure	7-36
Mach Indicator	1-87
Mach-Monitor Indicator Lamps	1-75
Magnetic Compass	1-91
Main Landing Gear Arrangement	1-77*
Malfunction, Cabin Pressurization	3-35
Malfunction Control Panel	4-76, 4-77*
Malfunction Indicator and Warning System	1-92
Pilot's Indicator Lamp System	1-92
Switches	1-92, 1-93
Test Button	1-92
Voice Warning System	1-93
Malfunction Detection and Switching	4-61
Maneuvering Flight	6-18
Manual Button	4-108
Manual Control Handle	4-108
Manual Data Request Button	4-91
Manual Fire Control Panel	4-108*
Manual Frequency Selector Knobs	4-25
Manual Groundspeed Correction Procedure	8-51
Map and Data Case, Pilot's	4-117
Master Caution Lamp	1-93
Master Warning Lamp	1-93
Maximum Airspeed Limit With Drag Chute Doors Open	5-6
Maximum Allowable Overspeed	5-1
Maximum Sinking Speed at Touchdown	5-29
Maximum Taxi Distance	5-21*
MB and LA-331A Pod	4-96*
MB Pod	4-97
MD-7 Scope Presentations	4-110*
Mechanical Release Handle	4-81
Microphone Buttons, Capsule	4-19
Microphone Buttons, Foot Operated	4-19
Minimum Airspeed for Control in a Crosswind	2-63*
Minimum Crew Requirements	5-1
Minimum Flying and Maneuver Speed	5-7, 5-7*
Minimum Flying Speed	6-4*
Minimum Forward Tank Fuel Quantity For Air Pressure Transfer to Reservoir Tank	7-13, 7-16*
Minimum Reaction Cocking Checklist	2-37
Minimum Reaction Posture	2-69
Minimum Reaction Scramble Checklist	2-38
Minimum Turning Radius and Ground Clearances	2-35, 5-23

	Page
Mirrors	4-118
Miscellaneous Emergency Equipment	3-40*
Miscellaneous Equipment	4-116, 4-116*
Missed Approach Procedures	9-9
Mission Flight Plan, Navigator's	8-6*
Mission Preparation	8-2, 8-4, 8-13
MM-3 Attitude Indicator	1-89
Mode Restrictions, Elevator Control Available	5-24
Modes, Autopilot	4-47, 4-51
Multiple Drift Procedure	8-50
Multiple Voltage Power Panels (Typical)	1-42*

N

	Page
Nacelle Cooling System	1-13
Navigation Control Panel	4-67, 4-67*
Navigation System, Tactical Air	4-31
Controls and Indicators	4-31
Normal Operation	4-34
Navigator's and DSO's Equipment Storage Case	4-117
Navigator's and DSO's Work Table	4-117
Navigator's Canopy Release Handles	1-100
Navigator's Checklist	8-13
Navigator's Duties	8-3
Navigator's Interphone Control Panel	4-18*
Navigator's Left Console	4-59
Navigator's Lighting Control Panel	4-41
Navigator's Right Console	4-60
Navigator's Station	4-57*
Negative Gravity Operation, Fuel Management	7-12
Night Flying	9-12
Normal Operation,	
Active Defense System	4-111
Air Conditioning System	4-10
Air Navigation Data Recording System	4-92
Air-to-Ground IFF Equipment	4-36
AN/ARC-34 Command Radio System	4-26
AN/ARC-74	4-27
AN/ARC-110	4-30
Anti-Icing System, Engine and Spike	4-15
Autopilot	4-50
Auxiliary Flight Reference System	4-56
BDE System	4-94
Communication System (AN/ARC-57)	4-22
Defogging System	4-13
Emergency Communications System	4-27
Instrument Landing System	4-34
Oxygen System	4-46
PI Beacon System	4-37
RV Beacon System	4-39
TACAN	4-34
Nose Wheel Ground Turning Limits	5-22*
Nose Wheel Steering Hydraulic System	1-81
Nose Wheel Steering System	1-81
Nose Wheel Uncontrolled Hardover Steering	3-8
NWS, A/R Disc, A/R Reset Button	1-82, 4-113

*Denotes Illustration

O

	Page
Offset and Storage Panel	4-69*
Oil Pressure, Engine	5-3
Oil Supply System	1-15
Oil System Emergency Procedures	3-17
Operation of Automatic Trim and Elevator Ratio Changer Computers	7-32*
Operational Center-of-Gravity Limits	5-9, 5-10*
Overspeed Limitations	5-1
Oxygen Duration, Normal System	4-43*
Oxygen Duration, Capsule System	4-44*
Oxygen Systems	4-43
Control Panel	4-45*, 4-46*
Controls	4-45
Emergency Operation	4-46
Emergency System	4-44
Indicators	4-45
Leakage	4-46
Normal Operation	4-46
Normal System	4-43
Preflight Check	4-46
Regulator	4-45

P

	Page
Paper Break Alarm Lamp	4-93
Parachute Deployment Handle, Manual	1-110
Parachute Disconnect Handle	1-111
Parking Break Handle	1-83
Penetration	8-47
Penetration, Prior to	2-52, 8-45
Personal Gear Connections	2-14*
Photo Reconnaissance System	4-103
Controls and Indicators	4-104
Operation	4-105
Pod Release System	4-103
Photo Recorder Coding	4-72*
Photo Run	8-31
PI Beacon Control Panel	4-37*
Pilot's Bomb Panel	4-82*
Pilot's Canopy Override Lever	1-99
Pilot's Communication Control Panel	4-16*
Pilot's Data Indicator	4-58*
Pilot's Duties	8-2
Pilot's Forward Left Console	1-80*
Pilot's Indicator Lamp System	1-92
Pilot's Left Sidewall Console	1-12*
Pilot's Lighting Control Panel	4-40*
Pilot's Lower Left Console	1-16*
Pilot's Lower Right Console	1-64*
Pilot's Main Instrument Panel	1-11*
Pilot's Map and Data Case	4-117
Pilot's Oxygen Control Panel	4-45*
Pilot's Station	1-4*
Pilot's Tunnel Anti-Glare Curtain	4-117
Pitot Anti-Icing System	4-13
Pitot-Static System	1-86
Malfunction	3-33
Pneumatic Power Supply Systems	1-60
Pneumatic Pressure Gage, Capsule	1-111
Pneumatic System, Brake Emergency	1-83
Pneumatic System, Landing Gear Emergency	1-81
Pneumatic System Pressure Gage, Canopy	1-100
Pod and DECM Power Caution Lamp	1-39
Pod Camera Control Panel	4-105*
Pod Lock Indicator, Photo Recon	4-105
Pod-to-Airplane Fuel Transfer System	1-20
Pod Transfer Pump Low Pressure Caution Lamps	1-32
Pods	
Drop	6-20
Drop, Upper	6-21
Fuel System	4-99
Fuel Tank Loading Limits	5-31*
Gross Weights	4-97
Jettisoning Procedures	2-45
Jettisoning, Lower Pod	2-47
MB	4-97
Mechanical Release Handle	4-81
Normal Jettison Limits, Lower Pod	5-4*, 5-6
Present Switch Monitor	4-102
Principal Dimensions	4-97
Ready Switch, Fuel Pod	4-103
Release System	4-99
Release System, Photo Recon	4-103
Restoring Electrical Power	3-16
Safety Lock Handle	4-80
Two Component	4-101
Upper	4-97
Position Indicating Beacon System	4-36
Emergency Operation	4-38
Indicator Lamps	4-37
Knobs	4-37
Mixing Switch	4-37
Normal Operation	4-37
Post Release Check, Bombing	8-40, 8-44
Postflight	2-68
Power-Off Interior Inspection	2-6, 8-14
Power-On Interior Inspection	2-9, 8-17
Power Source, External	1-40
Preflight Check	2-4, 8-14
Preparation for Flight	2-2
Pressure Gage, Canopy	1-100
Pressure Gage, Drag Chute	1-86
Pressure Gage, Oxygen	4-45
Pressurization Control	4-7
Pressurization System	1-25

*Denotes Illustration

	Page
Primary Navigation System	4-56
Astro Control Panel	4-65
Astrotracker	4-59
Auxiliary Control Panel	4-61
Auxiliary Flight Instrument Panel	4-63
Computation and Stabilization System	4-58
Doppler Radar	4-60
Indicator Panel	4-64*
Isolation Switches	4-79, 4-79*
Malfunction Control Panel	4-76, 4-77*
Malfunction Detection and Switching	4-61
Navigation Control Panel	4-67
Offset and Storage Panel	4-68
Operation	4-79
Radio Altimeter	4-61
Search Radar	4-60
Search Radar Indicator Panel	4-71
Search Radar Test Panel	4-75
Sighting and Test Panel	4-68, 4-70*
Tracking and Flight Control Unit	4-71
Principal Dimensions, Pod	4-97
Prohibited Maneuvers	5-8

R

	Page
Radar Approach	9-4*, 9-9
Radar, Doppler	4-60
Radar Fire Control Panel	4-107*
Radar Jamming	4-112
Radar Position Fix Procedure	8-50
Radar Scope	4-109
Radar, Search	4-60
Radio Altimeter	4-61
Radio Control Transfer Button	4-19
Rain	9-9
Rain Removal System	4-13
Ram Air Mode Limit Speed	5-6, 5-6*
Ram Air Operation	4-11
Ram Air Temperature Limits	5-3
Ratio Changer, Aileron	1-68
Ratio Changer, Elevator	1-66
RBS Tone Selector Switch	4-21
Ready Fire Lamp	4-109
Recorder Control Unit	4-89
Recorder, VGH	4-118
Recording Cycle, BDE	4-92
Recording System	4-88
Controls	4-90
Indicators	4-90
Recorder Control Unit	4-89
Refueling, Air	4-112
Relief Containers	4-116
Rendezvous Beacon System	4-38
Emergency Operation	4-39
Indicator Lamps	4-39
Knobs	4-38

	Page
Mixing Switch	4-39
Normal Operation	4-39
Reservoir Tank Automatic Filling System	1-20
Reservoir Tank Not Full Caution Lamp	1-32
Reservoir-to-Manifold Switches	1-26
Reset Button, Yaw	1-74
Restoring Electrical Power to Pod and DECM Equipment	3-16
Restricted High Speed	5-8
Restrictions, Flight	2-2
Resume Search Button	4-109
Right A-C and Multiple Weapons 28 Volt D-C Power Panels	1-38*
Roll Rate, Maximum Allowable	5-24
Ropes, Escape	1-96
Rope Transfer Line	4-118
Rudder	
Control System	1-68, 3-30
Damper Servo	1-69
Pedal Trim and Fuel System	1-68
Pedals	1-71
Position Indicator	1-75
Trim Switch	1-72
Runway Barrier Engagement	3-50
RV Beacon Control Panel	4-38*

S

	Page
Safety Belts	1-113
Safety Lock Handle	4-80
Safety Pins, Canopy	1-100
Safety Pins, Ground	1-111
Scavenge System, Fuel	1-25
Scavenging, Fuel Tank	7-12
Scramble/SRP Power-Off Scramble	2-31, 8-25
Search Radar	4-60
Search Radar Indicator Panel	4-71, 4-74*
Search Radar Test Panel	4-75, 4-76*
Seat Pan Adjustment Lever	1-110
Seat Pin Stowage Provisions	4-117
Secondary Pitot-Static System Deviation From Primary System	1-86*
Servicing Diagram	1-112*
Servo, Aileron Damper	1-68
Servo, Elevator Damper	1-67
Servo, Rudder Damper	1-69
Shoulder Harness, Escape Capsule	1-109
Sighting and Test Panel	4-68, 4-70*
Single-Point Refueling System	4-114
Controls	4-115
Operation	4-115
Small Weapons Arm Panel	4-81*
Small Weapon (B 43 Bomb)	4-94, 4-95*
Small Weapon Drop	6-22
Smoke and Fume Elimination	3-39
Spike Anti-Icing System	4-13
Spin Characteristics	6-6
Spin Recovery Procedures	3-28, 6-6

*Denotes Illustration

Index

Spins
Switches

	Page
Spins	6-6
SRP Power-Off Scramble	2-31, 8-25
SRP Power-On Cocking	2-33, 8-26
SRP Power-On Scramble	2-34, 8-27
Stability Augmentation	1-65
Stall Clearing, Compressor	3-13
Stall, Compressor	7-1
Stall Warning Indication	3-28
Stall Warning Lamp	1-91
Stalls	6-2
Standby Gains and Gain Adjustment System	7-37*
Standby Gain Operating Region	7-38*
Standby Gains System	1-69, 7-36
Star Lost Indicator Lamp	4-67
Starter Limits	5-4
Starter System, Engine	1-12
Starting Engines	2-15
Starting Engines, Cold Weather Procedures	9-13
Statically Stable System	6-12*
Strange Field Exterior Inspection	2-73, 2-73*
Strange Field Postflight Inspection	2-73
Strange Field Procedure	2-72
Structural Limit Speed	5-8
Subsonic Buffet Region	6-19
Switches	
Aileron Control Available	1-72
Aileron-Elevator Stick Trim	1-73
Airflow	4-9
Air Refueling Door	4-113
Airspeed Calibration	4-78
Airspeed Computer Malfunction	4-78
Airspeed Inertial	4-63
Altitude Malfunction	4-78
Anticollision Light	4-40
Anti-Skid Control	1-83
Arming Control	4-82
Arming Power	4-82
Astro Filter	4-66
Astrotracker Malfunction	4-78
Auto Release	4-81
Auto Steering	4-76
Automatic Radar Photography	4-70
Autopilot Airspeed Control	4-50
Autopilot Engage	4-49
Autopilot Trigger	4-50
Auxiliary Flight Reference System Power	4-55
Auxiliary Listen	4-20
Auxiliary Rapid Erect	4-77
Bailout Alert and Warning	1-96
Balance to Aft Tank Interconnect	1-28
Battery	1-39
BDE Power	4-94
Beta	4-74
Camera Operate	4-105
Camera Power	4-104
Cartridge Start	1-13
Control Stick Manual CG Shift	1-27

	Page
Control Stick Microphone	4-19
Coordinate Reference	4-68
Coriolis Malfunction	4-84
Damper	1-73
Data Review	4-91
Doppler Return	4-63
Doppler Transmitter	4-62
EBL, Air Refueling	4-113
Electrical Release, Bombing	4-81
Elevator Control Available Manual Adjust	1-72
Elevator Control Available Mode Selector	1-71
Emergency Boom Latch	4-113
Emergency Lighting, Pilot's	4-42
Emergency Override, LRC	4-30
Engine Anti-Ice	4-14
Engine Start	1-13
Flight Control Power	1-71, 4-49
Flight Reference Indicator Power	4-55
Flow	4-9
Fuel Dump	1-28
Fuel Gage Power	1-29
Fuel Pod Ready	4-103
Fuel Pod Release	4-103
Gain Selector	1-73
Generator Control	1-33
Generator Drive Decoupler	1-33
Heading, Autopilot	4-50
Heading Integrator Malfunction	4-79
Heading Selector, AFRS	4-54
Identification of Position	4-36
Ignition	1-12
Indicator Console Unit	4-75
Isolation, Primary Navigation	4-79
Landing Light	4-39
Mach-Altitude, Mach, Autopilot	4-50
Mach Indicator Malfunction	4-78
Malfunction and Indicator Lamp Dimming	1-92
Manual-Automatic Receiver Tuning	4-73
Manual-Preset-Guard	4-26
Map Light	4-42
Marker Beacon Mixing	4-34
Marker Generator	4-108
Master, Active Defense System	4-106
Microphone, Control Stick	4-19
Mixing, Interphone	4-20
Mixing, PI Beacon Equipment	4-37
Mixing, RV Equipment	4-39
Mixing, TACAN	4-32
Mode, Air-to-Ground IFF Equipment	4-36
Navigation Lights Control	4-40
Navigation Lights Mode	4-40
Nose Wheel Steering (NWS) Ratio Selector	1-82
Passageway Light	4-42
Pilot's Floodlight Selector	4-42
Pitot Anti-Ice	4-13
Plan Position Indicator	4-74
Pod Air Conditioning Control	4-105

*Denotes Illustration

	Page
Switches (Cont'd)	
Pod and DECM Power	1-33
Pod Tank Interconnect	1-29
Pod Warhead Control Selector	4-83
Polar/Non-Polar	4-68
Power, AFRS	4-55
Power, AN/ARC-74	4-27
Power, BDE	4-94
Power, LRC	4-29
Power, Recorder	4-90
Primary Navigation System Isolation	4-79
Primary Rapid Erect	4-77
Radar Bomb Scoring Tone	4-83
Radar Sighting	4-75
Radio Altimeter	4-62
RBS Tone Selector Switch	4-21
Reservoir Booster Pump	1-26
Reservoir to Manifold	1-26
Rudder Trim	1-72
RV Mixing	4-39
Safe-Fire	4-107
Search Antenna Malfunction	4-79
Search Power	4-62
Search Test Normal/Override	4-76
Seat Adjustment	1-110
Sight Malfunction	4-78
Single Point Refueling Floodlight	4-40
Small Weapon Jettison	4-82
Small Weapon Lock	4-81
Small Weapon Warhead Control Selector	4-83
Spike Position	1-16
Stick Trim Selector	1-73
Taxi Light	4-40
Time-to-Go, Servo Malfunction	4-84
Trail and Time-of-Fall Malfunction	4-85
Vertical Reference Selector	4-76
Vertical Velocity Malfunction	4-84
V/H Control Converter Power	4-104
V/H Control Selector	4-104
Voice Warning System Monitoring	1-94
Voice Warning System Power/Reset	1-93
Warhead Control Selector	4-83
Warning and Caution Indicator	1-92
Weapon Release	4-81
Weapon Selector	4-82
Windshield Defog	4-12
Windshield Rain Removal	4-12
Wing Heavy Control	1-74
Synchronization Indicator	4-55

T

	Page
T_2 Cutback	7-3
T_2 Cutback—Rpm vs Exhaust Gas Temperature	7-3*
T_2 Reset	7-2
T_2 Reset and Cutback Versus Engine Speed	7-2*
T_2 Reset or Manual Selected Overspeed	5-1
Tachometers	1-13
Tactical Air Navigation System	4-31
Controls	4-31
Indicators	4-31
Tail Turret	4-106
Takeoff	2-38, 9-16
Aborted	3-3
After	2-43, 8-29, 9-16
Checklist	2-41
Cold Weather	9-16
Crosswind	2-40
Data Card	2-3
Engine Failure During	3-4
Engine Fire During	3-4
EWO Takeoff and Climbout	2-41
Fuel Management During	7-9
Hot Weather	9-17
Instrument	9-3
Light Gross Weights	2-40
Monitoring Procedure (S_1/S_2)	2-38
One Engine Inoperative	3-8
Procedures and Techniques	2-39
Slippery Runway	2-41
Tire Failure During	3-6
Takeoff Emergencies	3-3
Abort	3-3
Engine Failure	3-4
Engine Fire	3-4
Landing Gear Will Not Retract	3-8
Nose Wheel Uncontrolled Hardover Steering	3-8
Takeoff With One Engine Inoperative	3-8
Tire Failure	3-6
Takeoff (Typical)	2-39*
Tank Scavenging, Fuel Management	7-12
Target Run, Photo Recon	8-31
Taxi-back Landing	2-65, 8-48
Taxi Distance, Maximum	5-21*
Taxi Limitations	5-22
Taxiing	2-35, 2-80, 8-28, 9-15
Taxiing Instructions, Cold Weather Procedures	9-15
Temperature Control Malfunction	3-35
Thermal Curtains	4-117
Three Engine Subsonic Flight	3-14
Throttles, Engine Fuel Control System	1-9
Throttle Lock Lever	1-9
Throttle Quadrant	1-8*
Throttle Retard Button	1-10
Thrust Variation With Engine RPM at Landing Speeds	2-60*
Thunderstorms, Turbulence and	9-11
Time Index Indicator Digitalizer	4-91
Time Limits, Engine Operation	5-3
Tire Failure During Takeoff	3-6
Tire Limit Speed	5-5*, 5-6
Tone Button	4-21, 4-25

*Denotes Illustration

	Page
Touch-and-Go Landing	2-64
Touchdown, Maximum Sinking Speed	5-29
Tracking and Flight Control Stick	4-71
Tracking and Flight Controller Unit	4-71, 4-73*
Transfer Rates Into Aft Tank for Dumping	7-12*
Transition Checklist	2-55
Transverse Entry	8-32
Transverse Exit	8-33
Trim Control Panel	1-74*
Trouble Shooting Procedure, Flight Control System	7-39*
Turbulence and Thunderstorms	9-11
Turbulence, Operation in	6-20
Turn and Slip Indicator	1-91
Turning Radius, Minimum	5-23
Turning Speed, Maximum	5-23
Two Component Pod	4-98*, 4-99
Typical Jet Penetration	9-2*
Typical Longitudinal Control Variations	6-14*
Typical Radar Approach	9-4*

U

	Page
UHF Command Radio System	4-17, 4-24
Uncocking	2-30, 8-24
Unlocked Canopy Indication During Flight	3-37
Unusable Fuel	7-13, 7-14*
Upper Door Release Latches	1-110
Upper Pod	4-99, 4-101
Upper Pod Drop (EWO)	6-21

V

	Page
Variable Exhaust Nozzle System	1-10
Variable Inlet Guide and Stator Vane System	1-10, 7-1
Variation of Power Required During Landing	2-57*
Vent and Pressurization System, Fuel	1-25
Vertical Gyro Fast Erect Button	4-55
Vertical Velocity Indicator	1-89
VGH Recorder	4-118
View From Closed Capsule	3-25*
Visual Phase of Instrument Approach	9-8*

	Page
Voice Warning System	1-93
Message Priority	1-94*
Override Button	1-94
Switches	1-93, 1-94
Voltmeter, A-C	1-35
Voltmeter, D-C	1-40

W

	Page
Warhead Arming and Fuzing System	4-99
Warning and Caution Lamp Panels	1-31*
Warning Lamps	
Ammo Temperature	4-111
Bailout	1-95
Landing Gear	1-79
Low Altitude	1-88
Manifold Low Pressure	1-31
Master	1-94, 4-86
Release System Activated	4-86
Stall	1-91
Target	4-109
Yaw Damper	1-76
Weapon Abort Procedure	8-41
Weapon Lock and Arm Panel	4-80*
Weapon Monitor and Release Panel	4-86*
Weapons Preparation for Release	8-36
Weapons Control System (AN/ASQ-42)	4-56
Weight and Balance	2-3
Weight Limitations	5-33
Weight, Gross	1-1
Windmilling, Airstart Speeds	3-12*
Windshield and Window Glass Panels	1-113
Windshield Rain Removal and Defog System	4-12
Wing Angle of Attack	5-30
Wing Heaviness	6-17
Wing Heavy Control System	1-69

Y

	Page
Yaw Damper Warning Lamp, Lighting of	3-31
Yaw Reset Button	1-74

*Denotes Illustration

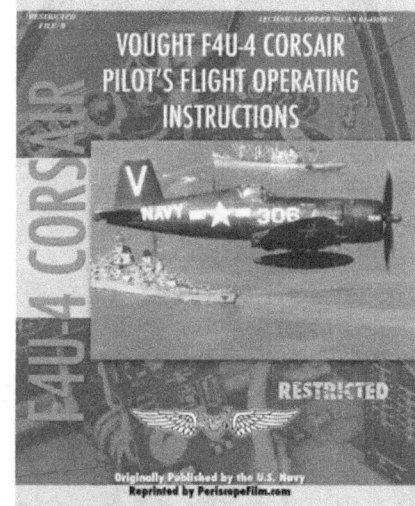
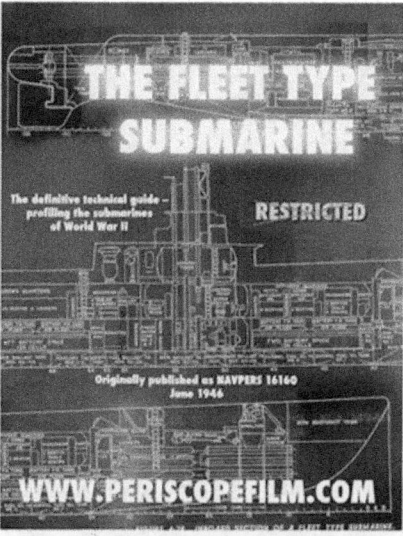
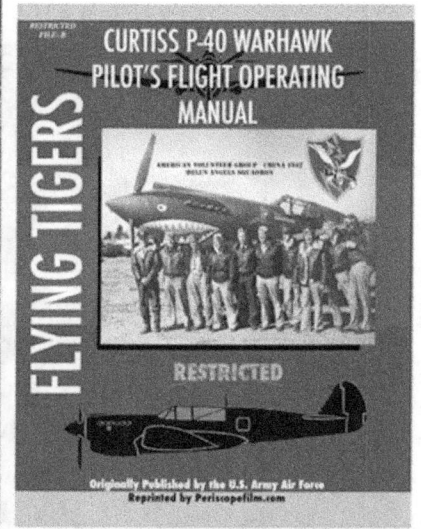

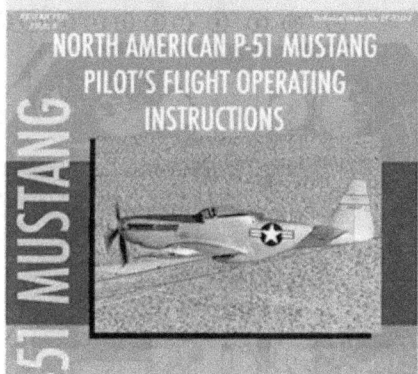

ALSO NOW AVAILABLE
FROM PERISCOPEFILM.COM

NASA
PROJECT GEMINI

FAMILIARIZATION MANUAL
Manned Satellite Capsule

Periscope Film LLC

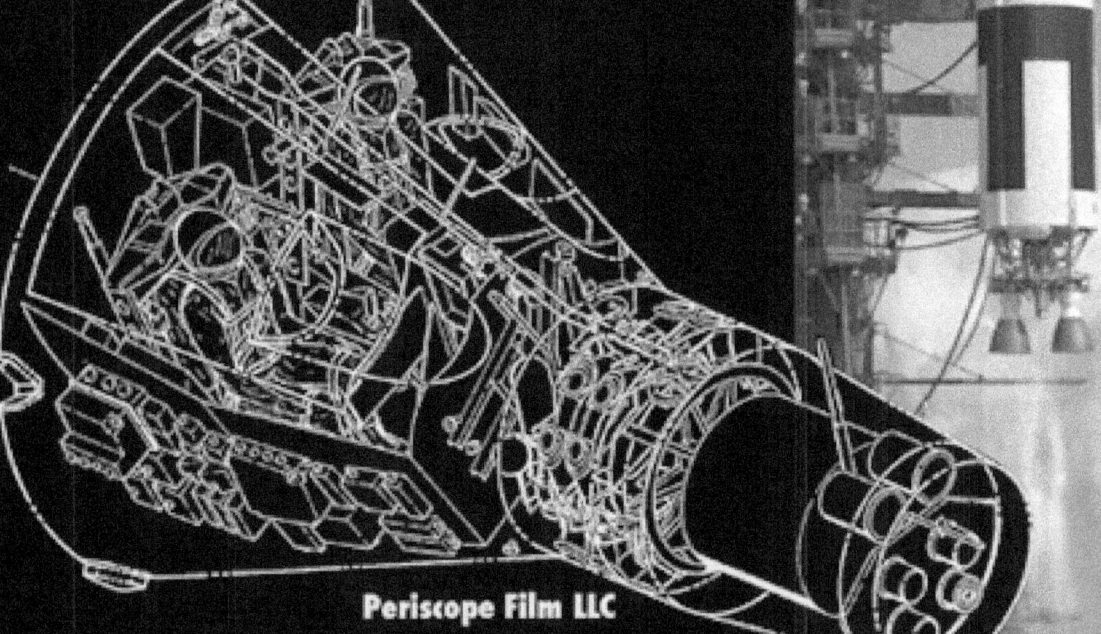

LMA 790-1

PROJECT APOLLO

lem
LUNAR EXCURSION MODULE

FIRST MANNED LUNAR LANDING
FAMILIARIZATION MANUAL

GRUMMAN AIRCRAFT ENGINEERING CORPORATION • BETHPAGE, L. I., N. Y.

©2008-2012 Periscope Film LLC
All Rights Reserved
ISBN #978-1-937684-93-8

www.ingramcontent.com/pod-product-compliance
Lightning Source LLC
Chambersburg PA
CBHW081753300426
44116CB00014B/2105